W9-COZ-705

FOR REFERENCE

Do Not Take From This Room

The American Dictionary of Criminal Justice

Key Terms and Major Court Cases

Third Edition

Dean John Champion

The Scarecrow Press, Inc.
Lanham, Maryland • Toronto • Oxford
2005

SCARECROW PRESS, INC.

Published in the United States of America by Scarecrow Press, Inc.
A wholly owned subsidiary of The Rowman & Littlefield Publishing Group, Inc.
4501 Forbes Boulevard, Suite 200, Lanham, Maryland 20706
www.scarecrowpress.com

PO Box 317
Oxford
OX2 9RU, UK

Copyright © 2005 Roxbury Publishing Company
First Scarecrow Press cloth edition 2005

British Library Cataloguing in Publication Information Available

Library of Congress Cataloging-in-Publication Data

The American dictionary of criminal justice: key terms and major court cases / Dean
J. Champion—3rd ed.
   p. cm.
Includes index.
   1. Criminal justice, administration of—Dictionaries. 2. Criminology—Dictionaries.
3. Criminal justice, administration of—United States—Cases. 4. Criminal law—United
States—Cases I. Title.

HB7411.C48 2004
364′.03—dc22

2004042836

ISBN 0-8108-5406-6 (alk. paper)

∞ The paper used in this publication meets the minimum requirements of
American National Standard for Information Sciences—Permanence of
Paper for Printed Library Materials, ANSI/NISO Z39.48-1992.

Manufactured in the United States of America.

Contents

Preface

The American Dictionary of Criminal Justice: Key Terms and Major Court Cases, Third Edition, will be useful to every student of the criminal justice system. Like any good dictionary, this resource will assist students in a variety of courses, as well as in writing papers and understanding terminology in journal articles. The book was written to enable the reader to quickly identify both key terms and leading United States Supreme Court cases in a single ready reference.

This dictionary is not intended to replace conventional legal dictionaries, such as *Black's Law Dictionary*, or to substitute for detailed expositions of how to do legal research and writing. Rather, the book attempts to pull together key terms and concepts from diverse areas, including criminology, criminal justice, corrections, probation/parole, juvenile justice, and policing. This interdisciplinary approach greatly enhances the dictionary's effectiveness as a "one-stop" resource. Students will no longer need to spend precious study time seeking out definitions in numerous specialized sources. The coverage greatly enhances the information provided in most standard textbook glossaries, as do the examples drawn from the research literature accompanying many definitions.

In many cases, terms that refer to similar phenomena have been grouped under a single definition or a series of definitions, with minor variations to reflect slight differences in application. One feature of this dictionary is the inclusion of the names of researchers and criminologists who have done important work and influenced the nature and direction of criminology and criminal justice. It is beyond the scope of this book to include *every* criminologist, however. Choices were made according to which theorists are most closely associated with various key terms, issues, and theories.

Conveniently alphabetized and indexed, the most recent and significant United States Supreme Court cases are summarized, offering students an easy-to-read account of the events leading to each case, how the Court decided the case, the rationale used in the decision, and the case's significance for criminal justice. An innovative feature of these listings is the full citation, including the first and last names of parties or organizations or boards. Two examples are "*Abel v. United States,* 362 U.S. 217, 80 S.Ct. 683 (1960) [**Rudolf Ivonovich ABEL, also known as 'Mark' and also known as Martin Collins and Emil R. Goldfus, Petitioner, v. UNITED STATES of America**] (**Fourth Amendment; Informants; Law Enforcement Officers or Agencies; Searches and Seizures; Searches Incident to an Arrest**)," and "*Gideon v. Wainwright,* 372 U.S. 335, 83 S.Ct. 792 (1963) [**Clarence Earl GIDEON, Petitioner, v. Louie L. WAINWRIGHT, Director, Division of Corrections**] (**Indigent Clients; Right to Counsel**)." In each of these cases, the full text of the citation is presented. This permits students to know who each of the principals is in the different cases. Also, one or more topics are provided in parentheses. These are key terms that are relevant to the case. Furthermore, each of these terms is matched to a case index term where that particular case is found. This topical breakdown is important for those wishing to look up and study cases in a particular subject category, such as "searches and seizures," "searches incident to an arrest," or "right to counsel."

The Supreme Court Cases section represents the most comprehensive and current assemblage of decisions to date. This eases instruction, eliminating the necessity of duplicating and distributing case summaries. Especially for students who do not have immediate access to a large legal library, the cases included here are critical and have wide application and relevance. Departing from other dictionaries, in which cases are grouped under particular amendment headings or subject matter designations, these cases have been arranged alphabetically. They have also been indexed into numerous important categories in order to permit those doing legal research to search out relevant and related topics more easily. A particular case may have relevance for more than one legal issue. Thus, in looking up a particular topic, the reader will find the most up-to-date cases associated with it.

The case compilation in *The American Dictionary of Criminal Justice* is considerably more extensive than that found in most standard textbooks. The coverage consists primarily of United States Supreme Court cases. This does not mean that the cases of circuit courts of appeal, state supreme courts, and district courts are not important. The opinions in this volume were chosen because they represent laws applicable throughout the United States, rather than to specific geographical areas.

The reader should note that some cases have been reported that were subsequently overturned, overruled, or replaced with new or revised interpretations. For the legal scholar, it is important not only to know where we are now, but where we have been in the past regarding the application of our laws. It is important for students to understand that case law is constantly changing. The United States Supreme Court is always refining old laws and views and providing us with exceptions, increasingly specific interpretations, and modifications of previous decisions governing how the police, courts, and corrections conduct their business with arrestees, defendants, convicted offenders, and clients.

Before studying these cases, it would be useful for students to read the discussion of case referencing under "Court Cases" at the beginning of the section. This will familiarize the reader with the abbreviations and numbers following cases and how to locate them in library collections. Furthermore, the examples of protocol to follow when referencing legal citations will help students in preparing research papers.

Although the author accepts full responsibility for any errors of fact or interpretations of United States Supreme Court cases, the criticisms and suggestions of several experts in the fields of criminal justice and criminology are gratefully acknowledged. Among those who examined the original proposal and helped to shape the project's nature and direction were Paul Cromwell, University of Miami; Chris W. Eskridge, University of Nebraska, Omaha; Frank R. Scarpitti, University of Delaware; and Richard A. Wright, University of Scranton. Also, my thanks are extended to those who read the manuscript in its entirety and offered constructive criticisms and suggestions: Mitchell B. Chamlin, University of Cincinnati; Frederic L. Faust, Florida State University; Charles B. Fields, California State University, San Bernardino; and William Geary, University of Florida. For the present edition, the following reviewers are gratefully acknowledged: Susan Blankenship, Kentucky State University; Michael Bogner, Chadron State College; Egan Kyle Green, University of Tennessee; James Jengeleski, Shippensburg University; G. Larry Mays, New Mexico State University; Robert D. McCrie, John Jay College of Criminal Justice; Heather Perfetti, Darton College; and Caryl Lynn Segal, University of Texas, Arlington.

Dean John Champion
Texas A&M International University

About the Author

Dean John Champion is a professor of criminal justice at Texas A&M International University in Laredo, TX. Dr. Champion has taught at the University of Tennessee–Knoxville, California State University–Long Beach, and Minot State University. He earned his Ph.D. from Purdue University and B.S. and M.A. degrees from Brigham Young University. He also completed several years of law school at the Nashville School of Law.

Dr. Champion has written more than 30 texts and edited works and maintains memberships in 11 professional organizations. He is a lifetime member of the American Society of Criminology, the Academy of Criminal Justice Sciences, and the American Sociological Association. He is former editor of the ACJS/Anderson series on *Issues in Crime and Justice* (1993–1996) and the *Journal of Crime and Justice* (1995–1998). He is a contributing author for the *Encarta Encyclopedia 2000* for Microsoft. He was the visiting scholar for the National Center for Juvenile Justice in 1992 and is president of the Midwestern Criminal Justice Association.

His published books for Prentice-Hall include *Basic Statistics for Social Research* (1970, 1981); *Research Methods for Criminal Justice and Criminology* (1993, 2000, 2006 forthcoming); *The Juvenile Justice System: Delinquency, Processing, and the Law* (1992, 1998, 2001, 2004); *Corrections in the United States: A Contemporary Perspective* (1990, 1998, 2001, 2005); *Criminal Courts* (with Gary Rabe, 2002, 2006 forthcoming); *Probation, Parole, and Community Corrections* (1990, 1996, 1999, 2002, 2005); *Policing in the Community* (with George Rush, 1996); and *The Administration of Justice Systems* (2001). Works from other publishers include *The Sociology of Organizations* (McGraw-Hill, 1975); *Research Methods in Social Relations* (John Wiley & Sons, 1976); *Sociology* (Holt, Rinehart, and Winston, 1984); *The U.S. Sentencing Guidelines* (Praeger, 1989); *Juvenile Transfer Hearings* (with Larry G. Mays, Praeger, 1991) *Measuring Offender Risk* (Greenwood Press, 1994); *The American Dictionary of Criminal Justice* (Roxbury, 1997, 2001, 2005); and *Criminal Justice in the United States, Second Edition* (Wadsworth, 1998). Dr. Champion's primary research interests relate to attorney use in juvenile-justice proceedings and plea bargaining. ✦

DICTIONARY
OF
TERMS

A

ABA models of court organization Schemes for organizing different state courts devised by the American Bar Association in 1962 and 1974. The 1962 model provides for a supreme court, an intermediate appellate court, a major trial court, and a minor trial court; the 1974 model simplifies the 1962 model, providing for a supreme court, an intermediate appellate court, and a trial court. *See also* **Pound's Model.**

abandonment Parents physically leaving their children with the intention of completely severing the parent-child relationship.

abate To declare null and void.

abating problems, nuisance abatement Reducing, minimizing, or eliminating problems such as drug houses and derelict properties.

ABA transit numbers Numerical codes devised by the American Banker's Association to route negotiable instruments (checks) to banks of origin.

abduction Unlawfully stealing or taking away another, with or without the use of force.

abet To encourage or assist an offender in the commission of a crime.

abeyance A temporary halting of an intended or continuing action; temporary termination of action where resolution is expected. Removal is prohibited by law.

ab inconvenient A term used in cases where, because of a significant impediment, the prosecution cannot present or establish one or more facts crucial to its case.

ab initio "From the beginning" (Latin); the commencement of a state or condition.

abnormal psychology The study of behavioral disorders, including mental retardation and illness, that focuses on the etiology of such disorders and examines physical and biochemical causal factors associated with such disorders.

abnormal sex A general term describing any unconventional sexual act or practice that has been criminalized, apart from adultery or fornication.

abolitionism The movement to abolish the death penalty as a form of punishment. Abolitionism was particularly strong in the twentieth century with the advent of DNA testing and its ability to exonerate the wrongfully convicted, including those awaiting execution. Also, the movement to abolish slavery in the U.S. prior to the Civil War.

abolitionists A term applied to those opposed to capital punishment; also, those opposed to slavery in the U.S. prior to the Civil War.

abortion Termination of a pregnancy by use of drugs or a medical operation. Abortions are performed for a variety of reasons and are either permitted or prohibited, depending on the jurisdiction. *See the leading abortion case,* **Roe v. Wade** (1973).

abortion law An act or prohibition on the termination of a pregnancy short of full-term birth for a variety of reasons, including voluntary termination by one or both parents, poten-tial health risks to the mother, or the possibility of substantial birth defects detected in an examination of the unborn fetus.

About Face Georgia boot camp program. *See also* **boot camp.**

abrasion collar A round hole with blackened margins made when a bullet pierces the skin. Such collars not only indicate to investigators that a wound was made by a firearm, but may also reveal the caliber of weapon, the distance from the shooter to the victim, and other forensic details.

abrogate To abolish or annul; to breach one's responsibilities by failing to live up to or discharge them.

ABSCAM A 1978–1980 federal detection of political corruption whereby FBI undercover agents posed as wealthy Arab businesspeople to identify politicians susceptible to bribes and other forms of wrongdoing. The name is an abreviation of "Abdul scam," after Abdul Enterprises, the name of the fictitious company.

abscond To flee a geographical area or jurisdiction prescribed by the conditions of one's probation or parole without authorization. To intentionally and unlawfully leave to avoid prosecution.

absolute certainty A level of evidence that is not required in any criminal or civil case.

absolute deterrent A legal control action intended to discourage or eliminate certain criminal acts.

absolute immunity Government officials are completely immune from lawsuits from probationers, parolees, or inmates for their actions.

absolute pardon A pardon for British subjects banished to Australia that restored their rights, including the right to return to England.

absolve To release a person from any penalties, obligations, or consequences arising from a criminal act; not necessarily equated with a declaration or finding of innocence.

Abt Associates A Cambridge, MA–based research and consulting firm founded in 1965 by Dr. Clark Abt that uses research to address a variety of social issues, and includes a law and policy area known as JUST. It undertakes many influential projects in criminal justice, including the development of software packages for neighborhood problem solving.

abuse, child, abuse, child sexual, abuse, spousal Intentional psychological or physical injury caused by one person to another. It may involve prohibited sexual relations or exploitation.

abused child Any child who has been intentionally physically, sexually, or mentally injured. Most jurisdictions consider a child abused when he or she is forced into delinquent conduct by a parent or guardian.

abuse excuse A defense in which someone claims that his or her own past physical or psychological abuse by others justifies or explains his or her own current criminal conduct. Abuse is sometimes considered a mitigating circumstance.

abuse of a corpse Misuse of a dead body, which may take many forms, including mishandling or storage of a dead body, or necrophilia, in which someone sexually abuses a dead body.

abusive home A dwelling where some type of physical, sexual, emotional, or verbal abuse occurs.

academic achievement Success in a school setting.

Academy of Criminal Justice Sciences (ACJS) An international organization founded in 1963 that serves to further the development of the criminal justice profession and whose membership is involved in various components of the criminal justice system and universities.

Academy of Experimental Criminology (AEC) A scholarly organization founded in 1999 to promote experimental design with random assignment in criminological and criminal justice research. Membership is by invitation and is based on the individual's contributions to experimental research in the field.

accelerant Any chemical that hastens the occurrence of an event; in forensics, for instance, a substance that speeds up a reaction. Any substance that quickens combustion, such as a fire-enhancing material or liquid employed by an arsonist.

acceptance of responsibility A genuine admission or acknowledgment of wrongdoing. In federal presentence investigation reports, for example, convicted offenders may write an explanation and apology for the crime(s) they committed. A provision that may be considered in deciding whether leniency should be extended to offenders during the sentencing phase of their processing.

access control A crime-prevention mechanism stressing "target-hardening" security measures, including alarm systems, making it more difficult for criminals to commit their crimes; also, computer-card systems that can control or restrict employee access within buildings or computer systems through card-keys, wireless keys, or biometrics, as well as track all access and use of such systems for subsequent analysis.

accessory A person who assists another to commit a crime.

accessory after the fact One who is indirectly involved in criminal conduct, facilitating such conduct once it has occurred, by assisting, aiding, or abetting the perpetrator(s) in various ways.

accessory before the fact Anyone who is indirectly involved in criminal conduct, facilitating such conduct before it has occurred, by assisting, aiding, or abetting the perpetrator(s) in various ways.

access to the courts A fundamental prisoner's right that is the key element for enforcement of other rights because it is the mechanism for gaining judicial protection of constitutional rights. This right includes protected contact with lawyers and provision of legal resources for case preparation.

accidental killing The unintentional taking of a human life; sometimes equated with involuntary manslaughter.

accident investigation (AI) A law enforcement protocol following any accident, including the collection of physical evidence, photographing the accident scene, and determining the cause or causes of the occurrence. It often includes a determination of fault for the occurrence.

accomplice One who helps another commit a crime.

accomplished characters Prison inmates good at providing diversions and entertainment.

accomplished gamblers Inmates whose gaming skills or luck enable them to acquire substantial winnings from other inmates, putting them in a position of power relative to the inmate economy.

accountability Responsibility of either adults or children for their actions, criminal or delinquent. It may involve restitution to victims, community service, or other forms of compensation to manifest one's acceptance of responsibility.

accountability and control Organizational subcomponents that greatly restrict individual discretion and lower-echelon decision making. A disciplinary mechanism whereby people can be employed to perform an exacting task.

accountability system Any method of dealing with law enforcement, prosecution, court, or correctional corruption by making superiors responsible for the behavior of their subordinates.

accreditation A prescribed program generally receiving the approval of a recognized group of professionals, where desired program components have been identified and are used to compare other programs in terms of their effectiveness. In law enforcement and corrections, any professional organizational approval of curriculum, training procedures, and instruction designed to train personnel to perform their jobs in a capable manner.

accusation An allegation of wrongdoing; a complaint alleging that a crime has been committed or a tort perpetrated. It may be a criminal information, grand jury presentment, or indictment.

accusation, modes of A person may be charged with a crime as the result of an indictment, presentment, or information through grand jury or prosecutorial action, or a complaint may be filed by one person against another.

accusatorial system A way of administering justice or law whereby the accuser and the accused as opposing parties can resolve their disputes through court action.

accusatory pleading A generic name for any legal document used to charge a person with a crime.

accusatory process All phases of the arrest and booking process, from the arrest of suspects to the filing of formal charges against them either through an indictment or information.

accusatory stage Any event in a criminal investigation in which a suspect has been identified and designated for prosecution. A suspect's rights attach at this stage and the *Miranda* warning must be given; the accused is entitled to an attorney and other constitutional rights and protections.

accused The person alleged to have committed a crime; the defendant in any criminal action.

accused persons, rights of Those charged with a criminal offense are entitled to representation by counsel and to a speedy trial by judge or jury, depending on the seriousness of the charge(s), and the right to confront and cross-examine witnesses, and to give testimony in their own behalf. The Bill of Rights attaches when any person is accused of a crime.

accuser One who brings an accusation against another in either civil or criminal proceedings.

achievement motivation theory Elaborated by David McClelland, a theory that holds that persons engage in goal-setting behaviors, in which the goals involve challenging work. Through aggressive action toward goal attainment, and through a problem-solving process, persons obtain important feedback from significant others, such as supervisors and other workers, about the quality of their work performance. The ultimate result for high achievers is the attainment of desired goals, such as promotions, advancements, and tangible recognition and rewards.

achievement-oriented leadership Involves goal-setting behavior and also reflects task-oriented leadership.

acquaintance rape The unlawful sexual violation of an individual by someone known to that person, sometimes known as date rape. A majority of rapes against girls and unmarried women are perpetrated by someone they know.

Acquired Immune Deficiency Syndrome *See* **AIDS (Acquired Immune Deficiency Syndrome).**

acquit To find a defendant not guilty. A finding may be by a judge, jury, or panel of judges.

acquittal Any judgment by the court, considering a jury verdict or a judicial determination of the factual basis for criminal charges, in which the defendant is declared not guilty of the offenses alleged.

action, actions at law A court proceeding, either civil, to enforce a right, or criminal, to punish an offender; court litigation in which opposing parties litigate an issue involving an alleged wrongdoing. Actions at law may be for the protection of a right or the prevention of a wrong.

active intrusion sensor Any device capable of detecting movement, usually of persons, on premises where persons should not be during particular periods.

active speech Expressing an opinion by speaking or writing; freedom of speech as a protected right under the First Amendment of the U.S. Constitution. *See also* **Bill of Rights.**

act of God An explanation for any naturally occurring phenomenon, such as a disaster (e.g., tornado, earthquake, hurricane) in which property is destroyed or persons are killed or injured, which limits personal or business liability for personal injuries or physical losses sustained.

Act of October 14, 1940 An act that prohibited the interstate transportation of all prison-made goods except agricultural commodities and goods produced for states and their political subdivisions.

Act to Regulate the Treatment and Control of Dependent, Neglected, and Delinquent Children An act passed by the Illinois legislature in 1899 that created the first juvenile court.

actual enforcement Implementation of the law at a level that reflects such factors as civil liberties, discretion, resources, and community values.

actuarial justice The traditional orientation of juvenile justice, rehabilitation and individualized treatment, that has been supplanted by the goal of efficient offender processing.

actuarial prediction The forecast of future inmate behavior based on a class of offenders similar to those considered for parole. It uses the principles of group prediction found in the insurance industry for setting rates based on known group attributes, e.g., rates of death or accident involvement.

actuarial records Public records concerning the demographic characteristics of the population served by the recordkeeping agency.

ACT UP (AIDS Coalition to Unleash Power) An aggressive organization expressly formed to protest a perceived lack of government funding for AIDS research. Its members have used disruptive tactics and occasionally resorted to civil disobedience as a means of promoting their cause.

actus reus "Guilty deed" (Latin); one component of a crime; any overt act that accompanies the intent to commit a crime (e.g., pulling out a pistol in front of a convenience store clerk while robbing the store would be an *actus reus,* or overt act, and drawing plans of a bank floor layout while conspiring to rob the bank would be an overt act in furtherance of the criminal conspiracy).

ad alium diem "At another day" (Latin).

ADAM (Arrestee Drug Abuse Monitoring) An expanded and redesigned version of drug use forecasting (DUF), which was methodologically upgraded and expanded in 1998. It was fully implemented in 2000 using new sampling procedures to improve data generalizability. The original DUF program was initiated in 1987 and was intended to estimate drug use prevalence among adult male and female arrestees. An earlier sampling plan was based on self-reported drug use and considered nonrandom. ADAM is based on probability-based sampling. Its measuring instruments were improved to more accurately compile descriptive data from those surveyed.

adamsite Diphenylaminochlorarsine, or DM; an incapacitating gas with a rapid rate of action developed during World War II by Roger Adams, an American; also called sneeze gas.

ad curiam "At or to a court" (Latin).

Addams, Jane (1860–1935) Founded Hull House, a shelter for runaways and others who were in need of housing, food, and clothing, in Chicago in the 1890s.

addict Anyone with an overwhelming physical or psychological need to continue taking a particular substance or drug or performing a particular act, like gambling.

addiction Dependence on drugs, alcohol, or a certain habit; may be psychological or physiological dependence.

addiction-prone personality The basis of the view that substance abuse may be traced to a personality that has a compulsion for mood-altering drugs.

ad hoc **committee** "To this" (Latin); any group established to investigate or handle a particular matter.

ad hominem "To a man" (Latin); an argument against another person involving a personal attack rather than an argument on the merits of the different positions taken.

adipocere A fatty, soaplike substance that can form when human or animal bodies decompose in moist, oxygen-deprived environments; sometimes referred to as grave wax or corpse fat.

adjective law Part of a law that prescribes methods or procedures for carrying out the rights and obligations of persons.

adjournment The conclusion or termination of a session; postponement to another time and place.

adjudge To rule upon judicially; to grant through judicial process.

adjudicate To judge; to decide a case; to conclude a matter.

adjudication The legal resolution of a dispute (e.g., when a juvenile is declared delinquent or a status offender, the matter has been resolved; when an offender has been convicted or acquitted, the matter at issue [guilt or innocence] has been concluded by either a judge or jury).

adjudication hearing, adjudication inquiry A formal proceeding involving a prosecuting attorney and a defense attorney in which evidence is presented and a juvenile's status or condition is determined by the juvenile-court judge.

adjudication petition A formal written request or application to juvenile court to take judicial action on a certain matter, to determine whether or not a juvenile is delinquent, filed by parent, school official, police officer, intake officer, or any other interested party.

adjudication withheld A cessation of court proceedings pending some alternative action, such as diversion or alternative dispute resolution. Conditions are imposed and jurisdiction is maintained over a person subject to compliance with conditions for a specified duration, such as one year. In some cases, persons may be released on their own recognizance unconditionally.

adjudicatory hearing *See* **adjudication hearing, adjudication inquiry.**

adjustment A settlement or conclusion such that opposing parties are in agreement without an official court intervention.

adjustment centers The euphemism applied to segregation units in California during the rehabilitation era.

Adler, Freda (1934–) Author of *Sisters in Crime: The Rise of the New Female Criminals* (1975); former president of the American Society of Criminology.

Admax Administrative maximum; a term used to describe high-security prisons where only the most dangerous prisoners are housed.

administration of justice, administration of criminal justice Covers such areas as police management, criminal procedure, pretrial services, arraignment and trial, prosecution and defense, court organization, pleadings, sentencing, appeals, probation, and parole.

administrative component That part of an organization charged with coordinating, facilitating, and supporting the activities of the rest of the organizational participants.

administrative courts Special courts in Europe that preside over all cases in which government or officers of government are involved. They exist as a separate hierarchy and apply administrative law, and they are intended to protect citizen interests, providing speedy justice and countermanding administrative orders that lack statutory authority.

administrative facilities Institutions with special missions, including Metropolitan Correctional Centers, Federal Medical Centers, and U.S. penitentiaries. Administrative facilities are capable of holding inmates in all security categories.

administrative judge The judicial officer supervising administrative functions and tasks for a given court whose duties include assigning cases, establishing court policies and procedures, and formulating budgets and personnel policies.

administrative law The branch of public law dealing with the powers and duties of government agencies.

administrative model A sentencing scheme in which control over sentence length is vested with correctional officials.

Administrative Office of United States Courts The organization that hires federal probation officers to supervise federal offenders and prepare presentence investigation reports about offenders at the request of a district judge. It also supervises pretrial divertees.

administrative regulations Rules created by governmental agencies to implement specific public policies.

administrative segregation Residential units in prison that isolate prisoners from the general population for non-disciplinary reasons.

administrative sentencing Awards of good time, pardons, or clemency to inmates who demonstrate good conduct or perform services. Such awards are made by the executive branch rather than the judicial branch.

administrative services The unit in a police department assigned police–community relations tasks and the selection and training of police personnel.

administrative succession The degree of turnover among organizational administrators during a given time interval, such as a year or longer.

administrator, administratrix Respectively, a male or female authorized by a court to administer an estate.

admin max Maximum-security prison such as the federal penitentiary at Florence, CO, intended to hold only the worst prisoners, who pose the greatest danger to other inmates and who are considered flight risks.

admiralty, admiralty courts, admiralty law Tribunals originating in England centuries ago to handle maritime cases (those involving sailors, ships, and activities on the high seas) and maritime law (dealing with ocean vessels and their regulation and commerce).

admiralty jurisdiction Authority involving cases under maritime law, concerned with piracy, collisions, wartime captures, and torts on the high seas.

admissibility The status of a statement or evidence that permits it to be used in criminal proceedings against a criminal defendant.

admissible An evidentiary term designating testimony or physical evidence that may be presented to the finders of fact (juries or judges) in criminal proceedings. Restrictions and conditions are usually articulated in federal or state rules of evidence.

admission, civil or criminal Acknowledgement of a material fact well below the threshold of confession (e.g., admitting to being in an area does not constitute confessing to the crime committed there, but may nevertheless be material circumstantial evidence that builds a case in the absence of a confession); a confession; a concession as to the truthfulness of one or more facts, usually associated with a crime that has been committed. The term may also apply to tort actions.

admission, corrections The entry of an offender into the legal jurisdiction of a corrections agency or the physical custody of a correctional facility.

admit To plead guilty, acknowledge culpability, or accept the accuracy of the facts alleged in either an adult or a juvenile proceeding; also, to allow into evidence.

admonish A judicial warning or reprimand, usually directed at those before the court whose behaviors are disrespectful or otherwise unacceptable.

adolescence A diffuse age range from puberty to adulthood, generally 12 to 18 or 21 years of age.

adolescence limiteds Delinquents who begin their offending career in their late teens and soon desist from crime.

adolescent court Limited jurisdictional handling of juvenile delinquents by unofficial and informal means or sanctions, and characterized by an absence of record keeping and labeling.

adult Depending on the jurisdiction, anyone who has reached the age of majority and is subject to criminal court laws.

Adult Basic Education (ABE) An educational program that stresses literacy and mathematical skills as a foundation for further education and training, generally viewed as a feeder system for GED preparatory classes.

Adult Children of Alcoholic Parents (ACAP) Offspring of adults with alcoholic dependencies; a support group that seeks to understand psychological and other types of problems stemming from being reared in households where parents are alcoholics.

Adult Education Act of 1964 A federal act that provided funding for programs targeting adults with deficiencies in communication, computation, or social relations that substantially impair their employment chances.

adulteration The modification of evidence so as to render it useless or inadmissible in court; some type of contamination of evidence collected from crime scenes, where such contamination makes the evidence unacceptable or unanalyzable for court purposes.

adultery Consensual sexual intercourse between persons at least one of whom is married to another person.

adultification The process of transforming the juvenile court into a criminal court–like atmosphere created, in part, by a proliferation of constitutional safeguards extended to juveniles that also pertain to adults.

Adult Inmate Management System (AIMS) A system used by South Carolina prison officials and those in other jurisdictions for purposes of classifying prisoners into three basic aggressiveness levels, the alphas, betas, and gammas; also known as the Quay system.

ad valorem **tax** "According to value" (Latin); a surcharge on a percentage of an item's value, including sales taxes and real-estate taxes.

advance sheets Published opinions of the U.S. Supreme Court distributed by West Publishing Company within a few weeks after the opinions are rendered. A series of 22 to 24 short, paperback volumes during each term are distributed to subscribers and eventually bound into interim volumes known as the *Supreme Court Reporter*. Final versions of the *Supreme Court Reporter* are published within two years of the distribution of interim volumes to allow time for Supreme Court justices to correct errors and language in the opinions rendered.

adversarial justice, adversarial proceedings Opponent-driven court litigation in which one side opposes the other: the prosecution seeks to convict or find the defendant guilty, while the defense counsel seeks to defend its client and obtain acquittal.

adversary One's opponent in the courtroom; the opposing party in a legal dispute.

adversary system of justice, procedure, process A legal system involving a contest between two opposing parties under a judge who is an impartial arbiter.

advertising, legal An American Bar Association ethical rule governing advertising for business by licensed attorneys, which was generally prohibited until 1977, when the U.S. Supreme Court declared that such a ban violated the free speech provisions of the First Amendment. It is presently common practice for attorneys to solicit business through various media forms, including television and newspaper advertising.

advisement training A preliminary protective or temporary custody hearing in which a court reviews the facts, determines whether removal of a child is justified, and notifies parents of the charges against them.

advisory board A panel of citizens, judges, or other public officials who act as advisers to the judiciary or some other agency in setting general policies or in determining aspects of services and administration.

Advisory Commission on Intergovernmental Affairs (ACIR) Created in 1959 by Congress, ACIR is a national bipartisan body that represents executive and legislative branches of federal, state, and local governments and the public. It attempts to mediate among federal, state, and local areas of potential friction. Publishes the quarterly magazine *Intergovernmental Perspective*.

advocate A proponent of some cause or issue. In law, any attorney who acts on behalf of a client.

affective violence Violence that is the result of highly charged emotions (e.g., someone who reacts violently to insults from another following excessive drinking).

affiance An agreement between parties wherein mutual expectations are articulated and observed.

affiant A person who makes an affidavit.

affidavit A statement in writing given under oath before someone who is authorized to administer an oath.

affirm The act of validating an earlier decision or ruling. When an appellate court affirms a decision by a lower court, that decision stands, unless a higher court overrules the appellate body.

affirmance A pronouncement by a higher court that a lower court decision on a specific matter was correctly decided. *See also* **stare decisis**.

affirmation In courts, an oath, or declaration in place of an oath for those whose religious beliefs prohibit oaths, to tell the truth and nothing but the truth when giving testimony.

affirmative action A formal program to correct previous discriminatory hiring practices through aggressive recruitment and promotion of previously disadvantaged groups.

affirmative defense A response to a criminal charge in which the defendant bears the burden of proof (e.g., automatism, intoxication, coercion, duress, mistake). It goes beyond simple denial of facts and gives new facts in favor of the defendant, if facts in the original complaint are true.

affray Any impromptu altercation or fight between two or more persons in public, where such a fight draws attention and results in disturbing the peace.

AFIS Automated Fingerprint Identification System.

aftercare A general term to describe a wide variety of programs and services available to both adult and juvenile parolees, including halfway houses, psychological counseling services, community-based correctional agencies, employment assistance, and medical treatment for offenders or ex-offenders.

agar, agar composition In forensics, a material used to make plaster casts of footprints or other tangible evidence at crime scenes.

age A legal factor in determining one's status as either a juvenile or an adult; the common-law presumption that infants under the age of 7 are presumed incapable of formulating criminal intent. Various jurisdictions have adopted other criteria to determine one's culpability for various types of offenses at different ages.

age composition of the population The breakdown of an entire population into age-specific categories. In criminological and corrections research, this is an important variable in the prediction of crime rates or incarceration rates, as younger groups are at greater risk.

Age Discrimination in Employment Act of 1967 A federal statute prohibiting discrimination in hiring, discharging, or promoting any employee over the age of 40. An employer may hire, discharge, or promote older employees based on age only if actual job qualifications are age-related.

age-graded theory A life-course theory positing that delinquency, deviance, or criminality develop early in the lives of adult criminals as a part of their cognitive development. Associated with the work of Robert Sampson and John Laub in *Crime in the Making* (1993).

agency theory The notion that subordinates act at the wishes and on the authority of others at their direction, and if subordinates commit offenses, the ultimate liability rests with their superiors.

agent Any individual, usually with legal expertise, who acts on behalf of another (called a principal); any officer of various federal and state law enforcement agencies, civil or criminal, who is empowered to enforce the laws of these agencies.

agent provocateur A spy or secret agent, usually in the employ of a government, who conducts surveillance of a group or organization; an undercover person, either a police officer or someone working on behalf of the police, who infiltrates a group for the purpose of learning about the group's illegal activities.

age of consent The age at which youths are legally adults and may be independent of parental control. When an adolescent reaches the age of consent, he or she may engage in sexual behaviors prohibited to youths.

age of majority The chronological age at which one reaches adulthood, usually either 18 or 21; when juveniles are no longer under the jurisdiction of the juvenile courts but rather, the criminal courts; also, the age of consent.

age of maximum criminality Based on criminal statistics, a particular age or age range during which persons are most likely to get into trouble with the law and commit delinquent acts or crimes. Property crimes are most likely committed by persons age 16 to 20, whereas older persons are more likely to engage in robbery or aggravated assault.

age of onset The age at which youths begin their delinquent careers. Early onset is believed to be linked with chronic offending patterns.

age-specific arrest rate The number of arrests per 100,000 persons in a given age category.

agglutinin Used in blood typing, an antibody substance in blood that causes clumping of blood cells or bacteria in a type of liquid suspension.

aggravated assault An unlawful attack by one person on another for the purpose of inflicting severe bodily injury, or the attempt or threat thereof.

aggravating circumstances Elements of a crime that may intensify the severity of punishment, including bodily injury, death to the victim, or the brutality of the act. *See box.*

Aggravating Circumstances

1. The crime involved death or serious bodily injury to one or more victims.
2. The crime was committed while the offender was out on bail facing other criminal charges.
3. The offender was on probation, parole, or work release at the time the crime was committed.
4. The offender was a recidivist and had committed several previous offenses for which he or she had been punished.
5. The offender was the leader in the commission of the offense involving two or more offenders.
6. The offense involved more than one victim and/or was a violent or nonviolent crime.
7. The offender treated the victim(s) with extreme cruelty during the commission of the offense.
8. The offender used a dangerous weapon in the commission of the crime and the risk to human life was high.

---

aggravation Any circumstance that enhances the penalties for a crime or makes the resolution of a conflict more difficult.

aggregate Persons who are in the same place at the same time but who have no sense of common identity or close interaction, or a portion of the population sharing similar characteristics and who do not necessarily have to be in a given place at the same time; may also refer to statistical populations.

aggregate data Information collected by agencies on how many crimes or dispositions they process. No individual-level data are collected, only summary statistics and counts.

aggression Any intentional act designed to bring harm to another.

aggressive patrol A police patrol strategy designed to maximize the number of police interventions and observations in the community.

aggressive preventive patrol Any police patrol technique designed to prevent crime before it occurs.

AGILE Program A National Institute of Justice program whose mission is to assist state and local law enforcement agencies to effectively and efficiently communicate with one another across agency and jurisdictional boundaries. It is dedicated to studying interoperability options and making valuable information available to law enforcement, firefighters, and emergency technicians in different jurisdictions across the country. It also helps to facilitate emergency communications among agencies by identifying, adopting, and developing interoperability solutions that include open architectural standards for voice, data, image, and video communication systems, thus allowing multiple parties to exchange information on the spot.

aging-out phenomenon, aging-out process The notion that criminals either diminish or discontinue their criminal conduct as they grow older through maturation, religious conversion, marriage, taking on more life responsibilities, or growing older, thus committing fewer crimes because of less energy and interest. James Q. Wilson and Richard Herrnstein have argued that an aging-out process is responsible for the decline of crime among persons as they grow older.

Agnew, Robert (1953–) A sociologist who has examined general strain theory (GST), which holds that crime results from negative affective states, in order to account for criminal behavior (1992).

agnomen Nickname or alias.

aiding and abetting Assisting in or otherwise furthering the commission of a crime.

aid panel Primarily found in New South Wales, Australia, a group consisting of a police officer, a solicitor, community members, and young persons who work with the court in identifying opportunities for youthful offenders.

AIDS (Acquired Immune Deficiency Syndrome) A condition in which the body's immune system is unable to fight illness and disease, making sufferers susceptible to a host of infections that otherwise do not affect healthy people. It is caused by the Human Immunodeficiency Virus (HIV), which is spread through exchange of certain bodily fluids.

AIDS Clearinghouse, National Institute of Justice Established in 1987, this organization collects, processes, and disseminates information about how AIDS is distributed or transmitted and affects criminal justice agencies.

Aid to Incarcerated Mothers (AIM) An organization formed in Massachusetts in 1980 to meet female offender needs by providing substance-abuse counseling, parenting courses, and parent-child relations.

AIMS (Adult Internal Management System) A self-administered questionnaire given to prison inmates to determine their psychological and emotional states.

air piracy The illegal commandeering of an aircraft by force or threat of force; sometimes known as skyjacking.

Airport Security Council (ASC) An organization, formed in 1968, responsible for development and administration of air cargo loss prevention. It includes anti-theft programming in various airports known for high incidence of cargo thefts.

ajuration An oath taken to forsake the realm forever, which was taken by an accused person who claimed sanctuary (circa 1400s).

AKA "Also known as"; a legal reference to an alias a criminal defendant might use instead of his or her real name.

Akers, Ronald (1939–) The sociologist and criminologist who wrote *Deviant Behavior: A Social Learning Approach* (1973, 1977), among other substantial writings; former president of the American Sociological Association; advocate of differential reinforcement theory, a revision of Edwin Sutherland's work on differential association theory.

AK-47 A Soviet-made, fully automatic assault rifle capable of discharging a large number of bullets rapidly that is widely used throughout the world in combat.

Al-Anon A support group for families and friends of alcoholics.

alarm A device that emits a sound or signal intended to alert someone in a building or automobile to some violation or intrusion.

alarm, class A A fire-protection provision requiring alarm operation even if power to the alarm is interrupted or terminated.

alarm, class B A fire-protection provision requiring detection of any break in a connection or line signal.

alarm station A device manually activated and installed at a location to give an alarm signal in response to an emergency such as a holdup at a bank. It may be connected to a local police department or a centrally located alarm company for rapid response.

alarm system Any electronic apparatus designed to alert persons that there are intruders or that an emergency exists that must be addressed.

Alaska Judicial Council The public council that evaluates judicial sentencing practices and assesses all matters pertinent to the Alaska judiciary.

Alateen A program for teenagers affected by alcoholic family members and friends; the teen counterpart to Al-Anon.

Albastone Material used for casting footprints or other indentations instead of plaster of Paris.

Alcatraz The island site of a former federal penitentiary in the San Francisco Bay area of California famous for inmates such as Al Capone, George "Machine Gun" Kelly, Alvin Karpis, and Robert "The Birdman" Stroud; a maximum-security facility that operated from 1934 to 1963, and subsequently reopened in 1973 as a tourist attraction.

alcohol Fermented or distilled liquids containing ethanol, an intoxicating substance.

Alcoholics Anonymous (AA) A voluntary organization founded in 1935 whose membership consists of people who are either addicted to alcohol or wish to avoid becoming addicted to alcohol. Groups meet informally and discuss family, personal, and social problems that contribute to alcohol abuse, and ways of overcoming such problems. AA employs a 12-step program with social support to avoid alcohol on a day-to-day basis. It is occasionally used in conjunction with state sanctions for individuals convicted of driving while intoxicated.

alcoholism A chronic, progressive, treatable disease of alcohol dependency or addiction with a high relapse rate.

Alford plea A *nolo contendere* plea whereby defendants plead "no contest" to the factual scenario as outlined in the charges; it originated with the case of *North Carolina v. Alford* (1970), in which a defendant did not wish to admit guilt, but entered a *nolo contendere plea,* admitting to certain facts as specified by the prosecution.

algolagnia Sexual pleasure derived from anticipated or actual infliction of pain on another; sadomasochism.

alias Any name by which someone is known other than his or her legal name on public documents. An alias is used to change identity for various purposes, legal or otherwise.

alias dictus "Otherwise called" (Latin).

alibi A defense to a criminal allegation that places an accused individual at some place other than the crime scene at the time the crime occurred.

alien One who is not a citizen or legal resident of a particular country.

alienate To transfer property or a right from one person to another.

alienation A social psychological state wherein a person feels varying levels of powerlessness, normlessness, self-estrangement, and meaninglessness; psychological detachment from society or other persons; a negative feeling toward someone, usually a person in authority. Some citizens may feel estranged from the police officers who patrol their neighborhoods and regulate their conduct.

alienative involvement One type of participation in Amitai Etzioni's compliance-involvement typology, which suggests that persons who are forced or coerced into doing something will become resentful and object to becoming involved, leading to poor work performance, low job satisfaction, and less organizational loyalty.

alien conspiracy theory The idea that organized crime was imported by Europeans and that criminal organizations limit their membership to people of their own ethnic background.

Alien Documentation, Identification, and Telecommunications (ADIT) A computer system operated by the Immigration and Naturalization Service.

alimony Financial support awarded to a party in a divorce action that is paid by the former partner. A variant, "palimony," refers to comparable support paid by one formerly cohabitating, but unmarried, partner to the other.

allegation An assertion or claim made by a party to a legal action.

allege To aver, assert, or claim. Usually, a prosecutor alleges certain facts in developing a case against a criminal defendant.

Allegheny Academy A Pennsylvania probation program with the general aim of changing the negative behavior of offenders that targets those juvenile offenders who have failed in other, traditional probation programs in Pennsylvania.

Allen charge Additional jury instructions from a judge when a jury is having difficulty reaching a verdict. It is not permitted in some state jurisdictions.

alley A highway or roadway no more than 25 feet wide that is used almost exclusively for rear or side entry to buildings or abutting property.

allocution The right of convicted offenders to address the court personally prior to the imposition of sentences.

Almighty Latin King Nation (ALKN) A gang formed by largely Hispanic inmates from Rikers Island in New York City in the mid-1970s, closely affiliated with the Latin Kings and considered one of the fastest-growing gangs in New York. Their colors are black and gold, and colored clothing is worn at funerals and other events. They actively recruit members from age 8 up, recruiting in schools. The gang operates according to a constitution which has 10 commandments, and its leadership is headed by a High Holy Inca, a Supreme Cacique, and a Royal Crown. Members also include warlords and enforcers. The gang is characterized by violent behavior, drug and weapons trafficking, and protection. Its common prayer is "Almighty Father, King of Kings, hear us as we come before you, one body, mind, and soul, true wisdom, knowledge and understanding. Give us strong brown wisdom, for we realize you are the best and wisest of all seeing eyes."

alpha A statistical concept in criminological research that represents the probability that a person will reoffend, which has been used in research about the deterrent effects of various legal punishments.

alpha code Authorized words standing for alphabet letters in an internationally recognized code: Alpha, Bravo, Charlie, Delta, Echo, Foxtrot, Gold, Hotel, India, Juliet, Kilo, Lima, Mike, November, Oscar, Papa, Quebec, Romeo, Sierra, Tango, Uniform, Victor, Whisky, X-ray, Yankee, and Zulu.

al Qaeda A Middle Eastern terrorist organization headed by Osama bin Laden. Al Qaeda is believed to be behind the September 11, 2001, World Trade Center towers' destruction and the air attack on the Pentagon on the same date. Its goals include driving the United States from Middle Eastern soil through terrorist acts.

Alston Wilkes Society A private organization, founded in 1962 in memory of a late Methodist minister, that assists prison inmates being paroled with their reintegration into mainstream society.

altercation A dispute between two or more parties that usually escalates into physical violence.

alter ego rule Canon of law holding that some persons can defend a third party only under certain circumstances and only to the degree that the third party can act in his or her own defense.

alternative care cases Borderline cases in which judges may sentence offenders to either incarceration or probation subject to compliance with various conditions.

alternative dispute resolution (ADR) A procedure whereby a criminal case is redefined as a civil one and the case is decided by an impartial arbiter, where both parties agree to amicable settlement. Usually reserved for minor offenses.

alternative facility An alternative place of limited confinement, such as a treatment center for drug-dependent offenders.

alternative sanctions The group of punishments falling between probation and prison; community-based sanctions, including house arrest and intensive supervision, that serve as an alternative to incarceration.

alternative sentencing When a judge imposes a sentence other than incarceration, often involving good works such as community service, restitution to victims, and other public-service activity. *See also* **creative sentencing.**

Alternative Work Sentencing Program (EARN-IT) A Massachusetts program that brings together a juvenile and his or her crime victim to develop an equitable work program to provide restitution to the victim.

alternative writ A request granted on *ex parte* affidavits that requires a person to perform a specific act or show cause for not doing so.

altruism Any behavior intended to benefit someone else; an unselfish act.

Alveolar Air Breath Alcohol System A device to test the breath of suspects stopped for driving under the influence to ascertain their blood-alcohol ratio.

AMA *See* **American Medical Association (AMA).**

AMBER Alert, AMBER Plan (America's Missing Broadcast Emergency Response) A voluntary partnership between law enforcement agencies and news broadcasters to activate an urgent bulletin in the most serious child-abduction cases with the hope that ordinary citizens will be able to aid in the search for abducted children. Also known as the AMBER Plan, the program was named for 9-year-old Amber Hagerman, who was kidnapped in 1996 and brutally murdered in Arlington, TX. The Dallas–Ft.Worth Association of Radio Managers (ARMS) developed an innovative emergency alert plan to help recover abducted children. The plan was eventually adopted by law enforcement agencies across the United States. The AMBER Alert not only helps to recover abducted children but also acts as a deterrent to this type of crime. Working in partnership with the AMBER Alert is the National Center for Missing and Exploited Children. On April 30, 2003, President George W. Bush signed into law a national AMBER Plan, which has been adopted by most states.

ambisexual Bisexual.

ambush A surprise attack perpetrated by someone unseen by the victim prior to the attack; lying in wait.

amenability issue The possibility that certain kinds of offenders are amenable or suited to a particular type of treatment.

amendment A modification, addition, or deletion; also, a change to the U.S. Constitution setting forth one or more rights.

amentia Insanity.

amercement A fine or other monetary penalty.

Amer-I-Can A project commenced in the 1990s by actor/sportsman James Brown. Brown and his associates function as intermediaries between rival gang members in South Central Los Angeles and attempt to repair interpersonal differences and minimize violence such as drive-by shootings.

American Academy for Professional Law Enforcement An organization established in 1973 to develop educational programs for law enforcement personnel and to establish and promulgate ethical and professional standards.

American Academy of Forensic Sciences (AAFS) An organization of physicians, criminalists, toxicologists, attorneys, document examiners, and others interested in forensic sciences headquartered in Colorado Springs, CO. Publishes the *Journal of Forensic Sciences.*

American Academy of Judicial Education Established by the American Judges Association to provide educational programs and services to state court judges.

American Association of Wardens and Superintendents Correctional administrators organized on a national level and providing survey information, consultation, and assistance to any correctional organization requesting such help.

American Bar Association (ABA) A professional organization of more than 400,000 lawyers headquartered in Chicago, IL. The ABA offers a variety of services, including law school accreditation, continuing legal education, and other programs designed to assist lawyers, judges, and other members of the legal profession.

American Bar Foundation (ABF) The funding and research arm of the American Bar Association, headquartered in Chicago, IL, and staffed by full-time employees and several visiting fellows. The ABF maintains a close working relationship with Northwestern University and the University of Chicago.

American Civil Liberties Union (ACLU) An organization founded in 1920 dedicated to guaranteeing civil rights of persons charged with crimes or persons who have been wronged, often by a government agency.

American common law Derived from English common law, and based on precedents established in particular localities; a body of unwritten law whereby persons' actions are regulated by prevailing custom. No common law exists at the federal level.

American Correctional Association (ACA) An association established in 1870 to disseminate information about correctional programs and training designed to foster professionalism throughout correctional communities.

American Criminal Justice Association (ACJA) An organization established in 1963 dedicated to promoting greater understanding of criminal and delinquent behavior and the criminal- and juvenile-justice systems. The international membership meets annually and exchanges ideas about criminal behaviors and processing offenders. Headquartered in Greenbelt, MD, it publishes *Justice Quarterly* and the *Journal of Criminal Justice Education.*

American District Telegraph Company (ADT) A burglar alarm company that offers various electronic protection devices to businesses and homes throughout the United States.

"American Dream" Describes the goal of accumulating material wealth under conditions of open competition. A "success at all costs" ethos causes those without the means to achieve goals to adopt criminal or deviant options to acquire wealth. The term is described by Steven Messner and Richard Rosenfeld (1993), although its origin in sociological theory occurred much earlier in the work of Ely Chinoy, author of *Automobile Workers and the American Dream* (1965).

American Federation of Labor (AFL) Samuel Gompers founded the AFL in 1886 as a labor union to represent skilled trades. It merged with the Congress of Industrial Organizations (CIO) in 1955.

American Federation of Labor–Congress of Industrial Organizations (AFL-CIO) Created in 1955 by the merger of the American Federation of Labor and the Congress of Industrial Organizations, the AFL-CIO represents the interests of labor union members.

American Federation of Police, Inc. An association of local, county, state, and federal law enforcement officers, including private security officers, established in 1966 to provide information and training services.

American Humane Association An organization established in 1876 committed to providing information, advice, and training to prevent both animal and child abuse.

American Indian Movement (AIM) Founded in Minneapolis in 1968 by Native Americans seeking to change the purpose and attitude of the Bureau of Indian Affairs toward Indians not living on reservations. The AIM seeks to deter or prevent discrimination by law enforcement personnel against Native American citizens.

American Institute for Research Established in 1946, the Institute emphasizes personnel development and training, selection and recruitment, and dissemination of factual information pertaining to law enforcement education.

American Jail Association (AJA) A national organization that supports those who operate and work in jails; headquartered in Hagerstown, MD. Publishes *American Jails.*

American Jails A journal published by the American Jail Association that deals with prison and jail issues.

American Judicature Society Established in 1913, the aim of this society is to improve administration of justice and court effectiveness.

American Justice Institute Established in 1959, its goals are to further the equality of treatment among minorities by law enforcement personnel.

American Law Enforcement Officers Association Established in 1976, this association includes law enforcement personnel of all ranks, and is dedicated to providing leadership and planning in cooperative programs among police, prosecutors, the courts, and corrections.

American Law Institute (ALI) An organization of lawyers and legal scholars whose purpose is to promote the clarification and simplification of the law. Established in 1923, the ALI has an elected membership of 3,000 lawyers, judges, and law professors, and has attempted to define the law by establishing a model penal code for professionals and laypersons.

American Medical Association (AMA) A national organization of physicians seeking to establish standards for improved health care and dispensing of medication.

American Municipal Association An organization of state leagues of municipalities that provides consultation services for those involved in municipal government.

American Outlaws Association An organized group of motorcyclists whose activities center on several types of criminal enterprises. Organized in 1935 in McCook, IL, the club stayed together during World War II and in 1950 changed its name to the Chicago Outlaws, as its headquarters had moved to that city. The club's logo consisted of a small skull with a winged motorcycle and Old English–style letters. The designs were embroidered on black shirts and hand-painted on leather jackets for members. The gang went national in 1964 and became known as the American Outlaws Association, with a logo of a skull and crossed pistons.

American Police Association (APA) A private nonprofit professional organization for law enforcement officers of all ranks that promotes professionalism and ethical standards.

American Prison Association (APA) An early name given to the American Correctional Association.

American Probation and Parole Association (APPA) A professional association for probation, parole, and community corrections workers. The APPA disseminates information about probation, parole, and community corrections to its members; provides technical assistance to community corrections agencies and governing bodies; conducts training; establishes and monitors professional standards; and provides a forum for a broad range of correctional issues and controversies. It is headquartered in Lexington, KY, and publishes *APPA Perspectives.*

American Psychological Association (APA) A scientific society of persons interested in psychology and psychiatry. Founded in 1892, its purpose is to advance psychology as a science and promote human welfare.

American Radio Relay League A privately organized group of amateur radio operators, or "hams," who occasionally assist police officers during emergencies when normal communications channels have been disrupted.

Americans for Effective Law Enforcement (AELE) Established in 1966, the AELE provides research and other forms of assistance relating to civil liability issues for law enforcement agency personnel and administrators.

American Society for Industrial Security (ASIS) An international organization of security professionals headquartered in Alexandria, VA, that works to increase the effectiveness of security through educational programs and materials. Publishes the magazine *Security Management.*

American Society of Criminology An international professional society of criminology founded in 1941 to enhance the status of the discipline.

Americans With Disabilities Act (ADA) A 1990 act that made it illegal to discriminate against persons with disabilities. These individuals are entitled to equal access to employment, including the processes of recruitment, hiring, promotion, and any other benefits and privileges of employment.

amicus curiae "A friend of the court" (Latin); a person allowed to appear in court or file a brief even though the person has no right to participate in the litigation otherwise. Persons may initiate petitions on behalf of others, perhaps for someone who is in prison. Such *amicus* briefs are designed to present legal arguments or facts on behalf of someone else.

amicus curiae **brief** A document filed by *amicus curiae* on behalf of one of the parties.

ammunition Cartridges, consisting of bullets, casings, and propellants, that can be used in firearms.

amnesia Partial or total loss of memory, often arising as the result of trauma to the brain.

Amnesty International An organization concerned with human rights and abuses that opposes capital punishment and carries on campaigns to reduce or abolish it.

amotivational syndrome A depiction of police officers who suffer from burnout, fatigue, and stress.

amphetamine/methamphetamine A synthetic drug consisting of Benzedrine sulfate, designed to stimulate the central nervous system; sometimes referred to as an "upper."

Amsterdam Workhouse An early Dutch workhouse for inmates.

anabolic steroids Drugs used by athletes and bodybuilders to enhance their muscle bulk and strength.

anamnestic prediction A method of forecasting one's likelihood of reoffending by considering circumstances prior to one's conviction and the circumstances of one's environment if paroled. If circumstances have changed favorably, then the offender will likely be paroled.

anarchism A political ideology in which overthrowing the government is advocated.

anarchist Someone who advocates the overthrow of any legitimized government or who promotes the idea of a lack of government.

anarchist ideology of punishment The beliefs that modern society is based on structured power relationships, that deviance is a product of fitting human relationships into hierarchical rules, and that the current punishment system preserves the power system while reducing human capacity for cooperation.

anarchy, criminal Advocacy of the overthrow of a government through the assassination of that government's leaders.

Anderson, Elijah (1943–) A social critic and sociologist who wrote about the siege mentality in *Streetwise: Race, Class and Change in an Urban Community* (1990).

androgen The principal male sex hormone.

androgynous A term that refers to persons who possess both male and female personality and/or sexual traits or characteristics.

anesthetic drugs Central nervous system depressants.

angel dust *See* **phencyclidine (PCP).**

angel of death A type of serial killer; usually someone who works in a medical profession such as a nurse, nurse's aide, or even a physician, who believes that he or she is relieving his or her victims of their pain and suffering by administering a lethal dose of a drug to end their lives prematurely.

anger rape Rape prompted by a rapist's desire to release pent-up anger and rage.

Animal Liberation Front (ALF) Headquartered in Memphis, TN, this organization carries out direct action against animal abuse in the form of rescuing animals and causing financial loss to animal exploiters, usually through damage and destruction of property. It consists of small, autonomous groups of people around the world who carry out direct action according to ALF guidelines: (1) to liberate animals from places of abuse (e.g., laboratories, factory farms); (2) to inflict economic damage on those who profit from the misery and exploitation of animals; (3) to reveal the horror and atrocities committed against animals behind locked doors by performing nonviolent direct actions and liberations; and (4) to take all necessary precautions against harming any animal, human or nonhuman. Any group of people who are vegetarians or vegans and who carry out actions according to ALF guidelines have the right to regard themselves as part of the ALF.

Animal Liberation Front Supporters Group (ALFSG) A group that supports the work of the Animal Liberation Front (ALF) by all lawful means possible, including supporting imprisoned activists, supporting and defending the ALF, educating the public as to the need and rationale of direct action, providing a communication forum through the *Supporters Group* newsletter, and raising funds for the group's activities. The North American organization is called the North American ALF Supporters Group.

animus "Will" (Latin); intention or motivation.

animus furandi "Intent to steal" (Latin); the intent to steal property or otherwise deprive the owner of it.

annoying calls Telephone calls made for the purpose of threatening, harassing, intimidating, or otherwise disturbing someone; may be called crank calls, prank calls, or obscene calls.

annulment The act of canceling or voiding a contract.

anomalies, physical Cesare Lombroso's identifying characteristics of criminal behavior, including peculiar shapes of various body parts, such as sloping foreheads, long earlobes, the proximity of one's eyes relative to one another, and other unusual features that he presumed to be associated with criminal behavior.

anomalous plea A court plea containing both positive and negative statements and arguments.

anomie, anomie theory Robert Merton's theory, influenced by Emile Durkheim, alleging that persons acquire desires for culturally approved goals, but adopt innovative, sometimes deviant, means to achieve these goals (e.g., someone may desire a nice home but lack or reject the institutionalized means to achieve this goal, instead using bank robbery, an innovative mean, to obtain money to realize the culturally approved goal); implies normlessness.

anonymity Concealed or not directly visible; disguising one's identity to minimize identification.

anorexia nervosa An eating disorder typified by the inability to consume sufficient nourishment; the perception of oneself as being overweight or unattractive physically; deliberately refraining from eating food to sustain oneself, thereby losing weight. Extreme cases may result in death from malnutrition.

anoxia The deprivation of oxygen from the body by some means. Significant brain damage occurs and death may result if anoxia persists or is prolonged.

answer A written response in relation to a filed complaint prepared by a litigant or defendant.

Antabuse therapy A method of treatment for alcohol users and addicts that employs a safe drug, disulfiram, which causes nausea and vomiting whenever alcohol is consumed.

Antebellum Plantation Model A farm organized in the manner of pre–Civil War plantations used as a model of prison design.

antecedent Prior to or preceding.

ante mortem "Before death" (Latin); occurring before death.

anthrax An acute infectious disease caused by the spore-forming bacterium *Bacillus anthracis*. Anthrax most commonly occurs in wild and domestic cattle, sheep, goats, camels, and antelopes, but it can occur in humans who are exposed to infected animals or to tissue from infected animals. It is not contagious. Spores can live in soil for many years, and can be spread by eating undercooked meat from infected animals. Types include cutaneous (skin), inhalation, and gastrointestinal. Spores can be used as a bioterrorist weapon that can be spread through the mail in a powdery form that can be inhaled. The fatality rate can be as high as 75 percent without appropriate antibiotic treatment.

anthropology The scientific study of humans and their development; the study of the history of human development, including natural history and physical evolution.

anthropometry The scientific study of body measurements for comparative purposes. *See also* **Bertillon identification.**

anthropophagy Cannibalism.

anticipatory socialization A reference group theory term referring to the tendency of some individuals to internalize the values and norms of a group or category to which they do not yet belong but with which they wish to be identified or to join.

Anti-Defamation League (ADL) A national organization committed to exposing and fighting anti-Semitism and other forms of hatred and bigotry, including white supremacism and Holocaust denial.

antidote Any substance that counters the influence or effects of a poison or other toxic substance.

anti-lynch bills Formal legislative actions designed to prevent lynchings of persons belonging to specific minority groups, such as blacks.

antipsychotic drugs Any drug, such as Thorazine, used to relieve or control the symptoms of delusions and hallucinations, but that does not cure psychiatric disorders.

Antiracketeering Act A 1934 law making it a crime to interfere with interstate commerce. It was especially aimed at organized crime in which large criminal organizations can create work stoppages and other forms of interference for extortion purposes.

antisocial behavior Behavior that does not conform to a society's standards of decency or acceptability.

antisocial personality disorder A condition characterized by callousness, impulsiveness, lack of loyalty, and a chronic indifference to and violation of the rights of others.

Antiterrorism and Effective Death Penalty Act of 1996 An act limiting death-penalty claims of sentenced inmates. It created standards for judging the granting of *habeas corpus* relief to death-row inmates, restricted the filing of successive *habeas corpus* petitions, and required dismissals of claims previously raised in prior petitions. *See Felker v. Turpin* (1996).

antitrust actions, antitrust cases Any cases designed to prevent large organizations from monopolizing particular industries.

antitrust laws Federal and state statutes designed to prevent price fixing and monopoly control.

AOD Alcohol and other drugs.

Apalachin Meeting A 1957 meeting of organized crime bosses from around the United States. Law enforcement authorities raided the estate where the meeting occurred and arrested numerous mob bosses. Subsequent evidence disclosed the existence of a Mafia, or an organized crime family. Sometimes referred to simply as Apalachin, NY.

apathy A sense of uncaring; lack of feeling about an issue or a person.

APB (All Points Bulletin) An announcement, usually issued by a law enforcement agency and broadcast to all other law enforcement agencies throughout a wide jurisdiction, to be on the lookout for specific persons, including suspected criminals or missing persons, or to advise of a law enforcement emergency.

aphrodisiac Any chemical substance designed to stimulate one's sexual interest or capability.

apocrypha Any writings or statements of doubtful authenticity or authorship.

apparent danger In a self-defense response to alleged criminal activity, the defendant can use this type of danger to justify self-preservation. The danger must be obvious, manifest, and clear.

appeal, appeal proceedings Any request by the defense or prosecution directed to a higher court to contest a decision or judgment by a lower court.

appeal bond The money or surety posted by one who requests a hearing before a higher court on a lower-court decision. The money or surety is provided to defray the costs of failed appeals.

appeal case A cause of action filed in appeals court for review following an original judgment or decision from a lower trial court.

appeal proceedings Steps whereby an appellate court hears a case from a lower court and makes a decision on the basis of facts presented in oral arguments.

appeals court Any court higher than the court of original jurisdiction where a case commences. Appeals are directed to appeals court for various purposes, usually to request reconsideration of the verdicts rendered.

appeal to higher loyalties A technique of neutralization that justifies a violation of the law by the demands of a group that is smaller than the whole society and that requires of its members conformity to standards that may be incompatible with the law.

appearance The act of coming into a court and submitting to the authority of that court.

appellant The person who initiates an appeal.

appellate court, judge A court hearing appeals emanating from lower courts. These courts typically do not try criminal cases.

appellate jurisdiction Authority to rehear cases from lower courts and alter, uphold, or overturn lower-court decisions.

appellate process The process that allows a convicted offender to have a case brought before a higher court for review.

appellate review A comprehensive rehearing of a case in a court other than that in which it was previously tried.

appellee The party who prevailed in lower court who argues on appeal against reversing the lower court's decision.

appointed counsel A private attorney appointed by the court to represent an indigent defendant; may be a public defender.

appointment on merit Promotion in organizations according to one's expertise and accomplishments, rather than on the basis of whom one knows.

appointment system A system used in employee hiring in which a pool of applicants meeting certain minimum requirements is developed but no examination is mandated. Agency administrators interview qualified candidates and select whomever they please from this group.

appose To examine an organization's business officer, especially when embezzlement is suspected.

apprehend To take into custody or arrest someone suspected of a crime; also, to understand or perceive.

apprenticeship Binding out a child to serve time with a master craftsman, either learning a trade or, in the case of involuntary apprenticeship, working as a servant or field hand.

Appriss Data Network (ADN) The nation's largest privately managed integrated criminal-justice information network, linking 1,400 criminal-justice agencies in 36 states and covering 58 percent of the nation's state and local inmate population. The ADN collects offender information in near–real time from hundreds of different jail and court management systems across the country, and receives, processes, and stores information for VINE (Victim Information and Notification Everyday) users. Headquartered in Louisville, KY, the ADN processes more than 13 million records a month.

approver Someone who confesses to a crime while simultaneously incriminating others as a way of minimizing his or her own culpability or fault.

appurtenance A right attached to something else, such as a right-of-way, as an accessory or adjunct.

aquaeroticism Sexual gratification derived from submersing one's head or body into water to produce a sensation of losing consciousness during orgasm.

arbitrage In business, the term may refer to the simultaneous purchase and sale of the same or equivalent commodity, contract, insurance, or foreign exchange on the same or different markets in order to profit from price discrepancies; also, subject to decision by arbitration.

arbitration A process through which labor-management disputes can be resolved, involving third-party arbiters who can decide disputes. Under binding arbitration, both sides are legally bound to accept the arbitrator's decision. Otherwise, the process may be a recommendation without legal force. Arbitration is sometimes used to resolve appeals over disciplinary matters.

arbitrator A third party who intervenes, conducts meetings between opposing parties, and decides unresolved issues or disputes.

arch A segment of a human fingerprint.

archives Public papers and/or records; records or documents preserved as evidence.

area, delinquency A city area marked as having a high delinquency rate compared with other geographical city areas.

area, metropolitan A geographical region that includes a large population concentration and where economic and social life is influenced largely by the central city.

argot A special language, vocabulary, or slang unique to a particular group, such as prison or jail inmates.

ARIMA (Autoregressive Integrated Moving Averages) A statistical technique for forecasting trends in data.

aristocracy The highest social classes, including a nation's governing or ruling classes.

Arkansas prison scandal The notorious illegal exploitation of inmates in the Tucker, AK, prison farm during the 1960s and 1970s. Prisoners were forced to work for private enterprises outside of the prison, and profits were paid to prison administrators. Prisoners were tortured with electrodes attached to their penises, nipples, or testicles and to an old crank-type telephone (the "Tucker Telephone") if they violated prison rules. These electrical shocks were sometimes fatal. Torture, malnutrition, starvation, and exploitation were eliminated with the entry of a new warden, Thomas O. Murton, who fired abusive officers and made living conditions at the Tucker prison farm more humane. Murton himself was later fired by the governor for uncovering the scandal and making it public.

armed robbery A theft in which valuables are taken from someone by force, and in which some type of weapon is used.

armory A storehouse for firearms and a place where military maneuvers are conducted.

arms, right to bear *See* **right to bear arms.**

Army Model Sometimes called the military model, this quasi-theory justifies the militarization of police action and allows police to claim exemption from civilian oversight based on their paramilitary organization and function. *See also* **boot camp.**

arousal theorists Delinquency experts who believe that aggression is a function of the level of an individual's need for stimulation or arousal from the environment. Those who require more stimulation may act in an aggressive manner to meet their needs.

arraignment, arraignment for trial An official proceeding in which a defendant is formally confronted by criminal charges and enters a plea, and a trial date is established. *See figures p. 16 and 17.*

array A group of persons summoned to court for potential jury duty; also, an order in which persons are selected or ranked in the jury box; venire; venireman list.

arrest The act of taking into custody and restraining an individual until he or she can be brought before the court to answer the charges against him or her.

arrest clearance The official removal by police officers of an active case following the arrest of a particular suspect.

arrestee A person who is arrested.

arrestee dispositions Law enforcement or prosecutorial actions that terminate or temporarily suspend actions against an arrested person before charges have been formally filed in court.

Arrestee Drug Abuse Monitoring (ADAM) A national program sponsored by the U.S. Department of Justice to routinely collect information about drug abuse by those who are arrested and jailed.

arrest order A written notice issued by either a probation or parole officer to arrest a parolee or probationer for a new offense or a technical violation of program rules.

arrest practices Various means whereby law enforcement officers effect arrests.

arrest rate The number of persons arrested in relation to the number of crimes reported or known to police during a given period (e.g., an arrest rate of .30 for 1996 would mean that of all crimes reported or known to police in 1996, arrests were made for 30 percent of these reported crimes).

arrest record A list of one's prior arrests, including dismissed or dropped charges as well as convictions.

arrest register A chronological record of all arrests made by members of a particular law enforcement agency for a period of time that contains the identities of all arrestees and charges filed at time of arrest. Contemporary records are electronically stored on computers for instant retrieval.

arrest report A document prepared by a law enforcement officer or other official articulating what led to an arrest. Information includes the arrestee's name, address, telephone number, occupation or profession, and prior record, if any, reasons for arrest, and personal observations and interpretations of events.

arrest upon hue and cry The common-law process of pursuing persons with horn and voice, usually suspected felons and others who have caused harm to one or more victims.

arrest upon order of magistrate An oral or written order from a judicial official or magistrate to command someone such as a police or court officer to arrest someone who has committed an offense in the presence of the magistrate.

A Federal Arraignment Order

DC 15
(Rev. 1/62)

NOTICE OF SETTING OF CASE FOR _____ ARRAIGNMENT _____

United States District Court
FOR THE

_____

THE UNITED STATES OF AMERICA
vs.

Criminal No.

To

☐ ¹ TAKE NOTICE that the above entitled case has been set for arraignment in said Court at Federal Courtroom   ,
on   , 19 , at

☐ ¹ As surety for the said defendant
you are required to produce   ² in said Court at said time, otherwise the bail may be forfeited.

_____, 19____   _____

¹ Sentences following boxes which have been checked are applicable.

² Insert "him," "her," as appropriate.

Alternative Procedures Leading to Arraignment

Waiver of right to preliminary hearing

Arrest (with or without warrant) → Initial appearance before magistrate (bail bond set, complaint prepared) → Preliminary hearing (establishment of probable cause) → Grand jury action

or

Grand jury action (indictment, presentment, information) → Summons, capias, arrest warrant → Arraignment (reading of the indictment, charges, plea entered, and trial date established)

---

arrest warrant A document issued by a court ordering law officers to arrest a specific individual. *See box.*

arsenic A poisonous white powder found in rat poisons and certain herbicides that was at one time commonly used to commit murder.

arson Any willful, malicious burning or attempt to burn, with or without intent to defraud, a dwelling house, public building, motor vehicle, aircraft, or the personal property of another.

Arson Investigators, International Association of An organization founded in 1949. Publishes *The Fire and Arson Investigator Quarterly.*

arsonist One who commits arson; a fire setter.

artificial presumption Any presumption based on law rather than on actual physical facts or events. In some jurisdictions, persons are presumed dead, even in the absence of physical evidence, if they have been missing for seven years or more.

art theft The taking of fine art, such as paintings or sculptures.

Aryan Brotherhood A white supremacist prison gang.

Aryan Nations A group of neo-Nazi extremists dedicated to the preservation of the white race.

Ashurst-Sumners Act Federal legislation passed in 1935 that ended the industrial prison era by limiting interstate commerce in prison-made goods.

asphyxia The deprivation of oxygen leading to unconsciousness, injury, or death.

asphyxiate To suffocate or cause unconsciousness as the result of interfering with the exchange of oxygen and carbon dioxide in the body.

aspiration of vomitus The breathing of regurgitated food into the respiratory tract, which cuts off the intake of air.

asportation The carrying away of something; in kidnapping, the carrying away of the victim; in larceny, the carrying away of a victim's property.

An Arrest Warrant Based on a Filed Complaint

FORM 4.
WARRANT OF ARREST ON COMPLAINT

(RCr 2.04, 2.06)
(Caption)

TO ALL PEACE OFFICERS IN THE COMMONWEALTH OF KENTUCKY:

You are hereby commanded to arrest _____
(Name of defendant)
and bring him forthwith before a judge of the District Court in Franklin County, Kentucky (or, if he be absent or unable to act, before the nearest available magistrate), to answer a complaint made by _____ charging him with the offense of reckless driving.
Issued at Frankfort, Franklin County, Kentucky, this _____ day of _____, 19__.

_____
Judge, District Court of Kentucky
Franklin County

(Indorsement as to bail)
The defendant may give bail in the amount of $_____.

_____
Judge, District Court of Kentucky
Franklin County

(Amended October 14, 19 , effective January 1, 19 .)

assailant One who commits, or is suspected of committing, assault.

assassin One who kills a public figure, such as a head of state or president.

assassination The murder of a head of state, government official, or other highly important public figure.

assault Any unlawful attempt with force or violence to harm or frighten another. *See also* **aggravated assault; simple assault.**

assault and battery An assault carried into effect by doing some violence to the victim.

assault on a law enforcement officer Simple or aggravated assault, in which the victim is a law enforcement officer involved in the performance of his or her duties.

assault weapon An automatic or semiautomatic firearm, generally with a large-capacity magazine, capable of discharging many bullets rapidly (e.g., an AK-47 rifle).

assault with a deadly weapon The unlawful intentional inflicting, or attempted or threatened inflicting, of injury or death with the use of a weapon capable of killing the victim.

assembly, lawful or unlawful Congregating in a particular place for a lawful or unlawful purpose.

assembly-line justice A term applied to an overworked, inadequately staffed court that is unsympathetic and unfair to criminal defendants; also, the presumptive process that includes plea bargaining, regardless of the competency or the sympathy of the individuals involved in the decision making.

assessment centers Organizations for selecting entry-level officers for correctional work. Assessment centers hire correctional officers and probation or parole officers, and are used in the promotion process, particularly for upper-level positions.

assessment facilities Secure premises responsible for orienting the juvenile to the correctional system in a particular state and to what the expectations are. These centers are responsible for conducting many types of testing and diagnoses of individual juveniles committed to the juvenile correctional authority.

asset-focused approach The identification and use of an offender's positive assets, such as family and community support, as opposed to focusing on risks and deficits.

asset forfeiture, asset seizure The governmental seizure of personal assets obtained from or used in a criminal enterprise (e.g., a yacht may be forfeited to the government if it was used to facilitate a crime, such as distributing narcotics).

assignation house A location where prostitution occurs.

assigned counsel, assigned counsel system A program wherein indigent clients charged with crimes may have defense attorneys appointed for them. These defense attorneys may be private attorneys who agree to be rotated to perform such services for a low rate of reimbursement from the city, county, or state.

assisted-living prisons Confinement facilities for those with serious illnesses or other debilitating conditions that require special medical services and assistance. They often cater to elderly offenders who have assorted chronic medical problems.

assisted suicide The taking of one's own life with the help of another, often a physician or medical professional. *See also* **Kevorkian, Jack.**

assisting in arrests, assisting officers in making arrests Civilians may come to the aid of officers making arrests of criminal suspects. Other officers who assist fellow officers in making arrests are credited with "assists."

association, differential *See* differential association.

assumpsit Lawsuit alleging breach of contract.

assumption A statement accepted as fact about the real world or events (e.g., "All societies have laws," "The greater the deviant conduct, the greater the group pressure on the deviant to conform to group norms").

asylum Sanctuary; a place of refuge; also, an institution of social relief for the unfortunate or a place used to house those with mental disorders.

asylum state A jurisdiction to which persons seeking to escape prosecution in other jurisdictions flee.

atavism, atavistic characteristics A positivist school of thought arguing that a biological condition renders some people incapable of living within the social constraints of a society. According to Cesare Lombroso, atavistic characteristics are the physical characteristics that distinguish born criminals from the general population, evolutionary throwbacks to animals or primitive people.

atavistic stigmata The physical human characteristics noted by Cesare Lombroso that distinguish born criminals from others in populations.

Atlanta serial murders On July 28, 1979, Atlanta, GA, police discovered the bodies of Alfred James Evans, 13, and Edward Hope Smith, 14. Over the next two years, Atlanta residents were terrorized by abductions and murders of 29 young African Americans. The FBI entered the case and subsequently questioned Wayne Bertram Williams in May 1981. Following questioning, a search warrant was issued and Williams' home, person, and automobile were searched and valuable incriminating evidence was discovered. Although suspected of the other murders, Williams was convicted on just two counts on February 26, 1982.

at-risk youths Any juveniles who are considered more susceptible to the influence of gangs and delinquent peers; any youths in danger of becoming a delinquent. They tend to be characterized as having less developed reading skills, greater immaturity, lower socioeconomic status, and parental dysfunction, and are otherwise disadvantaged by their socioeconomic and environmental circumstances;.

attachment A bond between persons and their families, friends, and school associates; a component of Travis Hirschi's social bond theory; in law, property seizure or asset forfeiture.

Attack on America A term used by politicians, the media, and others to describe the September 11, 2001, terrorist attacks that destroyed the World Trade Center and portions of the Pentagon.

attainder The loss of civil rights because of a felony conviction.

attaint To convict one of a crime.

attempt, criminal attempt An overt action associated with a crime and done with criminal intent; an act that goes beyond preparation but does not necessarily mean a criminal act has been completed.

attempted crime, attempt to commit a crime A criminal act that has not been completed.

attendant circumstances The facts surrounding an event.

attention center A detention facility for youth.

Attention Deficit Disorder (ADD), Attention Deficit Hyperactivity Disorder (ADHD) A syndrome characterized by impulsivity, hyperactivity, and an inappropriate lack of concentration associated with poor school performance and a lack of response to discipline.

attestation A verbal authentication that indicates truthfulness (e.g., a statement declaring that factual information and signatures in property documents are true and authentic).

Attica A state correctional facility in New York that became known for prison reform following a bloody riot between prisoners and correctional officers from September 9–13, 1971. Inmates protested overcrowding and racial discrimination, taking over cell blocks for four days of rioting. The uprising ended when police stormed the facility and regained control. Thirty-nine inmates died and 80 others were wounded in the process.

Attica revolt A name given to the riot that occurred at the Attica, NY, correctional facility in 1971.

attitude All of a person's inclinations, prejudices, ideas, fears, and convictions about a given topic; a tendency to act in a given way.

attorney, attorney at law, counsel, lawyer A person licensed to practice law; anyone admitted to practice before the bar in a given jurisdiction; any qualified and licensed person who can defend or prosecute someone in a court of law; an officer of the court; anyone trained in the law who has received a law degree from a recognized university and who is authorized to practice law in a given jurisdiction.

attorney-client privilege The confidentiality that exists between lawyers and those they represent; the traditional confidentiality that prevents disclosure of incriminating information to others, such as prosecutors.

attorney fees The part of an award paid to attorneys who prevail in actions at law.

attorney general The senior U.S. prosecutor in each federal district court; a cabinet member who heads the Justice Department; top prosecutors of states.

attractive nuisance A condition or establishment, such as a loosely managed bar, thought to represent an enticement to criminal activity; a public nuisance.

Auburn State Penitentiary A prison constructed in Auburn, NY, in 1816 that pioneered the use of "tiers" to house inmates on different floors or levels, usually according to the seriousness of their offenses. It introduced the congregate system, in which prisoners had opportunities to mingle with one another for work, dining, and recreation, and stereotypical striped uniforms for prisoners. A prison system was developed in New York during the nineteenth century that emulated this model and depended on mass prisons where prisoners were held in congregate fashion. *See also* **Auburn Style, Auburn System.**

Auburn Style, Auburn System A silent system introduced at the Auburn State Penitentiary in New York in 1825. Inmates were obligated to work in silence, housed at night in individual cells, and marched in groups to meals in a common eating area. Other penitentiaries and prisons used the Auburn System as a pattern for inmate supervision and discipline. This style of imprisonment was compared with the Pennsylvania System.

audit trail A series of financial documents that can support fiscal responsibility and uncover embezzlement, fraud, or other types of financial wrongdoing.

Augustus, John (1785–1859) The originator of probation in the United States in 1841. Considered the first informal probation officer, this Boston shoemaker and philanthropist, active in reforming petty offenders and alcoholics charged with crimes, assumed responsibility for them and posted their bail while attempting to reform them.

authentic document A paper bearing a real signature or seal attesting to the genuineness of the document.

authenticity The genuineness of private records.

authoritarianism A type of government with rigid hierarchy of authority and power distribution; also, a personality system with similarly rigid attributes, including a dogmatic style of behavior closed to new ideas or procedures and fixed, prejudicial ideas or views; also, a personality trait attributed to police officers by Jerome Skolnick and designated as their "working personality."

authoritarian model A prison management style characterized by a high degree of centralization of power and decision making that emphasizes a high degree of regimentation and inmate control; also, in nonprison settings, a supervisory style emphasizing a high degree of control over employees.

authority The power to delegate duties and responsibilities, which is usually vested in superordinates or supervisors, in relation to subordinates or lower-level participants; the influence to cause others to conform to one's wishes.

authority-conflict pathway The developmental path taken to delinquency that begins with stubborn or defiant behavior.

authority revolution The erosion in respect for authority, tradition, and adults by youths that began during the 1960s.

autocracy Dictatorship.

autoerotic asphyxia, autoerotic death, autoerotic fatality Accidental termination of one's life by strangulation during sexual intercourse. Sexual excitement is allegedly heightened by the life-threatening experience.

autoeroticism Self-arousal and sexual satisfaction by means of fantasy or genital stimulation.

automated case-level data Information collected by agencies at the individual case level. The data contain details of the offenders, victim, disposition, and other relevant items.

automated data processing (ADP) Data processing with a computer system; data storage, retrieval, and analysis performed by computer.

Automated Fingerprint Identification System (AFIS) A process that permits the electronic collection, storage, retrieval, and comparison of human fingerprints.

Automatic Data Processing Intelligence Network (ADPRIN) A computer network used by the U.S. Bureau of Customs to combat smuggling.

automatic fire Repeated fire from an automatic weapon. When the trigger of the weapon is depressed and held down, bullets are continuously discharged in rapid succession. This is distinguished from semiautomatic fire, in which a single trigger pull discharges a single round and rechambers a new one.

automatic transfer laws, automatic transfer waivers Jurisdictional laws that provide for automatic waivers of juveniles to criminal court for processing; a legislatively prescribed directive to transfer juveniles of specified ages who have committed especially serious offenses to the jurisdiction of criminal courts.

automatic weapons Firearms capable of firing multiple rounds with a single trigger pull.

automatism A set of actions taken during a state of unconsciousness.

automobile exception An exception to the prohibition of warrantless searches of vehicles where probable cause to conduct a search is present, as there is a high likelihood of a suspect moving an automobile and destroying incriminating illegal goods or substances. *See California v. Carney* (1985).

automonosexual perversion Sexual activities performed on oneself, including self-fellatio or self-mutilation.

autonomic nervous system The system that controls the body's involuntary functions, such as blood pressure and heart rate.

autonomous model of parole organization An organizational pattern in which parole decisions are made within an autonomous body not affiliated with other agencies of the criminal justice system; the most common pattern for adult paroling authority.

autonomy The state of being self-governing or self-directing.

autopsy Dissection of a body to determine the cause of death.

autosadism The infliction of pain on one's self for sexual gratification.

auto theft, automobile theft Any stealing of a motorized vehicle. *See also* **vehicular theft.**

auto theft deterrence Any method of preventing vehicle theft, including car alarms and systems such as the LoJack Stolen Vehicle Recovery System, designed to locate a stolen vehicle by emitting electronic signals that identify its whereabouts.

autrefois acquit, *autrefois* convict A plea of "formerly acquitted" or "formerly convicted" in not-guilty proceedings on double jeopardy grounds.

auxiliary police Trained and uniformed volunteer civilians who work with local police in law enforcement activities.

aversion therapy A method to alter a person's behavior by conditioning particular actions with painful or unpleasant stimuli.

avertable recidivist An offender who would still have been in prison serving a sentence at a time when a new offense was committed if he or she had not been released on parole or probation.

Aviation Crime Prevention Institute An organization established in 1986 designed to prevent airplane theft and crimes involving aircraft.

Avoider In the Muir Typology, a type of police officer who avoids work, just collects a paycheck, and is a shirker or slacker. The term was suggested by William Ker Muir, Jr.'s 1977 work *Police: Streetcorner Politicians. See also* **Muir Typology.**

avowtry Adultery.

avulsion The tearing away of a body part or tissue as the result of a trauma or a surgical procedure.

axiom, axiomatic theory A theoretical system that contains a set of concepts and definitions, a set of existence statements, a set of relational statements divided into postulates and theorems, and a logical system used to relate concepts to statements and to deduce theorems from axioms.

B

Baader-Meinhof Gang A group founded in the 1960s from a student protest movement by Andreas Baader and Ulrike Meinhof. The ideological basis of the gang was a commitment to violence in the service of the class struggle associated with Marxism. They developed an extensive network of underground guerrillas and left-wing sympathizers who claimed to be motivated by disgust with materialism and fascist tendencies in German society. The gang subsequently committed numerous terrorist acts against government leaders, including bombings, kidnappings, and robberies. Eventually, it evolved into the Red Army Faction.

baby boom A noticeable increase in birthrate within a relatively short period of time. Specifically, following World War II, there was a dramatic increase in childbirths when many returning veterans fathered children. The higher numbers of children in the population of baby boomers creates a potential for an increase in the crime rate when these baby boomers reach offending ages.

B.A.C.I.S. (Behavior Alert Classification Identification System) A method of distinguishing between inmates according to their risk and needs that separates mentally ill jail inmates from the rest of the jail population. Assessments are conducted by jail officers and other personnel.

back-door corrections, back-door solution An answer to the prison or jail overcrowding problem that involves court-ordered prison or jail population reductions, use of early release or parole, furloughs, work release, and administrative release.

back-dooring cases The judicial practice of sentencing borderline (low-risk) offenders to incarceration with the strong admonishment that they be encouraged to apply for intensive probation supervision programs.

back-door program A community program that functions as an early release mechanism for high-risk offenders who may or may not meet the criteria for regular parole.

backlog The number of impending cases awaiting adjudication that exceed the court's capacity and cannot be acted upon because the court is occupied with other cases.

back-to-the-people movement Community-oriented policing that focuses on foot patrols and neighborhood beats; proactive policing that stresses community wellness.

bad check A worthless negotiable instrument; a check written where insufficient funds are in the account to cover the amount of the check written.

badgering Harassment of a witness who gives testimony in court, often used by an opposing attorney to make a strong impression on the jury or to confuse a witness into making contradictory statements.

badges and shields, law enforcement Pentacles or metal stars worn by law enforcement officers to signify different branches of enforcement. The five-pointed pentacle signifies the U.S. Marshal's Service, and there are insignias for different military ranks. Sheriffs' stars are used extensively because of their manufacturing simplicity.

"bad-seed" hypothesis The theory that certain persons are born with the capacity to engage in evil behavior. This hypothesis, earlier dismissed, has begun to win greater credibility through sociobiological investigations.

bad-tendency test The rule articulated in *Gitlow v. New York* (1924) that authorizes legislative bodies to suppress speech that promotes revolution or armed uprisings that may upset prevailing government.

bad time Days added to one's sentence in a prison or jail for misconduct or rule violations.

bagging of finds The tying of paper bags around the hands of homicide victims in order to preserve evidence underneath their fingernails or on their skin surfaces.

bagnes Secure stockades established at French seaports to house slaves and others.

bail Surety provided by defendants or others to guarantee their subsequent appearance in court to face criminal charges. Bail is available to anyone entitled to it (not everyone is entitled to bail); it is denied when suspects are considered dangerous or likely to flee. *See also* **preventive detention;** *United States v. Salerno* (1987).

bail agent A person who finds and takes into custody those who have skipped out on bail bonds; a bounty hunter.

bail bond, bail bonding A written guarantee, often accompanied by money or other securities, that the person charged with an offense will remain within the court's jurisdiction to face trial at a time in the future. *See box.*

bail bondsman, bail bondsperson A person who is in the business of posting bail for criminal suspects, usually charging a percentage of whatever bail has been set.

bail-enforcement agent A professional who specializes in apprehending persons wanted by one or more jurisdictions, usually persons who have been placed on bail but who have fled their jurisdiction to avoid prosecution; also known as a bounty hunter. Depending on the amount of bail, an agent receives a portion of the bail money for capturing and returning to custody a wanted person.

Bailey, F. Lee (1933–) An attorney born in Waltham, MA, who achieved acclaim through his defense of Dr. Samuel Sheppard in Cleveland, OH, who had been convicted in 1954 of murdering his wife. Bailey successfully won retrial for Sheppard, showing that pretrial publicity had prejudiced his case, and Sheppard was acquitted. Bailey also assisted in defending O.J. Simpson in a double-murder trial in Los Angeles, CA, in the mid-1990s, in which Simpson was acquitted. Bailey is considered flamboyant and has frequently been censured for his trial conduct and demeanor.

bailiff A court officer who maintains order in the court while it is in session, oversees the jury during a trial proceeding, and sometimes has custody of prisoners while they are in the courtroom; also known as messengers.

bail reform A movement dedicated to making the practice of bail more equitable for the accused. Prior bail practices tended to discriminate against certain types of persons according to their race and socioeconomic status.

Bail Reform Act of 1984 An act to revise bail practices and to assure that all persons, regardless of their financial status, shall

---

A Bail Bond Form

BAIL BOND

(Caption)

_____being in custody charged with
(Name of defendant)
the offense of _____ and being admitted to bail in
the sum of $_____, we undertake that he will appear and
be amenable to the orders and process of this and any
other court in which this proceeding may be pending
hereafter for any and all purposes and at all stages of the
proceeding (including, in event of indictment, proceedings thereafter) in accordance with
(Name of defendant)
Executed this ___ day of _____, 19__.

_____   _____
(Name of defendant)   (Address)

_____   _____
(Name of surety)   (Address)
Taken and subscribed before me this
_____day of _____, 19__.

_____
(Signature)

_____
(Title)
I, _____, by entering into the (above) bond
obligation, do hereby submit to the jurisdiction of the
courts of   in which any forfeiture proceeding
arising out of my bail obligation may be pending, and do
further irrevocably appoint the clerk of such court as my
agent upon whom any process affecting my liability on
such bond may be served, such clerk to forthwith mail
copies to me at _____ City
(Street address)

of _____, County of _____, State
of _____, or at my last known address.
Date this ___ day of _____, 19__.

_____
(Name)

not needlessly be detained to answer criminal charges. The act does not mean that all persons are entitled to bail regardless of their alleged offense.

bail revocation A judicial decision denying previously granted bail for a defendant; the act of court withdrawing a defendant's previously granted release on bail.

bail system The practice of releasing defendants after they place a financial guarantee with the court to ensure their subsequent trial appearance. Usually, defendants may place the entire amount with the court or pay a premium to a bail bondsman.

bailiwick A jurisdiction or place of authority, usually in reference to a sheriff, constable, or police chief.

bait and switch A deceptive practice used by some retailers, who try to persuade a customer to buy a different, often more expensive, item rather than the advertised item that drew the customer into the store initially.

balance and restorative justice (BARJ) A new philosophy of juvenile justice that advocates accountability, community safety, and youth development in combination with restorative justice between offenders, victims, and communities.

balanced approach A probation orientation that simultaneously emphasizes community protection, offender accountability, individualization of treatments, and competency assessment and development.

Balanced Juvenile Justice and Crime Prevention Act of 1996 A law passed by Congress that embraces the punitive and accountability assumptions of the late 1970s and 1980s, reflecting the fundamental changes in assumptions about juveniles and juvenile justice.

balanced probation Programs that integrate community protection, accountability of the juvenile offender, competency, and individualized attention to the juvenile offender, based on the principle that juvenile offenders must accept responsibility for their illegal acts.

balance of sentence suspended A judicial sentencing option whereby convicted offenders are given credit for the time they have served and permitted to be free from jail, often accompanied by payment of a fine and court costs.

balancing-of-the-interest approach Efforts by the courts to balance the parent's natural right to rear a child with the child's right to grow into adulthood free from physical abuse or emotional harm.

balancing test A principle devised by courts and applied to corrections in the case of *Pell v. Procunier* (1974) that weighs the constitutional rights of inmates against the authority of the state to make laws or otherwise restrict a person's freedom to protect its interests and citizens.

ballistics The study of the motion, appearance, and modification of missiles (bullets) and other vehicles acted upon by propellants, wind, gravity, temperature, and any other modifying substance, condition, or force. *See also* **firearms identification.**

bandit One who violates the law by taking items of value from others by force or threats.

banditry Aggravated robbery; the illegal activity of a bandit.

Bandura, Albert (1925–) A psychologist and child development expert who has investigated social learning relevant to criminology. He has examined the stages of development among children and has concluded that criminal conduct develops at particular stages when certain interaction stimuli are present.

banishment The physical removal of undesirables, criminals, and political and religious dissidents to remote locations.

bank fraud Any scheme designed to swindle financial institutions of any monies, funds, assets, or securities through false pretenses, trickery, or misrepresentations.

bankruptcy fraud A scam in which individuals falsely attempt to claim bankruptcy (and thereby erase financial debts) by taking advantage of loopholes in the laws.

Bank Secrecy Act A federal statute protecting the confidentiality of banking transactions, but which makes certain information available to the government in connection with criminal proceedings.

bar An aggregate containing all attorneys admitted to practice law in every jurisdiction.

barbed wire Common metal perimeter wire with sharpened knots at closely spaced intervals designed to cut human flesh if touched forcefully. It is used by prisons or encampments to deter persons from escaping and to supplement prison walls as a security measure. It was patented in 1867 by William D. Hunt and subsequently perfected and distributed by J.F. Glidden in Illinois.

Barbie, Klaus (1913–1991) A former Nazi Gestapo commander during World War II who was charged with committing atrocities against Jewish prisoners. He was known as the "Butcher of Lyons" because of his especially cruel treatment of Jews living in that part of France.

barbiturates Any drug functioning as a depressant on the central nervous system; also known as "downers."

Barker **balancing test** The speedy-trial standard, where delays are considered in terms of the reason, length, existence of prejudice against the defendant by the prosecutor, and the assertion of the defendant's speedy-trial rights (from the case of *Barker v. Wingo* [1972]).

Barnes, Harry Elmer (1889–1968) A historian who chronicled the history of confinement, torture, and execution in his book *The Story of Punishment* (1972).

barretry Initiating groundless quarrels or disputes or lawsuits or frequently provoking lawsuits or arguments; in maritime law, any willful and unlawful act by a ship's master or crew intended to injure a ship's owners.

barrio A Latino term meaning neighborhood.

barrio gangs Neighborhood gangs organized in Mexican-American areas of California and elsewhere for mutual protection.

barrister In England, a counselor who has been admitted to the bar to practice law and becomes a client advocate.

barroom violence Any type of physical confrontation that occurs in or around a bar, tavern, or other establishment where liquor is sold for consumption on the premises.

BARS (Behaviorally Anchored Rating Scale) A method of evaluating one's job performance and effectiveness.

base penalty The modal sentence in a structured sentencing state, which can be enhanced or diminished to reflect aggravating or mitigating circumstances.

basic car plan A method of patrolling a particular neighborhood or geographical area of a city, in which a police cruiser is assigned to the neighborhood as the primary patrol vehicle. All calls for service in that neighborhood are directed to that patrol cruiser unless the cruiser officers request additional assistance from other cruisers and officers nearby. This plan furthers community-oriented policing, because police officers get to know neighborhood residents and have their confidence and respect.

Bastille An infamous Paris prison known for holding political prisoners that was destroyed by revolutionaries in 1789.

Bates, Sanford (1884–1972) Bates was appointed the first director of the U.S. Bureau of Prisons in 1929. He was a former Massachusetts legislator (1912–1917), commissioner of penal institutions in Boston (1917–1929), and chairman of Federal Prison Industries, Inc. (1934–1972).

baton The "nightstick" carried by police officers; a weighted club between one and two feet in length, designed as a defensive device for law enforcement officers involved in physical confrontations.

Battelle Law and Justice Center Established in 1971 by the Battelle Memorial Institute, the Center's goals are to collect and disseminate information concerning arson and white-collar crime.

battered child syndrome Emotional and physical injuries to children intentionally inflicted by others, usually by parents or guardians, often associated with psychological problems in coping with reality.

battered women's syndrome, battered wife's syndrome (BWS) Violent reactions by women who have been battered by men with whom they have had a close relationship. It has been successfully used as a defense in some cases in which women have been tried for the murder of their husbands.

battery A civil offense involving intentional touching or inflicting hurt on another.

Baumes' laws Similar to habitual-offender laws, these statutes provide for increasingly severe penalties for successive offenses. Sponsored by Caleb H. Baumes, chairman of the New York State Senate in 1926, they were the forerunners of three-strikes-and-you're-out laws, which impose life-without-parole sentences for a third or fourth felony offense.

bawdy house A dwelling where prostitution occurs.

bayonet A knife that attaches to the barrel of a rifle, often used as a weapon by youth gangs.

beam test A test to determine under microscopic conditions whether a substance is marijuana (cannabis) or some other substance.

Bean, Judge Roy (1825–1903) Born in Mason County, KY, Bean became an infamous frontier judge near the Pecos River in Texas. He regularly held court in a saloon and considered himself the "law west of the Pecos." He was removed from the bench in 1896 following a town vote. He had an early history of lawlessness and barroom brawls, and worked as a gold miner in his younger years. He was known to dispense rapid justice in his court, which often meant death by hanging.

beat The geographical area routinely patrolled by a law enforcement officer.

beat patrolling A police patrol style originating in the early 1900s designed to bring officers into closer physical contact with area residents. Beats are small geographical areas of neighborhoods or cities that are patrolled by individual officers, usually on foot.

Beccaria, Cesare Bonesana, Marchese di (1738–1794) Beccaria developed the classical school of criminology in writings including *An Essay on Crimes and Punishments* (1764). He believed that corporal punishment was unjust and ineffective and that crime could be prevented by clear legal codes specifying prohibited behaviors and punishments. He promoted the "just deserts" philosophy and endorsed a utilitarianistic approach to criminal conduct and its punishment by suggesting that useful, purposeful, and reasonable punishments ought to be formulated and applied. He viewed criminal conduct as pleasurable to criminals, and believed that as they sought pleasure and avoided pain, pain might function as a deterrent to criminal behavior. *See also* **Bentham, Jeremy; "just deserts" model.**

Becker, Howard S. (1928–) A criminologist and social psychologist who has studied deviance and criminality and wrote *Outsiders: Studies in the Sociology of Deviance* (1963). A labeling theorist, Becker believes or considers deviance relative to a particular group in a particular time and place.

behavioral approach A type of police discretion typified by a blend of sociology, psychology, and political science; a developmental scheme whereby police officers attempt to negotiate their way through each public encounter.

behavioral conditioning A psychological principle holding that the frequency of any behavior can be increased through reward, punishment, and association with other stimuli.

behavioral contracting The negotiation of a written agreement between inmates and corrections personnel that specifies that if the inmates behave in certain ways, they will be rewarded.

behavioral deep freeze of incarceration A lifestyle adopted by long-term inmates in which they either develop guarded or no relationships with other inmates. This is to avoid facing the devastation of having relationships terminated by transfer or releases.

behavioral modeling Learning how to behave by fashioning one's behavior after others'.

behavioral model of crime In criminology, the view that crime is explained by the individual pathology of an offender, the social pathology of society, or a combination of the two.

Behavioral Research Institute Established in 1974, this organization conducts research on crime, delinquency, drug abuse, alcoholism, and other current social problems. It is headquartered in Boulder, CO.

Behavioral Science Unit (BSU) The unit of the Federal Bureau of Investigation that uses in-depth crime-scene analyses, criminal personality profiling, and other scientific techniques to solve homicides and other violent and serial crimes.

behaviorism A branch of psychology concerned with the study of observable behavior, rather than unconscious motives, that focuses on the relationship between particular stimuli and persons' responses to them.

behavior modification A treatment program that attempts to change behavior, rather than personality, by rewarding favorable actions and punishing unfavorable ones.

Behavior Pattern Recognition (BPR) A system devised by air marshals in 2004 to profile suspicious persons at major airports that includes itemized lists of indicators and scale scores of suspicious behavior. Anyone with a high score is singled out for a thorough search and questioned before being permitted to board an aircraft. Suspicious conduct includes profuse sweating, loitering in an air terminal without luggage, wearing heavy clothes on a hot day, using peculiar hand signals unrelated to conventional communication, and observing airport security methods.

Beheler **admonition** A request made of someone who has been invited to a police station by a law enforcement officer to discuss a matter, usually a crime. The person invited to appear is not under arrest, although he or she may be a suspect. If the person voluntarily appears at the police station and is interviewed, he or she is not entitled to a *Miranda* warning. The *Beheler* admonition is considered a consensual encounter in which the person is free to leave at any time, and is thus considered a consent interrogation. It was named for the case of *California v. Beheler* (1983).

belief One of four elements of Travis Hirschi's social control theory of delinquency. *See also* **Hirschi, Travis; social control theory.**

belly chain A steel chain designed to pass through the belt loops of an individual in custody, and to which handcuffs are attached.

"Beltway bandits" Consulting firms located in and around Washington, DC, that lobby for federal contracts. The term is not limited to criminal-justice applications.

Beltway Sniper Case The fall 2002 serial sniper killings resulting in a total of 10 deaths and extortion by two drifters, one a juvenile, centering in and around the Washington, DC, Beltway. Sniper incidents and deaths also occurred in Maryland, Richmond, VA; Georgia; Louisiana; and Alabama. John Allen Muhammad, 42, was subsequently convicted in 2003 by a Virginia Beach, VA, jury for sniper-related deaths in Virginia and sentenced to death. Later in 2003, Lee Boyd Malvo, 18, was convicted of first-degree murder in a Virginia federal trial and sentenced to life imprisonment. Other states, such as Alabama, want to try Malvo on capital-murder charges and seek the death penalty against him.

bench The site where judges sit during a trial; an entire body of judges convening as a court.

bench parole, bench probation Action by a court to permit convicted offenders to remain free in their communities only under the jurisdiction of the sentencing judge.

bench trial A tribunal in which the guilt or innocence of a defendant is determined by the judge rather than a jury.

bench warrant A document issued by a judge and not requested by the police, demanding that a specified person be brought before the court without undue or unnecessary delay.

benefit of clergy An early form of clemency in England originally intended for clergy convicted in King's Courts but transferred to church jurisdiction for punishment. It was eventually extended to many nonclerics who could read or who claimed to be able to read, primarily as an escape from the death penalty.

Bentham, Jeremy (1748–1832) A British hedonist who wrote *Introduction to the Principles and Morals of Legislation* (1781). He believed that criminals could be deterred by minimizing pleasures derived from wrongdoing, and that punishment should be swift, certain, and painful.

benzidine test A forensic chemical test for the presence of blood on the surface of any object.

bequeath To provide in a will for the legal transfer of property or valuables to others.

Berkemer **rule** A rule named after Sheriff Harry J. Berkemer of Franklin County, OH, that states that routine traffic stops do not constitute custodial interrogations for purposes of issuing *Miranda* warnings to persons suspected of driving while intoxicated or under the influence of drugs. *See Berkemer v. McCarty* (1984).

Berkowitz, David (1953–) Serial killer known as the Son of Sam who used a .44 magnum pistol to kill several persons in the New York City area during the 1970s. He was caught and convicted, and sentenced to life without the possibility of parole. *See also* **Son of Sam laws.**

Bertillon, Alphonse (1853–1914) A French police records clerk who developed the Bertillon classification system.

Bertillon identification, Bertillon classification system, Bertillon method of identification A nineteenth-century identification method deriving its name from its inventor, Alphonse Bertillon, head of the Paris police. Bertillon used body measurements to compare persons and photographs to make positive identifications.

best-efforts standard A requirement of the federal Victims' Rights and Restitution Act of 1990 (also known as the Victims' Rights Act) that mandates that federal law enforcement officers, prosecutors, and corrections officials use their best efforts to ensure that victims receive basic rights and services during their encounter with the criminal-justice system.

best-evidence rule In the course of presenting evidence in court, this edict states that if factual information or tangible documents are offered as proof, the original information or documents are preferred. If such original information or documents are unavailable, then a reasonable facsimile is the next most preferred item (e.g., a photocopy of an unavailable automobile title would be the best evidence, in the event that the original automobile title was destroyed or missing).

bestiality Any act involving sexual intercourse between a human being and an animal.

best interests of the child A philosophical viewpoint that encourages the state to take control of wayward children and provide care, custody, and treatment to remedy delinquent behavior. *See also* ***parens patriae.***

betting Wagering or gambling on any type of activity, from horse racing, sporting events, dog races, card and dice games, or other activities.

beyond a reasonable doubt The standard used in criminal courts to establish the guilt of a criminal defendant.

bias Prejudice based on preconceptions about groups or individuals, usually couched in an ethnic or racial context; any predetermined opinion about someone based on one or more characteristics, such as gender, hair color, or some other physical attribute.

bias crime *See* **hate crime.**

bifurcated A type of juvenile court in which adjudication and disposition proceedings are held separately.

bifurcated process Juvenile terminology for separating the adjudicatory and dispositional hearings so that different levels of evidence can be heard at each.

bifurcated trial A tribunal in capital cases in which the jury is asked to make two decisions: first, to determine guilt or innocence of defendant; second, if the defendant is found guilty, to decide punishment, which may include the death penalty.

bigamy The crime of being married to more than one spouse at a time.

big brother plan A juvenile delinquency intervention strategy that uses adults to act as surrogate father figures to wayward youths to provide them with guidance and companionship. Its aim is to give youths stability and heighten their self-esteem and self-worth through interacting with father figures who give them guidance and attention.

Big Brothers/Big Sisters of America A federation of more than 500 agencies serving children and adolescents. Adults relate on a one-to-one basis with youths to promote their self-esteem and self-sufficiency. Volunteers attempt to instill responsibility, excellence, and leadership among assisted youths.

Big House A pre-1950s term for prison.

bill of attainder A legislative act imposing punishment without trial upon persons deemed guilty of treason or felonies. Such bills are currently prohibited by the United States Constitution.

bill of exceptions A written listing of the objections made by either the prosecution or the defense during a trial proceeding. Such bills may be used later if the case is appealed by either side.

bill of indictment A document submitted to a grand jury by the prosecutor asking it to take action and indict a suspect.

bill of information A written document, usually a charging document, used by prosecutors when a felony case is not taken before a grand jury. Such bills are sometimes used by prosecutors against defendants who are not going to contest the charges.

bill of pains and penalties A legislative conviction carrying a penalty of something less than death. Such bills are not enforceable in the United States.

bill of particulars A written statement that specifies additional facts about a charge.

Bill of Rights The first 10 Amendments to the U.S. Constitution, which set forth certain freedoms and guarantees to U.S. citizens. *See box p. 26.*

bill of sale A legal document transferring ownership or title of some property to another.

billy club A rodlike weapon, often fashioned from hardwood, used by law enforcement officers to subdue criminal suspects.

binding An element in the definition of an apprenticeship; also, a term used in labor union arbitration agreements, where it means that opposing parties are obligated to observe a settlement reached by a third-party arbiter, as in "binding arbitration."

bind over To cause a defendant, by a court action, to be tried on charges later in a criminal court, following a finding of probable cause that a crime has been committed and that the defendant committed it.

Binet, Alfred (1857–1911) A psychologist who designed tests to measure intelligence and suggested a high correlation between criminality and IQ.

binge drinkers Individuals who consume five or more alcoholic drinks on at least two occasions per month.

bin Laden, Osama (1957–) A terrorist leader of al Qaeda who is considered responsible for a number of terrorist acts against the United States, including the World Trade Center attacks on September 11, 2001.

bio-assay The estimation of a drug's potency by its peculiar action on a living organism.

biocriminology The subdiscipline of criminology that investigates biological and genetic factors and their relation to criminal behavior.

biographical method A research strategy in which the experiences of a single individual are examined in detail.

biological determinism, Biological School A view in criminology holding that criminal behavior has a physiological basis. The theory proposes that genes, foods and food additives, hormones, and inheritance all play a role in determining individual behavior, and genetic make-up causes certain behaviors to become manifest, such as criminality.

biological evidence Information that derives from the human body, such as blood or tissue. DNA testing can be performed on such evidence for purposes of identification.

biology and genetics A set of factors correlated with juvenile delinquency that focus on heredity and chemistry.

biometrics The science of making a personal identification through physical attributes such as fingerprints and other body measurements, usually in an electronic form and involving the use of multiple factors; the modern successor to anthropometry and the Bertillon system, phrenology, and physiognomy.

biometry The process of measuring or estimating the probable duration of a human life; also, the attempt to correlate crime frequency between parents and children or siblings.

biosocial criminology *See* **sociobiology.**

biosocial theory The view that both thought and behavior have biological and social bases.

bioterrorism The use of biological material, such as anthrax or botulin, to perpetrate terrorism. Biological weapons, such

---

Bill of Rights

Amendment I: Congress shall make no law respecting an establishment of religion, or prohibiting the free exercise thereof, or abridging the freedom of speech, or of the press; or the right of the people peaceably to assemble, and to petition the government for a redress of grievances.

Amendment II: A well-regulated militia, being necessary to the security of a free state, the right of the people to keep and bear arms, shall not be infringed.

Amendment III: No soldier shall, in time of peace be quartered in any house, without the consent of the owner, nor in time of war, but in a manner prescribed by law.

Amendment IV: The right of the people to be secure in their persons, houses, papers, and effects, against unreasonable searches and seizures, shall not be violated, and no warrants shall issue, but upon probable cause, supported by oath or affirmation, and particularly describing the place to be searched, and the persons or things to be seized.

Amendment V: No person shall be held to answer for a capital, or otherwise infamous crime, unless on a presentment or indictment of a grand jury, except in cases arising in the land or naval forces, or in the militia, when in actual service in time of war or public danger; nor shall any person be subject for the same offense to be twice put in jeopardy of life or limb; nor shall be compelled in any criminal case to be a witness against himself, nor be deprived of life, liberty, or property, without due process of law; nor shall private property be taken for public use, without just compensation.

Amendment VI: In all criminal prosecutions, the accused shall enjoy the right to a speedy and public trial, by an impartial jury of the state and district wherein the crime shall have been committed, which district shall have been previously ascertained by law, and to be informed of the nature and cause of the accusation; to be confronted with the witnesses against him; to have compulsory process for obtaining witnesses in his favor, and to have the assistance of counsel for his defense.

Amendment VII: In suits at common law, where the value in controversy shall exceed twenty dollars, the right of trial by jury shall be preserved, and no fact tried by a jury, shall be otherwise reexamined in any court of the United States, than according to the rules of common law.

Amendment VIII: Excessive bail shall not be required, nor excessive fines imposed, nor cruel and unusual punishments inflicted.

Amendment IX: The enumeration in the Constitution, of certain rights, shall not be construed to deny or disparage others retained by the people.

Amendment X: The powers not delegated to the United States by the Constitution, nor prohibited by it to the states, are reserved to the states respectively, or to the people.

The Fourteenth Amendment is often included when referencing the Bill of Rights. This amendment is as follows:

Amendment XIV: All persons born or naturalized in the United States, and subject to the jurisdiction thereof, are citizens of the United States and of the state wherein they reside. No state shall make or enforce any law which shall abridge the privileges or immunities of citizens of the United States; nor shall any state deprive any person of life, liberty, or property, without due process of law; nor deny to any person within its jurisdiction the equal protection of the laws.

---

as the dispersement of anthrax with a bomb or spray, can cause large numbers of deaths in a large geographical area in a matter of hours or days, for example.

birth cohort An aggregate consisting of all persons born in the same year.

birth order The sequence in which a person is born in relation to his or her siblings.

bisexuality Acts of persons who have sexual relations with persons of both their own and the opposite gender.

bite-mark identification Forensic determination of a perpetrator's identity by using impressions made by the perpetrator's teeth on the skin of a victim, or on food or other materials. *See also* **forensic odontology.**

Bittner, Egon (1921–) A sociologist who authored several major works on police organizations and functions, including *The Functions of Police in Modern Society* (1970), and has done work for the National Institutes of Mental Health.

Bivens **action** A civil suit arising from the case of *Bivens v. Six Unknown Named Defendants* (1971) brought against federal government officials for denying the constitutional rights of others.

Black, Hugo Lafayette (1886–1971) A former associate justice of the U.S. Supreme Court (1937–1971), appointed by Franklin D. Roosevelt. Black was a believer in civil rights as literally defined by the Bill of Rights, and considered the First Amendment rights of free speech, press, and religion to be absolutes. He was known for frequent intellectual confrontations with rights activists who promoted government authority over individual rights, and endorsed Roosevelt's plan to add additional justices to U.S. Supreme Court (known as the "court-packing plan").

Black Codes Penal codes especially developed to control black slaves in the pre–Civil War South that inflicted more severe punishments on slaves than on whites for many offenses.

Black Gangster Disciple Nation An alliance formed by two separate organizations, the Disciple Nation, whose president was David Barksdale, and the Gangster Nation, whose president was Larry "King" Hoover. It is made up largely of Chicago-based street gangs that formed during the 1950s and 1960s. Established in 1969 as the Black Gangster Disciple Nation, the gang has engaged in various community projects, including security work, welfare programming for the homeless, and political activism. Some members have been lost to the illegal drug trade. The gang has attempted to minimize violence and gain respectability throughout the community.

Black Gangster Disciples A Chicago-based street gang formed in the 1960s engaged in illegal drug and weapons trafficking. Its identifying symbols include the six-pointed star, the letters "BGD," and raised pitchforks.

Black Guerrilla Family (BGF) A black prison gang formed to protect and advance the position of the black race with a philosophy that advocates violence to achieve its objectives.

Black Hand An extortionist group that originated in Sicily and became active in the United States in the early twentieth century.

"black hat" A term used to describe a computer hacker or cracker, usually a former criminal convicted of one or more cybercrimes, who breaks into a computer system or network with malicious intent; originally derived from Western movies in which bandits or "bad guys" wore black hats, as opposed to heros, who wore white hats. Some corporations may hire a criminal hacker to break into the computer systems of others for various nefarious purposes, such as stealing company secrets, learning about new inventions in a competitive economic market, or copying protected designs or diagrams or formulae. *See also* **"gray hat"; "white hat."**

blackjack A short bludgeon consisting, at the striking end, of an encased piece of lead or some other heavy substance and, at the handle end, a strap or springy shaft that increases the force or impact when a person or object is struck; includes but is not limited to the billy club, sand club, sandbag, or slapjack.

black-light stamps A security device involving stamping the palm or hand with ink that reflects ultraviolet light and so is visible when black light is shone on it.

blacklist To deny privileges and rights to others because of their political or social beliefs or other criteria.

blackmail Extorting money or valuables by threatening to reveal or disclose information a person would not want generally known (e.g., if a public official has an illegitimate child and is running for political office).

black market The illegal trafficking in merchandise that is either in scarce supply or whose manufacture or distribution is heavily regulated.

Black Muslims An organization begun in America in the 1930s by blacks that combined the tenets of Islam and Christianity.

Black Panther Party Research Project (BPPRP) An organization created in 1997 to locate sources and develop aids to assist researchers and the general public with uncovering information about the Black Panther Party.

Black Panthers, Black Panther Party A group of dissident blacks organized in Oakland, CA, in October 1966 by Bobby Seale and Dr. Huey P. Newton in reaction to police brutality in the black community and to provide protection for blacks from the police. Their objective, with respect to inmates, was to unite all prisoner movement groups through an inclusive ideology emphasizing their similarities and minimizing their differences.

black rage The deep anger and hatred that blacks have felt over being subjected to more than three and a half centuries of humiliation, prejudice, and discrimination.

Blacks in Law Enforcement (BLE) Established in 1986 and headquartered in Memphis, TN. Publishes *Blacks in Law Enforcement*.

Blackstone Rangers A Chicago youth gang formed in the 1960s by 12- to 15-year-old youths from Blackstone Avenue in Woodlawn, a Chicago suburb. Its leader was Jeff Fort, who contended from the beginning of the gang's existence that it was an "organization" and not a "gang." It was the first Chicago gang to form gangs in other cities, including Cleveland, OH; Milwaukee, WI; and Gary, IN, by 1967. It was subsequently renamed the Black P. Stone Nation, as gang leadership adopted the Muslim faith, and later renamed El Rukus. It met in the Grand Temple, which was raided by police and demolished several years later. Fort and others were implicated in a conspiracy with Libyan terrorists.

Black Talon A special cartridge, outlawed in many jurisdictions, that causes extreme damage to human tissue due to sharp points that extend on impact.

black tar heroin A crudely refined form of heroin, usually imported from Mexico.

blameworthiness The amount of culpability or guilt a person maintains for participating in a particular criminal offense.

"blaming the victim" The stereotypical practice of charging the socially and psychologically handicapped with the lack of motivation; an attitude or belief that the adverse conditions and negative characteristics of a group, often a minority group, are the group's own fault.

blended families Nuclear families that are the product of divorce and remarriage that blend one parent from each of two families and their combined children into a single family unit.

blended sentencing Any type of sentencing procedure in which either a criminal or juvenile court judge can impose *both* juvenile and adult incarcerative penalties. *See figure p. 28.*

block officers Those responsible for supervising inmates in housing areas.

block watch A group of neighbors in a housing subdivision who band together for the purpose of watching for and reporting suspicious persons or activities to the police. Signs are sometimes posted stating that such watches are under way as a warning to potential criminals who may wish to burglarize dwellings in such neighborhoods. *See also* **Neighborhood Watch, neighborhood watch programs.**

blood alcohol The concentration of alcohol in blood, which is usually measured by grams per 100 milliliters of blood.

blood alcohol content (BAC) The amount of alcohol in blood as measured by various devices and by which intoxication can be inferred. BAC can be determined by breath, blood, or urine samples. Testing devices yield a percentage, such as .13, which means that there are 13/100ths of a part alcohol per 1,000 parts of blood. Generally, .08 or .10 are conventional BACs for determining that motorists are legally intoxicated. If a motorist registers .08 or higher in a state with a .08 standard, the motorist is legally intoxicated.

blood-borne pathogens Disease-causing organisms, including bacteria or viruses, carried through the circulatory system.

blood feud An ongoing conflict between two kinship groups.

Bloods A juvenile street gang seen as part of a new, more violent influx of gangs into prisons. The Bloods originated in

Southern California to defend against the Crips, and are aligned with People Nation. Bloods use the color red and red bandannas or rags to identify one another, and use the word "Piru," which is the original Blood gang term. Gang members cross out the letter *c* to show disrespect to Crips. Through migration, Bloods are found in most states with numerous affiliate gangs and individual gang members. Members commit many different forms of violence, and are known for trafficking in illegal drugs and weapons.

bloodstain Residue of blood that may reveal clues to criminal investigators about blood type, the position of the victim, and other crime details.

bludgeon A club similar to a short baseball bat used to attack an opponent.

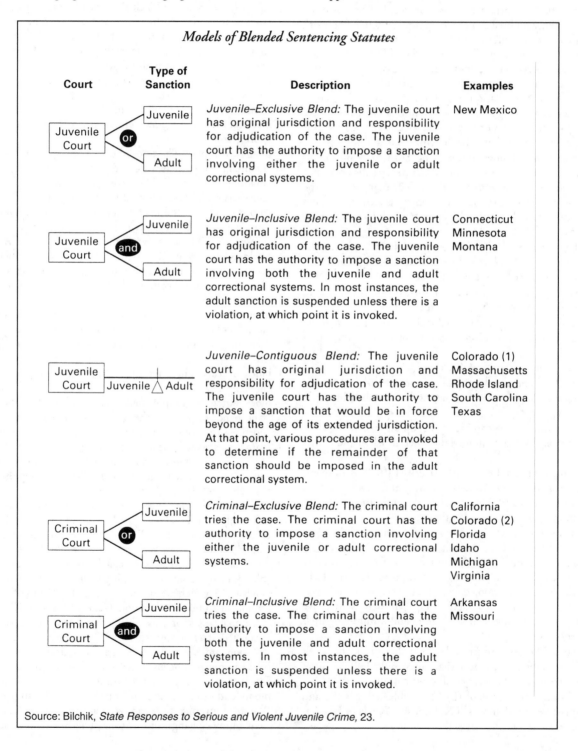

Models of Blended Sentencing Statutes

Court	Type of Sanction	Description	Examples
Juvenile Court	*or* Juvenile / Adult	**Juvenile–Exclusive Blend:** The juvenile court has original jurisdiction and responsibility for adjudication of the case. The juvenile court has the authority to impose a sanction involving either the juvenile or adult correctional systems.	New Mexico
Juvenile Court	*and* Juvenile / Adult	**Juvenile–Inclusive Blend:** The juvenile court has original jurisdiction and responsibility for adjudication of the case. The juvenile court has the authority to impose a sanction involving both the juvenile and adult correctional systems. In most instances, the adult sanction is suspended unless there is a violation, at which point it is invoked.	Connecticut Minnesota Montana
Juvenile Court	Juvenile △ Adult	**Juvenile–Contiguous Blend:** The juvenile court has original jurisdiction and responsibility for adjudication of the case. The juvenile court has the authority to impose a sanction that would be in force beyond the age of its extended jurisdiction. At that point, various procedures are invoked to determine if the remainder of that sanction should be imposed in the adult correctional system.	Colorado (1) Massachusetts Rhode Island South Carolina Texas
Criminal Court	*or* Juvenile / Adult	**Criminal–Exclusive Blend:** The criminal court tries the case. The criminal court has the authority to impose a sanction involving either the juvenile or adult correctional systems.	California Colorado (2) Florida Idaho Michigan Virginia
Criminal Court	*and* Juvenile / Adult	**Criminal–Inclusive Blend:** The criminal court tries the case. The criminal court has the authority to impose a sanction involving both the juvenile and adult correctional systems. In most instances, the adult sanction is suspended unless there is a violation, at which point it is invoked.	Arkansas Missouri

Source: Bilchik, *State Responses to Serious and Violent Juvenile Crime*, 23.

bluebeard A man who serially marries and then murders his wives, based on a fictional character in a novel by Charles Perrault.

blue-collar workers A term associated with employees who are factory workers, as distinguished from supervisory and administrative personnel who wear shirts with white collars, that signifies limited skills and nonsupervisory status. Many factory workers have worn traditional blue shirts.

blue curtain, blue wall, blue wall of silence The reluctance among police officials to punish one of their colleagues when a citizen complains. When police agencies "investigate their own," the very language used in such investigations is telling.

blue laws Any local laws or ordinances prohibiting store operations on Sunday, racetrack betting, or other activities that may be morally questionable if performed on Sunday. Blue laws in most jurisdictions have been overturned by the U.S. Supreme Court as unconstitutional.

Blueprints Model Programs Ten model prevention and intervention programs that meet scientific standards of proven program effectiveness. The programs identified focus on a variety of prevention methods and target several different populations for interventions.

blue-ribbon jury A jury considered by either side, prosecution or defense, to be ideal because of its perceived likelihood of rendering a verdict favorable to that side.

blue-sky laws Statutes intended to prevent sale of fraudulent securities. The term was coined by a Kansas bank commissioner who remarked that certain brokers and promoters were so skillful in their fraud that they could sell large blocks of blue sky to gullible clients. Presently the government requires companies that issue stock to file financial statements with banking commissioners in all jurisdictions.

board of pardons Special appointed boards in different jurisdictions that convene to hear requests from inmates to be pardoned or to receive executive clemency from governors.

board of parole Any body of persons, usually appointed by the governor or chief executive officer of any jurisdiction, that convenes for the purpose of determining an inmate's early release. Each state and the federal government has a parole board. Most state parole boards are gubernatorial appointments. Parole boards vary in size from three-person panels to as many as 10 to 12 members. No special qualifications are required for parole-board membership.

boards of review Special boards convened to review evidence and make recommendations. They may also make recommendations for citations or rewards. Law enforcement agencies have such boards in cases involving allegations of officer misconduct.

bobbies British police named for Sir Robert "Bobby" Peel, a British Home Secretary of the 1820s.

body armor Bullet-proof or bullet-resistant vests and other clothing designed to stop the penetration or lessen the impact of bullets.

Body Armor Safety Initiative A December 2003 National Institute of Justice–sponsored study of the effectiveness of body armor or bullet-proof vests and their reliability as defensive clothing to protect law enforcement officers from ballistic threats during shooting incidents. The study was prompted by an incident in Forest Hills, PA, in which a bullet penetrated the Zylon body armor of a police officer during a June 2003 shooting. The officer, who was wearing a Second Chance Ultima vest made of Zylon, was seriously injured when the bullet penetrated the armor. Companies involved in the manufacture of questionably effective body armor include Second Chance Body Armor, Inc. of Central Lake, MI, and Toyobo Co., Ltd. of Osaka, Japan. Despite the Forest Hills incident, body armor manufacturers claim that law enforcement officers who do not wear body armor have a risk of fatality 14 times greater than that of officers who do wear body armor.

body belt A restraining device worn by prisoners with wrist restraints at the center of the abdomen.

body cavity search Any inspection of the vagina, rectum, or other body orifice.

body types Early nineteenth- and twentieth-century theorists conjectured an association between one's physical features and criminal conduct. Typologies were invented showing patterns of association between body types and behaviors. The theory is currently outmoded.

Boesky, Ivan (1937–) An infamous Wall Street inside trader of the 1980s who used confidential stock information to illegally gain millions of dollars.

bogus False; not genuine.

boiler room, boiler room fraud An operation run by one or more stock traders and manipulators who, through deception and misleading sales techniques, seduce unsuspecting buyers into purchasing stocks in obscure and poorly financed corporations.

bombing incident The detonation or attempted detonation of an explosive or incendiary device with the willful disregard for others and for a criminal purpose.

bomb squad A unit of a law enforcement agency especially trained to safely handle, move, disarm, and/or detonate bombs and other explosives.

bomb training school A Department of Justice–initiated school, later replicated in certain state jurisdictions, where persons acquire knowledge about bombs, their construction and operation, and how to defuse them.

bona fide "In good faith" (Latin); without the attempt to defraud or deceive.

bona fide **occupational qualifications (BFOQ)** Job qualifications that are in and of themselves necessary for adequate performance of a particular job, and that can be used to exclude individuals who do not have them.

bona fide **religious belief or practice** A belief or practice that is found in a religion's published theology or expert testimony, which indicates that it is associated with a particular religion.

bond A written document indicating that defendants or sureties assure the presence of these defendants at a criminal proceeding. If the defendants fail to appear, the bond is forfeited.

bond act A common means of financing public construction with private funds by selling bonds to be paid back at moderate interest over a number of years. Bond financing drastically increases costs of construction, but also removes construction costs from yearly operating costs.

bondage Masochistic activities generally involving bindings and restraints, hoods, gags, and blindfolds. It may be practiced with partners or alone.

bond agent, bondsman *See* **bail bondsman, bail bondsperson.**

bonding, bonding theory A key concept in a number of theoretical formulations; Emile Durkheim's notion that deviant behavior is controlled to the degree that group members feel morally bound to one another, are committed to common goals, and share a collective conscience; in social control theory, the elements of attachment, commitment, involvement, and belief; an explanation of criminal behavior implying that criminality is the result of a loosening of bonds or attachments with society, which builds on differential association theory. The theory is primarily designed to account for juvenile delinquency.

Bonger, Willem Adrian (1876–1940) A Dutch theorist who advocated Marxist socialist views about crime and its causes. He believed that crime is of social origin rather than biological, that criminal behavior is within the boundaries of normal human behavior, and that methods to control crime should include punishment of sufficient severity to deter offenders, thus offsetting the gratifying element derived from committing crime. Bonger endorsed the Marxist view of class conflict, believing that law functions to benefit the ruling class (bourgeoisie) rather than the working class (proletariat). He wrote *Criminality and Economic Conditions* (1910).

boodle Gratuities accepted in exchange for use of political influence. The term was coined in New York City during the 1880s.

bookie A person who engages in the illegal practice of accepting bets relating to horse or dog races, athletic events, or any other contest or event whose outcome is in doubt.

booking The process of making a written report of an arrest, including the name and address of the arrested persons, the alleged crimes, arresting officers, the place and time of arrest, a physical description of the suspect, photographs (sometimes called "mug shots"), and fingerprints.

bookmaking The illegal activity of accepting bets or wagers on athletic events, races, Academy Award winners, and any other event whose outcome is in doubt.

booster A thief, particularly a shoplifter.

booster girdle An elastic band or similar device worn about the waist by a shoplifter, designed to hold stolen goods tightly against the body for the purpose of concealment.

boot camp A short-term institutional sentence, usually followed by probation, that puts the offender through a physical regimen designed to develop discipline and respect for authority. *See also* **shock probation.**

Booth, John Wilkes (1838–1865) Born in Bel Air, MD, Booth was an actor who assassinated President Abraham Lincoln at Ford's Theater in Washington, DC, on April 14, 1865. Booth was found on April 26, 1865, hiding in a barn in Bowling Green, VA. He was either killed by his captors or committed suicide.

bootlegger A person who engages in the illegal manufacture, sale, or transportation of alcohol.

bootlegging Illegally manufacturing alcohol or alcoholic beverages and/or transporting such contraband for sale.

Borden, Lizzie (1860–1927) A Fall River, MA, woman alleged to have viciously murdered her own parents with a hatchet in 1892. Borden was tried and found not guilty by a jury.

border A political dividing line establishing a geographical jurisdiction and demarking territory. Borders are usually associated with lines separating countries from one another geographically.

borderline personality disorder A psychological abnormality characterized by instability of relationships and impulsive behavior.

Border Patrol (BP) Established in 1924 with 450 officers, the BP was originally created to police the borders between the United States and Canada and Mexico. Under the McCarran Walter Act of 1952, the BP was charged with three goals: (1) the reunification of families; (2) the immigration of persons with needed labor skills; and (3) the protection of the domestic labor force.

born criminal In Cesare Lombroso's deterministic view, one who is born with genetically transmitted criminal characteristics and thereby destined to become a criminal; an atavist.

borstal A British facility for juveniles equivalent to U.S. industrial schools, where British juvenile offenders are sentenced to a term of supervision during which they may receive therapy, vocational or educational training, and remedial help.

borstal system European halfway houses used to temporarily house recently released inmates from prisons or jails, providing food, shelter, employment assistance, and other services.

Boston Children's Aid Society A privately funded philanthropic society founded by Rufus R. Cook in 1860 that catered to orphans and other minors who did not have adequate adult supervision. Volunteers assisted juvenile offenders.

Boston Massacre An incident that occurred in Boston in 1770 involving British troops who fired into a crowd of protesting men and boys in Boston Harbor, killing several.

Boston Offender Project (BOP) An experimental juvenile treatment program commenced in 1981 through the Massachusetts Department of Youth Services aimed at reducing recidivism, reintegrating youths, and increasing offender accountability.

Boston Police Strike A boycott by 75 percent of the Boston Police Department officers in September, 1919, prompted by the police commissioner's refusal to recognize the union recently established by police officers. Then-Governor Calvin Coolidge brought in the Massachusetts militia to temporarily police the city, declaring that no one has the right to strike against public safety at any time.

Boston Strangler *See* **DeSalvo, Albert.**

bot Under Anglo-Saxon law, the restitution paid for killing someone in an open fight.

botanical material Fragments of plants that can be used in solving crimes. Such material might be found on someone's shoes, on tire treads, or on other surfaces and can be used by forensics specialists to identify criminals.

Bounds violation The failure of a prison to provide an inmate with some form of legal assistance. The adverse consequences to the inmate must be demonstrable and include substantial shortcomings that would hinder his or her efforts to pursue nonfrivolous legal claims. *See Bounds v. Smith* (1977).

bounty Monetary rewards offered for the capture of persons who escape prosecution from a given jurisdiction.

bounty hunter Someone hired to apprehend a person who has posted a bond with a bonding company so that monies deposited with the courts by the bonding company can be recovered.

bourgeoisie In Marxist theory, owners of the means of production; the capitalist ruling class.

Bow Street Runners A small English organization of paid police officers that was established in 1754 to apprehend criminals.

Brace, Charles Loring (1826–1890) Established the New York Children's Aid Society in 1853.

brachioproticism Also known as brachioprotic eroticism, the practice involves inserting an arm into another's rectum for sexual gratification; also known as fisting.

Brady, James S. (1940–) Born in Centralia, IL, in 1940, Brady graduated from the University of Illinois in 1962 with a degree in communications and political science. He served as a staff member to Senator Everett Dirksen from 1961 to 1962, joined Delaware Senator William V. Roth, Jr.'s staff in 1977, became Press Secretary to then-presidential candidate Governor John Connally in 1979, was appointed by President Ronald Reagan as White House Press Secretary in 1981, and was shot and permanently disabled during John Hinckley's March 30, 1981, assassination attempt on President Ronald Reagan. In subsequent years, Brady and his wife, Sarah, lobbied for stronger gun laws, eventually leading President William Clinton to sign the Brady Bill, named in Brady's honor. Brady serves as a committee member for the Center to Prevent Handgun Violence and Handgun Control, Inc., and is vice-chairman of the National Organization on Disability. *See also* Brady Bill.

Brady Bill A piece of federal legislation named for former White House press secretary James S. Brady, who was shot and disabled in the 1981 assassination attempt on President Ronald Reagan. The bill was designed to reduce the opportunities for criminals to obtain handguns easily by requiring purchasers of handguns to undergo extensive criminal background checks and imposing a national waiting period on gun purchases.

Brady materials Exculpatory materials that must be disclosed through discovery to defense counsel by the prosecution when a defendant is to be tried for a crime. *See Brady v. Maryland* (1963).

Brady violation A violation of discovery rules when a prosecutor fails to turn over exculpatory materials acquired during a criminal investigation to defense counsel. A violation occurs whenever three conditions are met: (1) the evidence at issue is favorable to the accused, either because it is exculpatory, or because it is impeaching; (2) the evidence has been suppressed by the state, either willfully or inadvertently; and (3) prejudice has ensued.

brain dead, brain death A physical condition in which the brain has been deprived of oxygen to the extent that brain function ceases but the body continues to survive, usually through mechanical means and artificial life-support systems. A person is presumed dead with a brain death.

Bramshill The United Kingdom's senior police college.

Brandeis, Louis Dembitz (1856–1941) Associate Justice of the U.S. Supreme Court (1916–1939) appointed by President Woodrow Wilson in 1916. Brandeis achieved fame as a trial litigator in civil suits, and for the use of social and economic arguments to emphasize legal points. He advocated judicial restraint and helped to formulate the clear-and-present-danger test to judge the impact of speeches and published articles.

branding A method of torture whereby a mark is placed on an individual with a hot iron to label that person a criminal.

brank A cagelike instrument placed over a victim's head that contained metal spikes which extended into an inmate's mouth. Any movement by the victim caused spikes to gouge the mouth or tongue. It was used in the late eighteenth century as a disciplinary tool for unruly inmates.

brass knuckles A handheld device fashioned from brass rings or other cast-iron metals used to inflict greater harm when hitting someone with the fist.

Brawner rule, *Brawner* test The legal rule that a person will be found not guilty by reason of insanity "if at the time of such conduct as a result of mental disease or mental defect, he lacks substantial capacity either to appreciate the criminality of his conduct or to conform his conduct to the requirements of the law." The rule was adopted by the American Law Institute in 1972 and can be found in *United States v. Brawner,* 471 F.2d 969 (1972).

breach of the peace Any disruption of public decorum, such as loud noises, fighting, or any other interference with neighborhood equilibrium, can be the basis for a complaint to the police to intercede and stop the disruption.

breach of trust A contractual term implying a failure to comply with one or more terms of a contract or mutual agreement between parties; a criminal act involving a fiduciary, possibly embezzlement.

breaking, breaking and entering, break-in The forceful, unlawful entry into a building or conveyance.

Breathalyzer A product or device used to test the breath of suspected motorists or pedestrians to determine whether they are legally intoxicated by measuring blood-alcohol content.

breath-testing equipment Any device designed to ascertain the amount of alcohol in a person's body by measuring his or her breath.

bribe, bribery The crime of offering, giving, requesting, soliciting, or receiving something of value to influence a decision of a public official.

"bricks and mortar" Attempts to construct new or renovate existing jail or prison facilities to expand available bed space to house more inmates.

Bridewell Workhouse The first correctional institution in England. Both children and adults considered to be idle and disorderly were confined there.

bridle An iron cage that fit over the head and had a front plate that was sharpened or covered with spikes designed to fit into the mouth of an offender, used to punish individuals as well as to keep them from speaking.

brief A document filed by a party to a lawsuit to convince the court of the merits of that party's case.

Brink's Armored Car Service An organization established in 1859 in Chicago, IL, by Washington Perry Brink to transport money and other items of value from one location to another (e.g., between banking institutions and businesses).

British Crime Survey (BCS) An annual compilation of victimization figures for both England and Wales comparable to the National Crime Victimization Survey published in the United States.

British North America Act Legislation passed by the Canadian Parliament in 1867 that created the structure of the present Canadian criminal-justice system.

British Society of Criminology (BSC) A professional organization of criminologists in the United Kingdom with a membership of more than 800. It holds an annual conference and publishes the *British Journal of Criminology.*

broad community notification A type of law that permits states to disseminate information about sex offenders in the community to the public.

Brockway, Zebulon Reed (1827–1920) As the first superintendent of New York State Reformatory at Elmira in 1876, Brockway has been credited with arguably introducing the first "good-time" system in the United States, whereby inmates could have their sentences reduced or shortened by the number of good marks earned through good behavior.

Broderick Typology A classification of police officers into Idealists, who are college-educated, have high ideals, and believe in social order and commitment; Enforcers, who are ends-oriented and least likely to choose or recommend a police career; Optimists, who are people-oriented, management-aspiring "yes" persons; and Realists, who believe their work is "just a job," have a "hell with it" attitude, and are retired in place. The terms were defined by John Broderick in his 1977 work *Police in a Time of Change.*

broken home A home plagued by a variety of serious problems, including abuse, neglect, and/or divorce; a single-parent family. The term is usually associated with juvenile delinquency.

"broken windows" approach, broken window syndrome A form of police patrol that stresses better communication with citizens. Foot patrols, team policing, and other "back to the people" programs are consistent with this patrol form. The term is used to describe the role of the police as maintainers of community order and safety and the view that police attention to disorder (low-level offenses such as drunkenness or prostitution) will prevent or forestall acts of more serious crime.

broken windows probation A form of probation supervision grounded in the broken windows theory that helped create community policing. Such probation connects probation more closely with the problems and needs of the communities where probationers live and are supervised, focusing on programming that works.

brokerage model A probation or parole officer work-role orientation in which the officer functions as a referral service and supplies the offender-client with contacts to agencies that provide needed services. A probation or parole officer attempts to determine the needs of the probationer or parolee and refers him or her to the appropriate community agency for services.

Bronner, Augusta (1881–1966) Together with William Healy, she conducted a 1926 study of delinquent boys and reported that they were five to 10 times more likely to be subnormal in intelligence than nondelinquents.

brothel A house of prostitution, typically run by a madam who sets prices and handles "business."

brutalization effect, process The belief that capital punishment creates an atmosphere of brutality that enhances, rather than deters, the level of violence in society, and that the death penalty reinforces the view that violence is an appropriate response to violence.

***Bruton* rule** A rule prohibiting the introduction during joint trials of confessions of nontestifying codefendants that name a defendant as the perpetrator. The rule also extends to redacted or edited confessions in which the name of the defendant has been deleted. *See Bruton v. United States* (1968).

budget A plan for the accomplishment of programs relating to objectives and goals within a definite time period, including an estimate of financial resources required together with an estimate of resources available, usually compared with past periods and showing future requirements.

bug An electronic device enabling a listener to intercept conversations of other persons. Devices are usually secreted on premises or in a telephone device. Law enforcement officers must obtain judicial authorization to conduct such surveillance, also known as wiretapping.

buggery *See* **sodomy.**

building tender An inmate who achieves a supervisory position to assist prison officials with maintenance of an institution and the control of other inmates. *See also* **trusty.**

bulimia nervosa An eating disorder characterized by binge eating and then deliberately regurgitating or throwing up eaten food or taking excessive laxatives to purge the body of food. It is a psychologically based condition wherein a person strives to become slender or thin.

bull A prison guard; also, a woman who is masculine in appearance in a lesbian relationship (i.e., a mannish lesbian); also, an early twentieth-century term for a railroad police officer.

bull dyke A woman in a lesbian relationship who plays a masculine role and often has masculine features (e.g. large-bodied, short hair); also, prison slang for such a person.

bullet A projectile made for firing in a rifle or pistol or any firearm. It is usually seated in a brass casing filled with special gunpowder and a primer, and activated in the firearm when a hammer on the firearm strikes the primer, igniting the powder and discharging the projectile. Types of bullets include lead roundnose, jacketed hollowpoint, wadcutter and semi-wadcutter, metal piercing, and teflon-coated.

bullet jacket A sheath, usually made of copper, that encases a lead bullet for the purpose of reducing lead fouling of the inside of the gun barrel.

bullet-proof vest Any type of jacket worn, usually by a law enforcement officer, for the purpose of deflecting bullets; a protective covering worn about the upper torso that is impenetrable by bullets.

bullet track In forensics, the path made by a bullet entering and passing through the body.

bullpen A cagelike structure for holding nonviolent prisoners on a temporary basis, sometimes referred to as the drunk tank.

bullying Threatening or intimidating behavior, sometimes accompanied by physical violence, by some youths toward others, especially smaller or weaker children, and usually carried out on school grounds.

Bullying Prevention Program A program that targets bullies in elementary, middle, and high schools and vests school authorities with intervention powers to establish class rules for disciplining bullies and bullying behavior through student committees.

Bundy, Theodore ("Ted") (1946–1989) A serial killer of the 1970s who abducted and murdered numerous women in Washington, Utah, and Colorado. Also known as Chris Hagen, Bundy grew up in Tacoma, WA, did charity work, and campaigned for the Republican Party. He became assistant director of the Seattle Crime Prevention advisory committee. The former law student was eventually apprehended after murdering two women at a sorority house at Florida State University. Evidence disclosed that between 1973 and 1978 he went on a crime spree through a number of states, killing at least 36 women. He became a fugitive from justice but was apprehended in Florida on a routine traffic stop while driving a stolen car. Implicated in several Florida murders, he was subsequently executed in the Florida electric chair in 1989.

bunko game A trick devised to gain the confidence of a victim for the purpose of obtaining something of value, such as goods or money, from the victim; a confidence racket.

burden of proof The requirement to introduce evidence to prove an alleged fact or set of facts.

bureaucracy An organizational model that vests individuals with authority and spheres of competence in a predetermined hierarchy with abstract rules and selection by test.

bureaucratic-lawful model The bureaucratization of prisons and the establishment of elaborate chains of command linking prison administrators with their subordinates.

bureaucratic model, bureaucratic organizational model A way of viewing an organization as characterized by the following features: impersonal social relations, appointment and promotion on the basis of merit, previously specified authority obligations that inhere in the position, a hierarchy of authority, abstract rules or laws covering task assignments and decisions, and specialization of position.

bureaucratic model of legislation The orientation that laws are created or enacted as the result of legitimate power exerted by bureaucratic organizations.

bureaucratization The extension of the bureaucracy's spheres of activities and power either in its own interests or those of some of its elite. It tends toward greater regimentation of different areas of social life and some extent of displacement of its service goals in favor of various power interests or orientations.

Bureau of Alcohol, Tobacco, and Firearms (BATF) The BATF began as a subunit of the Internal Revenue Service in 1862, when certain alcohol and tobacco tax statutes were created. It was originally called the Alcohol, Tobacco, and Tax Unit and was later named the Alcohol, Tobacco, and Firearms Division within the IRS. In 1972, it became the current BATF under the direct control of the Department of the Treasury. Its general mission in combating crime is to reduce the illegal use of firearms and explosives. It also seeks to curtail arson-for-profit schemes, and its agents investigate scenes of fires with mysterious origins.

Bureau of Justice Assistance A bureau created in 1984 to make grants available to researchers for the purpose of learning more about crime prevention and control. It is known for block grants to criminal-justice agencies to fund operational costs of programs.

Bureau of Justice Statistics A bureau created in 1979 to distribute statistical information concerning crime, criminals, and crime trends.

Bureau of Narcotics and Dangerous Drugs Established in 1968 by the Bureau of Narcotics, the U.S. Department of the Treasury, and the Bureau of Drug Abuse Control of the Department of Health, Education, and Welfare. Headquartered in Washington, DC, the bureau conducts investigations and compiles statistics relative to illicit drug use in the United States and disseminates this information in government documents.

Bureau of Prisons Female Offenders An organization headquartered in Washington, DC, that monitors and oversees programs for federal female offenders.

bureaus of criminal identification (BCIs) Similar to the FBI, these state bureaus perform routine criminal investigation functions. When state police become involved in such operations, they usually perform supporting functions such as assisting state investigative agents. They may assist agents by making arrests of criminal suspects, interviewing witnesses, or gathering and securing evidence from crime scenes.

Burger, Warren Earl (1907–1995) A former chief justice of the U.S. Supreme Court (1969–1986), appointed by President Richard Nixon in 1969, Burger was a strict constructionist with law-and-order views. He was born in St. Paul, MN, and was a successful lawyer. In 1953, Burger was appointed attorney general of the United States by President Dwight D. Eisenhower. Known for his conservative views, Burger helped to define obscenity, supported busing programs and affirmative action, and helped force President Nixon to disclose the Watergate tapes.

Burger Court The United States Supreme Court under the leadership of Chief Justice Warren Burger, 1969–1986.

Burgess, Ernest W. (1886–1966) Burgess helped to form the Chicago School of thought, a social ecology view that related crime with various sectors or zones emanating from city centers. The concentric-zone hypothesis posited that different types of behavior or criminal conduct could be found in particular well-defined zones emanating away from the center of a city. Zones undergoing urban renewal, known as interstitial areas, were believed to contain a high degree of criminality because social disorganization was a key feature of such areas, with neighborhoods in transition and families in disarray, heightening conditions for criminal conduct.

burglar One who commits burglary or breaking and entering a dwelling for the purpose of committing another crime, such as theft.

burglar alarm An electronic device designed to emit a sound or signal alerting residents or car owners that a break-in has occurred.

burglary The unlawful entry of a structure to commit a felony or theft.

burglary tools Any devices or instruments used to gain illegal entry into a business or family dwelling.

burking Murder by asphyxia and smothering in such a way as to disguise the manner of death by leaving the victim unmarked.

burnese A form of highly concentrated cocaine.

burnout Usually the result of stress, burnout is a syndrome of emotional exhaustion, depersonalization, and reduced personal accomplishment; a progressive loss of idealism, energy, and purpose; a state of physical, emotional, and mental exhaustion marked by physical depletion and chronic fatigue; feelings of helplessness and hopelessness; the development of a negative self-concept; and negative attitudes toward work, life, and other people. *See also* **Maslach Burnout Inventory.**

Burns, William John (1861–1932) The founder of the Burns International Detective Agency and chief of the Federal Bureau of Investigation. Born in Baltimore, MD, Burns served in the U.S. Secret Service and the Department of the Interior. He formed Burns and Sheridan Detective Agency with William Sheridan in 1909 and subsequently, after Sheridan sold his interest in the business to Burns, founded the Burns International Detective Agency.

Burns International Security Services, Inc. Offers security services to public and private organizations and conducts investigations involving possible criminal activities of members of business and other organizations. Established by William Burns in 1909, it was originally called the Burns International Detective Agency.

Bursik, Robert A criminologist who collaborated with Janet Heitgerd (1987) in noting the phenomenon that as parts of communities undergo change, adjacent areas not undergoing change will experience a change in their crime rates.

business crime A wrongful act committed in the course of transacting business. *See also* **white-collar crime.**

business organization In criminology, a reference to any permanent structure that profits from extortion and the provision of illegal goods and services, more commonly called "organized crime"; in traditional usage, any legitimate enterprise.

bust An arrest.

butt The grip end of a handgun or stock end of a rifle opposite the muzzle end.

butterfly knife A folding pocketknife that can be spun or twirled in one's hand, opening and closing the blade with each revolution; also called a Balisong, after the town of its origin in the Philippines. This type of knife is unique in that it has two handles that counter-rotate around a tang. When the knife is opened and the two handles are locked together, it is as strong and reliable as a fixed-blade knife. These knives are often used by gang members in hand-to-hand fighting with rival gangs.

bystander Someone who is in close proximity to a crime or accident and who has the potential of being a witness or affecting the response to an incident.

"by the book" A reference to a strict legalistic approach to situations, without the exercise of discretion that takes into account the personal situations of the individuals involved. This approach eschews alternative means of problem solving. The term is usually applied to arrest-oriented police officers, but may be applied to all officials and functionaries.

C

CA An abbreviation for a U.S. Circuit Court of Appeals.

cache A collection of hidden contraband, often associated with an illegal storage of weaponry.

cadaver A dead body.

cadaveric spasm A physiological reaction that may occur soon after death in which a single muscle group becomes stiff and rigid.

cadet programs Programs designed to bring underage but otherwise qualified individuals into police service.

cadre Trained activists who form the core of an organization and who are capable of training others.

Cain The Old Testament farmer, son of Adam and Eve, known as the world's first murderer for killing his brother Abel.

calculative involvement The disposition of persons who believe that they will be rewarded for complying with a superior's request to do something. Rewards may be tangible or intangible (e.g., better working hours, pay, supervision, recognition, promotion or advancement).

calendar A court listing of pending cases to be heard; a docket.

caliber The diameter of a cartridge. Different calibers (e.g., .44, .44 special, .38, .22) are used to designate the sizes of cartridges fired by certain types of weapons.

Cali Cartel An illegal organization based in Cali, Colombia, believed at one time to control the vast majority of the world's cocaine distribution.

California Personality Inventory (CPI) A psychological device or instrument that purportedly measures personality dimensions such as anxiety, sociability, personal adjustment, and social adjustment.

California Youth Authority (CYA) The California state agency responsible for the confinement of youths aged 17 to 25 who have been remanded by juvenile courts.

Calley, William L., Jr (1943–) In March 1968, Lt. Calley was involved in the massacre of the village of My Lai, Vietnam, in which nearly 600 civilians were executed. They were believed to be supporters of the Viet Cong, the enemy soldiers fighting U.S. troops during the Vietnam war. Calley was subsequently charged with crimes stemming from the killings of these civilians, and convicted. Sentenced to life imprisonment, Calley was subsequently placed under house arrest, and later, his sentence was commuted.

call girls Prostitutes who make dates via the telephone and then service customers in hotel rooms or apartments. Call girls typically have a steady clientele of repeat customers.

callouts The taking of inmates from regularly scheduled activities for a special purpose, such as a dental appointment.

calls for service Reports of crime from citizens or requests for any other type of police assistance within the scope of police authority, duties, and responsibilities.

calumny A spoken degradation of some person; slander or malicious speech about someone or their qualities and personality.

Camarena, Enrique ("Kiki") (1948–1985) A DEA agent who assisted in a Mexican marijuana raid in 1984, Camarena was later kidnapped in Guadalajara and murdered. Two drug kingpins, Caro Quintero and Ernesto Carrillo, were arrested, charged, and convicted of Camarena's murder.

Cambridge-Somerville Youth Study An investigation of delinquency prevention that began in 1937 that was unique because it examined a large number of youth over a long period of time (a longitudinal study). Collected data included intelligence, personality characteristics, school progress, and neighborhood features.

cameras in the courtroom Use of video cameras in courtrooms to record proceedings, most often trials.

Camorra A secret underworld organization originating in Naples, Italy, in 1830 that existed until the early 1920s; a general term for a criminal syndicate or enterprise; an early version of the Mafia.

camp, farm, ranch In corrections, any of several types of similar correctional confinement facilities for adults or juveniles, usually located in rural areas.

Campaign for an Effective Crime Policy (CECP) An initiative by criminal-justice professionals to move toward a less politicized and more informed debate on criminal-justice policy. It questions unnecessarily long prison sentences, easy access to firearms, and the highly publicized nature of criminal trials, such as the O.J. Simpson trial.

Campbell and Stanley's threats to internal and external validity Based on D.T. Campbell and J.C. Stanley's 1963 *Experimental and Quasi-Experimental Designs for Research,* which identifies and examines several factors that influence the generalizability of social research findings, including factors such as history (pretest, posttest effects), maturation (aging, time of month, tiredness), testing (familiarity with test or scale might influence responses given), instrumentation (changing features of measuring instruments), statistical regression (incorrect classification of respondents for assignments to control and experimental groups), selection (individual differences between persons in experimental and control groups, personality factors), and interactions with selections (combination of maturation, history, and instrumentation effects).

campus crime Violations of the law committed in or around a college or university campus.

campus model, campus-style facilities A model for detention of female offenders stressing skill acquisition, including cosmetology, parenting, office skills, arts, and crafts.

Campus Pride A program implemented in various school districts throughout the United States that seeks to remove gang graffiti from school grounds. Police officers can assist school leaders in identifying gang slogans and symbols, and often, gang members themselves are ordered by juvenile courts to remove this graffiti. Otherwise, the students act in concert to keep their schools clean of gang graffiti and possible violence. Because gangs often define certain areas, including schools, as their "turf" or territory, the students, acting together, can force gang members out of their turf and into another.

campus unrest A term used to indicate a variety of disturbances occurring on or around a college or university campus.

Canadian Association for the Prevention of Crime Established in 1919, this organization works to prevent crime through public education, giving citizens greater input in government policy and program development, and provides for the exchange of ideas and information. It is headquartered in Ottawa, Ontario, Canada, and publishes the *Canadian Journal of Criminology.*

Canadian Centre for Justice Statistics An agency that annually reports the amount of crime in Canada, comparable to the Bureau of Justice Statistics in the United States.

canine (K-9) The detector dog unit of a police department. Dogs are used to sniff out illegal contraband, such as marijuana, from suspect vehicles and homes, and to inspect luggage at airports, ships, aircraft, and vessel cargo.

caning Punishment administered with a long branch or stick across one's back, buttocks, or hand.

cannabis, *cannabis sativa* The hemp plant that produces hashish and marijuana; the pharmaceutical term for the marijuana plant; also known as hemp.

cannabism Poisoning with hashish or hemp.

cannibalism The act of one human being eating the flesh of another.

canon A principle accepted as true and adopted as a guideline to regulate one's conduct in any organization.

canon law Church laws devised in the thirteenth century to regulate morality, marriage, and related matters.

canons of police ethics Standards and ethics adopted by the International Association of Chiefs of Police that embrace primary job responsibility, limitation of authority, duty to be familiar with the law, utilizing proper means to gain proper ends, and proper conduct toward the public.

canvass A process used by law enforcement officers to gather information about a crime or other incident under investigation by asking questions of witnesses, nearby residents, and other persons who are in proximity to a crime scene.

capacitance alarm device A crime-prevention device associated with burglar alarms. Such devices are activated by one's presence in proximity to the device, wherever it may be located on the premises. Approaching or walking near such a device activates an alarm elsewhere, which notifies surveillance or security personnel that an intruder is present.

capacity The mental state of being legally responsible; having the mental acuity to know the difference between right and wrong and to realize and appreciate the nature and consequences of particular actions.

capias "That you take" (Latin); a general term for various court orders requiring that some named person be taken into custody.

capital crime, capital offense Any crime punishable by death. *See table p. 37.*

capital punishment Imposition of the death penalty for the most serious crimes. It may be administered by electrocution, lethal injection, gas, hanging, or shooting.

Capone, Alphonse "Al" (1899–1947) A notorious organized crime figure during the 1920s in Chicago who rose through the ranks to become one of the most powerful mob bosses involved in bootlegging in the United States. He was subsequently convicted of income-tax evasion and sentenced to prison. He was eventually paroled and died of advanced symptoms of syphilis.

caporegima The head of a regiment or a lieutenant in an organized crime family.

capper An outdated term for persons who solicit business for lawyers.

CAPRA Clients, Analysis, Partners, Response, and Assessment; an acronym used by the Royal Canadian Mounted Police.

carabiniere An Italian policeman.

carbine A light, short-barreled rifle.

carbolfuchsin A dye that can be applied to various objects, including bands used to wrap currency. When touched, the dye stains the skin or clothing. Thus, when a robber is apprehended, the presence of carbolfuchsin is evidence implicating the person in the crime.

car bomb An explosive device planted in, under, or near a motor vehicle for the purpose of killing or seriously injuring those in or around the automobile.

carbon monoxide poisoning The result of inhaling odorless, poisonous carbon monoxide gas emitted in automobile exhaust. The victim loses consciousness and his or her skin flushes, breathing becomes deep, and pulse is rapid and full. It may result in death.

Cardozo, Benjamin Nathan (1870–1938) A jurist and liberal lawyer who influenced the U.S. Supreme Court, particularly in the New Deal legislation of the Franklin D. Roosevelt era. Cardozo was a New York Supreme Court Justice in 1913 who believed that historical law should guide justice and that the function of the judiciary was to apply established principles to current trends.

career criminal An offender who makes his or her living through crime, usually who commits offenses throughout his or her life; in law, an offender who has substantial convictions and qualifies as a habitual or chronic offender, which subjects him or her to enhanced penalties such as longer prison terms or life without parole.

career escalation Committing progressively more serious offenses; moving as a juvenile offender to progressively more serious offenses as new offenses are committed (e.g., committing new violent offenses after adjudications for property offenses).

career integrity workshops An in-service training program in the Los Angeles County Sheriff's Department. In-house instructors lead small groups of deputies into creating "questionable conduct" scenarios and facilitate group discussions that delve into possible causes of actions or inactions and possible results. Participants see behaviors more clearly and are more closely in tune with reality than in "canned" situations brought into the training environment.

career life cycle of police officers A depiction of a hypothetical police officer career divided into stages: Rookie (1–2 years), TV cop (3–4 years), Cynicism (5–10 years), Realism (11–15 years), and Retirement (16–20 years).

Cargo Criminal Apprehension Teams (Cargo CATS) County, state, and federal law enforcement officers who conduct investigations, apprehend, and prosecute cargo thieves at airports and other sites where large-scale commerce occurs.

carjacking A recent phenomenon emerging on a large scale in the mid-1980s in which persons stop motorists and illegally take their vehicles by force. Material elements include vehicular theft and robbery.

Carlos the Jackal *See* Sanchez, Ilich Ramirez.

carnal knowledge Sexual intercourse; the act of having sexual bodily connection or familiarity.

carotid choke hold, choke hold A controversial grip used by law enforcement officers to restrain violent arrestees in which pressure is applied with the arm or a baton to the carotid artery located below the jaw at the side of the neck, which causes unconsciousness. Sometimes deaths have occurred, and thus, this hold is now banned. The term also applies to a lateral carotid neck restraint that temporarily slows the flow of blood to the brain, but does not put pressure on the larynx or the vagus nerve. Choke holds are forbidden by many jurisdictions, but the lateral carotid technique is still taught.

Carrier's Case The legal precedent of 1483 that redefined larceny in England to cater to the interests of merchants.

Carroll Doctrine The U.S. Supreme Court's ruling in *Carroll v. United States* (1925), in which it was held that warrantless

Capital Offenses, by State, 2002

Alabama. Intentional murder with 18 aggravating factors (Ala. Stat. Ann. 13A-5-40(a)(1)-(18)).

Arizona*. First-degree murder accompanied by at least 1 of 10 aggravating factors (A.R.S. 13-703(F)).

Arkansas*. Capital murder (Ark. Code Ann. 5-10-101) with a finding of at least 1 of 10 aggravating circumstances; treason.

California. First-degree murder with special circumstances; train wrecking; treason; perjury causing execution.

Colorado*. First-degree murder with at least 1 of 15 aggravating factors; treason.

Connecticut*. Capital felony with 8 forms of aggravated homicide (C.G.S. 53a-54b).

Delaware*. First-degree murder with aggravating circumstances.

Florida*. First-degree murder; felony murder; capital drug trafficking; capital sexual battery.

Georgia*. Murder; kidnapping with bodily injury or ransom when the victim dies; aircraft hijacking; treason.

Idaho. First-degree murder with aggravating factors; aggravated kidnapping.

Illinois. First-degree murder with 1 of 15 aggravating circumstances.

Indiana*. Murder with 16 aggravating circumstances (IC 35-50-2-9).

Kansas*. Capital murder with 8 aggravating circumstances (KSA 21-3439).

Kentucky*. Murder with aggravating factors; kidnapping with aggravating factors (KRS 532.025).

Louisiana. First-degree murder; aggravated rape of victim under age 12; treason (La. R.S. 14:30, 14:42, and 14:113).

Maryland*. First-degree murder, either premeditated or during the commission of a felony, provided that certain death eligibility requirements are satisfied.

Mississippi. Capital murder (97-3-19(2) MCA); aircraft piracy (97-25-55(1) MCA).

Missouri*. First-degree murder (565.020 RSMO 1994).

Montana. Capital murder with 1 of 9 aggravating circumstances (46-18-303 MCA); capital sexual assault (45-5-503 MCA).

Nebraska*. First-degree murder with a finding of at least 1 statutorily defined aggravating circumstance.

Nevada. First-degree murder with at least 1 of 14 aggravating circumstances (NRS 200.030, 200.033, 200.035).

New Hampshire. Six categories of capital murder (RSA 630:1, RSA 630:5).

New Jersey. Knowing/purposeful murder by one's own conduct; contract murder; solicitation by command or threat in furtherance of a narcotics conspiracy (NJSA 2C:11-3C).

New Mexico*. First-degree murder with at least 1 of 7 statutorily defined aggravating circumstances (Section 30-2-1 A, NMSA).

New York*. First-degree murder with 1 of 12 aggravating factors (NY Penal Law §125.27).

North Carolina*. First-degree murder (NCGS §14-17).

Ohio. Aggravated murder with at least 1 of 9 aggravating circumstances (O.R.C. secs. 2903.01, 2929.02, and 2929.04).

Oklahoma. First-degree murder in conjunction with a finding of at least 1 of 8 statutorily defined aggravating circumstances.

Oregon. Aggravated murder (ORS 163.095).

Pennsylvania. First-degree murder with 18 aggravating circumstances.

South Carolina*. Murder with 1 of 10 aggravating circumstances (§ 16-3-20(C)a)).

South Dakota*. First-degree murder with 1 of 10 aggravating circumstances; aggravated kidnapping.

Tennessee*. First-degree murder with 1 of 15 aggravating circumstances (Tenn. Code Ann. § 39-13-204).

Texas. Criminal homicide with 1 of 8 aggravating circumstances (TX Penal Code 19.03).

Utah*. Aggravated murder (76-5-202, Utah Code Annotated).

Virginia. First-degree murder with 1 of 13 aggravating circumstances (VA Code § 18.2-31).

Washington*. Aggravated first-degree murder.

Wyoming. First-degree murder.

*Nineteen States excluded mentally retarded persons from capital sentencing as of December 31, 2002: Arizona, Arkansas, Colorado, Connecticut, Delaware, Florida, Georgia, Indiana, Kansas, Kentucky, Maryland, Missouri, Nebraska, New Mexico, New York, North Carolina, South Dakota, Tennessee, and Washington. Mental retardation is a mitigating factor in South Carolina and Utah.

Source: Bonczar and Snell, *Capital Punishment, 2002,* 2.

searches of vehicles are permissible where reasonable suspicion of illegal actions exists.

cartel An organized criminal enterprise that often specializes in a particular type of crime, such as drug manufacturing and trafficking or prostitution.

cartography, cartographic school An approach to the study of crime that uses official data to map or chart patterns of crime.

CASASTART Program A program that targets high-risk youths who are exposed to drugs and delinquent activity and seeks to decrease risk factors by greater community involvement.

case An incident investigated by law enforcement officers; also, a single charging document under the jurisdiction of a court; a single defendant.

case law Legal opinions having the status of law as enunciated by the courts (e.g., U.S. Supreme Court decisions become case law and govern identical or very similar cases that are subsequently heard in lower courts).

case-level sentencing The sentencing of specific offenders.

caseload The number of clients a probation or parole officer is assigned according to some standard such as cases per week, month, or year.

case study An analysis of any pertinent aspect of one unit of study, such as a person, a group, or an organization; an in-depth analysis of a small number of persons.

casework A treatment program designed to help offenders cope with specific problems they face; in social services, the term includes clients on welfare or under the jurisdiction of children's services, and who are supervised.

casework model, caseworker model In this model, the probation or parole officer serves primarily as a counselor, dispensing treatment to clients in a one-on-one therapeutic relationship.

cash bail bond A cash payment for situations in which charges are not serious and the scheduled bail is low. Defendants obtain release by paying in cash the full amount, which is recoverable after the required court appearances are made.

CASKU (Child Abduction and Serial Killer Unit) A special unit of the FBI.

cast A plaster mold made of some impression, such as a tire track or footprint.

castle doctrine "A man's home is his castle." In common law, the right to use whatever force is necessary to protect one's dwelling and its inhabitants from an unlawful entry or attack.

castration The removal or chemical neutralization of male testes, which has been employed in the treatment of sex offenders. *See also* **chemical castration.**

catamite A homosexual male prostitute.

cat burglar A thief who breaks into and enters a residence or business by stealth, usually at night, by means of an upper story of the dwelling.

Catch-22 A situational dilemma in which any decision made will have negative consequences, named for Joseph Heller's 1961 novel about World War II.

catchers Victims of sexual assaults in prisons; also known as punks or kids.

Catellammarese Wars A series of bloody conflicts in the 1920s between Sicilian Mafia factions headed by Salvatore Maranzano and Joe Masseria.

catharsis hypothesis The assertion that violence as reported or portrayed by the media permits the audience to vent its aggressive tendencies, thereby dispelling the impulse to actually engage in violent behavior.

cat-o-nine-tails A short lash at the end of a solid handle with sharp spikes worked into the knots used to whip unruly prison inmates during floggings.

causal factor Any variable that is said to cause another variable to change in value.

causal fallacy The misconception in a social policy intended to address crime when the underlying causes are not subject to such a policy.

causation A causal link between two or more factors, where one factor brings about the occurrence of one or more other factors.

cause Any matter brought before a court for a decision.

cause, challenges of jurors for In jury selection, the method used by either prosecution or defense attorneys to strike or remove prospective jurors from the available jury pool because of prejudices they might have, either toward the defendant or the prosecution. Prospective jurors may also be excused from jury duty because they are law enforcement officers, relatives of law enforcement officers, court officers, or relatives of court officers. Any obvious bias for or against a defendant may result in the exclusion of the biased prospective juror.

cause célèbre A major case receiving widespread media attention.

cause of death Injury or disease directly responsible for an individual's death.

cautioning Warnings issued to those who have committed minor crimes. Police use cautioning to warn persons rather than arrest them, especially if the criminal acts observed are not particularly serious.

caveat Notice served to a judge to refrain from engaging in certain actions.

caveat emptor "Let the buyer beware" (Latin); the concept is intended to enable sellers of goods to disavow the unreliability of the products they market and absolve them of legal responsibility in this regard.

CB Radio Patrol of American Federation of Police An organization established in 1976 and headquartered in Miami, FL, that consists of radio operators or "hams" who use their transmissions to assist police and emergency personnel in the performance of their duties. Publishes *Police Times.*

CCH *See* **computerized criminal history (CCH).**

CCR An abbrevation for computerized criminal record.

cease-and-desist, cease-and-desist order An injunction to discontinue a practice or refrain from continuing a particular action until a court can settle the pending issue.

celerity The speed with which a suspect is apprehended by police; also, the speed with which punishment is applied for offending.

cell A self-contained room in a lockup, jail, or prison where an inmate is housed.

cellblock A group of individual or multiple-inmate cells in a locked enclosure, such as a prison or jail.

Cellmark Laboratories A private organization located in Maryland that came into prominence during the late 1980s and early 1990s as one of a few agencies capable of analyzing DNA evidence for law enforcement purposes.

cellular telephone device An electronic monitoring device worn by probationers or parolees that emits a radio signal received by a local area monitor.

censorship A practice of forbidding the distribution of particular materials, books, or movies. Censorship may seek to limit speech so that certain issues are not raised.

censure The practice of punishing someone because of particular acts they have committed. If a judge has acted improperly, for instance, a higher judicial body may censure such conduct by issuing the judge an informal or formal reprimand. Censure differs from formal punishment for a criminal offense, such as a fine or term of confinement in jail or prison.

census tract A geographic area with a population between 3,000 and 6,000, which has been politically subdivided for statistical purposes. Some police departments have established "beats" to coincide with such geographical areas.

Center for Criminal Justice Established in 1969 at Harvard University and headquartered in Cambridge, MA, this organization conducts studies of different dimensions of the criminal- and juvenile-justice systems, court procedures, and sentences imposed on both adults and juveniles, and makes recommendations and supports public policies relating to these topics. Publishes the *Annual Report of the Center for Criminal Justice.*

Center for Criminal Justice Training and Research Affiliated with the College of Human Services and California State University–Long Beach, the center, headquartered in Long Beach, does research and postcertification training.

Center for Law and Justice Founded in 1976 by the University of Washington, Seattle, this criminal-justice research organization is dedicated to the study of the prevention of juvenile delinquency.

Center for Research in Criminology Established by Indiana University of Pennsylvania in 1983, the center's goals include the advancement of criminological research and criminal justice as a discipline. The research center, headquartered in Indiana, PA, provides consultants for national, state, and local criminal justice agencies.

Center for Studies in Criminal Justice Established in 1965 and headquartered in Chicago, IL, at the Chicago Law School, the center conducts research on various criminal justice subjects and periodically disseminates published results.

Center for Substance Abuse Prevention (CSAP) The division of the U.S. Department of Health and Human Services responsible for promoting preventive approaches for substance abuse. The CSAP makes grants available to state and local organizations.

Center for Substance Abuse Treatment (CSAT) The division of the U.S. Department of Health and Human Services responsible for promoting treatment approaches for substance abuse. Headquartered in Rockville, MD, it networks with private and public treatment providers to devise and support approaches, policies, and programs for persons who abuse alcohol and drugs.

Center for the Administration of Criminal Justice Created in 1967 and headquartered at the University of California–Davis, the Center seeks to improve the criminal-justice system by conducting various demonstration projects that combine law and social science skills.

Center for the Administration of Justice An organization that seeks to combine law and social science skills to develop demonstration programs and research activities to improve criminal-justice agency operation.

Center for the Prevention of School Violence Various states, such as North Carolina, have established such institutes and facilities designed to assure that every student will attend a school that is safe, secure, free of fear, and conducive to learning, and that every youth will live in a community that takes interest in, is involved with, and invests on behalf of its youth. Various violence prevention initiatives have been implemented by different states and supported from funds from the Office of Juvenile Justice and Delinquency Prevention. The North Carolina Center was established in 1993 and is funded by both state and federal monies. Its purposes include providing information, program assistance, and research evaluation and expertise to interested schools.

Center for the Study and Prevention of Violence (CSPV) An organization committed to conducting and disseminating research on violence. It maintains a literature database that is searchable online and lists blueprint programs for violence prevention initiatives whose effectiveness has been demonstrated through rigorous evaluation. It is headquartered at the University of Colorado–Boulder.

Center for the Study of Crime, Delinquency, and Corrections Established in 1961 by Southern Illinois University and headquartered in Carbondale, IL, this center conducts instruction and research in criminal justice and provides teaching internships at Marion Penitentiary in Marion, IL (a maximum-security federal facility).

Center for the Study of Law and Society Established in 1961 by the University of California–Berkeley, the Center analyzes legal institutions and the processes of legal change.

Centers for Disease Control and Prevention (CDC) The funding and research arm of the Public Health Service, known for overseeing an ambitious research agenda on many health problems, including homicide, suicide, and intentional injuries.

central core members Gang members with a very strong commitment to a gang, usually gang leaders and their close friends.

Central Intelligence Agency (CIA) Under the National Security Act of 1947, this organization was created to investigate matters of national security.

centralization Limited distribution of power among a few top staff members of an organization.

central station alarm system Any alarm system whose installation is connected with other alarm systems and is monitored by a central headquarters.

Centre of Criminology Library Established in 1963 by the University of Toronto in Canada, the Centre is a comprehensive library of criminological materials. Its resources are made available to interested persons seeking to learn more about the administration of justice.

centurions In the early Roman era, between about 100 B.C. and 200 A.D., centurions were soldiers used for policing purposes who usually commanded units of 100 men.

certainty The aspect of a penal sanction that guarantees its imposition.

certificate plan A system of legal aid in Ontario, Canada, in which a defendant is issued a certificate entitling him or her to choose any counsel, whose fee will be paid in whole or in part from public funds.

certification, juvenile *See* **waiver.**

certification, offender The social verification by the criminal-justice system or by conventional persons that an offender is rehabilitated.

certified copy Any document that has been notarized by a notary, which authenticates the veracity of the document's signer and attests to its truthfulness or accuracy.

certified court orders Orders certified by a judge committing convicted offenders to the custody of the department of corrections.

Certified Fraud Examiner (CFE) A person who specializes in the investigation of different types of fraudulent schemes, including embezzlement or misappropriation of funds by banking personnel. CFEs are often members of the National Association of Fraud Examiners, headquartered in Washington, DC.

certiorari *See* **writ of** *certiorari.*

chain gang A group of inmates, usually chained together, used by Southern county and state correctional agencies to clear highway rights-of-way. Currently used in Arizona and other jurisdictions as a punishment.

chain of custody In evidence gathering, the sequence of possession and transmission of evidence from one department, unit, or person to another. If the chain of custody of evidence is broken for any reason, the value of the evidence is tainted or reduced.

chains of command The pattern of authority relations in any organization showing vertical and horizontal power relations of different positions and roles relative to other positions or roles.

"chalk fairy" A police officer who feels compelled to draw a chalk outline around a homicide victim.

chalk lines, chalk outlines Lines drawn by authorized personnel with chalk around a victim at a crime scene to show the location and position of a suspected homicide victim.

challenge *See* **peremptory challenge.**

Challenge of Crime in a Free Society A 1968 report about the American criminal-justice system prepared by the President's Commission on Law Enforcement and the Administration of Justice. Its summary statement said that America's system of criminal justice is overcrowded and overworked, undermanned, underfinanced, and very often misunderstood, and that it needs more information and more knowledge, more financial and technical resources, more coordination among its many parts, more public support, the help of community programs and institutions in dealing with offenders and potential offenders, vision, and the willingness to re-examine its old ways of doing things, to reform itself, to experiment, and to run risks.

challenges of jurors Questions asked concerning jurors by the judge, prosecutor, or defense attorney relating to their qualifications as impartial finders of fact; a determination of juror bias one way or another for or against the defendant.

chambers Usually a judge's office in a courthouse.

Chambliss, William A criminological theorist who has written extensively about conflict theory and radical criminology. His works include *Law, Order and Power* (1971), a treatise that extends conflict theory and explains more precisely how rich and powerful interests are able to control less powerful interests. Political and economic factors are considered to be significant determinants of societal conflict.

champerty Joining a lawsuit in the name of another person with the expectation of deriving something of value as compensation, or for the purpose of sharing in the damages awarded from the lawsuit.

chancellors King's agents used to settle disputes between neighbors on the king's behalf, such as property boundary issues, trespass allegations, and child misconduct. An early equivalent of the chancellor, with similar duties and responsibilities, was the justice of the peace, dating back to about 1200 A.D.

chancery court A tribunal of equity rooted in early English common law in which civil disputes are resolved. Chancery courts are also responsible for juvenile matters and adjudicating family matters such as divorce and have jurisdiction over contract disputes, property boundary claims, and exchanges of goods disputes.

chancery procedure A process whereby chancellors acted on behalf of the King of England to settle matters involving women and children who were unable to protect themselves under existing laws.

change agent A person with some amount of expertise concerning individual, interpersonal, or organizational problems. Change agents may be consultants who are asked to solve organizational problems. They provide possible solutions to problems, and organizational members rely on their advice to remedy existing problems.

change of venue A change in the place of a trial, usually from one county or district to another. Changes of venue are often conducted to avoid prejudicial trial proceedings, where it is believed that a fair trial cannot be obtained in the specific jurisdiction where the crime was alleged to have been committed.

character One's background and general reputation, which can be established through the testimony of friends of a defendant who testify on his or her behalf.

characters Inmates who are good at providing humorous diversion by virtue of their storytelling abilities, dress, and general behavior.

charge A formal allegation filed against some defendant in which one or more crimes are alleged.

charge bargaining, charge-reduction bargaining A negotiation process between prosecutors and defense attorneys that involves the dismissal of one or more charges against a defendant in exchange for a guilty plea to the remaining charges, or in which the prosecutor downgrades the charges in return for a plea of guilty.

charge stacking A ploy by prosecutors to add numerous lesser included offenses to charges against a criminal suspect in an attempt to overwhelm the suspect with fear and cause him or her to plead guilty to certain principal charges in a subsequent plea-bargain agreement.

charging document A formal written accusation filed in court that alleges that one or more persons have committed a crime.

charisma, charismatic authority A term meaning "gift of grace"; attributed to persons who have strong personal qualities and who are able to attract others to do what they want.

Chase, Salmon P. (1808–1873) Chief justice of the U.S. Supreme Court (1864–1873). Born in New Hampshire and educated and given religious training at Cincinnati College, Chase eventually entered Dartmouth College, where he graduated in 1826. He moved to Washington, DC, to study law, and was admitted to the bar in 1829. He then settled in Cincinnati, OH, and practiced law, defending escaped slaves in local and federal courts, and helped to form the antislavery Liberty Party. During the Mexican War, Chase helped form the Free Soil Party, which was dedicated to the nonexpansion of slavery. He eventually joined the Republican Party and was elected governor of Ohio in 1855. President Abraham Lincoln appointed Chase Secretary of the Treasury in 1861, where he assisted in financing federal government operations during the Civil War, and established the national banking system in 1863. Considered an antislavery radical, he was appointed chief justice of the U.S. Supreme Court by Lincoln in 1864, where he supported civil rights petitions, presided over impeachment proceedings against Samuel Johnson, and presided over many cases dealing with the Civil War, Reconstruction, and government finance. He died of a paralytic stroke in 1873.

Chase, Samuel (1741–1811) An American Revolutionary patriot, signer of the Declaration of Independence, and subsequent associate justice of the U.S. Supreme Court (1796–1811). He was impeached in 1804 on a charge of political favoritism, but was acquitted.

chat room A public or private area on the Internet that allows one-on-one conversations between parties. Most of the time, the two-party conversation is relatively secure from outside observation or monitoring.

chattel The property of a landowner or another, including an inventory of farm animals and other stock; personal, tangible property; assets.

chattel mortgage Any lien on property in exchange for money.

cheating Fraudulently acting to obtain something of value from a victim.

cheating at common law The fraudulent taking of another's property through some false symbol, but which is nevertheless accepted by the public for what it represents.

cheating by false pretense A statute prohibiting knowingly taking the property of another with the intent to defraud.

check forging The criminal offense of making or altering a negotiable instrument, such as a check, in order to obtain money by fraud.

check fraud Issuance of a bad check, draft, or money order that is a legal formal document and signed by the account holder but with the previous knowledge that the bank or depository will refuse to honor the instrument because of insufficient funds or a closed account.

check kiting The deliberate criminal act of writing checks on nonexistent bank accounts, closed accounts, or accounts other than one's own, or otherwise an account with insufficient funds to cover the check written.

checks and balances Political balancing of the legislative, judicial, and executive branches of government, to ensure that one branch doesn't dominate the others; internal controls of government to regulate conduct of various branches.

chemical agents Gases or other substances that temporarily immobilize individuals subjected to them.

chemical castration The use of Depo-Provera, which contains female hormones, to diminish the sex drive of male sex offenders.

chemical imbalance Abnormal levels of certain chemicals in the human body that can cause behavioral changes and various mental disorders, such as depression and anxiety.

CHEMTREC (Chemical Transportation Emergency Center) Established and operated by the Manufacturing Chemists Association, the Center, headquartered in Washington, DC, disseminates information about hazardous chemicals that may be involved in accidents.

Cherry Hill The name given to a Philadelphia prison established in 1829 on the site of a cherry orchard. It was subsequently renamed Eastern Penitentiary and designated a solitary-confinement institution.

Chesney-Lind, Meda (1947–) A feminist criminologist who believes that criminology is largely male-focused. She has examined the relation between crime and the treatment of females in society, and attempts to balance coverage of both males and females in criminological research.

Chicago Area Project (CAP) A delinquency prevention program, commenced in 1934 by Clifford Shaw and Henry McKay, designed to establish recreational centers and counseling programs for high-risk youths.

Chicago Boys' Court Founded in 1914 in Illinois as the first special court for older boys aged 17 through 20, who were over the age of juvenile court jurisdiction in Chicago.

Chicago Crime Commission A citizen action group set up in Chicago to investigate problems in the criminal justice system and explore avenues for positive change.

Chicago Jury Project A series of in-depth studies of juries and jurors undertaken at the University of Chicago Law School during the 1950s and 1960s to shed light on the jury process.

Chicago Law Enforcement Study Group Established in 1970 and headquartered in Chicago, IL, this nonprofit organization and advocacy agency is interested in various criminal justice issues pertaining to law enforcement, the courts, and corrections as they affect local communities.

Chicago School The name given to sociologists at the University of Chicago during the 1920s; founded by Albion Small in 1892.

Chicago Seven A notorious group tried in federal court in 1970 in Chicago because of their attempt to disrupt the Democratic National Convention in 1968. The group consisted of Abbie Hoffman, Tom Hayden, Jerry Rubin, Lee Weiner, John Eroines, David Dellinger, and Renard Davis. They were originally known as the "Chicago Eight" and included Bobby Seales, who was subsequently ejected from court because of his disruptive and outrageous conduct.

chicanery Trickery.

Chicanos During the rehabilitation era, a term applied specifically to Mexican-American inmates from Los Angeles; now, more generally a Mexican-American.

chief deputy Second in command in a sheriff's department, usually in charge of day-to-day operations of department. Unlike the sheriff, who is often an elected politician, the chief deputy is often a career police officer.

chief justice The presiding or principal judge of a court, who possesses nominal authority over the other judges (e.g., the chief justice of the U.S. Supreme Court).

chief of police A local law enforcement officer who is the appointed or elected head of a police department.

Chiefs of Police National Drug Task Force An organization headquartered in Washington, DC, that provides education to assist neighborhoods in combatting drug problems. Its activities emphasize education, crime prevention, law enforcement, and active community involvement.

Chikatilo, Andrei (1936–1994) A Russian serial killer responsible for 52 deaths of adults and children. He was executed by gunshot in 1994.

child Any person under the age of legal majority. This age varies among states, but is 18 in most jurisdictions.

child abandonment The act of a parent deserting or giving up his or her child.

Child Abduction and Serial Killer Unit (CASKU) A Critical Incident Response Group of the Federal Bureau of Investigation that provides investigative support through the development of profiles, investigative strategies, and behavioral assessments, as well as offering expert testimony.

child abuse Any form of cruelty to the physical, moral, or mental well-being of a child; the sexual abuse, exploitation, negligent treatment, or maltreatment of a child by a person who is responsible for the child's welfare.

Child Abuse and Neglect Information, National Center for (NCCAN) Established in 1975 by the U.S. Department of Health and Human Services and headquartered in Washington, DC, this clearinghouse disseminates information relating to child welfare and tracks state laws about children and their supervision, child maltreatment, and child custody matters.

child delinquency law Originally passed in Colorado in April 1909, this law defined persons guilty who encouraged, caused, or contributed to the delinquency or neglect of a child or minor.

child endangerment Intentional or unintentional behavior by a parent, guardian, or caregiver that places a child in danger.

Childhelp USA/International Established in 1984 and headquartered in Woodland Hills, CA, this humanitarian agency is devoted to preventing or minimizing child neglect and abuse and publishes *Too Young at Sixteen, The Call That Came Too Late!*

child homicide Homicide in which the victim is a child.

child molestation Any one of several forms of handling, fondling, or other contact of a sexual nature with a child, which may include photographing children in lewd poses.

child molester One who sexually abuses a child. *See also* **child molestation.**

child neglect Any deliberate act by the parents or legal guardians of minors that deprives those minors of life's necessities, including protection, adequate sustenance, and behavioral regulation.

child pornography Any depiction of a minor under age 18 engaged in a sexual act or posing in a sexual manner.

children at risk *See* **at-risk youths.**

children in need of supervision (CHINS) Typically, unruly or incorrigible children who cannot be supervised well by their parents; also includes children from homes where parents are seldom present. State agencies exist to find housing for such children.

Children of Murdered Parents A group of those whose parents were victims of homicide.

Children's Aid Society Early child-saving organization that attempted to place homeless city youths with farm families.

Children's Bureau A U.S. agency operated between 1912 and 1940 charged with compiling statistical information about children and methods whereby delinquency could be prevented and treated.

children's courts, hearings, tribunals Judicial mechanisms to deal with errant and unruly children during the nineteenth century. They were replaced by juvenile courts commencing in Illinois in 1899.

Children's Defense Fund A private organization dedicated to advocating children's rights by examining treatment of children in social and justice agencies and dedicated to heightening citizen awareness of how children's problems and needs should be addressed.

children's rights A term with various referents, such as natural rights (those that are inalienable because they belong to all persons as human beings), civil rights (those conferred by legal enactment), nurturance rights (those things that nourish or sustain the person or promote human development), and self-determined rights (opportunities for children that allow them considerable self-control and autonomy).

children who witness violence Youth who suffer physical, mental, or emotional trauma as the result of witnessing homicide or other violent acts.

child savers Nineteenth-century reformers who promoted the rights of minors, helped create a separate juvenile court, developed programs for troubled youths, and influenced legislation creating the juvenile-justice system. Sometimes their efforts were viewed by critics as a form of social control and class conflict.

child sexual abuser *See* **child molester.**

child support Court-ordered monetary payments to maintain dependent children.

child welfare agency An agency licensed by the state to provide care and supervision for children; also, an agency that provides service to the juvenile court and that may accept legal custody. These agencies may also be licensed to accept guardianship, accept children for adoption, and license foster homes.

child welfare board In Sweden, panels of citizens responsible for investigating and resolving matters involving juveniles.

child witness A juvenile who is a witness to a crime.

chilling effect Law or policy that discourages persons from exercising their rights.

Chinese triads Secret Chinese organizations alleged to control organized crime in New York's Chinatown and other predominantly Chinese communities throughout the United States.

CHINS *See* **children in need of supervision (CHINS).**

Chiricos, Theodore A criminologist who has examined the relation between class and race bias and punishment in the criminal justice system (1970) and the relation between unemployment and crime.

chiva Powdered brown or tan heroin from Mexico, usually snorted or inhaled.

chivalry hypothesis An explanation for judicial leniency toward female offenders. It posits that much of the criminality among females is hidden because of the generally protective and benevolent attitudes toward them by police, prosecutors, juries, and judges.

choice theory The modern version of classical theory that emphasizes the rational weighing of the specific costs and gains in the decision-making process governing criminal events.

chop shop An illegal enterprise that dismantles stolen vehicles for their component parts, which are then sold on the black market.

chop wounds Traumas to human tissue made by the repeated application of a heavy cutting instrument.

chose **in action** Any issue in action, or the right to recover or receive a debt or damages through legal action or lawsuit.

Christopher Commission, Christopher Commission Report An investigatory body led by Warren Christopher that investigated the Los Angeles Police Department in the wake of the Rodney King beating. It concluded that police lacked adequate discipline and used excessive force. The public image of the police was tainted through the King incident. *See also* **King, Rodney.**

chromatograph In forensics, a device that measures and evaluates gaseous substances.

chromosomal aberration A deviation in the standard number or structure of chromosomes. One example is an extra Y chromosome causing the *XYY* sex chromosome pattern, also called "supermale," which is a controversial genetic view of male aggressiveness that has been used by some theorists to explain violent and antisocial behaviors among certain persons.

chromosomes Basic cellular structures containing genes.

chronic offenders, chronic delinquent offenders, chronic recidivists, chronic juvenile offenders Habitual offenders; repeat offenders; persistent offenders; youths who commit frequent delinquent acts.

chronic 6 percent A term used to describe the result of a birth cohort study by Marvin Wolfgang, Thorsten Sellin, and Robert Figlio, in which male birth cohorts from Philadelphia were studied over time, between 1945 and 1963. The study revealed that 6 percent of these males accounted for over 50 percent of all criminality and delinquency in the entire cohort.

church arson Any attempted or completed burning or bombing of a church.

Church of Satan Established in April 1966 by Anton Szandor LaVey, a former police photographer, the church is located in the Central Grotto area of San Francisco, CA.

churning Broker trading in which shares of stock are bought or sold on behalf of a client for the sole purpose of generating large commissions.

chuzaisho A Japanese "live-in" unit that provides accommodations for an officer's entire family. Staffed on a 24-hour basis, both *kobans* and *chuzaishos* are strategically located to ensure close contact between police officers and community residents.

CIA *See* **Central Intelligence Agency (CIA).**

circle sentencing A form of criminal sentencing derived from Native American practices in which offenders permit members of the community to express their feelings about the crime and to make their requirements known.

circuit, circuit courts Originally, courts that were held by judges who followed a circular path, hearing cases periodically in various communities. The term now refers to courts with several counties or districts within their jurisdiction. In the federal court organization, there are 13 federal circuit courts of appeal, having jurisdiction over U.S. district courts within specified states. *See table p. 44.*

circuit, class A In alarm system usage, a four-wire alarm circuit used to detect an alarm or line fault.

circuit, class B A four-wire alarm circuit connected to one or more alarm sensors. A trouble condition occurs whenever the alarm signal is interrupted.

circuit riders Judges who rode from jurisdiction to jurisdiction in remote locations of states or federal territories to hold trials on a regular basis, such as once a month or once every six months.

circumstantial evidence Material provided by a witness from which a jury must infer a fact.

citation, citation to appear Any document issued by a law enforcement or court officer directing one to present oneself in court on a specific date and time.

cite, citation Any legal reference in which a point of law is made; in law enforcement, a summons.

citizen action model A Youth Service Bureau model using community volunteers to actively intervene and assist in the lives of delinquency-prone youths.

citizen complaint Grievance filed by a citizen against a police officer for alleged misconduct.

citizen dispute settlement A mediated settlement by a third and neutral party. *See also* **alternative dispute resolution.**

Citizen Police Academy (CPA) A police-citizen awareness program designed to heighten citizen awareness of police operations and tactics; a community-oriented policing program which allows citizens to meet the police officers who serve them. It enables citizens to become educated about the "whys" and "hows" of law enforcement, and provides police officers the opportunity to meet and hear from the citizens they serve. CPA sessions are conducted over a specified period, such as 12 weekly sessions, including weekend ride-alongs and firearms demonstrations.

citizen's arrest The apprehension of a criminal suspect by a private citizen unaffiliated with any law enforcement agency.

Citizens United for Rehabilitation of Errants Established in 1972 and headquartered in Washington, DC, this organization advocates prison reforms and improvements in amenities for inmates, and aims to reduce crime through reform in the criminal-justice system.

citizen value system A parole board decision-making model appealing to public interests in seeing that community expectations are met by making appropriate early release decisions.

city courts Lower courts of special original jurisdiction. Rural counterparts are justice-of-the-peace courts.

civil As opposed to criminal. Penalties from civil actions result in monetary damage awards, not criminal punishments.

civil action Any lawsuit brought to enforce private rights and to remedy violations thereof.

Civil Aviation Security Service An organization headquartered in Washington, DC, that maintains information on all air carriers and about domestic and foreign hijacking and bomb threats. It investigates compliance with regulations and enforces violations of air safety rules.

civil case A judicial proceeding that results in an award of monetary damages rather than a criminal conviction.

civil commitment The legal confinement of a person to a hospital or other treatment facility for a period of time, usually to undergo examination or to receive some type of therapy.

civil commotion *See* **disturbing the peace.**

civil courts Tribunals that handle civil cases, as opposed to criminal cases. The objective of a civil case is to recover damages (money), whereas the object of a criminal case is to seek punishment of imprisonment and/or fines and victim restitution.

The Thirteen Federal Circuit Courts of Appeal		
Circuit	**Composition**	**Number of Circuit Judges**
District of Columbia	District of Columbia	12
First	Maine, Massachusetts, New Hampshire, Puerto Rico, Rhode Island	6
Second	Connecticut, New York, Vermont	13
Third	Delaware, New Jersey, Pennsylvania, Virgin Islands	14
Fourth	Maryland, North Carolina, South Carolina, Virginia, West Virginia	15
Fifth	Canal Zone, Louisiana, Mississippi, Texas	17
Sixth	Kentucky, Michigan, Ohio, Tennessee	16
Seventh	Illinois, Indiana, Wisconsin	11
Eighth	Arkansas, Iowa, Minnesota, Missouri, Nebraska, North Dakota, South Dakota	11
Ninth	Alaska, Arizona, California, Idaho, Montana, Nevada, Guam, Oregon, Washington, Hawaii	28
Tenth	Colorado, Kansas, New Mexico, Oklahoma, Utah, Wyoming	12
Eleventh	Alabama, Florida, Georgia	12
Federal	All Federal Judicial Districts	12
Total		179

Source: Administrative Office of the U.S. Courts. 2004. Title 28, U.S. Code, Sec. 44.

civil death The custom of terminating all civil rights of convicted felons (e.g., forbidding them the right to vote or to marry). No state uses civil death today.

civil disabilities Rights forfeited as the result of a criminal conviction (e.g., in some states, convicted offenders lose the right to vote).

civil disobedience Any public action that violates the law involving political demonstrations or picketing in order to protest a government action, law, or proclamation.

civil disturbances Riots; collective, aggravated public demonstrations resulting in physical injury and loss of property.

civil forfeiture The relinquishing of assets to the state as the consequence of crime.

civilian complaint review board, civilian review board An appointed board whose role is to objectively examine allegations of excessive force and other complaints of misconduct made by citizens against police officers; also, an advisory panel of citizens considered to be a more objective body in making decisions about whether police actions are abuses of discretionary authority. It can recommend sanctions or punishments.

civilianization Incorporating into police departments private citizens to perform particular law enforcement functions, such as directing traffic and office duties.

civil justice Civil law or law of civil procedure and the range of procedures and activities having to do with private rights and remedies sought by civil action.

civil law All state and federal law pertaining to noncriminal activities, also referred to as municipal law. Laws pertain to private rights and remedies. Also, a body of formal rules established by any society for its self-regulation.

civil liability In tort law, the basis for a cause of action to recover damages.

civil liberties Rights guaranteed by the U.S. Constitution and the Bill of Rights.

civil nature of juvenile proceedings The juvenile court is operated and proceeded as a civil court. Proceedings are much less formalized and due process does not apply.

civil process Orders and official documents issued by a court, such as summonses, subpoenas, or injunctions.

civil protection order A court order designed to protect one person from another.

civil remedy A judgment, other than an indictment in a criminal case, where the law awards monies to a victim against an offender.

civil rights Liberties possessed by citizens of a country and guaranteed by the government. In the United States, the Bill of Rights encompasses many of the liberties people enjoy as their civil rights.

Civil Rights Act Title 42, Section 1983 of the U.S. Code permitting inmates of prisons and jails as well as probationers and parolees the right to sue their administrators and/or supervisors under the "due process" and "equal protection" clauses of the Fourteenth Amendment. It may also pertain to civil suits filed by employees against their employers where discrimination is alleged.

Civil Rights Division, Civil Rights Enforcement That part of the U.S. Department of Justice, headquartered in Washington, DC, that handles cases involving violations of civil rights guaranteed by the Constitution and federal law. It prosecutes violations of the Civil Rights Act and assists federal agencies in identifying and minimizing gender discrimination and related forms of discrimination and inequalities.

Civil Rights Institute Established in 1992 and headquartered in Birmingham, AL, the Institute is a repository of information and artifacts relating civil rights violations, including actions by freedom riders, police misconduct, and other incidents from racially charged periods related to enforcing the equal-protection clause of the Fourteenth Amendment.

civil rights movement A multiracial movement commenced in the 1960s to combat racial injustice and inequality.

Civil Rights of Institutionalized Persons Act (CRIPA) A 1997 federal law granting authority to the Department of Justice to sue correctional institutions on behalf of inmates in an effort to safeguard their civil rights. It also assists in the development of inmate grievance procedures.

Civil Rights—Special Litigation An office under the U.S. Department of Justice responsible for protecting rights of persons under Title VI of the Civil Rights Act of 1964 prohibiting discrimination against persons confined in prisons and jails. It is headquartered in Washington, DC.

civil service Employment by a local, state, or federal government. Public employees are civil service employees.

civil suit A lawsuit to recover property, maintain a right or privilege, or satisfy various types of claims, such as wrongful death actions, tort actions, strict liability actions, negligence claims, and property and contract disputes.

clandestine A term used to describe actions or behaviors that are secret or concealed.

Clark, Benjamin C. (1839–1908) A philanthropist and "volunteer" probation officer who assisted courts with limited probation work during the 1860s, carrying on the work of John Augustus.

Clarke, Ronald V. A criminologist who wrote *Situational Crime Prevention* (1992), which describes three crime prevention tactics: increasing the effort required to commit crime, increasing the risk of committing crime, and reducing the rewards of committing crime. Clarke is an advocate of target-hardening and caller ID. Together with David Weisburd, Clarke has argued that crime displacement may occur through extinction, diffusion of benefits, and discouragement. Extinction occurs when burglarproof neighborhoods cause potential burglars to cease burglary and move to other forms of crime in other areas. Diffusion of benefits occurs whenever crime prevention measures calculated to prevent one type of crime may actually deter other types of crime in the same area. Discouragement occurs when criminals give up particular types of crime because they no longer pay.

class action, class-action suit Any lawsuit on behalf of a segment of the population with specific characteristics, namely that they are victims of whatever wrongs are alleged. The class of persons may persist over time and change, but the action is for all current and future members of the class.

classical conditioning A learning theory that states people learn by associating stimuli with certain responses.

Classical School of Criminology, classical criminology, classical philosophy of criminal law, classical theory A criminological perspective indicating that people have free will to choose either criminal or conventional behavior. People choose to commit crime for reasons of greed or personal need. Crime can be controlled by criminal sanctions, which should be proportionate to the guilt of the perpetrator.

classic research design An experimental design format, usually associated with research in the biological and social sciences, that consists of two comparable groups, an experimental and a control group. These two groups are equivalent except that the experimental group is exposed to the independent variable and the control group is not.

classification, classification of prisoners Inmate security designation based on psychological, social, and sociodemographic criteria and various types of instruments relating to one's potential dangerousness or risk posed to the public. It is used to categorize offenders according to the level of custody they require while incarcerated. It measures potential disruptiveness of prisoners and early release potential of inmates for parole consideration. Some offenders may be placed in particular vocational, educational, counseling, or other types of programming and treatment. No classification system has been demonstrably successful at effective prisoner or client placements.

classification center *See* **diagnostic center.**

classification committee A committee composed of several correctional staff who have the responsibility of classifying and periodically reclassifying inmates.

classification instrument Any paper-and-pencil instrument designed to assist correctional officials in determining inmate needs and problems and assigning them to appropriate institutions and programs.

classification of crimes Categories of misdemeanors and felonies facilitating the compilation of statistical information relating to such crimes.

Clayton Act of 1914 Congressional legislation exempting labor organizations from the Sherman Antitrust Act and narrowing the jurisdiction of the courts in labor disputes.

clearance The event in which a known occurrence of a crime is followed by an arrest or other decision that indicates a solved crime at the police level of reporting.

clearance rate The percentage of crimes known to the police that they believe have been solved by arrest. The statistic is used as a measure of a police department's productivity.

clear and convincing evidence That which indicates that the thing to be proved is highly probable or reasonably certain. The burden of proof is greater than that of the preponderance of evidence but less than that required to establish guilty beyond a reasonable doubt.

clear-and-present-danger doctrine In constitutional law, the doctrine that the First Amendment does not protect those forms of expression that pose an obvious and immediate danger of bringing about some substantive evil that government has a right to prevent.

cleared by arrest The term used by the FBI in *Uniform Crime Reports* to indicate that someone has been arrested for a reported crime. It does not necessarily mean that the crime has been solved or that the actual criminals who committed the crime have been apprehended or convicted.

clemency A grant of mercy by an executive official commuting a sentence or pardoning a criminal.

clerk of the court A court official who handles much of the routine paperwork associated with the administration of the court.

client Any person, convicted of a crime or not, who is under the direct supervision of a community corrections agency, whether it is a probation or parole office or a community services organization.

client-specific planning An alternative sentencing program involving selective tailoring of a sentence (other than imprisonment for each individual offender), depending on the offense committed. It requires judicial approval.

client system Either an individual, group, or an organization experiencing a problem which may be remedied by the services and intervention of a change agent.

Clinard, Marshal B. A prominent American criminologist of mid- to late twentieth century who was trained at the University of Chicago, taught at the University of Wisconsin, and investigated corporate crime, cross-cultural aspects of crime, and the development of criminal behavior typologies.

clinical criminology A field of study applying criminological findings to the assessment and treatment of offenders.

Clinical Pastoral Educational Movement A movement among the clergy that led to clinical training and that viewed prison chaplaincy as a specialty subgroup of the clergy.

clinical prediction The forecast of inmate behavior based on a professional's expert training and direct work with offenders.

Clink An early London prison near London Bridge; the term was subsequently used as a generic name for all prisons, as well as various brothels.

cliques Primary and semi-primary groups formed by prisoners, from the same tip or from several tips, who have regular contact and share an interest in some prison activity, subcultural orientation, or pre-prison experience.

Cloaca Maxima An ancient Roman prison constructed under the main sewers of Rome about 640 B.C. It was a vast series of interconnected dungeons.

close-custody inmates Those prisoners with past assaultive or escape histories who must be constantly supervised.

closed-ended question A question that offers respondents a set of answers from which they are asked to choose the one that most closely fits their views.

closed shop A labor agreement whereby employers will hire only persons who are union members. Such agreements are now considered illegal and discriminatory under federal law.

closed-system model Descriptive indicators of organizations that rely almost wholly on internal organizational processes to account for organizational behavior.

close-security facility Any type of prison facility classified as maximum security. Whenever inmates are not in their cells, they are under direct supervision from correctional officers.

closing argument An oral summation of a case presented to a judge, or to a judge and jury, by the prosecution or defense during a criminal trial.

Cloward, Richard (1926–2001) A sociologist who collaborated with Lloyd Ohlin in describing the theory of opportunity in *Delinquency and Opportunity* (1960), which posited that delinquent subcultures exist independent of but within mainstream society. Youth gangs emerge because there is a lack of opportunity for many youths to achieve socially approved and desirable goals. Slum children, therefore, may wish to conform to institutionalized or socially approved means to achieve culturally approved goals, but lack the means to do so. This is a prelude to deviance, delinquency, and criminality. This theory influenced President Lyndon B. Johnson's War on Poverty program by highlighting the disruptive effects of slum areas and poverty conditions in relation to delinquency and crime.

Club, The A steel bar with hooks fastened across the steering wheel of an automobile to prevent its theft.

club drugs Synthetic substances such as ecstasy and Rohypnol commonly used at nightclubs, bars, and raves.

Club Fed An informal name for the Federal Law Enforcement Training Center. *See* **Federal Law Enforcement Training Center (FLETC).**

cluster analysis A statistical technique designed to identify groups of cases under study.

clustered crime scene A scene of criminal investigation at which most of the crime-related activity has taken place, including the confrontation, the attack, any sexual assault, and the homicide, if applicable.

clustergeeking Computer terminology for a person who spends a great deal of time at a computer cluster doing computer homework.

Cluster-Type Vocational Training Courses Courses offered in 100-hour blocks of instruction in related but different subject areas of a given trade.

CN A standard type of tear gas.

coagulation The transformation of a liquid, such as blood, to a semisolid.

Coast Guard jurisdiction The territorial waters of the United States, where U.S. Coast Guard officers, including commissioned, warrant, and petty officers, are empowered to make inquiries, inspections, searches, and seizures on the high seas.

Coates Typology A classification of police officers as Legalistic-Abusive, who are extremely rigid and have to be right all the time; Task-Oriented, who are concerned that rules and regulations cover everything; and Community-Service, who are interested in documenting how the community is helped by police actions. The scheme was suggested by R.B. Coates in his 1972 work, *Dimensions of Police-Citizen Interaction.*

cocaine, crack cocaine A stimulant manufactured from the coca plant (an "upper" in the drug community). It is used as a pain reliever in certain forms. Crack cocaine consists of small crack "rocks" that result from powdered cocaine being dissolved in water and heated until the water evaporates.

Cocaine Anonymous A support group, similar to Alcoholics Anonymous, for persons addicted to cocaine.

co-corrections, co-correctional facilities, coed prisons Penal facilities where male and female prisoners live, supervised by female and male staff, and prisoners participate in all activities together. Sharing the same quarters is prohibited.

code A systematic collection of laws.

Code, Napoleonic *See* **Napoleonic Code.**

codefendants Two or more defendants charged with the same crime and tried in the same judicial proceeding.

codeine Methylmorphine, a strong sedative and pain-relieving drug derived from opium, used in the treatment of postoperative surgery or dental work, that is often abused.

code of ethics Regulations formulated by major professional societies that outline the specific problems and issues that are frequently encountered in the types of research carried out within a particular profession. It serves as a guide to ethical research practices.

Code of Hammurabi (circa 1792–1750 B.C.) Babylon's first written criminal code. It was preceded by the Sumerian Code of Ur-Nammu. It was believed to be the first and most important codification of law before the discovery of the Code of Lipit-Ishtar. *See box 48.*

Code of Lipit-Ishtar (circa 1868–1857 B.C.) Subsequent code of laws devised in Sumeria following the Code of Ur-Nammu. *See box p. 48.*

code of secrecy, code of silence A tacit agreement among police officers that discourages "whistle-blowing" regarding misconduct of fellow officers as negative and potentially self-destructive. It was suggested by Elizabeth Ruess-Ianni in her 1983 work *Two Cultures of Policing.* She describes police solidarity as endorsing feelings such as "don't give up on another cop; watch out for your partner first; if you get caught off base, don't implicate anyone else."

Code of Ur-Nammu (circa 2060–2050 B.C.) The earliest known written legal code, showing an advanced legal system with specialized judges, the giving of testimony under oath, the proper form of judicial decisions, and the ability of the judges to order that damages be paid to a victim of the guilty party. It allowed for the dismissal of corrupt men, protection for the poor, and a punishment system in which punishment is proportionate to the crime. Established circa 2060–2050 B.C., the code derives its name from the king of the ancient city of Ur, sometimes called Zur-Nammu or Ur-Engur, a part of the Sumerian dynasty. The prologue of the code describes the king as powerful and great and as having established justice throughout the land. One law provided that "if anyone bring an accusation against a man, the accused go to the river and leap in the river; if he sink in the river his accuser shall take possession of his house; but if the river prove that the accused is not guilty, and he unhurt, then he who had brought the accusation shall be put to death, while he who leaped into the river shall take possession of the house that had belonged to his accuser." Another states, "If a 'sister of God' [nun] open a tavern, or enter a tavern to drink, then shall this woman be burned to death."

Co-Dependents Anonymous An organization of persons who regard themselves as having low self-esteem and who unite because they are addicted to destructive interpersonal relationships. It is headquartered in Phoenix, AZ.

codicil A provision added to a will subsequent to its initial preparation, which amends the original document by adding or taking away certain provisions.

codification The act of rendering laws in written form.

CODIS (Combined DNA Index System) A three-tiered DNA system with separate local, state, and federal databases. Local and state labs can maintain their own DNA databases according to their own laws and needs, but they can also access the federal database for matches at the national level. A total of 175 crime labs in all 50 states and Puerto Rico, as well

Excerpts from the Code of Hammurabi

1. If a man charge a man with sorcery, but cannot convict him, he who is charged with sorcery shall go to the sacred river, and he shall throw himself into the river; if the river overcome him, his prosecutor shall take to himself his house. If the river show that man to be innocent and he come forth unharmed, he that charged him with sorcery shall be put to death. He who threw himself into the river shall take to himself the house of his accuser.

2. If a judge pronounce a judgment, render a decision, deliver a sealed verdict, and afterward reverse his judgment, they shall prosecute the judge for reversing the judgment which he has pronounced, and he shall pay twelvefold the damages which were (awarded) in said judgment; and publicly they shall expel him from his seat of judgment, and he shall not return, and with the judges in a case he shall not take his seat.

3. If a man steal ox or sheep, ass or pig, or boat—if it belonged to god or palace, he shall pay thirtyfold; if it belonged to a common man, he shall restore tenfold. If the thief have nothing wherewith to pay, he shall be put to death.

4. If a man aid a male or a female slave of the palace, or a male or a female slave of a common man, to escape from the city, he shall be put to death.

5. If a fire break out in a man's house and a man who goes to extinguish it cast his eye on the household property of the owner of the house, and take the household property of the owner of the house, that man shall be thrown into the fire.

6. If a man owe a debt and Adad [the storm god] inundate the field or the flood carry the produce away, or, through lack of water, grain have not grown in the field, in that year he shall not make any return of grain to the creditor, he shall alter his contract tablet and he need not pay the interest for that year.

7. If a man who is a tenant have paid the full amount of money for his rent for the year to the owner of the house, and he [the owner] say to him before "his days are full," "Vacate," the owner of the house, because he made the tenant move out of his house before "his days were full," shall lose the money which the tenant paid him.

8. If a man receive grain or silver from a merchant and do not have grain or silver to repay, but have personal property, whatever there is in his hand, when he brings it before witnesses, he shall give to the merchant. The merchant shall not refuse [it], he shall receive [it].

9. If the agent be careless and do not take a receipt for the money which he has given to the merchant, the money not receipted for shall not be placed to his account.

10. If a priestess or a nun who is not a resident in a convent open a wineshop or enter a wineshop for a drink, they shall burn that woman.

11. If the wife of a man be taken in lying with another man, they shall bind them and throw them into the water. If the husband of the woman spare the life of his wife, the king shall spare the life of his servant.

12. If a woman hate her husband and say, "Thou shalt not have me," her past shall be inquired into for any deficiency of hers; and if she have been careful and be without past sin and her husband have been going out and greatly belittling her, that woman has no blame. She shall take her dowry and go to her father's house.

13. If a man, after [the death of] his father, lie in the bosom of his mother, they shall burn both of them.

14. If a man take a wife and she bear him children and that woman die, her father may not lay claim to her dowry. Her dowry belongs to her children.

15. If a man destroy the eye of another man, they shall destroy his eye.

16. If he breaks a man's bone, they shall break his bone.

17. If a man knock out a tooth of a man of his own rank, they shall knock out his tooth.

18. If a man knock out a tooth of a common man, he shall pay one-third mana of silver.

19. If a man hire an ox and cause its death through neglect or abuse, he shall restore ox for ox to the owner of the ox.

20. If an ox when passing through the street gore a man and bring about his death, that case has no penalty.

Excerpts from the Code of Lipit-Ishtar

1. If a man entered the orchard of [another] man and was seized there for stealing, he shall pay ten shekels of silver.

2. If a man cut down a tree in the garden of [another] man, he shall pay one half mina of silver.

3. If adjacent to the house of a man the bare ground of [another] man has been neglected and the owner of the house has said to the owner of the bare ground, "Because your ground has been neglected someone may break into my house: strengthen your house," and this agreement has been confirmed by him, the owner of the bare ground shall restore to the owner of the house any of his property which is lost.

4. If a man married a wife and she bore him children and those children are living, and a slave also bore children for her master [but] the father granted freedom to the slave and her children, the children of the slave shall not divide the estate with the children of their [former] master.

5. If a man's wife has not borne him children but a harlot [from] the public square has borne him children, he shall provide grain, oil and clothing for that harlot; the children which the harlot has borne him shall be his heirs, and as long as his wife lives the harlot shall not live in the house with the wife.

6. If a man rented an ox and injured the flesh at the nose ring, he shall pay one-third of [its] price.

7. If a man rented an ox and damaged its eye, he shall pay one-half of [its] price.

8. If a man rented an ox and broke its horn, he shall pay one-fourth of [its] price.

9. If a man rented an ox and damaged its tail, he shall pay one-fourth of [its] price.

as the FBI Lab and the U.S. Army Crime Lab, are involved in CODIS. The system has been used successfully to solve various crimes including rape, murder, kidnapping, burglary, and assault and battery.

coeducational prison *See* **co-corrections.**

coerced confession Any admission to a crime extracted from a criminal suspect by force or involuntarily.

coerced treatment Any treatment for substance abuse, mental illness, or other problems that is mandated by judicial or administrative order.

coercion The use of force to compel another to do what one wants; the threat of application of sanctions to impose one's will on another.

coercive intervention In juvenile law, out-of-home placement of juveniles, detainment, or mandated therapy or counseling. For adults, it may include similarly court-ordered interventions for individual family members or entire family units.

coercive power A form of influence by which a superior elicits compliance by subordinates through threats of punishment.

cognitive approach Any treatment approach based on the assumption that incorrect thinking underlies and drives most behavior and that if the thinking is corrected, problem behaviors will be changed.

cognitive behavioral therapy A form of psychodynamic therapy that purports to alter dysfunctional thinking patterns in patients by presenting scenarios.

cognitive development theory Also called "developmental theory," this theory stresses stages of the learning process whereby persons acquire abilities to think and express themselves, respect the property and rights of others, and cultivate a set of moral values.

cognitive theory The study of the perception of reality; the mental processes required to understand the world in which we live.

cognomen Family name or surname.

cohabitation The act of living together as husband and wife without the benefit or authorization of a legitimate marriage.

Cohen, Albert K. A criminologist who developed the notion of delinquent subculture as a culture existing within the larger mainstream conventional culture. Delinquents develop their own value system, complete with rewards and punishments, which becomes inculcated in others seeking to become a part of the delinquent subculture. Strain arises because of the inability of persons to gain status and acceptance. Applied to juveniles, strain would be generated by not doing well in school or not being accepted into social groups. Thus, poor scholastic ability and interpersonal relations would lead persons toward deviant conduct as an alternative means to achieve goals.

Cohen, Lawrence A criminologist who, with Marcus Felson, developed routine activities theory. Their theory suggests that the motivation to commit crime and numbers of offenders are rather constant. Thus, it is inevitable that in every society there will, for diverse reasons, be someone willing to commit crime. Predatory crime, a vital component of their theory, rests on the existence of suitable targets (victims), capable guardians (police), and motivated offenders (criminals). *Rou-*

tine activities refers to the activities of the normal American lifestyle.

cohort Any statistical group of persons with unique identifying characteristics. *See also* **birth cohort.**

cohort effect The effect of belonging to a given generation (e.g., the '60s generation). Sometimes people mistakenly assume that a difference between people of different age groups is the result of biological aging when the difference is really due to the two groups having different backgrounds because they grew up in different eras.

cohort study Any examination over time of a segment of persons born in a given year for varied purposes. Criminologists seek to show that a certain percentage of persons born in a particular year will commit disproportionately larger numbers of crimes compared with others in the same cohort.

Cointelpro An abbreviation for counterintelligence program; an FBI initiative to infiltrate, disrupt, and discredit liberal organizations.

cold blood A term denoting premeditation and aggravation, usually in association with a homicide.

collateral attack The attempt to defeat the outcome of a judicial proceeding by challenging it in a different proceeding or court.

collateral consequences of conviction Disabilities that follow a conviction that are not directly imposed by a sentencing court, such as the loss of the right to vote, serve on a jury, practice certain occupations, or own a firearm.

collateral facts Any material fact not directly connected with the case in question.

collateral security A bond or deposit besides the principal amount or original security.

collective bargaining The process of negotiating wages, working conditions, hours of work, rest pauses, and other work-related variables between employees and management. Usually, union representation on behalf of employees bargains with management or company owners for employee benefits in exchange for certain employee concessions and agreements.

collective child abuse Attitudes held as a group by society that impede the psychological and physical development of children.

collective conscience A term used by the early sociologist Emile Durkheim to describe the beliefs held by a society's citizens.

collective efficacy The ability of communities to regulate the behavior of their residents through the influence of community institutions, such as the family and church. Residents in these communities share mutual trust and a willingness to intervene in the supervision of children and the maintenance of public order.

collective gang A type of gang that has a short history, limited size, and little defined territory.

collective incapacitation A policy of giving the same prison sentence to everyone convicted of a particular offense in order to reduce the crime rate.

collective violence Violent behavior that results from many persons coming together, even when many of the participants would not have been violent if acting alone.

collusion A conspiracy or compact between two or more persons to commit a crime or perpetrate a fraud.

Colonial Period The period of English rule over the American colonies that ended with the American Revolution.

colony, penal Any aggregate of prisoners kept in a secluded geographical area. The term may refer to actual geographic places used to confine prisoners for long periods, such as Devil's Island and van Dieman's Land.

color of authority In one's official capacity, usually as a law enforcement officer or judicial official.

color of law Officials in their capacity as officers representing law and legal authority; in one's official capacity, typically as a law enforcement officer or agent of the justice system.

"colors" Clothing used by gang members to demonstrate their affiliation with a particular gang.

Colquhoun, Patrick (1745–1820) A proponent of organized police agencies to combat crime. Colquhon created early training programs for police officers, stressed particular recruitment standards, and wrote *A Treatise on the Police of the Metropolis* (1795).

Colt, Samuel (1814–1862) The American inventor of a revolver that fires six shots that was adopted by the U.S. Army as its official handgun, and proved useful during the 1800s for mounted warfare.

Columbine massacre The infamous mass murder that occurred on April 20, 1999, at Columbine High School in Littleton, CO. High-school seniors Eric Harris and Dylan Klebold entered the school armed with semiautomatic weapons, shotguns, and homemade bombs, killed 15 people, and took their own lives.

combination sentence *See* **split sentencing.**

combined designs The merging of two or more research designs into a single study to increase the inferential powers of that study.

Combined Pre-Employment Screening System A process in which a written exam is used to screen candidates. Those who have qualifying scores are then placed on a list from which candidates are interviewed and selected.

comes stabuli "Officer of the stable" (Latin); early non-uniformed mounted law enforcement officers in medieval England. Early police forces were small and relatively unorganized but made effective use of local resources in the formation of posses for the pursuit of offenders.

comity An interjurisdictional judicial courtesy whereby one state recognizes the laws of another jurisdiction.

command Orders from a duly appointed official for officers to act in a given way, such as serving warrants or seizing property.

commercial crime Any crime committed against a company or business, as opposed to a crime against a particular individual.

commercial law Law pertaining to businesses and interstate commerce.

commissary The prison store; also, the incidental items sold to inmates; also, an inmate's account, which is debited when an item is purchased.

commission Power conferred by the chief executive of a jurisdiction upon someone; power vested in someone to perform particular tasks; also, a body of persons who convene and perform the duties of an organization or agency.

commissioner A person who heads a particular agency, federal, state, or local, under a commission form of government.

Commissioner of Deeds The officer who is authorized to administer oaths to others in those situations in which no special provisions are made according to law.

commission of inquiry A board comprised of persons appointed to investigate and report about a particular problem.

commission of interstate cooperation The first interstate commission to establish law enforcement procedures in the United States was the New Jersey Commission on Interstate Cooperation, created in 1935. Its duties included developing interstate cooperation relative to crime control, taxation, motor vehicles, and agriculture.

Commission on Accreditation for Corrections Established in 1974 as a private, nonprofit entity, this organization attempts to foster professionalism among its membership by implementing training courses, procedures, and standards that promote greater job performance and conduct. It is sponsored by the American Correctional Association.

Commission on Accreditation for Law Enforcement Agencies, Inc. (CALEA) A body of persons formed in 1979 by the International Association of Chiefs of Police, the National Organization of Black Law Enforcement Executives, the National Sheriffs' Association, and the Police Executive Research Forum to develop a set of law enforcement standards and to establish and administer an accreditation process through which law enforcement agencies could voluntarily demonstrate that they meet professionally recognized criteria for excellence in management and service delivery. It was subsequently replaced by the Peace Officer Standards and Training (POST) initiative, which established state and local training centers for law enforcement officers.

Commission on Civil Rights Established in 1957, this bipartisan commission investigates complaints of interfering with voting rights and registration, and it serves as a clearinghouse for civil rights information. It makes recommendations to Congress, issues criticisms of various federal agencies in terms of the speed with which compliance with federal mandates occurs, and issues periodic reports.

commitment A judicial action placing an individual in a particular type of confinement as authorized by law.

commitment rate The number of juveniles sent to secure correctional facilities per 100,000 juveniles in the population.

commitment to conformity A theoretical ingredient of social control positing that real, present, and logical reasons exist to obey the rules of society.

Committees of Vigilance Citizens' self-defense groups formed for mutual protection in the absence of stable, effective local law enforcement on the American frontier (circa 1850s).

commodity fraud Any deception involving the trading of goods or merchandise.

common law The authority based on court decrees and judgments that recognize, affirm, and enforce certain usages and customs of the people. Laws are determined by judges in accordance with their rulings.

common-law marriage After a man and a woman reside together in a common residence for a certain amount of time, sometimes seven years, the parties become married without an official ceremony but with all legal rights of married persons.

common pleas court In the United States, usually a court of general and original jurisdiction.

communal consensus model *See* **consensus approach, consensus model, consensus perspective, consensus view of crime.**

community aid panel A group consisting of a police officer, a solicitor, and responsible community members who assist offenders in addressing problems that led to their illegal behavior. Such panels are used in New South Wales, Australia, as a form of restorative justice.

Community Anti-Drug Coalitions of America Affiliated with the National Association of Drug Court Professionals, this organization is an advocacy agency that offers information and technical assistance in the development and strategic planning of public policy initiatives.

community-based corrections facilities, community-based corrections programs, community corrections Locally operated services offering minimum-security, limited-release, and work-release alternatives to prisoners about to be paroled. These programs may also serve probationers.

community-based policing An umbrella term encompassing any law enforcement agency or community citizen- or group-initiated plan or program to enable police officers and community residents to work cooperatively in creative ways that will reduce or control crime, fear of crime, and the incidence of victimizations; promote mutual understanding for the purpose of enhancing police officer/citizen co-production of community safety and security; and establish a police-citizen communications network through which mutual problems may be discussed and resolved.

community-based supervision Reintegrative programs operated publicly or privately to assist offenders by providing therapeutic, support, and supervision programs for criminals. Programs may include furloughs, probation, parole, community service, and restitution.

Community Board Program A civil mediation mechanism utilizing volunteers to mediate between victims and offenders.

community control A term used to denote various forms of community supervision, particularly in Florida, where electronic monitoring is used.

community correctional center An institution, usually located within an urban area, that houses inmates soon to be released. Such centers are designed to help inmates establish community ties and thus to promote their reintegration into society. They are also called community prerelease centers.

Community Corrections Act (CCA) A statewide mechanism included in legislation whereby funds are granted to local units of government and community agencies to develop and deliver "front-end" alternative sanctions in lieu of state incarceration.

community court A special court in which lay members of the community participate in developing a just disposition for the offender.

community custody The lowest custody level, ordinarily reserved for inmates who meet the qualifications for participation in community activities.

Community Diversion Incentive (CDI) A Virginia diversion program established in 1981 for prison-bound offenders. Participants were required to perform specified unpaid community services and make financial restitution to victims. Clients were also subject to intensive supervised probation.

Community Effort to Combat Auto Theft (CECAT) An organization operating as a task force, established in 1995 by the Los Angeles Police Department, dedicated to the investigation and eventual apprehension of car thieves.

community facility *See* **community correctional center.**

community justice A movement beginning in the late twentieth century to involve the community in the disposition of criminal cases, based on the premise that the community both gives rise to criminality and suffers the consequences.

community model A correctional model stressing community reintegration. Offenders are permitted brief furloughs or visits to the community from prison, work release, and limited exposure to community life. Eventually, their transition to the community from prison proceeds smoothly.

community notification An advisory to the community of the release or pending release of convicted offenders.

community organization A response to gangs that includes efforts to mobilize the community in an effort to deal with gangs.

community organization model A Youth Services Bureau model that uses citizens on a voluntary basis to assist delinquency-prone youth.

Community Patrol Officer Program (CPOP) A problem-oriented community policing effort involving other community agencies, which commenced as a pilot project in 1984 in New York City. Officers were assigned to foot patrols for 16- to 60-block beats. The most important function of CPOP was the prevention of street-level drug problems. Seventy-five precincts used the CPOP by 1989.

Community-Police Educational Program A program implemented by the Philadelphia Police Department in 1980 that was designed to educate citizens by explaining the necessity for certain police actions and to reduce their criticism of police performance.

community policing A philosophy rather than a specific tactic, community policing is a proactive, decentralized approach designed to reduce crime, disorder, and fear of crime by intensely involving the same officer in a community for a long term so that personal links are formed with residents. Its purpose is to stimulate and enhance citizen participation and strengthen informal social controls.

Community Policing Consortium A partnership of five police organizations in the United States, including the International Association of Chiefs of Police (IACP), the National

Organization of Black Law Enforcement Executives (NOBLE), the National Sheriffs' Association (NSA), the Police Executive Research Forum (PERF), and the Police Foundation. Sponsored and funded by the U.S. Department of Justice, it helps to advance the philosophy of community policing through research, training, and technical assistance.

Community Projects for Restoration A federal law enforcement and social welfare program begun under the first Bush Administration. In 1992, $18 million in federal funds was targeted for community policing, public housing assistance, and gang prevention efforts under the "weed and seed" program.

community prosecution The practice of strengthening the relation between district attorneys and the communities they serve; a process of connecting criminal justice services with neighborhoods.

Community Protection Program A New York State county-based program as an alternative to prison, in which prison-bound offenders are diverted to intensive supervision and treatment.

community reintegration, community reintegration model A process whereby an offender who has been incarcerated is able to live in the community under some supervision and gradually adjust to life outside of prison or jail.

community relations A partnership between police and citizens in any given community whereby the public image of police officers is influenced by progressive programs that decrease crime and increase community safety. Considerable input is received from community residents working cooperatively with police officers in various programs to solve community problems, usually of a criminal nature.

Community Relations Service (CRS) An agency of the U.S. Department of Justice whose primary goal is to resolve disputes relating to violations of antidiscrimination statutes.

community residential centers Transitional homes located in neighborhoods, which provide offenders with limited counseling, job placement services, food and shelter, and limited supervision.

community resource management model *See* **brokerage model.**

community resource management team model A form of brokerage model in which caseloads of probationers or parolees are pooled and served by more than one officer, each specializing in one or more areas, such as drug/alcohol services or employment. The officer specializing in a particular area develops linkages to community agencies that provide those services. Thus, a drug/alcohol specialist would assess the probationer's needs in the area of substance abuse, refer him or her to community agencies that provide substance abuse services, and monitor the offender's progress in that area.

community security facilities Nonsecure facilities that include prerelease centers, such as work release or educational release, halfway houses, and other nonsecure settings.

Community Service In the Coates Typology, the type of police officer who is interested in documenting how the community is helped by police action. *See also* **Coates Typology.**

community-service disposition A judicially imposed or parole board–imposed requirement as a condition of one's probation or parole program to perform a fixed number of hours of work for the community, usually as a part of one's punishment. These dispositions are intended to heighten offender accountability.

community-service officer Any police officer assigned the duty of handling noncrime-related matters for a police department.

community-service orders Judicially imposed restitution for those convicted of committing crimes. Some form of work must be performed to satisfy restitution requirements.

Community Service Program, Inc. (CSP, Inc.) Established in Orange County, CA, this program is designed to instill self-confidence in youths, reduce parental and familial dysfunction, and establish self-reliance and -esteem through family counseling therapy and sessions.

community-service restitution A program in which offenders are required to assist a worthwhile community organization for a period of time.

community services Local delinquency or adult criminal prevention services such as recreational programs and drug and alcohol information programs that help meet the community's needs for offenders.

community standard A phrase used by the U.S. Supreme Court in articulating the norms of a given community or geographical area as the measure of whether or not particular conduct is considered illegal or inconsistent with community values and ways of behaving.

community supervision officers Federal officers responsible for the supervision of parolees and mandatory releasees. These personnel prepare periodic reports about parolee progress and adjustment and make this information available to the U.S. Parole Commission.

community treatment Using nonsecure and noninstitutional residences, counseling services, victim restitution programs, and other community services to treat juveniles in their own communities.

Community Treatment Project The famous California Youth Authority program that released selected juveniles to aftercare immediately after reception. The project included classification by interpersonal maturity levels and attempted differential treatments based on classification.

community wellness A proactive collaborative effort between police departments and community residents to initiate watch and alert programs to inform police about possible criminal activities. As residents take a more active role in preventing crime, there are substantial decreases in crime observed in their neighborhoods over time.

commutation, commutation of sentence, commutation laws Reduction of a sentence to a less severe one, usually by administrative authority.

comorbidity The state of having two or more diseases or conditions at the same time.

compact An agreement between two or more jurisdictions to accept and supervise convicted offenders, such as parolees and probationers.

comparative corrections The study of similarities and differences in the correctional systems of other cultures, societies, and institutions.

comparative criminal/juvenile justice Analyses of criminal justice systems of other countries, studying their similarities and differences.

comparative criminologist One who studies crime and criminal justice on a cross-national level.

comparative criminology The study of crime on a cross-national level.

comparative justice The study of criminal justice systems across other countries and cultures.

comparative policing The study of police and policing across other countries and cultures.

comparative research A research strategy that looks at crime, policing, corrections, or any other common phenomena in societies with different cultures and different social structures.

comparison microscope Any magnification device capable of viewing two objects simultaneously for purposes of comparison.

comparison prints Fingerprints taken from possible suspects or others to be compared with latent prints found at a crime scene.

compelling government interest For correctional facilities, this means anything representing a serious threat to a prison's security, order, or discipline.

compelling interest A legal concept that provides the basis for suspicionless searches when public safety is at issue (e.g., urinalysis tests of train engineers).

compensation Money awarded to victims of crime to repay them in part for their losses and injuries; in research, subjects in the control group attempting to make up for being deprived of a desired treatment.

compensatory damages An award used to compensate injured parties in legal actions where injuries have been sustained.

competence, competency, competent The state of being fit to give testimony or stand trial.

competency hearing A court hearing to establish that a defendant is fit to stand trial.

competent evidence Any information presented at a trial that is admissible and has probative value. It is considered as proof that a particular act was committed or some behavior was observed to occur at a particular time and place.

competent to stand trial A finding by a court, when the defendant's sanity at the time of trial is at issue, that the defendant has sufficient present ability to consult with his or her attorney with a reasonable degree of rational understanding and that the defendant has a rational as well as a factual understanding of the proceedings against him or her.

complainant One who swears out a criminal complaint against another.

complainantless crime Victimless illegal conduct, such as prostitution or illegal gambling; victimless crime. Usually, the activity is engaged in by willing participants who have no interest in seeing the laws that prohibit such activity enforced.

complaint A written statement of essential facts constituting the offense alleged, made under oath before a magistrate or other qualified judicial officer.

complaint denied, granted The decision by a prosecutor to decline or grant a request that he or she seek an indictment or file an information or complaint against a specified person for a specific offense.

complaint desk The work location, usually of a deputy district attorney, where police reports or complaints are screened and several crucial decisions are made about arrested persons. Usually, reports are examined to determine if they are factually accurate and have sufficient evidence to support criminal charges, and if an officer's conduct is legal.

complaint requested A request by a law enforcement agency that a prosecutor should seek an indictment or information against a specified person for a specified offense.

complete count census The census of population and housing taken every 10 years, intended to reach every household in the country. It includes only basic demographic information on each member of the household, plus a few questions about the housing unit.

completed crime An illegal act that has already been carried out.

compliance-involvement scheme, typology A system devised by Amitai Etzioni in which a relation is drawn between the type of power used by a superior to elicit compliance from subordinates and the type of involvement resulting from power used. "Congruent" types would be reward-calculative, coercive-alienative, or normative-moral.

complicity Conspiratorial conduct whereby two or more persons plan a crime and attempt to commit it. Any effort by one person to assist or aid another who is about to commit or has committed a crime.

composite A sketch or picture of a criminal suspect, produced either manually or by computer.

compounding a crime, compounding a criminal offense The crime of receiving something of value in exchange for an agreement not to file a criminal complaint.

comprehension An important element of informed consent that refers to the confidence that the participant has provided knowing consent when the research procedure is associated with complex or subtle risks.

Comprehensive Crime Control Act of 1984 A significant act that authorized the establishment of the U.S. Sentencing Commission, instituted sentencing guidelines, provided for the abolition of federal parole, and devised new guidelines and goals for federal corrections.

compressed gang A relatively new type of gang with fewer than 50 members of about the same age that does not have a defined territory.

CompStat A crime analysis and police management process developed by the New York City Police Department dedicated to the collection, analysis, and mapping of crime data and other essential police performance measures on a regular basis for the purpose of holding police managers accountable for their performance as measured by these data. Its philosophy is accurate and timely intelligence, effective tactics, rapid deployment of personnel and resources, and relentless follow-up and assessment.

compulsion An irresistible impulse; the inability to control behavior that may be criminal.

Compulsory School Act Legislation passed in Colorado in 1899 directed to prevent truancy among juveniles. The act included juveniles who were habitually absent from school, who wandered the streets, and had no obvious business or occupation.

compurgation A method of trial used before the thirteenth century in which a person charged with a crime could be absolved by swearing to innocence and producing a number of other persons willing to swear that they believed the accused's declaration of innocence.

computer-aided dispatch (CAD) A computer-driven program capable of performing routine clerical tasks in dispatch offices, including filing and sorting information.

computer-assisted telephone interviewing (CATI) A type of telephone survey in which the interviewer sits at a computer terminal and, as a question flashes on the screen, asks it over the telephone. The respondent's answers are typed and coded directly on a disk.

computer crime Any form of crime in which a computer is used (e.g., illegally transferring funds from one account to another by means of a computer, or stealing software programs by means of computer copying).

Computer Crime Information Any newsworthy information that can be distributed by the Bureau of Justice or the Computer Security Institute, which is headquartered in Northborough, MA. The information pertains to computer security and related topics.

computer criminal A person who uses a computer to commit a crime.

Computer Emergency Response Team (CERT) Established in 1988 by the U.S. Department of Defense and headquartered in Pittsburgh, PA, this organization helps computer administrators detect security gaps and repair or rectify computer problems.

computer fraud Falsification of stored data or deception in legitimate transactions by manipulation of data or programming, including the unlawful acquisition of data or programs for purposes of financial gain.

computer geek, geek A person who has acquired considerable expertise in computer programming and hacking for either positive or negative ends or goals; one who eats (computer) bugs for a living; also known as a spod, terminal junkie, propeller head, turbo nerd, and turbo geek.

computer hacking In criminology, activities that include the gaining of unauthorized access to data banks for malicious though not necessarily destructive purposes, and for neither financial gain nor purposes of espionage.

computerized criminal history (CCH) An electronically stored and retrievable record of an offender's arrests and case dispositions.

Computer Protection Systems (CPS) Established in 1980 and headquartered in Plymouth, MA, this organization provides asset protection and loss prevention advice to private industries, banks, and various businesses.

Computer Security Institute Established in 1975 and headquartered in Northborough, MA, this organization collects information about computer security. Publishes the *Computer Security Journal.*

computer virus A computer program designed to severely invade systems and either modify how they operate or alter the information they store; a destructive software program that can vandalize computers.

Comte, Auguste (1798–1857) The French positivist considered to be the "father of sociology." He believed that social forces dominate individual behaviors and that the strict use of scientific methods ought to be used in order to understand the nature and implications of these forces upon individual behavior. He wrote *A System of Positive Reality* (1851).

con Short for convict.

concealment of birth Hiding the birth of a child.

concealment of death Hiding the death of a person.

concentric-zone hypothesis, concentric-zone theory A series of rings originating from a city center, such as Chicago, and emanating outward, forming various zones characterized by different socioeconomic conditions including areas of high delinquency and crime.

concept An abstraction representing an object, a property of an object, or a certain phenomenon that scientists use to describe the empirical world; a term that has a direct empirical referent.

conceptual framework A level of theory in which descriptive categories are systematically placed within a broad logical structure of explicit and assumed propositions.

conceptual replication An attempt to demonstrate an experimental phenomenon with an entirely new paradigm, or set of measures, or manipulations.

conciliation Indirect mediation between a victim and an offender.

conclusive evidence Any compelling evidence that is so strong that it cannot be disputed or discounted; proof establishing guilt beyond a reasonable doubt.

concordance rate The similarity of delinquent behavior.

concubinage Cohabitation; living together as husband and wife without benefit of marriage or legal wedding ceremony sanctioned by law.

concurrence Coexistence of an act in violation of the law and a culpable mental state.

concurrent At the same time.

concurrent jurisdiction A situation in which an offender may be held accountable in several different jurisdictions simultaneously; also, courts in the same jurisdiction.

concurrent sentence A sentence for two or more criminal acts that are served simultaneously, or run together; more than one sentence handed out on the same occasion to a convicted offender, to be served during a common time period while the offender is incarcerated, on probation, or on parole.

concurrent writs Two or more summonses or writs issued by judicial officials that run at the same time for the same purpose. City and county judges may issue independent writs against the same suspect charged with the same offense, seeking the suspect's arrest.

concurring opinion A judge's written opinion agreeing or adding additional justification for the result in the case, but disagreeing with the reasoning of the majority opinion.

condemn To find guilt or sentence a convicted offender to a particular punishment, especially death; in civil terminology, to find a dwelling unsuitable for habitation.

condemnation of the condemners A technique of neutralization that asserts that it is the motives and behaviors of the people who are condemning offenders, rather than offender motives and behaviors, that should be criticized.

conditional disposition A decision by a juvenile court judge authorizing payment of fines, community service, restitution, or some other penalty after an adjudication of delinquency has been made.

conditional diversion Suspension of prosecution in the pretrial stage, while specific conditions are met. If the conditions are satisfied, prosecution may be dismissed or the charges reduced in seriousness.

conditional pardon Any pardon action by a governor or pardon board in which program requirements are articulated.

conditional release Freedom of a defendant who agrees to meet specific conditions in addition to appearing in court later (e.g., remaining in the jurisdiction, maintaining steady employment, avoiding contact with victims or other known criminals).

conditional variable A contingency necessary for the occurrence of the relationship between the independent and dependent variables.

conditions of confinement One of two tests used by courts to determine whether cruel and unusual punishment exists within a facility. It examines whether basic human needs, such as food, health care, or sanitary conditions are being met in a constitutional manner.

conditions of criminality Conditions that make a person criminally responsible for committing a particular crime under common law. The person must be of a specific age, have criminal intent, have mental capacity, and act voluntarily.

conditions of probation or parole, conditions of release on probation or parole The general (state-ordered) and special (court-ordered or board-ordered) limits imposed on offenders who are released either on probation or parole. General conditions tend to be fixed by statute; special conditions are mandated by the sentencing authority and take into consideration the background of the offender and circumstances surrounding the offense.

conduct disorder A personality disorder that involves the commission of delinquent acts and little concern for the feelings and well-being of others.

conduct in need of supervision (CINS) Any misbehavior by a juvenile requiring parental or guardian intervention.

conduct norms Behaviors expected of social group members. If group norms conflict with those of the general culture, members of the group may find themselves described as outcasts or criminals.

confabulation A fictitious rendering of events by someone who is mentally disturbed.

confession An admission to a crime by a suspect.

confidence game, con game Obtaining of money by means of deception through the trust a victim places in the offender.

confidence man, con man One who operates a confidence game; one who cheats other persons out of their money or possessions.

confidentiality, confidential communication Protection of the identity of research participants; also, any privileged communication between a client and an attorney.

confidentiality and sealing restrictions A law that keeps juvenile records confidential.

confidentiality privilege The right between a defendant and his or her attorney where certain information cannot be disclosed to prosecutors or others because of the attorney-client relation. For juveniles, records are maintained under secure circumstances with limited access, and only then accessed by those in authority with a clear law enforcement purpose.

confinement, congregate or solitary Placement in a secure facility or area where an individual's movements are restricted or controlled.

confinement facility A correctional facility, usually a jail or prison, where inmates are not permitted to depart unaccompanied.

confiscation The seizure of private property without compensating its owner; taking possession of property because it is used in connection with an illegal act (e.g., government confiscation of a pleasure craft used in transporting cocaine from one location to another).

conflict, class Karl Marx's concept of clashes between the bourgeoisie and the proletariat classes over their different vested interests. The proletariat works for the bourgeoisie, who own the means of production.

conflict, social Any dispute between groups of people, often of different classes or cultures. It may include physical confrontation.

conflict criminology *See* **radical criminology.**

conflict gang A type of gang described by Richard Cloward and Lloyd Ohlin in *Delinquency and Opportunity* (1960), characterized by engagement in violence with other gangs or community residents; also known as "fighting gangs." These gangs' primary interest is not criminal activity. *See also* **criminal gang; retreatist gang** *for goal comparisons.*

conflict model, approach, perspective A legal model that asserts that the political power of interest groups and elites influences the content of the criminal law.

conflict of interest A situation in which a party to a legal matter or business transaction cannot participate due to a preexisting personal or professional relationship with another party.

conflict of laws A situation existing in which two different laws are seemingly incompatible but which nevertheless apply to the same case.

conflict resolution An interpersonal strategy whereby persons in a group resolve their differences through discussion and compromise.

conformity Robert K. Merton's mode of adaptation, characterized by persons who accept institutionalized means to achieve culturally approved goals.

confrontation In court, any direct meeting between an accused person and the accuser. The Fifth Amendment assures every citizen the right to confront and cross-examine his or her accuser. *See also* **Bill of Rights.**

congregate system The system introduced at Auburn State Penitentiary in New York in which prisoners worked and ate together in common work and recreational areas, but were segregated at night.

conjugal visits, visitation Programs, usually in jails or prisons, that permit inmates to have contact with their spouses or significant others to maintain positive relationships. Sexual contact is permitted between inmates and their spouses.

con man *See* **confidence man, con man.**

"connects" In prison slang, inmates whose prison assignments allow them to acquire scarce information and resources that can be used for personal gain.

conning In treatment, this involves inmates' attempts to fool a counselor or therapist into believing that the treatment received is causing positive changes in the person doing the conning. Its purpose is to achieve an early release.

connivance Conspiracy to commit a crime; involvement in a crime or an attempted crime.

conscientious objector A person who refuses military service on moral grounds.

consecutive sentences, sentencing More than one sentence imposed on the same occasion to a convicted offender, with the sentences to be served one after another and not concurrently.

consensual encounter Any voluntary exchange between a police officer and a citizen, with no restraint of individual liberty, because the police do not have any objective justification to stop, detain, or arrest. The citizen is free to leave at any time and free not to cooperate or answer any questions.

consensual transaction, exchange A mutually agreeable action between two or more parties (e.g., prostitution is a consensual transaction in which sex is exchanged for money).

consensus approach, consensus model, consensus perspective, consensus view of crime A model of criminal lawmaking that assumes that societal members agree on which conduct is right or wrong and that such law is codified to reflect agreed-upon societal values.

consent Voluntarily yielding to the will or desire of another person.

consent, implied Consent based on an agreement between parties. There is implied consent between a probation officer and a probationer to permit routine home or apartment searches and inspections whenever the probation officer believes the probationer may be secreting contraband or using drugs. The term is also used in conjunction with DUI offenses, in which a person who drives on a highway is presumed to have given consent to provide a breath or blood sample when operation under the influence is suspected. Such consent may be actively withdrawn, but it allows doctors to draw blood from unconscious patients for police lab analysis of BAC.

consent decree A formal agreement involving a child, parents, and the juvenile court in which the youth is placed under the court's supervision without an official finding of delinquency.

consenting adult One who is no longer a juvenile and who engages in certain deviant acts, often of a sexual nature, such as fellatio or anal intercourse.

consenting adult laws Statutes that permit particular behaviors otherwise unlawful but where both parties are adults and consent to performing the behaviors. Sodomy has been declared illegal in numerous jurisdictions, but if consenting adults engage in sodomy, such behavior is permissible.

consent interrogation Any questioning by law enforcement officers of a criminal suspect when the suspect appears voluntarily at the police station and gives a brief interview with police and is not detained; interrogations that are not subject to the *Miranda* warning.

consent of the victim Any voluntary yielding of the will of the victim, accompanied by his or her deliberation, agreeing to the act of the offending party.

consent search Any search of a dwelling, person, or vehicle in which the owner has given permission to search.

conservative The view or social position that persons act with free will and choice and that crime is a result of moral failure rather than due to political or social factors. Conservatives are generally in favor of harsher punishments for criminals and support capital punishment.

Conservative Vice Lords A Chicago-based gang that was a forerunner of the Vice Lords and the Vice Lords Nation. The gang originally started with a group of youths who were incarcerated in the St. Charles Correctional Facility in 1957. Members were largely from Lawndale on Chicago's West Side.

consigliere In organized crime, one who serves as an advisor to a boss.

consolateur A penis-shaped device or dildo which may be either battery operated or manually used for erotic genital stimulation.

consolidated laws A compendium of all laws of a given jurisdiction that are currently upheld, arranged according to subject.

Consolidated Parole Board Model Under this model, the parole board makes the release decision, but field parole services are in the state department of corrections and authority is split between these two administrative units.

consolidation model of parole organization An organizational pattern in which parole decisions are made by a central figure who has independent powers but who is organizationally situated in the overall department of corrections.

conspiracy The crime of two or more persons agreeing or planning to commit a crime. The overt act itself is a tangible indication of the furtherance of the conspiratorial act. *See also* **complicity.**

conspirator One who willingly participates in a conspiracy.

constables Favored noblemen of the king who commanded neighborhood groups; the forerunners of modern-day police officers. Latter-day constables are comparable to county sheriff's departments, doing patrol and criminal apprehension. They may be local officials with limited police powers.

constitution Fundamental laws contained in a state or federal document that outlines the design of the government and the basic rights of individuals. Prescribes the structure or organization and major duties of the legislative, executive, and judicial branches of government; allocates power between respective branches of government; and places restrictions on the exercise of that power, specifying what government may not do.

Constitution, U.S. The basis of law in the United States. Written in 1787 and ratified by the states in 1788, it has subsequently been amendend to grant specific rights. Modifications occur as new Amendments are added and existing laws are interpreted by Congress and the U.S. Supreme Court.

Constitution Act of 1867 This act bestowed the Canadian Parliament with the legislative authority to define all criminal law throughout the provinces. (It has since undergone extensive revision.)

constitutional court Any judicial body created under a specific provision of a constitution of a governmental body or legal authority.

constitutionalism The view that the power to govern others should be limited by precise principles so that the rights of individuals will not be infringed or violated; also, the philosophy that articulated principles of an organization or jurisdiction should be strictly interpreted and enforced as a regulatory medium for social action.

constitutional law An area of study in law schools involving the U.S. Constitution and its Amendments; an investigation and discussion of the principles articulated by the U.S. Supreme Court and its interpretations of the law in different legal contexts.

constitutional officer Any law enforcement officer specifically and expressly provided for in either the U.S. Constitution or a state constitution. The sheriff, constable, and coroner are constitutional officers in several states.

constitutional rights Rights guaranteed to all U.S. citizens by the U.S. Constitution and its Amendments. *See also* **Bill of Rights.**

constitutional theory Any theoretical perspective in criminology that focuses on the physical, biological, or mental constitution of a person.

constitutive criminology The study of the process whereby persons create an ideology of crime that sustains the notion of crime as a concrete reality.

construction Interpretation.

constructive breaking Where the law implies breaking into a dwelling or business (e.g., persons posing as city termite inspectors who enter a dwelling in order to commit theft, even though residents invited them in, are guilty of constructive breaking).

constructive contempt Contempt that occurs out of the court's presence, but which does not involve one's failure to appear in court.

constructive intent The finding of criminal liability for an unintentional act that is the result of negligence or recklessness.

constructive possession In the crime of larceny, willingly giving up temporary physical possession of property but retaining legal ownership; also, drug possession charges in which the owner of a property or the driver of a vehicle is presumed to be the owner of the contraband found therein, in the absence of any other acknowledgment of ownership, such as by one or more passengers.

consumer fraud Any deception perpetrated against those who purchase merchandise or services.

consumer protection Federal, state, and local laws governing business enterprises that regulate product quality in an effort to protect citizens who might consume the business's products.

consumers' rights movement A trend begun in the 1960s by various public groups to urge the adoption of higher standards governing the production of goods for consumer safety.

contact patrols A project funded by the British Home Office that promoted greater police officer contact with community residents through more continuous police presence in "beat" areas.

contact surveillance Any application of trace substances that attach to clothing or body parts when one comes into contact with these substances. It is useful in identifying persons who may have been at crime scenes and thus are considered suspects.

contact visits Prison visitations that permit visitors and inmates to have limited nonsexual physical contact.

contact wound Any injury that occurs when a firearm is discharged while in direct contact with the body.

contagion effect The negative, crime-promoting influence of deviant siblings on their brothers and sisters.

containment theory An explanation elaborated by Walter Reckless and others that positive self-image enables persons otherwise disposed toward criminal behavior to avoid criminal conduct and conform to societal values. Every person is a part of an external structure and has a protective internal structure providing defense, protection, and insulation against his or her peers, such as delinquents.

contamination of evidence Adulteration of evidence by the introduction of foreign substances, either deliberately or accidentally.

contemnor A person found to be in contempt of court.

contemporaneous Occurring at the same time.

contempt of court Disobeying orders from judges in their courtrooms; failing to observe the proper decorum of legal proceedings; crossing the line of proper conduct, either as a defense attorney or prosecutor (e.g., failing to give testimony when compelled to do so).

content analysis A set of qualitative data analysis techniques that permits the analysis of a text for terms, concepts, themes, or theoretical constructs.

context of justification The activities of scientists as they attempt logically and empirically to verify claims for knowledge.

contingency A factor that determines movement from one criminal role to another, and from one crime to another.

contingency question A question that applies only to a subgroup of respondents because it is relevant only to certain people.

contingency theory The view that effective leadership is dependent on the circumstances and work environment of the leader or administrator. If the work is highly structured and clearly spelled out by rules, such as are specified by the rules of criminal procedure in the courtroom environment, then managers (e.g., judges, court officers, and others) orient themselves toward subordinates in a task-directed fashion.

continuance An adjournment of a scheduled case until a future date.

continuing custody theory The view that the parolee remains in the custody of either the parole board or the prison and that his or her constitutional rights are limited. Release on parole is merely a change in the degree of custody.

continuity of crime The idea or theory that crime begins early in life and continues throughout the life course, and the best predictor of future criminality is past criminality.

continuous crime Any criminal act that extends over a prolonged period (e.g., possessing and driving a stolen car for several days).

continuous signalling device Electronic monitoring device that broadcasts an encoded signal that is received by a receiver-dialer in the offender's home.

continuum of care The seamless delivery of services to delinquents or children at risk.

contraband Any item, including weapons, drugs, or alcohol, the possession of which is illegal.

contract An enforceable agreement between two or more parties.

contract law The part of the law that governs agreements between parties, including individuals, companies, and corporations.

contract law enforcement An arrangement whereby small communities or businesses might contract with local law enforcement agencies to provide for police services and general protection from criminals.

contract prisoners Inmates held in jails or other incarceration facilities out of their own jurisdictions. Hawaiian prisoners might be housed in Texas jails, for instance, because of overcrowding. States or local jail officials contract with other jurisdictions to house a portion of their inmate overflow. These prisoners are also known as holdback inmates.

contract system, attorney A system that provides counsel to indigent offenders by retaining attorneys under contract to the county to handle some or all of these cases.

contract system, prison A system used in the early twentieth century in which inmates were leased out to private industry to work.

contract theory The view that parole represents a contract between the state and the parolee whereby the prisoner agrees to abide by certain conditions and terms in exchange for his or her release. Violation of the conditions represents a breach of contract that permits parole to be revoked.

contractual rights Any rights or privileges conveyed under a contract or legally enforceable document.

contraventions A French crime designation denoting petty offenses or violations comparable with misdemeanors in U.S. jurisdictions.

contrecoup contusion A contusion of the brain found opposite to the point of impact.

contributing to the delinquency of a minor Any act by an adult that induces a juvenile to engage in a criminal act.

contributory negligence The share of responsibility of a victim in any negligent act for which the victim's own lack of care is partially at fault.

control Close supervision or management of offenders while they are on probation or parole.

control conditions Rules imposed on all probationers and parolees, including obeying all laws, not associating with known criminals, and reporting regularly to the probation office.

control group A comparison group of subjects that does not receive a particular stimulus or program.

controlled substance Any bioactive or psychoactive chemical substance proscribed by law, which is ordinarily dispensed by a licensed physician for the specific treatment of a physical or mental condition.

Controlled Substances Act The Comprehensive Drug Abuse and Control Act of 1970, which sought to control drugs in the United States by classification and specification of penalties for possession or distribution. It was replaced by the Comprehensive Crime Control Act of 1984.

controller value system A parole board decision-making system that emphasizes the functions of parole supervision and management.

Controlling Customer Prison Industries Model Under this model, the private sector is the primary or exclusive customer of a business operating as part of a prison industries program that it owns or has helped to capitalize, which it may or may not manage.

control theories Any explanations of a person's conduct that rely on the cohesiveness of social ties and interpersonal obligations.

contumacious A situation in which one deliberately disobeys a court order; contempt of court.

contusion Any bruise caused by a blow or impact to the body.

conventional model, conventional model with geographic considerations A caseload assignment model in which probation or parole officers are randomly assigned clients. When geography is considered, assignments are based on the travel time required for probation officers to meet regularly with offender-clients.

convergence hypothesis The notion that as males and females move toward equality, the differences between their amount of criminal activity will decrease.

conversion The unlawful assumption of the rights of ownership to someone else's property without their permission.

conveyance, legal Any written document authorizing the transfer of property from one person to another.

convict An adult who has been found guilty of a crime; an inmate of a jail or prison.

convict code The dominant value system in the Big House, heavily influenced by the thieves' code, which includes the following values: do your own time; don't rat on another prisoner; and maintain your dignity and respect.

convicted innocent An individual who did not commit the crime but was convicted for it anyway.

conviction The state of being judged guilty of a crime in a court, either by a judge or jury.

convict labor The use of inmates to perform menial labor either inside or outside of prison.

convict lease system A system of prison industry in which a prison temporarily relinquishes supervision of its prisoners to a lessee. The lessee either employs the prisoners within the institution or transports them elsewhere in the state.

convict subculture The separate culture that exists in a prison that has its own set of rewards and behaviors. The traditional culture is now being replaced by a violent gang culture.

co-occurring disorders Contemperaneous conditions in which persons suffer from two or more social, physical, biological, or psychological problems, such as heroin addiction and paranoia.

co-offending Committing criminal acts in groups.

Cook, Rufus R. A social reformer associated with the Temperance Movement in the mid-1800s, who was dedicated to reforming alcoholics charged with crimes.

cook-chill method of food production A method that allows large quantities of food to be cooked in advance and then stored for later use in prison lunchrooms.

Cooley, Charles Horton (1864–1929) A sociologist who developed the concept of primary and secondary groups. Primary groups are face-to-face groups with whom we have close interaction. Secondary groups might be football teams or college fraternities or sororities. Cooley also developed the concept of the "looking-glass self," which consists of (1) our impressions of how others view us, (2) our interpretations of these impressions as either good or bad, and (3) our persistence or change in the behaviors eliciting the approval or disapproval of others.

cooling-off period The span of time between the offenses of a serial killer; also, the period between a person's application to purchase a firearm and when he or she actually takes possession, which is intended to permit any anger on the part of the purchaser to subside.

cool inmates, "cools" A term used to describe female inmates by other inmates. "Cools" are those females with prior records who attempt to violate prison rules and remain undetected.

Cooper, D.B. (?–1971?) A passenger aboard a Northwest Orient Airlines jet on November 24, 1971, who hijacked the plane for ransom and parachuted over Washington State. His body was never recovered, and some speculate that he successfully landed and escaped with over $200,000 in ransom money.

cooperating agencies model A Youth Service Bureau model in which several agencies act as a team to provide delinquency-prone youths with needed services.

cop-killer bullets A term given to Teflon-coated bullets capable of penetrating the typical bullet-proof vest and causing extensive damage to human tissue.

"copping out" Entering a plea of guilty, normally following plea bargaining. The copping-out ceremony consists of a series of questions that the judge asks defendants as to the voluntariness of their plea. Rule 11 of the Federal Rules of Criminal Procedure in the U.S. Code governs plea-agreement hearings and the litany judges must pronounce in order for guilty pleas and copping out to be accepted.

coprophilia Sexual obsession with feces.

coprophobia Fear of defecation or excreting.

COPS AHEAD (Accelerated Hiring, Education, and Deployment) Program Under the 1994 Crime Bill, 1,600 cities were authorized to immediately augment their police forces under an accelerated hiring, education, and deployment scheme. Cities with populations over 50,000 could start hiring and training a limited number of officers while their grant is pending. The program was designed to benefit departments by permitting them to fund hiring additional officers in numbers up to 3 percent of their sworn force. It was intended to benefit communities prepared to move forward with their community policing programs and underscores the U.S. attorney general's commitment to expedite assistance to communities by putting more police officers on the street quickly. City applicants cannot compromise the quality of their community policing strategies or reduce the scope of their officer screening and training procedures. Appropriations were made of up to $8.8 billion for police hiring through 2000.

COPS Fast Grant Program Under the Violent Crime and Law Enforcement Act of 1994, police departments may hire police officers under the "Cop on the Beats Program," with community-oriented policing as its base. The program is intended to encourage the development of police-citizen cooperation to control crime, maintain order, and improve the quality of life in various communities.

COPS MORE A grant program commenced in the mid-1990s to provide more advanced technology to police departments, such as sophisticated mobile laptop computers that permit more rapid officer access to information in order to do more effective police work, and computer-assisted dispatch systems. The program also funds other police-related activities, including additional personnel and their deployment procedures, and may include hiring civilians to perform routine office work to free police officers to work more directly with crime-prevention strategies with other officers on city streets.

COPS Universal Hiring Program Stemming from the 1994 Crime Bill, grants from the U.S. Department of Justice were made available to cities for the purpose of hiring additional police officers, with the ultimate objective of putting 100,000 new police officers on city streets. More than 10,000 policing agencies have subsequently hired 88,000 new officers to fight crime and assist citizens in community-oriented policing activities. The belief is that the greater the police visibility on city streets, the less crime.

copulatio analis Anal sodomy; contact of the penis with the anus.

copycat A person who copies the *modus operandi* of a publicized crime, often a murder, for secondary gain.

copycat syndrome The phenomenon of someone committing a crime simply to imitate other criminals; some offenders commit new crimes in the exact ways that other criminals have committed those crimes in the past.

COPY Kids (Community Opportunities Program for Youth) A Spokane, WA, program for disadvantaged youth commenced in 1992 that allows youth to participate in arts and crafts and learn valuable work skills.

copyright A legal registration signifying exclusive ownership of the right to make and distribute a particular work of art, device, or other product.

copyright infringement The unlawful reproduction or use of copyrighted material for profit.

core The approximate center of a fingerprint pattern.

"corner boy" A young man who is not a delinquent, but may engage in marginal behavior. Eventually he will marry a local girl and obtain a menial job with few prospects for advancement or success.

coroner A physician who performs autopsies or examines corpses to determine the manner and time of death.

corporal punishment The infliction of pain on the body by any device or method as a form of punishment.

corporate crime Crime committed by wealthy or powerful persons in the course of their professions or occupations, but in which liability is distributed throughout organizational leadership. It includes price-fixing, fraudulent stock manipulation, insider trading, and the establishment of illegal trusts. *See also* **white-collar crime.**

corporate gang A coalition of juveniles formed to emulate organized crime.

Corporate Prison Industries Model A logical extension of current efforts to operate prison industries using free-world business practices. This model establishes a quasi-independent corporation that operates and manages prison industries, yet is connected with the corrections department for security purposes.

corpse A dead body.

corpus delicti "Body of the crime" (Latin); the body of the crime made up of the *actus reus* and *mens rea;* the facts that prove a crime has been committed.

correctional agencies Publicly or privately operated organizations or facilities responsible for the supervision of convicted offenders. They may include prisons, penitentiaries, jails, community agencies, day programs, and probation and parole departments.

correctional client Any person, usually a convicted offender, who is assigned to a community correctional facility for treatment or supervision.

correctional day program Any publicly or privately operated supervision plan for convicted offenders. The term encompasses all community corrections agencies, including halfway houses, work release/study release plans, counseling centers, and probation/parole department activities.

correctional econometrics The study of the cost-effectiveness of various correctional programs and related reductions in the incidence of crime.

correctional facility, correctional institution A building or set of buildings designed to house convicted offenders or adjudicated delinquents.

correctional filter A diagrammatic portrayal of sentencing options and stages through which convicted offenders pass before they are ultimately placed in institutional or community corrections.

correctional funnel A method of describing the process whereby apprehended offenders may be screened out of the system at different points along the way. *See figure.*

correctional interest group A group that interacts with a correctional organization to protect its investment in correctional activities.

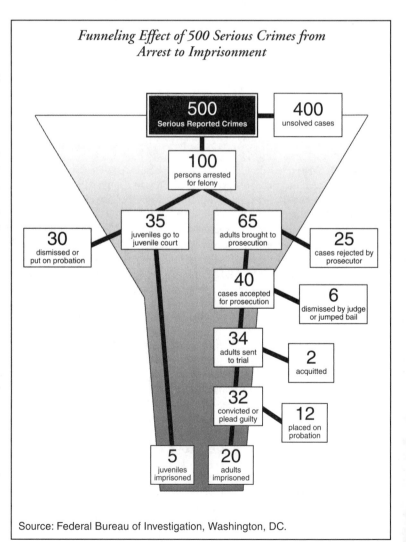

Funneling Effect of 500 Serious Crimes from Arrest to Imprisonment

| 500 Serious Reported Crimes | 400 unsolved cases |

100 persons arrested for felony

30 dismissed or put on probation

35 juveniles go to juvenile court

65 adults brought to prosecution

25 cases rejected by prosecutor

40 cases accepted for prosecution

6 dismissed by judge or jumped bail

34 adults sent to trial

2 acquitted

32 convicted or plead guilty

12 placed on probation

5 juveniles imprisoned

20 adults imprisoned

Source: Federal Bureau of Investigation, Washington, DC.

correctionalism The belief of Marxists and radical criminologists that most of the mainstream research conducted by criminologists is calculated to unmask weak and powerless members of society so that they may be more effectively dealt with by the legal system.

correctionalists Penal specialists, many with college degrees, who began to work in or study prisons during the rehabilitation era.

correctional network The collection of agencies and decision makers that funds, manages, and regulates the correctional process.

correctional officer personalities The personal characteristics of officers as well as their modes of adaptation to their jobs, institutional conditions, the requirements of staff subculture, and institutional expectations.

correctional officers, corrections officers Licensed personnel who supervise or manage inmates in jails or prisons.

correctional process The sequence of decisions and activities through which convicted offenders are processed until the completion of sentence.

Correctional Recovery Academy (CRA) A program offered by CiviGenics in Massachusetts that provides institutional programming and other services for inmates. They offer adult education, outpatient programs for drug and alcohol addiction, life skills, and literacy classes.

correctional supervision Authorized and required guidance, treatment, and regulation of the behavior of a person who is subject to adjudication or conviction, performed by a correctional agency.

corrections The aggregate of programs, services, facilities, and organizations responsible for the management of people who have been accused or convicted of criminal offenses.

corrections (correctional) officer task inventory A cataloging of skills and tasks of correctional officers to determine which tasks are considered most important or vital to the operation of an institution or which skills have been transmitted during officer training.

corrections professional A dedicated person of high moral character and personal integrity who is employed in the field of corrections and takes professionalism to heart.

Corrections Services of Canada The Canadian agency responsible for providing correctional services to all offenders serving terms of two or more years for their crimes.

corrections statistics Information about jail and prison inmates compiled by different agencies since the early 1800s, including age, gender, ethnicity/race, type of conviction offense, length of punishment, and other pertinent data. The information is distributed to interested persons or agencies, and can be used to justify corrections expenditures, such as building more prisons or jails and hiring more correctional officers.

Corrections Today A monthly magazine published by the American Correctional Association that features articles on different aspects of corrections.

corrections volunteer Any unpaid person who performs auxiliary, supplemental, augmentive, or any other work or services for any law enforcement or corrections agency.

corrective prevention The attempt to eliminate the conditions that lead to or cause criminal behavior; also called "primary prevention."

corrective works Productive labor in Soviet corrective-labor colonies.

correlates Variables that are related with one another are said to be correlated. Correlations are not necessarily causally related.

corroboration Evidence that strengthens the evidence already given.

corrupt Depraved; evil; debased; dishonest.

corrupt favoritism An informal control mechanism whereby guards granted special privileges to certain key inmates in exchange for their assistance in maintaining order.

corruption Behavior of public officials who accept money or other bribes for doing something they are under a duty to do anyway; exercising a legitimate discretion for improper reasons.

corruption of a minor A sex offense involving intercourse or other sexual contact by an adult with someone who is under age 18.

corruption of blood Under English common law, the fact of committing treason or another serious felony that could result in a convict's inability to possess property or convey it through inheritance to offspring.

Corrupt Practices Acts Legislation targeting political campaign and election abuses which commenced in 1925 and continues to the present.

cortical arousal The activation of the cerebral cortex, a structure of the brain responsible for higher intellectual functioning, information processing, and decision making.

Cosa Nostra *See* **La Cosa Nostra.**

cost overrun The practice of contractors knowingly exceeding estimated costs for merchandise or services.

CO subculture Norms, behaviors, and adaptations developed by correctional officers to cope with their work environment.

cottage industry Any type of productive work that can be done by an individual alone or in the confines of his or her cell.

cottage system, cottage plan The design of many prisons built with a series of cottage-like living facilities that surround the administration and other general-use buildings. The design was developed at the turn of the century to provide inmates with a homelike atmosphere that would preserve or create a family orientation.

Council of Europe Formed in 1949, the Council discusses issues including definitions of crime among different countries and extradition matters. Although Council activities have been largely informal, much international cooperation has been achieved to combat certain types of crime effectively.

Council of State Governments An organization established in 1933, headquartered in Lexington, KY, and associated with the American Probation and Parole Association. Its goal is to provide state governments with current research about problems in state governments.

counsel A lawyer who represents a party in either a civil or a criminal matter.

counselor A lawyer who gives advice about the law; someone who works with offenders to give them advice and coping information.

count The general name given to each separate offense of which a person is accused in an indictment or an information; also, in prison, a periodic roll call to determine that all prisoners are still in custody.

count, correctional or institutional The numerical tally at some time during the day in a penal institution when inmates are physically counted.

counterculture Associated with the "hippie movement" of the 1960s, a complex of ideas and behavior patterns running counter to, or in opposition to, prevailing, traditional society.

counterfeit Illegally reproduced.

counterfeiting Any unauthorized manufacture of currency or any item of value, such as artwork, precious coins, or artifacts.

counter performance The defendant's participation, in exchange for diversion, in a treatment, counseling, or educational program aimed at changing his or her behavior.

county A geographical area or political subdivision of a state derived from the English shire, the county equivalent. Its chief law enforcement officer is the sheriff.

county court A court whose jurisdiction is limited to the boundaries of a county. It may be either a court of special original jurisdiction or a court of general jurisdiction.

county home A site that provides social relief for indigents and youths who do not have means of supporting themselves in their communities.

coup d'état An overthrow of a government or political entity by another political force or body.

court A public judiciary body that applies the law to controversies and oversees the administration of justice.

court, adolescent A New York City–based type of juvenile court, characterized by informality and informal dispositions of delinquent conduct, in use during the 1960s and 1970s. Juveniles would often meet in a judge's home, not a courtroom, to determine what was best for the juvenile. Often the judge would prescribe victim restitution or community service in some form to promote juvenile offender accountability.

court, canonical An ecclesiastical court of the Middle Ages hearing both criminal and civil cases, often involving domestic disputes and family matters.

court, domestic relations A special court of limited jurisdiction that hears cases involving divorce, desertion, neglect, or child custody matters.

court, inferior Any lower-level court with misdemeanor jurisdiction or limited jurisdiction, such as a municipal court.

court, juvenile *See* **juvenile court.**

court, specialized Any court with limited jurisdiction to hear particular kinds of cases. Family court is a specialized court, as it can not hear criminal cases; criminal courts do not hear child custody cases.

court, superior Any court with the jurisdiction to try any felony case as well as any misdemeanor case.

court administrator Any individual who controls the operations of the court in a particular jurisdiction, and who may be in charge of scheduling, juries, and judicial assignment.

Court-Appointed Special Advocates (CASA) Volunteers appointed by the court to investigate a child's needs and help officers of the court ensure a safe placement.

court backlog A glut of cases awaiting disposition in a criminal court, some of which may be nearing the legal limits for a trial.

court calendar Docket; the schedule of events for any judicial official.

court clerk The court officer who may file pleadings, motions, or judgments, issue process, and keep general records of court proceedings.

court costs Fees assessed convicted offenders by a judge or magistrate to help recover the costs associated with court processing.

court decision Any determination by a court officer, usually a judge, of a finding of guilt or blameworthiness, whether the matter is criminal or civil.

Court Deference Era The period, beginning about 1987, in which the U.S. Supreme Court's rulings made it clear that lower courts should defer to the judgment of correctional administrators.

court delay The unnecessary prolonging of a judicial proceeding.

Court Delay Reduction Program A program commenced in Oregon designed to facilitate the processing of criminal cases, offering a streamlined version of speedy trials.

court disposition The final outcome of a judicial proceeding, referring to the punishment imposed, such as probation, confinement to a jail or prison, community service, restitution, fines, or electronic monitoring and house arrest.

Court Employment Project A project established in 1967, called the Manhattan Court Employment Project until 1970. Its goals are to provide counseling, employment, education, and legal and vocational services to youthful offenders, ages 14 to 21. It is headquartered in New York City.

courthouse An edifice or building in which all legal matters are heard or decided. It may include criminal courts or civil courts, chancery courts, juvenile courts, or other specialty courts.

court liaison service An Australian program that provides psychiatric assessment and intervention services for those appearing before the magistrate's court.

court intervention A recognition by judges during the mid-1960s that courts needed to intervene in prison operations to end many unconstitutional conditions.

court-martial, courts-martial A military court convened by senior commanders under authority of the Uniform Code of Military Justice for the purpose of trying members of the armed forces accused of violations of the Code.

court master An official appointed by a judge to oversee the implementation of an institutional order. Court masters are also appointed to hear various types of cases in different jurisdictions, such as divorce, child custody, and labor matters.

court of appellate jurisdiction *See* **appellate court.**

Court of Assizes The highest court of original jurisdiction in France, and the only French court in which a jury hears and assists in deciding a case against an accused and renders a verdict.

court of chancery *See* **chancery court.**

court of common pleas Any early court designed to try minor cases under prevailing common law.

Court of Customs and Patent Appeals A special court of limited jurisdiction established by Congress to oversee decisions made by the Customs Court, Patent Office, and Tariff Commission. Its decisions are subject to review by the U.S. Supreme Court.

court of equity *See* **chancery court.**

court of errors or appeals The court of last resort in New Jersey.

court of general jurisdiction *See* **trial court of general jurisdiction.**

court of general sessions A court similar to a municipal court. Its jurisdiction includes traffic violations and low-grade misdemeanor cases.

court of last resort The last court that may hear a case. In the United States the Supreme Court is the court of last resort for many kinds of cases.

court of limited jurisdiction *See* **trial court of limited jurisdiction.**

court of nonrecord Any court that does not make a written record of a trial. Many juvenile courts are courts of nonrecord.

court of primary jurisdiction Any court with originating jurisdiction to hear special types of cases.

court of record Any court in which a written record is kept of court proceedings.

court of special jurisdiction Any judicial body that has jurisdiction over limited matters, such as family, juvenile, or probate courts.

Court of Star Chamber An English court established to prevent obstruction of justice by lower courts. It was subsequently abolished when abuse of power was detected.

court order Any judicial proclamation or directive authorizing an officer to act on behalf of the court.

court-ordered prison population reductions Judicially mandated reductions in inmate populations of prisons or jails to comply with health and safety standards.

court packing Any attempt by a U.S. president to influence the composition or political climate of the U.S. Supreme Court by nominating persons with political and policy views similar to the president's.

court probation A criminal court requirement that defendants fulfill specified conditions of behavior in lieu of a sentence of confinement, but without assignment to a probation agency's supervisory caseload.

court report, pretrial or presentence A document submitted by a person designated by the court before the disposition of cases. It contains a social history of a child and a plan of rehabilitation, treatment, and/or care.

court reporter Court official who keeps a written word-for-word and/or tape-recorded record of court proceedings. *See also* **transcript.**

courtroom disruption Any outbreak or disturbance occurring while a court is in session; any activity that interrupts the work of the court while it convenes.

courtroom work group All parties in the adversary process who work together cooperatively to settle cases with the least amount of effort and conflict. The group includes judges, defense counsels, prosecutors, court clerks, bailiffs, and court reporters.

courts of appeals Any court authorized to hear appeals arising from lower courts, usually trial courts. In the U.S. federal system, circuit courts of appeal are appellate courts for district court decisions, whereas the U.S. Supreme Court is the court of last resort for decisions appealed from the circuit courts.

Court TV A television network that debuted in the 1990s and features regular televised coverage of criminal and civil trials, parole hearings, and other interesting legal occurrences.

court unification A proposal that seeks to centralize and integrate the diverse functions of all courts of general, concurrent, and exclusive jurisdiction into a more simplified and uncomplicated scheme.

court-watchers Private citizens who sit in courtrooms and observe judicial decision making to ensure that justice is done and that some defendants do not escape the full measure of the law when judges punish them.

courtyard design A recent prison design adaptable to a number of security settings in which buildings are arranged around the perimeter of an internal open space.

covenant Any legally binding document whereby two or more parties agree to abide by one or more conditions and fulfill particular obligations.

covert A term that describes any activity that is undertaken in secret.

covert pathway A path to a criminal career that begins with minor underhanded behavior and progresses to theft.

covert sensitization A behavior modification technique intended to change the effect associated with a deviant behavior by pairing an imagined stimulus with imagined dire consequences.

cover-up Any intentional concealment of wrongdoing.

coyote A person who smuggles undocumented aliens into the United States, especially along the U.S.-Mexico border.

CPR (cardiopulmonary resuscitation) The attempt to revive a person whose heart has stopped beating through cardiac arrest or collapse. It may include artificial respiration or external cardiac compression.

CPTED *See* **Crime Prevention Through Environmental Design (CPTED).**

crack A smokable form of purified cocaine that provides an immediate and powerful high.

crack baby An infant born addicted to crack cocaine as a consequence of his or her mother's drug abuse.

crack cocaine *See* **crack.**

crackdown Concentrating police resources on a particular problem area, such as street-level drug dealing, in order to eradicate or displace criminal activity.

cracker A person who breaks into a computer system's security. The term was coined by computer hackers in 1985 in defense against journalistic misuse of the word "hacker."

crack house Any dwelling, frequently vacant, in which crack addicts get high.

craft organization A small and relatively permanent group of two or three thieves or confidence tricksters, each of whom plays a well-defined role in a specific type of crime that the group commits.

crank Slang for methamphetamine.

Crank-Up Task Force A California agency within the Justice Department that is a part of the Clandestine Laboratory Enforcement Program. It is charged with the duty of establishing networks of law enforcement agencies to investigate and shut down secret laboratories that manufacture methamphetamine.

crazies Inmates who are unpredictable and considered dangerous.

"creaming" Taking only those offenders most likely to succeed into a rehabilitative program. These offenders are low-risk and unlikely to reoffend.

creative sentencing A broad class of punishments as alternatives to incarceration that are designed to fit the particular crimes. They may involve community service, restitution, fines, becoming involved in educational or vocational training programs, or becoming affiliated with other "good works" activity.

credit card fraud The use or attempted use of a credit card to obtain goods or services with intent to avoid payment.

Cressey, Donald R. (1919–1987) A criminologist who advocated the consensus modes of crime, suggesting that the public generally defines what is criminal behavior, then reacts to such behavior as repugnant. He suggested that the law is applicable to all persons, regardless of their status, and through enforcement and adherence of the law, the society persists over time.

crime An act or omission prohibited by law, by one who is held accountable by that law. It consists of legality, *actus reus, mens rea,* consensus, harm, causation, and prescribed punishment.

crime, companionate Crime committed by two or more persons against one or more victims.

crime, etiology of The study of the causes of criminal behavior.

crime analysis Any systematic effort to track crimes in various jurisdictions over time, according to specified criteria, such as age or race/ethnicity.

Crime Classification System (CCS) A system for collecting data on the severity of crimes and the effect those crimes have on victims.

crime clock A graph used in the *Uniform Crime Reports* compiled by the Federal Bureau of Investigation to show the number of specific types of crime committed according to some time standard such as minutes or seconds. Figures are

calculated by dividing the number of crimes reported annually by the number of minutes or seconds in a year. *See figure.*

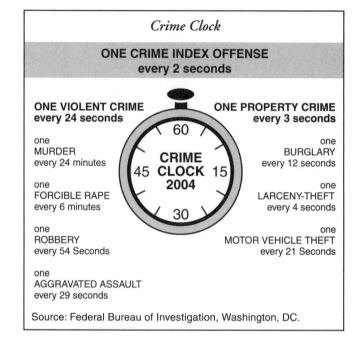

Crime Clock

ONE CRIME INDEX OFFENSE
every 2 seconds

ONE VIOLENT CRIME
every 24 seconds

CRIME CLOCK 2004

ONE PROPERTY CRIME
every 3 seconds

one MURDER every 24 minutes

one FORCIBLE RAPE every 6 minutes

one ROBBERY every 54 Seconds

one AGGRAVATED ASSAULT every 29 seconds

one BURGLARY every 12 seconds

one LARCENY-THEFT every 4 seconds

one MOTOR VEHICLE THEFT every 21 Seconds

Source: Federal Bureau of Investigation, Washington, DC.

crime construction A process whereby the police and prosecutor interpret information concerning the accused's behavior in order to determine whether a crime has been committed and to ascertain whether the legal elements necessary to prosecute are present.

crime control, crime-control model A model of criminal justice that emphasizes containment of dangerous offenders and societal protection. This criminal-justice system assumes that freedom is so important that every effort must be made to repress crime, and emphasizes efficiency and the capacity to apprehend, try, convict, and dispose of a high proportion of offenders. The model is attributed to Herbert Packer.

crime displacement An effect of crime-prevention efforts in which efforts to control crime in one area shift illegal activities to another.

crime fiction Any fictional plot revolving around the perpetration and solution of a crime, most often a homicide.

Crime Fighter In the White Typology, a type of police officer who is a zealot on a mission to wipe out a particular kind of crime. It was suggested by S.O. White in his 1972 work, *A Perspective on Police Professionalism. See also* **White Typology.**

crime fighter The proactive police style stressing dealing with violent crimes and arresting dangerous criminals.

crime forecasting The practice of using statistical techniques to predict future crime trends.

crime gradient The ecological distribution of crime; a profile of a curve using as its base information on the crime rates of consecutive geographical areas located along a straight line.

Crime Index Eight serious crimes identified by the FBI in the *Uniform Crime Reports* to chart crime trends: arson, murder and nonnegligent manslaughter, motor vehicle theft, theft/larceny, robbery, aggravated assault, forcible rape, and burglary.

crime in the suites A term describing white-collar or business crime.

crime mapping The practice of plotting crimes on a map, most often using computer software. This technique permits a visual inspection of crime patterns.

crimen fals A term that describes the class of offenses that involve the perpetration of a falsehood (e.g., forgery, perjury, counterfeiting).

crime of passion A spontaneous crime prompted by intense anger and emotion, often arising between spouses or lovers (e.g., during a heated argument, a wife may grab a nearby pistol and shoot her husband).

crime of violence *See* **violent crime.**

crime pact An agreement or interstate compact to cooperate in crime prevention and suppression. The first crime pact was between New York and New Jersey in 1833.

crime prevention, crime-prevention procedures Any overt activity conducted by individuals or groups to deter persons from committing crimes. Activities may include "target hardening" by making businesses and residences more difficult to burglarize; neighborhood watch programs, in which neighborhood residents monitor streets during evening hours for suspicious persons or automobiles; and equipping homes and businesses with devices to detect crime.

Crime Prevention Through Environmental Design (CPTED) C. Ray Jeffrey's concept of crime prevention which maintains that by eliminating the opportunities for crime inherent in the physical environment, many crimes can be prevented.

crime rate The number of reported crimes divided by the number of persons in an area, often expressed as a rate of crimes per 100,000 persons.

crime(s) against households A crime designation used by the National Crime Panel to describe household crimes, including burglary, household larceny, and motor vehicle theft.

crime(s) against property Nonviolent or passive crimes in which where no physical harm is inflicted upon victims, such as vehicular theft, burglary, and larceny.

crime(s) against the person Violent crimes, including all crimes committed in the victim's presence, such as murder, rape, robbery, and aggravated assault.

crime(s) against the state Any criminal act that victimizes a governmental body, such as treason or income-tax evasion.

crime(s) without complaints Victimless crimes, including prostitution and gambling (in jurisdictions where gambling is prohibited).

crime(s) without victims *See* **victimless crime.**

crime scene The physical area where a crime has occurred.

crime scene cards Placards placed at the scene of a crime to indicate that the area is restricted to authorized personnel.

crime scene contamination Activities, often unintentional, that destroy or alter physical evidence and compromise its value for prosecution purposes.

crime scene exception An attempt by police and prosecutors to justify warrantless searches of premises and the contents of suitcases and other containers subsequent to crimes being perpetrated on those premises. The U.S. Supreme Court held that warrants must be obtained for subsequent searches of premises following initial searches and investigations by police. *See Flippo v. West Virginia* (1999).

crimes known to the police All criminal offenses that have been reported to police for which the police have sufficient evidence to believe that the crimes were actually committed.

Crime Stoppers An organization commenced in Albuquerque, NM, in 1976, which offers rewards for information leading to the arrest and conviction of crime perpetrators.

Crime Watch, crime watch programs A crime reduction and control program facilitated through greater police presence in neighborhoods and the use of neighborhood observers; any program utilizing a cooperative alliance between police and citizens to prevent or control crime.

crime wave A period or trend of a higher amount of crime.

criminal Any person found guilty of either a misdemeanor or a felony.

criminal, pathological Anyone who deviates from normative behavior, usually as the result of some mental defect or deformity which may be the result of psychosis or insanity.

criminal action Any action at law involving prosecution of someone for a crime.

criminal anthropology The association of body types and other physical characteristics with the tendency toward engaging in crime.

Criminal Appeals Act Congressional action permitting the government to appeal cases in which lower courts have declared certain federal statutes to be unconstitutional in particular criminal cases.

criminal atavism The idea that delinquents and criminals manifest physical anomalies that make them biologically and physiologically similar to our primitive ancestors, savage throwbacks to an earlier stage of human evolution.

criminal attempt Any act or omission constituting a substantial step in a course of conduct planned to culminate in the commission of a crime.

criminal bankruptcy *See* **bankruptcy fraud.**

criminal behavior Any conduct involving committing a crime. If a person has the *mens rea* and *actus reus* involved in a criminal act, then criminal behavior is suspected, but he or she is not a criminal until adjudicated or convicted.

criminal behavior system A typology of crime devised by criminologists Marshall Clinard and Richard Quinney that includes violent personal, occasional property, occupational, corporate, political, public order, conventional, organized, and professional.

criminal biology The scientific study of heredity as it relates to or causes criminal behavior.

criminal career incapacitation An approach that would reduce crime by identifying and incarcerating classes of offenders who seem to be especially likely to remain active in crime.

criminal careers A concept describing the onset of criminal behavior, the types and amount of crime committed, and the termination of such activity.

criminal case Any action initiated by a law enforcement officer or other interested person in which one or more criminal accusations are made against one or more defendants.

criminal charge A criminal accusation; accusing someone of a crime. *See also* **charge.**

criminal contamination The belief that if criminals live together in halfway houses, they will breed more criminality and infect neighborhoods with their criminal behavior.

criminal conversation Adultery; illicit sexual relations between a married person and someone other than his or her spouse.

criminal courts Tribunals handling criminal cases. They may also handle civil cases, in which case they are called criminal courts only in reference to the criminal cases that they handle.

criminal culture A generalized set of values and standards followed by persons who consider themselves to be criminals; a subcultural phenomenon, in which a group of criminals follow particular behavior patterns and support those patterns that happen to be criminal.

Criminal Division The branch of the U.S. Justice Department that prosecutes federal criminal violations.

criminal-exclusive blend A form of sentencing by a criminal court judge in which either juvenile or adult sentences of incarceration can be imposed, but not both.

criminal gang One form of gang described by Richard Cloward and Lloyd Ohlin in their book *Delinquency and Opportunity* (1960). Such gangs recruit members to engage in illegal activity, which is their primary reason for existence. Members go through an apprenticeship and learn how to commit crimes. *See also* **conflict gang; retreatist gang** *for other gang goals.*

criminal history information Any background details of a person charged with a crime. The term refers to any legal actions, such as prior convictions, indictments, and arrests.

criminal homicide The name the *Uniform Crime Reports* gives to all offenses causing the death of another person without justification or excuse.

criminal identification Compiling information from a defendant, such as recording his or her fingerprints, for subsequent retrieval and for rapid identification if a subsequent crime is committed and identifying information is found as evidence of the defendant's identity.

criminal incident In *National Crime Victimization Survey* terminology, a criminal event involving one or more victims and one or more offenders.

criminal-inclusive blend A form of sentencing by a criminal court judge in which both juvenile and adult sentences can be imposed simultaneously.

criminal intent A necessary element of a crime; the evil intent or *mens rea* associated with the commission of a crime.

Criminal Investigation Division (CID) The Internal Revenue Service agency charged with responsibility for investigating violations of federal tax laws. The CID recommends prosecution against income-tax law violators and has arrest powers.

criminal investigative analysis Application of in-depth knowledge about a suspect's personality and behavior to identify and apprehend predatory and other types of violent offenders.

criminalist A police crime scene analyst or laboratory worker skilled in criminalistics; one who has expertise or scientific training consistent with performing laboratory work and crime scene investigations.

criminalistics The use of technology or scientific techniques derived from physics, chemistry, and biology to solve crimes in criminal investigations; the application of scientific techniques to the detection and evaluation of criminal evidence; also known as forensic science.

Criminalistics Laboratory Information System A computerized database of rifling characteristics, such as grooves on bullets, that can be used to identify the manufacturer and type of weapon used in the commission of a crime or to identify a specific weapon that fired a particular bullet.

criminality The quality of being criminal or having such characteristics.

criminal justice An interdisciplinary field studying the nature and operations of organizations providing justice services to society.

Criminal Justice Act of 1948 An act that authorizes the compilation, maintenance, and distribution of information about crime in England and Wales for both adults and juveniles.

criminal-justice agency, criminal-justice organization Any one of numerous organizations involved in processing defendants charged with crimes which conventionally include law enforcement, prosecution, the courts, and corrections.

Criminal Justice Archive and Information Network Created in 1978 by the Bureau of Justice Statistics, a subcomponent of the U.S. Department of Justice, this entity provides information about crime victimization, delinquency, and other important information about crimes and criminal characteristics. It is headquartered in Ann Arbor, MI.

Criminal Justice Audiovisual Materials Directory Headquartered in Rockville, MD, a compendium of materials for training and education in the field of criminal justice, including videotapes and other media that assist in one's understanding of the criminal-justice system and its different components.

Criminal Justice Center A Sam Houston State University–sponsored agency containing numerous reference works to assist anyone interested in conducting criminal-justice research. It is headquartered in Huntsville, TX.

criminal-justice funnel A heuristic device to show the large number of suspected or reported crimes and their attrition as they pass through various stages of the criminal justice system. *See figure p. 60.*

Criminal Justice National Council on Crime and Delinquency An agency established at Rutgers University in 1983 that compiles extensive library materials, which it makes available to interested persons. It is headquartered in Newark, NJ.

criminal-justice process, criminal-justice system An interrelated set of agencies and organizations designed to control criminal behavior, to detect crime, and to apprehend, process, prosecute, punish, or rehabilitate criminal offenders.

The processual aspect suggests that the interrelatedness implied by "system" may not be strong (e.g., judges might not contact jail or prison officials to inquire whether there is sufficient space before they sentence offenders to jail or prison terms).

criminal-justice professional Anyone interested in studying the criminal-justice system. Such a professional may have a Ph.D. or master's degree in criminal justice or a related field, or may be a practitioner, such as a police officer, corrections officer, probation or parole officer, prosecutor, or judge.

Criminal Justice Reference and Information Center An organization established by the Wisconsin Law School that provides information and documents pertaining to all areas of the criminal-justice system. It maintains an extensive library and makes reference works, including statistical information, available to interested persons or organizations. It is headquartered in Madison, WI.

criminal-justice standards Models, commentaries, and recommendations for the revision of criminal-justice procedures and practices.

Criminal Justice Statistics Association An association established in 1974 and supported by the Bureau of Justice Statistics. Its goals are to develop, collect, analyze, and use various criminal-justice statistical information for various state, interstate, or federal purposes, to further the administration, management, and planning of various agencies. It is headquartered in Washington, DC, and publishes a quarterly newsletter.

"criminal-justice wedding cake" A model of the criminal justice process in which criminal cases form a four-tiered hierarchy with a few celebrated cases at the top, and each succeeding layer increasing in size as its importance in the eyes of officials and the public diminishes.

criminal law The body of law that defines criminal offenses and prescribes punishments (substantive law) and that delineates criminal procedure (procedural law).

criminally insane A legal condition of mental derangement or defect leading to criminal conduct; the state of mind of being mentally incompetent; impaired to the extent that such an impairment may either induce or accompany violent and criminal conduct.

criminal mischief, malicious mischief *See* **vandalism.**

criminal negligence A failure to exercise the degree of caution necessary to avoid being charged with a crime.

criminal nuisance Any conduct that is unreasonable and that endangers the health and safety of others.

criminal offense Any conduct that is either a misdemeanor or a felony. It includes both an *actus reus* and a *mens rea,* and punishments include imprisonment and/or a fine.

criminaloid According to the nineteenth-century Italian criminologist Raffaele Garofalo, an offender who is motivated by emotion that, in combination with other factors, results in criminal conduct.

criminal organization *See* **organized crime.**

criminal procedure, criminal proceedings Rules of law governing the procedures by which crimes are investigated, prosecuted, adjudicated, and punished; activities in a court of law undertaken to determine the guilt or innocence of an adult accused of a crime.

criminal punishment *See* **criminal sanctions.**

criminal responsibility Any liability incurred as the result of committing a crime.

criminal sanctions The right of a state to punish persons who violate the rules set down in criminal codes. Also, the punishment connected to the commission of specific offenses.

criminal saturation A theory devised by Enrico Ferri, an Italian criminologist, that posits that every society has a number of criminals produced by particular societal conditions.

criminal statistics Information that has been tabulated, usually portrayed in numerical form, which represents the amount of crime committed, the number of criminals apprehended, prosecuted, and convicted, and the socioeconomic and sociodemographic distribution of criminals.

criminal subculture A pattern of behaviors shared by persons engaged in illegal activity that includes special jargon and gestures are used to convey meanings unknown to noncriminals; a standard of conduct and ideas within the mainstream culture that are adhered to by persons engaged in illegal activity.

criminal syndicalism The crime of advocating violence as a means to accomplish political change.

criminal tendencies Urges that lead to criminal conduct; irresistible impulses to commit crime, which may be genetically based. This controversial view maintains that given certain environmental, social, and psychological conditions, certain persons are predisposed to commit crime.

criminal trespass Crimes that are generally misdemeanors or violations, and are differentiated from burglary when breaking with criminal intent is absent or when the trespass involves property that has been fenced off in a manner designated to exclude intruders.

criminal trial An adversarial proceeding within a particular jurisdiction, in which a judicial determination of issues can be made, and in which a defendant's guilt or innocence can be impartially decided.

criminal tribes Collectivities within a given culture that approve or disapprove of behaviors toward those not a part of the culture that otherwise might not be approved or disapproved if committed against members of the collectivity itself.

criminal typologies Any categories devised by criminologists whereby offenders are classified. Once typologies have been generated, then theories can be fashioned to explain particular "types" of crime.

criminate To accuse a person of committing a crime.

criminogenic, criminogenic environment, crimogenic factors, criminogenic social conditions Variables thought to bring about criminal behavior in persons (e.g., imprisonment with other criminals is believed to be a criminogenic atmosphere).

criminological theory Any systematic attempt to explain the causes or etiology of crime.

criminologist A professional or scholar who studies crime, criminal law, criminals, and criminal behavior, examining the etiology of crime and criminal behavior and crime trends.

criminology The study of crime; the science of crime and criminal behavior, the forms of criminal behavior, the causes of crime, the definition of criminality, and the societal reaction to crime; an empirical social-behavioral science that investigates crime, criminals, and criminal justice.

Crips A California street gang seen as part of a more violent influx of street gangs into prisons. The gang originated in Los Angeles in the late 1960s, branched out into other parts of Los Angeles County during the 1970s, and eventually established gang affiliates in other states. The gang is identified with the color blue, and members wear blue handkerchiefs and other blue clothing to distinguish themselves from others. They are known for violence and extortion and are the enemies of the Bloods, another Los Angeles gang. They often wear athletic clothing with names of Los Angeles sports teams on jackets, shirts, or caps.

crisis intervention, crisis-intervention center An action intended to enable others to cope appropriately with stressful life situations; an agency established for such a purpose.

crisis-intervention units Particular programs for law enforcement officers who are trained to deal with domestic disturbances and other interpersonal conflicts. Educational training includes recognition of body language, psychology, conflict-resolution skills, and an awareness of various types of referral services.

critical criminology, critical criminologists A school of criminology that holds that criminal law and the criminal-justice system have been created to control the poor and have-nots of society. Crimes are defined depending on how much power is wielded in society by those defining crime.

critical ideologies, critical theory Philosophies that challenge the dominant ideology, typically by analyzing social control systems as behaviors emerging from particular political and economic structures. *See also* **radical criminology.**

critical phase The stage of an investigation by law enforcement officers at which a case moves from investigation to accusation against specific suspects.

critical stage Any decision or processing point made by a criminal-justice agency or its personnel that is so important that the U.S. Supreme Court has attached to it specific due-process rights.

criticize Making statements that question one's veracity or performance and effectiveness. Such statements may be constructive or destructive.

Crofton, Sir Walter (1815–1897) Director of Ireland's prison system during the 1850s, Crofton is considered the "father of parole" in various European countries. He established a system of early release for prisoners, issuing "tickets of leave" as an early version of parole.

cross-cultural corrections *See* **comparative corrections.**

cross-examination The questioning of one side's witnesses by the other side's attorney, either the prosecution or the defense.

cross-projection A sketch of a crime scene enabling investigators to determine the location of physical evidence on ceilings and walls in relation to floors; a forensics device to understand how and where a crime occurred.

cross-sectional study Any research that takes a one-time snapshot view of the phenomenon of interest.

crosswalk Any part of a roadway used for pedestrian crossing, usually marked with particular lines on the surface of the road.

crowds Loosely organized groups who share interests or activities.

crown attorney A Canadian prosecutor.

Crown Court In England, the criminal court that deals with adult offenders or juveniles who have been transferred from youth court.

Crown Prosecution Service The national agency in England that is in charge of all criminal prosecutions of juveniles and adults.

cruel and unusual punishment Punishment prohibited by the Eighth Amendment of U.S. Constitution. The concept is vague and unspecified by the U.S. Supreme Court and is subjectively interpreted on a case-by-case basis. The electric chair has been determined to be "cruel and unusual" punishment for purposes of administering the death penalty, whereas lethal injection has not been determined to be cruel and unusual. *See also* **Bill of Rights.**

cruelty to animals Gross neglect, abuse, or killing of domesticated animals.

cryptogram Secret writing or communication decodable only through associations with secret interpretive schemes.

cryptographer Someone who deciphers cryptograms or decodes any type of secret communication or language.

crystal meth The crystalline form of the drug methamphetamine.

CS A super tear gas that is approximately 10 times stronger than CN gas.

CSA The Covenant, Sword, and Arm of the Lord, a right-wing extremist group.

culpable, culpability The state of mind of persons who have committed an act that makes them liable for prosecution for that act.

culprit A perpetrator of a crime who has not been convicted.

cult A small, closely knit group loosely organized around some obscure religious dogma. The group may engage in ritualistic behavior, possibly murder and torture or sacrifice of animals.

cult killings Murders that occur when members of religious sects or cults are ordered to kill by their leaders. Some cults engage in devil worship and human sacrifice when such types of killings occur.

cultural deviance theories Explanations that posit that crime results from cultural values that permit, or even demand, behavior in violation of the law.

cultural diversity A recognition that it is neither necessary nor desirable for different ethnic groups to shed their cultural identities to participate in the larger community.

cultural transmission, cultural-transmission theory An explanation emphasizing transmission of criminal behavior through socialization. This theory views delinquency as socially learned behavior transmitted from one generation to the next in disorganized urban areas.

culture Shared norms and values of a society; the material and nonmaterial artifacts and language shared by members of a society.

culture conflict, culture conflict theory The view that two groups may clash when their conduct norms differ, resulting in criminal activity.

culture of poverty A culture characterized by helplessness, cynicism, and mistrust of authority as represented by schools and police described by the sociologist Oscar Lewis in 1966.

culture of terror A term used to describe the violent world of underground drug trafficking in large cities.

cumulative disadvantage The net effect of poverty, social disorganization, physical, sexual, or emotional abuse, or other problems associated with the inner city on those who live there.

cumulative effect The total result of combined risk factors, emphasizing that individual risk factors are not as important as the total effect.

cunnilingus Contact of the mouth or tongue with the female genitalia.

curative statute A legal remedy to correct an earlier deficiency or defect in a previously enacted law.

curfew A law that makes it a crime for a juvenile to be out in public after a certain hour or during certain times of the day or evening.

curfew violation A status offense for juveniles; the act of being a juvenile and in a public place after an hour at which such a presence is prohibited by statute or ordinance.

curfew violators Youths who violate laws and ordinances of communities prohibiting youths on the streets after certain evening hours, such as 10:00 p.m. Curfew itself is a delinquency prevention strategy.

curtilage The fields attached to a house. It may also include outbuildings and house grounds.

Custer syndrome A depiction of police officers who defend their police work, and who are opposed to or feel alienated from the rest of the system and nonpolice citizenry.

custodial care Services associated with agencies that accommodate physically or mentally impaired persons.

custodial convenience The principle of giving jailed inmates the minimum comforts required by law in order to contain the costs of incarceration.

custodial disposition The outcome by a juvenile judge following adjudication of a juvenile as delinquent. It includes nonsecure custody (in a foster home, community agency, farm, or camp) and secure custody (in a detention center or industrial or reform school).

custodial interrogation Questions posed by police officers to a suspect being held in custody in the pre-judicial stage of the justice process.

custodial model The suggested ideal type of arrangement for housing female offenders, where the main interest is confinement, containment, discipline, and uniformity.

custodial officer Any official vested with insuring the safety of incarcerated or hospitalized persons.

custodial processes Daily activities and procedures designed to control and keep track of inmates.

custodian A person to whom legal custody of a child has been transferred by the court, but not a person who has only physical custody; a person other than a parent or legal guardian who stands *in loco parentis* to the child or a person to whom legal custody of the child has been given by order of a court.

custody Restraint of a person held on suspicion of committing or charged with a criminal offense. It may include the use of handcuffs or leg irons or simple placement in a cell or locked room.

custody, close A method of supervising inmates by continuous monitoring.

custody, discharge from Legal release from custody. State statutes provide that a child shall be released to a parent, guardian, or legal custodian unless it is impractical, undesirable, or otherwise ordered by the court. The legal custodian serves as a guarantor that the child will appear in court and may be asked to sign a promise to that effect (this takes the place of bail in adult court).

custody, maximum Maximum-security maintenance of prisoners or patients in isolated cells or units with few amenities, for periods of up to 24 hours a day.

custody, medium Medium-security maintenance of prisoners or patients in cells with more amenities or freedoms. Inmates/patients have more privileges than those in maximum-security custody, such as access to the prison yard.

custody, minimum Minimum-security maintenance of prisoners or patients in the least restrictive, dormitory-like settings, with most privileges extended. Prisoners have more extensive freedoms encompassing access to the prison yard, workout areas, and more amenities.

custody, protective Any effort by a law enforcement agency to protect someone who may be harmed by a defendant or a defendant's friends or associates. Witnesses may be placed in protective custody so that they cannot be silenced by death.

custody, taking into The term used instead of "arrest" when an adult or child is taken by a law enforcement officer. State codes and laws prescribe that an adult or child may be taken into custody only under the following conditions: (1) whenever ordered by a judge for failure to obey a summons (petition); (2) whenever a law enforcement officer observes or has reasonable grounds to believe that the adult or child has broken a federal, state, or local law and deems it in the public interest; (3) whenever the officer removes children from conditions that threaten their welfare; (4) when the child is believed to be a runaway from parents or legal custody; or (5) whenever the child has violated the conditions of probation.

custody level The degree of staff supervision required to safely confine particular inmates.

customer model An approach to private business partnerships with prisons. In this model, a company contracts with a correctional institution to provide a finished product at an agreed-on price. The correctional institution owns and operates the business that employs the inmate work force.

customs Social conventions, mores, and folkways; common ways of behaving that are not ordinarily subject to legal sanctions; also, slang for the U.S. Customs Service.

Customs Court The judicial authority with exclusive jurisdiction in cases involving imported and exported goods, formerly called the Board of General Appraisers. Its decisions may be appealed to the Court of Customs and Patent Appeals.

Customs Service, U.S. The federal enforcement agency responsible for protecting U.S. borders. It combats smuggling using extensive land, air, and marine forces and investigates narcotics trafficking, prohibited animals and vegetation, pornography, cybercrime, and other types of criminal activity.

cut-purse English-style thievery of the eighteenth and early nineteenth centuries in which thieves surreptitiously emptied purses by cutting through the purse fabric with a sharp instrument without alerting the victim.

cut-throat, cutthroat Someone who kills by slitting a person's throat with a sharp instrument; an assassin; also, someone willing to do anything to accomplish a goal, regardless of the harm their actions may cause others.

CyberAngels An offshoot of New York City's Guardian Angels launched in 1998 to operate the Internet's largest cyber-safety program. The membership's goal is to promote online safety for young persons. The Internet is routinely scrutinized from members' homes for sites that may disseminate harmful or offensive subject matter.

cybercrime Computer crime; use of a computer to commit fraud, embezzlement, or fraudulent diversion of bank account monies to other accounts.

cyberstalking Using computers via the Internet to harass or invade the privacy of another individual.

cyberterrorism A form of terrorism that makes use of high technology, particularly computers and the Internet, in planning and carrying out acts of terrorism.

cycle menu A menu detailing daily meals and covering a relatively long time period, at the end of which the menu is repeated.

cycle of violence Exposure of children to violence by their families that in turn increases the likelihood that they will engage in violent behavior toward others, including their own children, when they grow older.

Czolgosz, Leon (1873–1901) An American anarchist who assassinated President William McKinley in Buffalo, NY, on September 6, 1901. He was executed by electric chair at Auburn State Prison.

D

dactyloscopy The use or study of fingerprints as a means of identification.

Dahmer, Jeffrey (1959–1994) A notorious serial killer who lived primarily in Milwaukee, WI, and preyed on predominantly young, gay, black males. Dahmer tortured his victims and dismembered them, keeping remains on his premises and eating some of them. He was convicted of 16 counts of murder and sentenced to life in a Wisconsin prison. He was subsequently murdered by another prison inmate, Christopher Scarver, who clubbed him to death in 1994. Scarver was considered deranged and later claimed that he was the "son of God" and was acting out his "father's" commands to kill Dahmer and another inmate on Dahmer's work detail.

Dahrendorf, Ralf (1929–) A conflict theorist who believes that society is organized into imperatively coordinated associations of two groups: one possesses authority and uses it for social domination, and the other lacks authority and is dominated. He believed that social conflict is pervasive and persistent, that coercion is the controlling element in social organization, that every person is an element potentially possessing the power to change society, and that every society is changeable. He wrote *Class and Conflict in Industrial Society* (1959).

daily sick call The process by which inmates who claim to have a health problem get permission to go to morning clinic sessions.

daisy chain scam An illegal operation in which companies create a chain of affiliates, each selling products to the others, in order to manipulate the product's price.

Dalkon Shield An intrauterine device (IUD) that was widely distributed and marketed by the A.H. Robbins Company despite the fact that it was responsible for the deaths of a number of women.

Dalton, Katharina Author of *The Premenstrual Syndrome* (1971) who pioneered the explanation of female antisocial, aggressive behavior attributable to PMS (premenstrual syndrome).

Daly, Katherine A feminist criminologist who regards criminology as mostly male-focused. She has researched the relation between crime and the treatment of females in society and attempted to balance the coverage of men and women in criminology.

damages Monetary sums awarded to prevailing litigants in civil actions.

danger law A regulation intended to prevent the pretrial release of defendants who are considered dangerous or who pose risks to themselves or others.

dangerous classes A population segment described by Terance Miethe and Charles Moore (1987) as young, single, poor urban males who are discriminated against by judges, prosecutors, and others in the criminal-justice system because of the belief that these persons pose a greater risk to society than those with different social characteristics.

dangerousness A concept defined differently in various jurisdictions. Characteristics include a prior record of serious offenses, the potential to commit future crimes if released, the predicted risk of being a convicted offender or prison or jail inmate, and the likelihood of inflicting harm upon others.

dangerous-tendency test Any subjective method of determining whether particular kinds of speeches are contrary to the public good.

D.A.R.E. (Drug Abuse Resistance Education) A school-based antidrug program initiated by the Los Angeles Police Department and now adopted throughout the United States.

dark figure of crime A metaphor that emphasizes the dangerous dimensions of crime that are never reported to the police (e.g., if someone steals a tire out of a pickup truck, the police won't recover it, so why report it? If someone rapes his daughter and no one knows about it, who will ever know?).

darkness One-half hour following sunset and one-half hour before sunrise, or any other time period when visibility is limited so that a person or vehicle cannot be seen at a distance of 1,000 feet.

DARPA (Defense Advanced Research Projects Agency) The central research and development organization for the Department of Defense. It manages and directs selected basic and applied research and development projects and pursues research and technology where risk and payoff are both very high and where success may provide dramatic advances for traditional military roles and missions.

Darrow, Clarence Seward (1857–1938) A renowned attorney born in Kinsman, OH. He studied law at the University of Michigan, obtained a law degree, and was admitted to the Ohio bar in 1878. He was known for his defense of highly visible and emotionally charged cases, such as the defense of Nathan Leopold and Richard Loeb, who killed a youth in Chicago for thrills, and defended John Scopes in the "Monkey Trial" in Tennessee in 1925. He subsequently headed the National Recovery Administration (NRA) in 1934. *See also* **Scopes, John T.**

Darwin, Charles (1809–1882) Author of *The Origin of Species* (1859), which described evolution. Several criminologists have used Darwin's theory to explain particular kinds of criminals who have particular sets of genetic attributes.

data, class I Computer data requiring off-site storage of backup copies under secure vault conditions.

data, class II Computer data requiring official storage of backup copies under conditions that resist accidental damage.

data, class III Computer data that require no off-site storage of backup copies, as data can be regenerated if needed. These data are not sufficiently important to require guarding.

data encryption The encoding of computerized information.

Data Encryption Standard (DES) The U.S. National Bureau of Standards' complex nonlinear ciphering algorithm capable of high-speed operation in hardware applications, used for classified data transmission within and between government agencies.

date rape Sexual intercourse without the consent of the victim, perpetrated by a person the victim has selected for a social occasion. The victim may have engaged voluntarily in some form of intimate interaction but did not agree to sexual intercourse.

date-rape drugs Substances used to render unwilling or unwitting victims susceptible to sexual advances and abuse. They include "roofies" (Rohypnol), "g-juice," (gamma-hydroxybutyrate, or GHB), and Vitamin K or Special K (both ketamine hydrochloride). They cause dizziness, hallucinations, memory loss, and even unconsciousness.

Daubert standard The test of scientific acceptability applicable to the gathering of evidence in criminal cases.

Daugherty, Harry M. (1860–1941) The U.S. attorney general from 1921–1924, who was accused of participating in the Teapot Dome Scandal involving oil lands. The case against Daugherty was dismissed. *See also* **Teapot Dome Scandal.**

Davis, David (1815–1886) An associate justice of the U.S. Supreme Court (1862–1877) who participated in various legal decisions contesting arbitrary military powers. He advocated the expansion of civil liberties and assisted Abraham Lincoln in his quest for the presidency.

day-fine programs Facilities operated in local, state, or federal jurisdictions in which offenders are assessed a certain amount of their earnings as a form of restitution to victims or victim compensation.

day fines Monetary sanctions geared to the average daily income of convicted offenders in an effort to bring equity to the sentencing process, or to compensate victims or the state (for court costs and supervisory fees).

day parole or day pass *See* **work (and educational) release, work/study release.**

day programs Any of a variety of programs entailing daily but nonresidential supervision of juvenile offenders.

day reporting A highly structured program that requires offenders to check in at a local community facility on a regular basis, such as daily, for supervision, sanctions, and services.

day reporting center A community correctional center where offenders report daily to comply with conditions of their sentence, probation, or parole program.

daytime The interval between sunrise and sunset when visibility is such that one's physical features can be discerned from a distance of 10 yards; the legal period covering a class of offenses committed with penalties that are substantially different from the same types of crimes committed during nighttime hours.

day treatment A rehabilitative alternative in which a convicted offender undergoes correctional treatment at a treatment center during the day, but returns to his or her home at night.

day watch In the 1500s, citizens were obligated to perform day- or night-watch duties in their villages on a rotating basis, comparable to modern-day shiftwork. Watchmen were expected to yell out a hue and cry in the event they detected a crime in progress or any other community disturbance.

dead body A corpse; a body deprived of life but not yet deteriorated.

dead letter A term that describes statutes on state or federal code compilations that are either no longer enforceable or obsolete from disuse.

deadly force Any force used by law enforcement officers or any other person (as in citizens' arrests) to apprehend those suspected of or engaging in unlawful acts. It may result in death or great bodily harm. *See also* **fleeing felon rule.**

deadly weapon Any instrument designed to inflict serious bodily injury or death, or capable of being used for such a purpose.

"dead man walking" An expression that conveys that a prisoner condemned to death is on his or her way to execution.

deathbed confession Revelations of criminal responsibility by someone who is about to die.

death certificate An official document issued by a coroner and signed by a physician attesting to the nature and cause of one's death.

death penalty *See* **capital punishment.**

death penalty, status of The number of persons executed during a given time interval or at a particular time; the number of persons under sentence of death on a given date or during a given time period. *See table.*

Death Penalty Focus of California A group opposing the death penalty headquartered in San Francisco, CA, made up of clergy, educators, physicians, and legal scholars.

death-qualified jury A jury whose members have been selected on the basis of their willingness to impose the death penalty in a capital case if the situation warrants such a decision. The term implies the exclusion of persons from possible jury duty who could not vote for a death penalty even if the defendant were guilty of a capital crime.

death row A place in a prison to accommodate any prisoner who has been sentenced to death for a capital offense. It is characterized by solitary cells and intensive supervision. The cells are usually in close proximity to where the execution will occur.

death-row inmate Any condemned person who is placed on death row and is awaiting execution for a capital offense. *See graph.*

death-row inmate characteristics The sociodemographic characteristics of persons who have been sentenced to death in those jurisdictions with capital punishment statutes. *See table p. 73.*

Death Row Support Project One program of the Washington Coalition to Abolish the Death Penalty. It seeks to match interested volunteers with pen pals who are prisoners on death row. It is headquartered in Seattle, WA.

Death Row, U.S.A. A monthly newsletter published by the NAACP Legal Defense and Educational Fund, Inc., which is headquartered in New York City.

death squads Politically sponsored groups or troops who are ordered to destroy political opponents or commit acts of terrorism against others for a variety of reasons.

death warrant A written document authorizing a time and place for the execution of a convicted offender sentenced to death for a capital offense.

Debs, Eugene V. (1855–1926) An advocate of industrial unionism and a pacifist who violated an injunction in a strike in Pullman, IL, in 1895. He ran for president of the United States on several occasions, and was regarded as a martyr.

debtor's prisons Incarcerative facilities established in the Middle Ages in England where people owing money were held until they or their friends paid their debts.

debureaucratization The reverse of bureaucratization, including the subversion of goals and activities of the bureaucracy in the interests of different groups with which it has close interaction (clients, patrons, interested parties). The specific characteristics of bureaucracy in terms of both its au-

Status of the Death Penalty, December 31, 2002

Executions during 2002		Number of prisoners under sentence of death		Jurisdictions without a death penalty
Texas	33	California	614	Alaska
Oklahoma	7	Texas	450	District of Columbia
Missouri	6	Florida	366	Hawaii
Georgia	4	Pennsylvania	241	Iowa
Virginia	4	North Carolina	206	Maine
Ohio	3	Ohio	205	Massachusetts
Florida	3	Alabama	191	Michigan
South Carolina	3	Illinois	159	Minnesota
Alabama	2	Arizona	120	North Dakota
Mississippi	2	Georgia	112	Rhode Island
North Carolina	2	Oklahoma	112	Vermont
Louisiana	1	Tennessee	95	West Virginia
California	1	Louisiana	86	Wisconsin
		25 other jurisdictions	600	
Total	71	Total	3,557	

Source: Bonczar and Snell, *Capital Punishment, 2002*, 1.

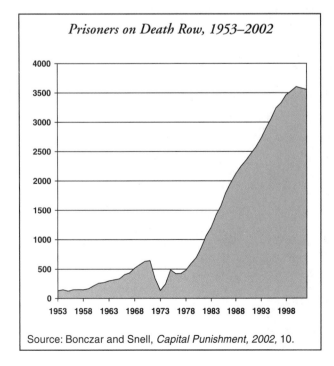

Prisoners on Death Row, 1953–2002

Source: Bonczar and Snell, *Capital Punishment, 2002*, 10.

Demographic Characteristics of Prisoners Under Sentence of Death, 2002

Characteristic	Prisoners Under Sentence of Death, 2002		
	Yearend	Admissions	Removals
Total number under sentence of death	3,557	159	179
Gender			
Male	98.6%	96.9%	97.2%
Female	1.4	3.1	2.8
Race			
White	54.3%	52.2%	67.0%
Black	43.7	45.9	31.8
All other races*	2.0	1.9	1.2
Hispanic origin			
Hispanic	11.5%	14.9%	9.5%
Non-Hispanic	88.5	85.1	90.5
Education			
8th grade or less	14.7%	21.4%	14.5%
9th–11th grade	37.1	34.9	36.2
High-school graduate/GED	38.5	37.3	36.2
Any college	9.7	6.3	13.1
Median	11th	11th	11th
Marital status			
Married	22.1%	25.8%	23.9%
Divorced/separated	20.8%	16.7	22.0
Widowed	2.8	6.8	3.1
Never married	54.3	50.7	50.9

Note: Calculations are based on those cases for which data were reported.
Missing data by category were as follows:

	Yearend	Admissions	Removals
Hispanic origin	399	38	21
Education	511	33	27
Marital status	342	27	20

* At yearend 2001, other races consisted of 27 American Indians, 32 Asians, and 12 self-identified Hispanics. During 2002, 2 Asians and 1 American Indian were admitted, and 1 Asian and 1 American Indian were removed.

Source: Bonczar and Snell, *Capital Punishment, 2002,* 6.

tonomy and its specific rules and goals are minimized, even up to the point at which its very functions and activities are taken over by other groups or organizations.

decarceration The prohibition of detention for juveniles; also, the removal of inmates from prisons or jails.

deceased Someone who is dead.

decedent Someone who has recently died.

decentralization Widespread distribution of power among many staff members. In prisons, limited power may be given to inmates as representatives of larger prisoner aggregates.

decentralized dining A system of feeding inmates under which they are fed in dayrooms, cell blocks, small satellite areas, or pods in new-generation jails.

deception, police Stratagems used by police authorities in order to elicit confessions or incriminating evidence from criminal suspects, such as pretending to have fingerprint evidence when, in fact, there is none. The deceit is intended to obtain information about a crime. *See also* entrapment.

deceptive advertising Any published advertisement intended to defraud or mislead potential consumers by offering products for sale that are not as advertised.

decertification The process of divesting arrest powers and law enforcement authority from police officers or sheriff's deputies for engaging in improper conduct or committing crimes; revoking one's power and authority as a law enforcement officer.

decision A court decree or resolution of an issue.

decision-making power The amount of freedom an employee has to determine how the work should be performed.

decision model A depiction of an organization consisting of three important components: (1) organizations are viewed as rational systems consisting of various parts; (2) each part, such as a department, makes decisions that affect relations with other parts and the organization as a whole; (3) organizational problems are accounted for, in part, by the quality of decisions pertaining to the utilization of organizational resources and personpower. The decision model has as its guiding theme the rational selection of the best action from several available alternatives with some calculated probability of predictable results.

decision tree concept A management idea that traces various types of decision-making processes from top administration to lower-level units. It consists of diagram with different branches, depending on different decisions made at strategic points. It is helpful and instructive in understanding why and how decisions are made and how different outcomes arise.

declaration An utterance or statement.

declaration of intent A legal step taken by an alien who wishes to become a U.S. citizen in which allegiance to his or her native country is renounced and the intention to become a U.S. citizen is expressed.

Declaration of Principles A set of principles for prison reform that were adopted at an 1870 conference. The principles advocated reform over punishment.

declarations of persons other than defendant Utterances committed to writing that have been made by persons who are dying, as dying declarations; any admissible declaration by someone who may or may not be present to give direct evidence in a courtroom; also, admissible evidence made by someone other than the defendant.

declaratory judgment A judicial resolution of a dispute, wherein the facts have been decided and a conclusion has been reached concerning the matter.

declaratory statute Any legal provision to make explicit the meaning of the law pertaining to a particular subject.

decomposition The natural breakdown of organic material when life ends.

deconstructionism The theory that terms used in everyday language are value-laden, as are rules and regulations. They reflect the inequities of the social structure, which is influenced directly by capitalism, making this theory is a type of radical criminology.

deconstructionist theory A view that challenges existing criminological perspectives to refute them and that acts toward replacing them with concepts more consistent with the postmodern era.

decoy A person, sometimes an undercover officer, who is in a position to be a crime victim, when in fact, the "victim" is under surveillance by other officers who will move in and make an arrest once a crime is attempted against the decoy.

decree A judicial proclamation, decision, or judgment.

decriminalization Legislative action whereby an act or omission, formerly criminal, is made noncriminal and without punitive sanctions.

dedicated line A telephone line that connects two points, usually for fire alarm signal reception. Sometimes called a direct-connect line, leased line, or direct wire.

dedicated security mode An automated data processing system exclusively used and controlled by users who process sensitive material.

deduction A logical inference in which conclusions are drawn from several given premises. Usually the premises consist of major and minor ones, together with a conclusion. An example might be, "All police officers are honest; John Jones is a police officer; therefore, John Jones is honest." Deductive arguments are sound to the extent that the premises are true.

deface To mar or damage the surface of property.

de facto "According to fact" (Latin); as a matter of fact.

defame To commit slander against another; to speak falsely or unduly critically about another.

default To fail to make good on an agreement; also, a failure to appear (in court).

defeminization The process whereby policewomen become enculturated into the police profession at the expense of their feminine identity.

defendant A person against whom a criminal proceeding is pending.

defendant dispositions Any one of several adjudication and dispositional options available to a judge at various points during a criminal proceeding, ranging from dismissal of the case to long-term imprisonment.

defendant's sentencing memorandum A version of events leading to the conviction offense in the words of the offender. This memorandum may be submitted together with a victim impact statement.

defense A response by defendants in criminal law or civil cases. It may consist only of a denial of the factual allegations of the prosecution (in a criminal case) or of the plaintiff (in a civil case). If the defense offers new factual allegations in an effort to negate the charges, this is called an affirmative defense.

defense attorney, counsel A lawyer who represents a client accused of a crime.

Defense Intelligence Agency (DIA) Headquartered at the Pentagon in Washington, DC, the DIA collects and disseminates defense intelligence at the pleasure of the Secretary of Defense and the Joint Chiefs of Staff. It is an agency within the Department of Defense.

Defense Investigative Service (DIS) A U.S. Department of Defense agency headquartered in Washington, DC, that provides personnel and security investigative services.

defense of accused person All persons accused of a crime are entitled to representation by counsel, and public defenders are appointed at no expense to indigent defendants.

defense-of-life standard Criteria by which law enforcement officers decide whether to use deadly force in effecting the arrest of criminal suspects. It involves discretion whether the officer's life or the lives of others are in jeopardy as the result of the suspect's actions. The standard was established in the leading case of *Tennessee v. Garner* (1985).

defenses to criminal charges Claims based on personal, special, and procedural considerations that defendants should not be held accountable for their actions, even though they may have acted in violation of the criminal laws.

Defense Supply Agency File An index of personnel cards collected by the Defense Supply Agency that contains security clearance information about individuals employed to do work in connection with various projects affiliated with the Department of Defense.

defense witness Any witness whose testimony is believed to be exculpatory to the defendant.

defensible space, defensible-space theory The principle that crime prevention can be achieved through modifying the physical environment to reduce the opportunity criminals have to commit crime; also, opportunities for surveillance that the physical environment offers. *See also* **target-hardening.**

defensive wounds Cuts or other injuries sustained by a crime victim from an attack by a perpetrator that are obtained by attempting to ward off the blows or strikes of a perpetrator.

deferred adjudication A form of probation that, after a plea of guilty or *nolo contendere,* defers further proceedings without an adjudication of guilt.

deferred prosecution The temporary halting of a prosecution against a defendant while he or she is subjected to a program with particular requirements for a short period. *See also* **diversion.**

deferred sentencing A mechanism whereby a judge postpones sentencing an offender until other actions have occurred. Sometimes, offenders are placed on various types of probation, and if their behavior is acceptable over a given time period, incarcerative penalties are waived.

deficiency judgment A creditor's claim against a debtor for the remaining monetary award not satisfied by sale of the debtor's property.

definite sentence A sentence consisting of a fixed term of confinement.

definition of crime Any act punishable by fine and/or imprisonment that is injurious to the public and prohibited by law.

defounding Artificially, through statistical means, reducing felonies to misdemeanors in cases in which the crimes have remained unsolved.

defraud To falsely deal with another; to cheat someone out of property or something of value by deviousness.

degenerate anomalies According to Cesare Lombroso, the primitive physical characteristics that make criminals animalistic and savage.

degradation ceremony Going to court, being scolded by a judge, or being found delinquent after a trial are examples of public ceremonies that can transform youthful offenders by degrading their self-image.

degree Ranking of crimes in order of their seriousness.

dei gratia "By the grace of God" (Latin).

deindividuation The process whereby an individual acting in concert with others as a group or mob loses his or her individual identity or responsibility for the acts of the group. The concept is sometimes used as a defense of a person who commits a crime while acting as a part of a larger group against one or more victims.

deinstitutionalization Providing programs in community-based settings instead of institutional ones.

deinstitutionalization of status offenses (DSO) Movement to remove nondelinquent juveniles from secure facilities by eliminating status offenses from the delinquency category and removing juveniles from or precluding their confinement in juvenile correction facilities; also, the process of removing status offenses from the jurisdiction of the juvenile court.

de jure "From the law" (Latin); as a matter of law.

delegated sentencing policy The practice by the legislature of permitting or authorizing the construction of sentencing policy by a group other than itself.

delegating style A mode of leadership that is task-oriented and requires supervisors to tell subordinates what to do and delegates tasks to those who are emotionally mature enough to perform them.

delegation model A form of participatory management stressing that input from all workers is valued.

deliberate, deliberately Willful; intentional.

deliberate indifference The attitude of prison or jail officials who ignore inmates with injuries or do not act as they should to prevent inmate abuse by other inmates. It is an intentional tort.

deliberation *See* **premeditation.**

delicts A crime category used by the French government to describe serious offenses, comparable to property crimes or felonies in U.S. jurisdictions.

delinquency control, delinquency repression The use of any justice program designed to prevent the occurrence of a future delinquent act.

delinquency prevention The activity of any nonjustice program or policy designed to prevent the occurrence of a future delinquent act.

delinquent, defective A minor who has some defect in his or her physical or mental condition that minimizes or excuses the delinquent act(s) committed.

delinquent, delinquent act, delinquent child, delinquency A child who has committed an offense that would be a crime if committed by an adult. In some states, status offenses are considered delinquent conduct and subject to identical punishments, including incarceration. The offense itself is the delinquent act. Also, a child of not more than a specified age who has violated criminal laws or engages in disobedient, indecent, or immoral conduct, and is in need of treatment, rehabilitation, or supervision. Delinquency is a status acquired through an adjudicatory proceeding by juvenile court.

delinquent subculture A subset of youth who are set apart from the rest of society because of their beliefs, values, and activities, which are often vastly different from those of conventional society.

delirium tremens "Trembling delirium" (Latin); a reaction of chronic alcoholics when they are deprived of alcohol. The reaction lasts several days and is manifested by vomiting, nausea, hallucinations, and violent cramping.

delit A particular grade or classification of crime (e.g., Class A, B, and C misdemeanors or felonies).

Delphi management technique A method of piecing together various diverse opinions to achieve consensus about the likelihood of some future event or occurrence.

delusion A psychological malady characterized by irrational beliefs about the real world.

delta That point on a ridge of a fingerprint at or near the point of divergence of two type lines.

demand reduction A drug-control policy that emphasizes reducing current and potential drug users' desire to take drugs.

demand waiver Requests by juveniles to have their cases transferred from juvenile courts to criminal courts.

demeanor The way in which persons outwardly manifest themselves to others. Police officers use the term to describe attitudes and actions that may arouse suspicion.

dementia Mental impairment.

de minimus Minimal.

demise Transfer of an estate to someone else; also, the death of a person.

democracy A form of government in which a nation's power rests in the hands of its citizens, who participate in the selection of those who will represent them and make decisions in their best interests.

demography The study of characteristics of human populations.

demonology The notion that some persons, including those who commit crime, are possessed by evil spirits that cause the criminal behavior.

demonstration, public A public gathering of varying size dedicated to promoting a particular view or ideology by various means, such as parading or carrying placards.

demonstrative evidence Material related to a crime that is apparent to the senses, in contrast to material presented by the testimony of other persons.

demoralization The shame and stigma suffered by a family when one of its members is convicted of a crime and imprisoned.

demur To take exception; to make an objection.

demurrage Detaining a vehicle or vessel beyond a time considered reasonable for loading or unloading; also, compensation for such detention.

demurrer A document challenging the legal sufficiency of a complaint or an indictment.

demystify The process whereby different theorists unmask the true purpose of the capitalist system's rules and laws.

denial A defense mechanism that refers to blocking out part of external rather than internal reality.

denial of injury A technique of neutralization that claims no one is hurt by an offender's crime, even if it technically violates the law.

denial of responsibility A technique of neutralization involving the denial of personal responsibility for actions that violate criminal laws.

denial of service (DOS) attacks Attempts to disable a computer by flooding a network, thereby preventing legitimate network traffic; attempts to disrupt connections between two machines, thereby preventing service; attempts to prevent a particular individual from accessing a service; attempts to disrupt service to a specific system or person. Most DOS attacks are against computer network activity and consist of consuming scarce, limited, or nonrenewable resources, destruction or alteration of configuration information, or physical destruction or alteration of network components.

denial of the victim A technique of neutralization that claims that a crime is justified as a rightful retaliation against the victim.

de novo "From the new" (Latin); anew; afresh; as if there had been no earlier decision.

density The number of persons per square mile in a given geographical area.

Denver Youth Survey A study designed to assess the level of juvenile crime and the correlates of juvenile crime.

deny To enter a plea of "not guilty" in juvenile proceedings.

department of corrections Any government agency that is headed by a politically appointed director who develops policy and oversees the operation of mandated correctional facilities and programs.

Department of Homeland Security On October 8, 2001, President George W. Bush announced the establishment of the United States Office of Homeland Security to coordinate homeland security efforts, to be headed by former Pennsylvania governor Tom Ridge with the title of Assistant to the President for Homeland Security. Its mission is to develop and coordinate the implementation of a comprehensive national strategy to secure the United States from terrorist threats or attacks. The office coordinates the executive branch's efforts to detect, prepare for, prevent, protect against, respond to, and recover from terrorist attacks within the United States. The office was established largely as the result of the terrorist attack on the two World Trade Center towers in New York City and the Pentagon in Washington, DC, on September 11, 2001.

Department of Homeland Security Advisory System A system created as a presidential directive to provide a comprehensive and effective means to disseminate information regarding the risk of terrorist acts to federal, state, and local authorities and the American people. It was implemented on March 12, 2002, following the terrorist attacks on the World Trade Center towers in New York on September 11, 2001.

Department of Justice (DoJ) The official legal arm of the government of the United States, headed by the attorney general, who is appointed by the president with Senate approval, this department controls and supervises all criminal prosecutions and represents the government in any legal suits in which it is a party. There are U.S. attorneys in each judicial district. Within the department are several law enforcement organizations that investigate violations of federal laws, including (1) the Federal Bureau of Investigation (FBI); (2) the Drug Enforcement Administration (DEA); (3) the Immigration and Naturalization Service (INS); and (4) the U.S. Marshals Service (USMS).

Department of the Treasury (DoT) An agency of the federal government, created in 1789, that supervises and manages the financial affairs of the government, including printing currency and minting coins for use in commercial transactions and exchanges. It analyzes taxation methods, controls licensing of vessels and vehicles used in foreign commerce, investigates counterfeiting, and oversees the Secret Service, which protects the president of the United States and other government figures.

dependency The legal status of juveniles over whom a juvenile court has assumed jurisdiction because the court has found their care by parents or guardians to be short of the standard of reasonable and proper care.

dependent, dependent child A child adjudged by the juvenile court to be without parent, guardian, or custodian; also, a child who needs special care and treatment because the parent, guardian, or custodian is unable to provide for his or her physical or mental condition; also, a child whose parents, guardian, or custodian desire to be relieved of legal custody for good cause; also, a child who is without necessary care or support through no fault of the parents, guardian, or custodian.

dependent variable Any factor or variable in a theory that is influenced by or is changed in value by another variable or factor.

depersonalization Efforts made by a killer to cover or otherwise obscure the identity of a victim; in organizational research, a psychological detachment of the worker from the actual work performed.

deponent A person who gives testimony through a deposition. If someone cannot physically attend a trial and give testimony under oath, then a deposition is taken and read into the court record.

Depo-Provera A hormone-based drug that reduces sex drive, used most effectively to treat sex offenders who are attracted to younger males.

deport To banish from a country. Aliens who commit crimes in the United States may be deported.

deposition A sworn written record of oral testimony.

depraved, depraved mind A serious moral deficiency; the highest level of malice.

depraved heart murder Extremely negligent or atrocious behavior that results in someone's death.

depraved-indifference murder Extremely negligent or violent behavior that causes death.

deprivation model, deprivation theory A suggested method of prisonization based on the idea that the prisoner subculture stems from how other inmates adapt to the severe psychological and physical losses imposed by imprisonment.

deprived child One who is without proper parental care or control, subsistence, education as required by law, or other care or control necessary for his or her physical, mental, or emotional health or morals, and whose deprivation is not due primarily to the lack of financial means of the parents, guardians, or other custodians.

deputy, deputy sheriff A subordinate to the sheriff, usually of a county; a law enforcement officer at the county level.

deringer, derringer A small pistol capable of firing one or two bullets. It was created by Henry Deringer in Philadelphia, PA, and was widely imitated by other manufacturers.

derivative evidence Information obtained as the result of previously discovered evidence (e.g., residue from an automobile tire may suggest that a crime was committed in a part of the city where such residue is found and police discover subsequent derivative evidence by investigating that area).

DeSalvo, Albert (1931–1973) Serial killer known as the Boston Strangler, alleged to have murdered at least 13 women in the Boston area from 1962 to 1964. Despite DeSalvo's confession, evidence later surfaced to indicate that he may not have been the perpetrator. He was eventually killed in prison by a fellow inmate.

descriptive guidelines Sentencing guidelines in which the sentence values are determined by studying the normal patterns for certain offenses and offender types. The sentence values in this case describe past practice.

descriptive statistics Any measure that typifies a group of persons or objects according to various properties, such as means, modes, medians, standard deviations, and other characteristics.

desecration Defacing or damaging of public structures, buildings, monuments, or religious shrines.

desegregation The integration of public toilets, various forms of travel, neighborhoods, and schools where prohibitions previously prevented minorities, especially black persons, from using the same facilities as white persons; action to reverse the "separate, but equal" doctrine.

desert-based sentences Sentences in which where the length is based on the seriousness of the criminal act and not the personal characteristics of the defendant or the deterrent impact of the law.

desertion Abandonment.

desert model *See* **justice model.**

deserts What someone deserves as the result of committing a crime.

design capacity The optimum number of inmates whom architects originally intended to be housed or accommodated by a jail or prison.

designer drug A substance which causes similar effects to a known narcotic or hallucinogen but has a slightly altered chemical makeups, usually to avoid classification as an illegal drug.

desistance Phenomenon whereby persons eventually refrain from wrongdoing as they grow older. It may also be attributed to religious conversion, marriage, or maturity. *See also* **aging-out phenomenon, aging-out process.**

detached street workers Social workers who go out into the community and establish close relations with juvenile gangs with the goal of modifying gang behavior to conform with conventional behaviors and to help gang members get jobs and educational opportunities.

detain To prevent someone from leaving a given area; to prevent one's freedom of action for a temporary period, such as an investigatory stop by police officers who wish to question persons, usually about a recently committed crime or one they think is about to be committed.

detainee A person held in local or very short-term confinement while awaiting consideration for pretrial release or an initial appearance for arraignment.

detainer, detainer warrant A hold order against a person incarcerated in another jurisdiction, which seeks, upon that person's release from current confinement, to take him or her into custody to answer other criminal charges; a notice of criminal charges or unserved sentences pending against a prisoner, usually authorized by one jurisdiction to be served on a prisoner held in another jurisdiction. After prisoners serve their sentences in one jurisdiction, they are usually transferred under detainer warrants to other jurisdictions where charges are pending against them.

detective A police officer assigned to investigate crimes after they have been reported; also, a special police officer who has been trained to gather evidence and identify perpetrators.

detector A probation or parole officer work-role orientation in which the probation or parole officer attempts to identify troublesome clients or those who are most likely to pose high community risk.

detention A period of temporary custody of juveniles before their case dispositions.

detention, preventive Holding persons in a place such as a jail pending trial or for some other investigative purpose, such as determining their identity. This has been upheld by the U.S. Supreme Court as valid for juveniles in the case of *Schall v. Martin* (1984) and for adults in *United States v. Salerno* (1987).

detention, protective The detention of persons who are believed to be in danger of losing their lives due to testimony they may provide against dangerous defendants. This is sometimes called protective custody, in which persons are detained and protected. Also, a policy of keeping certain types of offenders in custody for longer periods if these persons are believed to pose a danger to society. *See also* **selective incapacitation.**

detention center Any publicly or privately operated confinement facility for either adults or juveniles; usually, a secure facility designed to hold individuals for short periods, such as when they are awaiting trial on criminal charges.

detention hearing A judicial or quasi-judicial proceeding held to determine whether or not it is appropriate to continue to hold a juvenile in a shelter facility.

detention home Detention center.

detention rate The number of juveniles detained by the juvenile court in juvenile detention per 100,000 juveniles in the population.

deter To discourage criminals from committing crimes.

determinate sentencing A sanctioning scheme in which the court sentences an offender to incarceration for a fixed period, which must be served in full and without parole intervention, less any good time earned in prison.

determinism A concept holding that persons do not have free will but rather are subject to the influence of various forces over which they have little or no control.

deterrence, general or specific Actions that are designed to prevent crime before it occurs by threatening severe criminal penalties or sanctions. They may include safety measures to discourage potential lawbreakers such as elaborate security systems, electronic monitoring, and greater police officer visibility. Andenaes (1975) defines deterrence as influencing by fear, specifically fear of apprehension and punishment.

deterrence model A model of crime control based on the philosophy that stronger penalties imposed on criminals will cause potential offenders to refrain from crime. Three requirements must exist before any deterrence is successful: (1) severity of punishment, (2) certainty of punishment, and (3) swiftness of punishment.

detoxification The process whereby persons are cured of alcoholism or drug abuse.

detoxification center A place where persons are treated for alcohol or drug dependency.

Detroit Police Ministation Program Starting in the early 1980s, the Detroit, MI, Police Department placed small substations staffed by police officers, or ministations, in high-crime areas of Detroit. The intent of the program was to improve response time to calls for service from citizens whenever crimes were committed.

developed countries Countries recognized by the United Nations as the richest in the world.

developmental process At different stages of the life course, a variety of factors influence behavior. Factors influential at one stage of life may not be significant at another stage.

developmental theory, developmental view *See* **cognitive development theory.**

deviance Conduct that departs from accepted codes expected by society or by a particular group, including illegal behavior prohibited by statute.

deviance amplification Mislabeling a group's behavior as a consequence of certain biases or preconceptions about the group members.

Devil's Island A French penal colony off the coast of French Guiana in South America.

diagnosis Identifying the nature and cause of some phenomenon.

diagnostic center A functional unit within a correctional institution, or a separate facility, that holds persons kept in custody in order to determine to which correctional facility or program they should be committed.

Diagnostic and Statistical Manual (DSM-IV-R) A manual published by the American Psychiatric Association that contains a classification of mental disorders.

diagnostic committal Court action that places certain persons in a confinement facility or hospital so that their personal history and characteristics can be studied by psychiatrists and others. Often, such persons are accused of crimes, and a determination must be made as to whether they are competent to stand trial or are legally responsible for the crimes they are accused of committing.

dialed number recorder A device that can be used to identify numbers dialed on a telephone by printing out the numbers associated with sounds produced when someone dials a particular number.

dichotomy The division of something into two parts; male/female; upper class/lower class; religious/nonreligious; property offender/violent offender.

Dickerson's Rangers An antidrug program in the San Fernando Valley of Southern California that targets children ages 7 through 13. It operates in various city parks and recreational centers. Children meet weekly and discuss drug abuse in their schools and communities. Police officers advise them how to resist overtures made by drug dealers or their peers who might use drugs. Field trips are also sponsored that include speakers whose specialties include drug abuse and illicit drug prevention.

dicta, dictum "Utterances, utterance" (Latin); written portions of a judicial opinion that are not part of the actual ruling or holding of the court, and which therefore are not legally binding precedents for future court decisions.

Diderot, Denis (1713–1784) A French novelist, anarchist, and penal reformer who wrote about cruel and inhuman punishment in French prisons.

dies non From *dies non juridicus,* "nonjuridical day" (Latin); a day when courts do not transact business, such as weekends and holidays.

diethyltryptamine Psychedelic drug such as yopo; its street name is DET.

differential association, differential association reinforcement A theory of criminality based on the incorporation of psychological learning theory and differential association with social learning theory. Criminal behavior is learned through associations and is contained or discontinued as a result of positive or negative reinforcements.

differential identification theory A theory that people engage in criminal or delinquent behavior because they identify with real or imaginary persons from whose perspective their crime or delinquency seems acceptable.

differential involvement hypothesis The hypothesis that racially different incarceration rates are caused by different levels of involvement of different racial groups in specific types of crime.

differential opportunity, differential opportunity theory An explanation of criminality linking concepts of anomie and differential association by analyzing both the legitimate and illegitimate means of attaining goals (e.g., theft or hard work) available to persons. The theory suggests that these means are unequally distributed.

differential pressure sensor A perimeter protection device usually placed in the ground so that someone who steps on the device will activate sensors elsewhere and alert persons that someone is crossing off-limits grounds.

differential reinforcement theory An explanation that combines elements of labeling theory and a psychological phenomenon known as conditioning. Persons are rewarded for engaging in desirable behavior and punished for deviant conduct.

differential response A police patrol strategy that prioritizes calls for service and assigns various response options.

diffusion of benefits An effect that occurs when an effort to control one type of crime has the unexpected benefit of reducing the incidence of another.

diffusion of responsibility The situation that exists among groups of witnesses to an emergency or a crime, when people believe that someone should act but that it need not be themselves because other potential helpers are present.

diffusion of treatment Whenever the treatment given to an experimental group is spread to the control group by treatment group subjects (e.g., a professor hands out sample tests to one section of a class but not to the other, but students who get the sample test make copies and give them to their friends in the control group). It may result in a failure to observe any differences between groups, which leads to the false conclusion that the treatment has no effect.

digital crime Computer crime.

dilatory Any action intended to delay court proceedings, to postpone a court decision, or to gain more time, such as in preparing a case for prosecution or defense.

dilatory exceptions Motions filed to delay legal cases or proceedings but which do not overcome the charges filed against a defendant.

diminished capacity, responsibility A defense based on claims of a mental condition that may be insufficient to exonerate the defendant of guilt but that may have relevance for specific mental elements of certain crimes or degrees of crime.

dimorphism Possession of both male and female reproductive organs and sexual characteristics.

dingbats Crazy but harmless inmates.

diphenylaminochloroarsine A solid material dispersed by heat that produces skin and eye irritation, chest distress, or nausea and vomiting; a vomiting gas that is considered nontoxic.

diphenylcyanoarsine (DC) A riot-control gas with rapid rate of action and dissipation. It is nontoxic but produces debilitating physical effects, which make it useful in mob control.

diplomatic immunity The protection from prosecution enjoyed by various envoys or diplomats from foreign countries.

dipsomania An urge toward intoxication; alcoholism.

direct action Violence or intimidation in order to overwhelm authorities and seize power.

direct contempt of court Any act contrary to a court ruling or protocol committed in front of the bench within view of the court.

direct control External controls that depend on rules, restrictions, and punishments.

direct costs Operating expenses such as salary, fringe benefits, program services, equipment and contractual costs, plus expenses and capital costs.

directed leadership A style of leadership in which leaders spell out exactly what is expected of their subordinates and detail how organizational goals can be achieved by subordinate behaviors.

directed patrol A police patrol strategy designed to direct resources proactively to high-crime areas.

directed verdict An order by the court declaring that the prosecution has failed to produce sufficient evidence to show the defendant guilty beyond a reasonable doubt.

direct evidence Evidence offered by an eyewitness who testifies to what he or she saw or heard.

direct examination Questioning by an attorney of one's own (prosecution or defense) witness during a trial.

direct file Prosecutorial waiver of jurisdiction to a criminal court; an action taken against a juvenile who has committed an especially serious offense, in which that juvenile's case is transferred to criminal court for the purpose of a criminal prosecution.

direct loss The result of a crime in which a stock of useful things is reduced, as in arson or vandalism.

direct-sentencing policy The construction of sentencing policy directly by the legislature.

direct-supervision jails Temporary confinement facilities that eliminate many of the traditional barriers between inmates and correctional staff, allowing staff members the opportunity for greater interaction within, and control over, residents; also known as third-generation jails.

dirty urine A urine specimen containing prohibited drugs.

disability Any physical or mental impairment.

disaggregated The relationship between two or more independent variables (such as murder convictions and death sentences) analyzed while controlling for the influence of an independent variable, such as race or ethnicity.

disarmament The removal of arms from those who pose a threat to the safety and security of a community.

Disaster Squad An FBI-sponsored agency headquartered in Washington, DC, that conducts investigations and identifications of disaster victims.

discharge To release a convicted offender from supervision or confinement.

disciplinary detention (DD) Punishment given to an inmate found guilty of a serious rule violation. Usually, such inmates are placed in more secure units with restricted privileges.

disciplinary punishment Any punishment, such as prolonged solitary confinement or a withdrawal of privileges for a specified time, imposed on an inmate for violating institutional rules.

disciplinary report (DR) A written report citing an inmate's rule-breaking behavior or misconduct.

disclaimer Any denial or statement attempting to absolve oneself of responsibility for the operation or performance of a product.

disclosure of presentence investigation report The practice of sharing the contents of a presentence investigation report with defendant and counsel.

discouragement An effect that occurs when an effort made to eliminate one type of crime also controls others because it reduces the value of criminal activity by limiting access to desirable targets (e.g., pickpocketing). By placing more patrol officers on subway trains to discourage muggings, there are more police to prevent pickpocketing (nonviolent theft), which discourages assaults, muggings, and other violent theft.

discovery A procedure in which the prosecution shares information with the defense attorney and the defendant. Specific types of information are made available to the defendant before trial, including results of any tests conducted, psychiatric reports, and transcripts or tape-recorded statements made by the defendant. These are also known as "Brady materials," after *Brady v. Maryland* (1963).

discretion, general In the criminal-justice system, the authority to make decisions based on one's own judgment rather than on specified rules. The result may be inconsistent handling of offenders as well as positive actions tailored to individual circumstances.

discretion, police In accordance with the dictates of an intuitive grasp of situational exigencies, police have authority to use force to enforce the law, if, in the officer's opinion, the situation demands it. This has been discussed and elaborated by Egon Bittner and also Albert Reiss, who has postulated that police officers may choose not to arrest persons in lieu of finding better solutions than are offered by arrest. *See also* **behavioral approach; legal approach; organizational approach.**

discretionary judicial waivers, discretionary waivers Transfers of juveniles to criminal courts by judges, at their discretion or in their judgment. These are also known as judicial waivers.

discretionary justice The ability of law enforcement officers, prosecutors, and others in the criminal-justice system to use their own judgments about how or even whether to process offenders or cases.

discretionary parole The release of an inmate at the discretion of a parole board.

discretionary release Release of inmates from incarceration at the discretion of parole boards within the boundaries set by the sentence and the penal law.

discretionary review A form of appellate-court review of lower-court decisions that is not mandatory but occurs at the option of the appellate court.

discriminatory (discriminative) power A measure of each statement's ability on an attitudinal scale to separate persons who possess a characteristic to a high degree from those who possess the same characteristic to a low degree. It can be used in determining the internal consistency or reliability of an attitudinal measure.

disembowel To cut the abdomen in such a way as to permit the intestines to spill out or be exposed.

disfranchisement Withdrawing privileges and status from particular individuals, including prisoners who lose certain rights as the result of being convicted of a crime.

disinterment The act of exhuming a previously buried body.

dismemberment As a punishment, the practice of severing body parts; as a social condition, the adjustment made to the loss of a husband or other family member when such a loved one dies or is incarcerated for a lengthy period.

dismissal A decision by a judicial officer to terminate a case without a determination of guilt or innocence.

dismissal for want of prosecution A judicial decision to terminate proceedings against a criminal suspect because of the failure of prosecutors to present a case against the accused.

dismissal in the interests of justice A judicial decision to terminate proceedings against a criminal defendant because such a prosecution is unwarranted, evidence is nonexistent, or a wrongful prosecution has been discovered and must be corrected.

disorder Any public behavior that disturbs the peace; mob or rioting behavior.

disorderly conduct Any illegal behavior that disturbs the public peace or order.

disorderly house A house of prostitution or a drug house, where behaviors conducted on the premises undermine public morals, health, and safety.

disorderly person Someone who is guilty of disorderly conduct, such as a vagrant, beggar, homeless person, or transient.

disorganized neighborhood An inner-city area of extreme poverty where the critical social control mechanisms have broken down.

disorganized offender A serial killer who tends to be of low intellect or intelligence.

disparity In corrections, the failure to provide equal programming for both male and female inmates; in courts, the practice of imposing different sentences and punishments on persons convicted of committing identical offenses, usually on the basis of race, ethnicity, gender, or socioeconomic status.

displacement The transferral of an emotion, such as anger, to an object, person, or action other than that which caused the emotion.

displacement effect A change in the pattern of crime without a reduction in the total amount of crime that results from criminals' efforts to avoid punishment. Displacement may be from one target to another, from one area to another, or from one kind of offense to another.

disposition An action by a criminal or juvenile justice court or agency signifying that a portion of the justice process is completed and jurisdiction is relinquished or transferred to another agency or signifying that a decision has been reached on one aspect of a case and a different aspect comes under consideration, requiring a different kind of decision.

disposition hearing, dispositionary hearing A hearing in juvenile court, conducted after an adjudicatory hearing and a finding of delinquency, status offender, or dependent/neglected, to determine the most appropriate punishment, placement, or treatment for the juvenile.

disproportionate minority confinement The containment in detention, jail, prison, or other incarcerative facilities of minorities or juveniles in percentages out of proportion to their representation in the general population.

disputatiousness Seeking satisfaction through violent means. In the subculture of violence, this is considered appropriate behavior for a person who has been offended.

dispute resolution Resolving disagreements through third-party arbiters.

dispute resolution centers Informal hearing infrastructures designed to mediate interpersonal disputes without the need for more formal arrangements of criminal trial courts.

disqualification Withdrawing someone, either voluntarily or involuntarily, from a proceeding or meeting, usually because that person is prejudiced, biased, or incompetent, or has conducted him- or herself improperly to qualify for performing the necessary services that must be performed. *See also* **recusal.**

disruptive group An organization that has a common cause or symbol and engages in unlawful activities to disrupt community activities.

dissatisfiers Motivational factors contributing to work satisfaction and directly linked with working conditions, such as the nature of supervision, the supervisor-subordinate relation, salary, and work stress.

dissent, dissenting opinion Any judicial opinion disavowing or attacking the decision of a collegial court.

dissident Someone holding a contrary view from the majority.

dissolve To render null and void.

distress To hold the property of a person against the payment of debts.

distributed leadership Also known as multiple leadership, a mode of exercising control over others in which different persons in a group may have a special facility for calling the group to order, others may be able to quell a troublesome situation, others may be highly respected because of their judgment and character, and still others may be respected because of their expertise and because they have more facts to contribute than any other member.

district attorney A city, county, or state prosecutor who is charged with bringing offenders to justice and enforcing the laws of the state.

district courts Trial courts at the county, state, or federal level with general and original jurisdiction. Boundaries of their venue do not conform to standard political unit boundaries, but generally include several states or counties.

District of Columbia Preventive Detention Law A 1970 bill in Washington, DC, that authorized the placement of suspects in pretrial preventive detention for up to 60 days based on a forecast of their future dangerousness or risk posed to the public if freed. The U.S. Supreme Court subsequently upheld the law for juveniles in *Schall v. Martin* (1984) and for adults in *United States v. Salerno* (1987).

disturbing the peace Any act that disrupts the public decorum or neighborhood equilibrium; any noise or physical altercation sufficiently loud to warrant police officers to intercede.

diversion Removing a case from the criminal justice system, while a defendant is required to comply with various conditions (e.g., attending a school for drunk drivers, undergoing counseling, performing community service). It may result in expungement of record. Also, conditional removal of the prosecution of a case prior to its adjudication, usually as the result of an arrangement between the prosecutor and judge.

diversion, juvenile Directing of youths from the juvenile justice system, where they can remain with their families or guardians, attend school, and be subject to limited supervision on a regular basis by a juvenile probation officer.

Diversion Plus Program Established in Lexington, KY, in 1991, this program is designed to reduce recidivism and promote conformity to the law without stigmatization. Youths targeted included first offenders, low-risk delinquent offenders, and any youth without a prior juvenile record. The program consists of a series of weekly meetings and self-help sessions that stress self-esteem and self-control, substance-abuse prevention, independent living, one-on-one counseling, and small-group interaction.

diversion program One of several programs preceding a formal court adjudication of charges against defendants in which they participate in therapeutic, educational, and other helping programs. *See also* **diversion.**

diversion to civil court A procedure whereby a crime is reduced in seriousness to that of a tort action and placed for disposition in civil court rather than in criminal court. *See also* **alternative dispute resolution.**

diversity jurisdiction A type of jurisdiction used by the U.S. Supreme Court when it attempts to resolve suits between residents of different states.

divertee A person who participates in a diversion program or who is otherwise granted diversion.

divestiture of jurisdiction Juvenile court relinquishment of control over certain types of juveniles, such as status offenders.

Division of Investigation Act A 1934 Congressional action authorizing members of the Division of Investigation, an agency within the U.S. Department of Justice, to serve warrants and subpoenas, to make seizures subject to warrant, and to make arrests for felonies without a warrant, if probable cause exists to believe that a crime has been committed and the person to be arrested or seized committed it.

division of labor The organized distribution of positions and work roles in any organization, usually involving a hierarchy of authority and planned and predictable communication patterns.

divorce The legal dissolution of a marriage.

divorce, no fault The legal dissolution of a marriage where neither party is considered responsible for the dissolution.

dizygotic (DZ) twins Fraternal twins who develop from two separate eggs fertilized at the same time. *See also* **monozygotic twins.**

DNA The abbreviation for deoxyribonucleic acid; one of two nucleic acids found in all cells.

DNA fingerprinting Deoxyribonucleic acid (DNA) is an essential component of all living matter that carries hereditary patterning. Suspects can be detected according to their unique DNA patterning, as each person has a different DNA pattern. This is similar to fingerprint identification, in which no two persons have identical fingerprints.

DNA profiling The identification of criminal suspects by matching DNA samples taken from their person with specimens found at crime scenes.

DNA testing The use of DNA in criminal cases.

DOB Date of birth; an acronym used in various documents at the time of booking and arrest.

Doc Holliday syndrome A depiction of police officers who are suspicious of others, bitter, and quick-tempered, named after John Holliday (1852–1887), a dentist and skilled gunfighter who participated in the gunfight at the O.K. Corral in Tombstone, AZ, on October 26, 1881.

docket A court record of the cases scheduled to appear before the court.

doctrine of *parens patriae* *See parens patriae.*

document Any written paper, official or unofficial, having potential evidentiary importance.

document, class A An identification document that is considered reliable, such as a driver's license or passports.

document, class B An identification document that is considered reasonably reliable, such as a photo identification card issued by public or private organizations like a school, hospital, emergency services, or fire or police department. These items can be faked, as can class A documents, although class A documents are considered more reliable.

document, class C An identification document sometimes considered reliable, such as a birth certificate, insurance card, or credit card.

document, class D An identification document that is considered unreliable, such as a Social Security card, which is easily obtained and faked.

documentary evidence Any written evidence.

document examiner An expert who can determine the authenticity of a writing or written document.

Doe, John *See* **John Doe, Jane Doe.**

doing time Adapting to imprisonment by avoiding trouble.

domestic battery Physical abuse between married persons or persons who are living together as husband and wife without benefit of a legal marriage.

domestic murder The killing of an intimate, most often a spouse or significant other.

domestic relations courts Courts dealing with family problems, divorce, and separations.

domestic terrorism Terrorist acts committed on domestic soil, often by citizens.

domestic violence Any spousal altercation or intrafamilial conflict of sufficient nature to justify law enforcement intervention. Spousal abuse is the most frequently cited example, but domestic violence may involve parent-child conflict, either physical or psychological.

domestic violence court Judicial proceeding that specializes in cases involving domestic violence.

domestic violence shelter A house or other building maintained for the purpose of providing safe housing for women who have been physically or otherwise abused by their spouses or others in a domestic setting.

domicile One's place of residence or abode.

Do-Pops Half-trusties whose duties include popping doors open for superiors, cleaning buildings, waiting tables, and caring for animals.

double action A type of firearm that discharges a bullet when the trigger is pulled without requiring the hammer to be separately cocked.

double-bunking Placing two or more inmates in a cell originally designed to accommodate one inmate.

double-celling *See* **double-bunking.**

double jeopardy Subjecting persons to prosecution more than once in the same jurisdiction for the same offense, usually without new or vital evidence. It is prohibited by the Fifth Amendment. *See also* **Bill of Rights.**

double marginality The social burden African-American police officers carry by being both minority group members and law enforcement officers.

downers Slang for central nervous system depressants and other drugs known to have a calming or tranquilizing effect.

Draft Riots In 1863 in New York City, gangs revolted in protest of the recently enacted draft laws that went into effect during the Civil War. Stores were looted, buildings were burned, and over 100 persons were killed.

dramatization of evil The process of social typing that transforms an offender's identity from a doer of evil to an evil person.

dram law A liquor law that provides that someone who serves an intoxicated customer liquor may be liable for any injuries, damages, or deaths that result if that customer is subsequently involved in an accident.

Draper, John T. A Vietnam veteran who discovered in 1971 that a giveaway whistle in Cap'n Crunch cereal boxes could perfectly reproduce a 2600 hertz tone used by AT&T that could be used to make free long-distance telephone calls. Draper, nicknamed "Cap'n Crunch," was subsequently arrested and convicted of illegal use of the telephone system. *See also* **phone phreaking; phreaking.**

Dream Team The group of high-profile criminal defense attorneys who worked to defend O.J. Simpson against charges that he murdered Nicole Brown Simpson and Ronald

Goldman, including F. Lee Bailey, Johnnie Cochran, Robert Shapiro, and Alan Dershowitz.

Dreyfus, Alfred (1859–1935) A Jewish captain in the French army who was framed for passing secrets to the Germans during the 1890s. The subsequent scandal and legal events ultimately resulted in Dreyfus' acquittal and the award of the French Legion of Honor medal. Sometimes referred to as the Dreyfus Affair, the incident was subsequently sensationalized in a Hollywood movie, *What Price Glory?* (Kirk Douglas).

drift, drift theory David Matza's term denoting a state of limbo in which youths move in and out of delinquency and in which their lifestyles embrace both conventional and deviant values.

drive-by A situation in which a citizen sees a crime committed and notifies the police, who stop and detain a criminal suspect. Later, the citizen drives by with the police to identify the suspect who has been detained.

drive-by shooting Any gunfire directed at one or more pedestrians from a moving vehicle.

driver The person who is in physical control of a vehicle; in a crime, the person who transports criminals to and from the crime scene.

driver and pedestrian education A Department of Transportation–initiated program providing information and financial assistance to state and local agencies to improve driver safety and pedestrian education. It is headquartered in Washington, DC, and overseen by the National Highway Traffic Safety Administration.

driving record A licensed driver's driving history, including the number and type of tickets issued and driver's license suspensions and revocations, maintained by the Department of Motor Vehicles for a particular jurisdiction.

driving under the influence (DUI), driving while intoxicated (DWI) A term designating someone operating a vehicle while intoxicated or under the influence of a narcotic or drug, which may or may not be illegal.

Driving Under the Influence Cost Recovery Program Responsibility for damages resulting from operating a vehicle while under the influence of drugs or alcohol rests with the driver convicted of DUI. After commencing in California in 1989, the program has been mandated by a majority of the states.

"driving while black" An unfavorable expression describing the practice by law enforcement officers of stopping black motorists when there is no violation of the law to justify a stop.

driving while intoxicated (DWI) *See* **driving under the influence (DUI), driving while intoxicated (DWI).**

dropouts Youths who leave school before completing their required program of education.

dropsy testimony Perjured testimony made by police officers in an attempt to solidify a weak case. Defendants are often alleged to have "dropped" drugs on the ground during automobile stops for traffic violations, hence, "dropsy testimony." It became more prevalent after the exclusionary rule became the search and seizure standard following the case of *Mapp v. Ohio* (1963).

drowning Death caused by immersion in water.

Dr. Snow *See* **Lavin, Larry.**

drug Any chemical substance used for psychological or physical purposes.

drug abuse, drug-abuse violations Any offenses involving the use, possession, manufacture, or distribution of illegal or controlled substances (e.g., marijuana, cocaine or crack, heroin, and methamphetamine).

Drug Abuse Epidemiology Data Center An organization established in 1973 by the National Institute on Drug Abuse. Its goals are to collect survey data concerning drug research and to maintain an extensive library of drug-related documents and computer files containing drug literature. It is headquartered in Ft. Worth, TX.

Drug Abuse Warning Network (DAWN) A large-scale data-collection system sponsored by the Substance Abuse and Mental Health Services Administration (SAMHSA) that uses data reported by hospital emergency departments and medical examiners and collects information about drug deaths, overdoses, and other drug facts.

drug addiction Any dependency on a given substance, including narcotics, alcohol, and prescription medicines.

drug/alcohol dependent offenders Offenders with chemical dependencies, including addiction to illegal substances or drugs and alcoholic beverages.

Drug and Crime Data Center Clearinghouse An agency of the U.S. Department of Justice that provides crime statistics and publishes information about drug-related crimes and drug information. Databases are compiled and data research is conducted for interested persons and organizations. It is headquartered in Washington, DC.

drug cartel Any criminal organization whose activities include the cultivation, manufacture, distribution, and sale of illegal drugs.

drug courier One who transports illegal drugs or substances for someone else.

drug-courier profile A way of identifying drug runners based on their personal characteristics. Police may stop and question individuals based on how they fit the characteristics contained in the profile.

drug court A tribunal established exclusively for the purpose of hearing and deciding drug cases.

Drug Court Resource Center Sponsored by the Bureau of Justice Assistance, this agency provides technical support for drug court officials and disseminates information about drug courts to interested persons and agencies. It is headquartered at American University in Washington, DC.

drug czar A cabinet-level position, originally created during the Reagan presidency, that functions to organize federal drug-fighting efforts.

Drug Dealer Liability Act California legislation that provides for civil damage awards to persons victimized by illicit drug use. Victims may include drug users, their parents and employers, and government agencies that pay for drug-treatment programs. Its objective is to hold drug dealers accountable for such expenses and use seized funds and revenue from illegal drugs to fund civil damage awards.

drug-education materials Any information, audiovisual aids, or published documents made available to interested persons and agencies; sponsored by Drug Enforcement Administration, headquartered in Washington, DC.

Drug Enforcement Administration (DEA) An agency established to investigate violations of all federal drug-trafficking laws. It regulates the legal manufacture of drugs and other controlled substances.

drug-enforcement research DEA-sponsored research related to law enforcement investigations of drug trafficking and use. Information and support are provided to local jurisdictions to combat illicit drug use. The DEA is headquartered in Washington, DC.

drug-enforcement training Any practical hands-on work involving the education and preparation of persons, including law enforcement officers and researchers, who wish to learn more about and investigate illicit drug manufacture, distribution, and use. The Enforcement Training Division of the Drug Enforcement Administration is headquartered in Washington, DC.

DRUGFIRE program Computer technology that permits law enforcement officers to link firearms evidence in shooting investigations.

Drug Information Resources A comprehensive guide, published in 1990 and available to state and federal agencies, that offers documents and other materials related to illicit drug use and distribution. It is published in Rockville, MD.

drug kingpin Any head of a criminal organization whose principal activity is the distribution of illegal drugs.

drug-law violation(s) The unlawful sale, possession, purchase, distribution, manufacture, cultivation, transportation, or use of a controlled or prohibited drug, or the attempt to commit such an act.

drug legalization A movement to make the cultivation, possession, and use of certain drugs legal.

drug misuse Drug abuse; the use of any drug beyond the parameters of what the drug was originally prescribed to cure; recreational use of drugs prescribed for other purposes.

drug monitoring A patch used on bodies of drug abusers or those convicted of drug crimes that collects perspiration and detects whether or not the subject has used drugs or particular kinds of drugs within a given time interval. This is a nonintrusive method for controlling and monitoring offenders convicted of drug offenses or who are drug-dependent and are undergoing therapy or treatment for their drug addictions.

drugs of abuse Illegal drugs, and legal drugs that are taken in excess or for purposes other than which they were prescribed.

drug registration Under the Controlled Substances Act, all persons who manufacture, distribute, or dispense controlled substances must register annually with the registration branch of the Drug Enforcement Administration. Information is used to ensure compliance, specifically that the registrants are not dispensing extraordinary quantities of controlled substances which are unaccounted for through legitimate prescriptions.

drug testing Various means for determining whether someone has consumed various types of drugs in a recent period of time.

drug trafficking Selling and distributing narcotics and other drugs for profit.

drug types Classifications of drugs into useful categories for investigative purposes. Types include marijuana, synthetic drugs, nonnarcotic drugs, psychedelic drugs, and a host of other drug categories that are tabulated and monitored by different agencies.

Drug Use Forecasting Program (DUF) A Department of Justice program implemented in 1987 that compiled data on self-reported drug use by arrestees in selected cities. The program became ADAM (Arrestee Drug Abuse Monitoring) with a change in political administration. ADAM uses probability-based sampling methods for greater generalizability of findings, together with improved measures of social and demographic variables.

drunkard One who habitually is drunk.

drunk driving Operating a motor vehicle while under the influence of alcohol.

drunkenness Intoxication from alcohol, other than driving under the influence.

drunk tank A small holding facility in jails for persons who have been arrested for public drunkenness or driving while intoxicated.

druzhiny "People's volunteers" that functioned as tribunals for Soviet offenders.

DSM-IV-R See Diagnostic and Statistical Manual (DSM-IV-R).

dual citizenship The possession of citizenship in two or more jurisdictions.

dual court system A system consisting of a separate judicial structure for each state in addition to a federal court organization. Each case is tried in a court of the same jurisdiction as that of the law or laws broken. Separate lines of appeal exist for federal and state court matters. *See figure p. 85.*

dual diagnosis Having two problems in need of treatment at the same time.

dual-factor theory of motivation Victor Vroom's concept that one's desire to work originates from *satisfiers,* or events in one's work environment that contribute to one's satisfaction, such as work content and intrinsic interest of the work performed, the potential for advancement and recognition, and responsibility for important tasks; and *dissatisfiers,* or those events in one's work environment that contribute to one's dissatisfaction.

dualistic fallacy The mistaken notion that criminal populations under investigation are distinct from the general population, which is assumed to be comprised of noncriminals. The notion stems from the original belief that criminals were concentrated largely in the lower social classes.

dual-procedure offense An offense similar to a British hybrid offense, in which the prosecutor decides whether prosecution should proceed either by summary conviction or by indictment.

DUBAL Driving with an unlawful blood alcohol level.

duces tecum "Bring with you" (Latin); a court order obligating an attorney to bring to court all materials related to a given piece of evidence.

ducking stool A sixteenth-century colonial corporal punishment device in which the offender is placed in a chair at the end of a long lever and dunked in a pond until almost drowned. This punishment was often imposed for gossiping or wife-beating.

dueling The illegal practice of settling an argument between two parties by fighting to the death. In the eighteenth and nineteenth centuries, dueling was accomplished with pistols or swords.

due process The basic constitutional right to a fair trial, the presumption of innocence until guilt is proven beyond a reasonable doubt, and the opportunity to be heard, to be aware of a matter that is pending, to make an informed choice whether to acquiesce or contest, and to provide the reasons for such a choice before a judicial official. Actual due-process rights include timely notice of a hearing or trial that informs the accused of charges, the opportunity to confront one's accusers and to present evidence on one's own behalf before an impartial jury or judge, the presumption of innocence under which guilt must be proved by legally obtained evidence and the verdict must be supported by the evidence presented, the right of accused persons to be warned of their constitutional rights at the earliest stage of the criminal process, protection against self-incrimination, assistance of counsel at every critical stage of the criminal process, and the guarantee that individuals will not be tried more than once for the same offense.

due-process model A model of the criminal justice system that assumes that freedom is so important that every effort must be made to ensure that criminal justice decisions are based on reliable information. It emphasizes the adversarial process, the rights of defendants, and formal decision-making procedures.

due-process protection Protections extended to individuals being prosecuted by the criminal-justice system under the Fifth, Sixth, and Fourteenth Amendments. *See also* **Bill of Rights.**

due-process revolution The period during the 1960s and early 1970s when the U.S. Supreme Court made several rulings that created or applied additional due-process protections to criminals.

Dugdale, Richard (1841–1883) Author of *The Jukes: A Study in Crime, Pauperism, Disease, and Heredity* (1877), which advocated that heredity is responsible for the genetic transmission of criminal traits.

DUI *See* **driving under the influence (DUI), driving while intoxicated (DWI).**

dum-dum, dumdum, dumdum bullet A projectile designed to expand greatly on impact, causing severe tissue damage. Such bullets are illegal to use or possess.

dungeon A subterranean chamber used for confinement, torture, or execution of prisoners.

Duquenois reaction A chemical test to determine the presence of marijuana.

duress An affirmative defense used by defendants to show lack of criminal intent, alleging force, psychological or physical, from others as the stimulus for otherwise criminal conduct.

duress alarm device A fixed or portable device used to trigger an alarm, silent or audible, under a condition of stress, such as a holdup or robbery, fire, illness, or some other emergency.

duress and consent Any unlawful constraints exercised upon individuals forcing them to do some act that would not have been done otherwise.

Durham rule An insanity test requiring that it be shown that an accused person had either a mental disease or defect at the time a criminal act was committed. Such a showing would cause the accused

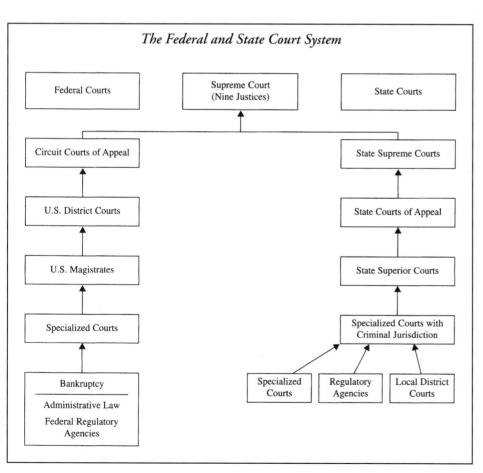

The Federal and State Court System

not to have to requisite *mens rea,* and thus criminal responsibility and liability could be avoided.

Durkheim, Emile (1858–1917) A French sociologist and positivist influenced by Auguste Comte. Durkheim believed crime to be prevalent as an integral part of human nature and even functional, and thus inevitable. He wrote *Suicide: A Study in Sociology* (1897), an elaborate theoretical scheme about various types of suicide originating from different conditions, such as anomie and either close or loose attachments or social bonds with others in society. He also wrote *The Division of Labor in Society* (1893), wherein he described various types of society, growing from rural, mechanistic society to more complex organic systems characteristic of urban environments.

duty An obligation that a person has by law or contract.

DWI *See* **driving under the influence (DUI), driving while intoxicated (DWI).**

dyathanasia Mercy killing by withdrawal of life support machinery from a dying patient.

Dyer Act A 1919 act prohibiting interstate transportation of stolen motor vehicles.

dye A substance used to color materials that is difficult to wash away.

dying declaration An oral or written statement made by someone who is about to die that may include accusatory or exculpatory information. An exception to the hearsay rule allows the introduction of an utterance by a person who knows he or she is dying, usually one identifying a criminal perpetrator.

dysfunctional family A family in which parent-parent and/or parent-child relationships are characterized by marital discord; physical, sexual, mental, or emotional abuse or problems; neglect; or other problems that prevent the family's normal social functioning.

E

Early Alliance Project A large-scale enterprise designed to promote coping and competence among youths and reduce their risk for conduct problems, aggression, substance abuse, delinquency, violence, and school failure. It was established in Columbia, SC, in 1997.

early onset A term referring to the assumption that a criminal career begins early in life and that people who are deviant at a very young age are those most likely to persist in crime.

early predelinquent intervention and prevention A range of programs designed to target children at risk of becoming delinquent based on the identification of early risk factors.

early release *See* **parole.**

early-release program Any inmate release process that includes early parole or sentence reductions.

Earth First! An organization with diffuse origins that suggest its first organized meetings occurred in Santa Cruz, CA, during 1982–1983. It is dedicated to preserving the natural environment and opposes anything that pollutes or undermines it, such as logging, plastics manufacturing, and animal hunting and trapping. It promoted a demonstration at a McDonald's in San Francisco to protest plastic packaging in 1985, and members demonstrated at a Bank of America in Santa Cruz to protest the actions of Big Creek Lumber Company, which sought to harvest wood from California forests. Early founders of Earth First! include Dave Foreman, Howie Wolke, and Mike Roselle, who allegedly established the organization in 1979. The organization has been linked with violent demonstrations and terrorist-like sabotage, such as blowing up power towers, blocking roadways, harassment, threats, and using gunfire to intimidate persons, groups, or organizations from engaging in operations that damage the natural environment. Publishes the *Earth First!* journal.

Earth Liberation Front (ELF) Labeled as the largest and most active U.S.-based terrorist group by the FBI, ELF members caused over $43 million in damage from 1995 to 2002, claiming responsibility for a Vail, CO, ski resort arson incident that caused $40 million in damage and were involved in burning down a 206-unit condominium in San Diego, CA, in August 2003. Also in August 2003, members destroyed or vandalized a large number of vehicles, primarily fuel-inefficient SUVs, at several Los Angeles car dealerships. Although elements of ELF are United Kingdom–based, U.S. ELF was started in the mid-1990s when Earth First! turned away from acts of sabotage in favor of more legally acceptable forms of protest and action. ELF is a highly decentralized organization with many cells, making it difficult for law enforcement officials to infiltrate. Three guiding principles of ELF include inflicting economic damage on those who profit from the destruction and exploitation of the natural environment; revealing to and educating the public on the atrocities committed against the environment and all species within it; and taking all necessary precautions against harming any animal, human or nonhuman. An early leader was Craig Rosebraugh. It is classified as an ecoterrorist organization that uses direct action (economic sabotage) to stop the exploitation and destruction of the natural environment.

Eastern Penitentiary at Cherry Hill Opened in 1829, this was the first penitentiary to put into effect the Pennsylvania System.

Eastern State Penitentiary A prison in Pennsylvania intended to provide both incarceration and labor. It opened in 1929 and became the model for many other prisons throughout the United States. It was closed in 1971.

Eastman Gang An Irish gang that controlled the Bowery and East River areas of New York City during the early 1900s. Its leader, Edward Eastman, was jailed for robbery and assault convictions.

eavesdropping Surveillance of various forms designed to intercept communications between others.

Ebbinghaus, Hermann (1850–1909) A psychologist who sought to quantify intelligence by designing tests to measure one's ability to memorize. He believed that a correlation exists between criminality and IQ.

ecclesiastical Pertaining to religious laws or institutions.

ecological environment A set of factors correlated with juvenile delinquency, focusing on the community and neighborhood.

ecological fallacy The mistaken tendency to draw inferences about individuals based on aggregate data descriptive of group characteristics.

ecological school of criminology One of several schools of criminology that focus on the spatial distribution of social problems such as crime and delinquency.

ecology The study of the distribution of persons and their activities in time and space.

ecology of crime The geographical and social distribution of crime, as well as the meaning of such distributions.

economic compulsive behavior Behavior that occurs when drug users resort to violence to gain funds to support their drug habits.

economic crime An act in violation of the criminal law designed to bring financial gain to offenders.

economic sanctions Any sanction imposed on convicted offenders that is economically based, such as restitution, fines, and requiring payment of court costs.

economism A policy of controlling white-collar crime through monetary incentives and sanctions.

ecotage Civil disobedience targeting environmental agencies or companies that exploit natural resources.

ecoterrorism Violent and property crimes committed in the name of preserving the environment and other natural resources.

ecoterrorist One who engages in ecoterrorism.

ECPA Electronic Communications Privacy Act.

Ecstasy (MDMA) A methamphetamine compound (3,4 methylene dioxymethamphetamine) that produces stimulation and psychedelic effects. It was used clinically until 1988, when it was classified as a controlled substance. It is presently a recreational illicit drug in tablet or capsule form. Also known as X or E.

ectomorph A body type characterized by thinness and delicacy described by William Sheldon. *See also* **Sheldon, William.**

Edmunds Act A congressional act passed in 1882 providing for the cessation of polygamy by Mormons in Utah. Anyone practicing polygamy was prohibited from holding public office, prosecuted, and punished.

educational environment A set of factors correlated with juvenile delinquency, focusing on the juvenile's school, attitudes toward education, academic behavior, and performance.

educational release Temporary unescorted leaves from prison or jail to attend courses at nearby schools. *See also* **work (and educational) release, work/study release.**

educator In probation and parole, a probation or parole officer who works with clients to improve their deficiencies, usually by networking with various community agencies and assisting clients in receiving needed services to meet their needs; in education, one trained in a specialized field of expertise who professes to or teaches others. An educator possesses academic credentials of at least a bachelor's degree in a given field, but more often possesses advanced or graduate degrees such as a master's degree, Ph.D., J.D., or Ed.D.

EFT crime Any violation of the law that would not have occurred except for the presence of an electronic fund transfer system.

e.g. (*exempli gratia*) "For example" (Latin).

egalitarian families Families in which husbands and wives share power at home. Daughters gain a kind of freedom similar to that of sons, and their law-violating behaviors mirror those of their brothers.

Egan's Rats An early Irish organized crime gang organized by Jellyroll Egan, which was the forerunner of St. Louis, MO's contemporary Cosa Nostra.

ego The part of one's personality that represents the identity of the individual and actual behavior.

ego identity According to psychologist Erik Erikson, ego identity is formed when persons develop a firm sense of who they are and what they stand for.

egress An exit location from a building or other structure.

eight ball One-eighth of an ounce of cocaine; also, a gang graffiti symbol that shows whether rival gangs such as the Crips and Black Gangster Disciples are aligned or in a state of friction. If the eight ball is drawn or displayed intact, the gangs are aligned; if it is cracked or drawn through, then there is dissension among the groups. When the hand sign for the Crips is brought together with the pitchfork hand sign, it forms an eight ball.

18th Street Gang A Los Angeles, CA, street gang considered the largest in Los Angeles County during the 1990s, with over 20,000 members. It is made up of a collection of about 20 smaller gangs, with the gang stronghold and oldest barrio located in the 18th Street barrios in South Los Angeles, between Vernon (north) and Slauson (south) along Vermont Avenue. The gang consists predominantly of Mexicans, Chicanos, Salvadoreans, and some African Americans. It has been linked with at least 154 homicides between 1985 and 1995, including the murder of a Los Angeles Police Department officer in September 1999. The Los Angeles district attorney's office obtained three gang injunctions against the 18th Street Gang in 2002, prompting greater scrutiny by law enforcement.

Eighth Amendment The amendment to the U.S. Constitution that prohibits excessive bail and cruel and unusual punishment. *See also* **Bill of Rights.**

e-jurors Prospective jurors who are notified of court appearances as veniremen via the Internet. The Internet can be used by such prospective jurors to request exemption from jury duty or to reschedule their court appearances. Such prospective jurors could also be blended in with traditionally selected prospective jurors to create diversity and minimize the biasing effects toward those possessing Internet access.

elaboration A method of introducing other variables to an analysis in order to determine the links between the independent and dependent variables.

elder abuse The physical, mental, or emotional abuse of an older person, most often a parent or grandparent.

electrical equipment conspiracy A major price-fixing conspiracy in the early 1960s by electrical equipment manufacturers, including General Electric and Westinghouse, that resulted in heavy fines and jail terms for various persons involved.

electric chair A device used to electrocute condemned prisoners through the application of high-voltage electricity. A condemned person is strapped into the chair and outfitted with arm, leg, and head devices that emit an electrical charge sufficient to pass through the body and bring about his or her death.

electrified fences Fences used around prison perimeters for security purposes. The wire used in the fencing is electrically charged to deter inmates from escaping.

electrocution One means by which offenders convicted of murder and sentenced to death are killed. Convicted offenders are strapped into chairs wired to an electrical power terminal and given a prolonged jolt of electricity that kills them.

electroencephalogram (EEG) A device that can record the electronic impulses given off by the brain, which are commonly called brain waves.

electronic monitoring (EM), electronic monitoring devices The use of electronic devices (usually anklets or wristlets) that emit electronic signals to monitor offenders, probationers, and parolees. The purpose of their use is to monitor an offender's presence in the environment in which the offender is required to remain or to verify the offender's whereabouts.

electrophoresis A method of separating large molecules, such as DNA fragments or proteins, from mixtures of similar molecules. Electric current is passed through a medium containing the mixture, and each kind of molecule travels through the medium at a different rate, depending on its electrical charge and size. The method is used in forensics for identifying DNA from one or more donors.

element of the offense Any conduct, circumstance, condition, or state of mind that, in combination with other conduct, circumstances, conditions, and states of mind, constitutes an unlawful act.

eligible for parole The qualification of an incarcerated person to be freed short of serving his or her full sentence. A parole board determines an inmate's early-release eligibility.

elimination prints Fingerprints taken from those who may have been in or around a crime scene to distinguish the prints of innocent persons from those of possible criminal suspects.

elite prisoners Convicts who are given special privileges and status by institutional authority.

Elizabethan Poor Law Statutes passed by the British Parliament in 1603 to provide for the poor by giving them financial assistance.

Elizabeth Fry Center A diversion program for female offenders operated in San Francisco, CA.

Elliott, Delbert Elliott, together with David Huizinga and Suzanne Ageton, developed the integrated theory, which holds that persons experience perceptions of strain, suffer from inadequate socialization, and live in socially disorganized areas. When these factors exist simultaneously, youths develop weak bonds with conventional groups and some seek out delinquent persons to emulate, to receive approval. Eventual bonding with delinquent peer groups completes the process whereby one becomes a delinquent. This theory is extensively discussed in *Explaining Delinquency and Drug Use* (1985).

Ellsworth, Oliver (1745–1807) Chief justice of the U.S. Supreme Court (1796–1800). Born in Windsor, CT, Ellsworth entered Yale in 1762 but transferred to the College of New Jersey (later Princeton) during his second year. He received an A.B. degree, worked on a law degree, and was admitted to the bar in 1771. He became Connecticut's state attorney, and subsequently became one of Connecticut's state representatives. He represented Connecticut at the Continental Congress, and was a signer of the Declaration of Independence in 1776. He worked on the Articles of Confederation and proposed an amendment to use "United States" as the official designation of the new country, and served on the first Committee of Five, which drafted the U.S. Constitution. He opposed the abolition of the foreign slave trade and framed a bill organizing the federal judiciary. Ellsworth was appointed chief justice of the U.S. Supreme Court in 1796, and served in that position until 1800. He was later appointed ambassador to France, after which he retired from public life and service in 1801, and died in 1807.

Elmira Reformatory The first true reformatory, built in 1876. Its first superintendent was Zebulon Brockway, a rehabilitation and reformation advocate who promoted educational training and cultivation of vocational skills and believed in prisoner reformation. The approach was questionably successful.

emancipation Giving up the care, custody, welfare, and financial support of a minor child by renouncing parental duties. Emancipated juveniles have more legal responsibilities equivalent to those of adults. An earlier use of the term stemmed from the 1863 Emancipation Proclamation, which freed slaves from bondage.

embargo Any governmental effort to restrict the flow of commerce, usually from a foreign country.

embedded Inserted into some group to report on its activities; in the military, news correspondents were embedded into various military units to report the news as it was happening during the Iraq war in 2003.

embezzlement A crime involving withholding or withdrawing, converting, or misappropriating, without consent, funds entrusted to an agent, such as a bank or bank officer.

embracery An attempt to influence a jury to vote a certain way in determining the guilt or innocence of the defendant, usually through bribes or promises.

embryo A human fetus in its first trimester following conception.

emergency crowding provisions Policies that alleviate prison overcrowding by making inmates eligible for release in a shorter time period.

Emergency Programs Center The office that coordinates activities of the U.S. Department of Justice relative to civil disorder, domestic terrorism, and extortion or theft and responds to security threats to public events. It is headquartered in Washington, DC.

emergency release procedure A legal means to reduce the prison population when it reaches a certain size, usually defined as a percentage of capacity, by permitting earlier-than-normal consideration for parole or earlier-than-specified mandatory release dates through the award of additional good time.

emergency searches Warrantless searches conducted by police officers that are justified on the basis of some immediate and overriding need, such as public safety, the likely escape of a dangerous suspect, or the removal or destruction of evidence.

emergency strikes Work stoppages that harm the public interest. Usually, such strikes are carried out by persons whose work directly affects the public interest, such as firemen, police officers, and sanitation workers.

eminent domain The legal authorization for government to commandeer private property for its own use.

emotional numbing A condition in which officers distance themselves from a stressful incident and make an effort not to feel anything. They deny having an emotional component, and therefore give the appearance that they are in a state of shock, but usually say, however, that they are in control and are having no problems dealing with the situation.

empathy The ability to sympathize with the feelings of another or to put oneself in another's place in order to feel like and be sympathetic toward that person.

empirical Amenable to the senses; based on scientific observation and established factual information.

empirical data Data based on observation, experience, or experiment.

empirical generalizations Facts; observable regularities of human or social behavior.

employee-assistance program A program used by some police departments to help police officers or their family members with problems such as drug abuse, alcoholism, and emotional difficulties.

employee crime An illegal act committed against a business or other organization by an employee of that business or organization.

employee-maturity theory A mode of leadership stressing the emotional and educational maturation of subordinates; a collaborative relation between supervisors and subordinates, in which subordinates are given emotional consideration and involved in decision making through feedback solicited by supervisors.

employee theft The unauthorized taking of goods or services from a business or organization by one who works for that organization.

Employer Prison Industries Model, employer model In this model, the private sector owns and manages the business employing inmates to produce its goods and services.

employment prison A prison for low-risk offenders that allows inmates to work at jobs outside the prison during the day, but requires them to return to prison after work. *See also* **work (and educational) release, work/study release.**

empowerment Empowerment is the essence of both organizational mission and value statements. It permits employees the latitude to perform at their highest levels, authorizing them to make any decisions within the scope of their work or employment.

empty hand control techniques Control techniques that do not involve weapons, ranging from gently guiding inmates, to techniques that temporarily immobilize them, to force such as kicks or strikes used against aggressive inmates.

enabler A probation or parole officer who seeks to instruct and assist offenders to deal with problems as they arise in the community and assists clients to find support groups and necessary therapy to overcome personal problems; also, someone who assists others to facilitate a crime or other enterprise.

en banc "In the bench" (French); a term referring to a session of the court, usually an appellate court, in which all of the judges assigned to the court participate.

endomorph A body type characterized by fatness and softness described by Sheldon William. *See also* **Sheldon, William.**

enforcement *See* **law enforcement.**

Enforcement Acts Congressional action passed in 1870–1871 to enforce the Fourteenth and Fifteenth Amendments. It was aimed at groups such as the Ku Klux Klan, an organization adhering to the belief that blacks are inferior to whites and should not be entitled to the same privileges, and provided for severe penalties for those convicted of acts against minorities.

enforcement costs The financial cost of crime that results from the money spent on various criminal-justice agencies.

Enforcer In the Muir Typology, a type of police officer who is both cynical and coercive (from William Ker Muir, Jr.'s 1977 work, *Police: Streetcorner Politicians*); in the Broderick Typology, a type of police officer who is ends-oriented and least likely to choose or recommend a police career (from J. Broderick's 1977 work, *Police in a Time of Change*). *See also* **Muir Typology; Broderick Typology.**

enforcer A probation or parole officer work-role orientation in which officers see themselves as enforcement officers charged with regulating client behaviors.

enforcer demeanor The negative attitude displayed by correctional officers in public because they believe it is expected of them.

Engels, Friedrich (1820–1895) An associate of Karl Marx who collaborated in the formulation of economic determinism and the conflict perspective and in the writing of the *Communist Manifesto* (1848). Engels also wrote *The Condition of the Working Class in England* in 1844. He was a German social revolutionary and a member of the Communist League, who viewed society as a class struggle between those who own the means of production (the bourgeoisie) and those who work for them (the proletariat). According to Engels, conflict arises between these two classes because of conflicting vested interests: profit versus survival. Crime is also a function of social demoralization: workers become caught up in a milieu of frustration leading to violence and crime; thus, the capitalist system turns workers into criminals despite their will to act in conventional ways.

English common law *See* **common law.**

English Penal Servitude Act An act passed by British Parliament in 1853 authorizing the establishment of rehabilitative programs for inmates and gradually eliminating transportation as a form of punishment.

enhancement Any specific aspect of a crime or a perpetrator's role in its commission that would add to the seriousness of the offense and possibly extend the period of punishment imposed upon conviction.

Enoch Arden law A statute permitting someone to remarry another, provided that one's spouse has been missing or absent for a period of seven successive years and is presumed dead.

entail The law originating in Medieval England providing for the transfer of property to one's bequeathed heirs upon his or her death.

enterprise Any person, partnership, corporation, organization, or association.

enterprise syndicate An organized crime group that profits from the sale of illegal goods and services, such as narcotics, pornography, and prostitution.

entrance wound An intrusion in human tissue created when penetrated by a bullet or other projectile, or a knife or other object.

entrapment Activity by law enforcement officers that suggests, encourages, or aids others in the commission of crimes that would ordinarily not have occurred without officer intervention; also, a defense used by defendants to show that an otherwise criminal act would not have occurred without police intervention, assistance, or encouragement.

entrepreneur One willing to take risks for profit in the marketplace.

entry, gaining entry Accessing any automobile, home, or business, legally or otherwise.

environmental crime(s) Destruction or contamination of the environment through neglect or purposeful action.

Environmental Protection Agency (EPA) An organization established in 1970 and charged with protecting the environment that investigates allegations of different types of pollution and is responsible for oversight and enforcement of legislation pertaining to environment and the health and safety of citizens stemming from environmental hazards. It is headquartered in Washington, DC.

ephedrine A stimulant closely related to methamphetamine, found in common cold and allergy medications such as Sudafed.

epidemic Widespread contagion of a disease or other socially harmful phenomenon such as crime in a specific area within a specified period of time.

episodic criminal A person who only occasionally engages in criminal conduct.

epistemology The study of the foundations of knowledge, especially with reference to its limits and validity.

equability The principle that justice is applied evenhandedly across a jurisdiction.

equal employment opportunity The policy of selection and advancement of personnel on the basis of merit, without regard to criteria such as race or gender. The Equal Employment Opportunity Commission (EEOC) was created in 1964 by Congress under Title VII of the Civil Rights Act of 1964 to enforce civil rights of employees.

Equal Employment Opportunity Commission (EEOC) The federal body that oversees the hiring of minority and female correctional officers and others to reduce discrimination.

equal protection The clause of the Fourteenth Amendment to the U.S. Constitution guaranteeing to all citizens equal protection of the law, without regard to race, color, gender, class, origin, or religion. *See also* **Bill of Rights.**

equilibrium model An explanation of organization processes that stresses the importance of motivational factors to encourage member participation in organizational activities.

equipotentiality The view that all people are equal at birth and are thereafter influenced by their environment.

equitable action Any lawsuit raised in a court of equity that pertains to a third party not directly involved in the lawsuit but who may benefit from the results of the litigation.

equitable right Any entitlement that is enforceable in a court of equity.

equity The concept that the relationships between men, women, and society should be just and fair and in accordance with contemporary morality.

Equity Fund scandal A corporate swindle in which the Equity Fund created thousands of fake insurance policies, resulting in reinsurers and stockholders losing millions of dollars.

equity jurisdiction The power of a court of equity to hear and decide certain types of civil cases.

equity of redemption The interest retained in property by a mortgagor.

equity theory A theory that posits that workers desire equitable treatment when performing their jobs and compare themselves with others who perform similar work tasks, that their work output is a product of their job input, and that rewards as outcomes should be equivalent to the rewards of others who expend similar energy to reach the same goals. Workers are content to the extent that they perceive that equity exists between all employees who perform similar work and are rewarded by the system equally.

equivalent group hypothesis A hypothesis similar to the victimization explanation of crime, which suggests a high-risk lifestyle places certain persons in positions where they may be victimized more easily. The notion is that victims and criminals share similar characteristics because they are not actually separate groups. Thus, retaliation by one victimized group or person is great because victim and offender are equivalent in their power to victimize each other.

equivocate To conceal the truth; to relate a version of events in a misleading way; to use ambiguous words.

error in fact Any error made in a court of law that may or may not affect a judicial decision or judgment.

error in law Any error made by the court that may affect the case outcome (e.g., permitting the prosecution to show numerous bloody photographs of a crime scene to inflame the jury and enhance a defendant's likelihood of being convicted and sentenced harshly). *See also* **harmless error; reversible error.**

escalation An increase in the amount of crime an offender commits as well as the progressive seriousness of offending.

escape Any flight or unauthorized departure of a confined person from any type of criminal-supervision facility, such as a jail or prison, community-corrections agency, probation or parole department, halfway house, or electronic-monitoring/house-arrest program.

escape artist One who is skilled in fleeing from secure places, such as jails or prisons, or from handcuffs or straightjackets.

escape from lawful imprisonment Fleeing from incarceration without authorization.

Escobedo, Danny (1938?–) The subject of *Escobedo v. Illinois* (1964), in which Escobedo's murder conviction was overturned because police refused him access to an attorney when he requested one (a constitutional right). Escobedo subsequently confessed to police about his involvement in the murder, but his confession was excluded and the murder conviction was overturned by the U.S. Supreme Court.

espionage Illegal acquisition of secret government information by a citizen who transmits such information to a foreign power. *See also* **industrial espionage.**

espionage, industrial The act of transmitting information from one company to another by an agent or employee of the first company, in exchange for money or other rewards or inducements. It may involve giving secret product formulae to a competing company.

Espionage Act A 1917 act limiting civil liberties which was passed by Congress during World War I as a result of war hysteria and fear. It provided for a 20-year incarceration term for those convicted of disloyalty or draft evasion.

essoiner A person who appears in court to present an excuse for the absence of the defendant.

establishment clause The portion of the First Amendment that prevents government support or endorsement of particular religions. *See also* **Bill of Rights.**

Estes scandal Billie Sol Estes, a Texas entrepeneur, was indicted in 1962 for rigging cotton-acreage allotments and contracts for storing government surpluses. Several federal officials were incriminated and Estes was convicted. His conviction was subsequently set aside because bias and undue media coverage of the trial prevented a fair trial.

estoppel A legal means of preventing someone from doing something.

ethics The science or philosophy of appropriate human conduct.

ethics, law enforcement Codes of honor tacitly or overtly observed by law enforcement officers, upholding both the spirit and letter of the law and fulfilling the mission statement of police agencies.

Ethics in Government Act A 1978 act requiring financial disclosures by public officials, showing where and how they obtained their money and property.

ethnic cleansing A policy of some countries or factions to systematically purge or annihilate members of certain races, ethnic groups, cultures, or national origins.

ethnic/racial organizations Ethnically or racially based prison organizations that focus on cultural awareness and education. They are largely populated by African Americans, Hispanics, and Native Americans.

ethnic succession theory The view that control of organized crime passes from one ethnic group to another.

ethnocentrism, ethnocentricity The perception that one's own culture or cultural group is the best culture or group.

ethnography The systematic description of social phenomena as the result of close observation and interaction.

etiology The study of the origins of events, such as crimes.

et ux "And wife" (Latin).

eugenics, eugenic criminology A science based on the principle of heredity, having for its purpose the improvement of the human race. It is largely discounted by contemporary theorists, who consider it pseudoscience.

European Police Office (Europol) The integrated police intelligence-gathering and -dissemination arm of the member nations of the European Union.

euthanasia "Mercy killing"; causing the death of persons suffering from incurable illnesses by administering lethal injections of deadly substances or withdrawing life-support systems from such persons with the intent of ending pain and suffering.

evaluation research Investigations that attempt to answer practical and applied questions; any investigation geared to test the efficacy of a strategy or intervention in relation to some event, such as delinquency or criminality.

Evarts Act of 1891 Introduced in 1891 and sponsored by New Jersey lawyer William M. Evarts, this act created circuit courts of appeal to hear appeals emanating from the U.S. district courts.

event history analysis A set of statistical methods used to analyze change of a phenomenon from one state to another.

evidence All materials or means admissible in a court of law to produce in the minds of the court or jury a belief concerning the matter at issue.

evidence, aliunde Extraneous evidence.

evidence, associative Any type of evidence linking a criminal suspect with the actual crime; any type of evidence found on a suspect's person that places him or her at the crime scene or indicates that he or she may be the crime's perpetrator. Such evidence is not considered conclusive of guilt, but merely shows that a suspect has knowledge about the crime or may have been present when it was committed.

evidence, corroborating Any collateral evidence that enhances the value of other evidence.

evidence, derivative Any evidence deduced from other evidence from a crime scene. It may be associative evidence.

evidence, material Germane evidence concerning a case or legal matter. It must relate to the issue or charge directly or indirectly.

evidence, prejudicial Any evidence presented in court that may overwhelm jurors in ways that cause them to view the case subjectively rather than objectively.

evidence given in a former proceeding Any admissible evidence that has been presented in a former trial or at some other legal proceeding, perhaps by a witness who is now dead who has made or given incriminating statements in the past that are in the record.

evidence rule, best *See* **best evidence rule.**

evidence wrongfully obtained Illegally obtained evidence may be tangible objects, written or oral admissions, or other forms of information or documentation that are admissible against defendants in a court of law. Some exceptions include evidence obtained that falls within the scope of the exclusionary rule or fruits of the poisonous tree doctrines.

evidentiary Pertaining to the rules of evidence or the evidence in a particular case.

evidentiary items Any secondary evidence not directly used in a crime but which may support a circumstantial case. It does not include contraband, weapons, or anything directly connected with the crime itself.

evil-causes-evil fallacy A faulty belief that evil products, such as delinquent behavior, must have evil antecedents, such as child abuse or emotional trauma.

eviscerate To remove the intestines of a victim.

evolutionary theory An explanation of the existence of aggression and violent behavior as positive adaptive behaviors in human evolution. These traits allowed their bearers to reproduce disproportionately, which has had an effect on the human gene pool.

examination, cross- *See* **cross-examination.**

examination, direct *See* **direct examination.**

examining trial A preliminary hearing; a hearing for the purpose of determining probable cause that a crime has been committed and some identified suspect has committed it.

exception An objection to a ruling or to comments made by the judge or attorneys.

exceptional circumstances doctrine Under this policy, courts hear only those cases brought by inmates in which the circumstances indicate a total disregard for human dignity and deny hearings to less serious abuses. Cases allowed access to the courts usually involve situations of total denial of medical care.

excessive force Any exceptional force extending beyond that necessary to disable suspects or take them into custody through arrest.

exchange A mutual transfer of resources; also, a balance of profits and deficits that flow from behavior based on decisions as to the values and costs of alternatives.

exchange rates An approach to sentencing implemented by a sentencing commission that emphasizes interchangeability of punishments. For instance, three days under house arrest might be considered equal to one day of incarceration.

excluded offenses Crimes, some minor and others very serious, that are automatically excluded from juvenile-court jurisdiction.

exclusionary rule A rule that provides that evidence obtained in violation of the privileges guaranteed by the U.S. Constitution may be excluded at trial. Dropsy testimony, stemming from *Mapp v. Ohio* (1963), suggests that some evidence obtained by police officers may be contrived in order to secure convictions against the accused. Such evidence may be suppressed or excluded because of this rule.

exclusive jurisdiction Specific jurisdiction over particular kinds of cases. The U.S. Supreme Court has authority to hear matters involving the diplomats of other countries who otherwise enjoy great immunity from most other courts. Family court may have exclusive jurisdiction to hear child custody cases.

ex-con A person who has served time in prison but is no longer incarcerated.

exculpatory evidence Evidence tending to exonerate a person of allegations of wrongdoing.

excusable homicide Death from some accident or misfortune that may occur during some lawful act.

excuse A defense to a criminal charge in which the accused person maintains that he or she lacked the intent to commit the crime.

execution A legal enforcement of the death penalty as a sentence against an offender convicted of a capital crime. *See table p. 93.*

execution, methods of Ways of terminating the life of a person convicted of a capital offense and who has been sentenced to death, including lethal injection, electrocution, lethal gas, hanging, and firing squad. *See table p. 93.*

execution, minimum age for The youngest age at which a person can commit a capital offense and suffer the death penalty in any jurisdiction that uses capital punishment. The U.S. Supreme Court declared in *Wilkins v. Missouri* (1989) and *Stanford v. Kentucky* (1989) that 16 is the minimum age at which one can commit a capital offense and then suffer the death penalty as the maximum punishment in those jurisdictions with death-penalty statutes. Individual states have different age minimums for death-penalty cases, such as 17 or 18. *See table p. 94.*

executioner One who puts condemned prisoners to death.

execution of a warrant, execution and return of a warrant Action by court officers to serve a warrant on a defendant in a court action; also, action of fulfilling the demands of a warrant, such as a warrant to search premises, persons, or personal effects and seize one or more items sought by the warrant.

execution trends in the United States A portrayal over time of the frequency of executions carried out in those states with capital punishment statutes, usually described on an annual basis. *See graph p. 95.*

executive branch That segment of government responsible for the administration, direction, control, and performance of government. Examples of executives are the president of the United States, state governors, and city mayors. Police and correctional subsystems are under the executive branch.

executive clemency or pardon The removal of punishment and legal disabilities of a person by order of an executive, usually the president or a governor. *See also* **pardon.**

executive management team A group of assistant superintendents who specialize in managing certain prison functions such as security, treatment programs, and business operations.

executive model of sentencing A formal statement of goals, a codification of criminal penalties consistent with the goals, and an explicit structure and stated process for implementing sentencing goals.

Methods of Execution, by State, 2002

Lethal Injection		Electrocution	Lethal Gas
Alabama[a]	Nevada	Alabama[a]	Arizona[a,b]
Arizona[a,b]	New Hampshire[a]	Arkansas[a,c]	California[a]
Arkansas[a,c]	New Jersey	Florida[a]	Missouri[a]
California[a]	New Mexico	Kentucky[a,d]	Wyoming[a,e]
Colorado	New York	Nebraska	
Connecticut	North Carolina	Oklahoma[f]	
Delaware[a,g]	Ohio	South Carolina[a]	
Florida[a]	Oklahoma[a]	Tennessee[a,h]	
Georgia	Oregon	Virginia[a]	
Idaho[a]	Pennsylvania		
Illinois	South Carolina[a]		
Indiana	South Dakota	**Hanging**	**Firing Squad**
Kansas	Tennessee[a,h]	Delaware[a,g]	Idaho[a]
Kentucky[a,d]	Texas	New Hampshire[a,i]	Oklahoma[f]
Louisiana	Utah[a]	Washington[a]	Utah[a]
Maryland	Virginia[a]		
Mississippi	Washington[a]		
Missouri[a]	Wyoming[a]		
Montana			

[a]Authorizes two methods of execution.

[b]Authorizes lethal injection for persons sentenced after 11/15/92; for those sentenced before that date, the condemned may select lethal injection or lethal gas.

[c]Authorizes lethal injection for those whose capital offense occurred on or after 7/4/83; for those whose offense occurred before that date, the condemned may select lethal injection or electrocution.

[d]Authorizes lethal injection for persons sentenced on or after 3/31/98; for those sentenced before that date, the condemned may select lethal injection or electrocution.

[e]Authorizes lethal gas if lethal injection is ever held to be unconstitutional.

[f]Authorizes electrocution if lethal injection is ever held to be unconstitutional, and firing squad if both lethal injection and electrocution are held to be unconstitutional.

[g]Authorizes lethal injection for those whose capital offense occurred after 6/13/86; for those whose before that date, the condemned may select lethal injection or hanging.

[h]Authorizes lethal injection for those whose capital offense occurred after 12/31/98; those before that date may select electrocution.

[i]Authorizes hanging only if lethal injection cannot be given.

Source: Bonczar and Snell, *Capital Punishment, 2002,* 4.

Number of Persons Executed, by Jurisdiction, 1930–2002

	Number Executed	
State	Since 1930	Since 1977
U.S. total	4,679	820
Texas	586	289
Georgia	397	31
New York	329	0
California	302	10
North Carolina	286	23
Florida	224	54
South Carolina	190	28
Virginia	179	87
Ohio	177	5
Louisiana	160	27
Alabama	160	25
Mississippi	160	6
Pennsylvania	155	3
Arkansas	142	24
Missouri	121	59
Oklahoma	115	55
Kentucky	105	2
Illinois	102	12
Tennessee	94	1
New Jersey	74	0
Maryland	71	3
Arizona	60	22
Washington	51	4
Indiana	50	9
Colorado	48	1
District of Columbia	40	0
West Virginia	40	0
Nevada	38	9
Federal system	35	2
Massachusetts	27	0
Delaware	25	13
Oregon	21	2
Connecticut	21	0
Utah	19	6
Iowa	18	0
Kansas	15	0
New Mexico	9	1
Montana	8	2
Wyoming	8	1
Nebraska	7	3
Idaho	4	1
Vermont	4	0
New Hampshire	1	0
South Dakota	1	0

Source: Bonczar and Snell, *Capital Punishment, 2002,* 9.

executive order Any presidential proclamation that becomes a law and legally binding.

executive privilege A preventive measure designed to protect the president or the president's staff from Congressional inquiries and interrogation.

executor A person appointed to fulfill the conditions of a will and carry out its provisions.

exemplar A sample of material evidence that may be used to verify the authenticity of other similar evidence.

exemplary project An activity deemed so promising or successful that it should be recognized as worthy of replication by other jurisdictions.

Exemplary Projects Program An initiative sponsored by the Law Enforcement Assistance Administration designed to recognize outstanding innovative efforts to combat crime and provide assistance to crime victims.

Exemplary Rehabilitation Certificates Awards from the Secretary of Labor to military personnel who have been separated from the service under nonhonorable conditions, when it has been determined that such persons have become rehabilitated since they have been discharged from military service.

ex facie "From the appearance" (Latin); apparently; evidently.

exhaustion requirement Under the Prison Litigation Reform Act of 1995, state prisoners are barred from bringing lawsuits against their prison systems in federal district courts until they have exhausted all available remedies for their causes of action in their state appellate courts.

exhibit A piece of evidence, usually obtained from an investigation, admissible for or against a defendant in a trial.

exhibitionism Exposure of one's sexual organs to others in a public place.

exhibitionist One who exposes one's sexual organs to others in a public place.

exhumation Process of removing human remains from their place of burial in order to conduct toxicological tests or other necessary investigative procedures, often to confirm the circumstances surrounding the person's death.

exigent circumstances Circumstances in which quick action is necessitated, such as searches for drugs and other contraband that might be easily destroyed. Such circumstances provide an exception to the exclusionary rule.

exile The expulsion, temporary or permanent, of an individual from a particular area or country as a punishment for wrongdoing; also, one who has been exiled.

exiting A successful disengagement from a previous pattern of criminal behavior.

exitus "Going out" (Latin); death.

exit wound The site and rupture in human tissue at the point where a projectile leaves the body.

ex-offender A probationer or parolee, usually someone who has been processed by the criminal justice system, tried and convicted, served a sentence, and is no longer under the jurisdiction of the criminal justice system.

ex officio "From office" (Latin); by virtue of the office.

Minimum Age Authorized for Capital Punishment, 2002

Age 16 or Less	Age 17	Age 18	None specified
Alabama (16)	Florida	California	Arizona
Arkansas (14)[a]	Georgia	Colorado	Idaho
Delaware (16)	New	Connecticut[b]	Louisiana
Kentucky(16)	Hampshire	Federal	Montana[d]
Mississippi(16)[e]	North	system	Pennsylvania
Missouri(16)	Carolina[c]	Illinois	South
Nevada(16)	Texas	Indiana	Carolina
Oklahoma (16)		Kansas	South
Utah (14)[g]		Maryland	Dakota[f]
Virginia(14)[g]		Nebraska	
Wyoming (16)		New Jersey	
		New Mexico	
		New York	
		Ohio	
		Oregon	
		Tennessee	
		Washington	

Note: Reporting by States reflects interpretations by State attorney generals' offices and may differ from previously reported ages.

[a]See Ark. Code Ann. 9-27-318(c)(2)(Supp. 2001).

[b]See Conn. Gen. Stat. 53a-46a(g)(1).

[c]Age required is 17 unless the murderer was incarcerated for murder when a subsequent murder occurred; then the age may be 14.

[d]Montana law specifies that offenders tried under the capital sexual assault statute be 18 or older. Age may be a mitigating factor for other capital crimes.

[e]The minimum age defined by statute is 13, but the effective age is 16 based on interpretation of U.S. Supreme Court decisions by the Mississippi Supreme Court.

[f]Juveniles may be transferred to adult court. Age can be a mitigating factor.

[g]The minimum age for transfer to adult court by statute is 14, but the effective age is 16 based on interpretation of U.S. Supreme Court decisions by the State attorney general's office.

Source: Bonczar and Snell, *Capital Punishment, 2002*, 4.

---

exonerate To absolve of blame, usually through trial and a finding of "not guilty."

exonerate bail To release a surety on a bail bond.

ex parte "From one side" (Latin); a hearing or examination in the presence of only one party in the case.

expatriation The act of abandoning or forsaking allegiance to one's country.

expectancy theory A theory that casts worker motivation to perform into a performance-outcome framework in which employees are taught by their organizations that hard work and following the rules will lead to desirable outcomes, such as promotion, advancement, and greater recognition.

experience programs Various activities for juveniles who have been adjudicated delinquent or status offenders, including wilderness experiences and other outdoors programs in

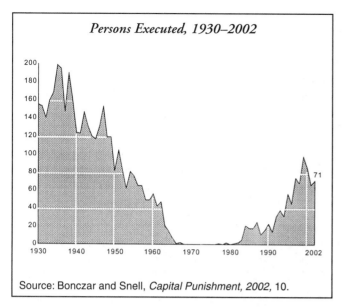

Persons Executed, 1930–2002

Source: Bonczar and Snell, *Capital Punishment, 2002,* 10.

which youths learn self-esteem, survival skills, self-respect, and respect toward others and authority.

experimental group The group receiving the experimental stimulus or program.

expert power Influence based on personal expertise or skills (e.g., one might listen to an expert on gangs and gang prevention in order to eliminate gangs, while a concerned parent might not have expert power there).

expert system Computer hardware and software intended to duplicate the decision-making processes used by skilled investigators in the analysis of evidence and in the recognition of patterns that such evidence might represent.

expert testimony Any oral evidence presented in court by someone who is considered proficient and learned in a given field when such evidence is relevant; testimony provided by an expert witness.

expert witness A witness with expertise or special knowledge in a relevant field pertaining to the case at trial; a witness who is qualified under the Federal Rules of Evidence to offer an opinion about the authenticity or accuracy of reports, who has special knowledge which is relevant to the proceeding; sometimes called a "hired gun."

expiation Offender punishments.

expiration of a sentence Completing the time imposed by a judge. An inmate who serves the entire sentence imposed following conviction experiences an expiration of that sentence.

explanation The systematic and empirical analysis of the antecedent factors that are responsible for the occurrence of an event or behavior.

explicit sentencing policy A formal statement of goals, a codification of criminal penalties consistent with the goals, and an explicit structure and stated process for implementing sentencing goals.

exploitation The use of someone or someone's services that takes advantage of that person, without adequate compensa-

tion or explanation; obtaining work from someone at a disadvantage or in a position where he or she is unable to object to being required to work.

explosive Any volatile material capable of detonating and causing considerable destruction.

explosive bullet Any projectile containing a substance that explodes on impact with a target. Some ammunition has been manufactured in the United States as safety slugs, which are teflon-coated cartridges designed to explode on impact. The result is massive destruction of flesh if a person is struck by such a bullet. These are sometimes known as Glaser Safety Slugs, named after the cartridge designer.

explosive D Named for B.W. Dunn, inventor of the explosive material dunnite, which consists of ammonium picrate. It is used in armor-piercing projectiles because of its low sensitivity to shock or friction when striking metal objects.

explosive ordnance disposal unit A unit whose members have special training and exploratory equipment and are capable of defusing bombs or other explosive devices, as well as supervising the removal of explosive substances to a site where they can be safely destroyed.

explosive residue Remnants of chemicals left behind after an explosion.

explosives classifications A designation system created by the U.S. Department of Transportation. Explosives are graded according to destructive power: Class A explosives include dynamite, nitroglycerin, picric acid, lead azide, and fulminate of mercury; Class B explosives are flammable materials used as propellants; and Class C explosives are less destructive devices containing smaller amounts of materials used in Class A or Class B explosives.

***ex post facto* laws** "From a thing done afterward" (Latin); statutes that retroactively make an act illegal or increase an existing crime's penalty. Such laws are unconstitutional.

expressive crime A crime having no purpose except to accomplish the behavior at hand, as opposed to creating monetary gain.

expressive violence Violence intended not for profit or gain but to vent rage, anger, or frustration.

expropriation State seizure of personal property.

expunge To delete one's arrest record from official sources. In most jurisdictions, juvenile delinquency records are expunged when one reaches the age of majority or adulthood. Records may be reopened at a later date under special circumstances.

***ex rel.* (*ex relatione*)** "By or on the information of" (Latin); used in legal case designations whenever the government acts on behalf of someone who is not in the position of initiating a legal action him- or herself, such as a minor child or a mentally incompetent person.

exsanguination Loss or draining of blood from the body.

extended jurisdiction The policy and practice of maintaining correctional jurisdiction over juveniles after they have reached the age of their majority, usually 18 years of age.

extenuating circumstances Conditions under which offenders might be excused from culpability in criminal conduct.

exterior ballistics The science of ballistics that investigates the motion of projectiles while in flight to determine drops or trajectories of different-sized bullets fired from different weapons with different powder loads over given distances.

extinction A condition in which a crime prevention effort has an immediate impact that then dissipates as criminals adjust to the new conditions.

extortion Unlawfully obtaining or attempting to obtain property of others by threats of eventual injury or death to others, or harm to their property.

extradition Surrender of a person by one jurisdiction to another for the purpose of a criminal prosecution.

extrajudicial Beyond the scope of the court jurisdiction.

extralegal factors Any element of a nonlegal nature. In determining whether law enforcement officers are influenced by particular factors when encountering juveniles on the streets, extralegal factors might include juvenile attitude, politeness, appearance, and dress. Legal factors might include age and specific prohibited acts observed by the officers.

extraneous evidence Document information that is derived from anything about a document other than the document's contents, such as fingerprints on the document or the type of paper used.

extraterritorial operation of laws Although crime is a localized phenomenon in a given country or locality at a particular time and place, persons may be liable for violations of the law in foreign jurisdictions even though they reside elsewhere. Conspiracies may occur across countries, and persons who commit crimes in one country but live in another are subject to prosecution in the country where the crime was committed and may be extradited for purposes of a criminal prosecution.

extremist group Any aggregate of persons whose purpose is to bring about radical changes in government or policies to which they are opposed. They may engage in violent conduct, even conduct resulting in death, to bring about the group's goals or ends.

extrinsic evidence Any external evidence not directly embodied within a document, agreement, or object.

extroversion Hans Eysenck's term meaning a dimension of the human personality describing individuals who are sensation-seeking, dominant, and assertive.

extrovert A person who behaves impulsively and doesn't have the ability to examine motives and behavior.

eyewitness A witness who actually saw a crime committed.

eyewitness testimony Information given in court by someone who saw a crime take place or has important information about who committed the crime.

Eysenck, Hans (1916–1997) A criminologist and psychologist who studied criminal personality systems, and the author of *Crime and Personality* (1977). He regards criminal behavior as conditioned reflexes in response to apprehension of either pleasure or pain.

F

facial reconstruction The process of using clay, hair, or other materials to restore a human skull as closely as possible to a likeness of a deceased victim for purposes of identification.

facilitators of crime Materials and conditions other than human agents (e.g., accomplices or accessories) that encourage or make possible the commission of crimes that might otherwise not occur. They include alcohol or drug ingestion, access to firearms, and conditions of ineffective guardianship.

facility security level The nature and number of physical design barriers designed to control inmate behavior and prevent escapes.

facsimile A copy of an original object or document.

fact A true statement; an actual event.

fact finder, finder of fact The jury in a case, criminal or otherwise. A judge may also be the fact finder in a bench trial. Arbitration proceedings may also use fact finders to conduct investigations.

fact finding, finding of fact In collective bargaining, the intervention of a third party to determine the source of a disagreement or impasse; also, gathering evidence for the purpose of resolving a disputed claim; also, a court's determination of the facts presented as evidence in a case, which have been affirmed by one party and denied by the other.

fact-finding hearing As applied to juvenile court, any hearing to determine whether the allegations in a petition are supported. *See also* **adjudication hearing, adjudication inquiry.**

factual question A question designed to elicit objective information from respondents regarding their background, environments, and habits.

failure to appear When a defendant fails to present him- or herself for trial or some other formal proceeding, such as arraignment or a preliminary hearing or examination.

Fair Housing and Equal Credit Opportunity A provision of Title VIII of the Civil Rights Act of 1968 to ensure equality of opportunity regarding the purchase, sale, rental, or financing of housing; an antidiscrimination measure to deter discrimination in anything related to the purchase, habitation, or sale of dwellings or other types of property.

fair sentencing Sentencing practices that incorporate fairness for both victims and offenders. Fairness is said to be achieved by implementing principles of proportionality, equity, social debt, and truth in sentencing.

fair-trade laws State statutes permitting manufacturers of brand-name goods to establish minimum prices for resale of products.

fait accompli "Accomplished fact" (French); an action after the fact not subject to subsequent litigation or negotiation.

faith-based programs In criminal justice, crime or delinquency prevention or intervention programs promoted by or affiliated with the faith community.

Faith in Families Multi-Systematic Therapy Program (MST) Operated by the Henry and Rilla White Foundation in Bronson, FL, this program attempts to modify youth behaviors by working with their interpersonal environment, including family, therapists, and peer groups. Subjects taught include self-control, anger management, self-reflectiveness, and problem-solving skills.

Falcon and Snowman Names given to Christopher Boyce and Andrew Dalton Lee, two spies who sold U.S. military secrets to the Soviets during the 1970s.

FALN A radical Puerto Rican group dedicated to achieving independence from the United States.

false advertising Commercial advertising that is deceptive and misleading.

false arrest Unlawful physical restraint of someone by a law enforcement officer. It may include confinement or brief detention in a jail for no valid legal reason.

False Claims Act Congressional action during and following the Civil War to provide incentives to whistle-blowers or persons who give information about misdeeds of their organizations or groups. Their action results in monetary awards of up to 30 percent of damage claims awarded by the government.

false confession An admission given to law enforcement officers by a person who did not commit the crime.

false impersonation Pretending to be someone else, usually to perpetrate a crime.

false imprisonment The act of unlawfully detaining or restraining a person.

false knuckles Any set of finger rings attached to a transverse piece, to be worn over the front of the hand for use as a weapon, and constructed in such a manner that when striking another person with the closed fist, considerable physical damage may be inflicted upon the person struck.

false negative error In research, a prediction that an event, such as delinquency, will not occur, but it does occur. *See also* **false positive error.**

false negatives Offenders who are predicted to be nonviolent or not dangerous according to various risk prediction devices, but who turn out to be dangerous or pose serious public risk.

false positive error In research, a prediction that an event, such as delinquency, will occur, but it does not occur. *See also* **false negative error.**

false positives Offenders who are predicted to be dangerous or who pose serious public risk according to various prediction devices and instruments, but who are not dangerous and do not pose public risks.

false pretenses, obtaining property by Inducing victims to part with their property through trickery, deceit, or misrepresentation.

familicide Mass murders where a spouse and one or more children are slain.

family courts Courts of original jurisdiction that typically handle the entire range of family problems, from juvenile delinquency to divorce cases.

family group conference, group conference A form of restorative justice that involves a meeting of the offender, the victim, their families, and other supportive persons to engage in a dialogue intended to bring about restoration and healing.

family group homes A combination of foster care and a group home in which a juvenile is placed in a private group home run by a single family rather than by a professional staff.

family model Established under the Juvenile Law of 1948, bodies exist in all Japanese jurisdictions and hear matters pertaining to juvenile delinquency, child abuse and neglect, and child custody matters. Both status offenders and delinquents appear before family court judges, who are similar to juvenile court judges in U.S. jurisdictions. Family court judges have considerable discretionary authority to decide cases within the *parens patriae* context.

family visits Private overnight visits between inmates and close family members, such as wives and husbands, parents, grandparents, and children.

fantasy A recurring mental image conjured up by many sex offenders and serial murderers as a prelude to an offense.

farm prisons Incarcerative facilities designed on farmland that are much like the plantations of the pre–Civil War era.

Farnham, Eliza (1815–1864) The matron at Mount Pleasant prison in 1844, which was the first separate prison for women in the United States. She transformed the prison into a model facility with a homelike environment.

Farrington, David P. (1944–) A criminologist who developed a theory of delinquent development describing both nonoffenders and desisters. He wrote about his theory in the *Cambridge Study in Delinquent Development* (1983), an examination of 411 London boys. Unemployment was found related to certain forms of offending. Desisting was associated with physical relocation. Considerable stress is given to childhood factors as predictors of teenage antisocial behavior. Adolescents are "energized" to act in deviant ways, and their life events influence their behavior. Offending is viewed as situational, and criminality is variable over time, as one ages. Adult behavior is a function of both internal and external factors.

fascism An autocratic form of government in which power is centralized in the hands of one or a few persons, and in which opposition to government policies is aggressively repressed, as in a dictatorship.

FAST Track Program A rural and urban intervention program targeting girls and boys of many ethnicities, designed to treat severe and chronic misconduct problems for high-risk children.

fat cats Persons who derive enormous profits from corporate crimes, including executives, attorneys, and others who benefit directly or indirectly from white-collar criminal enterprises.

FBI *See* **Federal Bureau of Investigation (FBI).**

FBI Academy Established in 1935 at Quantico, VA, to provide agents with training in a wide variety of areas, including firearms, fingerprinting, hostage negotiation, organized crime, computer fraud, and other topics. The Academy presently offers training programs to interested law enforcement agencies and officers.

FBI field training Any course work or activities offered by FBI agents/instructors relating to any and all topics taught at the FBI Academy.

FBI Laboratory A comprehensive facility headquartered in Washington, DC, that assists law enforcement agencies at all levels in criminal investigations with analysis of evidence, forensic examinations, and related matters.

FBI museum Headquartered in Washington, DC, a museum that features weapons, photographs, memorabilia, and other highlights of FBI investigations of historical significance.

FBI National Academy Founded on July 29, 1935, and headquartered in Quantico, VA, this program had graduated over 37,000 persons by 2003. It works to improve law enforcement standards, knowledge, and cooperation throughout the world and provides a wide range of leadership and specialized training, as well as the opportunity for professional law enforcement officers to share ideas, techniques, and experiences. Its curriculum focuses on leadership and management training and consists of courses related to leadership development, behavioral science, law, communication, forensic science, and health and fitness.

fear of crime The real or perceived extent to which the general citizenry is concerned about their chances of being victimized by criminals.

feasance Performing an act.

Federal Alcohol Control Board An organization established by Congress in 1933 to regulate, brand, and grade all alcoholic beverages and to regulate the interstate commerce of alcoholic beverages. It was renamed the Federal Alcohol Administration.

federal appeals courts Circuit courts of appeal in the federal government. There are 13 circuit courts of appeal that hear appeals from U.S. district courts, which are the basic trial courts for federal civil and criminal matters.

Federal Aviation Act A congressional act passed in 1968 that made it a crime to enter an aircraft with a concealed weapon.

Federal Aviation Administration (FAA) Established under the authority of the U.S. Department of Transportation, this organization promulgates safety regulations for the operation of aircraft, including standards for personnel who operate aircraft. It also regulates aircraft manufacture and air navigation facilities.

Federal Bureau of Investigation (FBI) The FBI was established in 1908 through the Department of Justice Appropriation Act as the department's enforcement arm. It is an investigative agency that enforces all federal criminal laws and annually compiles information for the *Uniform Crime Reports*. The FBI maintains extensive files on criminals and assists other law agencies. (The initials FBI also stand for fidelity, bravery, and integrity.)

Federal Bureau of Prisons (FBOP) Established in 1930 and charged with providing suitable quarters for prisoners and the safekeeping of all persons convicted of offenses against the United States. It also contracts with local jails and state prisons for confinement of federal prisoners where there are insufficient federal facilities in the geographical area in which the person has been convicted.

Federal Communications Commission (FCC) The agency regulating interstate communications and facilities, including telephone, telegraph, cable, radio, television, and computers. It is headquartered in Washington, DC.

federal court system The four-tiered structure of federal courts, including the U.S. Supreme Court, the circuit courts of appeal, the U.S. district courts, and the U.S. magistrate.

Federal Deposit Insurance Corporation (FDIC) An agency created in 1933 that provides insurance for all deposits in federally insured banks and investigates robberies or embezzlements in such banks and other federal criminal violations pertaining to banking and bank laws.

federal district courts Basic trial courts for the federal government that try all criminal cases and have extensive jurisdiction. District judges are appointed by the president of United States with the advice, counsel, and approval of the Senate. Cases from these courts are appealed to particular circuit courts of appeal. *See figure p. 99.*

Federal Drugs, Alcohol, and Crime Clearinghouse Network A Washington, DC–based organization providing information on a wide variety of crimes related to drugs and alcohol that furnishes publications to interested persons and organizations.

Federal Emergency Management Agency (FEMA) An organization established in 1983 to investigate arson-related crimes and disseminate information about arson. Since 1983, its duties have expanded to include furnishing temporary operations and control centers in the event of sudden loss of government ability to communicate with different agencies and the general public.

Federal Firearm Act A 1934 congressional act regulating the possession of automatic weapons and other firearms. The National Firearms Act was subsequently passed in 1938. The Gun Control Act, passed in 1968, prohibited interstate retailing of all firearms. The goal of the legislation was to prevent or deter persons who cannot legally own or possess firearms, such as convicted felons, from ordering firearms by mail under false names and identifications.

Federal *Habeas Corpus* Statute Title 28, Section 2241 of the U.S. Code, permitting probationers, parolees, and inmates of prisons and jails to challenge the fact, length, and conditions of their confinement, or placement in particular facilities or programs.

federal-interest computer A computer that is the property of the federal government, belongs to a financial institution, and is located in a state other than the one in which a criminal perpetrator is operating.

Federal Judicial Center A research and education center of the federal judicial system in the United States. Established in 1967 and controlled by a board chaired by the chief justice of the United States, it offers education and training programs for judges, attorneys, and nonjudicial court employees, including personnel of clerks and probation offices.

federal judicial system An organization of federal courts, including the U.S. Supreme Court, circuit courts of appeal, U.S. district courts, claims court, court of international trade, and administrative quasi-judicial agencies. *See figure p. 100.*

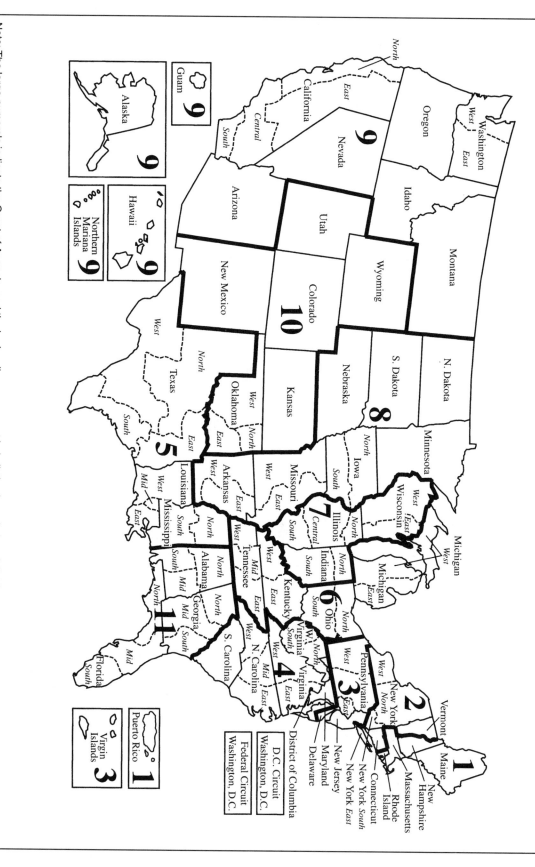

Federal District and Appellate Court Boundaries

Note: The large numerals indicate the Court of Appeals, and the broken lines represent jurisdiction boundaries of district courts.

Source: Administrative Office of the U.S. Courts. 2004. Title 28, U.S. Code, Sec. 44.

Federal Juvenile Delinquency Act Legislation passed in 1968 providing for optional probation to youthful offenders within federal jurisdiction. It was revised in 1972.

Federal Kidnapping Law A general kidnapping statute prompted by the abduction and death of Charles Lindbergh's child in the early 1930s that made kidnapping a federal offense punishable by either death or life without the possibility of parole; also known as the Lindbergh Law.

Federal Law Enforcement Training Center (FLETC) An interagency organization that provides basic training for law enforcement officers at all state and federal levels. It also provides advanced training and specialist activities for criminalistics, criminal investigation, forensics, and firearms training. Also kown as "Club Fed."

federal litigation procedures All federal rules of civil and criminal procedure outlined in the U.S. Code.

Federal Motor Vehicle Safety Standards A government requirement enforced by the Highway Traffic Safety Administration that automobiles operating on U.S. highways must meet certain minimum design and performance standards in order to be considered safe to operate. These standards are established under the auspices of the U.S. Department of Transportation.

federal prison A correctional facility operated by the Federal Bureau of Prisons for the confinement and punishment of persons convicted of federal crimes.

Federal Prison Industries (FPI, UNICOR) A profitable government-owned corporation that markets goods produced by prisoners in confinement. *See also* **UNICOR.**

Federal Programs Litigation Headquartered in Washington, DC, this agency handles any and all litigation filed against any U.S. government organization or its officials. It oversees enforcement and litigation targeting statutory or regulatory violations, employment policies and personnel actions, and any litigation relating to government records.

federal question Any significant issue involving the U.S. Constitution or its amendments; any argument involving a federal statute, civil or criminal.

Federal Register A government publication published by U.S. Government Printing Office that records and disseminates presidential proclamations or announcements, plans, executive orders, and proposals.

Federal Reserve banknotes Any currency printed by the U.S. government. The notes contain numbers and letters that identify one of 12 Federal Reserve Districts (1, A = Boston; 2, B = New York; 3, C = Philadelphia; 4, D = Cleveland; 5, E = Richmond; 6, F = Atlanta; 7, G = Chicago; 8, H = St. Louis;

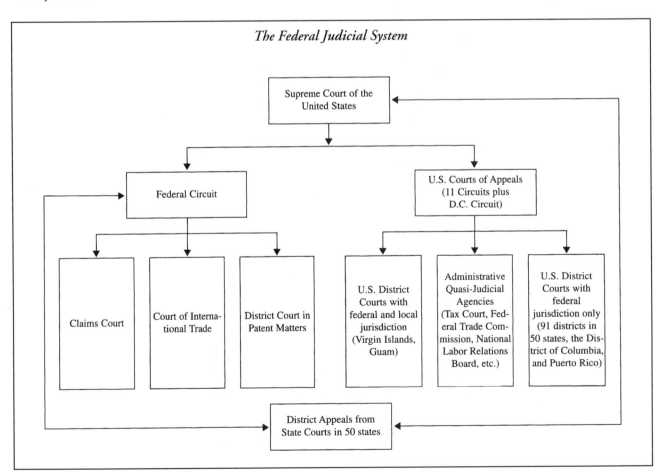

The Federal Judicial System

9, I = Minneapolis; 10, J = Kansas City; 11, K = Dallas; 12, L = San Francisco).

Federal Rules of Evidence A compendium of procedures to be followed when presenting evidence before a U.S. district court or other federal judiciary body.

Federal Tort Claims Act of 1946 Title 28, Section 2674 of the U.S. Code, provides that the United States shall be liable, respecting the provisions of this title relating to tort claims, in the same manner and to the same extent as a private individual under like circumstances, but shall not be liable for interest prior to judgment for punitive damages.

Federal Trade Commission (FTC) A five-member commission established in 1915, charged with enforcing laws pertaining to industrial practices, pricing, food and drug purity, labeling, packaging, and contents specification. The FTC may subject businesses to penalties for noncompliance with regulations. Its members are appointed by the U.S. president with the advice and consent of Congress.

federal trial court A U.S. district court in which civil and criminal proceedings occur.

Federal Witness Protection Program A program established under the Organized Crime Control Act of 1970 whereby those who give evidence against criminals and thereby place their lives in jeopardy are relocated under new names and identifications to other parts of the country in order to avoid retaliation or death from offenders convicted by their testimony.

feeblemindedness Defective mental abilities, which are believed responsible for criminal behavior.

fee splitting The illegal practice by physicians of making unnecessary referrals to specialists, who split their fees in exchange for these referrals.

fee system A system whereby county government pays a modest amount of money for each prisoner per day as an operating budget.

feigned accomplice A person who pretends to conspire with others in the planning or commission of a crime with the goal of obtaining incriminating information about the crime and the perpetrators and to provide evidence against them to prosecutors or law enforcement officers; an informant.

felicific calculus *See* **hedonistic calculus.**

felon One who commits a felony.

felonious Of or pertaining to felonies; with the intent to commit a felony.

felony A crime punishable by incarceration, usually in a state or federal prison, for periods of one year or longer.

felony murder, felony-murder doctrine, felony-murder rule Imposition of criminal liability on anyone who participates in a crime in which one or more victims are killed. Accomplices in a criminal scheme resulting in death do not actually have to be those who have killed others to be liable.

felony probation A procedure of not requiring felons to serve time in jail or prison, usually because of prison overcrowding. It involves a conditional sentence in lieu of incarceration.

Felson, Marcus (1947–) A criminologist who, together with Lawrence Cohen, developed routine activities theory. *See also* **Cohen, Lawrence.**

female auxiliary gang A female gang that is affiliated with a male gang and generally takes on a feminized version of the male gang's name.

female crime Illegal acts committed by women or girls.

femicide Killing of a woman.

feminist criminology, feminist theory A view that emphasizes gender issues in criminology.

fence A receiver of stolen property who resells the goods for profit.

fencing Negotiating the sale of stolen property.

Ferracuti, Franco A criminologist who collaborated with Marvin Wolfgang to devise the term *subculture of violence.*

Ferri, Enrico (1856–1929) A student of Cesare Lombroso, who believed that certain physical characteristics indicate a particular criminal nature and that forces external to the individual are responsible for criminal conduct. Ferri wrote *Criminal Sociology* (1917).

Fetal Alcohol Syndrome (FAS) A condition caused by the effect that alcohol has on a developing fetus.

feticide An abortion prohibited by law.

fetish, fetishism Any strong sexual attachment to particular objects, such as shoes or women's hose.

fetus An unborn child still in the womb.

feud An ongoing, violent conflict between two factions.

fiction Anything untrue or false, imaginary, or hypothetical.

fiduciary Someone authorized to act on behalf of another, in a position of trust, usually involving financial transactions.

field citation Citation and release in the field by police as an alternative to booking and pretrial detention. The practice reduces law enforcement costs as well as jail costs.

Fielding, Sir Henry (1707–1754) An eighteenth-century British novelist who laid the foundation for the first modern police force. He originated the Bow Street Runners, an early version of police, and wrote *An Inquiry Into the Cause of the Late Increase of Robbers* (1748).

field interview, interrogation law enforcement A question-answer session conducted between a law enforcement officer and a citizen.

field training officer (FTO) A senior police officer who trains other officers in the field, overseeing their on-the-job training.

fighting gang *See* **conflict gang.**

filicide The murder of one's child.

filing The commencement of criminal proceedings by entering a charging document into a court's official record.

filtering process A process whereby criminal-justice officials screen out certain cases while advancing other cases to the next level of decision making.

final A term used in fingerprint classification. The final is determined by ridge counts in the little finger. The right hand is used if there is a loop; if not, the left hand is used. If neither hand has a loop but each has a whorl, a ridge count is made between the delta and core on the right hand. *See also* **core; delta.**

final order A decree that ends litigation between two parties by determining all of their rights and disposing of all issues.

financial/community service model A restitution model for juveniles that stresses the offender's financial accountability and community service to pay for damages.

financial penalty A punishment that requires a defendant to pay money.

finder of fact *See* **fact finder, finder of fact.**

finding A holding or ruling by the court or judge.

finding of fact *See* **fact finding, finding of fact.**

fine A financial penalty imposed at the time of sentencing convicted offenders. Most criminal statutes contain provisions for the imposition of monetary penalties as sentencing options.

fingerprint The residual pattern left on surfaces by the application of human hands and fingers.

fingerprint, latent An occasional fingerprint left on the surface of an object.

fingerprint classification, fingerprint identification A system for classifying and identifying fingerprints according to unique patterns of whorls and ridges on the fingertips.

fingerprint conviction A guilty verdict against a criminal suspect obtained on the basis of matching the suspect's fingerprints to the crime scene to establish his or her presence, or on the murder weapon to determine his or her culpability. The first conviction obtained using fingerprint identification was that of Caesar Cella for burglary in New York City in March 1911.

fingerprint patterns Special configurations of ridges on finger surfaces, consisting of arches, whorls, and loops. Fingerprint patterns have been graded and stored on computer systems for instant retrieval, and used to identify possible suspects in criminal investigations. No two fingerprints are identical; thus, fingerprint evidence is admissible in court and is extremely persuasive as to one's identity. The first fingerprint system was adopted by the St. Louis (MO) Metropolitan Police Department in October 1904.

fire, classification A method of categorizing fires according to their seriousness and type of burning material: Class A fires involve burning wood, cloth, rubber, or plastic; Class B fires involve flammable liquids, such as gasoline, grease, or oil; Class C fires are electrical fires; and Class D fires involve combustible materials such as magnesium, titanium, zirconium, or potassium, where conventional fire extinguishing equipment is not useful and where a heat-absorbing extinguishing medium must be used.

firearm Any weapon capable of discharging a projectile, usually through an explosive mechanism.

firearms examination The in-depth examination of firearms suspected of being used in crimes.

firearms identification The process of matching known bullet samples to unknown ones. *See also* **ballistics.**

firearms trafficking The illegal sale and distribution of firearms.

Fireman's Rule Originating in 1892, this policy was established to protect from liability those who prevail upon firemen and police officers to put out fires or arrest persons, and where injuries to firemen or law enforcement officers occur in response to such citizen requests.

fire setter, fire starter One who engages in arson; an arsonist.

firing pin impressions The unique marks left on shell cases by firearms when cartridges are discharged. Firing pins of weapons strike primers, which explode when struck, igniting powder in the cartridge casing and propelling the bullet at a given speed toward a particular object. These unique impressions assist investigators in identifying the firearms used to discharge bullets and the owners of these firearms. Firing pins leave distinctive marks on primers of cartridge casings for easy identification.

firing squad A method of execution in which several persons shoot the condemned person to death, usually with rifles.

First Amendment The First Amendment guarantees that no laws will be enacted that restrict or abridge the freedom of religion, speech, or the press. *See also* **Bill of Rights.**

first appearance Initial appearance.

first offender, first-time offender A person who has never been convicted of a criminal offense prior to the current conviction.

first plea Initial plea.

fiscal year A financial reporting period covering a 12-month interval. A fiscal year does not have to coincide with the conventional calendar year, but may run from July 1 to June 30.

"fish" Prison slang for a new inmate in a jail or prison.

Fitness for Life A prisoner-oriented organization established in 1984 to provide athletic programs for inmates to improve their physical fitness. It is headquartered in Grand Rapids, MI.

fix Slang to indicate the use of influence to avoid or minimize the legal consequences of criminal, traffic, or other citations or to unlawfully influence the outcome of a sporting event.

fixed indeterminate sentencing A sentencing scheme whereby a judge sentences offenders to a single prison term that is treated as the maximum sentence for all practical purposes. A parole board may determine an early release date for the offender. *See also* **indeterminate sentencing.**

fixed sentencing *See* **determinate sentencing.**

fixed-time rule A policy in which people must be tried within a stated period after their arrest. *See also* **statute of limitations.**

flag A material emblem representing a particular country, usually made of cloth or some other more sturdy pliant material. The word derives from Anglo-Saxon *fleogan,* which means to fly in the wind.

flailing The practice of using split bamboo stalks to beat convicted offenders; caning.

flare, fuzee A device that, when ignited, produces bright light that burns for a short period of time, such as 30 minutes or an hour. Flares can be ignited and placed on highways to warn oncoming motorists of hazards.

flash bang A device that explodes with a loud noise and gives off a brilliant light to create a diversion, stunning one or more perpetrators.

flasher, flashing An exhibitionist; one who exposes his or her genitals to others, usually for sexual gratification; the sex-related crime of exposure of one's private parts (usually the genitals of men or the breasts and/or genitals of women) to unwilling witnesses, for shock value and gratification. At law, *indecent exposure* is the term used in most jurisdictions. Flashing is sometimes distinguished from indecent exposure because of the brief duration and intentional motivation of the act.

flash houses An eighteenth-century term describing public meeting places and taverns where thieves, pickpockets, and other criminals could congregate and exchange stolen goods.

flashover An arson term describing a fire phenomenon in which temperatures in a room reach 2,000 degrees and clothing and furniture burst into flame spontaneously. In past years, arson was suspected whenever such spontaneous combustion occurred, because it was almost always related to the use of an arsonist's gasoline or explosives. Current belief is that it may occur accidentally.

flat organizational structure A type of organizational hierarchical arrangement in which there are few levels of supervision.

flat sentence, flat term A specific, definite term for a conviction, not necessarily known in advance of sentencing.

flat time The actual amount of time required to be served by a convicted offender while incarcerated.

flawed execution Executions in which equipment fails to operate properly, such as a power failure for operating the electric chair or frayed rope in a hanging.

flaying The practice of skinning or removing the skin from the body by using a knife.

fleeing Attempting to elude or avoid apprehension by law enforcement authorities.

fleeing-felon rule A rule that allowed law enforcement officers were permitted to use deadly force to apprehend felons attempting to escape apprehension. It was rendered unconstitutional by the U.S. Supreme Court in 1985. *See also **Tennessee v. Garner** (1985).*

fleeting targets exception An exception to the exclusionary rule permitting law enforcement officers to search a motor vehicle based on probable cause but without a warrant. The exception is based on the idea that automobiles are highly mobile entities that can quickly leave the jurisdiction of the law enforcement agency.

FLETC model Graduated or escalating amounts of force, applied in accordance with the nature of suspect cooperation or resistance. Suspects who are cooperative are given verbal orders by officers, whereas other suspects may require varying degrees of force to subdue them. *See also **force continuum**.*

flex cuffs Plastic restraints that function to restrict one's movements, much like metal handcuffs.

flick-knife A British term for switchblade knife.

flight Any escape; fleeing from justice, especially by alleged offenders charged with an offense or who are awaiting sentencing following conviction.

floater A term for a deceased person who is floating in water.

flogging Whipping with a lash as a form of corporal punishment.

floodgate theory The notion that decriminalizing certain behavior will dramatically increase its adoption.

flopped Being denied parole by a parole board.

Florida Assessment Center An organization established in Dade County, FL, whose purpose is to train probation and parole officers for entry-level positions in probation and parole. *See also **assessment centers**.*

Floyd, Charles Arthur ("Pretty Boy") (1901–1934) A notorious gangster who robbed banks during the 1920s and 1930s in the Midwest. He was eventually killed by FBI agents in October 1934.

focal concerns According to Walter Miller, the value orientations of lower-class cultures whose features include the need for excitement, trouble, smartness, fate, and personal autonomy (1958).

folk crime Nonserious offenses that are motivated more by social sentiments than by greed, revenge, or other typical motives for crime.

Folk Nation, Folk Nation set A gang aggregate made up of over 50 different Chicago-based gangs formed during the 1950s and 1960s. Members are mostly prison inmates who have formed an association for self-protection against enemy gangs, including the People Nation. The Folk Nation gang set is made up of Black Gangster Disciples, Black Disciples, Gangster Disciples, Imperial Gangsters, La Raza, Spanish Cobras, Latin Eagles, Latin Disciples, and Two Sixers. The gang's members use a six-pointed star and a pitchfork as gang symbols, whereas the People Nation uses a five-pointed star or crown for identification. The large Los Angeles–based Crips gang is affiliated with the Folk Nation, whereas its rival gang, the Bloods, is affiliated with the People Nation set.

folkways Ways of doing things that are current in a society; generally followed customs without moral values attached to them (e.g., not interrupting people when they are speaking). The term was created by the sociologist William Graham Sumner.

Folsom Prison strike The longest of the prison demonstrations that was part of the prisoner movement. It occurred in 1968 and lasted 19 days, involving 2,400 inmates. Inmates refused to leave their cells after having smuggled out a list of 29 demands, and the warden locked the prison down. Despite outside assistance, the strike ended after two weeks when supplies ran low and the warden offered to lift the lockdown if inmates went back to work.

Food and Drug Administration (FDA) An organization established in 1907 responsible for overseeing the manufacture of foods and drugs and their purity. The FDA conducts research to determine the effects of certain drugs on patients to determine their safety and effectiveness and investigates claims by food and drug manufacturing companies concerning what their products can do. It is headquartered in Washington, DC.

footcandle A unit of measurement for the amount of illumination projected on a surface one foot away from the light source.

foot patrol A method of policing in which officers patrol communities by walking through them. Originally used in nineteenth- and early twentieth-century policing, more recent programs in Flint, MI, and elsewhere have been moderately successful in bringing community residents into closer touch with patrolling officers. *See also* **community policing.**

foot rail An alarm device, often set near cashier's stations in banks, which can be activated by one's foot in the event of a robbery or theft.

force, reasonable Any amount or degree of force necessary for persons to protect themselves from aggressive suspects. Law enforcement officers may use force no greater than that which is necessary to subdue crime suspects.

force continuum A subjective measure of the amount of force law enforcement officers apply in making arrests.

forced entry A break-in by a burglar or law enforcement officer.

forcible entry *See* **breaking and entering.**

forcible rape Sexual intercourse with persons forcibly and against their will. Assaults or attempts to commit rape by force or threat of force are also included.

Ford Pinto case A 1978 case in which the Ford Motor Company sold its Pinto model despite evidence from crash tests that showed that rear-end collisions would result in fuel tank explosions. Over 500 persons died as the result of such explosions. Lawsuits resulted in heavy damages paid to survivors by Ford.

Foreign Claims Settlement Commission A U.S. Department of Justice–sponsored commission that investigates claims made by foreign nationals against the U.S. government and its agencies for losses or injuries sustained. It is headquartered in Washington, DC.

Foreign Corrupt Practices Act A 1977 federal law prohibiting the payment of bribes to obtain business from foreign governments.

forensic anthropology The application of anthropological principles and techniques in criminal investigations.

forensic art Drawings or other illustrations applied to the investigation of crime and the identification of unidentified subjects, including composite drawings, facial reconstruction, and the use of computer-assisted composite programs.

forensic entomology The use of insects and their arthropod relatives that inhabit decomposing remains to aid legal investigations. Techniques may be used to detect abuse of children or the elderly, where parents and others intentionally use wasps or bees to sting their children as a punishment. Entomological evidence has been used to prove neglect and lack of proper care for wounds existing on the elderly under both private and institutional care. Insects can also affect the interpretation of blood spatter pattern analysis; thus, it is important to recognize and properly document the natural artifacts that may occur from the presence, feeding, and defecation of roaches, flies, and fleas. Insects that feed on living, decomposing, or dried vegetable material are submitted to forensic entomologists to determine their country or point of origin, or to conduct tests for the presence of human blood.

forensic medicine An area of study investigating crimes that involves anatomy, pathology, toxicology, chemistry, and other areas. Forensics medical personnel provide expert testimony in trials when their services are required.

forensic odontology A branch of forensics focusing on bite marks and bite mark patterns for the purpose of identifying potential perpetrators of crimes, usually murders or rapes.

forensic pathologist A medically trained professional who is an expert at determining the cause of death.

forensic psychiatrist, forensic psychologist Someone skilled in profiling those who have committed certain types of crimes who examines criminals to determine their sanity and criminal motives for the purpose of understanding their actions, and who furnishes expert testimony in court about the mental capabilities of criminal defendants.

Forensic Sciences Foundation An association of persons from different forensics fields who share newly emerging information about forensics topics. The organization, headquartered in Colorado Springs, CO, was created in 1969. Publishes *Forensic Serology News* and *News and Views in Forensic Toxicology.*

forensics, forensic science The study and identification of the causes of crimes, deaths, and crime-scene investigations.

Forest Service An organization established in 1905 under the U.S. Department of Agriculture to manage public lands in national forests and grasslands.

forfeiture, civil or criminal Seizure by the government of property and other assets derived from or used in criminal activity.

forgery The creation or alteration of a document such as a negotiable instrument; fraud by means of trickery and alteration of written documents that, if validly executed, would be legally binding transactions.

forget pill *See* **Rohypnol.**

formal communication network An information transmission mode in an organization that relies almost exclusively on the prescribed hierarchy of authority. Information is distributed to organizational membership through official channels.

formal control A social control governed by written rules and usually employing formal organizations for implementation.

formalization The extent to which communications and procedures in an organization are written down and filed; a measure of the extent to which rules, procedures, instructions, and communications are written.

formal social control An effort to bring about conformity to the law by agents of the criminal-justice system such as the police, the courts, and correctional institutions.

fornication Sexual intercourse between unmarried persons. It is an offense in some jurisdictions.

Fortune Society An organization established in 1967 to bring public attention to the conditions in prison systems and problems inmates experience. The Society also works with recently released prisoners to assist them in job placement and skills training and provides speakers to schools and other institutions for informative presentations. It is headquartered in New York City.

Fosdick, Raymond Blaine (1833–1872) An attorney and author born in Buffalo, NY, who received a law degree from NYU Law School and two doctorates from other schools. He accompanied military personnel during campaigns in different foreign lands and wrote about his experiences. Fosdick earned many honors during his lifetime, including the Distinguished Service Medal.

foster-care program A program in which juveniles who are orphans or whose parents cannot care for them are placed with families who provide the attention, guidance, and care they did not receive at home.

foster family Any surrogate family used temporarily to provide shelter to unsupervised youths.

foster grandparents program An association of persons over the age of 60 who work with children who have psychological problems or physical, mental, social, or emotional needs. These volunteers often furnish temporary housing to children in need of supervision, receiving a modest stipend from local government agencies. The program is part of the National Older Americans Volunteer Program, headquartered in Washington, DC.

foster home, foster group home A blend of group home and foster home initiatives. A foster home provides a "real family" and is run by a single family, not a professional. A group home facility is an unlocked facility, licensed by the state or local jurisdiction and operated by a person or couple, to provide care and maintenance for children, usually one to four such children.

Fourteenth Amendment The amendment to the U.S. Constitution that contains the equal-protection and due-process clauses that are applicable to state governments. *See also* **Bill of Rights.**

Fourth Amendment The amendment to the U.S. Constitution that protects people from unreasonable searches and seizures of their persons, property, homes, automobiles, and personal effects by law enforcement officers. *See also* **Bill of Rights.**

4-World Syndrome The notion holds that police officers must adjust to life in four worlds: the inner (defensive) world of policing; the outer (cooperative) world of the public; the street (quick response) world; and the station (paperwork) world. The idea was suggested by Elizabeth Reuss-Ianni in her 1984 work, *Two Cultures of Policing,* which describes and differentiates between street cops, station cops, us, and them.

frame of reference A way of looking at an organization or problem affecting persons, groups, or organizations.

frame-up An attempt to make it appear that another is responsible for a crime.

franchise fraud A scheme in which the defrauded person is led to believe that he or she can make large sums of money by purchasing what is really a bogus franchise.

frangible bullet A projectile made of plastic or some other brittle and nonlethal substance used for target practice. When such a bullet strikes a surface, it crumbles without penetrating, leaving a mark to show where a target has been hit.

frangible grenade An incendiary explosive device; a glass container containing flammable liquid, with some type of igniting device protruding from the container, such as a rag or piece of cloth or fuse; sometimes called a Molotov cocktail. When it strikes an object, the glass breaks and the fluid inside ignites.

Frankfurter, Felix (1882–1965) An associate justice of the U.S. Supreme Court (1939–1962) and former presidential advisor, Frankfurter received a law degree from Harvard Law School and taught there for several years. At the end of World War I, he was an advisor to the Paris Peace Conference, and he was appointed to the U.S. Supreme Court in 1939 by President Franklin D. Roosevelt. Frankfurter believed that the judiciary should play a minimal role in political governance.

frankpledge A tenth- to twelfth-century system that required loyalty to the King of England and shared law-and-order responsibilities among the public. The system directed that neighbors should form into small groups to assist and protect one another if they were victimized by criminals.

Fraternal Order of Police (FOP) A large union of nonexecutive law enforcement officers consisting of 288,000 members that promotes officer benefits and the protection of law enforcement officers.

fratricide Killing one's sister or brother.

fraud An act of trickery or deceit, especially involving misrepresentation.

fraud, charity Misappropriation and collection of funds from the public under the guise of representing a well-known charity, such as the United Way or the Red Cross. The National Charities Information Bureau, headquartered in New York City, disseminates information about fraudulent practices as well as a list of reputable charities and how to recognize them.

fraud, health-care A misappropriation of funds, often involving the prescription of unnecessary medications, the provision of unnecessary services, or claiming to provide medications or services when in fact they are not provided.

fraud, investment A crime involving persons who take money under false pretenses, claiming to invest such money in moneymaking stocks or securities. Profits are taken and victims receive little or no return on their invested money.

fraud, postal Any crime committed by persons who use the U.S. mails to solicit money or items of value from unsuspecting victims, for example by advertising defective or nonexistent goods by mail and receiving money from victims for such defective or nonexistent merchandise.

fraud, telemarketing Any crime committed through telephonic solicitation of money or items of value, or offering for sale defective, substandard, or nonexistent merchandise to unwary consumers.

fraud, toll Use of stolen telephone credit card numbers or business toll codes to obtain security or PIN numbers from which money can be obtained illegally from customer accounts.

fraud offense Any crime involving the use of misrepresentation or deception with the intent of depriving persons of money or valuables.

freebase Purified cocaine crystals that are crushed and smoked to provide a more powerful high than cocaine; also, a mix of cocaine and other agents.

freedom of assembly One of a U.S. citizen's constitutional rights involving the right to meet with others and discuss political issues.

Freedom of Information Act (FOIA) A mechanism legislatively created in 1967 whereby private citizens can obtain secret government files about them. Some information is confidential and cannot be released to private citizens, but most documented information must be disclosed to those making such requests.

freedom of religion A First Amendment right guaranteeing the right to worship as one chooses. *See also* **Bill of Rights.**

freedom of speech and the press A First Amendment right guaranteeing the right to free speech and the right to print news freely without disclosure of the sources for such news. Some restrictions on speech and the press have been created such that some speech may be illegal, and under certain circumstances the press may be compelled to reveal its source of information, particularly if an overwhelming government interest is demonstrated. *See also* **Bill of Rights.**

Freedom Riders A group of young men and women, black and white, who boarded buses, trains, and airplanes in 1961 and went to the Deep South to challenge that region's Jim Crow laws and noncompliance with U.S. Supreme Court decisions barring segregation of blacks and whites. They were trained in nonviolence by Martin Luther King Jr. The Freedom Riders encountered angry mobs in Alabama and other states, and many were arrested and jailed in Jackson, MI. The actions of the Freedom Riders led to major changes in transportation laws, which eventually banned segregation of all interstate public transportation facilities on the basis of race, color, or creed.

Freedom Summer Formed during the summer of 1964 in Mississippi and organized by a coalition of persons called the Mississippi Council of Federated Organizations, this organization promoted voter registration drives in various Mississippi cities in order to get more black persons to vote. Blacks were routinely denied the right to vote, despite having that right, through racial prejudice and intimidation by violent white supremacists. Freedom Schools were established in 30 communities to raise racial awareness and promote black history. Activists were threatened and harassed during the campaign, many black homes and churches were bombed and burned, and members were arrested for various minor offenses to discourage their voter registration efforts. Tragedy occurred on June 21, 1964, when three civil rights workers, James Chaney, Andrew Goodman, and Michael Schwerner, were murdered by various persons including some law enforcement officers. The 1988 feature film *Mississippi Burning* (Gene Hackman) was based on this civil rights initiative, which eventually led to the 1965 Voting Rights Act, federal legislation that prevented Southern states from using tactics to discourage voting among blacks.

free exercise clause That portion of the First Amendment to the U.S. Constitution that forbids government interference with people's religious beliefs and practices. *See also* **Bill of Rights.**

freelancers In prison, jailhouse lawyers who seek their own inmate clients.

free-venture program, free-venture system Privately run industries in prison settings in which inmates work for wages and goods are sold for profit. *See also* **UNICOR.**

freeway A major highway with limited access. Owners of abutting land have either no rights or limited rights concerning such land adjacent to these highways.

freeway patrol A law enforcement agency responsible for patrolling major highways and interstate thoroughfares, such as a state highway patrol.

free will The view that persons are in charge of their own destinies and are free to make personal behavior choices unencumbered by environmental factors.

French Connection A drug-smuggling operation of the early 1960s that involved large-scale heroin smuggling from France to the United States in various types of shipping containers. The discovery of smuggling operations by New York police detectives led to extensive investigation and arrests and convictions of several persons which was sensationalized in the 1971 feature film *The French Connection* (Gene Hackman, Roy Scheider).

fresh pursuit Continuous and uninterrupted chase of a fleeing suspect by police, which may cross jurisdictional boundaries of cities, counties, and states.

Freud, Sigmund (1856–1939) A psychologist who pioneered the fields of psychoanalysis and psychological theory. He theorized the Oedipus complex and the Electra complex, and devised terms such as the id, ego, superego, and libido, or sex drive. Freud studied psychoses and neuroses as related to criminal conduct.

Freudian theory The psychoanalytic theory advanced by Sigmund Freud that focuses on conflicts in the individual arising during childhood, some of which are believed to lead to criminal behavior.

friction, coefficient of The speed, weight of vehicle, and type of highway surface are factored to determine drag factor, or the coefficient of friction, which investigators can use to determine the circumstances of a traffic accident.

friction ridges Ridges on the skin on one's palms, fingertips, and feet that are necessary to grasp objects by providing friction. Ridges on the fingertips are fingerprints.

Friends Outside An organization established in 1955 to assist prison inmates and their families in dealing with the separation resulting from incarceration. It also works toward prison reform and the improvement of the conditions of one's confinement. It is headquartered in Salinas, CA.

frisk Patting down or running one's hands quickly over a person's body to determine whether the person has a weapon. *See also* ***Terry v. Ohio* (1968);** ***Sibron v. New York* (1968).**

frivolous lawsuit, frivolous suit A legal action brought by a complainant which has no foundation in fact. Such suits are usually initiated by lawyers and plaintiffs for publicity or political reasons, and may result in fines against plaintiffs or their counsel.

front-door corrections, front-door program, front-door solution A solution to prison or jail overcrowding occurring at the beginning of the criminal-justice process, which includes plea bargaining resulting in diversion, probation, community service, intermediate punishment, or some other nonincarcerative alternative.

frottage A compulsive act whereby persons derive sexual satisfaction by rubbing the clothing of another, particularly the clothing of strangers. Persons who commit frottage are called *frotteurs*. Criminally, it is a mild form of battery.

frotteurism Practice of rubbing or touching another without consent for sexual pleasure.

fruits of a crime Any objects, money, property, or instruments collected which are obtained through a criminal act.

fruits of the poisonous tree doctrine The U.S. Supreme Court decision in *Wong Sun v. United States* (1963) held that evidence which is spawned or directly derived from an illegal search or an illegal interrogation is generally inadmissible against a defendant because of its original taint. *See also Brown v. Illinois* (1975).

frumentarii Under the Roman empire, the first professional criminal investigative units in western history. They had three principal duties: to supervise grain distribution to Rome's needy, to oversee the personal delivery of messages among government officials, and to detect crime and prosecute offenders.

Fry, Elizabeth Gurney (1780–1845) An English Quaker women's prison reformer who toured the United States and other countries in the early 1800s attempting to implement prison reforms. She encouraged separate facilities for women, religious and secular education, improved classification systems for women, and reintegrative and rehabilitative programs.

Frye rule The legal requirement that scientific evidence introduced in court must have acceptance by the larger scientific community.

fugitive, fugitive from justice A person who has concealed him- or herself or has fled a given jurisdiction in order to avoid prosecution or confinement.

fugitive apprehension Determining the whereabouts and taking into custody persons wanted in one or more jurisdictions; actions taken to apprehend suspects or wanted criminals by bounty hunters. Contemporary bounty hunters refer to themselves as "fugitive-recovery agents" or "bail-enforcement agents." Monetary rewards are given for recovery of wanted persons and returning them to custody.

Fugitive Apprehension Unit (FAU) A department created by major law enforcement agencies in different jurisdictions to detect and apprehend violent criminals and probation and parole violators. FAUs also conduct operations to take into custody those named in arrest warrants or who have been placed on bail but who have fled their jurisdiction to avoid prosecution. The Texas Department of Safety devised such a unit in 1993 when over 17,500 parole violators were wanted, more than 3,800 of them violent offenders. Texas subsequently expanded FAU activities to include high-profile sex offenders and those convicted of crimes against children who have absconded from parole.

Fugitive Felon Acts Government laws passed in 1932 making interstate travel to commit a crime unlawful. They vest the FBI and other federal agencies with the authority to make arrests of such persons for violating federal laws.

Fugitive Interception Network Design A Philadelphia Police Department plan to prevent felons from escaping from major crime scenes.

fugitive-recovery agent A professional who seeks to capture and return to custody anyone wanted by one or more jurisdictions, usually through issuance of an arrest warrant or because of being placed on bail and fleeing the jurisdiction to avoid prosecution; also know as a bounty hunter. Monetary rewards are given for recovery of wanted persons and returning them to custody.

Fugitive Recovery Network An organization that provides professional service to bail bondspersons.

fugitive slave laws Prior to the Civil War, laws passed by Congress authorizing the capture and return of slaves to slave states when they escaped to nonslave states.

fugitive warrant Any written judicial order authorizing officers to arrest a particular person named in the warrant.

full enforcement A policy whereby the police are given the resources and support to enforce all laws within the limits imposed by the injunction to respect the civil liberties of citizens.

Fuller, Melville W. (1833–1910) Chief justice of the U.S. Supreme Court (1888–1910). Born in Maine and graduated from Bowdoin College, Fuller attended Harvard Law School and moved to Chicago in the 1850s. As a Democrat, he supported Stephen Douglas in the Presidential race against Abraham Lincoln. He practiced law in Chicago until being appointed chief justice of the U.S. Supreme Court by Grover Cleveland in 1888. He assisted Cleveland in his reelection campaign, although Cleveland lost. Fuller was opposed to efforts regulating business and property, and was known for writing Supreme Court opinions holding impermissible the use of the Sherman Antitrust Act against a sugar-manufacturing monopoly on the grounds that manufacture and commerce are distinctly different aspects of business. He also declared unconstitutional a direct tax imposed by the Income Tax Act of 1894. He married twice, in 1858 and again in 1866 after his first wife died, and died in 1910.

full pardon A pardon that frees the criminal without any condition whatever. It reaches both the punishment prescribed for the offense and the guilt of the offender.

full-time temporary release Unescorted leave from a prison or jail for a short period of time; a furlough to seek employment, reunite with family, obtain educational coursework, or seek various treatments or services.

functional approach to prison culture An explanation of the prison culture that focuses on the shared experience within the prison, such as inmate responses to the pains of imprisonment.

functional authority The power to complete tasks because of expertise or ability rather than because of one's title or rank.

functional incompetence or illiteracy The inability to read well enough to perform the basic skills necessary in a modern society.

functionalism The sociological view that deviant behaviors such as crime perform a necessary and useful function in society by reinforcing the norms against such behaviors, as each part of society makes a contribution to the maintenance of the whole. The view stresses social cooperation and consensus of values and beliefs among a majority of society's members.

functionally illiterate A condition in which an individual who may have completed middle or high school functions at a much lower level than his or her education would indicate, and does not have the skills to generally gain or maintain employment at wages sufficient to support dependents.

functional specialization A line-staff distinction in various criminal-justice organizations that is similar to the bureaucratic division of labor. Different departments and work roles perform specific duties and functions.

fundamental error In a judicial proceeding, an error that affects the substantial rights of the accused and is an affront to the integrity of the court.

fundamental fairness A legal doctrine supporting the idea that so long as a state's conduct maintains the basic elements of fairness, the Constitution has not been violated.

fundamental law A codified statute with the effective force of constitutional law.

funnel effect, funnelling effect The reduction occurring between the number of crimes committed annually and the number of arrests, prosecutions, and convictions. Only about 25 percent of all arrests in the United States result in convictions annually.

furlough, furlough program An authorized unescorted or unsupervised leave granted to inmates for home visits, work, or educational activity, usually from 24 to 72 hours; a temporary release program. Such a program was first used in Mississippi in 1918.

Furman **commutee** A death-row inmate whose sentence has been commuted as a result of the *Furman v. Georgia* (1972) decision.

G

G.A.A.P. Generally accepted accounting principles; norms for the proper auditing of financial records.

Gacy, John Wayne (1942–1994) A serial killer who operated in and around Chicago, IL, during the 1970s, Gacy was born in 1942 and had two sisters and an abusive father. He worked as a shoe salesman in his early years, and as a janitor in a mortuary. At age 11, he was struck in the head by a playground swing, which caused him to have occasional blackouts. He gradually developed a talent for salesmanship and eventually owned his own restaurant and later a construction firm. Gacy was arrested in Iowa in 1968 for sodomy with young men, and convicted. Sentenced to 10 years, he was paroled after 18 months and returned to Chicago. Gacy lured and murdered young men, subsequently burying them in the basement of

his own home. He drew the attention of police because he was the last person to see a missing boy alive in 1978. A background check disclosed his previous sodomy conviction, and caused police to look further into Gacy as a suspect. Eventually, police obtained a search warrant for Gacy's premises and discovered 32 bodies hidden in Gacy's basement. Gacy was tried and convicted of multiple murders and died by lethal injection in 1994. His last words were "Kiss my ass."

gag Any device used to muzzle an individual to keep him or her from speaking.

gag law Any prohibition against speaking or publicizing an event by a person or the press, typically used in conjunction with an ongoing criminal case. The law was designed to minimize pretrial publicity and prejudice of citizens before a trial is held and a defendant's guilt or innocence is determined.

gain time The amount of time deducted from the maximum time to be served in prison for participating in special projects or programs.

Gall, Franz Joseph (1758–1828) A phrenologist who studied the shapes of skulls in an effort to predict the type of criminality exhibited by persons possessing certain physical characteristics.

galleys Oar-driven ships used in commerce and warfare for hundreds of years until the seventeenth century by Mediterranean nations. During the Middle Ages, convicts and other undesirables were sentenced to galley servitude.

gallows A structure, most often constructed of wood, from which or on which a condemned person is executed by hanging.

Gallup Poll A public opinion survey based on a national sample of citizens who are interviewed concerning their views on a variety of subjects, often politically related. Sample results are considered representative of U.S. citizen public opinion on a given issue, with a small margin of error.

Galton, Sir Francis (1812–1911) A criminologist and social theorist who studied fingerprints and their uniqueness and was a pioneer in fingerprinting science.

galvanometer A device for measuring small amounts of electricity used in various lie detector or polygraph tests.

Gambino, Carlo (1902–1976) The boss of New York Italian organized crime for many years.

"gamblers" In prison, inmates of upper-middle-class status who obtain economic power by wagering their skills.

gambling, gaming Operating or playing a game for money in hopes of gaining more than the amount played; any wager between two or more persons.

game families Pseudofamilies found in female prisons. Each has a core group of 6 to 12 long termers and is a stable, well-recognized force within the prison.

gamma-hydroxybutyrate (GHB) An odorless and tasteless depressant that causes unconsciousness, which is referred to as the "date-rape" drug because it renders users susceptible to sexual advances. It may be introduced into a person's drink and takes about 15 to 20 minutes following ingestion to cause unconsciousness and memory loss. An excessive dose may induce coma or death, and there is no antidote. An excessive

Age of Gang Members, by Year of Gang Problem Onset, 1996 Survey

	Average Percentage of Gang Members			
Year of Onset	Under Age 15	Age 15–17	Age 18–24	Over Age 24
Before 1981 (n=78)	21	38	31	10
1981–85 (n=56)	20	41	31	9
1986–90 (n=303)	21	45	29	6
1991–92 (n=195)	21	47	27	5
1993–94 (n=224)	24	47	26	3
1995–96 (n=74)	22	54	23	1

Note: Percentages within each onset category may not total 100 because of rounding. The number of jurisdictions (n) varies because some respondents did not answer all of the survey's demographic questions. The percentages listed were estimated by reporting jurisdictions.

Gender of Gang Members, by Year of Gang Problem Onset, 1996 Survey

	Average Percentage of Gang Members	
Year of Onset	Male	Female
Before 1981 (n=79)	90	10
1981–85 (n=64)	89	11
1986–90 (n=337)	89	11
1991–92 (n=202)	90	10
1993–94 (n=247)	88	12
1995–96 (n=75)	86	14

Note: The number of jurisdictions (n) varies because some respondents did not answer all of the survey's demographic questions. The percentages listed were estimated by reporting jurisdictions.

Race/Ethnicity of Gang Members, by Year of Gang Problem Onset, 1996 Survey

	Average Percentage of Gang Members				
Year of Onset	African American	Hispanic	Asian	Caucasian	Other
Before 1981 (n=75)	21	58	7	10	3
1981–85 (n=62)	34	44	5	15	2
1986–90 (n=319)	35	34	7	24	1
1991–92 (n=198)	32	23	6	37	2
1993–94 (n=251)	30	23	5	39	2
1995–96 (n=80)	36	16	3	40	4

Note: Percentages within each onset category may not total 100 because of rounding. The number of jurisdictions (n) varies because some respondents did not answer all of the survey's demographic questions. The percentages listed were estimated by reporting jurisdictions.

Source: Howell, Egley, and Gleason, *Modern-Day Youth Gangs*, 3.

dose may induce coma or death, and there is no antidote for an overdose. Also known as g-juice and liquid X.

gang A group that forms an allegiance for a common purpose and engages in unlawful or criminal activity; any group gathered together on a continuing basis to engage in or commit antisocial behavior. *See tables.*

gang codes of conduct Gang norms that involve expected behavior and regulate member activities. They include secrecy and intense loyalty.

ganghood A concept emphasizing the significance of belonging to a gang.

gang hit, gang killing Any murder involving members of teenage gangs for whom violence is a part of their group activity.

gang member An individual who actively participates in the activities of a gang. *See tables.*

gang migration The movement of gangs from large metropolitan areas such as Los Angeles or Chicago to other areas of the country.

gang-motivated crime Any criminal activity that has been encouraged by a gang for one or more of its members, sometimes as an initiation ritual to complete gang entry or membership; one or more illegal acts to further gang-related interests, such as drug trafficking, drive-by shootings of rival gang members, or illicit gun trafficking.

gang-related crime Acts of delinquency in which the offender or the victim is a gang member.

Gang Resistance Education and Training (G.R.E.A.T.) A program developed by the Bureau of Alcohol, Tobacco, and Firearms (BATF) designed to assist youth in refraining from becoming involved in gangs. Law enforcement officers work in schools to teach students a specific anti-gang curriculum.

gang sets Alliances of various gangs organized along corporate lines for mutual protection. Gang sets include People Nation, Folk Nation, and Black Gangster Disciple Nation.

Gangster Disciples A Chicago-based street gang formed in the 1960s. By 1995, it had a membership of over 30,000 in 35 states. Originally led by Larry "King" Hoover, the gang operates a sophisticated illicit drug network worth $100 million a year. It is modeled after Chicago's Italian Mafia organization. Numerous imprisoned gang members, known by initials "GD," have formed prison gangs that have between 5,000 and 10,000 members. Gang organization consists of a chairman, a board of directors, regents and coordinators (who distribute drugs), and enforcers (who administer beatings and death to those violating gang rules). The gang lures young recruits from among the jobless and poor with the promise of easy cash. Hoover has attempted to improve the gang's public image by drafting rules for membership, which include avoiding addictive drugs and better dress standards.

Gantt chart An instrument created in World War I by Henry L. Gantt to graphically illustrate the work planned and the work accomplished within a given time frame.

Ganzer syndrome A depiction of police officers who exhibit a type of battle fatigue and who use humor to ward off the horror and dangers associated with their work roles.

gaol fever A set of illnesses in jails of the seventeenth and eighteenth centuries caused by unhygienic conditions. It included typhus as well as malignant forms of dysentery.

gaols Fifteenth-century English jails.

Gardner, Erle Stanley (1889–1970) A California attorney who wrote the Perry Mason novels. The books inspired radio and television programs around their fictitious hero, attorney Perry Mason. Gardner also originated Court of Last Resort, an organization that assisted persons believed to be wrongfully convicted of crimes.

garnishment A legal means of attaching someone's wages in order to pay a debt.

Garofalo, Raffaelo (1852–1934) A student of Cesare Lombroso who believed that physical characteristics or attributes are indicative of different types of criminal conduct; author of *Criminology* (1914).

Garrity **warning** Based on *Garrity v. New Jersey* (1967), internal investigations conducted by police agencies or other governmental organizations cannot compel their employees to give incriminating information if such information could be used to impose severe administrative sanctions, such as loss of one's job, or if the information could later be used in criminal proceedings against these employees. However, refusal to answer specific questions stemming from an internal investigation may permit inferences to be made about the employee's conduct, provided that other incriminating information exists. *See box.*

garrote To strangle a person, usually by a rope device or wire; also, the device used to strangle someone.

gas chamber A means of legal execution in which the condemned is placed in an air-tight chamber in which sulfuric acid and cyanide crystals are combined to form lethal gases that cause death.

gas chromatography A technique for analyzing a mixture of volatile substances in which the mixture is carried by an inert gas through a column packed with a selective absorbent and a detector records on a moving strip the conductivity of the gas leaving the tube. Peaks on the resulting graph indicate the presence of a particular component or element.

gate fever An emotional feeling experienced by some prison inmates scheduled for release, which includes anxiety about where they will live and how they will adapt to conditions outside of prison.

gatekeeper function Police discretionary actions (decisions to arrest or not arrest) that allow them to determine how far some individuals are processed in the criminal-justice system.

gatekeeping Tallying records and counting heads, such as prison counts; also, a process of restricting access to an organization or association by excluding or including certain persons as members.

gate money The money an inmate has when he or she is discharged from prison.

gateway drugs A series of drugs, such as includes alcohol, tobacco, marijuana, and inhalants, believed to lead to heavier drug use.

Gatling, Richard Jordan (1818–1903) Inventor of the Gatling gun, a machine gun capable of firing numerous bullets in a short period of time. The slang term "gat" was used in the 1920s and 1930s, when machine guns were used by gangsters to commit crimes and defend their territory.

The Garritty Warning

1. I am being questioned as part of an investigation by this agency into potential violations of department rules and regulations, or my fitness for duty. This investigation concerns

   _____

   _____

2. I have invoked my *Miranda* rights on the grounds that I might incriminate myself in a criminal matter.

3. I have been granted use immunity. No answer has been given by me, nor evidence derived from the answer, may be used against me in any criminal proceeding, except for perjury or false swearing.

4. I understand that I must now answer questions specifically, directly, and narrowly related to the performance of my official duties or my fitness for office.

5. If I refuse to answer, I may be subject to discipline for that refusal which can result in my dismissal from this agency.

6. Anything I say may be used against me in any subsequent department charges.

7. I have the right to consult with a representative of my collective bargaining unit, or another representative of my choice, and have him or her present during the interview.

Assistant Prosecutor/Deputy Attorney General Authorizing:

_____

Signature: _____

Date: _____   Time: _____

Location: _____

Witnessed by: _____

_____

gauge The means of measuring the bore of shotguns, such as 16 gauge or 20 gauge, with larger gauge corresponding to a smaller bore diameter.

gay Homosexual.

gay bashing The practice of assaulting gays or lesbians.

GED *See* **General Equivalency Diploma (GED).**

geek, computer geek A person who eats (computer) bugs for a living; a person who has acquired substantial expertise in the art of computer hacking and programming for positive or negative purposes; also also called turbo nerd, turbo geek, propeller head, terminal junkie, and spod.

geek out To say or do something highly technical relating to computers when you don't have time to explain what you are doing or saying to others. A computer user may say, "Pardon me while I geek out."

gendarme A member of an armed French police organization.

Gendarmerie Nationale A military force in France under the administrative control of the minister of armed forces.

gender bias Bias toward or discrimination against an individual on the basis of his or her gender.

gender courses Classes conducted for jail and prison officers to sensitize them to how they can work around women in ways that will not lead to sexual harassment. The classes are oriented toward respecting the work of persons of a different gender.

gender identity The gender characteristics individuals identify in their own behaviors. Members of both sexes who identify with masculine traits are more likely to engage in delinquent acts.

gender-schema theory The theory that our culture polarizes males and females, forcing them into exclusive gender roles of feminine and masculine. These gender scripts provide the basis for deviant behaviors.

gender-specific services Activities for at-risk youths and delinquent girls that meet their needs, in view of their particular age and development.

general adaptation syndrome (GAS) A stress response as a reaction involving all of a person's biological and psychological resources. The person typically experiences stress, is alarmed, resists the stress, and eventually becomes exhausted. Mental or emotional breakdowns are a common result of substantial stress.

general appearance file Law enforcement records containing photographs and other information about persons known to engage in crime.

general court martial The highest level of tribunal in the military, in which the most serious offenses are tried.

general deterrence The belief that punishment inflicted on one lawbreaker will deter others. *See also* **deterrence, general or specific.**

General Equivalency Diploma (GED) A certificate signifying satisfactory completion of coursework that is the equivalent of a high-school education. GEDs are usually attained by older persons who did not formally graduate from a high school in their earlier years.

general intent Actions that on their face indicate a criminal purpose (e.g., breaking into a locked building, trespassing on someone's property); also, willful wrongdoing where one's motive for committing the crime is inferred; used as a method of legal proof in court.

general jurisdiction The power of a court to hear a wide range of cases, both civil and criminal.

general law Any statute affecting all persons in all places. Rights conferred by the U.S. Constitution are general laws that apply to any U.S. citizen.

general members Gang members whose purpose in joining is for protection. Most are not as committed to gang values as hardcore gang members.

general strain theory An expanded version of anomie theory that focuses on both positive and negative sources of strain, the various dimensions of strain, strategies for coping with strain, and factors that determine whether strain will be coped with in a delinquent or nondelinquent fashion. The theory was described by sociologist Robert Agnew (1992).

general theory of crime A criminological theory advanced by Michael Gottfredson and Travis Hirschi that posits that offenders are those who are low in self-control and who selfishly pursue their own self-interest.

general verdict A finding of guilty or not guilty; the result of jury deliberations where the outcome is either a guilty or not guilty vote.

generation gap A belief once widely held, particularly during the 1960s, of extreme differences in attitudes between adults and adolescents. More recent evidence suggests that this gap has been exaggerated.

genetic fingerprint The unique genetic characteristics an individual possesses.

genocide The systematic killing of a people based on their race, ethnicity, religious beliefs, or some other criterion.

genome The entire collection of an organism's genes.

genomic DNA DNA found in an organism's genome that is passed on to offspring and is necessary for survival.

genomics The study of genomes, which includes gene sequencing and genome mapping; the study of an entire collection of genes.

Genovese, Kitty (1935–1964) A 28-year-old woman who was murdered in plain view of other citizens in New York City on March 14, 1964. She was stabbed repeatedly and screamed for help, but at least 38 nearby persons closed their windows and did not call police. The attacker fled, but then returned to finish killing Ms. Genovese. Her death signified the unfeeling, isolated dynamics attributed to urban life at the time.

gentrification The process of reclaiming and reconditioning deteriorated neighborhoods by refurbishing depressed real estate and then renting or selling the properties to upper-middle-class professionals.

geographical profiling The use of detailed information and specialized analytical tools, such as a Rigel geographical profiling system, to locate offenders.

geographic base files A coded database covering a geographical area, which contains information such as traffic violations, arrest records, and other pertinent data. Data may be retrieved by computer for subsequent analysis. These files are also useful for resource allocation and dispatching police officers to areas considered high-crime locations.

Georgia Intensive Supervision Probation Program, Georgia ISP model A program commenced in 1982 that established three phases of punitive probation conditions for probationers. Phases moved probationers through extensive monitoring and control to less extensive monitoring, ranging from six to 12 months. The program has demonstrated low rates of recidivism among participants.

geriatric prisoners Members of the growing population of older inmates between ages 55 and 70; also, those who have aged out of crime and no longer pose a threat to society.

Germanic law Customary laws of Teutonic origin. Such customary laws were the equivalent of common law in England, and they governed decisions in disputes based on prevailing norms.

get-tough movement, get-tough policies A general orientation toward criminals and juvenile delinquents that favors the maximum penalties and punishments for crime and delinquency; also, any action toward toughening or strengthening sentencing provisions or dispositions involving adults or juveniles.

GHB *See* **gamma-hydroxybutyrate (GHB).**

gibbet In England, an upright post with an extended arm from which executed criminals were displayed to the public.

Gideon, Clarence Earl (1910–1972) An indigent Florida criminal who was tried and convicted of breaking and entering without attorney representation, even though he asked for an attorney. The U.S. Supreme Court heard Gideon's appeal and reversed his Florida conviction. This landmark decision in defendant's rights granted attorney representation to indigents in serious cases (e.g., felonies) when they are in jeopardy of losing liberty. *Gideon v. Wainwright* (1963) was the first of several indigent rights cases.

gift *causa mortis* A gift of personal property made by someone who believes he or she is about to die.

gift *inter vivos* A gift conveyed from one living person to another.

g-juice *See* **gamma-hydroxybutyrate (GHB).**

glandular theory A theory linking abnormal or criminal behavior with thyroidal, adrenal, or other glandular malfunctions.

global fallacy The tendency to explain all crime with a specific theory.

Global Positioning Satellite (GPS) system A network of satellites used by the U.S. Department of Defense to pinpoint targets and guide bombs that is currently used in some jurisdictions to track probationers and parolees.

Glueck, Eleanor and Sheldon Criminologists who studied the life cycle of delinquent careers in their classic work *Unraveling Juvenile Delinquency* (1950). They regarded family relations as the primary factors in whether youths adopted delinquent behaviors, and believed that the earlier the onset of delinquency, the more deeply rooted would be the path of eventual criminal careers. Antisocial youths were more prone toward adult criminal careers than non-antisocial youths. Their research has influenced risk instruments and dangerousness forecasts for probation, parole board early-release decision making, and institutional placement, assigning higher risk scores when delinquency is first observed at younger ages.

goals model A view of an organization that makes the following assumptions: (1) the organization exists to achieve stated goals; (2) the organization develops a rational procedure for goal attainment; and (3) the organization is assessed in terms of the effectiveness of goal attainment.

Goddard, Henry H. (1866–1957) Goddard studied "feebleminded" persons in institutions in the 1920s and concluded that a majority of juvenile delinquents were feebleminded. His studies were later discounted for their lack of scientific integrity. He wrote *The Kallikak Family: A Study in the Heredity of Feeblemindedness* (1912).

Goffman, Erving (1922–1982) A criminologist and social psychologist who investigated the impact of stigma on social behavior. Goffman wrote *Presentation of Self in Everyday Life* (1959) and *Asylums* (1961). He suggested that others' reactions to one's stigma, such as a facial deformity, trigger deviant conduct among those with various stigmata, and thus, stigma itself is not a direct cause of deviant or criminal conduct.

going rate The local view of the appropriate sentence or punishment for a particular offense, in consideration of the defendant's prior record and other factors.

Golden Crescent The traditional area of opium poppy cultivation and production; the region encompassing Iran, Afghanistan, and Pakistan.

Golden Triangle A poppy-growing area in southeastern Asia in which a high grade of opium is cultivated and produced; the region encompassing Burman, Thailand, and Laos.

gold investment fraud A scam perpetrated during difficult economic times that lures unsuspecting investors into buying gold, silver, or other precious metals.

golf cart patrolling A method of officer surveillance of neighborhoods or city areas using golf carts as transportation instead of cruisers. Golf carts are used, especially in Tampa, FL, where golf cart patrolling was pioneered, to bring officers into closer touch with neighborhood and area residents. Such patrolling is often classified as a part of community-oriented policing.

good boys, bad boys Terms used to refer to the youth studied by Walter C. Reckless and Simon Dinitz in their attempt to test Reckless's containment theory in which schoolteachers were asked in the study to group male children in their classes into either good boys or bad boys.

"good cop, bad cop" An interrogation tactic used by law enforcement officers in which one officer plays the role of a hard-nosed investigator who is out to get the suspect, while the other officer pretends to be the suspect's friend.

"good-faith" exception An exception to the exclusionary rule when police officers with good or honest intentions conducted a search and seizure on the basis of a faulty warrant. Acting in "good faith" presumably excuses conduct.

good marks Credit obtained by prisoners in nineteenth-century England. Prisoners were given "marks" for participating in educational programs and other self-improvement activities.

good moral character The totality of virtues that forms the basis of one's reputation in the community.

good Samaritan A person other than a police officer who administers aid or assists someone who is involved in an accident or who has suffered injury. The person rendering assistance is not involved in the injury or responsible for its cause. Also, a person who assists police in apprehending a fleeing offender.

Good Samaritan Laws Statutes in some jurisdictions that obligate passersby to render aid or assistance to persons injured in car accidents and other mishaps.

goods and chattels Personal property of any kind other than real property.

"good time," "good-time" credits An amount of time deducted from the period of incarceration of a convicted offender, calculated as so many days per month on the basis of good behavior while incarcerated; credits earned by prisoners for good behavior. The system was introduced in the early 1800s by British penal authorities, including Alexander Maconochie and Sir Walter Crofton. *See table; see also* **good marks.**

Good-Time Credits for Different State Jurisdictions	
More than 30 days per month:	Alabama, Oklahoma, South Carolina, Texas
30 days per month:	Arkansas, Florida, Illinois, Indiana, Kansas, Louisiana, Nevada, New Mexico, Virginia, West Virginia
20 days per month:	Maryland, Massachusetts
15 days per month:	Arizona, California, Connecticut, Kentucky, Maine, Nebraska, New Jersey, Rhode Island, South Dakota, Vermont, Washington, Wyoming
Fewer than 15 days per month:	Alaska, Colorado, Delaware, District of Columbia, Federal Bureau of Prisons, Iowa, Michigan, Mississippi, Missouri, New Hampshire, New York, North Carolina, North Dakota, Oregon, Tennessee
No good-time credit given:	Georgia, Hawaii, Idaho, Minnesota, Ohio, Pennsylvania, Utah, Wisconsin
Source: Ching, "Credits as Personal Property: Beware of the New *Ex Post Facto* Clause," 1–16.	

"good-time" laws Laws that allow a reduction of a portion of a prisoner's sentence for good behavior while in prison.

Gordon Riots A five-day riot against the Irish in London in 1780, engineered by Lord Gordon to protest Parliament's Catholic Relief Act, which made Catholics eligible for service in the British Army (a means of attaining higher social respect). The riots were suppressed by the army with firearms. Revulsion at the sight of Englishmen killing Englishmen is attributed as one of the motivating forces behind the creation of the new police by Sir Robert Peel in 1829.

Goring, Charles Buckman (1870–1919) A British criminologist who wrote *The English Convict* (1902), an examination of the characteristics of 3,000 English convicts and their comparison with college students, hospital patients, and soldiers. Goring concluded that criminals were shorter and weighed less, and were "mentally defective."

GOSSlink *See* **electronic monitoring devices.**

goths Youth who wear black clothing, listen to dark music, and otherwise separate themselves from conventional high-school groups and activities.

Gotti, John (1940–2002) An organized crime leader during the 1980s and 1990s who worked his way up through the ranks of the mob. He was known as the "Dapper Don" because of his expensive clothing, and later as the "Teflon Don," because of the difficulty prosecutors had in securing convictions against him. Gotti was eventually convicted and died in prison.

government agency Any legitimate organization that is a part of the legislative, judicial, or executive branches of government, with the authority to act in various official matters on behalf of the government.

grace theory The view that parole is a privilege and a matter of grace or mercy by the executive. Parole confers no particular rights on the recipient and is subject to withdrawal at any time for one or more reasons, usually a violation of a parole program condition.

graduated sanctions A series of alternative punishments for convicted offenders, each of which is slightly more punitive and restrictive than the last.

graduate entry scheme A special course in England and Wales whereby prospective police recruits are selected on the basis of their performance of in-service work and law enforcement education.

graffiti Any wall writing, indoors or outdoors. Outdoors it is sometimes referred to as the "newspaper of the street."

Graffiti Removal Initiative Program A community program, designed as a condition of probation in cases of vandalism, in which youths remove graffiti from public buildings or houses in conjunction with other program conditions.

graft Bribes accepted in the course of one's police role in exchange for favors or concessions, usually involving violations of the law.

graft, honest A term used by Tammany Hall character George Plunkitt to designate the profit yielded from a politician's knowledge of public building projects and contracts.

Graham, Jack Gilbert (1932–1957) A bomber who constructed an explosive device and planted it in his mother's luggage before she boarded a United Airlines flight in Denver, CO. The plane exploded over Longmont, CO, on November 1, 1955, killing all 44 passengers and crew.

grain A unit of measurement to weigh gunpowder used the manufacture of cartridges for use in firearms. Charts exist to instruct those who load ammunition with powder how many grains of gunpowder to use to cause bullets to be expelled from firearms at given speeds over a given distance.

grandfather clause A clause used to exempt organizations or persons from certain laws passed as regulatory statutes or provisions. When new laws are enacted, persons or organizations employed or functioning prior to these new laws are exempt from having to comply with the new laws or be affected by them.

grand jury Investigative bodies whose numbers vary among states, and whose duties include determining probable cause regarding commission of a crime and returning formal charges against suspects. *See also* **true bill; no true bill.**

grand jury, charging A body of persons convened as a grand jury to decide whether to amend original charges against a particular defendant at the prosecutor's request.

grand jury, investigative A body of persons convened as a grand jury to investigate possible crimes in either state or federal jurisdictions. They may or may not issue true bills, indictments, or presentments.

grand larceny Theft of property with a value in excess of a given amount, such as $5,000. States vary on the specific amount. *See also* **petit larceny.**

grand theft Grand larceny.

grand theft auto Stealing an automobile, which is considered to be a felony.

granny bashing Abuse of the elderly, particularly one's parents.

grant of probation Any court declaration sentencing a convicted person to probation.

grapevines Informal communication patterns that exist within the formal communication network. Informal leaders emerge who do not have the same degree of formal job status as formal leaders but who nevertheless exert significant influence on employees' attitudes toward their jobs. Every organization creates an informal structure, and the process of modifying organizational goals is effected through such structures.

graphology Handwriting analysis.

"grass eaters" Slang for police officers who accept payoffs when their everyday duties place them in a position to be solicited by the public.

grassroots movement A movement that starts with the general public and not the political arena.

gratuity Any present in exchange for a service.

gravity knife Any knife with a blade that is released from the handle by the force of gravity or the application of centrifugal force, and that when so released is locked in place by means of a button, spring, lever, or other locking or catching device.

"gray hat" A computer hacker who is like a white hat hacker in most situations but uses his or her knowledge for less than noble purposes on occasion; that is, one who may be thought of as a white hat hacker who wears a black hat at times to accomplish his or her own agenda. Also, persons who have engaged in criminal conduct with computer systems but are hired by corporations to assist them in improving the security of their systems. *See also* **"black hat"; "white hat."**

GREAT (Gang Resistance Education and Training) A program established in Phoenix, AZ, in which police officers visit schools and help youths understand how to cope with peer pressure to commit delinquent acts. Topics of educational programs include victim rights, drugs and neighborhoods, conflict resolution, and need fulfillment.

Great Law of Pennsylvania A law established by William Penn in 1682, designed to make prison and jail conditions more humane by banning branding, stocks and pillories, and other forms of corporal punishment. It was repealed when Penn died, and corporal punishments were restored.

great man approach A leadership notion similar to charismatic leadership that vests particular persons with significant power to influence others on the basis of their natural ability and will. Such a leader is similar to a natural-born leader.

Greek law Law derived from the writings of Socrates, Plato, and Aristotle, who influenced legal reasoning. Such law was once referred to as the reasonable person doctrine.

Green Haven Prison A New York incarceration facility constructed initially as a military prison during World War II. In 1949, it was designed by New York officials as an escape-proof prison.

Greenpeace Founded in 1971, Greenpeace consists of activists who use nonviolent direct action and creative communication to expose global environmental problems and to promote solutions that are essential to a green and peaceful future. In 1971, a small group of activists boarded an aging 80-foot boat and slowly made their way through the North Pacific waters off Alaska to bear witness to the destructive nuclear weapons testing planned for Amchitka Island. Subsequently, Greenpeace became the largest environmental movement in the world. Its goals are to save ancient forests, stop global warming, eliminate persistent organic pollutants, protect the oceans, eliminate the threat of genetic engineering, and end the nuclear age. There are over 250,000 U.S. members and 2.5 million worldwide members who contribute unsolicited funds for Greenpeace's perpetuation.

Green River Killer A serial murderer responsible for the deaths of 48 women found in and around the Green River in Washington between 1982 and 1984, and some murders in the 1990s. The cases were solved in 2003, when Gary Leon Ridgway, a 54-year-old former truck painter, confessed to 48 murders. Ridgway was first arrested in November 2001, after detectives linked his sperm through DNA with three of his victims. In a plea-bargain agreement in which Ridgway agreed to assist authorities in finding the bodies of his victims, he was sentenced to life without the possibility of parole by a Washington court in December 2003. Ridgway told the court that he killed these women because he hated prostitutes and didn't want to pay them for sex. He said that he killed so many women that he had a hard time keeping them straight.

Green River laws Statutes prohibiting door-to-door sales.

Green River Task Force The body of persons convened to investigate the Green River murders of women in and around the Seattle, WA, area. The group of Task Force members consisted of 56 law enforcement officers at the local, state, and federal levels.

Greenwood Scale A scale to measure future dangerousness devised by RAND researcher Peter Greenwood. The scale is used as a classification measure for determining the level of custody for certain persons who are to be incarcerated. Greenwood advocates selective incapacitation as a crime-reduction strategy, and conducted empirical investigations of the effectiveness of the "three strikes and you're out" strategy for crime prevention and control.

grid search A technique for searching crime scenes for evidence. Areas are searched by means of a strip method, whereby plots of land area are marked off by tape at right angles and searched in minute detail.

grievance, grievance procedure A formalized arrangement, usually involving a neutral hearing board, whereby institutionalized individuals have the opportunity to register complaints about the conditions of their confinement.

grievous bodily harm Serious physical injury as the result of a criminal act.

grifter One who conducts a confidence game.

grooming A course of acts and words taken by molesters to encourage children to consider sexual acts with the molester.

groove diameter The actual diameter of the bore of a firearm as determined from the distance from one groove at the bottom of the bore to a groove at the top of the bore.

grooves and lands The spiraling lines within the barrel of a firearm. Unique marks on a projectile are examined by forensic specialists to determine whether a particular firearm fired the projectile.

gross misdemeanor A hybrid offense classification in some jurisdictions that allows for greater penalties than are ordinarily imposed for typical misdemeanors, such as a jail sentence exceeding one year in duration, without invoking civil disabilities that accompany felony convictions.

gross negligence A tort wherein someone fails to provide the standard of care required in a given situation.

grounded-theory approach In field research, the development of a theory that is closely and directly relevant to the particular setting under study whereby the researcher first develops conceptual categories from data and then makes new observations to clarify and elaborate these categories. Concepts and tentative hypotheses are then developed directly from the data.

group autonomy The independence of a group and its separation from other cultural groups, which are achieved by maintaining the subcultural values and attitudes that reinforce the group's independence.

group cohesiveness The tendency of group members to stick together, which can be measured by the number of times group members use "we" when referring to their group activities, the number of in-group sociometric choices, the degree of willingness of group members to leave the group, the number of times that a work group will process grievances jointly before administrative higher-ups, and the attraction of members to the group in terms of the strength of forces on the individual member to remain in the group and to resist leaving the group.

group conference *See* **family group conference, group conference.**

group counseling, group therapy A treatment program that allows several inmates to be treated at the same time and at a low cost. It involves the discussion of feelings or attitudes in an effort to create mutual acceptance and a supportive environment. Group interaction is used as a therapeutic device.

group home A nonsecure custodial facility for juveniles that provides limited supervision and support. Juveniles live in a homelike environment with other juveniles and participate in therapeutic programs and counseling. *See also* **foster home.**

grouping A collective of individuals who interact in the workplace but, because of shifting membership, do not develop into a work group.

group process A perspective applied to juvenile gangs that sees this form of delinquency as being produced primarily by status strivings within the gang itself, rather than by external strains or lower-class focal concerns.

guaranty A promise by one person to another to repay a debt owed to a third party.

guard Once the preferred term to refer to those who supervise inmates in prisons, penitentiaries, and jails. Currently, the preferred term is "correctional officer."

guardian Any person placed in legal control of another either temporarily or permanently and who is responsible for the other person's welfare.

guardian *ad litem* "For the suit" (Latin); a court-appointed attorney who protects the interests of children in cases involving their welfare and who works with the children during the litigation period.

Guardian Angels A New York–based organization consisting of young men and women who monitor subways and city streets to protect citizens from muggers. It was founded in 1979 by Curtis Sliwa as a voluntary organization to protect and offer assistance to New York City citizens who are potential victims of thieves, pickpockets, and muggers. Members wear red berets that symbolize courage in the quest for street safety. Various members make presentations in school classrooms and offer their protective services to different groups. *See also* **CyberAngels.**

Guerry, Andre-Michel (1802–1866) Guerry assisted in the establishment of the cartographic school of criminology, which posited that social factors, including gender and age, influence crime rates significantly. Factors such as season, climate, population composition, and poverty also were believed to be correlated with criminality.

guided discretion Decision making bounded by general guidelines, rules, or laws.

guided group interaction (GGI) A group dynamics treatment process stressing the use of a youth reference group and changes in group norms to change behavior. *See also* **Provo Experiment.**

guidelines-based sentencing *See* **sentencing guidelines.**

guillotine An instrument, devised in France, used for beheading people as a punishment.

guilt The state of having committed a crime.

guilt by association Any inference of one's culpability as the result of being in the company of someone who has committed a crime or is suspected of having committed a crime.

guilty Legally responsible for committing a crime.

guilty but mentally ill A legal status in which the suspect is considered legally responsible for the criminal act but acknowledges that his or her mental state is compromised by mental problems or illness.

guilty plea A defendant's formal affirmation of guilt in court to charges contained in a complaint, information, or indictment claiming that the defendant committed the offenses listed.

guilty verdict A decision of guilt by a judge in a bench trial or a jury in a jury trial of the guilt of defendants, based on evidence beyond a reasonable doubt for a conviction.

gulags From the 1930s to the 1980s, a chain of prisons, labor camps, insane asylums, and villages operated in the Siberian region of Russia where those opposed to the government were confined and exiled.

gun Any type of firearm, including handheld weapons as well as rifles; a broad class of firearms, including pistols, revolvers, semiautomatic pistols, rifles, shotguns, and other similar devices.

gun buy-back program A program that offers incentives, such as cash, to turn firearms over to authorities.

gun control, gun-control laws Any regulatory mechanism governing the sale, transfer, manufacture, or exchange of firearms, including screening mechanisms for determining one's background and possible disqualifications for acquiring a firearm.

gun court A specialty court designed to more quickly process offenders whose crimes involved the possession or use of firearms.

gun lobby Organizations in the United States, such as the National Rifle Association (NRA), who work to preserve the Second Amendment of the U.S. Constitution and the right of citizens to bear arms or possess firearms.

gun meltdown The practice of taking confiscated firearms and melting them in a foundry to prevent their future recirculation and use by criminals.

gunshot The report given off by a firearm.

gunshot wound Any trauma to human tissue caused by the impact of a bullet or other projectile discharged from a firearm.

H

habeas corpus "You have the body" (Latin); a writ used by prisoners to challenge the nature and length of their confinement.

habeas corpus petition A petition filed by or on behalf of an inmate challenging the legitimacy of his or her confinement and the nature of that confinement. The document commands authorities to show cause why an inmate should be confined in either a prison or a jail. It also includes challenges of the nature of confinement. Also, a written order by the court to any person, including a law enforcement officer, directing that person to bring the named individual before the court so that it can determine if there is adequate cause for continued detention.

habitual-criminal laws, habitual-offender statutes Statutes vary among states. They generally provide life imprisonment as a mandatory sentence for chronic offenders who have been convicted of three or more serious felonies within a specific time period.

habitual offender Any person who has been convicted of two or more felonies and may be sentenced under a habitual offender statute for an aggravated or longer prison term.

habituation Psychological dependence on a substance such as tobacco, which may include drug dependence. Withdrawal from these substances is more psychological than physical.

hacker A computer hobbyist who has advanced computer skills; a person capable of accessing confidential information from another's computer by remote electronic means; a person who enjoys exploring the details of programmable systems and how to stretch their capabilities. The term is believed to have originated in the 1960s at the MIT Artificial Intelligence (AI) Lab, but was possibly used earlier in association with teenage radio hams and electronics tinkerers.

hacking run A hacking session by a computer hacker extending long outside of normal working times, especially a session lasting longer than 12 hours; a term analogous to "bombing run" or "speed run."

hacks Jail and prison guards.

hair trigger The action device of a firearm, most often a pistol or revolver, that requires relatively little pressure to bring about the firearm's discharge.

half-steppers A term used to describe black inmates during the prisoner movement era who leaned toward revolutionary ideas but were unwilling to adopt the regimented and spartan lifestyle of true revolutionaries.

half-trusties In the Arkansas prison system circa 1940s–1970s, inmates who had a status between trusties and rank men. Their duties allowed them to avoid working in the fields.

halfway house A community-based center or home operated either publicly or privately, staffed by professionals, paraprofessionals, or volunteers, which is designed to provide housing, food, clothing, job assistance, and counseling to ex-prisoners and others in order to assist parolees in making the transition from prison to the community.

halfway-in house A home used as an alternative to prison commitment for probationers.

halfway-out house A halfway house designed for newly paroled inmates and used as an intermediate step between the regimentation of prison life and community living.

hallucinogens Natural or synthetic substances that produce vivid distortions of the senses without greatly disturbing consciousness.

haloperidol A nonaddictive drug used for treatment programs involving withdrawal from drugs such as heroin.

Hamas A movement that evolved from cells of the Muslim Brotherhood in Egypt in 1928. After the Six-Day War between Palestine and Israel in 1967, Hamas grew in power and popularity as an anti-Israeli organization. In 1978, under the spiritual leadership of Sheikh Ahmed Yassin, the movement was legally registered. Funds for the movement derive from Middle Eastern oil-producing states and leftist groups that promote Palestinian nationalism. Hamas wants to establish a transitional state under the rule of Islam. Successful attacks against Israel and the U.S. by other organizations during the 1980s and 1990s strengthened Hamas, which took credit for suicide bombings in Jerusalem in 2002. Hamas continues to threaten peace and stability in the Middle East and seeks to interfere with peaceful relations between Israel and other Middle Eastern countries.

Hand, Learned (1872–1961) A jurist and scholar who held posts as a federal and appellate judge, and wrote numerous commentaries on the law and how it should be interpreted.

handcuffs Mechanical devices that fasten about the wrists and are designed to restrain the mobility of an offender. They are most often made of metal, but are sometimes plastic.

handgun Any small, easily concealed firearm designed to be held and fired with one hand.

Handgun Control, Inc. An organization founded in 1974 and headquartered in Washington, DC, that promotes gun safety legislation. It is difficult to research because of the secrecy of its membership and headquarters. It was originally formed by Edward O. Welles, who was the first chairman of the National Council to Ban Handguns (NCBH), later renamed Handgun Control, Inc. Its national committee consists of numerous Hollywood stars. The founding chair is Nelson T. Shields III, and the chair is Sarah Brady, wife of James Brady, the presidential aide who was permanently disabled in John Hinckley's assassination attempt against President Ronald Reagan. The organization advocates banning military-style assault weapons, prohibiting the manufacture and distribution of Saturday night specials or cheap handguns sold at gun shows, barring multiple handgun sales, and requiring stringent safety classes for those who buy guns, and mandates strict reporting requirements for the theft of handguns from gun dealers and gun owners.

hand sign Any method of communication used by gang members that uses the hands and identifies the particular gang or gang terms.

hands-off approach, hands-off doctrine, hands-off policy The doctrine practiced by state and federal judiciary up until the 1940s whereby matters pertaining to inmate rights were left up to jail and prison administrators to resolve. These were considered "internal" matters in which no court intervention was required or desired. For corrections, the leading case establishing the doctrine was *Griffin v. Commonwealth* (1871). The doctrine was challenged in *Ex parte Hull* (1941). In juvenile matters, the doctrine was typical of the attitiude of the U.S. Supreme Court toward appeals stemming from juvenile-court decisions. The tendency was to let juvenile courts manage themselves until *Kent v. United States* (1966).

hands-on approach, hands-on doctrine, hands-on policy The approach by the courts, after the hands-off approach was discarded during the 1960s, of dealing with prison conditions and juvenile matters. The courts recognized that prisoners and juveniles had certain constitutional rights, and intervention was necessary to insure that those rights were observed.

hanging A method of administering the death penalty in capital punishment cases. A condemned offender is placed on a scaffold with a rope around his or her neck, and a trap door opens, causing the condemned to fall a designated distance, at which time the rope tightens and his or her neck breaks, causing death.

harassing calls Telephone communications in which the intent of the caller is to intimidate or threaten the recipient of the call; nuisance calls which may include sexually suggestive calls.

harassment Any continuous course of conduct that annoys or alarms another person. *See also* **stalking.**

harbormaster An administrator vested with the responsibility of enforcing state or federal harbor laws in accordance with city or state or federal statutes.

hardcore members Gang members who wield the majority of power through violence.

hardened criminal An offender considered beyond rehabilitation or redemption.

hard labor A form of punishment in which a convicted offender's sentence includes vigorous physical work.

hard time A sentence served under conditions that create relatively severe discomfort. The term is used to describe actual imprisonment for a specified period.

Harlan, John Marshall (1833–1911) An associate justice of the U.S. Supreme Court (1877–1911) noted for his decisions against racial discrimination and segregation. Harlan was appointed to the U.S. Supreme Court by President Rutherford B. Hayes in 1877. He was considered a liberal by his contemporaries, and was the only dissenter in the U.S. Supreme Court opinion in *Plessy v. Ferguson* (1896), which established the separate, but equal doctrine in 1896.

harmful error An error made by a judge that may be prejudicial to a defendant's case, and which may lead to a reversal of conviction against the defendant and a new trial.

harmless error An error of a minor or trivial nature that is not deemed sufficient to harm the rights of parties in a legal action. Cases are not reversed on the basis of harmless errors.

harms Under the U.S. Sentencing Guidelines, any aspect of a crime or its commission by a federal offender that would result in a sentence enhancement, such as the use of a firearm during the commission of a felony, providing someone with a firearm to commit a crime, a prior felony conviction, or being a member of a street gang when committing a crime.

Harrison Act, Harrison Narcotics Act The first federal antidrug legislation, enacted in 1914.

Harris Poll Surveys of households from data provided by the U.S. Bureau of the Census from at least 100 different locations throughout the nation. Interviews with persons in these samples are believed to be representative of public opinion within a small margin of error.

hashish A product of the hemp plant used for its hallucinogenic effects, hashish is a depressant that acts on the central nervous system. It is similar to but more powerful than marijuana, and may be smoked or chewed to produce desired effects.

Hatch Act of 1939 A congressional action to guard against politicians seeking to intimidate voters and persuade them to vote certain ways in federal elections. The act also prohibits bribes for votes and other forms of special consideration related to the way one votes. It is also called the Federal Corrupt Practices Act of 1939.

hate crime A crime committed against a victim because of his or her membership in a specific ethnic or racial category.

Hauptmann, Bruno Richard (1899–1936) A German immigrant executed in 1936 after his conviction for allegedly kidnapping the child of Charles Lindbergh. Contemporary evidence suggests that Hauptmann was wrongfully convicted by a politically motivated court and police officials. His conviction was based almost exclusively on circumstantial evidence. Some authorities believe the real kidnappers escaped punishment and that Hauptmann was convicted and executed because he was of German descent at a time when the United States was on poor terms with Nazi Germany.

Hawes-Cooper Act of 1929 Legislation that allowed states to block the importation of prison-made goods.

Hawthorne effect The impact of being observed. Persons who know they are being observed will act differently than they do when they don't know they are being observed.

Hawthorne studies An experiment conducted in the 1920s at the Hawthorne plant of the Western Electric Company that involved bank wiring for telephones. Workers were given special attention by observers and behaved differently compared with their behavior when not being observed.

Hayes, Rutherford B. (1822–1893) The first president of the American Correctional Association (originally called the National Prison Association). He later served as U.S. President (1877–1881).

Haymarket Massacre A bombing and shooting incident in May 1886 involving striking workers at the McCormick Reaper Works in Chicago. Strikebreakers attacked strikers with police assistance, and clubs and guns were used to disperse strikers, some of whom were killed. At least seven police officers were killed, and 60 others were wounded. An unknown number of civilians was killed during the strike.

Healy, William Together with Augusta Bronner, Healy studied delinquent boys and IQ in Chicago and Boston in 1926. They found that delinquents were 5 to 10 times more likely to have subnormal intelligence than were nondelinquents.

hearing Any formal proceeding in which the court hears evidence from prosecutors and defense and resolves a dispute or issue.

hearing, probable cause A proceeding in which arguments, evidence, or witnesses are presented and in which it is determined whether there is sufficient cause to hold the accused for trial or whether the case should be dismissed.

hearsay Information that is not based on the personal knowledge of a witness.

hearsay evidence Evidence that is not firsthand but is based on an account given by another.

hearsay rule The courtroom precedent that hearsay cannot be used in court. Rather than accepting testimony on hearsay, the trial process asks that persons who were the original source of the hearsay information be brought into court to be questioned and cross-examined. Exceptions to the hearsay rule may occur when persons with direct knowledge are either dead or otherwise unable to testify.

Hearst, Patricia (1955–) The daughter of newspaper tycoon William Randolph Hearst who was kidnapped by Symbionese Liberation Army (SLA) members in 1974. Hearst was subsequently involved in one or more bank robberies and was observed holding a weapon. Eventually, the SLA members were killed or captured, including Hearst, who was charged with and convicted of bank robbery in 1976. She was subsequently pardoned by President Gerald Ford.

hebephile A pedophile who is attracted to children at their age of puberty and adolescence.

***Heck* rule** A holding by the U.S. Supreme Court in *Heck v. Humphrey* (1994) establishing that whenever Section 1983 civil rights actions are filed by persons such as inmates against corrections officials or others, in order for the plaintiff to recover damages from the defendant, the plaintiff must prove that the conviction or sentence (1) has been reversed on direct appeal, (2) was expunged by executive order, (3) was declared invalid by a state tribunal authorized to make such a determination, or (4) was called into question by a federal court's issuance of a writ of *habeas corpus*.

hedonism Jeremy Bentham's term indicating that people avoid pain and pursue pleasure. *See also* **Bentham, Jeremy.**

hedonistic calculus Jeremy Bentham's term referring to thought processes of persons who calculate the benefits of pleasure derived from various acts and the minimization of pain; applied to criminality, the process by which persons may weigh the positive and negative benefits accruing from engaging in crime or deviance.

hedonistic gang A type of gang primarily involved in using drugs and getting high, with little involvement in crime.

heir at law Someone entitled by law to inherit a decedent's estate and property.

Hell's Angels An organized group of motorcycle enthusiasts, headquartered in California, allegedly involved in criminal activity, including protection schemes, drug trafficking, murder for hire, prostitution, and various property crimes. Founded in Fontana, CA, in 1948, the group was named after a bomber group that flew during World War II. Arvid Olsen, a World War II squadron leader, was one of the group's original founders. The group's color is red, and its insignia is the copyrighted "Deathhead" that can be traced to the 85th Fighter Squadron and 552nd Medium Bomber Squadron designs from World War II.

hematoporphyrin test A test for traces of blood (e.g., on clothing retrieved from a crime scene).

hemp Slang for marijuana; also, the plant that hasish and marijuana come from.

Hennard, George, Jr. (1956—1991) A 35-year-old Killeen, TX, man who drove his pickup truck through a Luby's cafeteria window in October 1991 and shot and killed 22 persons, wounding 23 others. He committed suicide before being captured.

Henry system A fingerprint classification system created by Sir Edward Henry, a former London police commissioner, in 1901. The system uses a combination of loops, arches, whorls, and composites. It is widely used by law enforcement agencies throughout the world.

hepatitis C (HCV) A liver disease that is the most common blood-borne infection in the United States, with 8,000 to 10,000 persons dying from it each year.

hereditary criminal propensities Biologically transmitted criminal inclinations or tendencies.

heredity theory A theory that postulates that behaviors result from genetically transmitted characteristics. Criminal behaviors would be explained according to inherited genes from parents or ancestors who are criminal or who have criminal propensities.

heroin A highly addictive opiate, usually injected into the bloodstream with syringes.

Herrnstein, Richard (1930—1994) A criminologist who collaborated with James Q. Wilson to write *Crime and Human Nature* (1985). They argued that personal traits, such as genetic makeup, intelligence, and body build, may actually outweigh social variables as predictors of criminal conduct. Herrnstein proposed an integrated theory of criminal behavior that includes biosocial makeup, personality, rational choice, structure, and social process.

Herzberg's motivation-maintenance theory The view that different job conditions and characteristics contribute to job satisfaction or dissatisfaction. The presence of certain conditions does not necessarily improve job satisfaction, nor does the absence of certain factors does not necessarily create job dissatisfaction; thus, satisfiers and dissatisfiers as variables were identified and used by Frederick Herzberg in explaining worker motivation. He wrote *Motivation to Work* (1959).

hesitation marks Shallow, slashing-type wounds found on some suicide victims that run parallel to a deeper, fatal wound caused by a knife or other sharp object.

Hezbollah, Hizbollah, Hizbullah A militant Shia political party in Lebanon that began as a guerilla group fighting against the Israeli occupation of southern Lebanon in 1982. Despite Israel's withdrawal from Lebanon in 2000, the group still maintains an active militia, known as the Islamic Resistance. A terrorist organization, the organization has killed more than 300 American citizens. It is headed by Sheik Hassan Nasrallah and is known or suspected to have been involved in numerous attacks on American targets in Lebanon during the 1980s, including bombings of the U.S. embassy and U.S. marine barracks in Beirut in September 1984, which killed 63 people, including 18 Americans. Elements of the group have been linked to kidnappings and detentions of Americans and other Western hostages in Lebanon. The group continues to fight Israel because it occupies the Shebaa Farms area, which, although within the UN-agreed Israeli border, is claimed as Lebanese territory. The UN rejects the group's claim, verifying that Israel has thoroughly withdrawn from Lebanon. The group operates its own satellite television station from Lebanon, called Al-Manar TV, meaning "Lighthouse." Israelis contend that the television station is a propaganda machine for Hezbollah.

hidden crime Crime not reported to police and thus not measured by official crime statistics.

hidden delinquency Infractions reported by surveys of high-school youths. It is considered "hidden" because it most often is undetected by police officers, but is disclosed in self-report surveys.

hierarchical linear modeling (HLM) A set of statistical techniques permitting the simultaneous analysis of variables representing different levels of analysis.

hierarchical model, hierarchy of authority A predetermined arrangement of superior-subordinate relations involving the distribution of power in any organization. Lower-level employees or workers report or are responsible to higher-level employees or managers.

hierarchy of needs A motivational scheme devised by Abraham Maslow that envisions basic physiological needs as the basis for developing other needs, including safety and security, belongingness, self-esteem, and self-actualization.

hierarchy rule A standard *Uniform Crime Reports* scoring practice in which only the most serious offense is counted in a multiple-offense situation.

high crimes and misdemeanors A term applied to offenses committed by public officials that are considered sufficiently serious to justify their impeachment by the U.S. House of Representatives.

higher courts Appellate courts and sometimes trial courts of record, as distinguished from lower courts.

higher law doctrine The view that natural law is superior to positive law; an alternative view that some laws are more important than statutory law, such as the rights set forth in the U.S. Constitution.

High Mask Lighting A system used as a part of a prison's perimeter security system. Usually five to eight lights, each illuminating a large area, are placed on poles 100 to 120 feet to completely light the prison compound and its perimeter.

high-risk entry Law enforcement officer intrusion into premises where there is a strong likelihood of encountering armed resistance by the occupants.

High School Senior Survey A National Institute on Drug Abuse–sponsored continuing study of 15,000 to 17,000 high school seniors that investigates the prevalence of drugs among them. Research that surveys information and tracks findings is conducted on a regular basis.

high-seas law enforcement U.S. Coast Guard-enforced laws within U.S. territorial waters. Investigations of smuggling and illegal fishing are conducted.

high-security institution A U.S. penitentiary with highly secure perimeters, multiple- and single-occupant cell housing, and close staff supervision and movement controls.

high sheriff A sheriff or chief county law enforcement officer.

high-speed pursuit The practice of law enforcement officers engaging in motor-vehicle chases of suspects at high rates of speed in order to capture them.

High Street Jail The first jail constructed under the Great Law of Pennsylvania on High Street in Philadelphia.

high-technology crime A violation of criminal law whose commission depends on or makes use of sophisticated and advanced technology.

high treason Betrayal of one's country.

highway A publicly maintained roadway traversed by motor vehicles.

Highway Patrol A state law enforcement agency whose primary function is to enforce motor vehicle laws on state and interstate highways.

highway statistics A compilation of accident information, driver's license information, and any other information relating to automobile travel on the nation's highways.

hijack alert system A method of alerting organizations that trucks are being hijacked on roadways. Other truck drivers are alerted and keep a lookout for hijacked trucks.

hijacking Taking over any mode of transportation by force. Automobiles, ships, and aircraft are the most common targets, although trains and buses have also been hijacked.

Hinckley, John W., Jr. (1955–) The man who unsuccessfully attempted to assassinate President Ronald Reagan on March 30, 1981. Hinckley had become obsessed with actress Jody Foster. He is now confined to a mental institution.

Hindelang, Michael (1946–1982) A criminologist who has studied juvenile delinquency and its causes. He described delinquents as extroverted, and generally finds support for the studies and theories of Hans Eysenck. Hindelang has investigated the relation between IQ and criminality, collaborating with Travis Hirschi, and has found support for the association between IQ and criminal behavior.

hippies Young persons during the 1960s and 1970s who rejected the values and ideas of mainstream society in regard to money, work, and material goods, dressed distinctively, grew long hair, ate vegetarian food, experimented with drugs, opposed the Vietnam War, and argued that love and peace could change the world. Many refused to work at traditional jobs, and they often lived in communes and wandered from place to place. They were sometimes called "flower children."

Hire a Gang Leader An El Monte, CA, delinquency prevention program established in 1975. Ssponsored by members of the local police department, groups of 10 to 15 gang leaders met with police officers and designed a program to provide job opportunities for gang members who were unemployed. The program taught gang members that police officers are not always their enemies, and it gave them a different view of the police officer role as an "enabler" and "facilitator," as there were numerous successful job placements.

Hirschi, Travis (1935–) A criminologist who examined delinquency in *The Causes of Delinquency* (1969), and the processes whereby persons acquire deviant behaviors. Hirschi described social control theory, positing that social ties and bonds in society become weakened. All persons in society are assumed to be potential law violators, but most are law-abiding because of fear of loss of close relations with friends, employment, and neighbors. Without such strong bonds, persons become detached from others and are more willing to engage in behaviors that will damage their reputations. Individual differences among society's members cause differential reaction to society's moral and ethical codes; thus, some persons become more susceptible to criminal conduct. Social bond elements include attachment (sensitivity to and interest in others), commitment (time, energy, and effort expended in conventional activities), involvement (social inclusion in ongoing group activities), and belief (sharing a common set of moral values with others). Hirschi also wrote *A General Theory of Crime* (1990) with Michael Gottfredson, which examined self-control as an essential feature in their refinement of social control theory. The criminal offender and criminal act are separate concepts. Crime may be situational and impulsive for some persons predisposed to criminal conduct, but self-control is a stabilizing force. Effective parenting and early socialization are mechanisms that influence how one decides to engage in criminal conduct.

histology Study of human tissue.

historical research A research strategy that examines the same society at different times and looks at the way crime has changed with economic and social development.

history All events occurring during the time of the research that might affect the individuals studied and provide a rival explanation for the change in the dependent variable. History may be a possible contaminant to the validity of a measure.

hit Slang term for murder for hire or by order.

hit-and-run An incident in which the driver of a vehicle strikes a pedestrian or motor vehicle and leaves the scene without staying to provide identifying information for establishing responsibility for the act.

hit man One who performs murder for hire or under the orders of a superior in organized crime.

HITS *See* **Homicide Investigation Tracking System (HITS)**.

HIV *See* **Human Immunodeficiency Virus (HIV)**.

hoax A fraud or purposeful deception motivated either by humorous or malicious intent.

Hobbs Act Antiracketeering legislation, passed in 1947, intended to control interference with interstate commerce.

hobby cop A part-time police officer whose full-time employment is in a different position; a reserve officer. Some jurisdictions use private-sector citizens to perform law enforcement roles on a voluntary or part-time basis, such as the Organized Reserve Officers attached to the Knox County, TN, Sheriff's Department.

Hoffa, James Riddle (1913–1975?) The Teamsters Union president elected in 1957 who was convicted of evidence tampering in 1967. After his release from prison he mysteriously disappeared, and is assumed murdered.

hog A prison or jail inmate.

holdback jail inmates Prisoners held in jails who are being accommodated for state and federal prisons that are overcrowded; also known as contract prisoners.

holding The legal principle drawn from a judicial decision; whatever a court, usually an appellate court, decides when cases are appealed from lower courts. When an appellate court "holds" a particular decision, it may uphold the original conviction, set it aside, or overturn in part and uphold in part.

holding cell A small area designed to confine a suspect temporarily.

holding facilities Places also known as lockups that contain arrestees for up to 48 hours. They are often located in police stations or local jails for the convenience of arresting officers.

hole An inmate term for solitary confinement.

holistic approach A comprehensive approach targeting multiple aspects of a problem using multiple agencies and groups instead of a single intervention method.

Holmes, Oliver Wendell, Jr. (1841–1935) A jurist and associate justice of the U.S. Supreme Court (1902–1932) appointed by President Theodore Roosevelt. Holmes was known as the "great dissenter" because of his opposition to judicial power. He believed in judicial self-restraint, formulated the "clear and present danger" doctrine, and advocated the First Amendment rights of free speech and press.

Holocaust The experience of Jews during World War II under Adolf Hitler's Nazi program to exterminate them. Approximately 6 million Jews are believed to have been executed between 1939 and 1945. A major tenet of white-supremacy groups is Holocaust denial.

holograph A handwritten will; any document in the handwriting of the person who has signed it, with legal force in court to insure that the will provisions are enforced.

Homans, George (1910–1989) A sociologist who developed modern social exchange theory, based on principles elaborated by George Herbert Mead and Georg Simmel, and author of *The Human Group* (1950). He considered social exchange as a primary ingredient to establishing societal conformity, viewing interactions in terms of rewards and costs.

homeboy A term applied to individuals who share some common experience, such as coming from the same town or neighborhood, having the same ethnic-minority status, or being a member of the same youth gang.

homeboy connection A pattern of prison gang membership based on relationships formed outside of prison, usually based on coming from the same neighborhood or having been boyhood friends.

homeboy pattern Illustrated by the Mexican Mafia pattern of formation, this refers to gangs formed from a nucleus that shares ethnicity, a subculture, and a membership in a youth gang.

home confinement, home detention, home incarceration Housing of offenders in their own homes with or without electronic monitoring devices, which reduces prison overcrowding and prisoner costs. This is sometimes an intermediate punishment involving the use of offender residences for mandatory incarceration during evening hours after a curfew and on weekends, which is also called "house arrest."

home invasion A hybrid crime, similar to carjacking, that combines burglary with robbery. It is usually accomplished by persons who kick or force their way into a home and terrorize the residents into giving up their valuables and other property.

homeless Persons, often unemployed and sometimes suffering from mental illness, who do not have stable living arrangements and who live on city streets.

home rule The ability of local government to manage its own affairs. States have little or no power relating to the regulation or affairs of city or town policies and ways of conducting business.

homestead A filing process protecting property against most debts.

Homestead Massacre An 1892 conflict between striking workers and company guards at Carnegie Steel Company in Homestead, PA. Three hundred Pinkerton guards were ordered to the strike site to protect strikebreakers. Pinkerton guards met with resistance by strikers, which resulted in 10 guard and striker deaths. The state militia eventually arrived to restore order.

Homeward Bound A program established in Massachusetts in 1970 designed to provide juveniles with mature responsibilities through the acquisition of survival skills and wilderness experiences. A six-week training program subjected 32 youths to endurance training, physical fitness, and performing community service.

homicide The killing of one person by another.

homicide, criminal Causing the death of another without justification or excuse.

homicide, excusable The intentional but justifiable causing of death, which is a noncriminal action.

homicide, felonious Any killing of a human being under circumstances that make it a crime subject to punishment.

homicide, justifiable The intentional causing of another's death in the legal performance of one's duty or under circumstances defined by law as constituting legal justification; also, any killing of a human being that is not criminal, but is committed in such a way that it is unavoidable. This is used in self-defense cases to defend against murder charges.

homicide, willful The intentional causing the death of another, with or without legal justification.

homicide investigation Any law enforcement inquiry into the death of one or more persons who have been killed.

Homicide Investigation Tracking System (HITS) A program operated by the attorney general of the state of Washington to track and investigate homicides and other violent crimes having similar methods of operation.

homicidomania An aberrant desire to commit murder.

homophobia Fear or hatred of homosexual persons.

homosexuality The practice of sexual relations between persons of the same gender.

honor block A dormitory area within a prison reserved for inmates who have maintained good behavior over long periods of time. In such areas, inmates have more privileges.

hooch An alcoholic beverage made in prison.

hoodlum A street offender, most often a young person.

hooker Slang for prostitute.

hooligan, hooliganism A term used by the Soviets to describe a broad range of criminal conduct including disorderly conduct, alcohol or drug abuse, prostitution, and loitering.

"Hoosiers" Dull, backward, and provincial individuals with little knowledge of crime who come from rural areas.

Hooton, Earnest (1887–1954) A neo-Lombrosian and anthropologist who wrote *Crime and the Man* (1939), in which he claimed that on the basis of various physical characteristics, criminals could be differentiated from noncriminals. Hooton believed that criminality was caused by physical inferiority.

Hoover, John Edgar (1895–1972) A former director of the Federal Bureau of Investigation. In 1924, he became director of the Bureau of Investigation, which was renamed the Federal Bureau of Investigation in 1935. Hoover created the FBI Academy for training federal agents in 1935. He required early agents to be attorneys or certified public accountants as prerequisites for special agent positions.

Hoover Commissions From 1947 to 1949 and 1953 to 1955, these commissions were established to determine the causes of bureaucratic waste, corruption, and paralysis in government. They were named for President Herbert Hoover, who was concerned with government waste and duplication of function.

horizontal complexity The lateral differentiation of functions that may be duplicated at all levels of authority in corporate organizations.

horizontal differentiation A division of labor in which there is a proliferation of subunits at the same level and numerous departments at approximately the equivalent rank or status of other departments within an organization.

hormonal imbalance A condition in which an excess or insufficient amount of a particular hormone can be responsible for criminal behavior.

hormones Substances produced by the body that control such bodily functions as central nervous system functioning and reproduction.

Horney, Julie Horney wrote about premenstrual syndrome (PMS) in 1978 and established a link between PMS and criminality. She believes that psychological and physical stress trigger early menstruation and violent conduct rather than simply menstruation.

horses in law enforcement Police officers use horses to conduct patrols in certain jurisdictions such as New York City.

hospice An interdisciplinary, comfort-oriented care unit that allows seriously ill and dying prisoners to die with dignity and humanity in an environment that provides mental and spiritual preparation for the natural process of dying.

Hospice of San Michele, Hospital of Saint Michael A custodial institution established at the request of the Pope in Rome in 1704 to provide for unruly youths and others who violated the law. Youths were assigned tasks, including semi-skilled and skilled labor, which enabled them to get jobs when released.

hostage A person who is held until ransom is paid or some other condition of release is met.

hostage negotiation The art of working to bring about a peaceful solution to a hostage situation, which usually involves negotiations between criminals and law enforcement officers compromising for the subsequent release of hostages.

hostage-taking The act of holding a person for ransom or some other demand.

hostile witness A person in a criminal case who gives evidence but who fails to cooperate with the side that subpoenaed him or her.

hot pursuit A chase of suspects by law enforcement officers. A chase is often used to justify search and seizure when a suspect is eventually apprehended.

hot spot, hot spot of crime According to the criminologist Lawrence W. Sherman, a significant portion of police calls originate from only a few city locations, which include taverns and housing projects, so-called "hot spots"; a place typified by a high rate of criminal activity.

***houdoud* crimes, *hudud* crimes** Serious violations of Islamic law regarded as offenses against God, including such behavior as theft, adultery, sodomy, drinking alcohol, and robbery; Islamic punishment as a crime deterrent, which may involve amputation of a thief's hand.

hours of work The particular shift time when an employee reports for work and completes his or her responsibilities and duties. Typically, persons work in eight-hour shifts.

house arrest *See* **home confinement, home detention, home incarceration.**

housebreaking Breaking and entering a dwelling with the intent to commit theft or some other crime; burglary.

Household Survey *See* **National Survey on Drug Abuse.**

house of corrections Any county correctional institution generally used for the incarceration of more serious misdemeanants, whose sentences are usually less than one year.

houses of refuge Workhouses, the first of which was established in 1824 as a means of separating juveniles from the adult correctional process.

Howard, John (1726–1790) An early English prison reformer and sheriff of Bedfordshire, England. He was influenced by other European countries such as France to lobby for prison reforms.

Huber Act, Huber Law Legislation that established the first work-release programs in 1913.

Huberty, James Oliver (1942–1984) An unemployed security guard who entered a McDonald's restaurant in July 1984, shooting and killing 21 persons. Huberty was subsequently killed by a sharpshooter from a rooftop several hundred feet away.

hue and cry In the 1500s, a warning shouted by village watchmen if a crime was observed. *See also* **Statute of Winchester.**

Hughes, Charles E. (1862–1948) Chief justice of the U.S. Supreme Court (1930–1941). Born in Glen Falls, NY, Hughes graduated from Columbia Law School and was admitted to the bar in 1884. He practiced law in New York City and served in 1905 as counsel for a committee of the New York Legislature investigating gas companies. He also helped to expose corrupt practices of insurance companies during 1905–1906 on another state investigating committee. He was elected Republican governor of New York in 1907 and appointed an associate justice to the U.S. Supreme Court by President William Taft in 1910. He left the Supreme Court in 1916 to campaign for president as a Republican, and was defeated by Woodrow Wilson. He continued to practice law in New York, but in 1921 was appointed Secretary of State by President Warren G. Harding, and continued in that position under President Calvin Coolidge. He directed negotiations in several important foreign treaties and greatly improved the prestige of the U.S. Department of State. He was a member of the permanent Court of Arbitration (1926–1930), and a judge of the Permanent Court of International Justice (1928–1930). President Herbert Hoover appointed Hughes chief justice of the U.S. Supreme Court in 1930, where he served until voluntary retirement in 1941. Considered a moderately conservative justice, he was often the swing vote on freedom of speech issues, and helped to void all laws permitting prior restraint of press publication. He supported President Franklin D. Roosevelt's New Deal policies, but he found the act that created the National Recovery Administration (NRA) to be unconstitutional. He vigorously opposed Roosevelt's unsuccessful attempt to reorganize the U.S. Supreme Court in 1937. He died in 1948.

hulks Mothballed ships that were used to house prisoners in eighteenth-century England.

Hull House A settlement home established by Jane Addams, a reformer. It was financed by philanthropists and operated as a home for children of immigrant families in Chicago, who were taught religious principles, morality, and ethics.

human ecology The study of the relation between people and the physical space in which they live.

human identification The art of establishing the identify of a person by reconstructing human remains.

Human Immunodeficiency Virus (HIV) The virus that causes AIDS. It infects and destroys the body's ability to fight disease.

humanitarianism In penal philosophy, the doctrine advocating the removal of harsh, severe, and painful conditions in penal institutions.

human relations A school of organizational behavior stressing personal qualities of those in roles such as police officers. Apart from impersonal relations with citizens, human relations stresses persons as personality systems with emotional components.

human relations model A model of organizations devised by Elton Mayo in the early 1930s, which emphasized recognition of individual differences among employees. Individual motivation is critical, and human dignity and personality characteristics are important. This model is often contrasted with bureaucracy. *See also* **bureaucracy** *for comparison.*

human relations school A body of thought emphasizing the importance of social contacts and influence in organizations. It de-emphasizes adherence to rules and order maintenance, as suggested by bureaucracy, and focuses on emotional and affective factors as most important for encouraging employees to carry out organizational rules.

human rights Privileges considered so universal that they belong to all persons.

human rights violations Different acts that deprive persons of universal privileges to which they are entitled.

Human Rights Watch An international organization headquartered in New York City and dedicated to protecting human rights throughout the world. It conducts investigations into alleged human-rights violations and periodically publishes statistics on executions, torture, and other violations.

human sacrifice The practice of ritualistically killing a person, often for religious reasons.

human-services approach The philosophy of some corrections officers, either in prisons or jails, whereby they regard each inmate as a human being with feelings or emotions. Actions toward inmates are in terms of how those inmates' needs can be met, apart from simply viewing inmates as objects to be guarded or confined.

hundred In medieval England, a group of one hundred families that had the responsibility to maintain order and try minor offenses.

hung jury A jury that cannot agree on a verdict.

husband beating Spousal abuse in which a wife assaults her husband.

hustle, hustling The underground prison economy; also, an attempt to defraud.

hybrid offense A case involving a hybrid offense may be heard either by magistrates or by other courts, depending on prosecutorial discretion. Such an offense may or may not be indictable, and is greatly influenced by situational factors such as a defendant's lack of a prior record, circumstances surrounding the commission of the offense, and harm inflicted upon the victims. Sometimes the term refers to a gross misdemeanor, which is punishable by an extraordinary term of incarceration in excess of one year without invoking civil disabilities that usually accompany felony convictions.

hydrodynamics of blood drops and splashes The science of studying patterns, shapes, and sizes of blood drops and splashes at crime scenes to determine the site of death or violence. This study may assist in determining the type of weapon used to commit a violent act, the angle of the weapon used, the height of the person using the weapon, and other relevant information.

hydroplaning The process whereby an automobile loses traction on a roadway as the result of water or oil on the road surface. Control of the vehicle is lost, possibly causing it to crash.

hyperactivity Excessive activity characterized by symptoms such as impulsiveness, restlessness, fighting, short attention span, erratic behavior, and aggressiveness.

hypnosis A sleeplike state in which a person is susceptible to suggestions from the hypnotist.

hypoglycemia A condition occurring in susceptible individuals in which their level of blood sugar falls below an acceptable range, causing anxiety, headaches, confusion, fatigue, and aggressive behavior.

hypomania A less severe form of a mania.

hypothalamic region The part of the human brain that controls body temperature, thirst and hunger, and other functions.

hypothecation The right of creditors to obtain the property of their debtors. Property of debtors is eventually awarded to creditors so that it may be sold for money.

hypothesis A statement derived from theory that is subject to empirical test; a statement of theory in testable form; a proposition set forth for some specific phenomenon.

hypothetical construct An entity that cannot be observed directly with present technology (e.g., love, motivation, short-term memory).

hypothetical question A question based on an assumed set of facts.

hysteria A psychological reaction to a shocking event, characterized by extreme fear, laughter, or some other highly emotional outburst.

I

I-Adam International Arrestee Drug Abuse Monitoring program; a comprehensive program begun in the mid-1980s to track trends in the prevalence and types of hardcore drug use, such as cocaine, heroin, marijuana, and methamphetamine among booked arrestees. The program uses interviews and urine specimen testing to assess the U.S. drug abuse problem and studies links between drug use and crime and other social problems.

ice A processed form of methamphetamine that resembles chips of clear ice.

ICPSR *See* **Inter-University Consortium for Political and Social Research (ICPSR).**

id Sigmund Freud's term to depict the part of personality concerned with individual gratification; the "I want" part of a person formed in the early years.

Idealist In the Broderick Typology, the type of police officer who is college-educated, has high ideals, and is committed to social order. *See also* **Broderick Typology.**

identification In psychology, the incorporation in one person's personality of the features of another person's personality.

identification numbers Numbers used to designate a file for a person charged with a crime. The FBI uses such numbers for fingerprint identification.

identification parade a British term for lineup.

identification record One's criminal record.

identify To determine the identity of someone. In criminal investigations, to recognize something or someone relating to a crime.

Identi-Kit A kit containing numerous facial features on overlapping transparencies used by law enforcement officers to identify suspects, witnesses, and other unknown persons of interest in criminal, missing person, or other investigations.

identity crisis A psychological state in which youth face inner turmoil and uncertainty about life roles.

identity theft The assumption of another person's identity through the use of the victim's credit cards, Social Security number, driver's license, or other personal data. The common core is one person's representation of him- or herself as another, with or without stolen documentation, for criminal purposes, usually theft, but also to avoid apprehension for other crimes.

ideology A tightly knit set of beliefs, often with political implications, that justify a particular action system.

"I except" A phrase used in court as an objection to a ruling. The ruling becomes a possible point of argument to pursue if the case is subsequently appealed.

ignition interlock A device connected to the ignition of a motor vehicle that prohibits an intoxicated driver from operating it.

ignorance A weak defense to a criminal charge; admission by a suspect that he or she didn't know that his or her act was wrong or illegal; similar to mistake of fact.

I-level classification (Interpersonal Maturity Level Classification) A psychological assessment of convicted offenders that uses developmental and psychoanalytical theories to determine on which level or stage offenders can function and cope with interpersonal problems. The higher the I-level, the better-adjusted the offender.

illegal alien One who enters and remains in a country without proper authorization; a pejorative term for any alien in the United States without proper authorization and documentation, especially one entering from Mexico in search of employment. More recently, the term "undocumented alien" has been used.

illegal detention Similar to false arrest, when one has been detained by law enforcement officers without probable cause or reasonable suspicion.

illegal expenditures The costs of crimes that divert money from the legitimate economy and represent a loss of potential revenue for people who produce and supply legal goods and services.

illegally seized evidence Any tangible information or evidence seized in violation of the Fourth Amendment. *See also* **Bill of Rights.**

illegal search and seizure Any act in violation of the Fourth Amendment of the U.S. Constitution, which guarantees "[t]he right of the people to be secure in their persons, houses, papers and effects, against unreasonable searches and seizures, shall not be violated, and no warrants shall issue, but upon probable cause, supported by oath or affirmation, and particularly describing the place to be searched and the persons or things to be seized." *See also* **Bill of Rights.**

illegitimacy The condition of a child being born out of wedlock. In early times, illegitimacy was closely linked to inheritance of property. Illegitimate children, or "bastards," could inherit neither property nor title, and were conceivably at risk of becoming wards of the state.

illegitimate opportunity structure Neighborhood structures as established criminal enterprises and criminal mentors that lead youths to become criminals.

Illinois Juvenile Court Act (1899) Legislation establishing the first juvenile court in the United States.

Illinois Plan A bail plan.

illiteracy Lack of reading, writing, and computational skills required to function adequately in society.

Imam A Muslim clergyman.

imitator Copycat.

immediate family member A parent, brother, sister, spouse, or other close relative related by blood or marriage.

Immigration and Naturalization Service (INS) A division of the U.S. Department of Justice that conducts inspections and investigations related to immigrants.

immigration laws Any statutes governing foreign nationals and their entry into the United States. Certain classes of persons are denied entry, including prostitutes, felons, diseased persons, beggars, and illegal aliens.

imminent-peril standard A defense used by defendants who kill another person in the belief that there is an apparent, present, and immediate threat to their life and safety that must be instantly dealt with, or must so appear at the time to a reasonable person.

immunity, immunity from prosecution Exemption from a civil suit or criminal prosecution, usually through an agreement with prosecutors to testify or give evidence of value to the prosecutors' case.

immunity, transactional A grant of immunity applying to offenses to which a witness' testimony relates (e.g., one who conspires with others to commit a crime may testify against the coconspirators without fear of being prosecuted for the crime contemplated).

immunity, use A grant of immunity forbidding prosecutors from using immunized testimony as evidence against witnesses in criminal prosecutions.

Immunity Act A 1954 action that requires witnesses to appear in national security cases and where such persons are granted immunity from prosecution in exchange for their testimony against others.

immunity bath A prosecutorial decision to exempt certain persons in a group from prosecution in exchange for their testimony or assistance in the conviction of others.

IMPACT (Intensive Motivational Program of Alternative Correctional Treatment) A boot camp program operated in New York that incorporates educational training with strict physical and behavioral requirements.

impanel To select and swear in a jury in a civil or criminal case.

impeach Questioning by the prosecution or defense to challenge the credibility or veracity of each other's witnesses; also, an action taken to remove someone such as a president or a judge from public office for a high crime or misdemeanor.

impeaching credit of witness A challenge of the credibility of information about a witness by producing one or more other persons who know the bad reputation of the witness and will testify to that effect.

impeachment exception to exclusionary rule This exception provides that prosecutors may introduce illegally seized evidence to impeach the testimony of defendants but not the testimony of others. *See James v. Illinois* (1990).

imperfect self-defense standard An argument used by a person who kills another person in the honest but unreasonable belief in the necessity to defend against imminent peril to life or great bodily injury. While the killing is still unlawful, the offender is not guilty of murder. When fear is unreasonable but nevertheless genuine, the crime is reduced from murder to voluntary manslaughter.

impersonating an officer A crime, usually committed by a citizen who wears the clothing of and pretends to be a police officer for a variety of reasons. It may involve simply carrying a badge and identifying oneself as a police officer in order to gain entry to a dwelling or seduce a victim.

implicit plea bargaining A defendant pleading guilty with the expectation of receiving a more lenient sentence. *See also* **plea bargaining.**

implicit sentencing policy A legislative orientation to sentencing that must be inferred from its other actions.

importation hypothesis Explanations of the prison culture that focus on the background of inmates rather than their current prison experience as a source of values and attitudes.

importation model The view that the violent prison culture reflects the criminal culture of the outside world and is neither developed in nor unique to prisons.

importuning Soliciting for sexual purposes.

imprisonment Incarceration of a convicted offender. *See also* **false imprisonment.**

imprisonment for debt A civil form of commitment of persons who are indebted to others financially and attempt to evade repayment of their debt.

impulse, irresistible A type of insanity in which the offender is acting under a compulsion over which he or she has little or no control.

impulsivity A component of a theory that a particular trait produces criminal behavior. Impulsive people lack self-control.

impunity State of not being subject to retaliation or consequences.

inadmissible An evidentiary term used to describe something that cannot be used as evidence during a trial.

inalienable rights Rights under natural law that are conferred on persons and cannot be transferred to others.

in articulo mortis At the point of death.

in camera In a judge's chambers.

incapable Unable to act in a particular way (e.g., unable to strangle a victim because of paralysis in hands or arms).

incapacitate To render one unable to act; to deprive someone of his or her ability to resist, either through imprisonment or by court decree.

incapacitation, isolation A philosophy of corrections espousing loss of freedom proportional to the seriousness of the offense; the belief that the function of punishment is to separate offenders from other society members and prevent them from committing additional criminal acts.

incarceration Imprisonment in either a jail or a prison.

incendiary Any highly flammable device; a bomb intended to cause a fire.

incest Sexual relations between close relatives other than husband and wife.

Incest Anonymous Headquartered in Long Beach, CA, an organization of persons who have been victims of incest; a support group to counsel and assist those victims of incestuous relations.

inchoate offenses Conduct made criminal even though it has not yet produced the harm that the law seeks to prevent, such as offenses preparatory to committing other crimes (e.g., conspiracy, attempt, or solicitation); also associated with the felony murder rule and agency theory.

incidence, incidence of crime The frequency with which offenders commit crime, or the average number of offenses per offender, measured by dividing the number of offenses by the number of offenders.

incident A specific criminal act involving one or more victims.

incident-based reporting A less restrictive and more expansive method of collecting crime data (as opposed to summary reporting) in which all the analytical elements associated with an offense or arrest are compiled by a central collection agency on an incident-by-incident basis.

incident-driven policing A technocratic product, whereby police officers have traditionally responded or reacted to calls for service.

incised wound A trauma to the skin caused by a cutting instrument.

incite To provoke or set in motion.

inciting a riot The crime of instigating persons to riot, usually against some governmental policy or issue.

included offense An offense that is made up of elements that are a subset of the elements of another offense having a greater statutory penalty, and the occurrence of which is established by the same evidence or by some portion of the evidence that has been offered to establish the occurrence of the greater offense.

income-tax evasion The intentional failure to report income at the time of filing federal or other tax returns.

incommunicado A state in which a person charged with a crime is held without being allowing to communicate with anyone, including an attorney.

incompetent evidence Evidence inadmissible because it is flawed in various respects (e.g., a copy of an original document that appears to have been altered to project a particular viewpoint favorable to one side or the other).

incompetent to stand trial The finding by a criminal court that a defendant is mentally incapable of understanding the nature of the charges and proceedings against him or her, of consulting with an attorney, and of aiding in his or her own defense.

incorporation The extension of the due-process clause of the Fourteenth Amendment to make binding on state governments the rights guaranteed in the first 10 amendments to the U.S. Constitution. Often, rights are conveyed in limited ways and under certain circumstances, based on subsequent court decisions. *See also* **Bill of Rights.**

incorrigible Unmanageable; a term applicable to unruly children who are often placed in foster care, in nonsecure or secure circumstances, where they can be governed, controlled, and supervised.

incriminate To indicate guilt.

inculpate To incriminate or show one's possible guilt. Incriminating factors are inculpatory.

in custody Under arrest; in corrections, the second-highest level of custody assigned to an inmate, requiring the second-highest level of security and staff supervision. Inmates are assigned to regular quarters and are eligible for all regular work assignments and activities under a normal level of supervision. They are not eligible for work detail outside the institution.

indecent Sexually explicit material or actions that offend the sensibilities of the average person.

indecent exposure Exhibitionism; exposure of one's sexual organs to others in a public place.

indefinite sentence *See* **indeterminate sentencing.**

in delicto Fault, as to a crime or happening; a finding that one is at fault in causing an accident or committing a crime.

indemnify To compensate for losses or injuries in a tort action or actual compensation for such losses or injuries.

indentured servant system A system whereby persons paid for their passage to the American colonies from England by selling their services for a period of seven years, considered a "voluntary slave" migration pattern.

Independent Parole Board Model Autonomous units that have the power to make parole release decisions and to supervise all conditionally released inmates.

"independents" In corrections, inmates who do not affiliate with a gang or other such group.

independent state grounds A state's legislature may enact laws that provide greater protections for juveniles than the minimum required by the Constitution and the U.S. Supreme Court's interpretation of it.

independent-untainted-source doctrine A U.S. Supreme Court ruling permitting the government the opportunity of proving one's guilt through the introduction of evidence wholly untainted by police misconduct. *See United States v. Crews* (1980).

independent variable In statistical analysis, any variable or factor that explains the occurrence of another factor or variable, or causes it to change in value.

indeterminate punishment *See* **indeterminate sentencing.**

indeterminate sentencing A sentencing scheme in which a period is set by judges between the earliest date for a parole decision and the latest date for completion of the sentence. In holding that the time necessary for treatment cannot be set exactly, the indeterminate sentence is closely associated with rehabilitation.

index crimes, major and minor offenses Type I offenses are eight felonies used by the Federal Bureau of Investigation in the *Uniform Crime Reports* to chart crime trends, including aggravated assault, larceny, burglary, vehicular theft, arson, robbery, forcible rape, and murder; Type II offenses are misdemeanors or less serious crimes.

indict To formally charge, based on a decision by a grand jury.

indictable offense An offense in either Canada or Great Britain that includes violations of the criminal code or federal statutes.

indictment, bill of A charge or written accusation found and presented by a grand jury that a particular defendant probably committed a crime.

indigent, indigent client, indigent defendant Poor; anyone who cannot afford legal services or representation. *See also Gideon v. Wainwright* (1963).

indirect control Behavioral influence arising from an individual's identification with noncriminals and desire to conform to societal norms.

indirect costs Costs to support an operation, such as central office administration and expenses incurred by other departments in supporting corrections.

indirect evidence Circumstantial evidence; material information from which facts of a crime and its commission may be inferred.

individual deterrence *See* **specific deterrence.**

individualized treatment model The view that each sentence must be tailored to the individual needs of an offender.

individual level of analysis, individual unit of analysis A study of organizations in which personality systems and attitudes are considered as primary factors in determining what is going on in organizations and why. Key elements of analysis are persons and their dispositions and sentiments.

individual rights In criminal justice, any rights guaranteed to criminal defendants facing formal processing by the system. The preservation of the rights of criminal defendants is important to society because it is through the exercise of such rights that the values of our culture are most clearly and directly expressed.

individual-rights advocate One who seeks to protect personal freedoms within the criminal-justice process.

individual therapy A method of treatment commonly used in prison in which psychiatrists, psychologists, or psychiatric social workers help offenders solve psychological problems that are thought to be the cause of criminal behavior.

induction Creation of a general rule by seeing similarities among several specific situations.

industrial espionage Obtaining a company's secrets or formulae for a product or idea, usually with the help of a company employee or officer.

industrial prison Any prison in which the principal activity is industrial labor by the inmates; also, prisons in the period from 1900 to 1930, when the focus of most prisons in the United States was on the production of goods.

industrial school A secure facility designed for juvenile delinquents where the principal functions are to equip youths with employable work skills.

Industrial Security Organization *See* **American Society for Industrial Security.**

industrial shop and school officers Those that ensure efficient use of training and educational resources within a prison.

inebriate One who is drunk; someone under the influence of alcohol; also, to make one drunk or intoxicated.

inevitable discovery, inevitable discovery rule A rule of law stating that evidence that would have almost assuredly been independently discovered can be used in a court of law, even when it was obtained in violation of certain legal rules and practices.

in extremis "In the extreme" (Latin); at the point of death.

in facto "In deed" (Latin); in fact.

infamous crime Any crime that is so heinous in its commission as to deserve national, even international, notoriety; any crime involving a highly visible public or private figure.

infamous punishment Imprisonment at hard labor in a prison or penitentiary.

infant According to Black (1990), a legal term applicable to juveniles who have not attained the age of majority. In most states, the age of majority is 18.

infanticide The killing of a newborn baby.

infantophilia Propensity to regard young children with strong sexual interest.

inference A way of concluding something from a given set of facts. Juries make inferences about things based on facts presented by both sides in a criminal case.

inferential statistics Any numerical techniques for estimating population values (e.g., the average age of a group of persons or the average height of probation officers in Ohio).

inferior courts Lower courts, courts of limited jurisdiction.

inferiority complex A psychological condition in which a person's self-perception is weak and the person believes that he or she is not equal in competence or capable enough compared with others to perform particular tasks or to solve particular problems.

infibulation Torture of the genitals.

in-field show-up A situation in which a citizen observes a crime committed and reports the suspect to police. Police later stop and detain the suspect, who is subsequently identified by the citizen who originally reported the crime. The citizen drives by the detained suspect with police and makes a visual identification of the suspect.

infirmaries The most common type of medical facility in a prison or jail. They provide bed care for inmates, and some have round-the-clock nursing care.

in flagrante delicto "While the crime is blazing" (Latin); caught in the act. The fact that the perpetrator of a crime was caught during the crime's commission is direct evidence of guilt.

influence Power on the part of any organizational member to obtain compliance from others.

informal communication network A grapevine of information transmission that is unauthorized by the existing formal hierarchy of authority; how rumors generated by social groups unrelated to the power hierarchy are spread in an organization.

informal probation Also known as informal adjustments or deferred prosecution; a procedure whereby a juvenile agrees to meet certain requirements in exchange for having a case dismissed.

informal social control The reactions of individuals and groups that bring about conformity to norms and laws, including peer and community pressure, bystander intervention in a crime, and collective responses such as citizen patrol groups.

informant One who supplies information to police officers about others who are engaged in illegal activities.

in forma pauperis "In the manner of a pauper" (Latin); a term referring to the waiver of filing costs and other fees associated with judicial proceedings in order to allow indigent persons to proceed with their cases.

information, criminal information A written accusation made by a public prosecutor against a person for some criminal offense, usually restricted to minor crimes or misdemeanors, without an indictment.

informed consent An agreement to participate in an activity based on full knowledge and understanding of what will take place.

infraction An offense punishable by a fine or other penalty, but not normally by incarceration.

infrared light Any light having a wavelength greater than the visible red, in the region of 8,000 to 9,000 angstroms. It can be used to read writing that has been erased or obliterated.

infrared motion detector A sensor that detects movement whenever infrared light intensity is changed in a given direction by the movement of an intruder.

inhalants Volatile liquids that give off a vapor, which, if inhaled, produces short-term excitement and euphoria followed by a period of disorientation.

inherent coercion Those tactics used by police interviewers that fall short of physical abuse but nonetheless pressure suspects to divulge information.

inheritance school An early form of biological theory that held that deviant behavior was inherited and therefore ran in families, being passed on from one generation to the next.

initial appearance A formal proceeding during which the judge advises the defendant of the charges, including a recitation of the defendant's rights and a bail decision.

initial classification analysis A classification device created in 1983 by the Missouri Department of Corrections to determine the treatment plan and institutional assignments for both male and female offenders.

initial plea At the time of an initial appearance, a defendant's declaration of guilt or innocence in response to the charges against him or her.

initiating structure A view of supervisory behavior that the leader facilitates group interaction toward goal attainment. This involves planning, scheduling, criticizing, and initiating ideas.

injunction A court order prohibiting someone from doing some specified act or commanding someone to undo some wrong or injury.

injunction order A written notice by the court to a party, prohibiting that party from committing some act.

injunctive relief A command to either end or desist a practice or to have one activated.

in loco parentis "In the place of the parent" (Latin); rights given to schools that allow them to assume parental duties in disciplining students.

inmate A prisoner of a jail or prison.

inmate accounts Similar to bank accounts, but managed by prison personnel. Such accounts contain any money that has been sent to an inmate from others or that the inmate has earned through working at a prison job.

inmate classification Any attempt or method of assigning prison or jail inmates to particular areas based on their measured risk or dangerousness.

inmate code, inmate subculture An informal set of rules reflecting the values of the prison culture or society.

inmate control model A scheme that proposes the establishment of inmate grievance committees and inmate boards to investigate and decide issues pertaining to inmate grievances.

inmate credit cards Cards issued by some jurisdictions in an attempt to cut down on the illegal economy of prisons. Inmate credit cards that can be used to make commissary purchases replace money, which is declared contraband.

inmate custody category The degree of staff supervision necessary to ensure adequate control of an inmate.

inmate disciplinary councils Internal inmate grievance procedures established by inmates themselves in either prisons or jails.

inmate grievance procedure A mandatory administrative grievance procedure in all state and federal prisons whereby inmates may bring grievances to the attention of wardens and other supervisory personnel.

inmate handbook A booklet containing information with which inmates should be familiar concerning the rules and regulations of prisons and jails.

inmate litigation explosion *See* **litigation explosion.**

inmate self-government Any prison management system that provides formal inmate participation or control over some decisions regarding routine, discipline, and program.

inmate social code, inmate social world An informal set of rules that governs inmates.

inmate subculture Ways of thinking, feeling, and acting about all aspects of prison life that help inmates cope with the special circumstances of prison life.

inmate suicide The taking of one's own life by an inmate of a jail or prison, or under detention in any other type of facility.

innocent bystander A pedestrian or person who has nothing to do with a crime but who gets injured or killed as a result of it.

innocent-owner defense Under federal asset forfeiture laws, the government has the right to seize any property used for the purpose of criminal activity. Sometimes property seized belongs to others who may be ignorant of the illegal activity in which their property is put to use. An innocent-owner defense may be raised to prevent government seizure of one's assets where crimes have been perpetrated by others. *See* **Bennis v. Michigan** (1996), *the leading case on this defense.*

innovation In social theory, the mode of adaptation formulated by Robert K. Merton in which cultural goals are accepted, but the means used to achieve these goals are considered unacceptable and possibly criminal; also, devising new solutions to old problems.

Innovations Project A project implemented by the Ninth Circuit Court of Appeals in which cases are presented without oral argument; a "submission-without-argument" program intended to streamline case processing and backlogs.

innovative adaptation An alternative name for Merton's anomie theory that stresses the "innovation" mode of adaptation in the goals/means relation.

Innovative Neighborhood Oriented Policing (INOP) A program designed by the Bureau of Justice Assistance to further community-based demand reduction. It is grounded in the importance of community, including community-policing patterns.

in-presence requirement The legal principle that police officers cannot make an arrest in a misdemeanor case unless the crime is committed in their presence.

inquisitorial justice, inquisitory system A system in which defendants must prove their innocence, as opposed to an adversary system, which presumes defendants innocent until proven guilty by the prosecutor.

in re "In the matter of" (Latin); a term referring to cases filed for juveniles who must have an adult act on their behalf when filing motions or appeals.

in rem "Against a thing" (Latin).

insane A legal term meaning that an offender did not understand that what he or she was doing was wrong or was operating under such compulsion that he or she could not change his or her behavior or conform to the requirements of the law.

insanity A degree of mental illness that negates the legal capacity or responsibility of the affected person.

insanity defense A defense that seeks to exonerate an accused person by showing that he or she was insane when the crime was committed.

Insanity Defense Reform Act of 1984 An act aimed to obligate the defense to prove a defendant insane as an affirmative defense. Previously, prosecutors in federal district courts bore the burden of showing that the defendant was not insane. This act was triggered by the attempted assassination of President Ronald Reagan by John Hinckley, who pleaded insanity and was acquitted thereby.

insanity plea A plea entered as a defense to a crime. The defendant admits guilt but assigns responsibility for the criminal act to the condition of insanity presumably existing when the crime was committed.

inside cell block design A design in which cells are built back-to-back, sometimes five tiers high, in a hollow building. These cells have doors that open onto galleries or walkways 8 to 10 feet from the outer wall of the building.

inside cells Prison cells constructed back-to-back, with corridors running along the outside shell of the cell house.

insider trading Using material nonpublic financial information to obtain unfair advantage over others when trading securities and stocks.

inspectional services The particular bureau in a police department charged with investigations of other officers, sometimes known as the internal affairs division.

instanter Immediately; the term used by courts when issuing a *capias* or arrest warrant to order that the person named in the warrant be arrested immediately.

instant offense The present offense with which a defendant is charged.

Institute for Court Management Established in 1971 and sponsored by the National Center for State Courts, this organization provides training, education, and certification for court officers and administrators, and publishes the *Justice System Journal*. It is headquartered in Williamsburg, VA.

Institute for Law and Justice (ILJ) A private research and policy organization that undertakes criminal-justice studies, performs policy analyses, and consults on various matters related to criminal sentencing.

Institute for Law and Social Research (INSLAW) Established in 1973, INSLAW's goals are to support criminal-justice administration research and assist criminal-justice agencies in their more efficient organization and operations. It is headquartered in Washington, DC, and publishes *Promis Newsletter.*

Institute for Youth Development (IYD) A nonprofit organization that promotes the avoidance of alcohol, drugs, sex, tobacco, and violence. Its philosophy is that youths are capable of making appropriate choices, especially if they receive social and psychological support from their families.

Institute of Criminal Law and Procedure Established in 1965 and headquartered in Washington, DC, an organization based at Georgetown University that conducts legal research and the administration of justice. It maintains compendiums of data relating to plea bargaining, victim assistance, and other criminal justice–related matters and issues.

Institute of Governmental Studies Library Established in 1920 and headquartered at the University of California–Berkeley, this organization collects data and documents pertaining to all dimensions of criminal justice, and publishes *Public Affairs Report.*

Institute of Judicial Administration Established in 1952 and headquartered at New York University, this organization sponsors research that examines ways of improving the court system and case management, networks with different bar associations throughout the United States to improve judicial systems, and publishes the *IJA Report.*

institutional capacity The rated capacity of a prison or other facility, indicating the number of beds available and how many individuals can be lawfully accommodated.

institutional child abuse The approved use of force and violence against children in schools; the denial of children's due-process rights in institutions run by different levels of government.

institutionalization The process that occurs in people during prolonged periods of confinement in a prison, which results in their inability to cope with mainstream life outside of the institution.

institutionalized personality A nonclinical term denoting someone who has adapted to institutional life to the extent that freedom in noninstitutional living is more difficult. Long-term patients in mental hospitals or prisoners serving lengthy prison terms have this sort of personality system and find it hard to adapt to social living when released into their communities.

institutional model of parole organization An organizational pattern in which parole release decisions are made primarily within the institution. Advocates of the institutional model believe that because institutional staff are most familiar with an offender and his or her response to institutional rules and programs, they are the most sensitive to the optimal time for release. This model is most commonly used in juvenile corrections.

institutional needs Prison administration interests recognized by the courts as justifying some restrictions on the constitutional rights of prisoners, such as maintenance of institutional order, security and safety of prisoners and staff, and rehabilitation of inmates.

institutional orders Also known as court decrees, the judicial orders applied to an institution to correct the conditions or practices that infringe on inmate rights.

instrumental crimes Illegal acts whose purpose is to obtain funds to secure goods and services; offenses in which committing the act is not an end in itself.

instrumental gang A type of gang that is primarily involved in committing property crime and is actively involved in using drugs.

instrumental Marxism, instrumental Marxist theory The view that capitalist institutions, such as the criminal-justice system, have as their main purpose the control of the poor in order to maintain the hegemony of the wealthy.

instrumental violence Violence that is designed to improve the financial or social position of the criminal.

insubordination Defiance of authority; deliberately disobeying orders of superiors.

insufficient evidence Inadequate evidence to show guilt beyond a reasonable doubt; if a prosecutor presents a case without sufficient incriminating evidence, the case may be dismissed.

insurance fraud Any deception involving bogus claims made to an insurance company based on a contrived loss.

insurgency A revolt against a constituted government.

insurrection A full-fledged uprising or rebellion in which a group opposes or resists the legitimate government or state authority.

intake, intake screening The process of screening juveniles who have been charged with offenses. Dispositions include release to parents pending further juvenile-court action, dismissal of charges against the juvenile, detention, and treatment by some community agency. Also, a critical phase in which a determination is made by a juvenile probation officer or other official as to whether to release a juvenile to his or her parent's custody, to detain the juvenile in a formal detention facility for a later court appearance, or to release the juvenile to parents pending a later court appearance.

intake decision Review of a case by a juvenile or criminal court official. Screening of cases includes weeding out weak cases. In juvenile cases, intake involves the reception of a juvenile against whom complaints have been made. The decision to proceed or dismiss the case is made at this stage.

intake hearings Proceedings in which a juvenile probation officer conducts an informal investigation of the charges against a juvenile and determines whether the juvenile should be moved forward into the juvenile justice system for further processing.

intake officer An officer who conducts screening of juveniles.

intake process The overall admissions process into a jail or prison.

intake unit A government agency that receives juvenile referrals from police, other government agencies, private agencies, or persons and screens them, which results in closing of the case, referral to care or supervision, or filing of a petition in juvenile court.

intangible losses Costs such as fear, pain and suffering, or reduced quality of life that accrue to crime victims as a result of their victimization.

intangible property Property with no tangible value (e.g., bonds, promissory notes, and stock certificates).

integrated contract model When guilt of an offender has been determined and before a judge has passed sentence, the judge considers the prisoner's choice of sentence for incarceration or reintegration. A contract is negotiated involving informed disposition by the offender, defense counsel, and the prosecutor, which is approved and signed by all parties. The objective is to achieve predefined rehabilitative goals by a predetermined time.

Integrated Criminal Apprehension Program Established in 1976 and headquartered in Washington, DC, this program aims to plan, investigate, or improve patrol operations, increase the clearance rate of violent and property crimes, and improve the deployment of law enforcement resources in crime prevention.

integrated structural theory Criminologists Mark Colvin and John Pauly devised this theory, which views crime as the direct result of socialization within families (1983). Families characterized by despair and coercive relations are criminal behavior antecedents. Negative social relations at home carry over into school relations and scholastic performance is adversely affected, feelings of alienation and strain develop, and delinquency is a result.

integrated theory, integrated theoretical model A perspective that seeks to expand and synthesize earlier positions into a modern analytical device with great explanatory and predictive power; a blend of seemingly independent concepts into coherent explanations of criminality. *See also* **multifactor theories.**

integration model A blend of importation theory and deprivation theory; the belief that in childhood, some inmates acquired, usually from peers, values that support law-violating behavior, but that the norms and standards in a prison also affect an inmate.

integrative shaming The social process of shunning or avoiding those found guilty of various offenses, with the intention of humiliating them through social condemnation and isolation.

integrative theory A criminological theory that seeks to combine and reconcile two or more existing theoretical perspectives into a more comprehensive, unified perspective.

intelligence In policing, information about a crime and its occurrence.

intelligence officer The individual responsible for collection of intelligence information or who is in charge of an intelligence unit.

intelligence unit A correctional organization's unit responsible for the collection of strategic information that can be used to deal with potential prison security problems.

Intensive Aftercare Program (IAP) A Philadelphia-based intervention for serious youthful offenders involving intensive counseling and training for acquiring self-help skills. Recidivism of participants was greatly reduced during the study period of 1980–1990.

intensive offender A person who engages in criminal activity that begins at an early age and is sustained over time, consciously planned, persistent, skilled, and frequent.

intensive probation supervision (IPS) *See* **intensive supervised probation/parole.**

intensive supervised probation/parole (ISP) No specific guidelines exist across all jurisdictions, but ISP usually means lower caseloads for probation officers, less than 10 clients per month, regular drug tests, and other intensive supervision measures. *See box p. 132.*

intensive supervision program A probation or parole program in which the officer-offender ratio is low, offenders receive frequent visits from their officer-supervisors, and continuous communication is maintained by the supervising agency or authority.

intent A state of mind, the *mens rea,* in which a person seeks to accomplish a given result, such as a crime, through a given course of action.

intent, constructive A deliberate plan to implement an illegal act that injures other persons unrelated to the crime in the process.

intent, specific A purposeful state of mind to commit a specific illegal act; an element of certain crimes, such as conspiracy to distribute stolen property and transport it interstate.

intent in cases of negligence Deliberate failure to perform a duty to others; culpable omission; the state of mind to commit a negligent act.

intentional injury Any physical harm caused through purposeful action by another.

intentional torts Any actions filed when it can be shown that there is an intention on the part of a person to bring physical or psychological harm to someone else.

interactional or interactionist theory The notion that interaction with institutions and events during the life course determines criminal behavior patterns and that crimogenic influences evolve over time. Terence Thornberry applies this concept in describing the onset of delinquency and criminality. It is viewed as age-graded and couched in a cognitive developmental context, as deviance either emerges or doesn't emerge during various stages in which reasoning and sophistication develop and mature.

interactionist perspective The view that one's perception of reality is significantly influenced by one's interpretations of the reactions of others to similar events and stimuli.

interaction process analysis A set of 12 categories used to code interaction in groups; a highly structured observational technique, using both structured observational categories and a structured laboratory setting, that was established by the social psychologist Robert Bales.

Interagency Agreement Plan An early intervention plan instituted in San Diego County, CA, in 1982 for the purpose of reducing delinquency. Graduated sanctions are used for repeat offenders. Youths are held accountable for their actions, and there is a gradual increase of services and punishments for repeat offenders.

inter alia "Among others" (Latin); among other things.

interception of prisoners' mail Prison administration's reading of mail intended for inmates in jails or prisons in order to prevent communications from others that will jeopardize the safety and security of the institution.

interdict To intercept, prohibit, or prevent.

interdisciplinary theory A view that integrates a variety of theoretical approaches in an attempt to explain crime.

interested adult law Any law that requires the advisement and consent of any waiver of Fifth and Sixth Amendment rights by some adult who has a concern in a minor's welfare. More than a few jurisdictions require custodial parents or guardians to give their consent before a juvenile is interrogated by police without the presence of an attorney.

interest groups Private organizations formed to influence government policies so that they will coincide with the desires of their members.

interior ballistics The science of projectile movement with a firearm's bore, considering powder combustion, pressure, and other elements, to determine the effect of rifling, size, weight, and other factors.

interlocutory Temporary; not final; a temporary court order.

interlocutory appeal An appeal during a trial proceeding in which the judgment of the trial court is suspended pending the success of an appeal.

interlocutory decision A temporary judgment pending the resolution of the facts at issue.

intermediate appellate courts The third level of state courts; appellate courts between trial courts and courts of last resort.

intermediate punishments, intermediate sanctions Punishments involving sanctions existing somewhere between incarceration and probation on a continuum of criminal penalties. They may include home confinement and electronic monitoring.

intermittent confinement, intermittent sentence An imposed punishment in which an offender must serve a portion of his or her sentence in jail, perhaps on weekends or specific evenings. It is considered similar to probation with limited incarceration. *See also* **split sentencing.**

intermittent offender A person who engages in irregular and opportunistic crimes with low payoffs and great risks, and who does not think of him- or herself as a professional criminal.

Conditions of the New Jersey Intensive Supervision Program (ISP)

You have been placed on the Intensive Supervision Program (ISP) by the ISP Resentencing Panel for a trial period of 90 days subject to your compliance with your case plan and the conditions listed below. If you are arrested for a new offense, the ISP Resentencing Panel may issue a warrant to detain you in custody, without bail, to await disposition on the new charges.

1. I will obey the laws of the United States, and the laws and ordinances of any jurisdiction in which I may be residing.

2. I am required to promptly notify my ISP Officer if I am arrested, questioned, or contacted by any law enforcement official whether summoned, indicted, or charged with any offense or violation.

3. I will report as directed to the Court or to my ISP Officer.

4. I will permit the ISP Officer to visit my home.

5. I will answer promptly, truthfully, and completely all inquiries made by my ISP Officer and must obtain approval prior to any residence change. If the change of address or residence is outside the region in which I am under supervision, I will request approval at least 30 days in advance.

6. I will participate in any medical and/or psychological examinations, tests, and/or counseling as directed.

7. I will support my dependents, meet my family responsibilities, and continue full-time (35 hours or more per week), gainful employment. I will notify my ISP Officer prior to any change in my employment or if I become unemployed.

8. I will not leave the State of New Jersey without permission of my ISP Officer.

9. If I abscond from supervision (keep my whereabouts unknown to my ISP Officer), I may be charged with a new crime of Escape under 2C: 29-5, which may subject me to an additional sentence of up to five years consecutive to any ISP violation time.

10. I will not have in my possession any firearm or other dangerous weapon.

11. I will perform community service of at least 16 hours per month, unless modified by the ISP Resentencing Panel.

12. I will participate in ISP group activities as directed.

13. I will maintain a daily diary of my activities and a weekly budget while under supervision.

14. I will not borrow any money, loan any money or make credit purchases without permission of my ISP Officer. I may be required to surrender any credit cards in my possession to my officer.

15. I will maintain weekly contact with my community sponsor and network team.

16. I will comply with the required curfew of 6 p.m. to 6 a.m. unless modified by my ISP Officer. If unemployed, I will abide by a 6 p.m. curfew unless modified by my ISP Officer.

17. I will submit at any time to a search of my person, places, or things under my immediate control by my ISP Officer.

18. I will abstain from all illegal drug use and consumption of alcohol (including nonalcoholic beer) and submit to drug and/or alcohol testing as directed. I also will not ingest any product containing poppy seeds. I will not use any medications, including over-the-counter medications, which contain alcohol.

19. I will notify my employer of my participation in ISP within 30 days after commencing employment.

20. I will not ingest any medication prescribed to someone else and will inform my ISP Officer of any medication prescribed to me by a physician or dentist.

21. I will file my Federal and State tax returns by the lawfully prescribed date and provide copies of the returns to my ISP Officer.

22. In accordance with State law, I cannot vote in any public election while under ISP supervision.

23. I will maintain telephone service at my approved residence. If the telephone service is discontinued, I will notify my ISP Officer immediately. I am not permitted to have a caller ID or call forwarding services on my telephone.

24. I cannot collect unemployment benefits, disability assistance, or welfare benefits without permission.

25. I cannot possess a pager (beeper) and/or cellular telephone unless approved by my ISP Officer.

26. I cannot visit inmates in county or state correctional facilities until I have completed six months of satisfactory ISP supervision and with the permission of the ISP Regional Supervisor.

27. I may not serve in the capacity of an informant for a law enforcement agency. If requested to do so, I must decline and inform my ISP Officer of the request.

28. I will not engage in any gambling including the purchase of lottery tickets. I will not enter a gambling establishment (casino) unless employed at such an establishment or given permission to visit such establishment by my ISP Officer.

29. I will turn in to my ISP Officer my driver's license (if driving privileges have been revoked), firearms ID card, and hunting license if any of them are in my possession.

30. I will comply with any and all directives from the ISP Resentencing Panel or my officer.

intern To confine to a particular space; also, someone who works under others to learn more about a particular profession.

internal affairs, internal affairs unit A department within a police agency charged with the responsibility to investigate misconduct and possible criminal behavior on the part of police officers.

internalized control Self-regulation of behavior and conformity to societal norms through guilt feelings arising from the conscience.

internal process model A perspective on organizations that places high value on predictability and control and uses structures that make activities more predictable.

Internal Revenue Service (IRS) A federal agency, part of the U.S. Department of the Treasury, responsible for enforcing provisions of the Internal Revenue Code and collecting income taxes.

International Association for Civilian Oversight of Law Enforcement (IACOLE) A volunteer-based nonprofit organization headquartered in Evanston, IL, that publishes a newsletter, investigates police misconduct and other related incidents, and reports its findings.

International Association for Property and Evidence, Inc. This association, headquartered in Burbank, CA, was established to learn about proper procedures for storing property and evidence from crime scenes, and conducts seminars and training.

International Association of Asian Crime Investigators (IAACI) Established in 1987 and headquartered at the University of Chicago, this organization consists of persons who investigate crimes committed by persons of Asian descent, such as gang activity and organized crime.

International Association of Auto Theft Investigators (IAATI) This organization, established in 1931, publishes the journal *Training and Education.*

International Association of Bomb Technicians and Investigators Established in 1973 and headquartered in Colorado Springs, CO, the association's membership consists of professionals concerned with the manufacture and use of explosive devices and related matters. Publishes *The Detonator Magazine.*

International Association of Campus Law Enforcement Administrators Established in 1958 and headquartered in Hartford, CT, the assocation's international membership includes heads of campus police organizations. Publishes the *Campus Law Enforcement Journal.*

International Association of Chiefs of Police (IACP) An organization of police executives from throughout the world that sponsors research, and training and holds annual conferences.

International Association of Correctional Officers (IACO) An organization that brings together correctional experts and personnel from many areas around the world.

International Association of Law Enforcement Intelligence Analysts Established in 1981 and headquartered in Washington, DC, this association works to process crime information and disseminate findings to interested agencies and persons. Publishes *Intelscope.*

International Brotherhood of Police Officers (IBPO) Established in 1964 and headquartered in Washington, DC, this police union is dedicated to acquiring more benefits for its membership from different police organizations. It has affiliate chapters in various cities throughout the world.

International Brotherhood of Teamsters The largest labor union in the United States. It represents members of police and sheriff's departments in some cities.

International City/County Management Association (ICMA) Established in 1934 and headquartered in Washington, DC, this organization is a professional association of city and county managers. It publishes newsletters and relevant information pertaining to city and county organization, operations, and policies.

International Code A list of words used by law enforcement and emergency agencies to clarify alphabet letters when using the telephone or radio: A = Alpha; B = Bravo; C = Charlie; D = Delta; E = Echo; F = Foxtrot; G = Gold; H = Hotel; I = India; J = Juliette; K = Kilo; L = Lima; M = Mike; N = November; O = Oscar; P = Papa; Q = Quebec; R =Romeo; S = Sierra; T = Tango; U = Uniform; V = Victor; W = Whiskey; X = X-ray; Y= Yankee; Z = Zulu.

International Conference of Police Chaplains An organization headquartered in Livingston, TX, established to provide assistance to members of the ministry in law enforcement agencies.

International Court of Justice A body formed to establish some degree of jurisdiction over international crime.

international crimes Major criminal offenses so designated by the community of nations for the protection of interests common to all world citizens.

international extradition Treaties between different countries to return fugitives to the countries in which they have been charged with crimes.

International Guide to Missing Treasures (IGMT) An art dealer compendium of missing or stolen pieces of art consisting of special reports and bulletins to make dealers aware of stolen art objects that may be offered for sale.

International Halfway House Association (IHHA) A public organization established in Chicago in 1964 whose membership operates halfway houses throughout the world.

international law A global body of rules and regulations that the principal nations of the world abide by; a pact among nations to respect and observe particular laws governing trade, commerce, and trafficking in illegal contraband. Also, an agreement to condemn terrorism and give up terrorists who seek asylum in particular countries.

International Law Enforcement Instructors Agency The goal of this association, founded in 1976 and headquartered in Concord, MA, is to train and develop personnel in criminal-justice organizations and equip them with standards that maximize their effectiveness in the performance of their work roles.

International Narcotic Enforcement Officers Association Established in 1960 and headquartered in Albany, NY, this organization studies problems of narcotics distribution and control, conducts conferences and seminars, and publishes *Narc Officer.*

International Personnel Management Association This association, founded in 1973 and headquartered in Alexandria, VA, provides advisory services to organizations relating to personnel administration, job analyses, and other personnel matters, and publishes *IPMA News* and *Public Personnel Management.*

international police forces Military forces from various countries placed under United Nations control. Their intent is to provide police services in countries where there is organized protest and revolt.

international terrorism Any terrorism or violent act that transcends the boundaries of any single country into another.

International Union of Police Administration (IUPA) A police union established in 1978 that seeks to obtain more benefits for its membership from local police organizations.

internships These programs are generally three-unit, upper-division offerings for graduating seniors to allow them practical exposure to the criminal-justice system. Several universities make an internship mandatory, requiring up to 160 contact hours per 16-week semester.

interobserver reliability An index of the degree to which different raters give the same behavior similar ratings.

interpersonal level of analysis, interpersonal unit of analysis A study of organizations in which the principal object of inquiry is the group. The emphasis is on group structure and process as well as group influence on the organization itself and individuals within the group. Small work groups are considered primary targets of inquiry for organizational researchers who use this level of analysis for the approach to what is happening in organizations and why.

INTERPOL (International Criminal Police Organization) This organization is attributed to Baron Pasquier, prefect of the Paris police in 1809. It was formally established in 1923 and is dedicated to combating world crime.

interpretive approach The belief that the phenomena of focal concern to the sociobehavioral scientist are far less stable than those of interest to the natural scientist.

interrogation A method of acquiring evidence in the form of information or confessions from suspects by police; questioning, which has been restricted because of concern about the use of brutal and coercive methods and an interest in protecting against self-incrimination.

interrogatory, interrogatories A set of questions prepared by both prosecution and defense and administered to potential witnesses for either side.

intersection Places where two roadways intersect or join one another.

Interstate Commerce Commission (ICC) A former government agency that regulated common carriers on U.S. roadways. It disbanded in 1955.

interstate compact An agreement between two or more states to transfer prisoners, parolees, or probationers from the supervisory control of one state to another.

Interstate Compact for the Supervision of Parolees and Probationers An agreement among the states to supervise probationers and parolees for each other.

interstate extradition The process of returning a fugitive residing in another state to a state in which he or she has been charged with a crime.

interstitial area In the concentric-zone hypothesis, the area nearest the center of a city undergoing change, such as urban renewal, that is characterized by high rates of crime.

interstitial group A delinquent group that fills a crack in the social fabric and maintains standard group practices.

intersubjectivity A norm of scientific methodology that states that knowledge must be transmittable so that scientists can understand and evaluate the methods of other scientists and perform similar observations in order to verify empirical generalizations.

Inter-University Consortium for Political and Social Research (ICPSR) A membership organization of colleges and universities established in 1962 and headquartered at the University of Michigan at Ann Arbor. It maintains extensive archives of social science data sets and offers training in quantitative methods and technical assistance to researchers using ICPSR data.

intestate Without having made a will.

intimate violence Any physical altercation between those living together who may or may not be married.

in toto "In all" (Latin); completely, entirely.

intoxication The state of being incapable of performing certain tasks legally, such as operating a motor vehicle or boat. Intoxication can be induced through consumption of alcoholic beverages, inhaling toxic fumes from petroleum products, or consumption of drug substances.

intoximeter A device used to test the breath for determining presence of alcohol. *See also* **Breathalyzer.**

intrafamily conflict An environment of discord within the family unit. Children who grow up in dysfunctional homes often exhibit delinquent behaviors, having learned at a young age that aggression pays off.

intrinsic evidence Actual information or documentation. Any inculpatory or exculpatory information or material that is self-explanatory or requires no elaboration or comment (e.g., fingerprints on a murder weapon).

intruder One who purposefully breaks into and enters the premises of another.

invalidate To annul, negate, or set aside.

inventory exception The doctrine that allows warrantless searches of an automobile to be conducted whenever police officers have towed or seized a vehicle to a police impound facility. Inventories of an automobile's contents are for the purpose of verifying the nature and type of property in the automobile to ensure its proper return to the owner of the vehicle when it is later retrieved.

inventory shrinkage The loss of a company's inventory due to employee theft.

investigation An inquiry concerning suspected criminal behavior for purposes of identifying offenders or gathering information or further evidence to assist the prosecution of apprehended offenders.

investigator One who conducts an investigation, such as an attempt to solve a crime.

investigatory stage That stage of a criminal investigation in which law enforcement officers are collecting information and evidence and in which no charges have been brought against any particular suspect.

involuntary manslaughter Homicide in which the perpetrator unintentionally but recklessly causes the death of another person by consciously taking a grave risk that endangers the person's life.

involuntary servitude Slavery; a practice in which children were sold into service to a businessperson or wealthy person for service. In exchange for money, parents would essentially give up all rights to their children.

involvement A variable used by Travis Hirschi to describe an individual's participation in conventional activities.

iodine A chemical element whose fumes can be used to ascertain fingerprints on a paper surface.

IP (Internet Protocol) address The unique numerical protocol assigned to a computer machine that accesses the Internet. It is a configuration (such as 26.415.82.236) used to identify and possibly locate the host computer accessing the Internet. It identifies one computer from others on the Internet. An IP address may be static, meaning that it never changes from one Internet session to the next, or dynamic, meaning that each time a computer logs onto the Internet, a new IP address is assigned for that particular Internet session. *See also* **TCP/IP (Transmission Control Protocol/Internet Protocol).**

ipso facto "By that very fact" (Latin); by the fact itself (e.g., "We can assume, *ipso facto,* that if the defendant was observed beating another person in a bar by 10 witnesses, then he is likely guilty of the beating inflicted on the victim").

IQ Intelligence quotient. It is usually measured by some intelligence scale.

IRA *See* **Irish Republican Army (IRA).**

Iran-Contra affair A scandal during President Ronald Reagan's administration in which the U.S. government sold arms to Iran in exchange for the safe return of American hostages. The money received was used to fund Nicaraguan Contras or rebels. Both the sale of arms and giving money to the Contras were against the law.

Irish Republican Army (IRA) Spawned from the 1790 United Irishmen movement against British rule, the IRA was gradually established in 1914 as the Irish Volunteers, who carried out frequent attacks on British soldiers and authorities in Dublin and other Irish cities. Following World War I, Irish guerrillas formed the IRA in 1921, which has struggled for Irish independence since. The IRA has continued to carry out violence against British leaders and soldiers, despite various factions of the IRA splitting to form their own organizations with different goals. In an attempt to reach an amicable settlement with British authorities, cessation of military actions against England occurred in August 1994. Subsequently, military operations by IRA members resumed where IRA leaders cited continued British abuse of Irish citizens.

Irish System Sir Walter Crofton's correctional methods involving tickets-of-leave for prisoners serving long sentences. Prisoners could gain early release (parole) through acquisition of tickets-of-leave. It provided a method of obtaining compliance from inmates and rewarding them by releasing them short of serving their full sentences.

Iron Law of Prison Commitments The propensity of government to fill all available prison and jail cells as soon as prisons and jails are built.

irresistible impulse, irresistible impulse test A desire that cannot be resisted due to impairment of the will by mental disease or defect; a compulsion to commit a crime. The "irresistible impulse test" is an insanity defense requiring a showing that although an accused person knew right from wrong, he or she was unable to control an irresistible impulse to commit the crime.

irritant gas Any nonlethal gas that causes skin irritation or eyes to water; one of several items used for crowd control.

Isaac T. Hopper Home A halfway house established in New York City in 1845.

Islamic Jihad A militant Palestinian group.

Islamic jihad Islamic holy war.

Islamic law A system of laws based on the Muslim religion and the holy book known as the Koran.

isolated organizations Correctional organizations that have weak ties to both centralized and local sources of policy and resources.

isolation A sentencing philosophy seeking to separate an offender from others in confinement by placing the prisoner in a cell with no communication with others; also known as solitary confinement. It originated in the Walnut Street Jail in Philadelphia, PA, in the late 1700s. Also, the segregation of offenders from society by incarceration.

isomorphism Similarity or identity in structure.

issuance of warrants, issuance of writs Any authorization by a judicial officer directing a law enforcement officer to act, including search warrants or seizure orders.

issue A legal fact to be resolved.

issue of fact A question of fact to be determined by a jury.

issue of law A matter to be decided by a judge or the court.

Italian school The school of thought developed by Cesare Lombroso linking criminal behavior with abnormal, unusual physical characteristics.

J

Jackal *See* **Sanchez, Ilich Ramirez.**

Jackson rule The rule says that once a defendant invokes the Sixth Amendment right to counsel, any waiver of that right, even if voluntary, knowing, and intelligent under traditional standards, is presumed invalid if given in a police-initiated discussion, and that evidence obtained pursuant to that waiver is inadmissible in the prosecution's case in chief. However, suspect-initiated statements can be used to impeach testimony given by defendants on cross-examination. *See Michigan v. Jackson* (1986).

Jack the Ripper The name given to a serial murderer who killed several prostitutes in London's Whitechapel district in 1888. The murders were never solved.

jail A facility operated and financed by a city or county to contain offenders serving short sentences or awaiting further processing. Jails also house more serious prisoners from state or federal prisons through contracts to alleviate overcrowding as well as witnesses, juveniles, vagrants, and others. *See box.*

jail as a condition of probation A sentence in which the judge imposes limited jail time to be served before commencement of probation. *See also* **split sentencing.**

jail boot camp A program similar to boot camp but operated for a wider age range of clientele; a short-term program designed to foster discipline, self-improvement, and self-image. *See also* **boot camp.**

jailbreak An escape from a jail, lockup, or similar holding facility.

jail commitment A sentence of commitment to the jurisdiction of a confinement facility system for adults that is administered by an agency of local government and of which the custodial authority is usually limited to persons sentenced to a year or less of confinement.

jail confinement rate The number of persons confined in jails, both as detainees awaiting trial and as misdemeanants serving short sentences, per 100,000 persons in the general civilian population.

jail design Any one of several architectural designs used in the construction of jails. *See figure p. 137.*

jail diversion, jail diversion program A method of channeling mentally ill persons or substance abusers to local mental-health services where they can be closely monitored and their recidivism diminished.

"jail fever" Typhus, a common ailment suffered by inmates in prisons that were unsanitary and poorly run. It was found in Ukrainian prisons in the 1770s and described by John Howard.

jailhouse lawyer An inmate in a prison or jail who becomes skilled in the law; an inmate who learns about the law and assists other prisoners in filing suits against the prison or jail administration.

jailhouse turnouts Inmates who are introduced to homosexuality while in prison.

jailing An adaptation to imprisonment generally adopted by a state-raised youth. These prisoners almost completely orient themselves to the prison, which becomes the world around which their lives revolve.

Jail Removal Initiative An action sponsored by the Office of Juvenile Justice and Delinquency Prevention and the Juvenile Justice and Delinquency Prevention Act of 1974 to deinstitutionalize juveniles from secure facilities, such as jails.

jail sentence Penalty of commitment to a jail facility for a specified period.

Jails

1. Receive individuals pending arraignment and hold them awaiting trial, conviction, or sentencing.
2. Readmit probation, parole, and bailbond violators and absconders.
3. Temporarily detain juveniles pending transfer to juvenile authorities.
4. Hold mentally ill persons pending their movement to appropriate health facilities.
5. Hold individuals for the military, for protective custody, for contempt, and for the courts as witnesses.
6. Release convicted inmates to the community upon completion of sentence.
7. Transfer inmates to federal, state, or other authorities.
8. House inmates for federal, state, or other authorities because of crowding of their facilities.
9. Sometimes operate community-based programs as alternatives to incarceration.
10. Hold inmates sentenced to short terms (generally under one year).

Source: Harrison, and Karberg, *Prison and Jail Inmates at Midyear 2002,* 7.

---

jail time Credit allowed on a sentence for time spent in jail awaiting trial or mandate on appeal.

James, Jesse Woodson (1847–1882) An infamous leader of an outlaw gang in the mid- to late 1800s that robbed banks and trains. He was killed by one of his own gang members, Robert Ford, for a reward.

Jay, John (1745–1829) The first chief justice of the U.S. Supreme Court (1789–1795). Jay was born in New York City. He was a delegate to the Continental Congress and an author of essays in the *Federalist.* He subsequently served as governor of New York.

Jellinek's Curve A graph depicting the progression of alcoholism along 43 different steps or stages that identify the subphases of alcohol addiction.

jeopardy Imminent danger of conviction or potential loss of liberty.

Jesse James Act The federal government passed legislation in the 1860s mandating a 25-year prison term for anyone convicted of armed robbery of a postal facility. It was named after Jesse James, a western outlaw.

jihad An Islamic holy war against a person, group, or nation; also, more recently, any concerted effort by a group or organization to protest acts of unfairness or policies that are perceived as poorly conceived or bad (e.g., a media jihad, pertaining to actions against various media outlets for biased or unfair or unbalanced coverage of newsworthy events).

Jim Crow laws Any number of ordinances that were passed, primarily in southern states and municipalities in the 1880s, legalizing segregation of blacks and whites. *Plessy v. Ferguson* (1896) was a major "separate, but equal" ruling, in which the

U.S. Supreme Court actually endorsed the legality of such laws.

"jitterbugs" The term used by adult or older inmates to describe many youthful inmates.

"jive bitches" Inmates who tend to be manipulative and unstable, causing problems for other inmates and staff.

job action Organized activity by law enforcement members to pressure their departments or the government to meet certain union demands in the context of collective bargaining.

job bidding A practice that allows senior correctional officers to bid for certain jobs within their institutions.

job enrichment Infusing tasks with problem-solving activities and more complex and challenging duties that require thinking and creativity. This strategy seems to work better for those employees with greater amounts of education.

job satisfaction Degree of contentment with work performed.

job status A ranking determined by one's position in the hierarchy of authority. People tend to evaluate one another in an organization according to the amount of power they can wield over others. Higher or lower positions or greater or lesser amounts of power possessed determine one's status.

"jockers" Sexual aggressors who take the traditional masculine role in oral or anal intercourse during a homosexual encounter.

Joe Friday A character originally portrayed by Jack Webb on the radio and television program *Dragnet*. Detective Sergeant Friday was known to go "by the book" in his application of the law and pursuit of justice against criminals. The name became a slang term to refer to police officers who do their jobs in a manner that is impersonal and legalistic. *See also* **legalistic model.**

Johari window A model for examining interpersonal disclosure and feedback that consists of four "windows," in which certain facts about a person are distributed as follows: facts that are known to others but not known by the person; known to the person but not known to others; known to the person and known to others; and not known to the person or to others.

"john" Slang for a man who solicits the sexual services of a prostitute.

John Birch Society A right-wing organization of extremists established by Robert Welch in 1958 in Indianapolis. The society opposes communism, questions the integrity of political leaders, opposes all forms of internationalism, and is supportive of traditional police practices.

John Doe, Jane Doe A name used for a criminal suspect or dead body when the true name of the person is unknown.

John Doe warrant A warrant or *capias* issued when a suspect's name is unknown, but an otherwise accurate description and location of the suspect have been provided.

John Howard Association, John Howard Society An organization formed in 1901 that is known for pressing for prison reforms.

John Wayne syndrome A depiction of police officers who tend to be overserious and cold and have tunnel-vision.

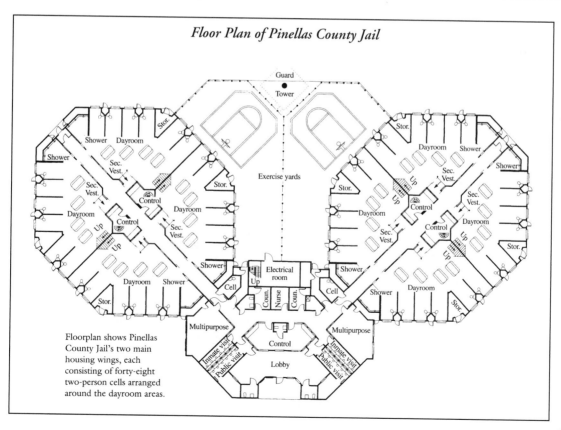

Floor Plan of Pinellas County Jail

Floorplan shows Pinellas County Jail's two main housing wings, each consisting of forty-eight two-person cells arranged around the dayroom areas.

joinder Coupling two or more criminal prosecutions (e.g., in a case in which two or more persons have allegedly committed a crime together, they may be tried in a single trial proceeding through a joinder).

Join Together Online Substance abuse links on the Internet. The group provides site information for studies of drug use and abuse and resources for combatting illicit drug use. It is headquartered in Boston, MA.

joint trial calendar system A method of case processing used by judges in certain jurisdictions, in which several judges share a common court calendar with the shared objective and responsibility of trying all cases on the calendar within a specified period.

Joliet Site of the famous Stateville Correctional Center in Illinois. Inmates housed there included John Wayne Gacy and Richard Speck.

joyriding Temporarily taking a motorized vehicle without the intent to permanently deprive the owner of it.

judge A political officer who has been elected or appointed to preside over a court of law, whose position has been created by statute or by constitution, and whose decisions in criminal and juvenile cases may only be reviewed by a judge or a higher court and may not be reviewed *de novo*.

Judge Advocate General (JAG) The chief legal counsel of any military branch, which conducts military tribunals and other military court proceedings.

judge-made law Common law resulting from court decrees; reliance on judicial decisions where the law has been interpreted according to prevailing standards in society not necessarily consistent with existing statutory authority; proclamations made by judges where no statutes exist.

judge *pro tem* A replacement judge who sits in for another judge because of scheduling conflicts or illness or some other reason causing the original judge's absence. The temporary judge has the full range of powers of the original judge who is not present.

judgment The final determination of a case; a proclamation stating one's guilt or innocence in relation to criminal offenses alleged; in tort law, a finding in favor of or against the plaintiff; in civil cases, the amount of monetary damages awarded.

judgment-suspending sentence A court-ordered sentencing alternative that results in the convicted offender being placed on probation.

judicial activism The U.S. Supreme Court's use of its power to accomplish social goals. Judicial activism is often imputed to courts by persons who disagree with court decisions.

judicial adjuncts Lawyers and others who assist courts and judges on a temporary basis in minor offense cases. Judicial adjuncts maintain law practices while performing these temporary duties.

judicial branch That segment of government charged with interpreting the law and administering justice. Examples include the U.S. Supreme Court; state supreme, superior, and appellate courts; county courts; and magistrates' courts. The court subsystem falls under this branch of government.

judicial circuit A specific jurisdiction served by a judge or court, as defined by given geographical boundaries.

judicial discretion The inherent ability of a judge to make subjective decisions about cases before the court.

judicial misconduct Any behavior perpetrated by a judge in the official performance of his or her duties that would be inconsistent with propriety or proper conduct.

judicial model of sentencing A sentencing scheme in which control over type and duration of sentence is left in the hands of the trial judge.

judicial notice An exclusively judicial determination or acknowledgment of facts in evidence apart from any persuasion by the defense or prosecution.

judicial officer A judge or magistrate who presides in a given jurisdiction.

judicial order A court order that involves the exercise of judicial discretion and affects the final result of litigation.

judicial plea bargaining The recommended sentence by a judge who offers a specific sentence or fine in exchange for a guilty plea. *See also* **plea bargaining, plea negotiation.**

judicial powers Court jurisdiction to act in certain cases and decide punishments.

judicial process The sequence of procedures designed to resolve disputes or conclude a criminal case.

judicial reprieve Temporary relief or postponement of the imposition of a sentence. The practice commenced during the Middle Ages at the discretion of judges to permit defendants more time to gather evidence of their innocence and to allow them to demonstrate that they had reformed their behavior.

judicial restraint The U.S. Supreme Court's deference to legislative and executive decisions, unless a clear constitutional right has been violated.

judicial review The authority of a court to limit the power of the executive and legislative branches of government by deciding whether their acts defy rights established by the state and federal constitutions. *See Marbury v. Madison* (1803).

Judicial Sentencing Institute An educational or training session for judges on issues relevant to sentencing.

judicial system The entire organization of federal, state, and local courts and their operations.

judicial waiver A decision by a juvenile judge to waive a juvenile to the jurisdiction of a criminal court.

Judiciary Act of 1789 A congressional act that provided for three levels of courts: (1) 13 federal district courts, each presided over by a district judge; (2) three higher circuit courts of appeal, each comprising two justices of the Supreme Court and one district judge; and (3) a Supreme Court, consisting of a chief justice and five associate justices.

Judiciary Act of 1891 The congressional act that created the contemporary United States circuit court scheme for federal appellate review.

judicious nonintervention Similar to a "do nothing" policy of delinquency nonintervention.

"juice" Possessing information and influence that come through a job or relationship with authority figures. It allows inmates to circumvent rules or avoid delays to get things done.

Jukes, the A family used in attempts to illustrate the idea that criminal tendencies are inherited, which was promoted by the questionable research of Henry Goddard, who compared the Jukes family and their descendants with another family, the Kallikaks. One family, the Jukes, supposedly had numerous deviant offspring, whereas the Kallikaks had more normal offspring. The notion was subsequently discarded as a legitimate explanation of criminal conduct because of the questionable research practices and data collected by Goddard.

JUMP *See* **Juvenile Mentoring Program (JUMP).**

jump bail The act by a defendant of leaving the jurisdiction in which a trial was to be held in an attempt to avoid prosecution on criminal charges.

jural postulates Propositions developed by the jurist Roscoe Pound holding that the law reflects the shared needs without which members of society could not coexist. Pound's jural postulates are often linked to the idea that the law can be used to engineer the structure of society in order to predetermine certain kinds of outcomes, as property rights embodied in the law of theft do in capitalist societies.

jurat A certificate showing that an affidavit was properly executed before a particular authority.

juridical Pertaining to the office and functions of a judge.

juridical days Particular days when a court is in session.

jurisdiction, court The power of a court to hear and determine a particular type of case; also, the territory within which a court may exercise authority, such as a city, county, or state.

jurisdiction, original The lawful authority of a court or an administrative agency to hear or act upon a case from its beginning and to pass judgment on it.

jurisdiction, police The established geographical boundaries in which the police of a political subdivision have authority.

jurisdictional age limit The age at which a juvenile court no longer has jurisdiction over a juvenile offender, usually between 19 and 21.

jurisprudence The application of the law in any jurisdiction.

jurist A person who is skilled or well-versed in the law, usually a lawyer or judge.

jurist value system A category of decision making by parole boards in which parole decisions are regarded as a natural part of the criminal-justice process in which fairness and equity predominate.

juror A person who serves on a jury; a citizen selected from a list of registered voters or some other official compilation of persons, who sits on a jury that will decide the guilt or innocence of someone accused of a crime.

jury *See* **petit jury.**

jury, grand *See* **grand jury.**

jury, hung *See* **hung jury.**

jury deliberation Discussion among jury members concerning the weight and sufficiency of witness testimony and other evidence presented by both the prosecution and defense; an attempt to arrive at a verdict. *See figure.*

jury duty The practice and obligation of citizens to serve on juries for local courts.

jury instructions Verbal advice given by a judge to jurors before they begin their deliberations.

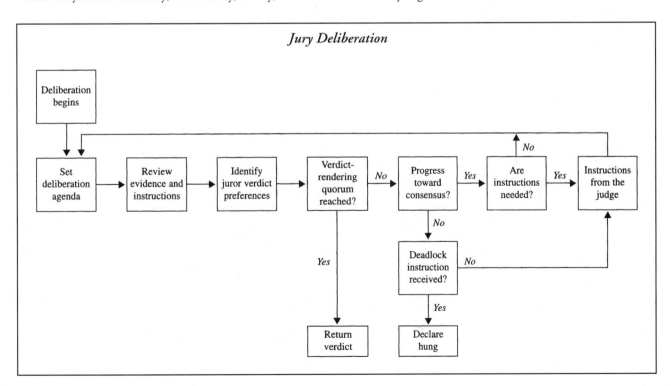

Jury Deliberation

jury nullification An outcome in which the jury refuses to accept the validity of evidence at trial and acquits or convicts for a lesser offense (e.g., although all of the elements for murder are proved, a jury may acquit a defendant who killed his or her spouse allegedly as an act of mercy killing).

jury panel A list of jurors summoned to serve on possible jury duty at a particular court. From the jury panel, the petit jury is selected.

jury poll A poll conducted by a judicial officer or by the clerk of the court after a jury has stated its verdict but before that verdict has been entered into the record of the court, asking each juror individually whether the stated verdict is his or her own verdict.

jury school Established in 1937 in Newark, NJ, to educate citizens about their responsibilities and duties as jurors, the school provides instruction on proper juror behavior.

jury selection The process whereby jurors are selected for either a civil or a criminal trial.

jury sentencing The process of determining one's sentence in which a jury imposes a particular penalty or makes a recommendation to the judge that a particular penalty should be imposed.

jury size Although there are traditionally 12 members on a jury at the federal level and at many state and local levels, the number may vary between six and 12 at the state and local levels.

jury system A method of justice using a body comprised of one's peers, which hears the facts and decides one's guilt or innocence as a result.

jury tampering A criminal offense involving an attempt to threaten, intimidate, bribe, or otherwise influence one or more members of an impaneled jury.

jury trial A trial in which guilt or innocence of the defendant is determined by a jury instead of by the judge.

jury wheel A device for deriving the names of jurors who should be summoned as the venire for a particular court case.

jus gentium "Law of nations" (Latin); a compendium of law developed by Roman jurists for use in trials involving Roman citizens and noncitizens.

just deserts The view that someone should be punished in proportion to the offense committed.

"just-deserts" model A correctional model stressing equating punishment with the severity of the crime. The model is based on Cesare Beccaria's ideas about punishment.

justice A judge, particularly a supreme court judge; also, an ideal concerning the maintenance of right and the correction of wrong in the relations of human beings.

justice, sporting theory of An adversarial method of administering justice. Both sides present their cases, which are then decided by the judge. It is similar to bench trial.

justice administration The description and elaboration of the structural, functional, and managerial processes involved in coordinating activities related to determining the incidence of criminal conduct, the detection and apprehension of alleged criminals, an assessment of the credibility of evidence against the accused, a formal judgment about that conduct, and how that conduct is punished.

Justice Fellowship An organization established in 1983 by Christians who support reforms in criminal justice and headquartered in Washington, DC. Its goals are to develop system of punishing criminals fairly, compensating victims for their losses and protecting communities and citizens from criminals.

Justice Management Institute An organization headquartered in Denver, CO, that was established to investigate and report about court management issues.

justice model A philosophy that emphasizes punishment as a primary objective of sentencing, fixed sentences, abolition of parole, and an abandonment of the rehabilitative ideal.

justice of the peace A minor judicial official who oversees trivial offenses.

justice of the peace court A court, usually rural, possessing special original jurisdiction in most instances and certain quasi-judicial powers.

Justice of the Peace Act An English act of 1361 that created a local magistrate to oversee constables and the watch, and also to resolve local disputes under authority of the Crown.

Justice Research and Statistics Association (JRSA) A national organization whose membership primarily consists of statistical analysis center (SAC) directors and that provides specialized training in criminal justice data analysis techniques, holds an annual meeting, and publishes *Justice Research and Policy.*

justifiable homicide A homicide permitted by law in defense of a legal right or mandate.

justifiable use of force Correctional officers or police officers can use force in self-defense and in defense of others to prevent a crime.

justification Defense to a criminal charge in which defendants maintain that their actions were appropriate or non-criminal according to the circumstances, and therefore, that they should not be held criminally liable.

Just Say No An anti-drug program during the 1980s that was based on the idea that youth and other potential drug users would refrain from the use of drugs simply by the repetition of this phrase.

juvenile One who is under the age of consent for a particular jurisdiction. Usually, someone under the age of 18 or 21 is considered a juvenile for legal purposes.

juvenile bindover The transfer of certain youths to adult court because of the seriousness of their offenses.

juvenile-contiguous blend A form of blended sentencing in which a juvenile-court judge can impose a disposition beyond the normal jurisdictional range for juvenile offenders (e.g., a judge may impose a 30-year term on a 14-year-old offender, but the juvenile is entitled to a hearing when he or she reaches the age of majority to determine whether the remainder of the sentence shall be served).

juvenile court A term for any court that has original jurisdiction over persons statutorily defined as juveniles and alleged to be delinquents, status offenders, or dependents.

juvenile-court judge A person elected or appointed to preside over juvenile cases, and whose decisions can only be reviewed by a judge of a higher court.

juvenile-court judgment A juvenile-court decision terminating an adjudication hearing that the juvenile is delinquent, a status offender, or dependent, or that the allegations in a petition are not sustained.

juvenile-court jurisdiction Authority to decide juvenile matters by juvenile court. It usually applies to juveniles between 10 or 12 and 18 years of age, although ages vary among states.

juvenile-court records A formal or informal statement concerning an adjudication hearing involving sustained allegations against a juvenile; a written document of one's prior delinquency or status offending.

juvenile-defense attorneys Lawyers who represent juveniles in juvenile court and play an active role at all stages of the proceedings.

juvenile delinquency An act committed by a youth that would be a crime if an adult committed the same offense.

juvenile delinquent A person under the age of majority who commits an act that would be a crime if an adult committed it.

juvenile detention center A temporary holding facility for youthful offenders.

juvenile disposition A decision by a juvenile court, concluding a disposition hearing, that an adjudicated juvenile be committed to a juvenile correctional facility; placed in a juvenile residence, shelter, care, or treatment program; required to meet certain standards of conduct; or released.

juvenile diversion *See* **diversion, juvenile.**

juvenile diversion/noncustody intake program A California juvenile program implemented in 1982 targeted at more serious juvenile offenders. It is characterized by intensive supervised probation, required school attendance, employment, and counseling.

juvenile diversion program Any program for juvenile offenders that, similarly to an adult diversion program, temporarily suspends their processing by the juvenile-justice system; also, a program established in 1981 in New Orleans, LA, by the district attorney's office in which youths could receive treatment before being petitioned and adjudicated delinquent. *See also* **diversion, juvenile.**

juvenile-exclusive blend A blended sentencing form in which a juvenile-court judge can impose either adult or juvenile incarceration as a disposition and sentence, but not both.

juvenile facility Any institution in which juveniles are detained or incarcerated for variable periods, such as halfway houses, group homes, boot camps, diagnostic centers, and assessment centers.

Juvenile Firesetters Program Headquartered in Washington, DC, these seminars train fire investigators and others about the etiology of fire-starting behavior among youths and how it can be prevented.

juvenile gang A loosely organized group of youths who band together for protection, social interaction, and sometimes criminal or delinquent activity.

juvenile-inclusive blend A form of blended sentencing in which a juvenile-court judge can impose *both* adult and juvenile incarceration simultaneously.

juvenile information source A directory of organizations that provide information about different aspects of the juvenile justice system. It is part of the National Directory of Children and Youth Services and publishes the *Child Protection Report.* It is headquartered in Washington, DC.

Juvenile Intensive Supervised Probation (JISP) An Ohio-operated program for youthful offenders that includes home confinement, electronic monitoring, and other intensive probation supervision methods.

juvenile justice The entire system designed to process and meet the needs of offenders who are under the age of their majority. *See box p. 142.*

juvenile-justice administrative body An organization responsible for the administration and management of juvenile justice within a state.

juvenile-justice agency Any governmental or private agency of which the functions are the investigation, supervision, adjudication, care, or confinement of juveniles whose conduct or condition has brought or could bring them within the jurisdiction of a juvenile court.

Juvenile Justice and Delinquency Prevention Act of 1974 An act passed by Congress in 1974 and amended numerous times, including in 1984, encouraging states to deal differently with their juvenile offenders. The act promotes community-based treatment programs and discourages incarceration of juveniles in detention centers, industrial schools, or reform schools.

Juvenile Justice Reform Act of 1977 A Washington State statute that created mandatory sentencing for juvenile offenders based on their age, the crime, and their prior history as offenders.

juvenile-justice system, juvenile-justice process The system through which juveniles are processed, sentenced, and corrected after arrest for juvenile delinquency. *See diagram p. 143.*

juvenile locators services Operated by the Youth Department of Health and Human Services, the National Runaway Switchboard offers services to youths who are runaways. Services include facilitating contact with one's parents and other types of assistance, including shelter and food.

Juvenile Mentoring Program (JUMP) A grant program sponsored by the Office of Juvenile Justice and Delinquency Prevention (OJJDP) designed to promote mentoring specifically to address poor school performance and dropping out of school.

juvenile offender Any youth who is under the age of majority when charged with a status or delinquent offense.

juvenile-offender laws Regulations providing for automatic transfer of juveniles of certain ages to criminal courts for processing, provided they have committed especially serious crimes.

juvenile officers Police officers who specialize in dealing with juvenile offenders. They may operate alone or as part of a juvenile police unit within the department.

juvenile petition *See* **petition.**

Juvenile Probation Camps (**JPCs**) California county-operated camps for delinquent youth placed on probation in the early 1980s, which included physical activities, community contacts, and academic training.

juvenile-probation department The agency in charge of monitoring all juveniles on probation within a given jurisdiction.

juvenile-probation officer An officer of the juvenile court involved in all four stages of the court process—intake, predisposition, postadjudication, and postdisposition—who assists the court and supervises juveniles placed on probation.

juvenile prosecutor A government attorney responsible for representing the interests of the state and bringing a case against an accused juvenile.

juvenile record An official record containing, at a minimum, summary information pertaining to an identified juvenile concerning juvenile-court proceedings, and, if applicable, detention and correctional processes. Such records may be ex-

---

Chronological Summary of Major Events in Juvenile Justice

1791 Bill of Rights is passed by U.S. Congress

1825 New York House of Refuge is established

1839 *Ex parte Crouse* establishes the right of juvenile court to intervene in parent-child matters

1841 John Augustus initiates probation in Boston

1853 New York Children's Aid Society is established

1855 Death penalty is imposed on 10-year-old James Arcene in Arkansas, for robbery and murder; the earliest juvenile execution was of Thomas Graunger, aged 16, for sodomizing a horse and cow in 1642

1866 Massachusetts statute is passed giving juvenile court the power to intervene and take custody if parents are unfit

1868 Fourteenth Amendment is passed by U.S. Congress, establishing the right to due process and equal protection under the law

1874 Massachusetts establishes the first Children's Tribunal to deal with youthful offenders

1889 Indiana establishes children's guardians to have jurisdiction over neglected and dependent children

1889 Hull House is established in Chicago by Jane Addams to assist unsupervised children of immigrant parents

1899 Compulsory School Act, Colorado; statutory regulation of truants

1899 Illinois Act to Regulate the Treatment and Control of Dependent, Neglected, and Delinquent Children; first juvenile court is established in the United States

1901 Juvenile court is established in Denver, CO

1907 Separate juvenile court with original jurisdiction in juvenile matters is established in Denver, CO

1912 Creation of U.S. Children's Bureau, charged with compiling statistical information about juvenile offenders; it existed from 1912 to 1940

1918 Chicago slums are studied by Shaw and McKay; delinquency was related to the urban environment and transitional neighborhoods

1938 Federal Juvenile Delinquency Act is passed

1966 *Kent v. United States* establishes a juvenile's right to a hearing before transfer to criminal court, the right to assis-

tance of counsel during police interrogations, and the right to reports and records related to transfer

1967 *In re Gault* establishes a juvenile's right to an attorney, the right to notice of charges, the right to confront and cross-examine witnesses, and the right against self-incrimination

1970 *In re Winship* establishes a juvenile's right to the criminal-court standard of "beyond a reasonable doubt" when loss of freedom is a possible penalty

1971 *McKeiver v. Pennsylvania* establishes that a juvenile's right to a trial by jury is not absolute

1974 Juvenile Justice and Delinquency Prevention Act is passed by U.S. Congress

1974 Office of Juvenile Justice and Delinquency Prevention is founded, and becomes instrumental in promoting deinstitutionalization of status offenders

1975 *Breed v. Jones* establishes that double jeopardy exists if a juvenile is adjudicated as delinquent in juvenile court and later tried for the same offense in criminal court; prohibits double jeopardy

1982 *Eddings v. Oklahoma* establishes that the death penalty applied to juveniles is not cruel and unusual punishment *per se.*

1984 *Schall v. Martin* establishes the constitutionality of the preventive detention of juveniles

1985 *New Jersey v. T.L.O.* establishes a lesser standard of search and seizure on school property; searches and seizures are permissible without probable cause or warrant

1988 *Thompson v. Oklahoma* establishes that applying the death penalty to juveniles convicted of murder who were under age 16 at the time of the murder is cruel and unusual punishment

1989 *Stanford v. Kentucky* and *Wilkins v. Missouri* establish that the death penalty is not cruel and unusual punishment when applied to juveniles convicted of murder who were aged 16 or 17 at the time the murder was committed

---

Source: Compiled by author.

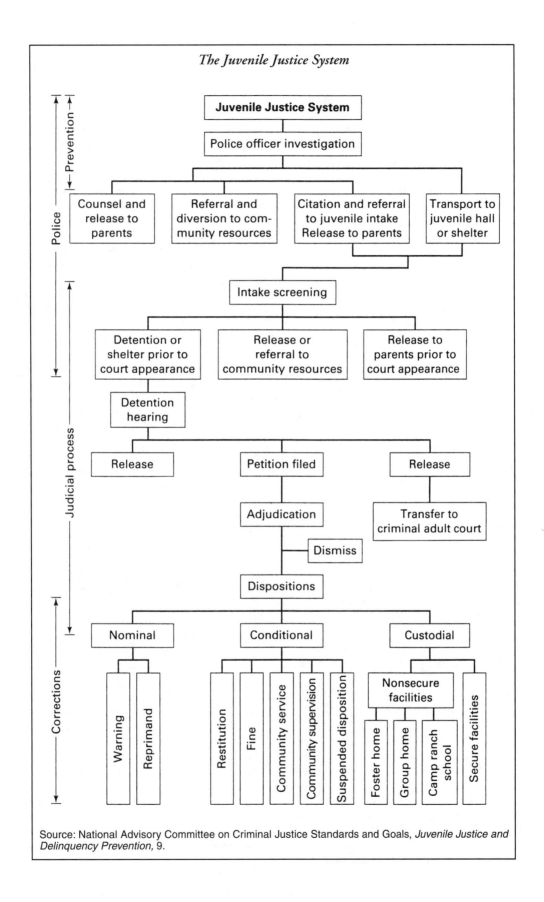

The Juvenile Justice System

Source: National Advisory Committee on Criminal Justice Standards and Goals, *Juvenile Justice and Delinquency Prevention,* 9.

punged or sealed when a youth reaches age 18 or 21 in most jurisdictions. The records may be reopened later under special circumstances.

juvenile rights All constitutional rights that attach when a juvenile appears before a juvenile court, an adjudicatory proceeding, or at any stage of juvenile offender processing. *See table p. 145.*

juvenile sex offender A youth who has committed one or more sex offenses.

juvenile transfer A waiver of a juvenile from the jurisdiction of juvenile court to criminal court.

juvenile waiver A transfer of a juvenile from the jurisdiction of juvenile court to criminal court.

K

Kaczynski, Theodore (1942–) A former university professor known as the Unabomber who killed three and wounded 26 with package bombs in 16 incidents between 1978 and 1995. He was born in Chicago in 1942, and studied at Harvard University. Kaczynski was eventually caught and sentenced to life without the possibility of parole in 1998.

Kairos Prison Ministry (KPM) An organization that emanates from mainline churches. It puts on seminars to teach inmates religious principles and provides significant transitional services to inmates.

Kales plan A 1914 version of the Missouri Plan, in which a committee of experts creates a list of qualified persons for judgeships and makes recommendations to the governor. *See also* **Missouri Plan.**

Kallikaks, the A family supposedly studied by Henry Goddard that was compared with another family, the Jukes, to support the idea that criminal traits are inherited. Goddard's work has been largely discounted because of his questionable research practices.

kangaroo court An unofficial court, often held by a mob or vigilante group, whose judgment is biased against the accused.

Kansas City Experiment, Kansas City Preventive Patrol Experiment, Kansas City Study A controversial study conducted in the early 1970s in Kansas City, which showed no relation between crime and the intensity of police patrolling in various city areas.

Katz, Jack (1944–) A criminologist who devised the term "seductions of crime" to indicate immediate benefits accruing from criminal activity. Situational inducements may propel persons otherwise exhibiting conventional behavior toward criminal conduct if they perceive sufficient rewards. The phenomenon may be related to need-fulfillment and doing something pleasurable and exciting, regardless of whether it is criminal.

Keeper's Voice A newsletter published by the International Association of Correctional Officers (IACO) that provides a forum for correctional officers.

"keestering" drugs Conceal drugs or contraband in one's rectum.

Kefauver Commission, Kefauver Committee, Kefauver Investigation A special Senate committee during the period 1950–1951 that targeted organized crime in the United States. With exciting courtroom drama, its disclosures demonstrated the extent to which racketeers had established themselves in American society.

Kelly-Frye motion A defense tactic to move to suppress evidence believed to be faulty. Such a motion usually challenges the scientific basis for establishing the credibility of evidence, as was done in early DNA cases because of the newness of this identification procedure.

Kent **criteria** Factors established by the U.S. Supreme Court in *Kent v. United States* (1966) that juvenile-court judges should take into consideration when deciding whether or not to waive a juvenile to criminal court for processing as an adult offender.

Kent State University The site at Kent, OH, where Ohio National Guardsmen fired on students during a student demonstration on May 4, 1970, killing four and wounding 11. The shootings led to a formal investigation into what caused the incident and how such incidents could be prevented in the future.

Kerner Commission The National Commission on Civil Disorders, chaired by Senator Otto Kerner, was formed in federal response to the racial unrest of the 1960s, and reported its findings in 1968.

ketamine hydrochloride A date-rape drug known as Special K or Vitamin K that is colorless, odorless, and can be slipped into a person's drink for the purpose of rendering him or her susceptible to sexual advances and abuse. Persons who ingest the substance experience a trancelike state, accompanied by dizziness, hallucinations, and unconsciousness.

Kevlar A synthetic material from which body armor capable of repelling bullets is made.

Kevorkian, Jack (1928–) A physician and pathologist known for his assistance of elderly terminally ill patients in committing suicide to end their pain and suffering. He was convicted and imprisoned in Michigan.

key In fingerprint classification, the ridge count in the first loop appearing in a set of fingerprints.

kickback Payment to an official by a contractor for favoritism in awarding a contract.

"kid" In prison, an individual, usually very young and weak, who has been coerced or forced into being another inmate's sex slave.

kiddie porn Any photographic images of small children in lewd poses; generally, any photographs of children under the age of 18, who may or may not be engaged in any type of sexual activity, and that are used for the sexual stimulation and gratification of an adult. The Internet is a growing source of such pornography.

Juvenile and Adult Rights Relating to Delinquency and Crime[a]

Right	Adults	Juveniles
1. "Beyond a reasonable doubt" standard used in court	Yes	Yes
2. Right against double jeopardy	Yes	Yes
3. Right to assistance of counsel	Yes	Yes
4. Right to notice of charges	Yes	Yes
5. Right to a transcript of court proceedings	Yes	No
6. Right against self-incrimination	Yes	Yes
7. Right to trial by jury	Yes	No in most states
8. Right to defense counsel in court proceedings	Yes	No
9. Right to due process	Yes	No*
10. Right to bail	Yes	No, with exceptions
11. Right to cross-examine witnesses	Yes	Yes
12. Right of confrontation	Yes	Yes
13. Standards relating to searches and seizures:		
a. "Probable cause" and warrants required for searches and seizures	Yes, with exceptions	No
b. "Reasonable suspicion" required for searches and seizures without warrant	No	Yes
14. Right to hearing prior to transfer to criminal court or to a reverse waiver hearing in states with automatic transfer provisions	NA	Yes
15. Right to a speedy trial	Yes	No
16. Right to *habeas corpus* relief in correctional settings	Yes	No
17. Right to rehabilitation	No	No
18. Criminal evidentiary standards	Yes	Yes
19. Right to hearing for parole or probation revocation	Yes	No
20. Bifurcated trial, death-penalty cases	Yes	Yes
21. Right to discovery	Yes	Limited
22. Fingerprinting, photographing at booking	Yes	No, with exceptions
23. Right to appeal	Yes	Limited
24. Waivers of rights		
a. Adults	Knowingly, intelligently	
b. Juveniles		Totality of circumstances
25. Right to hearing for parole or probation revocation	Yes	No, with exceptions
26. "Equal protection" clause of Fourteenth Amendment applicable	Yes	No, with exceptions
27. Right to court-appointed attorney if indigent	Yes	No, with exceptions
28. Transcript required of criminal/delinquency trial proceedings	Yes	No, with exceptions
29. Pretrial detention permitted	Yes	Yes
30. Plea bargaining	Yes, with exceptions	No, with exceptions
31. Burden of proof borne by prosecution	Yes	No, with exceptions**
32. Public access to trials	Yes	Limited
33. Conviction/adjudication results in criminal record	Yes	No

[a]Compiled by author.
*Minimal, not full, due-process safeguards assured.
**Burden of proof is borne by prosecutor in 23 state juvenile courts, while the rest make no provision or mention of who bears the burden of proof.

kidnapping A felony consisting of the seizure and abduction of someone by force or threat of force and against the victim's will. Under federal law, victims of a kidnapping are those who have been taken across state lines and held for ransom.

kill To bring about the cessation of one's life.

kilhas Subgroups of same-aged youths in Hispanic gangs that remain together and have separate names and a unique identity within the gang.

King, Martin Luther, Jr. (1929–1968) A black civil rights leader who was awarded the Nobel Peace Prize in 1964. He headed efforts to promote civil rights for black citizens and was assassinated by James Earl Ray in Memphis, TN, on April 4, 1968.

King, Rodney (1965–) A Los Angeles motorist who was stopped for a routine traffic violation and beaten by Los Angeles Police Department officers on March 3, 1991, in a videotaped incident. In 1992, four of the officers were acquitted by an all-white jury in nearby Simi Valley, which sparked several days of rioting that resulted in more than 50 deaths and hundreds of millions of dollars in property damage. Two of the officers were later convicted in federal court of violating King's civil rights. The case led to a commission to investigate police officers in the LAPD.

kingpin The head of a criminal organization, often one involved with drug trafficking.

King's Peace A fifteenth- and sixteenth-century law by which the king extended his protection to those in his presence and in the local area in which he was staying.

Kirchheimer, Otto (1905–1965) A critical criminologist who has written extensively about Marxist criminology. He views internal societal clashes as the result of unequal distribution of wealth and power. Kirchheimer collaborated with Georg Rusche in investigating societal conflict.

kite An anonymous note to a guard's superior detailing his past dereliction of duty.

kiting, check Writing checks from one bank to cover checks written on another bank, where insufficient funds exist in either bank to cover the check amounts. Delays in check processing enable persons to defraud banks of large monetary sums.

Kleck, Gary (1951–) A criminologist who has written extensively about gun control and conducted numerous surveys about gun control and gun ownership. Kleck determined that there are over 2 million defensive gun uses per year by law-abiding citizens. He has published numerous articles and books of factual information concerning firearms use and abuse in the United States, and published *The Illegitimacy of One-Sided Speculation: Getting the Defensive Gun Use Estimate Down* (1998) with Marc Gertz. Kleck has been critical of the *National Crime Victimization Survey,* which has, in his opinion, seriously underestimated the number of defensive gun uses in United States annually. He claims that government interviewers intimidate citizens during interviews designed to collect such information, and that underestimates of defensive gun use arise because citizens are reluctant or afraid to disclose that they have used firearms for defensive purposes to government officials.

kleptomania A psychological compulsion to steal.

Knapp Commission A public body created in 1970 in New York City that led the investigation into police corruption and uncovered a widespread network of payoffs and bribes among regular patrol officers, detectives, and administrators.

knout A Russian wooden-handled whip typically consisting of several rawhide thongs twisted together and terminating in a single strand. Sometimes the hide was plaited with wire, dipped in liquid, and then frozen before use, or the thongs had hooks or rings attached to the ends.

known groups technique Determining the validity of a measure by seeing whether groups known to differ on a characteristic differ on a measure of that characteristic (e.g., ministers should differ from atheists on a measure of religiosity).

known specimen Physical evidence obtained from a known source (e.g., a particular knife taken from a particular individual's knife collection is a known specimen).

Koga method A way of self-defense named after Robert Koga, a martial arts specialist and former Los Angeles Police Department officer, that involves minimal force to reduce likelihood of injuries to arrestees. It uses the martial art aikido and uses distraction to achieve control over arrestees.

Kohlberg, Lawrence (1927–1987) A psychologist who developed stages of cognitive development as an explanation for why persons adopt conventional and nonconventional behaviors in their early years. Different stages of moral development are crucial in determining whether or not someone acquires the cognitive means to avoid unconventional conduct and to realize that whatever conduct is contemplated might be criminal or wrong.

Kretschmer, Ernst (1888–1964) A criminologist and anthropologist who believed that physical characteristics were highly correlated with criminality. He wrote *Physique and Character* (1926) and advocated that various body types were associated with various forms of criminality.

Krisberg, Barry A criminologist who has declared as a part of a conflict theoretical perspective that crime is a function of privilege, in which crimes are created by powerful interests to perpetuate their domination of those less powerful or powerless. His theory is elaborated in *Crime and Privilege: Toward a New Criminology* (1975).

KRUM A Swedish association for advancing the cause of more humane treatment for prisoners. It was formed in 1966 to provide legal assistance for furtherance of inmate rights.

Ku Klux Klan An organization of white supremacists and racists, found mostly in the South, dedicated to asserting the superiority of whites over racial, ethnic, religious, and other minorities, including African Americans, Jews, gays, and lesbians.

L

labeling, labeling model, labeling perspective, labeling theory A theory, attributed to Edwin Lemert, that persons acquire self-definitions that are deviant or criminal. Persons perceive themselves as deviant or criminal through labels applied to them by others; thus, the more people are involved in the criminal-justice system, the more they acquire self-definitions consistent with the criminal label.

labor camp A place where sentenced offenders are required to perform physical labor.

labor relations Interactions between employers and employees, usually through collective bargaining, in which each side seeks concessions from the other relating to wages, vacations, retirement benefits, and other matters.

labor turnover The number of persons who leave an organization within some time interval, such as each year.

labor union Any organization of workers dedicated to furthering their interests as employees in a given company. A union's goals include obtaining more benefits for workers.

La Cosa Nostra "Our thing" (Italian); a secret criminal organization of Sicilian origin; the Mafia.

landmark case, landmark decision A decision handed down by U.S. Supreme Court that becomes the law of the land and serves as a precedent for subsequent similar legal issues in lower courts.

lands The ridges between the rifling grooves in the barrel of a firearm.

Lansky, Meyer (1902–1983) A major Jewish mobster during the mid-twentieth century; a head of organized crime who competed with others, often resulting in bloody shootouts and deaths.

La Nuestra Familia (NF) A gang formed by Mexican American prisoners from Northern California to protect themselves from members of the Mexican Mafia. Today this group is considered an organized crime group and has units both inside and outside of California prisons.

larceny, larceny-theft The unlawful taking, carrying, leading, or riding away of property from the possession or constructive possession of another. It includes shoplifting, pick-pocketing, thefts from motor vehicles, and thefts of motor vehicle parts or accessories.

large jails Jails with 250–999 beds.

laser (Light Amplification by Stimulated Emission Radiation) A device that produces a very narrow beam of light, useful for detecting speeds of motorists on highways.

latchkey children Children left unsupervised after school by working parents.

latency theory The theory that various needs are hidden in one's subconscious until they are triggered or activated by an event (e.g., latent homosexuality that may manifest itself in a situation in which the suggestion of a homosexual relation is made or under conditions that are conducive to such a liaison).

latent delinquents Youths whose troubled family life leads them to seek immediate gratification without consideration of right and wrong or the feelings of others.

latent functions Hidden or unintended functions of an action.

latent prints Fingerprints lifted from surfaces other than the hands bearing prints.

latent social identities Personality dispositions and attitudes that individuals bring with them to an organization. Persons cannot separate themselves from their thoughts and beliefs outside of the work setting. When they are working at their jobs, their behaviors are influenced by their previous experiences and encounters outside of the workplace.

latent trait theory, latent trait view An explanation of crime over time throughout the life cycle. It assumes that persons possess a dormant characteristic controlling their propensity to offend, and when opportunities arise that awaken such characteristics they cause manifestations of criminal behavior. Thus, the predisposition to act in criminal ways is a stable phenomenon, whereas the opportunity to commit crime fluctuates depending on situational circumstances. The term is associated with David Rowe, D. Wayne Osgood, and W. Alan Nicewander (1990).

Latin Kings, Latin King Nation (LK, LKN) The oldest and largest Hispanic gang in Chicago, established in the mid-1970s. The gang originated in the South Chicago and Humboldt Park areas. Its main goal is to protect its neighborhood or turf from other gangs. They are considered very violent. Elements of the gang have been found in New York City, Connecticut, New Jersey, Wisconsin, Iowa, Indiana, and Florida. Their colors are black and gold, and members wear tattoos to signify gang affiliation. Members also wear a medallion, known as "la Virgin," inside their clothing, and use special hand signs and unique jargon to communicate with one another. They are involved in drug sales and trafficking, weapons trafficking, and providing protection. Female members are referred to as Queens. The gang is linked with the Almighty Latin King Nation. Members are recruited from age 8 up.

Laub, John A criminologist who collaborated with Robert Sampson to devise the age-graded theory and establish the significance of turning points throughout the life course. Marriage and career are viewed by these researchers as crucial in enabling adults to refrain from engaging in criminal activity. Their theory is elaborated in *Crime in the Making* (1993).

laundering money Concealing illegally obtained money in different ways; fraudulent accounting practices that enable criminals to conceal their illicit income from the government.

Lavater, J.K. (1741–1801) A physiognomist who believed that facial features of criminals could be used to predict their potential for criminal conduct.

Lavin, Larry A dentist known as "Dr. Snow" who distributed over 60 kilos of cocaine per year in Philadelphia, PA. Considered a drug kingpin, he made more than $6 million from his drug operations. He was indicted in 1984 and sentenced to 22 years for drug offenses and an additional 20 years for income-tax evasion.

law The body of rules of specific conduct, prescribed by existing, legitimate authority, in a particular jurisdiction, and at a particular point in time.

law and order A political ideology and slogan that seeks a return to the morality and values of earlier times and rejects the growing permissiveness in government and social affairs.

law assessors In Sweden, citizens under age 70, with or without legal training, who sit with judges in hearing certain cases.

law clerk In corrections, an inmate assigned by the prison, as a jailhouse lawyer, to litigation tasks.

law enforcement The activities of various public and private agencies at the local, state, and federal levels that are designed to ensure compliance with formal rules of society that regulate social conduct; the component of the criminal-justice system concerned with enforcing laws and statutes. It conducts investigations of crimes, has arrest powers, and includes personnel and agencies dedicated to upholding the criminal laws.

law enforcement agency A local, state, or federal organization, such as a police department, sheriff's department, or federal agency such as the Federal Bureau of Investigation, whose personnel uphold the laws of their respective jurisdictions.

law enforcement assistance Any monies, equipment, information, or training designed to improve the effectiveness of law enforcement agencies and their personnel.

Law Enforcement Assistance Administration (LEAA) An outgrowth of the President's Crime Commission of 1965–1967, a time of great social unrest and civil disobedience. It was created by Congress in 1968 under Title I of the Omnibus Crime Control and Safe Streets Act, and terminated in 1982. The LEAA was designed to provide resources, leadership, and coordination to state and local law enforcement agencies to prevent or reduce adult crime and juvenile delinquency. It allocated millions of dollars to researchers and police departments over the next decade for various purposes. Many experiments were conducted with these monies, which led to innovative patrolling strategies in some communities. It also made funds available to schools and other organizations for the purpose of improving criminal-justice agency functions, funded numerous studies to improve law enforcement agency effectiveness, and provided monies for training of police officers in college or university settings.

law enforcement emergency Any uncommon situation that threatens to become serious, and that local law enforcement resources are not equipped to handle. The situation may require temporary imposition of strict laws and regulations.

law enforcement equipment Any device used by law enforcement agencies to perform their regulatory functions of keeping the peace and enforcing the law. These may include various products such as radar, Breathalyzers, special clothing, and surveillance cameras.

law enforcement intelligence units Agencies within law enforcement organizations that provide information to police officers and detectives about crimes that have been or are about to be committed by persons or groups.

law enforcement officer An employee of a local, state, or federal governmental agency sworn to carry out law enforcement duties; a sworn employee of a prosecutorial agency who primarily performs investigative functions.

law enforcer An officer policing style characterized by playing it by the book and enforcing all laws.

law guardian, legal guardian A person with the legal authority and duty of taking care of someone and managing their property and rights, if the person is incapable of administering his or her affairs personally.

law of effect A learning theory concept postulating that persons will learn behaviors leading to satisfaction rather than habits leading to dissatisfaction.

law of nations International law or public law.

law of precedent *See stare decisis.*

law of the sea International regulations governing vessels at sea, including commercial vessels of all types, marine research, and exploration for oil and gas resources.

law of the situation A management term meaning that people should pool their intelligence and resources in order to arrive at a common solution to a problem rather than unilaterally ordering another person to do a particular thing.

law reform Any legislative action designed to modify existing laws, which may include abolishing certain laws, creating new laws, or modifying existing laws.

Law Reform Commission Act 1 An act implemented by the Canadian legislature in 1990 to keep pace with changing Canadian society and to make appropriate reform recommendations to the legislature.

law-related education A large-scale coordinated effort to lessen youth violence and delinquency by involving youths in learning about the law and developing alternatives to violence.

laws, sumptuary All laws governing a person's expenditures for food, clothing, and other consumer goods, and taxation of such goods and items.

laws of imitation An explanation of crime as learned behavior. Individuals are thought to emulate the behavior patterns of others with whom they have contact.

lawsuit syndrome Similar to the litigation explosion, in which jail and prison inmates deluge the courts with numerous frivolous filings of writs and motions; a means whereby inmates can harass jail and prison officials and officers.

lawyer *See* **attorney, attorney at law, counsel, lawyer.**

"lawyering up" An action by an arrested person who demands a lawyer before being interrogated by police.

lay witness An eyewitness, character witness, or any other person called upon to testify who is not considered an expert. Lay witnesses must testify to the facts alone and may not draw conclusions or express opinions.

leader in a particular situation An explanation of why certain persons emerge as group or organizational leaders based on their particular abilities and skills relative to tasks assigned and regardless of their rank within the organizational hierarchy.

leadership The ability of one person to evoke conformity to organizational rules or solicit compliance to directives from one or more others.

leadership behavior The action of obtaining compliance from others in accordance with what one wants. It may stem from personal qualities, one's ability to sanction or punish nonconformity, and a number of other factors.

leadership styles Modes of conduct that emphasize how particular leaders will orient themselves toward subordinates.

Leadership styles include (1) laissez-faire, (2) democratic, and (3) autocratic.

leading question In an interrogation of a witness during a trial, a question that suggests a particular answer that might not otherwise be given by the witness. A question structured to lead the respondent to give the answer the questioner wants (e.g., "You like this book, don't you?").

LEAP (Law Enforcement Against Prohibition) An organization of law enforcement officers started in 1998 under the leadership of former law enforcement officers Peter Christ, Mark Greer, Jack Cole, Howard Wooldridge, and Daniel Solano. After three decades of a war on drugs with half a trillion dollars and increasingly punitive punishments, the U.S. court system has been glutted with ever-increasing prosecutions of nonviolent drug violators and prison populations have quadrupled. More than 2.2 million citizens have been arrested and 1.6 million are arrested each year for nonviolent drug offenses. LEAP's goal is to change U.S. drug policy. Its mission is to (1) educate the public, media, and policymakers to the failure of current drug policies by showing a true picture of the history, causes, and effects of drug abuse and crimes related to drug prohibition; (2) create a speakers bureau staffed with knowledgeable and articulate former drug warriors who describe the impact of current drug policies on police/community relations, safety of law enforcement officers and suspects, police corruption and misconduct, and financial and human costs of drug policies; (3) restore the public's respect for law enforcement, which has been greatly diminished by its involvement in imposing drug prohibition; and (4) reduce the multitude of harms resulting from fighting the war on drugs and lessen the incidence of death, disease, and addiction by ultimately ending drug prohibition. LEAP believes that a system of regulation and control relating to drug use is more effective than one of prohibition.

learned leadership The view that the ability to invoke wanted behaviors from others can be acquired through gaining knowledge and education.

learning disability (LD) A neurological dysfunction that prevents an individual from learning to his or her potential.

learning theories Any explanation for human behavior that suggests that behaviors are the product of associating with others and acquiring behaviors from the process of social interaction and social experience.

lease system A form of prison industry under which contractors assumed complete control over prisoners.

least detrimental alternative A program chosen for a child that will best foster the child's growth and development.

least developed countries Countries recognized by the United Nations as being the poorest in the world and suffering from long-term barriers to economic growth.

least restrictive alternative A program chosen as the least restrictive or secure setting that will best benefit the child.

Least Restrictive Means Test for RFRA Cases Prison officials can only ban legitimate practices that are an important part of a religion if they can show the restriction is based on a compelling government interest related to prison security or inmate safety.

leather restraints Bonds used to formally restrain agitated inmates.

leftist One who seeks radical change in society and who advocates a form of socialism in which radicals attempt to change or influence social policy.

left realism A branch of conflict theory that holds that crime is a "real" social problem experienced by the lower classes, and that radical criminologists have ignored the victimization of the working class to focus on upper-class crime. Fear of violence among the lower classes has allowed the right wing to seize the law-and-order issue for political control. The theory posits that lower-class concerns about crime must be addressed by radical scholars. Community-based crime prevention strategies are regarded as desirable as crime control techniques that do not disenfranchise any particular societal aggregate.

left-wing political group A political group espousing a socialist or communist political philosophy.

legal aid Any form of assistance wherein an agency or person assists another, usually indigent, in a legal matter by providing legal representation.

legal aid society A private, nonprofit organization of attorneys that exists to represent indigent defendants.

legal approach A type of police discretion characterized by codifications of discretion according to legal proscriptions. Discretionary behavior is measured by amount of deviation from proscribed rules.

legal assistant A paralegal.

legal cause A legally recognized cause.

legal dose The amount of a drug recommended to treat a medical condition.

legal ethics A code of conduct generally accepted by those admitted to the bar for the purpose of practicing law. One ethic is to avoid a personal and intimate relation with a client; another is to avoid assisting a client in violating the law by conspiring with the client to taint evidence or fabricate evidence to make the defense case stronger.

legal factors Variables influencing the intake decision relating to the factual information about delinquent acts, such as crime seriousness, type of crime committed, prior record of delinquency adjudications, and evidence of inculpatory or exculpatory nature.

legal fiction Some idea assumed to be true in the minds of court officials, such as judges or lawyers, but for which no statutes exist or laws have been formulated.

Legalistic-Abusive In the Coates Typology, a type of police officer who is extremely rigid and has to be right all the time. *See also* **Coates Typlogy.**

legalistic model A law enforcement model that emphasizes the importance of written procedure and limited individual officer discretion. It promotes a "Joe Friday" or "strictly-by-the-book," "only the facts" mentality among law enforcement officers.

legalistic style A mode of policing characterized by strict concern with law enforcement.

legalization Removal of all criminal penalties from a previously outlawed act.

legalization of drugs Decriminalizing drug use to reduce the association between drug use and crime.

legal opinion An informed interpretation of the law based on statutes and judicial precedents.

legal personality A status vested in a corporation entitling it to act authoritatively as though it were a person with rights. A corporation may sue and suffer liabilities for its actions, although these actions are abstractions.

Legal Points Monthly publication of the ICAP Police Legal Center, headquartered in Washington, DC. It contains information about interesting legal facts and court interpretations of statutes.

legal-rational authority Max Weber's concept wherein authority is based in law, and persons are vested with rights to order others to comply with directives. It is the most common authority form for bureaucracies.

legal realism A phenomenon that assists persons in distinguishing between the letter and spirit of the law. It investigates the gap between what the law says and how societal changes compare with law applications.

legal responsibility The accountability of persons for a crime because of the perpetrator's characteristics and the circumstances of the illegal act.

legal screening An investigation to determine the nature of the offense, whether a youth has previously committed offenses, and whether he or she is currently under some type of probationary supervision. The term may also be applied to prosecutorial prioritizing of pending cases against criminal suspects.

Legal Services for Children (LSC) A law firm headquartered in San Francisco, CA, dedicated to protecting the legal rights of juveniles. It provides *pro bono* services to juveniles and families with limited resources for legal fees.

Legal Services for the Elderly (LSE) An organization headquartered in New York City, established in 1969, that provides legal services at low or no cost to elderly persons who are in need of legal assistance but who have limited resources or may be indigent. Publishes the *Progress Report.*

legal sufficiency The presence of the minimum legal elements necessary for prosecution of a case. When a prosecutor's decision to prosecute a case is based on legal sufficiency, most cases are accepted for prosecution, but the majority of them are disposed of by plea bargaining or dismissal.

leg irons Restraints or manacles designed for use on the legs; heavy metal restraints that constrained a person's ability to run away.

legislation Any legal product from a lawmaking body; statutes and acts passed by Congress or other duly constituted lawmaking bodies.

legislative branch, legislature That segment of government responsible for the consideration, drafting, and enactment of the law (e.g., the U.S. Congress, state legislatures, county commissioners, and city councils).

legislative exclusion The legislature excludes from juvenile-court jurisdiction certain offenses usually either very minor, such as traffic or fishing violations, or very serious, such as murder or rape.

legislative model, legislative model of sentencing A sentencing structure in which the legislature retains most discretion, and does not permit a great deal of judicial or executive flexibility in fixing terms.

legislative power The right to make law or policy. Legislatures and Congress are authorized to pass laws that apply to all citizens. Other bodies, such as the executive branch and the judiciary, are not vested with lawmaking powers. However, both the president and judges create laws in different ways through their pronouncements and interpretations of cases.

legislative waiver A provision that compels a juvenile court to remand certain youths to criminal courts because of specific offenses that have been committed or alleged.

legitimacy, legitimate authority Any method of obtaining compliance from others that is predetermined or approved by an organization or system. Max Weber identified three types of legitimate authority, including legal-rational authority, traditional authority, and charismatic authority.

legitimate correctional objectives Institutional objectives that are seen as a constitutionally acceptable basis for prisons' placing restrictions on prisoners' rights because they are necessary to maintain prison security.

legitimate penological objectives The realistic concerns that correctional officers and administrators have for the integrity and security of the correctional institution and the safety of staff and inmates.

legitimate power A form of power based on the belief that a superior has a right to compel subordinates to follow orders.

legitimate prison economic system Inmate funds and goods obtained through approved channels. Inmates can acquire money from relatives and friends, work assignments, veterans' benefits, or hobbies.

legitimate submission hold A term borrowed from wrestling and used to describe the police officer tactic of restraining a violent arrestee with an appropriate use of force necessary to render the arrestee submissive and compliant, such as holding or twisting an arrestee's arm behind his or her back to obtain compliant behavior while making an arrest or subduing suspects.

Leisure Education Model In corrections, a Therapeutic Recreation (TR) model that encompasses value clarification, in which inmates learn to identify their needs for praise and belonging.

Lemert, Edwin M. (1912–1996) A sociologist who wrote *Social Pathology* (1951) and *Human Deviance, Social Problems, and Social Control* (1967). He promoted labeling theory, which posits that persons acquire deviant perceptions of themselves through labels applied to them by others. The labeling process includes primary deviance, which may not be serious, but may nevertheless trigger the labeling process and secondary deviance. One's chances of becoming labeled are enhanced as the result of lower socioeconomic status, racial and ethnic minority status, and other factors.

Leopold and Loeb Nathan F. Leopold, Jr. (1904–1971) and Richard A. Loeb (1905–1936), convicted of murdering 14-year-old Bobby Franks in 1924 in Chicago, IL, as a thrill killing. The sons of prominent persons, they believed that they had committed the perfect crime, but were subsequently foiled by police, prosecuted, and convicted.

Lepine, Marc (1964–1989) A Canadian mass murderer who shot and killed 14 female students, wounded 13 more, and then killed himself at the University of Montreal in 1989.

lesbianism Female homosexuality.

lesser included offense A less important crime that is also a part of a more serious offense (e.g., in a vehicular homicide charge, if the defendant had been drinking alcoholic beverages a DWI charge might be a lesser included offense).

less-than-lethal force The next level of force after empty-hand control techniques; the use of impact weapons such as batons, chemical agents, and electrical shocking devices, to temporarily disable inmates but not inflict permanent injuries; a category of weapons and instruments used to apprehend criminals and extract prisoners from particular locations. They may be lethal if mishandled but are designed to operate and be effective below the threshold of inflicting death or serious bodily injury (e.g., TASERs, capture nets, and pepper spray).

lethal chamber The place within a prison where prisoners convicted of capital crimes are executed.

lethal force Any physical effort used by law enforcement personnel, prison correctional officers, and other criminal justice officials that could result in the death of suspects or inmates in their custody.

lethal gas A combination of cyanide and sulfuric acid used to execute condemned prisoners.

lethal injection A form of capital punishment in which lethal amounts of paralyzing drugs that induce cardiac arrest and death (suxamethonium chloride, pancuronium bromide, or tubocurarine chloride) are administered to a condemned person until life ceases.

letter of the law A strictly legalistic approach to law enforcement; a zero-tolerance interpretation of the law.

leuco-malachite test A forensic test to determine the presence of blood on a surface.

level of aspiration The goal or aim established by a worker in an organization which may be a position sought or a particular salary level or fringe benefit.

level of custody The security level in which a prisoner is placed according to his or her risk or dangerousness. Levels include minimum, medium, and maximum security.

level of government The federal, state, regional, county, or city location of administrative and major funding responsibility of a given agency.

level of proof The standard of evidence that needs to be established in a legal proceeding.

levels of analysis, units of analysis Three strata for examining organizational phenomena that focus on one of the following dimensions: (1) the individual; (2) the small interpersonal work group; or (3) the formal organization.

levels of authority The degree of vertical differentiation within an organization. Levels connotes layers of different positions, each layer constituting a homogeneous aggregate of employees.

lewd and lascivious conduct Moral depravity, immorality, or gross depravity.

lewdness Degenerate conduct in sexual behavior that is so well-known that it may result in the corruption of public decency.

Lewis, Oscar (1914–1970) A sociologist who wrote about the culture of poverty in 1966. As a part of the culture of poverty, "at-risk" children were described, who were economically and culturally disadvantaged, conditions tending to generate violence and criminality.

lex non scripta "Law not written" (Latin); unwritten or common law; law not written down in a codified form.

Lexow Commission A committee appointed by the New York State Legislature in 1894 to investigate corruption in the New York Police Department. Its findings led to extensive police reforms.

lex salica The custom of atonement for wrongs by payment to appease the family of a victim.

lex talionis "Law of retaliation" (Latin); the law of retaliation or retribution; a form of revenge dating back to the Apostle Paul and used up until the Middle Ages.

libel A tort of defamation through published writing or pictures critical of others.

liberal approach The perspective that crime can be reduced by attacking its underlying causes through social reforms.

liberal feminism, liberal feminist theory Freda Adler, who wrote *Sisters in Crime* (1975), and Rita Simon, who wrote *The Contemporary Woman and Crime* (1975), have both advocated that low crime rates among women are attributable to their "second-class" economic and social position relative to men, and that as these economic and social positions converge over time because of greater rights and opportunities for women, crime rates for both men and women will tend to converge. Their writing has given rise to "the new female criminal," a disputed term to depict today's female offender population.

liberal ideals Liberalism as an ideology and related policies aimed at social reform designed to increase equality and democratic participation in governance. Liberals advocate the use of state power to aid disadvantaged individuals and groups, and believe that much criminal activity has roots in the social fabric.

liberals Persons who advocate social reforms that increase citizen equality and greater democratic participation in political decision making. They promote softer policies relating to criminal punishments, such as alternative sentencing and more extensive use of probation and community corrections, and emphasize due process and individual rights.

liberty interest Interests that require due-process protections and are defined by the Constitution, court orders, and statutes. Inmate freedoms are jeopardized if constitutional rights are violated.

libido Sigmund Freud's term describing the sex drive he believed was innate in everyone.

Librium A prescription tranquilizer that is often sold without prescription on the street as a recreational drug.

license The authority granted by a public official to perform particular acts, which usually involves passing a qualifying examination (e.g., securing a driver's license for automobile operation).

lie detector An apparatus that records blood pressure and various other sensory responses and records reactions by means of paper and a moving marker. It is designed to determine whether one is telling the truth during an interrogation. It is also known as a polygraph. Results of tests are not admissible in court.

"life" A habitual female offender in prison who engages in deviant behavior with little or no regard for punitive consequences; also, a prison sentence of incarceration for the duration of one's human existence.

life-course persisters Delinquent youth who begin their offending career quite early and persist into their childhood.

life-course theory The study of changes in criminal offending patterns over a person's entire life. Are there conditions or events that occur later in life that influence the way people behave, or is behavior predetermined by social or personal conditions at birth? The theory was presented by Rolf Loeber and Marc LeBlanc, who endorsed a developmental view of criminal conduct (1990). They focus criminological attention on questions such as "Why do people begin to act antisocially?" and "Why do some persons escalate to more serious forms of crime?"

life-cycle theory A management leadership style suggesting that supervision should be based on the maturity of the subordinates supervised. Maturity level is often measured as the amount of education acquired, the desire to work, and the willingness to accept responsibilities to perform tasks.

life history A research method using experiences of persons as the unit of analysis (e.g., using the life experience of individual gang members to understand the natural history of gang membership).

LifeLog A DARPA-sponsored project to track volunteers through their life courses, creating an individual database.

"lifer" Slang for someone serving a life sentence of imprisonment.

life sentence A judicially imposed term of imprisonment equal to the life of the sentenced offender.

Life Skills Programs Educational programs that provide inmates with practical knowledge in employability/job search skills, consumer skills, the use of community resources, health and safety skills, parenting and family child skills, and civic skills.

lifestyle An organized pattern of behaviors, attitudes, and outcomes adopted by a person.

lifestyle violent juveniles Youths who have become more violent when exposed to more serious offenders in institutions.

lifetime appointments Royal judges in England served "at the King's pleasure during good behavior," the equivalent of serving for life. This practice is still followed in all U.S. federal district and appellate courts and in some states, where judges are appointed for life or until they decide to retire.

life-without-parole (LWOP) sentence A penalty imposed as the maximum punishment in states that do not have the death penalty. It provides for permanent incarceration of offenders in prisons, without parole eligibility. Early release may be attained through accumulation of good-time credits.

Likert scale An ordinal-level measure consisting of summing weights assigned to graduated responses (e.g., strongly agree, agree, disagree, strongly disagree) to various questionnaire items, permitting researchers to draw inferences about the intensity with which certain attitudes are possessed; also known as a summated rating scale.

limitations of actions The period of time following a crime's commission that an indictment must be presented; statute of limitations.

limited jurisdiction The restriction of a court to handling certain types of cases, such as probate matters or juvenile offenses; also known as special jurisdiction.

limited-risk control model A model of supervising offenders based on anticipated future criminal conduct that uses risk assessment devices to place offenders in an effective control range.

limit line Solid white line on highway not less than 12 inches nor more than 24 inches wide to indicate at which point a vehicle must stop before proceeding forward.

Lindbergh Law A law named for Charles Lindbergh, whose baby was kidnapped in the early 1930s. It forbids interstate transportation of anyone who has been kidnapped or held for ransom. Violating this law is a capital crime.

line The aggregate of persons at the lowest levels in an organizational hierarchy who perform different tasks that fulfill the goals of the organization. They typically do not have administrative authority to determine company policy or influence organizational affairs.

linear A relationship between an independent and a dependent variable that is graphically represented by a straight line.

linear design A penological term designating a type of prison architecture in which inmate cells are aligned along corridors. Prison correctional officers may walk along corridors and observe inmates in their cells, which are adjacent to the corridors.

linear design supervision Leadership in jails and prisons in which cells are constructed in long straight rows aligned with corridors where correctional staff walk from cell to cell to intermittently supervise inmate activities.

line functions Police work including patrol, traffic, juvenile, and detective investigation.

line personnel Operational personnel who carry out the primary goals of an organization; in police agencies, full- or part-time sworn officers who respond to calls for service.

line supervision Supervisors in police departments and other paramilitary organizations at the rank of sergeant.

line units Police components that perform the direct operations and carry out the basic functions of patrol, investigation, traffic, vice, and juvenile.

lineup A procedure in which police ask suspects to submit to being viewed by witnesses to a crime together with others who resemble their personal characteristics. Identification in a lineup can later be used as evidence in court.

LONGITUDINAL STUDIES   **153**

linkage blindness The inability of law enforcement officers to make connections between related crimes.

link network diagrams Patterns drawn by police investigators to determine associations between different criminals and their organizations; a way of depicting the structure of an organized crime family; any technique to show name associations between telephone numbers and other items designated by numbers.

liquid X *See* **gamma-hydroxybutyrate (GHB).**

liquor laws, liquor law violations State or local law violations relating to alcohol, except drunkenness and driving under the influence (e.g., consuming alcoholic beverages on the streets is prohibited in some cities). Infractions committed by liquor-serving establishments, such as serving minors, serving intoxicated persons, or serving intoxicating beverages after hours, are also included.

literacy Possession of skills required to function effectively in society.

literacy programs Educational programs that focus on providing basic skills to low-level readers and nonreaders.

litigation Civil prosecution in which proceedings are maintained against wrongdoers, as opposed to criminal proceedings.

litigation explosion The sudden increase in inmate suits against administrators and officers in prisons and jails during the late 1960s and continuing through the 1980s. Suits usually challenged the nature and length of confinement or torts allegedly committed by administration, and usually seek monetary or other forms of relief.

littering An offense, usually a misdemeanor, involving discarding trash or other materials in public areas such as roadways or parks.

Little Rock riots Civil disorders arising out of efforts to desegregate the Little Rock, AR, city schools following a 1957 court order following the *Brown v. Board of Education* (1954) decision.

LiveScan A patented electronic system for scanning human fingerprints that assists in the identification of criminal suspects.

livestock theft Stealing any kind of livestock, such as cattle, horses, sheep, pigs, and other farm animals; cattle rustling; a crime involving stealing livestock that is punishable by imprisonment and/or fine.

lividity In forensics, a term describing the condition of tissue of a dead person. Red and purple blotches form when blood settles at the lowest portions of the body after death. Lividity may indicate whether a corpse has been repositioned, determine the time of death, and otherwise aid an investigation.

Livingston, Edward (1764–1836) An American penologist and critic of penal systems who wrote extensively about different conditions in penal systems and sought to improve them for inmate health and safety. He served briefly as Secretary of State and was a minister to France under President Andrew Jackson.

loan shark Anyone who lends money to others at various interest rates, usually exorbitant, or above what are lawfully prescribed. The activity also includes the occasional use of force

and intimidation to insure collection. It is often linked to organized crime and racketeering.

lobotomy A psychosurgical procedure involving a cut made into the frontal lobe of the brain, rendering the patient less violent and more docile.

local corrections A system of facilities and programs dealing with convicted misdemeanant offenders and pretrial detainees.

local legal culture Norms shared by members of a court community as to case handling and a participant's behavior in the judicial process.

local union Any organization of workers existing independent of an employer, with mutual interests, and having the ability to negotiate with organizations and management for worker benefits and work agreements.

lockdown A complete removal of inmate privileges and permanent confinement in cells that usually follows a prison riot or other serious prison disturbance.

Locke, John (1632–1704) An English philosopher whose writings included *Essay Concerning Human Understanding* (1690) and *Second Treatise on Government* (1690). He advocated the application of reason, humanitarianism, and secularism to problems of philosophy and political theory.

lockstep A formation in which convicts were marched from place to place in close order, single file, each looking over the next man's shoulder with their faces pointed to the right to prevent conversation and with their feet moving in unison.

lockup Facility sometimes counted as a jails, intended to hold prisoners for public drunkenness for short periods such as 24 or 48 hours.

loco parentis *See* **in loco parentis.**

Loeber, Rolf A criminologist who has suggested the pathways to crime theory, which holds that persons follow different roads or paths as a means of acquiring criminal behaviors (1993).

log A record of events, meetings, visits, and other activities of an individual over a given period of time.

logistics Activity of police operations pertaining to supplies, facilities, and personnel support and maintenance.

logo In gang culture, a descriptive emblem used to identify a gang member. Logos may include a group of Roman numerals, the gang's initials, or pictures such as pitchforks, crowns, or the Playboy bunny.

loitering Standing around idly; "hanging around." The term is often used as a provocation by police officers to stop and question citizens who appear "suspicious," and to describe vagrants, persons who are in public places with no visible means of support.

Lombroso, Cesare (1835–1909) An Italian physician and criminologist who asserted that criminals were throwbacks to an earlier form of human. He emphasized the systematic collection of data and is known as the father of criminology.

long gun A firearm with a stock and long barrel, such as a rifle or shotgun.

longitudinal studies Investigations or research designs that entail repeated measures over time. For example, a cohort may be measured at several points over their life course to determine risk factors for chronic offending.

long-term facility Any incarcerative institution for either juveniles or adults that is designed to provide prolonged treatment and confinement, usually for periods of one year or longer.

long-term offender Any inmate serving a lengthy prison term of 25 years to life; also, someone who offends for an extended period of time, usually called a career offender.

lookout One who keeps watch for others while they commit a crime.

loop Part of a human fingerprint.

loose protocol effect Variations in procedure because the written procedures (the protocol) are not sufficiently detailed. These variations in procedure may result in researcher bias.

lower-class culture *See* focal concerns.

lower courts Courts of special original jurisdiction and sometimes trial courts, as opposed to higher or appellate courts.

LoJack A brand name for an electronic device installed in a motor vehicle that enables authorities to locate and track it if it is later lost or stolen.

low-security institution A level of security that is higher than minimum security, with a higher staff-to-inmate ratio and strong work and program components for inmates.

low-visibility decision making Decisions made by public officials in the criminal- and juvenile-justice systems that the public is not in a position to understand, regulate, or criticize.

LSD (lysergic acid diethylamide) A substance derived from rye that acts as a hallucinogenic drug.

lust murder A form of homicide that is primarily motivated by aberrant sexual fantasies.

lynch To hang without a trial. Mobs in the 1930s and 1940s and earlier lynched persons suspected of committing crimes. The term is often associated with hanging African Americans in the South during a period of great racial tension and discord.

M

M-2 Sponsors Program A program in which community volunteers were trained to function as visitors for inmates who had no family or friends to visit them.

MacDonald, Jeffrey (1943–) A Green Beret captain convicted of slaying his wife and two daughters in 1970 at Fort Bragg, NC, who was sentenced to three consecutive life terms.

mace A type of tear gas that is the least incapacitating of the gases currently used to subdue prisoners.

machine model This organizational conceptualization stresses the maximization of organizational effectiveness. Therefore, attention is directed to those aspects of organizations that can be rearranged and structured to fulfill this objective. Certain management principles should be applied, such as a division of labor, authority, discipline, unity of command and direction, subordination of individual interest to general interest, remuneration of personnel, centralization, a chain of command, order, equity, stability of tenure of personnel, initiative, and esprit de corps. One outcome of the application of these principles is the maximization of efficiency. Two variations of the machine model are scientific management and bureaucracy.

machismo The demonstration of masculinity through the manipulation and exploitation of women.

Mack, Julian W. (1866–1943) A juvenile-court innovator and advocate. Born in San Francisco and Harvard-educated, Mack was a Cook County, IL, judge in Chicago's Juvenile Court. He became the first juvenile-court judge in Illinois when the first juvenile court was established in 1899.

Maconochie, Alexander (1787–1860) A prison reformer and superintendent of the British penal colony at Norfolk Island and governor of Birmingham Borough Prison. Maconochie was known for his humanitarian treatment of prisoners and the issuance of "marks of commendation" to prisoners that led to their early release, which are considered the forerunner of indeterminate sentencing in the United States

MADD (Mothers Against Drunk Driving) An organization founded in 1980 by Candy Lightner after her daughter was killed by a drunk driver with multiple drunk-driving convictions. MADD is headquartered in Marlboro, MA.

Mafia Organized crime syndicates, originated in Sicily, that operate in the United States and elsewhere.

magazine A detachable container that holds cartridges for a firearm.

Magdelen Society A women's prison reform society formed in 1830.

magistrate A judge who handles cases in pretrial stages and usually presides over misdemeanor cases; an officer of the lower courts.

magistrate courts Courts of special jurisdiction, usually urban.

magistrature assise In French court, a judge.

magistrature debout In French court, a prosecutor.

MAGLOCLEN Middle Atlantic–Great Lakes Organized Crime Law Enforcement Network.

Magna Carta The "Great Charter" signed by King John in 1215, which guaranteed the legal rights of English subjects. It is generally considered the foundation of Anglo-American constitutionalism.

magnetic ink character recognition (MICR) A process originated in late 1950s by the American Bankers Association (ABA) that uses magnetic ink at the bottoms of checks and other negotiable instruments for automatic data processing, making the transfer of funds from accounts more efficient and improving the speed of accounting. The Bank of America in California was one of the first banks to use MICR extensively. The numbers at bottoms of checks and deposit slips indicate an ABA routing number, bank number, account number, and check amounts.

mail fraud, mail-order fraud Use of the United States mails to commit a crime, such as fraudulent advertising, shipping stolen merchandise by mail, or sending threatening letters to others.

maim To inflict bodily injury on another willfully, usually resulting in loss of an organ or limb.

Main Customer Prison Industries Model A system in which the private sector buys a substantial portion of the output of a prison-owned and -operated business but has no other connection with it.

main effect The overall or average effect of an independent variable.

mainstreaming The practice of placing individuals with special needs in the general population of a prison facility.

major crimes Part I offenses in the *Uniform Crime Reports.*

majority A greater number, more than half; in legal opinions, the prevalent court opinion; in juvenile matters, the age of accountability or adulthood.

make-believe families Peer units containing mother and father figures formed by women in prison to compensate for the loss of family and loved ones.

maladministration Public corruption.

mala fides "Bad faith" (Latin).

mala in se **crimes** Illegal acts that are inherently wrong or intrinsically evil (e.g., murder, rape, or arson). *See also malum in se.*

mala prohibita **crimes** Illegal acts that have been codified or reduced to writing. Offenses defined by legislatures as crimes. Many state and federal criminal statutes are *mala prohibita. See also malum prohibitum.*

Malcolm X (1925–1965) Born Malcolm Little in Nebraska in 1925, Little joined the Black Muslims and took the name Malcolm X. He advocated the black nationalist cause and formed the Organization of Afro-American Unity. Malcolm X was assassinated on February 21, 1965, in New York.

male prostitute A man or boy who exchanges sexual acts for money, drugs, other forms of currency, or anything of value.

malfeasance Misconduct by public officials; engaging in acts that are prohibited while serving in public office.

malice The intent to commit a wrongful act without a legitimate reason or legal justification. Express malice is overt or actual malice; general malice is wickedness or tendency toward wrongdoing; implied malice is inferred from a person's behavior; legal malice is intentional or purposeful crime.

malice aforethought The *mens rea* requirement for murder, consisting of the intention to kill with the awareness that there is no right to kill. *See also mens rea.*

malicious act An unlawful act resulting from malice toward another.

malicious arrest Taking someone into custody without probable cause.

malicious mischief The crime of willfully destroying another's property.

malicious prosecution Prosecutorial action against someone without probable cause or reasonable suspicion.

malpractice Incompetent representation from an attorney who provides substandard legal representation; in medicine, inappropriate or incompetent treatment for an illness or disease.

malum in se "Bad in and of itself" (Latin).

malum prohibitum "Bad because it has been prohibited" (Latin).

Malvo, Lee Boyd (1985–) The youthful sniper, 18, who was convicted of first-degree murder by a federal court in Virginia for the murders of several persons in a Virginia suburb during the fall of 2002. Malvo was one of a pair known as the Beltway Snipers. He committed these and other murders with his convicted accomplice, John Allen Muhammad, 42. Muhammad was convicted in November 2003 and sentenced to death. Malvo was convicted in December 2003 and sentenced to life without the possibility of parole, largely because of his age at the time he committed the murders (17). *See also* **Muhammad, John Allen.**

Mamertine Prison An ancient prison constructed about 640 B.C. under the Cloaca Maxima, the main sewer of Rome, by Ancus Martius. It consisted of a series of dungeons constructed to house a variety of offenders.

manacles Restraint devices, such as handcuffs or leg irons.

managed care Programs that attempt to control health-care costs for prison inmates.

management by objectives (MBO) An organizational strategy used in the early 1970s whereby administrators could cope successfully with various organizational problems. MBO was achieved by effective goal-setting and creating a system of accountability whereby one's performance could be measured over time. Feedback from higher-ups was considered essential.

management by walking around A management style in which administrators go out into the institution or prison to obtain a firsthand look and a real feel for what is actually going on among inmates at the institution.

management cops A type described in Elizabeth Reuss-Ianni's 1984 analysis of the New York Police Department, *Two Cultures of Policing: Street Cops and Management Cops.*

management functions Tasks that are regarded as supervisory duties, including planning, organizing, directing, policy formulation, and other administrative matters.

management variables Variables used to temper computer scores with human decision making when determining the appropriate security-level institution for a specific inmate.

managerial style grid A measurement device in administration that evaluates a supervisor according to how he or she balances production with employee needs. The grid consists of 81 blocks, with nine "concern for people" blocks and nine "concern for productivity" blocks. The number of blocks on either side is used to determine whether an administrator is people-centered or production-centered.

mandamus See **writ of** *mandamus.*

mandate A command or an order (e.g., a governor has a mandate to approve emergency legislation in state disaster situations).

mandate law A statute imposing a legal duty on a public official to act in a given way without discretion; similar to *mandamus.*

mandatory arrest A policy in which police officers must arrest one of two sparring parties in a domestic violence situation.

mandatory conditional release Usually, the conditional release of a prisoner through accumulation of good-time credits.

mandatory death penalty A death sentence that the legislature has required to be imposed on persons convicted of certain offenses. Such sentences are no longer constitutional.

mandatory judicial waiver A type of judicial waiver in which a juvenile-court judge must waive a juvenile to criminal court if the judge finds probable cause that the juvenile committed the offense.

mandatory minimum sentencing A flat-time sentence that must be imposed such that a minimum amount of time must be served before an inmate becomes eligible for parole.

mandatory parole Obligatory early release for inmates.

mandatory release The required release of inmates from incarceration upon the expiration of a certain time period, as stipulated by a determinate sentencing law or parole guidelines.

mandatory sentencing Sentencing in which the court is required to impose an incarcerative sentence of a specified length, without the option for probation, suspended sentence, or immediate parole eligibility.

mandatory waiver The automatic transfer of certain juveniles to criminal court on the basis of (1) their age and (2) the seriousness of their offense (e.g., a 17-year-old in Illinois who allegedly committed homicide would be subject to mandatory transfer to criminal court for the purpose of a criminal prosecution).

Manhattan Bail Project An experiment in bail reform carried out from 1961 to 1964 that introduced and successfully tested the concept of "release on own recognizance." It led to significant bail reforms.

Manhattan Court Employment Project Project operated by the Vera Institute between 1967 and 1970 in New York City that provided vocational training and job placement services to petty offenders and some minor felons. It was discontinued after high recidivism rates were observed.

manhunt An organized search by law enforcement or corrections officers for an escaped or otherwise wanted offender.

manic-depression A mental disorder characterized by experiences involving wide mood swings between elevated happiness and depression.

manifest function An intended or recognized function; in probation and parole, the manifest function is to facilitate offenders' reintegration into society.

manipulation A procedure allowing the researcher in an experimental setting to have some form of control over the introduction of the independent variable. This procedure allows for the determination that the independent variable preceded the dependent variable.

Mann Act A federal act passed in 1910 to prohibit the transportation of women from the United States to serve in brothels in other countries. It also prohibited using women from other countries in U.S. brothels, coerced prostitution generally, and transporting persons across state boundaries for purposes of prostitution.

manner of death The way in which a person dies.

Mannheim, Herman An academic criminologist of the twentieth century affiliated with the London School of Economics.

Mano Nera *See* **Black Hand.**

Manpower Prison Industries Model A system in which a private-sector partner manages the industry shops and supervises the inmate workers, but a public agency administers the programs and pays the inmates.

manslaughter Criminal homicide without malice, committed intentionally after provocation (voluntary manslaughter) or recklessly (involuntary manslaughter).

manslaughter, involuntary *See* **involuntary manslaughter.**

manslaughter, vehicular *See* **vehicular manslaughter.**

manslaughter, voluntary *See* **voluntary manslaughter.**

Manson, Charles (1934–) Leader of the Manson Family, which was was responsible for the murders of numerous people, including actress Sharon Tate. Manson and his followers were sentenced to death, but their death sentences were commuted to life with the possibility of parole in 1972 following the U.S. Supreme Court decision in *Furman v. Georgia* (1972).

Mapp, Dollree A Cleveland woman whose home was unreasonably searched without a warrant and who was charged with and convicted of possession of obscene material (pencil drawings) discovered as the result of the search, which led to the U.S. Supreme Court case *Mapp v. Ohio* (1961) and the classic clarification of the exclusionary rule declaring inadmissible into evidence anything that was illegally seized by police.

marbling In forensics, a *post mortem* effect on the human body produced by the hemolysis of blood vessels in reaction with hemoglobin and hydrogen sulfide. The condition includes green, purple, and/or red discoloration of the skin.

marginal deterrent effect The extent to which crime rates respond to incremental changes in the threat of sanctions.

marginal members Peripheral members of a gang who are called on when the gang needs to present a strong show of force or power.

Mariel Boatlift The five-month exodus of more than 125,000 Cubans who fled to the United States between April and August 1980 after Fidel Castro relaxed barriers to leaving the country. It was notorious for the Castro regime, which opened the country's prisons, sending numerous prisoners and mentally ill persons to the United States as a part of the exodus, which caused an upsurge in criminal acts in cities where Marielitos landed.

Marielitos Those who fled Cuba by boat from the port of Mariel between April and August 1980. *See also* **Mariela Boatlift.**

marijuana A substance from the leaves of the hemp plant. Ingestion through eating or smoking causes euphoria. It is considered a "downer" in the drug community, and known as reefer, maryjane, bud, chronic, and pot.

Marion The federal prison in Marion, IL, considered an admin max prison holding the most violent and dangerous offenders.

marital rape Sexual intercourse forced upon one spouse by the other.

mark Slang for the intended victim of a swindle or confidence game.

marks of commendation Point rewards given to inmates of the Birmingham Borough Prison by Alexander Maconochie in the 1850s.

mark system A system devised by Sir Walter Crofton in which inmates earned credit for time served, which was applied against their original sentences, thereby permitting them to gain early release.

marriage, consanguineous The marital union of two persons closely related by blood, such as siblings or cousins.

marshal A sworn officer who performs civil duties of the courts, such as the delivery of papers to begin civil proceedings. Some jurisdictions obligate these persons to serve papers for the arrest of criminal suspects and escort prisoners from jail to court or into the community when they are permitted to leave the jail or prison temporarily.

Marshall, John (1755–1835) The fourth chief justice of the U.S. Supreme Court (1801–1835), appointed by President John Adams. He was prominent in establishing the separation-of-powers doctrine, and strengthened U.S. Supreme Court powers and the U.S. Constitution.

martial law The usurpation of civilian authority by the military. It is usually invoked during disasters or riot situations to prevent looting of demolished businesses and to control unruly crowds.

Martinson, Robert (1927–) A criminological critic who wrote numerous essays about the futility of rehabilitative and reintegrative programs. Martinson is associated with the "nothing works" philosophy and the belief that correctional programs are only as good as the persons who run them and the adherence to policies that guide such programs.

Marx, Karl (1818–1883) A German theorist who believed that society was a continuous class struggle between those who own the means of production (the bourgeoisie) and those who work for those who own the means of production (the proletariat). The different vested interests of these two "classes" (survival for the proletariat and profit for the bourgeoisie) make class conflict inevitable and perpetual. His ideas are also known as economic determinism, as economic forces and their control were viewed as governing social interaction. Marx collaborated with Friedrich Engels in writing *The Communist Manifesto* (1848). Marx's ideas were later adopted, interpreted, and described by subsequent generations of scholars known as critical criminologists, Marxists, and conflict theorists or radical criminologists.

Marxian ideology of punishment The beliefs that capitalist society has built-in conflicts between capital and labor, that deviance is a result of class structure, and that the punishment system protects the unequal distribution of resources.

Marxist criminology, Marxist position *See* **radical criminology.**

Marxist feminists Those who view gender inequality as stemming from the unequal power of men and women in a capitalist society. Gender inequality stems from exploitation of females by fathers and husbands. Female criminality is a response to the subordination of women and male aggression.

masculinity hypothesis The view that women who commit crimes have biological and psychological traits similar to those of men. Cesare Lombroso believed that a few "masculine" females were responsible for the handful of crimes committed by women.

mask of sanity A term used by psychologist Hervey Cleckley to describe the seemingly normal persona of a sociopath.

Maslach Burnout Inventory An inventory measuring a disorder, "burnout," characterized by a loss of motivation and commitment related to task performance. Burnout among police is measured by the Maslach Burnout Inventory and other psychological devices that test the degree of commitment to the job and the level of motivation to be successful.

Maslow's hierarchy of needs Essential psychological and biological needs that have been suggested by Abraham Maslow. They include biological needs, safety needs, belongingness needs, esteem needs, and self-actualization. Maslow believed that these needs exist in a pyramid form, and that the most basic biological needs must be fulfilled before higher needs in the pyramid become important to a person (i.e., one must feel that he or she belongs before he or she has the need for esteem or self-actualization; one must satisfy biological needs of hunger and thirst before acquiring the need to belong). Maslow conjectured that need fulfillment explained certain behaviors manifested by persons (i.e., certain acts could be interpreted as need-fulfilling behaviors).

masochism The practice of deriving sexual pleasure from having pain inflicted.

Massachusetts Model A centralized model in which a high degree of control over offenders is exercised. Use of this model has led to less than 15 percent recidivism. It requires additional conditions besides close monitoring, including community service, victim restitution, curfew, and drug and alcohol tests. Because of its stringent selection criteria, the model has a limited clientele.

Massachusetts Prison Commission An investigative body appointed by the governor of Massachusetts in 1817 to examine prison conditions and prisoner early-release options and to make recommendations about policy issues. The commission is noted for originating the concept of the halfway house.

massacre The killing of many persons in a single incident.

massage parlor A business offering massages that is often a front for prostitution services.

mass murder The killing of more than one person as a part of a single act or transaction, by one or more perpetrators.

mass spectrometer A machine used in forensics laboratories to identify chemical compositions of substances.

master status The situation in which other aspects of a person's behavior become submerged in a particular social identity, such as that of a deviant.

masturbation Sexual gratification by self-stimulation of one's genitals.

material fact An important, relevant finding; a necessary element; evidence that is relevant to a criminal case.

material witness Any witness who has relevant testimony about a crime.

matricide The murder of one's mother.

MATRIX (Multistate Anti-Terrorism Information Exchange) This initiative, launched in 2003 with $12 million in federal funds, is a crime and terrorism database project intended to function as a quick-access information repository that combines state records with 20 billion pieces of data maintained by a private company, Seisint, Inc. The database is intended to furnish information about millions of persons drawn from a variety of public sources. It includes information about one's criminal and correctional history; motor vehicle, pilot, and boat licenses and registrations; federal and local weapons, hunting, and fishing licenses; voter registration; digitized photos; property ownership, address history, and utility records; U.S. directory listings; bankruptcies; and U.S. domain names. In 2004, states involved included Florida, Connecticut, Pennsylvania, Ohio, New York, and Michigan. The goal of MATRIX is eventually to involve all states in this information-sharing endeavor. It is controversial among civil rights groups because of privacy concerns.

matron In early women's prisons, the woman who was the chief supervisor of the women's prison or unit.

Mattachine Society Founded by Henry Hay in the 1940s, this organization is dedicated to protecting the rights of homosexuals.

maturation The biological, psychological, and social processes that produce changes in the individuals or units studied with the passage of time. These changes could possibly influence the dependent variable and lead to erroneous inferences.

mature offenders Older inmates.

Matza, David In collaboration with Gresham Sykes, Matza developed neutralization theory (1957), which posits that criminal behavior is learned. Although persons who acquire and inculcate societal values are considered normal, they are able to neutralize these normal values with illegitimate and unconventional behaviors. Such persons can drift between conventional, law-abiding behavior and criminal conduct for varying periods of time.

maxi-maxi prison A prison such as the federal penitentiary at Marion, IL, where offenders are confined in individual cells for up to 23 hours per day, under continuous monitoring and supervision, with no more than three prisoners per guard.

maximum-custody inmates Those inmates deemed most likely to pose the most serious threat to prison security or who are high escape risks. They are confined in single cells with restricted privileges.

maximum expiration date The date when one's sentence has been served in its entirety.

maximum security, maximum-security prison A designation given to a prison in which inmates are maintained in the highest degree of custody and supervision. Inmates are ordinarily segregated from one another and have restricted visitation privileges.

maximum sentence Under law, the most severe sentence a judge can impose on a convicted offender.

mayhem In common law, the crime of injuring someone so as to render them less able to fight.

mayor's court A local court presided over by the mayor of a town or municipality, which usually hears minor criminal and traffic cases.

McAdoo, William (1853–1930) A court reformer born in Ireland who practiced law in New Jersey and New York. He reorganized the municipal court system of New York after serving as police commissioner and chief magistrate.

McCarthyism The tendency to label all left-wing views as communistic. The term stems from the McCarthy hearings of 1954, in which Senator Joseph McCarthy questioned the patriotism and loyalty of many persons, causing many of them to be blacklisted from their jobs. The hearings involved a number of celebrities, and ruined many lives. McCarthy was subsequently disgraced and his investigative work terminated.

McClellan Commission A U.S. Senate commission convened to investigate organized crime.

McGruff the Crime Dog A cartoon dog used as a campaign symbol for national crime prevention. A catch phrase was coined, "help take a bite out of crime," and McGruff's picture was posted in places offering shelter to persons in need.

McKay, Henry A sociologist who collaborated with Clifford R. Shaw in describing social disorganization theory in the 1920s, which posited a link between transitional slum areas and crime rates. McKay was strongly influenced by the Chicago School and the work of Ernest Burgess and Robert E. Park.

McLaughlin Rule A rule that established a 48-hour interval within which probable cause must be determined after a suspect is arrested. The intent of the rule is to prevent unnecessary or undue delay in processing criminal defendants. *See County of Riverside v. McLaughlin* (1991).

McNaughten's Rule, McNaughten case, McNagten Rule The insanity defense, formulated in 1843, by which a defendant claims that when he or she committed a criminal act, he or she didn't know what he or she was doing, or if he or she did know, didn't know that the act was wrong. Currently, persons raising such a defense claim they did not know the difference between right and wrong.

McVeigh, Timothy (1968–2001) A U.S. Army veteran who perpetrated the Oklahoma City bombing on April 19, 1995. He was convicted of more than 160 counts of murder and executed by lethal injection in 2001.

Mead, George Herbert (1863–1931) A sociologist who elaborated the term "symbolic interactionism" (developed earlier by Georg Simmel), a view that explains social behaviors as responses to social stimuli. Mead also developed the term "generalized other" as an abstract conformity medium, as "our impression of what we think others think of us and how we ought to behave," "a generalized conception of others' expectations of us" regardless of whether such conceptions are true or false.

meaninglessness A lack of clarity about what one ought to believe, uncertainty about criteria for making important decisions.

meat eaters A term used to describe police officers who actively solicit bribes and vigorously engage in corrupt practices.

mechanical jurisprudence The belief that everything is known and that therefore, the laws can be made in advance to cover every situation.

mechanical prevention Efforts directed toward target hardening to make particular offenses difficult or impossible to commit.

mechanical solidarity A unity based on shared values and norms and on the similarity of functions performed by all members of a society.

mechanic's lien Contractor recourse for obtaining money owed from a debtor, involving attaching the debtor's property or equipment.

Medellín Cartel A powerful narcotics trafficking organization based in Medellín, Colombia.

media Newspapers, radio, television, and the Internet; any service that delivers information to the public.

media jihad A concerted effort to protest unfair coverage and reporting of various events and issues by the media, which is usually perceived as biased, prejudiced, or intent on slanting the news in favor of a political or social position with which certain groups of persons take offense or oppose. For example, the Media Jihad website publishes information about different social, political, and economic events, including what occurred and how it was reported in the media, for the purpose of showing media bias and prejudicial reporting.

mediajihad.com An Internet site devoted to illustrating media coverage of different political, social, or economic events and how such coverage is tainted or slanted in prejudicial or unfavorable ways. It is a nonprofit, noncommercial project that uses "copyleft" instead of "copyright" to indicate its contrary position to government regulations. It is edited by Brent Jesiek, and in 2003 was being transformed into the Riedsrow Omnimedia Network.

mediation Informal conflict resolution through the intervention of a trained negotiator who seeks a mutually agreeable resolution between disputing parties.

mediation committees Chinese civilian dispute resolution groups found throughout the country. Mediation committees successfully divert many minor offenders from handling by the more formal methods of justice.

mediator A probation or parole officer who seeks to intervene in disputes between clients and others (e.g., a client may not be able to pay rent on time and the mediator, a probation officer, may negotiate with landlord to permit the client to make periodic payments until the rent is paid). The term also includes dispute resolution responsibilities, labor negotiations, and restorative justice.

media violence Any violent acts portrayed in various print or electronic media.

medical examiner A qualified physician who examines bodies and performs autopsies. Such persons, usually employed by state or local agencies, examine those who have been killed in violent crimes and conduct examinations into how deaths resulted.

medical jurisprudence The science of applying medical knowledge in the administration and application of the law.

medical marijuana Marijuana legally prescribed by a physician to alleviate the discomfort or other symptoms of a disease, usually cancer.

medical model A model that considers criminal behavior as an illness to be treated; "treatment model."

medical treatment The care given to victims who have sustained treatable injuries or illnesses.

medicide Termination of life by a physician; euthanasia; mercy killing.

medium-custody inmates Prisoners who move about the institution during the day within sight of correctional officers. They are eligible for all programs and activities within the main prison perimeter.

medium jails Jails with 50 to 249 beds.

medium security, medium-security prison The designation given to a prison in which some direct supervision of inmates is maintained but prisoners are eligible for recreational activities. Visitation privileges are more relaxed than in maximum-security prisons.

Meese Commission A body convened in 1985 and headed by Attorney General Edwin Meese to investigate pornography.

megajail Any jail facility that has 1,000 or more beds.

Megan's Law The Sex Offender Registration Act, a 1996 federal law requiring convicted sex offenders to register with local law enforcement authorities upon their release from prison. The law is named for Megan Kanka of New Jersey, a 7-year-old murdered in 1994 by a convicted sex offender living across the street.

Megargee inmate typology A measure of inmate adjustment to prison life devised from items from the Minnesota Multiphasic Personality Inventory, a psychological personality assessment device; permits classification of prisoners into different risk levels.

memorandum of understanding A document used in collective bargaining that outlines terms of agreement between a union and a company; a negotiated settlement document outlining what each party will do for the other.

Menendez brothers Erik and Lyle Menendez, brothers who murdered their parents in California in 1989 and maintained that they had been subjected to sexual abuse by their father for years. They were convicted after their first trials resulted in hung juries.

mens rea "Guilty mind" (Latin); the intent to commit a crime.

mental deficiency Feeblemindedness or disease that reduces one's ability to differentiate between right and wrong, or minimizes one's capacity to understand the law; low IQ; any disease or defect of the mind that makes one unable to conform his or her behavior to the requirements of the law.

mental element in crime *Mens rea;* the intent to commit a criminal act.

mental-health court A special court designed to ensure the appropriate treatment of defendants afflicted with mental illness.

mentally disordered, mentally handicapped, mentally ill Persons who cannot conform their conduct according to the law, who don't know the difference between right and wrong, or who have a mental disease or defect.

mental retardation A condition characterized by significant subaverage general intellectual functioning that exists concurrently with deficits in adaptive behavior.

mentoring program A program that teams an at-risk youth with a caring and nurturing adult in the community for the purpose of promoting positive role modeling, reduction in family and youth violence, and avoidance of drug use.

merchants Inmates who obtain or manufacture scarce luxury items, both legal and illegal, to be sold or traded in the inmate economy.

mercy Compassion toward offenders, shown by judges and others, manifested by reduced or lighter sentences than otherwise would have been imposed.

mercy killing The killing of someone because of their intense pain and suffering as a part of a terminal illness or condition. A potentially criminal act whereby life-support system maintenance of a person is removed so that the person dies.

mere evidence Evidence collected at a crime scene that is cumulative to show one's possible guilt but that does not show any material gain.

merger of offenses Joining two or more offenses that are related by statute (e.g., stealing an object of high value might be both theft and grand theft; both offenses would be combined and grand theft would be charged as the more serious offense alleged).

merit selection A reform plan in which judges are nominated by a committee and appointed by the governor for a given period. When the term expires, the voters are asked to signify their approval or disapproval of the judge for a succeeding term. If the judge is disapproved, the committee nominates a successor for the governor's appointment.

merit system A system used in employee hiring that requires applicants to qualify for a specific job by meeting certain minimum requirements for that job and scoring above a certain level on a written exam.

Merton, Robert King (1910–2003) Merton wrote extensively about the theory of anomie and strain (1938), and was influenced by Emile Durkheim and his theory of anomie. He wrote *Social Theory and Social Structure* (1957), and argued that societal emphasis on success goals cannot be achieved by all persons; thus, those who are less successful than others will turn to alternative means, perhaps criminal, to achieve these culturally desirable and approved goals.

mescaline The primary active ingredient in the peyote cactus; a strong hallucinogen.

mesomorph A body type suggested by William Sheldon that is characterized by muscularity and was once thought to characterize aggressive criminals. *See also* **Sheldon, William.**

mesne process A writ issued between the beginning and the conclusion of a case; an intermediate or intervening writ.

Mesopotamian laws, codes The earliest written laws or statutes from Mesopotamia, which include the Babylonian Code of Hammurabi (1760 B.C.). *See also* **Code of Hammurabi.**

Messner, Steven F. (1951–) A criminologist who wrote about social ecology and its relation to suicide (1985). He also collaborated with Richard Rosenfeld in describing the American Dream, a phenomenon not altogether different from Robert Merton's discussion of anomie and its link to crime.

meta-analysis A methodological technique of surveying a large number of research articles for the purpose of determining commonalities or parallel findings where the same or similar subject matter is studied.

metallic knuckles *See* **false knuckles.**

methadone Dolophine, a synthetic narcotic that is used as a substitute for heroin in drug-control efforts.

methadone diversion A program designed to divert heroin-addicted persons from regular criminal-justice processing.

methadone maintenance A treatment program for heroin addicts that uses an addictive drug that does not produce euphoria if taken orally in regular doses, but satisfies cravings and blocks the euphoric effects of any heroin that is used.

methamphetamine A synthetic derivative of amphetamine whose effects include increased alertness, euphoria, and decreased appetite.

methaqualone A strong depressant often used to calm the effects of other drug highs. Prescribed under the trademark Quaalude, it is known on the street as "ludes."

methodology A system of explicit rules and procedures on which research is based and against which claims for knowledge are evaluated.

methylene blue A dye, packets of which are inserted into bank money bags. The packets burst upon opening, leaving the thief covered in dye which is difficult to remove or wash away. The subsequent stains can be used as evidence of guilt.

methylphenidate Ritalin; a substance used to treat narcolepsy or the tendency to abruptly fall asleep, as well as for treatment of hyperactive children. It is related to amphetamines, and works on the central nervous system.

Metropolitan Police Act of 1829 The act that empowered Sir Robert Peel to select and organize the Metropolitan Police of London.

Metropolitan Police Force Project Act of 1981 A law authorizing a Toronto complaint review to investigate citizen complaints against police.

Metropolitan Police of London A police force organized in 1829 by Sir Robert Peel, a prominent British government official. Its duties were influenced by an emphasis on close interaction with the public and maintenance of proper attitudes and temperament.

Metropolitan Statistical Areas (MSAs) A U.S. Census Bureau designation for measuring population. MSAs are intended to show population concentrations or shifts in particular geographical areas which can be used for political reapportionments and redistricting efforts and to determine the number of electoral votes per state.

Mexican Mafia A California prison gang formed in the early 1960s by a group of Mexican-American inmates, including inmate leader Joe Morgan, who was serving time at the Duel Vocational Institute in Tracy, CA. Its members are drawn largely from the Marvilla section of East Los Angeles. Gang members are found in many prisons throughout the United States. The gang's symbols include XIII, X3, 13, and 3 dots, referring to 13th letter of alphabet, "M," which stands for Mexican Mafia. The gang is often aligned with the Ayran Brotherhood, Black Guerilla Family, and La Nuestra Familia as a Southern California inmate gang for mutual protection against Northern California gangs. Members also use words such as "Sureno" (Spanish for Southerner), "Sur," and "Southerner."

Mexikanemi A Texas gang that was an offshoot of the Mexican Mafia.

mickey Slang for a substance usually inserted into drinks for the purpose of rendering unwilling victims unconscious or unable to resist sexual advances and abuse. The term is often used as slang in reference to one of several date-rape drugs, such as Rohypnol, GHB (gamma-hydroxybutyrate), or Special K (ketamine hydrochloride). *See also* **Rohypnol; GHB; Special K; Vitamin K.**

microchemistry The field of chemistry concerned with testing and analyzing extremely small quantities of substances.

microscope, comparison In forensics, a microscope capable of showing parallel views of two objects for comparative purposes. It can be used to compare grooves in bullets fired from weapons and determine if the bullets were fired from the same weapon, which may be used as proof of a crime or one's guilt in court.

microscopy Any investigation involving the use of a microscope.

middle-class measuring rods According to Albert Cohen, the standards by which teachers and other representatives of state authority evaluate lower-class youths. Because they cannot live up to middle-class standards, lower-class youths are bound to fail, which gives rise to frustration and anger at conventional society.

middle managers Supervisors responsible for overseeing the delivery of specific services, such as education, in a prison or other organization.

midnight basketball A delinquency prevention program mentioned in the 1994 Crime Bill. It was promoted with good intentions but ridiculed for its simplistic and unsubstantiated approach to delinquency prevention.

midnight judges Judicial appointments made by John Adams shortly before midnight of the expiration of his presidential term in 1801, ostensibly to preserve the powers of his political party, the Federalists. *See Marbury v. Madison* (1803).

mildly retarded Individuals who have IQs ranging from 55 to 69 (based on a Wechsler Adult Intelligence Scale IQ) but who can essentially function on an independent basis.

milieu management, milieu therapy A treatment that capitalizes on environmental conditions or persons in the surroundings as instruments of rehabilitation. This strategy is used to create a supportive, caring atmosphere so as to encourage the formation of constructive values, a positive self-concept, and behavioral change.

military justice, military law The system of justice used by any branch of the armed forces.

military police Law enforcement authorities of any branch of the armed forces.

military prison Any incarceration facility where members of armed forces are held during or following their trials for military crimes; a stockade, brig, or penitentiary for military personnel convicted of crimes.

military syndrome The propensity of police organizations to organize and operate police departments according to military organization and protocol, including use of ranks and similar hierarchies of authority.

militia An armed force of citizens primarily used for domestic defense or civil defense in emergencies.

Milken, Michael (1946–) An infamous inside trader during the 1980s who was convicted and sentenced to serve 10 years for illegal stock practices.

Miller, Walter B. (1920–) A criminologist who has investigated gang delinquency (1958). He describes the unique value system of lower-class culture and focal concerns, which gradually develop or evolve to fit conditions in slum areas.

minimal brain dysfunction (MBD) An attention-deficit disorder that may produce such antisocial behaviors as impulsivity, hyperactivity, and aggressiveness.

minimal necessities of civilized life Factors considered by the courts in making decisions about the constitutionality of the totality of prison living conditions, including food, shelter, sanitation, health care, and personal safety.

minimization of penetration A form of diversion that keeps an offender from going further into the criminal-justice system.

minimum age of juvenile-court adjudication The lower age limit for which the juvenile court might hear a case.

minimum-custody inmates Prisoners who do not pose the risk to others associated with higher custody levels. Inmates can move about the facility within the view of the staff, are eligible for all inside jobs and supervised assignments outside the prison's perimeter, and have access to all programs and activities.

minimum due process, minimum due-process rights *See* **due process.**

minimum-maximum determinate sentencing Judicially imposed punishment consisting of a minimum and maximum amount of time to be served by a convicted offender. Following the minimum sentence, the offender becomes eligible for parole, which may be granted by a parole board, depending on the convicted offender's eligibility.

minimum security, minimum-security prisons A designation given to prisons in which inmates are housed in efficiency apartments and permitted extensive freedoms and activities, under little supervision by correctional officers. They are designated for nonviolent, low-risk offenders.

mini-stations Small police stations strategically located in high-crime-rate neighborhoods, staffed by one or more police officers.

Minnesota Multiphasic Personality Inventory (MMPI) A personality assessment measure that purportedly assesses a number of personality traits including anxiety, authoritarianism, and sociability.

Minnesota sentencing grid Sentencing guidelines established by the Minnesota legislature in 1980 and used by judges to sentence offenders. The grid contains criminal history score, offense seriousness, and presumptive sentences to be imposed. Judges may depart from the guidelines upward or downward depending on aggravating or mitigating circumstances.

minor Any person not of legal age of age of majority; any juvenile or infant.

minor in need of supervision (MINS) Any juvenile who is without parent supervision or some form of guardian direction.

minority overrepresentation The disproportionate number of minorities in criminal-justice populations, especially those in confinement.

minute order The official record of findings by a court.

minutes The written record of what transpires during a meeting of a group or organization or court.

Miranda, Ernesto After being convicted of kidnapping and rape in Arizona in early 1960s, Miranda's conviction was reversed in *Miranda v. Arizona* (1966) when it was shown that the government had failed to advise Miranda of his right to counsel before being interrogated by police. The case led to the Miranda warning presently used by law enforcement officers when arresting criminal suspects.

Miranda **triggers** Dual principles of custody and interrogation in which a suspect must be informed of his or her *Miranda* rights.

Miranda **rights,** *Miranda* **warning** The warning, named for the landmark case of *Miranda v. Arizona* (1966), given to suspects by police officers advising suspects of their legal rights to counsel, to refuse to answer questions, to avoid self-incrimination, and other privileges. *See box.*

The Miranda Warning

You have the right to remain silent and refuse to answer questions. Do you understand?

Anything you say may be used against you in a court of law. Do you understand?

You have the right to consult an attorney before speaking to the police and to have an attorney present during questioning now or in the future. Do you understand?

If you cannot afford an attorney, one will be appointed for you before any questioning if you wish. Do you understand?

If you decide to answer questions now without an attorney present you will still have the right to stop answering at any time until you talk to an attorney. Do you understand?

Knowing and understanding your rights as I have explained them to you, are you willing to answer my questions without an attorney present?

---

misanthropic A descriptor of the behavior of persons who are distrustful of or hostile to others.

miscarriage of justice Decision by a court that is inconsistent with the legal rights of a party in the case.

miscegenation laws Outmoded laws forbidding interracial marriages which were declared unconstitutional in 1967.

miscellaneous docket The U.S. Supreme Court docket of cases filed by *in forma pauperis* appellants.

misconduct in office Any conduct in the performance of one's official duties that is criminal behavior or a violation of ethical standards.

misdemeanant A person who commits a misdemeanor.

misdemeanor A crime punishable by fines and/or imprisonment, usually in a city or county jail, for periods of less than one year.

misfeasance The improper performance of public duties.

misnomer An improper name given to something, including an incorrect name given to someone who is charged with a crime, or a misleading or false description of someone.

misogynist A person who dislikes females.

misprision Concealment of a crime; any criminal act that doesn't have a specific name. Negative misprision is concealing something that ought to be revealed; positive misprision is committing an act that should not have been committed.

misprision of felony The crime of concealing a felony committed by another.

misprision of treason Knowingly concealing any act of treason.

misrepresentation An untrue statement of fact made to deceive or mislead.

missing children acts Any one of a series of acts by Congress to maintain central files on missing youths; a centralized effort to identify and locate missing youths.

Missing Person Locator A service in over 90 countries furnished by the Salvation Army that facilitates searches for persons who are missing and cannot be located by conventional means.

missing person Any person who is unaccounted for following a 24-hour period.

mission statement The goals and orientation statement of an organization designed to disclose its purposes and responsibilities. A mission statment can be used to vest employees with direction and motivation.

Missouri Plan A method of selecting judges in which a merit system for appointments is used, which is believed to reduce political influence in the selection of judges.

mistake In law, an affirmative defense that alleges that an act was not criminal because the person charged did not know the act was a prohibited one.

mistake of fact Unconscious ignorance of a fact or the belief in the existence of something that does not exist.

mistake of law An erroneous opinion of legal principles applied to a given set of facts. A judge may rule on a given court issue and the ruling may be wrong because the judge misunderstands the meaning of the law and how it should be applied.

mistrial A trial that cannot stand, that is invalid. Judges may call a mistrial for reasons such as errors on the part of prosecutors or defense counsel, the death of a juror or counsel, or a hung jury.

mitigating circumstances, mitigating factors Circumstances about a crime that may lessen the severity of the sentence imposed by the judge. Cooperating with police to apprehend others involved, youthfulness or old age of a defendant, mental instability, and having no prior record are considered mitigating circumstances. *See box.*

mitigation Anything that minimizes an act's seriousness.

mittimus An order by the court to an officer to bring someone named in the order directly to jail.

mix Behavior and associations that got the inmate into trouble on the outside and that can keep him or her in trouble within the institution.

mixed control organization A correctional organization in which policy making and resource supply are shared by centralized and local resources.

mixed sentence Two or more separate sentences imposed after an offender has been convicted of two or more crimes in the same adjudication proceeding. *See also* **split sentence.**

MMPI *See* **Minnesota Multiphasic Personality Inventory.**

M'Naghten Rule *See* **McNaughten's Rule, McNaughten case, McNagten Rule.**

MO *See modus operandi.*

mob Any violent crowd with a nefarious purpose.

mobile command post A law enforcement vehicle containing communications equipment permitting the unit to control the activities of officers in other vehicles operating in the same geographical area.

mobile crime laboratory A van equipped with numerous instruments and other devices used in the investigation of crime scenes and the analysis of evidence.

mobile patrols Vehicles manned by armed correctional officers that are used to patrol the perimeter of a prison compound.

mobility impaired A condition in which an individual requires assistance to get around.

mob justice The practice of a mob of meting out punishment to one they believe has committed a crime.

mock prison A prisonlike setting in which students or other experimental subjects experience the organizational and interpersonal dynamics of prison life for research purposes.

mode In statistics, the most frequently occurring number in a set; in a frequency distribution of scores, the midpoint of the interval containing the largest number of frequencies.

model An abstraction that serves to order and simplify reality while still representing its essential characteristics.

modeling A learning theory that states that people learn by imitating the behavior of others.

model of criminal sentencing A strategy or system for imposing criminal sanctions.

Model Penal Code A protocol developed by the American Law Institute clarifying crimes and accompanying punishments. No jurisdictions are obligated to adhere to it.

Mitigating Circumstances

1. The offender did not cause serious bodily injury by his or her conduct during the commission of the crime.

2. The convicted defendant did not contemplate that his or her criminal conduct would inflict serious bodily injury on anyone.

3. The offender acted under duress or extreme provocation.

4. The offender's conduct was possibly justified under the circumstances.

5. The offender was suffering from mental incapacitation or a physical condition that significantly reduced his or her culpability in the offense.

6. The offender cooperated with authorities in apprehending other participants in the crime or in making restitution to the victims for losses suffered.

7. The offender committed the crime through motivation to provide necessities for him- or herself or his or her family.

8. The offender did not have a previous criminal record.

---

model policies Written policies composed by national organizations in an effort to standardize operating procedures at the local level.

models Conceptions of how organizations are structured or organized and function; views of organizations that enable researchers to determine and chart predictable patterns involving communication and power. Examples are bureaucracy, human relations, professional, and systems.

mode of adaptation A way that persons who occupy a particular social position adjust to cultural goals and the institutionalized means to reach those goals. *See also* **strain theory.**

moderately retarded Individuals who have IQs between 40 and 54 (based on a Wechsler Adult Intelligence Scale IQ) and can learn to care for themselves but are not likely to function independently.

modification of probation A judicial change in one's probation program that usually results whenever one or more program violations are detected or following a prolonged period of good behavior. It may involve less restrictive conditions.

modified index The crime index together with the offense of arson.

modus operandi "Manner of operating" (Latin); the characteristic method a person uses in the performance of repeated criminal acts; method of operation.

Moffitt, Terrie E. Moffitt wrote about neurophysiology, a study of brain activity, in 1990, arguing that neurological and physical abnormalities are acquired during the fetal stage and then control behavior throughout one's lifespan.

mole An undercover operative who collects information to be used in subsequent investigations or prosecutions.

molestation Making improper sexual advances.

molester One who engages in molestation.

Mollen Commission An investigative unit set up to inquire into police corruption in New York in the 1990s.

Molly Maguires A powerful secret organization made up of mine workers in 1870s Pennsylvania, considered terrorists by mine bosses.

Molotov cocktail A firebomb used like hand grenade, made from a glass container filled with flammable liquid with a protruding rag or cloth that is ignited and thrown at an object. When the glass breaks, the fluid is ignited, causing extensive burning of the object.

monasteries Religious facilities used to house members of religious orders.

monetary restitution *See* **restitution.**

money laundering A process whereby money derived from illegal activities is placed in secret bank accounts and subsequently transferred as legal funds to United States banks or institutions.

monitored release Any form of recognizance release with the additional minimal supervision of service (e.g., defendants may be sworn to keep a pretrial services agency informed of their whereabouts, and the agency reminds these defendants of court dates and verifies their subsequent court appearance).

Monitoring the Future Survey An annual study of 3,000 high school students by the Institute for Social Research at the University of Michigan that attempts to discover hidden delinquency not ordinarily disclosed by published public reports.

monogamy Having only one spouse, as distinct from bigamy or polygamy.

monotony Work routine and boredom from repetitiveness.

monozygotic (MZ) twins Identical twins who develop from a single fertilized egg that divides into two embryos. *See also* **dizygotic twins.**

Montesquieu, Charles-Louis de Secondat, Baron de La Brede et de (1689–1755) A lawyer, philosopher, and author who wrote *The Spirit of the Laws* (1748). He was a penal reformer who wrote about inhuman punishments at Devil's Island in French Guiana.

mood disorders Another name for affective disorders such as depression.

moonlighting The practice of holding after-hours jobs in addition to full-time employment (e.g., police officers may also work in private security or other related professions).

Moorish Science Temple of America A hybrid offshoot of the Black Muslim movement.

moot A term used to describe a controversy that has ended or evolved to a stage at which a court decision on that particular case is no longer relevant or necessary. This is a limitation on the power of courts to decide cases.

moot court A court created and used by law students to practice what they have learned in class; a mock court in which students act as witnesses, the judge, jury, and prosecutors and defense counsel.

moot question A question that, because of situational factors, is no longer relevant. During testimony, a question may have been answered indirectly, thus rendering it moot.

moral A value considered prevalent in a community; anything good or virtuous, honest, and upright.

moral crusade Efforts by interest-group members to stamp out behavior they find objectionable. Typically, moral crusades are directed at public-order crimes, such as drug abuse or pornography.

moral development, moral-development theory A view of criminality that holds that criminals have an underdeveloped moral sense preventing them from making the correct behavior choices in a given situation.

moral enterprise The process undertaken by an advocacy group to have its values legitimated and embodied in law.

moral entrepreneurs Persons who use their influence to shape the legal process in ways they see fit.

moral involvement The disposition of persons who believe in complying with a superior's requests because it is the right and proper thing to do. Persons who become involved in their work because of a moral sense of obligation or duty believe that their administrators or supervisors have a legitimate right to issue orders to them to behave in particular ways.

moral panic The elevation of a social issue that previously received little attention to national prominence (e.g., Phil Jenkins' treatment of the sex offender as a moral panic). The term was coined by Stanley Cohen in his 1972 work *Folk Devils and Moral Panics.* Cohen says that over time, there have been several panics over a variety of issues, including crime, youth activities, and sexual freedom, each considered a threat to the moral fiber of society. Any newspaper headline that warns of some new danger triggers a potential moral panic, such as the "drug culture" of the 1960s. Any occurrence characterized by stylized and stereotypical representations by the mass media, and a tendency for those in different power positions (politicians, bishops, newspaper editors) to man the "moral barricades" and pronounce judgment can become a moral panic. In 1990s, drugs and pedophilia became moral panics leading to the establishment of the National Sex Offenders Register in response to growing concern and panic over child sex offenses.

moral turpitude Depravity or baseness of conduct.

mores Ways of behaving in a society with a moral connotation attached.

mortification process The process whereby prison routines deprive individuals of key aspects important for maintaining their self-concept.

MOSOP Missouri Sexual Offender Program, targeted to serve the needs of incarcerated, nonpsychotic sex offenders.

mother-child programs Activities that help to maintain the bond between a female inmate and her child.

motion An oral or written request to a judge that asks the court to make a specific ruling, finding, decision, or order. A motion may be presented at any appropriate point from an arrest until the end of a trial.

motion for a bill of particulars An action before the court asking that the details of the state's case against a defendant be made known to the defense. *See also* **discovery.**

motion for continuance An action before the court asking that the trial or hearing or proceeding be postponed to a later date.

motion for summary judgment A request granted by a judge who has read the plaintiff's and defendant's versions of events, and reached a decision holding for the defendant.

motion *in limine* A pretrial motion, generally to obtain judicial approval to admit certain items into evidence that might otherwise be considered prejudicial or inflammatory.

motion to dismiss An action before the court requesting that the judge refuse to hear a suit. A motion to dismiss is usually granted when a person who files a petition fails to state a claim upon which relief can be granted.

motive Reason for committing a crime.

motor vehicle A motorized self-propelled conveyance used to carry one or more persons from one place to another. The term excludes bicycles, wheelchairs, or other self-propelled devices.

motor-vehicle theft Stealing or attempting to steal an automobile or any other mode of transportation powered by gasoline or diesel fuel, such as snowmobiles, trucks, buses, motor scooters, and motorcycles. *See also* **carjacking.**

Motor Vehicle Theft Law Enforcement Act A 1984 law requiring manufacturers to equip their motor vehicles with a 17-character antitheft identification number on various car components, including the dash, engine, hood, bumpers, and other less conspicuous places. This facilitates investigations of motor-vehicle thefts and tracing motor vehicles or their components.

moulage Molding and casting in investigative work. Forensics specialists make casts of tire prints or footprints left at crime scenes so that they can be matched later and used in court against criminal suspects.

Mount Pleasant Female Prison The first prison for female offenders, established in 1835 in New York.

move In law, to make a motion in court.

MOVE A radically militant black separatist group opposed to social and political institutions that promotes radical religious beliefs and social/political ideals. Founded by John Africa in Philadelphia, PA, in the early 1970s.

movement A collective enterprise intended to bring about a desired social result; also, in corrections, a transfer of status or location from one place to another in a prison.

muckrakers A term given to writers in the early 1900s who exposed political and social corruption, crime, delinquency, prostitution, and other social problems. They were noted for revealing shocking information about persons or groups.

mugger One who assaults his victims in order to rob them of things of value.

mug shot A photograph of a criminal suspect taken by police when the suspect is booked following an arrest.

Muhammad, John Allen (1960–) The convicted 42-year-old Beltway Sniper who helped to kill at least 10 persons with a juvenile, 17-year-old Lee Boyd Malvo, during the fall of 2002. Muhammad was convicted of first-degree murder in Virginia in November 2003 and sentenced to death. He has been persuasively linked to other deaths in several states, including Alabama, Georgia, and Louisiana. *See also* **Malvo, Lee Boyd.**

Muir Typology A categorization of police officers into four types: Professionals, who use proper integration of coercion and sympathy in law enforcement practice; Enforcers, who are both cynical and coercive; Reciprocators, who are wishywashy, oversympathetic, and can't make up their minds; and Avoiders, who avoid work, just collect their paychecks, and are shirkers and slackers. William Ker Muir, Jr. outlined his typology in his 1977 work *Police: Streetcorner Politicians.*

"mules" In smuggling, a name given to couriers and smugglers of drugs and other illegal contraband, especially from other countries into the United States. Mules often swallow large quantities of heroin or cocaine in glassine envelopes in an originating country. After crossing U.S. borders, they defecate to retrieve the illegal contraband. Mules are paid nominal amounts for such smuggling.

mulet Fine; a deprivation as a part of punishment.

multiculturalism *See* **cultural diversity.**

multifactor theories Explanations of criminal behavior that combine the influences of structural, socialization, conflict, and individual variables. *See also* **integrated theory.**

multiple homicide The killing of many victims by an offender or a set of offenders within a short period of time.

multiple leadership Perhaps the most realistic view of leadership in organizations, multiple leadership involves considering various group needs and relying on several persons to fulfill leadership roles specifically designed to meet each need rather than depending on a single person to perform such an overwhelming diversification of tasks. It is a leadership division of labor, in which some persons are responsible for certain tasks while others see to different tasks. No single person performs or assumes all leadership functions, but rather, these duties are distributed to various group members.

multiple personality disorder Split personality in which a person evidences two or more different personality systems, each with its own identity, manner of speech, ideas, and behaviors; a form of schizophrenia.

multisystemic treatment, multisystemic therapy (MST) A form of therapy that addresses a variety of family, peer, and psychological problems by focusing on problem solving and communication skills training.

mummification The drying of a corpse due to burial in a dry place or exposure to a dry climate.

municipal charter An act that confers powers of state upon local organizations and governments to regulate themselves.

municipal corporation Any public organization established as a part of a state for local governmental purposes.

municipal courts Courts of special jurisdiction whose jurisdiction follows the political boundaries of a municipality or city.

municipal home rule A plan that provides political autonomy to a city that is organized under a charter bestowed by state government.

municipality Any local jurisdiction, such as a town or county.

municipal law Any statutes of local governmental bodies authorized through the power of a larger government, such as a state or nation.

municipal liability theory A theory that says a city is liable when its police officers or other agents act to cause unreasonable harm to citizens; a theory of agency whereby a city assumes responsibility for the actions of its employees, including the police.

municipal officer An official who is a part of a municipality and empowered to make certain types of administrative decisions.

municipal ordinance A statute established by a local government to regulate the conduct of local inhabitants.

municipal reform Any organized or semi-organized attempt to change the mechanics of localized political control and the administration of local political power.

murder Intentionally causing the death of another without reasonable provocation or legal justification, or causing the death of another while committing or attempting to commit another crime.

Murder Castle A name given to the home of serial killer Herman Mudgett, who lured more than 200 female victims to their deaths in his castle-like residence in the late 1800s. Mudgett was convicted of torturing and killing the women, and was subsequently executed.

Murder, Inc. A group of organized criminals in the 1940s who carried out contract killings for the Mafia.

murder in the first degree A killing done with premeditation and deliberation or, by statute, in the presence of other aggravating circumstances.

murder in the second degree A killing done with intent to cause death but without premeditation and deliberation.

murder spree Killings at two or more locations by the same individual(s) resulting from a single event. Persons may engage in killing for the sake of killing in a murder rampage, or they may kill different persons while eluding police after a crime's commission.

murder transaction The concept that murder is usually a result of behavior interactions between victims and offenders.

Murph the Surf A nickname given to Jack Murphy who, with an accomplice, burglarized New York's Museum of Natural History and stole a number of precious gems in 1964. He was later caught and convicted.

"mushrooms" A term given by youth gang members to innocent-bystander victims of drive-by shootings. The term comes from the video game *Centipede,* in which the object is to "kill" or "mash" mushrooms that grow into threatening game enemies. When gang members discuss how many rival gang members were shot, they may say, "We got a few mushrooms too," meaning that they hurt or killed innocent bystanders as well.

mushrooms *See* **psilocybin.**

Muslim Community A name used by the Sunni Muslim community, which consists largely of Middle Eastern immigrants and African Americans and is the largest group of Muslims in the United States. They identify with one Islamic leader.

mutilation Any form of punishment in which the individual is mutilated, such as dismemberment.

mutiny An uprising by sailors or soldiers against their superiors; a revolt, usually on a military vessel or craft, by military personnel, in which an attempt is made to overthrow or subvert superior authority.

mutual-agreement program Any formal agreement between inmates and penitentiary or parole-board administrators or members whereby the inmate voluntarily enters a course of study or therapy designed for self-improvement such that a definite parole date can be established. If the inmate complies with the requirements of the agreement through completing educational, vocational, or any other prescribed endeavor, the parole board will be influenced favorably to consider the inmate's early release from prison.

mutual aid A contractual agreement between different law enforcement bodies to provide assistance to one another if needed in emergency situations.

mutual pledge A system of internal policing established by England's Alfred the Great (849–901) that organized the people into tithings, hundreds, and shires. The system persisted to 1500 A.D.

mutual transfer Contact of objects with one another in which trace evidence is transferred. The suspicion is that over 80 percent of all U.S. currency in circulation has cocaine residue merely from bills rubbing one another during handling in bank transactions. Bills are sometimes claimed by certain law enforcement agencies to be "drug money" because of the presence of drug residue, rendering them subject to seizure or confiscation.

muzzle The open end of a firearm's barrel, from which a bullet exits.

muzzle stamp The outline on a shooting victim's skin of the front sight and muzzle of a gun barrel. A muzzle stamp occurs whenever the gun barrel is in contact with the skin, and the body cavity immediately beneath the skin allows for the infusion of gases from the discharge of the gun.

Myers-Briggs Type Indicator (MBTI) A method of determining correctional managers' leadership style, behaviors, and work orientations.

Myrdal, Gunnar (1898–1987) The Scandinavian sociologist who wrote *An American Dilemma* in 1944. He contended that U.S. race relations could be understood best from the point of view of persons outside of the United States, who might be more objective in their assessments. Myrdal's own biases were evident from his work, which strongly suggested that cultural differences may not outweigh racial ones when evaluating race relations in other cultures.

mysoped A child molester who is especially aggressive and sadistic.

mystery A crime novel in which the identity of the perpetrator is not revealed until the end of the book.

N

naive check forgers Edwin Lemert's term for amateurs who forge checks and do not believe that their actions will harm anyone. They are often from middle-class families and resort to forgery as a hasty reaction to some financial setback, often rationalizing their conduct. This latter behavior is called "closure."

naline test A test administered to persons to detect narcotics.

Napoleonic Code Laws enacted in France during the regime of Napoleon Bonaparte, between 1810 and 1819, which were subsequently adopted by various European countries.

"narc" Slang for "narcotics officer."

narcissistic personality disorder A psychological problem characterized by feelings of grandiosity and entitlement.

narcoterrorism A political alliance between terrorist groups and drug-supplying cartels. The cartels provide financing for the terrorists, who in turn provide quasi-military protection to the drug dealers.

narcotic Any drug capable of producing euphoria, pain relief, or some other psychologically desirable condition, that is a controlled substance and prohibited without a prescription.

Narcotics Anonymous An organization similar to Alcoholics Anonymous whose members band together to avoid the use of narcotics and other drugs. It is headquartered in Van Nuys, CA.

narrative In corrections, a portion of a presentence investigation report prepared by a probation officer or private agency that provides a description of an offense and the offender. It culminates in and justifies a recommendation for a specific sentence to be imposed on the offender by judges.

National Advisory Commission on Civil Disorders Also known as the Kerner Commission, this commission was established in 1968 to investigate civil disorders in the United States, their causes, and possible solutions.

National Advisory Commission on Criminal Justice Standards and Goals This organization promulgated several important goals for police departments in order to clarify their policing functions, including maintenance of order, enforcement of the law, prevention of criminal activity, detection of criminal activity, apprehension of criminals, participation in court proceedings, protection of constitutional guarantees, assistance to those who cannot care for themselves or who are in danger of physical harm, control of traffic, resolution of day-to-day conflicts among family, friends, and neighbors, creation and maintenance of a feeling of security in the community, and promotion and preservation of civil order.

national agency check and inquiry An investigative step in hiring personnel for various government jobs conducted by the Office of Personnel Management. It includes background information requests about one's former employers, references, schools attended, and criminal record, if any.

National Alliance for Model State Drug Laws Congressional action led to the forming of this organization headquartered in Alexandria, VA, which seeks to codify and standardize state drug laws and punishments.

National Archive of Criminal Justice Data (NACJD) A repository of crime- and justice-related data sets at the University of Michigan that provides no-cost access to hundreds of criminal-justice data sets. It receives financial support from the Bureau of Justice Statistics.

National Association of Blacks in Criminal Justice (NABCJ) An association of criminal justice scholars and other professionals established in 1972 and headquartered in Washington, DC, that investigates the impact of criminal justice policies and practices on the minority community and compiles information and statistics about black involvement in the criminal justice field. Publishes the *Local Criminal Justice Newsletter* and the *NABCJ Minority Criminal Justice Personnel Directory.*

National Association of Drug Court Professionals Established from and affiliated with the Anti-Drug Coalitions of America, this agency seeks to encourage drug courts to place drug offenders in treatment programs rather than incarceration. It is headquartered in Alexandria, VA.

National Association of Juvenile Correctional Agencies (NAJCA) Established in 1953, this organization eventually became a part of the Association of State Juvenile Justice Administrators. It is headquartered in Bow, NH.

National Association of Legal Assistants, Inc. (NALA) Established in 1975 and headquartered in Tulsa, OK, this organization consists of paralegals and other legal assistants who wish to improve their education and skills through credentialing. Its credentialing process is approved by the American Bar Association and other professional legal groups. Certifications are offered in a wide variety of areas, including real estate law, bankruptcy, and business law.

National Association of Police Organizations (NAPO) A lobbying organization for law enforcement officers that seeks more benefits associated with law enforcement employment. It is headquartered in Washington, DC.

National Automobile Theft Bureau (NATB) Organized in 1912, the NATB is a nonprofit agency supported by insurance companies to assist law enforcement organizations in minimizing or preventing theft of automobiles and other types of motor vehicles.

National Bomb Data Center Established in 1970, an organization that provides various types of technical information about explosive devices to law enforcement agencies. It is affiliated with the International Association of Chiefs of Police (IACP).

National Bureau of Document Examiners An organization established in 1984 and headquartered in New York City that consists of experts who examine documents and testify in court as to their authenticity. Publishes *The Exemplar.*

National Burglar and Fire Alarm Association A clearinghouse established in 1948 and headquartered in Washington, DC, for information related to security alarm systems and services.

National Center for Citizen Involvement Established in 1979 by volunteers and headquartered in Arlington, VA, an organization that promotes the exchange of information among various volunteer programs. Publishes *Voluntary Action and Volunteering.*

National Center for Community Anti-Crime Established in 1981 and headquartered in Norfolk, VA, the Center has as its goal the training of community citizens for the planning, development, and implementation of various crime prevention programs.

National Center for Community Policing Headquartered in East Lansing, MI, at Michigan State University, this center provides seminars and training for police agencies and community groups to promote community policing efforts in cities and towns.

National Center for Health Statistics (NCHS) A unit within the Centers for Disease Control and Prevention that provides statistics that ultimately improve the health of Americans. It conducts both ongoing and periodic surveys, and serves as a repository of a vast amount of health-related data, including those related to intentional injury or death.

National Center for Juvenile Justice (NCJJ) The juvenile-justice research arm of the National Council of Juvenile and Family Court Judges. Located in Pittsburgh, PA, it is a non-profit organization that engages in applied research, legal research, and systems research applied to juveniles.

National Center for Missing and Exploited Children A center dedicated to locating missing children throughout the United States. It was established by Adam Walsh in 1981.

National Center for State Courts (NCSC) A nonprofit organization founded in 1971 that provides leadership and service to state courts and assists courts with case flow management and court technology. It is headquartered in Williamsburg, VA.

National Center for the Analysis of Violent Crime (NCAVC) A division of the FBI Critical Incident Response Group that investigates unusual or repetitive crimes. Its programs include the Violent Criminal Apprehension Program (VICAP).

National Center for the Prevention and Control of Rape An organization founded in 1976 by the U.S. Department of Health and Human Services that conducts research and disseminates information about rape's causes, sexual assault data, the consequences of rape, and the status and treatment of victims. It is headquartered in Rockville, MD.

National Center for Victims of Crime (NCVC) A national organization committed to helping crime victims rebuild their lives that advocates for victims' rights and resources.

National Center on Institutions and Alternatives (NCIA) A nonprofit organization headquartered in Alexandria, VA, that promotes humane alternatives for offenders.

National Clearinghouse for Alcohol and Drug Information A general information service about drug abuse and substance abuse prevention, treatment programs, and education.

National Clearinghouse for Alcohol Information Library An organization created by the U.S. Department of Health and Human Services in 1972 to collect and disseminate information about alcoholism. Publishes *Alcohol Health and Research World,* a quarterly publication.

National Clearinghouse for Drug Abuse Information Established by the National Institute of Health, this agency headquartered in Chevy Chase, MD, publishes documents and distributes information about drugs and drug abuse to interested persons and organizations.

National Coalition Against the Death Penalty An agency opposed to the death penalty headquartered in Washington, DC. It is an information center that disseminates death penalty information to interested persons, advocates the abolition of the death penalty, coordinates local citizen groups that oppose use of the death penalty, and publishes *Lifelines.*

National Coalition for Drug-Free School Zones Sponsored by the Chiefs of Police National Drug Task Force, headquartered in Washington, DC. Its goals are to assist in the recognition and use of drugs in schools in order to prevent their use on school grounds or near schools.

National Coalition for Jail Reform Established in 1978 and headquartered at Rutgers University in Newark, NJ, this organization seeks to change the nation's jails and improve their physical plants and other amenities to improve conditions for inmates.

National College of District Attorneys Headquartered in Houston, TX, and established in 1970, this group consists of district attorneys and interested persons who provide continuing education in legal developments and case law for prosecuting attorneys through workshops and seminars.

National Commission on Correctional Health Care (NCCHC) A commission comprised of representatives from 36 organizations that have an interest in correctional health care, who set standards for prison medical services.

National Commission on Law Observance and Enforcement A commission created by President Herbert Hoover in 1929 to investigate law enforcement practices and standards.

National Commission on the Causes and Prevention of Violence An organization convened by President Lyndon Johnson in response to the social violence of the 1960s. Its methods for collecting relevant data included citizen surveys and the analysis of archival data.

National Commission on Terrorist Attacks Upon the United States (9/11 Commission) A commission formed in late 2002 by Congressional legislation and signed by President George W. Bush. It was chaired by Thomas H. Kean and comprised of five Democrats and five Republicans, and was charged with preparing a full and complete account of the circumstances surrounding the September 11, 2001, terrorist attacks on the New York World Trade Center towers. It reviewed 2.5 million pages of documents, interviewed 1,200 persons in 10 countries, and analyzed the social and political milieu prevalent prior to the attacks. The commission discovered evidence of increased contact between Iran and al Qaeda, and that Iraqi government officials had met with al Qaeda leadership prior to the attacks, although Saddam Hussein did not appear to have assisted al Qaeda in the U.S. attack. The commission also found that the CIA and FBI had not shared information about terrorists, and that this fragmented intelligence gathering contributed to the lack of preparedness of the U.S. relating to potential terrorist threats. Recommendations of the commission include the centralization of intelligence-gathering agencies where information about terrorist activities can be coordinated and swift counter-terrorist actions can be taken. A report was issued June 16, 2004, and distributed to the general public in July 2004.

National Correctional Recreation Organization A professional association of full-time professional correctional personnel who are committed to promoting professional programs and services that assist inmates in eliminating barriers to leisure, in developing leisure skills and attitudes, and in optimizing leisure participation.

National Council of Juvenile and Family Court Judges, Inc. Established in 1937, this organization seeks to investigate and improve the juvenile-justice system. It is headquartered in Reno, NV, and publishes the *Juvenile and Family Court Journal.*

National Council on Crime and Delinquency A private national agency that promotes efforts at crime control through research, citizen involvement, and public information.

National Council on Organized Crime An organization established in 1970 by President Richard M. Nixon for the purpose of controlling organized crime. It authorized the attorney general of the United States to investigate and initiate arrests of persons affiliated with organized crime.

National Crime Information Center (NCIC) The NCIC was established by the FBI in 1967 as a central information source for stolen vehicles, accident information, stolen property, arrested persons, fingerprint information, criminal offenses, and criminal offenders and their whereabouts.

National Crime Panel Reports, National Crime Panel Survey Reports Criminal victimization surveys conducted for the Law Enforcement Assistance Administration by the U.S. Bureau of the Census that gauge the extent to which persons age 12 and over, households, and businesses have been victims of certain types of crime, and describe the nature of the criminal incidents and their victims. *See also **National Crime Victimization Survey** (NCVS).*

National Crime Prevention Council Headquartered in Washington, DC, this organization provides communities with various forms of assistance in crime prevention and information about drug abuse, and disseminates educational materials that are useful in crime-prevention strategies. Publishes *The Catalyst.*

*National Crime Survey (NCS) See **National Crime Victimization Survey** (NCVS).*

National Crime Victimization Survey (NCVS) A random survey of 60,000 households, including 127,000 persons 12 years of age or older and 50,000 businesses, published in cooperation with the U.S. Bureau of the Census. It measures crime committed against specific victims interviewed and not necessarily reported to law enforcement officers. Prior to 1991, the survey was known as the *National Crime Survey (NCS).*

National Criminal Justice Association (NCJA) A nonprofit organization headquartered in Washington, DC, whose members include state planning agencies and other criminal justice professionals.

National Criminal Justice Reference Service (NCJRS) A service of the U.S. Department of Justice that makes available a wide range of documents and bibliographical sources regarding crime and criminal justice.

National Disabled Law Officers Association (NDLOA) Organized in 1971 and headquartered in Nutley, NJ, this organization consists of law enforcement officers who have been wounded or disabled while performing their jobs and who are otherwise unable to perform their jobs effectively.

National District Attorney's Association (NDAA) A nonprofit organization that represents the interests of prosecutors and engages in a variety of activities to improve the effectiveness and professional standing of district attorneys.

National Drug Enforcement Board Established in 1984 under the National Narcotics Act of 1984, this board facilitates and coordinates drug policies and enforcement among different federal law enforcement agencies and departments.

National Drug Prosecution Center Part of the American Prosecutors Research Institute, this center provides education and technical assistance in identifying and evaluating drug control and demand-reduction methods. It is an anti–drug abuse program that assists in promoting enabling antidrug legislation.

National Firearms Act Legislation passed in 1934 that restricted interstate commerce in machine guns and other types of nonconventional weapons, and imposed a high tax on such weapons.

National Forensic Center Established in 1978 and headquartered in Lawrenceville, NJ, this organization's membership consists of forensics personnel and other interested persons who wish to share and learn about new developments in forensics sciences. Publishes *The Expert and the Law.*

National Gang Crime Research Center Headquartered in Chicago, IL, this center collects and distributes information about gangs and gang activities in the United States, and publishes *Gang Journal.*

National Guard A state-based voluntary militia authorized by governors to act to protect states in the event of emergencies. It supplements military and law enforcement units in restoring order during conditions of rioting and civil disobedience.

National Incident-Based Reporting System (NIBRS) A reporting system in which the police describe each offense in a crime incident together with the data describing the offender, victim, and property. It is designed to replace the more limited *Uniform Crime Reports.*

National Instant Criminal Background Check System A national computerized database used to screen handgun buyers that grew out of the Brady Handgun Violence Prevention Act of 1993. The instant check makes it possible for law enforcement authorities to conduct background checks on those trying to purchase handguns.

National Institute of Corrections (NIC) Headquartered in Washington, DC, the NIC provides technical assistance and training, disseminates information about correctional programs, and works to establish policies and standards for interested persons, educators, and corrections personnel and their agencies.

National Institute of Corrections' Model Classification Project A risk and needs assessment project established by the federal government to enable juvenile judges to make more informed sentencing decisions.

National Institute of Justice (NIJ) The NIJ was created in 1979 to provide for and encourage research to improve federal, state, and local criminal-justice systems, prevent or reduce the incidence of crime, and identify effective programs.

National Institute of Mental Health (NIMH) A major division of the Alcohol, Drug Abuse, and Mental Health Administration of the U.S. Department of Health and Human Services that conducts and supports empirical research on delinquency and crime, substance abuse, alcoholism, narcotics addiction, and other social problems. It is headquartered in Washington, DC.

National Institute on Drug Abuse (NIDA) A federal organization that conducts and promotes research on drug abuse and addiction.

National Insurance Crime Bureau (NICB) The aim of this organization, established in 1992, is to combat insurance fraud in the automobile industry. It investigates potentially false insurance claims filed by persons seeking to profit from injuries that they haven't suffered or collect for damages to property that did not exist.

National Judicial College Headquartered in Reno, NV, this college offers training for judges to enable them to understand court protocol, motions, and other matters related to court proceedings.

National Juvenile Court Data Archive A compendium of national statistical information and databases about juvenile delinquency available through the National Center for Juvenile Justice, under the sponsorship of the Office of Juvenile Justice and Delinquency Prevention (OJJDP), that acquires court dispositional records and publishes periodic reports of juvenile offenses and adjudicatory outcomes from various jurisdictions.

National Juvenile Detention Association Established in 1968 and headquartered in Richmond, KY, and Lansing, MI, this organization seeks to improve juvenile detention centers, their physical plants, and their vocational and educational programming.

National Legal Aid and Defenders Association Established in 1911, this organization strives to furnish adequate legal representation to indigents accused of crimes and assists those in need of legal assistance in finding quality representation. It is headquartered in Washington, DC, and publishes *Cornerstone* and *Briefcase*.

National Military Intelligence Association Established in 1974 and headquartered in Gaithersburg, MD, this organization compiles information about different military concerns. Its members are intelligence officers affiliated with intelligence offices in various military organizations. Publishes the *American Intelligence Journal.*

National Mounted Services Organization An association of law enforcement personnel who patrol their cities or towns on horseback, headquartered in Sparkhill, NY.

National Narcotics Border Interdiction System This organization coordinates drug intelligence and issues reports concerning illicit drug trafficking internationally, and investigates money laundering in relation to illegal drugs, coordinating with the DEA, CIA, and INS in their drug-fighting efforts.

National Night Out An annual crime prevention event sponsored by the National Association of Town Watch to emphasize the right of citizens to enjoy their communities without fear of criminal victimization.

National Ombudsman A Swedish representative of the people, elected by the Parliament for a four-year term, who oversees and intercedes in prisoner complaints and public grievances. The ombudsman may resolve disputes about judicial sentencing decisions and conduct inspections of Swedish prisons.

National Opinion Research Center (NORC) A University of Chicago–sponsored social science organization that conducts numerous national and regional surveys, some of which directly or indirectly address crime- and justice-related topics.

National Organization for the Reform of Marijuana Laws (NORML) A national membership organization dedicated to lessening the severity of laws prohibiting the manufacture, cultivation, sale, and especially the use of marijuana.

National Organization for Victim Assistance (NOVA) Headquartered in Washington, DC, this organization is dedicated to recognizing and implementing victims' rights and services. It established victim-compensation programs and promoted victim input in the criminal-justice process.

National Organization of Black Law Enforcement Executives (NOBLE) Established in 1976 and headquartered in Alexandria, VA, an organization whose national membership includes black law enforcement officials in all state and federal jurisdictions. Publishes *NOBLE Actions.*

National Police Agency Japanese national police and recentralized police operations throughout the 47 prefectures, including three additional prefecture-equivalent agencies in Tokyo and Hokkaido.

National Polygraph Association Headquartered in Chattanooga, TN, an organization established in 1966 whose members consist of polygraph examiners who meet to exchange new ideas about lie-detector tests, recent developments, and other related matters of interest.

National Prison Association Founded in 1870, this association later became the American Prison Association, and then the American Correctional Association. Its first president was future U.S. President Rutherford B. Hayes. *See also* **American Correctional Association.**

National Rifle Association (NRA) A nonprofit organization headquartered in Virginia whose mission is to protect the rights of gun owners and sportsmen in the United States. It contributes to the political campaigns of politicians whose views favor gun freedoms and emphasizes responsible gun ownership and harsh penalties for those convicted of using firearms during crimes. The organization was formed in 1871 by Civil War General Ambrose Burnside, who was also a former governor of Rhode Island and a U.S. Senator, and who became the NRA's first president.

National Sheriffs Association (NSA) A national organization of county sheriffs headquartered in Alexandria, VA. The NSA promotes professionalism among sheriffs and assists them in obtaining federal and state funding.

National Stolen Property Act Congressional action in 1934 that prohibited all interstate trafficking in stolen securities and property, such as checks, bonds, stock certificates, and currency. It extended provisions of the earlier National Motor Vehicles Theft Act.

National Survey on Drug Abuse A household survey of prevalence of drug use in the United States that canvasses 8,000 households every few years to examine trends in drug use, geographical patterns of use and trafficking, and provide information and disseminate literature about illicit drug use to schools, agencies, and interested persons.

National Youth Gang Survey (NYGS) A survey conducted annually since 1995 to identify and describe critical gang components and characteristics.

National Youth Survey (NYS) A program for gathering data on crime by interviewing adolescents over a five-year period. The program has been structured to overcome many of the criticisms of other self-report studies.

Nation of Islam The name given to the original Black Muslim movement in the United States by its founder, Elijah Muhammad.

natural areas of crime Inner-city areas of extreme poverty in which the critical social control mechanisms have broken down.

naturalization A means whereby persons may attain United States citizenship, usually after completing various requirements, swearing allegiance to the United States, and agreeing to obey its laws.

natural law A body of principles and rules, imposed by some higher power than is person-made law, considered to be uniquely fitting for and binding on any community of rational beings.

natural rights Inalienable rights enjoyed by individuals independent of government-imposed laws. Theorists, writers, and political thinkers have used this abstraction to measure democracy and its effects, or to describe tyranny and other conditions that infringe or seek to infringe one's pursuit of happiness.

natural-system model A model in which organizations are perceived as systems made up of independent parts, each part functioning so that the entire system is perpetuated and survives over time. The system draws its nourishment or energy from sources in its external environment. The system has built-in mechanisms for maintaining it and for regulating the relations between its component parts. In the context of the organic analogy, the system develops and grows, becoming increasingly complex. Each of the parts adjusts to the contributions of the other parts so that a type of homeostasis is generated. The major assumption is that the organization is a natural whole. The component structures of the system are emergent institutions that can be understood only in relation to the diverse needs of the total system. The component parts of an organization are interdependent. The organization is an end in itself. The realization of goals of the system as a whole is but one of several important needs to which the organization is oriented. The organization serves to link parts of the system and to provide avenues for controlling and integrating them. Organizational structures are viewed as spontaneously and homeostatically maintained where the system depends greatly on the conforming behavior of group members. Changes in organizational patterns are considered the results of cumulative, unplanned, adaptive responses to threats to the equilibrium of the system as a whole. Responses to problems are creatively developed defense mechanisms that are constantly shaped by shared values which are deeply internalized in the members.

nature-nurture debate The ongoing controversy over whether crime is due to biological causes or environmental causes, including child rearing.

nature theory A theory that holds that low intelligence is genetically determined and inherited.

Nazi war criminals Officials and military personnel who escaped punishment following World War II but who are believed to be responsible for the atrocities committed against 6 million Jews and other minorities in Europe during World War II.

NCVS See *National Crime Victimization Survey (NCVS)*.

near groups Relatively unstructured short-term groups with fluid membership.

necessarily included offense An offense committed for the purpose of committing another offense (e.g., trespass committed for the purpose of committing burglary).

necessity A condition that compels someone to act because of perceived needs. An affirmative defense (e.g., when someone's automobile breaks down during a snowstorm and an unoccupied cabin is nearby, breaking into the cabin to save oneself from freezing to death is acting out of necessity and would be a defense to breaking and entering charges).

necrophagia The practice of eating the flesh of dead persons.

necrophilia A fixation on death and dead persons. Sometimes fetishes may encompass having sexual relations with dead bodies.

need for treatment The criteria on which juvenile dispositions are based. Ideally, juveniles are treated according to their individual needs for treatment and not the seriousness of the delinquent acts they commit.

needs assessment, needs-assessment device A paper-and-pencil instrument used for various purposes by community and institutional corrections to determine which types of services are needed for offenders who have psychological problems or drug or alcohol dependencies.

needs-based supervision A form of community supervision in which interventions by the correctional staff are designed to meet specific needs attributed to or claimed by the offender.

ne exeat "Let him not go" (Latin); a writ to restrain someone from departing.

negative affective states Sociologist Robert Agnew has described strain theory with this variant condition (1992), characterized by failure to achieve positively valued goals, disjunction of expectations and achievements, removal of positively valued stimuli, and exposure to negative stimuli.

negative reinforcements Punishments administered by superiors to subordinate police officers and others to prevent particular kinds of undesirable conduct.

neglect Either passive or active, with or without the intent or a parent of guardian, the act of failing to protect or give care to a child.

neglected child An infant adjudged in need of supervision by the juvenile court if they are abandoned, without proper care, or without substance, education, or health care because of neglect or the refusal of a parent, guardian, or custodian.

negligence Liability accruing to prison or correctional program administrators, probation or parole officers, police officers, and any other officials as the result of a failure to perform a duty owed to clients, inmates, or arrestees, or the improper or inadequate performance of that duty. It may include negligent entrustment, negligent training, negligent assignment, negligent retention, or negligent supervision (e.g., providing probation or parole officers with revolvers and not providing them with firearms training).

negligence tort Breach of a common-law or statutory duty to act reasonably toward those who may foreseeably be harmed by one's conduct.

negligent Failing to perform a duty to others or acting in a way so as to harm others; failure to exercise due care; blame arising from acting carelessly.

negligent assignment Placement of correctional officers, probation or parole officers, or other staff members in a position for which they are unqualified.

negligent entrustment Administrators' failure to monitor guards supplied with items they have not yet been trained to use, such as firearms.

negligent hiring and selection A basis for a civil lawsuit that arises when incompetent persons have been selected to perform important tasks, such as police work, and injuries to victims are caused by such incompetent persons.

negligent retention Administrators' maintaining officers determined unfit for their jobs in those jobs.

negligent training A basis for a civil lawsuit that arises when a clear duty to train employees (e.g., to use firearms) is not met.

negotiable Capable of being transferred by endorsement or assignment.

negotiable instrument Any written document promising to pay a certain amount of money (e.g., a check, money order, or promissory note).

Neighborhood Justice Centers Facilities in which volunteer mediators act as hearing officers and attempt to resolve minor disputes between citizens that otherwise might end up in court.

Neighborhood Police Posts Police posts in Singapore, similar to mini-stations or substations such as those found in Detroit, MI.

neighborhood policing Any law enforcement patrol style emphasizing "beats" or regular patrols of the same city blocks or town territories for the purpose of allowing officers to become better acquainted with the public they serve.

Neighborhood Watch, neighborhood-watch programs An organization of residents maintaining surveillance over a given area, where neighbors are encouraged to report suspicious circumstances to police and take precautions to prevent crime.

neoclassical school of criminology, neoclassicism A school of thought that maintained that the accused should be exempted from conviction if circumstances prevented the exercise of free will.

neonaticide Killing of a newborn child.

nepotism The practice of hiring one's relatives or close friends, regardless of their qualifications.

net widening Pulling anyone into a program who would not otherwise be targeted for such a program (also known as "widening the net"). Under ordinary conditions, when police officers confront people on the street, the officers may be inclined to issue verbal warnings and release them. However, if a community program is created that caters to particular kinds of clients, officers may arrest these same people and involve them in these programs simply because the programs exist, thus needlessly bringing them into the program.

networking, networks Ties among individual members of groups or among different groups.

neurological Related to the brain and nervous system structure.

neurophysiology The study of brain activity. *See also* **Moffitt, Terrie.**

neuroticism A personality disorder characterized by low self-esteem, high anxiety, and variable mood swings.

neutralization techniques A set of attitudes and beliefs that allow would-be delinquents to negate any moral apprehension they may have about committing a crime so that they may freely engage in antisocial behavior without regret.

neutralization theory This explanation holds that delinquents experience guilt when involved in delinquent activities and that they respect leaders of the legitimate social order. Their delinquency is episodic rather than chronic, and they adhere to conventional values while "drifting" into periods of illegal behavior. In order to drift, the delinquent must first neutralize legal and moral values.

neutron activation analysis A forensic test using radioactive chemicals to analyze poisonous substances or to trace evidence on clothing or hands of suspects to determine from the presence of cartridge discharge residue if they have recently discharged a firearm.

newbie Derived from military slang, this term refers to a Usenet neophyte who has recently acquired sufficient computer expertise to engage in hacking and intricate programming.

new-generation jails *See* **direct-supervision jails.**

New Jersey Intensive Probation Supervision Program (IPS) A plan commenced in 1983 to serve low-risk incarcerated offenders, which draws clients from inmate volunteers. The program's selectivity limits participants through a seven-stage selection process. Participants must serve at least four months in prison or jail before being admitted to the program, which monitors their progress extensively. It is similar the to Georgia Intensive Probation Supervision Program in success and low recidivism scores among participants.

newly discovered evidence Any new or material fact disclosed either during or following a trial that may alter the trial's outcome and verdict.

new-offense violation Arrest and prosecution for the commission of a new crime by a parolee.

New Penology Model A plan under which persistent pressures for more human practices and programs to reform offenders were applied. The movement traced its origins to an 1870 meeting of the National Prison Association.

New Police Also known as the Metropolitan Police of London, the agency formed in 1829 under the command of Sir Robert Peel that became the model for modern-day police forces throughout the Western world.

new trial A tribunal *de novo*. After a hung jury or a case is set aside or overturned by a higher court, a new trial is held to determine one's guilt or innocence.

New York House of Refuge Established in New York City in 1825 by the Society for the Prevention of Pauperism, this school largely managed status offenders. Compulsory education was provided, and a strict prisonlike regimen was considered detrimental to youthful clientele.

"New York Jack" Slang term for heroin.

next friend A person who files or enters a case on behalf of an infant.

next of kin The nearest living relative to an arrested, injured, or deceased person.

Nicewander, W. Alan (1939–) Nicewander proposed the concept of the latent trait theory together with David Rowe and D. Wayne Osgood.

niche In corrections, a way of adapting to the prison community that stresses finding one's place in the system, rather than fighting for one's individual rights.

nicotine A powerful stimulant ingested by smoking or chewing a tobacco product.

Nidal, Abu (1937–2002) A terrorist born Sabri I. Banna in Jaffa who became a Palestinian politician and guerilla leader responsible for carrying out terrorist attacks in the Middle East and other parts of the world. He joined the Baath Party in Jordan in 1955, and became a secret member of Al Fatah, a guerilla organization. Nidal was sent to Baghdad, Iraq, as an Al Fatah representative, and was subsequently accused by Al Fatah of murder plots against their leadership and sentenced to death. He then moved to Syria, and helped to hinder an agreement between Jordan, Israel, and the Palestinian Liberation Organization. Nidal died in Baghdad in August 2002 under mysterious circumstances. Some claim he was assassinated.

Niederhoffer, Arthur (1917–1981) An authority on police work and methods, Niederhoffer was an attorney who practiced in New York. He wrote extensively about police-community relations and was subsequently a professor at John Jay College of Criminal Justice and a member of the American Society of Criminology.

night court A court convened at night that presides over many people arrested for public drunkenness or lewdness, offenses which often occur at night. Such courts hear and resolve petty offenses and make bail decisions. Some courts, such as exist in New York City, are called "after-hours" courts, but arrestees also refer to them as "night courts."

night prosecutor's program An enterprise in which prosecutors hear and attempt to settle disputes after normal working hours without the formal filing of criminal charges. This program is particularly useful in resolving domestic violence disputes and altercations between neighbors that have led to assaults.

nightstick A baton used by police officers as a defensive device against suspects who assault them.

night watch An early English watchman program designed to report crime.

night watchman A thirteenth-century untrained citizen who patrolled at night on the lookout for disturbances; currently, a usually privately employed officer who maintains a vigilance on the premises of private or public buildings.

nihil "Nothing" (Latin).

nihilism A position that rejects laws and their application; the belief that the use of force is necessary against those in authority.

NIMBY Syndrome "Not in my backyard"; refers to objections citizens have about having any kind of correctional facility built in or near their neighborhoods or communities; conveys sentiments of neighborhood residents who oppose any type of institutional or residential facility that houses inmates, probationers, or parolees near their own homes, because of the belief that property values will be adversely affected and the risk of victimization will be greater with criminals housed nearby.

9-1-1 An emergency telephone number used nationwide to solicit assistance from medical or law enforcement personnel in emergency situations.

1980 Refugee Act Legislation that radically expanded the definition of those eligible for political asylum. Because it has been poorly enforced and easily abused, it helped bring on today's growing demand for new limits on aliens.

1983 lawsuit *See* **Section 1983 actions.**

no bill *See* **no true bill.**

no contest A plea entered by the defendant in criminal court in which the defendant agrees with the facts stated in the complaint but technically makes no admission of guilt. Also called a *nolo contendere* plea, it is treated as a guilty plea for all practical purposes.

"no knock" law A regulation empowering law enforcement officers to enter homes or public places with a proper court order without knocking or announcing their intent to enter, in order to obtain evidence that might otherwise be destroyed or to protect themselves against persons who might otherwise imperil their safety.

nolle prosequi "To be unwilling to prosecute" (Latin); disposition of a criminal case in which the prosecutor decides not to prosecute.

nolo contendere "I do not wish to contend" (Latin); a plea of "no contest" to charges. The defendant does not dispute the facts, although issue may be taken with the legality or constitutionality of the law allegedly violated. Such a plea is treated as a guilty plea. It is also known as an "Alford plea," from the leading case of *North Carolina v. Alford* (1970).

nomadic killer A serial killer who roams from location to location to find and kill victims.

nominal brain dysfunction (NBD) Damage to the brain itself that causes antisocial behavior injurious to the individual's lifestyle and social adjustment.

nominal damages Token sums awarded to plaintiffs when there is no substantial loss or injury.

nominal disposition A juvenile-court outcome in which a juvenile is warned or verbally reprimanded but returned to the custody of his or her parents.

nonavertable recidivist An offender whose prior sentence would not have affected the commission of new crimes.

non compos mentis "Not in control of the mind" (Latin); not of sound mind.

noncontact visitation Prison visitation in which visitors and prisoners are not permitted any physical touching or contact and are separated by glass partition.

nonfeasance Failure to carry out official duties.

noninstitutional corrections *See* **community corrections.**

nonintervention The philosophy popularized by Edwin M. Schur in his 1973 book *Radical Nonintervention,* which rests on the assumption that the juvenile-justice system and other such systems often do more harm than good.

nonjudicial disposition A decision in a juvenile case by an authority other than a judge or court of law (e.g., an intake officer). It is usually an informal method of determining the most appropriate disposition in handling a juvenile.

nonjuror Anyone called for jury service who refuses to take the required oath to act in the capacity of a juror.

nonlethal force Any power exerted to subdue criminal suspects that does not involve death, such as verbal judo, use of TASER weapons, rubber bullets, tear gas, and Mace; any method of subduing another person without risk of serious injury or death.

nonlethal weapons Instruments that are designed to incapacitate rather than kill (e.g., stun guns, TASERs, or pistols that shoot rubber bullets).

nonpartisan election An election in which candidates who are not endorsed by political parties are presented to the voters for selection.

nonpayment of child support A criminal charge stemming from the failure of a parent or legal guardian to pay child support that was previously ordered by a court.

non prosequitor One who does not prosecute another.

nonrational model Characterizations of organizations that incorporate unplanned and spontaneous dimensions, in which order is attained apart from rules and regulations. Personality systems are primary, and individual differences account for employee performance and excellence rather than obedience to abstract rules under a bureaucratic model.

nonreporting probation A form of probation in which the probationer does not have to check in with his or her probation officer. Most often, such persons mail in monthly reports of their employment and law-abiding behavior to probation offices.

nonresidential program A plan allowing youths to remain in their homes or foster homes while receiving services.

nonsecure custody, nonsecure facility, nonsecure setting A facility that emphasizes the care and treatment of youths without the need to place constraints to ensure public protection.

non sequitur "It does not follow" (Latin); an argument with false or unfounded conclusions, or no conclusions.

nonsuit A judgment in favor of a defendant because of the failure of the plaintiff to state a case upon which relief can be granted.

nonviolence A policy of protest groups that involves refraining from the use of physical force or resistance. Persons may chain themselves to the gates of political buildings or lie down in front of doorways to protest particular policies. Police are obligated to carry these persons away from these locations, usually without resistance.

nonviolent offense A crime against property in which no physical injury to victims is sustained (e.g., embezzlement, fraud, forgery, larceny, burglary, vehicular theft).

no paper *Nolle prosequi;* a prosecutor declines to prosecute a case.

"no pros" *See* **nolle prosequi.**

normative power The allocation of esteem and prestige symbols for the benefit of subordinates to enlist their compliance.

normlessness A situation in which social guideposts or rules have eroded or become ineffective for regulating conduct. In this condition, sometimes called anomie, delinquent behavior or criminal activities may be seen as justifying illegitimate routes to goal achievement. *See also* **Durkheim, Emile; Merton, Robert King.**

norms Standards of conduct that are current in a society.

North American Man-Boy Love Association (NAMBLA) A U.S.-based organization of pedophiles founded in the early 1980s claiming that sexual intercourse between grown men and boys is often beneficial for the boys and should be legalized. Some convicted child molesters are thought to have been involved in the organization, including Paul Shanley, a Roman Catholic priest from Boston, MA, who was accused of raping boys. A similar organization in the Netherlands is MARTIJN (for acceptance of pedophilia), which was founded in 1982.

North American Police Work Dog Association Established in 1977 and headquartered in Adrian, MI, an organization that consists of persons who train dogs to work in connection with investigative police activities, such as drug sniffing or searches for illegal contraband in vehicles or on persons. Some dogs can be trained to attack criminal suspects who pose a danger to arresting officers.

notary, notary public A person empowered by law to administer oaths, to certify things or documents as true, and to perform various minor official acts.

not guilty, not-guilty plea A defense plea that the defendant has not committed the crime with which he or she is charged.

not guilty by reason of insanity The plea of a defendant or the verdict of a jury or judge in a criminal proceeding that the defendant is not guilty of the offense charged because at the time the crimes were committed, the defendant did not have the mental capacity to be held criminally responsible for his or her actions.

nothing-works doctrine Robert Martinson's belief, articulated in the 1970s, that virtually every correctional treatment program is ineffective in rehabilitating offenders.

notice An official document advising someone of a proceeding, which usually requires their attendance.

"not in my backyard" *See* NIMBY syndrome.

no true bill A grand jury decision that insufficient evidence exists to establish probable cause that a crime was committed and that a specific person committed it.

nuclear family A family unit composed of parents and their children. This smaller family structure is subject to great stress due to the intense, close contact between parents and children.

nuisance An unlawful or unreasonable use of a person's property resulting in injury to another or to the public (e.g., someone who lets his dog roam freely about the community, where it may bite someone or cause physical harm, would be considered a nuisance).

nuisance abatement A method to deal with gangs that defines their behavior as a public nuisance and forbids certain legal and illegal behaviors.

null No legal force; not binding.

nullen crimen, nulla poena, sine lege "There is no crime, there is no punishment, without law" (Latin).

null hypothesis A statement believed not to be true but which is nevertheless used to contradict the true hypothesis statement. It is used as a conventional test of a hypothesis in social research. Rejecting the null hypothesis statement leads to support of the research hypothesis, which is logically derived from a theory and is believed to be true. The use of a null hypothesis is intended to show research objectivity in establishing truth or knowledge about something.

numbers-game model A caseload assignment model for probation or parole officers in which the total number of offender/clients is divided by the number of officers.

numbers racket An illegal lottery game in which persons pay to bet on certain sets of numbers in hope sof winning a large sum of money.

nunchaku A flailing instrument consisting of two or more rigid parts, connected by a chain, cable, rope, or other non-rigid, flexible, or springy material, constructed in such a manner as to allow the rigid parts to swing freely, so that one rigid part may be used as a handle and the other rigid part may be used as the striking end.

Nuremberg principle The idea that those faced with carrying out orders should disobey those orders if they are unjust.

Nuremberg trials A series of trials held in Nuremberg, Germany, following World War II, to determine the guilt or innocence of Nazi war criminals and their conspirators believed to have killed numerous Jews and other minorities.

nurture theory The theory that intelligence is partly biological but mostly sociological. Negative environmental factors encourage delinquent behavior and depress intelligence scores for many youths.

O

oath An affirmation of truth of statements given or about to be given sworn in advance of giving testimony in court.

obit "He died" (Latin).

obiter "In passing" (Latin); incidental opinion rather than the primary question.

obiter dictum "Something said in passing" (Latin); a belief or opinion delivered by a judicial official regarding his or her decision in case.

objective classification system An approach to classification that provides more accurate information on the characteristics of the prison population than subjective systems. Projections are made about security, custody, and staffing needs for new institutions and the expansion of existing prisons.

objective parole criteria General qualifying conditions that permit parole boards to make nonsubjective parole decisions without regard to an inmate's race, religion, gender, age, or socioeconomic status.

objective test An experiment for identifying entrapment. The test assumes that suspects have criminal records or are disposed to a particular type of crime, and whatever means police wish to use to elicit behavior are acceptable.

objectivity Detached neutrality; scientific finding of fact without bias or prejudice.

obligatory Having the effect of being binding; bound by duty of office or through allegiance.

obscene material Sexually explicit books, videotapes, or other documents or media that lack a serious purpose and appeal solely to the prurient interest of viewers. Although nudity *per se* is not usually considered obscene, open sex behavior, masturbation, and exhibition of the genitals are banned in many communities. Local community standards most often define obscenity among different jurisdictions..

obscene phone call A telephone call made by one whose purpose is to utter obscenities, sometimes for sexual gratification.

obscenity Offensive photos, movies, Internet-generated depictions, or other works, often sexual in content, that are judged immoral by community standards; work totally lacking in literary or artistic value.

OBSCIS Offender-Based State Corrections Information System; a multi-state program to develop a prisoner-information system for state corrections agencies.

observation A research strategy that involves the careful and systematic watching of behavior.

obstruction of justice Impeding or preventing law enforcement officers from doing their job; interfering with the administration of justice.

OBTS (Offender-Based Transaction Statistics) A new means of reporting crime information more systematically by establishing interagency networks of information exchange.

occasional criminal One who does not define him- or herself as a criminal but who commits infrequent crimes, usually property crimes; the opposite of a career criminal, who commits crime regularly and for a living.

occasional property crime A wrongful act committed by an occasional criminal. An occasional offender often commits crimes on the spur of moment; crime is not a usual pattern or customary occurrence for him or her.

occult Pertaining to the supernatural.

occult crime An offense perpetrated by a person or persons as an element of practicing witchcraft or the occult arts.

occupational crime Offenses committed by persons for their own benefit in the course of performing their jobs.

occupational deviance Unusual behavior engaged in during the course of a legitimate occupation.

Occupational Safety and Health Administration (OSHA) An organization headquartered in Washington, DC, that was established in 1970 to develop workplace standards and safety to protect workers. It enforces laws and regulations, and may inspect workplaces to insure compliance with federal laws.

occupational stressors Factors associated with a job that make people feel uncomfortable, overwhelmed, unhappy, fearful, or anxious.

o'clock Points on a target or at a crime scene when compared with a clock face. Twelve o'clock refers to the topmost point of a target, and six o'clock the bottommost point.

odometer tampering Interfering with or modifying an automobile's mileage indicator, which measures the distance traveled by vehicle, in violation of federal law. The National Highway Safety Administration prohibits altering the mileage on an automobile's odometer. The prohibition was prompted by used-car salespersons and mechanics who turn back automobile odometers to indicate lower mileage than had actually been recorded. False readings give buyers the impression that a vehicle is less used than would be disclosed by an unaltered odometer.

odontology *See* **forensic odontology.**

off-duty weapon A firearm, most often a handgun, carried by a law enforcement officer when not on duty.

offender One who has been convicted of one or more crimes.

offender, alleged One who has been charged with a specific offense by a law enforcement agency or court but has not been convicted.

offender, convicted An adult who has been found guilty of one or more criminal offenses.

offender, sex One who has committed a sex crime, including rape, statutory rape, child sexual abuse, exhibitionism, sodomy, or similar acts.

offender-based presentence investigation report A presentence investigation report that seeks to understand an offender and the circumstances that led to the offense and to evaluate the potential of the offender to become a law-abiding and productive citizen.

offender control The amount of supervision given to any probationer, parolee, or institutionalized prison inmate.

offender rehabilitation The condition achieved when criminals are reintegrated into their communities and refrain from further criminal activity. *See also* **rehabilitate.**

offense A felony, misdemeanor, or delinquent act.

offense against the family or children Any offense pertaining to abandonment, spousal neglect or abuse, child abuse, or nonpayment of alimony or child support.

offense-based presentence investigation report A presentence investigation report that focuses primarily on the offense that was committed, the offender's culpability, and the offender's criminal history.

offense escalation The progression of less serious adult or juvenile offenders to more serious types of crimes.

offense seriousness Crimes with greater punishments associated with their commission; the degree of gravity of the conviction offense (e.g., felonies are more serious than misdemeanors).

offenses, Part I *See* **Part I offenses.**

offenses, Part II *See* **Part II offenses.**

offenses known to the police Reported occurrences of offenses in the *Uniform Crime Reports* which have been verified at the police level.

Office for Victims of Crime (OVC) A branch of the U.S. Department of Justice's Office of Justice Programs that administers grant programs intended to assist victims and victim advocate organizations in the states and territories.

Office of Community Oriented Policing Services (OCOPS, COPS) A federal office within the Office of Justice Programs charged with promoting community policing that oversees grant programs, including the funding of a number of regional community policing institutes throughout the country. OCOPS was implemented in 1994 with an $8.8 billion expenditure over an eight-year period to accelerate the hiring, education, and deployment of 100,000 police officers in major U.S. cities.

Office of Foreign Litigation A U.S. Department of Justice agency headquartered in Washington, DC, that represents the U.S. government before foreign tribunals in civil cases. It also represents the government in domestic cases where questions of international law are raised.

Office of Homeland Security *See* **Department of Homeland Security.**

Office of Justice Assistance, Research and Statistics (OJARS) A federal criminal-justice funding agency comprised of the National Institute of Justice, the Bureau of Justice Statistics, and the Law Enforcement Assistance Administration. Prior to 1979, it was known as the Law Enforcement Assistance Administration.

Office of Justice Programs (OJP) Created in 1984 to replace the Law Enforcement Assistance Administration, the OJP holds similar powers and duties. It administers grants designed to assist the criminal-justice systems. It is also the umbrella division in the Department of Justice that houses the National Institute of Justice, the Bureau of Justice Assistance, the Bureau of Justice Statistics, and the Office of Juvenile Justice and Delinquency Prevention.

Office of Juvenile Justice and Delinquency Prevention (OJJDP) Established by Congress under the Juvenile Justice and Delinquency Prevention Act of 1974, the OJJDP was designed to remove status offenders from the jurisdiction of juvenile courts and dispose of their cases less formally.

Office of National Drug Control Policy (ONDCP) A federal office located administratively within the Executive Office of the President charged with developing and overseeing the administration's antidrug policies. The office's emphasis of is to reduce drug use, manufacturing, and trafficking.

officer subculture The correctional officer subculture, consisting of norms and values expected of such officers.

official crime Criminal behavior that has been recorded by the police.

official criminal statistics Enumerations of crimes that come to the attention of law enforcement agencies; arrest compilations and characteristics of offenders and crimes based on arrest, judicial, and prison records.

official data In criminal justice, any data collected by law enforcement agencies, courts, and other governmental sources. The principal sources of official juvenile delinquency and crime data are the *Uniform Crime Reports* and the *National Crime Victimization Survey.*

official delinquency Delinquent acts that result in arrest by local police and that are reported to the FBI for inclusion in the *Uniform Crime Reports.*

official records In criminal justice, statistics and data collected by law enforcement agencies, courts, and correctional institutions.

Ohio experience A program for juvenile delinquents in various Ohio counties in which home confinement, electronic monitoring, and other forms of intensive supervised probation are used. The emphasis is on public safety, offender accountability, and offender rehabilitation.

Ohlin, Lloyd (1918–) A criminologist who collaborated with Richard Cloward to write *Delinquency and Opportunity* (1960), which described strain theory and opportunity theory. The authors posited that deviance, delinquency, and crime are precipitated whenever disadvantaged youths are deprived of or lack the legitimate means to achieve culturally approved or desired goals. They described criminal gangs, conflict gangs, and retreatist gangs.

Oklahoma City bombing The 1995 bombing of the Alfred P. Murrah federal office building, which resulted in 168 deaths. Timothy McVeigh and Terry L. Nichols were convicted of committing the crime, and McVeigh was executed in 2001.

Old Bailey A famous historical trial court in London.

older inmates Inmates age 50 or older, as defined by the National Institute of Corrections.

ombudsman *See* **National Ombudsman.**

omerta Oath of silence sworn by those who join the Mafia, an organized crime family.

omission The failure to do whatever the law prescribes or requires a person to do.

Omnibus Crime Control and Safe Streets Act of 1968 A piece of federal law-and-order legislation that was viewed by some as a political maneuver aimed at allaying fears of crime rather than bringing about criminal-justice reform.

"once an adult, always an adult" provision The ruling that once a juvenile has been transferred to criminal court to be prosecuted as an adult, regardless of the criminal-court outcome, the juvenile can never be subject to the jurisdiction of juvenile courts in the future. In short, the juvenile, once transferred, will always be treated as an adult if he or she commits future crimes, even if the youth is still not of adult age.

180 Degrees, Inc. A program operated by the Minnesota Department of Corrections, commencing in 1973 and comparable to a halfway house, for sex offense parolees with no previous treatment for their sex offenses, who are willing to admit that they have committed one or more sex offenses and who can function as group members in productive discussions about their sexual conduct.

on-the-job training Informal training of correctional officers or police officers, accomplished while they work, via daily interactions with older veteran officers.

"on the pad" An expression denoting a police officer who receives regular payoffs for ignoring vice-related cases.

open court Any court in which spectators may gather.

opening statement Remarks made by the prosecution and defense attorneys to the jury at the commencement of trial proceedings. These statements usually set forth what each side intends to show by the evidence to be presented.

open institutions Prisons without walls, such as correctional camps, ranches, and farms.

open-systems model A perspective on organizations that places high value on resource acquisition and growth through the use of flexible structures that can respond to opportunities.

operant conditioning theory A theory that explains behavior by reference to overt action and its conditioning by external stimuli, particularly the reinforcing or punishing consequences of one's actions.

operational capacity The total number of inmates that can be accommodated based on the size of a jail or prison facility's staff, programs, and other services.

operational or tactical intelligence A means of obtaining information about the current activity of an individual or group.

Operation Blockade An Immigration and Naturalization Service (INS) experiment launched with $250,000 in extra overtime funds and agents stationed in inland posts in El Paso, TX, to prevent the influx of illegal aliens into the United States. Presently, the blockade ranges from San Diego to South Texas. It uses military reconnaissance aircraft with infrared capabilities to conduct surveillance at night, as well as electronic sensors and other detection equipment, night-vision scopes, and high-tech communications equipment to detect illegal immigrants seeking entry into the United States.

Operation Borderline A 1988 sting operation of the U.S. Customs Bureau in which pedophiles were arrested when they ordered child pornography from a phony mail-order house.

Operation Brilab An FBI sting operation involving organized crime in Louisiana and Texas.

Operation Cease-Fire A project in Chicago designed to prevent and respond to incidents of gun violence that involved the Chicago Police Department and various community institutions.

Operation Chaos A special operations group of the Central Intelligence Agency whose purpose was to investigate foreign influence in protest activities within the United States.

Operation El Dorado A task force established in 1992, headquartered in New York City, and affiliated with the U.S. Department of the Treasury, designed to interdict drug-generated bulk cash transfers and money laundering.

Operation Greylord A Cook County, IL, FBI undercover operation in 1985 calculated to identify corruption in the Illinois judiciary. Many judges were caught accepting bribes in exchange for particular court decisions and case fixing. Nearly 30 persons, including six judges and 13 lawyers, were indicted.

Operation Guatemalan Auto Theft Enforcement (GATE) An undercover operation conducted in 1995 by interstate authorities to recover stolen vehicles. It operated between Texas, California, New Mexico, and Arizona.

Operation Identification A program sponsored by local police and other agencies to assist citizens in identifying their personal property if it is stolen. It also includes fingerprinting children for later identification if they are lost or kidnapped.

Operation Ill Wind An FBI operation focusing on Department of Defense contracts. DoD personnel collaborated with defense contractors to defraud the United States government of millions of dollars, which led to the conviction of Pentagon officials, contractors, and others.

Operation Intercept U.S.-Mexico border activity commenced in 1969 to stem the flow of illicit narcotics and other types of drug trafficking across the border. Tons of drugs were seized and a large quantity of money was recovered from activities of various federal agencies, including the DEA, Border Patrol, and INS.

Operation Mongoose An attempt by the Central Intelligence Agency to enlist organized criminals to assassinate Cuban Premier Fidel Castro.

Operation Polar Cap A 1989–1991 investigation by the FBI and other federal agencies to interdict drugs and drug money transported between Colombia and the United States. It led to seizures of large quantities of drugs and money from the Colombian Medellín cartel, whose illegal activity was a national operation extending from California to New York. Over $300 million was seized in a vast money-laundering scheme.

Operation Rescue An aggressive antiabortion group, founded by Randall Terry, that uses civil disobedience and passive resistance to alter or shut down abortion clinics and operations.

operations Any activity derived from planning and regulating the activities of a police force or other law enforcement agency; also, the communications center of a law enforcement agency or other criminal-justice organization.

Operation Underworld A World War II U.S. Navy program in which the Navy received assistance from organized crime figures to protect U.S. docks from espionage.

Operation UNIRAC An FBI sting operation investigating organized crime connected with longshoremen and shipping companies.

opiate Any drug capable of relieving pain and creating a psychological euphoria.

opinion The official announcement of a court's decision and the reasons for that decision; in research methods, the verbal expression of an attitude.

opinion evidence Witness testimony given that reflects the opinion of the giver rather than an actual fact or scientific conclusion. It may or may not be admissible in court, depending on the expertise of the witness.

opinion of the court An opinion summarizing the views of the majority of judges participating in a judicial decision; a ruling or holding by a court official.

opium A substance derived from the poppy plant used to manufacture heroin, a highly addictive narcotic.

Opium Wars Conflicts between the Chinese and Europeans from 1839 to 1842 over the ability to trade in opium.

opportunist robber One who steals small amounts whenever a vulnerable target presents itself.

opportunities provision A response to gangs that involves efforts to deal with gangs through employment, job training, and education.

opportunity theory The theory proposes that individuals of low socioeconomic status are more likely to engage in criminal acts because they have fewer legitimate opportunities.

Optimist In the Broderick Typology, a type of police officer who is people-oriented, management-aspiring, and a "yes" person. *See also* **Broderick Typology.**

O.R. On one's own recognizance. In bail decision making, persons released on O.R. are released under their own supervision and do not have to post bail.

Oraflex A drug marketed by the Eli Lilly Company in 1985 despite knowledge that it had deadly side effects.

oral argument A verbal presentation made to an appellate court by the prosecution or defense in order to persuade the court to affirm, reverse, or modify a lower-court decision.

oral evidence Testimony given in court that stems from verbal statements from an expert witness or an eyewitness. It is sometimes called parol evidence.

Orange County Peer Court A teen court established in Orange County, CA, that consists of high-school students who volunteer for different court positions, including prosecutors, defense counsel, and jurors. Its intent is to vest youths with responsibility and accountability in deciding through a jury process whether other youths charged with delinquency or status offenses are guilty or innocent. A judge presides, together with community volunteers.

ordeal by water A medieval torture process in which prisoners were strapped down on their backs and had a funnel forced into their mouths into which a steady stream of water was poured.

order Any written declaration or proclamation by a judge authorizing officials to act.

order maintenance The police function of preventing behavior that disturbs or threatens to disturb the public peace or that involves face-to-face conflict between two or more persons. In such situations, police exercise discretion in deciding whether a law has been broken.

order *nisi* Conditional order.

Order of Misericordia A group founded in Florence, Italy, in 1488 to provide assistance and consultation to offenders condemned to death.

order of recognizance or bail Any directive setting forth bail amount or simple release of persons on their own recognizance.

order to show cause A court directive that one side must give a reason why a request or motion from the other side should not be granted.

ordinance Any enactment of a local governing body such as a city council or commission.

ordinary care The degree of care exercised by a prudent person; reasonable treatment expected.

ordnance Any weapon, ammunition, explosives, or vehicles used in law enforcement or war.

Oregon boot A correctional device used to disable prisoners who work on chain gangs. It usually consists of metal anklets linked by a short chain to impede walking or running.

Oregon Coalition to Abolish the Death Penalty Headquartered in Portland, OR, this organization consists of interested persons who wish to abolish the death penalty. It disseminates information about the death penalty, wrongful convictions, and other relevant death-penalty information.

Oregon model A probation development project devised by the Edna McConnell Clark Foundation that uses risk scores for selecting clients, relying heavily on former drug abuse and violence as criteria which exclude offenders from participation. It attempts to select middle-range offenders, who are subject to "shock incarceration" for 30 days or more as part of the program. *See also* **shock probation.**

organic brain dysfunction Brain damage that can influence an individual's susceptibility to engage in criminal conduct.

organic disorders Mental disorders caused by damage to the central nervous system.

organic law General fundamental law or constitution.

organic solidarity A unity based on an independence of functions, much as in a complex biological organism. *See also* Weber, Max.

organizational approach A type of police discretion whereby police administrators provide officers with a list of priorities and explicitly clarify how police should handle encounters with citizens.

organizational behavior Any characteristic referring to a dimension or feature of an organization that personifies it, such as an aggressive organization or an efficient organization.

organizational change and development A response to gangs that involves organizational adaptations that facilitate the application of gang control strategies.

organizational chart A diagrammatic portrayal of the vertical and horizontal interrelatedness of all roles in an organization, from the highest level of administration to the lowest level and frontline employees. Each role is represented by a box, and interconnecting lines are drawn to show the superior-subordinate or horizontal relations between boxes (roles).

organizational climate Somewhat like personality for a person; the perceptions that people have of an organization that produce its image in their minds. Some organizations are bustling and efficient, whereas others are easygoing. Some are quite human, whereas others are hard and cold. Organizations change slowly, being influenced by their leaders and their environment.

organizational complexity Two types of complexity have been identified: horizontal and vertical. Horizontal complexity is the lateral differentiation of functions that in corporate organizations may be duplicated at all levels of authority. Vertical complexity refers to the extent to which there is differentiated depth or organizational penetration below the most inclusive level (e.g., an organization that includes three or four different levels—national, regional, state, local—is more vertically differentiated and complex than one that has no additional levels below the national).

organizational conflict The amount of friction between persons or departments within an organization; also, different departmental or personal goals that may be inconsistent with one another and in conflict.

organizational control Any variable that is central to the planning and coordinating of tasks within the overall division of labor of an organization. The initiation of directives to subordinate personnel and the formulation and implementation of policy decisions fall within the control realm.

organizational crime Crime that involves large corporations and their efforts to control the marketplace and earn huge profits through unlawful bidding, unfair advertising, monopolistic practices, and other illegal means.

organizational development An organizational change strategy that seeks to revitalize the culture of the organization by developing teamwork and sensitivity to workers' needs while improving organizational performance. It usually starts at the top of the organization and uses expert outside consultants to assist in the change process.

organizational deviance Any unusual conduct engaged in by employees of an organization on behalf of the organization.

organizational effectiveness The degree to which any organization is able to achieve its goals or objectives.

organizational flexibility The extent to which an organization can adapt to changes from within the internal environment and from the external environment; the adaptability of an organization to change.

organizational goals The ends which organizations strive to achieve; objectives and aims articulated by organizations in either written or unwritten form.

organizational growth The increase of the number of employees in an organization over a specified time period, such as one year or longer. The term may also refer to an expansion of the division of labor or additional levels in the hierarchy of authority.

organizational model Any explanation of what is occurring in an organization that focuses on specific features or characteristics of organizations as key explanatory factors.

organizational size The number of personnel on the organization payroll; the total number of full-fledged members in the association.

organizational smarts Inmates who enter prison with skills in interpersonal relations, managing bureaucracies, and common courtesy are said to have organizational smarts.

organizational structure Variables that tend to describe the arrangement of formalized positions or departments within an organization. They also describe the amount of differentiation and specialization within it. Three key variables pertaining to structure are (1) size, (2) complexity, and (3) formalization.

organizational typologies Ways of describing or labeling differences among organizations. Certain relationships among variables may be true within one type of organization but not necessarily within another. Typologies considered useful because they contribute to explanations of differences between organizations.

organizational unit of analysis, level of analysis A study of organizations in which the focus of a researcher's interest is the organization itself. The work group, interpersonal relations, and individuals within the organization are considered secondary to organizational factors, which include organization size, structure, complexity, effectiveness, and change.

organizational values Standards imparted by organizations to membership designed to instill in them work motivation and goals.

organized crime Those self-perpetuating, structured associations of individuals and groups combined for the purpose of profiting in whole or in part from by illegal means, while protecting their activities through a pattern of graft and corruption.

Organized Crime and Racketeering Section (OCR) A Kefauver Committee conclusion in 1951 that the Mafia existed as an organized crime family led to the founding of the OCR office at the U.S. Department of Justice, headquartered in Washington, DC. The OCR collects and disseminates information about organized crime in the United States and conducts intelligence operations related to drug trafficking, loan sharking, prostitution, gambling, corrupt labor practices, and illicit political practices with links to organized crime.

Organized Crime Control Act of 1970 Congressional action initiated by President Richard M. Nixon that broadened the law to fight organized crime. It made a special charge to the FBI to investigate bombing of federal property or any other enterprise receiving government assistance.

Organized Crime Drug Enforcement Task Force Program A joint federal, state, and local law enforcement initiative against high-level drug trafficking organizations.

organized crime syndicate A sophisticated self-perpetuating organized crime group.

organized deception of the public Crimes against ethics and trust involving persons in higher political offices.

organized offender A criminal offender whose crimes give evidence of a methodical, planned offense rather than a haphazard, spontaneous, or unplanned one.

organized robbery and gang theft Highly skilled criminal activities using or threatening to use force, violence, coercion, and property damage, and accompanied by planning, surprise, and speed to diminish the risks of apprehension.

organoleptic Identification or testing through the senses, such as touching, smelling, or tasting.

orientation process In corrections, the period during which inmates in prisons and jails are provided with information about what is expected of them and what they can anticipate from their institutional experience.

original jurisdiction First authority over a case or cause, as opposed to appellate jurisdiction.

orphanages Places, either public or private, in which parentless or wayward children can be placed and raised until they can be placed in homes for care and supervision.

orphan's court A probate court whose functions include guardianship matters involving minors, as well as estate administration.

orphan train A practice of the Children's Aid Society in which urban youths were sent West on trains for adoption by local farm couples (circa 1850s–1920s).

Orwellian A term derived from the name George Orwell, author of *1984* (1949), a novel that detailed the oppressive conditions in a society in which the government was able to monitor the activities of all of its citizens.

Osborn, Albert Sherman (1858–1946) A handwriting analyst whose testimony was influential in obtaining a conviction against Bruno Richard Hauptmann, who was convicted of kidnapping Charles Lindbergh's child in early 1930s. *See also* **Hauptmann, Bruno Richard.**

Osgood, D. Wayne He proposed latent trait theory, together with David Rowe and W. Alan Nicewander.

ostracism Punishment within a local group or community consisting of shunning a rule violator socially. Sex offenders are often ostracized by their communities when they attempt to relocate for purposes of rehabilitation and reintegration.

O.T.B., OTB (Off-Track Betting) Private persons or organizations that accept bets on horse racing or sporting events. Depending on the jurisdiction, it may or may not be legal.

other crimes A reference to crimes that may or may not have been committed by the person presently charged with a crime, and that do not have any relation to present crimes charged. Certain crimes may be mentioned in court to show a pattern of crimes allegedly committed by the accused.

other-report study A form of criminological research in which an investigator asks subjects about the criminal or deviant behavior of others.

outcomes and opportunities The results of a particular lifestyle adapted by a person. Low-risk lifestyles lead to different outcomes and opportunities than high-risk lifestyles.

out custody The second-lowest level of custody assigned to an inmate, requiring the second-lowest level of security and staff supervision. Inmates may be assigned to less secure housing and be eligible for work details outside of the institution.

outlaw motorcycle gang (OMG) Any group of motorcycle enthusiasts who have voluntarily made a commitment to band together and abide by their organization's rigorous rules enforced by violence, who engage in activities that bring them and their club into serious conflict with society and the law. OMGs are involved in many types of illegal activities, including drug trafficking, money laundering, murder, fraud, theft, prostitution, telemarketing, and trafficking in illegal weapons and contraband.

outlawry In old Anglo-Saxon law, the process by which a criminal was declared an outlaw and placed outside the protection and aid of the law.

outreach centers Substations or satellite offices of regular probation and parole agencies.

outside cell blocks Cells, which may be several tiers high, that line the outside wall of each unit with doors that open into a central corridor.

outsiders A term used by Howard Becker to describe those who, on being labeled by society and denied the legitimate means to carry on their lives, turn to illegitimate activities, including crime.

Outward Bound Wilderness programs for juvenile offenders and other youths. The programs' intent is to teach survival skills, coping skills, self-respect, self-esteem, and respect for others and authority.

overbreadth doctrine A First Amendment doctrine holding that a law is invalid if it can be applied to punish people for engaging in constitutionally protected expression, such as speech or religious rituals. *See also* **Bill of Rights.**

overcharging Filing charges against a defendant that are more serious than the prosecutor believes are justified by the evidence and charging more or more serious counts than those on which the prosecutor wants a conviction; in plea bargaining, the ritual of trading away the "loaded on" charges in return for a guilty plea to a higher charge than might otherwise occur.

overclassification The practice of assigning prisoners or juveniles to higher levels of custody than they deserve (e.g., placing someone in maximum-security custody when he or she could be placed in less expensive minimum-security custody instead).

overcriminalization The use of criminal sanctions to deter behavior that is acceptable to substantial portions of society.

overcrowding The condition that exists when numbers of prisoners exceed the space allocations for which a jail or prison is designed. The condition is often associated with double-bunking.

overdose An amount of a drug that exceeds the recommended or safe dosage.

overkill The practice of continuing to shoot, stab, or bludgeon someone after death has obviously occurred.

override An action by an authority in an institution or agency that overrules a score or assessment made of a client or inmate. Raw scores or assessments or recommendations can be overruled. The function of an override is to upgrade or downgrade the seriousness of an offense status, thus changing the level of custody at which an inmate is maintained in secure confinement. An override may also affect the type and nature of community programming for a particular offender.

overrule To reverse or annul by subsequent action (e.g., judges may overrule objections from prosecutors and defense attorneys in court, nullifying these objections; lower court decisions may be overruled by higher courts when a case is appealed).

overt act Any action undertaken by a criminal suspect that may further a crime's commission (e.g., mere planning of a bank robbery to further its occurrence without actually carrying out the robbery would be considered an overt act).

Overtown riot A civil disturbance in the Overtown area of Miami, FL, as a result of police officer William Lozano shooting Clement Anthony Lloyd, who was driving towards him on a motorcycle. The motorcycle crashed, killing Lloyd and Allan Blanchard, his passenger. The subsequent riots lasted four days. Lozano was subsequently convicted of manslaughter in 1991, but a new trial led to his acquittal in 1993.

overt pathway The developmental path taken to delinquency that begins with violent outbursts and bullying.

"oyez" "Hear ye" (Middle English); a phrase used to begin court sessions.

P

PACT (Prisoner and Community Together) *See* **alternative dispute resolution; Victim/Offender Reconciliation Project (VORP).**

paedophilia *See* **pedophilia.**

pains of imprisonment The deprivations associated with imprisonment, including loss of freedom, autonomy, goods and services, security, and heterosexual relationships.

Palestine Liberation Organization (PLO) A group of Palestinian nationalists, headed by Yasir Arafat, dedicated to the liberation of Palestine. Founded in 1964, the group ceded its negotiation and administrative roles to the Palestinian Authority (PA) after the 1993 concord between the PLO and Israel, but still exists as an umbrella organization.

panacea A quick fix; a cure-all. In juvenile delinquency prevention, these types of programs are often short-term, not individualized, and offer nothing in the way of follow-up or aftercare services.

pandering Procuring another person for the purpose of prostitution.

panel A set of jurors or prospective jurors; a set of judges assigned to hear a case; in research, a design in survey research that offers a close approximation of the before-after condition of experimental designs by interviewing the same group at two or more points in time.

panhandle, panhandler To beg for money in a public place. One who begs for money in public.

panopticon, panoptican plan A prison, whose design is credited to Jeremy Bentham, in which multitiered cells are built around a hub so that correctional personnel can view all inmates at the same time.

pansexual One who engages in diverse sexual relations.

"paper-hanging" A slang term for someone who knowingly writes bad checks or forges checks.

paper trail The chain of documents that links an offender to an offense, especially in financial crimes such as embezzlement.

paradigm A set of assumptions, propositions, and concepts in research that suggest a model for viewing an organization or particular action.

paraffin test A technique in which a person's hands or clothing are coated with melted paraffin. When the paraffin hardens it is removed, and the inside surface is coated with diphenylamine solution. If nitrates are present, they indicate that the person has recently fired a weapon. The test discloses gun powder residue on a person or clothing and may serve to implicate that person in a crime.

paralegal A person with some legal training who assists attorneys with their business. A paralegal may look up legal cases, brief cases, and conduct interviews and interrogatories.

parameter In statistics, a characteristic or an attribute of a population of elements, such as the population average age; any measurable quantity whose magnitude may vary.

paramilitary Describing a group organized along the lines of a military unit. The term is often used in the field of terrorism and counterterrorism.

paramilitary model A structure followed by the Texas Syndicate and other prison gangs. Its organizational structure is hierarchical, and when a leader leaves, a new leader is chosen by vote.

paranoia Psychotic behavior wherein a person (1) has delusions of grandeur and (2) is fearful of others and feels persecuted.

paraphilias Bizarre or abnormal sexual practices that may involve recurrent sexual urges focused on objects, humiliation, or children.

paraprofessional One who works in a community agency or public organization; one who has some skills relating to corrections, but is not certified or has not completed any formal course of study culminating in a corrections certificate or degree.

Parchman Farm A Mississippi prison farm known for its racists and inhuman conditions. It changed in the 1960s in response to court orders.

pardon The unconditional release of an inmate, usually by the governor or chief executive officer of a jurisdiction.

Pardon Attorney A federal office headquartered in Chevy Chase, MD, that hears appeals for executive clemency. Recommendations for clemency are prepared for sentence reductions, full pardons, or commutations.

parens patriae "Parent of the country" (Latin); a phrase referring to the doctrine that the state oversees the welfare of youth. The concept was originally established by the King of England and administered through chancellors.

parent abuse Intentional battery or other physical abuse of a parent by a child.

parental banishment The act of parents prohibiting their children from coming back to their homes after being unmanageable, incorrigible, or running away.

parental liability The idea that parents are held responsible to varying degrees for their children's conduct.

parenteral Introducing a substance into the human body other than by means of ingestion, including by needle, bite, cut, or abrasion.

parenticide Killing of one's parents.

parenting programs In prison settings, these programs improve parenting skills through a series of educational activities that may include special events involving inmates and their children.

Parents of Murdered Children (POMC) A national organization headquartered in Cincinnati, OH, dedicated to providing emotional support for those who have lost loved ones to homicide.

parity In corrections, equality in programming and distribution of resources between female and male inmates.

parity pay Identical pay for the same job and job classification, regardless of one's gender, race, socioeconomic status, or ethnicity.

Park, Robert Ezra (1864–1944) Park assisted in developing the "Chicago School," in which theorists focused on the functions of social institutions and their breakdown. They closely associated crime with particular neighborhoods and neighborhood conditions. Some neighborhoods form "natural areas" of affluence or poverty. Further, different types of crime can be associated with different types of neighborhoods. Chicago School researchers examined "concentric zones" adjacent to Chicago and its suburban communities. They considered areas of urban renewal as "interstitial areas," or zones of transitions. The concentric-zone hypothesis, a defining feature of the Chicago School, noted that different neighborhood zones emanating away from the "Loop," or downtown Chicago, exhibited different characteristics as well as different forms of criminal behavior. Park collaborated with Edwin Sutherland, Louis Wirth, and Ernest W. Burgess.

Parker, Isaac C. (1838–1896) A notorious Fort Smith, AR, judge who sentenced persons convicted of various crimes to be hanged. He was noted for mass hangings, in which more than one person was hung at once at a public execution.

Parker, William H. (1902–1966) A Los Angeles, CA, law enforcement officer who became chief of police of the Los Angeles Police Department (LAPD) in 1950. Parker was born in Lead, SD, and came to California in 1930. He participated in World War II and reorganized postwar police forces in Europe. Parker was known for strict discipline over police officers during his administration. LAPD headquarters was renamed Parker Center in his memory.

Parker syndrome A depiction of police officers who believe they must defend a thin blue line and who tend to have antisociety attitudes. Named for William H. Parker, former chief of the LAPD.

Park Police U.S. Department of the Interior–sponsored law enforcement officers, assigned to Washington, DC, and all national park service areas, vested with arrest powers.

Park Rangers Persons in the National Park Service who are charged with protecting plant and animal life. They are vested with police powers to enforce federal laws and regulate park visitor conduct, and are headquartered in Washington, DC.

parole Prerelease from prison short of serving a full sentence; the status of an offender conditionally released from a confinement facility prior to the expiration of the sentence and placed under the supervision of a parole agency.

parole agency Any corrections panel or agency that may or may not include parole boards. Its primary functions are prerelease investigations, parole-plan preparation, and supervision of adults or juveniles on parole status.

parole board, paroling authority A body of persons, either appointed by governors or others or elected, that determines whether those currently incarcerated in prisons should be granted parole or early release.

parole clinic Any facility that furnishes parolees with therapy and other health services when such services are required as a part of their parole programs.

parole contract An agreement between a parolee and the parole board outlining what parole program conditions are to be obeyed. Failure to obey these conditions may subject the offender to reincarceration or revocation of parole, which may mean a change in parole conditions or requirements, such as a change from standard parole to intensive supervised parole. *See box.*

parole d'honneur "Word of honor" (French); term from which the English word "parole" is derived.

parolee A convicted offender who has been released from prison short of serving the full sentence originally imposed, and who usually must abide by conditions established by the parole board or paroling authority. *See table p. 184.*

parole eligibility date The earliest date on which an inmate might be paroled.

parole guidelines Protocol to be followed in making parole release decisions. Most guidelines prescribe a presumptive term for each class of convicted inmate depending on both offense and offender characteristics.

parole officer A correctional official who supervises parolees.

Ohio Parole Contract

In consideration of having been granted supervision on December 1, 2001, I agree to report to my probation/parole officer within 48 hours or according to the written instructions I have received and to the following conditions:

1. I will obey federal, state, and local laws and ordinances, and all rules and regulations of the Fifth Common Pleas Court or the Department of Rehabilitation and Correction.

2. I will always keep my probation/parole officer informed of my residence and place of employment. I will obtain permission from my probation/parole officer before changing my residence or my employment.

3. I will not leave the state without written permission of the Adult Parole Authority.

4. I will not enter upon the grounds of any correctional facility nor attempt to visit any prisoner without the written permission of my probation/parole officer nor will I communicate with any prisoner without first informing my probation/parole officer of the reason for such communication.

5. I will comply with all orders given to me by my probation/parole officer or other authorized representative of the court, the Department of Rehabilitation and Correction or the Adult Parole Authority, including any written instructions issued at any time during the period of supervision.

6. I will not purchase, possess, own, use, or have under my control, any firearms, deadly weapons, ammunition, or dangerous ordnance.

7. I will not possess, use, purchase, or have under my control any narcotic drug or other controlled substance, including any instrument, device, or other object used to administer drugs or to prepare them for administration, unless it is lawfully prescribed for me by a licensed physician. I agree to inform my probation/parole officer promptly of any such prescription and I agree to submit to drug testing if required by the Adult Parole Authority.

8. I will report any arrest, citation of a violation of the law, conviction or any other contact with a law enforcement officer to my probation/parole officer no later than the next business day, and I will not enter into any agreement or other arrangement with any law enforcement agency which might place me in the position of violating any law or condition of my supervision unless I have obtained permission in writing from the Adult Parole Authority, or from the court if I am a probationer.

9. I agree to a search without warrant of my person, my motor vehicle, or my place of residence by a probation/parole officer at any time.

10. I agree to sign a release of confidential information from any public or private agency if requested to do so by a probation/parole officer.

11. I agree and understand that if I am arrested in any other state or territory of the United States or in any foreign country, my signature as witnessed at the end of the page will be deemed to be a waiver of extradition and that no other formalities will be required for authorized agents of the State of Ohio to bring about my return to this state for revocation proceedings.

12. I also agree to the following Special Conditions as imposed by the court or the Adult Parole Authority:

I have read or had read to me, the foregoing conditions of my parole. I fully understand these conditions, I agree to comply with them, and I understand that violation of any of these conditions may result in the revocation of my parole. In addition, I understand that I will be subject to the foregoing conditions until I have received a certificate from the Adult Parole Authority or a Journal Entry from the Court if I am a probationer, stating that I have been discharged from supervision.

The parolee signs this form and a witness also signs.

Source: Adapted from the Ohio Parole Board, *Ohio Parole Program and Requirements.*

parole prediction An estimate of the probability of violation or nonviolation of parole on the basis of experience tables, developed with regard to groups of offenders with similar characteristics.

parole program The specific conditions under which inmates are granted early release.

parole revocation A two-stage proceeding that may result in a parolee's reincarceration in jail or prison. The first stage is a preliminary hearing to determine whether the parolee violated any specific parole condition. The second stage determines whether parole should be canceled and the offender reincarcerated.

parole revocation hearing A formal proceeding in which a parole board decides whether a parolee's parole program should be terminated or changed because of one or more program infractions.

parole rules The conditions upon which an inmate is granted early release. These may require inmates to report regularly to parole officers, to refrain from criminal conduct, to avoid contact with other convicted offenders, to maintain and support their families, to abstain from alcoholic beverages and drugs, or to remain within the jurisdiction. Violating any one or more of these rules may result in parole revocation. *See box p. 183.*

parole supervision Guidance, treatment, or regulation of the behavior of a convicted adult who is obliged to fulfill conditions of parole or conditional release. Parole supervision is authorized and required by statute and performed by a parole agency, and it occurs after a period of prison confinement.

parole supervisory caseload The total number of clients a parole agency or officer has on a given date or during a specified time period.

parole suspended Withdrawal of one's parole status, usually accompanied by a change in one's parole conditions or reincarceration.

parol evidence Any information given orally in court; orally presented information.

parole violation A parolee's act against or failure to act in relation to the conditions of his or her parole program.

parole violator A parolee who has not complied with one or more terms of his or her parole program.

paroling authority An administrative body, such as a parole board, empowered to decide whether inmates shall be conditionally released from prison before the completion of their entire sentences, to revoke parole, and to discharge from parole those who have satisfactorily completed their terms.

parricide Murder of one's guardian, mother, or father.

parsimonious Explaining a broad range of phenomena with only a few principles.

partial confinement An alternative to traditional jail sentences consisting of "weekend" sentences that permit offenders to spend the workweek in the community or in school. *See also* **work (and educational) release, work/study release; furlough, furlough program.**

partial deterrent A legal measure designed to restrict or control, rather than to eliminate, an undesirable act.

Characteristics of Adults on Parole, 1995, 2000, and 2002

Characteristics of adults on parole, 1995, 2000, and 2002

Characteristic	1995	2000	2002
Total	100%	100%	100%
Gender			
Male	90%	88%	86%
Female	10	12	14
Race			
White	34%	38%	39%
Black	45	40	42
Hispanic	21	21	18
American Indian/ Alaska Native	1	1	1
Asian/Pacific Islander[a]	--	--	--
Status of supervision			
Active	78%	83%	82%
Inactive	11	4	4
Absconded	6	7	8
Supervised out of State	4	5	5
Other	--	1	2
Sentence length			
Less than 1 year	6%	3%	4%
1 year or more	94	97	96
Type of offense			
Violent	**	**	24%
Property	**	**	26
Drug	**	**	40
Other	**	**	10
Adults entering parole			
Discretionary parole	50%	37%	39%
Mandatory parole	45	54	52
Reinstatement	4	6	7
Other	2	2	2
Adults leaving parole			
Successful completion	45%	43%	45%
Returned to incarceration	41	42	41
With new sentence	12	11	11
Other	29	31	30
Absconder[b]	**	9	9
Other unsuccessful[b]	**	2	2
Transferred	2	1	1
Death	1	1	1
Other	10	2	1

Note: For every characteristic there were persons of unknown status or type. Detail may not sum to total because of rounding.
**Not available.
--Less than 0.5%.
[a]Includes Native Hawaiians.
[b]In 1995 absconder and "other unsuccessful" statuses were reported among "other."

Source: Glaze, *Probation and Parole in the United States, 2002,* 6.

---

participant observation A research methodology in which the researcher interacts with those studied; collecting information through involvement in the social life of a group the researcher is studying.

participating style A leadership mode devised by Hershey and Blanchard (1977) in which supervisors are task-oriented and tell subordinates what to do and a collaborative relation between subordinates and supervisors exists. Subordinates are given emotional consideration and are involved in decision making through feedback solicited by supervisors.

participation hypothesis, participative organizational model The idea that the more subordinates participate in making decisions that affect their work, the more they will like their work and comply with orders from superiors.

participative leadership, participative management A mode of leadership which stresses involvement of subordinates in decisions affecting their work. Supervisors solicit input from subordinates in the decision-making process, with the anticipated result of greater work satisfaction and commitment to organizational goals. The theory of organizations in which employees have some input or "say" regarding departmental operations.

particularity The requirement that a search warrant must state precisely where the search is to take place and what items are to be seized.

parties to offenses All people associated with the crime, either before or after it was committed, whether they actually committed the crime or assisted in some way in its planning. Such parties may include those who assist criminals in eluding capture.

partisan election An election in which candidates endorsed by political parties are presented to the voters for selection.

Part I offenses Crimes designated by the FBI as "most serious" and compiled in terms of the number of reports made by law enforcement agencies and the number of arrests reported. This category includes homicide, robbery, forcible rape, aggravated assault, burglary, motor-vehicle theft, arson, and larceny. *See also table p. 258.*

Part II offenses Crimes designated by the FBI as "less serious" and compiled in terms of the number of reports made to law enforcement agencies and the number of arrests made. This category includes simple assault, fraud, embezzlement, disorderly conduct, vagrancy, runaways, curfew and loitering violations, suspicion, drunkenness, liquor law violations, drug abuse violations, gambling, prostitution, and several other offenses.

party A person who is associated with one side of a legal issue; a person who assists or joins with another in a contractual agreement.

party-dominated process An adversarial system wherein a judge assumes a passive role in deciding a case. The opposing parties litigate factual issues and determine the legal boundaries of the case.

passing bad checks Issuance of checks when the issuer knows there are insufficient funds to cover.

passive intrusion sensor A passive sensor in an intrusion alarm system that detects an intruder within the range of the sensor.

passive alcohol sensor An alcohol-detection device used by Japanese police and others in drunk-driving investigations to detect the presence of alcohol in exhaled breath. Officers wave a wand in the car, and the presence of alcohol causes it to change color.

passive speech A form of expression protected by the First Amendment but not associated with actually speaking words. Examples include wearing symbols or protest messages on buttons or signs. *See also* **Bill of Rights.**

pastoral counseling A field promoting professionalism in religious counseling in hospitals, the military, or prisons that includes courses of study to advance one's expertise as counselor in giving aid and assistance psychologically and socially to those in need of such assistance.

pat-down search A frisk involving a law enforcement officer moving his or her hands along the outside of a suspect's clothing with the intent of determining whether the person is carrying a dangerous weapon.

patent A property right vested in an inventor of a new product. It vests the owner of the patent with the exclusive right to distribute and profit from the invented product.

paternalism Male domination (e.g., a paternalistic family is one in which the father is the dominant authority figure); in a broader sense, paternalism involves actions or attitudes intended for the betterment of others, even though attended by a patronizing belief in the moral superiority of the actor. Paternalistic actions have at least some anchor in the welfare of the person the action is done for (or to).

paternalism hypothesis *See* **chivalry hypothesis.**

paternalistic family A family style wherein the father is the final authority on all family matters and exercises complete control over his wife and children.

path analysis A statistical technique of identifying key variables that bring about a given result. Coefficients are determined to represent associations between causal variables in a pattern, showing influence or independent variables on a dependent variable (e.g., path analysis is used to show which variables exert the greatest impact on an officer's decision to make an arrest, for example, to show how police discretion is affected in a domestic violence situation).

path-goal theory A leadership view holding that there are goals sought by the organization and paths designated that are directly influenced by administrators; thus, administrators can influence goal attainment in specific ways by exercising different styles of leadership over subordinates.

pathogenic Causing a disease.

pathologist An expert trained in pathology, which involves the study of the etiology and development of a disease.

pathology The science of diseases.

PATHS Program (Promoting Alternative Thinking Strategies) A program intended to promote emotional and social competencies and to reduce aggression and related emotional and behavioral problems among elementary-school children.

pathways, pathways to crime A part of life-course theory suggesting that more than one road leads to criminal conduct. The "authority-conflict pathway" proposes that criminal conduct begins in one's early years with parental defiance and stubborn behavior. The "covert pathway" proposes that crime begins with minor offending and status offending. The "overt pathway" proposes that various acts escalate from less to more serious, and eventually to criminal violence. Pathway theory was suggested by Rolf Loeber (1993).

patriarchy A male-dominated system. *See also* **paternalism.**

patricide The killing of one's father.

PATRIOT Act, USA PATRIOT Act Officially, the Uniting and Strengthening America by Providing Appropriate Tools Required to Intercept and Obstruct Terrorism Act of 2001; enacted by Congress in October 2001, this act provides expanded law enforcement authority to enhance the federal government's efforts to detect and deter acts of terrorism in the United States or against U.S. interests abroad. The act was prompted by the September 11, 2001, terrorist acts on the World Trade Center towers in New York City and the Pentagon, in which airplanes were used as destructive weapons to kill innocent civilians. The act also vests the inspector general in the U.S. Department of Justice (DOJ) to undertake various actions related to claims of civil rights or civil liberties violations allegedly committed by DOJ employees. The act also requires semiannual reports to Congress on the implementation of the inspector general's responsibilities under the act. A person commits the crime of domestic terrorism if within the United States he or she engages in activity that involves acts dangerous to human life that violate the laws of the United States or any state and appear to be intended to (1) intimidate or coerce a civilian population, (2) influence the policy of a government by intimidation or coercion, and (3) affect the conduct of a government by mass destruction, assassination, or kidnapping.

patrol A means of deploying police officers in ways that give them responsibility for policing activity in defined areas and that usually requires them to make regular circuits of those areas.

patrol beat A geographical area to which police officers are assigned on a regular basis.

patrol car Police car; an automobile equipped with special devices, including lights, siren, communications gear, special bumpers, and radar.

patrol car video cameras Videotape units in police vehicles used for various purposes (e.g., to tape arrests of suspected drunk drivers, to illustrate causes for stops and arrests of motorists for various charges).

patrol district A geographical area usually including a police or sheriff's station in which more than one patrol car is assigned.

patrol officer A police officer whose duties include peacekeeping, service, and law enforcement in a particular area of a jurisdiction, and who may cover the jurisdiction by foot, car, air, or by another method.

patrol wagon A police van capable of holding several arrestees.

patronage, political A promise of jobs by a political official to to those who support his or her candidacy and election.

patterns of crime A research strategy that involves the use of data to determine where crime is committed, who commits

crime, who is victimized, and the major dimensions of the criminal act.

pauper One without money or means to support him- or herself.

payola A bribe offered in exchange for a favor by a politician or other official.

PCP *See* **phencyclidine (PCP).**

peace bond A fixed bail amount as determined by a magistrate to ensure that someone will appear later in court for trial.

peaceful picketing The protected right of citizens to picket as approved by Congress in 1935. Congress also prohibited persons from being employed by organizations in which their purpose would be to interfere with or break up peaceful picketers.

peacekeeping, peacekeeping role The function of police involving keeping order within communities and seeing that societies operate in a smooth and conventional fashion; also, overseas policing of countries in transition, such as Kosovo and Cambodia.

peacemaker One who asserts that peace and humanism can reduce crime and offers a new approach to crime control through mediation; also a gun, the Colt .45 Peacemaker.

peacemaking criminology The view that the main purpose of criminology is to promote a peaceful and just society; an attempt to find humanistic solutions to social problems and crime rather than punishment and imprisonment.

peace officer Any law enforcement officer at the state or local level, such as a sheriff or deputy, constable, or a member of a city police force, whose primary responsibility is to enforce and preserve the public peace.

Peace Officers' Memorial Day A day of national observance established in 1962; May 15th of each year, during Police Week.

Peace Officer Standards and Training (POST) A commission established to administer training programs for prospective law enforcement officers nationwide, which include mandatory training requirements for hiring police officers and those entering other aspects of law enforcement.

peculate To embezzle.

pecuniary value Monetary value.

pederasty Anal intercourse, usually between a man and a boy.

pedestrian Any person who travels on foot, or a physically handicapped person who travels about in a wheelchair or a self-propelled conveyance.

pedomania Pedophilia.

pedophile A molester of children.

pedophilia An unnatural fondness for children, particularly for sexual intercourse.

Peel, Sir Robert (1788–1850) British Home Secretary in 1829, Peel founded the Metropolitan Police of London, one of the first organized police forces in the world.

peeling A method used by burglars of safes in which safes are opened by peeling off the safe facing to access the locking device.

Peeping Tom One who looks in windows of others for the purpose of sexual gratification. *See also* **voyeurism.**

peer An "equal." A trial by a jury of one's peers is, theoretically, a trial composed of persons with characteristics similar to the defendant.

peer counseling program A plan utilized by some police departments in which certain police officers are used to counsel others. They are intended to be nonthreatening and to help officers overcome their problems.

peer tutors In prison, inmates, usually with a GED or high school diploma, who tutor other inmates with lower academic skills.

penal Of or pertaining to punishment.

penal administration Management of prisons or jails.

Penal Code of 1907 In Japan, a code of law that initially defined a broad range of crimes and punishments Although there is no formal distinction between felonies and misdemeanors such as that made in the United States, the Japanese Penal Code defines traditional crimes, including homicide, rape, burglary, robbery, and vehicular theft. The age of criminal responsibility was set at 14, although persons age 20 or over are considered adults. Those between the ages of 14 and 19 are usually treated as juveniles in independent juvenile proceedings.

penal codes, penal laws Any statutes pertaining to crimes and prescribed punishments.

penal colony A separate tract of land, often an island or other remote location, where convicts are placed.

penal institution A prison.

penal philosophy An ideology relating to the punishment and treatment of offenders.

penal reform Organized efforts to lessen the severity or inhumanity of criminal sanctions, especially imprisonment.

penal sanction Any legal consequence stemming from a criminal conviction, especially one involving incarceration or control.

penal servitude, penal slavery The condition of being put to work at hard labor under conditions of confinement.

penalty A punishment prescribed by law or judicial decision for the commission of a particular offense, which may be death, imprisonment, fine, or loss of civil privileges.

Pendleton Act An 1883 act that set forth a merit system for promotions and other types of advancements for public officials.

penetration A sexual act involving insertion of the penis into a woman's vagina or other orifice; an element of the crime of rape.

Penile Plethysmograph A device sometimes used in the behavior modification of sex offenders that measures penile erection.

penis envy According to Sigmund Freud, women are envious of the male sex organ and unconsciously wish that they were men.

penitentiary A term used interchangeably with "prison" to refer to long-term facilities in which high custody levels are observed, including solitary confinement or single-cell occupancy, in which prisoners are segregated from one another during evening hours.

Penitentiary Act of 1779 Legislation passed by England's House of Commons in 1779 that authorized the creation of new facilities to house prisoners, where they could be productive. Prisoners would be well-fed, well-treated, well-clothed, housed in safe and sanitary units, and trained to perform skilled tasks.

penitentiary movement A movement which focused political and social attention on debates about the most effective penitentiary design. During this time (1790–1830), the first major prisons were built in the eastern United States.

penitentiary science The scientific study of penal institutions.

Penn, William (1644–1718) A Quaker, penal reformer, and founder of Pennsylvania who established the "Great Law of Pennsylvania" and abolished corporal punishments in favor of fines and incarceration, using jails to confine offenders.

Pennsylvania school of criminology A tradition of criminological research originating at the University of Pennsylvania. Its most influential exponents were Thorsten Sellin and Marvin Wolfgang.

Pennsylvania System A system devised and used in the Walnut Street Jail in 1790 to place prisoners in solitary confinement. It was a predecessor to modern prisons that used solitude to increase penitence and prevent cross-infection of prisoners. The system encouraged behavioral improvements.

penologist A social scientist who studies and applies the theory and methods of punishment for crime.

penology A branch of criminology dealing with the management of prisons and inmate treatment.

pen register A dialed number recorder; a manual system of recording numbers dialed from a particular telephone.

Pentagon Papers case A collection of classified documents showing U.S. involvement in the Vietnam War was published in June 1971 in the *New York Times* and the *Washington Post*. They led to the espionage trial of Dr. Daniel Ellsberg, but the case was dismissed following the disclosure that White House officers had burglarized Ellsberg's private files to obtain evidence against him.

penumbral right A constitutional right not especially articulated, although guaranteed by implication through other rights.

peonage Enforced servitude; imposed labor to repay a debt or obligation, in which laborers perform work against their will.

People for the Ethical Treatment of Animals (PETA) An organization founded in 1980 and headquartered in Virginia to protect the rights of all animals. Its principle is that animals are not ours to eat, wear, experiment on, or use for entertainment. PETA claims to have 800,000 members worldwide, and is the largest animal rights organization in the world. Some members of PETA have been linked with terrorist-like attacks on laboratories and other facilities where animals are used in experiments, or with the intimidation of persons who manufacture various articles of clothing from animals. PETA conducted an early undercover investigation of a Maryland laboratory that resulted in the conviction of an animal experimenter on charges of animal abuse, convinced the fast-food giant Burger King to improve conditions for millions of animals on factory farms, and produces educational tapes, documents, and other materials for distribution to schools, corporations, and interested persons.

People Nation, People Nation set A multiracial 25,000-member alliance formed largely from several Chicago-based street gangs that came into existence during the 1950s and 1960s. People Nation is comprised of a number of smaller gangs and was established largely in prisons for mutual protection against rival gangs. Its enemies are members of the Folk Nation set. People Nation members identify themselves with a five-pointed star or crown, whereas the Folk Nation uses a six-pointed star. Gang activities consist of illegal drug trafficking, which has led to the incarceration of numerous gang members. A large Los Angeles–based street gang, the Bloods, are affiliated with People Nation set, whereas their rival gang, the Crips, identify with the Folk Nation set. Major People Nation gangs include the Latin Kings, Vice Lords, Spanish Lords, El Rukus, Bishops, Gaylords, Latin Counts, and Kents.

Pepinsky, Harold (Hal) (1945–) An advocate of peacemaking as the primary function of criminology. Pepinsky proposes that establishing social justice would eliminate all forms of predatory behavior.

pepper spray An aerosol containing capsicum oleoresin, the essence of chili peppers, which is designed to temporarily blind or disable without permanent damage. It can be used in mob control or self-defense.

per annum "By the year" (Latin).

per capita "By the head" (Latin); by person; for each person.

percentage bail A publicly managed bail service arrangement that allows defendants to deposit a percentage (about 10 percent) of the amount of bail with the court clerk.

perceptual research A line of research that asks subjects their beliefs about how likely they would be to get caught and punished if they broke specific laws and then whether they would commit the crime anyway.

per curiam "By the court" (Latin); a phrase used to distinguish an opinion rendered by the whole court as opposed to one expressed by a single judge.

per diem "By the day" (Latin); the cost per day, here the daily cost of housing inmates, which may include daily rates of meals and hotels for researchers and other professionals permitted by various states and the federal government.

peremptory challenge The rejection of a juror by either the prosecution or the defense in which no reason needs to be provided for excusing the juror from jury duty. Each side has a limited number of these challenges. The more serious the offense, the more peremptory challenges are given each side.

perfidious Untrustworthy; false; disloyal.

perfidity Faithlessness; treachery.

perimeter security Structures and processes consisting of secure walls, protected windows, and controlled access to points of entrance and exit from prisons or jails.

perimeter security officers Those correctional officers assigned to security towers, wall posts, and perimeter patrols.

peripheral members Gang members who are generally paranoid about their position in the gang. They are very careful not to say or do the wrong thing.

perjury Lying under oath in court.

"perks," perquisites Anything of value deriving from one's position, such as an expense account, company car, and other amenities associated with one's job.

permanent circuit An alarm circuit that is hardwired and capable of transmitting an alarm signal whether the alarm signal is in access mode or secure mode. Permanent circuits are used in tamper switches, foiled fixed windows, and supervisory lines.

permanent protection A system of alarm devices such as burglar alarm pads connected in a permanent circuit so as to provide protection whether the control unit is in access or secure mode.

permit An official document or paper identifying a person as having authority to exercise a privilege under the law.

"perp," perpetrator One who commits or attempts to commit a crime.

"perp walk" The practice of parading arrestees, usually those of prominent social status or those accused of heinous crimes, before the public news media for photographs. This practice has been criticized by some persons as a form of shaming and violating the presumption of innocence, which is an integral part of one's due-process rights.

Perry Preschool Program A Michigan-based program that provides high-level early childhood education to disadvantaged children in order to improve their later school life and performance.

per se "By itself" (Latin); in itself (e.g., the death penalty is not unconstitutional *per se*, but a particular method of administering the death penalty may be unconstitutional in some states).

per se **attorney laws** Laws that require a juvenile to have an attorney present during interrogation or other critical police proceedings.

per se **test** Any test required by a court in all circumstances regardless of the facts of the case.

persistence The process by which juvenile offenders continue in their delinquent careers rather than aging out of crime.

persistent felony offender A habitual offenders who commits felonies with a high recidivism rate.

persister A criminals who does not age out of crime; a chronic delinquent who continues offending into adulthood. *See also* **recidivism.**

person A human being considered a legal unit with rights and responsibilities, who may litigate claims or be prosecuted or adjudicated. Presently, the status of a person who has been born alive, although some challenge whether fetuses and zygotes should be considered persons from the moment of conception.

personal choice A perspective that sees all delinquent and criminal behavior as emanating from responsible individuals rather than from the social conditions in which they reside. Such persons must be held accountable for their actions, and their defective thinking must be corrected by firm and consistent approaches.

personal crime An illegal act in which the offender confronts the victim.

personality The sum total of social and psychological characteristics that define a person; also, a set of factors that are correlated with juvenile delinquency, focusing on psychological makeup and attitudes.

personality disorder An inflexible and maladaptive pattern of behavior, associated with antisocial behavior, developed early in life and causing significant impairment in overall functioning.

personal larceny Theft.

personally secured bail or bond Security that is put up by a defendant or the defendant's family. This arrangement is generally out of the reach of less affluent defendants.

personal property Money or goods or all movable property as distinguished from real property, such as land or fixed buildings.

personal retaliation A remedy for wrongs committed against a person or a person's property that consists of simple revenge against the perpetrator by the victim.

personate To impersonate with intent to defraud.

person in need of supervision A youth characterized as ungovernable, incorrigible, truant, or habitually disobedient. *See also* **PINS, CHINS, JINS, MINS.**

personnel security Protocol seeking to protect employees, records, technology, and other materials from loss or embezzlement.

perversion An unnatural tendency toward a certain type of behavior, especially of a sexual nature.

Pestalozzi, Henrich (1746–1827) A Swiss educator who developed private institutions dedicated to the reform and training of wayward and destitute children.

petechial hemorrhage Pinpoint hemorrhages of the eyes indicative of death by strangulation.

Peter Principle A theory formulated by Laurence Peter that each person is promoted in an organization to the level where he or she becomes incompetent to perform more responsible tasks, so that every person rises to the level of his or her own incompetence.

petition A document filed in juvenile court alleging that a juvenile is a delinquent, a status offender, or a dependent, and asking that the court assume jurisdiction over the juvenile or that the juvenile be transferred to a criminal court to be prosecuted as an adult.

petitioner One who brings a petition before the court.

petition not sustained A finding by a juvenile court at an adjudicatory hearing that there is insufficient evidence to sustain an allegation that a juvenile is a delinquent, status offender, or dependent.

petit jury, petite jury The trier of fact in a criminal case; the jury of one's peers called to hear the evidence and decide the defendant's guilt or innocence. Petit jury size varies among states.

petit larceny, petit theft Any theft of small amounts; a misdemeanor consisting of illegally taking goods or services in an amount less than that required to qualify for a felony.

petty offense Minor infraction or crime; misdemeanor. Petty offenses are usually punishable by fines or short terms of imprisonment.

petty larceny *See* **petit larceny, petit theft.**

petty theft *See* **petit larceny, petit theft.**

peyote A substance from a cactus of the same name that is used for its hallucinogenic effects. It is a narcotic and an illegal substance.

phantom effect The deterrence of crime in the absence of actual police presence; the belief of burglars and thieves that police may be patrolling a particular area causing them to avoid that area. This effect has been used to explain the findings of the Kansas City Preventive Patrol Experiment.

pharmacognogy The identification of plant materials used in pharmacy by means of their microscopic appearance.

pharmacology A branch of science dealing with the study of drugs and their human or animal effects.

phencyclidine (PCP) A psychedelic surgical anesthetic that can be ingested, smoked, sniffed, or injected that triggers psychotic attacks and may cause dramatic changes in personality which lead toward greater aggressiveness. It may be ingested by tablet, capsule, liquid, flake, or spray.

phenobarbital A barbiturate that has hypnotic or sedative properties.

phenolphthalein test A crude test to determine whether a substance is blood.

phenomenological criminology A perspective on crime causation that holds that the significance of criminal behavior is ultimately knowable only to those who participate in it. Central to this school of thought is the belief that social actors endow their behavior with meaning and purpose. Hence, a crime might mean one thing to the person who commits it, quite another to the victim, and something far different still to professional participants in the justice system.

Philadelphia House of Industry A halfway house established in Philadelphia in 1889.

Philadelphia Society for Alleviating the Miseries of Public Prisons A society, established in 1787, made up of prominent Philadelphia citizens, philanthropists, and religious reformers who believed that prison conditions ought to be changed and made more humane.

phone phreaking The art and science of cracking a telephone network for the purpose of making free long-distance telephone calls. *See also* **phreaking.**

phonoscopy The study of voice prints, voice-print analysis, and identification.

phony accident claim Insurance fraud.

photoelectric alarm system A detection system using a light beam and photoelectric sensors to provide a line of protection. Interruption of the beam by an intruder activates the alarm.

photoengraving A way of producing etched printing plates, such as for currency production, by photographic methods.

photogrammetry A method of obtaining measurements from photographs using two cameras to produce photo images from two different reference points. Precise measurements can be made from the composite prints obtained.

photomacrograph A photograph of something large enough to be seen by the naked eye but in which the lens of a microscope enlarges the object's size and detail.

photomicrograph A photograph taken through a microscope of something too small to be seen by the naked eye.

Photostat A camera that makes a copy of a letter or document.

phreaking An activity closely related to computer hacking that uses a computer or other device to trick a phone system; using a telephone by trickery to make free calls or to have telephone calls made to a different account. The term has been extended to security cracking in any other context, such as hacking into communications networks.

phrenology An outmoded system of analysis that claimed to be able to determined one's character and development of faculties based on the shape and protuberances of one's skull.

physical dependence An addiction to drugs such that increased amounts are needed to obtain desired effects.

physical evidence Any tangible materials that offer the potential of solving a crime and bringing those responsible to justice.

physical location analysis A simple observation that focuses on how individuals use their bodies in a social space.

physical security That area of security concerned with the physical means to safeguard someone; use of bodyguards to maintain custody over something or protect someone from others.

physical stigma Any physical characteristic or abnormality, considered indicative of criminality.

physical trace evidence In forensics, the same as physical evidence; any tangible material from which inferences can be made as to the cause of death or the identity of the perpetrator.

physiognomy An outmoded study of the relation between facial features and human behavior.

picaresque organization A relatively permanent gang under the leadership of a single person who sometimes relies on the support and advice of a few officers.

pickpocket One who steals money or valuables directly from the garments of a victim.

PIE (Prison Industry Enhancement) A certification program authorizing states to market prison-made goods on the open market; a private-sector operation for the purpose of marketing prison-made goods.

piece-price system, Piece-Price Prison Industries System A variation of the contract system of prison industry in which the contractor supplies the raw material and receives the finished product, paying the prison a specified amount for each piece produced.

"pigeon" The target of a swindle or con.

"pigeon drop" A confidence game in which a mark is convinced to deposit a sum of money to share in a larger share of recovered monies.

pilferage Theft by employees through stealth or deception. *See also* **shrinkage.**

Pill Addicts Anonymous Headquartered in Reading, PA, a self-help organization to assist those addicted to various medications.

pillory A device similar to the stocks, by which an individual could be punished by being secured by his or her wrists and neck. These devices, used in the Middle Ages, were usually placed in the town square so that the offender would suffer public humiliation.

pimp A procurer or manager of prostitutes who provides access to prostitutes, protects them, and lives off their proceeds.

Pine Ridge Reservation *See* **Wounded Knee II.**

Pinkerton, Allan (1819–1884) Born in Glasgow, Scotland, Pinkerton moved to the United States in 1842 and became the first professional detective. He founded the Pinkerton National Detective Agency and helped to organize the first secret service division in the American military during the Civil War. Pinkerton saved Abraham Lincoln's life on occasion by uncovering assassination plots.

Pinkerton Rule A test enunciated by the U.S. Supreme Court in *Pinkerton v. United States* (1946), which held that a member of a conspiracy is liable for all offenses committed in furtherance of the conspiracy.

PINS, CHINS, JINS, MINS "Person in need of supervision," "child in need of supervision," "juvenile in need of supervision," and "minors in need of supervision"; juveniles who are either status offenders or are thought to be incorrigible or on the verge of becoming delinquent.

PINS Diversion Program A New York program established in 1987 to divert youths in need of supervision to out-of-home placements, such as foster care.

piquer A criminal who uses sharp objects with to stab his or her victims.

piquerism The sexual proclivity toward the cutting, stabbing, puncturing, or tearing of human flesh.

piracy Raiding or seizing vessels on the high seas illegally and by force; also, obtaining software or other licensed computer information by illegal means.

pirate One who steals from another. An early meaning referred to robbery on the high seas. Today, a "film pirate" is one who traffics in stolen and copyrighted motion pictures or videotapes.

pistol A small firearm designed to be held and fired in one hand.

Pitchess motion A request to have access to the personnel file of the arresting police officer in a criminal case. It usually involves an examination of the officer's history of complaints made by citizens of police brutality or misconduct.

Pittsburgh Youth Study (PYS) A longitudinal investigation of 1,517 inner-city boys conducted between 1986 and 1996 that studied factors involved in what caused delinquency among some youths while others did not become delinquent.

Pizza Connection An FBI case investigated during the early 1980s involving the smuggling and distribution of narcotics in Asia's Golden Triangle by the Sicilian Mafia. Subsequently, money from narcotics sales was distributed to pizza parlors in New York City. Numerous persons were indicted in 1984 as the result of the FBI investigation.

PKPA The Parental Kidnapping Prevention Act, designed to deter or prevent "child snatching" by noncustodial parents.

placed A judicial disposition in which a juvenile is disposed to a group or foster home, another type of out-of-home care, or secure confinement in an industrial school or comparable facility.

placement A sentence or disposition involving confinement to a facility or institution.

plagiarism Passing off another's written work as one's own.

plain arch A fingerprint pattern in which the ridges of the fingerprint come in from one side and go out the other side without recurving or turning back in loops.

plainclothesman A detective who does not wear a uniform.

plain error Any error occurring during a trial that may have substantially affected its outcome. The standard used is legal impropriety affecting the defendant's substantial rights that is sufficiently serious to bring about an unjust result.

plain sight *See* **plain view, plain-view doctrine, plain-view rule.**

plaintiff The person or party who initiates a legal action against someone or some party in a civil court.

plain view, plain-view doctrine, plain-view rule Officers conducting a search may seize any contraband or illegal substances or items that are in the immediate vision of the officers. Evidence may be introduced in a trial whether the original search was lawful or unlawful, to the extent that the unlawful search was the result of a good-faith error.

plain whorl A fingerprint pattern.

planning The process of identifying goals and objectives and the means to achieve them based on previously obtained information.

plantations In corrections, prisons organized in the manner of pre–Civil War plantations; also called farm prisons.

plant security Any form of business protection using various means, including alarms and police personnel; protection from theft, fire, or other type of liability.

plaster of paris A substance used to make surface impressions of tire prints, footprints, or any indentations in soil. The material is poured into the indentations, where it hardens and forms a pattern identical to the indentations. Such casts can be used as identifying evidence in court.

plasticized white phosphorus (PWP) A common component of incendiary devices, which is produced by melting white phosphorus and pouring it into cold water. Small granules are produced and mixed with synthetic rubber. The rubbery mass disperses upon detonation.

platoon system The division of police officers into shifts or groups, each of which performs duty for a fixed period, such as a 12- or 24-hour shift.

Platt, Anthony Author of *The Child Savers* (1969). Platt wrote that criminologists themselves have helped to reinforce stereotypical notions about poor and minority-group criminals. He believed that criminology must redefine its goals and definitions more in line with humanistic properties and ac-

cept the reality of a legal system founded on power and privilege.

"playing the game" Conning by a prisoner.

plea An answer to charges by a defendant. Pleas vary among jurisdictions. Not guilty, guilty, *nolo contendere,* not guilty by reason of insanity, and guilty but mentally ill are possible pleas.

plea, final The last plea to a given charge.

plea, guilty A defendant's formal answer in court to the charges in a complaint, information, or indictment in which the defendant states that the charges are true and that he or she has committed the offense(s) as charged. *See box p. 192.*

plea, initial The first plea in response to a given charge entered in a court record by or for a defendant.

plea, *nolo contendere* *See* ***nolo contendere.***

plea, not guilty A defendant's formal answer in court to the charges in a complaint or information or indictment, in which the defendant states that he or she has not committed the offense(s) as charged.

plea-agreement hearing A meeting presided over by a trial judge to determine the accuracy of a guilty plea and the acceptability of the general conditions of a plea-bargain agreement between the prosecution and defense attorneys.

plea bargaining, plea negotiation A preconviction deal-making process between the state and the accused in which the defendant exchanges a plea of guilty or *nolo contendere* for a reduction in charges, a promise of sentencing leniency, or some other concession from full, maximum implementation of the conviction and sentencing authority of the court. Types of plea bargaining include implicit plea bargaining, charge reduction bargaining, sentence recommendation bargaining, and judicial plea bargaining.

plead To respond to a criminal charge.

plea negotiation *See* **plea bargaining, plea negotiation.**

pleasure-pain principle The utilitarian view that persons pursue pleasure and avoid pain, which helps to explain why persons commit crime.

pledge, legal The process of delivering property or securities to be held by a creditor until one's debt is paid.

pledge system An early method of law enforcement following the Norman Conquest of England in 1066 that relied on self-help and mutual aid.

plenary Entire; full; complete.

pluralistic ignorance A situation in which witnesses in a group fail to help the victim of an emergency or a crime because they interpret the failure of other witnesses to help as a sign that no help is needed.

pluralistic prison environment The inmate world of the contemporary prison, which is characterized by ethnic and cultural diversity.

plurality opinion An opinion of an appellate court that is joined by more judges than have joined any concurring opinion, although not by a majority of judges in the court.

PMS *See* **premenstrual syndrome (PMS).**

PO An abbreviation for probation or parole officer.

poacher One who illegally hunts and traps on another's property without permission; one who illegally captures or kills game or protected wildlife.

podular direct, podular direct supervision A process of inmate supervision that requires correctional officers to be in direct contact with inmates who are not confined to cells.

Guilty Plea Acceptance Form for New Orleans, LA:
Alternative Procedure for Accepting Guilty Pleas Used by Local Judges

CRIMINAL DISTRICT COURT
PARISH OF ORLEAN
STATE OF LOUISIANA
SECTION "D"

STATE OF LOUISIANA

vs.

_____

JUDGE: FRANK A. MARULLO, JR.

NO. _____

VIO: _____

PLEA OF GUILTY

I, _____, defendant in the above case informed the Court that I wanted to plead guilty and do plead guilty to the crime of _____ and have been informed and understand the charge to which I am pleading guilty. (_____)

The acts which make up the crime to which I am pleading have been explained to me as well as the fact that for this crime I could possibly receive a sentence of _____. (_____)

I understand that in pleading guilty in this matter I waive the following rights:

(1) To a trial by either a judge or a jury and that further the right to a trial by judge extends until the first witness is sworn, and the right to a trial by jury extends until the first juror is sworn, and if convicted the right to an appeal.
Please specify: Judge trial or Jury trial   (_____)

(2) To face and cross-examine the witnesses who accuse me of the crime charged.   (_____)

(3) The privilege against self-incrimination or having to take the stand myself and testify.   (_____)

(4) To have the Court compel my witness to appear and testify.   (_____)

I am entering a plea of guilty to this crime because I am, in fact, guilty of this crime. I have not been forced, threatened, or intimidated into making this plea, nor has anyone made me promises in order that I enter a plea. I am fully satisfied with the handling of my case by my attorney and the way in which he has represented me. I am satisfied with the way the Court has handled this matter. (_____)

_____
DEFENDANT

_____
JUDGE

_____
ATTORNEY FOR DEFENDANT

DATE: _____

NOTE: Defendant is to place his initials in the blocks provided for same.
Defendant is to block out Judge trial or Jury trial as it applies.

podular indirect, podular indirect supervision A process of supervision wherein inmates are not confined to cells, and correctional officers can observe inmates but are physically separated from them.

podular remote surveillance Surveillance in jails and prisons with pods housing various numbers of inmates that are arranged to permit observation of activities from a central, protected control room.

podular units Separate jail or prison areas where various numbers of prisoners can be observed from a single central location.

pogrom A slaughter or massacre originated by a governmental power and directed against certain persons because of prejudice or hatred.

points of identification In fingerprint identification, a matching of ridges for particular fingers. Usually, a minimum of 12 points of identification is required to show that someone's fingerprint matches one found at a crime scene.

poisoning The intentional act of administering toxic substances to someone for the purpose of harming or killing that person.

police Persons whose responsibility is to enforce the criminal laws and ensure public safety.

police advisory board A board made up of citizens from the community to oversee police policies and the administration of police procedures.

Police and Criminal Evidence Act of 1984 A British act authorizing the establishment of an independent Police Complaints Authority in 1985.

Police Athletic League (PAL) A police program, sponsored to provide recreation and sports, designed to reduce delinquency and increase youths' commitment to law-abiding behaviors.

police brutality Any unnecessary physical force used by police officers against citizens from which injuries to citizens are sustained.

Police Bureau of Criminal Alien Identification A unit of police departments created in 1930 for the purpose of identifying undesirable aliens in order to deport them under immigration laws.

Police Bureau of Identification A bureau created in 1884 by Captain Michael Evans of the Chicago Police Department for the use of different forensic techniques to combat crime and identify possible criminal suspects.

police cadet program Any program designed for older adolescents and college students that allows participants to perform some police tasks and learn about law enforcement.

police cautioning The verbal warning by a law enforcement officer to a person who may have committed or attempted to commit a crime.

police-civilian review board A body of citizens and police personnel that investigates citizen complaints against police officers, including allegations of police misconduct and brutality, and recommends sanctions for officers where guilt is established.

police-community awareness academies Schools established to teach citizens how police agencies operate. The idea originated in England, specifically in the Devon and Cornwall Constabulary, Middlemoor Exeter, at the request of local citizens. In 1977, two small British municipal police agencies established a Police Night School, a concept that in the United States has come to be known as the Citizens Police Academy.

police-community relations A generic concept that includes any program designed to promote or make more visible law enforcement strategies that are aimed at crime prevention and control and in which varying degrees of proactive citizen involvement are solicited.

Police Complaints Authority An independent English investigative body that examines the validity of citizen complaints against police, and which is capable of imposing appropriate administrative sanctions against offending officers.

police corruption Misconduct by police officers in the form of illegal activities for economic gain, including accepting gratuities, favors, or unlawful payment for services that police are sworn to carry out as a part of their peacekeeping role. The term is not applied to officer conduct while off duty.

police court A municipal tribunal trying those accused of violating city ordinances (e.g., vagrancy or public drunkenness).

police cynicism The notion held by some police officers that all people are motivated by selfishness and evil.

police decoys Undercover officers who pose as drunks, tourists, prostitutes, and others to encourage criminals to attack them. They are placed in high-crime areas as a crime detection and prevention measure.

police department A local law enforcement agency directed by a chief of police or a commissioner. *See diagram p.194.*

police discretion The ability of police officers to select behaviors from among alternatives in citizen-police encounters.

police diversion A program that allows police to recommend to juvenile suspects that they enroll in a program that offers counseling or training.

police ethics The special responsibility for observing moral duty and obligation that is police work.

Police Executive Research Forum (PERF) A national organization of police executives dedicated to improving policing and advancing professionalism through research and involvement in public policy debate. The organization depends on private grants and contracts for funding.

police explorer posts A police program for younger adolescents, often associated with Boy Scouting, designed to teach youths about policing.

Police Foundation A nonprofit organization headquartered in Washington, DC, that was founded in 1970 and is dedicated to improving policy through research, technical assistance, and technology.

police jury The administrative board of a Louisiana parish. It is similar to a county police commission.

police management The administrative duties associated with controlling, directing, and coordinating police personnel in police departments.

police misconduct Any one of several different types of illegal or improper behavior of police officers, including acceptance of graft, falsifying police reports, and perjury.

police mission Either implicit or explicit statements of general goals and objectives of police departments and officers.

police officer A local law enforcement officer employed by a police department.

police officer style The belief that the large aggregate of police officers can be classified into ideal personality types. Popular style types include supercops, who desire to enforce only serious crimes, such as robbery and rape; service-oriented officers, who see their job as that of a helping profession; and avoiders, who do as little as possible. The actual existence of ideal police officer types has never been conclusively proven.

police power The influence of government to legislate to protect public health, safety, welfare, and morality.

police presence The almost certain presence of police officers in places of business for the crime deterrent effects it affords.

police probation A program requiring juvenile troublemakers to report to police regularly, attend school, make restitution, and maintain a neat personal appearance.

police professionalism The increasing formalization of police work and the rise in public acceptance of the police that accompanies it. It includes a well-focused code of ethics, equitable recruitment and selection practices, and informed promotional strategies among many agencies.

police protection Security services offered by law enforcement officers to witnesses and others whose lives may be in danger.

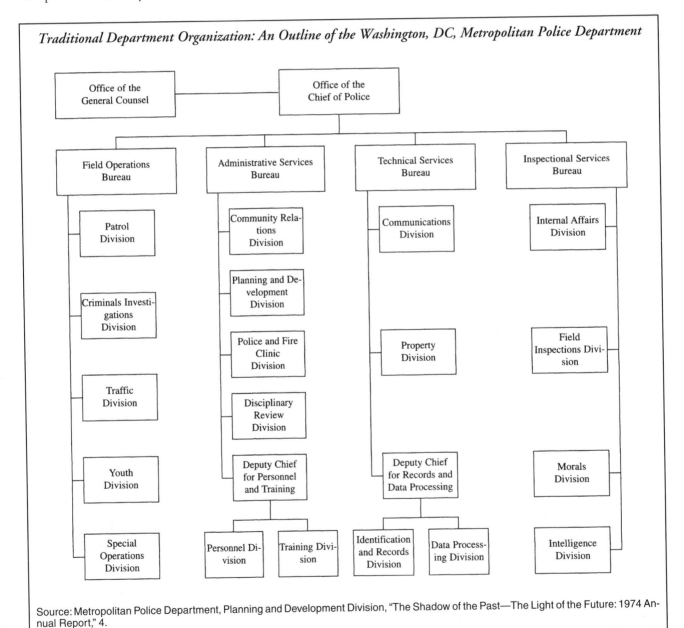

Traditional Department Organization: An Outline of the Washington, DC, Metropolitan Police Department

Source: Metropolitan Police Department, Planning and Development Division, "The Shadow of the Past—The Light of the Future: 1974 Annual Report," 4.

police review boards Bodies of citizens who convene to investigate allegations of police misconduct and recommend punishments if it is detected or proved.

police role The position assumed by a police officer working in the community or the courts, and probation or parole officers.

police-school liaison program A program initiated in 1995, after a public forum on safety, that places law enforcement officers within schools to help prevent juvenile delinquency and to improve community relations. Officers routinely handle in-school behavior problems, investigate crimes, act as counselors, provide security, and help maintain a safe school environment. In some jurisdictions, the program is called "adopt-a-cop." *See also* **school resource officer.**

police state A government in which special powers are given to the police to investigate private individuals and obtain information about them. Police powers are extensive, whereas citizen rights and powers are minimal.

police subculture The result of socialization and bonding among police officers because of their stress and job-related anxiety; the unofficial norms and values possessed by coteries of police in different agencies, formed by their peculiar working hours and job stress.

police union An organized group that represents police interests and seeks additional benefits for police personnel. It may engage in negotiations with police administration and political authorities for concessions relating to working hours, pay increases, retirement benefits, and other work-related topics.

Police Week The second or third week of May each year, Police Week was established in 1962 to honor police officers who protect and serve the public.

police working personality *See* **working personality.**

policy-centered approach A method of thinking and planning for intermediate sanctions that draws together key stakeholders from inside and outside the corrections agency that will implement the sanction.

policy-level sentencing decisions Sentencing decisions by the legislature or its delegate about the goals and structure of sentencing.

political considerations Matters taken into account in the formulation of public policies and the making of choices among competing values.

political crimes Acts that constitute threats against the state, including treason, sedition, or espionage.

political espionage Spying carried out for political purposes.

political policing Secret policing practices used by law enforcement officers to control or suppress unpopular or alleged subversive views or activities.

political prisoners Individual inmates imprisoned for engaging in particular political activities, from simple political dissent to murder.

political question Any issue in a case that the court believes should be decided by a nonjudicial unit of government.

political terrorism Domestic terrorism.

politicians Inmates who work for key officials or occupy positions in administrative offices and whose position gives them the ability to influence decisions affecting other inmates.

polling the jury *See* **jury poll.**

pollution control Any effort on the part of a federal or state agency to regulate air quality and the general pollution of water and highways.

polyandry The practice of a woman having more than one husband at the same time.

polygamy Plural marriage; having more than one spouse at the same time.

polygraph test *See* **lie detector.**

polygyny The practice of a man having more than one wife at the same time.

polymerase chain reaction The first practical system for *in vitro* amplification of DNA and as such one of the most important recent developments in molecular biology. Two synthetic oligonucleotide primers, which are complementary to two regions of the target DNA to be amplified, are added to the target DNA in the presence of excess deoxynucleotides and Taq polymerase, a heat-stable DNA polymerase. In a series of temperature cycles, the target DNA is repeatedly denatured and annealed to the primers, and a daughter strand extended from the primers. As the daughter strands themselves act as templates for subsequent cycles, DNA fragments matching both primers are amplified exponentially, rather than linearly. The original DNA need thus be neither pure nor abundant and the polymerase chain reaction has accordingly become widely used not only in research, but in clinical diagnostics and forensic science to aid in criminal investigations.

Ponzi, Charles (1882–1949) A Boston clerk who made money in the 1920s by buying foreign postal coupons and selling them for large profits in the United States to investors as a get-rich-quick scheme. He guaranteed investors a 50 percent return on their money, but in reality paid off old investors with money from new investors. This type of pyramid scheme became known as a "Ponzi scheme."

poor laws Seventeenth-century laws binding out vagrants and abandoned children as indentured servants.

popular justice The creation of community courts to operate in lieu of duly constituted courts as a means of dispensing justice informally. Informal nonbureaucratic organizations have been designed to fulfill the official functions of courts and police (e.g., citizen patrols who oversee neighborhood safety without sanction or approval from a police department).

population A large group of persons under study about which the researcher wants to draw certain conclusions.

population caps Limits placed by the courts or by statute on the number of inmates that can be legally housed in a jail, prison, or prison system.

population movement In corrections, the entries and exits of adjudicated persons, or persons subject to judicial proceedings, into or from correctional facilities or programs.

pornography The portrayal, by whatever means, of lewd or obscene sexually explicit material prohibited by law.

poroscopy The scientific study of sweat pores, their arrangement and configuration, that can be examined through fingerprint impressions.

portrait parle A speaking likeness; a method of recording persons' descriptions.

port warden Person who safeguards harbors or ports and keeps them safe against various types of hazards.

POSDCORB An organizational acronym for the primary management functions of planning, organizing, staffing, directing, coordinating, reporting, and budgeting.

positive evidence Any information, document, or object that directly proves a particular fact at a given point in time.

positive identification Verification of the identity of a suspect, witness, or missing person of interest to authorities.

positive law Any system of regulative rules of human conduct with accompanying sanctions (punishments or rewards) for deviance or conformity.

positive peer culture (PPC) A counseling program in which peer leaders encourage other group members to modify their behavior and peers help reinforce acceptable behaviors.

positive reinforcements Rewards given by administrators to lower-level police officers for good conduct or otherwise conforming to the requirements set forth in the police mission.

positive school (of criminology) A school of criminological thought emphasizing analysis of criminal behaviors through empirical indicators such as physical features compared with biochemical explanations. It postulates that human behavior is a product of social, biological, psychological, and economic forces. It is also known as the "Italian School."

positivism A branch of social science that uses the scientific method of the natural sciences and that suggests that human behavior is a product of social, biological, psychological, and economic factors.

positivist criminology *See* **positive school (of criminology)**.

posse A group of persons empowered by a law officer to pursue criminal suspects. The term may refer to a loose and informal gang.

posse comitatus The power of a police officer or other law enforcement officer to form a posse or request assistance from anyone over age 18 to assist him or her in effecting an arrest of a criminal perpetrator.

Posse Comitatus Act of 1878 A prohibition against the use of military personnel to assist civilian personnel in civil law enforcement. The act does not bar a state's National Guard from supplementing local police forces in times of crisis or emergencies.

possession A charge for having a quantity of prohibited drugs or stolen property.

possession, writ of Designates any writ whereby a sheriff or other officer is ordered to place someone in possession of real or personal property.

post Position; the location of assignment of an officer; afterward, in time.

POST Peace Officer Standards and Training.

postconviction relief Various mechanisms whereby offenders may challenge their conviction after other appeal attempts have been exhausted.

posterity Descendants or offspring.

post facto After the fact.

posthumous Occurring after death.

postmodern criminology A view of criminology that builds on the tenets of postmodern social thought, based on the premise that reality is a subjective construct of each individual.

post mortem "After death" (Latin).

post mortem **lividity** Discoloration of human tissue caused by the effects of gravity pulling the blood to the lowest parts of the body of the deceased.

postpartum defense A tactic used by some women charged with certain violent crimes, including the murder of their newborn children, asserting that during the period of recovery from childbirth, physical, mental, and emotional changes in the mother occur and prompt erratic behavior that would be unusual under normal circumstances.

postrelease control Form of supervision for those released from prison.

posttest A subsequent analysis of a phenomenon under study.

posttrauma strategies Officer support programs designed to provide individual or group counseling for officers involved in stressful events, such as shootings.

posttraumatic stress disorder (PTSD) A mental disorder characterized by intense distress, greater arousal, and dampened enthusiasm for life, triggered by crisis such as a war or violence. PTSD is suffered by veterans of the Vietnam War, the Iraqi war, and other conflicts. Also, a severe disorder suffered by those who have experienced such traumatic, violent stress, such as combat, that they later lose orientation and kill or engage in other violent behavior, believing that they have returned to the traumatic situation. Some argue that victims of this disorder should not be held criminally responsible for crimes they commit as a result of it.

potency The strength of drug activity on a living organism; the amount of a drug desired to produce predictable effects.

potential member Someone suspected of being a gang member.

Pound's model A plan of court organization with three tiers: a supreme court, a major trial court, and a minor trial court. *See figure p. 197.*

powder, black A propellant used in reloading or charging firearms ammunition. Grains of powder can be measured to project a bullet at a certain speed for a given distance.

powder burn, powder pattern The arrangement of gunpowder on an object, such as clothing or human skin, that discloses the proximity of the discharged weapon to the object or skin. The closer the muzzle of the firearm to the object or skin, the greater the powder pattern or burn.

powder pattern test A forensic test to determine from gunpowder residue the distance of a firearm's muzzle from clothing or skin when it was discharged.

powders Types of propellant used in ammunition loading, which include black, semi-smokeless, and smokeless. Powders burn at differing rates and are therefore designated for different types of cartridges to be fired in particular types of weapons. Charts are used to gauge the amount of particular powders needed for particular bullets, distances, and speeds.

power One person's ability to influence another person to carry out orders.

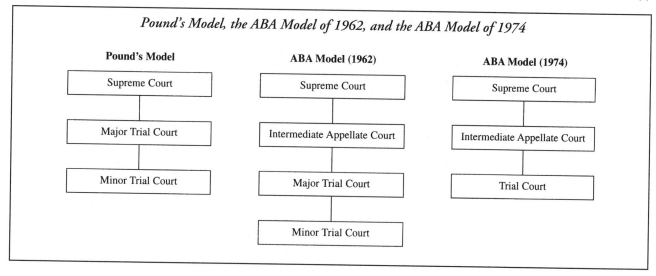

Pound's Model, the ABA Model of 1962, and the ABA Model of 1974

power clusters Issue networks and vested interest groups that have a stake in correctional organizations and correctional agencies, and that work in collaboration with other interest groups to bring about a particular end and ensure that their interests are protected.

power-control theory The theory holds that gender differences in the delinquency rate are a function of class differences and economic conditions that influence the structure of family life.

power elite Sociologist C. Wright Mills' concept for those who have political and financial control in society.

power group A criminal organization that does not provide services or illegal goods but trades exclusively in violence and extortion. *See also* **power syndicate.**

powerlessness A person's belief or expectation that his or her actions cannot determine outcomes or the future; a perception of the loss of personal influence over one's life or destiny, which is viewed as being controlled by powerful external forces.

power of attorney The authority given to another to act in one's place.

power rape A rape motivated by the need for sexual conquest.

power syndicate An organized crime group that uses force and violence to extort money from legitimate businesses and other criminal groups engaged in illegal business enterprises. *See also* **power group.**

praxis The application of a theory to action. Marxist criminology applies this idea to explain revolution.

prearraignment lockup Preventive detention; a place for preventive detention.

prebriefing conference program A method of streamlining case processing in court, in which attorneys file appeals and discuss the structure and length of these appeals prior to their presentation before appellate courts.

precedent The principle that how a previous case was decided should serve as a guide for how a similar case currently under consideration ought to be decided.

precinct community councils (PCCs) Established as liaisons between police officers and local residents, these face-to-face councils have done much to foster better police-community cooperation and create better conditions of community crime control.

precipe "Give rules" (Latin); a document containing the particulars of a writ.

precipitant reaction test A forensic test to determine whether blood is from a human or an animal.

precipitation hypothesis The view that violence as reported and portrayed by the media actually creates violent behavior in society.

precocious sexuality Sexual experimentation in early adolescence.

predator Any offender who actively stalks or otherwise pursues his or her victims; any criminal who victimizes others repeatedly and without remorse, especially in the crimes of robbery, rape, and murder. Predators in the animal kingdom are used as a metaphor for criminal behavior.

predatory crimes Violent crimes against persons and crimes in which an offender attempts to steal an object directly from its holder.

predatory gang A gang actively involved in committing violent acts, such as drive-by shootings.

predatory violence Purposeful action on the part of a predator to bring about physical injuries or death.

prediction An assessment of some expected future behavior of a person including criminal acts, arrests, or convictions.

prediction scales, predictions of dangerousness, predictions of risk Any device or instrument that purports to estimate an offender's chances of posing serious public danger if released from custody.

prediction table A device used by correctional personnel to predict the future risk of recidivism by using past behaviors and personal characteristics as predictor variables.

predisposition investigation, predisposition report, predispositional investigation, predispositional report A report prepared by a juvenile intake officer to furnish a juvenile judge with background about a juvenile so the judge can make a more informed sentencing decision. It is similar to a presentence investigation report.

preempt To move into an area or take particular action before others move into that area or take action.

prejudicial error A wrongful procedure that substantially affects the rights of parties and thus may result in the reversal of a case.

preliminary examination, preliminary hearing A hearing by a magistrate or other judicial officer to determine if a person charged with a crime should be held for trial; a proceeding to establish probable cause. A preliminary hearing does not determine guilt or innocence.

preliminary injunction Temporary relief granted by the courts at the beginning of a lawsuit to prevent officials from continuing to engage in certain conduct or to keep an inmate in a designated status that is in dispute.

preliminary jurisdiction The initial court with jurisdiction over a case, which may be moved to a different court following a hearing to determine the type of case to be heard and the seriousness of the offense. A U.S. magistrate may direct a case to a district court, where more extensive powers and jurisdiction reside, if a case warrants.

premeditation A deliberate decision by a perpetrator to commit a crime; any kind of planning beforehand to commit or carry out a crime.

premenstrual syndrome (PMS) A set of symptoms associated with the onset of menstruation, including fatigue, tension, nervousness, irritability, and depressed moods. It can be a defense of criminal conduct based on chemical or hormonal imbalances.

preplea conference A discussion in which all parties participate openly to determine ways of bringing about an agreement on a sentence in return for a plea of guilty.

preponderance of evidence The civil standard whereby the weight of the exculpatory or inculpatory information is in favor of or against the defendant. The greater the weight of information favoring the defendant, the greater the likelihood of a finding in favor of the defendant.

prerelease classification The final classification decisions prior to release for the purpose of allocating inmates to transition programs.

prerelease programs in prison Programs within the institution that are designed to prepare the inmate for release, usually including assistance in applying for a job and locating a suitable residence.

prescription Acquiring advantage to property as the result of possession for a particular time period; time limitations set forth for different types of offenses and that govern time limits within which a prosecution may be conducted against one or more suspects; also, a legitimate written authorization from a physician for medicine for use in the treatment of an illness or medical condition.

prescriptive guidelines Sentencing guidelines in which the sentence values are determined on the basis of value judgments about appropriateness, rather than on the basis of past practice.

presentence investigation An examination of a convicted offender by a probation officer, usually requested or ordered by the court, including a victim impact statement, prior arrest records, and the offender's employment and educational history.

presentence investigation report, presentence report (PSI) A report filed by a probation or parole officer appointed by the court containing background information, socioeconomic data, and demographic data relative to a defendant. Facts in the case are included. It is used to influence the sentence imposed by a judge, and by a parole board considering an inmate for early release.

presentment An accusation, initiated by the grand jury on its own authority, from its own knowledge or observation, which functions as an instruction for the preparation of an indictment.

preservice training Any form of training occurring before a person assumes the day-to-day responsibilities of his or her position.

President's Commission on Campus Unrest A nine-member panel convened in 1970 to study causes of campus violence and unrest, created in response to the student shootings at Kent State University in Ohio that same year. Its recommendations included several strategies for combatting student unrest. The Commission was chaired by William Scranton, former governor of Pennsylvania.

President's Commission on Law Enforcement and the Administration of Justice, President's Crime Commission A commission created in 1967 to establish and promote standards for the selection of police officers and correctional employees. It led to the establishment of the Law Enforcement Assistance Administration.

presiding judge The title of the judicial officer formally designated for some period as the chief judicial officer of the court.

pressure The force exerted in a cartridge chamber and the bore of a firearm by powder gasses, measured by pounds per square inch.

pressure alarm system Any protection device for a vault in which a predetermined air pressure differential exists between the inside and outside of the vault. An alarm signal is activated when the pressure differential is changed, absent any authorized vault opening.

prestige crime Stealing from or assaulting someone to gain prestige, which is often part of a gang initiation rite.

presumed dead An artificial presumption in which a person who is missing for seven or more years is considered deceased. A person is also presumed dead if evidence exists of foul play but a body cannot be found.

presumption An inference drawn from a set of facts; a logical deduction from a set of related statements.

presumption, legal A law permitting the judiciary to draw certain facts from a given set of circumstances.

presumption, rebuttable A legal assumption that may be disproved with contrary proof.

presumption of innocence The premise that a defendant is innocent unless proven guilty beyond a reasonable doubt, which is fundamental to the adversary system.

presumption of validity In constitutional law, the premise that a statute is valid until it is demonstrated otherwise.

presumptive evidence The assumption of the incapacity of a minor to act; any evidence that may be disproved by contrary information or facts.

presumptive fixed sentence A fixed determinate sentence within a limited range established by statute.

presumptive parole date The presumed release date stipulated by parole guidelines should the offender serve time without disciplinary or other infractions or incidents.

presumptive sentencing A statutory sentencing method that specifies normal sentences of particular lengths with limited judicial leeway to shorten or lengthen the term of the sentence.

presumptive waiver A type of judicial waiver wherein the burden of proof shifts from the state to the juvenile to contest whether the youth is transferred to criminal court.

pretermit Pass by; disregard; take no action concerning.

pretest In social research, the administration of a survey, test, or other measure to a sample before an intervention or treatment variable is administered.

pretext carstop Any stop of a motor vehicle by police when probable cause exists to believe that a traffic violation has occurred, but when the real purpose of the vehicle stop is to see who is in the car or to find a way to search the vehicle if more serious criminal activity is suspected.

pretrial conference A meeting between opposing parties in a lawsuit or criminal trial for purposes of stipulating things that are agreed on and thus narrowing the trial to the things that are in dispute, disclosing the required information about witnesses and evidence, making motions, and generally organizing the presentation of motions, witnesses, and evidence.

pretrial detention *See* **preventive detention.**

pretrial discovery *See* **discovery.**

pretrial diversion *See* **diversion.**

pretrial hearing A court proceeding at which motions are made and pleas are entered and considered.

pretrial intervention *See* **diversion.**

pretrial motion *See* **motion** *in limine.*

pretrial publicity Media attention given to a case before it is tried in court. Pretrial publicity may have a chilling effect on the court's ability to impanel an unbiased jury, and often leads to a requests for a change of venue in high-profile trials.

pretrial release The release of an accused person from custody for all or part of the time before or during prosecution upon his or her promise to appear in court when required.

Pretrial Services Resource Center A Washington, DC–based nonprofit organization providing information about pretrial issues for criminal-justice professionals and others. The center works to improve the criminal-justice system at the pretrial stage, to improve safety, services, and appearance rates, and reduce recidivism. Its services include an information clearinghouse, providing technical assistance, and promoting the best practices.

pretrial status Any status in which an accused individual finds him- or herself while awaiting court processing.

prevalence The proportion of a population that commits crime in a given period, measured by the number of offenders divided by the size of the population.

prevalence of crime The extent to which crime exists in a given geographical area or in a given population at a particular time.

prevention A philosophy of corrections that believes the aim of punishment should be to prevent crime.

prevention and protection costs The financial costs of crimes that result from expenditures on alarm systems, spotlights, locks, other target-hardening devices, and insurance premiums to cover potential theft losses.

preventive detention, preventive pretrial detention A constitutionally approved method of detaining those charged with crimes when the likelihood exists that they either pose a serious risk to others if released or will flee the jurisdiction to avoid prosecution.

preventive patrol A scheme by police officers inspired by the belief that high police officer visibility effectively deters crime.

price fixing An illegal conspiracy between two or more corporations to set the prices of merchandise or services to minimize competition and maximize mutual profits.

price-tag justice Fines for criminal offenses instead of confinement.

PRIDE Prison Rehabilitative Industries and Diversified Enterprise; a nonprofit corporation that runs Florida's prison industries.

prima facie **case** "On its face" (Latin); a case for which there is as much evidence as would warrant the conviction of defendants if properly proved in court; a case that meets the evidentiary requirements for a grand jury indictment.

prima facie **evidence** "On its face" (Latin); any proof offered to support a fact or set of facts.

primary classification Initial categorization of fingerprints for subsequent specific identification.

primary crime scene In a criminal case, the site where the crime occurred and where the body was found.

primary deviance, primary deviation Minor violations of the law that are frequently overlooked by police (e.g., "streaking" or swimming in a public pool after-hours).

primary evidence Firsthand evidence, eyewitness testimony, or tangible incriminating evidence.

primary group Charles Horton Cooley's term denoting a small and relatively permanent group characterized by intimate relationships.

primary prevention *See* **corrective prevention.**

prime beneficiary typology A typology based on the principle of who benefits by the particular organizational activity. The four classes or types of beneficiaries are (1) members or rank-and-file participants; (2) owners and managers; (3) clients; and (4) the general public. The scheme was created and described by Peter Blau and Richard Scott.

primitive term A concept so basic that it cannot be defined by any other concept.

primogeniture During the Middle Ages, the right of a first-born son to inherit lands and titles, leaving his brothers the option of a military or religious career.

Principle of Least Eligibility The principle that prisoners should not be given programs and services or live under conditions that are better than those of the lowest classes of the noncriminal population in society.

principal A perpetrator of a criminal act.

principal in the first degree The person who actually commits a crime.

principal in the second degree A person who participates in a crime but does not actually carry it out (e.g., the driver of a getaway car in a robbery).

principal registration A system of classifying and identifying fingerprints based on impressions of all 10 fingers of one's hands.

principal's liability for acts of agent The liability that attaches to a person who assents or authorizes another to act on his or her behalf in committing a crime without actually being present at the crime scene. Such liability may not exist if the act is carried out without the principal's knowledge or approval.

prior record Criminal history information concerning any law enforcement, court, or correctional proceedings that have occurred before the current investigation of or proceedings against a person; statistical descriptions of the criminal histories of a set of persons.

prison A state- or federally operated facility to house long-term offenders, usually designed to house inmates serving incarcerative terms of one or more years. Prisons are self-contained facilities sometimes called total institutions. *See also* **penitentiary.**

prison, receiving An assessment center where inmates are first placed in order to classify them according to particular psychological and social characteristics for their long-term placement in a particular level of custody. Assessment varies from several days to two weeks or longer.

prison administration A group of individuals that runs a prison, comprised of a warden, a superintendent, and their assistants.

prison argot The slang characteristic of prison subcultures and prison life.

Prison-Ashram Project An organization founded in 1973 and headquartered in Durham, NC, that holds workshops in prisons and universities. Its pen pal project is designed to match inmates with noncriminals on the basis of spiritual interests. Ashrams are like monasteries.

prison camp A correctional facility located in a rural area where the physical facilities usually consist of a barracks, tents, or similar temporary construction.

prison capacity The size of the correctional population an institution can effectively hold. The term may refer to rated capacity, design capacity, or operating capacity. *See tables p. 201.*

prison chaplains Ministers of particular faiths who are typically employed and paid by a jurisdiction to administer, supervise, and plan all religious activities and services in a prison or jail.

prison classification *See* **classification.**

prison code A set of norms and values among prison inmates.

prison commitment The period of time a sentenced offender must serve, imposed by a judge following conviction for a crime; time, usually expressed in terms of months or years, that may be served in either jail or prison, depending upon the offense seriousness and space availability.

prison community The subcultural association of inmates in a penitentiary that includes social structure and hierarchy of authority among inmates, a leadership system, folkways and customs, and other aspects of inmate culture.

prison crowding A condition wherein the number of inmates held in a prison exceeds its rated capacity.

prison discipline Punishments meted out by prison authorities for violations of institutional rules, which may include loss of privileges, solitary confinement, and extended incarceration beyond the original sentence.

prisoner Anyone held in a county or city jail, prison, or penitentiary.

Prisoner Litigation Reform Act of 1995 (PLRA) Legislation designed to decrease the sheer numbers of inmate lawsuits filed against prison systems in federal courts by limiting government subsidies for case filing fees and other litigation expenses previously paid for on behalf of prisoners by the state.

Prisoner Movement, prisoner rights movement, prisoner rights revolution Activity inspired by the changes that occurred during the 1960s that focused on reforming prison conditions.

prisoners' rights movement A diffuse movement among prisoners and groups supporting prisoners' rights in which means are examined whereby prisoners can exercise their legal rights in court and challenge jail and prison administration policies. The movement started in the late 1960s and continues, with growing numbers of petitions filed by inmates in state and federal courts annually.

Prisoners' Rights Union An organization founded in 1971 and headquartered in Sacramento, CA, that advocates improved conditions for inmates by improving prison physical plants and more extensive inmate amenities. Publishes *California Prisoner.*

prison escape A situation in which one or more inmates flee the confines of a prison institution without permission and become fugitives.

prison farm A large custodial facility for inmates that may include agricultural areas where prisoners can grow their own fruit and vegetables. There are several different types, which vary in terms of offenders housed and length of confinement.

prison fellowship A prison ministry that recruits and trains volunteers and provides teaching, mentoring, and aftercare programs for released inmates.

Prison Fellowship International Established in 1976 and headquartered in Washington, DC, this Christian ministry for inmates in various communities consists of family members of inmates and other interested persons. Publishes *World Report.*

Reported Federal and State Prison Capacities, Yearend 2002

Region and jurisdiction	Type of capacity measure			Custody population as a percent of —	
	Rated	Operational	Design	Highest capacity[a]	Lowest capacity[a]
Federal	103,897	...	...	133 %	133 %
Northeast					
Connecticut[b]	...	...	...	...	...
Maine	1,779	1,779	1,779	104 %	104 %
Massachusetts	...	...	7,721	128	128
New Hampshire	2,419	2,238	2,213	102	112
New Jersey	...	...	17,122	138	138
New York	61,265	63,531	54,210	105	123
Pennsylvania	34,583	34,583	27,113	113	145
Rhode Island	3,907	3,907	4,061	86	89
Vermont	1,286	1,286	1,226	106	111
Midwest					
Illinois	31,351	31,351	27,256	136 %	157 %
Indiana	15,859	21,039	...	93	123
Iowa	6,772	6,772	6,772	124	124
Kansas	9,114	...	...	98	98
Michigan	...	51,429	...	97	97
Minnesota	7,064	7,064	7,064	97	97
Missouri	...	30,580	...	97	97
Nebraska	...	3,924	3,139	103	129
North Dakota	1,005	952	1,005	109	115
Ohio	36,270	...	...	120	120
South Dakota	...	2,827	...	102	102
Wisconsin	...	15,559	...	117	117
South					
Alabama	...	...	12,459	201 %	201 %
Arkansas[c]	11,972	12,189	11,299	95	103
Delaware	...	4,206	3,192	164	216
Florida	...	78,805	58,396	95	129
Georgia	...	47,706	...	99	99
Kentucky	...	12,162	...	87	87
Louisiana	19,688	20,010	...	98	100
Maryland	...	24,263	...	99	99
Mississippi[c]	...	21,011	...	73	73
North Carolina	...	28,284	...	117	117
Oklahoma[c]	...	23,566	...	93	93
South Carolina	...	22,600	22,955	100	101
Tennessee[c]	19,138	18,691	...	96	98
Texas[c,d]	159,667	154,999	159,667	85	88
Virginia	30,925	...	...	95	95
West Virginia	...	3,539	3,189	101	112
West					
Alaska	3,098	3,206	...	93 %	97 %
Arizona	26,228	29,406	25,346	100	116
California	...	155,087	80,587	103	198
Colorado	...	13,925	12,593	116	129
Hawaii	...	3,487	2,451	107	152
Idaho	5,871	5,544	4,564	71	92
Montana	...	2,460	...	78	78
Nevada[c]	10,532	...	8,315	96	121
New Mexico[c]	6,245	6,239	5,985	94	98
Oregon	...	11,556	11,556	101	101
Utah	...	4,196	4,419	97	102
Washington	9,898	12,793	12,793	127	164
Wyoming	1,111	1,051	1,141	98	106

...Data not available.
[a]Population counts are based on the number of inmates held in facilities operated by the jurisdiction. Excludes inmates held in local jails, in other States, or in private facilities.
[b]Connecticut no longer reports capacity because of a law passed in 1995.
[c]Includes capacity of private and contract facilities and inmates housed in them.
[d]Excludes capacity of county facilities and inmates housed in them.

Source: Harrison and Beck, *Prisoners in 2002*, 7.

Prison Fellowship Ministries An organization founded in 1976 by former Watergate figure Chuck Colson and headquartered in Merrifield, VA. It promotes the spiritual healing of offenders, their families, victims, and entire communities, and publishes *Justice* and *Justice Report*.

prison furlough A short-term, unescorted leave away from prison, which may be granted for various purposes.

prison incarceration rate The number of persons serving sentences in federal and state prisons per 100,000 people in the general population.

prison industrial complex The extensive financial and political enterprise represented by the correctional system.

prison industries Employment of prisoners in a business enterprise, often with market restrictions.

Prison Industry Enhancement Certification Program (PIECP) A provision of the Justice System Improvement Act of 1979 that establishes partnerships between state and local prison industries and the private sector.

prison information General statistical compilations about prisoner characteristics, inmate population data, historical information, and other pertinent documents describing prison life and inmate characteristics.

State Prison Population as a Percent of Capacity, 1995–2002

	State prisons
Highest capacity	1,161,262
Lowest capacity	1,005,466
Population as a percent of capacity*	
Highest	
1995	114
2000	100
2001	101
2002	101
Lowest	
1995	125
2000	115
2001	116
2002	117

*Excludes inmates sentenced to prison but held in local jails and inmates in private facilities (unless included in the reported capacity). See *Jurisdiction notes*.

Source: Harrison and Beck, *Prisoners in 2002*, 7.

prison intelligentsia A group of inmates who, during the rehabilitation era, took advantage of educational programs to develop their academic skills and eventually came to enjoy reading.

prisonization The social process whereby inmates determine where other inmates should be placed in the inmate subculture according to their strength, fighting ability, attractiveness, age, social connections, race, ethnicity, and other criteria.

prison labor Any manufacture of goods or performance of services by prisoners.

prison population The number of inmates held in state or federal prisons and in local jails for a specific year. *See table.*

prison psychosis Any attitudes among certain inmates that develop in response to rigid controls exerted by prison officials. Characteristics include apathy, aggressiveness, agitation, violence, and defeatism. Inmate reactions are affected by the amount of time they are incarcerated. Prison psychosis creates difficulties for the prisoner in adjusting to noninstitutional life when he or she is released from confinement.

"prison queen" An inmate who is openly homosexual and manifests feminine characteristics in dress and manner.

prison reform Any activity designed to improve prison conditions, usually sponsored or initiated by organized groups interested in prisoner welfare and rehabilitation.

prison riot Any uncontrolled mob action by inmates in prisons, which sometimes results in deaths of inmates and prison personnel.

prison rules All institutional regulations, which are required to be constitutionally acceptable, and should be clear, intelligible, and prohibit only behavior that threatens important institutional interests, such as order and inmate safety.

prison sentence *See* **prison commitment.**

prisons for profit Any custodial facilities that are owned and operated by private corporations, such as Corrections Corporation of America.

prison smarts Knowledge concerning how to manage the prison community's resources that inmates learn through experience. Such knowledge permits them to live their lives in prison on their own terms.

prison stupor Referred to as prison psychosis, this is a mental escape from the deprivations of prison life.

prison subculture An inmate code of conduct independent from prison rules and regulations. It is characterized by special hand or verbal signals and gestures, particular conduct, and a pecking-order system of status from high to low, depending on one's strength or access to scarce goods or contraband.

Number of Persons Held in State or Federal Prisons or in Local Jails, 1995–2002

	Total inmates in custody	Prisoners in custody on December 31		Inmates in jail on June 30	Incarceration rate[a]
		Federal	State		
1995	1,585,586	89,538	989,004	507,044	601
1996	1,646,020	95,088	1,032,440	518,492	618
1997	1,743,643	101,755	1,074,809	567,079	648
1998	1,816,931	110,793	1,113,676	592,462	669
1999[b]	1,893,115	125,682	1,161,490	605,943	691
2000[c]	1,937,482	133,921	1,176,269	621,149	684
2001[c]	1,961,247	143,337	1,180,155	631,240	685
2002[c]	2,033,331	151,618	1,209,640	665,475	701
Percent change, 2001-2002	3.7%	5.8%	2.5%	5.4%	
Average annual increase, 1995-2002	3.6%	7.8%	2.9%	4.0%	

Note: Counts include all inmates held in public and private adult correctional facilities.
[a]Number of prison and jail inmates per 100,000 U.S. residents at yearend.
[b]In 1999, 15 States expanded their reporting criteria to include inmates held in privately operated correctional facilities. For comparisons with previous years, the State count 1,137,544 and the total count 1,869,169 should be used.
[c]Total counts include Federal inmates in nonsecure, privately operated facilities (6,598 in 2002, 6,515 in 2001 and 6,143 in 2000).

Source: Harrison and Beck, *Prisoners in 2002*, 2.

prison toughs An inmate who manifests a constant hostility toward prison officials, conventional society, and most other prisoners.

privacy, right to A constitutional right of all United States citizens relating to the Fourth Amendment, which protects persons against unreasonable searches and seizures of their persons and homes. *See also* **Bill of Rights.**

Private Benefit Prison Industry System A system of prison industry in which a private entity derives profits from its involvement in the industry.

private facilities Correctional institutions run by private corporations or individuals.

private law Statutes that regulate relations among individuals.

privately commissioned presentence investigation reports PSIs prepared by private individuals, usually employed by private corporations who provide such services; unofficial reports that supplement official PSIs preceding one's sentencing.

privately secured bail An arrangement similar to the bail bondsman system, except that bail is provided without cost to the defendant. A private organization may provide bail for indigent arrestees who meet its eligibility requirements.

private person arrest Citizen-initiated arrest of a criminal suspect; citizen arrest or arrest of a suspect by private security personnel.

private police All nonpublic law enforcement officers including guards, watchmen, doorkeepers, crossing guards, bridge tenders, private detectives, and investigators.

private prisons Correctional facilities operated by private firms on behalf of local and state governments.

private protective services Proprietary commercial organizations that provide protective services to employers on a contractual basis.

private rehabilitation agency Any one of a number of different kinds of privatized services for probationers, parolees, and ex-offenders, including juveniles, providing temporary housing, job assistance, and other services.

private right Entitlement by an individual under the law. The Bill of Rights conveys numerous private rights.

private sector People or businesses not affiliated with the government (the "public sector").

private sector involvement in corrections Some jurisdictions contract with private companies to provide specific services such as food or to manage or build a facility.

private security, private security agencies Those self-employed individuals and privately funded businesses and organizations providing security-related services to specific clientele for a fee, for the individual or entity that retains or employs them, or for themselves, in order to protect their persons, private property, or interests from various hazards. Organizations that provide security for individuals and organizations.

private wrongs Torts or civil wrongs.

privatization of prison management Delegation of the ownership and operation of prisons and jails to private corporations. Privatization is believed to be more economical than public ownership and operation methods.

privilege A term associated with instrumental Marxism, defined as the possession of that which is valued by a particular social group in a given historical period, including life, liberty and happiness, material goods and wealth, luxuries, and land. Barry Krisberg has written extensively about this phenomenon in his book *Crime and Privilege: Toward a New Criminology* (1975).

privilege, absolute Insulation from prosecution for criminal liability, regardless of malice, bestowed on certain government officials such as representatives or congressmen.

privileged communication A verbal exchange between two or more people that the court cannot require either to disclose. Examples include doctor-patient relations, therapist-client interactions, and priest-penitent relations.

proactive Acting in anticipation of an event.

proactive management An approach to management that involves trying to anticipate and correct problems before they develop by continually evaluating programs and planning for and creating opportunities for the organization to develop the capacity to pursue its mission.

proactive patrol, proactive police work An active search for offenders by police in the absence of reports of violations of the law. Arrests for crimes without victims are usually proactive, as opposed to reactive.

probable cause Reasonable suspicion or belief that a crime has been committed and that a particular person committed it.

probable evidence Any information that is presumptive.

probate To prove or establish a will.

probate court, surrogate's court A judicial proceeding in which wills are administered or executed.

probatio "Test" (Latin); a period of proving, trial, or forgiveness.

probation An alternative sentence to incarceration in which the convict stays under the state's authority. It involves conditions and retention of authority by the sentencing court to modify the conditions of sentence or to resentence the offender if the offender violates the conditions. Such a sentence should not involve or require suspension of the imposition or execution of any other sentence. *See box p. 204.*

probation, juvenile A sentence of supervised, conditional release of a juvenile for a specified period, usually under supervision of a juvenile probation officer.

probation agency, probationary department Any correctional agency of which the principal functions are juvenile intake, the supervision of adults or juveniles placed on probation status, and the investigation of adults or juveniles for the purpose of preparing presentence or predisposition reports to assist the court in determining the proper sentence or juvenile-court disposition.

probation agreement A document outlining the general conditions of probation for either juveniles or adults, indicating any special conditions or requirements, and in force as long as the offender abides by its conditions.

probationary employees Rookies or new recruits who are in training for a given period. Following their training, they become regular full-time employees or officers.

probation caseload The number of persons supervised by a probation officer.

probation contract An agreement between a probation officer and a probationer specifying what conditions should be met as a part of one's probation program. *See box p. 205.*

probation counselor Anyone who supervises a juvenile while the juvenile is on probation.

probationer A convicted offender sentenced to a nonincarcerative alternative such as supervised release in the community, restitution, community service, fines, or other conditions. *See table p. 206.*

probation officer A professional who supervises probationers.

probation revocation The process of declaring that a sentenced offender violated one or more terms of a probation program imposed by the court or probation agency. If probation involved a suspended prison or jail sentence, the revocation may mean that the original sentence is invoked and the individual is sent to prison or jail.

probation supervision fees Monetary amounts set by statute that are required of probationers to contribute to their own supervision.

probation supervisory population movement Entries and exits from the probation population over a given time interval.

probation termination The ending of the probation status of a probationer because of routine expiration of the probationary period, early termination by the court, or some program violation involving probation revocation.

probation violation Any act or failure to act of a probationer that does not conform to the conditions of his or her probation.

probation violator A probationer who has failed to obey one or more of his or her probation conditions.

probation without adjudication Deferred prosecution, which allows judges to withhold adjudication in the interests of reducing the penetration of offenders into the criminal-justice system.

probation workload The total set of activities required in order to carry out the probation agency functions of intake screening of juveniles cases, referral of cases to other service agencies, investigation of juveniles and adults for the purpose of preparing predisposition or presentence reports, supervision or treatment of juveniles and adults granted probation, assisting in the enforcement of court orders concerning family problems such as abandonment and nonsupport cases, and such other functions as may be assigned by statute or court order.

probative Tending to prove the truth or falsehood of a proposition. A witness may give testimony that has probative value if it shows the truthfulness or the untruthfulness of another witness or defendant.

probing The technique used by an interviewer to stimulate discussion and obtain more information.

problem behavior syndrome (PBS) A clustering of antisocial behaviors including substance abuse, smoking, precocious sexuality and early pregnancy, educational underachievement, suicide attempts, and thrill seeking, that some consider to be a precursor to criminality.

Major Developments in the History of Probation in the United States

1791 Passage of Bill of Rights

1817 New York passes first good-time statute

1824 New York House of Refuge is founded

1830 Judge Peter Oxenbridge Thatcher in Boston introduces release on one's own recognizance

1836 Massachusetts passes first recognizance with monetary sureties law

1841 John Augustus introduces probation in the United States in Boston

1863 Gaylord Hubbell, warden of the State Correctional Facility at Ossining, NY, (Sing Sing), visits Ireland and is influenced by Walter Crofton's ticket of leave or mark system, which later led to good-time credits earned by prisoners for early release

1869 Elmira Reformatory is established in New York, with early release dates set by the board of managers

1870 Establishment of the National Prison Association (later the American Correctional Association), emphasizing indeterminate sentencing and early release

1876 Zebulon Brockway releases inmates on parole from Elmira Reformatory

1878 First probation law is passed by Massachusetts

1899 Illinois passes first juvenile-court act, creating special juvenile courts

1906 Work release originates in Vermont through informal sheriff action

1913 Huber Law, the first work-release statute, originates in Wisconsin

1916 U.S. Supreme Court declares that sentences cannot be indefinitely suspended by courts; rather, this right is a legislative right

1918 Furlough program begins in Mississippi

1932 44 states have parole mechanisms

1954 All states have parole mechanisms

1965 Prisoner Rehabilitation Act applicable to federal prisoners is passed by Congress

1967 *Mempa v. Rhay* case is decided involving a probationer; court-appointed counsel must be appointed for probationers who are in jeopardy of having their probation programs revoked; any indigent must be represented by counsel at any stage where substantial rights of accused may be affected

1972 *Morrissey v. Brewer,* a U.S. Supreme Court case involving a parolee, declares parolees entitled to minimum due-process rights before parole programs are revoked; also requires two-stage hearings for parole revocations, to determine if allegations are true and what punishment(s) should be imposed

1973 *Gagnon v. Scarpelli,* a U.S. Supreme Court case involving probationer, equates probation revocation with parole revocation; entitles probationers to a two-stage hearing before probation is revoked

1976 Maine abolishes parole

1983 In *Bearden v. Georgia,* U.S. Supreme Court declares that probationers who are indigent and can not pay fines can not have their probation programs revoked solely on that basis

1984 Sentencing Reform Act is passed, creating the U.S. Sentencing Guidelines, implemented in 1987; federal probation use is reduced from 65 percent to 10 percent as the result of newly implemented presumptive guidelines

1985 In *Black v. Romano,* U.S. Supreme Court declares that judges are not obligated to consider options other than incarceration for probationers whose programs are revoked

1987 In *Board of Pardons v. Allen,* U.S. Supreme Court declares that parolees are entitled to a statement of reasons for parole denial from parole board

1998 In *Pennsylvania Board of Probation and Parole v. Scott,* U.S. Supreme Court declares Fourth Amendment right not applicable in parole revocation proceedings, where parole officer enters one's premises without a warrant and seizes incriminating evidence which is later used in parole revocation action

problem-oriented policing A policing technique employing citizen involvement in defining community crime problems and suggesting solutions for them.

Problem Solver In the White Typology, the type of police officer who pays attention to citizen needs described in S.O. White's 1972 work *A Perspective on Police Professionalism. See also* **White Typology.**

problem-solving policing *See* **problem-oriented policing.**

pro bono "For the good" (Latin); in law practice, legal services provided at no cost to the defendant (e.g., indigent clients receive assistance from defense attorneys on a *pro bono* basis).

procedural criminal law, procedural law Rules that specify how statutes should be applied against those who violate the law; procedures whereby the substantive laws may be implemented.

procedural defense A defense claiming that the defendant was in some significant way discriminated against in the justice process or that some aspect of official procedure was not followed in the investigation or prosecution of the crime alleged.

procedural due process The constitutional requirement that all persons be treated fairly and justly by government officials. Accused persons can be arrested, prosecuted, tried, and punished only in accordance with procedures prescribed by law.

procedural rights Those rights that govern or dictate the process by which a hearing or court action will proceed.

procedure Court protocol developing from custom.

proceeding Any official meeting, such as a court, for the purpose of settling a case or dispute or finding guilt or innocence; an official inquiry.

Florida Probation Conditions

1. Probationer must report to the probation supervisor as directed.
2. Probationer must permit supervisors to visit him or her at his or her home or elsewhere.
3. Probationer must work faithfully at suitable employment insofar as may be possible.
4. Probationer must remain within a specified place.
5. Probationer must make reparation or restitution to the aggrieved party for the damage or loss caused by his or her offense in an amount to be determined by the court.
6. Probationer must make payment of the debt due and owing to a county or municipal detention facility for medical care, treatment, hospitalization, or transportation received by the probationer while in that detention facility.
7. Probationer must support his or her legal dependents to the best of his or her ability.
8. Probationer must make payment of debt due and owing to the state subject to modification based on change in circumstances.
9. Probationer must pay any application fee assessed and attorney's fees and costs assessed subject to modification based on change of circumstances.
10. Probationer must not associate with persons engaged in criminal activities.

11. Probationer must submit to random testing as directed by the correctional probation officer or the professional staff of the treatment center where he or she is receiving treatment to determine the presence of alcohol or use of alcohol or controlled substances.
12. Probationer is prohibited from possessing, carrying, or owning any firearm unless authorized by the court and consented to by the probation officer.
13. Probationer is prohibited from using any intoxicants to excess or possessing any drugs or narcotics unless prescribed by a physician. The probationer shall not knowingly visit places where intoxicants, drugs, or other dangerous substances are unlawfully sold, dispensed, or used.
14. Probationer will attend an HIV/AIDS awareness program consisting of a class of not less than 2 hours or more than 4 hours in length, the cost of which shall be paid by the offender, if such a program is available in the county of the offender's residence.
15. Probationer shall pay not more than $1 per month during the term of probation to a nonprofit organization established for the sole purpose of supplementing the rehabilitative efforts of the Department of Corrections.

Special Conditions of Probation

1. Probationer is required to be intensively supervised and under probation officer surveillance.
2. Probationer is required to maintain specified contact with the probation officer.
3. Probationer shall be confined to an agreed-upon residence during hours away from employment and public service activities.
4. Probationer shall perform mandatory public service.
5. Probationer shall be supervised by means of an electronic monitoring device.

6. Probationer placed on electronic monitoring shall be monitored 24 hours a day.
7. Probationers placed on electronic monitoring will be subject to investigation and supervision by a probation officer 24 hours a day.
8. The court shall receive a diagnosis and evaluation of any probationer for appropriate community treatment.

Source: Florida Department of Corrections, *Probation Guidelines.*

Characteristics of Adults on Probation, 1995, 2000, and 2002

Characteristic of adults on probation	1995	2000	2002
Total	100%	100%	100%
Gender			
Male	79%	78%	77%
Female	21	22	23
Race			
White	53%	54%	55%
Black	31	31	31
Hispanic	14	13	12
American Indian/ Alaska Native	1	1	1
Asian/Pacific Islander[a]	--	1	1
Status of probation			
Direct imposition	48%	56%	60%
Split sentence	15	11	9
Sentence suspended	26	25	22
Imposition suspended	6	7	9
Other	4	1	1
Status of supervision			
Active	79%	76%	75%
Inactive	8	9	10
Absconded	9	9	11
Supervised out of State	2	3	2
Other	2	3	2
Type of offense			
Felony	54%	52%	50%
Misdemeanor	44	46	49
Other infractions	2	2	1
Most serious offense			
Sexual assault	**	**	2%
Domestic violence	**	**	7
Other assault	**	**	10
Burglary	**	**	8
Larceny/theft	**	**	13
Fraud	**	**	5
Drug law violations	**	24	24
Driving while intoxicated	16	18	17
Minor traffic offenses	**	6	6
Other	84	52	8
Adults entering probation			
Without incarceration	72%	79%	83%
With incarceration	13	16	14
Other types	15	5	2
Adults leaving probation			
Successful completions	62%	60%	62%
Returned to incarceration	21	15	14
With new sentence	5	3	3
With the same sentence	13	8	6
Unknown	3	4	4
Absconder[b]	**	3	3
Other unsuccessful[b]	**	11	13
Death	1	1	--
Other	16	11	9

(cont'd)

Note: For every characteristic there were persons of unknown status or type. Detail may not sum to total because of rounding.
**Not available.
--Less than 0.5%.
[a]Includes Native Hawaiians.
[b]In 1995 absconder and "other unsuccessful" statuses were reported among "other."

Source: Glaze, *Probation and Parole in the United States, 2002,* 4.

process A summons requiring the appearance of someone in court.

process in practice A writ or summons issued by a judge to gain jurisdiction over a person or property; to expedite a judgment or cause of action.

procuracy, procuratorate A term used in many countries to refer to agencies with powers and responsibilities similar to those of prosecutors' offices in the United States.

procurement policy An expressed or written statement defining conditions and terms under which a law enforcement agency or other body obtains goods or services.

productivity Either measured or unmeasured output by officers, including numbers of arrests, time on duty, tickets issued, and participation in public events.

profession Any career for which a recognized specialized course of study is required in order to belong to a special class known as professionals.

Professional In the Muir Typology, the type of police officer who enforces the law with integration of coercion and sympathy described in William Ker Muir, Jr.'s 1977 work *Police: Streetcorner Politicians. See also* **Muir Typology.**

professional Having the characteristics of a profession; usually measured by acquiring education and expertise relating to a given field, such as corrections or law enforcement; possessing body of knowledge, skills, and legitimacy through licensing, to act in certain ways.

Professional, Reciprocator, Enforcer, and Avoider The four typologies of police officers in William Ker Muir, Jr.'s 1977 work *Police: Streetcorner Politicians.* Professionals enforce the law with proper integration of coercion and sympathy; Enforcers are cynical and coercive; Reciprocators are wishy-washy, can't make up their minds, and are oversympathetic with citizens in law enforcement situations; and Avoiders avoid work, collect paychecks, and are considered shirkers and slackers. This classification scheme is also known as the Muir Typology.

professional criminal *See* **career criminal.**

Professional Education Council A group created by the American Correctional Association for the purpose of devising a common curriculum leading to an associate degree in corrections for corrections officers, including jail guards. A degree is not obligatory in most jurisdictions.

professionalization The process of acquiring standards, greater education, practical skills, certification, and recognition from approved bodies, which promotes more ethical behavior and a commitment to excellent community service and quality of life.

professionalization movement Efforts by various interests to encourage higher standards of selection for police officers, including more formal education and training.

professional model An explanation of organizations focusing on increased specialization within the organization as a means of attaining greater flexibility in managing organizational problems. Expanding the training of organizational members to deal with problematic events more flexibly is professionalizing them. Professional persons are typically identified as persons trained in professional schools, possessing complex skills and special knowledge, and equipped with internalized control mechanisms.

professional period The era in law enforcement (early 1900s) when the goal was to increase the professionalization of policing, thus removing it from political pressures.

professional thief A skilled offender who is committed to crime as an occupation and thinks of him- or herself as a criminal.

profiler One who attempts to describe the psychological and personal characteristics of unknown criminals.

profiling The process of using past information about offenders and their behavior to track, identify, or apprehend other such offenders.

profit-making firm An organization that charges greater than cost for services rendered and returns the surplus value to its owners.

pro forma "As a matter of form" (Latin); according to form; a matter of policy or procedure; following specific rules.

program-centered approach A method of planning intermediate sanctions in which planning for a program is usually undertaken by a single agency, which develops and funds the program.

Program for Female Offenders, Inc. A community-based corrections program designed to reform female offenders and create economically independent clients.

programmed contact devices An electronic monitoring system in which telephonic contact is made at random times with the offender, whose voice is electronically verified by a computer.

Program on Human Development in Chicago Neighborhoods (PHDCN) A large-scale research project designed to assess the many causes of delinquency, crime, substance abuse, and violence. The program researches families and individuals, and devises community measures.

progressives Early-twentieth-century American reformers who believed that state action could relieve human ills.

Prohibition The era between 1919, when the Eighteenth Amendment to the Constitution prohibited liquor in the United States, and 1933, when the Twenty-First Amendment allowed it once more.

prohibition A ban of a particular act or set of actions or behaviors, such as barring consumption of certain goods or acceptance of services of particular types.

Prohibitory Act of 1940 A law that prohibited the interstate transport of all prison-made goods except agricultural commodities and goods produced for states and their political subdivisions.

Project Heavy A program located in Los Angeles County involving peer and group counseling for children and youths ages 8 to 18. Youth leaders are targeted for change so that they can set good examples for others.

projection A psychological defense mechanism by which the blame for unacceptable thoughts or behavior is directed at another person or group.

Project Newgate A program commenced in the 1970s to bring the first years of college to prisons together with instructors and curriculum.

Project New Pride Established in Denver, CO, in 1973, this program blends education, counseling, employment, and cultural education for children ages 14 through 17. Eligible juveniles include those with two prior adjudications for serious misdemeanors or felonies. The program's goals are to reintegrate juveniles into their communities through school participation and employment and thereby reduce recidivism.

project organization A group of several criminals who come together to commit one or a series of acts of robbery, burglary, fraud, or smuggling.

Project Outward Bound *See* **Outward Bound; wilderness experiments.**

Project Rio A multiagency program operated by the Texas Department of Criminal Justice. While in prison, inmates are assessed and referred to appropriate academic or vocational programs. Upon release, they are referred to the Texas Employment Commission to continue training or for job placement.

proletariat In Marxism, the working class, which is dominated by the bourgeoisie in a capitalist society. Under socialism, the working class would ideally also be the owners of production, thus leading to a classless society.

PROMIS *See* **Prosecutor's Management Information System (PROMIS).**

promiscuity Indiscriminately engaging in sexual relations with multiple partners.

promulgate To officially put forth, as in a document containing rules and regulations.

proof beyond a reasonable doubt The standard of proof to convict in a criminal case.

propeller head A term used by computer hackers to describe a computer geek.

property Any tangible item of value, including real property, land, or personal effects. It may also include rights, privileges, or entitlements.

property bond Setting bail in the form of land, houses, stocks, or other tangible property. In the event the defendant absconds prior to trial, the bond becomes the property of the court.

property clerk A police officer or other law enforcement employee who is responsible for all property delivered to a police station, and who is expected to catalog property and store it for safekeeping.

property crime A nonviolent felony involving criminal acts against property including but not limited to larceny, burglary, and vehicular theft.

property-crime index Property crimes included in Part I offenses, including burglary, motor-vehicle theft, larceny/theft, and arson.

Property Crime Program (Sting) An undercover program initiated by law enforcement agencies in 1974 to penetrate fencing operations and recover stolen property. Fictitious businesses are created by law enforcement agencies and publicize that they will buy stolen merchandise. Perpetrators of crimes are arrested when they bring stolen property to sell to these fictitious business operations.

property in service The eighteenth-century practice of selling control of inmates to shipmasters who would then transport them to colonies for sale as indentured servants.

property rights Common-law entitlements to ownership of private property against public restraints.

prop friendship A close relation between two inmates, one of whom may be stronger than the other, who back one another up in violent confrontations.

proponent One who is in favor of a given view or proposal.

proportionality A sentencing principle that holds that the severity of sanctions should be in direct relation to the seriousness of the crime committed.

propositions Statements about the real world that lack the high degree of certainty associated with assumptions (e.g., "Burnout among probation officers may be mitigated or lessened through job enlargement and giving officers greater input in organizational decision making" and "Two officer patrol units are less susceptible to misconduct and corruption than one officer patrol units").

proprietary alarm system Any detection device that is similar to a central alarm system except that the equipment is centrally located and under constant guard by security personnel. Guards monitor the system and respond to intruders or alarm activations.

proscribe To forbid or prohibit.

pro se "For himself" (Latin); acting as one's own defense attorney in criminal proceedings; representing oneself.

prosecute To move forward with a criminal proceeding against one or more suspects and bring the matter to court for resolution.

prosecuting attorney *See* **prosecutor.**

prosecution Carrying forth of criminal proceedings against a person, culminating in a trial or other final disposition such as a plea of guilty in lieu of trial.

prosecution agency, prosecutorial agency Any local, state, or federal body charged with carrying forth actions against criminals; state legal representatives, such as district attorneys or U.S. Attorneys and their assistants, who seek to convict persons charged with crimes.

prosecution witness One who has information about a crime that incriminates a defendant, and who testifies against the defendant, supporting the district attorney's legal case.

prosecutor A court official who commences civil and criminal proceedings against defendants, and who represents state or government interest, prosecuting defendants on behalf of the state or government.

prosecutorial bluffing An attempt by the prosecution to bluff a defendant into believing a case is much stronger than it really is. This tactic may be used to elicit a guilty plea from a defendant to avoid a lengthy trial where proof of the defendant's guilt may be difficult to establish.

prosecutorial discretion The decision-making power of prosecutors based on the wide range of choices available to them in the handling of criminal defendants, the scheduling of cases for trial, and the acceptance of bargained pleas. The most important form of prosecutorial discretion lies in the power to charge or not to charge a person with an offense.

prosecutorial misconduct Any immoral, unethical, or illegal acts associated with prosecutorial duties (e.g., it is unethical for a prosecutor to pursue a case against a defendant when the prosecutor knows the defendant is innocent).

prosecutorial waiver Prosecutors in juvenile cases having those cases transferred to the jurisdiction of criminal court.

prosecutor's information A charging document, usually involving a minor misdemeanor offense, initiated by the prosecutor against one or more criminal suspects.

Prosecutor's Management Information System (PROMIS) An early management information system devised for the scheduling of federal criminal cases, the management of witnesses, and the evaluation of prosecution services.

prosecutrix A female prosecutor; also, a female victim who makes a criminal complaint against a perpetrator of a crime.

prosocial bonds The attachment a child has with positive elements of society such as schools, parents, and peers.

prostitute One who engages in sexual acts in exchange for something of value.

prostitution The practice of engaging in sexual activities for hire.

protection order A judicial order intended to keep a threatened or vulnerable individual safe from another.

protection racket An illegal enterprise in which business owners are encouraged to pay for protection against robbery, assault, arson, or other crimes that could negatively affect their businesses. Those selling such protection indicate that such crimes will occur if the payments are not made.

protective custody Segregation of a variety of inmates who are in serious danger of being harmed for reasons that include their offense (e.g., child molestation), gambling debts, homosexual triangles, or being identified as a snitch.

protective factors A range of variables that research has found to protect or insulate a juvenile from becoming a delinquent.

protective neighboring A combination of cooperative surveillance and willingness to intervene in a crime by the residents of a community.

protective-sweep doctrine The rule that when police officers execute an arrest on or outside private premises, they may conduct a warrantless examination of the entire premises for other persons whose presence would pose a threat, either to their safety or to evidence capable of being removed or destroyed.

protest Collective action taken by a group to show disapproval of a public policy or legislative action, which may involve violent or nonviolent conduct and is more or less organized.

Protestant Ethic A moral principle that requires that everyone should work hard. *See also* **Weber, Max.**

provincial courts Criminal courts of limited jurisdiction in Canada.

provisional exit An authorized temporary leave from prison to attend a legal proceeding or appear in court, for the purpose of being a witness to a criminal case or for purposes of filing an appeal.

provocation Any action by one party designed to cause another person to act in a particular way, such as assault.

Provo Experiment A community-based delinquency rehabilitation program in Provo, UT, designed to curb recidivism through group therapy and other group activities.

provost marshal A military officer whose authority is similar to that of a chief of police.

prowl car A police cruiser that patrols neighborhoods looking for crime.

proximate cause The factor that is closest to actually causing an event such as the death of a victim.

proximity hypothesis A view devised by Rodney Stark and others that persons become crime victims because they live or work in high-crime areas with large criminal populations.

proxy Someone acting on behalf of someone else in any legal proceeding, civil or criminal.

PR-24 A nightstick fashioned of synthetic material with a handle attached perpendicular to the main shaft.

"pruno" Also called "Raisin Jack," this is an intoxicating brew made by accumulating sugar, grains, fruit, or potatoes, adding yeast, and allowing the mixture to ferment for several days or weeks.

prurient interest An excessive or unnatural interest in sex.

pseudofamilies Adaptive groupings of female inmates that involve family-like relationships. Each individual within the group adopts a role as one of the family members.

psilocybin *Psilocybe mexicana;* a hallucinogenic drug known as the "magic mushroom" of Mexico that produces effects similar to LSD, but less potent.

psychedelic drugs Any narcotics capable of creating hallucinogenic experiences or euphoria.

psychiatric disability, psychologic disability Any type of mental disturbance.

Psychiatric Emergency Coordinating Committee This group formulated a comprehensive Memorandum of Agreement that took effect on April 1, 1985. The administrator of each participating agency agreed in writing to a list of specific actions. Their plan was designed to divert mentally ill persons involved in minor criminal behavior from the criminal-justice system into the health-care system, where they could receive more appropriate care.

psychiatric social worker Someone trained to work with psychiatrists and psychologists to assist in treating patients with mental disorders. Their role includes interviewing patients to determine their symptoms, counseling patients' families, and assisting patients in their rehabilitative efforts.

psychiatry The study of medical practice that deals with the diagnosis, treatment, and prevention of mental and emotional disorders.

psychoactive drug, psychoactive substance A chemical substance that affects cognition, feeling, and/or awareness.

psychoanalysis A method of dealing with human behavior, based on the writings of Sigmund Freud, that views personality as a complex composite of interacting mental entities.

psychoanalytic perspective, psychoanalytic theory Sigmund Freud's theory of personality formation through the id, ego, and superego at various stages of childhood. The theory maintains that early life experiences influence adult behavior.

psychological autopsy The art of analyzing the personality and mental condition of a person after his or her death.

psychological fact A mentally perceived statement believed true mentally rather than through proof by written statements or tangible physical evidence.

psychological manipulation Actions based on subtle forms of intimidation and control that are used by police interviewers to pressure suspects to disclose incriminating information.

psychological profiling An attempt to categorize, understand, and predict behavior of certain types of offenders based on behavioral clues that they provide.

Psychological School A perspective on criminological thought that views offensive and deviant conduct as the products of dysfunctional personality systems. The conscious, and especially the subconscious, contents of the human psyche are identified by psychological thinkers as major determinants of behavior.

psychological screening The administration of tests or assessment devices designed to exclude potential police officers whose personal behaviors and personalities may be unsuitable for police work.

psychological theories Explanations linking criminal behavior with mental states or conditions, antisocial personality traits, and early psychological moral development.

psychoneurosis Any one of a number of emotional disorders thought to stem from problems of tension or anxiety. The term is commonly shortened to "neurosis."

psychopathic behavior Chronic asocial behavior rooted in severe deficiencies in the development of the conscience; actions virtually lacking in conscience.

psychopathic killer One who kills, often repeatedly, with no apparent remorse.

psychopathic personality A person lacking in warmth and affection, exhibiting inappropriate behavior responses, and unable to learn from experience.

psychopathology The science and study of mental disorders.

psychopathy A condition in which a person appears to be psychologically normal but in reality has no sense of responsibility, shows disregard for others, is insincere, and feels no sense of shame, guilt, or humiliation.

Psychopathy Check List—Revised (PCL-R) A psychometric instrument developed by Robert D. Hare to assess the extent to which an individual possesses antisocial tendencies and traits.

psychopharmacological A descriptive term used to depict actions of persons who have ingested mood-altering drugs (e.g., violence may be psychopharmacological if the perpetrator ingested LSD or PCP).

psychosis, psychotic disorder A mental illness characterized by a loss of contact with reality.

psychosurgery Any type of brain surgery designed to treat mental disorders.

psychotherapy Highly structured counseling in which a skilled therapist helps a client solve conflicts and a make more positive adjustment to society.

psychotic A person whose id has broken free and now dominates his or her personality. Psychotics suffer from delusions and experience hallucinations and sudden mood shifts.

psychoticism A dimension of the human personality describing persons who are aggressive, egocentric, and impulsive.

PTL scandal A 1988–1989 scam by evangelists Jim and Tammy Bakker of the Praise the Lord organization, a televangelistic church. The Bakkers collected millions of dollars in donations from followers and used the money largely for their own purposes. Jim Bakker was convicted and served less than five years of a 45-year sentence.

public defender An attorney appointed by the court to represent an indigent defendant.

public-defender agency, public-defender organization Any local, state, or federal organization, public or private, established to provide a defense to indigent clients or those who otherwise cannot afford to pay for their own defense against criminal charges. Because everyone is entitled to counsel, whether or not counsel can be afforded, such services exist to meet the needs of those without funds to hire their own private counsel.

public disclosure Information about police agencies and officers disseminated by a public relations officer.

public enemy A dangerous and notorious criminal. Several public enemies in past years include John Dillinger, Al Capone, and Bugsy Siegel.

public housing Government-subsidized residences for low-income families.

public humiliation A method of publicly shaming offenders as a punishment.

public-interest disputes Commonweal strikes (by police officers or firefighters) that may jeopardize public safety.

public-interest law A general legal term covering quasi-legal activities that may be undertaken to protect a large group of persons or a community rather than isolated individuals, such as class-action suits involving environmental disputes and consumer protection.

public intoxication The condition of being severely under the influence of alcohol or drugs in a public place to the degree that one may endanger persons or property.

public law A general classification of law consisting of constitutional, administrative, international, and criminal law.

public nuisance Any action or condition that adversely affects the public in a community.

public opinion The feelings and preferences of citizens, often measured by a survey.

public-order advocate One who suggests that under certain circumstances involving a criminal threat to public safety, the interests of society should take precedence over individual rights.

public-order crime, public-order offense Any breach of the peace or disturbance of community order. Such offenses include sit-in demonstrations at abortion clinics, rioting behavior, and disturbing the peace.

public-order mandate The government's task of maintaining law and order and protecting society from crime and criminals.

public relations Persons or bureaus involved in creating more effective and pleasant interactions and working associations between citizens, police officers, and agencies.

public-safety department Any agency organized at the state or local level to incorporate various emergency service functions in potential disaster situations.

public-safety doctrine, public-safety exception The holding that police can legally question an arrested suspect without giving the *Miranda* warning if the information they need is essential for maintaining public safety.

public-sector union Any organized labor union representing employees working within some branch of local, state, or federal government.

public-works system A system of prison industry in which prisoners are employed in the construction of public buildings, roads, and parks.

public wrongs Actions considered crimes in preliterate societies, such as sacrilege and other offenses against religion, treason, and witchcraft.

publisher-only rule A court ruling mandating that inmates can only receive hardback books if they are mailed directly by publishers, book clubs, or bookstores.

pugilistic attitude In forensics, the position of a burned body that resembles a boxer, with arms extended as if engaged in a boxing match.

pulling method The safe-cracking craft of using a screw-type device with a long handle to penetrate a safe door and pull the combination wheel and its attached spindle from the safe.

Pullman Strike An 1894 strike in Pullman, IL, involving the Pullman Palace Car Company. Wages had been cut without reducing workers' rents. The striking railway workers paralyzed railroads in more than half of all states. The U.S. government used the Sherman Antitrust Act to issue an injunction against the union and quell the strike, thus restoring order until the matter could be legally resolved.

Pulse Check A periodic data collection effort of the Office of National Drug Control Policy to keep up to date on current trends in drug use in the United States.

punching tool A device used by safe burglars to batter away a safe's lock and spindle so that the locking bars can be accessed and removed and the safe opened.

punishment Any penalty imposed for committing delinquency or a crime.

punishment, capital *See* **capital punishment**.

punishment gap The discovery that juveniles waived to adult court for the first time are usually given leniency accorded to first-time adult offenders.

punitive damages Monetary awards made over and above what would compensate a plaintiff for his or her losses.

punitive intent standard A standard that distinguishes incarceration from other forms of confinement, such as detention, on the grounds of a demonstrable alternative purpose for the confinement, and reasonable relationships between the confinement practice and the alternate purpose.

punitive model of juvenile justice The current model of juvenile justice, which holds that juveniles are just as responsible as adults for their delinquent behavior and that they should be held accountable and punished.

punitive prevention The use of the threat of punishment to forestall criminal acts.

"punks" In corrections, young inmates who are seduced by gifts or favors, and who, by threat or force, become the sex slaves of stronger inmates.

Pure Food and Drug Act A federal law enacted in 1906 to regulate food preparation industries and ensure adequate food quality. Subsequently, the law affected statements that could be placed on drugs and foods stating their benefits and potential effects.

purge The complete removal of arrest, criminal, or juvenile record information from a given record system.

purge fluid A product of decomposition that may drain from the mouth or nose of a deceased person.

Puritans A religious group in early America who essentially believed that through hard work, religion, and education, a person could get closer to God. These ideals served as the foundation for the creation of early institutions of juvenile justice in the United States.

pursuit An attempt by police to apprehend a traffic offender or a criminal suspect, usually in a vehicle.

putrefaction Decomposition of a corpse.

pyromania A psychological condition that includes the compulsion to start fires, often for sexual gratification.

Q

qualified immunity A defense to a Civil Rights Act suit that claims the right violated was not clearly enunciated and therefore the violation was unintentional and the official should not be liable for damages.

quality circles An application of total quality management. This approach encourages workers classified similarly (e.g., dispatchers, detectives, or patrol) to interact with one another in group settings to resolve problems common to their particular work specialties. Acting as a team, these personnel can often offer recommendations leading to savings in labor and time, enhanced service, and improved working conditions.

quality of life In community policing, an umbrella term referring to the absence of petty annoyances, and hence, a good quality of life, usually in urban locales. Petty annoyances can range from drug-dealing to abandoned cars and barking dogs.

Quantico, VA The site of the Federal Bureau of Investigation National Academy on the U.S. Marine Corps base at Quantico. It includes the FBI training camp and also contains a crime laboratory and a critical-response team.

quarter-session courts Originally, courts that met four times a year, usually to try serious cases. Where this old title is still used, it is in connection with a higher or trial court.

quash To vacate a sentence or annul a motion.

quasi-experiment A study resembling an experiment except that random assignment is not used to determine which subjects receive which level of treatment. Quasi-experiemnts usually have less internal validity than experiments.

quasi-judicial immunity A type of insulation from lawsuits enjoyed by probation officers who work directly for judges when preparing presentence investigation reports. Officers may include erroneous information in their reports that may be harmful to probationers, but the officers enjoy some immunity within the scope of their duties under the power of the judges with whom they work.

quasi-judicial powers Lawmaking authority established by Congress to administer regulatory agencies.

Quasimilitary Model Auburn-type prisons were organized in military fashion, which included a rigid daily schedule, with inmates wearing striped uniforms and being marched to and from all activities, and harsh discipline.

Queer Nation An organization of gay men formed in 1990 in New York City following the terrorist bombing of an allegedly gay nightclub. The group advocates gay rights and promotes demonstrations to further gay rights.

questioned specimens Any physical evidence the origin or ownership of which is unknown.

questionnaire A paper-and-pencil document consisting of questions, administered by mail, in person, or by telephone, requesting information from particular respondents. It may include sociodemographic and attitudinal measures. Questionnaires are a major means of data collection for subsequent analysis and one of several popular data collection methods.

Quetelet, Lambert Adolphe Jacques (1796–1874) Belgian mathematician who was one of the first to use statistics to analyze social data, particularly criminological data. Quetelet founded the cartographic school of criminology, in which factors such as season, climate, gender, and age were believed to be relevant variables influencing the occurrence of crime. He wrote *Treatise on Man and the Development of His Faculties* (1835).

Quinney, Richard (1934–) Quinney wrote *The Social Reality of Crime* (1970). His theory consists of six propositions: (1) definition of crime (crime is a definition of human conduct created by authorized agents in a politically organized society); (2) formulation of criminal definition (such definitions describe behaviors that conflict with interests of that segment of society interested in shaping public policy); (3) application of criminal definitions (criminal labels are applied by persons who have political power); (4) development of behavior patterns in relation to criminal definitions (people engage in actions likely to be defined as criminal); (5) construction of criminal conceptions (conceptions of crime are diffused in the segments of society by communication); and (6) the social reality of crime (constructed by the formulation and applications of criminal definitions, the development of criminal behavior patterns, and the construction of criminal conceptions). Quinney is also known for viewing criminology for its peacemaking potential. He sees peacemaking as a key criminology goal and believes that the establishment of social justice is the way to eliminate all forms of predatory behavior.

qui tam suit An action taken by an individual against a contractor of the U.S. government alleging criminal or unethical conduct.

Qur'an The holy book of Islam.

R

rabble hypothesis A theory suggested by John Irwin that persons of lower socioeconomic statuses are placed in jails to rid society of their presence. Homeless, detached, or disreputable persons are often selected by police officers for confinement. The objective is to remove these undesirables from society so that other social classes will not have to interact with them.

rabble management The control of persons whose noncriminal behavior is offensive to the community, such as public nuisances, derelicts, junkies, drunks, vagrants, and the mentally ill.

race relations An area of study focusing on the behaviors and customs of particular ethnic groups as a means of understanding them better to improve relations between police and members of these different groups; also, the process of bringing members of different ethnic or genetic backgrounds together to promote harmony and goodwill.

racial profiling The practice of law enforcement officers stopping minority citizens when no offense has been committed.

racist One who believes in the superiority of a particular race and hates members of other races, ethnicities, and/or religious groups.

Racketeer Influenced and Corrupt Organizations Act (RICO) A federal statute permitting law enforcement officers to charge or sue criminal enterprises or organizations, passed by Congress in 1970 to attack and prosecute organized crime. The act also authorizes both civil and criminal asset forfeiture.

racketeering Any organized crime (e.g., organized gambling, prostitution, illegal regulation of commerce).

radar Ra(dio) d(etecting) a(nd) r(anging); radio-frequency energy used to measure distance, depth, or altitude. Police officers use radar systems to detect speeders in vehicles on highways.

radial design The physical design associated with the Pennsylvania system of prison housing units, usually untiered cells on outside walls radiating from a central control hub.

radical One who advocates abrupt and basic changes in present laws pertaining to economic and social conditions.

radical approach A perspective that focuses on crime by both the underprivileged and the privileged, and attributes crime by both groups to the conditions of a capitalist society.

radical criminology A school of thought that stresses control of the poor by the wealthy and powerful. Crime is defined by those in political and economic power in such a way as to control the lower socioeconomic classes (e.g., vagrancy statutes are manifestations of control by the wealthy over the poor).

radical feminists Also known as Marxist feminists, radical feminists hold that gender inequality stems from the unequal power of men and women and the subsequent exploitation of women by men. The cause of female delinquency originates with the onset of male supremacy and the efforts of males to control females' sexuality.

radical groups In corrections, left-wing groups that focus on changing society rather than helping inmates or changing prison conditions.

radicalism An attitude that goes to the basis of a problem or situation, questions the fundamentals of an economic or governmental system, and advocates immediate change in various political and social institutions.

radical nonintervention The principle of doing the minimum legally possible to a criminal offender. This approach attempts to minimize the stigma attached by the justice system (e.g., preferring diversion to a formal criminal procedure).

radio frequency motion detector A sensor that detects the motion of an intruder through radiated radio frequency or an electromagnetic field.

radio watch Citizen band (CB) radio operators who supplement police organizations and emergency personnel by monitoring and surveilling, passing important information to relevant agencies for action.

railroad police One of the largest private police organizations, whose function is to protect railroad cargo, passengers, property, and general railway integrity.

Railroad Strike An 1877 strike involving railroad workers on two-thirds of all U.S. rail lines. The strike lasted two weeks, during which 100 persons were killed and millions of dollars in property were destroyed.

rampage killings Multiple-victim killings that are random in nature, characterized by violent and quick outbursts on the part of one or two suspects seemingly without reason or motive.

Ramsey, JonBenet (1990–1996) A young girl and regular beauty pageant contestant from a prominent Boulder, CO, family who was found murdered in her home over Christmas in 1997. A subsequent investigation yielded few suspects, and the crime remains unsolved.

Rand Corporation A private institution located in Santa Monica, CA, that conducts investigations and surveys of criminals and examines a wide variety of social issues. It distributes literature to many criminal justice agencies and contracts with and conducts research for other institutions.

Randolph, Edmund (1753–1813) A Williamsburg, VA, native who became the first U.S. attorney general under President George Washington in 1793 and secretary of state from 1794–1795. He was placed on trial for treason, where Aaron Burr defended him, and acquitted.

Randolph Plan Sometimes called the Virginia Plan, a court system consisting of superior and inferior courts, with the former having considerable appellate authority over the latter. It evolved from England's royal court system.

randomization Selection of elements from a population in such a way that each element has an equal and an independent chance of being included in a subsequent sample; in social experiments, a method of assigning subjects to experimental and control groups.

randomized experimental design Considered the standard of evaluation designs to measure the effects of a program on crime or delinquency or other outcomes, this design involves randomly assigning subjects either to receive the program or stimulus (the experimental group) or not to receive it (the control group).

rank-and-file building tenders In Texas prisons, the head building tender's assistants.

rank men The lowest level of inmate in the Arkansas prison farms; farm laborers.

ransom Money or valuable property demanded in exchange for something of value in someone else's possession.

ransom note A document left by kidnappers indicating their demands.

rape, rape, forcible Traditionally, the felony of sexual intercourse forced by a man on a woman (not his wife) against her will by violence or the threat of violence. The stipulation that the woman not be the man's wife is omitted in modern statutes. More generally, sexual intercourse or attempted sexual intercourse with persons against their will, by force or threat of force. The concept stems from common law. The traditional man-against-woman definition has been replaced by a gender-neutral one, aggravated felonious sexual assault, in most U.S. jurisdictions.

rape, sadistic Illegal sexual intercourse by force that is motivated by the offender's desire to torment and abuse the victim.

rape, statutory *See* **statutory rape.**

rape kit A package of products to facilitate the collection and preservation of semen, hairs, and other physical evidence taken from a rape victim.

rape shield laws Regulations protecting the identity of a rape victim or preventing disclosure of a victim's sexual history.

rape trauma syndrome Predictable reactions of rape victims, including an initial acute reaction in which the victim's life is disrupted seriously, followed by a long-term phase in which the victim's symptoms decrease and then a period of readjustment and reconstruction.

rape without force or consent Sexual intercourse with a person who is legally of age but who is either unconscious or whose ability to judge or control his or her behavior is impaired by mental defect or intoxicating substances.

"rapos" Also called abnormal sex offenders, these are sex offenders sentenced for incest and child molestation.

rap sheet An acronym for record of arrests and prior convictions (sometimes prosecutions).

rasphouses Workhouses in which the major form of work involved the rasping of bark off of logs to produce materials that could be used in making dyes.

rated capacity The number of beds or inmates assigned by a rating official to a jail or prison.

rational choice, rational-choice theory The theory that crime is the result of a decision-making process in which an offender weighs the potential penalties and rewards of committing a crime.

rational goal model A perspective on organizations that places high values on productivity and efficiency and achieves these through goal planning, technological development, and evaluation.

rationalism A school of thought that holds that the totality of knowledge can be acquired only by strict adherence to the forms and rules of logic.

rationalization A defense mechanism by which one justifies one's behavior with socially acceptable reasons.

rational model Any characterization of an organization that stresses planned and coordinated activities and rules that lead to goal attainment and greater organizational effectiveness (e.g., scientific management and bureaucracy).

ratio scale In statistics, the level of measurement entitling the use of any mathematical formula without restriction. It assumes absolute zero as the base of scale score.

"rats" Inmates known to inform on others to the staff.

rattle watchmen In the fifteenth century, persons equipped with noise-making rattles who were expected to shout and rattle their rattles in the event that they observed crimes in progress or fleeing suspects.

rave An all-night party, often located in a downtown bar or warehouse, that usually involves significant drug and alcohol use.

Ray, James Earl (1928–1998) Ray assassinated Martin Luther King, Jr. in Memphis, TN, on April 4, 1968. He was convicted and sentenced to life imprisonment, and died in prison of liver disease.

RCMP *See* **Royal Canadian Mounted Police (RCMP).**

reaction formation An individual response to anxiety in which one reacts to a stimulus with abnormal intensity or inappropriate conduct. It is an act of rejecting that which a person desires but cannot have.

reaction time (RT) The interval between introducing a stimulus and observing a reaction to the stimulus. It can be used as a measure of the effects of alcohol on the body as a way of showing impairment when driving while intoxicated.

reactive management Waiting until an incident manifests itself before taking action.

reactive patrols, reactive police Police activity occurring in response to a stimulus, such as a reported crime incident or notification that a crime has been committed; the opposite of proactive police work.

reactive units Police youth squad units that respond to calls for service whenever gangs are terrorizing neighborhoods.

real evidence Physical evidence such as a weapon, records, fingerprints, or stolen property.

Realist In the Broderick Typology, the type of police officer who has "just a job" or "the hell with it" attitude about work, who is, so to speak, retired in place. *See also* **Broderick Typology.**

reality therapy, reality therapy model The equivalent of shock probation, in which short incarcerative sentences are believed to provide "shock" value for juvenile offenders and scare them from reoffending.

real property Land and buildings permanently attached thereto.

rearrest An indicator of recidivism; taking a parolee or probationer into custody for investigation in relation to crimes committed. Rearrest is not necessarily indicative of new crimes committed by probationers or parolees, as it may be the result of police officer suspicion.

reasonable competence The standard by which legal representation is judged gauging whether the defendant received a reasonable level of legal aid.

reasonable doubt Standard used by jurors to decide if the prosecution has provided sufficient evidence for conviction. Jurors vote for acquittal if they have reasonable doubt that the accused committed the crime.

reasonable force The amount of force necessary to subdue suspects and that is not considered excessive.

reasonable man A concept and standard whereby normal and appropriate conduct is gauged to determine whether one's actions or inactions were criminal or otherwise violated some civil duty.

reasonableness test A judicial criterion that mandates that there be a valid rational connection between a prison rule restricting inmates' rights and the legitimate government interests put forth to justify it or that there be alternative means of exercising this right; also, criterion used by the U.S. Supreme Court to determine whether inmate petitions that protest correctional institution policies and practices should be heard. The interests of jail/prison officials are contrasted with those of inmates in determining what is best for all concerned. Institutional safety considerations usually outweigh inmate interests and allegations of legal rights violations.

reasonable suspicion Warranted suspicion (short of probable cause) that a person may be engaged in criminal conduct.

rebellion A mode of strain adaptation in which people reject cultural goals and develop a new set of goals, and reject institutionalized means to reach cultural goals and develop a new set of means; also, behavior by which a person seeks to create a new social structure that will more effectively allow people to meet what the rebel considers appropriate goals.

rebutting evidence, rebutting testimony Any questioning or presentation of evidence designed to offset, outweigh, or overwhelm evidence presented by the other side or question the veracity or truthfulness of witnesses.

recall A procedure for dismissing elected officials from public office.

receiver Someone legally appointed to possess property of others pending formal judicial action.

receiving stolen goods, receiving stolen property An offense consisting of accepting merchandise or other goods known to be or suspected of being stolen.

reception, reception and diagnostic center, reception center, reception process A separate unit on prison grounds apart from regular prison cells and the inmate population that receives inmates from the court for their initial classification.

recidivism The return to criminality, including rearrest, reconviction, and reincarceration of previously convicted felons or misdemeanants.

recidivism rate The proportion of offenders who, when released from probation or parole, commit further crimes.

recidivism statutes Habitual-offender laws, three-strikes-and-you're-out laws, persistent felony offender laws, and repeat offender laws, all of which involve limitations on the number of convictions one can obtain before the next violation triggers a separate offense with a mandatory punishment of life without the possibility of parole.

recidivist Repeat offender.

Reciprocator In the Muir Typology, the type of police officer who is wishy-washy, can't make up his or her mind, and is oversympathetic in enforcement of the law, described in William Ker Muir, Jr.'s 1977 work, *Police: Streetcorner Politicians. See also* **Muir Typology.**

Reckless, Walter A criminologist who has described containment theory (1957, 1961), which suggests that youths have the ability to resist criminal inducements ("containments"), but that there are prevalent crime-inducing forces at work: "internal pushes" (discontent, anxiety, rebellion, mental conflict), "external pressures" (relative deprivation, limited opportunities, unemployment, insecurity), and "external pulls" (deviant peer group influence, mass media).

reckless behavior, reckless endangerment An activity that increases the risk of harm.

reclassification The periodic reassessment of an inmate during the period of incarceration.

recognizance Personal responsibility to return to court on a given date and at a given time.

reconviction The situation in which a former convicted offenders are found guilty of new crimes by a judge or jury. Reconviction is a measure of recidivism.

record The compilation of one's prior offenses; a collection of information about a criminal or suspected criminal; collected information about a given person for background purposes.

record expungement An order by a governor, president, or other executive to obliterate one's arrest and/or criminal conviction or delinquency adjudication.

record piracy The illegal reproduction and distribution of copyrighted sound recordings.

recoupment Forcing indigents to repay the state for at least a part of their legal fees.

recreational drug user One who experiments with drugs infrequently and in social settings where occasional drug use is acceptable, for pleasure, and not for dependency.

recreational killer A serial killer whose primary motivation to kill is pleasure.

recreational law enforcement Policing activities in areas where the public engages in recreational activities, such as hiking, snowmobiling, and boating.

recusal The act of judges excusing themselves from proceedings, especially those in which they have an apparent conflict of interest in the case being tried.

Red Army Faction (RAF) Spawned from the Baader-Meinhof Gang in Germany, the RAF was founded in 1970 by Andreas Baader and Ulrike Meinhof. It eventually became one of Europe's most feared terrorist organizations. Although numerous arrests of RAF leaders occurred during the 1980s and 1990s, the group continues and is responsible for many bombings, kidnappings, assassinations, and other acts of violence against German, U.S., and NATO organizations and officials. The name "Red Army Faction" is probably derived from a note received by press following escape of Andreas Baader from a Berlin prison in May 1970, which said, among other things, "Build up the Red Army!" Actually, the Red Army Faction was named after the Red Army, a Japanese leftist terrorist organization, and the word "faction" was used to suggest that the group was a part of a larger, international Marxist struggle.

red-handed Caught in the act of committing a crime.

Red Hannah The whipping post used by Delaware prison authorities to flog inmates until the state's corporal punishment statute was repealed in 1973.

redirect examination Questioning of a witness following the adversary's questioning under cross-examination.

Red Light Abatement Law A statute enacted in California in 1913 abating or preventing the operation of any business or residence used as a place of illegal gambling, lewdness, or prostitution, and causing such a business or residence to be closed.

red-light district Any neighborhood in a community where prostitution is known to exist and flourish. In early times, red lights were hung outside of homes known for having prostitutes on premises.

redress of grievances Correction or amelioration of government abuses. Individuals may seek such relief if they believe one or more of their constitutional rights have been violated.

reductionism A British procedure for removing petty offenders from imprisonment to make room for more serious offenders.

reentry court A court that manages the return to the community of individuals released from prison.

reeves Chief law enforcement officers of English shires or counties (circa 900s–1600s), who were the forerunners of county sheriffs.

referee A lawyer who serves part-time or full-time to handle simple, routine juvenile cases; a lower-level judicial official.

reference relationship A person, group, or entity that a person takes into account when making decisions. These relationships are key sources of values, norms, attitudes, and aspirations.

referent power A form of influence based on friendship, in which subordinates comply because they like or identify with their superior.

referral Any citation of a juvenile to juvenile court by a law enforcement officer, interested citizen, family member, or school official. Referrals are usually based on law violations, delinquency, or unruly conduct. *See box p. 216.*

referral to intake The process of transferring a juvenile from the custody of law enforcement officers or a social welfare agency to the custody of an intake officer or juvenile probation officer who will conduct a preliminary screening to determine whether the juvenile should move forward to juvenile court and be charged.

reflective role taking A process whereby youths take on antisocial roles assigned to them by others.

reformation The idea that prison will change inmates by instilling a new sense of morality and purpose in them.

reformatory A detention facility designed to change criminal behavior or reform it.

reformatory concept, reformatory style A late-nineteenth-century correctional model based on the use of the indeterminate sentence and a belief in the possibility of rehabilitation, especially of youthful offenders. This concept faded with the emergence of industrial prisons around the turn of the century.

reformatory model A plan of custody for women stressing reformation, reintegration, skill acquisition, and moral and social improvement.

reform schools An antiquated term designating juvenile facilities geared to improve the conduct of those forcibly detained within them.

refreshing one's memory, reminding During testimony, witnesses may have their memories refreshed by rereading some document or looking at pictures to enable them to recall with greater clarity something that happened some time ago.

refugee One who flees from his or her original country to seek sanctuary in another country; a person displaced because of war or social upheaval.

refused admittance requirement A federal requirement that before law enforcement officers may enter one's premises by force with a valid search warrant, they must reasonably suspect that the inhabitant has refused to admit them or that exigent circumstances exist to justify their forced intrusion into the premises. This requirement was articulated in *United States v. Banks* (2003).

Regimented Inmate Discipline Program (RID) An Oklahoma Department of Corrections program operated in Lexington, OK, for juveniles, stressing military-type discipline and accountability. Its facilities are secure and privately operated.

Regional Information Sharing System (RISS) A program consisting of six regional centers that share criminal intelligence information that focuses on narcotics trafficking, violent crime, and gang activities. Its membership ranges between 500 and 1300 agencies.

regionalization Attempts to save money and improve services by consolidating certain functions, such as dispatch and prisoner transportation and emergency medical services, on a regional rather than a local basis. Some jurisdictions have established regional jails to more effectively hold inmates from remote geographical locations in states. Sites for regionalization of different activities include San Diego, CA; Marion County, IN; and Jacksonville, FL. *See also* **regional jail.**

regional jail A jail built and run using the combined resources of several contiguous jurisdictions, such as counties or cities. Certain areas of Virginia have established such facilities to reduce the costs of incarceration.

regression A defense mechanism in which threatening impulses, wishes, and feelings are automatically kept from consciousness.

regulation Legal rules created by government agencies.

rehabilitate To correct criminal behavior through educational and other means, usually associated with prisons.

rehabilitation The process of reforming offenders through vocational and educational training, counseling, and other services.

Rehabilitation Act of 1973 Congressional action prohibiting discrimination in bidding on government contracts or other federal financial assistance programs because of any disability. The act requires affirmative action in allocating such contracts.

rehabilitation era Loosely defined as 1870–1920, beginning with the founding of the Elmira Reformatory, although efforts to rehabilitate prisoners continue.

rehabilitation model, rehabilitative model A plan of corrections emphasizing the provision of treatment programs designed to reform offenders.

rehabilitation policy A correctional system with high concern for the individual offender and low concern for the community, using identification strategies to help the offender mature.

rehabilitative ideal The ideology in corrections that the ultimate goal is to cause offenders to become law abiding by learning useful skills and means of coping with life in mainstream society.

Rehnquist, William Hubbs (1924–) Chief justice of the U.S. Supreme Court (1986–). Rehnquist served in the U.S. Army Air Corps (1943–1946), and achieved the rank of sergeant. He attended Stanford University (B.A., M.A., 1948) and Harvard University (M.A., 1950), and earned a law degree from Stanford University in 1952. He engaged in private law practice in Phoenix, AZ, from 1953 to 1969, emphasizing civil litigation. He was nominated an associate justice of the U.S. Supreme Court by President Richard Nixon in 1971, and was sworn in in 1972. He became chief justice of the U.S. Supreme Court in 1986 under President Ronald Reagan. He is active in professional, civil, and church affairs, and has written numerous articles on various legal subjects for professional periodicals. He is considered an anti-choice advocate concerning abortion, and has consistently called for *Roe v. Wade* (1973) to be overruled. In 2004, he was the second-oldest member of the U.S. Supreme Court at 80. It has been thought that he would retire in recent years, but he has defied expectations.

Rehnquist Court The U.S. Supreme Court under the leadership of Chief Justice William Rehnquist (1986–present).

Reiman, Jeffrey (1942–) A criminologist who advocates a conflict perspective model. He believes that criminalized acts are threats to the wealthy and powerful and that such acts are

---

Referral Form Used by New Mexico JPPOs to Refer Youths into an Early Intervention Program

REFERRAL FORM

Date: _____ File #: _____ Cause # (if appl.): _____

Client's Name: _____ DOB: _____ Age: _____

Address: _____ Zip: _____ Phone #: _____

Ethnicity: _____ Gender: _____ SS#: _____

Referral Source: _____ Primary Language Spoken: _____

Guardian's Name: _____ Relationship: _____

Guardian's Legal Status: _____

Current Offense: _____

School: _____ Grade: _____ Reg. Ed. _____ Special Ed. _____

Client's Mental Health Issues (meds, if any): _____

_____

_____

_____

Guardian's Mental Health Issues (meds, if any): _____

_____

_____

_____

Directions to client's residence:

Source: New Mexico Juvenile Division (2003).

prevalent among the poor, that the criminal-justice system fails in its attempt to deal with street crime, and that white-collar offenses should be punished as harshly as street crime. Reiman wrote *The Rich Get Richer and the Poor Get Prison* (1984).

reincarceration Return to prison or jail for one or more reasons including parole or probation violations and revocations, rearrests, and reconvictions.

reinforcement In social learning theory, strengthening or increasing the likelihood of the future occurrence of some voluntary act. Positive reinforcement is produced by rewarding behavior, negative reinforcement by an unpleasant or punishing stimulus. Differential reinforcement is produced when a person comes to prefer one behavior over another as the result of more rewards and less punishment. Self-reinforcement refers to self-imposed positive or negative sanctions.

reintegration A punishment philosophy that promotes programs that lead offenders back into their communities. Reintegrative programs include furloughs, work release, and halfway houses.

reintegration model A correctional model that emphasizes the maintenance of offender ties with family and community as a method of personal reform, in recognition of the fact that the offender will be returning to the community.

reintegrative shaming A method of correction elaborated by John Braithwaite in *Crime, Shame, and Reintegration* (1989), that encourages offenders to confront their misdeeds, experience shame because of the harm they caused, and then be brought back into society.

relabeling Redefinition of juvenile behaviors as more or less serious than previously defined. An example would be police officers who relabel or redefine certain juvenile behaviors, such as curfew violation, as loitering for purposes of committing a felony, such as burglary or robbery. Relabeling is associated with political jurisdictions that have deinstitutionalized status offenders or have divested juvenile courts of their authority over specific types of juvenile offenders. As one result, police officers lose power, or their discretionary authority, to warn such juveniles or take them into custody. A new law may mandate removing such juveniles to community social services rather than to jails. In retaliation, some officers may relabel status behaviors as criminal ones, in order to preserve their discretionary authority over juveniles.

relapse prevention A treatment strategy that prepares the individual to deal with the various circumstances that can lead to resumption of the condition being treated.

relation A joint occurrence or covariation between two or more variables.

relative deprivation A condition existing when people of wealth and poverty live in close proximity. Feelings of envy or envious indignation may arise whenever persons see others with goods or lifestyles that they feel they deserve but don't have. Some criminologists attribute crime-rate differentials to relative deprivation.

release, pretrial A procedure whereby accused persons who have been taken into custody may be freed before and during their trials.

release from detention The authorized exit from detention of a person subject to criminal- or juvenile-justice proceedings.

release from prison Any lawful exit from a federal or state confinement facility primarily intended for adults serving sentences of one year or longer, including all conditional and unconditional releases, deaths, and transfers to other jurisdictions.

release on bail Release by a judicial officer of an accused person who has been taken into custody, upon the accused's promise to pay a certain sum of money or property if he or she fails to reappear later in court as required, a promise that may or may not be secured by the deposit of an actual sum of money or property.

release on own recognizance (ROR) An arrangement in which a defendant is temporarily set free to await later trial without having to post a bail bond. Persons with ROR status are usually well-known or have strong ties to the community and have not been charged with serious crimes.

release to parole Setting free from prison inmates who have become entitled to early release by virtue of serving their minimum time; conditional release subject to parole officer supervision and other requirements.

release to third party The release by a judicial officer of an accused person who has been taken into custody to a third party who promises to return the accused to court for criminal proceedings.

relevant evidence Information tending to prove or disprove a fact.

reliability In research, the property of a measure to assess consistently whatever it says it is measuring.

relief officers Experienced correctional officers who know and can perform almost any custody role within the institution, used to temporarily replace officers who are sick or on vacation or to meet staff shortages.

Religious Freedom Restoration Act (RFRA) Federal legislation passed in 1993 requiring that the government shall not substantially burden a person's exercise of religion unless it is in furtherance of a more compelling government interest.

remand To send back (e.g., the U.S. Supreme Court may remand a case to the lower trial court in which it was originally tried, where it is usually retried or revised).

remedial Ameliorative; curative; describing work taken to make up for some deficiency.

remedy Any declared solution to a dispute between parties (e.g., if someone is found guilty of slashing another's automobile tires, the remedy may be to cause the convicted offender to compensate the victim with money for the full value of the destroyed tires).

remission Reverting to an original condition; a release or pardon for an offense.

remote supervision Surveillance such as is observed in podular facilities; direct supervision jail surveillance.

removal *See* **waiver.**

removal of landmarks The relocation of monuments or other markings that designate property lines or boundaries for the purpose of fraudulently reducing the owner's interest in lands and estates.

removal proceedings The process of transferring a defendant in one court to another court, where the case may be heard and adjudicated.

remunerative power Influence vested in the ability of the supervisor or superordinate to reward subordinates or others; obtaining compliance from others by enticing them with rewards.

reparations Monetary damages awarded to victims that must be paid by criminals for any injuries suffered or property damaged.

reparole The process of placing an inmate on parole who has previously been on parole. The parolee has violated one or more parole conditions, has had his parole program terminated, but has qualified to be paroled again.

repeal A legislative act removing a law from the statute books.

repeat offender Any juvenile or adult with a prior record of delinquency or criminality.

repeat victimization A phenomenon wherein a small number of victims of crime are victimized more than once, in disproportionate numbers. This phenomenon is similar to the observation that a small number of high-volume offenders commit a disproportionately high number of crimes, or that criminal acts are concentrated in hot spots.

replevin An action in court by a person to recover possessions which have been unlawfully seized.

replication research Conducting a subsequent study based on the general guidelines of a previous study; an attempt to obtain the same results from a different sample by conducting fresh research at a later point in time; repetition of experiments or studies that utilize the same methodology.

report Documentation of an event; a written or oral record of an incident or meeting.

reported crime Official crime information collected by individual police and sheriff's departments and sent to the FBI for tabulation and distribution; crimes known to the police.

"representing" Tossing or flashing gang signs in the presence of rivals, often escalating into a verbal or physical confrontation.

reprieve An executive act temporarily suspending the execution of a sentence, usually a death sentence. A reprieve differs from other suspensions of sentence not only in that it almost always applies to temporary withdrawal of a death sentence, but also in that it is usually an act of clemency intended to provide the prisoner with time to secure amelioration of the sentence.

request for proposals (RFP) A solicitation from a public or private organization for research plans to investigate particular topics of interest to the organization. The U.S. Department of Justice and the Office of Juvenile Justice and Delinquency Prevention Programs distribute these requests regularly, with guidelines and formats to follow. These solicitations lead to research proposal submissions, which may or may not eventually be funded.

requisition A demand made from one state governor to another to return a specific fugitive from justice to the originating state.

research Any activity undertaken in an objective fashion to discover relationships between two or more variables; scientific investigation of a problem.

res gestae "Things done" (Latin); events that speak for themselves.

resident In corrections, a person required by law to reside in a particular place, such as a mental hospital, for the purpose of confinement, supervision, and care.

residential child care facility A dwelling other than a detention or shelter facility providing care, treatment, and maintenance for children.

residential commitment A sentence to a correctional facility for a period of time. The facility is nonsecure, requiring the client to reside in the facility at night. The person is permitted to work during daytime hours and move about the community unsupervised.

residential community center, residential treatment center A government facility serving juveniles whose behavior does not necessitate the strict confinement of a training school, often allowing them greater contact with the community.

residential facility Any home or correctional facility in which residents are only obligated to stay during evening hours, such as a halfway house. Such facilities usually offer programs involving counseling, skills development, and other therapeutic activities.

residential programs A community-based program that requires clients to live in a facility while participating in the program.

resistance In corrections, actions manifested by a prisoner who is attempting to evade an officer's efforts to control him or her.

resisting arrest The crime of obstructing or opposing a police officer making an arrest.

res judicata "The thing has been judged" (Latin); matters already decided in court, which are not subject to relitigation.

resource broker A probation officer acting as a referral agent and advocate for his or her clients.

resource dilution As the number of children in a family increases, the social and economic resources available to raise them are spread thinner and become less effective.

respondeat superior "Let the superior answer" (Latin); a doctrine under which liability is imposed on an employer for the acts of his or her employees that are committed in the course and scope of their employment.

respondent A person asked to respond in a lawsuit or writ.

response time The interval between receipt of information and action taken by officials or authorities.

responsible A condition of being legally accountable for one's actions and obligations.

ressentiment Systematic self-poisoning of the mind that is created by repression of internalized emotion. Ressentiment is found in members of highly structured work organizations with numerous explicit rules and edicts. Persons with this condition may contemplate seeking revenge against their superiors. Theorist Max Scheler used this concept to describe police officer response to the highly regimented work environment of police departments.

restitution A stipulation by a court that offenders must compensate victims for their financial losses resulting from crime; compensation to a victim for psychological, physical, or financial loss. Restitution may be imposed as a part of an incarcerative sentence.

restoration A goal of criminal sentencing that attempts to make the victim "whole again."

restorative justice Mediation between victims and offenders whereby offenders accept responsibility for their actions and agree to reimburse victims for their losses, It may involve community service and other penalties agreeable to both parties in a form of arbitration with a neutral third party acting as arbiter.

restorative policing Police-based family group conferencing uses police, victims, youths, and their families to discuss the harm caused by the youth and creates an agreement to repair the harm; similar to restorative justice.

Restrained Hands-On Doctrine A modification of the hands-on doctrine of the mid-1970s that recognized that whereas inmates do not forfeit all constitutional rights, their rights are not as broad as those enjoyed by nonprisoners.

restraining order A requirement by the court prohibiting contact between one person and another.

restraint policy A correctional system with low concern for the offender and the community, which uses no strategy to influence offender behavior; a holding strategy.

restraints Any device, such as handcuffs, a belly chain, leg irons, or a straitjacket, used to subdue an inmate temporarily.

restrictive deterrence The effect of a penalty that causes people to limit their violations of the law in order to minimize the risk of punishment.

retained counsel An attorney, not employed or compensated by a government agency or subunit or assigned by the court, who is privately hired to represent a person in a criminal proceeding.

retaliation Revenge for wrongs, real or perceived.

retentionist One who favors capital punishment.

rethermalization unit In corrections, any mobile unit that is used to bring food to the appropriate serving temperature.

Retired Senior Volunteer Program A national effort that places retirees in community volunteer positions. The program has been received in many quarters as one approach to augment police manpower shortages.

retreatism A mode of strain adaptation in which cultural goals are abandoned and institutionalized means are also rejected.

retreatist gang A gang whose members retreat into drugs and alcohol use.

retreatist subculture A concept from opportunity theory in which youths relinquish cultural goals by withdrawing from society. Rejected by members of both criminal and conflict subcultures, these youngsters seek status and outlets such as drugs.

retreat to the wall A legal term referring to the obligation of a victim of aggression to escape from some location by any means possible to avoid harming or killing the aggressor.

retribution Revenge.

retributionist philosophy A view of punishment that says offenders should be punished as a form of revenge for the wrongs that have committed against others.

retribution model *See* "**just-deserts**" **model**.

retroactive A term referring to things past (e.g., making a new law applicable to a previous time period, which is currently an unconstitutional action).

return The deliverance of a previously issued writ to the originator of the writ, such as a judge.

reus "Defendant" (Latin); the person formally charged with a crime.

Reuss-Ianni Typology Also known as the 4-World Syndrome, this classification scheme is a version of the "we-they" mentality that anthropologists call the world view. It divides officers into "street cop," "station cop," "us," and "them." The street versus station distinction refers to whether or not the officer has a patrolman's mentality (e.g., if an officer assigned to the station most of the time, a sergeant, still keeps and uses a patrol car); "us" refers to a willingness to work with the public. The 4-World Syndrome holds that officers must adjust to life in all four worlds: the inner (defensive) world of policing; the outer (cooperative) world of the public; the street (quick response) world; and the station (paperwork) world. The scheme was suggested by Elizabeth Reuss-Ianni in her 1984 work *Two Cultures of Policing*.

revenge A motive or act of getting even with someone else for some real or perceived wrong.

reversal An action by a higher court to overturn, set aside, or vacate a particular conviction of a matter being appealed.

reverse certification A situation in which a criminal court has exclusive jurisdiction and transfers a case to a juvenile court.

reverse waiver A motion to transfer a juvenile's case from criminal court to juvenile court following a legislative or automatic waiver action.

reverse waiver hearing, reverse waiver action A formal proceeding used in jurisdictions with automatic transfer laws to contest the automatic transfer of a juvenile to the jurisdiction of a criminal courts.

reversible error Errors committed by judges during trial that may result in reversal of convictions against defendants.

review The procedure whereby a higher court examines one or more issues emanating from a lower court on an appeal by the prosecution or defense.

review, writ of Any form of process issuing from an appellate court and directing someone to bring up for review a record or decision from a lower court.

review hearing A periodic meeting to determine whether the conditions of the case plan for an abused child are being met by the parents or guardians of the child.

revocation, probation or parole *See* **probation revocation; parole revocation**.

revocation hearing A two-stage proceeding conducted to determine whether a probationer's or parolee's program should be terminated or modified. The first stage determines whether an infraction occurred and whether it is a violation of one or more of the probationer's or parolee's program conditions. The second stage determines the punishment, which for probationers may be termination or modification of probation, transfer to a more intensive supervised probation program, or placement in a jail. For parolees, it may be return to prison, more intensive parole supervision, or transfer to a different type of parole program.

revoke To terminate a probation or parole order, because of either a rule violation or the commission of a new offense, and force the offender to begin or continue serving his or her sentence.

revolution Radical change of society through violent or nonviolent action.

revolutionary science The abrupt development of a new paradigm that is accepted only gradually by a scientific community.

revolver A handgun in which bullets are contained in a cylinder.

reward A bounty or monetary sum paid by a government to someone who performs a particular service for that government, usually to someone who furnishes information to the government about someone else, leading to the recovery of money or property that legally belongs to the government through forfeiture or fine or other penalty.

reward power Influence based on the ability of a superior to reward subordinates.

Reynolds, James Bronson An early prison reformer who established the University Settlement in 1886 in New York.

RFRA *See* **Religious Freedom Restoration Act (RFRA).**

ricin A toxic protein derived from the beans of the castor plant. Castor beans are found worldwide, and the toxin is fairly easily produced, thus making it useful as a potential weapon for bioterrorists. Also, it can be spread easily through the air, thus heightening the risk of respiratory exposure. Symptoms include weakness, fever, cough, and pulmonary edema, which occur within 18 to 24 hours of exposure, followed by severe respiratory distress and death from hypoxemia within 36 to 72 hours.

RICO *See* **Racketeer Influenced and Corrupt Organizations Act (RICO).**

"ride the medical pony" A correctional term concerning the abuse of the prison medical system by inmates who deliberately fake symptoms of illnesses in order to gain attention.

ridge A mark or line making up part of one's fingerprint.

Ridgway, Gary Leon (1949–) The Green River Killer, originally arrested on November 30, 2001, when DNA from sperm on the victims' bodies was linked to him, who confessed to murdering 48 women between 1982 and 1984, and even into the 1990s. Ridgway, 54, was a former truck painter who picked up prostitutes in the Green River area near Seattle, WA, raped and murdered them, and dumped their bodies in the Green River. Prosecutors originally charged Ridgway with seven murders and had given up hope of finding evidence linking him with the others. Through a negotiated plea bargain, in exchange for showing authorities where bodies could be found, Ridgway was sentenced to life without the possibility of parole in December 2003. Ridgway told the court at his sentencing hearing that he hated prostitutes because he didn't like to pay for sex. He said he dumped some bodies in the Green River, and disposed of others in remote areas near Seattle.

rifling *See* **spiral rifling.**

Rigel geographical system A system of geographical profiling that uses a criminal geographic targeting algorithm that shows the proximity of criminals' homes to crimes committed. Developed by Environmental Criminal Research, Inc. of Vancouver, B.C.

"right guy" An inmate code referring to any inmate who honors the prisoners' social codes.

rightist One who is a conservative or a reactionary.

right of allocution A defendant's right to speak before his or her sentence is pronounced.

rights of accused Persons accused of crimes are entitled to a court-appointed attorney if they cannot afford one; they may elect to refrain from conversing with police officers and remain silent; they may give evidence in their own behalf; they may cross-examine their accusers; and have other rights articulated in the Bill of Rights and the *Miranda* warning.

rights of defendant Constitutional guarantees to all persons charged with crimes, including representation by counsel at various critical stages, such as when being charged with crimes and at preliminary hearings, arraignments, trials, and appeals.

right to bear arms The controversial right to carry firearms under the Second Amendment. The U.S. Supreme Court has maintained that this is not a specific individual right, but rather a right of a state to maintain an armed militia. Individual states regulate whether persons may possess and use firearms. *See also* **Bill of Rights.**

right to counsel The right to be represented by an attorney at critical stages of the criminal-justice system. Indigent defendants have the right to counsel provided by the state.

Right to Keep and Bear Arms An organization headquartered in Round Rock, TX, dedicated to the preservation and promotion of the Second Amendment right to keep and bear arms under the U.S. Constitution.

right-to-know laws Any statutes entitling persons from radio, television, or newspapers and other citizens to attend official meetings, trials, or other sessions or to obtain information about such events. Some proceedings, because of the confidentiality guaranteed participants, are closed to the public.

right to privacy The freedom of individuals to choose for themselves the time, circumstances, and extent to which their beliefs and behavior are to be shared or withheld from others.

right to release on bail Certain persons have the right to post bail as a surety that they will reappear later for trial when they have been accused of a crime and do not pose a risk to others or are unlikely to flee the jurisdiction.

right to treatment The assumption, usually by prison inmates, that inmates must be maintained in sanitary and comfortable settings, receive therapy or counseling if mentally unbalanced, and receive medical attention if injured.

right-wing political group A conservative or reactionary element of a political party or other organization.

rigor mortis "Stiffness of death" (Latin); temporary muscular rigidity in a deceased person.

Riker's Island Penitentiary A large New York City prison constructed in 1933 and consisting of six different sections, each housing different types of offenders.

Riksdagen Swedish Parliament.

Ring of Fire A handful of gun manufacturing companies located in and around Los Angeles, CA, including Bryco Arms, noted for its production of cheap handguns or junk guns or Saturday night specials. The group also includes Raven Arms, Davis Industries, Phoenix Arms, Lorcin, and Sundance Industries. Their weapons are cheaply made from inferior materials and mass-produced compared with weapons from more mainline companies such as Smith & Wesson and Colt. Lorcin boasts, for instance, that it makes the world's most affordable handguns for as little as $38. "Ring of Fire" was first applied to these companies by Dr. Garen J. Wintemute, a public health professor at the University of California–Davis, who studies links between guns and crime.

riot A civil or public disturbance involving acts of violence, usually by three or more persons.

Riot Act An English statute intended to disperse persons who are assembling for the purpose of social upheaval and tumultuous conduct. It identifies 12 or more persons engaged in concert to bring about social discord as an imminent threat to society and orders their dispersal.

riot-control agent Any device or chemical product that produces temporary conditions that incapacitate participants in a riot or a group that is out of control.

riot grenade An explosive device consisting of plastic or other nonfragmenting material that releases tear gas or another nonlethal debilitating substance. These devices are intended to cause groups of persons to disperse.

riot gun A firearm, usually a shotgun with a short barrel, designed to intimidate rioters or quell riots.

ripping method A safecracking method involving pulling the metal facing off a safe to gain entry.

risk assessment, risk assessment device or instrument, risk prediction scale The process of forecasting one's likelihood of reoffending if released from prison on parole or placed on probation by a judge. Any instrument designed to predict or anticipate one's future behavior based on past circumstances or answers given to questions on questionnaires.

risk factors A range of variables correlated with juvenile delinquency. Drug-related risk factors might include psychological, behavioral, family, social, and environmental characteristics that are associated with a higher probability of drug use among youths.

risk-focused approach The development of prevention and intervention programs for youth based on their risk of engaging in problem behaviors.

risk management Loss prevention and loss control; a business function that limits liability and casualty insurance and processing of claims.

risk/needs assessment instrument A predictive device intended to forecast offender propensity to commit new offenses or recidivate.

ritualism A mode of strain adaptation in which cultural goals are scaled down or given up, while norms about the institutionalized means to reach cultural goals are accepted.

RNA Ribonucleic acid; single-strand molecules of a type of nucleic acid.

roadblock A temporary barrier to stop vehicles, which can be created by police officers to stop fleeing offenders or to check for escaped prisoners.

road deputy A sheriff's deputy generally responsible for conducting patrol activities within his or her jurisdiction.

road gang A group of prison or jail inmates who work on highways, parks, or other public or governmental properties.

road rage Extreme anger and its associated violence by motorists.

robber baron A wealthy person who uses power and influence to control industries through such tactics as manipulation and intimidation of competitors.

robbery The taking or attempt to take anything of value from the care, custody, or control of a person or persons by force or the threat of force or violence or by putting the victim in fear.

ROBO-PO A contemporary view of probation and parole officers who see their role as law enforcers and regulators which represents a move away from the traditional rehabilitation and reintegrative goals practiced by many probation and parole officers.

Rochester Youth Development Study An investigation designed to assess the level of juvenile crime and the correlates of juvenile crime.

Rochin **exception** This exception relates to shocking conduct exhibited by police officers in their zealousness to recover contraband from suspects. Criminal suspect Rochin was made to vomit in order for police to recover capsules containing drugs, which were later used as evidence against Rochin in court to convict him. The U.S. Supreme Court said that such conduct is unconstitutional and overturned Rochin's conviction. See *Rochin v. California* (1952).

R.O.C.K. (Reaching Out, Convicts and Kids) Established by the Tulare County Probation Department in 1992, this antiburglary program uses volunteer ex-convicts to assist juvenile delinquents, transmit coping skills, and channel youth behavior toward law-abiding acts.

Rohypnol A date-rape drug; a tasteless, odorless illegal substance that can be slipped into an unsuspecting person's drink for the purpose of rendering the individual defenseless against sexual advances. Also known as the "forget pill" and "roofie," Rohypnol has debilitating effects 15 to 20 minutes following ingestion. Persons who take the drug cannot remember what has happened or where they have been.

role The normal pattern of behavior expected of one holding a particular social position.

role ambiguity Lack of clarity about work expectations; unfamiliarity with correctional tasks.

role clarity The extent to which one knows what is expected of him or her in the performance of work tasks in an organization.

role conflict This term pertains to (1) conflict lying in the disparity between the demands of two roles which an individual performs; (2) conflict arising when a person assumes so many roles that he or she cannot possibly fulfill all of the obligations involved; (3) conflict internal to a given role, where (a) a person accepts a role and finds that he or she does not have time to meet the demands and doesn't know how to get out of them, and where (b) a person accepts a role for which he or she has time but feels neither the interest nor the ability to carry out its obligations; and (4) conflict arising because of different expectations about how one's role should be carried out.

role diffusion A situation in which youths spread themselves too thin, experience personal uncertainty, and place themselves at the mercy of leaders who promise to give them a sense of identity they cannot develop for themselves.

role dispossession Separation of inmates from many of the roles they normally occupy in the outside world.

role playing Organizational activity to encourage empathy among members by having them act out roles played by others in organizations. Persons are required to put themselves in the places of others to understand to a better degree the others' frustrations and problems associated with their job performance. Role playing is an effective training device to help assist persons acquire more effective problem-solving skills in interpersonal relations.

role specificity The perceived degree of familiarity with the requirements of one's work role in an organization; role clarity; role expectations.

Roman legal system This system was based on social status. Laws similar to the Babylonian system were codified and formally adopted to systematize the law and judicial decision making. There was an attempt by lawmakers to resolve conflict-of-law questions.

roofie *See* **Rohypnol.**

rookie A new, inexperienced police officer, usually in the first year of his or her service for a police department; any new person performing a particular job for the first time.

ROR *See* **release on own recognizance.**

Rosenfeld, Richard A criminologist who has collaborated with Steven F. Messner and written about the American Dream, a concept not altogether different from Robert K. Merton's discussion of anomie and its association with criminality.

rotten pocket Corrupt police officers who band together for illegal gain.

rout At common law, a disturbance of the peace similar to a riot but without carrying out the intended purpose.

routine activities approach, routine activities perspective, routine activities theory An explanation devised by Lawrence Cohen and Marcus Felson that states that an increase or decrease in crime rates can be explained by changes in the daily habits of potential victims. The theory is based on the expectation that crimes will occur where there is a suitable target unprotected by guardians. The motivation to commit crime and the numbers of offenders are considered rather constant. Thus, it is inevitable that in every society there will be someone willing to commit crime for some reason. Predatory crime, a vital component of their theory, rests on the existence of suitable targets (victims), capable guardians (police), and motivated offenders (criminals). "Routine activities" are the activities of the typical American lifestyle.

Rowe, David Rowe proposed latent trait theory, together with D. Wayne Osgood and W. Alan Nicewander.

Royal Canadian Mounted Police (RCMP) The federal police of Canada, a national police force with general jurisdiction in all provinces.

Ruby Ridge The name given to an incident occurring in Northern Idaho in August 1992 involving a white antigovernment separatist family and the FBI. Randy Weaver and his wife and children lived in a cabin he built just 40 miles south of the Canadian border in Idaho on Ruby Ridge. The cabin had no electricity or running water. The Weavers wanted to be left alone, but 400 FBI agents and other law enforcement officers and military personnel converged on Weaver's cabin, which led to an 11-day standoff and ended with the death of Weaver's wife and son and a federal marshal. The incident was subsequently investigated by Attorney General Janet Reno to determine what happened and why.

Rule Applier In the White Typology, the type of police officer who goes strictly by the book and would give his or her own mother a speeding ticket, described by S.O. White in *A Perspective on Police Professionalism* (1972). *See also* **White Typology.**

Rule of Four A U.S. Supreme Court rule whereby the Court grants *certiorari* only on the agreement of at least four justices.

rule of law The willingness of persons to accept and order their behavior according to rules and procedures that are prescribed by political and social institutions.

rule of thumb Although believed by some to stem from a legal standard allowing husbands to hit their wives with a cane no thicker than their thumbs, the phrase's actual origin is in carpentry, where carpenters used their thumbs as measures. However, domestic violence applications of the phrase are sometimes encountered. According to folk writer Henry Kelly, the phrase has been used in a "handful" of legal cases historically, and is considered without exceptional legal merit.

rules Standards, written or oral, agreed on by members of a society or organization that govern one's conduct in the organization.

Rules of Civil Procedure Rules governing civil cases in which compensatory damages are sought; rules governing courts of equity.

Rules of Criminal Procedure Rules legislatively established by which a criminal case is conducted. Law enforcement officers, prosecutors, and judges use rules of criminal procedure in discretionary actions against suspects and defendants. *See table p. 223.*

runaway Any juvenile who leaves his or her home for long-term periods without parental consent or supervision.

rural crime Any crime occurring in a rural area, particularly those offenses having to do with cattle rustling, illegal hunting, and theft of gasoline from farm tanks.

rural programs Specific recreational and work opportunities provided for juveniles in a rural setting, such as a forestry camp, a farm, or a ranch.

Rusche, Georg A criminologist and conflict theorist who views society as consisting of two basic classes, those with power and those without it. He extends Marxist theory to include an unequal distribution of wealth and power.

Rush, Dr. Benjamin (1745–1813) A Quaker penal and religious reformer and physician. Rush helped with the organization and operation of Philadelphia's Walnut Street Jail for the benefit of prisoners and encouraged the humane treatment of inmates.

Russian mafia Organized crime activity based in Russia or dominated by Russians. There is a significant presence of Russian-dominated organized crime in the United States.

Rust Belt Any city or region of the country in which the loss of local industry has harmed the economy, raised unemployment, and brought attendant problems such as urban decay and crime.

Rutledge, John (1739–1800) Chief justice of the U.S. Supreme Court (1795). Born in Charleston, SC, Rutledge studied law at London's Middle Temple in 1760 and returned to Charleston, where he became wealthy off his plantation holdings and slaves. He became politically active in 1761, and was appointed provincial attorney general in 1764 for a short period. He supported self-government of the colonies and opposed British attempts to subjugate the colonists. He was sent to the Continental Congress in 1774 by South Carolina, and signed the Declaration of Independence. Rutledge's property was eventually seized by the British, who invaded and captured South Carolina. He subsequently aided the Continental Army in recovering South Carolina and became a delegate to the Constitutional Convention. He was appointed an associate justice of the U.S. Supreme Court in 1789 by President George Washington, but resigned for reasons of mental health. He was then appointed chief justice by Washington in 1795, and served only that year. He opposed John Jay's treaty efforts, and died in 1800.

S

sabotage Any act willfully committed by someone against either an organization or a government. Sabotage may involve destruction of property or transmittal of information to parties not entitled to possess it.

Sacco-Vanzetti case Two Italian immigrants and reputed anarchists, Nicola Sacco, a fish peddler, and Bartolomeo Vanzetti, a factory worker, were arrested and charged with an April 15, 1920, robbery and murder occurring at a company payroll office in South Braintree, MA. Following the conclusion of World War I, the political, social, and economic climate of the United States was such that these persons, as members of a minority group, were targets of considerable discrimination. Nearly indigent, the defendants had difficulty with the English language and could not satisfactorily account for their whereabouts at the time of the robbery and murder. In a highly prejudicial trial, they were convicted on July 14, 1921, and subsequently executed on August 23, 1927. Perjured testimony, questionable judicial rulings and misconduct, and interjurisdictional disputes over who should

Rule	Subject	Stage
3	Complaint	Preliminary proceedings
4	Arrest warrant	Preliminary proceedings
5	Appearance	Preliminary proceedings
5.1	Preliminary examination	Preliminary proceedings
6	Grand jury	Indictment/information
7	Indictment	Indictment/information
8	Joinder/offenses	Indictment/information
9	Warrant/summons	Indictment/information
10	Arraignment	Arraignment/trial preparation
11	Pleas	Arraignment/trial preparation
12	Pleadings/motions	Arraignment/trial preparation
15	Depositions	Arraignment/trial preparation
16	Discovery	Arraignment/trial preparation
17	Subpoena	Arraignment/trial preparation
23	Trial by jury	Trial proceedings
24	Trial jurors	Trial proceedings
26	Taking testimony	Trial proceedings
30	Instructions	Trial proceedings
31	Verdict	Trial proceedings
32	Sentences/judgments	Judgments
33	New trial	Judgments
34	Arrest judgment	Judgments
35	Corrections/sentences	Judgments

Selected Federal Rules of Criminal Procedure

Several rules have been omitted because of their incidental nature to this process or because of their special application to particular motions or technicalities.

Source: Title 18, U.S. Code, 2004.

share in the glory of their capture and prosecution caused more than a few civil rights groups to protest their case and launch ineffective appeals. It is debatable whether the wrong persons were convicted, and their case has been sensationalized by several Hollywood movies sympathizing with their ordeals. Likely scapegoats of the corrupt criminal-justice system of the time, these persons symbolized everything that was wrong with the system and highlighted the pervasive prejudice of the times against immigrants.

SADD Students Against Destructive Decisions.

sadism Derivation of pleasure from inflicting pain or suffering on someone else.

sadomasochism A psychosexual condition in which sexual partners inflict pleasure and pain on one another simultaneously, usually for sexual gratification.

safe An insulated security filing cabinet constructed so as to withstand forced entry. Different classes of safes have been constructed with various types of burglarproof systems. Safe classifications are rated in terms of minutes taken to breach their security devices and gain entry.

Safe Futures Initiative An OJJDP-sponsored program designed to create a continuum of care in communities to prevent and control delinquency.

safe house A dwelling used by law enforcement officers or other criminal-justice authorities to hide and protect witnesses or others who may be in danger.

Safer Society Program A national clearinghouse on sexual abuse prevention, including assessment and treatment programs, headquartered in Orwell, VT.

Safe Schools/Healthy Students Initiative The U.S. Congress appropriated $40 million in 1999 to fund a program for prevention of violence in schools. The current initiative is a grant program designed to develop real-world knowledge about what works best to reduce school violence. School districts are using the funds to help communities design and implement comprehensive educational, mental health, social service, law enforcement, and juvenile-justice services for youth. These services are intended to promote healthy childhood development, foster resilience, and prevent youth violence. Principles include combining security with healthy childhood development; approaching school violence as a public health issue; offering comprehensive, coordinated services along the path of childhood development; encouraging partnerships among school districts, law enforcement agencies, and local mental health agencies; and replicating services known to work.

Safety Town A crime-prevention program in which youths learn how to be safe in their communities, including how to cross streets, what to do in case of fire, and what to do if approached by a stranger.

Saint Valentine's Day Massacre The Chicago, IL, murders of a gang of bootleggers carried out against the notorious gangster "Bugs" Moran by Al Capone and his gang in 1929. Capone's gangsters posed as police officers and raided a garage in which several of Moran's gang were working. Moran's men were machine-gunned to death in the garage. The murders remain unsolved.

Salient Factor Score, SFS 76, SFS 81 A score used by parole boards and agencies to forecast an offender's risk to the public and future dangerousness; the numerical classification that predicts the probability of a parolee's success if parole is granted. The different versions (SFS 76, SFS 81) refer to the years they were devised.

sally port A prison area with double gates; an area enclosed by double gates to allows for searches of suspected contraband or weapons. Persons are allowed to enter the facility through one gate, but they are prevented from proceeding further by another gate. The second gate is opened once prisoners are searched.

Sam Browne belt A leather waistband worn by police officers and designed to carry a pistol, extra ammunition, handcuffs, a baton, Mace, keys, and other items.

Samenow, Stanton (1941–) A criminologist who advocated rational choice theory in his work *Inside the Criminal Mind* (1984). Samenow believes that criminals are characterized as being chronic liars, having intense anger, and being artful at manipulativeness. He also wrote, with S. Yochelson, *The Criminal Personality* (1976, 1977).

same-sex abuse Physical, mental, or emotional abuse by a person toward another of the same gender.

sample In research and statistics, a smaller part of the general population or a method of obtaining a portion of population elements. In forensics or evidentiary matters, a specimen.

Sampson, Robert A criminologist who collaborated with John Laub to develop age-graded theory and highlight the significance of turning points. Life-course theory is elaborated in his book *Crime in the Making* (1993).

Sanchez, Ilich Ramirez (1949–) A Venezuela-born assassin known as "Carlos the Jackal" because of his ability to disguise himself and get near enough to high-profile political leaders to assassinate them and escape. He purportedly studied in the Soviet Union under the KGB or secret police, and trained in Cuba under Fidel Castro's protection. He may have been involved in the terrorist attack on Israeli athletes at the Munich Olympics in 1972, and has been linked to numerous bombings. Carlos subsequently stayed in Syria for a time, but he was ejected in 1990 and moved to Sudan, where he was arrested in 1994. Linked to more than 80 deaths, Carlos was convicted for many of these murders and sentenced to life imprisonment.

sanction A penalty or punishment that is imposed on persons in order to enforce the law.

sanctioner value system A plan used by parole boards in early-release decision making in which amount of time served is equated with seriousness of conviction offense.

sanctuary A medieval practice that allowed protection of those accused of crimes who entered a city or a special building, such as a temple or church, which could not be lawfully entered by law enforcement officers.

San Francisco Project A research project that compared recidivism rates of probationers supervised by POs with caseloads of 20 and 40 respectively and found no significant differences in recidivism rates of probationers.

sanguinary laws Laws in the late 1600s and early 1700s providing for harsh punishments, including capital punishment, for burglary, rape, maiming, and witchcraft.

sanity hearing A formal proceeding designed to determine whether a criminal defendant is sane or insane.

San Quentin A California state prison located in San Quentin; the oldest of California's prisons, built in 1852, and famous for its use of gas chamber to execute condemned prisoners.

sans "Without" (French).

sap Heavy, leather-clap weapon used to strike a person, usually in the head.

SARA model (Scanning, Analysis, Response, and Assessment) A method suggested by professor Herman Goldstein to systematically document and evaluate problems in a community.

satanic cult A quasi-religious group whose practices and ceremonies center on the worship of Satan.

Satanism A belief in the occult, centering on the worship of the devil.

Satanist One who worships Satan or otherwise practices the black arts of witchcraft.

satisfactory evidence Any information that is sufficient to allow someone to conclude that something is true; tangible objects or testimony about something that is considered reliable and relevant, and that helps to establish the truthfulness of a belief.

satisfiers An integral part of Victor Vroom's dual-factor theory of motivation; those factors related directly to job content, such as the intrinsic interest in work performed, the potential for advancement and recognition, and the responsibility of the tasks.

Saturday night special A cheap, easily acquired handgun, frequently used by criminals.

saving clause An exception to a class of items covered in a statute.

scaffold A platform upon which condemned persons stand when they are to be executed by hanging.

scale of measurement, nominal, ordinal, interval, ratio A distinction between numbers according to the properties they possess. Nominal measurement uses numbers to classify information into discrete categories with no implication of greater or less; ordinal measurement allows graduated positioning of numbers on a scale to reflect greater or less, but not how much greater or less; interval measurement identifies equal spacing between numbers on a scale; and ratio measurement has a scale with an absolute zero. Different scales of measurement permit different arithmetic and statistical operations. The most limited scales are nominal, which permit only percentaging, whereas ratio-level scales permit all mathematical and statistical functions.

scale of patrol The scope of a police officer's routine geographical patrol responsibilities.

scapegoat A person or group that is assigned blame, deserved or otherwise, for a particular act. This phenomenon is often indicative of racial or ethnic prejudice, so that a minority group or person becomes the target of ridicule or blame.

Scared Straight A delinquency deterrent program whose purpose is to scare youthful offenders in ways that will deter them from committing further delinquent acts or pursuing crime as adults. Juvenile offenders are taken through a prison where they are confronted by prisoners on a firsthand basis and told about the harshness of prison life.

Scarman Centre The department of criminology at the University of Leicester, England, formerly the Scarman Centre, was established in 1988 and undertakes research, teaching, professional training, and consultancy in the study of policing, public disorder, crime and punishment, racism and ethnicity, crime prevention, security, risk, crisis and disaster management, community safety, and health and safety management.

Scarman Report A document detailing the causes of the 1981 Brixton riots in South London, England, critical of the police actions prior to and during the events. The investigation by Lord Scarman revealed that rioting was caused by a spontaneous crowd reaction to police action, rightly or wrongly believed to be harassment of black persons, and it had not been planned. As a result of the investigation, Lord Scarman called for a new emphasis on community policing and proposed that more people from ethnic minorities should be recruited into police work. In 1985, there were further riots in Brixton when a police officer accidentally shot and wounded a black woman during a police raid. In 1995, another riot occurred in the same area following the death of a young black man while in police custody. The Scarman Report is comparable to reports about the rioting that followed the acquittal of several police officers in the beating of a motorist, Rodney King, in the early 1990s in Southern California.

scavenger gang A juvenile coalition formed primarily as a means of socializing and for mutual protection.

schizophrenia A type of psychosis often characterized by bizarre behavior, hallucinations, loss of thought control, and inappropriate emotional responses.

schizophrenic A person suffering from schizophrenia.

school-based probation A model in which the probation officer works and is housed within the walls of a school.

school crime Any illegal activity committed in or around a school.

school failure Failing to achieve success in school, which can result in frustration, anger, and reduced self-esteem, which in turn may contribute to delinquent behavior.

school resource officer (SRO) A law enforcement officer assigned to a school for purposes of preventing delinquency and diverting youths from contact with the juvenile-justice system; a certified law enforcement officer who is permanently assigned to provide coverage to a school or a set of schools and who is specifically trained to perform three roles: law enforcement officer, law-related counselor, and law-related education teacher.

school safety A general term that includes any program or movement intended to ensure the protection of students, teachers, and staff from intentional harm from others.

schouts and rattles Early New Yorkers who were equipped with actual noise-making rattles and who were expected to shout and rattle their rattles in the event they observed crimes in progress or fleeing suspects.

scientific jury selection   A method of using correlational techniques from the social sciences to obtain jurors favorable to either the prosecution or the defense.

scientific management   A scheme for supervising workers devised by Frederick Taylor (1911), who believed that organizational effectiveness could be maximized by dividing all production-related tasks into a series of simple movements and operations. Each worker could be trained to perform a few simple operations, and the combined efforts of all workers laboring for the common good would maximize efficiency and productivity. Taylor believed also that the average worker is incapable of being self-motivated. Workers are interested in doing only whatever is minimally required by management. Therefore, in addition to redesigning and simplifying tasks, increased productivity could be achieved by establishing incentives to work harder during the work period.

scientific misconduct   Illegal or unethical research or publication practices during the performance of conducting scientific research.

scientific police management   The application of social scientific techniques to the study of police administration for the purpose of increasing effectiveness, reducing the frequency of citizen complaints, and enhancing the efficient use of available resources. The heyday of scientific police management probably occurred during the 1970s, when federal monies were far more readily available to support such studies than they are currently.

scintilla of evidence   Any shred or bit of evidence or information that enables a jury to establish an issue.

scope of sentencing policy   The breadth of sanctions covered by sentencing policy. The most important distinction is between broad policies that address probation as well as prison terms and narrow policies that address only length of incarceration, not whether to incarcerate.

Scopes, John T. (1900–1970)   A Dayton, TN, schoolteacher who taught biology and evolution. The conservative community put Scopes on trial, which later became known as the Monkey Trial. Clarence Darrow and William Jennings Bryant respectively defended and prosecuted Scopes, who was ultimately found guilty on July 21, 1925, and fined $100. Scopes' conviction was subsequently reversed on technical grounds by the Tennessee Supreme Court.

Scotland Yard   A London Metropolitan Police investigative division established in 1829 and located on Victoria Street. Its name derives from the rear of the premises on Whitehall Place, named Scotland Yard after a medieval palace where visiting Scottish royalty resided.

Scots verdict   A United Kingdom verdict that denotes "not proved," indicating the likelihood that the accused was in fact guilty of a crime, but that the Crown could not prove guilt beyond a reasonable doubt; a middle finding between conviction and exoneration of a criminal charge, ultimately resulting in a "not guilty" finding.

Scottsboro Boys   Nine black youths ranging in age from 13 to 21 who were charged with the rape of two women on a freight car in Alabama. Most were convicted by an all-white jury in a one-day trial on March 31, 1931, and sentenced to life imprisonment. Retrials for these youths were conducted on the basis that they were denied adequate counsel and that the juries were prejudiced. Appeals of these cases dragged on for seven years. Several were subsequently paroled, one escaped, and the rest were ultimately released. *See Powell v. Alabama* (1932).

screening   A procedure used by a prosecutor to define which cases have prosecutive merit and which ones do not. Some screening bureaus are made up of police and lawyers with trial experience. Also, in juvenile justice, an intake procedure to determine which youth cases are more serious than others and to keep the least serious cases from further involvement in the system.

"screws"   Prison or jail guards.

scrip   Nonlegal tender or money created for special situations. Some prison systems issue their own scrip, which inmates are required to use to buy goods at the prison commissary.

seal   To close from public inspection any record of an arrest, judgment, or adjudication, either criminal or juvenile.

sealing   The legal concealment of a person's criminal (or juvenile) record so that it cannot be opened except by order of the court.

search and seizure   A legal term contained in the Fourth Amendment of the U.S. Constitution referring to the searching for and carrying away of evidence by police during a criminal investigation. *See also* **Bill of Rights**.

SEARCH, Inc.   An organization operating since the early 1970s that has promoted the development of criminal-justice information systems in the United States. It is headquartered in Sacramento, CA, and receives considerable funding from the Bureau of Justice Statistics.

search incident to an arrest   The authority of an arresting law enforcement officer to search immediate areas within the control of an arrestee. If a suspect is arrested in his or her living room, police authority does not extend to searches of other areas not immediately within the control of the arrestee, such as an attic or back porch, detached garage, or basement.

search pattern   Any of several systematic ways whereby investigators can comb crime scenes for evidence of a crime. Search patterns include spiral, wheel, grid, and zone methods.

search warrant   An order of the court directing law enforcement officers to search designated places for specific persons or items to be seized.

Second Amendment   The part of the Bill of Rights of the U.S. Constitution that contains provisions for the right of citizens to bear arms. *See also* **Bill of Rights**.

secondary classification   A fingerprint classification term; a two-letter code that describes the fingerprint pattern for each of the index fingers.

secondary conflict   In culture-conflict theory, the type of conflict developing in society wherein it becomes more heterogeneous and groups become more differentiated and develop their own distinct values. Eventually these values clash with other groups.

secondary deviance, secondary deviation Law violations that have become incorporated into a person's lifestyle or behavior pattern.

secondary group A group that is usually larger, more complex, and less intimate than a primary group.

secondary prevention An approach that focuses on changing the behavior of individuals likely to become delinquent. It includes punitive prevention.

secondary sociopath An individual who is biologically normal but who exhibits antisocial behavior due to negative life experiences.

secondary victim Anyone who indirectly suffers as the result of a crime, such as a friend or relative of the victim.

Second Chance Body Armor, Inc. A company in Central Lake, MI, that manufactures bullet-resistant fabric made of Zylon, which consists of a yarn strength designed to prevent bullets from penetrating body armor worn by law enforcement officers. The company makes Second Chance Ultima body armor.

Second Chance Program A probation program operated in Iowa in the early 1990s to provide delinquent youths with opportunities to acquire skills, vocational and educational training, preemployment training, and job placement services.

Second Chance Ultima Body armor manufactured by Second Chance Body Armor Inc. in Central Lake, MI, and marketed to law enforcement officers as bullet-resistant. It is made of Zylon, which is a fabric designed in different yarn strengths to withstand penetration of bullets of different calibers.

second-degree murder Taking of a human life without premeditation.

second-generation jails Jail facilities constructed in the early 1980s designed to improve on the physical plants of earlier jails.

secondhand evidence Hearsay.

secret Hidden information about something; any information that is concealed and known only to designated persons; information considered sensitive and well-guarded.

secretor In forensics, one who secretes blood type A, B, or AB antigens in the bodily fluids.

secret police Law enforcement authorities in totalitarian governments who investigate and accuse, frequently without evidence.

Secret Service An agency created in 1865 under the Department of the Treasury with the primary function of investigating the counterfeiting of U.S. currency. After the 1901 assassination of President William McKinley, it was given responsibility for guarding U.S. presidents and other dignitaries. In 2002, the agency was incorporated into the Department of Homeland Security.

Section 1983 actions Legal actions under Title 42, Section 1983 of the U.S. Code, which sets forth grounds for actions involving civil rights violations by police officers against citizens.

sector search Zone search.

secure confinement, secure custody Incarceration of a juvenile offender in a facility that restricts movement in the community. It is similar to confinement in an adult penal facility involving total incarceration.

secure setting An environment that places constraints on youths for their care and treatment and for the protection of the public.

Securities and Exchange Commission (SEC) A federal agency that supervises the securities industry, including brokers and investment companies. The SEC investigates securities fraud and preserves the integrity of the securities industry. It was established in 1934 and is headquartered in Washington, DC.

securities fraud, securities violation Any deceptive practice designed to enable one to profit illegally from the manipulation of stocks or other securities.

security The degree of restriction of inmate movement within a correctional facility, which is usually divided into maximum, medium, and minimum levels.

security and privacy standards Sets of principles and procedures developed to ensure the security and confidentiality of criminal or juvenile record information in order to protect the privacy of persons identified in such records.

security classification An internal corrections system of categorizing offenders into different supervisory or custody levels (e.g., minimum, medium, and maximum security).

security for costs Any surety required of a plaintiff by a defendant when the plaintiff does not reside in the jurisdiction of the court.

security for good behavior A recognizance or bond given to the court by a defendant before or after conviction conditioned on his or her being "on good behavior" or keeping the peace for a prescribed period of time.

security guard A privately employed person who protects people or property for a living.

security threat group (STG) An administrative prison term used to refer to a gang that poses a threat to institutional security and inmate safety.

security threat individual Any person deemed to pose a potential threat of a dangerous act and who threatens the safety of others.

sedative A drug of the barbiturate family that depress the central nervous system into a sleeplike condition.

sedition Actions or speech that could promote rebellion against the government or other officials.

seditious conspiracy Any agreement between two or more persons that involves undermining or changing the government by force or encouraging law violations in order to induce disloyalty to the government.

seduction The common-law crime of inducing an individual of previously innocent character to have sexual relations.

"seduction of the innocent" A phrase used by Fredric Wertham, who wrote in 1953 about the influence of comic books, crime thrillers, horror, and police stories on juvenile delinquency. He attempted to establish a causal relation between violence in popular television programs and actual violence in society among youths. Wertham's assumptions were tenuous at best. Because of his wide use of the opinions of self-styled experts in criminal and delinquent behavior, his ideas were not believed to be scientific or thoroughly documented and were subsequently discounted as unscientific and unconvincing as an explanation for contemporary violence.

seductions of crime The visceral and emotional appeal that the situation of crime has for those who engage in illegal acts. *See also* **Katz, Jack.**

See Our Side (SOS) A juvenile aversion program in Prince George's County, MD, designed to prevent delinquency.

segregated incarceration The practice of housing juveniles convicted in adult court in a separate prison facility for younger offenders, usually those between the ages of 18 and 25.

segregation A correctional practice whereby certain types of offenders are separated either according to their institutional violations or for their own safety.

Seidmann, Robert A criminologist who collaborated with William Chambliss in writing *Law, Order, and Power* (1971); a conflict theorist who has extended Marxist philosophy to explain in greater detail how rich and powerful economic and political interests dominate the lower classes.

seizin Possession of real property or real estate.

seizure The act of taking into custody a person or thing believed connected with illegal activity.

selective enforcement The act by police officers of prioritizing particular offenses or offenders and enforcing some laws and not enforcing others.

selective incapacitation The process of incarcerating certain offenders who are defined by various criteria as having a strong propensity to repeat serious crimes. The practice is based on the belief that offenders who are recidivists or who have prior criminality should be incapacitated with relatively long prison sentences.

selective incorporation A process whereby due process aspects of the Fourteenth Amendment of the U.S. Constitution were incorporated into other amendments. *See also* **Bill of Rights.**

self-actualization Abraham Maslow's concept of developing one's ultimate potential, which he placed at the top of his hierarchy of needs; a personality trait indicative of attaining ultimate fulfillment.

self-assessment A method of enhancing self-understanding; identifying one's unique characteristics, what one does well, what is important to one, and what one likes to do, clearly and accurately.

self-concept theory Any criminological theory that emphasizes the importance of a youth's self-concept as a cause of delinquency.

self-control The ability to control one's own behavior.

self-defense An affirmative defense in which defendants explain otherwise criminal conduct by showing a necessity to defend themselves against aggressive victims.

self-estrangement A form of alienation in which persons see themselves as "aliens" or "strangers." Such individuals tend to view their actions in terms of external consequences instead of intrinsic pleasure or self-satisfaction and to see themselves

as falling far short of what might have been high personal ideals.

self-fulfilling prophecy That which occurs whenever persons live up to the labels they are given by others. Whatever is believed to be true will be true as a consequence.

self-help group An association formed by persons dependent on drugs or alcohol or some other addiction, such as gambling.

self-incrimination The act of exposing oneself to prosecution by answering questions that may demonstrate involvement in illegal behavior. Coerced self-incrimination is not allowed under the Fifth Amendment. In any criminal proceeding, the prosecution must prove the charges by means of evidence other than the testimony of the accused.

self-labeling The process whereby a person who has been negatively labeled accepts the label as a personal role or identity.

self-made person A social myth that glorifies individual accomplishment to the exclusion or underestimation of the relevance of social structure to a person's life chances.

self-mutilation In corrections, self-inflicted injuries by inmates designed to remove them from the harsh conditions that exist in their prison systems.

self-report crime, self-report data Information disclosed by persons who have committed crimes of which the police are unaware; any statistical compilations of crimes reported by persons and where such persons have not been caught and prosecuted for these crimes.

self-report survey A method whereby researchers ask persons directly about various types of offenses they have committed, regardless of whether they have been arrested or charged with those offenses.

self-representation *See pro se.*

Sellin, Thorsten A criminologist of the twentieth century, educated at the University of Pennsylvania, who is best known for his work for the Social Science Research Council, *Culture Conflict and Crime* (1938) and *Delinquency in a Birth Cohort* (coauthored with Marvin E. Wolfgang and Robert Figlio). Sellin posited that different values present in segments of society may lead to persons engaging in criminal conduct. In turn, this serves as the basis for conflict. Normative conflict between various ethnic groups might generate criminal conduct, as diverse ethnic norms clash.

Sellin Center for Studies in Criminology and Criminal Law A foundation established in 1960 that conducts research on crime, delinquency, and other criminal-justice topics. It is headquartered at the University of Pennsylvania in Philadelphia, and named after Thorsten Sellin.

selling style A leadership mode emphasizing a collaborative relation between supervisors and subordinates, in which subordinates are given emotional consideration and involvement in decisions affecting their work through feedback solicited from supervisors.

semiautomatic weapon A firearm designed to discharge and rechamber a new round with the single pull of the trigger. These weapons have high-capacity magazines and are capable of shooting a large number of bullets within a short time interval.

Senate crime investigations Periodic inquiries into organized crime and other perceived federal law violations by various U.S. Senate crime committees.

sense of community A psychological milieu established between police officers and citizens in which citizens acquire a feeling of security and safety among their own in individual neighborhoods.

sense of inequity The belief that one's social position is not in as great a ratio to one's efforts as the social positions and efforts of others.

sensitivity training A management technique that teaches group dynamics techniques for problem formulation and resolution. The techniques lead personnel to become more empathetic with the needs and interests of others, and provide feedback to encourage open information exchanges, which ultimately improve individual and organizational performance. The groups are sometimes designated as T-groups (for training groups).

sentence A penalty imposed on a convicted person for a crime. Penalties may include incarceration, fine, both, or some other alternative. *See also* **mandatory sentencing; presumptive sentencing; indeterminate sentencing; determinate sentencing.**

sentence, determinate *See* **determinate sentencing.**

sentence, flat A term of incarceration that must be served in its entirety without early release, sometimes called flat time; the actual amount of time served.

sentence, indeterminate *See* **indeterminate sentencing.**

sentence, maximum The upper limit of time one must serve in incarceration.

sentence, minimum The least amount of time one must serve in incarceration before being freed.

sentence, suspended A period of time of incarceration imposed by a judge but the implementation of which is withheld temporarily while the person serves probation in lieu of incarceration.

sentence bargaining Any negotiation between prosecutors and defense attorneys for the prosecutor's recommendation of a reduced sentence in exchange for a guilty plea to a lesser charge from a defendant.

sentence credits, sentence credit time Time deducted from an inmate's sentence that he or she has already served on the basis of good-time credits earned by the inmate.

sentence disparity *See* **sentencing disparity.**

sentence effective date The particular time when one's sentence is calculated, which may include days held in pretrial detention while awaiting trial; a benchmark to indicate how much time remains to be served on one's sentence.

sentence hearing *See* **sentencing hearing.**

sentence-recommendation bargaining A negotiation in which the prosecutor proposes a sentence in exchange for a guilty plea. *See also* **plea bargaining, plea negotiation.**

sentence review The reconsideration of a sentence imposed on a person convicted of a crime, either by the same court that imposed the sentence or by a higher appellate court.

sentencing The process of imposing a punishment on a defendant convicted of one or more crimes.

sentencing circle A form of restorative justice based on Native American tradition. The perpetrator, the victim, family members, and interested community citizens meet for the purpose of healing both the perpetrator and the victim.

sentencing commission A group commissioned by the legislature to determine sentencing policy and usually to monitor implementation of that policy.

sentencing conference An informal meeting prior to a sentencing hearing involving the judge, the prosecutor, the defense attorney, and a probation officer to discuss sentence recommendations.

sentencing council The meeting of a panel of judges in a multi-judge court to discuss sentencing of pending cases. Such a council is designed to temper individual decisions by comparison to group norms.

sentencing discount Reduction in an offender's sentence in exchange for a guilty plea.

sentencing disparity Inconsistency in the sentencing of convicted offenders, in which those committing similar crimes under similar circumstances are given widely disparate sentences by the same judge, usually on the basis of gender, race, ethnicity, or socioeconomic factors.

sentencing dispositions Any punishments imposed by judges following a conviction or adjudication. Punishments may include probation, incarceration of some specified duration, fines, and/or other conditions (e.g., attending counseling or Alcoholics Anonymous meetings, victim compensation).

sentencing guidelines Instruments developed by the federal government and various states to assist judges in assessing fair and consistent lengths of incarceration for various crimes and past criminal histories. Use of these guidelines is referred to as "presumptive sentencing" in some jurisdictions.

sentencing hearing An optional hearing held in many jurisdictions in which defendants and victims can hear the contents of presentence investigation reports prepared by probation officers. Defendants and victims may respond to a report orally, in writing, or both. The hearing precedes the sentence imposed by the judge.

sentencing jury A body of persons, the trial jury, responsible for imposing one's sentence on a finding of guilty.

sentencing memorandum A court decision that furnishes a ruling or finding and orders it to be implemented relative to convicted offenders. This document does not necessarily include reasons or a rationale for the sentence imposed.

sentencing postponed The delay of punishment for a period of time. Usually, delays in sentencing are intended to place the convicted offender in a conditional nonincarcerative program to show good behavior. An incarcerative penalty may or may not be imposed later, depending on the conduct of the convicted offender.

Sentencing Project, The An organization headquartered in Washington, DC, that promotes the development of sentencing alternatives. It publishes numerous reports, many indicating the inequitable and discriminatory treatment of minorities in the criminal-justice system.

Sentencing Reform Act of 1984 An act that provided federal judges and others with considerable discretionary powers to provide alternative sentencing and other provisions in their sentencing of offenders.

sentencing review procedures Any set of arrangements employed to reduce sentencing inconsistencies or disparities.

sentencing structure The division of decision authority at the individual case level of sentencing. Sentencing structure Provides the formal relationships by which to implement policy.

sentinel One who stands guard and warns of danger if a threatening situation arises.

sentry One who performs the task of being a lookout; one who keeps watch while others do their particular activities, legal or otherwise.

separate, but equal doctrine Set forth in *Plessy v. Ferguson* (1896), a decision involving a black person who attempted to board a train car in Louisiana that was designated exclusively for whites. The U.S. Supreme Court upheld the constitutionality of the "separate, but equal doctrine," which held that as long as blacks were provided with separate, but equivalent amenities or facilities, segregation of those amenities on the basis of race was constitutional. *Brown v. Board of Education* (1954) was the first of several U.S. Supreme Court decisions that invalidated the separate, but equal doctrine when it was held that school segregation on the basis of race was unconstitutional. In short, the separate, but equal doctrine did not pertain to schools.

separate confinement, separate system A penitentiary system developed in Pennsylvania and in practice from 1820 to 1900, in which each inmate was held in isolation from other inmates. All activities, including craftwork, were carried out in individual cells. Also, solitary confinement in an isolated cell for the purpose of eliminating evil association in congregate quarters.

separation-of-powers doctrine The principle that power is distributed among three branches of government—the judicial, legislative, and executive—for the purpose of ensuring that no one person will make the law, interpret the law, and apply the law; a process of checks and balances, whereby one branch of government regulates or counters the influence of the other branches.

sepulcher A burial vault.

sequester, sequestration The insulation of jurors from the outside world so that their decision making cannot be influenced or affected by extralegal factors.

sequestered jury A jury that is isolated from the public during the course of a trial and throughout the deliberation process.

sergeant A quasi-military rank used by law enforcement or corrections organizations to denote someone who is higher in formal authority than a patrol officer but lower than a lieutenant.

serial arson The occurrence of two or more instances of arson by the same perpetrator.

serial arsonist One who engages in serial arson.

serial killer One who commits serial murder; one who kills numerous persons, but usually individually over a given time period.

serial murder The killing of a large number of people over time by an offender who seeks to escape detection; also, ho-micides that are committed over a period of time and involving a sequence of victims killed by the same perpetrator.

serial murderer *See* **serial killer.**

serious delinquents, serious offenders Delinquents or criminals who persist in offending; those committing offenses that cause serious bodily injuries, possibly resulting in maiming or death.

serious medical need Any condition requiring the immediate services of a physician.

serious misdemeanor Any class of misdemeanors that carry maximum penalties of a year less a day, or 11 months, 29 days.

seriousness scaling The use of psychophysical scaling techniques to assess the perceived seriousness of criminal, delinquent, or deviant acts. The concept was introduced by Thorsten Sellin and Marvin E. Wolfgang in their work *The Measurement of Delinquency* (1964).

serology The study of blood.

serotonin A compound in the blood that acts as a neurotransmitter.

Serpico, Frank (1934–) A former New York City police officer who exposed widespread corruption among detectives and police officers in his division during the 1970s. Serpico was subsequently wounded under suspicious circumstances and retired from police work shortly thereafter. Allegations against the NYPD led to the formation of the Knapp Commission, whose investigation into police corruption and misconduct eventually led to numerous convictions against officers. The incident was eventually made into a 1973 motion picture, *Serpico* (Al Pacino).

service The police function of providing assistance to the public, usually with regard to matters unrelated to crime.

service model A model in which services are designed to meet community needs and expectations and are therefore shaped by them.

service of process The act of serving a summons on someone notifying him or her to appear in court at a particular time.

service revolver A weapon carried by a law enforcement officer while on duty, usually a pistol or handgun.

service style A style of policing that is marked by a concern with helping rather than strict enforcement. Service-oriented agencies are more likely to take advantage of community resources, such as drug-treatment programs, than are other types of departments.

service weapon Service revolver.

session Meeting; the duration of a court proceeding, legislature, or other authoritative body.

settlement houses Homes or shelters established between 1886 and 1900 to furnish food, clothing, and temporary lodging to wayward or disadvantaged youths. They were operated by charitable and religious organizations and staffed by volunteers.

Seven Steps One of the earliest of self-help organizations, modeled after the 12-step program of Alcoholics Anonymous.

severance Separation of related cases so that they can be tried separately in different courts.

severity The degree of punitiveness of a criminal sanction.

sex offender An individual who commits a sexual act prohibited by law. Sex offenders include rapists, prostitutes, voyeurs, and child molesters.

sex-offender notification system, sex-offender registration A requirement under the law that sex offenders must register with local authorities whenever they relocate to new communities or neighborhoods.

Sex Offender Registry Under Megan's Law and similar revised laws, sex offenders are required to register their addresses and workplaces with local police departments. Some registries are available to the public for scrutiny in the interests of public safety. In other registries, police are required to notify neighbors of the presence of the sex offender in their community or neighborhood. Some registries are available for viewing via the Internet.

sex offense One of several offenses involving sexual misconduct, including rape, statutory rape, child sexual abuse or molestation, and prostitution.

"sexploitation" Slang to describe the commercialization of sex through the production and distribution of sexually explicit materials and pornography.

sex slave A human captive who is forced to engage in sexual relations with his or her captor.

sex trade The selling and transportation of females for use in prostitution.

sexual abuse Illegal sex acts performed against a minor by a parent, guardian, relative, or acquaintance.

sexual assault *See* **sexual battery.**

sexual battery In modern statutes, the unlawful oral, anal, or vaginal penetration by or union with the sexual organ of another.

sexual deviance Any unusual sexual practice.

sexual harassment Unequal or offensive treatment in the workplace on the basis of gender.

sexual homicide A killing for which the perpetrator's motive is primarily sexual.

sexual misconduct Any type of improper sexual conduct.

Sexual Offender Treatment Program (SOT) A treatment program for juvenile offenders adjudicated delinquent on sex charges. The program includes psycho-social-educational interventions, therapies, and counseling.

sexual predator A sex offender who chronically commits sex offenses.

sexual psychopath A sex offender who is considered predatory and beyond redemption.

sexual sadist One who derives considerable sexual pleasure from inflicting pain on his or her victims.

sexual safety A sexist rationalization offered by male officers for not assigning women to direct-contact positions in male prisons.

shackles Metal restraints that close around the ankles or wrists to prevent movement.

shadow board A pegboard on which tools can be hung that has an outline of each item making it easy to recognize when an item is missing. They are used in correctional settings to determine whether tools have been stolen or misplaced.

shakedown An intensive search conducted of inmate cells for the purpose of discovering weapons or contraband; also, a form of police corruption in which money or valuables are extorted from criminals by police officers in exchange for the criminals not being arrested.

shall A legal command meaning "must"; a definitive requirement stemming from a judicial pronouncement.

shaming penalty Consequences for a crime in which the offender is subject to the community's disapproval. The criminal is usually ostracized from the community by social isolation.

sham religious group Association of persons in a prison setting claiming to belong to a religious organization that does not meet the requirements for constituting a religion.

"shanghai" To subdue someone by force or to get someone intoxicated, or otherwise impaired so as to bring the person aboard a ship or other sailing vessel illegally to work as a seaman.

"shank" A slang term for a homemade knife, often used by prisoners for defensive or offensive purposes.

SHAPE-UP A diversion program in which juveniles spend two days over a two-week period at Colorado State Penitentiary to discuss confinement with prisoners. The shock value of prison life seems to be therapeutic for youths and diverts them from further delinquent conduct.

shared-powers model A plan of prison administration stressing prisoner participation in administration of prison affairs.

Shaw, Clifford R. (1895–1957) A sociologist who collaborated with Henry McKay in developing social disorganization theory, positing a relation between transitional slum areas and high crime rates during the 1920s.

Sheldon, William (1898–1977) A physician who wrote about the relation between physique and criminal behavior. Sheldon developed the somatotype notion that different physiques tend to manifest different criminal behaviors. His typology included mesomorphs, who are well-developed and muscular, tending to commit robbery and assault; endomorphs, heavily built persons who are sluggish and have a propensity toward sex crimes; and ectomorphs, tall and thin persons believed to have a propensity toward embezzlement and property crimes.

"shell game" A confidence game or game of chance in which the player must guess the location of a pea under one of three shells. These games are often rigged so that no player ever wins.

shelter A confinement or community facility for the care of juveniles, usually those held pending adjudication; also, place to provide food and other necessities to those who are homeless or victims of domestic violence.

shelter care, shelter-care facility A nonsecure or unlocked place of care and custody for children awaiting court appearances and those who have already been adjudicated and are awaiting disposition.

sheriff The chief executive officer of a county, who appoints jailers and other jail personnel and hires deputies to enforce county laws.

sheriff, deputy A law enforcement officer employed by a county sheriff's department.

sheriff's department A law enforcement agency organized and exercising its law enforcement functions at the county level, usually within unincorporated areas, and which operates the county jail in most jurisdictions.

Sherman, Lawrence W. (1949–) A criminologist who has done extensive work relating to various law enforcement practices, including the study of hot spots. He is the author of the Sherman Report on Police Education and also conducted a Minneapolis experiment on domestic violence.

Sherman Antitrust Act An 1890 act of Congress prohibiting any contract, conspiracy, or combination of business interests in restraint of foreign or interstate trade.

Sherman Report A 1984 national review of law enforcement education programs that found that a liberal arts–related curriculum was the most appropriate for training police officers.

shield laws Statutes that protect professional persons from disclosing facts about their clients to the public. Psychiatrists have the right to refuse to disclose information about those they are treating for neurotic or psychotic conditions, for example. *See also* **rape shield laws.**

Shining Path A Peruvian communist guerrilla force founded in 1970 by Abimael Guzman Reynoso as an offshoot of the Peruvian Communist Party. Several thousand guerrilla fighters were subsequently recruited and began significant acts of terrorism in the late 1980s. Guzman was eventually captured and convicted of various crimes and sentenced to life imprisonment. Between 1988 and 2003 more than 25,000 persons, mostly civilians, were killed as the result of fighting and acts of terrorism committed by Shining Path members.

shire reeve In early England, the senior law enforcement figure in a county; the forerunner of today's sheriff.

shires Early English counties.

"shiv" A make-shift knife made from an ordinary utensil, such as a fork or a toothbrush, by an inmate in a prison or jail.

shock incarceration *See* **shock probation.**

shock parole *See* **shock probation.**

shock probation The practice of sentencing offenders to prison or jail for a brief period, primarily to give them a taste or "shock" of prison or jail life, and then releasing them into the custody of a probation or parole officer through a resentencing project.

shock treatment A medical procedure in which a mental patient is given an electroconvulsive shock to restore him or her to better mental health.

shoot To discharge a firearm or other weapon; also, to inject drugs into one's body with a syringe.

shooting gallery Any location where drug addicts go to ingest or inject (shoot) their drugs out of public view, often in abandoned buildings.

shoplifting Stealing goods from stores or markets by persons not employed by those establishments.

short ridge A fingerprint pattern that is a short, broken ridge or line.

short-run hedonism According to Albert Cohen, the desire of lower-class gang youths to engage in behavior that will give them immediate gratification and excitement but in the long run will be dysfunctional and negativistic.

short-term confinement Placement in any incarcerative institution for either adults or juveniles for a period of confinement less than one year.

short-term facility Any incarcerative institution for either adults or juveniles where confinement is for a period of less than one year. Jails are considered short-term facilities.

shotgun A firearm with a smooth bore that fires numerous pellets.

shot pattern The dispersion of pellets fired from a shotgun at a given distance from a target.

show cause, show cause order Any order to appear in court and indicate to the court why an event has not occurred or why some disposition should not be made in a given case.

showing consideration A view of supervisory behavior reflecting the degree to which the leader establishes two-way communication, mutual respect, and acknowledgment of the feelings of subordinates. Essentially, it represents a human relations orientation toward leadership.

showup *See* **lineup.**

shrapnel Fragments from devices that detonate; metal fragments that are dispersed when an explosive is discharged. The intent of shrapnel is to maim or disable enemies.

shrinkage In private sector retail, the difference between the amount of goods shown on inventory lists and the lesser amount of goods on hand. The difference is usually attributed to shoplifting or pilferage, but may also stem in part from erroneously diverted goods and errors in accounting for inventory.

shunning Socially isolating deviants in a group or society; avoiding those who have violated the law.

siege The process of surrounding a fortified place to obtain the surrender of persons who are defending the facility. It may involve depriving persons in the place under siege of water and electricity, so as to make the fortified place uninhabitable and encourage the defenders to surrender more quickly.

siege mentality A term developed by Elijah Anderson, who wrote *Streetwise: Race, Class and Change in an Urban Community* (1990). It refers to general mistrust of social institutions, such as businesses, schools, and government, to deal effectively with poverty. Aggregates in neighborhoods, such as African Americans, might believe generally that secret plans exist for their eradication through dispersion of drugs, AIDS, police brutality, and other adverse phenomena. The outside world is viewed as the "enemy" when, in fact, such may not be the case. Such beliefs are reinforced when police ignore crime in poor areas, when they are violent or corrupt, or whenever policies are enacted that adversely affect the poor and the communities in which they live.

sight and sound separated The concept that juveniles should not be able to see or hear adult offenders when they are taken into custody by police officers and detained for brief periods in lockups or jails.

signal Any transmitted electronic impulse; a type of message consisting of one or more words or letters, characters, flags, visual displays, or special sounds, transmitted by visual, acoustic, or electrical means.

signal security Any communications security or electronic security.

signature A distinguishing mark of a serial killer or other offender that is apparent from the appearance of the crime scene or the victim(s).

silencer Any device capable of suppressing the sound of a firearm when discharged. Such devices attach to the barrels of firearms, either by screwing on or by overlapping barrels and being tightened by screws on the silencers themselves.

silent system *See* **Pennsylvania System.**

Silkwood, Karen (1946–1974) An employee at Kerr-McGee's plutonium fuels production plant in Crescent, OK, who accused the company of health and safety violations. On November 13, 1974, she was killed in an automobile accident under suspicious circumstances as she was taking evidence of the crime and wrongdoing to an investigator.

silver-platter doctrine A doctrine derived from the fact that federal authorities must obtain a search warrant before seizing property or conducting searches in criminal cases. When they conduct such searches and seizures without a warrant, their collected evidence is inadmissible in federal court, but they may give their evidence "on a silver platter" to state officials, and the state officials can use this evidence against the same persons legally in state proceedings. This doctrine was discarded as the result of *Elkins v. United States* (1960) and *Mapp v. Ohio* (1961). *See also* **exclusionary rule.**

similarity of values The extent to which work groups share the same interests and attitudes about their work.

Simon, Rita (1931–) A sociologist who has written about feminist criminology in her work *Women and Crime* (1975). She argues that the women's movement has created greater economic opportunities for women. A "liberation hypothesis" suggests that women are in positions of committing the same types of crimes as men.

simple assault An attack inflicting little or no physical harm on a victim.

Simpson, O.J. (1947–) A football hero and Heisman trophy winner who played for the University of Southern California, a sports commentator, and an actor. Simpson was accused in the 1994 double murder of Ronald Goldman and Simpson's ex-wife, Nicole Brown Simpson. He was defended by the "dream team" of F. Lee Bailey, Johnnie Cochran, and others, and was acquitted. Simpson was successfully sued in civil court for causing the deaths of the victims and assessed substantial monetary damages.

simulated forgery Any writing that is intended to appear as genuine, but that is not written by the originating writer of the authentic writing, usually prepared by a forger or an accomplished person who imitates the writing of others.

simulation A model constructed by an investigator seeking to illustrate hypotheses or theoretical tests; an artificial illustration of how something should operate properly. Automobile safety companies utilize portions of automobiles to simulate car crashes or impacts with fixed surfaces, such as walls or metal poles, to show the effects of an impact of an actual automobile in an accident.

simultaneity A reciprocal cause-effect relation between two variables (e.g., sanctions by the criminal-justice system may affect the crime rate, but the crime rate may also affect the sanctions that are meted out by the criminal-justice system).

sine qua non "Without which it could not be" (Latin); indispensable necessity.

single action A type of firearm requiring pulling back of the hammer before pulling the trigger to discharge a cartridge. Single-action revolvers cannot be discharged by simply pulling the trigger unless the hammer is pulled back first, as opposed to double-action revolvers, for which a trigger pull alone can turn the cylinder, which automatically pulls back the hammer and fires the weapon.

single-fingerprint registration A way of classifying fingerprints so as to allow for identification of fingerprints left at crime scenes.

Sing Sing The New York State prison near Ossining infamous as a tough prison and known for holding many dangerous and notorious offenders.

Sirhan Sirhan (1944–) The man convicted of assassinating Senator Robert F. Kennedy on June 5, 1968, at the Ambassador Hotel in Los Angeles during a political function. He was sentenced to life imprisonment and continues to be denied parole.

situational crime prevention A method of crime prevention stressing tactics and strategies to eliminate or reduce particular crimes in narrow settings (e.g., reducing burglaries in a housing project by increasing lighting and installing security alarms). This approach is associated with the work of Ron Clarke.

situational inducements Opportunities that maximize one's likelihood of engaging in criminal conduct. Where risk taking is unlikely to result in apprehension and arrest, criminal conduct may occur for various incentives, usually monetary or thrill seeking.

situationally based discretion Options exercised by police officers during police-citizen encounters. Such options may or may not include letter-of-the-law interpretations of events.

situational offender A first-time offender who has committed only one offense, for which he or she was apprehended and prosecuted, but who is unlikely to commit future crimes.

"skeezer" A prostitute who trades sex for drugs, usually crack.

sketch artist One who paints or draws pictures of criminal suspects based on recollections of eyewitnesses.

sketching Drawing objects, places, or activities to show relevant details. Crime scenes may be sketched to assist in investigations. Faces of suspects may be sketched from memories of victims or witnesses so that others may be able to identify possible suspects.

skewness In statistics, the tendency of a bell-shaped curve, which is ordinarily symmetrical, to taper more in one direction than the other. Scores or values that bunch up in the left area of a curve and for which the curve tapers off toward the right are considered positively skewed, whereas scores or values that bunch up in the right part of the curve and for which the curve tapers off toward the left are negatively skewed.

skid A slide by a vehicle resulting from loss of contact with a road's surface. A skid may be controlled or uncontrolled, and may leave rubber markings, called skid marks.

skid marks Rubber traces or imprints from tires left on roadways that are indicative of an automobile skid. Investigators can determine from such marks the speed at which a car was traveling, given other factors, such as car weight and type, tire width, and road conditions (wet, dry).

skimming Concealing profits in order to avoid paying taxes or simply for personal gain.

skinhead A member of a white supremacist gang, identified by a shaved skull and Nazi or Ku Klux Klan markings.

Skinner, B.F. (1904–1990) A psychologist who promoted behavior modification as a way of regulating criminal conduct. Through positive or negative reinforcement of behaviors, desirable or undesirable behaviors can be encouraged or discouraged.

skip tracer One who tracks down alleged offenders who have fled the jurisdiction to avoid prosecution. *See also* **bounty hunter.**

skyjacking Taking over an airplane by force, often with the intent to extort money from the airline or some other organization by using passengers as hostages.

sky marshals Armed officers who travel aboard airplanes to protect against skyjacking.

slander The tort of defaming one's character through verbal statements.

slap jack A leather, lead-filled device used for hitting someone, usually on the head.

slavery Involuntary servitude in which one is held against his or her will and forced to work for another.

"slaves of the state" Slang for prison or jail inmates.

slum A run-down or blighted area of a community known for high drug use, poverty, and violent activity.

"smack" Slang for heroin.

Small, Albion (1854–1926) A sociologist and originator of the "Chicago School" in 1892.

small arms Firearms that are capable of being concealed on one's person, usually pistols or revolvers.

small-claims court A specialized court for resolving claims not exceeding a particular dollar amount (e.g., not more than $1,000 or $2,500, depending on the jurisdiction). Claims are mostly civil and involve contractual disputes that can be resolved quickly by a judicial airing of the opposing parties' differences and facts presented.

small jail Short-term incarcerative facility with 49 or fewer beds.

smallpox A serious, contagious, fatal infectious disease with no specific treatment indicated other than vaccination. Its scientific name, *variola,* derives from the Latin word for "spotted" and refers to raised bumps that appear on the face and body of an infected person. The last known case of smallpox in the United States was in 1949, and the last world case was in Somalia in 1977. However, bioterrorism has increased the likelihood of the use of smallpox against specific popula-

tions. Smallpox is caused by the *variola* virus, which emerged in human populations thousands of years ago. The *variola* virus has been eliminated, except for laboratory stockpiles. Usually, direct and fairly prolonged face-to-face contact is required to spread smallpox from one person to another; however, direct contact with the bodily fluids of an infected person can spread this disease.

smart sentencing *See* **creative sentencing.**

Smith, Susan (1971–) A woman who murdered her two children by rolling her car into a lake in South Carolina. She was convicted of first-degree murder and sentenced to life imprisonment.

Smith & Wesson A large manufacturer and distributor of firearms in the United States, headquartered in Massachusetts.

smoke bomb, smoke grenade An explosive device that emits considerable smoke to obscure movements of persons under conditions of conflict with others, such as war. A dense white smoke is emitted from the bomb's contents, which usually include white phosphorus. A smoke bomb may ignite paper or clothing if the device comes into contact with such articles. In war conditions, such devices are used to screen troop movements.

smuggle To import or export goods without paying a duty on the goods.

smuggling The unlawful movement of goods or persons across a national frontier or state boundary or into or out of a correctional facility.

sneeze gas An airborne substance that causes sneezing and disables certain persons; a riot dispersal nonlethal weapon, diphenylchlorarsine.

sniperscope An electronic device used on rifles that permits shooters to aim at a target during nighttime hours through a combination telescopic sight and a fluorescent screen in which objects appear to be green.

"snitch" Any inmate informer in a jail or prison.

snuff film A motion picture showing someone being killed; the actual murder of someone while the act is being filmed, which is thought to be sexually gratifying to the viewer.

social bond A bond that ties a person to the institutions and processes of society. Elements of the bond include attachment, commitment, involvement, and belief.

social bond theory A criminological view that the strength of a person's bonds to society affect the likelihood of his or her becoming involved in delinquency and crime.

social capital Positive relations with individuals and institutions that are life-sustaining. Relations include positive interpersonal relations with other persons and institutions. Marriage and a career are considered integral features of social capital.

social casework Services provided by social workers for members of families who have various types of personal or social problems. Social workers may provide counseling services to individuals or entire families as a form of therapy to improve family conditions and functioning.

social class The socioeconomic level of one's family, usually measured by profession or occupation, wealth, and type of neighborhood where one lives.

social conflict theories Explanations that assume criminal law and the criminal-justice system are primarily means of controlling the poor and disenfranchised.

social control Informal and formal methods of getting members of society to conform to norms, folkways, and mores.

social control theory An explanation of criminal behavior that focuses on control mechanisms, techniques and strategies for regulating human behavior that lead to conformity or obedience to society's rules, and that posits that deviance results when social controls are weakened or break down, so that individuals are not motivated to conform to them.

social debt A sentencing principle that takes into account an offender's criminal history in sentencing decisions.

social defense A nonviolent, nonmilitary response to aggression. Demonstrations and boycotts are preferred to the use of weapons and force.

social development model (SDM) An array of personal, psychological, and community-level risk factors that make some children susceptible to development of antisocial behaviors.

social disorganization theory The theory that criminal behavior is caused by a breakdown of neighborhood solidarity and community organization. Social disorganization is often observed in zones in transition, such as areas of urban renewal, or areas in inner cities suffering decay and economic decline, where conditions are created that increase the incidence of crime.

social ecology A view that focuses on misbehaviors of lower-class youths and considers delinquency primarily to be the result of social disorganization.

social environment A set of factors correlated with juvenile delinquency, focusing on one's peers, social class, activities, and interests.

social indicators Statistical information provided by the U.S. Bureau of the Census about societal characteristics, including age patterns, gender characteristics, race/ethnicity, socioeconomic status, and other factors.

social injustice A collective sense of social inequality perceived by the poor toward the wealthy in describing relative deprivation.

social intervention A response to gangs that involves counseling and other direct attempts to change the values of youth in order to make gang involvement less likely.

social-investigation report A document consisting of a clinical diagnosis of the juvenile and his or her need for court assistance, relevant environmental and personality factors, and any other information that would assist the court in developing a treatment plan for the juvenile; also known as a predispositional report, developed by juvenile probation officers.

social isolation Feelings of loneliness, rejection, or social distance from others; a sense that one does not belong and that no one cares.

socialization The process of learning values and norms of society or the subculture to which the individual belongs; learning through interaction with others.

socialized delinquency Youthful behavior that violates the expectations of society but conforms to the expectations of other youths, particularly delinquent ones.

social justice Fair distribution of important goods and services, such as housing, education, and health care.

social-learning theory Applied to criminal behavior, a theory stressing the importance of learning through modeling others who are criminal. Criminal behavior is a function of copying or learning criminal conduct from others.

socially disorganized neighborhood An area in a community marked by cultural conflict, lack of cohesiveness, a transient population, and insufficient social organizations. These problems are reflected in the problems at schools in these areas.

social norms *See* **norms.**

social-order advocate One who suggests that under circumstances involving criminal threats to public safety, the interests of society should take precedence over individual rights.

social pathology Behavior in society that has negative consequences, such as crime.

social-process theories Theories that view criminality as normal behavior. Everyone has the potential to become a criminal, depending on the influences that impel him or her toward or away from crime and how he or she is regarded by others.

Social Psychological School A perspective on criminological thought that highlights the role played in crime causation by weakened self-esteem and meaningless social roles. Social-psychological thinkers stress the relationship of the individual to the social group as the underlying cause of behavior.

social screening The acquisition of a child's case history, consisting of the child's relationship with his or her family, the child's demeanor, school records, and medical and psychological history.

Social Security numbers Identifying nine-digit numbers used for taxation purposes by the Internal Revenue Service and by other government and private agencies for various identifying purposes. The numbers were first used in 1936 when the Social Security Administration was established. The first three digits of the number usually indicate the state where the number was issued. Social Security numbers are required by employers, who use them to report employee income to the IRS and other agencies.

social structure Recurrent, stable patterns of interaction among persons.

social-structure theories Theories that explain criminal conduct according to the creation of a lower-class culture based on poverty and deprivation, and the response of the poor to this situation.

social therapeutic institutions Facilities for convicted offenders that emphasize treatment over punishment.

Society for Laws Against Molesters (SLAM) An organization devoted to creating tougher legislation against child molesters.

Society for the Prevention of Pauperism A philanthropic society that established the first public reformatory for juveniles in the nation, the New York House of Refuge, in 1825.

Society for the Reformation of Juvenile Delinquents The organization that opened the House of Refuge in New York City in 1824; first organization to attempt to remove children from prisons and jails and provide them with food, shelter, and services.

Society of Forensics Toxicologists Established in 1970 and headquartered in Mesa, AZ, this association consists of forensics personnel and other interested persons who study poisons and other harmful substances that may cause serious bodily injury or death if ingested.

sociobiology The scientific study of the causal relation between genetic structure and social behavior.

socioeconomic status The level of income of neighborhood residents and their general social standing or prominence.

sociological explanations, sociological theories Theories of criminal conduct that emphasize social conditions that bear on the individual as the causes of criminal behavior.

sociological law Scientifically established statements about the social world that are largely unrefuted; causal relations between social variables that have been tested to the extent that their relation is largely undisputed.

sociology The scientific study of social interaction.

sociopath One who has an antisocial personality; one who appears to accept and be comfortable with social interactions, but who cynically regards such interactions as a means to other ends, usually personal gain or other selfish motives. *See also* **psychopath.**

sodium amytal Truth serum; a drug that lowers inhibitions so that a person will disclose private details or secrets about him- or herself.

sodomy Sexual penetration of the mouth or anus, a felony at common law. Sodomy laws were overturned by the U.S. Supreme Court in *Lawrence v. Texas* (2003).

software piracy The unauthorized duplication of computer programs and data from one storage medium to another.

solicitation The inchoate offense of requesting or encouraging someone to engage in illegal conduct.

solicitor In England, a lawyer who is qualified to advise clients and provide instruction to barristers.

solicitor general A functionary who conducts and supervises litigation in the U.S. Supreme Court, who may be a high-ranking officer which is the equivalent of an attorney general.

solitary confinement *See* **isolation.**

somatotype Body type, which results from embryonic development.

somatotype school of criminology A criminological perspective that relates body build to behavioral tendencies, temperament, susceptibility to disease, and life expectancy.

Son of Sam *See* **Berkowitz, David.**

Son of Sam laws Legislated rules prohibiting criminals from profiting from their crimes through sales or publications of their stories to or through the media. The name stems from David ("Son of Sam") Berkowitz, who sold his life story for profit.

sororicide The killing of a sister by a sibling.

sound-sensing detection system An alarm device that detects audible sounds produced by someone seeking unlawful entry into a business or residence or other dwelling. Microphones and control units are placed in different locations and equipped with a power supply. Controls may be adjusted to tune out ambient noise so that normal sounds will not activate the alarm.

Sourcebook of Criminal Justice Statistics A compendium of statistical information about juvenile and adult offenders, court facts, statistics, and trends, probation and parole figures, and considerable additional information. It is published annually by the Hindelang Criminal Justice Research Center at the State University of New York at Albany, and funded by grant from the U.S. Department of Justice, Bureau of Justice Statistics.

Southern Police Institute A law enforcement education and training center affiliated with the Department of Justice Administration at the University of Louisville, KY.

Southern Poverty Law Center A legal organization headquartered in Montgomery, AL, that keeps track of white supremacists and other hate groups and promotes litigation against them.

souvenirs In a serial murder case, one or more objects taken by the killer from each victim to function as mementos of the crime.

sovereign immunity The principle that the state cannot be sued in its own courts or in any other court without its consent and permission.

SP State police.

span of control The number of persons or departments under the direct control of a supervisor or individual department. Span of control may also refer to the managerial or supervisory responsibilities and power relative to subordinates in different organizational units.

SpeakerID Program An electronic voice-verification system used as a part of electronic monitoring to verify the identity of a person called by a probation or parole agency.

special conditions of probation Extra requirements written into a standard probation agreement, including possible vocational or educational training, counseling, drug or alcohol treatment, attendance at meetings, restitution, and community service.

special court martial The military court that is second in the three grades of court martial in terms of the severity of the penalty that can be imposed.

specialization An organizational principle of bureaucracy indicating that each person should be highly trained to perform a certain function. This specialized training enhances a person's productivity and effectiveness.

specialized caseloads model A probation or parole officer caseload model based on the officer's unique skills and knowledge relative to offender drug or alcohol problems. Some probation and parole officers are assigned particular clients with unique problems that require more than average officer expertise.

Specialized Offender Accountability Program (SOAP) A program operated by the Lexington Correctional Center in Oklahoma for juveniles under 22 years of age. It is based on a military disciplinary model. Individualized treatment is provided, although a strict military regimen is observed.

special judge A judicial official who is appointed to hear certain types of cases; an independent judge who can decide unique cases, usually serving temporarily as a supplemental judge to regularly appointed or elected judges, called upon because of his or her particular expertise and objectivity in the matter before the court.

special jurisdiction This term indicates that a court is restricted to handling certain types of cases such as probating wills or adjudicating juvenile offenders.

Special K *See* **ketamine hydrochloride.**

special master A person appointed by the court to oversee court orders or injunctions.

special-needs inmate A prisoner who requires specific treatment or care because he or she suffers from mental illness, chemical dependency (drug or alcohol abuse), or a communicable disease.

special prevention *See* **secondary prevention.**

specialty court Any court designed to address a specific social issue or offender problem, such as drugs, guns, domestic violence, or mental health. *See also* **domestic violence court; drug court; gun court.**

special verdict A decision by a jury as the fact finder, where judgment in the case is decided by the judge.

specification A circumstance of a crime that carries an additional mandatory term of confinement for those convicted.

specific deterrence Punishment that causes one particular person upon whom the punishment is inflicted to refrain from committing new crimes. *See also* **deterrence, general or specific.**

specific intent The intent to accomplish a specific purpose as an element of a crime (e.g., breaking into someone's house for the purpose of stealing jewelry).

specific learning disabilities Handicaps believed to be related to a minimal brain disorder, resulting in perceptual distortions that inhibit proper learning of reading, writing, and other skills.

specimen A piece of physical evidence that can be examined by a crime laboratory. Investigation of physical evidence can determine what it is and where it came from.

Speck, Richard (1941–1991) A mass murderer who was convicted of stabbing and strangling eight student nurses in Chicago in 1966. He subsequently died in prison.

spectator violence Any physically rough activity engaged in by those attending sporting events.

spectrograph A device used to photograph elements of the light spectrum. The device is used to identify certain small or minuscule quantities of materials in inorganic substances.

speedball A mixture of cocaine and heroin giving a dual and opposite effect of stimulation and depression.

speedy trial A concept defined by federal law and applicable to federal district courts, where a defendant must be tried within 100 days of an arrest. Every state has speedy-trial provisions that are within reasonable ranges of the federal standard, which was originally established to comply with the Sixth Amendment of the U.S. Constitution. The longest state speedy-trial provision is New Mexico's, at 180 days.

Speedy Trial Act of 1974 (amended 1979, 1984) An act to ensure compliance with the Sixth Amendment provision for a citizen to be brought to trial without undue delay 30 to 70 days from the date of formal specification of charges, usually in an arraignment proceeding.

Spencer, Herbert (1820–1903) A British sociologist who wrote *Social Statics* (1855). Spencer was a devotee of Charles Darwin and believed in social evolution through a similar process to the one described by Darwin for biological evolution. Thus, "survival of the fittest" was a dominant theme in Spencer's writing. He believed that society is governed by laws of conflict, out of which emerge criminality and conformity as competing interests.

Spike Strip Stop Stick; a long triangular steel box filled with spikes designed to puncture the tires of fleeing suspects in automobiles on open highways.

spindle A component of the combination-lock mechanism on a safe. Its function is to turn the locking mechanism whenever the dial is rotated in one direction or the other.

spin house An early Dutch workhouse for women.

spiral rifling Cutting of spiral grooves in the bore of a firearm barrel. The purpose of such rifling is to give a discharging bullet a spinning motion as it exits the barrel, which is intended to maintain a straight trajectory of the bullet during its travel from the muzzle of the firearm to the target it strikes. Rifling leaves unique marks on a bullet that can be used to identify the particular firearm and possibly the identity of the perpetrator of a crime in which the firearm was used.

spirit of the law Efforts by police officers to exhibit leniency where law violations are observed. First offenders may receive leniency because of extenuating circumstances.

Spitzer, Stephen A structural Marxist who contended that laws are used to maintain long-term interests of the powerful and to control those persons who oppose or threaten these interests. Deviants are considered by structural Marxists as anyone who calls into question or criticizes capitalist modes of appropriating the product of human labor, social conditions under which capitalist production occurs, patterns of distribution and consumption in capitalist society, the process of socialization for productive and nonproductive roles, and the ideology supporting capitalist society.

split sentence A punishment imposed by a criminal court that consists of a term of confinement together with conditional release, such as probation.

split sentencing The procedure whereby a judge imposes a sentence of incarceration for a fixed period, followed by a probationary period of a fixed duration; similar to shock probation.

spod A computer geek who communicates almost exclusively over the Internet; a computer geek who has no interest in computers *per se.*

spoils system The practice of rewarding political supporters with various government appointments and positions, regardless of their qualifications or lack thereof for such positions.

spontaneous declaration An excited utterance, such as confessing to a crime during emotional stress at the crime scene.

spontaneous remission The aging-out process. Offenders become too old to commit crime or become less interested in committing crime.

spoofing Compromising or defeating an alarm system by short-circuiting some or all of the wires in a series circuit; entering false signals into an alarm system to reduce its sensitivity.

sporting theory of justice An idea conceived by Dean Wigmore that describes a criminal trial in which two highly skilled lawyers attempt to prosecute and defend a client, with the judge acting as an impartial referee.

sport violence Physical altercations between players during athletic events.

spot protection Maximizing the security measures taken to safeguard particular objects or anything of value, such as art objects, in a building where such items are displayed or stored.

spousal abuse The psychological or physical mistreatment of one spouse by another.

spree murder Killing of three or more persons within 30 days. Spree murder is often associated with felony homicides.

spur The ridge detail of a fingerprint; a small branch stemming from a single ridge line; a hooklike ridge appearing in a fingerprint.

spuriousness An apparent relation between two variables that is subsequently explained by the presence of a third, unknown variable; a false relationship that can be explained away by other variables.

Spurzheim, Johann K. (1776–1832) A phrenologist who studied head shapes and bumps and contours of the head in an effort to predict the types of criminal behaviors persons with such physical characteristics might manifest.

spy One who secretly collects and reports information about the activities or movements of an enemy or competitor.

"square" An inmates who is a noncriminal type and is considered a situational offender. This type of inmate does not conform to the inmate code.

"square John" An accidental offender, or one who committed only a few crimes, who is often better educated than most inmates. Square Johns are not considered criminals by the inmate population, and are oriented toward conventional society.

SRO School resource officer; also single-room occupancy, a type of boarding house.

stability of punishment hypothesis The hypothesis that the rate of punishment in a given society will remain stable, despite fluctuations in the crime rate.

stable slum A neighborhood in which the population shifts have slowed down, permitting patterns of behavior and traditions to develop over a number of years.

staff A component of an organization consisting of personnel in administrative positions charged with planning, coordinating, advising, and investigating.

staff functions Civilian work including clerks and professionals who coordinate internal organizational activities in police departments.

staff personnel Support personnel consisting of the dispatchers, secretarial help, and other ancillary employees who facilitate the performance of police officer tasks, including communication, training, property, and records.

staging a crime scene The arrangement of a corpse, weapon, or other evidence to mislead investigators about how a crime occurred.

stale misdemeanor rule When someone commits a misdemeanor in the presence of a police officer, the officer must arrest the person right after the misdemeanor is committed, not at some later date more convenient for the police officer. Thus, a substantial delay between the commission of the misdemeanor and the arrest will cause the officer to lose jurisdiction. To effect an arrest at a later date, the officer must first obtain an arrest warrant from a judicial official.

stalking Following another person with the intent to harass, intimidate, or harm physically. Often, the person being stalked is unaware of the stalker's presence.

standard deviation A statistical term that defines a fixed proportion of scores that lie within a given distance on either side of the mean of a distribution of scores. A normal or bell-shaped curve characterizes the distributions of scores. This measure is the distance from the mean that must be traversed in order to include a fixed proportion of scores. The interval within one standard deviation on either side of the mean of a distribution usually encompasses approximately 68 percent of the total scores in the distribution.

standard diversion *See* **unconditional diversion.**

standardization of personnel The selection and training of personnel to increase uniformity in knowledge, skill, or decisions.

standardization of work The planning of work routines and practices to increase uniformity of processes and outcomes.

standard muzzle velocity The particular speed at which a bullet leaves the muzzle of a firearm, depending on the weight and type of bullet, the gunpowder load used, and the type of firearm.

standard of proof Norms used by courts to determine the validity of claims or allegations of wrongdoing against offenders. Civil standards of proof are "clear and convincing evidence" and "preponderance of evidence," whereas the criminal standard is "beyond a reasonable doubt."

standard probation A type of supervision in which probationers conform to all terms of their probation program, but their contact with probation officers is minimal. Often, their contact is by telephone or letter once or twice a month.

standing A doctrine mandating that courts may not recognize a party to a suit unless that person has a personal stake or direct interest in the outcome of the suit.

standing order Any directive remaining in force indefinitely until it is cancelled or rescinded.

Star Chamber An early English court that met secretly to try and punish offenders, usually in political matters.

star chamber proceeding A secret tribunal in which a group of judges decides one's fate without formality and without providing the person the opportunity to defend him- or herself or give his or her side or argument.

stare decisis "To stand by a decision" (Latin); a legal precedent; the principle whereby lower courts issue rulings consistent with those of higher courts, where the same types of cases and facts are at issue. The principle of leaving undisturbed a settled point of law or a particular precedent.

Stark, Rodney A criminological theorist who has devised the proximity hypothesis, which posits that persons who live in socially disorganized, high-crime areas have the greatest risk of coming into contact with criminal offenders, regardless of their own behavior or lifestyle. Victims do not encourage crime, but rather, are simply in the wrong place at the wrong time. "Deviant" places are depicted by Stark as poor, densely populated, highly transient neighborhoods in transition. In a sense, this theory is an offshoot of the concentric-zone hypothesis devised by the Chicago School and Ernest Burgess and Robert Park.

Starkweather, Charles (1938–1959) A spree killer who went on a murder rampage in the Midwest during the late 1950s with a 14-year-old female accomplice, Carol Ann Fugate. Starkweather was executed in 1959.

starring The star-shaped rupture of human flesh caused by the pressure of exploding gases during a contact gunshot wound.

state account system A form of prison industry in which inmate production is directed by prison officials, goods are sold on the open market, and inmates receive a share of the profits.

state action doctrine The traditional legal principle that only government officials or their representatives in the criminal-justice process could be held accountable for the violation of an individual's constitutional civil rights.

state administering agency Any state agency that administers federal formula or block grant programs such as are sponsored by the Office of Juvenile Justice and Delinquency Prevention or the Bureau of Justice Assistance.

state attorney general The chief legal officer of a state responsible for both civil and criminal matters.

state constitution An official document that sets forth all rights and laws enjoyed by persons who reside in a particular state and grants or limits powers of persons holding official positions in different departments or divisions of state government.

state court administrator The person who coordinates case-flow management, operating funds, budgeting, and court docket administration.

state courts Civil or criminal tribunals in which cases at the state level are decided through an adversarial proceeding. State courts are created by state authority without federal jurisdiction. Their case decisions may be appealed through the state court system and eventually to the U.S. Supreme Court or the court of last resort.

state court system A state judicial structure. *See diagram p. 240.*

state highway patrol A state law enforcement agency whose principal functions are the prevention, detection, and investigation of motor-vehicle offenses and the apprehension of motor-vehicle traffic offenders.

state institution, state school In juvenile corrections, a self-contained facility that provides a variety of services for juveniles including rehabilitation, health, education, counseling, recreation, employment, and training.

State Justice Institute (SJI) A private, nonprofit organization established in 1984 by Congress to bring about improvements in state court operations. The SJI awards grants to organizations and governmental agencies to address court-related problems or to undertake innovative practices.

state legislature An elected body with powers to enact state civil and criminal laws but prohibited from violating the U.S. Constitution.

state planning agency A unit of state government officially charged with overseeing criminal-justice planning and policy development throughout the state, which usually administers federal funds for different state criminal-justice projects.

state police A state law enforcement agency whose principal functions may include police communications, aiding local police in criminal investigations, training police, guarding state property, and patrolling highways.

state prison Any correctional facility operated by a state to house convicted felons; a long-term confinement facility for a state jurisdiction; a state penitentiary.

state-raised youth Individuals who are raised by state agencies, who have spent most of their lives in institutions or foster care. They are at home in prisons and form tightly knit cliques that threaten and use violence for protection and to increase their power.

state's attorney An elected or appointed person in a local or state jurisdiction with the authority to issue informations and secure indictments who represents the state in criminal prosecutions.

state's evidence Testimony given by those involved in crimes that incriminate others involved in the crime, usually in exchange for leniency or some other consideration, such as immunity from further prosecution.

states' rights This term refers to the fact that states retain any powers not specifically delegated to the federal government by the U.S. Constitution.

states' sovereign domain Those areas of government over which a state has exclusive control.

state-use prison industries system, state-use system A form of inmate labor in which items produced by inmates are salable only by or to state offices. Items that only the state can sell include such things as license plates and hunting licenses. Items sold only to state offices include furniture and cleaning supplies.

stationary killer A serial killer who commits his or her crimes within a small geographical area.

station cop In Reuss-Ianni's 4-World Syndrome, the type of police officer who is content to stay at the police station and do routine paperwork, but who still keeps and uses a patrol car, described by E. Reuss-Ianni in her 1984 work *Two Cultures of Policing. See also* **Reuss-Ianni Typology.**

stationhouse adjustment, stationhouse release A decision by police officers to deal informally with an arrestee, often at a police station. Such actions often do not involve arrests, but warnings.

stationhouse citation An alternative to pretrial detention, whereby the arrestee is escorted to the precinct police station or headquarters rather than the pretrial detention facility. Release, which may occur before or after booking, is contingent upon the defendant's written promise to appear in court later as specified on the release form.

station world In Reuss-Ianni's 4-World Syndrome, the type of police orientation embodied by an officer who is primarily involved in police-department paperwork, described by E. Reuss-Ianni in her 1984 work *Two Cultures of Policing. See also* **Reuss-Ianni Typology.**

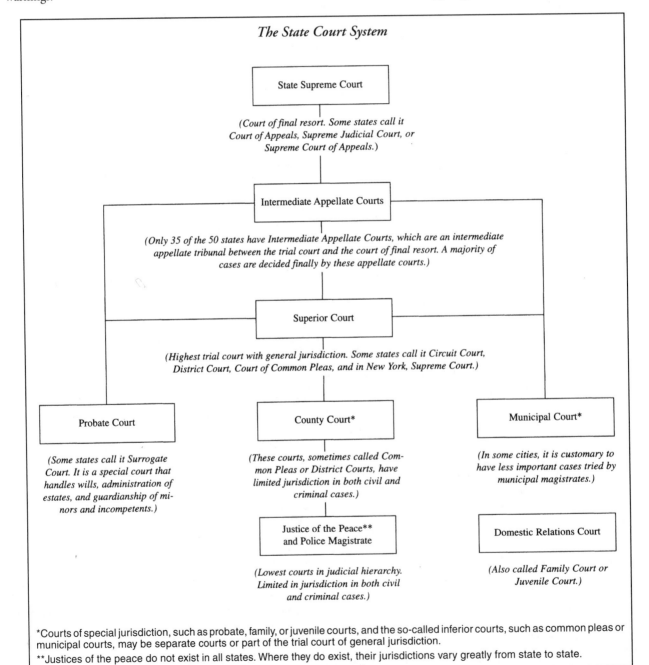

The State Court System

State Supreme Court

(Court of final resort. Some states call it Court of Appeals, Supreme Judicial Court, or Supreme Court of Appeals.)

Intermediate Appellate Courts

(Only 35 of the 50 states have Intermediate Appellate Courts, which are an intermediate appellate tribunal between the trial court and the court of final resort. A majority of cases are decided finally by these appellate courts.)

Superior Court

(Highest trial court with general jurisdiction. Some states call it Circuit Court, District Court, Court of Common Pleas, and in New York, Supreme Court.)

Probate Court

(Some states call it Surrogate Court. It is a special court that handles wills, administration of estates, and guardianship of minors and incompetents.)

County Court*

(These courts, sometimes called Common Pleas or District Courts, have limited jurisdiction in both civil and criminal cases.)

Municipal Court*

(In some cities, it is customary to have less important cases tried by municipal magistrates.)

Justice of the Peace**
and Police Magistrate

(Lowest courts in judicial hierarchy. Limited in jurisdiction in both civil and criminal cases.)

Domestic Relations Court

(Also called Family Court or Juvenile Court.)

*Courts of special jurisdiction, such as probate, family, or juvenile courts, and the so-called inferior courts, such as common pleas or municipal courts, may be separate courts or part of the trial court of general jurisdiction.

**Justices of the peace do not exist in all states. Where they do exist, their jurisdictions vary greatly from state to state.

statistical analysis The application of particular formulae in hypothesis tests or to analyze distributions of scores representing attitudes and other social or psychological phenomena from a group of persons.

statistical analysis center (SAC) An organizational unit in most states established for the purpose of collecting, analyzing, maintaining, and disseminating various types of criminal-justice data.

statistical hypothesis A statement that can be tested and potentially refuted; an assertion of a particular population value, a parameter, which is compared with an actual value from a sample of persons, a statistic, taken from the population. Tentative conclusions may be drawn about the truthfulness or falsity of a statement from observed results of a statistical test.

statistical inference The process of making inferences about population values based on sample values taken from a sample of persons from the population. The process usually utilizes inferential statistics, which contain a probability about the likelihood that the population value has been accurately estimated.

statistical model An artificial mathematical equation showing relationships between variables, which is intended to represent how actual variables would react under real conditions; a prediction made that is subsequently tested to determine its accuracy; a method of testing hypotheses and ultimately the theory from which the hypotheses were derived.

statistical prediction The use of statistical variables to predict the likelihood of some event.

statistical significance A probabilistic interpretation of numerical results of a hypothesis test, in which the likelihood is determined that a hypothesis is true. Sample size affects statistical significance in that as sample size increases, statistical significance of observed differences increases. This is because the size of standard error term is substantially reduced, thus producing an inflated numerical result giving a false impression of the actual substantive significance of the difference between what is expected according to chance and what is actually observed.

statistics Characteristics of a sample of persons or elements; also, an assemblage of tests and procedures from which one can describe and make inferences about samples taken from populations.

status frustration Feelings of anger and hopelessness brought about by membership in a powerless segment of society. This condition is linked to lower socioeconomic status.

status offender Any juvenile who has committed an offense that would not be considered a crime if committed by an adult (e.g., a curfew violation would not be a criminal action if committed by an adult, but such an act is a status offense if engaged in by a juvenile).

status offense Any act committed by a juvenile that would not be a crime if committed by an adult.

statute of limitations The period of time after which a crime that has been committed cannot be prosecuted. No statute of limitations exists for capital crimes.

Statute of Winchester A law written in 1285 that created a watch and ward system in English cities and towns and that codified early police practices. It also required all citizens to keep arms for defense, establishing the hue and cry as a mandatory service under the constable.

statutes Laws passed by legislatures. Statutory definitions of criminal offenses are embodied in penal codes.

statutory Having to do with law or anything protected by law.

statutory exclusion, statutory exclusion provisions Provisions that automatically exclude certain juveniles and offenses from the jurisdiction of the juvenile courts (e.g., murder, aggravated rape, and armed robbery).

statutory law Authority based on enactments of state legislatures; also, laws passed by legislatures.

statutory rape Having consensual sexual intercourse with another person who is under the statutory age of consent for sexual intercourse.

statutory release A state's obligation to release an inmate who has served his or her full sentence.

stay A court order suspending proceedings or the enforcement of an order (e.g., a stay of execution for a prisoner who is about to be put to death).

stay *ad interim* "For the meantime" (Latin); a temporary halting of proceedings, usually pending the conclusion of some other proceeding or action.

stay of execution The temporary cessation of a capital sentence to be carried out against a person sentenced to the death penalty. A stay of execution is ordinarily issued by an appellate judge or a governor and is in effect until the issue or issues resulting in the delay of the sentence of death can be heard and resolved.

steal To make off with the property of another; to appropriate the property of another without his or her consent or approval.

Steering Committee Model An organizational structure preferred by the Aryan Brotherhood in U.S. prisons. A committee comprising an odd number of members who founded the organization governs it. When a committee member dies, the council chooses his replacement.

stellate A star-shaped wound caused by a contact gunshot to the head or body. Gases expand under the skin, causing a ragged wound resembling a star or cross.

stereotype A preconceived perception of a group, regardless of individual differences. Stereotypes may be either negative or positive, but they are often emotional and groundless.

stet "Let it stand" (Latin); leave it alone.

stickup boy A small-time armed robber.

stigmata Unfavorable physical or behavioral characteristics that set a person apart from others and that cause others to avoid social contact.

stigmatization A social process whereby offenders acquire undesirable characteristics as the result of imprisonment or court appearances. Undesirable criminal or delinquent labels are assigned to those who are processed through the criminal- and juvenile-justice systems.

stimulants Synthetic substances that produce an intense physical reaction by stimulating the central nervous system.

sting, sting operation An undercover program wherein police officers attract likely perpetrators by posing as criminals.

stipend An amount of money as payment for completing a task; a fixed sum to be paid for performing a service.

stippling Tattooing oneself; getting a tattoo.

stipulation An agreement between counsel to accept certain evidence or testimony as factual without it actually being presented formally in court; a time-saving measure intended to facilitate the resolution of a civil or criminal case.

Stockholm syndrome An occurrence wherein a hostage begins to identify with and acquire sympathy for his or her captor and become antagonistic toward the authorities.

stock manipulation An illegal practice among brokers, in which they lead their clients to believe the price of a particular stock will rise, thus creating an artificial demand for it.

stocks A device similar to a pillory, by which individuals were punished by having their wrists and heads secured in a wooden apparatus placed in a public square where they could be seen by others and suffer public humiliation.

stolen property Any unlawfully obtained material objects that have been taken from another without consent or approval.

stolen-property offenses Any crime involving the exchange or transfer of property or contraband that has been taken by theft. Persons accepting such property who know it has been obtained by illegal means may be prosecuted for receiving and concealing such contraband or merchandise.

Stone, Harlan Fiske (1872–1946) A jurist who was chief justice of the U.S. Supreme Court (1941–1946). He practiced law in New York City in 1899 and was appointed an associate justice of the U.S. Supreme Court in 1925. During World War II, he presided over martial law and treason cases.

stoner gang A group of white youths who have a strong interest in heavy metal music and marijuana use.

Stonewall riots Considered the beginning of the gay rights movement, this riot began in June 1969 when the New York City Police Department conducted a raid of a gay bar in Greenwich Village. A warrant stated that liquor was being sold in violation of the existing premises permit, but patrons of the bar resisted, claiming routine harassment. In the ensuing melee that became the Stonewall riots, four police officers were seriously injured and 13 patrons were arrested.

"stooper" A petty criminal who earns his or her living by retrieving winning tickets that are accidentally discarded by race track patrons.

STOP *See* **Stop Turning Out Prisoners (STOP)**.

stop-and-frisk A situation in which police officers who are suspicious of an individual will run their hands lightly over the suspect's outer clothing to determine if the person possesses a concealed weapon. Such a search, also called a "patdown" or "threshold inquiry," is intended to stop short of any activity that would be considered a violation of the Fourth Amendment clause pertinent to reasonable searches and seizures. *See Terry v. Ohio* (1968); *Sibron v. New York* (1968).

Stop Assaultive Children Program (SAC) A program started in Phoenix, AZ, in the late 1980s designed for youths who have committed serious family violence. Children are detained in a juvenile facility for a short time, and their release is contingent upon being law abiding, observing curfew, and other conditions. Their prosecution is deferred, and they must participate in counseling. The program may include volunteer work.

stoppage in transit The right of a merchandiser or seller to prevent sold goods in transit from being delivered to a buyer.

Stop Stick *See* **Spike Strip**.

Stop Turning Out Prisoners (STOP) An organization originating in Florida to reduce or prevent the release of violent prison inmates into communities.

straight adult incarceration The practice of housing juveniles convicted in criminal court in the general adult prison population.

strain Emotional turmoil and conflict caused when persons believe they cannot achieve their desires and goals through legitimate means.

strain-sensitive cable Any electrical wire designed to trigger a signal whenever it is stretched. Such wire is used as a perimeter defense and is used to detect intruders or as an antitrespass device. It may be placed underground or fastened to a fence or wall.

strain theory A criminological theory positing that a gap between culturally approved goals and legitimate means of achieving them causes frustration that leads to criminal behavior.

stranger abduction A kidnapping by some individual unknown to the victim.

stranger homicide Criminal homicide committed by a person unknown and unrelated to the victim.

strangling The act of squeezing one's throat, thereby cutting off the air supply and eventually resulting in serious injury or death.

strap A leather strap attached to a handle and used for inflicting whippings.

strategic analysis A perspective holding that delinquency is best explained by assuming that human beings are rational individuals seeking to further personal interests and fulfill their goals by the most efficient means.

strategic intelligence The development of a detailed information base about the characteristics of a particular group or individual.

strategic leniency Less harsh dispositions meted out to certain offenders believed to be nonviolent and least likely to reoffend.

strategic policing A style of policing that embodies the traditional police objective of professional crime fighting but expands the enforcement target to include nontraditional criminals, such as serial offenders, gangs, and criminal associations.

stratification Grouping society into classes based on the unequal distribution of scarce resources.

stratified society The view that society can be separated into levels based on socioeconomic factors, ranging from the wealthy classes to the permanent underclass.

straw theory An oversimplified version of an existing theory. Opponents of a theory may present and attack a "straw" version of that theory but claim they have attacked the theory itself.

street A publicly maintained highway used for vehicular travel.

street attitudes The feelings of jail or prison correctional officers who fail to do their jobs or follow their job descriptions, or perform their duties poorly. The term includes those with personal prejudices toward racial or ethnic minorities.

street cop In E. Reuss-Ianni's 4-World Syndrome, the type of police officer who has a patrolman mentality, described in her 1984 work *Two Cultures of Policing*. *See also* **Reuss-Ianni Typology.**

street crime Illegal acts designed to prey on the public through theft, damage, and violence. Street crimes include mugging and robbery.

street justice When police decide to deal with a status offense or some other minor crime in their own way, usually by ignoring it; also, the illegitimate and unreported use of police force as an informal, extralegal punishment.

street-outreach model A Youth Service Bureau model establishing neighborhood centers for youths who are delinquency-prone, where youths can have things to do other than hang out on the streets.

street world The type of police officer orientation described by E. Reuss-Ianni in her 1984 work, *Two Cultures of Policing,* who favors a quick response world. *See also* **Reuss-Ianni Typology.**

stress, police stress The body's nonspecific response to any demand placed upon it. Police stress refers to negative anxiety accompanied by an alarm reaction, resistance, and exhaustion. Anxiety contributes to heart disease, headaches, high blood pressure, and ulcers.

stressors Factors that cause stress, including boredom, constant threats to officer health and safety, responsibility for protecting the lives of others, and the fragmented nature of police work.

stress vs. nonstress training Teaching police officers methods of coping with stress caused by role strain and conflict.

strict construction The idea that the U.S. Constitution should be literally interpreted.

strict liability Responsibility for a crime or violation imposed without regard to the actor's guilt; criminal liability without *mens rea.*

strict-liability crimes Illegal acts whose elements do not contain the need for intent or *mens rea.* These are usually acts that endanger the public welfare, such as illegal dumping of toxic wastes.

strict-liability tort Any civil wrong, typically pursued via a lawsuit seeking monetary recovery for injuries caused by another person or corporation; violation of a duty imposed by law or the existence of a legal duty to a plaintiff. A breach of that duty leads to damages as a result of the breach.

strike Any collective action by workers to refuse to work. It may be a protest regarding some issue, such as proposed wage increases or changes in working conditions that are unfavorably viewed by those who refuse to work.

stripes Chevrons on military or police or corrections officer uniforms indicative of one's rank.

strip search A search conducted of prisoners and visitors, who are asked to strip and their persons are searched. Thoroughness varies among jurisdictions, but such a search may include X rays or visual inspection of body cavities.

struck jury A trial jury obtained following actions by opposing counsel to strike prospective jury members from jury duty for various reasons, such as for cause or through peremptory challenge.

structural Marxist theory The view that the legal and justice systems are designed to maintain the capitalist system and that members of both the owner and worker classes whose behavior threatens the stability of the system will be sanctioned. Stephen Spitzer has elaborated these views as an extension of the Marxian theory of deviance.

structural theory A view that emphasizes the role of immutable structures in society in the origination and transmission of crime and delinquency.

structured conflicts In corrections, conflicts between guards and inmates that arise from differences in their organizational roles.

structured discretion Judicial sentencing decisions for which guidelines exist to limit the severity or leniency of sentences imposed. The intention is to standardize sentences and create greater fairness in the courts. The term also applies to early-release decisions by parole boards.

structured sentencing A method of punishment that includes determinate and commission-created presumptive sentencing schemes.

strychnine A bitter poison made from *nux vomica* and certain other plants. It is usually available in white crystalline pellets or powder.

Students for a Democratic Society (SDS) A student organization originating during the 1960s that was opposed to the draft and war. The Vietnam War galvanized the SDS into various actions to protest war, poverty, and social conditions. During the early 1970s, the SDS became more aggressive and violent, engaging in bombings, assaults, and other types of offensive action.

student threat Any verbal warning or intimidation made by a student against teachers, the school, or even other students.

study release *See* **work (and educational) release, work/study release.**

stun belt An electric security belt that adminsters a shock to its wearer by remote control.

stun bomb A nonlethal explosive device intended to disorient and disable for a short period. The concussive effects of the bomb induce a temporary inability to function or move about purposefully. Stun bombs are used in riot control and in military actions against enemy forces.

stun gun A TASER weapon that uses electrical charges to disable unruly suspects or inmates.

subculture The social clique and behavior patterns of a selected group, such as a gang.

subculture of violence A subculture with values that demand the overt use of violence in certain social situations. Marvin Wolfgang and Franco Ferracuti devised this concept to depict a set of norms apart from mainstream conventional society, in which the theme of violence is pervasive and dominant. These norms are learned through socialization with others as an alternative lifestyle.

subculture theory Any criminological theory that focuses on the distinguishing characteristics or criminogenic effects of a subculture.

subject One who is suspected of a crime and is under investigation; in forensics, an object that can be reproduced through a cast.

subjective test A way of determining whether entrapment has occurred. The test assumes that whatever record a suspect may have is irrelevant, and that police misconduct is reprehensible *per se* and should not be tolerated as a means of eliciting crime.

subject-matter specialization, subject-matter jurisdiction A term applied when certain judges have exclusive jurisdiction over particular crimes.

subjudicial officer Any judicial officer who is invested with certain judicial powers and functions but whose decisions in criminal and juvenile cases are subject to *de novo* review by a judge.

subjustice Under the authority of a judge or court; undetermined.

sublimation The channeling of energy, such as that generated by hostility, into socially acceptable or culturally creative outlets.

Submission-Without-Argument Program A plan designed to streamline case processing. Cases are presented without oral argument.

suboptimization The practice by organizational subunits of valuing unit objectives over organizational objectives.

subornation of perjury The crime of procuring someone to lie under oath.

subpoena A document issued by a judge ordering a named person to appear in court at a particular time to either answer to charges or to testify in a case.

subrogation Substituting one person for another in a legal claim.

sub rosa Privately; not generally available for public view or knowledge; done surreptitiously.

sub rosa **economic system,** *sub rosa* **inmate economy** Informal economic system among inmates in which contraband dealings and gambling exist under a strict set of inmate-created rules.

sub rosa **indictment** A sealed or secret indictment.

substance abuse Using drugs or alcohol in such a way as to cause physical, emotional, or psychological harm to oneself.

Substance Abuse and Mental Health Services Administration (SAMHSA) A large division of the U.S. Department of Health and Human Services responsible for establishing and promoting programs and funding for substance-abuse and mental-health issues.

substantial (impermissible) burden on religious freedom Pressuring an individual to commit an act forbidden by his or her religion or preventing him or her from engaging in conduct or having a religious experience that the faith mandates.

substantial capacity test A definition of insanity that has as its core the view that insane persons lack the ability to understand the wrongfulness of their acts.

substantive criminal law Legislated rule that governs behaviors that are required or prohibited. Such law, usually enacted by legislatures, also specifies punishments accompanying law violations.

substantive due process The practice of having substantive law conform to the principles of fairness set forth in the U.S. Constitution.

substantive evidence Any oral, written, or tangible information that is used to prove a given fact and not intended for witness impeachment.

substantive felony A separate felony charged, which is unrelated to other felonies charged against other defendants who may be conspirators in a criminal enterprise.

substantive law A body of law that creates, discovers, and defines the rights and obligations of each person in society. Substantive law prescribes behavior, whereas procedural law prescribes how harmful behavior is handled.

substantive predicates Language that delineates specific conditions or requirements.

substantive rights Those rights that protect an individual against arbitrary and unreasonable actions (e.g., those in the Bill of Rights).

substitutionary evidence Any information introduced in court that is a substitute for the original evidence, and that shows the truthfulness of an assertion.

subterfuge Any activity disguised for the purpose of taking advantage of another or gaining an unfair position in relation to another. It may be an action undertaken to avoid something unpleasant.

subterranean behaviors, subterranean values Values or ideals that are subordinate or below the surface in the dominant value system and are sought by most people only occasionally and in appropriate circumstances (e.g., 1960s deviance, social problems, beatniks, hippies, drug culture, gangs).

suburb A geographical location outside of the city limits that is in close proximity to downtown; usually, residential and business locations near city centers but without the amount of traffic and congestion typical of city centers.

subversion Destruction; demolition; an attempt to overthrow a government by various means, hidden or overt.

sue To file a lawsuit against another to recover damages, usually money or property.

sufficiency of bail An amount of surety required for bail bond, in order to insure the appearance of a defendant later at a trial.

sufficient condition A factor that is always followed by a phenomenon of which it is a cause.

sufficient evidence Adequate information to justify a particular legal action, such as a finding of guilt and imposing a particular sentence on the convicted offender; enough information to show by a preponderance of evidence that a particular accusation or assertion is true.

suffocation A condition caused by the interruption of the flow of air for breathing.

suicide The intentional taking of one's own life.

"suicide by cop" An intentional effort by someone to force a police officer to shoot. Some suspects charge police with their own weapons, intending for the police to shoot and kill them.

suit A claim initiated in a civil court in order to recover damages, either property or money or both.

suitable target According to routine-activities theory, a target for crime that is relatively valuable, easily transportable, and not adequately guarded.

Sullivan Act A 1911 New York law passed to criminalize the possession of a weapon without legal authority to do so.

Summary Admission Report An account of the legal aspects of an inmate's case; a summary of his or her criminal history, demographics, family, and personal history data.

summary court martial The military court that is the lowest of the three grades of court martial in terms of the severity of the penalty that it can impose.

summary judgment Any granted motion following the presentation of a case against a defendant in a civil court; any argument countering the plaintiff's presented evidence. A summary judgment is usually the result of failing to state a claim upon which relief can be granted.

summary jurisdiction Jurisdiction of a court to make an instant judgment, such as contempt of court, and impose an immediate penalty, such as incarceration in jail for a specified period.

summary justice A trial held by a court of limited jurisdiction, without benefit of a jury trial.

summary offense In Britain, a minor offense, equivalent to a misdemeanor, that may be adjudicated by a local magistrate in lieu of a trial; the least serious British law violation, involving a petty criminal infraction.

summary proceeding Any judicial pronouncement or action taken without a formal hearing in the matter.

summons A summons takes the same form as a warrant, except that it commands a defendant to appear before the magistrate at a particular time and place. In many jurisdictions, law enforcement officers may issue a summons in lieu of an arrest, whereas judges issue warrants that require actions by the police to arrest or search. Issuances of summonses are discretionary, according to police officers, whereas warrants must be served. *See box.*

Sumner, William Graham (1840–1910) A sociologist who developed the terms "folkways" and "mores," ways of doing things in a society, without moral attachment (folkways) and with moral attachment (mores). A functionalist and consensus theorist, he wrote *Folkways* (1906).

sunset law A provision created by a legislature that requires disbanding or termination of an agency after a specified period of existence. Special commissions may be established to operate for a fixed period of time, and when that time expires, the commission disbands and no longer exists.

sunshine legislation Public access to legislative proceedings; open proceedings compared with closed and private meetings of legislative bodies.

superego Sigmund Freud's label for that part of personality concerned with moral values.

superintendent The chief executive officer of a prison or penitentiary.

A Summons on Complaint

FORM 2.
SUMMONS ON COMPLAINT
(RCr 2.04, 2.06)

DISTRICT COURT OF KENTUCKY

Franklin County

COMMONWEALTH OF KENTUCKY
V.   SUMMONS
_____
             Defendant.

TO THE ABOVE NAMED DEFENDANT:

You are hereby summoned to appear before the District Court, in the Franklin County Court House at Frankfort, Kentucky, at 9:00 A.M. (Eastern Standard Time) on Wednesday, October 31, 19 , to answer a complaint made by _____ charging you with the offense of reckless driving.
    Issued at Frankfort, Franklin County, Kentucky, this _____ day of _____, 19__.

_____
Judge, District Court of Kentucky
Franklin County
(Amended October 14, 19 , effective January 1, 19 .)

FORM 3. SUMMONS IN INDICTMENT
          (RCr 6.52, 6.54)
(Caption)

TO THE ABOVE NAMED DEFENDANT:

You are hereby summoned to appear before the Franklin Circuit Court in the Franklin County Court House at Frankfort, Kentucky, at 9:00 A.M. (Eastern Standard Time) on Wednesday, October 31, 19 , to answer an indictment charging you with the offenses of (1) malicious shooting and wounding with intent to kill and (2) carrying concealed a deadly weapon.
    Issued at Frankfort, Franklin County, Kentucky, this _____ day of _____, 19__.

_____
Clerk, Franklin Circuit Court
By _____
Deputy Clerk

superior court A court of record or trial court.

supermale A person displaying the XYY chromosomatic structure. *See also* **chromosomal aberration.**

supermax facility, supermax housing, supermax prison A freestanding facility, or a distinct unit within a facility, that provides for management and secure control of inmates who have been officially designated as exhibiting violent or serious or disruptive behavior while incarcerated.

superpredator A juvenile who is coming of age in actual and moral poverty without parents, teachers, coaches, or clergy to teach right from wrong, and who turns to violent criminal activity; one of the most violent juveniles, who commits the most violent crimes.

supersede To annul or set aside.

supervised pretrial release The release of a defendant without bail but under the supervision of a pretrial release agency or other supervising party.

supervised probation Any conditional sentence by a judge upon a convicted offender that includes monitoring by a probation officer.

supervised release A type of release requiring more frequent contact than monitored release does. Typically, various conditions are imposed and supervision is aimed at enforcing these conditions and providing services as needed. Some form of monetary bail may also be attached as a condition of supervised release, especially in high-risk cases.

supervision Management of clients, prisoners, or patients by authorized personnel who oversee their behaviors.

supervisory alarm system Any alarm device that is designed to detect irregularities in scheduled patrols of guards or behaviors of persons under observation. Irregularities trigger the alarm and alert officials to check to see if security has been breached, or if a person's condition has changed.

supervisory style Predominantly an independent variable in formal organizational research, connotes initiating activity for subordinates in the work setting. Leaders must obtain the compliance of lower-level participants in the organization. Different managers or leaders obtain compliance from subordinates in different ways, characterized as their "style."

Supplementary Homicide Reports (*SHRs*) An addendum to a criminal homicide reported routinely by local law enforcement agencies as a part of their participation in the *Uniform Crime Reports* data collection program.

supporting evidence Any information that contributes to and reinforces an assertion or factual statement or observation; circumstantial evidence that strengthens one's case against the accused or supports a particular argument or position.

supportive leadership Any type of supervisory behavior that encourages greater employee involvement in decision making, in which administrators consider a worker's feelings and emotions and respect his or her knowledge of the work to be performed.

suppression A response to gangs that involves the use of the criminal-justice system to reduce gang behavior through the use of formal social control including arrest and incarceration.

suppression doctrine *See* **exclusionary rule.**

suppression effect A reduction in the number of arrests per year for youths who have been incarcerated or otherwise punished.

suppression hearing A session held before a judge who presides at a trial. The purpose of the session is to determine which evidentiary documents or statements will be permitted later at trial. Motions are heard from both the defense and the prosecution to keep out or put in particular evidence, and the judge decides which evidence can and cannot be introduced at trial.

supra "Above" (Latin); in U.S. Supreme Court written opinions, references are made to earlier statements (e.g., "in the case of *Doe, supra,* the matter was concluded in a particular way").

Supreme Court The federal court of last resort as specified by the U.S. Constitution; at the state level, any court of last resort in most kinds of cases.

surety, sureties During the Middle Ages, people who made themselves responsible for the behavior of offenders released to their care.

surety bond A sum of money or property that is posted or guaranteed by a party to ensure the future court appearance of another person. *See also* **bail bond.**

suretyship An action undertaken to account for a debt or default of another.

surplus value The Marxist view that laboring classes produce wealth that far exceeds their wages and goes to the capitalist class as profits.

surrebuttal Introducing witnesses during a criminal trial in order to disprove damaging testimony by other witnesses.

surreptitious Concealed; hidden; disguised.

surrogate In jurisprudence, a judge who has jurisdiction of probating wills and settling estates.

surveillance Visual or electronic eavesdropping for the purpose of monitoring one's presence, conversation, or behaviors.

surveillance cameras Any monitoring device that permits others to view different parts of premises from strategically placed cameras that transmit happenings to a central monitoring location in real time.

survey A systematic collection of data or information by asking questions in questionnaires or interviews.

survival analysis A statistical technique used to measure the time interval between the onset of a disease and a terminal outcome.

survivalist One who has radical views and is often heavily armed, fears government takeover of society, and stockpiles provisions, weapons, and other materials to be used in the event that mainstream society must be defended.

survivor A living victim of a crime.

suspect Any person believed by a law enforcement agency to have committed a crime.

suspected member An official designation for a person believed to be a gang member.

suspended sentence A jail or prison term that is delayed while the defendant undergoes a period of community treatment.

If treatment is successful, the jail or prison sentence is terminated.

suspension of judgment A temporary action by a judge to refrain from imposing a penalty, either a fine or incarceration or both, or some other decision, pending other action. A judgment may be reinstated at a later time, depending on circumstances, or judgment may be put off indefinitely.

suspicion A reasonable belief that a crime has been committed and that a particular person or persons have committed the crime. However, the level of incriminating evidence is such that probable cause cannot be established for the purpose of making an arrest.

suspicionless search A search conducted by law enforcement officers without a warrant and without suspicion. Such searches are only permissible if based on an overriding concern for public safety.

sustain To uphold (e.g., "the conviction was sustained by a higher appellate court").

sustained petition Adjudication resulting in a finding that the facts alleged in a petition are true; a finding that a juvenile committed the offenses alleged, which resulted in an adjudication and disposition.

Sutherland, Edwin (1883–1950) Sutherland is known primarily for originating and elaborating differential-association theory in his book *Principles of Criminology* (1934). This theory posits that persons acquire criminal behaviors not simply by associating with other criminals, but rather, through associations that are characterized as intense, of long duration, frequent, and with greater priority. Thus, intensity, duration, frequency, and priority are key concepts. Sutherland believed that criminal behavior is learned, and is acquired by the fairly elaborate interplay of factors noted above. He also described various types of career criminals in his classic work *The Professional Thief* (1937).

Sutton, Willie (1901–1980) Alias "the actor," Sutton robbed banks using various disguises during the 1940s and 1950s, and was considered the most infamous bank robber in the United States.

SWAT (Special Weapons and Tactics) SWAT teams are used in high-crime areas to conduct antiterrorist activities, rescue hostages, and eliminate public danger posed by dangerous armed persons.

sweat box A torture device consisting of a coffinlike cell with just enough space to accommodate a man standing erect, used in the 1800s and early 1900s. Generally made of wood or tin, it was completely closed except for a hole two inches in diameter at nose level. In the heat of the Southern sun, temperature levels in these devices reached 120 degrees or more.

sweatshops Exploitative businesses and industries that employ child labor and demand long work hours for low pay.

swindler Someone who cheats someone else out of money or property; someone who engages in deception or deceit to obtain something of value from another.

swindling The deceptive practice of cheating someone out of money or other things of value.

switchblade A spring-loaded knife designed to open quickly with the push of a button, also known as a snap-blade or spring-blade knife; any knife whose blade is released automatically by a spring mechanism or any other type of mechanical device.

sworn officers Police employees who have taken an oath and been given powers by the state to make arrests, use force, and transverse property, in accordance with their duties.

Sykes, Gresham (1922–) A developer of naturalization theory, in collaboration with David Matza.

Symbionese Liberation Army (SLA) An American-based terrorist group that committed several murders and acts of violence during the 1970s. It formed following the escape of "Cinque" (Donald DeFreeze) from Soledad State Prison (CA) in March 1973. DeFreeze joined with others in the San Francisco Bay area to form the SLA, which carried out their first revolutionary action in November 1973 by killing Oakland, CA, School Superintendent Dr. Marcus Foster. The SLA subsequently kidnapped Patricia Hearst, daughter of a newspaper publisher. After a robbery spree and other violent acts, SLA members were trapped in a home in Los Angeles that was raided by a Los Angeles Police Department SWAT team. When the shooting was over, among the dead were Donald DeFreeze, Patricia Soltysik, Camilla Hall, Nancy Ling Perry, William Wolfe, and Angela Atwood. Other SLA members were captured and convicted of various crimes. Subsequently, in August 1975, Kathleen Soliah failed in her attempt to kill LAPD officers when her bombs failed to detonate. She remained a fugitive until 1999, and in 2001 she pled guilty to possession of explosives with intent to murder and was sentenced to two 10-years-to-life terms. In January 2002, first-degree murder charges were filed against Emily and William Harris, Kathleen Soliah, Michael Bortin, and James Kilgore. In February 2003, sentences ranging from eight to 14 years were imposed for the shooting death of a bank customer, Myrna Opsahl, which occurred during an SLA bank robbery in April 1975.

symbolic interaction The sociological view that people communicate through symbolic exchange, interpreting symbolic communication and incorporating it within their personalities. Their view of reality, then, depends on their particular interpretation of symbolic gestures.

sympathizers Inmates who have no desire to join a gang but who share a gang's beliefs.

Synanist A person receiving treatment within a Synanon program.

Synanon A long-term residential drug treatment program, using the therapeutic community approach, that is still in operation today.

syndicate An organized crime organization.

synomie A societal state, the opposite of anomie, marked by social cohesion achieved through the sharing of values. The concept is associated with Freda Adler.

syntality The personality of a group.

system A complex whole consisting of interdependent parts whose operations are directed toward goals and are influenced by the environment within which they function.

systematic forger, systematic check forger Edwin Lemert's term for a professional who earns his or her living by forging checks or passing bad or bogus negotiable instruments.

system boundaries The division between a system and its environment. In human systems, the boundary is often permeable and changing.

system components The separate subroutines or activities that contribute to total system objectives.

system efficiency The operation of the prosecutor's office in such a way as to effect speedy and early dispositions of cases in response to caseload pressures within the system. Weak cases are screened at intake, and other nontrial alternatives are used as primary means of disposition.

systemic link Violent behavior that results from the conflict inherent in the drug trade; a bond between violent crime and substance abuse forged by drug sellers and users.

system objectives The measured performance of a total system, rather than its parts; the joint products of system components.

system resources Items a system may change and use to achieve objectives.

systems approach An analytical method that focuses on systemic properties and processes.

systems-modification model A Youth Service Bureau model involving the establishment of community-based facilities for delinquency-prone youths; associations of churches, schools, and neighborhood businesses organizing to assist youths.

T

table A group tactic to delay action on a motion pending further investigation; also, a visual two-dimensional illustration presenting an organized array of facts.

tactical intelligence The daily routine of gathering and processing information; in corrections, teams gather such information to anticipate escapes, planned violence, and other inmate activities.

tactical response team Also known as a Correctional Emergency Response Team and a Hostage Recovery Team, a special unit trained in hand-to-hand combat, firearms, and other skills designed to put down jail or prison rioting and inmate disturbances and to rescue hostages from prisons or jails.

Taft, William Howard (1857–1930) Chief justice of the U.S. Supreme Court (1920–1930). Taft was born in Ohio, graduated from Yale, and eventually studied and practiced law in Cincinnati. He rose quickly in Republican politics, and was appointed a federal circuit judge in 1891. President Theodore Roosevelt appointed Taft Secretary of War in 1903, and in 1907 decided that Taft should succeed him as president. Taft beat William Jennings Bryan, and served as U.S. President from 1909 to 1913. Taft antagonized the Progressive Party by defending high tariff rates on imported goods, and attempted to push through a trade agreement with Canada that was rejected. Progressives were further alienated by Taft's failure to carry out Roosevelt's conservation policies. Taft ran for reelection, but was defeated by Woodrow Wilson. Largely ignored by politicians were the facts that Taft had initiated more than 80 antitrust suits and that Congress had submitted amendments to the states for a federal income tax and the direct election of senators, that a postal savings system had been established, and that the Interstate Commerce Commission had been directed to set railroad rates. Taft subsequently served as a professor of law at Yale. President Warren G. Harding appointed Taft chief justice of the U.S. Supreme Court in 1921. Taft considered Supreme Court appointment to be his greatest honor, and declared that he couldn't remember that he had ever been president of the United States.

tagging Use of graffiti to demonstrate to others the control of territory; in corrections, being placed on electronic monitoring.

Tailhook scandal An incident involving U.S. Navy personnel in which male officers assaulted 26 females at a convention of the Tailhook Association in Las Vegas, NV, in 1992.

tailing Following another person, generally in a motor vehicle, for purposes of surveillance; maintaining visual contact or determining the person's ultimate destination or purpose.

take into custody Police action to physically apprehend a child engaged in status offending or delinquent conduct, which sometimes may include physical apprehension of a juvenile by a probation officer, social caseworker, aftercare worker, or child welfare worker.

tales Persons who are summoned as jurors; a list of veniremen.

talesman Someone who is selected for jury service but who is not necessarily present in court when called for such service.

tall organizational structure Any hierarchy of authority with many supervisory levels.

tampering with evidence Any intentional illegal removal, destruction, or alteration of evidence in a criminal case.

Taney, Roger Brooke (1771–1864) Chief justice of the U.S. Supreme Court (1836–1864) appointed by President Andrew Jackson and a key participant in the Dred Scott decision in 1857. That decision, which was highly controversial, deprived blacks of citizenship and other constitutional rights.

tangible losses Costs such as medical expenses, lost wages, and property losses that accrue to crime victims as a result of their victimization.

tangible property Possessions that have physical form and substance and value in and of themselves (e.g., houses, automobiles, jewelry).

"tanks" In the Texas prison system, the housing units or cell blocks in its prisons.

Tannenbaum, Frank (1893–1969) A criminologist who investigated labeling theory and wrote *Crime and the Community* (1938). Tannenbaum believed that socially powerful groups define and react to deviant conduct. The acts themselves are not inherently criminal until defined as such by a particular power aggregate. Therefore, deviant behavior is defined according to particular times and places, as are the consequences of such conduct.

Tarde, Gabriel (1843–1904) A French sociologist who promoted the view that imitation was a crucial factor influencing various forms of conduct, including suicide and criminality. Tarde espoused the theory of imitation, holding that criminals imitate "superiors" they admire and respect, in *The Laws of Imitation* (1903). He also wrote *Penal Philosophy* (1912).

target hardening, target-hardening technique Making residences and businesses less susceptible to breaking and entering through better security measures.

target removal Efforts to eliminate the potential object of a criminal's intentions or goals.

TASC *See* **Treatment Alternatives to Street Crime (TASC).**

TASER (Tom Swift's Electronic Rifle) A nonlethal weapon used to disable a suspect by sending an electrical charge through wires that are fired into the suspect's skin with a pistol-like weapon.

Task Force on Juvenile Justice and Delinquency Prevention A task force established in 1975 following the Juvenile Justice and Delinquency Prevention Act of 1974, comprised of persons interested in juvenile-justice issues and charged with the duties of developing national standards for the processing, care, and treatment of juvenile offenders.

Task-Oriented In the Coates Typology, the type of police officer who is concerned that rules and regulations cover everything. *See also* **Coates Typology.**

tattooing Altering the skin by placing dyes and other substances under the skin surface that are not easily removed; causing designs to be placed on the skin to signify gang membership or for some other identifying purpose.

taxonomy A level of theory consisting of a system of categories constructed to fit the empirical observations so that relationships among categories can be described.

tazirat **crimes,** *tazir* **crimes** Minor violations of Islamic law regarded as offenses against society, not God.

TCP/IP (Transmission Control Protocol/Internet Protocol) A numerical identifier that serves to identify a computer and distinguish it from other computers accessing the Internet. When one connects to the Internet, one is assigned an IP address, either via a service provider (e.g., AOL, Road Runner, Prodigy), which may be static, meaning that it never changes, or dynamic, meaning that each time one dials or logs in, one is assigned a new IP address for that session.

Teague **exception** The result of *Teague v. Lane* (1989), which decreed that the U.S. Supreme Court will not disturb a final state conviction or sentence unless it can be said that, at the time the conviction or sentence became final, a state court would have acted objectively unreasonably by not extending the relief later sought in federal court. *Teague* requires a federal *habeas* court to determine the date on which the conviction became final and to consider whether a state court considering the defendant's claim at the time it became final would have felt compelled by existing precedent to conclude that the rule he or she seeks was required by the Constitution. If not, the court must determine whether that new rule none-

theless falls within certain exceptions. *See Teague v. Lane* (1989).

team policing The practice of assigning investigative teams of police officers, detectives, and other personnel to a particular community area to work together in solving crimes that occur in that area.

Teapot Dome Scandal A conspiracy between Harry S. Sinclair's Mammoth Oil Company, Edward L. Doheny's Pan-American Petroleum and Transport Company, and Senator Albert Fall of New York, who had become Secretary of the Interior under President Warren G. Harding, to lease rich oil reserves in Teapot Dome, WY, and Buena Vista, CA, for financial kickbacks. Fall was convicted, sentenced to prison, and fined.

tear gas A nonlethal aerosol spray causing eye irritation. Tear gas is intended to disable and can be used to disperse crowds during unruly demonstrations. Law enforcement officers use such gas to encourage criminals to give up and exit premises when they are barricaded inside to evade capture by police.

"tearoom trade" Impersonal homosexual activity in public restrooms or other public places.

technical services A bureau in a police department or similar organization responsible for records maintenance, communications, identification, and laboratory duties.

technical violation In probation or parole programs, infractions of program rules unrelated to the commission of crimes (e.g., curfew violation, testing positive for alcohol use, or leaving work early without permission).

techniques of neutralization According to neutralization theory, the ability of delinquent youths to neutralize moral constraints so that they may drift into criminal acts. Such techniques include denial of responsibility, denial of injury, denial of the victim, condemnation of the condemners, and an appeal to higher loyalties.

technology The mechanisms or processes whereby an organization turns out its product or services.

teen courts Tribunals consisting of teenagers who judge other teens charged with minor offenses. Teen courts, also known as youth courts, are much like regular juries in criminal courts: juvenile prosecutors and defense counsel argue cases against specific juvenile offenders and juries decide punishment with judicial approval.

Tejanos Mexican-Americans raised in Texas.

telemarketing fraud Illegal solicitation of donations or business by telephone that results in undervalued or no merchandise for the purchaser.

telemedicine A practice that uses advanced video technology to link an inmate in a correctional setting with a physician who could be hundreds of miles away.

telephone pole design A prison design that replaced the block design for maximum-security units. A long central corridor is crossed by several shorter living unit and program buildings.

telling style A leadership mode that is task oriented, requires supervisors to tell employees or subordinates what to do, and involves delegating tasks to subordinates who are emotional enough to perform them.

TEMPEST A U.S. government code word for a once-classified set of standards for limiting electric or electromagnetic radiation emanations from electronic equipment, such as microchips, monitors, and printers.

temporal precedence The coming or happening of one thing before another in time. In attempting to establish causality, one must establish temporal precedence, that is, that the causal factor must have been introduced before the effect occurred.

temporary restraining order A preliminary injunction forbidding contact between two or more parties.

tender To offer money in payment of a debt or to fulfill a contract.

terminal junkie Computer jargon for an early-stage hacker who spends a great deal of time wandering the directory tree on a computer and writing programs simply to have the experience of spending time on the computer.

termination of parental rights Termination by the court, upon petition, of all rights to a minor by his or her parents. Parents may be judged incapable and their rights terminated because of the following: debauchery, use of drugs and alcohol, conviction of a felony, lewd or lascivious behavior, or mental illness.

territorial district courts Federal trial courts corresponding to the United States district courts, but located in the territories.

territorial gang A group of youths organized to defend a fixed amount of territory, such as several city blocks.

territorial jealousy Interagency rivalry, such as between the FBI and local law enforcement, when a particularly popular or sensational investigation is under way. Cooperation between different law enforcement agencies is hampered because of this phenomenon.

territorial jurisdiction The right of a state or other government to exercise control over any event or activity transpiring in a given geographical area, which may include either land or waterways.

territorial killer A serial killer who commits crimes within an identifiable, circumscribed geographical area.

territorial waters Any waterway under the jurisdiction of a government. Water boundaries of the United States are under U.S. jurisdiction for a distance of 12 miles, for example. Such boundaries are intended to deter spying by other countries and allow enforcement efforts against illicit drug smuggling and other illegal enterprises.

terrorism A violent act or an act dangerous to human life, in violation of the criminal laws of the United States or of any state, intended to intimidate or coerce a government, the civilian population, or any segment thereof, in furtherance of a political or social objective.

Terrorism Awareness Programs offered on the Internet and through various agencies to dispel many of the myths and misconceptions that accompany the ongoing threat of terrorism and to provide a basic understanding of the types of threats faced by a country, why terrorists select specific targets, and how they select their targets.

terrorist A politically or socially motivated person with diverse goals, but who most often attempts to cause public incidents and promote fear among people through deadly acts, including bombing airplanes, public transportation and public buildings, and assassinations. Any one of several loosely organized factions that commit acts of terrorism.

Terry stop A term derived from the case of *Terry v. Ohio* (1968) that refers to the stop-and-frisk of a suspicious person.

tertiary prevention The third level of prevention of recidivism, which focuses on preventing further delinquent acts by youths already identified as delinquents.

testamentary Regarding or relating to a will or testament; obtained through a will.

testimony Oral evidence provided by legally competent witnesses during trial proceedings.

tetrahydrocannabinol (THC) The active ingredient in all marijuana-derived products.

Texas model Also known as the "traditional" model of state court organization, which has two "supreme" courts, one for civil appeals and one for criminal appeals, and five tiers of district, county, and municipal courts.

Texas Rangers Founded by Stephen Austin in 1823, the first territorial police agency in the United States.

Texas Syndicate A Texan prison gang made up of persons of Mexican-American descent.

thanatology The study of death and dying.

Thanatos Sigmund Freud's concept of an instinctual drive toward aggression and violence.

theft The crime of taking the property of another without permission.

theft by deception Illegally acquiring property from another by using lies or other forms of deceit.

theft of computer time, theft of hardware, theft of software The unauthorized use of computer time and software services, unauthorized copying of software programs, or outright theft of computer equipment.

them A type of police orientation described by E. Reuss-Ianni in her 1984 work, *Two Cultures of Policing*. The term describes the distance some police feel between themselves and the citizenry with which they must interact. *See also* **Reuss-Ianni Typology.**

theoretical range The units or levels of analysis and explanation that might be sought by a particular theory.

theoretical system Systematic combinations of taxonomies, conceptual frameworks, descriptions, explanations, and predictions in a manner that provides structure for a complete explanation of empirical phenomena.

theory A set of propositions from which a large number of new observations can be deduced; an integrated body of definitions, assumptions, and propositions related in such a way as to explain and predict relations between two or more variables.

Theory X Advanced by Douglas McGregor, a view of motivating workers based on the assumption that persons have an inherent dislike of work and will avoid it if they can. Because of this human characteristic of dislike of work, most people must be coerced, controlled, directed, and threatened with punishment to get them to put forth sufficient effort toward the achievement of organizational objectives. The average human being prefers to be directed, wishes to avoid responsibility, has relatively little ambition, and wants security above all.

Theory *Y* An explanation of worker motivation devised by Douglas McGregor, postulating that the expenditure of physical and mental effort in work is as natural as play or rest. External control and the threat of punishment are not the only means for bring about effort toward organizational objectives. Workers will exercise self-direction and self-control in the service of objectives to which they are committed. Commitment to objectives is a function of the rewards associated with their achievement. The average human being learns, under proper conditions, not only to accept but to seek responsibility. The capacity to exercise a relatively high degree of imagination, ingenuity, and creativity in the solutions of organizational problems is widely, not narrowly, distributed in the population.

Theory *Z* An explanation of worker motivation that emphasized employee job security; participatory decision making; group responsibility and teamwork; increased product and services quality; slower evaluation and promotion policies; broader career paths; and a greater concern for employees' work and familial welfare. This theory was devised by William Ouchi (1981).

therapee One who receives therapy.

Therapeutic Communities of America (TCA) A network of facilities designed to treat substance abusers and others who are lacking in vocational skills and education. TCA provides total family support services and offers out-patient programs. It is headquartered in Washington, DC.

therapeutic community A residential treatment unit that promotes change through communal processes of norm building, inmate participation in decisions, and group responsibility.

therapeutic community drug-treatment programs Highly structured, long-term residential programs that help residents face the fact that they are addicted to drugs and their associated lifestyle.

therapeutic intervention A juvenile probation strategy in which a probation officer may make visits to a juvenile's home, inspect the premises, and check with school officials on the juvenile's progress.

therapeutic jurisprudence An approach to the use of the law as a potential therapeutic agent. The approach rests on the assumption that the law has the power to bring about significant social consequences, and that those consequences should be studied and evaluated.

therapeutic program (TP) Any program that includes individual and group therapy and counseling under the direction of psychologists and psychiatrists.

therapeutic recreation Any recreational program that concentrates on the knowledge of leisure and recreation as they relate to achieving optimal health for inmates.

thermic law of crime Adolphe Quetelet's assertion that crimes against persons tend to occur in warmer climates, whereas property crimes tend to occur in colder climates.

thief-takers In early England, persons who were "fleet of foot" and were selected to pursue and apprehend fleeing criminals for a fee; more generally, citizens who receive a reward for the apprehension of criminals.

third degree An interrogation technique involving the illegal use of coercive force by police to extract confessions from suspects. This practice was condemned by the 1931 Wickersham Commission.

third-generation jail Sometimes called a direct-supervision jail; a jail in which inmates are housed in small groups in pods staffed 24 hours a day by specially trained officers. Officers interact with inmates to help change behavior. Bars and metal doors are absent, reducing noise and dehumanization. This approach to jail construction emerged during the late 1970s.

third-party release A release to another person who has the responsibility to assure the defendant's subsequent appearance in court. The third party may be a person known to the defendant or a volunteer.

Thomas, W.I. (1863–1947) Author of *The Unadjusted Girl* (1928). Thomas developed the concept of "Four Wishes," including response (love), recognition, new experience, and security. He used the term "definition of the situation," meaning that "whatever is perceived as real will be real in its consequences." The four-wishes conception has been used to explain both conventional and unconventional (deviant) conduct, in which one form of new experience is conceivably criminal conduct.

THOR (Target Hardening and Opportunity Reduction) A community crime-prevention program originating in Atlanta, GA, and several other cities and sponsored by the Law Enforcement Assistance Administration.

Thornberry, Terence (1945–) A criminologist who has proposed an age-graded view of crime contending that crime emerges as social bonds deteriorate in one's early years. Serious delinquent youths form belief systems that are consistent with their deviant lifestyles. They seek out others like themselves and adopt their behaviors. They reinforce the delinquent behaviors of others through their own social approval and emulation of them. Age gradation is a key component closely attached to cognitive developmental stages, as one acquires reasoning ability and greater sophistication. Family attachment is crucial in one's early years in order to avoid delinquent and criminal behavior patterns.

threat An assertion by someone against another to cause harm, or expression of unlawful intent to cause injury to another, with the ability to carry out the act.

Three Prisons Act Congressional action in 1891 to establish three federal penitentiaries: Leavenworth, KS, in 1895; Atlanta, GA, in 1902; and McNeil Island, WA, in 1907.

three-strikes-and-you're-out philosophy, three-strikes laws A crime-prevention and control strategy that proposes to incarcerate those offenders who commit and are convicted of three or more serious or violent offenses. The usual penalty is life imprisonment or the life-without-parole option. The intent is to incarcerate high-rate offenders to reduce crime in society. *See also* **habitual-criminal laws, habitual-offender statutes.**

threshold inquiry *See* **stop-and-frisk.**

thrill killing Impulsive violence motivated by a murderer's decision to kill a stranger during a moment of recklessness or daring.

"throwaways" In corrections, inmates who are considered expendable and are used by a gang to do jobs that involve high risk of injury, death, or apprehension.

ticket-of-leave An early form of conditional release used in the English and Irish prison systems.

ticket-of-leave man A convict who has obtained a ticket-of-leave.

tier system A method of establishing various floors for cells where prisoners of different types can be housed started at Auburn State Penitentiary in 1816.

time, place, and manner doctrine A First Amendment doctrine holding that government may impose reasonable limitations on the time, place, and manner of expressive activities. *See also* **Bill of Rights.**

time series analysis A statistical technique used to forecast future trends in crime rates, correctional populations, or other criminal-justice applications.

time served Total time spent in confinement by a convicted adult before and after sentencing, or only the time spent in confinement after a sentence of commitment to a confinement facility.

Time-To-Think (TTT) A cognitive skills training program that is one component of the Living Skills Program. TTT addresses thinking and social skills such as problem solving, negotiation, communication, creative thinking, management of emotions, and critical reasoning.

TIPS (Teaching Individuals Protective Strategies) A program established by the U.S. Department of Education for grades K–8 to enable youths to acquire skills to avoid being victimized by other children. Children learn how to say no to drugs and other illicit activities.

tire marks Surface impressions made by a motor vehicle's tires.

tithing In Anglo-Saxon law, an association of 10 families bound together by a frankpledge for purposes of crime control.

toe tag An identifying tag affixed to the toe of a dead person by a coroner or other official.

token economy A means of exchange used by residents in a therapeutic community.

tokenism The action of allowing limited numbers of minority persons to be placed in schools, neighborhoods, or occupations/professions so as to meet minimum requirements of civil rights action or legislation.

Tongs Chinese criminal organizations that engage in various organized illegal enterprises, such as extortion, kidnapping, and murder.

Tonnies, Ferdinand (1855–1936) The German sociologist who pioneered the terms *gemeinschaft* and *gesellschaft* to depict two societal forms. The former characterizes societies founded on kinship and family, the latter those founded on contractual relations and formality. Criminal conduct is controlled through social ostracism in *gemeinschaft* societies, whereas crime is formally punished with specific sanctions and penalties in *gesellschaft* societies.

tool-mark identification The analysis of scratches and other marks found in metal and other hard materials at crime scenes.

TOPS (Teens on Patrol) A program implemented in the early 1980s in Rochester, NY, in which police officers decided to use teens themselves to "police" other teens. Police officers selected about 125 youths to maintain security and patrol city parks and recreational areas. Subsequently, some of the TOPS became cops and were hired by the Rochester Police Department.

top secret Government information that is considered most important and is accessible only to those with highest security clearance. The information may pertain to recently developed high-tech weaponry or international policy.

Top 10 Most Wanted Criminals The FBI list of the 10 most wanted persons who have committed federal crimes. Photographs of these persons are posted in U.S. Post Offices and elsewhere. Most wanted criminals have been featured in the 1980s, 1990s, and 2000s on the *America's Most Wanted* television program.

torch A professional arsonist.

tort A private or civil wrong or injury, other than breach of contract, for which the court will provide a remedy in the form of an action for damages; a violation of a duty imposed by law.

tort law The field of law that provides the basis for civil lawsuits seeking damages for personal injuries or property damages.

torture Infliction of pain and suffering upon another, either by psychological or physical means.

total enforcement A policy whereby the police are given the resources and support to enforce all laws without regard to the civil liberties of citizens.

total incapacitation Any form of punishment that prevents an offender from ever doing the crime again (e.g., capital punishment, life without the possibility of parole).

Total Information Awareness Resource Center A project of the Information Awareness Office (IAO), which is under the Defense Advanced Research Projects Agency (DARPA), part of the Department of Defense. The project's mission is to imagine, develop, apply, integrate, demonstrate, and transition information technologies, components, and prototype closed-loop information systems that will counter asymmetric threats by achieving total information awareness useful for preemption, national security warning, and national security decision making. Its purpose is to develop new surveillance technologies in the wake of the September 11, 2001, attacks on New York City's World Trade Center and the Pentagon.

total institution Erving Goffman's term describing places that completely encapsulate the lives of those who work and live within them. Rules govern behavior, and the group is split into two parts, one of which controls the lives of the other.

totality of circumstances, totality-of-circumstances doctrine An exception to the exclusionary rule, whereby officers may make warrantless searches of property and seizures of illegal contraband on the basis of the entire set of suspicious circumstances.

totality-of-circumstances test A test that replaced the two-pronged standard for informant credibility in the issuance of search warrants established by *Aguilar v. Texas* (1964). Information from an unknown informant is regarded as reliable and credible to the extent that the entire set of circumstances associated with a criminal act suggest probable cause to issue a search warrant. The totality-of-circumstances standard was established in *Illinois v. Gates* (1983).

totality of conditions A standard to be used in evaluating whether prison conditions are cruel and unusual.

total quality management (TQM) An organizational method of involving subordinates in decision-making procedures to give them greater responsibility and encourage greater loyalty and devotion among them toward the company (e.g., in policing, encouraging rank-and-file police officers to take a more active role in decision making about their jobs and work assignments and become more involved in community activities).

Tough Cop In the White Typology, a type of police officer who is outcome-oriented, described in S.O. White's 1972 work *A Perspective on Police Professionalism. See also* **White Typology.**

tough-time institution (TTI) Any prison that is an alternative to prison for nonviolent offenders. TTIs include the Spartan conditions of boot camps without the military aspects. Programs are characterized by long days emphasizing physical conditioning and other hard-labor activities.

tourniquet sentencing Intensive supervised probation or parole.

toxic criminals Corporations that create environmental disasters through illegal dumping of hazardous waste.

toxicology The study of poisons and other lethal substances.

Toyobo Co., Ltd. A company based in Osaka, Japan, that manufactures a number of nylon and other fabric products, including body armor made of Zylon. Body armor is used by law enforcement officers as a means of minimizing bullet penetration during shooting incidents.

traced forgery Any false document created by tracing genuine writing onto another document.

trace elements Minuscule quantities of a substance present on objects, bodies, or materials, that can be analyzed by laboratories, identified, and subsequently used as evidence.

trace evidence Any physical evidence left behind at a crime scene.

tracking In education, the practice of assigning students to groups or classes based on an assessment of their ability or potential. Tracks are classified by level of difficulty, which can result in the stigmatization of lower-track children and snobbery by higher-track children, who are likely to be college-bound.

tracking device Any electronic device associated with electronic monitoring that can enable authorities to determine an offender's whereabouts.

tracks Scars from repeated needle injections found on the bodies of certain drug addicts. Tracks are especially associated with heroin users and are usually found along the veins of the arms and legs.

Trademark Counterfeiting Act of 1984 Legislation providing that whoever knowingly traffics in goods or services that have counterfeit trademarks shall be fined up to $250,000 or imprisoned for up to five years. The act was designed to deter marketing counterfeit goods.

traditional agrarian values The ideas and beliefs shared by those who worked the land and espoused Puritan or Quaker values. The idea was that the city was a source of many juveniles' evil ways, and that the best way to change a child was to remove him or her from the city and place him or her in a remote rural location where the child could perform hard work and become reformed.

traditional authority A type of power that adheres in kinship and follows rules of descent, such as the rights of the father passing to the oldest male child at the time of the father's death; power exerted through custom rather than through bureaucratic prescription.

traditional model Applied to organizations, the view that organizations are like machines, and that just as we build a mechanical device with given specifications to accomplish a specific task, so also do we construct an organization according to a blueprint to achieve a given purpose; applied to court organization, also known as the Texas Model, featuring two courts of last resort: (1) the Supreme Court, which hears cases of a civil nature and juvenile matters; and (2) the court of criminal appeals, which has final appellate jurisdiction in criminal cases.

traditional political period The era in law enforcement marked by political corruption and political control of policing (roughly, the 1880s–1930s).

traditional prosecution The most common method of allocating prosecutorial resources, in which when a criminal suspect is charged, prosecutors are assigned specific jobs through a division of labor: one prosecutor handles one segment of the prosecution and another prosecutor handles another segment of it.

traditional rehabilitation model *See* **rehabilitate.**

traffic Any aggregate of pedestrians, vehicles, or other conveyances using a highway for travel purposes; also, to deal in and exchange stolen merchandise or illicit drugs.

traffic offense Any one of several ordinances governing automobiles and their operation on public highways, which include speeding, reckless driving, and driving under the influence.

training school A correctional facility for juveniles adjudicated to be delinquents or status offenders and committed to confinement by a juvenile court.

trait approach A leadership theory that holds that leaders have inborn characteristics, qualities, or specific genetic attributes that vest them with power over others. The theory assumes that such traits cannot be learned or transmitted socially.

trait theory The theory that youths engage in delinquent or criminal behavior due to aberrant physical or psychological traits that govern their behavioral choices. Delinquent actions are impulsive or instinctive rather than rational choices.

trajectory The path of a bullet or other projectile.

tranquilizers Drugs that reduce anxiety and promote relaxation.

transactional immunity *See* **immunity, transactional.**

transcript A written record of a trial or hearing.

transfer The movement of a person from one facility to another, such as in a prisoner transfer or relocation. In forensics, the process whereby a substance rubs off of one object to another (e.g., most U.S. currency has cocaine residue from everyday circulation, where bills rub against one another when stored in cash drawers or bundled; that residue occurs as the result of transfer); also, a method whereby a juvenile is waived to the jurisdiction of a criminal court for purposes of a criminal prosecution.

transfer hearing, transfer proceeding, transfer process A proceeding to determine whether juveniles should be certified as adults for purposes of being subjected to the jurisdiction of adult criminal courts where more severe penalties may be imposed. This process is also known as "certification" or "waiver."

transfer of property The cost of crimes in which property is transferred from one person to another, such as from the victim of a theft to the thief.

transferred intent If an illegal yet unintended act results from the intent to commit a crime, that act is also considered illegal.

transfer to adult court *See* **transfer.**

transient One who temporarily resides in a given location and moves to another location; one known for moving from place to place frequently without any permanent home location.

transitional neighborhood An area undergoing a shift in population and structure, usually from middle-class residential to lower-class mixed use.

transit police Officers who oversee the safety and security of passengers who use public transportation, such as subways or buses.

transnational crime A criminal act or transaction violating the laws of more than one country, or having an impact on a foreign country.

transponder warrant A search warrant permitting law enforcement officers to place a transponder or beeper on an automobile, a person, or property to track its movement and locate its whereabouts.

transportation *See* **banishment.**

transportation officers Authorized persons in charge of transporting inmates to correctional institutions, usually to the state prison system after sentencing.

trap In home security, a switch device used in an alarm system that provides a secondary backup in the event a perimeter alarm system is successfully breached; also, a tracing device placed on a telephone to identify the originating point of a telephone call.

Trasler, Gordon (1929–2002) A criminologist and psychologist who wrote *The Explanation of Criminality* (1962). Trasler was as a student of B.F. Skinner, who believed that conditioned anxiety or fear of punishment inhibits persons from engaging in criminal behavior.

traverse method A way of sketching an outdoor scene, particularly where contours, distances, and locations of objects need to be observed and noted. A sketch board, compass, and telescopic surveying instrument are used.

treason The crime of attempting by overt acts to overthrow the government, or of betraying the government to a foreign power.

treater value system A parole board decision-making system which emphasizes rehabilitation, and where early release decisions are made on the basis of what will best suit an offender.

Treatment Alternatives to Street Crime (TASC) A series of projects sponsored by the Law Enforcement Assistance Administration during the 1970s designed to treat offenders with drug dependencies.

treatment model *See* **medical model.**

treble damages, triple damages Monetary awards in civil court in which a plaintiff may recover up to three times the actual amount of the loss from the defendant.

trespass Any unlawful interference with one's person or property.

triad A collaboration between a sheriff, police chief, and senior citizens' group in the community to band together for the purpose of reducing victimization and more effectively meeting the needs of retired and other older persons. *See also* **Chinese triads.**

trial An adversarial proceeding within a particular jurisdiction, in which a judicial examination and determination of issues can be made, and in which a criminal defendant's guilt or innocence can be decided impartially by either a judge or jury. *See also* **bench trial; jury trial.**

trial court of general jurisdiction A criminal court that has jurisdiction over all offenses, including felonies, and may in some states also hear appeals from lower courts.

trial court of limited jurisdiction A criminal court whose trial jurisdiction either includes no felonies or is limited to some category of felony. Such courts have jurisdiction over misdemeanor cases, probable-cause hearings in felony cases, and sometimes, felony trials that may result in penalties below a specific limit.

trial *de novo* A new judicial hearing or proceeding; a new adversarial proceeding occurring as though there had never been a first trial or proceeding, usually granted to defendants where egregious wrongs or misconduct occurred to nullify former adjudicatory proceedings.

trial judge *See* **judge.**

trial jury *See* **petit jury.**

trial process, criminal All procedures that occur against a defendant from the point of an indictment, presentment, or information through a conviction or an acquittal. *See figure.*

trial sufficiency The presence of sufficient legal elements to ensure successful prosecution of a case. When a prosecutor's decision to prosecute a case is customarily based on trial sufficiency, only cases that seem certain to result in conviction at trial are accepted for prosecution. Use of plea bargaining is minimal. Good police work and court capacity are required.

triangulation The use of multiple data collection strategies in gathering information about people and their behaviors, attitudes, and other characteristics; in forensics, a method of obtaining measurements at a crime scene, often recorded on graph paper. Two points are chosen, and measurements are taken from each point and transferred to a sketch. The location of a particular object is disclosed by where the lines in the sketch intersect.

tribunal A court; a place where judges sit; a judicial weighing of information leading to a decision about a case; in the military, official court proceedings.

tricking Prostitution; in women's prisons, sexual promiscuity for economic gain.

trifurcation A single ridge in a fingerprint that divides into three separate lines.

Trojan horse A destructive computer program that masquerades as a benign application. Unlike viruses, Trojan horses do not replicate themselves, although they can be just as destructive. One of the most insidious types of Trojan horse is a program that claims to rid your computer of viruses but instead introduces viruses onto your computer.

Trojanowicz, Robert (1941–1994) A late professor of criminal justice at Michigan State University who studied community policing and foot patrols extensively.

truancy Staying out of school without permission.

truant A juvenile who absents him- or herself from school without a valid excuse.

truant officer An officer of the juvenile court who apprehends truants.

true bill A grand-jury decision that sufficient evidence exists that a crime has been committed and that a specific suspect committed it; a charge of an alleged crime; an indictment.

true crimes Extremely serious offenses in France, comparable to serious felonies in the United States; violent offenses.

true diversion A form of diversion that keeps an offender out of the system and avoids formal prosecution and labeling.

truly disadvantaged A term created by William Julius Wilson to describe those at the lowest level of the underclass. Such persons are described as victims of discrimination dwelling in urban inner cities. They live in areas where social disorganiza-

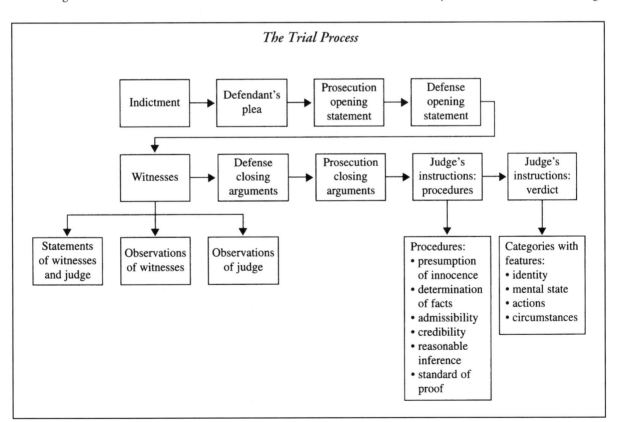

The Trial Process

Indictment → Defendant's plea → Prosecution opening statement → Defense opening statement →

Witnesses → Defense closing arguments → Prosecution closing arguments → Judge's instructions: procedures → Judge's instructions: verdict

Witnesses →
- Statements of witnesses and judge
- Observations of witnesses
- Observations of judge

Judge's instructions: procedures →
Procedures:
- presumption of innocence
- determination of facts
- admissibility
- credibility
- reasonable inference
- standard of proof

Judge's instructions: verdict →
Categories with features:
- identity
- mental state
- actions
- circumstances

tion has affected housing, schools, and employment, and which manifest a ghetto culture and behavior marked by criminality and violence. Since they seldom come into contact with the politically powerful, the source of their plight, they direct their rage and frustration inward toward others around them.

truncheon A short, clublike weapon carried by a police officer and used to subdue criminal suspects, usually by striking them on the head or other vital part of the body.

trustee Any person entrusted to handle the affairs of another.

trusty A prisoner entrusted with authority to supervise other prisoners in exchange for certain privileges and status.

trusty security A level of security permitting greater freedom for the trusty.

trusty servant A trusty inmate who performs household chores and other duties for prison officials.

trusty shooter An armed trusty guard.

Truth-in-Lending Act Congressional action in 1968 designed to protect consumers by causing lenders to advise prospective borrowers of the exact interest to be charged over time on various principal amounts borrowed or extended on credit.

truth in sentencing, truth-in-sentencing laws Close correspondence between the sentence imposed and the sentence actually served; federal policy and admonition advocated in the Crime Bill of 1994.

tuberculosis An infectious disease spread by bacteria in the air resulting from coughs or sneezes from infected individuals.

Tucker Telephone A torture device used in the 1960s at the Arkansas State Prison to electrically shock prisoners. Electrodes were attached to inmates' testicles, toes, and penises, and the electrical portion of a hand-crank telephone was used to administer shocks, often resulting in permanent physical and psychological damage.

Turk, Austin (1934–) A sociologist and criminologist who has written extensively about the conflict perspective. Turk suggests that persons are different in their understandings and commitments, that divergence leads to conflict, that each conflicting party manifests diverse and conflicting interests, that persons with similar beliefs join forces to counter those with opposing views, that continuing conflicts lead to routinization of activities, which in turn foster economic exploitation, and that continual conflict is inevitable.

Turner Diaries, The A book written by William Pierce, published in 1980 under the name Andrew McDonald. It is an example of neo-Nazi propaganda, espousing revolution against the U.S. government, which has been protective and supportive of Jews and other minorities.

turning points Life events that alter the development of a criminal career; a part of the age-graded theory devised by Robert Sampson and John Laub in their work *Crime in the Making* (1993). Turning points include marriage and career, which tend to function as deterrents to criminal conduct or cause predisposed persons to desist from criminal behavior. Social capital is also important.

turnkey approach Contracts with private interests to design, finance, construct, and operate facilities for the detention of juveniles, illegal aliens, and others.

turnkeys Inmates responsible for opening and closing riot gates.

tutelage Instruction or socialization in criminal motives and skills, including how to spot opportunities for theft, how to plan thefts, and how to carry out thefts.

Tweed, William Marcy (1823–1878) Known as "Boss Tweed," an influential, corrupt political figure who dominated Tammany Hall in Democratic Party politics in New York City from 1866 to 1871.

Twinkie defense A defense successfully used by Dan White, the confessed killer of San Francisco Mayor George Moscone and city councilman Harvey Milk, who claimed he killed because of his addiction to sugar-laden junk foods such as Twinkies; a biochemical explanation for criminal conduct.

twin studies Any criminological research using identical twins to test for the possible genetic transmission of criminal characteristics.

two-pronged test of informant reliability A standard for obtaining search warrants when information has been received by law enforcement officers from informants. The prongs relate to (1) the capacity in which the officers know the informant, and (2) the reliability of the information provided by the informant in the past. The standard established in *Aguilar v. Texas* (1964) but modified by the totality-of-circumstances test in *Illinois v. Gates* (1983).

Tyburn free Gallows erected outside of London, England, in the nineteenth century.

Type A personality The profile of someone who is highly competitive and impatient; a workaholic who sustains considerable stress from a high level of work output.

Type B personality The profile of someone who exhibits considerable patience, has the ability to react to stressful situations in productive ways, and is more easygoing than a Type A personality.

Type I minimum-security facility A facility designated for inmates who have a short period before release, facilitating reintegration into their communities. These facilities provide little or no programming.

Type II minimum-security facility A facility designed for inmates posing no security risk, with release or parole dates of 18 months or less. These facilities provide extensive programming.

Type I offenses *See* **index crimes, major and minor offenses.**

Type II offenses *See* **index crimes, major and minor offenses.**

typical prisoner The undistinguished majority of prisoners in prisons and jails in the United States, who have middle-class status in the prison, no or few work skills, and are deserving of little respect.

typographic printing In paper currency manufacture, a process of imprinting permanent figures or features onto paper, including serial numbers, signatures, and seals.

typology A set of categories.

U

UCR *See Uniform Crime Reports (UCR).*

U curve Also known as the J curve, the graphed pattern of inmate value distance from staff values as a prison sentence progresses. Inmates first entering prison have values most similar to those of staff. Inmates in the middle of their sentences have values least like those of staff. Inmates preparing for release have values closer to staff, but not as similar as those just entering prison.

ulnar loop Fingerprint pattern.

ultrasonic motion detector A sensor that can detect the motion of an intruder through the use of ultrasound-generating equipment. Ultrasonic waves fill a space, such as a room, and when that space is disturbed, an alarm is activated somewhere prompting an investigation of what caused the disturbance.

ultraviolet light A particular light form beyond the violet end of the visible spectrum. It is used in forensics to detect fluorescent substances such as semen, invisible writing or ink, and other things that are not ordinarily visible to the naked eye.

ultra vires "Beyond powers" (Latin); beyond the scope of one's prescribed authority.

Unabomber *See* **Kaczynksi, Theodore.**

unauthorized use of a motor vehicle A criminal offense involving the taking of a motor vehicle without the consent of the owner.

unconditional discharge A posttrial disposition, essentially the same as unconditional diversion. No savings are obtained in criminal-justice processing costs, but jail populations may be reduced. Conditions of release are imposed for an offense in which the defendant's involvement has been established.

unconditional diversion (standard diversion) program A diversion program requiring minimal or no contact with a probation department. It may include a minimum maintenance fee paid regularly for a specified period such as one year. No treatment program is indicated.

unconditional release The final release of an offender from the jurisdiction of a correctional agency; also, a final release from the jurisdiction of a court.

unconstitutionally vague A term used by the U.S. Supreme Court to declare a particular law lacking in specificity and failing to describe specific actions or behaviors that are prohibited, such as municipal vagrancy laws.

underachiever One who does not achieve success, usually in school, at the level expected.

underboss The second-highest-ranking official in an organized crime family, directly under the main boss or leader.

underclass According to Gunnar Myrdal, a permanent lower class that becomes institutionalized in a welfare state.

underclassification Placement of an inmate in a lower level of supervision and control than required.

undercover officer A law enforcement officer who poses as a criminal to infiltrate criminal organizations or gangs for the purpose of acquiring incriminating information.

undercover operation Any criminal investigation that uses law enforcement officers who pose as criminals as a means of gaining access to an organization or gang.

undercriminalization The tendency of the law not to treat seriously certain socially harmful behaviors.

underground Persons who carry out secret operations without being discovered by government officials.

underground economy Untaxed and unreported economic exchanges, legal and illegal, which occur outside of the official economy. Such exchanges include illicit drug and narcotics trafficking.

underground press Newspapers that express antigovernment views and are ordinarily suppressed by government agencies if detected. They are usually devoted to exposés of government officials and others whose acts are often scandalous, illegal, or improper.

underworld A broad class of criminals who operate outside of public view in activities such as organized prostitution or gambling; racketeers.

undisciplined child Any youth who is beyond parental control and who refuses to obey teachers or school officials.

undocumented alien Any foreign national who enters a country illegally and without proper legal authorization. The term is sometimes used to refer to those entering the United States from Mexico in search of work, but without proper authority or documentation to do so.

unfair and deceptive practices Actions by business firms that intentionally mislead consumers by making false claims about their product effectiveness. Such actions are prohibited by Congressional action and policies implemented by the Federal Trade Commission.

unfounding Declarations that certain unsolved crimes were never crimes in the first place.

UNICOR A federal prison industry that manufactures goods for profit, using prisoners who are paid the prevailing wage. Such work is considered a rehabilitative tool.

unification In the court system, an effort to organize all courts in a jurisdiction under a single administrative head.

Uniform Code of Military Justice The collection of criminal laws governing the behavior of armed services personnel in the United States.

Uniform Crime Reports (UCR) An annual publication of the Federal Bureau of Investigation that describes crime from all reporting law enforcement agencies in the United States. A new format in 1988 identified incident-based reporting compared with other reporting schemes used in past years. *See table p. 258.*

Uniform Juvenile Court Act A 1968 Congressional act proposing standards for processing juvenile delinquents and status offenders. The act eventually led to the Juvenile Justice and Delinquency Prevention Act of 1974.

uniform state laws Model penal and civil statutes enacted by various states to harmonize conflicting interstate statutes to facilitate interstate law enforcement.

Unione Corse A French organized crime enterprise similar to the Italian Mafia.

Unitarian Universalist Service Committee Established in 1975 and headquartered in Washington, DC, this organization advocates cessation of new prison construction and a thorough examination of alternatives to incarceration.

unit cost The cost to provide services or products expressed in some standard measure (e.g., such as cost of probation supervision per probationer per year).

United Bamboo A Taiwanese crime organization.

United Kingdom model A rigorous recruitment and training program used in England and Wales for the purpose of police officer selection and training.

United Nations Information Centre Established in 1946 and headquartered in New York City, this organization seeks minimum standards whereby inmates in different prisons can be maintained according to accepted standards, and it disseminates information to interested persons and organizations about prison conditions and inmate problems.

United Nations Standard Minimum Rules for the Treatment of Prisoners Regulations created in 1955 to seek improvements in inmate living conditions in prisons and jails by recommending minimum standards for all prisons to follow.

United States Attorneys (USAs) Officials responsible for the prosecution of crimes that violate the laws of the United States. They are appointed by the president and assigned to a United States district court jurisdiction.

United States circuit courts of appeal, United States courts of appeals The federal circuit courts of appellate jurisdiction.

As of 2004, there were 13 Circuit Courts of Appeal zoned throughout the United States and its territories.

United States Code, United States Code Annotated A comprehensive compendium of federal laws and statutes, including landmark cases and discussions of law applications. The annotated version contains paragraphs of contemporary cases summarizing court decisions applying specific statutes.

United States commissioners *See* **United States magistrates.**

United States Customs Service The agency authorized to conduct searches and inspections of all ships, aircraft, and vehicles entering United States borders.

United States District Courts The basic trial courts for federal civil and criminal actions.

United States magistrates Judges who fulfill the pretrial judicial obligations of the federal courts; formerly, United States Commissioners.

United States Parole Commission Established in 1930, this commission is responsible for the management and monitoring of all federal prisoners released on parole, as well as the classification and placement of parolees and maintenance of reports of their progress.

United States Sentencing Guidelines Rules implemented by federal courts in November 1987 obligating federal judges to impose presumptive sentences on all convicted offenders. The guidelines are based on offense seriousness and offender characteristics. Judges may depart from guidelines only by justifying their departures in writing.

Uniform Crime Reports, Part I: Crimes and Their Definitions

Crime	Definition
Murder and nonnegligent manslaughter	Willful (nonnegligent) killing of one human being by another
Forcible rape	Carnal knowledge of a female, forcibly and against her will; assaults or attempts to commit rape by force or threat of force are included
Robbery	Taking or attempting to take anything of value from the care, custody, or control of a person or persons by force or threat of force or violence and/or by putting the victim in fear
Aggravated assault	Unlawful attack by one person upon another for the purpose of inflicting severe or aggravated bodily injury
Burglary	Unlawful entry into a structure to commit a felony or theft
Larceny-theft	Unlawful taking, carrying, leading, or riding away of property from the possession or constructive possession of another, including shoplifting, pocket picking, purse snatching, and thefts of motor vehicle parts or accessories
Motor vehicle theft	Theft or attempted theft of a motor vehicle, including automobiles, trucks, buses, motorscooters, and snowmobiles
Arson	Any willful or malicious burning or attempt to burn, with or without intent to defraud, a dwelling house, public building, motor vehicle or aircraft, and the personal property of another

Source: U.S. Department of Justice, Federal Bureau of Investigation, *Crime in the United States.*

United States Supreme Court The court of last resort; the highest appellate court in the United States, which consists of nine justices and rules on constitutional issues. Its rulings are binding on all courts. *See box.*

United States Supreme Court retroactive principle Ordinarily, cases decided subsequent to other similar cases are not applied retroactively to affect earlier court decisions. There are limited exceptions. *See Teague v. Lane* (1989).

unit management, unit-management system A concept referring to semiautonomous teams of prison workers who assist inmates in their educational and vocational training and counseling.

units of analysis Three levels of analysis for studying organizations, including the individual, the group, and the organization itself. These are abstractions used for theorizing and constructing explanations for what is going on in an organization and why.

unity of command The view that workers should have to report directly to one boss.

universal precautions Basic medical standards of safety and care to reduce the spread of infectious diseases.

University Settlement A privately operated facility in New York commenced in 1893 by James Bronson Reynolds to provide assistance and job-referral services to community residents. The settlement became involved in probation work in 1901.

unlawful assembly Any prohibited gathering of persons in a particular public place.

unlawful entry Illegally opening an unlocked door without permission and entering the premises. A lesser included offense of burglary, or breaking and entering.

unlawful flight to avoid giving testimony The felonious action of traveling out of a state or country to avoid giving incriminating testimony as a material witness in a case.

unlawful flight to avoid prosecution The deliberate absence from a state or nation of a defendant who flees to escape prosecution for a felony.

unobtrusive measures Research techniques that do not involve direct contact or interviews with persons. Examples include content analysis, researching archival data, accretion measures, erosion measures, and analysis of letters and other documents or other types of secondary sources.

unreasonableness A search by law enforcement officers not conforming to the boundaries of propriety as prescribed by the courts (e.g., pumping a suspect's stomach in order to retrieve evidence).

unreported crime The amount of crime that occurs in a jurisdiction that is not reported to law enforcement agencies.

unsecured bail A form of release differing from release on own recognizance only in that defendants are subject to paying the amount of bail if they default. Unsecured bail permits release without a deposit or purchase of a bondsman's services.

unsolved crime Any crime for which a perpetrator has not been either apprehended or convicted.

U.S. Supreme Court Justices		
Justice	**Year of Appointment**	**President**
William H. Rehnquist, Chief Justice	1986	Ronald Reagan
John Paul Stevens	1975	Gerald Ford
Sandra Day O'Connor	1981	Ronald Reagan
Antonin Scalia	1986	Ronald Reagan
Anthony M. Kennedy	1988	Ronald Reagan
David H. Souter	1990	William Clinton
Clarence Thomas	1991	George H. W. Bush
Ruth Bader Ginsburg	1993	George H. W. Bush
Stephen G. Breyer	1994	William Clinton

UOC Uniform Offense Classification; an FBI automated classification system.

"uppers" Slang for stimulant drugs such as methamphetamines.

upperworld crime Conduct in violation of the law engaged in during the course of business activity (e.g., tax evasion, price-fixing). Perpetrators often view their offenses as shrewd business practices that are not really criminal.

UPR (Uniform Parole Reports) Published statistical information about parolees, parole decision making, and parole agency workloads compiled by the Bureau of Justice Statistics.

Urban Institute A private organization created in 1968 through the sponsorship of President Lyndon Johnson and headquartered in Washington, DC, that conducts research and offers consulting services on a wide variety of criminal justice issues. The Urban Institute is a nonprofit, nonpartisan policy research and education agency established to examine social, economic, and governance problems facing the nation. It is dedicated to raising citizen understanding of issues and trade-offs in policy making. Project funding comes from government agencies, foundations, multilateral organizations, and the World Bank.

urbanization Increasing population density in urban centers; the spread of industry and business in small geographical areas.

urban renewal Destruction of older buildings and rundown properties and the construction of modern buildings, businesses, and residences.

urban riots Mob rioting in cities; large public protests of government actions; major civil disturbances (e.g., the rioting after police officers were acquitted of beating California motorist Rodney King in 1992).

urinalysis Chemical analysis of urine to determine the presence of drugs or other prohibited substances.

Ur-Nammu, Code of *See* **Code of Ur-Nammu.**

us Type of police orientation described by E. Reuss-Ianni in her 1984 work, *Two Cultures of Policing,* describing officers who have a willingness to work with the public. *See also* **Reuss-Ianni Typology.**

USA PATRIOT Act *See* **PATRIOT Act, USA PATRIOT Act.**

use immunity *See* **immunity, use.**

usury The taking of or contracting to take interest on a loan at a rate that exceeds the level established by law.

utilitarian One who believes that people weigh the benefits and consequences of their future actions before deciding on a course of behavior.

utilitarianism, utilitarian model A criminological theory that crime prevention and criminal justice must serve the end of providing the greatest good for the greatest number. The theory is based on the assumed rationality of lawgivers, law enforcers, and the public at large.

utilitarian justification of punishment A justification that promises an empirical benefit from the exercise of punishment, such as deterrence, incapacitation, and rehabilitation.

uttering a forged instrument The crime of passing a false or worthless instrument, such as a check, with the intent to defraud or injure the recipient.

V

vacate To annul, set aside, or rescind.

vacated sentence Any sentence that has been nullified by action of a court.

Vacutainer A blood-alcohol testing system.

vagrancy The offense of living without any visible means of support. Most vagrancy laws have been declared unconstitutionally vague.

vagrant One without visible means of support; an unattached, itinerant person. Such persons are sometimes called homeless, hobos, tramps, or bums.

validated member A gang member who has met the criteria for being officially designated as a gang member by correctional officials.

Valium A prescription tranquilizer that is often sold without prescription on the street as a recreational drug.

value Something that is considered worthy, desirable, or proper.

value clarification Part of the Leisure Education Model, in which inmates identify their need for praise, belonging, and acceptance. Next, they look at methods for satisfying these values within themselves.

value isolation A condition sometimes considered cultural estrangement, in which low rewards are attached to commonly held social values such as good grades, a high-school diploma, or a steady job.

values Moral standards and guides for personal conduct, usually imparted to persons through socialization.

vandalism Destroying or damaging, or attempting to destroy or damage, the property of another without his or her consent, except by burning, which is arson.

variable Any quantity that can assume more than one value. Examples include gender, power, organizational size, complexity, and bureaucratization.

VASCAR (Visual Average Speed Computer and Recorder) A device used by law enforcement to determine the speed of oncoming vehicles on public highways for the purpose of traffic-law enforcement.

vaults Large repositories for money, securities, and other valuables, which are often used by banks for storing large quantities of money. Classes of vaults are graded according to the time taken to break into them.

vehicle Any conveyance, usually motorized, which is designated for travel on roadways or highways or streets used by a person to move about from one place to another.

vehicle identification number (VIN) A permanent numerical designation affixed to various places on all manufactured vehicles to aid in their identification. The VIN usually indicates the vehicle's model, engine displacement, place and year of manufacture, and other details.

vehicular homicide Death resulting from the unlawful and negligent operation of a motorized vehicle.

vehicular manslaughter Causing the death of another by grossly negligent operation of a motor vehicle.

vehicular theft Taking the vehicle of another without his or her authorization or permission.

vendetta A series of revenge acts or attacks committed by persons who have been wronged by their intended victims.

vengeance A private and personal response to a wrong, not involving an established authority.

venire, veniremen, veniremen list From *venire facias,* "you should cause to come" (Latin); a list of prospective jurors made up from registered voters, vehicle driver's licenses, and tax assessors' records, who must reside within the particular jurisdiction where a jury trial is held; persons who are potential jurors in a given jurisdiction.

venue The area over which a judge exercises authority to act in an official capacity; the place where a trial is held.

venue, change of Relocation of a trial from one site to another, usually because of some pretrial publicity making it possible that a jury might be biased and that a fair trial will be difficult to obtain.

Vera Institute of Justice A large, nonprofit organization in New York dedicated to improving the administration of justice through innovative research and practices.

verbal direction Using communication skills to control inmate resistance and obtain compliance.

"verbal judo" Techniques used by law enforcement officers to engage criminals in conversation intended to cause them to surrender or become compliant so that an arrest can be made without resorting to physical force; spoken commands to induce compliance.

verdict The decision by judge or jury concerning the guilt or innocence of a defendant.

verdict, guilty In criminal proceedings, the decision made by a jury in a jury trial, or by a judicial officer in a bench trial, that defendants are guilty of the offense(s) for which they have been tried.

verdict, not guilty In criminal proceedings, the decision made by a jury in a jury trial, or by the judge in a bench trial, that defendants are not guilty of the offense(s) for which they have been tried.

verstehen "Understand" (German); understanding; the notion that social scientists can understand human behavior through empathy.

vertical differentiation A proliferation of supervisory levels or numerous levels of supervision.

vertical prosecution A particular district attorney or his or her assistant handling a criminal case from its inception through prosecution and trial. No division of labor exists as it does in traditional prosecution.

vibration detection system An alarm system attached to a surface and capable of detecting excessive levels of vibration. The alarm unit contains a microphone, an amplifier, and an accumulator, together with a power supply. The unit can be regulated or adjusted to distinguish between ambient noise and normal vibrations and excessive noise or vibration.

vicarious liability A doctrine under which liability is imposed on an employer for the acts of employees that are committed in the course and scope of their employment.

Vice Lords The oldest and second-largest black Chicago-based gang, established by youths incarcerated in the St. Charles Correctional Facility in 1957. The group started in Lawndale, a Chicago West Side suburb. It was headed by Bobby Gore, who was subsequently arrested for murder. During the 1960s, the Vice Lords obtained government grants and engaged in political activism and community improvements. They were originally called the Conservative Vice Lords, and subsequently adopted Islamic doctrines in the 1960s. Later, they formed the Vice Lords Nation, consisting of over 20,000 prisoners and street-gang members. The gang has been linked with narcotics trafficking, drive-by shootings, murder, carjacking, assault, and kidnapping, and is notorious for intergang factional fighting and rivalries.

Vice Lords Nation A largely black Chicago-based gang of over 20,000 inmates and street gang members spawned from the Vice Lords and Conservative Vice Lords of the late 1950s and early 1960s. The gang is linked with narcotics trafficking, murder, assault, drive-by shootings, and kidnapping.

vice Any moral violation, such as gambling, prostitution, or drugs.

vice squad Police officers assigned to enforce morally tinged laws, such as those on prostitution, gambling, and pornography.

vicinage The county, subdivision, or district in which a court has jurisdiction to hear particular types of cases.

victim One who has suffered either death or serious physical or mental suffering, or loss of property resulting from actual or attempted criminal actions committed by others.

victim advocate A social worker or other person who assists crime victims in obtaining counseling and other services, and who helps navigate them through the criminal-justice system.

Victim and Witness Protection Act of 1984 A congressional act designed to prevent intimidation of witnesses in criminal cases. It also provides for establishing new identities for persons who have testified against powerful crime figures so as to conceal their whereabouts and protect them from subsequent retaliation.

victim-assistance program One of many programs in various states seeking to compensate victims of crimes for their losses.

victim compensation Any financial restitution payable to victims by either the state or convicted offenders.

victim-compensation program Any plan for assisting crime victims in making social, emotional, and economic adjustments.

victim-impact statement Information or a version of events filed voluntarily by the victim of a crime, appended to the presentence investigation report as a supplement for judicial consideration in sentencing the offender. It describes injuries to victims resulting from the convicted offender's actions.

victimization A basic measure of the occurrence of a crime; also, a specific criminal act affecting a specific victim.

victimization data Information collected about persons who are targets of criminal activity.

victimization rate The number of victimizations per 1,000 persons or households as reported by the *National Crime Victimization Survey. See table p. 262.*

victimization risk Vulnerability to aggressive actions from others because of a particular lifestyle (e.g., attending a neighborhood high school with a high crime rate).

victimization survey A survey of respondents who have been victimized that measures the extent of crime by interviewing persons about their experiences as victims.

victimless crime Crime committed in which there are no apparent victims, or in which victims are willing participants in the criminal activity (e.g., gambling and prostitution).

victim notification Notification to victims of the release or pending release of convicted offenders who have harmed them.

victim/offender mediation A meeting between a criminal and a person suffering loss or injury from that criminal whereby a third-party arbiter, such as a judge, attorney, or other neutral party decides what is best for all parties. All parties must agree to the decision of the third-party arbiter. The technique is used for both juvenile and adult offenders.

Victim/Offender Reconciliation Project (VORP) A form of alternative dispute resolution, whereby a civil resolution is made by mutual consent between the victim and an offender. Objectives are to provide restitution to victims, hold offenders accountable for crime committed, and reduce recidivism.

victimogenesis The contributory background of a victim as a result of which he or she becomes prone to victimization.

victimology A criminological subdiscipline that examines the role played by the victim in a criminal incident and in the criminal process.

victim-precipitated crime, victim precipitation The situation that exists when a person who suffers eventual harm from a crime plays a direct role in causing the crime.

victim-proneness The tendency for certain people to be victimized repeatedly; the degree of a person's likelihood of victimization. *See also* **victim-precipitated crime, victim precipitation.**

Rates of Criminal Victimization and Percent Change, 1993–2002

Type of crime	Victimization rates (per 1,000 persons age 12 or older or per 1,000 households)		Percent change[a,b]
	1993	2002	1993-2002
Personal crimes[c]	52.2	23.7	-54.6%*
Crimes of violence	49.9	23.1	-53.7*
Completed violence	15.0	7.6	-49.3*
Attempted/threatened violence	34.9	15.5	-55.6*
Rape/sexual assault	2.5	1.1	-56.0*
Rape/attempted rape	1.6	0.7	-56.3*
Rape	1.0	0.4	-60.0*
Attempted rape	0.7	0.3	-57.1*
Sexual assault	0.8	0.3	-62.5*
Robbery	6.0	2.2	-63.3*
Completed robbery	3.8	1.7	-55.3*
With injury	1.3	0.7	-46.2*
Without injury	2.5	0.9	-64.0*
Attempted robbery	2.2	0.5	-77.3*
With injury	0.4	0.2	-50.0*
Without injury	1.8	0.4	-77.8*
Assault	41.4	19.8	-52.2*
Aggravated	12.0	4.3	-64.2*
With injury	3.4	1.4	-58.8*
Threatened with weapon	8.6	2.9	-66.3*
Simple	29.4	15.5	-47.3*
With minor injury	6.1	3.9	-36.1*
Without injury	23.3	11.6	-50.2*
Personal theft[d]	2.3	0.7	-69.6*
Property crimes	318.9	159.0	-50.1%*
Household burglary	58.2	27.7	-52.4*
Completed	47.2	23.5	-50.2*
Forcible entry	18.1	9.2	-49.2*
Unlawful entry without force	29.1	14.3	-50.9*
Attempted forcible entry	10.9	4.2	-61.5*
Motor vehicle theft	19.0	9.0	-52.6*
Completed	12.4	7.1	-42.7*
Attempted	6.6	1.9	-71.2*
Theft	241.7	122.3	-49.4*
Completed[e]	230.1	118.2	-48.6*
Less than $50	98.7	37.9	-61.6*
$50-$249	76.1	40.4	-46.9*
$250 or more	41.6	29.6	-28.8*
Attempted	11.6	4.1	-64.7*

Note: Victimization rates may differ from those reported previously because estimates are now based on data collected in each calendar year rather than data about events within a calendar year.
Completed violent crimes include rape, sexual assault, robbery with or without injury, aggravated assault with injury, and simple assault with minor injury.
In 1993 the total population age 12 or older was 211,524,770; and in 2002; 231,589,260. The total number of households in 1993 was 99,927,410; and in 2002, 110,323,840.
*The difference between the indicated years is significant at the 95%-confidence level.

(cont'd)

[a]Differences between the annual rates shown do not take into account changes that may have occurred during interim years.
[b]Percent change was calculated using unrounded rates.
[c]The NCVS is based on interviews with victims and therefore cannot measure murder.
[d]Includes pocket picking, purse snatching, and attempted purse snatching.
[e]Includes thefts with unknown losses.

Source: Rennison and Rand, *Criminal Victimization, 2002,* 5.

victim-reparations model A restitution model for juveniles in which juveniles compensate their victims directly for their offenses.

victim restitution Having criminals pay back the victims of their crimes as an alternative to more serious sanctions.

Victims' Bill of Rights, victims' rights Entitlements established by the New York State Compensation Board outlining specific rights of crime victims, including notification of offender status and custody, case disposition, and incarceration/nonincarceration details. *See box p. 263.*

victim service restitution Restitution in which an offender is required to provide some type of service directly to the crime victim.

victims known as survivors Victims who survived a crime when others did not.

Victims of Crime Act (VOCA) Congressional action in 1984 to establish a crime victims' fund for the purpose of reimbursing crime victims for some or all of their monetary loses or costs of injuries resulting from crime.

victim-witness assistance program A plan available to prospective witnesses to explain court procedures and inform them of court dates, and to assist witnesses in providing better testimony in court.

victim-witness relocation program *See* **Witness Protection Plan.**

video mug shots Images of arrestees at the time of booking that integrate computer graphics and video footage.

video piracy Any illegal reproduction, distribution, or sale of unauthorized copies of commercial videotapes for profit.

video surveillance Any camera observation of areas where cameras are hidden from view and can see real-time activities. Video surveillance may be used in traffic enforcement and other activities, such as viewing organized crime operations.

vigilante One who is alert, a watchman, on guard, cautious, suspicious, or ready to take action to preserve the peace. The term currently refers to citizens who take the law into their own hands in an effort to apprehend and punish criminals. Historically, it is derived from Committees of Vigilance on the American frontier, citizens' self-defense groups formed in the absence of stable, effective law enforcement.

vigilante justice Informal retribution taken against a criminal, including beatings or even death, by citizens who believe that the perpetrator may escape proper justice in the court system.

vigilantism The illegal practice of citizens assuming police roles, functioning as prosecutors, judges, and executioners in capturing and punishing offenders without benefit of due process or a trial.

VINE (Victim Identification and Notification Everyday) The nation's leading crime-victim notification solution, allowing crime victims across the country to obtain timely and reliable information about criminal cases and the custody status of offenders, 24 hours a day, over the phone, on the Internet, through VINElink, VineWatch, or by email. It also provides Court Event Notification. Devised by Appriss Data Network headquartered in Louisville, KY.

VINELink This Appriss Data Network service is a web-based extension of the VINE service, where victims and other members of the public can register for notification or look up inmate information.

VINEWatch A secure Internet site that registers victims, obtains usage and other status reports, and prints notification letters that are mailed to victims to inform them of offenders' court appearances and release dates; a part of the Appriss Data Network.

Vinson, Frederick Moore (1890–1953) A U.S. Supreme Court chief justice (1946–1953) who began the practice of law in Kentucky in 1911 and was appointed to the U.S. Supreme Court by President Harry S. Truman. Vinson supported the New Deal policy of Franklin D. Roosevelt in the 1930s.

violation A minor criminal offense, usually under city ordinances, commonly subject only to fines.

violation of privacy Any unlawful trespass, interception, observation, eavesdropping, or other surveillance that serves to infringe on the private rights of others.

violence Any force used by one person against another producing injury, which may include the bombing of an unoccupied building or terrorism.

violent crime, violent personal crime A law violation characterized by extreme physical force including murder or homicide, forcible rape or child sexual abuse, assault and battery by means of a dangerous weapon, robbery, and arson.

Violent Crime Control and Law Enforcement Act of 1994 An act that made available increased funding for juvenile justice and delinquency prevention.

Violent Criminal Apprehension Program (VICAP) An FBI initiative consisting of a computerized database of detailed information about homicides, sexual assaults, and other violent crimes, contributed by various local law enforcement agencies.

Violent Juvenile Offender Programs (VJOPs) Procedures designed to provide positive interventions and treatments; reintegrative programs, including transitional residential programs for those youths who have been subject to long-term detention that provide for social networking, educational opportunities, social learning, and goal-oriented behavioral skills.

Victims' Bill of Rights

The following rights are hereby granted to victims in all prosecutions for crimes and juvenile delinquency proceedings:

1. The right to be reasonably protected from the criminal defendant or the convicted criminal throughout the criminal-justice process; decisions as to the pretrial release of the defendant are to be based on the principle of reasonable protection of the victim and the public; any person arrested for a crime for which the People have set a mandatory minimum sentence shall not be released prior to trial unless a court determines by clear and convincing evidence that the person will not commit new criminal offenses while on release.

2. The right to be present at, and be heard at, and, upon specific request, to be informed in advance of any critical stage of the proceedings where the criminal defendant is present, including trial.

3. The right, upon request, to information about the conviction, sentence, imprisonment, criminal history and future release from physical custody of the criminal defendant or convicted criminal.

4. The right to refuse an interview, deposition or other discovery request by the defendant, the defendant's attorney, or other person acting on behalf of the defendant.

5. The right to receive prompt restitution from the person or persons convicted of the future criminal conduct that caused the victim's loss or injury.

6. The right to have all relevant evidence admissible against the criminal defendant.

7. The right, in a criminal prosecution, to a public trial without delay by a jury selected from registered voters and composed of persons who have not been convicted of a felony or served a felony sentence within the last 15 years, except that no court shall hold that a jury is required in juvenile-court delinquency proceedings.

8. The right to have 11 members of the jury render a verdict of guilty of aggravated murder or murder, notwithstanding any other law or provision.

9. The right to have a copy of a transcript of any court proceeding, if one is otherwise prepared.

10. The right that no law shall permit a sentence imposed by a judge in open court to be set aside or otherwise not carried out except through the reprieve, commutation, and pardon power of the governor or pursuant to appellate or post-conviction relief.

11. The right that no law shall limit the court's authority to sentence a criminal defendant consecutively for crimes against different victims.

12. The right to have all charges against a criminal defendant tried in a single trial, subject to rules regarding venue.

13. The right to be consulted, upon request, regarding plea negotiations involving any violent felony.

14. The right to be informed of these rights as soon as reasonably practicable.

Virginia Plan A scheme deriving from England's royal court system, projecting superior and inferior courts; also called the "Randolph Plan."

virulency A stage in a violent career in which criminals develop a violent identity that makes them feared. They consequently enjoy hurting others.

visible crimes Offenses against persons and property committed primarily by members of the lower class. Often referred to as "street crime" or "ordinary crime," these are the offenses most upsetting to the public.

VisionQuest A carefully regulated, intensive supervision program designed to improve the social and psychological experiences of juveniles. It provides a reintegrative wilderness program to improve educational and social skills.

visitation The practice of allowing friends and relatives to visit inmates in prisons or jails.

visiting cottage program A scheme established by the Massachusetts Department of Corrections in which female offenders with children may have lengthy visits with their children in "cottages" on the prison premises.

visiting rules Penal institutions typically have rules that specify who can visit, their mode of dress, the items that can be brought in, the frequency and length of visits, and the extent of the contact.

visitor center An agency that provides a variety of services to the family members of inmates who visit them in prison. These services include transportation, child care, emergency clothing, information on visiting regulations and processes, referral to other agencies and services, emergency food, crisis intervention, and a sheltered area to use before and after visitation.

Vitamin K *See* **ketamine hydrochloride.**

VNS (Victim Notification System) A U.S. Department of Justice notification system designed to provide victims with information about criminals, their confinement status, court appearances, release dates, and other material information; links the FBI, U.S. Attorneys' Offices, and the U.S. Federal Bureau of Prisons to provide timely information to victims of federal crimes via telephone, letter, email, fax, and pager. The program was designed in partnership with AT&T Government Solutions, Inc., and the Appriss Data Network.

vocational training Education in a specific marketable skill.

voice identification Electronic detection of particular voice patterns.

voiceprint The unique pattern of impulses that is associated with particular persons' speaking voices; a spectrographic record of the energy output by the sound of words and other utterances of a particular person. Like fingerprints, each person's voiceprint is unique.

voice-stress analysis A method for determining truthfulness or deception in human speech; a competitor of the polygraph test or lie-detector test, with results that are similarly suspect or unreliable in court; an electronic means of understanding and charting voice patterns to detect deception or lies.

void-for-vagueness doctrine *See* **unconstitutionally vague.**

voir dire "To speak truly" (French); the interrogation process whereby prospective jurors are questioned by either the judge or the prosecution or defense attorneys to determine their biases and prejudices.

Vold, George (1896–1967) A conflict theorist who believed in a definite link between conflict theory and crime. He is considered the primary contributor to this particular view. The law is created by the ruling class to dominate the lower classes. Thus, Marxist philosophy fits Vold's view of society well. Conflict between classes is pervasive, fundamental, and persistent, and crime occurs when different classes clash over competing and opposing vested interests. Vold wrote *Theoretical Criminology* (1958).

Vollmer, August (1876–1955) Berkeley, CA, chief of police who professionalized policing by recommending educational training for police officers. Vollmer relied heavily on academic specialists in various forensics areas. He pioneered an informal academic regimen of police training, including investigative techniques, photography, fingerprinting, and anatomy, among other academic subject areas.

Volstead Act Legislation passed in 1919 to prohibit possession or consumption of alcoholic beverages. The act was repealed in 1933. *See also* **Prohibition.**

Voltaire, Francois-Marie Arouet (1694–1778) A French philosopher and writer who wrote about French injustices and corporal punishments.

voluntariness The willingness of a defendant to enter a plea or make an agreement in a plea-bargain proceeding. Judges must determine the voluntariness of a plea to determine that it was not coerced.

voluntarism The freedom of participants to choose whether or not to take part in a research experiment or project and the guarantee that exposure to known risks is voluntarily undertaken.

voluntary manslaughter Homicide in which the perpetrator intentionally, but without malice, causes the death of another person, as in the heat of passion, in response to strong provocation, or possibly under severe intoxication.

voluntary sentencing guidelines Recommended sentencing policies that are not required by law. They serve as a guide and are based on past sentencing practices. The legislature has not mandated their use. Voluntary or advisory guidelines may use either indeterminate or determinate sentencing structures.

volunteer Any citizen who wishes to donate time to assist in the supervision, education, counseling, or training of probationers, parolees, or divertees.

volunteerism The propensity of citizens to become actively involved in various auxiliary police functions, such as Neighborhood Watch.

Volunteers in Probation (VIP) A program in which citizen volunteers assist probation officers in performing their duties and meeting the needs of probationer-clients.

vomiting agents Any one of several types of gases or substances intended to induce vomiting; war or riot-control gases, such as DA, DM, or DC.

Von Hentig, Hans (1887–1974) A proponent of physical characteristics as indicative of criminal propensities. He wrote a treatise on this subject in 1948.

Von Hirsch, Andrew (1934–) A criminologist and classicist; author of *Doing Justice* (1976). Von Hirsch advocated "just-desert" philosophy, in which punishment is designed to fit the crime committed. Blameworthiness of an offense should not be changed for different persons who commit the same offense. Thus, committing the same offense should result in identical punishments, regardless of one's past criminal record, race, ethnicity, gender, or age.

vote of no confidence An action by an organization to express disapproval of organizational leadership. Such a vote is considered extralegal and not binding. Votes may influence persons to resign or change their policies to those more favored by the organization's membership.

voyeurism The surreptitious observance of an exposed body or sexual act. *See also* **Peeping Tom.**

W

WAIS (Wechsler Adult Intelligence Scale) An individually administered intelligence test.

wait, lie in To conceal oneself for purposes of attacking someone else.

Waite, Morrison Remick (1816–1888) A U.S. Supreme Court chief justice (1874–1888) appointed by President Ulysses S. Grant. Waite was educated at Yale, practiced law in Ohio, and was successful as a lawyer for banks and railroads.

waiver, waiver of jurisdiction, waiver provision, waiver to adult court Made by motion, the transfer of jurisdiction over a juvenile to a criminal court in which the juvenile is subject to adult criminal penalties. The process includes judicial, prosecutorial, and legislative waivers, and is also known as certification or transfer. *See table.*

waiver motion, waiver hearing A motion by a prosecutor to transfer a juvenile charged with various offenses to a criminal or adult court for prosecution, making it possible to sustain adult criminal penalties.

Walker spy ring Espionage perpetrated by John Walker, his son, brother, and his son's friend. The ring passed information to the Soviet government between the 1960s and the 1980s. The information resulted in numerous American deaths.

walking line An imaginary line fitting different persons' walking profiles that under normal walking conditions fuses with a direction line and runs along the inner sides of both heel prints.

walking picture A study of footprint characteristics, which may be used to identify types of shoes worn at a crime scene.

wall of silence *See* **blue curtain.**

Walnut Street Jail Considered the first American prison seeking to correct offenders, the Walnut Street Jail was built in 1776 in Philadelphia, PA, and was one of the first penal facilities to segregate female from male offenders and children from adults. It introduced solitary confinement of prisoners

Minimum Age for Transferring Juveniles to Adult Court	
Minimum Age	**States**
None	Arizona, Florida, Georgia, Indiana, Maine, Maryland, Nebraska, Nevada, New Hampshire, Oklahoma, Pennsylvania, Rhode Island, South Carolina, South Dakota, Tennessee, Washington, West Virginia
10	Vermont, Wisconsin
12	Colorado, Missouri, Montana, Oregon
13	Illinois, Mississippi, New York, North Carolina, Wyoming
14	Alabama, Arkansas, California, Connecticut, Iowa, Kansas, Kentucky, Louisiana, Massachusetts, Michigan, Minnesota, New Jersey, New Mexico, North Dakota, Texas, Utah, Virginia
15	District of Columbia
16	Hawaii

and separated them according to their offense severity. The jail operated on the basis that inmates could perform useful services to defray the costs of confinement. It operated one of the first prison industry programs. Inmates grew much of their own fruit through gardening.

Walsh-Healy Act of 1936 Legislation that prohibited the use of prison labor to fulfill general government contracts that exceeded $10,000.

"wanna-be" A young rookie gang member looking for opportunities to break into the gang's core; a youth who is not a gang members but who wants to join a gang; in computer jargon, someone who aspires to become a computer hacker or cracker but who lacks the technological sophistication to accomplish hacking tasks.

wanton and unnecessary In corrections, actions of corrections personnel to control or deal with inmates that are characterized by reckless and unreasonable disregard of the rights and safety of others or evil intent and not required by the circumstances of the situation.

war crimes Any crimes committed during war that violate international law.

warden The chief administrator of a prison or penitentiary.

WarDriving An early meaning of this term referred to persons who would run many telephone numbers in order to connect to other computers for some illicit purpose. Dial-in telephone numbers would enable hackers to access information from schools, businesses, or other networks they shouldn't have access to. A later meaning refers to scanning large numbers of IP addresses on the Internet looking for computers that are running certain types of servers. WarDriving originally applied to crackers who drove around in cars equipped with wireless gear looking for unsecured wireless networks, to gain illicit access.

warehousing An imprisonment strategy that confines prisoners simply to segregate them from society and prevent recurrent crime, without any attempt to rehabilitate, counsel, or train them.

War on Drugs An initiative by the federal government and state authorities to control the supply and distribution of illegal drugs in the United States.

warrant A written order directing a suspect's arrest and issued by an official with the authority to issue the warrant. A warrant commands that a suspect be arrested and brought before the nearest magistrate.

warrant, arrest A document issued by a judge that directs a law enforcement officer to arrest a person who has been accused of an offense.

warrant, bench A document issued by a judge directing that a person who has failed to obey an order or notice to appear be brought before the court without undue delay.

warrant, search A document issued by a judicial official, based on probable cause, directing law enforcement officers to conduct an inspection of an individual, automobile, or building with the intent of locating particular contraband or incriminating evidence as set forth in the document.

warrantless search and seizure An examination of a dwelling unit, person, or automobile without obtaining a search warrant from a magistrate or judge based upon probable cause and under oath.

Warren, Earl (1891–1974) A U.S. Supreme Court chief justice (1953–1969) appointed to the Court by President Dwight D. Eisenhower. Warren was considered to be a conservative influence on the Supreme Court, which greatly limited the scope of search-and-seizure powers of police officers through several decisions over which he presided, including *Mapp v. Ohio* (1961).

Warren Commission A federal commission chaired by Earl Warren to investigate the assassination of President John F. Kennedy in 1963. The commission concluded that Lee Harvey Oswald, a gunman, acted alone and that there was no conspiracy by others to assist him in Kennedy's assassination.

Warren Court The U.S. Supreme Court under the leadership of Chief Justice Earl Warren (1953–1969).

wartime trade violations The prohibited sale or exchange of specific goods reserved for the war effort.

Washington Coalition to Abolish the Death Penalty Headquartered in Seattle, WA, this advocacy organization is opposed to the death penalty and seeks its abolition. It consists of interested citizens and disseminates information pertinent to the death penalty, wrongful convictions, and other related data.

watchdog committee An oversight committee established by Congress to monitor and investigate lobbying activities, corrupt practices, campaign irregularities, and other possible government misconduct.

watchman model, watchman style A style of policing that is marked by a concern for order maintenance. It is characteristic of lower-class communities where informal police intervention into the lives of residents is employed in the service of keeping the peace.

watchmen Citizens in early England who were paid to observe their neighborhoods for possible criminal activity.

watch system During the Middle Ages in England, men were organized in church parishes to guard at night against disturbances and breaches of the peace under the direction of the local constable.

Watergate, Watergate affair An infamous incident occurring in 1972, in which the Democratic National Committee headquarters at the Watergate Hotel in Washington, DC, was burglarized. The burglars were subsequently linked with President Richard M. Nixon. Many indictments and convictions were forthcoming, as well as President Nixon's resignation.

watermark A design in paper, usually paper currency, that is inserted by the manufacturer to assist in determining whether money is authentic or counterfeit.

Watson, John (1878–1958) A psychologist who promoted the concept of behavior modification. Watson believed in operant conditioning, viewing behavior as the result of chains of stimuli and responses. Criminality is one response to stimuli that are found rewarding in connection with criminal conduct.

Watts An African-American section of Los Angeles, CA, that was the scene of widespread rioting in 1965.

wayward minors An early legal designation of youths who violate the law because of their minority status, now referred to as status offenders.

weapon Any tool, instrument, or firearm used in fighting, either defensively or offensively, capable of inflicting serious injury upon another.

weapon identification A means of identifying the make and type of weapon used in committing a crime.

weapons, carrying concealed The illegal carrying of firearms on one's person in public places.

weapons, firing, in public Discharging firearms in a populated area where there is a risk that someone might be injured or killed as a result.

weapons offenses The unlawful sale, distribution, manufacture, alteration, transportation, possession, or use or the attempted sale, distribution, manufacture, alteration, transportation, possession, or use of deadly or dangerous weapons or accessories.

Weathermen A group formed by militant members of Students for a Democratic Society (SDS) formed at Ann Arbor, MI, in 1969, that conducted violent antiwar protests during the Vietnam War.

Weber, Max (1864–1920) A German sociologist who authored many works, including *The Protestant Ethic and the Spirit of Capitalism* (1906). Weber elaborated on the concept of *verstehen*, which is interpreted literally as meaning "at the level of understanding." Thus, through *verstehen*, sociologists can acquire a better understanding of their social world. He also pioneered work on bureaucracy, an organizational model that has been used in establishing police and correctional systems. Bureaucracy incorporates characteristics including selection by test, prearranged hierarchy of authority, expertise, nonoverlapping functional departments or limited spheres of competence, abstract rules, and promotion according to ability. Weber advocated a value-free approach to research.

We Care Established in 1983 and headquartered in Atmore, AL, this organization is dedicated to delinquency prevention. The group often meets with delinquent or potentially delinquent at-risk youths and shows them videotapes of executions, or documentaries of imprisoned offenders. Sometimes organization uses convicted offenders to address youths and tell about their own experiences in prison and what led them to a life of crime. The organization publishes *We Care,* a newsletter.

Wedtech A New York business and defense contractor that cheated the U.S. government out of millions of dollars between 1980 and 1985.

Weed and Seed Operations A program created in 1992 dedicated to weeding out undesirable elements or persons in particular communities and seeding neighborhoods with economic revitalization and restoration. The program operates in communities throughout the United States. Its efforts are coordinated with law enforcement, neighborhood leaders, social services, and community redevelopment programs.

weekenders Misdemeanants who are permitted to serve their short sentences on weekends so that they may retain their jobs during the week.

weekend sentence A form of intermittent sentence in which the time is served on weekends.

Wehrli, Johann Jakob (1790–1855) A Swiss educator who helped to establish early private institutions for wayward and destitute children.

weight of the evidence The preponderance of evidence; a civil standard in determining liability.

Welch, Joseph Nye (1890–1960) A Harvard Law School graduate and special counsel for the U.S. Army in 1954. During Senator Joseph McCarthy's hearings into communism and communist conspiracies in 1954, Welch publicly asked McCarthy if he had no sense of decency. The hearings ultimately led to McCarthy's downfall.

wergild Under medieval law, the money paid by offenders to compensate victims and the state for a criminal offense.

Werther effect A copycat syndrome in which persons commit suicide as the result of media coverage of suicides by others. The name is taken from Johann Wolfgang von Goethe's novel *The Sorrows of Young Werther* (1774), in which the protagonist commits suicide. That literary suicide was said to result in subsequent suicides by others throughout Europe. Some social theorists, such as Gabriel Tarde, a Frenchman, used imitation to explain the suicide phenomenon. The theory is generally discounted by other social theorists, although some contemporary suicides, especially among teenagers, are attributable to imitation.

Western States Information Network A 1981 Congressional act that established six regional intelligence systems to improve federal narcotics investigations and enforcement of drug laws.

we-they A concept suggested by Jerome Skolnick as a part of his work on the working personality of police officers. It describes the attitude of police officers who feel isolated from society to the extent that they believe that they live in a fishbowl and that any indiscretions on their part, such as drinking too much alcohol at a party, would be viewed by nonpolice as hypocritical. Because of this, they socialize together and begin to count on each other for support. Police acquire a hostile attitude toward nonpolice, thus reinforcing their feelings of isolation.

WETIP (We Turn in Pushers) An organization established in 1972 and headquartered in Alta Loma, CA, that consists of persons who attempt to report known drug activity, drug traffickers, and users.

Wharton's rule Named after Francis Wharton, a well-known commentator on criminal law, this rule holds that two people cannot conspire to commit a crime such as adultery, incest, or bigamy, inasmuch as these offenses involve only two participants.

whipping Also known as flogging or scourging, this is one of the oldest, most widely used means of corporal punishment. It dates back to Egyptian times.

whistle-blower One who reports organizational or corporate wrongdoing to the authorities. The reporting person usually works for the organization allegedly engaged in wrongdoing.

White, Edward Douglas (1845–1921) A chief justice of the U.S. Supreme Court (1910–1921) appointed by President Grover S. Cleveland. White was a political conservative who consistently dissented in income-tax cases.

white-collar crime A law violation committed by persons of higher socioeconomic status in the course of their businesses, occupations, or professions (e.g., a banker who embezzles).

"white hat" A computer hacker who breaks into a computer system for some positive purpose, such as to disclose potential security weaknesses and thereby improve the soundness and security of the computer system. Some corporations hire former hacker criminals to improve their own systems, as in "using a thief to catch a thief." White hats do not have criminal or nefarious intentions when breaking into computer systems or hacking. The name derives from early Western movies featuring heros who often wore white hats, as differentiated from bandits who typically wore black hats. *See also* **"black hat"; "gray hat."**

White Night On May 21, 1979, thousands of gay men in San Francisco attacked City Hall, torched police cars, and smashed store windows following the murder of Mayor George Moscone and gay supervisor Harvey Milk. Police retaliation involved storming the Castro, San Francisco's gay ghetto.

white slavery The exploitation of females who are kidnapped and coerced into lives of prostitution.

White Typology A classification of police officers as Tough Cop, who is outcome oriented; Problem Solver, who pays attention to people's needs; Crime Fighter, who is a zealot on a mission to wipe out a certain type of crime; and Rule Applier, who goes strictly by the book and would give his or her own mother a ticket for speeding. The typology was suggested by

S.O. White in his 1972 work, *A Perspective on Police Professionalization.*

Whitman, Charles (1941–1966) A former U.S. Marine who shot and killed 16 persons and wounded 30 others at the University of Texas–Austin campus in 1966. He climbed the University of Texas tower and randomly opened fire until being overwhelmed by a SWAT team and killed.

whorl A circle-like segment of a human fingerprint.

Wichern, Johann Hinrich (1808–1881) A Swiss educator who assisted in developing private institutions for wayward and destitute children.

Wickersham Commission, Wickersham Reports A 1929 commission established to investigate police agencies and the state of training and education among police officers. The commission was generally critical of contemporary methods of police organization and operation. Its conclusions were published by the National Commission on Law Observance and Enforcement, chaired by George W. Wickersham.

widening the net *See* **net widening.**

wife beating Physical assault of a wife by the husband.

wilderness camp A remote camp located in a wooded setting that is designed as a correctional alternative for youthful offenders.

wilderness experiments Experience programs that include a wide array of outdoor programs designed to improve a juvenile's self-worth, self-concept, pride, and trust in others.

wilderness probation A program involving outdoor expeditions that provide opportunities for juveniles to confront the difficulties of their lives while achieving positive personal satisfaction.

Williams, Wayne (1938–) A serial killer believed responsible for the deaths of 28 black men and boys in the Atlanta, GA, area during the early 1980s.

Wilson, Edmund O. (1929–) Wilson espouses the influence and interplay of biological and genetic factors on perception and learning and held that one's conduct, including criminal conduct, is influenced to a great degree by one's genetic makeup. Societal factors exist to create conventional behavior patterns, but the genetic element is strong. Among his works is *Sociobiology: The New Synthesis* (1975).

Wilson, James Q. (1931–) A political scientist and criminologist; author of *Thinking About Crime* (1975), a policy analysis approach to crime. Wilson is critical of positivist thought, in which crime is believed to be a function of external forces. He believes, rather, that crime can be controlled more effectively by reducing criminal opportunities and selectively incapacitating known chronic recidivists. Wislon chaired numerous videotaped panels as a part of an educational series for the National Institute of Justice during the mid- to late 1980s that focused on crime-prevention strategies and the effectiveness of current tactics to deal with criminals at different phases of criminal-justice processing. He also authored *The Moral Sense* (1993), which details how hormones, enzymes, and neurotransmitters might be keys to understanding human behavior. He suggests that testosterone levels help to explain the aging-out process among criminals, and that there is a relation between violence and hormonal imbalances. Wilson collaborated with Richard Herrnstein to write *Crime and Human Nature* (1985), a controversial work linking criminal conduct with genetic factors. He maintains an integrated theoretical view attributing criminality to biosocial makeup, personality, rational choice, and social structure and process.

Wilson, Orlando W. (1900–1972) A former police chief in Wichita, KS and Chicago, IL, and the first Dean of the School of Criminology at the University of California–Berkeley, in 1950. Wilson was successful in centralizing police administration and created command decision making, not only in Berkeley but in many other cities during the 1950s and 1960s.

Wilson, William Julius (1935–) A criminologist who wrote *The Truly Disadvantaged* (1987). Wilson discusses persons who are isolated in urban society and who are at the bottom rung of the social ladder. The "truly disadvantaged" cannot attack the source of their frustration, the elite society, and thus direct their rage and frustration at others around them. This becomes a vicious cycle of loss of self-confidence, frustration, anger, helplessness, and violence.

Windham School District A nongeographical school district established in Texas specifically for conducting educational programs at the Texas Department of Criminal Justice correctional facilities.

wiretapping The practice of intercepting telephone transmissions for the purpose of gathering evidence for possible criminal prosecution.

Wirth, Louis (1897–1952) Wirth helped to establish the Chicago School during the 1920s, examining zones in and around Chicago, rings emanating from the city center outward toward the suburbs, in which different social patterns existed and different types of crime were observed. Zones undergoing urban renewal or rapid social change were increasingly disorganized and ripe for high degrees of criminality. Wirth collaborated with Edwin Sutherland, Robert Park, and Ernest Burgess.

wite Under medieval law, the portion of the *wergild* that went to the victim's family. *See also* **wergild.**

withdrawal An alternative to joining a gang or adopting a convict identity chosen by many inmates. The inmate withdraws from associating with the larger prison population, thereby guaranteeing his or her safety.

W.I. Thomas' four wishes A scheme devised by social psychologist W.I. Thomas that described four needs or wishes persons have. These wishes are motivating factors to behave in certain ways. The wishes include the wish for response or love, recognition, new experience, and security. Thomas presumed that persons are motivated to achieve these needs and that this action explains their conduct.

without prejudice Charges dismissed without prejudice can later be brought again against the same defendant.

without undue or unnecessary delay A standard used to determine whether a suspect has been brought before a magistrate or other judicial authority in a timely manner after being arrested. The definition of undue delay varies among jurisdictions. Circumstances of arrest, availability of a judge, and time of arrest are factors that determine reasonableness of delay.

with prejudice Charges dismissed with prejudice cannot later be brought again against the same defendant.

witness One who has relevant information about the commission of a crime; any person who has seen or heard inculpatory or exculpatory evidence that may incriminate or exonerate a defendant.

witness, character A person called in court to testify about the good character of the defendant.

witness, expert Someone called by the defense or prosecution in a criminal case, or by either side in a civil case, who has specialized knowledge and expertise resulting from his or her training, who can give critical testimony about certain factual issues.

witness intimidation The illegal act of threatening witnesses with harm if they do not testify in ways favorable to a particular side in a trial.

witness list A compilation of all persons that either side in a case intends to call as witnesses. Witness lists are usually disclosed by the process of discovery.

Witness Protection Plan A federal program established in 1970 under the Organized Crime Control Act that provides for the health, safety, and welfare of witnesses against criminals in federal cases. Witnesses and their families are given new identities and placed in faraway communities where they can live without fear of being killed by those against whom they testify.

witness stand A platform with a low wall behind it in the courtroom where witnesses sit and testify.

wobblers Crimes that may be considered either misdemeanors or felonies depending on how they are interpreted at the discretion of district attorneys or their assistants.

wobbler statutes Laws that allow prosecutors to charge particular offenses as misdemeanors or felonies, depending on how they wish to interpret the offense (e.g., if the crime of "petty theft" is committed, the prosecutor may treat this crime as a misdemeanor if it is a "first offense," or if it is "petty theft with a prior conviction for another offense," the prosecutor may decide to treat the petty theft as a felony for the purpose of a criminal prosecution). *See also Ewing v. California* (2003).

Wolfgang, Marvin (1924–1998) Author of *Patterns in Criminal Homicide* (1958), a landmark analysis of homicide and the relation between offenders and their victims. Wolfgang has elaborated on the white-collar crime concepts of Edwin Sutherland. He also published *Delinquency in a Birth Cohort* with Thorsten Sellin and Robert Figlio (1972), which examined two male birth cohorts from Philadelphia in 1945 and 1963. The study led these researchers to conclude that 6 percent of these persons, who became known as the "chronic 6 percent," accounted for 54 percent of all delinquency and criminal activity. They also formulated the concept of the "subculture of violence," which depicts a culture within a culture in which the theme of violence is an integral part of one's lifestyle and one learns through socialization to value this conduct more highly than conventional behavior. Albert Co-

hen is credited with extending the subculture notion to delinquent behavior.

Woman's Self-Help Center Justice Outreach Program An intermediate punishment program for women located in St. Louis, MO, offering diversion and other supervisory services.

Woolf Report A 1996 document prepared by Lord Woolf about the access to justice in Britain.

work (and educational) release, work/study release A community-based program whereby persons about to be paroled work in the community at jobs during the day, but return to a facility at night and receive limited supervision; any program that provides for prison labor in the community, under conditions of relaxed supervision, and for which prisoners are paid adequate wages.

work detail supervisors Those that oversee the work of individual inmates and inmate work crews.

work furlough *See* **work (and educational) release, work/study release.**

workhouse An early penal facility that operated in English shires in mid-sixteenth century and later, which was designed to use prison labor for profit by private interests.

working ideology The development of an officer work style as a result of beliefs developed from interactions with other groups in a correctional institution.

working personality A term used to describe police officers as having similar and distinctive cognitive tendencies and behavioral responses, including a particular "life style." The concept is associated with the work of Jerome Skolnick. At the time the term was coined, the police behaviors that were under criticism were the product of particular conditions of their work environment and not necessarily inherent attributes of the individuals themselves.

workplace violence Any physical altercation resulting in death or serious bodily injury occurring at or near the place of employment of the perpetrator, who is an employee or former employee.

work routine Monotonous and repetitive labor in organizational settings; doing the same things over and over again in a repetitive fashion; a work pattern.

World Association of Document Examiners Established in 1973 and headquartered in Chicago, IL, this association consists of experts on documentation throughout the world who examine documents, determine their authenticity, and testify in courts of law concerning such documents.

World Court Formerly the International Court of Justice. Formed in 1945 at the conclusion of World War II, this court resolves disputes involving international law. Cases resolved by the World Court may or may not be accepted by different countries, despite sanction or approval by the United Nations.

World Trade Center disaster The 110-story Twin Towers in New York City were attacked and destroyed by terrorists, who flew large passenger jets into these buildings on the morning of September 11, 2001, resulting in approximately 3,000 deaths of private citizens, police officers, and firefighters. The attack was the action of the terrorist group al Qaeda.

worldview A mentality or cognitive orientation involving how people see themselves and others. Police are said to have a "we-they" or "us-them" worldview. Solidarity is associated with the idea of a police subculture, but in practice, the term *culture* is commonly used to describe everything police have in common.

Wounded Knee II The site of an 1890 massacre between Indians and federal officials, as well as the Pine Ridge Reservation. Between February 27 and May 8, 1973, 200 Native Americans, led by leaders of the American Indian Movement (AIM), congregated to demonstrate against the elected tribal council head, Richard (Dick) Wilson, whose administration was alleged to be corrupt and inclined to silence its opponents with violence and intimidation. Sioux traditionalists rejected an Indian Reorganization Act government as represented by Wilson and engaged in organized protest. Local authorities attempted to break up the protest but were unsuccessful, and eventually 2,000 Native Americans were drawn to Wounded Knee as well as numerous FBI agents and other law enforcement officials. The site was surrounded by armed officers and armored personnel carriers, and the siege ended when the two sides began shooting at one another. Two Native Americans, Frank Clearwater and Buddy Lamont, were killed. A negotiated settlement was later concluded by both sides. In the aftermath of Wounded Knee II, the government embarked upon a campaign to neutralize Native American resistance and arrested 562 persons, issuing 185 indictments against AIM leaders and others. Between March 1973 and March 1976, at least 342 assaults were inflicted on AIM members by government agents, and at least 69 AIM members were killed. Despite eyewitness testimony, these deaths were never solved by the FBI, who denied any involvement in the incidents.

Wournos, Aileen (1956–2002) A serial killer who murdered several men in Florida during the 1980s. Wournos used prostitution to lure men whom she then robbed and killed. She was executed in 2002.

writ A document issued by a judicial officer ordering or forbidding the performance of a specific act.

writ of assistance An ancient writ issuing from the Court of Exchequer ordering sheriffs to assist in collecting debts owed to the British Crown. Prior to the American Revolution, writs of assistance gave agents of the Crown in the American colonies the unlimited right to search for smuggled goods. In modern practice, the term refers to judicial orders to put someone in possession of particular property.

writ of *audita querela* "The complaint having been heard" (Latin); arrest of judgment; a remedy setting aside the execution of an order because of an injustice by a party obtaining a judgment against another but which could not be pleaded at the time of trial.

writ of *certiorari* "[We wish] to be informed" (Latin); an order of a superior court requesting that the record of an inferior court (or administrative body) be brought forward for review or inspection; a means of accessing the U.S. Supreme Court in order for a case to be heard.

writ of detainer An official notice from a government agency to a correctional organization noting that a particular person is wanted by the first agency and requesting that he or she not be released or discharged without notifying the first agency and giving it the opportunity to respond.

writ of *distringas* "That you distrain" (Latin); a writ issued to a sheriff to seize a defendant's goods as well as the defendant. It is designed so that the sheriff can have the defendant in custody when it is time for the defendant to appear before a judicial officer.

writ of error A writ issued by an appellate court for the purpose of correcting an error revealed in the record of a lower court proceeding.

writ of *habeas corpus* *See* **habeas corpus.**

writ of *mandamus* "We order" (Latin); an order of a superior court commanding that a lower court, administrative body, or executive body perform a specific function. A writ of *mandamus* is commonly used to restore rights and privileges lost to a defendant through illegal means.

writ of prohibition An appellate court order that prevents a lower court from exercising its jurisdiction in a particular case.

writ of *supersedeas* "You must desist" (Latin); an order to temporarily suspend a proceeding.

wrongful conviction The actual finding of guilt of an accused person who, in fact, did not commit the offense.

wrongful execution The putting to death of an innocent person falsely convicted of a capital crime.

Wyatt Earp syndrome A depiction of police officers who are badge-heavy, who consider themselves macho and are victims of their image. Named for the famous 1870s sheriff of Tombstone, AZ.

X

xenophobe One who is afraid of or hates anyone from a foreign country.

XYY syndrome A theory of criminal behavior suggesting that some criminals are born with an extra Y chromosome, characterized as the "aggressive" chromosome compared with the "passive" X chromosome. The extra Y chromosome produces greater agitation, greater aggressiveness, and criminal propensities. *See also* **supermale.**

Y

Yablonsky, Lewis (1924–) A criminologist who has studied gangs and gang patterns. Yablonsky is particularly known for his observations of fighting gangs in studies of New York City gangs during late 1950s and early 1960s.

yard A feature of the big-house prison, typically enclosed by cell blocks and the prison's exterior wall. It is used for prisoner recreation.

Yippies (Youth International Party) An organization formed by Jerry Rubin and Abbie Hoffman in the 1960s which gained notoriety by announcing that it would put LSD in the Chicago water supply to send all Chicago residents on an acid trip. They demonstrated at the Chicago National Democratic Convention in 1968, after which the group's leaders were arrested and convicted for inciting rioting and other crimes. The group advocated free speech and a vague, anarchist government with no central authority and no currency, just one big commune with free goods and services. They also advocated revolt against society. Rubin and Hoffman were original members of the Chicago Eight, which became the Chicago Seven after one defendant was ejected from the trial proceeding.

Yochelson, Samuel (1906–1976) A criminologist who conducted extensive studies of the criminal personality in his work coauthored with Stanton Samenow, *The Criminal Personality* (1976, 1977).

Young Americans for Freedom (YAF) A national conservative youth organization formed in the early 1960s and supported by William F. Buckley. The group subsequently received support from Ronald Reagan, who became the YAF Honorary Chairman in the 1990s. They supported the Vietnam War and advocate active resistance to communism in Asia and throughout the world. Members formed a Truth Squad during Clarence Thomas' confirmation hearings as a Supreme Court justice to expose Anita Hill and lies she allegedly told about him. The group supports Republican ideologies and publishes *New Guard* magazine.

Young Lords A prison gang that emerged from a street gang in Chicago in 1969. It was revolutionary in nature and guided by Marxist/Leninist/Maoist principles.

Youngstown Gang An infamous group of criminals in the Youngstown, OH, area during the 1960s and 1970s. They committed many burglaries, robberies, and other property and violent crimes, with the support of both organized crime figures and local police officials.

youthful offender Any person who is an infant, juvenile, or minor, who has not yet reached the age of majority or adulthood, and over whom the juvenile court has jurisdiction. Youthful offender status varies according to each jurisdiction.

youth correction authority Any administrative agency responsible for the treatment, supervision, and housing of adjudicated youthful offenders.

Youth Correction Authority Act A model act conceived by the American Law Institute in 1940. Its nonbinding provisions were implemented by some states where youths are overseen by youth authorities until age 25. For example, the California Youth Authority has jurisdiction over youths ages 17–25.

Youth Crime Watch of America An organization headquartered in Miami, FL, dedicated to training students, teachers, and school administrators about crime-prevention methods.

Youth for Justice An Ohio-based enterprise to involve schoolchildren in trying to reduce violence and other types of crime.

youth gang A self-formed association of youths distinguished from other types of youth groups by their routine participation in illegal activities.

Youth Risk Behavior Survey (YRBS) A biannual survey of high school youth that studies their dietary habits, substance abuse, fighting, and other behaviors that might adversely affect their health.

youth services bureau A diversion program for juvenile courts that eliminates noncriminal cases and petty first offenses from the courts' consideration by providing a resource to help young persons become less troubled or less troubling; a neighborhood agency that coordinates all community services for young people, especially designed for the predelinquent or early delinquent.

Youth Services/Diversion (YS/D) Program A program established in Orange County, CA, with the goals of reducing family dysfunction, teaching youth responsibility, and instilling self-esteem and self-confidence through family counseling sessions.

youth squad A team of police officers in a police department whose responsibility is to focus on particular delinquency problems and resolve them.

Youth-to-Victim Restitution Project A program operated by the juvenile court in Lincoln, NE, based on the principle that youths must repay whatever damages they inflicted on victims. Enforcement of restitution orders decreased recidivism among delinquent offenders.

Z

Zebra killings Murders that occurred in the San Francisco Bay area between 1972 and 1974, leaving 71 dead. The killings were traced to five African Americans, called the "Death Angels," who were members of Farrakhan's Nation of Islam. They killed whites, whom they did not consider human beings, to earn their way to heaven. Some were convicted, but not all were caught, and some have been released from prison. The murders were dubbed the Zebra killings because of the radio channel police used to investigate cases—Channel Z.

zero-based budgeting A method of accounting by various criminal-justice agencies and departments requiring them to justify all annual expenditures without relying on funding allocations from prior years. Each year's budgeting is based on projected organizational needs and proposed expenditures, including agency goals and objectives.

zero tolerance A policy whereby law enforcement officials do not tolerate any disorder, especially public order offenses such as vagrancy, disorderly conduct, or soliciting for prostitution;

a federal antidrug measure that permits the confiscation of planes, vessels, or vehicles found to be carrying a controlled substance, with no amount of drugs or illegal contraband allowable or acceptable.

zero-tolerance policy Mandating specific consequences or punishments for delinquent acts or crimes and not allowing anyone to avoid those consequences.

Zidovudine (AZT)/Didanosine Antiviral medication used for preemptive or early intervention treatment of AIDS.

Zionist Occupational Government (ZOG) A name used by extremist Anti-Semitic groups who believe that the U.S. government is controlled by Zionists.

zip gun A device or combination of devices that was not originally a firearm and is adapted to expel a projectile through a smooth-bore or rifled-bore barrel by using the energy generated by an explosion or burning substance.

Zodiac killer A serial killer who was never apprehended, presumed responsible for 40 deaths in Southern California and the San Francisco Bay area during the 1960s and 1970s.

zone of transition An area nearest a city center undergoing rapid social change. Such areas are believed to contain high rates of crime and delinquency. The term comes from Burgess and Park's concentric-zone theory. *See also* **Burgess, Ernest W.; Park, Robert Ezra.**

zone search A method of searching crime scenes in which the area to be searched is divided according to sectors, and each is carefully examined.

zoning Division of communities into different districts, where each district is governed according to statute. Different districts are established for either residential or business use.

zoophilia A strong attachment to animals in which sexual pleasure is derived through petting or stroking them.

zoosadism Deriving sexual pleasure from torturing or killing animals.

Zylon A fabric used in the body armor used by law enforcement officers to protect them from bullets during shooting incidents. Zylon is manufactured by Toyobo Co., Ltd., and Second Chance Body Armor Inc. ✦

U.S. SUPREME
COURT CASES

Reading Citations in Cases

Abbreviations

BIA	Board of Immigration
DEA	Drug Enforcement Administration
DUI	Driving Under the Influence (of alcohol or drugs)
DWI	Driving While Intoxicated
FBI	Federal Bureau of Investigation
INS	Immigration and Naturalization Service
IRS	Internal Revenue Service
LEA	Law enforcement agency
NAACP	National Association for the Advancement of Colored People
RICO	Racketeer Influenced and Corrupt Organizations
SC	U.S. Supreme Court
VIS	Victim impact statement

The United States Supreme Court cases listed in this section, as well as cases from United States district courts, circuit courts of appeal, and state courts, are cited by the names of persons involved in the cases as well as the volume numbers and page numbers where the cases can be found. A hypothetical citation might appear as follows:

Smith v. Jones, 358 U.S. 437, 112 S.Ct. 229 (1993).

Or a citation might appear as:

Smith v. Jones, 226 F.Supp. 1 (1992)

or

Smith v. Jones, 442 P.2d 433 (1989).

These "cites" are important to anyone interested in legal research or learning about what the law says and how it should be interpreted or applied. They specify particular sources or *reporters* in which these cases can be found. A reporter is a collection of books containing published opinions of different courts. In the cases discussed in this book, most are United States Supreme Court cases, but several are from state supreme courts. The first number in each citation above specifies a *volume number,* and the second number is a *page number* in the volume. In the hypothetical example above, *Smith v. Jones* is found in the 358th volume of the *United States Reports* on page 437. The same case can also be found in Volume 112 of the *Supreme Court Reporter* on page 229. Below are several rules or guidelines governing citations and information about what is contained them.

U.S. Supreme Court Opinions

All Supreme Court opinions and decisions are printed in various sources. The official source for all Supreme Court opinions is the *United States Reports,* abbreviated as *U.S.,* and it is published by the United States Government Printing Office. The Supreme Court convenes annually for a *term,* such as the 1995 term or the 1996 term, during which cases are heard and decided. All Supreme Court actions are recorded in the *United States Reports.* There is a substantial time lag between the time the Supreme Court delivers its opinions and when cases are published in the *United States Reports,* however. This lag time may be up to a year. Other sources distribute these opinions in a more timely fashion to interested lawyers and researchers.

Parallel Citations and Unofficial Sources

Unofficial sources also print Supreme Court opinions in bound volumes on an annual basis. These include West Publishing Company's *Supreme Court Reporter* and the Lawyer's Cooperative's *United States Supreme Court Reports, Lawyer's Edition.* The *Supreme Court Reporter* is abbreviated as *S.Ct.,* and the *United States Supreme Court Reports, Lawyer's Edition* is abbreviated as *L.Ed.* Within days following a particular ruling by the United States Supreme Court, unofficial versions of the entire text of Supreme Court opinions are published by West Publishing Company and the Lawyer's Cooperative. For instance, West Publishing Company distributes *advance sheets,* booklets published every two or three weeks that contain recent Supreme Court actions, to its subscribers. During any given Supreme Court term, as many as 24 booklets or advance sheets will be sent to subscribers.

Another source is *United States Law Week,* which is published by the Bureau of National Affairs, Inc., and the *United States Supreme Court Bulletin,* published by Commerce Clearing House, Inc. The *United States Law Week* is abbreviated as *U.S.L.W.* Its major strength is that the most recent opinions are made available within days following decisions.

Many scholars use *parallel citations* to indicate where any given case can be found. For instance, a case with typical parallel citations might be *Brewer v. Williams,* 430 U.S. 387, 97 S.Ct. 1232, 51 L.Ed.2d 424 (1977). According to the Harvard Law Review Association in Cambridge, MA, as well as Kunz et al., *The Process of Legal Research* (2000), it is proper to rely exclusively on the official reporter, which is the *United States Reports* in Supreme Court cases. Thus, we would only need to cite *Brewer v. Williams,* 430 U.S. 387 (1977) to comply with legal protocol. However, because of the time lag between Supreme Court opinions and the publication of the *United States Reports,* it is proper to cite the next most recently available unofficial source. This would involve a citation from the *Supreme Court Reporter* published by West. Thus, if we didn't know the *United States Reports* cite yet, but we knew the *Supreme Court Reporter* cite, we could cite as follows: *Brewer v. Williams,* ___U.S.___, 97 S.Ct. 1232 (1977). The blank spaces indicate that we do not yet know the volume or page number of *Brewer v. Williams* in the *United States Reports.* Later, when the *United States Reports* is published as the official version, we can supply the appropriate page numbers.

There are several hundred volumes of each of these reporters. Obviously, it would be very expensive for any college or university library to acquire each of these compendiums. Many libraries subscribe to the *United States Reports;* others receive the *Supreme Court Reporter.* Some might subscribe to the *United States Supreme Court Reports, Lawyer's Edition.* Large law school libraries have all of these volumes and more. However, many colleges and universities cannot afford to maintain all three versions, and as these are parallel citations and virtually identical opinions, it makes little sense for an average library to purchase three different compendiums of opinions that say the same thing. Scholars sometimes give three standard parallel citations whenever cases are cited. Thus, researchers can look up the same opinion in any one of these sources, depending on which version is maintained by their libraries.

Legal Citations in Introductory Criminal Justice or Criminology Textbooks

When students read introductory textbooks in criminology or criminal justice, it should not be considered unusual or confusing to see the *same* case in different books with *different* citations. For example, one criminology book may cite *Brewer v. Williams,* 97 S.Ct. 1232 (1977), whereas another will refer to *Brewer v. Williams,* 430 U.S. 387 (1977). Yet another book may use the Lawyer's Cooperative version and cite *Brewer v. Williams,* 51 L.Ed.2d 424 (1977). All of these citations are considered proper. When an author provides *all three* parallel citations, it may not be necessary, but it can be helpful to those with access to only particular sets of Supreme Court volumes.

The Meaning of 2d and 3d

When "2d" or "3d" follow a reporter, this does not indicate that a new edition of the source has been published. Rather, it means that the publishing company has "started over" with a fresh numbering system. For instance, *Brewer v. Williams,* 51 L.Ed.2d (1977), denotes that the case can be found in Volume 51 of the *United States Supreme Court Reports, Lawyer's Edition, Second Series.* There are no fixed rules governing when publishing companies commence new series for their volume renumbering.

Lower Federal Court and State Supreme Court Opinions

There are *no* official sources for reporting the opinions of lower *federal* courts, such as the different circuit courts of appeal or United States district courts. However, West Publishing Company publishes the *Federal Reporter,* abbreviated as F., or F.2d, in which various opinions can be found for the United States circuit courts of appeal. Not all of these opinions are published each year. The selection of opinions is at the discretion of the publisher, and often the decision to include or

not to include particular circuit court of appeals opinions is influenced by their constitutional relevance. Another source, also published by West, is the *Federal Supplement,* abbreviated as F.Supp. This source publishes selected opinions from United States district courts, United States customs courts, and the United States Court of International Trade.

Separate state supreme court reporters are published. Several publishing companies, including West, publish state supreme court opinions. The chart provided below shows which outlets publish which state supreme court opinions and the abbreviations used for such compilations.

The Inconsistency of U.S. Supreme Court Case Coverage

Is There Consistency to How the Supreme Court Reports Its Opinions? Yes, more or less. Each case contains a consistent citation format, a summary of what the Court decided, and names of justices concurring or dissenting. However, concerning the actual presentation of each case, there is as much variation as there are cases.

Does Each Supreme Court Case Have the Same Amount of Factual Detail? No. Most cases in this book have been summarized from original cases reported in the *Supreme Court Reporter.* Opinions written by the Supreme Court vary in length and complexity from one case to the next. Because all of these cases are appeals, summaries of original trial proceedings are not reproduced. Thus, there is considerable variation in the amount of detail provided. With many exceptions, reported cases contain a *syllabus,* or synopsis, of the facts leading to the appeal. Some cases have extensive and informative syllabi, whereas others offer scant information.

Is the Criminal Justice Significance of a Case Outlined by the United States Supreme Court? No. The Supreme Court does not articulate the significance of each case for criminal justice. This chore is left for those who read and interpret these cases. Very often, the cases deal with a single question or issue.

Can Different Scholars Make Different Interpretations of the Same Case? Yes. It is entirely possible for two or more people reading a given case to have different opinions about the case and its significance. The decision rendered by the Supreme Court is only about the single question addressed, and the Court does not elaborate to say why a particular case is significant. The Court decides and interprets impartially and confines itself to the facts. The Court is supposedly devoid of emotion when rendering its opinions, although scholars cite ample instances of emotionally written opinions by various justices about different constitutional issues.

A good example of how individuals interpret the same case differently is as follows. It is popularly assumed that in the case of *Furman v. Georgia* (1972), the Supreme Court declared the death penalty in Georgia to be "cruel and unusual" punishment, and thus unconstitutional. This is not entirely true. Actually, the Court declared that the death penalty *as it was then being administered in Georgia* constituted cruel and unusual punishment, because it was applied in a racially discrimi-

Reporter	States Included
Atlantic Reporter (A. or A.2d)	Connecticut, Delaware, Maine, Maryland, New Hampshire, New Jersey, Pennsylvania, Rhode Island, Vermont, and District of Columbia
Northeastern Reporter (N.E. or N.E.2d)	Illinois, Indiana, Massachusetts, New York, and Ohio
Northwestern Reporter (N.W. or N.W.2d)	Iowa, Michigan, Minnesota, Nebraska, North Dakota, South Dakota, and Wisconsin
Pacific Reporter (P. or P.2d)	Alaska, Arizona, California, Colorado, Hawaii, Idaho, Kansas, Montana, Nevada, New Mexico, Oklahoma, Oregon, Utah, Washington, and Wyoming
Southeastern Reporter (S.E. or S.E.2d)	Georgia, North Carolina, South Carolina, Virginia, and West Virginia
Southwestern Reporter (S.W. or S.W.2d)	Arkansas, Kentucky, Missouri, Tennessee, Texas, and Indian Territories
Southern Reporter (So. or So.2d)	Alabama, Florida, Louisiana, and Mississippi

natory manner. Besides Georgia, all other states with death penalties suspended them until their legislatures could closely examine the procedures leading to death sentences. These investigations were intended to determine whether their particular death penalty provisions were racially discriminatory. California commuted all death sentences at the time to life imprisonment. Charles Manson was one California inmate spared the death penalty, largely because of the *Furman* decision (see below). The fact is that no other state wanted to be criticized by the Supreme Court as Georgia had been. Quite simply, the Supreme Court found something wrong with the way the death penalty was being applied in Georgia. All other states with death penalties wished to comply with whatever the Court believed to be a constitutional application of the death penalty.

A solution to this problem was found in 1976, again in Georgia, when the Court decided the case of *Gregg v. Georgia,* wherein new procedures for death sentences were implemented. The Court declared that the new procedures enacted by the Georgia legislature did not violate constitutional rights. Specifically, the *Gregg* case established a two-stage trial proceeding in which guilt or innocence would be established in the first phase and the punishment would be decided in the second phase. In the second phase, specific aggravating and mitigating factors would be considered and weighed. If the number of aggravating circumstances were greater than the number of mitigating circumstances, then the jury would recommend the death penalty. If the number of mitigating circumstances were equal to or greater than the number of aggravating ones, then the jury would recommend life imprisonment. This new procedure was approved by the Supreme Court, in part because it removed race as a consideration in whether the death penalty should be imposed.

Therefore, the United States Supreme Court did *not* say in *Furman v. Georgia,* "the death penalty is hereby unconstitutional and abolished." Further, the Court did *not* say in *Gregg*

v. Georgia, "The death penalty is hereby constitutional and can be used." The death penalty has *never* been abolished by the United States Supreme Court, despite the many different and conflicting interpretations scholars have attributed to the *Furman* decision. The question decided by the United States Supreme Court at the time was again a very narrow one: Is the application of the death penalty in Georgia constitutional? Yes or no? If yes, why? If no, why not?

Does the Supreme Court Reverse Itself Often in Deciding Cases? No. Only rarely does the Court rule an opinion rendered by an earlier Court as wrong. Usually the Court modifies, shapes, and focuses opinions by earlier Courts. One area undergoing continual modification and refinement is the Fourth Amendment provision against unreasonable searches and seizures. The Court is always considering different "search and seizure" scenarios that are considered "unreasonable" by appellants. All convicted offenders sentenced to death automatically become appellants, as all death penalties are appealed.

A good example of how the Supreme Court does not reverse itself, particularly on a sensitive issue, is the case of *Plessy v. Ferguson* (1896). In 1896, the Court decided that a black man's (Plessy's) rights were not violated in Louisiana when he was denied entry to a railroad dining car designated for whites only. The Court said then that as long as "separate but equal" facilities were provided for blacks as well as for whites (the railroad company provided all-black dining cars as well as all-white), blacks could not claim that their Fourteenth Amendment rights were being violated under the "equal-protection" clause.

Later, in 1954, the Court decided the case of *Brown v. Board of Education,* in which the issue was that black children were denied admission to all-white schools in violation of their Fourteenth Amendment equal-protection clause rights because "separate but equal" educational facilities were provided for black children. In a landmark decision, the Court ruled that the "separate but equal" doctrine *does not apply to schools.*

The Court did *not* say that the concept or doctrine of "separate but equal" was unconstitutional, just that it did not apply to schools. Later, the Court declared that the "separate but equal" doctrine did not apply to many other areas, such as public transportation, drinking fountains, and housing.

Interestingly, the "separate but equal" doctrine, inherently discriminatory, has *never* been reversed by the Court. No subsequent Court has proclaimed that the 1896 Court was wrong and that the "separate but equal" doctrine was unconstitutional. Rather, later Courts have stated that the "separate but equal" doctrine does not apply to this or that situation. Such is the narrowness of opinions delivered by the Court.

What About Cases Decided by State Supreme Courts? Some of the cases in this compilation are *state* supreme court cases. Whenever there is no United States Supreme Court case law to cite, the next best source is a state supreme court decision. Although the decisions of state supreme courts are not binding on other states, these decisions provide other state jurisdictions with guidance whenever similar issues are addressed by appellants. ◆

A

Abel v. United States, 362 U.S. 217, 80 S.Ct. 683 (1960) [Rudolf Ivonovich ABEL, also known as "Mark" and also known as Martin Collins and Emil R. Goldfus, Petitioner, v. UNITED STATES of America] (Fourth Amendment; Informants; Law Enforcement Officers or Agencies; Searches and Seizures; Searches Incident to an Arrest) Abel was a foreign national living in a New York hotel and suspected of espionage. Reliable informants gave FBI and INS agents sufficient information to incriminate him. INS agents obtained an administrative deportation warrant seeking to deport him as an undocumented or unregistered alien. They went to Abel's hotel with their warrant, seeking first to obtain his cooperation regarding his espionage activities. FBI agents accompanied INS agents but without a search or arrest warrant. When INS agents entered Abel's apartment, they placed him under arrest and proceeded to search the premises. The search, with FBI agents acting only as "observers," yielded a false birth certificate and other forged identities used by Abel in his espionage activities. This evidence was subsequently turned over to the United States Attorney for investigation and prosecution. Abel was subsequently convicted. He appealed, alleging that the items seized should have been suppressed because the FBI had not obtained a valid search warrant. The SC upheld Abel's conviction, contending that the INS had every right to search his premises following reliable evidence of his culpability as an unregistered alien and spy. The INS justified the search based on the administrative deportation warrant. As the evidence was obtained by INS agents during the lawful discharge of their responsibilities, it was not subject to suppression.

Adams v. Texas, 448 U.S. 38, 100 S.Ct. 2521 (1969) [Randall Dale ADAMS, Petitioner, v. State of TEXAS] (Aggravating and Mitigating Circumstances; Death Penalty) Adams was charged in Texas with killing a police officer. He maintained his innocence, but he was prosecuted and found guilty in a two-stage jury trial. The second phase of the trial led to the jury considering whether (1) Adams' act was deliberate, (2) his conduct in the future would cause a continuing threat to society, and (3) his conduct in the killing of the victim was unreasonable, given the victim's provocation, if any. If the jurors responded yes to all three questions, then the death penalty would be imposed. In this case, they did respond yes to all questions, and Adams was sentenced to death. He sought to have his conviction overturned because certain jurors had been excluded from his jury when they expressed opposition to the death penalty and their belief that their opposition might impair their judgment when deciding his case. The SC upheld Adams' murder conviction. (Years later, exculpatory circumstances concerning Adams' involvement in the murder were discovered. In 1989, his conviction was overturned, and he was released from the Texas Department of Corrections.)

Adams v. Williams, 407 U.S. 143, 92 S.Ct. 1921 (1972) [Frederick E. ADAMS, Warden, Petitioner, v. Robert WILLIAMS] (Fourth Amendment; Law Enforcement Officers or Agencies; Plain-View Rule; Search and Seizure; Searches Incident to an Arrest; Stop and Frisk) An informant known to a police officer told the officer that Williams, who was seated in his car, was carrying narcotics and, further, had a gun in his waistband. The officer approached the car and asked Williams to roll down his window. After Williams complied, the officer saw the gun in plain view, where the informant had said it would be. He therefore made an arrest, which then led to a "search incident to an arrest," in which he discovered heroin and other weapons in Williams' possession. Williams was convicted. He appealed on the grounds that the officer had not seen him do anything wrong and so should not have arrested him. Police officers may not have sufficient *probable cause* to arrest a defendant, but they must have *reasonable cause* to stop and frisk suspects for an officer's safety. Stop and frisk procedures need not be based on an officer's personal observation but on information supplied by another person. Because the officer was acting on information given by someone known to him, the SC upheld the conviction. The significance of the case is that officers do not always have to observe illegal conduct before making an arrest. Rather, informants who have been reliable in the past may justify an officer's investigation of suspicious suspects.

Adamson v. California, 332 U.S. 46, 67 S.Ct. 1672 (1947) [Admiral Dewey ADAMSON v. People of State of CALIFORNIA] (Corrections; Death Penalty; Fourteenth Amendment) Adamson was charged with murder in California. During his trial, he elected not to testify in his own defense, inasmuch as to do so would open the door for the prosecutor to question him about his past criminal record. Nevertheless, his refusal either to explain or deny the accusations against him was commented on by the judge and considered by the jury, who convicted him. He was sentenced to death. Adamson appealed to the SC, contending that this California court provision was unconstitutional under the Fourteenth Amendment. The SC upheld Adamson's death sentence and declared that the California provision was *not* unconstitutional.

Addington v. Texas, 441 U.S. 418, 99 S.Ct. 1804 (1979) [Frank O'Neal ADDINGTON, Appellant, v. State of TEXAS] (Mental Capacity) Addington's mother filed a petition in civil court for Addington's indefinite commitment to a mental institution. The state trial court determined that, based on *clear and convincing evidence,* Addington was mentally ill and should be indefinitely confined. Addington appealed, arguing that the *beyond-a-reasonable-doubt* standard should have been used to determine whether he was mentally ill and whether he should be indefinitely committed. The SC set aside Addington's commitment, holding that although the beyond-a-reasonable-doubt standard is not required in a civil proceeding, proof *stronger than preponderance of the evidence* is required. For this reason, the SC held that a standard stronger than preponderance of the evidence but less than beyond a reasonable doubt should govern whether juries may indefinitely commit individuals accused of being mentally ill.

Adickes v. S.H. Kress and Company, 398 U.S. 144, 90 S.Ct. 1598 (1970) [Sandra ADICKES, Petitioner, v. S.H. KRESS AND COMPANY] (Civil Rights, Section 1983

Claims) A white schoolteacher, Adickes, accompanied several black people to a Kress store in Hattiesburg, MS, to have lunch. Kress employees refused to serve Adickes because she was in the company of black people. She became belligerent, left the store, and was subsequently arrested for vagrancy by Hattiesburg police, who were alleged to be in a conspiracy with a Kress manager. The court found for Kress, denying a petition filed subsequently by Adickes wherein she alleged racial discrimination. Subsequently, however, the SC overturned the summary judgment and ordered a new trial for Adickes, in which she would have the opportunity to show that (1) a state-enforced custom of segregating the races in public eating places existed at the time of the incident, and (2) Kress was motivated to refuse her service as the result of that state-enforced custom. The SC declared that if such circumstances were found, then Kress would be in violation of Adickes' civil rights under Title 42 U.S.C. Section 1983.

Aguilar v. Texas, 378 U.S. 108, 84 S.Ct. 1509 (1964) [Nick Alford AGUILAR, Petitioner, v. State of TEXAS] **(Fourteenth Amendment; Fourth Amendment; Informants; Law Enforcement Officers or Agencies; Searches and Seizures)** On the basis of an informant's information, police in Texas obtained a search warrant to search the home of Aguilar for possible heroin, marijuana, and other narcotics. The police searched Aguilar's home and found large quantities of narcotics. After Aguilar was convicted, he appealed, contending that there was no probable cause on which a valid search warrant could be issued. The SC overturned Aguilar's conviction, saying that whenever information supplied by an informant is used as the basis for a search warrant, some information must be provided to the issuing magistrate that supports the credibility and reliability of the informant. That is, in what capacity do officers know the informant, and has the informant provided reliable information in the past? This, in short, is the *two-pronged test of informant reliability.* Thus, the SC established that the standard for obtaining a search warrant by state officers is the same as applies under the Fourth and Fourteenth Amendments; a search warrant may be defective when it does not specify any factual basis for the magistrate to form a decision regarding issuance; officers need to outline the factual basis for the search. This test of informant reliability as the basis for a valid search warrant was effectively rejected in the case of *Illinois v. Gates* (1983), which opened the door to a totality-of-circumstances test where the identity of the informant was unknown to police.

Ake v. Oklahoma, 470 U.S. 68, 105 S.Ct. 1087 (1985) [Glen Burton AKE, Petitioner, v. OKLAHOMA] **(Aggravating and Mitigating Circumstances; Death Penalty; Indigent Clients; Sentencing)** Ake was charged with two counts of first-degree murder. He declared that he was indigent, and counsel was appointed for him. He also requested the assistance of a competent psychiatrist to determine whether he was sane. Ake's defense was that he was insane, and thus it would be the state's obligation to furnish him with a psychiatrist to examine him and make a determination. A psychiatrist did so and found Ake to be incompetent to stand trial. He was confined in a mental hospital for a period of time. After six weeks

of treatment, he was found to be competent to stand trial. His attorney asked for another psychiatric evaluation, independent of the state-provided one, but the judge denied this request, claiming that the expense was prohibitive. Ake was convicted. No testimony was given by psychiatrists during the sentencing phase of his trial. The death penalty was imposed when the state psychiatrist indicated that Ake's future dangerousness warranted it. Ake appealed. The SC reversed his conviction, holding that when a defendant has made a preliminary showing that his sanity at the time of the offense is likely to be a significant factor, the state must provide access to a psychiatrist's assistance on this issue if the defendant cannot otherwise afford one.

Alabama v. Bozeman, 533 U.S. 146, 121 S.Ct. 2079 (2001) [ALABAMA, Petitioner, v. Michael Herman BOZEMAN] **(Detainer Warrants)** Bozeman was a federal prisoner serving a sentence in Florida and who had been transferred to the custody of Alabama authorities for a single day to be arraigned on state firearms charges. After spending the evening in Covington County, AL, Bozeman was transferred back to the Florida federal prison. About a month later, he was brought back to Covington County for trial. Bozeman's counsel sought to dismiss the Alabama charges because of a provision of an Interstate Agreement on Detainers (IAD). The IAD creates uniform procedures for lodging and executing a detainer, i.e., a legal order requiring a state to hold a currently imprisoned individual when he or she has finished serving his or her sentence so that he or she may be tried in another state for another crime. The IAD further provides that a state that obtains a prisoner for purposes of trial must try him or her within 120 days of arrival, and if it returns him or her to his or her "original place of confinement" prior to that trial, charges "shall" be dismissed with prejudice. The trial judge rejected the defense's motion to dismiss the charges and Bozeman was convicted. He appealed to the Alabama Supreme Court, which overturned his conviction, citing the IAD provision to support its decision. Alabama prosecutors appealed to the SC, who heard the case. The SC affirmed the Alabama Supreme Court and upheld the dismissal of the state charges against Bozeman. The SC said that the language of the IAD clearly bars any further criminal proceedings when a defendant is returned to the original place of imprisonment before a trial.

Alabama v. Shelton, ___U.S.___, 122 S.Ct. 1764 (2002) [ALABAMA, Petitioner, v. LeReed SHELTON] **(Probation and Parole; Sixth Amendment)** Shelton represented himself in an Alabama criminal court on one count of misdemeanor assault. At no time was Shelton advised of his right to counsel, nor was he offered counsel for his defense because he was indigent. He was convicted of the charge and sentenced to a 30-day jail sentence, which was suspended. The judge ordered Shelton placed on two years' unsupervised probation. The case was appealed to the Alabama Supreme Court, which reversed the trial court, holding that provision of counsel must be made in any petty offense, misdemeanor, or felony prosecution. The Alabama Supreme Court further declared that because Shelton could not be imprisoned absent provision of counsel, his suspended sentence could never be activated and was therefore invalid. The state appealed to the SC, which affirmed the Alabama Supreme Court. The SC declared that the controlling rule is that absent a knowing and intelligent waiver, no person may be imprisoned for any offense unless he or she was represented by counsel. A suspended sentence that may end up in the actual deprivation of a person's liberty may not be imposed unless the defendant was accorded the guiding hand of counsel in the prosecution for the crime charged. The controlling rule is that absent a knowing and intelligent waiver, no person may be imprisoned for any offense unless he or she was represented by counsel at trial. Applying this actual imprisonment rule, the SC rejected the argument that failure to appoint counsel to an indigent defendant does not bar the imposition of a suspended or probationary sentence upon conviction of a misdemeanor, even though the defendant might be incarcerated in the event probation is revoked. The Sixth Amendment does not permit activation of a suspended sentence upon an indigent defendant's violation of the terms of his or her probation where the State does not provide him or her with counsel during the prosecution of the offense for which he or she is imprisoned. A suspended sentence is a prison term imposed for the offense of conviction. Once the prison term is triggered, the defendant is incarcerated not for the probation violation, but for the underlying offense. The uncounseled conviction at that point results in imprisonment; it ends up in the actual deprivation of a person's liberty. This is precisely what the Sixth Amendment does not allow. A defendant who receives a suspended or probated sentence to imprisonment has a constitutional right to counsel.

Alabama v. Smith, 490 U.S. 794, 109 S.Ct. 2201 (1989) [ALABAMA, Petitioner, v. James Lewis SMITH] (**Plea Bargaining**) A grand jury indicted Smith for burglary, rape, sodomy, and assault. He entered a guilty plea in exchange for a 30-year sentence and the dropping of the sodomy charge. He was convicted of first-degree burglary and rape. The judge sentenced Smith to concurrent terms of 30 years in prison on each of the other charges. Later, Smith was successful in having his guilty plea vacated and a trial was held on the three original charges. The jury found him guilty on all counts, and this time the judge sentenced him to life imprisonment for the burglary and sodomy convictions and to a 150-year term for the rape conviction. The judge explained the different sentence this time because he had not previously been fully aware of the circumstances under which these terrible crimes had occurred. Smith appealed, alleging the sentence was vindictive. The SC rejected Smith's claim that the new sentence was vindictive, as it could not be demonstrated that the judge deliberately enhanced these sentences because of the previous vacating of Smith's earlier guilty plea. The SC also stressed that in cases that go to trial, greater and more detailed information is available to sentencing judges compared with the information received as a part of a plea-bargain agreement.

Alabama v. White, 496 U.S. 325, 110 S.Ct. 2412 (1990) [ALABAMA, Petitioner, v. Vanessa Rose WHITE] (**Law Enforcement Officers or Agencies; Stop and Frisk**) An anonymous tipster told police that a woman, White, would be leaving her apartment at a particular time with a brown briefcase

containing cocaine and that she would get in a particular type of car and drive to a particular motel. Watching her apartment, police saw White emerge and enter the described vehicle. They followed her to the motel and stopped her car. They advised her that she was suspected of carrying cocaine. At their request, she permitted them to search her vehicle, where they discovered the described briefcase. They asked her to open it, whereupon they found some marijuana and arrested her. A search of her purse incident to her arrest disclosed a quantity of cocaine. She was charged and convicted of possessing illegal substances. She appealed, arguing that the police lacked *reasonable suspicion* to stop her initially and therefore the discovered drugs were inadmissible as evidence against her. The SC disagreed, holding that the anonymous tip and the totality of circumstances of subsequent police surveillance more than satisfied the less demanding standard of reasonable suspicion contrasted with the more demanding standard of *probable cause.* (*See especially **Illinois v. Gates** [1983] for a more extensive discussion of anonymous informants and the totality of circumstances justifying police stops and searches of suspicious persons and their effects.*)

Alderman v. United States, 394 U.S. 165, 89 S.Ct. 961 (1969) [Willie Israel ALDERMAN et al., Petitioners, v. UNITED STATES. Igor A. Ivanov, Petitioner, v. United States. John William Butenko, Petitioner, v. United States] (**Electronic Surveillance, Wiretapping; Searches and Seizures**) Government officials had obtained information through unauthorized wiretaps of offices where Alderman did business. Alderman himself was not a party to the conversations, in which others conspired to transmit murderous threats in interstate commerce, but because he owned the premises, he as well as the others was considered culpable. He sought to overturn his conviction, alleging that the information used against him had been obtained illegally, through unauthorized wiretaps without probable cause. The SC overturned Alderman's conviction, concluding that it had resulted from an illegal wiretap and surveillance. Furthermore, no evidence existed to show that Alderman actually participated in these illegally obtained conversations. Any surveillance records illegally obtained by the government, said the SC, should be turned over to the petitioners before being presented to a trial judge.

Alexander v. Louisiana, 405 U.S. 625, 92 S.Ct. 1221 (1972) [Claude ALEXANDER, Petitioner, v. State of LOUISIANA] (**Discrimination; Grand Juries; Indictments**) Alexander, a black man, was convicted of rape and sentenced to life imprisonment. He had been indicted by a grand jury consisting of men, mostly white, women having been excluded. The SC heard the case. Electing not to decide the key constitutional issue of whether the grand jury was discriminatory by excluding black jurors, and noting that Alexander's conviction was set aside on other grounds, the SC said that it was up to the state to decide whether Alexander should be retried, whether a *properly constituted grand jury* would return a new indictment, and whether Alexander might be convicted again.

Alexander v. United Sates, 509 U.S. 544, 113 S.Ct. 2766 (1993) [Ferris J. ALEXANDER, Sr., Petitioner, v. UNITED STATES] (**Asset Forfeiture; Cruel and Unusual Punish-**

ment; Eighth Amendment; Fines; Obscenity Laws) Alexander ran a store selling sexually explicit materials. He was charged with tax and obscenity offenses and violating the RICO statute governing racketeer influenced and corrupt organization activities. He was subsequently convicted and his assets were seized. He appealed, arguing that the seizure of his assets was unusually severe, in violation of the Eighth Amendment right against cruel and unusual punishments and "excessive fines." The SC reversed his conviction, saying that the appellate court should have considered whether the asset forfeiture in his case was "excessive." The significance of this case is that convicted offenders who have their assets seized can appeal the severity of their sentences under the excessive-fines provision of the Eighth Amendment.

Allen v. Illinois, 478 U.S. 364, 106 S.Ct. 2988 (1986) [**Terry B. ALLEN, Petitioner, v. ILLINOIS**] (**Fifth Amendment; Self-Incrimination**) Allen was charged with committing crimes of unlawful restraint and deviant sexual assault. The state filed a petition to have him declared a sexually dangerous person within the meaning of the Illinois Sexually Dangerous Persons Act, and the court ordered a compulsory psychiatric examination. When two examining psychiatrists testified later about Allen's sexual propensities, on the basis of information he disclosed to them, Allen sought to suppress this testimony, claiming it violated his Fifth Amendment right against self-incrimination. The court allowed the psychiatric testimony, and Allen himself did not testify. He was found to be "sexually dangerous" by the trial court and appealed on Fifth Amendment grounds. The SC heard his case and upheld the trial finding, holding that proceedings under the Illinois Sexually Dangerous Persons Act are not "criminal" within the meaning of the Fifth Amendment's guarantee against compulsory self-incrimination. Thus, the Fifth Amendment attaches only in criminal proceedings, not civil ones.

Allen v. Wright, 468 U.S. 737, 104 S.Ct. 3315 (1984) [**W. Wayne ALLEN, Petitioner, v. Inez WRIGHT, etc., et al. Donald T. Regan, Secretary of the Treasury, et al., Petitioner, v. Inez Wright, et al.**] (**Discrimination**) Allen and other parents of black children attending private schools under court order brought a class-action suit against those schools to remove racially discriminatory policies and procedures. They alleged that their children had not been receiving quality instruction from certain public schools because the IRS had failed to apply standards to, and remove tax exempt status from, private institutions with discriminatory policies that indirectly hinder black children in public schools. In hearing this class action suit, the SC held that the parents had *no standing* in suits against private schools filed on behalf of public schools.

Almeida-Sanchez v. United States, 413 U.S. 266, 93 S.Ct. 2535 (1973) [**Condrado ALMEIDA-SANCHEZ, Petitioner, v. UNITED STATES**] (**Border Searches; Fourth Amendment; Law Enforcement Officers or Agencies; Searches and Seizures**) Almeida-Sanchez, a Mexican citizen with a valid work permit, was driving 25 miles from the Mexican border. Border Patrol officers stopped his car without probable cause or consent, not even "reasonable suspicion," discovered mari-

juana, and charged him with possession of a controlled substance. He was subsequently convicted. When he appealed, the SC overturned his conviction, holding that the Border Patrol had not been conducting a "border search" because the highway he was traversing ran east–west, not north–south, and did not approach Mexico. Almeida-Sanchez's right against unreasonable searches and seizures had been violated when these officers, without warrant, probable cause, or even "reasonable suspicion," stopped his automobile for no reason and searched it extensively. The fact that marijuana was discovered did not justify this warrantless and groundless search.

Amos v. United States, 255 U.S. 313, 41 S.Ct. 266 (1921) [**Lawrence AMOS v. UNITED STATES**] (**Consent Searches; Fourth Amendment; Law Enforcement Officers or Agencies**) Amos, a suspected bootlegger of illegal whiskey, was under surveillance by local authorities. One day these "deputy collectors of internal revenue" went to his home without an arrest or search warrant. Amos was not there, but his wife admitted them after they advised her that they were there to "search for violations of the revenue law." They found some bottled whiskey, evidence that was used to bring Amos to trial. A jury was selected, but before the case actually started, Amos petitioned the court for the "return of illegally seized property," namely his whiskey. The court denied the motion and Amos was convicted. The SC heard Amos' appeal and reversed the conviction. The officers admitted that they had gone to Amos' home without an arrest or search warrant. The SC said that the officers were not entitled to continue with their search, despite the wife's permitting them to enter. The wife could not waive her husband's constitutional right against an unreasonable search and seizure, particularly since the search was conducted under "implied coercion."

Andresen v. Maryland, 427 U.S. 463, 96 S.Ct. 2737 (1976) [**Peter C. ANDRESEN, Petitioner, v. State of MARYLAND**] (**Fifth Amendment; Fourth Amendment; Law Enforcement Officers or Agencies; Searches Incident to an Arrest; Self-Incrimination**) Andresen, a settlement attorney in Maryland who represented certain real estate interests, knowingly sold property to another individual where the title to the property was not clear because of two outstanding property liens. Investigating authorities asked for warrants to search Andresen's business premises, looking particularly for documents pertaining to "Lot 13T," the lot allegedly sold without clear title. Interviews with the purchaser and mortgage holder had been used as the basis for probable cause to obtain the search warrants. Andresen and his attorney were present at his office when the authorities conducted their search and seized the relevant documents. Andresen was tried and convicted of fraudulent misappropriation of funds. He appealed his conviction, alleging among other things that the search warrants were vague and that his presence constituted a form of self-incrimination, in violation of his Fifth Amendment rights. The SC upheld his conviction, holding the warrants to be proper. It ruled that statements voluntarily committed to writing by Andresen could be used against him. He was not compelled to say anything to officers while they conducted their search; thus his Fifth Amendment right was preserved.

Apodaca v. Oregon, 406 U.S. 404, 92 S.Ct. 1628 (1972) [Robert APODACA et al., Petitioners, v. OREGON] (Fourteenth Amendment; Juries; Jury Voting; Sixth Amendment) Apodaca and others were found guilty of various serious crimes by less than unanimous jury verdicts. Oregon has a statute mandating a conviction or acquittal on the basis of a 10-to-2 vote, or what is referred to by the Oregon Legislature as a 10-of-12 vote. In Apodaca's case, the vote favoring conviction was 11 to 1. Apodaca challenged this vote as not being unanimous, and the SC heard the case contemporaneously with the case of *Johnson v. Louisiana* (1972) on an identical issue. In Apodaca's case, the SC upheld the constitutionality of the Oregon jury voting provision, declaring that votes of these kinds do not violate one's right to due process under either the Sixth or the Fourteenth Amendment. The significance of this case is that less than unanimous jury votes among the states are constitutional and do not violate one's right to due process.

Apprendi v. New Jersey, 530 U.S. 466, 120 S.Ct. 2348 (2000) [Charles C. APPRENDI, Jr., Petitioner, v. NEW JERSEY] (Sentence Enhancements; Sentencing; Hate Crimes) Apprendi fired several shots into the New Jersey home of an African-American family and made a statement that he didn't want the family in his neighborhood because of their race. Under New Jersey law, Apprendi was charged with second-degree possession of a firearm for an unlawful purpose, which carries a prison term of from five to 10 years. New Jersey also has an enhanced-sentence statute that applies to cases designated as hate crimes. Under this statute, sentences may be enhanced if the trial judge finds, by a preponderance of evidence, that the defendant committed the crime with a purpose to intimidate a person or group because of their race. In a later trial, Apprendi was convicted of the firearm possession charge, and the judge found that the shooting was racially motivated. For this reason, he enhanced Apprendi's sentence and sentenced Apprendi to 12 years. Apprendi appealed, contending that the enhanced sentence violated his due-process rights. The SC heard the case and reversed the trial court, setting aside the enhanced sentence. The SC held that the question of whether Apprendi committed the crime with a purpose to intimidate others according to their race was an issue to be determined by the jury on the basis of the beyond-a-reasonable-doubt standard. Because the judge made this determination on his own and never submitted this additional factual information to the jury for their consideration, this violated Apprendi's Fourteenth Amendment right to due process. By using the "hate crime" element as a basis for a sentence enhancement, the judge created an additional element of the offense that had to be proved in court by the prosecution beyond a reasonable doubt. The Fourteenth Amendment right to due process and the Sixth Amendment right to a trial by jury, taken together, entitle a criminal defendant to a jury determination that he or she is guilty of every element of the crime with which he or she is charged, beyond a reasonable doubt. The judge's role in sentencing is constrained at its outer limits by facts alleged in indictment and found by jury. (*See also Ring v. Arizona* [2002].)

Arave v. Creech, 507 U.S. 463, 113 S.Ct. 1534 (1993) [A.J. ARAVE, Warden, Petitioner, v. Thomas E. CREECH] (Aggravating and Mitigating Circumstances; Death Penalty; *Habeas Corpus* Petitions) Creech, confined in the Idaho Penitentiary, was convicted of the murder of another inmate. At his trial, the judge sentenced him to death, basing his decision, in part, on aggravating circumstances. He used the phrases "utter disregard" and "the cold-blooded pitiless slayer." Creech appealed the sentence, contending that the phrase "utter disregard" was invalid. The SC upheld Creech's conviction, holding that the phrase "utter disregard" did not violate any constitutional provisions.

Argersinger v. Hamlin, 407 U.S. 25, 92 S.Ct. 2006 (1972) [Jon Richard ARGERSINGER, Petitioner, v. Raymond HAMLIN, Sheriff, Leon County, Florida] (Indigent Clients; Right to Counsel) Argersinger was an indigent charged with carrying a concealed weapon. In Florida, this crime is a misdemeanor punishable by imprisonment of up to six months and a $1,000 fine. Argersinger was not allowed to have court appointed counsel, as required for a *felony,* because his crime was not a felony (*see Gideon v. Wainwright* [1963]). He was convicted of the misdemeanor and sentenced to 90 days in jail. He appealed, and the SC overturned his misdemeanor conviction. The SC said that any indigent defendant is entitled to counsel for *any* offense involving imprisonment, regardless of the shortness of the length of incarceration. Thus it extended the *Gideon* decision to include misdemeanor offenses, holding that no sentence involving the loss of liberty (incarceration) can be imposed where there has been a denial of counsel; defendants have a right to counsel when imprisonment might result.

Arizona v. Evans, 514 U.S. 1, 115 S.Ct. 1185 (1995) [ARIZONA, Petitioner, v. Isaac EVANS] (Exclusionary Rule; Fourth Amendment; Good-Faith Exception; Law Enforcement Officers or Agencies) Evans was arrested by Phoenix police during a routine traffic stop when it was discovered there was an outstanding arrest warrant against him. In the search incident to his arrest, police found marijuana in his trunk and charged him with marijuana possession. He was convicted. Later, it was determined that computer errors had implicated him wrongly by associating an outstanding arrest warrant for another person with a similar name. Thus, police officers had arrested the wrong man and had searched the wrong man's automobile trunk. Evans sought to have his conviction overturned, because, he said, his Fourth Amendment right against an unreasonable search and seizure had been violated. After various appeals to the state court and an appeal to the Ninth Circuit Court of Appeals, Evans' conviction was overturned. The government appealed to the SC, which reinstated Evans' original conviction, saying simply that the "good-faith" exception to the exclusionary rule was in effect, inasmuch as arresting officers had been acting appropriately and not engaging in misconduct. The police had had no knowledge of computer errors. The significance of this case is that even if an arrest is later found to be illegal or unsubstantiated by the facts, such as computer errors, if police, acting in "good faith," discover contraband or controlled substances incident to their arrest of the wrong person, the evidence they discover may be admissible against the suspect later in court. The primary function of the exclusionary rule is to guard against police misconduct. In this case, there was no police misconduct, only clerical error unattributable to police.

Arizona v. Fulminante, 499 U.S. 279, 111 S.Ct. 1246 (1991) [ARIZONA, Petitioner, v. Oreste C. FULMINANTE] (Confessions; Informants; Law Enforcement Officers or Agencies) Fulminante was suspected of killing his daughter. Insufficient evidence existed to charge him, and he left the state of Arizona and traveled to New Jersey, where he was arrested and convicted for another crime. In prison, his cellmate, Sarivola, advised Fulminante that other inmates had heard that Fulminante was a "child murderer," and thus, his life was in jeopardy. Sarivola offered him protection in exchange for his confession to the murder of Fulminante's daughter. Fulminante confessed to Sarivola and later to Sarivola's wife. Later, he was charged in Arizona with the murder of his daughter, and the Sarivolas, who were also government informants, testified against him. Fulminante was convicted. He appealed on the ground that his confession had been coerced, because Sarivola had implied a threat. The SC overturned his conviction on the basis of this argument. It ordered a new trial without the use of the confessions he had given to the Sarivolas. The SC stressed that the "harmless error" doctrine exists to govern involuntary confessions. However, the government had failed to show harmless error beyond a reasonable doubt. The trial judge had erred by permitting a coerced confession to be used against Fulminante. The judge's error would not have resulted in a reversal of a conviction, but it must be judged as harmless by using the beyond-a-reasonable-doubt standard.

Arizona v. Hicks, 480 U.S. 321, 107 S.Ct. 1149 (1987) [ARIZONA, Petitioner, v. James Thomas HICKS] (Fourth Amendment; Law Enforcement Officers or Agencies; Open-Fields Doctrine; Plain-View Rule; Searches and Seizures; Searches Incident to an Arrest) One evening, persons in an apartment reported that someone from an above apartment had fired a bullet through their ceiling, injuring one of the lower apartment's occupants. Police investigated the upstairs apartment, rented by Hicks. While investigating, they discovered weapons and a stocking-cap mask. Also, they noted that the apartment was run-down but new stereo equipment stood in plain view. They wrote down serial numbers of the stereo equipment. In order to see the serial numbers, however, they had to move the equipment. Later, when compared with another crime report, these stereo items were found to have been stolen. A search warrant was obtained for Hicks' apartment. Hicks was arrested, charged with robbery, and convicted. He sought to suppress the evidence against him, alleging that his Fourth Amendment rights had been violated. The SC overturned Hicks' conviction, saying that in order for police officers to invoke the plain-view rule regarding the stereo equipment, they required probable cause to believe the equipment was stolen. Because the police used reasonable suspicion when moving the equipment, their act became a search requiring a

proper warrant based on probable cause. Reasonable suspicion does not, however, rise to the level of probable cause.

Arizona v. Mauro, 481 U.S. 520, 107 S.Ct. 1931 (1986) [ARIZONA, Petitioner, v. William Carl MAURO] (Confessions; Custodial Interrogations; *Miranda* Warning) Mauro went into a store and said he had killed his son. When the police arrived, Mauro admitted the killing and led officers to his son's body. The police arrested Mauro and took him to the police station for questioning. They advised him of his Miranda rights twice, and he told them that he did not wish to answer further questions without an attorney present. His wife arrived and asked to speak with him. The police agreed, saying that they would tape record the conversation with an officer present in the room. Despite a plea of temporary insanity, nullified by a number of statements in the conversation with his wife, Mauro was subsequently convicted of murder. He appealed, contending that his conversation with his wife should have been suppressed as evidence against him. The SC disagreed, saying that the conversation had not been an interrogation, despite the officer's presence and the taping of the conversation by police, because it had not been initiated by the police. Thus, the evidence was constitutionally proper and admissible. The significance of this case was that it further delineated what is or is not a custodial interrogation.

Arizona v. Roberson, 486 U.S. 675, 108 S.Ct. 2093 (1988) [ARIZONA, Petitioner, v. Ronald William ROBERSON] (Confessions; Law Enforcement Officers or Agencies; *Miranda* Warning) Roberson was arrested for a burglary and advised of his *Miranda* rights. He said he wanted to remain silent until he could speak to an attorney. A few days later, another officer approached Roberson in jail and asked to speak with him about another unrelated crime. The officer gave Roberson his *Miranda* warning before beginning that interrogation. Roberson made a full confession and was subsequently convicted. On appeal, he requested that his confession be suppressed. The prosecution countered by saying that he had confessed to another separate crime after being given his *Miranda* warning by another officer. However, the SC set aside Roberson's conviction, saying that police may not interrogate a suspect following his invocation of the right to silence and without his attorney present. The fact that the confession involved another crime did not matter. This second interrogation constituted a police-initiated custodial interrogation following an initial right invoked by the defendant to remain silent. The decision did not, however, bar defendants from initiating further conversation with police on their own, where their confessions and incriminating statements would be admissible in court.

Arizona v. Rumsey, 467 U.S. 203, 104 S.Ct. 2305 (1984) [ARIZONA, Petitioner, v. Dennis Wayne RUMSEY] (Aggravating and Mitigating Circumstances; Death Penalty; Reconvictions and Resentencing) Rumsey, convicted of murder, was sentenced to life imprisonment by the judge. His case was overturned and set for retrial. A new trial also resulted in a conviction for murder. This time, the death penalty was imposed by the judge, who cited aggravating factors that outweighed mitigating ones. Rumsey appealed on the ground that the second penalty was stiffer than the first. The SC overturned the death-penalty sentence, saying that in capital cases in resentencing proceedings, the punishment cannot be greater than that imposed in the first sentencing. Thus, states cannot impose the death penalty on convicted murderers following prior trials where life imprisonment was imposed. The SC declared that the first judge's refusal to impose the death penalty operated as an acquittal of that punishment, not the offense itself. Thus, judges who impose life sentences in lieu of the death penalty cannot later impose the death penalty as a greater punishment. (*See Bullington v. Missouri* [1981] *for a comparable case involving a* jury *decision about the same issue*.)

Arizona v. Washington, 434 U.S. 497, 98 S.Ct. 824 (1978) [ARIZONA, Richard Boykin, Sheriff, Pima County, Petitioner, v. George WASHINGTON, Jr.] (Discovery; Double Jeopardy; *Habeas Corpus* Petitions) Washington was convicted of murder, but an Arizona court granted him a new trial because the prosecution had withheld exculpatory evidence. At the beginning of the second trial, the defense counsel made various remarks about "hidden" information from the first trial. The prosecutor moved for a mistrial, which was granted. Washington was subsequently convicted in a third trial. Later, as a prison inmate, he filed a *habeas corpus* petition seeking to have his conviction overturned because the second judge's decision to declare a mistrial had been erroneous and had led to his being placed in double jeopardy by a third trial. The SC rejected Washington's arguments, holding that the mistrial had been proper. Thus, no previous trial had been concluded with an acquittal and so Washington was not being tried again for the same offense.

Arizona v. Youngblood, 488 U.S. 51, 109 S.Ct. 333 (1988) [ARIZONA, Petitioner, v. Larry YOUNGBLOOD] (Evidence Preservation) Youngblood was accused of child molestation, kidnapping, and sexual assault. Earlier, a 10-year-old boy had been sodomized by a middle-aged man, later identified as Youngblood (on the basis, in part, of semen samples collected from the child's anus). After a laboratory analysis, the semen samples had not been preserved by the police. Expert witnesses who testified on Youngblood's behalf at the trial said that he might have been exonerated if the samples had been preserved for more careful analysis. Youngblood was convicted. He appealed to have his conviction overturned, because, he argued, the police had showed bad faith in failing to preserve crucial evidence in his defense. The SC rejected Youngblood's appeal, holding that the failure of the police to preserve potentially useful evidence was not a denial of due process unless the defendant could actually show bad faith on the part of police. Youngblood's conviction stood, because he was unable to demonstrate this.

Arkansas v. Sanders, 442 U.S. 753, 99 S.Ct. 2586 (1979) [State of ARKANSAS, Petitioner, v. Lonnie James SANDERS] (Closed Container Searches; Exigent Circumstances; Fourth Amendment; Law Enforcement Officers or Agencies; Searches and Seizures) Sanders was stopped in a cab after leaving an airport. An informant had provided a tip to police to watch out for a person carrying a green suitcase containing marijuana. A description of Sanders was also provided. When Sanders arrived at the airport, he was carrying a green suitcase. He entered a cab and the suitcase was placed in the trunk. When police stopped the cab, they opened the suitcase and discovered marijuana. This evidence was used to convict Sanders of marijuana possession. Sanders appealed his conviction, contending that police should have obtained a warrant before opening his luggage. The SC agreed, overturned Sanders' conviction, and said that absent exigent circumstances, police are required to obtain a search warrant before searching luggage taken from an automobile properly stopped and searched for contraband. The SC said that one's luggage is a repository for one's personal effects, and thus some expectation of privacy exists. Therefore, a search warrant is required for such luggage searches. Thus, the significance of this case is that there were no compelling circumstances for police officers to act quickly. They had had time to obtain a warrant and had failed to do so. (*See also California v. Acevedo* [1991], *in which this doctrine was modified to include warrantless searches of large containers, including luggage.*)

Arkansas v. Sullivan, 532 U.S. 769, 121 S.Ct. 1876 (2001) [ARKANSAS v. Kenneth Andrew SULLIVAN] (Fourth Amendment; Inventory Searches; Searches and Seizures; Vehicle Searches) Sullivan was stopped for speeding in Conway, Arkansas. When Sullivan unsuccessfully attempted to produce his driver's license and registration for the officer, the officer recognized Sullivan's name as linked with narcotics. Further, when Sullivan opened his car door, the office noticed a rusted roofing hatchet on the car's floorboard. The officer then arrested Sullivan for speeding, driving without his registration and insurance documentation, carrying a weapon (the roofing hatchet), and improper window tinting. Subsequently, an inventory search of Sullivan's car led to the discovery of a bag containing a substance that appeared to be methamphetamine, as well as numerous other items suspected of being drug paraphernalia. As a result of the search, Sullivan was charged with various state-law drug offenses, unlawful possession of a weapon, and speeding. Sullivan moved to suppress the evidence seized from his vehicle, alleging Fourth and Fourteenth Amendment violations. Sullivan claimed that the evidence seized from his vehicle was the result of an arrest which was merely a pretext and sham to search him and his vehicle. The trial court granted the suppression motion and the state appealed, although the Arkansas Supreme Court affirmed the trial court's decision. The Arkansas Supreme Court claimed that a Fourth Amendment violation occurred because of the police officer's improper subjective motivation for making the traffic stop. Prosecutors petitioned the SC to hear the case. The SC reversed the Arkansas Supreme Court and remanded the case to the trial court, holding that Fourth Amendment challenges based on the actual motivations of individual officers, including their subjective intentions, play no role in ordinary probable-cause Fourth Amendment analysis.

Ashcraft v. Tennessee, 322 U.S. 143, 64 S.Ct. 921 (1944) [E.E. ASHCRAFT et al. v. State of TENNESSEE] (Confessions; Custodial Interrogations; Law Enforcement Officers or Agencies) Ashcraft and another man, Ware, allegedly conspired to kill Ashcraft's wife. They were arrested following her murder and interrogated at length. Specifically, officers interrogated Ashcraft first for about eight hours, from 6:00 p.m. on the day of the murder until about 2:00 a.m. the next morning. Several days later, on a Saturday, officers again took Ashcraft into custody and interrogated him in "relays" from Saturday evening at 7:00 p.m. until Monday morning at 9:30 a.m. During this period of intensive interrogation, Ashcraft was given no rest and only one five-minute respite. He confessed and was convicted. He appealed, alleging that his confession was coerced. The SC reversed Ashcraft's conviction, saying that his confession was not voluntary, but rather, compelled after 36 hours of interrogation. Thus, it was not admissible during his trial.

Ashe v. Swenson, 397 U.S. 436, 90 S.Ct. 1189 (1970) [Bob Fred ASHE, Petitioner, v. Harold R. SWENSON, Warden] (Double Jeopardy; Fifth Amendment) Several armed men broke into a room and robbed Roberts and five other men who were playing poker. Later, four men, including Ashe, were arrested and charged with robbery. Ashe was subsequently acquitted of the robbery because of weak identification evidence and contradictory testimony. Six weeks later, he was charged again with robbing Roberts. This time, Ashe was convicted, despite his contention that this was a clear case of double jeopardy. He appealed to the SC, which heard his case and agreed, reversing his conviction, holding that one cannot be tried for the same offense by using each and every victim of the robbery as a separate trial target. If that had been done, Ashe conceivably could have faced six separate trials for robbery involving each of the six poker players. After having been acquitted of the robbery charge involving at least one player, Ashe became effectively insulated from further prosecutions under the double-jeopardy clause of the Fifth Amendment.

Atkins v. Virginia, ___U.S.___, 122 S.Ct. 2242 (2002) [Daryl Renard ATKINS, Petitioner, v. VIRGINIA] (Cruel and Unusual Punishment; Death Penalty; Eighth Amendment; Mental Capacity) Atkins was convicted of capital murder by a Virginia jury and sentenced to death. Atkins, together with William Jones, abducted Eric Nesbitt in August 1996 and robbed and killed him. Both Jones and Atkins implicated one another at the subsequent murder trial. After a jury finding of guilt, Atkins was subjected to the penalty phase of the trial, where his defense counsel offered the testimony of Dr. Evan Nelson, a forensic psychologist, who testified that Atkins was mildly mentally retarded and had an IQ of 59. Virginia rebutted this testimony with their own expert, who gave the opinion that Atkins was not mentally retarded but rather was of average intelligence, although he had an antisocial personality disorder. Subsequently Atkins was sentenced to death and appealed, contending that the execution of a mentally retarded offender is a violation of his or her Eighth Amendment right against cruel and unusual punishment. The Virginia Supreme Court affirmed Atkins' conviction and sentence, and Atkins appealed to the SC, who heard the case. The SC reversed Atkins' death sentence, holding that the execution of mentally retarded criminals will not measurably advance the deterrent or retributive purpose of the death penalty, and that such punishment is excessive.

Atwater v. City of Lago Vista, 532 U.S. 318, 121 S.Ct. 1536 (2001) [Gail ATWATER, et al., Petitioners, v. CITY OF LAGO VISTA et al.] (Civil Rights, Section 1983 Claims; Fourth Amendment) Gail Atwater was a Texas motorist driving down a Texas road with her three children sitting in the front seat. None of the persons was wearing a seat belt. Atwater was stopped by a Lago Vista, TX, police officer because she was not wearing a seat belt. The officer pulled Atwater over, berated her, handcuffed her, and placed her in his squad car. He took her to the police station, where she was made to remove her jewelry and eyeglasses and empty her pockets. She was photographed and placed alone in a jail cell for about an hour, then released. She pleaded no contest to violating Texas' seat belt law and paid a $50 fine. Subsequently, she filed a Section 1983 civil rights claim in federal district court alleging that the City of Lago Vista had violated her Fourth Amendment right to be free from unreasonable seizure. The court granted the city a summary judgment, which was affirmed by the Fifth Circuit Court of Appeals. Atwater appealed finally to the SC, who heard the case. The SC upheld the lower courts, declaring that the Fourth Amendment does not forbid a warrantless arrest for a minor criminal offense, such as a misdemeanor seat belt violation punishable only by a fine. The SC noted further that no one disputed the fact that the officer had probable cause to pull Atwater over, and there was no evidence that the arrest was conducted in an extraordinary manner, unusually harmful to Atwater's privacy interests. Thus, according to the Fourth Amendment, the arrest and short-term detention of Atwater was not unreasonable.

Austin v. United States, 509 U.S. 602, 113 S.Ct. 2801 (1993) [Richard Lyle AUSTIN, Petitioner, v. UNITED STATES] (Asset Forfeiture; Eighth Amendment; Fines) The *Austin* case decided by the SC declared that there are limits on governmental authority to use forfeiture laws against drug criminals, finding that seizure of their property must not be excessive when compared with the seriousness of the offense charged. Austin was convicted of cocaine possession with intent to distribute. The federal government seized his mobile home and body shop as a part of their "asset forfeiture" program, in which assets used in the furtherance of the crime can be seized. Austin thought the seizure of his property and business was excessive in proportion to the amount of cocaine he had possessed. He also believed that the asset forfeiture violated his Eighth Amendment right against excessive fines. The government held that asset forfeiture in criminal cases should not be relevant for the excessive-fines clause of the Eighth Amendment; Austin argued that it *is* relevant. The SC reversed the judgment against Austin and sent the case back to the United States District Court to determine if the seizures of his home and business were excessive and cruel and unusual punishment.

B

Bailey v. United States, 516 U.S. 137, 116 S.Ct. 501 (1995) [Roland J. BAILEY, Petitioner, v. UNITED STATES. Candisha Summerita Robinson, aka Candysha Robinson, Petitioner, v. United States] (Law Enforcement Officers or Agencies; Plain-View Rule; Searches and Seizures; Sentencing; Vehicle Searches) A police officer stopped Bailey's vehicle in the District of Columbia because it lacked an inspection sticker and a front license plate. When he failed to produce a valid driver's license, Bailey was ordered from the car. At that time the officer saw something in plain view between the two front seats. A bag was produced, yielding 30 grams of cocaine. Bailey was subsequently convicted of drug charges. His sentence was enhanced by a federal district court judge when it was determined that during the discovery of the cocaine the police had found a firearm in the vehicle trunk. An appeal to the SC resulted in the sentence enhancement being overturned. The SC noted that the federal provision allowing enhancing sentences for using firearms during the commission of a federal crime refers to an active employment of the firearm by the defendant. In this case, the firearm, though loaded, was in a bag inside the locked vehicle trunk. Thus, the prosecution would have had to prove that Bailey was actively using his firearm during his possession and transportation of cocaine. The prosecution failed to show that Bailey intended such active employment of the firearm. (*See Robinson v. United States* [1995] *for a similar opinion.*)

Baker v. McCollan, 443 U.S. 137, 99 S.Ct. 2689 (1979) [T.L. BAKER, Petitioner, v. Linnie Carol McCOLLAN] (Good-Faith Exception) McCollan was stopped in Dallas, TX, for running a red light. A cursory check of records revealed that he was wanted in another county on separate charges. He was transported to the other county, where he was jailed for several days. Initially, he protested that this arrest and detention was a case of mistaken identity. Eventually, photographs of the wanted man and McCollan were compared and it was obvious that police had arrested the wrong person. They released McCollan and he sued for false imprisonment under a civil rights statute. Initially, the court gave him a summary judgment against the county sheriff, and the government appealed. The SC heard the case and reversed the lower court. In sum, they ruled *against* McCollan, declaring that the Constitution does not guarantee that only the guilty will be arrested. McCollan had failed to state a claim upon which relief could be granted. As long as police were acting in good faith and provided the accused with due-process rights, the arrest and detention were lawful. As soon as they recognized their mistake, they corrected it immediately.

Baldasar v. Illinois, 446 U.S. 222, 100 S.Ct. 1585 (1980) [Thomas BALDASAR, Petitioner, v. State of ILLINOIS] (Indigent Clients; Right to Counsel; Sixth Amendment) Baldasar was convicted in a theft of property not exceeding $150 in value. Although this offense was a misdemeanor, it was Baldasar's second offense, and therefore, it became a felony. He was sentenced to one to three years in prison. He appealed, claiming that he had not been represented by counsel at the time of his first conviction. Therefore, the enhanced penalty from the second conviction was not constitutional. The SC agreed with Baldasar and overturned his conviction, holding that no indigent criminal defendant shall be sentenced to a term of imprisonment unless the state has afforded him the right to assistance of counsel. Baldasar had requested but had been denied counsel in the trial for his original misdemeanor, which became a crucial step in enhancing the penalty resulting from his second conviction.

Baldwin v. Alabama, 472 U.S. 372, 105 S.Ct. 2727 (1985) [Brian Keith BALDWIN, Petitioner, v. ALABAMA] (Aggravating and Mitigating Circumstances; Cruel and Unusual Punishment; Death Penalty; Juries) Baldwin and another man, both of whom had escaped from a North Carolina prison, came upon a 16-year-old girl who was having car difficulty. They forcibly took her with them in their car, attempted to rape her, committed sodomy, and attempted to choke her to death. Then they ran over her with their car, locked her body in the trunk, and drove on through Georgia and Alabama. Twice on their journey when they heard her cry out, they opened the trunk and stabbed her repeatedly with knives. They took the still living girl from the trunk and ran over her again in a truck Baldwin had stolen. Finally, they cut her throat with a hatchet and she died after the 40-hour ordeal. Baldwin was convicted of robbery and murder. Alabama's 1975 statute concerning the death penalty (later repealed) required that penalty to be recommended if specified aggravating factors existed. Accordingly, the jury recommended the death penalty, and the judge, after considering the recommendation, imposed it. Baldwin appealed both verdict and penalty to the SC, contending that the "mandatory" nature of the sentence violated his constitutional rights, and that the judge's consideration of various background factors in his life was capricious and arbitrary as well. The SC rejected these arguments and affirmed Baldwin's death sentence, holding that judges may consider death-penalty recommendations from juries but are not obligated to follow them. These judges may weigh the mitigating and aggravating factors accordingly and decide on the best sentence. This procedure is constitutional.

Baldwin v. New York, 399 U.S. 66, 90 S.Ct. 1886 (1970) [Robert BALDWIN, Appellant, v. State of NEW YORK] (Jury Trials) Baldwin was arrested and prosecuted for "jostling" (picking pockets), a Class A misdemeanor punishable by a maximum term of imprisonment of one year in New York. According to New York law at the time, this was a petty offense not entitling a defendant to a jury trial. Baldwin asked for and was denied a jury trial. He then appealed. The SC declared that petty offenses carrying a one-year prison term are serious in that jury trials are required if requested. Specifically, the months of imprisonment constituted serious time. The SC said that a potential sentence in excess of six months' imprisonment is sufficiently severe by itself to take an offense out of the category of "petty" as respects right to jury trial (at 1886,

1891). The SC overturned Baldwin's conviction and sent the case back to the lower court for a jury trial.

Ballew v. Georgia, 435 U.S. 223, 98 S.Ct. 1029 (1978) [**Claude D. BALLEW, Petitioner, v. State of GEORGIA**] (**Fourteenth Amendment; Juries; Sixth Amendment**) Ballew was a theater manager in Atlanta. He showed a sexually explicit movie, *Behind the Green Door,* in his theater in violation of an Atlanta ordinance. The film was seized, but Ballew obtained another copy of the film and continued to exhibit it. He was arrested, charged, and convicted of violating a Georgia ordinance prohibiting distribution of obscene materials. He appealed, alleging his Sixth and Fourteenth Amendment rights were violated, since his conviction was by a five-member jury. The SC reversed Ballew's conviction, holding that a five-member jury deprived him of the right to a trial by jury guaranteed by the Sixth and Fourteenth Amendments. The significance of *Ballew* is that the SC effectively set the lower limit of a jury size at six. No upper limit of a jury size has ever been determined by the SC.

Banks v. Dretke, ___U.S.___, 124 S.Ct. 1256 (2004) [**Delma BANKS, Jr., Petitioner, v. Doug DRETKE, Director, Texas Department of Criminal Justice, Correctional Institutions Division**] (**Discovery; Postconviction Relief; Prosecutorial Misconduct**) Delma Banks was convicted of capital murder in the death of 16-year-old Richard Whitehead, which occurred in mid-April 1980. Banks was originally implicated in the murder by two associates, Jefferson and Farr, who were working with the county sheriff, Willie Huff, as informants. Unknown to Banks before and during the trial was the allegation that Jefferson and Farr were testifying against Banks in order to avoid drug charges which were threatened by the sheriff and prosecutor. At the same time, a confidential informant, Cook, also furnished the prosecution with incriminating circumstantial evidence against Banks. This information was also withheld from Banks pursuant to a motion for discovery. Although Banks had no prior criminal record, testimony from Farr and Jefferson provided the jury with innuendo that Banks had an unsavory and criminal past, which was untrue. Banks' efforts to impeach Farr and Jefferson were undermined because of his own witnesses, who were themselves impeached on cross-examination. Banks was sentenced to death and sought postconviction relief, alleging that the prosecution failed to disclose exculpatory evidence as required by *Brady v. Maryland* (1963), including the threats made to Farr and Jefferson as well as the confidential informant, Cook. In its answer, the state claimed that nothing had been kept secret from Banks and no deals had been made with government witnesses, including Cook. In 1993 Banks' postconviction claims were denied outright by an appellate court. Following this loss, Banks filed for *habeas corpus* relief in a U.S. district court, which granted relief on Banks' death sentence. In 1999 Banks filed discovery and evidentiary hearing motions, both supported by affidavits sworn to by Farr and Jefferson that the prosecution had wrongly withheld crucial exculpatory and impeaching evidence. The federal court determined that the state, indeed, had failed to disclose Farr's informant status during the original discovery phase of Banks' trial. Therefore, a writ of *habeas corpus* was granted Banks with respect to his death sentence, but not to his conviction. Banks petitioned the SC, who heard the case. The SC reiterated that under *Brady,* a prosecutorial misconduct claim must establish three things: (1) the evidence at issue must be favorable to the accused, either because it is exculpatory, or because it is impeaching; (2) that evidence must have been suppressed by the state, either willfully or inadvertently; and (3) prejudice must have ensued. In its response, the state contended that "it can lie and conceal and the prisoner still has the burden to discover the evidence." The SC ruled this assertion to be untenable and a violation of Banks' due-process rights. Banks presented sufficient evidence to support his *Brady* claim and was thus entitled to a full evidentiary hearing and a certification of appealability.

Barber v. Page, 390 U.S. 719, 88 S.Ct. 1318 (1968) [**Jack Allen BARBER, Petitioner, v. Ray H. PAGE, Warden**] (**Confrontation Clause; Sixth Amendment**) Barber was convicted of a crime in Oklahoma in part from testimony taken from a transcript of a preliminary hearing. A witness, Woods, was a prisoner in a federal prison in Texas. Oklahoma officials made no effort to find the witness to testify and used his transcripted testimony instead. Barber, represented by counsel, objected and appealed the conviction, contending that the right of cross-examination as set forth in the Sixth Amendment had been violated. The SC overturned the conviction, because the state had made no effort to secure Woods in court and had treated lightly Barber's right to cross-examine his accuser.

Barclay v. Florida, 463 U.S. 939, 103 S.Ct. 3418 (1983) [**Elwood BARCLAY, Petitioner, v. FLORIDA**] (**Aggravating and Mitigating Circumstances; Death Penalty**) Barclay and others had driven around Jacksonville, FL, streets looking for white people to kill. It was their intention to start a race war. In the process, they killed a white hitchhiker. Barclay was convicted of murder by a jury trial. In a second phase of the jury deliberations, the jury advised the judge to give Barclay life imprisonment; however, the judge noted from the presentence investigation report various statutory aggravating factors, and he imposed the death penalty. Among the aggravating factors were an extensive prior criminal record, committing the murder during an act of kidnapping, and knowingly creating a risk of death to many persons. The Florida Supreme Court vacated the judgment of the lower court and the case was retried in order to give Barclay the opportunity to rebut the aggravating factors cited by the sentencing judge. One of the aggravating factors cited, Barclay's prior record, was not an aggravating factor, according to statute. The other factors, however, were. The second trial ended like the first: Barclay was convicted and sentenced to death. The SC heard the case and upheld the death sentence, saying that although the original judge had erred by listing a nonstatutory aggravating factor, the other factors were aggravating according to statute and thus, the death penalty was proper. There was no reversible error in citing nonstatutory aggravating factors, as long as there were one or more statutory aggravating factors not outweighed by any mitigating ones.

Barefoot v. Estelle, 463 U.S. 880, 103 S.Ct. 3383 (1983) [**Thomas A. BAREFOOT, Petitioner, v. W.J. ESTELLE, Jr., Director, Texas Department of Corrections**] (**Bifurcated Trials;** *Habeas Corpus* **Petitions**) Barefoot was convicted of murder following a jury trial. A bifurcated proceeding was conducted, in which the first stage established Barefoot's guilt and the second stage determined his punishment. A part of the second phase involved psychiatrist testimony about Barefoot's potential for dangerousness in the future. The testimony concluded that Barefoot would pose a threat to others, so he was given the death penalty. He appealed, contending that such psychiatric testimony was unconstitutional. The SC disagreed, saying that the use of such testimony at sentencing hearings is constitutional. Thus, the testimony of psychiatrists about Barefoot's future dangerousness was not a violation of his due-process rights.

Barker v. Wingo, 407 U.S. 514, 92 S.Ct. 2182 (1972) [**Willie Mae BARKER, Petitioner, v. John W. WINGO, Warden**] (**Sixth Amendment; Speedy Trials**) Barker and Manning were alleged to have shot an elderly couple in Kentucky in July 1958. They were arrested later and a grand jury indicted them in September 1958. Kentucky prosecutors sought 16 continuances to prolong Barker's trial. Manning was subjected to five different trials, each with a hung jury until the fifth trial, in which Manning was convicted. Then, Barker's trial was scheduled. During these five trials, Barker made no attempt to protest or to encourage a trial on his own behalf. After postponement for various reasons, his trial was finally held in October 1963, when he was convicted. He appealed, alleging a violation of his right to a speedy trial. The SC heard the case and declared that as from every apparent circumstance Barker did not want a speedy trial, he was not entitled to one. The principle is that defendants must assert their desire to have a speedy trial in order to invoke the speedy trial provision and have their Amendment rights enforceable.

Barron v. Baltimore, 7 Pet. 243 (1833) [**John BARRON v. Mayor and City Council of BALTIMORE**] (**Bill of Rights; Fourteenth Amendment**) The owner of a wharf in Baltimore, MD, challenged a local action that seriously impaired the value of his wharf. He maintained that the government had taken his property without providing just compensation, in violation of the Fifth Amendment. At that time, state and local governments were exempt from the Bill of Rights, which pertained only to encroachments by the federal government, so he lost the case. Later, the Fourteenth Amendment (1868) changed this considerably and through the equal-protection clause and due-process provision extended the Bill of Rights and other amendments to all government levels.

Batson v. Kentucky, 476 U.S. 79, 106 S.Ct. 1712 (1986) [**James Kirkland BATSON, Petitioner, v. KENTUCKY**] (**Discrimination; Juries; Peremptory Challenges**) In Kentucky, a black man, Batson, was convicted by an all white jury of second-degree burglary. The prosecutor had used all of his peremptory challenges to exclude the few black prospective jurors from the jury pool. Ordinarily, peremptory challenges may be used to strike particular jurors without the prosecutor's having to provide a reason for doing so. In this case, the use of

peremptory challenges was rather transparent, and Batson appealed. In a landmark case, the SC decided that peremptory challenges may not be used for a racially discriminatory purpose. Thus, creating an all white jury by deliberately eliminating all prospective black candidates was discriminatory. The SC ruled in favor of Batson.

Baxstrom v. Herold, 383 U.S. 107, 86 S.Ct. 760 (1966) [**Johnnie K. BAXSTROM, Petitioner, v. R.E. HEROLD, Director, Dannemora State Hospital**] (**Corrections; Fourteenth Amendment**) Baxstrom was convicted of second-degree assault and sentenced to two-and-a-half years in prison. Later, he was certified as insane and placed in a state institution for the mentally ill. When his original sentence was about to expire, the doctor in charge of the institution filed a petition seeking a civil commitment of Baxstrom for a prolonged period. Eventually, Baxstrom filed an appeal, which reached the SC. The SC ruled that Baxstrom had been denied equal protection of the laws under the Fourteenth Amendment. Thus, the case was remanded in order for a jury review to determine his mental condition and the prospects for a civil commitment.

Baxter v. Palmigiano, 425 U.S. 308, 96 S.Ct. 1551 (1976) [**Joseph BAXTER et al., Petitioners, v. Nicholas A. PALMIGIANO, Jerry J. Enomoto et al., Petitioners, v. John Wesley Clutchette et al.**] (**Civil Rights, Section 1983 Claims; Corrections; Inmate Rights**) In a Rhode Island prison, a convicted murderer, Palmigiano, was serving a life sentence. During his confinement, he allegedly incited other prisoners to riot, and he was summoned before the Prison Disciplinary Board. He was advised that he might be prosecuted independently by the state for inciting other prisoners to riot, but for the time being, the board would hear and determine the factual nature of the charges against him. He was advised that his attorney could not be present during this hearing but that he himself could consult counsel substitutes. Palmigiano was forbidden to cross-examine persons giving testimony against him. He was also advised that he could remain silent but that his silence could lead the board to regard him unfavorably. He remained silent, evidence was presented, and the board placed him in punitive segregation for 30 days. He filed a Title 42 U.S.C. Section 1983 civil rights action, contending that the disciplinary hearing had violated his due-process rights. The SC upheld the decision of the board, declaring that prison inmates do not have a right to court-appointed or private counsel in disciplinary hearings. Also, they cannot confront and cross-examine witnesses at all times. Although criminal defendants usually have the right to remain silent without incurring negative inference, in an inmate's case, silence is incriminating.

Bearden v. Georgia, 461 U.S. 660, 103 S.Ct. 2064 (1983) [**Danny R. BEARDEN, Petitioner, v. GEORGIA**] (**Corrections; Indigent Clients; Probation and Parole**) Bearden's probation was revoked by Georgia authorities because he failed to pay a fine and make restitution to his victim as required by the court. He claimed he was indigent, but the court rejected his claim. The SC disagreed. It ruled that probation may not be revoked in the case of indigent probationers who have failed to pay their fines or make restitution. It further suggested alternatives for restitution and punishments that were more compatible with the abilities and economic resources of indigent probationers (e.g., community service). In short, the probationer should not be penalized where a reasonable effort has been made to pay court-ordered fines and restitution.

Beck v. Alabama, 447 U.S. 625, 100 S.Ct. 2382 (1980) [Gilbert Franklin BECK, Petitioner, v. State of ALABAMA] (Death Penalty; Jury Instructions) Beck was charged with murder during the course of a robbery. When the judge issued instructions to the jury, he did not advise it that felony murder is a lesser included offense than the capital crime of robbery with intentional killing. Rather, he gave instructions that the jury must either convict Beck of first-degree murder or acquit him. The jury convicted him. Beck appealed to the SC, contending that the judge should have issued instructions to the jury on the lesser included charge, for which evidence existed. The SC reversed Beck's conviction, saying that the judge erred in failing to issue such a jury instruction. The death penalty may not be imposed constitutionally after a jury verdict of guilt in a capital trial where the jury was not permitted to consider a verdict of guilt of a lesser included offense.

Beck v. Ohio, 379 U.S. 89, 85 S.Ct. 223 (1964) [William BECK, Petitioner, v. State of OHIO] (Fourth Amendment; Law Enforcement Officers or Agencies; Searches and Seizures) Beck, who had a prior record of criminal activity, was driving down a street in Cleveland, OH, when police officers stopped him without probable cause. They did not have a warrant, nor was Beck doing anything to arouse suspicions of criminal activity. They took him to the police station, where they searched him and his car. Some betting slips were found in his socks. He was charged with possessing "clearinghouse" (betting) slips in violation of state law and convicted. Beck appealed, contending that the clearinghouse slips had been illegally seized, because no lawful search warrant had been obtained and the officers had had no probable cause to stop him initially. The SC agreed with Beck and overturned his conviction, saying that the officers had no probable cause to stop him, search him or his car, or detain him for any length of time at the police station. That something illegal was discovered as the result of this warrantless search lacking probable cause did not justify the search. Police must have probable cause before stopping anyone and conducting any sort of search of the person or the automobile.

Becker v. Montgomery, 532 U.S. 757, 121 S.Ct. 1801 (2001) [Dale G. BECKER, Petitioner, v. Betty MONTGOMERY, Attorney General of Ohio, et al.] (Civil Rights, Section 1983 Claims; Conditions of Confinement; Corrections) Becker was an Ohio state prisoner who instituted a *pro se* civil rights action in federal court contesting the conditions of his confinement under Title 42 U.S.C. Section 1983. The federal district court dismissed the complaint because of Becker's failure to state a claim for relief. In a timely manner, within 30 days of the federal court action, Becker appealed, filing a *pro se* notice of appeal with the Sixth Circuit Court of Appeals. However, Becker failed to sign the appeal form. The form contained no requirement indicating that it should be signed. The Sixth Circuit dismissed Becker's appeal because it was unsigned. The Sixth Circuit further declared that Becker's notice of appeal was fatally defective and deemed this defect jurisdictional and therefore not curable outside the time allowed to file the notice of appeal. No court officer had earlier called Becker's attention to the need for a signature. Becker appealed to the SC. The SC reversed the Sixth Circuit, holding that when a party files a timely notice of appeal, the failure to sign the appeal does not require the court of appeals to dismiss the appeal. The SC stated further that imperfections in noticing an appeal should not be fatal where no genuine doubt exists about who is appealing, from what judgment, and to which appellate court.

Beckwith v. United States, 425 U.S. 341, 96 S.Ct. 1612 (1976) [Alvin A. BECKWITH, Jr., Petitioner, v. UNITED STATES] (Custodial Interrogations; *Miranda* Warning) Beckwith was interviewed in his home by visiting IRS agents. During this noncustodial questioning, he made various incriminating statements that were later used against him in a case involving criminal income tax evasion. Beckwith was convicted. He sought to suppress the statements he had made to IRS agents earlier, because, he alleged, they had failed to give him the *Miranda* warning. The SC disagreed and said that IRS interviews in field offices do not constitute custodial interrogations for purposes of administering the *Miranda* warning to taxpayers. Being interviewed in one's home and without mention of criminal charges does not constitute custodial interrogations for *Miranda* purposes. Although Beckwith may have felt that the interview was coercive, it wasn't.

Beecham v. United States, 511 U.S. 368, 114 S.Ct. 1669 (1994) [Lenard Ray BEECHAM, Petitioner, v. UNITED STATES. Kirby Lee Jones, Petitioner, v. United States] (Inmate Rights) Beecham was a convicted felon who had a prior felony conviction in Tennessee and a federal conviction for interstate transportation of stolen property. Subsequently, Tennessee reinstated Beecham's civil rights for purposes of voting and other matters. However, he was apprehended by federal agents for being a convicted felon in possession of a firearm. He was convicted and he appealed, arguing that the fact that Tennessee had reinstated his civil rights entitled him to possess a firearm. The SC disagreed, saying that although the State of Tennessee had restored his civil rights, his loss of rights stemming from his federal conviction for interstate transportation of stolen property had not been restored; thus, Beecham was in violation of a federal statute. His restoration of rights in Tennessee had nothing to do with his federal felony conviction. The significance of this case is that states can restore a convicted offender's civil rights, but if they are convicted federal felons, they are still in violation of federal laws such as "being a convicted felon in possession of a firearm."

Bell v. Cone, ___U.S.___, 122 S.Ct. 1843 (2002) [Ricky BELL, Warden, Petitioner, v. Gary Bradford CONE] (*Habeas Corpus* Petitions; Sixth Amendment) Cone was convicted in a Tennessee court for first-degree murder, murder in the perpetration of a burglary, assault with intent to commit murder, and robbery by use of deadly force, and he was given the death penalty. During the trial phase, the prosecution had presented numerous aggravating circumstances, while the defense relied upon testimony from Cone's mother and a psychiatrist that Cone was not guilty by reason of insanity due to substance abuse, that he was suffering from post-traumatic stress syndrome from his Vietnam military service, and that when he returned from war, he was a "changed person." During the sentencing phase, a junior prosecutor gave a weak closing, but restated four aggravating factors that outweighed no mitigating ones. Cone's attorney waived his final argument, denying the lead prosecutor, an extremely effective advocate, from arguing in rebuttal. Cone was sentenced to death and appealed, but his appeals were rejected. Subsequently, he filed a *habeas corpus* action, alleging defense counsel incompetence because he did not subject the prosecutor's final argument to meaningful adversarial testing. The Sixth Circuit Court of Appeals reversed with respect to Cone's sentence, agreeing with Cone. The appellate court further stated that Cone suffered a Sixth Amendment violation because the state court decision was "contrary to" and "an unreasonable application of clearly established Federal law" articulated in *Strickland v. Washington* (1984). The government appealed and the SC heard the case.

The SC reversed the circuit court of appeals, holding that Cone's claim was not governed by *Strickland,* and that the state court's decision neither was "contrary to" nor involved "an unreasonable application of clearly established Federal law" established in *Strickland.* Under *Strickland,* a two-part test for evaluating claims that counsel performed so incompetently that a defendant's sentence or conviction should be reversed must show that counsel's representation fell below an objective reasonableness standard and that there is a reasonable probability that, but for counsel's unprofessional error, the proceeding's final result would have been different. In defense of Cone's counsel, the SC noted that the counsel faced the onerous task of defending a client who had committed a brutal and senseless crime, and who, despite a normal upbringing, became a drug addict and robber. Counsel reasonably could have concluded that the substance of the medical expert's testimony during the guilt phase of the trial was still fresh to the jury during the sentencing phase, and that Cone's mother had not made a good witness at the guilt stage. Counsel also feared that the prosecution might elicit information about Cone's criminal history from other witnesses that he could have called, and that testimony about Cone's normal youth might cut the other way in the jury's eyes. Counsel's final argument options were to make a closing argument and reprise for the jury the primary mitigating evidence, plead for his client's life, and impress upon the jury other, less significant facts, knowing that it would give the persuasive lead prosecutor the chance to depict his client as a heartless killer just before the jurors began deliberation; or to prevent the lead prosecutor from arguing by waiving his own summation and relying on the jurors' familiarity with the case and his opening plea for life made just a few hours before. Neither option so clearly outweighs the other that it was objectively unreasonable for the state court to deem his choice a tactical decision about which competent lawyers might disagree.

Bell v. Wolfish, 441 U.S. 520, 99 S.Ct. 1861 (1979) [**Griffin B. BELL et al., Petitioners, v. Louis WOLFISH et al.**] (**Corrections; Eighth Amendment; Inmate Rights**) This case involved the minimum-security Metropolitan Correctional Center in New York City, a facility operated by the United States Bureau of Prisons and designed to accommodate 449 federal prisoners, including many pretrial detainees. It had been constructed in 1975 and was considered architecturally progressive and modern, generally a comfortable facility. Originally, the facility was designed to house inmates in individual cells. But soon, the capacity of the facility was exceeded by inmate overpopulation. Inmates were obliged to share their cells with other inmates. This double-bunking and other issues related to overcrowding eventually led to a class-action suit against the facility by several of the pretrial detainees and prisoners, including Bell. A lower court ruled in favor of the prisoners, holding that "compelling necessity" had not been demonstrated by prison officials in their handling of the overcrowding situation. But the SC overturned the lower court and said that the "intent" of prison officials should decide whether double-bunking was intended as "punishment" or a simple deprivation because of necessity. Since no "intent" to punish pretrial detainees could be demonstrated, there was no punishment. Hence, the Eighth Amendment was not violated.

Bennis v. Michigan, 516 U.S. 442, 116 S.Ct. 994 (1996) [**Tina B. BENNIS, Petitioner, v. MICHIGAN**] (**Asset Forfeiture; Innocent-Owner Defense**) Tina Bennis jointly owned an automobile with her husband, John Bennis. John Bennis was observed by Detroit police officers engaging in a sexual act with a prostitute in his car on a Detroit city street in public view. He was arrested and convicted of gross indecency. The automobile was seized as a public nuisance under a Michigan statute. Tina Bennis sued for recovery of her jointly owned vehicle, claiming that she was an innocent owner of the car and didn't know that it would be used for illegal purposes. The SC heard the case, rejected Mrs. Bennis' innocent-owner defense, and upheld Michigan's seizure of the vehicle as a public nuisance, defined as any object or place that was kept for the use of prostitutes. The SC referred to a long and unbroken line of cases (as precedent) that hold that an owner's interest in property may be forfeited by reason of the use to which the property is put, even though the owner did not know that it was to be put to such use.

Benton v. Maryland, 395 U.S. 784, 89 S.Ct. 2056 (1969) [**John Dalmer BENTON, Petitioner, v. State of MARYLAND**] (**Double Jeopardy; Self-Incrimination**) Benton was tried and convicted of burglary in a Maryland state court. He was acquitted on a larceny charge. Because of grand and petit jury irregularities, he was given the option of being retried by jury on both counts, burglary and larceny. He sought to have his burglary conviction set aside. A subsequent jury found him guilty of both burglary and larceny, the same larceny count of which he had been acquitted in an earlier trial. He appealed, contending that his right against double jeopardy had been violated. The SC reversed his conviction for larceny, saying that this was a clear case of double jeopardy. The state cannot set aside acquittals resulting from void grand-jury indictments.

Berger v. New York, 388 U.S. 41, 87 S.Ct. 1873 (1967) [Ralph BERGER, Petitioner, v. State of NEW YORK] (Electronic Surveillance, Wiretapping; Fourth Amendment; Law Enforcement Officers or Agencies; Searches and Seizures) Berger was a conspirator who was suspected of attempting to bribe a member of the New York State Liquor Authority. His telephone calls were monitored and recorded, according to a New York State statute authorizing such electronic eavesdropping. Placements of bugs or electronic wiretaps of telephones could be authorized by any police officer at the rank of sergeant or above. Nothing was specified in the order in the Berger case, only to record whatever was said. Berger was ultimately indicted and convicted. He appealed, contending that the wiretap was a violation of his Fourth Amendment rights. The SC overturned Berger's conviction because the New York statute was overly broad and contained little to safeguard the public against unreasonable searches and seizures. The SC declared that to be valid, a search warrant obtained for wiretapping purposes must be based on probable cause, specific as to conversation to be recorded, and for a limited period during which a suspected crime is committed. In addition, it must include a provision for reporting to the court what, if any, information was recorded, must name the person or persons to be wiretapped, and must end whenever the incriminating information has been recorded. In 1968, the Omnibus Crime Control and Safe Streets Act was passed by Congress, which spelled out these basic requirements for search warrants authorizing wiretaps or electronic surveillance of criminal suspects.

Berkemer v. McCarty, 468 U.S. 104, 104 S.Ct. 3138 (1984) [Harry J. BERKEMER, Sheriff of Franklin County, Ohio, Petitioner, v. Richard N. McCARTY] (Confessions; Custodial Interrogations; Law Enforcement Officers or Agencies; *Miranda* Warning) McCarty was stopped on suspicion of DUI by the Ohio State Highway Patrol. He made several incriminating statements to police, including the facts that he had formerly consumed two beers and smoked some marijuana. He was then placed under arrest and taken to the Highway Patrol station for further interrogation. At no time was he administered the *Miranda* warning. Police subsequently checked his blood-alcohol content (BAC) and found no alcohol. Nevertheless, McCarty pleaded "no contest" and was convicted of DUI. He appealed, arguing that his incriminating statements to police should have been suppressed as evidence against him. His conviction was overturned by a lower court and the SC affirmed the reversal, holding that whereas an ordinary traffic stop does not constitute a custodial interrogation for purposes of giving *Miranda* warnings to DUI suspects, subsequent interrogation when the suspect is in custody does require such a warning. In McCarty's case, this warning was never given; thus, his incriminating statements were inadmissible against him later in court. This Berkemer Rule, as it is known (named after Sheriff Harry J. Berkemer of Franklin County, OH), states that routine traffic stops do not constitute custodial interrogations for purposes of issuing *Miranda* warnings to persons suspected of driving while intoxicated or under the influence of drugs.

Betts v. Brady, 316 U.S. 455, 62 S.Ct. 1252 (1942) [Smith BETTS v. Patrick J. BRADY, Warden] (Death Penalty; Indigent Clients) Betts claimed that he was indigent and thus demanded a court-appointed attorney to defend him on a robbery charge. The court said that Betts could be appointed counsel only in rape or murder cases, and denied his request. He appealed. The SC ruled that in felony cases in which life or death is not an issue, the states are not required to furnish counsel in every case; many states at this time, however, provide counsel because it is required by their own constitutions or by court rulings in state courts. This decision was overturned as the result of the ruling in *Gideon v. Wainwright* (1963), in which the SC concluded that in all felony cases, state or federal, indigent defendants are entitled to counsel.

Bivens v. Six Unknown Named Agents of Federal Bureau of Narcotics, 403 U.S. 383, 91 S.Ct. 1999 (1971) [Webster BIVENS, Petitioner, v. SIX UNKNOWN NAMED AGENTS OF FEDERAL BUREAU OF NARCOTICS] (Fourth Amendment; Searches and Seizures) Bivens and others were subjected to an illegal search by federal narcotics agents who broke into his apartment, arrested Bivens and others, and searched the apartment for narcotics, all without a warrant. Bivens was convicted, but the conviction was reversed because of the warrantless arrest and search. Bivens and others then filed suit against federal narcotics officers, seeking damages. Their original suit was dismissed because the trial court said that they "lacked standing" and had failed to state a cause of action. The SC overturned the decision of the lower court, saying that in a federal cause of action, damages are recoverable upon proof shown of injuries resulting from agents' violation of the Fourth Amendment. (*See Carlson v. Green* [1980] *and Correctional Services Corporation v. Malesko* [2001] *for subsequent similar cases.*)

Black v. Romano, 471 U.S. 606, 105 S.Ct. 2254 (1985) [Lee Roy BLACK, Director, Missouri Department of Corrections and Human Resources, and Dick D. Moore, Chairman, Missouri Board of Probation and Parole, Petitioners, v. Nicholas J. ROMANO] (Corrections; Probation and Parole) Romano, a probationer, had his probation revoked by the sentencing judge because of alleged program violations. The defendant had left the scene of an automobile accident, a felony in the jurisdiction where the alleged offense occurred. The judge gave reasons for the revocation but did not indicate that he had considered any option other than incarceration. The SC ruled that judges are not generally obligated to consider alternatives to incarceration before they revoke an offender's probation and place him in jail or prison. Probationers and parolees have obtained substantial rights since 1985. SC decisions have provided them with several important constitutional rights that invalidate the arbitrary and capricious revocation of their probation or parole programs by judges or parole boards. The two-stage hearing is extremely important to probationers and parolees, in that it permits ample airing of the allegations against the offender, cross-examinations by counsel, and testimony from individual offenders.

Blackburn v. Alabama, 361 U.S. 199, 80 S.Ct. 274 (1960) [Jesse BLACKBURN, Petitioner, v. State of ALABAMA]

(Confessions; Custodial Interrogations; Fourteenth Amendment; Insanity Pleas) Blackburn, a mentally ill person, was charged with robbery in an Alabama court. He pleaded not guilty by reason of insanity. In fact, he had been absent from a mental ward in a hospital at the time the robbery was committed. Doctors and other experts confirmed that he was incompetent. Nevertheless, he confessed to the crime after an extensive interrogation, and on that basis he was convicted. Blackburn appealed, maintaining that he had been forced into making the confession. The SC heard the case, including evidence that the confession had been extorted after eight or nine hours of intense interrogation in a crowded sheriff's room. The SC overturned the conviction, saying the coercive conditions under which it had been obtained were unconstitutional and violated the due-process clause of the Fourteenth Amendment. Involuntary confessions to crimes are inadmissible as evidence against criminal suspects.

Blanton v. North Las Vegas, 489 U.S. 538, 109 S.Ct. 1289 (1989) [**Melvin R. BLANTON and Mark D. Fraley, Petitioners, v. City of NORTH LAS VEGAS, Nevada**] (**Jury Trials**) Blanton was convicted in Nevada of operating a motor vehicle while under the influence of alcohol, a petty offense. He then demanded a jury trial. Defendants can obtain jury trials in petty-offense cases only when they can show that the additional penalties (e.g., community service, fines) viewed together with the maximum prison term are so severe that the legislature clearly determines that the offense is a "serious one." Blanton had been convicted under Nevada law, where the maximum prison term is six months. That he lost his driver's license for 90 days, that he was required to attend courses on alcohol abuse, and that he had to pay a fine of $1,000 and perform 48 hours of community service did not amount to severe punishment. The SC declared Blanton's offense to be petty and not deserving of a jury trial. (*See United States v. Nachtigal* [1993] *for a comparable case.*)

Block v. Rutherford, 468 U.S. 576, 104 S.Ct. 3227 (1984) [**Sherman BLOCK, Sheriff of the County of Los Angeles, et al., Petitioners, v. Dennis RUTHERFORD et al.**] (**Civil Rights, Section 1983 Claims; Corrections; Inmate Rights**) Rutherford and other pretrial detainees at the Los Angeles County Jail protested that they were being denied contact visits with their spouses and that they were not permitted to observe shakedowns of their cells by jail correctional officers. A Title 42 U.S.C. Section 1983 action was filed against the county sheriff by Rutherford. The SC ruled that jail inmates have no constitutional right to contact visits with others and no constitutional right to observe correctional officers conducting cell shakedowns (searches for contraband). A primary consideration of the SC is whether a significant penological interest, such as security and safety of the institution, is served by such regulations. In this case, the SC said a significant penological interest existed for the Los Angeles County Jail to maintain such a policy.

Blockburger v. United States, 284 U.S. 299, 52 S.Ct. 180 (1932) [**Harry BLOCKBURGER, Petitioner, v. UNITED STATES**] (**Double Jeopardy; Fifth Amendment**) Blockburger was charged with violating the Harrison Narcotic Act.

Specifically, he allegedly sold morphine to particular persons over several days, and he was charged on each separate offense. He was convicted of each offense and appealed to the SC, arguing that his sales represented a single, continuous transaction, and therefore, only one offense should be punishable under the law rather than several offenses. The appeal sought to overturn the separate convictions for morphine sales under the double-jeopardy clause of the Fifth Amendment, which prohibits successive prosecutions for the same criminal act or transaction under two criminal statutes whenever each statute does not "require proof of a fact which the other does not." The SC upheld Blockburger's separate convictions, holding that separate sales of morphine to the same purchaser on successive days are separate offenses for purposes of punishment, and double jeopardy does not attach.

Bloom v. Illinois, 391 U.S. 194, 88 S.Ct. 1477 (1968) [**S. Edward BLOOM, Petitioner, v. State of ILLINOIS**] (**Aggravating and Mitigating Circumstances; Jury Trials; Right to Counsel; Sixth Amendment**) Bloom was held in contempt of court for allegedly filing a false will for probate. He was sentenced to imprisonment for 24 months. He requested a jury trial but was denied. Then he appealed to the SC, which reversed his conviction for contempt, holding that whether a jury trial is a constitutional right turns on the seriousness of the penalty actually imposed. A 24-month incarcerative term is indeed serious. It was clear that Bloom was entitled to a jury trial and it was constitutional error to deny him that right.

Blumhagen v. Sabes, 834 F.Supp. 1347 (D.Wyo.) (1993) (**Inmate Rights**) A Wyoming inmate filed a lawsuit against the Wyoming prison system for screening all inmates for tuberculosis but failing to isolate them once they were identified. In this instance, Wyoming officials responded that they treated TB-infected inmates with particular medications, and thus, it was unnecessary to isolate them from the entire prison population. The circuit court of appeals agreed with Wyoming and rejected the lawsuit. However, the court did note that the inmates might have a claim for malpractice under Wyoming tort law and suggested that inmates examine that avenue as a possible remedy.

Blystone v. Pennsylvania, 494 U.S. 299, 110 S.Ct. 1078 (1990) [**Scott Wayne BLYSTONE, Petitioner, v. PENNSYLVANIA**] (**Aggravating and Mitigating Circumstances; Corrections; Death Penalty**) Blystone was convicted of first-degree murder, robbery, and criminal conspiracy to commit homicide. The sentencing jury was instructed to consider aggravating and mitigating circumstances and to impose the death penalty if aggravating circumstances outweighed the mitigating ones. The death penalty was imposed on Blystone, and he appealed, contending that the weighing procedure of aggravating and mitigating circumstances made the death penalty a mandatory penalty and thus unconstitutional. The SC rejected Blystone's argument, saying that the Pennsylvania statute of weighing the aggravating and mitigating circumstances was not unconstitutional.

Board of Pardons v. Allen, 482 U.S. 369, 107 S.Ct. 2415 (1987) [**BOARD OF PARDONS and Harry Burgess, Petitioners, v. George ALLEN and Dale Jacobsen, etc.**] (**Corrections; Pardons; Probation and Parole) Allen was a Montana state prison inmate who filed suit against the Board of Pardons for denying him due process by failing to apply statutorily mandated parole criteria and failing to explain in writing the reasons for his denial of parole. The parole law in Montana said that the parole board shall release on parole certain persons who qualify according to specified criteria. Allen believed that he was parole-eligible and should be granted parole according to the phraseology of the Montana statute. Montana authorities disagreed. Allen appealed. The SC upheld Allen's right to have a substantial liberty interest in the statute as stated. Thus, Montana was obligated because of "shall" to apply the standards established for early release in Allen's case. At the very least, it became incumbent upon Montana to provide Allen with full due process to determine whether he should receive early release.

Bond v. United States, 529 U.S. 334, 120 S.Ct. 1462 (2000) [Steven Dewayne BOND, Petitioner, v. UNITED STATES] (Border Searches; Fourth Amendment; Searches and Seizures) Bond was a passenger on a bus traveling from California to Little Rock, AR. Border Patrol officers in Sierra Blanca, TX, boarded the bus to check the immigration status of passengers. One officer squeezed carry-on luggage in the overhead compartments of various passengers, including Bond. The officer detected a "brick-like" object and asked Bond if he could look inside the bag. The officer discovered a brick of methamphetamine that had been wrapped in duct tape and clothing. Bond was arrested and subsequently convicted in federal court with conspiracy to possess and possession with intent to distribute methamphetamine. Bond moved to suppress the methamphetamine as evidence against him, arguing that it was discovered as the result of an illegal search under the Fourth Amendment. The federal judge denied the motion, and Bond was convicted and sentenced to 57 months in prison. The court of appeals upheld the federal judge. Bond appealed to the SC, where the case was heard. The SC overturned Bond's conviction, holding that the Border Patrol agent's physical manipulation of Bond's bag violated his Fourth Amendment rights. The SC noted that whereas passengers expect that bus employees will, from time to time, handle their baggage, the passengers have a reasonable expectation of privacy in that bus employees will not physically manipulate luggage in an exploratory manner. Further, passengers, including Bond, express their desire for privacy of their personal effects by storing them in opaque bags and placing them directly above their seats. Thus, a traveler's personal luggage is an "effect" protected by the Fourth Amendment to be secure against unreasonable searches and seizures. Further, bus passengers have a privacy interest in bags carried aboard buses.

Booth v. Maryland, 482 U.S. 496, 107 S.Ct. 2529 (1987) [John BOOTH, Petitioner, v. MARYLAND] (Corrections; Cruel and Unusual Punishment; Death Penalty; Eighth Amendment; Victim Impact Statements) Booth was convicted of first-degree murder in a Baltimore court. During his sentencing, a victim impact statement (VIS) was read so that his sentence might be intensified. Following the sentence of

death, Booth appealed, alleging that the VIS was a violation of his Eighth Amendment right against cruel and unusual punishment. The SC agreed and said that during the sentencing phase of a capital murder trial, the introduction of a VIS is unconstitutional. Among its reasons for this opinion, the SC said that a VIS creates an unacceptable risk that a jury may impose the death penalty in an arbitrary and capricious manner. Thus, VIS information may be totally unrelated to the blameworthiness of the offender.

Bordenkircher v. Hayes, 434 U.S. 357, 98 S.Ct. 663 (1978) [Don BORDENKIRCHER, Superintendent, Kentucky State Penitentiary, Petitioner, v. Paul Lewis HAYES] (Plea Bargaining) Hayes was indicted for check forgery in Fayette County, KY. The punishment for such an offense was from two to 10 years, while a habitual-offender statute carried a mandatory life imprisonment sentence for those with prior felony convictions. Hayes also had several prior felony convictions; thus he qualified as a habitual offender and could be prosecuted under that statute. The prosecutor told Hayes that if he pleaded guilty to the forgery charge, the prosecutor would not charge him with violating the habitual-offender statute. Hayes decided to plead not guilty and was convicted of the forgery charge. Then, however, the prosecutor brought habitual-offender charges against Hayes, who was ultimately convicted and sentenced to life imprisonment. He appealed, alleging that he had been coerced to plead guilty by the threat of prosecution as a habitual offender. The SC disagreed with Hayes, saying that it is not a violation of due process for a prosecutor to threaten defendants with other criminal prosecutions so long as the prosecutor has probable cause to believe that the accused has committed an offense defined by statute. The significance of the case is that prosecutors may use additional charges as threats in plea bargaining with criminal defendants, as long as there is a basis for these charges. It would be improper and unconstitutional if a prosecutor threatened to bring charges for which there was no probable cause.

Bounds v. Smith, 430 U.S. 817, 97 S.Ct. 1491 (1977) [Vernon Lee BOUNDS, etc., et al., Petitioners, v. Robert (Bobby) SMITH et al.] (Corrections; Inmate Rights) Prison inmates have the right of access to adequate law libraries or to the assistance of those trained in the law. In a landmark case in North Carolina in 1977, Bounds and other prisoners alleged that prison officials were denying them reasonable access to the courts and equal protection by failing to provide them with adequate legal library facilities. The state then proposed to create seven libraries for offenders to be available to 13,000 prisoners housed in 77 prison units in 67 counties. The SC said this plan was not proper because it did not create a library for each prison, but the SC offered prison systems alternatives or forms of legal assistance besides law libraries. They can provide paralegals, train inmates to become paralegals working under a lawyer's supervision, hire attorneys on a part-time basis, or actually hire full-time attorneys for inmates on-site. The case is significant because it declared these other avenues of access to the law acceptable.

Bourjaily v. United States, 483 U.S. 171, 107 S.Ct. 2775 (1987) [William John BOURJAILY, Petitioner, v.

UNITED STATES] (Confrontation Clause; Sixth Amendment) Bourjaily was charged in United States district court with conspiring to distribute and of possession of cocaine. Various friends of Bourjaily were implicated, and he had become a suspect through evidence obtained in tape-recorded telephone conversations between him and undercover FBI agents. An FBI informant, Lonardo, also implicated Bourjaily. At his trial, Bourjaily protested that the government had accepted Lonardo's statements as proof of a conspiracy to distribute cocaine. Further, he argued that Lonardo's statements supported the conspiracy only according to a preponderance-of-the-evidence standard. Finally, Lonardo himself had not testified, but his statements had been read into the record against Bourjaily. Bourjaily was convicted. He appealed, alleging that his Sixth Amendment rights had been violated because he had been unable to cross-examine Lonardo. He also alleged that Lonardo's statements amounted to hearsay and were thus excludable as evidence against him. The SC decided otherwise and upheld his conviction. The SC declared that evidence of a coconspirator, Lonardo, is not hearsay if such evidence is obtained during the course and in the furtherance of a conspiracy. Thus, Lonardo's out-of-court statements were admissible against Bourjaily. Further, out-of-court statements may be proven by the offering party (the prosecution) only on the basis of the preponderance of the evidence.

Bowers v. Hardwick, 478 U.S. 186, 106 S.Ct. 2841 (1986) [Michael J. BOWERS, Attorney General of Georgia, Petitioner, v. Michael HARDWICK, and John and Mary Doe] (Sodomy Laws) In August 1982, Hardwick was charged with violating the Georgia statute criminalizing sodomy by committing that act with another adult male in the bedroom of his home. Hardwick filed suit challenging the constitutionality of Georgia's sodomy law. The SC declared that there is no fundamental right to commit sodomy among homosexuals. State laws prohibiting such behavior are constitutional if they otherwise meet constitutional standards. This case was overturned in 2003 in the case of *Lawrence v. Texas.*

Boyd v. United States, 116 U.S. 616, 6 S.Ct. 524 (1886) [E.A. BOYD & Sons and others, Claimants, etc., v. UNITED STATES] (Law Enforcement Officers or Agencies; Self-Incrimination) Fraudulently imported goods were seized by customs inspectors, and Boyd, one of the owners of the goods, requested to have his goods returned. The court required him to produce evidence, specifically invoices for previous shipments, in order to determine the value of the seized property in question. Boyd objected to having to produce such documents, because, he alleged, some of the documents might be incriminating. Nevertheless, he produced the documents under protest, and the court ruled against him. He appealed. The SC overturned the lower court's decision, saying that the notice to produce the invoices in this case, the order by virtue of which it was issued, and the law which authorized the order, were unconstitutional and void. The owner of property may be cited as a witness in a proceeding to forfeit his property. A witness, as well as a party, is protected by law from being compelled to give evidence that tends to incriminate him or her. Thus, persons who are subject to property forfeiture should be entitled to all privileges given to someone charged with committing a criminal offense.

Boyde v. California, 494 U.S. 370, 110 S.Ct. 1190 (1990) [Richard BOYDE, Petitioner, v. CALIFORNIA] (Aggravating and Mitigating Circumstances; Death Penalty; Eighth Amendment) Boyde was charged with robbery, kidnapping for robbery, and first-degree murder; convicted; and sentenced to death. During the sentencing phase of the trial, the jury was given instructions by the judge including the phrase, "shall consider, take into account and be guided by" in determining whether the death penalty ought to be imposed. Boyde appealed, challenging this phrase as mandatory phraseology and thus illegal in death-penalty cases, because mandatory death penalties are illegal (in that aggravating and mitigating circumstances cannot be weighed by the jury). Boyde also claimed that such instructions were "ambiguous and erroneous." The SC upheld Boyde's conviction and death sentence, holding that the judicial instruction did not violate the Eighth Amendment claim made by Boyde that the mandatory nature of the phraseology prevented the jury from making an individualized assessment of the death penalty's appropriateness. States are free to structure and shape consideration of mitigating evidence to achieve a more rational and equitable administration of the death penalty.

Boykin v. Alabama, 395 U.S. 238, 89 S.Ct. 1709 (1969) [Edward BOYKIN, Jr., Petitioner, v. State of ALABAMA] (Death Penalty) Boykin was arrested for common-law robbery. At his trial, which had no jury, he entered a guilty plea. He was convicted and sentenced to death, and he appealed. The SC overturned Boykin's conviction, largely because there was no evidence to show whether his guilty plea was voluntary or made knowingly. As the SC declared, it was reversible error for the trial judge to accept the petitioner's guilty plea without an affirmative statement showing that it was intelligent and voluntary. Thus, the significance of this case is that when guilty pleas are entered by criminal defendants, judges must determine from them whether their pleas are knowingly entered and completely voluntary; that is, that they are effectively waiving various rights to confront their accusers and cross-examine them and to give testimony on their own behalf.

Bracy v. Gramley, 520 U.S. 899, 117 S.Ct. 1793 (1997) [William BRACY, Petitioner, v. Richard B. GRAMLEY, Warden] (Discovery; *Habeas Corpus* Petitions; Judicial Misconduct) Bracy was tried, convicted, and sentenced to death in an Illinois court presided over by Judge Thomas J. Maloney. Maloney was subsequently convicted of taking bribes for fixing other murder cases in Operation Greylord, a federal sting operation intended to detect and prosecute judicial corruption. Bracy appealed his conviction and filed a *habeas corpus* action, arguing that Judge Maloney had a vested interest in Bracy's conviction in order to deflect suspicion that he was taking bribes in other cases. Further, Bracy alleged that Maloney had deliberately suppressed exculpatory evidence that may have mitigated Bracy's sentence. His *habeas corpus* appeals were denied and he appealed directly to the SC, where the case was heard. The SC reversed Bracy's conviction, holding that Bracy, who was convicted before a judge who was himself later convicted of taking bribes from defendants in criminal cases, showed "good cause" for discovery on his due process claim of actual judicial bias in his own case.

Brady v. Maryland, 373 U.S. 83, 83 S.Ct. 1194 (1963) [**John L. BRADY, Petitioner, v. State of MARYLAND**] **(Discovery)** Brady was charged with murder. He took the stand in his own defense and admitted to participating in the crime, but he declared that his confederate, Boblit, was the one who actually killed the victim. Various statements had been made to police and prosecution by Boblit. The prosecutor denied Brady access to these statements, alleging confidentiality. Following Brady's conviction, some of this evidence came to light and proved favorable and exculpatory to Brady. He sought an appeal, claiming that he had been denied due process because these important statements had been withheld during his trial. The SC agreed with Brady and overturned his murder conviction, saying that "suppression by prosecution of evidence favorable to an accused upon request violates due process where evidence is material either to guilt or to punishment, irrespective of good faith or bad faith of prosecution." Presently there are three components of a true *Brady* violation: (1) the evidence at issue must be favorable to the accused, either because it is exculpatory, or because it is impeaching; (2) the evidence must have been suppressed by the state, either willfully or inadvertently; and (3) prejudice must have ensued (*Strickler v. Greene* [1999]).

Brady v. United States, 397 U.S. 742, 90 S.Ct. 1463 (1970) [**Robert M. BRADY, Petitioner, v. UNITED STATES**] **(Death Penalty; Plea Bargaining)** Brady and a co-defendant were charged with kidnapping. The offense carried a maximum penalty of death. Brady initially entered a not-guilty plea, but his codefendant pleaded guilty under a plea-bargain arrangement. When Brady learned that his companion had confessed and agreed to testify against him, Brady changed his plea to guilty in exchange for a lengthy prison sentence. He knew that if the case proceeded through trial, the jury could impose the death penalty. After he received a 50-year sentence, it was commuted to 30 years. Brady appealed, claiming that his plea of guilty had been involuntarily given and that he had so pleaded only to avoid the possible imposition of the death penalty. The SC upheld Brady's conviction and sentence, saying that the guilty plea had not been coerced. The SC stated that a plea of guilty is not invalid merely because it is entered to avoid the possibility of a death penalty. Thus, although Brady's plea of guilty may well have been motivated in part by a desire to avoid a possible death penalty, the court was convinced that his plea was voluntary and intelligently made and it had no reason to doubt that his solemn admission of guilt was truthful.

Branzburg v. Hayes, 408 U.S. 665, 92 S.Ct. 2646 (1972) [**Paul M. BRANZBURG, Petitioner, v. John P. HAYES, Judge, etc., et al., In the Matter of Paul Pappas, Petitioner. United States, Petitioner, v. Earl Caldwell**] **(Media Rights)** Newspaper persons have no constitutional right to maintain the confidentiality of their news sources when subpoenaed before grand juries and are compelled to give testimony. They must disclose the identity of their sources if questioned about them.

Braxton v. United States, 500 U.S. 344, 111 S.Ct. 1854 (1991) [**Thomas BRAXTON, Petitioner, v. UNITED STATES**] **(Acceptance of Responsibility; Plea Bargaining; U.S. Sentencing Guidelines)** Braxton entered guilty pleas to charges of assaulting federal officers but pleaded not guilty to the more serious charge of intent to kill a United States marshal. The government accepted these pleas, but when applying the United States Sentencing Guidelines, it applied an enhancement more applicable to the charge to which Braxton had pleaded not guilty. Thus Braxton was sentenced as though he had actually committed the crime of "intentionally attempting to kill a United States marshal." The government argued that Braxton had "stipulated" to the essence of the charge, that he had deliberately fired a shotgun through his front door when United States marshals came to arrest him. Braxton appealed the more severe sentence. The SC heard the appeal and vacated the sentence, holding that there was nothing in Braxton's stipulation that he ever intended to kill a United States marshal. Because this was a necessary element of an "intent to kill a United States marshal" charge, the sentence had to be vacated and the case remanded for resentencing.

Brecht v. Abrahamson, 507 U.S. 619, 113 S.Ct. 1710 (1993) [**Todd A. BRECHT, Petitioner, v. Gordon A. ABRAHAMSON, Superintendent, Dodge Correctional Institution**] **(*Miranda* Warning; Prosecutorial Misconduct)** At a murder trial in a Wisconsin court, Brecht admitted shooting the victim but claimed it was accidental. State prosecutors in their jury arguments cited Brecht's pre-*Miranda* statements that he failed to tell anyone of the accidental nature of the shooting. More important, a prosecutor commented on his silence following the *Miranda* warning. The jury convicted Brecht and he appealed, arguing that the errors committed by the prosecutor were prejudicial. The SC upheld Brecht's conviction, holding that the prosecution statements did not have a substantial or injurious effect or influence in determining the jury's verdict.

Breed v. Jones, 421 U.S. 519, 95 S.Ct. 1779 (1975) [**Allen F. BREED, Etc., Petitioner, v. Gary Steven JONES**] **(Double Jeopardy; Juvenile Law)** On February 8, 1971, in Los Angeles, Jones, 17 years old and armed with a deadly weapon, allegedly committed robbery. He was apprehended and an adjudicatory hearing in juvenile court was held on March 1. Jones was declared delinquent for robbery. The judge transferred him to criminal court to stand trial on these same charges. Jones was subsequently convicted of robbery. He appealed the decision and the SC reversed the conviction, concluding that the robbery adjudication in juvenile court was considered the equivalent of a criminal trial on the same charges. The juvenile court judge should either have placed Jones in secure confinement following his adjudication or simply have waived jurisdiction over Jones initially to criminal court. To find a juvenile delinquent in juvenile court and then waive him to criminal court on the same charges was unconstitutional because it put him in double jeopardy.

Brewer v. Williams, 430 U.S. 387, 97 S.Ct. 1232 (1977) [Lou V. BREWER, Warden, Petitioner, v. Robert Anthony WILLIAMS, aka Anthony Erthel Williams] (Confessions; Custodial Interrogations; Law Enforcement Officers or Agencies; Right to Counsel) Williams was a suspect in the disappearance of a 10-year-old girl from a YMCA building on Christmas Eve, in Des Moines, IA. He was seen leaving the building with something wrapped in a blanket, with skinny legs sticking out. Williams' car was spotted later about 150 miles from Des Moines, and he was apprehended in Davenport. Des Moines police went to Davenport to bring Williams back to Des Moines, and during their return trip they asked him various questions. As it was beginning to snow heavily, they speculated out loud that a small girl's body would be difficult to find out in the snow and that the girl should at least have a proper "Christian burial." Williams broke down, admitted to the crime of murder, and led police to the girl's body. He was subsequently convicted of murder, but he appealed and his conviction was overturned because police had interrogated him without an attorney present during their trip back to Des Moines. A subsequent retrial resulted in Williams' conviction on other grounds, as there was additional incriminating evidence in his automobile. But the "Christian burial case," as it is known, clearly illustrates that police officers may not conduct interrogations of suspects without first advising them of their right to counsel. (*See the follow-up case, Nix v. Williams* [1984].)

Brinegar v. United States, 338 U.S. 160, 69 S.Ct.1302 (1949) [Virgil T. BRINEGAR, Petitioner, v. UNITED STATES] (Law Enforcement Officers or Agencies; Plain-View Rule; Searches and Seizures; Vehicle Searches) Brinegar was known by police to be a bootlegger of illegal liquor and to transport it frequently across state lines. Federal revenue agents observed him driving his car in Oklahoma, five miles west of the Missouri line. They noticed that it was weighed down in the back and was speeding. After a short chase, they forced Brinegar off the road and observed in plain view a case of liquor in his car. Twelve more cases of untaxed liquor were found under the car seats. Brinegar was convicted of transporting illegal liquor across state lines. He appealed, arguing that the officers had lacked probable cause to stop him and search his vehicle. The SC disagreed and adopted a totality-of-circumstances type of test in this situation. The officers who surveilled Brinegar's car knew who he was and what he did from past observation and experience. They knew various contact points where illegal liquor was obtained. Given all the events they observed, combined with reasonably trustworthy information, the SC believed that the officers had had probable cause to intercept Brinegar and search his vehicle. His conviction was thus upheld. (*See Carroll v. United States* [1925] *for a comparable case.*)

Briscoe v. LaHue, 460 U.S. 325, 103 S.Ct. 1108 (1983) [Carlisle W. BRISCOE, Chris P. Vickers, Sr., and James N. Ballard, Petitioners, v. Martin LaHUE and James W. Hunley, etc.] (Civil Rights, Section 1983 Claims; Immunity; Law Enforcement Officers or Agencies) Briscoe was convicted of burglary. He later sued a police officer who had

given perjured testimony against him, according to Title 42 U.S.C. Section 1983, a civil rights section. The SC held that police officers enjoy *absolute immunity* from civil prosecutions when they have given testimony, even perjured testimony, against criminal defendants. Officers who allegedly commit perjury are not immune from possible criminal penalties against them if their testimony is determined to be perjured.

Brooks v. Tennessee, 406 U.S. 605, 92 S.Ct. 1891 (1972) [Donald L. BROOKS, Petitioner, v. State of TENNESSEE] (Fifth Amendment; Self-Incrimination) Brooks was charged with armed robbery and unlawful possession of a pistol. At his trial, he desired to give testimony. Tennessee law mandated that if a defendant in a criminal case wishes to give testimony, he must do so before any other defense witnesses are called. After Brooks was convicted, he appealed, alleging that this protocol had violated his due-process rights as well as his right against self-incrimination under the Fifth Amendment. The SC heard his appeal and reversed his conviction, saying that the Tennessee statute was unconstitutional. Criminal defendants may or may not wish to testify after hearing other defense witnesses testify. It is the privilege of defendants to decide whether to testify in their own behalf. Thus, compelling a defendant who wishes to testify to speak first violates his right against self-incrimination. The significance of this case is that defendants in criminal cases may testify at any stage of the defense case or not testify at all, if they so choose.

Brower v. County of Inyo, 489 U.S. 593, 109 S.Ct. 1378 (1991) [Georgia BROWER, Individually and as Administrator of the Estate of William James Caldwell (Brower), Deceased, et al., Petitioners, v. COUNTY OF INYO et al.] (Civil Rights, Section 1983 Claims; Fourth Amendment; Law Enforcement Officers or Agencies; Searches and Seizures) Brower was a suspect who had stolen a car, leading police on a 20-mile chase down a major highway. In an effort to stop him, police caused an 18-wheel tractor-trailer rig to be placed across the highway ahead of him. Police headlights were turned toward Brower, thus preventing him from seeing the truck across the road. He crashed into the truck and was killed. His family filed a Title 42 U.S.C. Section 1983 civil rights action against police, alleging that Brower had been the subject of an unreasonable seizure. Liability was not decided by this case, but the SC declared that the roadblock established by police in this case was unreasonable and thus constituted an unreasonable seizure, violating Brower's Fourth Amendment rights. The police measures clearly exceeded the reasonableness necessary to stop a fleeing thief. It was a property crime, the punishment for which would probably have been a short prison term, certainly not the death penalty. Because the officers knew or should have known that the roadblock and blinding headlights would probably cause Brower's death, they were clearly using excessive force, which was unconstitutional.

Brown v. Board of Education, 347 U.S. 483, 74 S.Ct. 686 (1954) [BROWN et al., v. BOARD OF EDUCATION of Topeka, Shawnee County, Kansas, et al.] (Discrimination) In 1954, Brown brought a class-action suit challenging the separate-but-equal doctrine as it pertained to elementary schools. At the time, especially in the South, separate educational facilities were provided for black children that were allegedly of the same quality as those provided for white children. White and black children could not, however, attend the same schools. The SC heard the case and decided that as far as education is concerned, the separate-but-equal doctrine does not apply. Thus, the original *Plessy v. Ferguson* (1896) decision on this matter was partially set aside. It is unconstitutional to have separate but equal schools for blacks and whites.

Brown v. Illinois, 422 U.S. 590, 95 S.Ct. 2254 (1975) [Richard BROWN, Petitioner, v. State of ILLINOIS] (Law Enforcement Officers or Agencies; *Miranda* Warning; Self-Incrimination) Brown was arrested in Illinois without probable cause or a warrant and taken to a police station, where he was told his *Miranda* rights. While at the police station, he gave at least two incriminating statements, linking him with a murder. At his trial, he sought to suppress these statements. However, they were ruled admissible and Brown was convicted. He appealed, and the SC overturned his conviction, concluding that because his arrest was warrantless and lacking probable cause, the *Miranda* warning and Brown's statements were inadmissible. It cited the fruits-of-the-poisonous-tree doctrine, which says that if the arrest was illegal, its illegality taints the "fruits" of the arrest, or confessions given later.

Brown v. Mississippi, 287 U.S. 278, 56 S.Ct. 461 (1936) [Ed BROWN et al. v. State of MISSISSIPPI] (Confessions; Fourteenth Amendment; Law Enforcement Officers or Agencies) Brown was a suspect in a murder. He was visited at his home by a deputy sheriff and brought to the murder scene. He denied committing the murder. The deputy and others hanged him from a tree, let him down, and then hanged him again. Later they tied him to a tree and beat him. A few days later the deputy came to his home again and arrested him. Brown was taken to jail, where he was beaten repeatedly and told that the beatings would continue until he confessed. He confessed to the murder and was subsequently convicted and sentenced to death. He filed an appeal on the grounds that he had been denied due process under the Fourteenth Amendment. The SC agreed. It argued further that the brutality of police officers had rendered his confession and other statements inadmissible in court against him. Coerced confessions to crimes are unconstitutional. His conviction was overturned.

Brown v. Texas, 443 U.S. 47, 99 S.Ct. 2637 (1979) [Zackary C. BROWN, Appellant, v. State of TEXAS] (Law Enforcement Officers or Agencies) Brown was stopped by two Texas police officers, who asked him to identify himself and explain his presence to them. The officers had no suspicion that Brown was involved in anything illegal. He refused their request, was charged with refusing to cooperate with police, and was convicted. He appealed. The SC overturned his conviction, because persons may not be punished for refusing to identify themselves if police have no suspicion of their being involved in any type of criminal or suspicious activity.

Bruton v. United States, 391 U.S. 123, 88 S.Ct. 1620 (1968) [George William BRUTON, Petitioner, v. UNITED STATES] (Confrontation Clause; Sixth Amendment) Bruton and Evans were charged with armed postal robbery. The accomplice, Evans, gave police a confession implicating Bruton. Evans was not called to testify, although his confession was admitted against Bruton. Thus, Bruton's attorney could not cross-examine Evans. The trial judge instructed the jury that Evans' confession was significant evidence against Evans but should not be considered evidence against Bruton. Bruton was convicted. He appealed, and the SC overturned the conviction, saying that the jury instructions by the trial judge to disregard that part of Evans' confession implicating Bruton were insufficient to cure the error of not permitting Evans to be cross-examined. The significance of this case is that a defendant is entitled to cross-examine his accuser, even if it is an accomplice who confesses and implicates the defendant. It is insufficient for a judge to permit a confession into evidence where a party other than the confessor is implicated, without giving the other party an opportunity to confront his accuser in court. Bruton's Sixth Amendment right to cross-examine witnesses against him had clearly been violated in this case. (*See Harrington v. California* [1969] *for a similar case with a different holding under different circumstances.*)

Buchanan v. Kentucky, 483 U.S. 402, 107 S.Ct. 2906 (1987) [David BUCHANAN, Petitioner, v. KENTUCKY] (Death Penalty; Death-Qualified Juries; Fifth Amendment; Juvenile Law; Self-Incrimination; Sixth Amendment) Police discovered the body of Barbel Poore in an automobile; she had been shot twice in the head and sexually assaulted. (*See Stanford v. Kentucky* [1989] *for a discussion of the crime's details.*) Three persons were subsequently arrested, including Buchanan, a juvenile. Confessions from the other participants implicated Buchanan as the criminal events were reconstructed. He and an accomplice, Stanford, were transferred to criminal court for trial on the murder charges. The two were tried jointly. A "death-qualified" jury was selected. Objections from defense counsel were overruled. During the trial, Buchanan raised a mental-status defense, and the state used the results of a psychiatric report about him to rebut this defense. Both suspects were convicted. Buchanan appealed, alleging that his Fifth and Sixth Amendment rights had been violated, first because the jury was death-qualified and thus did not represent a fair cross-section of the community, and second because the report from the state psychiatrist was based on an evaluation of Buchanan during which his attorney had not been present. The SC rejected both of Buchanan's claims. It said that the use of a death-qualified jury for a joint trial in which the death penalty was sought only against Stanford, the codefendant, did not violate Buchanan's Sixth Amendment right to an impartial jury. Further, the state's use of a psychiatric report about Buchanan solely to rebut Buchanan's mental-status defense did not violate Buchanan's Fifth or Sixth Amendment rights.

Buck v. Bell, 274 U.S. 200, 47 S.Ct. 584 (1927) [Carrie BUCK v. J.H. BELL, Superintendent of State Colony for Epileptics and Feeble Minded] (Fourteenth Amendment; Mental Capacity) Carrie Buck was an 18-year-old "feeble-minded" woman who was committed to a mental-health facility in Virginia. A Virginia statute declared at that time that such mentally deficient persons should be sterilized. Buck's lawyer appealed, arguing that the Virginia statute was unconstitutional. The SC upheld the constitutionality of that statute, saying that "it is far better to prevent those who are manifestly unfit from continuing their kind . . . three generations of imbeciles are enough" (at 585). (*See Skinner v. Oklahoma* [1942] *for an opinion about another type of sterilization issue and a contrary holding on grounds involving the equal-protection clause of the Fourteenth Amendment.*)

Buckley v. Fitzsimmons, 509 U.S. 259, 113 S.Ct. 2606 (1993) [Stephen BUCKLEY, Petitioner, v. Michael FITZSIMMONS et al.] (Civil Rights, Section 1983 Claims; Immunity; Prosecutorial Misconduct) Buckley was charged with murder. Prosecutors made various statements surrounding the indictment of Buckley for the murder, including several untrue statements. Subsequently, the charges against Buckley were dropped, and he sued the prosecutors under Title 42 U.S.C. Section 1983, alleging that his civil rights had been violated by this prosecutorial misconduct. The prosecutors sought absolute immunity from this suit and the SC heard the case. The SC upheld Buckley's right to sue the prosecutor, who only enjoyed *qualified* immunity from such suits. Prosecutors are liable for statements they make publicly if such statements are false and they result in harm to defendants who are innocent of criminal wrongdoing.

Buford v. United States, 532 U.S. 59, 121 S.Ct. 1276 (2001) [Paula L. BUFORD, Petitioner, v. UNITED STATES]. (U.S. Sentencing Guidelines) Paula Buford was convicted of armed bank robbery and sentenced to 188 months after a finding by the federal district court judge that she was a career offender. Buford had five prior convictions, four relating to a series of gas station robberies. The fifth conviction was for a drug offense. The sentencing judge consolidated these prior convictions in determining whether Buford was a career offender and should receive the maximum sentence under the U.S. sentencing guidelines. Buford challenged the consolidation of these convictions, where the drug offense was included in order to determine her career offender status. Buford did not contest the factual circumstances of each of the prior convictions. State criminal courts in Wisconsin had previously sentenced Buford to three prison terms for the five crimes (six years for the drug crime, 12 years for two robberies, and 15 years for the other two robberies), and the courts had ordered that all three sentences should run concurrently. However, she raised a procedural issue that would seek to clarify the consolidation-related legal principles and bring consistency to her sentence. Thus, she challenged the right of the appellate court to review her sentence deferentially rather than *de novo*. The SC heard the case and affirmed the right of the appellate court to review Buford's case deferentially. Buford's 188-month sentence remained unchanged.

Bullington v. Missouri, 451 U.S. 430, 101 S.Ct. 1852 (1981) [Robert BULLINGTON, Petitioner, v. State of MISSOURI] (Death Penalty; Reconvictions and Resentencing) Bullington was charged with capital murder. His case was heard by a jury, who found him guilty. In the sentencing phase, the jury had to decide between the death penalty and life imprisonment as a punishment, and they recommended the latter. Subsequently, Bullington's conviction was

reversed and a new trial resulted. Bullington was again convicted. This time, the jury decided in favor of the death penalty. Bullington appealed and the SC heard his case. It set his death-penalty sentence aside, saying that the first jury's refusal to impose the death penalty was an acquittal for that form of punishment. A subsequent trial cannot result in a punishment greater than that imposed by the first in a capital case. (*See Arizona v. Rumsey* [1984] *and Caspari v. Bohlen* [1984] *for comparable cases.*)

Bumper v. North Carolina, 391 U.S. 543, 88 S.Ct. 1788 (1968) [Wayne Darnell BUMPER, Petitioner, v. State of NORTH CAROLINA] (Law Enforcement Officers or Agencies; Searches and Seizures) Bumper was a suspect in a rape case. Police went to his home and advised his grandmother that they had a search warrant and wanted to come in and look around. The police did *not* have any warrant. Nevertheless, the grandmother gave her consent, and police entered the home and found evidence that later incriminated Bumper in the rape. He was convicted and appealed, arguing that the evidence, a rifle, should have been suppressed because police did not have a warrant. The prosecutor countered by saying that they were conducting a valid search of Bumper's premises consistent with the consent to search given by the grandmother. The SC disagreed with the prosecutor, holding that misrepresentation by police that they have a valid search warrant and the giving of consent as the result of that misrepresentation do not justify a subsequent warrantless search. The incriminating evidence was suppressed, and Bumper's conviction was overturned.

Bunkley v. Florida, ___U.S.___, 123 S.Ct. 2020 (2003) [Clyde Timothy BUNKLEY v. FLORIDA] (Retroactive Rules) Bunkley was convicted in 1986 of committing burglary in the first degree and sentenced to life imprisonment. This was because Bunkley possessed a pocketknife, which was deemed a dangerous weapon by Florida law. No evidence was presented that Bunkley ever used the pocketknife or threatened anyone with it. If the pocketknife had not been considered a dangerous weapon, then Bunkley would have been charged with burglary in the third degree. The difference between first-degree burglary and third-degree burglary is a life sentence in the former and a five-year sentence in the latter. At that time, Florida excepted "common pocketknives" from its "dangerous weapons" list. In 1997 the Florida Supreme Court interpreted the meaning of "common pocketknife" for the first time in a case where a pocketknife was used. The court determined that a pocketknife with a blade of four inches or less clearly fell in the category of "common pocketknife." The case, *L.B. v. State,* 700 So.2d 370 (1997), resulted in the Florida Supreme Court vacating L.B.'s conviction because the knife in question was a common pocketknife and not a dangerous weapon within the meaning of the dangerous weapon statute. Bunkley therefore appealed for postconviction relief, as his pocketknife was within the scope of Florida's definition of a "common pocketknife." Florida denied Bunkley relief, because the court refused to apply the new definition of common pocketknife retroactively. The Florida Supreme Court declared that because this (i.e., the evolution of the meaning of the term *common pocketknife*) was a change in the law, retroactive application of this change was not possible. The SC subsequently heard Bunkley's appeal and vacated the decision, remanding the case for further proceedings. The Florida Supreme Court's legal error in using its change-of-law determination as the basis for resolving Bunkley's due-process question required remand for determination of the extent to which the term *common pocketknife* had evolved as of the date Bunkley's conviction became final, and whether, based on the understanding of that term at the time, Bunkley's possession of such a pocketknife satisfied the elements of Florida's first-degree burglary statute. Clarifications of the law are different from changes in the law, and the consequences of each action must be evaluated. Thus, if the law was merely clarified, Bunkley would not be guilty of first-degree burglary because the dangerous-weapons element would be absent.

Burch v. Louisiana, 441 U.S. 357, 99 S.Ct. 1623 (1979) [Daniel BURCH et al., Petitioners, v. State of LOUISIANA] (Jury Size; Jury Trials; Fourteenth Amendment; Right to Counsel; Sixth Amendment) Burch was convicted 5–1 by a six-person jury on charges of exhibiting obscene motion pictures. He appealed to the SC, which overturned his conviction. The SC used precedent to justify its action in which a less-than-unanimous six-person jury is unconstitutional (*see Duncan v. Louisiana* [1968] *and Ballew v. Georgia* [1978]). After an overly lengthy opinion (in view of the fact that the matter had already been settled in two landmark cases earlier), the SC said, again, that six-person juries must be unanimous; if they are not, then the defendant has been deprived of the right to a fair jury trial under the Sixth and Fourteenth Amendments.

Burks v. United States, 437 U.S. 1, 98 S.Ct. 2141 (1978) [David Wayne BURKS, Petitioner, v. UNITED STATES] (Double Jeopardy; Insanity Pleas) Burks was charged with robbery in a United States district court in Tennessee. During his trial, expert testimony of his insanity was offered. The government rebutted with expert and lay testimony of Burks' sanity. The jury found Burks guilty. A motion by Burks for a new trial was denied. However, an appellate court found that the government's proof to counter Burks' claim of insanity was insufficient, and his conviction was reversed. The appellate court sent the case back to the district court, where the judge could determine whether a directed verdict of acquittal was in order or if a second trial should be held. Burks contested the notion of a second trial. An appeal from Burks to the SC resulted in the following decision. The SC said that for the purposes of determining whether the double-jeopardy clause precludes a second trial after the reversal of a conviction, a reversal based on insufficiency of evidence is tantamount to an acquittal. This is to be distinguished from reversal due to trial error. In holding that evidence is insufficient to prove guilt beyond a reasonable doubt, the appellate court is giving the requirements for an entry of a judgment of acquittal. Burks was thereby acquitted of the robbery.

Butterworth v. Smith, 494 U.S. 624, 110 S.Ct 1376 (1990) [Robert A. BUTTERWORTH, Jr., Attorney General of Florida, et al., Petitioners, v. Michael SMITH] (First Amendment; Free Speech; Grand Juries) Smith, a reporter for a Florida newspaper, gave evidence before a grand jury in a criminal matter involving certain public officials. Subsequently, he wanted to write an article about his testimony and the subject matter of the events. However, a Florida statute barred him from disclosing grand-jury statements he made publicly, and Smith sued, alleging a violation of his First Amendment right of free speech. The SC eventually ruled that laws prohibiting disclosures of grand-jury testimony are unconstitutional to the extent that they pertain to witnesses who wish to speak about their own testimony after the grand jury has been terminated.

C

Cabana v. Bullock, 474 U.S. 376, 106 S.Ct. 689 (1986) [Donald A. CABANA, Superintendent, Mississippi State Penitentiary, et al., Petitioners, v. Crawford BULLOCK, Jr.] (Death Penalty; *Habeas Corpus* Petitions; Jury Instructions) Bullock and a friend, Tucker, were offered a ride by Dickson. An argument developed, and Dickson was killed by Tucker. Bullock and Tucker disposed of Dickson's body, but they were apprehended and charged with first-degree murder and robbery in a Mississippi court. Bullock was convicted, and during the sentencing phase of his trial, the judge issued confusing instructions to the jury. According to Mississippi law, Bullock could receive the death penalty if he had been found by the jury to have killed Dickson, intended to kill him, and/or intended to use lethal force against him. This factual prerequisite was not made clear to the jury; rather, mere presence at a scene involving a murder makes the partner equally guilty with the perpetrator who commits the murder, in this case Tucker. The jury sentenced him to death. Bullock filed a *habeas corpus* petition challenging his sentence, contending that the jury instructions had been faulty and that his role had been insufficient to warrant the death penalty. The SC heard his case and vacated the death sentence, remanding the case to a Mississippi trial court, where the jury could be given the choice of either imposing a sentence of life imprisonment on Bullock or determining the factual question of whether Bullock had killed, attempted to kill, or intended to use lethal force against Dickson. If it was determined that Bullock possessed the requisite culpability, then the death sentence could be reimposed.

Cabell v. Chavez-Salido, 454 U.S. 432, 102 S.Ct. 735 (1982) [Clarence E. CABELL et al., Appellants, v. Jose CHAVEZ-SALIDO et al.] (Corrections; Probation and Parole) Several resident aliens, including Chavez-Salido, attempted to secure jobs as probation officers in California. California has a statute requiring that all public employees declared by law to be police officers must be United States citizens. The resident aliens filed suit, alleging that they were constitutionally entitled to these jobs. The SC upheld the right of California to impose such a statute as a requirement for holding these law enforcement positions. That right does not mean that resident alien status disqualifies persons from any public positions. Rather, it pertains to law enforcement and probation and parole work.

Cady v. Dombrowski, 413 U.S. 433, 93 S.Ct. 2523 (1973) [**Elmer O. CADY, Warden, Petitioner, v. Chester J. DOMBROWSKI**] (**Inventory Searches; Law Enforcement Officers or Agencies; Searches and Seizures; Vehicle Searches**) Dombrowski was a Chicago police officer who became drunk and had an automobile accident in Wisconsin. He was transported from his disabled vehicle by another party to a nearby town, where he called the police and had them drive him back to his vehicle. The Wisconsin police officers were aware of Dombrowski's status as a police officer from Chicago and knew that officers carried firearms. Thus, when they returned to his car, they searched it for a weapon. Dombrowski had been drinking heavily and they considered him drunk. They arrested him for drunken driving and jailed him. In the meantime, the wrecked vehicle was towed to a garage, where its contents were inventoried. A revolver was found, together with some bloody clothing. Further investigation linked this clothing and pistol with a murder recently committed in nearby Fond du Lac County. Dombrowski was charged with murder and convicted, largely on circumstantial evidence. He sought to suppress the evidence resulting from the officer's inventory search of the vehicle. The SC upheld Dombrowski's conviction, saying that the warrantless search for the pistol was legitimate on the basis of what the officers knew about Dombrowski's police officer status, and that a subsequent search with a warrant disclosing incriminating bloody clothing was also valid. The original search of the vehicle by police was valid because the officers had exercised a form of custody over the car and removed it from the road as a possible traffic hazard. Police had also acted to protect innocent citizens who might have discovered Dombrowski's service revolver by accident and become injured.

Cage v. Louisiana, 498 U.S. 39, 111 S.Ct. 328 (1990) [**Tommy CAGE v. LOUISIANA**] (**Death Penalty; Jury Instructions**) Cage was convicted of first-degree murder in a New Orleans court. The judge issued instructions to the jury concerning the interpretation of "beyond a reasonable doubt." His definition of the phrase included words such as "it must be such doubt as would give rise to a grave uncertainty," "an actual substantial doubt," and "a moral certainty." Cage was sentenced to death. He appealed the conviction and sentence, and the SC overturned his conviction. The SC concluded by saying that phrases such as "grave uncertainty" and "moral certainty" suggest a higher degree of doubt than is required for acquittal under the reasonable doubt standard (at 329–330).

Calcano-Martinez v. Immigration and Naturalization Service, 533 U.S. 348, 121 S.Ct. 2268 (2001) [**Deboris CALCANO-MARTINEZ et al., Petitioners, v. IMMIGRATION AND NATURALIZATION SERVICE**] (**Deportation; *Habeas Corpus* Petitions**) Calcano-Martinez, Sergio Madrid, and Fazila Khan were lawful permanent residents of the United States from other countries who were convicted of aggravated felonies. Because of their felony convictions, they

were subject to deportation. The Immigration and Naturalization Service (INS) moved to have them deported according to the provisions of the Immigration and Nationality Act of 1996 (INA). They filed a petition for review with the Second Circuit Court of Appeals and a *habeas corpus* petition with the federal district court in order to challenge the Board of Immigration Appeals' determination that they were ineligible to apply for a discretionary waiver of deportation under 28 U.S.C. Section 2241 of the INA. The Second Circuit dismissed their petitions, holding that they could nevertheless pursue their claims in federal district court. They appealed to the SC, who heard their cases. The SC held that whereas the Second Circuit had no jurisdiction to hear their petitions for direct review, they were permitted to proceed with their *habeas corpus* petitions in federal district court. The INA expressly precludes courts of appeals from exercising jurisdiction to review a final removal order against an alien removable by reason of a conviction for an aggravated felony. (*See also Immigration and Naturalization Service v. St. Cyr* [2001].)

Calderon v. Coleman, 525 U.S. 141, 119 S.Ct. 500 (1998) [**Arthur CALDERON, Warden, v. Russell COLEMAN**] (**Death Penalty; *Habeas Corpus* Petitions; Jury Instructions**) Coleman was convicted of the rape, sodomy, and murder of Shirley Hill in 1979 in California. Coleman sought *habeas corpus* relief on the basis that the trial judge erred when giving jury instructions as to the governor's potential power to commute death sentences to life without parole or life with parole. The trial judge concluded by admonishing the jury to ignore the governor's commutation power in rendering its verdict as to sentence. The SC held that although the trial court gave ambiguous instructions, tests should have first been applied to determine whether the error had a substantial and injurious effect of influence in determining the jury's verdict. Although a federal court subsequently granted *habeas corpus* relief to Coleman as to the sentence but not to the conviction, it did so erroneously, because it did so without first applying the harmless-error standard. (*See Boyde v. California* [1990] and *Brecht v. Abrahamson* [1993] *for comparison.*)

Caldwell v. Mississippi, 472 U.S. 320, 105 S.Ct. 2633 (1985) [**Bobby CALDWELL, Petitioner, v. MISSISSIPPI**] (**Death Penalty; Eighth Amendment; Prosecutorial Misconduct**) Caldwell had shot and killed the owner of a small grocery store while robbing it. After he was apprehended and tried, the defense and prosecution gave their summations. The prosecution told the jury not to view itself as finally determining whether Caldwell would die, because a death sentence would be reviewed for correctness by the Mississippi Supreme Court. Caldwell was convicted and sentenced to death. He appealed, arguing that the prosecutor's remarks during summation had been improper and had misled the jury into believing that they would not be responsible for the death of Caldwell. The SC reversed his conviction, holding that the prosecutor's remarks had been improper because they were inaccurate and misleading in a manner that diminished the jury's sense of responsibility. Thus, the SC concluded, these prosecutorial remarks and the jury's subsequent recommendation for the death penalty had violated Caldwell's Eighth Amendment right to due process.

California v. Acevedo, 500 U.S. 565, 111 S.Ct. 1982 (1991) [CALIFORNIA, Petitioner, v. Charles Steven ACEVEDO] (Closed Container Searches; Law Enforcement Officers or Agencies; Searches and Seizures; Vehicle Searches) DEA agents discovered a Federal Express package shipped from Hawaii to California that contained a large quantity of marijuana. They allowed Federal Express personnel to deliver the package to a house and placed the house under surveillance. Subsequently, a man entered the house and left later carrying a tote bag. They intercepted him and found about a pound of marijuana in the bag. Later they observed Acevedo arrive at the house and leave later carrying a brown paper bag about the size of the tote bag. Police officers stopped Acevedo's car thereafter, searched the brown paper bag without a warrant, and discovered marijuana. The police lacked probable cause to search the vehicle itself, although they did have probable cause to believe that the paper bag held marijuana. Acevedo was convicted and he appealed. The SC upheld Acevedo's conviction, saying that probable cause to believe that a container has contraband may enable officers to search that container, even if it is in a vehicle that they lack probable cause to search. This case modified greatly two other cases, *United States v. Chadwick* (1977) and *Arkansas v. Sanders* (1979), because it permitted officers to open containers, even large ones, if there was probable cause to do so, even if those containers were in vehicles that police lacked probable cause to search in their entirety.

California v. Beheler, 463 U.S. 1121, 103 S.Ct. 3517 (1983) [CALIFORNIA, Petitioner, v. Jerry Lain BEHELER] (Custodial Interrogations; *Miranda* Warning) Jerry Beheler and several acquaintances attempted to steal some hashish from Peggy Dean, who was selling the drug in the parking lot of a liquor store. Dean was subsequently gunned down and killed by Beheler's stepbrother, Danny Wilbanks. Beheler called the police and told them that Wilbanks had killed Dean. Further, Beheler told police that Wilbanks had hidden the gun in Beheler's backyard, where the gun was eventually retrieved after consent was given to search the premises. Police officers invited Beheler to the police station later to talk about the crime, although they specifically told him that he was not under arrest. Beheler was not Mirandized. Beheler voluntarily went to the police station and talked with police about the murder, where he was again not Mirandized. After giving his voluntary statement to police, he was allowed to return home. Five days later, after prosecutors had an opportunity to review his voluntary statement, they had police arrest Beheler and charged him with aiding and abetting first-degree murder in Dean's death. At that time, Beheler was Mirandized and gave a confession admitting that his earlier interview with the police had been given voluntarily. Thus, both of Beheler's statements were admitted into his subsequent trial as evidence against him. Beheler appealed, seeking to have his statements excluded as evidence against him. Subsequently, the California Supreme Court reversed Beheler's convictions for aiding and abetting first-degree murder, because his first interview with

police was considered a custodial interrogation under the circumstances. Because police failed to Mirandize Beheler, his statements were declared inadmissible as evidence against him. California prosecutors appealed and the SC heard the case. The SC reversed the California Supreme Court and reinstated Beheler's convictions, as it was beyond doubt that Beheler was neither taken into custody nor significantly deprived of his freedom of action in his first interview with police. Thus, defendants, although criminal suspects, who are not placed under arrest and who voluntarily come to a police station, give brief interviews, and are allowed to leave unhindered after being interviewed, are not subject to *Miranda* warnings by police. Thus, their statements made are legally admissible against them in court later.

California v. Brown, 479 U.S. 538, 107 S.Ct. 837 (1987) [CALIFORNIA, Petitioner, v. Albert Greenwood BROWN, Jr.] (Bifurcated Trials; Eighth Amendment; Fourteenth Amendment; Jury Instructions) Brown was convicted of the forcible rape and first-degree murder of Susan J., a 15-year-old girl in Riverside, CA. During the penalty phase of the two-phased trial, the judge issued the following jury instruction: "You must not be swayed by mere sentiment, conjecture, sympathy, passion, prejudice, public opinion or public feeling." The jury imposed the death sentence. An automatic appeal resulted in the California Supreme Court reversing Brown's conviction on the grounds that the judge's jury instruction had violated Brown's Eighth and Fourteenth Amendment rights to due process. The SC heard the state's appeal and reversed the California Supreme Court, reinstating Brown's conviction and death sentence. The SC held that because the jury instruction had been given during the sentencing phase of Brown's trial, it did not violate either the Eighth or Fourteenth Amendment rights of Brown. Further, the jury instruction was reasonable because it emphasized to jurors the extraneous nature of factors unrelated to the factual circumstances of the murder itself. The instructions from the judge merely limited the jury's sentencing considerations to "record evidence."

California v. Byers, 402 U.S. 424, 91 S.Ct. 1535 (1971) [CALIFORNIA, Petitioner, v. Jonathan Todd BYERS] (Confessions; Fifth Amendment; Self-Incrimination) Byers was involved in an automobile accident and left the scene without first giving his name and address to the police. He claimed the privilege under the Fifth Amendment that such information given would be self-incriminating and thus would violate his rights. A California court granted an appeal of a writ of prohibition, preventing the court from proceeding against Byers on the hit-and-run charge. The government appealed and the SC vacated the judgment, holding that the constitutional privilege against compulsory self-incrimination had not been infringed by the state statute that required motorists involved in accidents to stop at the scene and give their name and address.

California v. Carney, 471 U.S. 386, 105 S.Ct. 2066 (1985) [CALIFORNIA, Petitioner, v. Charles R. CARNEY] (Fourth Amendment; Law Enforcement Officers or Agencies; Searches and Seizures; Vehicle Searches) Carney was believed to be exchanging marijuana for sex in a motor home parked in a vacant lot. Police had heard rumors, not from reliable informants, about his activities, and placed his motor home under surveillance. They observed a young boy enter it and leave a while later. They intercepted the boy and asked him whether Carney was exchanging sex for marijuana. The boy admitted it, so police entered Carney's motor home without a warrant and without Carney's consent. They found marijuana and arrested Carney. They impounded his motor home and searched it extensively at the police station, discovering more marijuana. He was subsequently convicted. He appealed, alleging that police had made an unlawful search of his vehicle in violation of his Fourth Amendment rights. The SC upheld Carney's conviction, stating in brief that it considered his motor home, for all practical purposes, to be the same as an automobile; thus, police were entitled to search it, with probable cause and without a warrant. This case is significant because it caused motor homes to fall under the so-called *automobile exception* to warrantless searches of vehicles whenever probable cause is present.

California v. Ciraolo, 476 U.S. 207, 106 S.Ct. 1809 (1986) [CALIFORNIA, Petitioner, v. CIRAOLO] (Fourth Amendment; Informants; Law Enforcement Officers or Agencies; Open Field Searches; Plain-View Rule) Ciraolo was growing marijuana in his backyard, according to an anonymous tip received by police. The yard could not be seen from the street, so police flew over Ciraolo's home in an airplane and photographed the backyard. After viewing photographs and detecting marijuana plants, officers obtained a search warrant for Ciraolo's premises, where they found growing marijuana plants. Ciraolo was convicted of cultivating marijuana. He appealed, contending that he had a reasonable expectation of privacy, which included his backyard, and that planes flying over his yard viewing it constituted a Fourth Amendment unreasonable search. The SC upheld the use of aerial photography in identifying illegal contraband, such as growing marijuana. It declared that one's property, such as a backyard, cannot be barred from public view from the air; thus, anything such as marijuana or other illegal contraband is subject to being viewed and seized.

California v. Greenwood, 486 U.S. 35, 108 S.Ct. 1625 (1988) [CALIFORNIA, Petitioner, v. Billy GREENWOOD and Dyanne Van Houten] (Law Enforcement Officers or Agencies; Searches and Seizures; Trash Searches) Greenwood, a suspected drug dealer, was under surveillance by the police. They observed that from time to time, he would place out trash for trash collectors. They inspected some of his trash and discovered sufficient incriminating evidence to obtain a search warrant of the premises based on probable cause. A search yielded large quantities of cocaine and hashish and resulted in Greenwood's arrest and conviction for various drug violations. He appealed, contending that his trash should have been subject to a search warrant before police inspected it, and thus, the evidence later discovered and used against him in court should have been excluded. The SC disagreed and said that warrantless searches of trash or garbage are permissible, because persons give up their right to privacy of refuse when-

ever they place it in public places in trash containers, readily accessible to others.

California v. Hodari D., 499 U.S. 621, 111 S.Ct. 1547 (1991) [CALIFORNIA, Petitioner, v. HODARI D.] (Juvenile Law; Law Enforcement Officers or Agencies; Searches and Seizures) Hodari was a juvenile who was observed by police late at night with others huddled around a vehicle in a high-crime neighborhood of Oakland. Everyone fled in different directions when they saw the approaching police vehicle. One officer, Petroso, drove around the block to intercept one of the fleeing persons, Hodari. Hodari ran into Pertoso and a brief scuffle ensued. Hodari broke free, began to run away again, and threw away what appeared to be a small rock. The officer tackled Hodari and arrested him. The recovered rock turned out to be crack cocaine. After Hodari was convicted, he appealed, contending that he had been seized unreasonably and that Petroso had lacked probable cause to arrest him and use the thrown-away cocaine against him. The SC disagreed with Hodari and upheld his conviction, saying that the thrown-away cocaine constituted *abandonment,* that Petroso had not *seized* Hodari before this abandonment, and thus, that the cocaine was admissible against Hodari. If Petroso had tackled Hodari and arrested him before Hodari threw away the crack cocaine, then the eventual discovery of cocaine would have been excluded as evidence against Hodari because Petroso would not have been able to establish probable cause for his arrest.

California v. Prysock, 453 U.S. 355, 101 S.Ct. 2806 (1981) [State of CALIFORNIA, Petitioner, v. Randall James PRYSOCK] (Confessions; *Miranda* Warning; Self-Incrimination) In January 1978, Prysock and another man murdered a woman, Erickson. Prysock and his companion were arrested shortly thereafter and taken to a police station for questioning. The questioning was preceded by an extemporaneous *Miranda* warning, in which the officers covered the general points. Prysock indicated a desire to talk with police but without a tape recorder. He also asked if he could have an attorney present *later,* after talking with police. They said he could have one. He gave incriminating statements to police without the attorney present, at his own insistence, and he was subsequently convicted. He appealed, arguing that the *Miranda* warning had not been recited precisely and thus his confession ought to have been excluded and his conviction overturned. An appellate court agreed, and the government appealed. The SC reinstated his murder conviction, holding that the *Miranda* warning need not be a virtual incantation of the precise language contained in the *Miranda* opinion; such a rigid rule is not mandated by *Miranda* or any other decision of the SC. Essentially, Prysock's constitutional rights had not been violated when police gave him the *Miranda* warning in a general way.

California v. Ramos, 463 U.S. 992, 103 S.Ct. 3446 (1983) [CALIFORNIA, Petitioner, v. Marcelino RAMOS] (Cruel and Unusual Punishment; Death Penalty; Eighth Amendment; Fourteenth Amendment; Jury Instructions) Ramos was convicted of murder, robbery, and attempted murder. During the penalty phase of his trial, the judge was obligated to advise the jury that a sentence of life imprisonment without possibility of parole may be commuted by the governor to a sentence that includes the possibility of parole (this is known as the *Briggs Instruction*). Subsequently, the jury gave the death penalty. Ramos appealed, claiming that the jury instruction had violated his due-process rights and constituted cruel and unusual punishment under the Eighth and Fourteenth Amendments. The SC rejected Ramos' appeal outright, holding that there is no federal prohibition against a judge instructing a jury to consider the governor's power to commute a life sentence without parole to one where parole is a possibility. A further assertion by Ramos concerned a statement given by a psychiatrist about Ramos' future dangerousness. The claim that such commentary by a psychiatrist is unconstitutional was also rejected. (*See Jurek v. Texas* [1976].)

California v. Trombetta, 467 U.S. 97, 104 S.Ct. 2528 (1984) [**CALIFORNIA,** Petitioner, **v.** Albert Walter **TROMBETTA** et al.] (**Evidence Preservation; Fourteenth Amendment; Law Enforcement Officers or Agencies**) Trombetta was stopped on suspicion that he was driving while intoxicated (DWI). Police administered a breath-analysis test to Trombetta to determine his blood-alcohol level. Contrary to custom, the breath sample they took was not preserved. Trombetta later sought to suppress the breath-analysis results, claiming that an independent examination of the sample might have led other experts to different conclusions about his alleged level of intoxication. A lower appellate court ruled in favor of Trombetta, obligating California officers to preserve breath samples that they planned to use against motorists on DWI charges in court. However, the SC reversed the lower court and ruled that it is not in violation of the Fourteenth Amendment due-process clause for law enforcement agencies not to preserve breath samples from DWI suspects. Put another way, it is not necessary for California or any other state to preserve breath samples taken from DWI suspects. This practice does not violate any constitutional right of DWI defendants to due process. Currently, California law advises DWI suspects that breath samples will not be preserved, but their results may be used against them in DWI court actions later. California offers defendants a urinalysis test and a blood test as options to a breath test to determine their level of intoxication for prosecution purposes. Defendants may choose their option, although a refusal to take any of the options will result in automatic revocation of their driver's licenses.

California Department of Corrections v. Morales, 514 U.S. 499, 115 S.Ct. 1597 (1995) [**CALIFORNIA DEPARTMENT OF CORRECTIONS** et al., Petitioners, **v.** Jose Ramon **MORALES**] (**Aggravating and Mitigating Circumstances; Corrections; Probation and Parole**) Morales had shot his girlfriend in the head, neck, and abdomen. He was convicted of first-degree murder in 1971 and was sentenced to life in prison. In 1980, he was paroled to a halfway house, where he became acquainted with a 75-year-old woman, Washabaugh. He married her shortly thereafter. The couple planned to move to Los Angeles. Washabaugh's family didn't hear from her and reported her missing after several days. A human hand found on the Hollywood Freeway in Los Angeles

was later identified as Washabaugh's. The body was never recovered, and Morales was subsequently arrested and charged with her murder. He pleaded *nolo contendere* to second-degree murder and was sentenced to 15 years to life. Morales became eligible for parole in 1990. At his parole-eligibility hearing in July 1989, the Board of Prison Terms found him unsuitable for release in 1990, citing numerous aggravating factors to justify their denial of parole. When Morales was originally convicted for Washabaugh's murder in 1980, California had a policy of reviewing a person's parole eligibility on an annual basis. However, in 1981 the policy changed to allow these reviews every three years. Thus, when Morales was denied parole in 1989, the board set his next hearing for 1992. He appealed, seeking an annual parole review and arguing that his three-year review resulted from an *ex post facto* policy decision. The SC upheld the California policy decision as applied to Morales, saying that the *ex post facto* clause is aimed at laws that retroactively alter the definition of crimes or increase punishment for criminal acts. The policy change in California only altered the method to be followed in fixing parole release dates.

Camara v. Municipal Court of the City and County of San Francisco, 387 U.S. 523, 87 S.Ct. 1727 (1967) [**Roland CAMARA,** Appellant, **v. MUNICIPAL COURT OF THE CITY AND COUNTY OF SAN FRANCISCO**] (**Fourth Amendment; Law Enforcement Officers or Agencies; Probation and Parole**) In November 1963, the Division of Housing Inspection of the San Francisco Department of Public Health entered an apartment building to make a routine annual inspection of possible violations of the city's housing code. Camara rented an apartment on the ground floor. Housing inspectors advised him that under the city building code, ground floor apartments were not for residential purposes and asked to enter the apartment. Camara denied them entry, saying that they needed a search warrant. Later, they attempted to enter his apartment without a warrant and were again refused. They charged him under a criminal code for refusing to permit a lawful inspection of a dwelling. Camara appealed. The SC supported Camara, holding that administrative searches of the kind at issue in this case are significant intrusions upon the interests protected by the Fourth Amendment. Further, no immediate need for such a search had been stated by city officials. The significance of the case is that Camara had a constitutional right to demand a search warrant from the city officials and could not be convicted of a crime for refusing to consent to a city inspection.

Campbell v. Louisiana, 523 U.S. 392, 118 S.Ct. 1419 (1998) [**Terry CAMPBELL,** Petitioner, **v. LOUISIANA**] (**Discrimination; Fourteenth Amendment; Grand Juries; Sixth Amendment**) Campbell, who is white, was convicted of second-degree murder in Louisiana. He appealed, contending that Louisiana grand juries have excluded black persons as grand jurors and as grand-jury forepersons for over 16 years, and that this exclusion policy violated his equal-protection and due-process rights under the Fourteenth Amendment and the Sixth Amendment's fair cross-section requirement. Because Campbell is white, the Louisiana SC rejected his claims, holding that Campbell lacked standing to allege discrimination against blacks in the selection of grand juries. The SC reversed the Louisiana SC and held that a white criminal defendant has a third-party standing to raise equal-protection challenges to discrimination against black persons in the selection of grand jurors, regardless of his or her skin color, and that a defendant suffers significant injury in fact when the composition of a grand jury is tainted by racial discrimination.

Campbell v. United States, 365 U.S. 85, 81 S.Ct. 421 (1961) [**Alvin R. CAMPBELL, Arnold S. Campbell and Donald Lester, Petitioners, v. UNITED STATES**] (Discovery) Campbell was charged with bank robbery. During the testimony of a government witness, it became known that a previous statement had been made by that witness. The defense sought to obtain that statement, but the court denied them access to it. The government also denied the *existence* of the statement, when, in fact, it actually existed. Campbell was convicted. He appealed, arguing that under the Jencks Act, he was entitled to discovery of the prior statement given by the government witness in order to impeach the witness. The SC overturned his conviction and held that under the Jencks Act, such information is discoverable and should be turned over to the defense by government attorneys. Thus, Campbell had been deprived of the right to a fair trial.

Cardwell v. Lewis, 417 U.S. 583, 94 S.Ct. 2464 (1974) [**Harold J. CARDWELL, Warden, Petitioner, v. Arthur Ben LEWIS**] (**Fourth Amendment; Law Enforcement Officers or Agencies; Searches and Seizures**) Lewis was suspected of a murder. Police interviewed him five days later and viewed his automobile, which was thought to have been used to accomplish the crime. While the automobile was in a public parking lot, police obtained an arrest warrant for Lewis and towed his car to the police station, where they made plaster casts of the car's tires, and obtained some paint scrapings from the outside of the car. Nothing was obtained from the interior. All of this external examination of the car was done without a warrant. Subsequently, Lewis was charged with the murder and convicted. He appealed, arguing that the search of his automobile without a warrant had violated his Fourth Amendment rights. A lower court excluded the evidence police had obtained. The SC reversed this decision, upholding Lewis' conviction, concluding that the external view of Lewis' car was not unreasonable, and that its towing to a lot for further search, based on probable cause, was not unreasonable; thus, Lewis' Fourth Amendment rights had not been violated.

Carlisle v. United States, 517 U.S. 416, 116 S.Ct. 1460 (1996) [**Charles CARLISLE, Petitioner, v. UNITED STATES**] (**Motion Deadlines**) Carlisle was convicted in federal district court on a federal marijuana charge. Following the jury trial and several days after the prescribed time limit of seven days following the jury verdict to file a motion for a judgment of acquittal, Carlisle filed such a motion. Carlisle argued that there was insufficient evidence to sustain his conviction. The motion was granted. The Sixth Circuit Court of Appeals reversed the judgment and reinstated the verdict against Carlisle. He appealed to the SC, who heard the case. The SC affirmed the Sixth Circuit and held that the federal district court did not have the authority to grant Carlisle's untimely motion for a judgment of acquittal. Such motions must be filed within the prescribed time period governing the filing of such motions.

Carlson v. Green, 446 U.S. 14, 100 S.Ct. 1468 (1980) [**Norman A. CARLSON, Director, Federal Bureau of Prisons, et al., Petitioners, v. Marie GREEN, Administratrix of the Estate of Joseph Jones, Jr.**] (**Corrections; Cruel and Unusual Punishment; Eighth Amendment; Federal Tort Claims Act**) Jones suffered personal injuries while incarcerated in a federal prison in Indiana. Prison officials failed to give him proper medical attention, and he died. His mother, Green, as administratrix of his estate, filed suit, alleging that prison officials had subjected him to cruel and unusual punishment, violating his due-process, equal-protection, and Eighth Amendment rights. The trial court dismissed the complaint, saying Green had no right to sue on behalf of her dead son. Green appealed, and the Seventh Circuit Court of Appeals reversed the dismissal and remanded the case. The government appealed. The SC ruled in favor of Green, holding that a remedy was available to the administratrix, even though her allegation could also support a suit against the United States under the Federal Tort Claims Act and survival of her cause of action was governed by federal common law rather than state statute. In short, Green had the right to sue as established by *Bivens v. Six Unknown Federal Narcotics Agents* (1971).

Carmell v. Texas, 529 U.S. 513, 120 S.Ct. 1620 (2000) [**Scott Leslie CARMELL, Petitioner, v. TEXAS**] (**Ex Post Facto Laws**) In 1996, Carmell was convicted in Texas on 15 counts of sexual offenses against his stepdaughter from 1991 to 1995, when she was 12 to 16 years old. Before September 1993, Texas law specified that a victim's testimony about a sexual offense could not support a conviction unless corroborated by other evidence or the victim informed another person of the offense within six months of its occurrence, but that, if the victim was under 14 at the time of the offense, the victim's testimony alone could support the conviction. A 1993 amendment allowed the victim's testimony alone to support a conviction if the victim was under age 18. Carmell appealed four of his 15 convictions, contending that these four offenses occurred before the 1993 amendment went into effect, and that his victim was under 14 at the time and had not corroborated her assaults by informing others within the prescribed six-month time period. Thus, Carmell argued, these four convictions should be overturned because they violated the *ex post facto* clause of the Constitution. The Texas Court of Appeals affirmed all of Carmell's convictions, and he appealed to the SC, where the case was heard. The SC reversed the four appealed convictions, holding that Texas' application of the new 1993 amendment to pre-1993 offenses amounted to an *ex post facto* application of the law. The Texas amendment authorizing conviction of certain sexual offenses on the victim's testimony alone, where a conviction was not previously permitted, was a law that altered the legal rules of evidence and required less evidence to obtain a conviction. Further, any law that alters the legal rules of evidence and requires less evidence to obtain a conviction is an *ex post facto* law. Thus, convictions that relied solely on the testimony of a victim who was 14 or younger at the time the offenses were committed are barred by the *ex post facto* clause of the Constitution.

Carnley v. Cochran, 369 U.S. 506, 82 S.Ct. 43 (1962) [Willard CARNLEY, Petitioner, v. H.G. COCHRAN, Jr., Director of the Division of Corrections] (Right to Counsel; Sixth Amendment) Trial judges must advise defendants of their right to counsel in plea-bargain proceedings, and a defendant's failure to request counsel is not equivalent to a waiver of that right to counsel.

Carroll v. United States, 267 U.S. 132, 45 S.Ct. 280 (1925) [George CARROLL et al., Petitioners, v. UNITED STATES] (Fourth Amendment; Law Enforcement Officers or Agencies; Searches and Seizures; Vehicle Searches) Carroll was a suspected bootlegger of illegal liquor. Police had tried several times to stop his car but had failed to do so. One evening officers saw Carroll's car returning to Grand Rapids from Detroit. They stopped the car and proceeded, without warrant, to search it extensively. Eventually, after tearing apart seats and other automobile components, they discovered illegal whiskey. Carroll was convicted of transporting intoxicating liquor. He appealed, arguing that the whiskey evidence was the result of an illegal search of his vehicle without probable cause and also without a valid search warrant. The SC upheld his conviction, saying that officers did, indeed, have probable cause to stop him and did not need a search warrant. It stressed that automobiles, unlike houses, are highly mobile entities, and therefore the police were authorized to search Carroll's car before its occupants could destroy any illegal contraband.

Carter v. Kentucky, 450 U.S. 288, 101 S.Ct. 1112 (1981) [Lonnie Joe CARTER, Petitioner, v. Commonwealth of KENTUCKY] (Prosecutorial Misconduct; Sixth Amendment) Carter was charged with a serious crime. He asked the judge to instruct the jury that the defendant's refusal to testify should not lead to an inference of guilt nor prejudice the jury against him in any way. The judge refused, and Carter was found guilty. He appealed, alleging that he had been denied a fair trial because the trial judge failed to issue those instructions to the jury after being asked to do so in a timely manner. The SC agreed with Carter and overturned his conviction on those grounds. It said that the state trial judge has a constitutional obligation, upon proper request from defense, to give a no-adverse-inference instruction to the jury before they deliberate on a defendant's guilt or innocence.

Carter v. People of State of Illinois, 329 U.S. 173, 67 S.Ct. 216 (1946) [Harice Leroy CARTER v. PEOPLE OF STATE OF ILLINOIS] (Corrections; Death Penalty; *Habeas Corpus* Petitions; Plea Bargaining; Right to Counsel) In 1928, Carter pleaded guilty to murder and was sentenced to a 99-year prison term. At the time he entered his plea, he was advised of his right to counsel, but he gave up that right knowingly and voluntarily. He also waived other rights normally waived during plea bargaining and the entering of guilty pleas. In 1945, Carter filed a writ of *habeas corpus,* alleging that he had been denied counsel during the sentencing phase of his trial. A reading of the 1925 record is clear, that Carter knowingly and intelligently gave up his right to an attorney when

entering his initial guilty plea. Only many years later did he express a concern about the absence of counsel, which he had never requested, at his sentencing. The SC upheld Carter's murder conviction, holding that his due-process rights had not been violated when he was sentenced without the presence of counsel. His own waiver of counsel, knowingly, intelligently, and voluntarily, defeated his contention that he was denied counsel.

Caspari v. Bohlen, 510 U.S. 383, 114 S.Ct. 948 (1994) [Paul CASPARI, Superintendent, Missouri Eastern Correctional Center et al., Petitioners, v. Christopher BOHLEN] (Double Jeopardy; Fifth Amendment) Bohlen and others were convicted of robbing a jewelry store in Missouri in 1981. The judge determined that Bohlen was also a persistent offender and was thus in violation of Missouri's persistent-offender statute. The jury convicted him of first-degree robbery, and the judge sentenced him to three consecutive terms of 15 years in prison. Bohlen appealed and the Missouri Supreme Court overturned his conviction, because no proof of his being a persistent offender had been presented at his trial. The case was retried, this time to allow the prosecution the opportunity of showing proof of Bohlen's four prior felony convictions and his status as a persistent offender for a commensurate sentence. Again, the trial judge sentenced Bohlen to three consecutive terms of 15 years in prison. Again, Bohlen appealed on the grounds that the second trial had violated his Fifth Amendment right against double jeopardy. Bohlen's conviction and consecutive sentences were upheld by the SC, who said that it is well established that there is no double-jeopardy bar to the use of prior convictions in sentencing persistent offenders (at 954). The significance of this case is that the double-jeopardy issue does not apply in resentencing proceedings in noncapital cases. (*See comparable cases such as* **Bullington v. Missouri** [1981] *and Arizona v. Rumsey* [1984].)

Chambers v. Florida, 309 U.S. 227, 60 S.Ct. 472 (1940) [Isiah (Izell) CHAMBERS et al., Petitioners, v. State of FLORIDA] (Confessions; Custodial Interrogations; Fourteenth Amendment) Following a murder and robbery in May 1933, Florida police arrested Chambers and other black men without warrants and confined them in the Broward County Jail for investigation. They underwent persistent questioning from the afternoon of May 20 until the sunrise of May 21. Chambers had also been questioned during the daytime all week leading up to the overnight interrogation. Others involved in the murder apparently implicated Chambers, who was subsequently indicted for the murder. He confessed under intense pressure from the sheriff's investigators, who used physical violence against him. He was sentenced to death. He appealed, alleging that his confession had been coerced. The SC agreed and overturned his conviction, ruling that his due-process rights had to be preserved at all times, and that dragnet methods of arrest on suspicion without warrant, protracted questioning and cross-questioning, and physical violence against a person being questioned over a five-day period are unconstitutional. Chambers was black and the murder victim was white. The equal-protection clause of the Fourteenth Amendment should have protected Chambers but had been violated. Chambers' case was sent back to the originating trial court for a possible retrial, this time without the benefit of a coerced confession from Chambers.

Chambers v. Maroney, 399 U.S. 42, 90 S.Ct. 1975 (1970) [Frank CHAMBERS, Petitioner, v. James F. MARONEY, Superintendent, State Correctional Institution] (Exclusionary Rule; Law Enforcement Officers or Agencies; Searches and Seizures; Searches Incident to an Arrest; Vehicle Searches) Chambers and three other men in a station wagon fit the description given to the police by eyewitnesses following a gas station robbery. The police stopped Chambers' car and placed them under arrest, asserting probable cause based on the profile of the perpetrators and their escaping vehicle. The officers had the car towed to the police station, where it was more extensively searched. The search yielded the money from the gas station, some weapons, and other incriminating material. The police then obtained a search warrant for Chambers' home, where they found further incriminating evidence of his involvement in the robbery. Chambers was convicted. He appealed, seeking to suppress the evidence disclosed by the search of his car by police at the police station. The SC upheld his conviction, saying that police may search vehicles at their convenience when they have arrested criminal suspects with probable cause that they are the likely perpetrators. The police were entitled to search the vehicle when they initially stopped Chambers on the highway as a search incident to an arrest. The fact that they chose to search the car at the police station did not nullify the legality of their search.

Chambers v. Mississippi, 410 U.S. 284, 93 S.Ct. 1038 (1973) [Leon CHAMBERS, Petitioner, v. State of MISSISSIPPI] (Fifth Amendment; Jury Trials; Sixth Amendment) Chambers was charged with murdering a police officer. It was known during the trial that three witnesses had heard another man, McDonald, admit to killing the officer. However, a Mississippi law prohibited the testimony of these witnesses because it considered such testimony to be hearsay. Chambers then sought to call McDonald so that he could cross-examine him. The Mississippi law also forbade calling McDonald because he was not considered to be an adverse witness. Chambers was convicted. He appealed. The SC overturned his conviction, saying that the Mississippi law was unconstitutional and had deprived Chambers of a fair trial by denying him the opportunity of cross-examining material witnesses.

Chandler v. Florida, 449 U.S. 560, 101 S.Ct. 802 (1976) [Noel CHANDLER and Robert Granger, Appellants, v. State of FLORIDA] (Jury Trials; Media Rights) The Florida Supreme Court placed a ban on televised broadcasting of judicial proceedings, respecting the right of criminal suspects to a fair trial. The ban was challenged. The SC ruled that a defendant must show something more than the jurors' awareness that a trial has attracted media attention in order to prevent broadcasting that might prejudice jurors.

Chapman v. California, 386 U.S. 18, 87 S.Ct. 824 (1967) [Ruth Elizabeth CHAPMAN and Thomas LeRoy Teale, Petitioners, v. State of CALIFORNIA] (Exclusionary Rule; Fifth Amendment; Law Enforcement Officers or Agencies; Prosecutorial Misconduct) Chapman and a confederate,

Teale, were charged with robbing, kidnapping, and murdering a bartender. During the trial, Chapman did not testify. At that time, California had a statute permitting the judge and prosecutor to comment on the fact that the defendant did not testify in his or her own defense and that inferences about guilt could be drawn from that failure to testify. The trial judge told the jury that they could draw adverse inferences from the defendant's failure to testify, and Chapman was convicted. Before she appealed, the SC decided another case, *Griffin v. California* (1965), which held that commentary by a judge or prosecutor about a defendant's refusal to testify in a criminal case must not infringe on his or her right not to be compelled to be a witness against him- or herself guaranteed by the Fifth Amendment. The California Supreme Court, therefore, admitted that Chapman had been denied a federal constitutional right because of the judge's instructions to the jury about that silence, but it held that the error was *harmless.* Chapman appealed. The SC reversed Chapman's conviction, holding that the error was *not harmless* when the state prosecutor's argument and the trial judge's jury instructions continuously and repeatedly impressed the jury that the refusal of the defendant to testify required inferences to be drawn in the state's favor. Chapman was granted a new trial, in which judicial and prosecutorial commentary on her refusal to testify in her own case were prohibited.

Chapman v. United States, 365 U.S. 610, 81 S.Ct. 776 (1961) [Elmer Samuel CHAPMAN, Petitioner, v. UNITED STATES of America] (Consent Searches; Fourth Amendment; Law Enforcement Officers or Agencies; Searches and Seizures) Chapman rented a dwelling in a wooded area near Macon, GA. The landlord went to the house to invite him to church. Chapman wasn't home and the landlord smelled "sour mash," a whiskey odor. He advised police, who went to the house and entered it through a window, without a warrant, although the landlord had given his permission for police to enter. The police found a distillery and 1,300 gallons of whiskey. Subsequently, federal officers were summoned to the house. Their investigation led to Chapman's arrest and conviction for making illegal whiskey. He appealed, alleging that the police should have obtained a valid warrant before entering his premises, and that the landlord had no right to admit officers to the dwelling he was renting. The SC reversed Chapman's conviction, holding that the warrantless search was unjustified. The federal officers had had time to obtain a warrant but had failed to do so. Even the search by Georgia police was in violation of the Fourth Amendment provision against unreasonable searches and seizures, because they had not known at the time that the premises were being used for illegal whiskey manufacture. A Georgia ordinance provides that an information must be filed by the solicitor general before a "public nuisance" can be abated, such as the dwelling where the whiskey was being manufactured illegally. (*See Weeks v. United States* [1914] *for a comparable case.*)

Chavez v. Martinez, ___U.S.___, 123 S.Ct. 1994 (2003) [Ben CHAVEZ, Petitioner, v. Oliverio MARTINEZ] (Civil Rights, Section 1983 Claims; Custodial Interrogations; Immunity) Martinez was being treated for gunshot wounds following an altercation with police officers and was interrogated by Chavez, a patrol supervisor. Under questioning, Martinez admitted to using heroin and that he had taken an officer's pistol during an altercation with police. At no time was Martinez given a *Miranda* warning. Although he was never charged with a crime and his answers were never used against him in court later, Martinez filed a Section 1983 civil rights action against Chavez, alleging that his due-process rights had been violated by Chavez's coercive questioning. Chavez claimed qualified immunity, but this claim was rejected by the court, which ruled in Martinez's favor. Chavez appealed, and the Ninth Circuit Court affirmed. Chavez's case was then heard by the SC. The SC reversed the lower courts, holding that Martinez's Fifth Amendment right against self-incrimination was not violated, as his statements were never used against him. Furthermore, the failure of Chavez to Mirandize Martinez did not violate Martinez's constitutional rights, as he was never charged with a crime. Also, because Chavez did not violate Martinez's constitutional rights, he is entitled to qualified immunity.

Cheek v. United States, 498 U.S. 192, 111 S.Ct. 604 (1990) [**John L. CHEEK, Petitioner, v. UNITED STATES**] (*Mens Rea*) Cheek was charged with income-tax evasion in a federal district court. He protested, citing his reasonable belief that the income-tax laws are unconstitutional because he had formerly been told so by a group believing the tax laws are unconstitutional. Thus, he had not paid income tax for various years. The judge instructed the jury that an honest but unreasonable belief that tax laws violate one's rights does not constitute a good-faith misunderstanding of the law. Cheek appealed. The SC overturned his conviction, saying that it was an error to instruct the jury to disregard evidence of the defendant's understanding about whether to pay income taxes. The SC held that a good-faith misunderstanding of the law or a good-faith belief that one is not violating the law negates willfulness, whether or not the claimed belief or misunderstanding is objectively reasonable.

Chimel v. California, 395 U.S. 752, 89 S.Ct. 2034 (1969) [**Ted Steven CHIMEL, Petitioner, v. State of CALIFORNIA**] (**Exclusionary Rule; Law Enforcement Officers or Agencies; Searches and Seizures; Searches Incident to an Arrest**) Chimel was suspected of being involved in the burglary of a coin company in California. Police officers obtained a valid arrest warrant and went to his home to arrest him. When Chimel returned from work, police were waiting for him. They placed him under arrest and then proceeded to search his entire house, as a "search incident to an arrest." In Chimel's attic, they found some of the stolen coins, which were used against him in court. He was convicted of burglary. Chimel appealed. The SC overturned his conviction, arguing that the police search of Chimel's residence was well beyond the scope of the *arrest* warrant. The police should have obtained a *search* warrant, but they had not. The SC said that in a search incident to an arrest under the circumstances in *Chimel,* police are permitted to search only the defendant's person and the area within the immediate vicinity. Thus, they may search the room where the suspect is arrested but cannot extend their search to other areas of his residence without a valid search warrant. (*See Cupp v. Murphy* [1973] *and Schmerber v. California* [1966] *for related issues.*)

City of Canton v. Harris, 489 U.S. 378, 109 S.Ct. 1197 (1989) [**CITY OF CANTON, Ohio, Petitioner, v. Geraldine HARRIS et al.**] (**Civil Rights, Section 1983 Claims; Immunity; Law Enforcement Officers or Agencies**) Harris was arrested and taken to a police station in a patrol wagon. During the trip, she apparently fell to the floor and was observed sitting on the floor when the police arrived at the station. While at the station, Harris fell several times, was incoherent, and eventually was left on the floor unattended. Police officials never gave her aid or medical attention. Her family later arrived and transported her to a hospital, where she was diagnosed with several emotional ailments and hospitalized. They later sued police officials and the municipality under Title 42 U.S.C. Section 1983, alleging that her civil rights had been violated because of deliberate indifference by police to her emotional and physical condition. The municipality claimed immunity from such a suit and alleged inadequate police training, for which the municipality denied responsibility. The SC disagreed, saying that the municipality was liable to such suits. However, the SC said that in order for plaintiffs to prevail, they must show (1) that the city had deliberately failed to train their officers, (2) that such training was municipality policy, and (3) that the identified deficiency in officer training was directly related to injuries sustained by victims.

City of Chicago v. Morales, 527 U.S. 41, 119 S.Ct. 1849 (1999) [**CITY OF CHICAGO, Petitioner, v. Jesus MORALES et al.**] (**First Amendment; Free Speech**) Chicago passed a Gang Congregation Ordinance (GCO) in 1992 that prohibited criminal street gang members from loitering in public places. The clear objective of the GCO was to discourage and decrease gang presence in public places in Chicago, where much gang violence existed. Morales and others were observed by police to be loitering on a public street in Chicago and were arrested and convicted for violating the GCO and sentenced to jail terms. Morales appealed, contending that the GCO was unconstitutionally vague in that it failed to delineate what precise behavior was prohibited. The Illinois Supreme Court reversed Morales' conviction, holding the Chicago ordinance to be unconstitutionally vague. The government appealed to the SC, who heard the case. The SC upheld the Illinois Supreme Court, holding that the GCO was unconstitutionally vague on at least two counts: (1) it failed to provide fair notice of prohibited conduct; and (2) the ordinance was impermissibly vague in failing to establish minimal guidelines for enforcement. The GCO violated the First Amendment right to free speech and association.

City of Indianapolis v. Edmond, 531 U.S. 32, 121 S.Ct. 447 (2000) [**CITY OF INDIANAPOLIS et al., Petitioners, v. James EDMOND et al.** (**Fourth Amendment; Searches and Seizures; Sobriety Checkpoints**) In August 1998, the Indianapolis, IN, Police Department began to operate vehicle checkpoints on city roads to interdict drug traffickers. Approximately 30 officers were deployed at each checkpoint and stopped a predetermined number of vehicles, usually 15 or 20, after which other vehicles were permitted to pass the checkpoint without being stopped. One officer would approach a vehicle and advise the driver that he or she was being stopped at a drug checkpoint, and ask the driver to produce a license and registration. Also, the officer would look for signs of impairment (e.g., DWI) and conduct an open-view examination of the vehicle from the outside. A narcotics-detection dog would walk around the outside of each stopped vehicle sniffing for drugs. The total duration of each stop averaged five minutes or less. Officers were advised to search vehicles more thoroughly if particularized suspicion developed or if consent to search was given by the driver. Motorists James Edmond and Joell Palmer were each stopped in late September 1998. Subsequently, they filed a class-action suit on behalf of all stopped drivers against the City of Indianapolis, claiming that the roadblocks violated the Fourth Amendment and the search and seizure provision. They sought an injunction against the police department to prevent it from establishing such checkpoints in the future. A U.S. district court denied injunctive relief to Edmond and Palmer, and they appealed. The Seventh Circuit Court of Appeals reversed, granting the injunction, and holding that the checkpoint stops violated the Fourth Amendment. The City of Indianapolis appealed and the SC heard the case. The SC affirmed the appellate court, holding the checkpoint stops by Indianapolis police to be in violation of the Fourth Amendment. Because the checkpoint program's primary purpose is indistinguishable from the general interest in crime control, the checkpoints violate the Fourth Amendment. The SC also noted that the checkpoint program's primary purpose of narcotics detection was not justified by the lawful secondary purposes of keeping alcohol-impaired drivers off the road and verifying licenses and registrations. (*See Delaware v. Prouse* [1979], *United States v. Martinez-Fuerte* [1976], *and Michigan Department of State Police v. Sitz* [1990] *for comparison.*)

Cleavinger v. Saxner, 474 U.S. 193, 106 S.Ct. 496 (1985) [Theodore CLEAVINGER, Marvin Marcadis, and Tom P. Lockett, Petitioners, v. David SAXNER and Alfred Cain, Jr.] (Corrections; Immunity; Inmate Rights; Probation and Parole) Saxner was an inmate at the Federal Correctional Institution in Indiana. He was found guilty by a prison disciplinary board of encouraging work stoppage by other inmates. He was placed in administrative detention and had to forfeit a certain number of "good-time" days that are normally used to reduce the maximum sentence to be served. Saxner was subsequently paroled. He filed suit against the prison disciplinary board and was awarded damages. Board members appealed, alleging that they were entitled to absolute immunity in such suits. The SC said that these board members were not the equivalent of parole board members and did not have absolute immunity; although they had qualified immunity, it did not protect them from such suits as that instigated by Saxner.

Clemons v. Mississippi, 494 U.S. 738, 110 S.Ct. 1441 (1990) [Chandler CLEMONS, Petitioner, v. MISSISSIPPI] (Aggravating and Mitigating Circumstances; Death Penalty; Mental Capacity) Clemons was accused of capital murder. During the sentencing phase of the trial, the judge instructed the jury that if the act was "especially heinous, atrocious or cruel," then this fact would be considered as a statutory aggravating factor. Clemons was convicted. When the appellate court in Mississippi heard his appeal, it reweighed the aggravating and mitigating circumstances, essentially upholding the originally imposed death sentence. Clemons then appealed to the SC, which reversed the Mississippi appeals court on the grounds that the record was "unclear" as to how the Mississippi court intended to reinterpret and reweigh the aggravating and mitigating factors and the judge's instructions to the jury. Thus, the death sentence was vacated and the case remanded to the Mississippi Supreme Court to clarify its intent relative to its decision and the harmless-error analysis of the case.

Coker v. Georgia, 433 U.S. 584, 97 S.Ct. 2861 (1977) [Ehrlich Anthony COKER, Petitioner, v. State of GEORGIA] (Corrections; Cruel and Unusual Punishment; Death Penalty; Eighth Amendment) Coker was convicted of raping a woman and he was sentenced to death. He appealed. The SC overturned his death sentence, saying that death sentences are inappropriate punishments for rape where the life of the rape victim is not taken.

Coleman v. Alabama, 399 U.S. 1, 90 S.Ct. 1999 (1970) [John Henry COLEMAN and Otis Stephens, Petitioners, v. State of ALABAMA] (Indigent Clients; Sixth Amendment) Several defendants, including Coleman, were accused of assault with intent to commit murder. As indigents, they were denied counsel at their preliminary hearing, with the Alabama judge declaring that nothing that happened at the preliminary hearing would influence the trial later. Coleman was convicted, and appealed. The SC ruled that preliminary hearings are critical stages. Because indigent defendants are entitled to counsel at critical stages, which Coleman had been denied, his conviction was overturned.

Colorado v. Bertine, 479 U.S. 367, 107 S.Ct. 738 (1987) [COLORADO, Petitioner, v. Steven Lee BERTINE] (Consent Searches; Inventory Searches; Law Enforcement Officers or Agencies; Vehicle Searches) Bertine was arrested for DWI. Police officers conducted a "routine" inventory of his van's contents, which yielded illegal drugs. The van was towed to the police impound lot, and Bertine was subsequently convicted of cocaine possession. He appealed. The police argued that the departmental policy and routine investigation without warrant was to protect a car owner's property and to insure against any claims of loss following a car's impoundment. The SC upheld Bertine's conviction, thus condoning the police policy of conducting warrantless inventories of impounded vehicles.

Colorado v. Connelly, 479 U.S. 157, 107 S.Ct. 515 (1986) [COLORADO, Petitioner, v. Francis Barry CONNELLY] (Confessions; *Miranda* Warning) Connelly approached a uniformed Denver police officer and began to confess to a murder committed in 1982. The officer advised him of his *Miranda* rights, but Connelly acknowledged that he understood and he continued his confession. Later, a detective arrived and advised Connelly of his *Miranda* rights again; Connelly continued to confess. In fact, he led officers to where the murder had been committed and furnished them with incriminating details. He said that he was "following the advice of God" by confessing. Psychiatrists examined Connelly and found him incompetent to assist in his own defense, but they also found him competent to stand trial. He was convicted and appealed, contending that his mental state rendered him incompetent to be properly advised of his *Miranda* rights. The SC disagreed and upheld his conviction, saying that his belief that he was confessing because of God's advice did not automatically exclude his confession as admissible evidence against him.

Colorado v. Spring, 479 U.S. 564, 107 S.Ct. 851 (1987) [COLORADO v. John Leroy SPRING] (Confessions; *Miranda* Warning) Spring was involved in a shooting of a man during a hunting trip in Colorado. Furthermore, he was involved in an illegal enterprise involving interstate transportation of stolen firearms. He was arrested in Kansas City by the FBI, who advised him of his *Miranda* rights and interrogated him about the stolen firearms. At various points during the interrogation, Spring was read his *Miranda* rights again, and he signed several statements to that effect. Subsequently, visiting Colorado officers continued to interrogate Spring, asking him if he had been involved in the murder of the man on the hunting trip earlier. Spring confessed and signed a written confession. He was convicted of murder. He appealed, arguing that his confession to the murder ought to have been suppressed as evidence against him because his *Miranda* warnings had been given only in relation to the stolen firearms charges. The SC disagreed and upheld his murder conviction. It said that once *Miranda* warnings have been given, police are not limited to maintain the scope of questioning only to one crime but can ask about other crimes. A waiver of a person's *Miranda* rights while police are asking questions about one crime continues and applies when police ask suspects about other crimes during the same custodial interrogation.

Conley v. Gibson, 355 U.S. 41, 78 S.Ct. 99 (1957) [J.D. CONLEY et al., Petitioners, v. Pat J. GIBSON, General Chairman of Locals 6051 and 28, etc., et al.] (Law Enforcement Officers or Agencies; Searches and Seizures) A black railway employee, Conley, was among those who suffered a loss of protection and seniority from a renewed contract between the railroad and the union. Conley sued, claiming that jobs had been "abolished," resulting in many blacks losing their jobs, while whites were hired as "new employees" to perform these old "abolished" jobs. The suit was dismissed by a lower court, but the SC heard Conley's case. The SC overruled the lower court and stated that the complaint filed against the union sufficiently alleged breach of contract and the union's statutory duty to represent fairly and without hostility all of the employees in the union, including Conley.

Connally v. Georgia, 429 U.S. 245, 97 S.Ct. 546 (1977) [John CONNALLY v. State of GEORGIA] (Fourteenth Amendment; Fourth Amendment; Law Enforcement Officers or Agencies) During a drug investigation, an informant had given the Georgia police information about Connally's involvement in marijuana distribution. Police officers secured a search warrant from an unsalaried justice of the peace, who received a fee for issuing search warrants but who did not receive any fee for denying them. Connally was convicted. He appealed, alleging that the particular fee system used in Georgia led to the issuance of a warrant without probable cause and that the judge was biased in issuing one because of the fee he would be paid. The SC agreed with Connally and reversed his conviction on these grounds. It said that a situation in which a judge benefits financially from issuing search warrants is in violation of the Fourth and Fourteenth Amendments.

Connecticut v. Barrett, 479 U.S. 523, 107 S.Ct. 828 (1987) [CONNECTICUT, Petitioner, v. William BARRETT] (Confessions; *Miranda* Warning) Barrett was a suspect in a sexual assault. He was arrested and told his *Miranda* rights. He acknowledged his *Miranda* rights, asked for an attorney, and advised police that he would not make any kind of written statement but wanted to make an oral statement. He was told his *Miranda* rights several times at different points during the interrogation. A defective tape recorder meant that the police had only one written record of the conversation, which was compiled by one of the interrogating officers. Subsequently, the oral confession was used against Barrett in obtaining a conviction. He appealed, contending that the "writings" kept of his oral and voluntary incriminating statements should have been excluded, because he had never waived his right to an attorney or to make written statements about what he had done. The SC upheld his conviction, saying that voluntary confessions are admissible even though a suspect has not waived his right to an attorney or to making a written confession. Therefore, if suspects wish to discuss their involvement in crimes with police voluntarily after they have heard their *Miranda* rights, their incriminating statements may, indeed, be used against them in a court of law.

Connecticut Board of Pardons v. Dumschat, 452 U.S. 458, 101 S.Ct. 2460 (1981) [CONNECTICUT BOARD OF PARDONS et al., Petitioners, v. David DUMSCHAT et al.] (Corrections; Fourteenth Amendment; Parole Hearings; Pardons; Probation and Parole) Dumschat was a prisoner serving a life term for murder in 1964. The Connecticut Board of Pardons was vested with the authority to commute such sentences and parole inmates after they had served minimum terms. Dumschat applied numerous times to have his sentence commuted, but the board refused. At no time were reasons given for these refusals. Dumschat filed suit against the board, alleging that his due-process rights under the Fourteenth Amendment were being violated because the board was not giving reasons for refusing to commute his sentence. He also noted that the board had granted commutations to more than three-fourths of prior applicants. The SC upheld the Connecticut Board of Pardons, saying that inmates eligible for commutations of their sentences are not guaranteed such commutations because of previous board actions. Furthermore, inmates are not entitled to a statement of reasons for the rejection of their applications. However, inmates seeking parole are entitled to statements from their parole boards about why their parole is denied.

Connecticut Department of Public Safety v. Doe, ___U.S.___, 123 S.Ct. 1160 (2003) [CONNECTICUT DEPARTMENT OF PUBLIC SAFETY et al., Petitioners,

v. John DOE, individually and on behalf of all others similarly situated] (**Civil Rights, Section 1983 Petitions**) Connecticut enacted a sex-offender law that required the Department of Public Safety (DPS) to post a sex-offender registry containing registrants' names, addresses, photographs, and descriptions on an Internet web site and to make the registry available to the public. Doe and other convicted sex offenders who were subject to the provisions of the act filed a civil rights Section 1983 claim alleging that Connecticut's sex-offender registration law deprived sex offenders of a liberty interest and also violated their due-process rights under the Fourteenth Amendment. Doe et al. claimed that they were entitled to a hearing to determine whether they posed a continuing danger to their community, and that the new law deprived them of this opportunity to be heard. A U.S. district court judge granted Doe et al. a summary judgment and the state appealed. The circuit court affirmed and the SC subsequently heard the case. The SC reversed the lower courts, holding that the due-process clause does not entitle sex offenders to a hearing to determine whether they are currently dangerous before their inclusion in publicly disseminated sex-offender registries. Furthermore, in order for the plaintiffs to assert the right to a hearing under the due-process clause, they must show that the facts they seek to establish in that hearing are relevant under the statutory scheme. In this instance, they failed to do so.

Coolidge v. New Hampshire, 403 U.S. 443, 91 S.Ct. 2022 (1971) [**Edward H. COOLIDGE, Jr., Petitioner, v. NEW HAMPSHIRE**] (**Law Enforcement Officers or Agencies; Searches and Seizures; Vehicle Searches**) Coolidge was a suspect in the murder of a 14-year-old girl. She had been called by a man who wanted her to work as a babysitter. She soon was missing but her body was not discovered until 13 days later. Coolidge was questioned by police and took a lie-detector test. Simultaneously, as the result of a search warrant issued by the state attorney general, police seized his vehicle, which they searched several times over a period of days. They also went to Coolidge's home and asked his wife for any guns in the home and for the clothes Coolidge was wearing the night the girl disappeared. Coolidge's wife turned several guns over to police as well as the clothes. This evidence, together with trace evidence from Coolidge's vehicle, was sufficient to convict him of the girl's murder. Coolidge appealed, contending that *all* evidence seized should have been excluded. The SC agreed in part and disagreed in part. It suppressed the evidence seized on the basis of the search warrant because it had not been issued by a neutral and detached magistrate. The SC stressed the fact that the attorney general was not a "neutral and detached" party and thus was not in the position of issuing a valid search warrant in this particular case. However, it allowed the evidence provided by Coolidge's wife, because it was the result of consent and did not require a warrant. Coolidge's conviction was upheld.

Cooper v. California, 386 U.S. 58, 87 S.Ct. 788 (1967) [**Joe Nathan COOPER, Petitioner, v. State of CALIFORNIA**] (**Fourth Amendment; Inventory Searches; Law Enforcement Officers or Agencies; Searches and Seizures; Vehicle Searches**) Cooper was suspected of selling heroin. A police informant provided sufficient information for police to arrest

Cooper. About a week later, his vehicle was impounded by police, who routinely searched it for inventory purposes. The search yielded a piece of a brown paper sack that matched a sack containing heroin that the police had earlier seized from Cooper. This evidence was introduced at Cooper's trial and he was convicted. He appealed, contending that the impoundment of his vehicle and subsequent warrantless search of it had violated his right under the Fourth Amendment against unreasonable searches and seizures. The SC upheld his conviction, noting that the nature of the inventory and warrantless search was not unreasonable or in violation of Cooper's Fourth Amendment rights.

Cooper v. Pate, 378 U.S. 546, 84 S.Ct. 1733 (1964) [**COOPER v. PATE, Warden**] (**Corrections; First Amendment; Fourteenth Amendment; Inmate Rights**) Cooper, a prisoner in the Illinois State Penitentiary, desired to purchase some religious periodicals. The warden refused, and Cooper sued, alleging a violation of his First Amendment religious rights. Appeals courts denied his petition, but the SC vacated these lower court rulings. Prisoners are entitled to the protection of the Civil Rights Act of 1871 and may challenge conditions of their confinement in federal courts. The SC held that Cooper was entitled under the First and Fourteenth Amendments to purchase religious materials.

Correctional Services Corporation v. Malesko, 534 U.S. 61, 122 S.Ct. 515 (2001) [**CORRECTIONAL SERVICES CORPORATION, Petitioner, v. John E. MALESKO**] (**Federal Tort Claims**) John Malesko was a federal offender convicted of securities fraud in December 1992. He was sentenced to a term of 18 months. During his imprisonment, Malesko was diagnosed with a heart condition. In February 1993, the Federal Bureau of Prisons assigned Malesko to Le Marquis Community Correctional Center, a privately operated halfway house. The halfway house was operated by Correctional Services Corporation (CSC), and it provided services exclusively to federal inmates. CSC had a policy that any offender who was assigned a bedroom below the sixth floor of the halfway house had to use the stairs rather than the elevator provided for those living on higher floors. Malesko was exempted from this policy and was entitled to use the elevator. However, one day a CSC employee refused to let Malesko use the elevator and made Malesko walk up the stairs to his bedroom. He suffered a heart attack while climbing the stairs, fell, and was injured. Three years following the incident, Malesko filed suit for damages against individual employees and CSC, alleging violations of his constitutional rights. The federal court dismissed his claim against individual employees because the suit was brought well beyond the statute of limitations. Further, it dismissed his claim against CSC. An appellate court reversed the federal district court ruling, holding that private entities such as CSC should be held liable. CSC appealed to the SC and the SC reversed the appellate court. Malesko was barred from recovering damages from a private agency acting under color of federal law and on behalf of the Federal Bureau of Prisons. The SC relied on *Bivens v. Six Unknown Federal Narcotics Agents* (1971), which held that private actions for damages against federal officers who allegedly violate a citizen's constitutional rights are valid. However, the SC refused to extend *Bivens* to include organizational entities such as CSC as liable in such lawsuits.

Costello v. United States, 350 U.S. 359, 76 S.Ct. 406 (1956) [**Frank COSTELLO, Petitioner, v. UNITED STATES of America**] (**Grand Juries; Informants**) Racketeer and mobster Costello was indicted by a federal grand jury following hearsay statements from various FBI agents who estimated his net worth and gave scenarios they derived from their informants. He was convicted. Later, he appealed, alleging that the hearsay statements should not have been included in grand-jury testimony and thus the indictments were defective and the conviction should be overturned. The SC disagreed and upheld his conviction, saying that grand juries may hear and consider hearsay evidence to determine whether to indict particular persons.

Couch v. United States, 409 U.S. 322, 93 S.Ct. 611 (1973) [**Lillian V. COUCH, Petitioner, v. UNITED STATES and Edward F. Jennings, etc.**] (**Fifth Amendment; Law Enforcement Officers or Agencies; Searches and Seizures; Self-Incrimination**) A taxpayer, Couch, was investigated by the IRS for possible tax fraud. When her records were requested, she told investigators that her records were in the possession of an accountant and had been for several years. When a summons was delivered to the accountant, the accountant said that the records had been delivered to Couch's attorney. Couch invoked the right against self-incrimination under the Fifth Amendment as a reason for refusing to turn over her records to the IRS. The SC heard the case and decided in the government's favor, holding that the right of self-incrimination doesn't exist where records are in the hands of a third party, such as an accountant. Thus, there is no reasonable expectation of privacy once a defendant has turned over records to an accountant or an attorney. There is no confidential accountant-client privilege.

County of Riverside v. McLaughlin, 500 U.S. 44, 111 S.Ct. 1661 (1991) [**COUNTY OF RIVERSIDE and Cois Byrd, Sheriff of Riverside County, Petitioners, v. Donald Lee McLAUGHLIN et al.**] (**Law Enforcement Officers or Agencies**) McLaughlin was arrested without a warrant and detained for several days over a weekend in the Riverside County Jail in California. The policy of arrest and detention in Riverside County provided for arraignments, without unnecessary or undue delay, within 48 hours after persons are arrested, excluding weekends and holidays. The SC heard the case and determined that a 48-hour period is presumptively reasonable, provided that an arraignment immediately follows. If not, then the government bears the burden of showing why a period beyond 48 hours is reasonable detention of an accused person. If the period is less than 48 hours, the burden shifts to the accused to show unreasonable delay.

County of Sacramento v. Lewis, 523 U.S. 833, 118 S.Ct. 1708 (1998) [**COUNTY OF SACRAMENTO et al., Petitioners, v. Teri LEWIS and Thomas Lewis, personal representative of the Estate of Philip Lewis, Deceased**] (**Civil Rights, Section 1983 Claims; Deadly Force; Fourteenth Amendment; Fourth Amendment**) James Smith and another county deputy, Officer Murray Stapp, were on patrol in separate cruisers when they observed a motorcycle approaching at high speed, driven by Brian Willard and carrying Philip Lewis. Smith and Stapp attempted to stop the speeding motorcycle by flashing their cruiser lights and maneuvering their cruisers to pen the cycle in. However, Willard maneuvered between the two police cruisers and sped off. Smith and Stapp turned on their emergency lights and began a high-speed pursuit. The chase proceeded through various neighborhoods and city streets at speeds in excess of 100 miles per hour. The chase ended a few miles later, when Willard crashed his motorcycle. Willard was thrown clear, but Lewis was thrown onto the road, into the path of the pursuing cruiser driven by Smith. Smith slammed on his brakes but could not prevent his vehicle from skidding into Lewis, killing him. Lewis' parents brought a Section 1983 suit against Sacramento County and the sheriff's deputies, alleging that the pursuit was undertaken with deliberate indifference and reckless disregard for the lives of Willard and Lewis. A federal court granted summary judgment in favor of Smith, but the Ninth Circuit Court of Appeals reversed, holding that the appropriate degree of fault for substantive due process liability for high-speed police pursuits is deliberate indifference to, or reckless disregard for, a person's right to life and personal security. Sacramento County and Smith appealed to the SC, where the case was heard. The SC reversed the Ninth Circuit, holding that a police officer does not violate substantive due process by causing death through deliberate or reckless indifference to life in a high-speed automobile chase aimed at apprehending a suspected offender. High-speed chases with no intent to harm suspects physically or to worsen their legal plight do not give rise to due-process liability. Smith was faced with a course of lawless behavior for which the police were not to blame. They had done nothing to cause Willard's high speed in the first place, nothing to excuse his flouting of the commonly understood police authority to control traffic, and nothing to encourage him to race through traffic at breakneck speed. Willard's outrageous behavior was practically instantaneous, and so was Smith's instinctive response to do his job, not to induce Willard's lawlessness, or to terrorize, harm, or kill. Thus, Lewis' Fourteenth Amendment substantive due-process rights were not violated by the officers' conduct.

Cox v. Louisiana, 379 U.S. 536, 85 S.Ct. 453 (1965) [**R. Elton COX, Appellant, v. State of LOUISIANA**] (**First Amendment; Fourteenth Amendment; Free Speech**) The First and Fourteenth Amendments do not afford the same kind of freedom to those who communicate ideas by marching, picketing, or patrolling on streets and highways that they do to those who communicate by speech alone.

Coy v. Iowa, 487 U.S. 1012, 108 S.Ct. 2798 (1988) [**John Avery COY, Appellant, v. IOWA**] (**Confrontation Clause; Sixth Amendment**) Coy was arrested for sexually assaulting two 13-year-old girls who were camping in a neighboring yard. The girls identified him as their attacker, and he was arrested. During the trial, a screen was erected between the witness stand and the defense table, so that Coy could not observe the girls directly when they testified against him. Following his conviction on two counts of lascivious acts with children, he appealed, alleging that his Sixth Amendment right to confront his accusers and cross-examine them in open court had been violated. The SC overturned his conviction, holding that his constitutional right to face-to-face confrontation was violated when the Iowa court placed a screen between him and his accusers.

Crane v. Kentucky, 476 U.S. 683, 106 S.Ct. 2142 (1986) [**Major CRANE, Petitioner, v. KENTUCKY**] (**Custodial Interrogations; Law Enforcement Officers or Agencies**) In August 1981, Crane allegedly shot to death a liquor store clerk in Louisville. He was 16 years old and was taken into custody by police for an unrelated charge. During interrogation by police, "out of a clear blue sky," Crane began to confess numerous crimes, including the murder of the liquor store clerk. Subsequently, Crane was indicted for murder, but he moved to suppress his confession to police on the grounds that it had been "coerced." The court denied his motion, noting that it had been given voluntarily, and Crane was convicted. He appealed, claiming that the judge had denied him the opportunity to present evidence that his confession had been coerced. A portion of that testimony would have been the circumstances under which Crane was interrogated, the size of the interrogation room, the number of officers present, the time interval over which the interrogation occurred, and other environmental factors. The SC heard the case and reversed Crane's murder conviction on the grounds that the judge had erred by denying the admissibility of evidence about the confession circumstances. The SC declared that evidence about the circumstances under which the confession had been given was central to the defense's case, as there was no physical evidence linking Crane with the murder and his confession was the only evidence presented by the state. Thus, the defense is entitled to rebut the credibility of a confession, particularly where such evidence is so central to the defendant's claim of innocence.

Crawford v. Washington, ___U.S.___, 124 S.Ct. 1354 (2004) [**Michael D. CRAWFORD, Petitioner, v. WASHINGTON**] (**Confrontation Clause; Sixth Amendment**) In August 1999, Michael Crawford and his wife, Sylvia, went to the apartment of Kenneth Lee, alleged by Sylvia to have attempted to rape her. Michael Crawford confronted Lee and a scuffle ensued, resulting in Crawford stabbing Lee in the torso. Crawford claimed self-defense, alleging that Lee was reaching for a knife in his pocket. Police officers at the scene interviewed both Crawford and his wife, who gave contradictory statements about what had transpired. Michael Crawford claimed he was cut on the hand by a knife carried by Lee, while Sylvia Crawford said that she saw no knife produced by Lee. Michael Crawford was charged with first-degree assault while armed with a deadly weapon, and convicted. Although Sylvia, his wife, did not testify against him because of marital privilege, the court allowed her prior statements given to police to be introduced as evidence against her husband. Michael Crawford's attorney objected to these statements as hearsay, and asserted that such statements should be barred because the witness who gave these statements was not allowed to be con-

fronted by the accused in court. The Washington Supreme Court upheld Crawford's conviction, permitting the admission of Sylvia's statements to police, relying on *Ohio v. Roberts* (1986), which permitted statements from unavailable witnesses where such statements bore guarantees of trustworthiness and reliability as determined by the presiding judge. The SC heard the case and overturned Crawford's conviction. The SC relied on the original meaning of the confrontation clause of the Sixth Amendment, which directs that the reliability of testimonial statements must be tested by cross-examination, not by a mere judicial determination of reliability. The SC was also critical of the *Ohio v. Roberts* case, which was said to have the unpardonable vice of admitting into evidence core testimonial statements that the confrontation clause plainly meant to exclude.

Crist v. Bretz, 437 U.S. 28, 98 S.Ct. 2156 (1978) [**Roger CRIST, as Warden of the Montana State Penitentiary, Deer Lodge, Montana, et al., Appellants, v. L.R. BRETZ et al.**] (**Corrections; Double Jeopardy; Fourteenth Amendment; *Habeas Corpus* Petitions**) Bretz and a codefendant, Cline, were charged with grand larceny, offering false evidence, and obtaining money and property under false pretenses. After the jury was selected, but before any witnesses could testify, Bretz filed a motion to have one of the charges dropped, as the Montana legislature had repealed the law they were accused of violating two weeks before they actually violated it. Actually, a typographical error had made the date appear as 1974 when, in fact, the year of their alleged illegal act was 1973. Thus, their act *would* fall within the repealed statute. The false-pretenses charge was dropped against a prosecutorial protest. Bretz then made a motion to dismiss the entire criminal information so that a new charge could be filed. The motion was granted, and the judge dismissed the jury. Subsequently, prosecutors filed revised charges against Bretz and Cline based on new information. After a second jury had been impaneled, Bretz sought to have the case against him dismissed on the grounds of double jeopardy. The motion was denied, and Bretz was subsequently convicted and sentenced. He then filed a *habeas corpus* petition. The SC overturned his conviction, holding that jeopardy attaches in a jury trial when the jury is impaneled and sworn, and not before any witnesses testify. The Montana statute reading that "jeopardy does not attach until the first witness is sworn in a jury trial" is unconstitutional under the Fifth and Fourteenth Amendments. Thus, Bretz was freed because of double jeopardy.

Crosby v. United States, 506 U.S. 255, 113 S.Ct. 748 (1993) [**Michael CROSBY, Petitioner, v. UNITED STATES**] (**Jury Trials**) Crosby and others were indicted by a federal grand jury in Minnesota on charges of mail fraud. Crosby appeared and posted a $100,000 bond. His trial was scheduled for a date in October 1988, but he failed to appear. He was tried *in absentia* and convicted, together with another codefendant. He was apprehended six months later in Florida and was returned to Minnesota. He was sentenced to 20 years in prison and appealed his conviction *in absentia*. The SC heard his appeal and overturned his sentence, holding that persons may not be tried *in absentia,* even if their absence is the result of fleeing the jurisdiction or escape.

Cruz v. Beto, 405 U.S. 319, 92 S.Ct. 1079 (1972) [Fred A. CRUZ v. George J. BETO, Director, Texas Department of Corrections] (Civil Rights, Section 1983 Claims; Corrections; First Amendment; Freedom of Religion; Inmate Rights) Cruz, a Buddhist, was a prisoner in the Texas Department of Corrections. He was prohibited from using the prison chapel, from communicating with his prison inmate Buddhist representative, and from reading newspapers or obtaining news from any other sources. He was placed in solitary confinement on a diet of bread and water for two weeks as a punishment for sharing some magazines about Buddhism with other inmates. He filed suit against the Texas Department of Corrections under Title 42 U.S.C. Section 1983 for violating his First Amendment freedom of religion rights. The SC agreed with Cruz that indeed, the Texas Department of Corrections had violated his religious rights. Inmates with unconventional religious beliefs must be given a reasonable opportunity to exercise those beliefs, comparable to the opportunities of other inmates to exercise their own religious beliefs.

Cruz v. New York, 481 U.S. 186, 107 S.Ct. 1714 (1987) [Eulogio CRUZ, Petitioner, v. NEW YORK] (Confessions; Confrontation Clause; Sixth Amendment) Two brothers, Eulogio and Benjamin Cruz, were implicated in the second-degree murder of a Bronx gas station attendant in 1982. They were tried jointly, despite Eulogio's request that he be given a separate trial. Although Benjamin did not testify, he had previously implicated Eulogio in a videotaped confession that was used in court. Eulogio's earlier confession was also read into the court record. The judge instructed the jury to disregard those portions of Benjamin's testimony that pertained to Eulogio. Eulogio Cruz was convicted. He appealed, alleging that his Sixth Amendment right to confront and cross-examine a witness had been violated when his brother's videotaped confession was played in front of the jury. The SC reversed his conviction, holding that Eulogio Cruz's Sixth Amendment right had been violated. The Court said that the confrontation clause bars admission of a nontestifying codefendant's confession incriminating the defendant at their joint trial, even if the jury is instructed not to consider it, and even if the defendant's own confession is admitted against him. Eulogio was entitled to a new trial without Benjamin's confession read into the record.

Culombe v. Connecticut, 367 U.S. 568, 81 S.Ct. 1860 (1961) [Arthur CULOMBE, Petitioner, v. CONNECTICUT] (Confessions; Self-Incrimination) Culombe was suspected of committing several burglaries and homicides. He was taken into custody on unrelated charges of disturbing the peace and held for four days, during which he was extensively interrogated about the burglaries and homicides. His detention for disturbing the peace was admitted by police to be a ruse to keep him in custody to interrogate him. Eventually, he confessed to the crimes and was convicted. He appealed. The SC ruled that his confession had been involuntarily given. It said that when an interrogation is so lengthy and protracted, the process becomes the equivalent of extortion to obtain a confession; thus, such an exploitation of questioning, whatever its usefulness, is not permitted. Culombe's conviction was reversed.

Cupp v. Murphy, 412 U.S. 291, 93 S.Ct. 2000 (1973) [Hoyt C. CUPP, Superintendent, Oregon State Penitentiary, Petitioner, v. Daniel P. MURPHY] (Law Enforcement Officers or Agencies; Searches and Seizures) Murphy voluntarily went to a police station for questioning after his estranged wife had been found dead. At the station, he was questioned by police, who noted a dark spot on one of his fingers. They asked him what it was, and Murphy began to wipe it off. Police asked him if they could take some scrapings of the dark spot from under his fingernails and examine them. Murphy refused and continued to rub off the dark spot. Police moved immediately to restrain him and obtain samples of the dark substance without his permission or a warrant. The specimens turned out to be blood matching his wife's blood as well as bits of fabric from her nightgown. Murphy was charged with second-degree murder on the basis of this evidence and convicted. He appealed, arguing that since he had not been formally arrested while at the police station, police officers should have obtained a valid search warrant to seize samples of the dark substance on his fingers. The SC upheld Murphy's conviction, saying that exigent circumstances existed and police had to move quickly before Murphy could remove or destroy these specimens. The delay involved in getting a warrant could have given him time to get rid of the incriminating evidence. (*See Chimel v. California* [1969].)

Custis v. United States, 511 U.S. 485, 114 S.Ct. 1732 (1994) [Darren J. CUSTIS, Petitioner, v. UNITED STATES] (*Habeas Corpus* Petitions; Sentencing) Custis was convicted in federal court for possession of firearms and cocaine. He had three previous state convictions, and under the Armed Career Criminal Act, he received an enhanced sentence. He appealed, contending that the convictions in Maryland had been the result of ineffective assistance of counsel. Thus, his federal sentence should not have been enhanced. The SC upheld his conviction and sentence enhancements, noting that Custis had not raised the issue of attorney competence at either of his previous Maryland convictions. Further, he had plea bargained and knowingly and intelligently waived his rights when entering guilty pleas. Thus, the SC declared, only if Custis had been convicted and denied counsel at those times could he challenge such convictions. Defendants in federal proceedings have no right collaterally to attack the validity of previous state convictions used to enhance their sentences under the Armed Career Criminal Act. However, if Custis wished to challenge his state convictions, he could do so not in federal court but rather in state court through federal *habeas corpus* review.

Cuyler v. Adams, 449 U.S. 433, 101 S.Ct. 703 (1981) [Julius T. CUYLER, Superintendent, State Correctional Institution, et al., Petitioners, v. John ADAMS] (Inmate Rights) Adams was a prisoner in a Pennsylvania prison. As part of an Interstate Agreement on Detainers, an order was issued to try him in New Jersey for other crimes, and he was scheduled for transfer to a New Jersey prison. He appealed the transfer order. The SC ruled that inmates are entitled to a hearing on the matter of whether they should be transferred from a prison in one state to another prison in another state under the Interstate Agreement on Detainers; thus, Adams was entitled to a hearing.

Cuyler v. Sullivan, 446 U.S. 335, 100 S.Ct. 1708 (1980) [John T. CUYLER, Superintendent, etc., et al., Petitioners, v. John SULLIVAN] (Multiple Defendants) Sullivan was one of three defendants charged with a crime. The three defendants were represented by two different attorneys. Sullivan was convicted. He appealed, alleging conflict of interest because two different attorneys were representing three clients. The SC declared that trial courts are obligated to investigate allegations of conflicts of interest provided that they are made in a timely fashion. In this case, the timeliness of the appeal was poor, and no evidence was presented to cause serious question whether multiple counsel amounted to a conflict of interest.

D

Dalia v. United States, 441 U.S. 238, 99 S.Ct. 1682 (1979) [Lawrence DALIA, Petitioner, v. UNITED STATES] (Law Enforcement Officers or Agencies; Searches and Seizures) Dalia was suspected by FBI agents of transporting stolen goods in interstate commerce. Armed with a court order, they entered Dalia's office late one evening and planted bugging equipment. On the basis of subsequent incriminating statements obtained through such surveillance, Dalia was convicted. He appealed, contending that the incriminating evidence against him ought to have been suppressed because the issuing judge had not specifically authorized unlawful entry into his office when approving the initial surveillance. The SC held that such specific authorization was not required under a separate warrant and upheld Dalia's conviction. Thus, when courts authorize bugging of suspect offices or dwellings, such orders do not need to contain separate provisions for how entry into these offices or dwellings should be conducted.

Daniels v. United States, 532 U.S. 374, 121 S.Ct. 1578 (2001) [Earthy D. DANIELS, Jr., Petitioner, v. UNITED STATES] (Armed Career Criminal Act [ACCA]; *Habeas Corpus* Petitions) Daniels was convicted in federal court of being a felon in possession of a firearm and his sentence was enhanced under the Armed Career Criminal Act (ACCA) of 1984. This act imposes a mandatory minimum 15-year sentence if anyone who violates it has three previous convictions for a violent felony or serious drug offense. Daniels had been convicted four previous times in California state court: in 1978 and 1981 for robbery, and in 1977 and 1979 for first-degree burglary. Daniels filed a *habeas corpus* petition to vacate, set aside, or correct his federal sentence, alleging in part that the two burglary convictions did not qualify under the ACCA. Daniels further alleged that at least two of his earlier convictions were themselves unconstitutional because they were both based on guilty pleas that were not knowing and voluntary,

and because the 1981 conviction was also the product of ineffective assistance of counsel. The district court denied Daniels' motion and the Ninth Circuit Court of Appeals affirmed. Daniels therefore appealed to the SC, who heard his case. The SC affirmed the Ninth Circuit, holding that Daniels had failed to challenge the constitutionality of his prior convictions within a proper time interval, or if he did challenge them, he did so unsuccessfully. Daniels is without recourse and may not collaterally attack prior convictions through a motion to vacate, set aside, or correct a sentence.

Daniels v. Williams, 474 U.S. 327, 106 S.Ct. 662 (1986) [Roy E. DANIELS, Petitioner, v. Andrew WILLIAMS] (Civil Rights, Section 1983 Claims; Corrections; Fourteenth Amendment; Inmate Rights) Daniels was an inmate at the Richmond, VA, jail. He slipped on a pillow left on some stairs and injured his back. He filed a lawsuit (Title 42 U.S.C. Section 1983 civil rights action) against Williams, a sheriff's deputy who worked at the jail and had left the pillow on the stairs. Daniels alleged that Williams' negligence had deprived him of his "liberty" interest and due process according to the Fourteenth Amendment. The SC disagreed, saying that due process is not violated merely because of an official's negligent act that causes an unintentional loss of life, liberty, or property.

Darden v. Wainwright, 477 U.S. 168, 106 S.Ct. 2464 (1986) [Willie Jasper DARDEN, Petitioner, v. Louie L. WAINWRIGHT, Secretary, Florida Department of Corrections] (Death Penalty; *Habeas Corpus* Petitions; Prosecutorial Misconduct; Sixth Amendment) Darden was a convicted murderer under sentence of death. He filed a *habeas corpus* petition challenging the exclusion of a juror from his earlier trial, allegedly improper remarks made by the prosecutor during his summation to the jury, and ineffective assistance of counsel. One prospective juror had been excused by the judge when the juror declared a moral and religious opposition to the death penalty, which was one option in Darden's case. The prosecutor had referred to him as an "animal." Darden thought the one-half hour preparation by his attorney between the trial's guilt phase and the penalty phase insufficient to prepare an adequate mitigation statement. The SC rejected all of Darden's arguments. It held that jurors may be excused from death-penalty cases if their religious views or moral feelings would render them unable to vote for such a penalty. Further, the emotional rhetoric from the prosecutor was insufficient to deprive Darden of a fair trial. Finally, evidence showed that the defense counsel had spent considerable preparatory time for both the trial and mitigation statement during the penalty phase.

Davidson v. Cannon, 474 U.S. 344, 106 S.Ct. 668 (1986) [Robert DAVIDSON, Petitioner, v. Joseph CANNON et al.] (Civil Rights, Section 1983 Claims; Corrections) Davidson, a New Jersey prison inmate, was threatened with assault by other inmates. He alerted the warden and other officials of the impending harm from these other prisoners. The officers failed to act on the warning, and subsequently Davidson was injured. He brought a Title 42 U.S.C. Section 1983 civil rights action against prison authorities for negligence that led to his injuries under the theory of "deliberate indifference." The SC rejected Davidson's argument that the prison officers had been abusively negligent. It held that the officers had not regarded the matter as particularly serious, in their opinion, and a lack of due care does not approach the seriousness of deliberate indifference.

Davis v. Alaska, 415 U.S. 308, 94 S.Ct. 1105 (1974) [Joshaway DAVIS, Petitioner, v. State of ALASKA] (Fourteenth Amendment; Juvenile Law; Sixth Amendment) Davis was charged with grand larceny in an Alaska court. A key witness against him was a juvenile, Green. Green was protected from extensive cross-examination by Davis' defense counsel through a special Alaska confidentiality law protecting a juvenile's status. Specifically, the defense counsel was barred from asking Green about his juvenile delinquency history. Green had previously been judged delinquent on a burglary charge. Davis was convicted, and he appealed. The SC decided that Davis' attorney should have been able to cross-examine the juvenile witness, despite the Alaskan law to the contrary. Thus, in a criminal trial, the accused is guaranteed the right to cross-examine and confront witnesses against him under both the Sixth and Fourteenth Amendments. These rights prevail over state policies or laws to the contrary.

Davis v. Georgia, 429 U.S. 122, 97 S.Ct. 399 (1976) [Curfew DAVIS v. State of GEORGIA] (Death Penalty; Eighth Amendment; Right to Counsel; Sixth Amendment) Davis was charged with murder. When his jury was being selected, one prospective and eligible juror expressed some doubt as to whether he could vote for the death penalty. After some questioning, he said that he could vote for the death penalty, although he didn't particularly favor it. He was excluded by the prosecutor. Davis was convicted and given a death sentence. He appealed, alleging that his Eighth Amendment right had been violated when an eligible juror had deliberately been excluded by the prosecution. The SC agreed with Davis and reversed his death sentence, holding that unless a prospective juror is irrevocably committed before trial to vote against the death penalty regardless of the facts and circumstances of the case, he or she may not be excluded, and if the juror is improperly excluded even though not so committed, any subsequently imposed death penalty cannot stand.

Davis v. Mississippi, 394 U.S. 721, 89 S.Ct. 1394 (1969) [John DAVIS, Petitioner, v. State of MISSISSIPPI] (Fourth Amendment; Law Enforcement Officers or Agencies; Searches and Seizures) Davis was one of 25 black youths who were picked up for questioning about a rape in December 1965 in Meridian, MS. The rapist had been described as black. Police began a systematic process of picking up black men, without arrest warrants or probable cause, taking them to police headquarters, interrogating and fingerprinting them, and then releasing them. Davis became a suspect when his fingerprints matched those of the rapist that had been left on the woman's home window. He was convicted on the testimony of the rape victim and the fingerprint evidence. He appealed, seeking to suppress the fingerprint evidence. The SC overturned his conviction, holding that where fingerprints are obtained without a warrant or probable cause, they are invalid as evidence against criminal suspects. Thus, the SC determined

that Davis' Fourth Amendment right against unreasonable searches and seizures had been violated.

Davis v. United States, 328 U.S. 582, 66 S.Ct. 1256 (1946) [Jack DAVIS, Petitioner, v. UNITED STATES] (Consent Searches; Law Enforcement Officers or Agencies) Davis owned a gas station in New York City under a company named Davis Auto Laundry Corporation. He was suspected of selling gasoline on the black market without rationing coupons, which were required during World War II. Two federal agents purchased gasoline from an attendant at Davis' gas station without using the required coupons. The attendant was arrested and Davis was later ordered to open his gasoline pumps so that agents could verify whether he had sufficient coupons to cover the gasoline purchases. He said that his records were in a locked office, and the federal agents threatened to knock the door down unless Davis permitted them to enter. Later, because of evidence seized as a result of a warrantless search of Davis' office, he was convicted of unlawful possession of gasoline coupons. He appealed, saying that the evidence from his office should have been obtained with a warrant. The SC upheld his conviction, saying that insufficient evidence existed to support his contention that he was forced into disclosing the contents of his office records. Thus, the SC held that the search was consensual rather than coerced. The officers also wanted to inspect public documents, not private ones. Thus, their demand of Davis was within their right.

Dawson v. Delaware, 503 U.S. 159, 112 S.Ct. 1093 (1992) [David DAWSON, Petitioner, v. DELAWARE] (Aggravating and Mitigating Circumstances; Death Penalty; Eighth Amendment; First Amendment; Fourteenth Amendment) Dawson was convicted of first-degree murder. During the penalty phase of his trial, a stipulation was read into the record about his membership in the Ayran Brotherhood, a white racist prison gang. The jury found sufficient aggravating factors outweighing the mitigating ones and recommended the death penalty. On appeal, Dawson contended that his First Amendment right had been violated when it was disclosed that he was a member of the Ayran Brotherhood; therefore, his death sentence ought to be reversed. The SC agreed with Dawson, holding that his First and Fourteenth Amendment rights had been violated by the admission of the Aryan Brotherhood evidence in the case, because the evidence had no relevance to the issues being decided and serious prejudicial effects had stemmed from it. His death sentence was vacated.

Deal v. United States, 508 U.S. 129, 113 S.Ct. 1993 (1993) [Thomas Lee DEAL, Petitioner, v. UNITED STATES] (Sentencing) Deal was convicted of six different bank robberies. He was also convicted of possessing and using a firearm in each of the six robberies. These convictions yielded sentences of 20 years and five years for each of the offenses to run consecutively. Deal appealed, arguing that the convictions and sentences were excessive. The SC upheld the constitutionality of the 105-year sentence, saying that it is not glaringly unjust to refuse to give the offender a lesser sentence merely because he escaped apprehension and conviction until the sixth crime had been committed. Thus, convicted offenders may incur sentence enhancements for various crimes they have committed but for which they have not been caught or convicted.

Delaware v. Fensterer, 474 U.S. 15, 106 S.Ct. 292 (1985) [**DELAWARE, Petitioner, v. William A. FENSTERER**] (**Confrontation Clause; Sixth Amendment**) Fensterer was accused of killing his fiancee. Circumstantial evidence was used, including a cat leash used to strangle the woman and hair fibers that matched those of Fensterer. FBI Special Agent Robillard testified at Fensterer's trial about the hair analysis but could not recall precisely which detection method had been used to establish the hair match. An expert for the defense gave a contrary opinion. Fensterer was convicted. On appeal to the Delaware Supreme Court, he argued that he had been denied adequate cross-examination of the FBI agent, because the agent could not recall the method for examining the hair fibers. The Delaware Supreme Court overturned Fensterer's conviction on the ground that "Fensterer was denied his right to effectively cross-examine a key state witness." The state appealed. The SC reversed the Delaware Supreme Court by holding that the agent's testimony should be evaluated according to its weight, not according to its admissibility. The expert opinion was admissible, and the fact that the agent couldn't recall the precise method of hair determination did not bar such an opinion from the jury; rather, the jury could give that opinion more or less weight in their determination of facts relevant to Fensterer's guilt or innocence. Fensterer's right to a fair trial and to cross-examination of witnesses against him had not been infringed.

Delaware v. Prouse, 440 U.S. 648, 99 S.Ct. 1391 (1979) [**State of DELAWARE, Petitioner, v. William J. PROUSE, III**] (**Law Enforcement Officers or Agencies; Plain-View Rule; Searches and Seizures**) Prouse was randomly stopped by a police officer, who observed nothing illegal about Prouse's vehicle or the way Prouse was driving it. The officer asked Prouse for his driver's license and vehicle registration. While doing so, the officer smelled marijuana and saw it in plain view on the floor of the vehicle. Prouse was subsequently convicted of marijuana possession. He appealed, contending that the officer had had no probable cause to stop him in the first place, so all evidence found should have been suppressed. The SC agreed with Prouse, saying that officers must have probable cause in order to stop vehicles; they may not stop vehicles randomly for spot checks. This case did not make spot checks of vehicles unconstitutional. The SC allowed for states to devise schemes whereby spot checks could be made less intrusively, such as DWI stops, which are currently permitted.

Delaware v. Van Arsdall, 475 U.S. 673, 106 S.Ct. 1431 (1986) [**DELAWARE, Petitioner, v. Robert E. VAN ARSDALL**] (**Confrontation Clause; Sixth Amendment**) Epps was stabbed to death following a New Year's Eve party in Smyrna, DE. On the basis of circumstantial evidence, Van Arsdall was charged with first-degree murder, because he had been one of two remaining guests at the party when Epps was killed. Various witnesses testified for the state, and evidence was introduced to show that Van Arsdall had bloodstained clothing matching the blood of the victim. A witness, Fleetwood, gave incriminating testimony against Van Arsdall.

On cross-examination, the defense counsel attempted to question Fleetwood about a deal he had made with prosecutors to give testimony in the case in exchange for dropping public drunkenness charges. The court permitted the cross-examination but outside of the jury's presence. Van Arsdall was convicted of murder. He appealed on the grounds that he had been denied a fair trial because of the violation of the confrontation clause of the Sixth Amendment. The Delaware Supreme Court reversed his conviction and the state appealed. The SC heard the case and vacated the Delaware Supreme Court judgment, remanding the case to the lower court for a determination as to whether the potential bias of the prosecution witness was actually harmless error or sufficiently important to have denied Van Arsdall a fair trial. Thus, the SC said, the correct inquiry was whether, assuming that the damaging potential of the cross-examination was fully realized, a reviewing court might nonetheless say that the error was harmless beyond a reasonable doubt.

Delo v. Lashley, 507 U.S. 272, 113 S.Ct. 1222 (1993) [**Paul DELO, Superintendent, Potosi Correctional Center, Petitioner, v. Frederick LASHLEY**] (**Death Penalty; Eighth Amendment;** *Habeas Corpus* **Petitions; Jury Instructions**) Lashley, aged 17, had brutally beaten and stabbed to death his 55-year-old physically impaired cousin. He was tried and found guilty of capital murder. At a conference held before the sentencing phase of his trial, the defense counsel sought to have the judge instruct the jury that Lashley had no significant history of prior criminal activity as a mitigating circumstance. At the same time, the counsel moved to have Lashley's juvenile record barred from the jury. The judge did not expressly rule on the latter motion. However, the judge indicated that Lashley would not be entitled to the requested assertion about his lack of prior criminal activity without appropriate evidence. Subsequently, the jury heard *no* evidence about Lashley's lack of prior criminal history. It gave the death sentence. Lashley filed a *habeas corpus* petition alleging that his due-process rights had been violated by the judge when he failed to issue this jury instruction. The SC rejected Lashley's appeal, holding that he was not entitled to the punishment-phase instruction that he was presumed innocent of other crimes as a mitigating factor without some proof offered by defense counsel.

Delo v. Stokes, 495 U.S. 320, 110 S.Ct. 1880 (1990) [**Paul DELO, Superintendent, Potosi Correctional Center, v. Winford STOKES**] (**Eighth Amendment;** *Habeas Corpus* **Petitions**) Stokes was convicted of capital murder and sentenced to death. Following several *habeas corpus* petitions in which Stokes raised several issues on appeal, he was granted a stay of execution. Missouri prosecutors appealed to the SC. The SC reversed the United States district judge's stay of execution. It was determined that Stokes had raised four *habeas corpus* petitions earlier and that he could have raised the present issue as a part of one of his earlier petitions. Thus, the SC said, it was abuse of judicial discretion for the federal judge to grant a stay of execution to Stokes when he filed his fourth petition. Thus, the application from the state to vacate the stay of execution was granted.

Demarest v. Manspeaker, 498 U.S. 184, 111 S.Ct. 599 (1991) [Richard DEMAREST, Petitioner, v. James MANSPEAKER et al.] (Corrections; *Habeas Corpus* Petitions) Demarest, a state prisoner in Colorado, was subpoenaed to appear as a witness in a federal trial. He was held in a local jail for eight days while waiting to testify. Later, he sought to be compensated for a *witness fee* of $30 per day ordinarily extended to other witnesses. He sought such fees as the result of being ordered to testify under a writ of *habeas corpus ad testificandum* ("you have the body to testify"). Lower courts rejected his claim, but the SC heard his case and ordered that the court must pay him the $30 per day witness fee, especially in view of the *habeas corpus ad testificandum* writ. The SC said that inmates are not otherwise excluded from collecting such fees, because they are subject to subpoena as is any private citizen.

Demosthenes v. Baal, 495 U.S. 731, 110 S.Ct. 2223 (1990) [Peter DEMOSTHENES, Warden, et al. v. Edwin and Doris BAAL] (Death Penalty; *Habeas Corpus* Petitions; Insanity Pleas; *Miranda* Warning) Baal had attempted to rob a woman in Nevada and subsequently stabbed her repeatedly, causing her death, stolen her car, and fled. Following Baal's subsequent arrest in Reno in February 1988, he was given his *Miranda* warnings and confessed. Two psychiatrists examined him in March 1988 and determined that he was competent to stand trial for the first-degree murder charges. He entered a plea of not guilty by reason of insanity. Before his trial, he was examined by other psychiatrists, who confirmed the earlier psychiatric diagnosis that Baal was "disturbed" but competent. Baal thus withdrew his not guilty by reason of insanity plea and pleaded guilty to first-degree murder and robbery, both with a deadly weapon. A three-judge Nevada panel accepted his guilty plea and sentenced him to death. On appeal, he won a stay of execution from the Nevada Supreme Court. Then he tried to waive a federal review of his claim to insanity. In May 1990, Edwin and Doris Baal, his parents, filed a *habeas corpus* petition on his behalf, asserting that Baal was not "competent" to waive the federal review. The SC rejected the petition, concluding that federal *habeas corpus* statutes to interfere with the course of state proceedings must occur only in specified circumstances, which in this case were clearly lacking. The Nevada Supreme Court had granted the stay of execution without finding that Baal was not competent to waive further proceedings. The SC, therefore, vacated the stay of execution and entitled Nevada to proceed with his execution as scheduled.

Dempsey v. Martin, 528 U.S. 7, 120 S.Ct. 3 (1999) [John B. DEMPSEY v. Ralph MARTIN, District Attorney for Suffolk County] (Frivolous Lawsuits; Inmate Rights) John B. Dempsey filed an *in forma pauperis* motion concerning a noncriminal matter. The SC denied Dempsey's motion, noting that Dempsey had previously filed 19 *in forma pauperis* petitions for *certiorari* or extraordinary writs, all of which were denied because they were deemed frivolous. Dempsey was barred from filing any future motions regarding noncriminal matters unless he first paid the required docketing fees. However, Dempsey was not barred from filing petitions challenging criminal sanctions that might be imposed on him. (*See also*

Judd v. United States District Court of Texas [1999] *and Prunty v. Brooks* [1999].)

Dickerson v. United States, 530 U.S. 428, 120 S.Ct. 2326 (2000) [Charles Thomas DICKERSON, Petitioner, v. UNITED STATES] (Confessions; *Miranda* Warning) Dickerson was indicted for bank robbery, conspiracy to commit bank robbery, and using a firearm in the course of committing a crime of violence. FBI agents interviewed Dickerson, who gave several incriminating statements voluntarily without a *Miranda* warning being given. Subsequently, the government sought to introduced Dickerson's statements against him in a criminal trial in a U.S. district court. Dickerson moved to suppress the statements, as they had been given prior to Dickerson receiving the *Miranda* warning from the FBI agents. Dickerson's motion to suppress the incriminating statements was granted. The government appealed, and the Fourth Circuit Court of Appeals reversed the district court's suppression order. Dickerson appealed to the SC, where the case was heard. The SC reversed the Fourth Circuit and allowed the suppression order to stand. The SC noted that Congress had passed a law, Title 18 U.S.C. Section 3501, that made the admissibility of statements such as Dickerson's turn solely on whether they were made voluntarily, regardless of whether or not a suspect had been given the *Miranda* warning. This law was interpreted by the SC as an attempt to overrule *Miranda* and its influence on confessions of suspects. The SC held that Congress may not legislatively supersede its decisions when interpreting and applying the constitution. The *Miranda* warning is constitutionally based on two grounds. First, it protects suspects by observing their right against self-incrimination. Second, the due-process clause of the Fourteenth Amendment probes the voluntariness of confessions through a consideration of the totality of circumstances under which confessions are given. The SC also stressed the principle of *stare decisis* and noted that the *Miranda* warning has become embedded in routine police practice to the point where the warnings have become a part of the national culture. The SC declined to overrule *Miranda,* holding that any departure from precedent should be supported by some special justification. In the Dickerson case, such justification was not demonstrated.

Dickey v. Florida, 398 U.S. 30, 90 S.Ct. 1564 (1970) [Robert Dean DICKEY, Petitioner, v. State of FLORIDA] (Speedy Trials) Dickey was charged in 1968 with various crimes allegedly committed in 1960. He tried several times to have an immediate trial, but for various reasons, his trial was delayed until 1968. Between 1960 and 1968, some witnesses died and others became unavailable. Also, some relevant police records were destroyed or misplaced. He was convicted. He appealed, arguing that his rights to a speedy trial had been violated. The SC overturned his conviction, saying that prompt inquiry is a fundamental right, and the charging authority has a duty to provide a prompt trial to ensure the availability of records, recollection of witnesses, and availability of testimony.

Dillingham v. United States, 423 U.S. 64, 96 S.Ct. 303 (1975) [Edward Earl DILLINGHAM v. UNITED STATES] (Sixth Amendment; Speedy Trials) Dillingham was arrested for a crime. After a 22-month interval, he was indicted, and 12 months after that, he was brought to trial and was convicted. He appealed, arguing that the 22-month interval between his arrest and indictment had violated his right to a speedy trial under the Sixth Amendment. The SC declared that invocation of the speedy-trial provision need not await indictment, information, or other formal charge. Thus, the delay between Dillingham's arrest, indictment, and trial was unreasonable under the Sixth Amendment; his conviction was overturned.

Dobbert v. Florida, 432 U.S. 282, 97 S.Ct. 2290 (1977) [Ernest John DOBBERT, Jr., Petitioner, v. State of FLORIDA] (Death Penalty; Eighth Amendment; Fourteenth Amendment; Publicity) Dobbert was convicted of first-degree murder, second-degree murder, child torture, and child abuse and sentenced to death. He appealed, alleging that changes in the jury decision to recommend mercy instead of the death penalty without review by a trial judge had jeopardized his chances of receiving a life sentence. Further, he claimed that there was no death penalty "in effect" in Florida at the time he was convicted, because an earlier death-penalty statute had been held to be invalid when *Furman v. Georgia* (1972) had been decided. Dobbert also claimed that excessive pretrial publicity denied him the right to a fair trial. The SC rejected all of his arguments, saying that changes in the death-penalty statute were simply procedural, and thus there was no rights violation. Further, new statutes provided convicted offenders with *more* procedural safeguards rather than fewer of them. Dobbert's equal-protection rights under the Fourteenth Amendment were not violated either, because the new statute did not deny him such protection. Finally, the pretrial publicity, in view of the "totality of circumstances," was insufficient to conclude that he was denied a fair trial. The SC upheld his conviction and sentence.

Doe v. United States, 487 U.S. 201, 108 S.Ct. 2341 (1988) [John DOE, Petitioner, v. UNITED STATES] (Confessions; Fifth Amendment; Self-Incrimination) An unnamed person, John Doe, was a target of a federal grand-jury inquiry into possible federal offenses involving fraudulent manipulation of oil cargoes and receipt of unreported income. The grand jury compelled Doe to disclose records of bank accounts he maintained in Bermuda and the Cayman Islands. He refused to give additional information and was cited for contempt and jailed. The contempt charge stemmed from the fact that he was asked to order the banks in question to disclose bank account sums, not necessarily the names of persons on those bank accounts. Doe claimed that to have done so would have violated his right against self-incrimination under the Fifth Amendment. He appealed. The SC ruled that authorizing foreign banks to disclose records of accounts without identifying the actual documents or acknowledging their existence does not violate a person's Fifth Amendment privilege against self-incrimination.

Doggett v. United States, 505 U.S. 647, 112 S.Ct. 2686 (1992) [Marc Gilbert DOGGETT, Petitioner, v. UNITED STATES] (Sixth Amendment; Speedy Trials) Doggett was charged in a United States district court with conspiracy to distribute cocaine. Because of various delays, mostly caused by the government, his trial was not held for eight and one-half years. He was convicted. He appealed, contending that the eight-and-one-half-year delay before his case was tried violated his speedy-trial rights under the Sixth Amendment. The SC overturned Doggett's conviction, concluding that the eight-and-one-half-year delay in his trial, largely because of government causes, violated his Sixth Amendment rights.

Douglas v. Buder, 412 U.S. 430, 93 S.Ct. 2199 (1973) [James R. DOUGLAS v. William E. BUDER, Judge] (Corrections; Probation and Parole) Douglas was a probationer whose probation was revoked because he had been in an automobile accident and had received a traffic citation. He did not report this citation for several days, and technically, he was in violation of his probation program, which required notification of his probation officer of any arrest without undue delay. Douglas appealed the revocation, contending that it was unreasonable. The SC reversed his revocation, holding that the issuance of a traffic citation is not an arrest, and thus the idea of reporting a traffic ticket is so devoid of evidentiary support as to be invalid under the due-process clause of the Fourteenth Amendment.

Douglas v. California, 372 U.S. 353, 83 S.Ct. 814 (1963) [William DOUGLAS and Bennie Will Meyes, Petitioners, v. The People of the State of CALIFORNIA] (Corrections; Fourteenth Amendment; Inmate Rights) Douglas was convicted of several felonies. He appealed, alleging that because of indigence, an attorney had not been appointed to represent him. An appellate court ruled that appointment of counsel would have been of no value to him. The SC overturned the appellate court decision, saying that where defendants have exhausted their state remedies for appeals of convictions, they are entitled to further discretionary review by the Supreme Court of California. Further, Douglas' Fourteenth Amendment right of equal protection under the law had been violated when counsel was not provided for his state appeal.

Dow Chemical Co. v. United States, 476 U.S. 227, 106 S.Ct. 1819 (1986) [DOW CHEMICAL COMPANY, Petitioner, v. UNITED STATES, etc.] (Aerial Surveillance; Fourth Amendment; Law Enforcement Officers or Agencies; Plain-View Rule) Dow Chemical brought suit against the United States government for conducting an unreasonable aerial surveillance of Dow's 2,000-acre property by the Environmental Protection Agency as a part of the Clean Air Act. Dow, which was subject to fines for various Clean Air Act violations, claimed that its Fourth Amendment right had been violated. The SC disagreed, holding that site inspections by aerial photography are reasonable and do not constitute a "search" in the context of the Fourth Amendment provisions.

Downum v. United States, 372 U.S. 734, 83 S.Ct. 1033 (1963) [Raymond DOWNUM, Petitioner, v. UNITED STATES] (Double Jeopardy; Fifth Amendment) Downum was charged on six counts of stealing from the mail and forging checks. In April 1961, he appeared for trial, and a jury was sworn in. Before the actual process of witness testimony began, the prosecutor moved that the jury should be discharged because one of his crucial witnesses was not present. The jury was discharged. Two days later another jury was impaneled and trial was held, whereupon Downum was convicted. He appealed on the grounds that his right against double jeopardy under the Fifth Amendment had been violated. The SC agreed with Downum and overturned his conviction. (*See* Christ v. Bretz [1978] *for a similar case and holding.*)

Doyle v. Ohio, 426 U.S. 610, 96 S.Ct. 2240 (1976) [Jefferson DOYLE, Petitioner, v. State of OHIO. Richard Wood, Petitioner, v. State of Ohio] (Fourteenth Amendment; *Miranda* Warning; Self-Incrimination) Doyle and another person were arrested for selling marijuana. At the time of their arrest, they were told their *Miranda* rights and elected to remain silent. However, during their trial, they gave exculpatory testimony that had been unknown by the prosecution. When cross-examined by prosecutors as to why they had not disclosed such exculpatory information at the time of their arrest, Doyle and his friend said that according to their *Miranda* rights, they had the right to remain silent. They were convicted and appealed, alleging a violation of their due-process rights under the Fourteenth Amendment. The SC reversed their convictions, saying that the government had had no right to impeach their exculpatory testimony at trial because of their invocation of the silence privilege under *Miranda.* Thus, the due-process rights of Doyle and his codefendant had been violated.

Draper v. United States, 358 U.S. 307, 79 S.Ct. 329 (1959) [James Alonzo DRAPER, Petitioner, v. UNITED STATES of America] (Law Enforcement Officers or Agencies; Searches and Seizures) An informant whose information had been reliable and accurate in the past gave a federal agent a description of Draper, time of arrival, and other information that was corroborated by the agent, which resulted in Draper's arrest. The subsequent search uncovered heroin in Draper's possession. He was convicted. He appealed, arguing that the information given by the informant, who died before Draper's trial and was unable to offer testimony, was hearsay and thus had not justified the eventual search incident to Draper's arrest. However, the SC reasoned that such hearsay from a previously reliable informant was sufficient to establish probable cause to stop and search Draper.

Duckworth v. Eagan, 492 U.S. 195, 109 S.Ct. 2875 (1989) [Jack R. DUCKWORTH, Petitioner, v. Gary James EAGAN] (Confessions; *Miranda* Warning; Self-Incrimination) Eagan, a murder suspect, was interrogated by Indiana officials, who gave him a general *Miranda* statement to sign. The form did not contain the full litany of the *Miranda* warning, but it was sufficiently specific to advise Eagan of his right to an attorney, and that if he could not afford one, an attorney would be provided free if and when the case went to court. Eagan made several incriminating statements. The following day, he was given another *Miranda* form to sign and did so. He was interrogated, confessed, and was convicted of the murder. He appealed, contending that his first waiver was not "valid" because it was not the exact *Miranda* warning carried by police officers for guidance when arresting suspects. Thus, he argued, his later confession was inadmissible as well, as it was prompted by his initial statements. The SC disagreed and said that the *Miranda* "general" warning was sufficiently specific to

constitute a valid warning for lawful and constitutional police interrogations. The SC declared that the *Miranda* warning is not required to be read to suspects in the exact form as contained in the *Miranda* case. The evidence obtained against Eagan in both interrogations was admissible against him, and his murder conviction was upheld.

Duckworth v. Serrano, 454 U.S. 1, 102 S.Ct. 18 (1981) [Jack DUCKWORTH, Warden, v. Isadore SERRANO] (Corrections; *Habeas Corpus* Petitions; Inmate Rights) A prisoner, Serrano, sought to challenge his conviction through a *habeas corpus* petition. He alleged that he had been denied effective assistance of counsel at his trial, and thus his due-process rights had been violated. Serrano had not sought relief in state courts *first,* however. The SC took significant notice of the fact that he had commenced his petition with the Seventh Circuit Court of Appeals, a federal appellate body, rather than in an Indiana state court. The SC dismissed his petition because he had failed to exhaust all state remedies. The significance of this case is that any petitioner who has been convicted of a state crime must first exhaust all state remedies before attempting to file petitions in federal courts. This is considered a landmark case because it obligates prisoners to direct their *habeas corpus* petitions first to state courts before they pursue federal remedies. This decision is no doubt calculated to reduce crowded federal court dockets.

Dumbra v. United States, 268 U.S. 435, 45 S.Ct. 546 (1925) [Domenico DUMBRA et al., Petitioners, v. UNITED STATES] (Law Enforcement Officers or Agencies; Stop and Frisk) During Prohibition, Dumbra operated a winery. Revenue agents observed an undercover Prohibition agent buy two gallons of wine from Dumbra. Several other transactions were completed with illegal liquor being exchanged for money. In each case, Dumbra was observed walking to the back of a store and returning with illegal liquor in gallon bottles. Subsequently, officials obtained a search warrant and raided Dumbra's premises, confiscating a large quantity of liquor. Dumbra was convicted. He appealed, saying that there was no probable cause as the basis for the search warrant issued. The SC disagreed with Dumbra and upheld his conviction, saying that under the circumstances of the ready availability of liquor on the premises and the frequent sales to agents by various Dumbra family members, sufficient probable cause existed to justify the issuance of the search warrant.

Dunaway v. New York, 442 U.S. 200, 99 S.Ct. 2248 (1979) [Irving Jerome DUNAWAY, Petitioner, v. State of NEW YORK] (Exclusionary Rule; Law Enforcement Officers or Agencies) Dunaway was involved in a murder according to a reliable informant; however, sufficient evidence could not be presented to obtain an arrest warrant. Police officers picked up Dunaway anyway (not formally arresting him) and took him to police headquarters, where he was interrogated for several hours. Subsequently, he made several incriminating statements that led to his being charged with and convicted of murder. Dunaway appealed, contending that police had lacked probable cause to arrest him initially. The SC agreed and overturned his conviction. The significance of *Dunaway* is that police officers cannot take persons into custody and interrogate them for purposes of criminal prosecution without showing probable cause. The SC declared that Dunaway's detention and interrogation at the station house by police were both illegal, and thus his subsequent confession was inadmissible in court.

Duncan v. Louisiana, 391 U.S. 145, 88 S.Ct. 1444 (1968) [Gary DUNCAN, Appellant, v. State of LOUISIANA] (Juries; Jury Trials; Sixth Amendment) Duncan was convicted in a bench trial of simple battery in a Louisiana court. The crime was punishable as a misdemeanor, with two years' imprisonment and a fine of $300. In Duncan's case, he was sentenced to only 60 days and a fine of $150. He appealed, saying that he had demanded a jury trial and none was provided. The SC agreed with Duncan, saying that a crime with a potential punishment of two years is a serious crime, despite the sentence of 60 days imposed. Thus, for serious crimes, under the Sixth Amendment, Duncan was entitled to a jury trial.

Duncan v. Walker, 533 U.S. 167, 121 S.Ct. 2120 (2001) [George DUNCAN, Superintendent, Great Meadow Correctional Facility, Petitioner, v. Sherman WALKER] (Antiterrorism and Effective Death Penalty Act of 1996; *Habeas Corpus* Petitions) In 1992, Sherman Walker was convicted of several counts of robbery in New York state courts. Walker was sentenced to seven to 14 years in prison for robbery in the first degree. Walker unsuccessfully petitioned various state remedies in connection with his convictions. Walker's last conviction became final on March 18, 1996, prior to April 24, 1996, the effective date of the Antiterrorism and Effective Death Penalty Act (AEDPA). Walker filed a *habeas corpus* petition in a U.S. district court on April 9, 1996, but on July 9, 1996, the court dismissed the complaint and petition without prejudice. The reason for dismissing the complaint was that it was not apparent that Walker had exhausted all of his state remedies. Further, he had failed to specify the claims litigated in the state appellate proceedings relating to his robbery convictions. On May 20, 1997, more than one year after the passage of the AEDPA, Walker filed another *habeas corpus* petition in the same federal district court. Walker had not returned to a state court to contest any charges subsequent to his March 18, 1996, conviction. In May 1998, the district court dismissed his petition because Walker had not filed the petition within a reasonable time from AEDPA's effective date. The Second Circuit Court of Appeals reversed the district court and reinstated the *habeas corpus* petition. The SC heard the case and reversed the Second Circuit Court of Appeals, holding that an application for federal *habeas corpus* review is not an application for state post-conviction or other collateral review, and therefore it did not toll the limitation period during the pendency of Walker's first federal *habeas corpus* petition. The case was remanded to the trial court for further proceedings consistent with this opinion.

Duren v. Missouri, 439 U.S. 357, 99 S.Ct. 664 (1979) [Billy DUREN, Petitioner, v. State of MISSOURI] (Juries; Right to Counsel; Sixth Amendment) Duren was charged with various crimes in a Missouri court. At the beginning of his trial, a jury was selected under a jury system that automatically exempted women from jury duty if they so chose to be ex-

empted. He was convicted. He appealed, contending that the jury-selection process that excluded women had deprived him of a fair trial, as it denied him the opportunity to be tried by a jury of his peers as a cross-section of the community. The SC agreed with Duren that he had indeed been deprived of a fair trial. Specifically, the SC said that if women, who are "sufficiently numerous and distinct from men," are systematically excluded from venires, the fair-cross-section requirement for jury selection cannot be satisfied. Thus, Duren's conviction was overturned on the basis of a deliberate pattern of underrepresentation of women on juries in Missouri.

Dusenbery v. United States, ___U.S.___, 122 S.Ct. 694 (2002) [Larry Dean DUSENBERY, Petitioner, v. UNITED STATES] (Asset Forfeiture; Fourteenth Amendment) Dusenbery was convicted on federal drug charges. While he was in prison, the FBI began an administrative process to seize his cash and other assets. The FBI notified Dusenbery at the prison where he was confined of their intent to seize his assets and cash. They also sent notification of asset forfeiture procedures to his last known address and to an address where his mother lived. Subsequently, they seized his assets. Dusenbery filed a motion for the return of his seized property and cash. The federal court denied his motion, but the Sixth Circuit court vacated and remanded. On remand, the federal district court granted the government summary judgment on their motion to retain the property seized, ruling that its sending notice by certified mail to Dusenbery's place of incarceration satisfied Dusenbery's due-process rights. Dusenbery appealed to the SC, who heard the case. The SC affirmed the summary judgment of the district court, holding that the FBI's notice of the cash forfeiture satisfied due process. Assets of convicted felons may be seized in accordance with strict notification procedures by the government, provided they were instruments of or derived from the crime(s) committed.

E

Early v. Packer, ___U.S.___, 123 S.Ct. 362 (2002) [Richard E. EARLY, Warden, et al., v. William PACKER] (*Habeas Corpus* Petitions; Juries; Jury Instructions) William Packer was found guilty in a California court of second-degree murder, two counts of attempted murder, two counts of robbery, two counts of assault with a deadly weapon, and one count of assault with a firearm. He was acquitted on 10 other counts. The jury had a difficult time in certain of its deliberations, with one juror in particular claiming illness, indecisiveness, and fatigue. At various points during jury deliberations, the trial judge requested information from the jury foreman about the status of jury voting, and he questioned the particular female juror at some length. The judge repeated various instructions to the jury as to their deliberations, including that they should follow the law, determine whether or not the elements of the offense were present, and find unanimously whether Packer was guilty or not guilty of each of those offenses. Subsequently, the jury rendered its verdicts as noted above and Packer appealed, filing a *habeas corpus* petition. The petition alleged that the trial judge coerced the female juror into agreeing with the majority of other jurors in reaching their guilty verdicts on the above counts. Thus, he claimed, he was denied his due-process right to a fair and impartial jury. The Ninth Circuit Court of Appeals granted Packer's petition and reversed his convictions. California appealed and the SC heard the case. The SC reinstated Packer's convictions, holding that the trial judge's remarks and instructions to jurors were not coercive, nor were they unreasonable or contrary to established federal law. Thus, it is not unconstitutional for a trial judge to urge a jury to continue deliberating as long as the judge does not attempt to coerce a particular type of jury verdict. In this instance, all of the judge's remarks clearly admonished jurors to follow and apply the law objectively and to make their decisions about Packer's guilt or innocence consistent with that objectivity.

Eddings v. Oklahoma, 455 U.S. 104, 102 S.Ct. 869 (1982) [Monty Lee EDDINGS, Petitioner, v. OKLAHOMA] (Aggravating and Mitigating Circumstances; Bifurcated Trials; Cruel and Unusual Punishment; Death Penalty; Eighth Amendment; Juvenile Law) On April 4, 1977, Eddings and several other companions ran away from their Missouri homes. In a car owned by Eddings' older brother, they drove, without direction or purpose, eventually reaching the Oklahoma Turnpike. Eddings had several firearms in the car, including rifles that he had stolen from his father. At one point, he lost control of the car and was stopped by an Oklahoma State Highway Patrol officer. When the officer approached the car, Eddings stuck a shotgun out of the window and killed the officer outright. When Eddings was subsequently apprehended, he was sent to criminal court on a prosecutorial motion. Efforts by Eddings and his attorney to oppose that action failed. In a subsequent two-stage trial, several aggravating circumstances were introduced and alleged, while several mitigating circumstances, including Eddings' youth, mental state, and potential for treatment, were considered by the trial judge. However, the judge did not consider Eddings' "unhappy upbringing and emotional disturbance" as significant mitigating factors to offset the aggravating ones. Eddings' attorney filed an appeal that eventually reached the SC. Although the Oklahoma Court of Criminal Appeals reversed the trial judge's ruling, the SC reversed the Oklahoma Court of Criminal Appeals. The reversal pivoted on whether the trial judge had erred by refusing to consider the "unhappy upbringing and emotionally disturbed state" of Eddings. The trial judge had previously acknowledged the boy's youth as a mitigating factor. The *fact* of Eddings' age, 16, was significant, precisely because the majority of justices did not consider it significant. Rather, they focused on the issue of introduction of mitigating circumstances specifically outlined in Eddings' appeal. They decided Oklahoma could lawfully impose the death penalty on a juvenile who was 16 years old at the time he committed murder. The case raised the question of whether the death penalty as applied to juveniles was "cruel and unusual" punish-

ment under the Eighth Amendment of the Constitution. The SC avoided the issue. The justices did *not* say it was "cruel and unusual punishment," but they also did *not* say it wasn't. What they said was that the youthfulness of the offender is a mitigating factor of great weight that must be considered. Thus, many jurisdictions were left to make their own interpretations of the high court opinion.

Edwards v. Arizona, 451 U.S. 477, 101 S.Ct. 1880 (1981) [Robert EDWARDS, Petitioner, v. State of ARIZONA] (Confessions; Law Enforcement Officers or Agencies; *Miranda* Warning) Edwards was implicated in a crime by an accomplice who gave police a taped confession. Edwards was given his *Miranda* warning. He wanted to strike a deal with police, but he also wanted an attorney. At that point, his interrogation stopped and an attorney was appointed. The next day, two officers visited Edwards in his cell and gave him his *Miranda* warning again. They asked him if he would talk to them. After indicating that he didn't want to talk with them, he asked if he could hear the taped confession of his accomplice. After hearing this, he gave incriminating statements to police. Edwards was charged with and convicted of various crimes, with his confession used as evidence against him in court. He appealed, seeking to suppress his confession. The SC overturned his conviction and threw out the confession, saying that once he had requested an attorney, police interrogation should have ceased entirely, even though he had been told his *Miranda* rights a second time before he gave the incriminating statements. His attorney had not been present during the second custodial interrogation. Edwards had already advised police of his desire not to say anything, but they had persisted. Thus, police may not continue a custodial interrogation of a suspect represented by an attorney who requests to remain silent, even though the *Miranda* warning is given more than once and preceding any subsequent interrogation. Suspect-initiated conversation, however, may be used for incrimination purposes.

Elder v. Holloway, 510 U.S. 510, 114 S.Ct. 1019 (1994) [Charles K. ELDER, Petitioner, v. R.D. HOLLOWAY et al.] (Civil Rights, Section 1983 Claims; Immunity) Elder was arrested without warrant by Idaho police because they believed he was wanted in Florida on a criminal charge. At first, they planned to arrest him in his workplace, which was a public area, where an arrest warrant is not required. However, they found that Elder had left work early and gone home. They continued to his home, where they surrounded the dwelling and ordered him out of the house. Authorities instructed Elder to crawl out of the house, but Elder, who suffered from epilepsy, walked out of the house instead and immediately experienced an epileptic seizure. He fell to the ground, where his head struck the pavement, causing him to suffer permanent brain trauma and paralysis. Subsequently, Elder filed suit against the police officers under Title 42 U.S.C. Section 1983, alleging that the officers had violated his civil rights by arresting him in his home without a suitable warrant. The United States district court granted the officers a summary judgment on the grounds of their qualified immunity from such suits. Elder appealed. The SC overturned the summary judgment and ordered the case sent back to district court for a trial resolution of factual questions. However, it did not offer an opinion or ruling on the qualified-immunity defense. Rather, it placed the matter in the circuit court of appeals to resolve the issue in light of all prevailing law and authority.

Elkins v. United States, 364 U.S. 206, 80 S.Ct. 1437 (1960) [**James Butler ELKINS and Raymond Frederick Clark, Petitioners, v. UNITED STATES of America**] (**Law Enforcement Officers or Agencies; Searches and Seizures**) The SC overturned the so-called silver-platter doctrine, which had previously allowed state authorities who discovered evidence of a federal crime in an illegal search to turn the evidence over to federal agencies for prosecution, as long as federal agents did not participate in the search.

Enmund v. Florida, 458 U.S. 782, 102 S.Ct. 3368 (1982) [**Earl ENMUND, Petitioner v. FLORIDA**] (**Corrections; Cruel and Unusual Punishment; Death Penalty; Eighth Amendment**) Enmund was the driver of a vehicle in which his codefendants committed first-degree murder. Under a felony-murder statute, he was treated by the court as though he had committed the murder with the other two defendants, and he was convicted and sentenced to death. He appealed. The SC reversed Enmund's conviction, saying that where the defendant did not take a life or use or attempt to use lethal force, the death penalty was too severe a punishment.

Escobedo v. Illinois, 378 U.S. 478, 84 S.Ct. 1758 (1963) [**Danny ESCOBEDO, Petitioner, v. State of ILLINOIS**] (**Custodial Interrogations; Law Enforcement Officers or Agencies; Right to Counsel**) An informant told police that Escobedo had murdered someone. Without an arrest warrant, the police arrested Escobedo and commenced to interrogate him, without benefit of counsel, on his way to the police station. Escobedo asked to speak with an attorney on several occasions during a subsequent long interrogation period. At certain points, he was escorted about the station to various rooms, and at these times, he would see his attorney at a distance down the hall. The attorney was denied access to his client, who was told that his attorney "did not wish to see him" or was "unavailable." After many hours of intensive interrogation, Escobedo eventually confessed to murder and was convicted. He appealed. The SC overturned the conviction on the grounds that Escobedo had been denied counsel and that interrogation had proceeded despite his plea to have counsel present. Thus, the denial of counsel to Escobedo when he requested it had violated his right to due process. The case is also significant because the SC stressed the fact that initially, police officers were merely investigating a murder. At some early point, their mode shifted to accusation, and they accused Escobedo of murder. Thus, whenever police officers shift their questioning from investigatory to accusatory, defendants are entitled to counsel and to refrain from conversing with officers unless counsel is present.

Espinosa v. Florida, 505 U.S. 1079, 112 S.Ct. 2926 (1992) [**Henry Jose ESPINOSA, Petitioner, v. FLORIDA**] (**Aggravating and Mitigating Circumstances; Death Penalty; Eighth Amendment**) Espinosa was convicted of first-degree murder, second-degree murder, attempted murder, grand theft, and burglary, and was sentenced to death. He appealed. One of the aggravating circumstances articulated by the judge to the jury during the penalty phase of the trial included the words "especially wicked, evil, atrocious or cruel." This particular phrase had been declared unconstitutionally vague in several prior cases, including *Stringer v. Black* (1992), *Clemons v. Mississippi* (1990), and *Maynard v. Cartwright* (1988). Thus, it was an invalid aggravating factor. Nevertheless, it was used and given "great weight" in finding Espinosa eligible for the death penalty. The SC held that the jury must not be permitted to weigh invalid aggravating circumstances and vacated the death penalty. Thus, Espinosa's due-process rights had been violated.

Estelle v. Gamble, 429 U.S. 97, 97 S.Ct. 285 (1976) [**W.J. ESTELLE, Jr., Director, Texas Department of Corrections, et al., Petitioners, v. J.W. GAMBLE**] (**Civil Rights, Section 1983 Claims; Corrections; Cruel and Unusual Punishment; Inmate Rights**) Gamble was an inmate in a Texas prison. He was injured while performing an inmate work assignment. During the next several months, he saw medical personnel on at least 17 occasions and subsequently was declared fit to work. He continued to refuse work assignments and eventually filed a Title 42 U.S.C. Section 1983 action alleging cruel and unusual punishment. Gamble alleged that personnel had not X-rayed his back and other body areas to determine whether bones were broken. The SC said that whenever prison authorities ignore a prisoner's medical ailments or complaints, they are inflicting constitute cruel and unusual punishment by their deliberate indifference to inmate medical needs. But in Gamble's case, it was clear that officials had not expressed deliberate indifference to Gamble's medical complaints; they had not acted negligently.

Estelle v. Smith, 451 U.S. 454, 101 S.Ct. 1866 (1981) [**W.J. ESTELLE, Jr., Director, Texas Department of Corrections, Petitioner, v. Ernest Benjamin SMITH**] (**Death Penalty; Fifth Amendment;** *Habeas Corpus* **Petitions; Right to Counsel; Self-Incrimination; Sixth Amendment**) Smith was a Texas prisoner who had been convicted of murder and given a death sentence. He sought through *habeas corpus* to have his conviction and death sentence overturned on the basis that the prosecution, without his attorney's knowledge, had used statements from a psychiatrist who had examined Smith, and to whom Smith had confided various incriminating facts that would lead the psychiatrist to believe that Smith would pose a danger to others in the future. The SC reversed his conviction and death sentence, holding that the admission of the doctor's testimony at the penalty phase of the trial had violated Smith's Fifth Amendment right against self-incrimination, as he had not been advised before the examination that his statements could or would be used against him in court. Further, the fact that the doctor gave testimony about the future dangerousness of Smith without Smith's attorney's knowledge violated Smith's Sixth Amendment right to effective assistance of counsel.

Estelle v. Williams, 425 U.S. 501, 96 S.Ct. 1691 (1976) [**W.J. ESTELLE, Jr., Director, Texas Department of Corrections, Petitioner, v. Harry Lee WILLIAMS**] (**Corrections;**

Discovery; Fourteenth Amendment; Inmate Rights) Williams was charged with assault with intent to commit murder and stood trial for the offense in his prison clothing. After he was convicted, he appealed, contending that he should not have had to stand trial in such clothing because it biased the case against him and violated the equal-protection clause of the Fourteenth Amendment. The SC agreed that Williams should not have been tried while wearing prison attire; however, because he had not objected during the trial to wearing this clothing, his appeal was negated. This case is significant because although Williams didn't win his point, he caused subsequent courts to be sensitive to how defendants should be dressed during their trials. Currently, defendants cannot be compelled to wear prison clothing during their trials, but they must make timely and proper objections.

Evitts v. Lucey, 469 U.S. 387, 105 S.Ct. 830 (1985) [Ralph W. EVITTS, Superintendent, Blackburn Correctional Complex, and David L. Armstrong, Attorney General, Petitioners, v. Keith E. LUCEY] (*Habeas Corpus* Petitions; Right to Counsel; Sixth Amendment) Lucey was convicted in a Kentucky court of trafficking in controlled substances. He filed an appeal, without representation by counsel; it was later dismissed. Eventually, Lucey sought *habeas corpus* relief, contending that he had been denied the effective assistance of counsel on his first appeal. The SC granted his petition and reinstated his appeal as a matter of right, holding that as an integral part of due process, Lucey was entitled to be represented by an attorney in his initial appeal of his conviction. Because he had not been permitted counsel on the appeal, the dismissal of his appeal was unconstitutional.

Ewing v. California, ___U.S.___, 123 S.Ct. 1179 (2003) [Gary Albert EWING, Petitioner, v. CALIFORNIA] (Cruel and Unusual Punishment; Eighth Amendment; Habitual Offender Statutes) Gary Ewing, a parolee, was arrested for stealing three golf clubs from the El Segundo Golf Course in March 2000. A subsequent check of Ewing's criminal record disclosed numerous felony convictions dating back to 1984. He was subsequently prosecuted under California's three-strikes law and convicted. The judge sentenced Ewing to a term of 25 years to life. Ewing appealed, contending that this was cruel and unusual punishment in violation of his Eighth Amendment rights, and that such a sentence was disproportionate punishment given the nature of his conviction offense. The SC heard Ewing's case and upheld his conviction and sentence, holding that Ewing's sentence of 25 years to life, imposed for the offense of felony grand theft under the three-strikes law, is not grossly disproportionate and therefore does not violate the Eighth Amendment's prohibition on cruel and unusual punishments.

Ex parte Crouse, 4 Wharton (Pa.) 9 (1838) [Ex parte CROUSE] (Juvenile Law) A girl was committed to the Philadelphia House of Detention by the court because she was considered unmanageable. She was not given a trial by jury. Rather, her commitment was made arbitrarily by a presiding judge. The father tried to secure her release, claiming that parental control of children is exclusive, natural, and proper. A higher court rejected the father's claim, upholding the power

of the state to exercise necessary reforms and restraints to protect children from themselves and their environments. In effect, children were temporarily deprived of any legal standing to challenge decisions made by the state in their behalf. Although this decision was only applicable to Pennsylvania citizens and their children, other states took note of it and sought to invoke similar controls over errant children in their jurisdictions.

Ex parte Hawk, 321 U.S. 114, 64 S.Ct. 448 (1944) [Ex parte Henry HAWK] (Corrections; *Habeas Corpus* Petitions; Inmate Rights) Hawk was convicted in a Nebraska court of a crime. He filed a *habeas corpus* petition, alleging various trial irregularities. He first filed his action in federal court, which rejected his appeal. He then appealed to the SC, which also rejected him, holding that Hawk had not exhausted all of the state remedies at his disposal. Hawk should have sought relief first in Nebraska courts, but had not done so.

Ex parte Hull, 312 U.S. 546, 61 S.Ct. 640 (1941) [Ex parte Cleio HULL] (Corrections; Inmate Rights) In 1941, prison and jail officials carefully screened all outgoing inmate mail, including legal documents and petitions addressed to state or federal courts. Petitions by inmates to the court for virtually any grievance or complaint, founded or unfounded, were often conveniently trashed by prison officials, who claimed that these petitions were improperly prepared and thus ineligible for court action. Prison and jail policies permitted the disposal of such materials. In *Hull,* the SC declared that no state or its officers may abridge or impair a prisoner's right to have access to federal courts. The court, not prison or jail officials, would determine whether petitions were properly prepared. Although the original *Hull* decision pertained to a particular class of legal petitions, it was eventually extended to include access to the courts for all petitions.

F

Fare v. Michael C., 442 U.S. 707, 99 S.Ct. 2560 (1979) [Kenneth F. FARE, etc., Petitioner, v. MICHAEL C.] (Confessions; Fifth Amendment; Juvenile Law; Law Enforcement Officers or Agencies; *Miranda* Warning; Self-Incrimination) Trial court judges must evaluate the voluntariness of confessions by juveniles by examining the totality of circumstances. Michael C. was a juvenile murder suspect who was taken into custody by police, told his *Miranda* rights, and questioned. When asked if he wanted an attorney, he asked to have his probation officer present. Police advised him that they would contact his probation officer later, and then they asked him if he wanted to answer some of their questions. Michael C. made subsequent incriminating statements and police charged him with murder. He was convicted. He appealed, alleging that his request for a probation officer was the equivalent of asking for an attorney, and thus, his Fifth Amendment right against self-incrimination had been violated when police did not provide him with a probation officer. The SC disagreed and concluded that when he was told his *Miranda* rights, he had given up his right to remain silent because he had not specifically asked for an attorney to be present during further questioning and he had given incriminating statements voluntarily. Probation officers do not perform the same functions as attorneys and so are irrelevant concerning the *Miranda* warning given to criminal suspects.

Faretta v. California, 422 U.S. 806, 95 S.Ct. 2525 (1975) [**Anthony Pasquall FARETTA, Petitioner, v. State of CALIFORNIA**] (**Right to Counsel**) Faretta, who was charged with grand theft, desired to represent himself. The judge ruled that he had no constitutional right to represent himself in the case and appointed a public defender to defend him. Faretta was convicted. He appealed, arguing that he had a right to represent himself. The SC overturned his conviction, holding that Faretta indeed had a right knowingly and intelligently to waive his right to counsel and represent himself in the criminal proceeding. Thus, he had been denied his constitutional right to act as his own counsel.

Felker v. Turpin, 518 U.S. 651, 116 S.Ct. 2333 (1996) [**Ellis Wayne FELKER, Petitioner, v. Tony TURPIN, Warden**] (**Antiterrorism and Effective Death Penalty Act of 1996;** *Habeas Corpus* **Petitions**) Felker was convicted of capital murder, aggravated sodomy, rape, and false imprisonment in a Georgia state court. Felker filed several *habeas corpus* appeals, which were denied. Subsequently, the Antiterrorism and Effective Death Penalty Act of 1996 was passed, which limited successive *habeas corpus* appeals filed by inmates sentenced to death. Felker sought appellate review by filing yet another *habeas corpus* claim, alleging that the Act amounts to a suspension of the writ of *habeas corpus*, and that exceptional circumstances exist to show why Felker should not be executed. The SC heard the case and rejected Felker's claims, holding that the Act does not amount to a "suspension" of the writ of *habeas corpus* and that Felker had failed to demonstrate any arguments that raised exceptional circumstances not previously raised in prior rejected filings.

Fellers v. United States, ___U.S.___, 124 S.Ct. 1019 (2004) **John J. FELLERS, Petitioner, v. UNITED STATES**] (**Custodial Interrogations; Sixth Amendment**) John Fellers was indicted by a federal grand jury in Lincoln, NE, on charges of conspiracy to distribute methamphetamine. A Lincoln police officer and a Lancaster County deputy sheriff were sent to arrest Fellers. When the officers arrived at Fellers' home, they advised him that they had a warrant for his arrest pursuant to the indictment, but prior to taking him to jail to be processed, they asked him several incriminating questions concerning his involvement in the distribution of methamphetamines for about 15 minutes. During that time, the officers did not Mirandize Fellers, nor did they advise him of his Sixth Amendment right to have counsel present during his questioning. Later, at the jail, Fellers was Mirandized, although he made further statements stemming from his earlier home questioning. He was subsequently convicted in a jury trial in which the jail statements were used as evidence against him. Although the district court judge suppressed the state-

ments Fellers gave to police at his home, he nevertheless permitted the statements given by Fellers at the jail later. Fellers appealed and the Eighth Circuit Court of Appeals upheld his conviction, holding that the jail interrogation following Fellers' *Miranda* warning, although stemming largely from the earlier home questioning, was not fruits of previous questioning in violation of Sixth Amendment standards. Fellers appealed further, and the SC heard the case. The SC reversed Fellers' conviction, holding that the officers violated Fellers' Sixth Amendment rights by deliberately eliciting information from him during their postindictment visit to his home absent counsel or waiver of counsel, regardless of whether the officers' conduct constituted an "interrogation."

Ferguson v. City of Charleston, 532 U.S. 67, 121 S.Ct. 1281 (2001) [**Crystal M. FERGUSON et al., Petitioners, v. CITY OF CHARLESTON et al.**] (**Fourth Amendment**) Several obstetrics patients at a state hospital in South Carolina filed suit against the hospital and the City of Charleston following their arrest by police officers when the hospital informed the officers that these patients had tested positive for cocaine from urine specimens the women had provided. It was the state hospital policy to reveal to the police anyone who tested positive for illegal drugs in the course of their obstetrics examinations and urinalyses. None of the women knew that their urine specimens were subsequently going to be used for a law enforcement purpose (e.g., to determine whether they had been using illegal drugs). The women filed a federal suit against the hospital, contending that the hospital had conducted an unreasonable search and seizure of their urine without their consent. The district court ruled in favor of the hospital and the appellate court affirmed the decision. Thus, the plaintiffs took their case to the SC. The SC overturned the lower court judgment for the City of Charleston, holding that urine tests were searches within the meaning of the Fourth Amendment, and that the tests, and reporting of positive test results to police, were unreasonable searches absent the patients' consent, in view of the policy's law enforcement purpose. Thus, searches unsupported by either a warrant or probable cause are unconstitutional where members of state hospital staff are functioning as government actors subject to the strictures of the Fourth Amendment.

Ferguson v. Georgia, 365 U.S. 570, 81 S.Ct. 756 (1961) [**Billy FERGUSON, Appellant, v. State of GEORGIA**] (**Fourteenth Amendment; Right to Counsel**) Ferguson was charged with murder. During his trial, he requested that he be questioned by his attorney while on the witness stand, but the Georgia court prohibited him from testifying according to an incompetency statute. Ferguson was subsequently convicted of murder. He appealed. The SC said that the denial of the right to have Ferguson's attorney ask him questions was a denial of counsel and in violation of his due-process rights guaranteed by the Fourteenth Amendment.

Fex v. Michigan, 507 U.S. 43, 113 S.Ct.1085 (1993) [**William FEX, Petitioner, v. MICHIGAN**] (**Speedy Trials**) Fex, a prisoner in Indiana, was brought to trial in Michigan 196 days following his trial request to Michigan officials and 177 days after the request was received by Michigan prosecutors. He was convicted. He appealed, alleging that the 180-day limit for a speedy trial had been violated. The SC upheld his conviction, noting that the statutory 180-day period had not begun until the Michigan prosecutor received his request. The SC said that if the warden in Indiana delayed the forwarding of a prisoner's request for a speedy trial, that merely postponed the starting of the 180-day clock, which is triggered by the prosecutor's receipt of notice.

Fiore v. White, 531 U.S. 225, 121 S.Ct. 712 (2001) **[William FIORE, Petitioner, v. Gregory WHITE, Warden, et al.]** **(Due Process; Wrongful Convictions)** William Fiore was the owner of a hazardous waste facility in Pennsylvania. He was arrested and subsequently convicted of operating a hazardous waste facility without a permit and sentenced to prison. Fiore petitioned for relief with a writ of *habeas corpus* filed in the U.S. district court. The court granted the writ, but the circuit court of appeals reversed. Subsequently, the Supreme Court of Pennsylvania interpreted the statute pertaining to hazardous waste operations and determined that Fiore had not violated that statute. Fiore possessed a hazardous waste permit. Nevertheless, Pennsylvania prosecutors contended, Fiore departed so dramatically from the permit's terms that he nonetheless had violated the statute. Fiore appealed to the SC, which reversed Fiore's conviction, holding that the conviction and continued incarceration of a defendant based on conduct that the state statute did not prohibit violated his due-process rights.

Fisher v. United States, 425 U.S. 391, 96 S.Ct. 1569 (1976) **[Solomon FISHER et al., Petitioners, v. UNITED STATES et al. United States et al., Petitioners, v. C.D. Kasmir and Jerry A. Candy]** **(Fifth Amendment; Law Enforcement Officers or Agencies; Searches and Seizures; Self-Incrimination)** Fisher was under investigation by the IRS for income tax fraud. His accountant placed Fisher's papers in the hands of Fisher's attorney, and the government subpoenaed the papers. Subsequently, Fisher was convicted. He appealed, alleging that his Fifth Amendment right against self-incrimination had been violated. The SC upheld his conviction, saying that there was no confidential disclosure made between Fisher and his attorney; thus, Fisher's Fifth Amendment rights had not been violated as the result of some vague attorney-client privilege he presumed existed, simply by a possession of important documents. Fisher had merely sought legal advice, not an opportunity to make disclosures normally covered under the ideal attorney-client privilege scenario.

Fitzpatrick v. Bitzer, 427 U.S. 445, 96 S.Ct. 2666 (1976) **[Garland M. FITZPATRICK et al., Petitioners, v. Frederick BITZER, etc., et al. Frederick Bitzer, etc., et al., Petitioners, v. Donald Matthews et al.]** **(Corrections; Inmate Rights)** Present and retired female employees of the State of Connecticut brought a suit against the state, alleging that a state benefit plan discriminated against them. The petitioners requested a back-pay award and reasonable attorney's fees for filing the suit. The lower court denied them relief, and the SC heard their case. The SC ruled in their favor, saying that under the Eleventh Amendment, they should not be prevented from seeking back-pay awards from the state. The SC held that the current version of the state's retirement plan was discriminatory against them because of their gender.

Fletcher v. Weir, 455 U.S. 603, 102 S.Ct. 1309 (1982) **[Lloyd FLETCHER, Superintendent, Bell County Forestry Camp, v. Eric WEIR]** **(Fifth Amendment; Prosecutorial Misconduct; Self-Incrimination; Sixth Amendment)** Weir was in a fight with Buchanan outside a nightclub and stabbed Buchanan, who died. Weir fled the scene. Later, when apprehended by the police, he said nothing about the incident. However, during the trial, he took the stand in his own defense and for the first time alleged self-defense as the reason for stabbing Buchanan. The prosecutor sought to discredit him by referring to his prearrest silence. When Weir was convicted, he appealed, alleging a violation of his Fifth Amendment rights against self-incrimination by the prosecutor's effort to impeach his testimony in court. The SC ruled that for impeachment purposes, it is proper for prosecutors to make such comments about the defendant's prearrest silence, particularly if the defendant raises self-defense as his defense. Thus, Weir's right against self-incrimination had not been jeopardized by the prosecutor who cross-examined him regarding his prearrest silence.

Flippo v. West Virginia, 528 U.S. 11, 120 S.Ct. 7 (1999) **[James Michael FLIPPO v. WEST VIRGINIA]** **(Closed Container Searches; Law Enforcement Officers or Agencies; Searches and Seizures)** James Michael Flippo was convicted of murdering his wife. The prosecution's case was supported in large part from the discovery of photographs of James Flippo and another man, Joel Boggess, engaged in sexual acts together. The facts were that Flippo, a minister, and his wife were vacationing at a cabin in a West Virginia state park one night in 1996. Subsequently, Flippo called 911 and reported that he and his wife had been attacked. Investigating police found the body of Flippo's wife, with fatal head wounds. There were no footprints or signs of forced entry into the cabin. Police closed off the cabin area, photographed the crime scene, collected evidence, and searched the cabin. Several hours later, the police returned to the cabin to "process the crime scene," and discovered a briefcase, which they opened. The briefcase contained numerous photographs and negatives of James Flippo and Joel Boggess. Boggess was a member of Flippo's congregation. Police surmised that Mrs. Flippo had discovered the photographs and negatives and become upset, and that Flippo had murdered her because of her displeasure. Prosecutors used these photographs and negatives against Flippo at his subsequent trial. Flippo sought to suppress these photos and negatives, as they had been seized without warrant. Prosecutors and police argued that because police were searching a crime scene, even at different points in time, they were not required to obtain a search warrant to enter and search the cabin premises. Thus, the prosecution invoked a "crime scene exception" to a warrantless search. The prosecution also stated that the briefcase and its contents were subject to search under the plain view rule and a routine inventory of the crime scene, although these latter reasons were not mentioned in Flippo's trial. The SC rejected the prosecution's argument, saying that there is no "crime scene exception" to a warrantless search. Police officers should have obtained a valid search warrant to resume their search of the murder scene and the contents of containers found therein. Thus, the SC ordered the photographs and negatives suppressed. The SC further noted that both the plain view and inventory exceptions to the warrantless search were not mentioned at trial and thus were unsuitable as arguments to counter Flippo's instant appeal.

Florida v. Bostick, 501 U.S. 429, 111 S.Ct. 2382 (1991) [FLORIDA, Petitioner, v. Terrance BOSTICK] (**Fourth Amendment; Law Enforcement Officers or Agencies; Searches and Seizures**) Bostick was a passenger on a bus from Miami to Atlanta. Florida police boarded the bus without any suspicion but rather with a simple intent to catch drug smugglers. They approached Bostick, asked him a few questions, asked to see his ticket, and then asked if they could search his bag. They advised Bostick he had a right to refuse, but he gave his consent. They discovered cocaine in his bag and he was subsequently convicted of cocaine possession. He appealed and the SC upheld the conviction, because given the totality of circumstances, Bostick had not been under arrest and had given his consent at the time of the search. Further, the fact that Bostick was on a bus did not constitute a "seizure" in the Fourth Amendment context. The SC concluded that the governing test is whether a reasonable person would feel free to decline the police offer to search his or her luggage, given the totality of circumstances.

Florida v. Jimeno, 499 U.S. 934, 111 S.Ct. 1801 (1991) [FLORIDA, Petitioner, v. Enio JIMENO et al.] (**Closed Container Searches; Consent Searches; Law Enforcement Officers or Agencies; Vehicle Searches**) Jimeno was overheard arranging a drug transaction over the telephone by a police officer. The officer followed Jimeno and stopped his car when Jimeno made an illegal traffic movement. He advised Jimeno that he believed Jimeno had narcotics in his possession and asked if he could search Jimeno's car. Jimeno consented, and the officer found narcotics in a closed container within the car. Later Jimeno was convicted. He appealed, moving to suppress the evidence in the closed container, arguing that it had been beyond the scope of the warrantless and consensual search of his vehicle. The SC upheld his conviction, stressing that police had had Jimeno's permission to search the car and that this permission had not been qualified to exclude containers that might contain illegal narcotics. (*See United States v. Ross* [1982].)

Florida v. J.L., 529 U.S. 266, 120 S.Ct. 1375 (2000) [FLORIDA, Petitioner, v. J.L.] (**Juvenile Law, Searches and Seizures**) In October 1995, in Miami, an anonymous tip was received by police that a young black male was standing at a particular bus stop wearing a plaid shirt and carrying a gun. Police arrived at the scene and saw several black males standing at the bus stop, one of whom was wearing a plaid shirt. The officers saw no firearm, nor did they observe any illegal conduct. However, they approached one of the boys, J.L., 15, and made him put his hands up, whereupon they conducted a frisk of his person. They seized a gun from his pocket and arrested him for carrying a concealed weapon. Later, at J.L.'s trial, J.L. sought to suppress the weapon as the fruit of an unlawful search. The

trial court granted the motion and suppressed the weapon as evidence against J.L.; however, the appellate court reversed the trial court. The Florida Supreme Court reversed the appellate court, holding that tips from unknown informants can form the basis for reasonable suspicion only if accompanied by specific indicators of reliability, such as the correct forecast of a suspect's "not easily predicted" movements. Because the tip leading to J.L.'s search and weapon seizure did not provide any such predictions, nor did it contain any other qualifying indicators of reliability, the police were not justified in subjecting J.L. to a search or pat-down and frisk. Florida prosecutors appealed to the SC, which heard the case. The SC upheld the Florida Supreme Court, holding that anonymous tips lacking any indicators of reliability do not justify stops and frisks whenever and however they allege the illegal possession of a firearm.

Florida v. Riley, 488 U.S. 445, 109 S.Ct. 693 (1989) [FLORIDA, Petitioner, v. Michael A. RILEY] (**Aerial Surveillance; Law Enforcement Officers or Agencies; Fourth Amendment; Open-Fields Doctrine; Plain-View Rule**) Riley was growing marijuana on his property, which was partially blocked from view by a greenhouse. A helicopter surveillance of Riley's yard by sheriff's officers revealed marijuana plants in plain view. A search warrant was obtained based on these observations, and Riley's home was searched and the plants seized. Riley was subsequently convicted of growing marijuana. He appealed, contending that the helicopter surveillance constituted a "search" of his premises and thus a search warrant was required to conduct it. The SC upheld Riley's conviction, noting that helicopter observations of ground structures in plain view do not constitute searches as set forth in the Fourth Amendment. Thus, the warrant had been lawfully obtained on the basis of probable cause. Search warrants are not required by police who travel the airways and who observe contraband in plain view with the naked eye.

Florida v. Royer, 460 U.S. 491, 103 S.Ct. 1319 (1983) [FLORIDA, Petitioner, v. Mark ROYER] (**Fourth Amendment; Law Enforcement Officers or Agencies; Searches and Seizures**) Royer was an airline passenger in the Miami airport. DEA agents thought he fit a "drug-courier profile," inasmuch as he bought a one-way ticket for cash and under an assumed name; he also was young, nervous, casually dressed, with heavy luggage. He gave police his driver's license with his correct name when requested. He also followed them to a room, again at their request, where they asked him if they could look through his luggage. He consented. They found marijuana, and Royer was eventually found guilty. He appealed, alleging that his Fourth Amendment rights had been violated because of the unreasonableness of his original stop and detention and the subsequent search. The SC agreed and overturned his conviction, saying that it is insufficient for police merely to have consent, without probable cause, to make a warrantless search of personal effects, such as luggage. The SC stressed Royer's lengthy detention and noted it was a serious intrusion into his privacy, especially as police had no probable cause to engage him in further searches. Consent given after an illegal act by police is tainted by the illegal act.

Florida v. Thomas, 532 U.S. 774, 121 S.Ct. 1905 (2001) [FLORIDA, Petitioner, v. Robert A. THOMAS] (**Fourth Amendment; Searches and Seizures; Vehicle Searches**) Thomas was suspected of making illicit marijuana sales. Police officers staked out his home and when he drove to his residence, he exited his vehicle and walked toward the back of the car. A police officer met him there and asked him to produce his driver's license. When Thomas complied, the officer determined that Thomas had an outstanding warrant for another offense and arrested him, handcuffed him, and took him inside Thomas' home. Then the officer went back outside, alone, and searched Thomas' automobile, finding several bags containing methamphetamine. Thomas was charged with possession of that drug and related offenses. Thomas moved to have the drug evidence suppressed because it was seized from his automobile without a warrant. The trial court granted his motion and the state appealed. The Florida Court of Appeals reversed the trial judge, finding the search to be valid according to the SC holding in *New York v. Belton* (1981). In *Belton,* the SC had established a bright-line rule permitting an officer who has made a lawful custodial arrest of a car's occupant to search the car's passenger compartment as a contemporaneous incident of the arrest. Thomas appealed, and the Florida Supreme Court reversed, holding that the bright-line rule only applies whenever a police officer initiates contact with a vehicle's occupant while that person remains in the vehicle. Further, the Florida Supreme Court remanded the case to the trial court to determine whether the vehicle search was justified under *Chimel v. California* (1969). Florida prosecutors appealed to the SC, which granted *certiorari.* However, the SC decided that it lacked jurisdiction to decide the question because there had been no final judgment from the trial court regarding Thomas' guilt in the drug possession charges. The SC is authorized to hear final judgments from state supreme courts, and as the Florida Supreme Court had not ruled decisively, the SC lacked jurisdiction to decide the case.

Florida v. Wells, 495 U.S. 1, 110 S.Ct. 1632 (1989) [FLORIDA, Petitioner, v. Martin Leslie WELLS] (**Inventory Searches; Law Enforcement Officers or Agencies; Searches and Seizures; Vehicle Searches**) Wells was stopped and arrested for DWI. After his car was impounded by police, they asked him if they could inventory its contents. Wells gave them permission. They found and pried open a large trunk, in which they discovered a large quantity of marijuana. Wells was convicted of possessing a controlled substance. He appealed. The SC overturned his conviction, saying that so-called inventory searches are not for the purpose of discovering evidence of a crime. Further, no department policy existed that would permit such intrusions into Wells' automobile. Had there been such a policy in effect, it is likely that the marijuana evidence would have been successfully used against him. The SC stressed the significance of an absence of police department policy relating to inventory searches of impounded vehicles.

Florida v. White, 526 U.S. 559, 119 S.Ct. 1555 (1999) [FLORIDA, Petitioner, v. Tyvessel Tyvorus WHITE] (**Asset Forfeiture; Fourth Amendment; Inventory Searches; Searches and Seizures; Vehicle Searches**) White was observed by police using his car to deliver cocaine to others. He was arrested at his workplace and his car was seized under the Florida Contraband Forfeiture Act (FCFA), which permits Florida officials to seize any assets used to commit crimes, such as drug distribution and sales. An inventory search of the vehicle yielded cocaine, and White was charged with cocaine possession. White sought to suppress the cocaine charge, arguing that the warrantless seizure of his automobile violated his Fourth Amendment rights, and thus, according to the "fruits of the poisonous tree" doctrine, the cocaine would be inadmissible against him in court. The trial court denied his motion to suppress the cocaine, and he was convicted on state drug charges. The Florida Supreme Court overturned White's conviction, holding that, absent exigent circumstances, the seizure of his automobile under the FCFA violated his Fourth Amendment rights. The government appealed, and the SC heard the case. The SC reversed the Florida Supreme Court and held that the Fourth Amendment does not require the police to obtain a warrant before seizing an automobile from a public place when they have probable cause to believe that it is forfeitable contraband. In this instance, the automobile was seizable contraband, as it was an instrument used in the furtherance of criminal activity, namely cocaine distribution. Although the police lacked probable cause to believe that White's automobile contained drugs, they did have probable cause to believe that the automobile itself was contraband under the FCFA, therefore justifying the seizure. The "fruits of the poisonous tree" doctrine does not apply when the seizure of contraband is lawful and yields further evidence of criminal activity.

Ford v. Wainwright, 477 U.S. 399, 106 S.Ct. 2595 (1986) [Alvin Bernard FORD, etc., Petitioner, v. Louie L. WAINWRIGHT, Secretary, Florida Department of Corrections] (**Corrections; Death Penalty**) Ford was convicted of murder in Florida in 1974 and sentenced to death. At no time during his trial had he shown any signs of being mentally incompetent. However, when he appealed in 1982, he was examined by two psychiatrists over a period of time and determined to be mentally incompetent. His condition deteriorated to such an extent that he was almost catatonic. Nevertheless, the governor of Florida appointed three other psychiatrists to examine Ford, and they found him sane enough to be executed. However, the SC decided in Ford's favor, holding that insane persons cannot be executed. Furthermore, the SC held that Florida's procedures for determining a person's competence were inadequate. This is an interesting case, because Ford was sane when he committed the offense and was convicted of it; he became insane afterward.

Forrester v. White, 484 U.S. 219, 108 S.Ct. 538 (1988) [Cynthia A. FORRESTER, Petitioner, v. Howard Lee WHITE] (**Corrections; Fourteenth Amendment; Immunity; Probation and Parole**) Forrester, a female probation officer, was demoted and discharged from her job by a judge, White. Forrester alleged that the judge had fired her because of her gender, in violation of the Fourteenth Amendment equal-protection clause. White disagreed, saying that he had absolute immunity from such litigation by Forrester because of his judicial status. The SC said otherwise, concluding that the act of firing Forrester was not a judicial one, and thus White did not enjoy absolute immunity because of his judicial position. The judge was subject to suits by those employees under him who believe they were unfairly treated or discriminated against.

Forsyth County, Ga., v. Nationalist Movement, 505 U.S. 123, 112 S.Ct. 2395 (1992) [FORSYTH COUNTY, GEORGIA, Petitioner, v. The NATIONALIST MOVEMENT] (First Amendment; Free Speech) An ordinance in Forsyth County, GA, provided for the payment of variable fees depending on events and the types of marches or assemblies planned. The Nationalist Movement filed suit to challenge the validity of this ordinance and the fees it imposed on a sliding scale. The SC declared the Forsyth County ordinance to be invalid, because it unconstitutionally tied the amount of fees to the content of speeches and lacked adequate procedural safeguards; no limit on such a fee could remedy these constitutional violations.

Foster v. California, 394 U.S. 440, 89 S.Ct. 1127 (1969) [Walter B. FOSTER, Petitioner, v. CALIFORNIA] (Law Enforcement Officers or Agencies; Lineups) Foster confessed to police the day following a robbery and gave information about the other two robbers who had participated. He was placed in a lineup with other men, all of whom were shorter. Foster was wearing a jacket similar to the one he had worn in the robbery. The eyewitness couldn't be sure that Foster was the robber and asked police if he could speak with Foster. After conversing with him in a private room, the witness still could not positively identify him as one of the robbers. A week later, the witness viewed another lineup, this time with Foster and four different persons from those in the first lineup. This time the witness positively identified Foster. Foster was convicted of the robbery. He appealed. The SC overturned Foster's conviction (despite his admission) and said that the police methods used were improper, because such lineups biased witness identifications of suspects. In this case, the police had violated Foster's right to due process by biasing the lineup for an eyewitness.

Foucha v. Louisiana, 504 U.S. 71, 112 S.Ct. 1780 (1992) [Terry FOUCHA, Petitioner, v. LOUISIANA] (Insanity Pleas) Foucha was charged with aggravated burglary and the discharge of a firearm. He pleaded not guilty by reason of insanity. Examining doctors found him lacking mental capacity, and he was acquitted on this basis. Subsequently, he was committed to the East Feliciana Forensic Facility until such time as doctors recommended that he be released or until further court order. Five years later, several doctors recommended to the judge that Foucha should be released from the mental health facility, but one doctor believed that Foucha continued to present a danger to either himself or to others. The judicial decision was to order the continued confinement of Foucha. He appealed. The SC ruled that the Louisiana statute requiring the continued confinement of someone acquitted by reason of insanity following a hospital review committee recommendation to release the person after a finding of no mental

illness was a violation of Foucha's due-process rights. Foucha was ordered released.

Francis v. Franklin, 471 U.S. 307, 105 S.Ct. 1965 (1985) [Robert FRANCIS, Warden, Petitioner, v. Raymond Lee FRANKLIN] (Jury Instructions) Franklin was convicted of murder by a Georgia court and sent to prison. He was awaiting treatment at a dentist's office outside the prison when he attempted to escape. He stole a pistol and shot and killed the resident of a nearby house, but he was apprehended shortly thereafter and charged with murder. When the trial was concluded and the jury was given instructions from the judge, the judge advised the jury, among other things, that Franklin's acts were "presumed to be the product of a person's will, but the presumption may be rebutted. A person of sound mind and discretion is presumed to intend the natural and probable consequences of his acts." This phraseology shifted the burden of proving at least one of the elements of the criminal offense of malicious murder to the defendant rather than the prosecution. Franklin was convicted. The SC heard his appeal and overturned his conviction, holding that it had been a harmful and irreversible error for the judge to have instructed the jury as to Franklin's *intent* to commit the crime. The SC said that a jury instruction that creates a mandatory presumption, whereby the jury must infer the presumed fact if the state proves certain predicate facts, violates the due-process clause if it relieves the state of the burden of persuasion on an element of an offense. The state, not the defendant, must prove intent.

Francis v. Henderson, 425 U.S. 536, 96 S.Ct. 1708 (1976) [Abraham FRANCIS, Petitioner, v. C. Murray HENDERSON, Warden] (Corrections; Grand Juries; *Habeas Corpus* Petitions; Sixth Amendment) Francis, a black man, was convicted in Louisiana of felony murder. He did not appeal. But six years later, he filed a *habeas corpus* petition, alleging that blacks had been excluded from the grand jury that had indicted him, and thus he had been deprived of a fair trial. The SC upheld his conviction, reasoning that his request failed to conform to the state requirement that any objection to the composition of the grand jury must be made in advance of the trial.

Franks v. Delaware, 438 U.S. 154, 98 S.Ct. 2674 (1978) [Jerome FRANKS, Petitioner, v. State of DELAWARE] (Fourth Amendment; Law Enforcement Officers or Agencies; Searches and Seizures) Franks was suspected of first-degree rape, second-degree kidnapping, and first-degree burglary. Authorities obtained a search warrant for Franks' premises. When police officers gave a sworn affidavit supporting the warrant, they gave misstatements and untruths. Franks' defense counsel sought to introduce evidence that the search warrant was illegally obtained on the basis of deliberate lies by police, but the judge denied his request. Franks was convicted. He appealed, contending that the search leading to the incriminating evidence against him had been prefaced by an illegal search warrant containing deliberate untruths from police officers under oath. The SC overturned his convictions on these grounds. The SC said if, after a hearing, Franks established by a preponderance of evidence that false statements led to the issuance of a search warrant and were intentionally made, and if the false statements were necessary to establish probable cause to justify the search warrant's issuance, then the search warrant had to be voided and the fruits of the search excluded from the trial to the same extent as if probable cause had been lacking on the face of the affidavit.

Frazier v. Cupp, 394 U.S. 731, 89 S.Ct. 1420 (1969) [**Martin Rene FRAZIER, Petitioner, v. H.C. CUPP, Warden**] (**Consent Searches;** *Habeas Corpus* **Petitions; Law Enforcement Officers or Agencies;** *Miranda* **Warning**) Frazier was indicted together with his cousin, Rawls, for murder in Oregon. Some question arose about whether Rawls, who pleaded guilty, would actually testify against Frazier, and whether the prosecutor ought to rely on such testimony. The prosecutor made statements to the jury about what they could expect to hear from Rawls. This and other statements by the prosecutor were regarded as prejudicial to Frazier, especially a reference to a "confession" made by Rawls implicating Frazier. Also, when Frazier was being questioned by police, he had said in passing, "I had better get a lawyer," but he had continued to answer questions. He was convicted. His appeal to the SC through a writ of *habeas corpus* was that his *Miranda* rights had not been observed and that there was prosecutorial misconduct and that his due-process rights had been violated. The SC upheld his conviction. The prosecutor's comments were harmless errors and Frazier had been advised of his *Miranda* rights but had simply failed to exercise them.

Frisbie v. Collins, 342 U.S. 519, 72 S.Ct. 509 (1952) [**FRISBIE, Petitioner, v. Shirley COLLINS**] (**Exclusionary Rule; Law Enforcement Officers or Agencies**) Collins, living in Chicago, was a suspect in a murder investigation in Michigan. Michigan authorities found Collins in Chicago and forcibly brought him back to Michigan to stand trial. Collins was convicted. He appealed, arguing that the officers had had no right to "kidnap" him in Chicago and strong-arm him back into Michigan. The SC heard Collins' case. Although the arrest appeared to be invalid, irregular, and perhaps illegal, Collins' return to Michigan placed him within the jurisdiction where he stood accused of murder. The SC upheld Collins' conviction, saying that nothing permits a guilty person rightfully convicted to escape justice because he is brought to trial against his will. Bounty hunters perform similar tasks by bringing persons back into jurisdictions from which they have fled to avoid prosecution. Thus, the case significance is that unlawful arrests of criminal suspects do not jeopardize their convictions in subsequent trials where they have been brought forcibly into jurisdictions where criminal charges have been brought against them.

Fuller v. Oregon, 417 U.S. 40, 94 S.Ct. 2116 (1974) [**Prince Eric FULLER, Petitioner, v. State of OREGON**] (**Indigent Clients; Probation and Parole**) Fuller was accused of third-degree sodomy. He entered a guilty plea and was sentenced to a five-year probation term, contingent on his successfully completing a jail work-release program that permitted him to attend a nearby college and on his reimbursing the county for fees involving an attorney and an investigator because of his indigency. Fuller appealed, alleging that the state could not constitutionally impose as a condition of his proba-

tion the repayment of legal fees and court costs. The SC upheld his conviction and probation program conditions, holding that Oregon's recoupment statute merely provides that a convicted person who later becomes able to pay for his counsel may be required to do so. This obligation may be imposed on persons with a foreseeable ability to meet it, and it is enforced only against those who actually become able to meet it without hardship. Indigent offenders who cannot repay these court costs cannot have their probationary terms revoked simply because of their inability to pay. In Fuller's case, however, he had the ability to repay the costs incurred for his court activity, and thus Oregon was able to enforce the recoupment statute against him.

Furman v. Georgia, 408 U.S. 238, 92 S.Ct. 2726 (1972) [**William Henry FURMAN, Petitioner, v. State of GEORGIA. Lucious Jackson, Jr., Petitioner, v. State of Georgia. Elmer Branch, Petitioner, v. State of Texas**] (**Cruel and Unusual Punishment; Death Penalty; Fourteenth Amendment**) Furman, a black man, was accused of murder. Evidence that he was mentally deficient was presented at his trial. Despite this defense and others, Furman was convicted and sentenced to death. He appealed the sentence on the grounds that his Fourteenth Amendment rights were being violated. At the time, disproportionately more black murderers were receiving the death penalty than were white murderers. The SC set Furman's death penalty aside, saying that the racially discriminatory way in which the death penalty was being administered in Georgia constituted cruel and unusual punishment. It is important to note that the SC never said that the death penalty was *per se* unconstitutional; rather, the manner in which it was being administered was unconstitutional because it violated the Eighth and Fourteenth Amendments.

G

Gagnon v. Scarpelli, 411 U.S. 778, 93 S.Ct. 1756 (1973) [**John R. GAGNON, Warden, Petitioner, v. Gerald H. SCARPELLI**] (**Corrections;** *Habeas Corpus* **Petitions; Indigent Clients; Probation and Parole**) Scarpelli pleaded guilty to a charge of robbery in July 1965 in a Wisconsin court. He was sentenced to 15 years in prison. But the judge suspended this sentence on August 5, 1965, and placed Scarpelli on probation for seven years. The next day, August 6, Scarpelli was arrested and charged with burglary. His probation was revoked without a hearing, and he was placed in the Wisconsin State Reformatory to serve his 15-year term. About three years later, Scarpelli was paroled. Shortly before his parole, he filed a *habeas corpus* petition, alleging that his probation revocation had been invoked without a hearing and without benefit of counsel; thus he had been denied due process. Following his parole, the SC acted on his petition and ruled in his favor. Specifically, it said that Scarpelli had been denied his right to due process, because no revocation hearing had been held and he had not been represented by court-appointed counsel as an indigent. In effect, the Court, referring to *Morrissey v. Brewer* (1972), said that "a probation revocation, like parole revocation, is not a stage of a criminal prosecution, but does result in loss of liberty. . . . We hold that a probationer, like a parolee, is entitled to a preliminary hearing and a final revocation hearing in the conditions specified in *Morrissey v. Brewer*." The significance of this case is that it equated probation with parole as well as equating the respective revocation proceedings. Although the Court did not say that all parolees and probationers have a right to representation by counsel in all probation and parole revocation proceedings, it did say that counsel should be provided in cases in which the probationer or parolee makes a timely claim contesting the allegations. No constitutional basis exists for providing counsel in all probation or parole revocation proceedings, but subsequent probation and parole revocation hearings usually involve defense counsel if legitimately requested. The SC declaration has been liberally interpreted in subsequent cases.

Gardner v. Broderick, 392 U.S. 273, 88 S.Ct. 1913 (1968) [Robert Vincent GARDNER, Appellant, v. Vincent L. BRODERICK, as Police Commissioner of the City of New York, et al.] (Fifth Amendment; Self-Incrimination) Gardner was a police officer who was dismissed from the force for refusing to waive his right against self-incrimination before a grand jury investigating police corruption. Gardner appealed his dismissal, alleging that the department had no right to dismiss him for invoking his Fifth Amendment privilege. The SC agreed, declaring it unlawful to compel testimony from persons when their jobs are in jeopardy for refusing to testify or give incriminating information. Thus attempts to compel testimony from persons at the expense of their constitutional rights are unconstitutional and a violation of their due-process rights.

Gardner v. Florida, 430 U.S. 349, 97 S.Ct. 1197 (1977) [Daniel Wilbur GARDNER, Petitioner, v. State of FLORIDA] (Aggravating and Mitigating Circumstances; Corrections; Death Penalty; Discovery; Fourteenth Amendment) Gardner was convicted of first-degree murder. Following the conviction, a sentencing hearing was held in which the jury recommended life imprisonment. However, the judge cited aggravating factors and imposed the death penalty. It was important that portions of the presentence investigation relied on by the judge for his knowledge of aggravating factors were not given to the defense under discovery. Apparently, there were several mitigating factors cited in the report favorable to Gardner but ignored by the judge. Gardner appealed. The SC overturned his conviction, acknowledging that the government had not complied with the discovery law by failing to give Gardner a complete presentence investigation report. The report contained information to support a life sentence rather than the death penalty. The SC declared that the failure of the Florida Supreme Court to consider or even read the confidential portion of the report violated Gardner's right to due process under the Fourteenth Amendment.

Garner v. Jones, 529 U.S. 244, 120 S.Ct. 1362 (2000) [J. Wayne GARNER, Former Chairman of the State Board of Pardons and Paroles of Georgia, et al., Petitioners, v. Robert J. JONES] (Parole Hearings; Probation and Parole) Robert Jones was convicted of murder in 1974 and began serving a life sentence in a Georgia state prison. He escaped in 1979 but was recaptured in 1982. While he was free, he committed a second murder and was subsequently convicted and sentenced to a second life term. When Jones was convicted of his second murder, the Georgia Parole Board had an internal policy requiring parole consideration after inmates serving life sentences had served seven years. If parole was denied, then reconsiderations for parole were to occur every three years thereafter. In 1985, the Georgia Parole Board changed its policy governing parole reconsideration for inmates serving life sentences to eight-year intervals subsequent to their earlier parole denials. Jones filed suit against the Georgia Parole Board, contending that its policy change violated the *ex post facto* clause and thus unconstitutionally extended the length of his incarceration by creating longer intervals between parole reconsiderations. A federal court granted summary judgment in favor of the Georgia Parole Board, but the Court of Appeals reversed the district court, holding that the *ex post facto* clause had indeed been violated. The SC heard the appeal from the Georgia Parole Board and reversed the Circuit Court of Appeals. The SC said that the *ex post facto* clause had not been violated, because internal parole board policy changes are consistent with their broad discretionary powers. Further, the fact of changing the frequency of required parole reconsideration hearings for inmates serving life sentences from every three years to every eight years did not lengthen the inmate's time of actual imprisonment, and the board had the discretion to act in accordance with its assessment of each inmate's likelihood of release between parole reconsideration dates. Finally, only through a showing of "gross abuse of discretion" can an inmate challenge a parole denial.

Garner v. United States, 424 U.S. 648, 96 S.Ct. 1178 (1976) [Ray D. GARNER, Petitioner, v. UNITED STATES] (Corrections; Probation and Parole; Self-Incrimination) Garner was charged in a United States district court in California with violating various federal gambling statutes. His tax returns were introduced as evidence against him, showing him to be a "professional gambler." He was convicted. Garner appealed, arguing that his tax returns were privileged documents and that to reveal their contents to a jury would be self-incriminating. The SC upheld his conviction, saying that he should have exercised his right against self-incrimination at the time his tax returns were prepared and when he stated his profession as "gambling." Thus, the SC gave considerable significance to the timeliness of asserting the Fifth Amendment self-incrimination claim.

Garrity v. New Jersey, 385 U.S. 493, 87 S.Ct. 616 (1967) [Edward J. GARRITY et al., Appellants, v. State of NEW JERSEY] (Fifth Amendment; Fourteenth Amendment; Self-Incrimination) Garrity and other police officers were suspected of fixing traffic tickets. Garrity was advised that any statement he made could be used against him and that if he refused to answer any question, he would be fired. Therefore, Garrity made various incriminating statements. He was convicted of conspiracy to violate state traffic laws. He appealed, alleging that his Fifth Amendment right against self-incrimination had been violated because his disclosures had been inherently coerced. The SC overturned his conviction, saying that circumstances in which a person may lose his job if he fails to give incriminating information are the equivalent of coercion and therefore not voluntary. Thus, the Fourteenth Amendment prohibits the use of such coerced evidence in a subsequent criminal proceeding if the statements were obtained under threat of removal from office; this privilege is extended to all public employees, including police officers.

Geders v. United States, 425 U.S. 80, 96 S.Ct. 1330 (1976) [**John A. GEDERS, Petitioner, v. UNITED STATES**] **(Right to Counsel; Sixth Amendment)** Geders was charged in a United States district court with possessing marijuana and illegally importing controlled substances. During a 17-hour overnight recess of his trial, Geders asked to speak with his attorney, but his request was denied by the federal district judge. He was convicted. He appealed, alleging a violation of his Sixth Amendment right to counsel. The SC agreed and overturned Geders' conviction, holding that the federal judge's order to deprive Geders of seeing his counsel between his direct examinations and cross-examination by the government had deprived Geders of the effective assistance of counsel. The federal judge had attempted to sequester the defendant, and though sequestration of witnesses is within the broad powers of federal judges, they are prohibited from sequestering defendants from seeing their own attorneys.

Gelbard v. United States, 408 U.S. 41, 92 S.Ct. 2357 (1972) [**David GELBARD and Sidney Parnas, Petitioners, v. UNITED STATES. United States, Petitioner, v. Jogues Egan and Anne Elizabeth Walsh**] **(Electronic Surveillance, Wiretapping)** Gelbard was subpoenaed to testify before a grand jury based on information disclosed from a judge-authorized wiretap of Gelbard's home. Gelbard refused to answer grand-jury questions, contending that he had a right to privacy in his telephonic communications. Because of the existence of a statute forbidding such intercepted telephonic transmissions, he was able to avoid a contempt charge for refusing to provide testimony to the grand jury.

Georgia v. McCollum, 505 U.S. 42, 112 S.Ct. 2348 (1992) [**GEORGIA, Petitioner, v. Thomas McCOLLUM and Ella Hampton McCollum**] **(Peremptory Challenges)** McCollum was indicted on charges of aggravated assault and simple battery. During jury selection, his attorney used his peremptory challenges to strike certain prospective jurors from jury duty because of their race. McCollum was acquitted. The state challenged the use of these peremptory challenges, arguing that they had created a biased jury as in *Batson v. Kentucky* (1986), in which the prosecutor used peremptory challenges for racial-bias purposes. The SC agreed with the state and rejected the defendant's attorney's use of peremptory challenges for racial purposes. Thus, according to *Batson* and *McCollum,* neither prosecutors nor defense attorneys may deliberately use their peremptory challenges to excuse jurors on the basis of their race.

Gerstein v. Pugh, 420 U.S. 103, 95 S.Ct. 854 (1975) [**Richard E. GERSTEIN, State Attorney for Eleventh Judicial Circuit of Florida, Petitioner, v. Robert PUGH et al.**] **(Fourth Amendment; Law Enforcement Officers or Agencies; Right to Counsel; Searches and Seizures)** Pugh and Henderson were arrested in Dade County, FL. They were charged with robbery and carrying a concealed weapon. The prosecutor alone determined the issue of probable cause in holding them without bail. Pugh and Henderson were convicted. They filed a *habeas corpus* petition with the court, declaring that a judge should have determined whether probable cause existed for pretrial detention in a hearing. The SC upheld their conviction, holding that it is not necessarily the case that judicial oversight to determine probable cause for pretrial detention is essential. The SC said that because of its limited function and its nonadversarial nature, the probable-cause determination is not a "critical stage" in the prosecution that would require appointed counsel. However, the Fourth Amendment requires a timely judicial determination of probable cause as a prerequisite to detention. It is not necessary, however, for counsel to be present in such a determination.

Gertz v. Robert Welch, Inc., 418 U.S. 323, 94 S.Ct. 2997 (1974) [**Elmer GERTZ, Petitioner, v. ROBERT WELCH, INC.**] **(Media Rights)** A Chicago police officer, Nuccio, was convicted of murder. The victim's family retained Gertz, a prominent attorney, to represent them in a civil action against Nuccio. An article appeared in a magazine shortly thereafter, alleging that the murder had been part of a Communist conspiracy to discredit local police. The article went on to blame Gertz, the attorney, for "framing" Nuccio. It further alleged that Gertz had a criminal record, and it labeled him a "Communist-fronter." Gertz sued the magazine because of the untrue defamatory statements. The trial court determined that Gertz had not proved that the defamatory statements were published with a knowledge of their falsity or in reckless disregard for the truth. The court decided in favor of the magazine. The SC overturned the lower court, holding that magazines may not claim constitutional privilege against liability arising from suits from persons who are not public officials or public figures. The media are not immune from suits from private individuals whom they have defamed.

Gideon v. Wainwright, 372 U.S. 335, 83 S.Ct. 792 (1963) [**Clarence Earl GIDEON, Petitioner, v. Louie L. WAINWRIGHT, Director, Division of Corrections**] **(Indigent Clients; Right to Counsel)** Gideon broke into a poolroom allegedly with the intent to commit larceny. This act was regarded as a felony in Florida. Gideon was indigent and asked for a lawyer to represent him. He was advised by the judge that counsel could only be appointed to persons if the offense involved the death penalty. Therefore, Gideon represented himself and was convicted. He appealed. The SC overturned his conviction, saying that all indigent defendants are entitled to court-appointed counsel in felony cases. (*See Argersinger v. Hamlin* [1972] *for a narrowing of this provision to minor crimes or misdemeanor cases.*)

Gilbert v. California, 388 U.S. 263, 87 S.Ct. 1951 (1967) [**Jesse James GILBERT, Petitioner, v. State of CALIFOR-**

NIA] (Fifth Amendment; Self-Incrimination) Gilbert was first arrested by an FBI agent on charges that he had robbed a bank in Alhambra, CA, and had killed an investigating police officer. During the robbery, Gilbert had given the bank tellers a note demanding money. When the FBI agent interviewed Gilbert following his arrest without an attorney present, Gilbert gave the agent some handwriting samples. These were incriminating, because they matched the writing in the note at the bank robbery scene. Gilbert was convicted. He appealed, arguing that his Fifth Amendment right against self-incrimination had been violated when he gave samples of his handwriting to the FBI agent. The SC upheld Gilbert's conviction and rejected his Fifth Amendment claim, noting that handwriting samples are mere physical evidence, not evidence of "self-incrimination." Self-incrimination pertains to utterances and documents that contain incriminating statements or content-specific information.

Gilmore v. Utah, 429 U.S. 1012, 97 S.Ct. 436 (1976) [Bessie GILMORE, Applicant and Next Friend of Gary Mark Gilmore, Applicant, v. State of UTAH] (Corrections; Death Penalty) Gilmore, a convicted murderer, was ordered executed in Utah. Shortly thereafter, he waived his right to appeal and asked for a speedy execution. Several of his friends interceded on his behalf and moved for a stay of execution. The stay was granted, and Gilmore promptly moved to have the stay terminated. The SC heard Gilmore's case and removed the stay of execution, arguing that whenever a convicted murderer has been sentenced to death and has made a knowing and intelligent waiver of any and all federal rights that he might have asserted after the sentence was imposed, a stay of execution may be terminated over any objections from family members or friends. Thus, if death-row inmates wish intelligently and knowingly to waive their rights to appeal death sentences, they may do so over objections from friends and relatives.

Gitlow v. New York, 268 U.S. 652, 45 S.Ct. 625 (1924) [Benjamin GITLOW v. People of the State of NEW YORK] (First Amendment; Free Speech) Gitlow, a member of the Socialist Party, was convicted of violating a New York sedition law by distributing leaflets advocating the overthrow of the government. He appealed. Although the SC did not overturn Gitlow's conviction, it did specify that the First Amendment right of free speech was applicable to states as well as the federal government. The case established the bad-tendency test, which authorized legislative suppression of speech designed to inflame or incite persons to revolution.

Glover v. United States, 531 U.S. 198, 121 S.Ct. 696 (2001) [Paul L. GLOVER, Petitioner, v. UNITED STATES] (Ineffective Assistance of Counsel; Sixth Amendment) Paul Glover was the vice president and general counsel of the Chicago Truck Drivers in the 1980s and 1990s. He and several coconspirators were convicted of racketeering, money laundering, and tax evasion. The federal probation officer recommended that the three convictions should be grouped together under the U.S. Sentencing Commission Guidelines, which allowed the grouping of counts involving "substantially the same harm." However, the government objected, and the money laundering counts were separated from the other offenses. As a result, Glover's offense level was increased by two levels, yielding a concomitant increase in the sentencing range of from 6 to 21 months. Glover was sentenced to 84 months, which is the middle of the sentencing range of 78 to 97 months. Glover appealed, contending that because his counsel failed to argue for grouping of certain offenses under the Sentencing Guidelines, this constituted ineffective assistance of counsel. Both the trial court and circuit court denied his appeal and the SC heard his case. The SC reversed the lower courts, holding that Glover had demonstrated ineffective assistance of counsel by showing their failure to contest the erroneous sentence increase of from 6 to 21 months. The case was remanded to the trial court to correct the sentencing error. The significance of this case is that if defense counsels fail to raise arguments contesting unfair sentencing practices, then their conduct falls below the reasonable standard expected of effective counsels. This failure to act creates prejudice against defendants, who are subsequently penalized unfairly.

Go-Bart Importing Company v. United States, 282 U.S. 344, 51 S.Ct. 153 (1931) [GO-BART IMPORTING COMPANY et al., Petitioners, v. UNITED STATES] (Fourth Amendment; Law Enforcement Officers or Agencies; Searches and Seizures) Gowens and Bartels, owners of the Go-Bart Importing Company, were suspected of possessing, selling, and importing intoxicating liquor in violation of the Prohibition Act. Federal officers went to their place of business with arrest warrants. There, they told a secretary that they had a search warrant, a false statement as they had no such warrant. O'Brien, the government agent who falsely stated that he had a search warrant, proceeded to search the premises and discovered various incriminating documents, which led to the conviction of Gowens and Bartels. They appealed, arguing that no search warrant had been obtained and that this was an unreasonable search in violation of their Fourth Amendment rights. The SC overturned their convictions and ordered the prosecutor to suppress any seized evidence emanating from the illegal search.

Godfrey v. Georgia, 446 U.S. 420, 100 S.Ct. 1759 (1980) [Robert Franklin GODFREY, Petitioner, v. State of GEORGIA] (Aggravating and Mitigating Circumstances; Corrections; Cruel and Unusual Punishment; Death Penalty; Eighth Amendment) Godfrey shot and killed his mother-in-law and wife by firing a gun through a window. He subsequently chased his daughter and beat her with the butt of the gun. Following his conviction, at his sentencing hearing, the judge said that his crimes were outrageously or wantonly vile, horrible, or inhuman in that they involved torture, depravity of mind, or aggravated battery of the victim (at 1760). Godfrey appealed, arguing that such phraseology was a violation of the cruel-and-unusual-punishment provision of the Eighth Amendment. The SC overturned his conviction, saying that this broad and vague construction of statutory aggravating circumstances suggested an arbitrary and capricious infliction of the death sentence. Thus, the judge's language in sentencing was interpreted as arbitrary and capricious, inconsistent with the defendant's rights under the Eighth Amendment. A state's responsibility, the SC said, was to authorize capital punishment in such ways as to provide clear, objective, and rational standards for such sentencing.

Godinez v. Moran, 509 U.S. 389, 113 S.Ct. 2680 (1993) [Salvador GODINEZ, Warden, Petitioner, v. Richard Allan MORAN] (Death Penalty; *Habeas Corpus* Petitions; Insanity Pleas; Right to Counsel) Moran was charged with several murders, although he had entered a plea of not guilty by reason of insanity. Several doctors reported test results that indicated Moran was competent to stand trial. Following these psychiatric reports, Moran advised the Nevada court that he wished to dismiss his attorneys and plead guilty to the multiple murders. The court determined that Moran made these guilty pleas knowingly, intelligently, and voluntarily. Further, Moran waived his right to assistance of counsel and other rights associated with guilty pleas. Subsequently, after he was convicted and sentenced to death, he filed a *habeas corpus* petition alleging that even though he had earlier requested to represent himself, he was incompetent to do so. The SC upheld the conviction and death sentence, holding that the competency standard for pleading guilty or waiving the right to counsel is the same as the competency standard for standing trial. Moran had been found competent in both instances and had knowingly and intelligently waived the rights he was now alleging had been violated.

Gomez v. United States District Court, 503 U.S. 653, 112 S.Ct. 1652 (1992) [James GOMEZ and Daniel Vasquez v. UNITED STATES DISTRICT COURT for the Northern District of California et al.] (Cruel and Unusual Punishment; Death Penalty; Eighth Amendment; *Habeas Corpus* Petitions) Gomez was convicted of capital murder and sentenced to death in California. He was to die in the gas chamber, but he lodged an appeal with the SC, alleging that death by cyanide gas was cruel and unusual punishment. The SC heard his appeal and rejected it. It is significant to note that Gomez had made several prior *habeas corpus* appeals, in which this particular allegation had not been included. Thus, the SC stressed Gomez's last-minute attempt to manipulate the judicial process as one reason for not ruling favorably for him. In effect, the SC did not rule precisely on whether death by cyanide gas was cruel and unusual, but only that Gomez had not properly raised such an issue in his previous *habeas corpus* petitions.

Grady v. Corbin, 495 U.S. 508, 110 S.Ct. 2084 (1990) [William V. GRADY, District Attorney of Dutchess County, Petitioner, v. Thomas J. CORBIN] (Double Jeopardy; Fifth Amendment; Grand Juries; Self-Incrimination) Corbin was a motorist involved in the death of one person and injury to another. He pleaded guilty to driving while intoxicated. Subsequently, he was indicted by a grand jury on charges of reckless manslaughter, criminally negligent homicide, and third-degree reckless assault stemming from the same incident. It is important to note that driving while intoxicated is an element establishing each of these other offenses. Because Corbin had already pleaded guilty to DWI and been convicted, he sought to dismiss the indictment on the grounds of double jeopardy. An appellate court dismissed the indictment, and the state

sought to challenge this dismissal with an appeal to the SC. The SC affirmed the dismissal on double-jeopardy grounds. The SC said that the double-jeopardy clause bars a subsequent prosecution if, to establish an essential element of an offense charged in that prosecution, the government will prove conduct that constitutes an offense for which the defendant has already been prosecuted.

Graham v. Connor, 490 U.S. 396, 109 S.Ct. 1865 (1989) [Dethorne GRAHAM, Petitioner, v. M.S. CONNOR et al.] (Civil Rights, Section 1983 Claims; Law Enforcement Officers or Agencies) Graham was a diabetic who asked his daughter to drive him to the store to buy orange juice for his condition. When he entered the store, there were long lines, and Graham hurried back out and told his daughter to drive him to another store. A police officer observed Graham's quick entry and exit at the store, became suspicious, and stopped Graham's daughter as an "investigative stop" while he determined to find out "what happened" back at the store. In the meantime, Graham became belligerent and was handcuffed by police. He sustained further "injuries" while handcuffed. When police found that nothing had happened at the store, they released Graham, who filed a Title 42 U.S.C. Section 1983 civil rights suit against the officers for using excessive force unnecessarily against him. The SC declared that police officers are liable whenever they use excessive force, and that the standard they should use is objective reasonableness rather than substantive due process when they subdue suspicious persons. This is tantamount to a totality-of-circumstances test applied to discretionary actions of police officers in the field when they are dealing with situations in which only partial information exists that a crime may have been committed. The reasonableness of the situation and force used is determined on the spot, considering all circumstances.

Gray v. Maryland, 523 U.S. 185, 118 S.Ct. 1151 (1998) [Kevin D. GRAY, Petitioner, v. MARYLAND] (Confessions; Confrontation Clause; Sixth Amendment) Gray and another man, Bell, were indicted in the beating death of Stacy Williams in Maryland. At the trial, where they were tried jointly, Bell's confession was read into the record by a detective, where the confession omitted references to Gray and substituted words such as "deleted" or "deletion." Both defendants were convicted of involuntary manslaughter and Gray appealed, contending that the *Bruton* rule prohibited the introduction during a joint trial of the confession of a nontestifying codefendant which names the defendant as perpetrator. (*See for reference Bruton v. United States* [1968].) The Maryland Court of Special Appeals reversed Gray's conviction, but the Maryland Supreme Court reinstated it, holding that the *Bruton* rule does not apply to redacted confessions in which the name of the defendant has been deleted. Gray appealed to the SC, who heard the case. The SC vacated Gray's conviction, holding that the *Bruton* rule prohibiting the introduction during joint trials of confessions of nontestifying codefendants that name the defendant as perpetrator extends also to redacted or edited confessions in which the name of the defendant has been deleted.

Gray v. Mississippi, 481 U.S. 648, 107 S.Ct. 2045 (1987) [David Randolph GRAY, Petitioner, v. MISSISSIPPI] (Death Penalty; Jury Trials) In June 1982, Gray was indicted for murder in the stabbing death of a man during a kidnapping. When the jury was being selected, the prosecution excluded for cause a prospective juror, who had equivocated but ultimately stated that she could consider the death penalty under appropriate circumstances. Gray was convicted of the murder and the death penalty was imposed. Gray appealed, alleging that he had been deprived of a fair trial because a prospective juror had been excused for cause, which was improper under the law. The SC overturned Gray's conviction on the grounds that the juror had been unlawfully and improperly excused from jury duty. Thus, this exclusion was not only improper but potentially prejudicial to the trial outcome and death sentence.

Green v. Georgia, 442 U.S. 95, 99 S.Ct. 2150 (1979) [Roosevelt GREEN, Jr., v. State of GEORGIA] (Death Penalty) Green was charged with the murder of a woman, Allen. During the trial, it was disclosed that he and an accomplice, Moore, had raped and murdered Allen. Green was convicted. Moore had been tried separately and convicted, receiving the death penalty. During the penalty phase of Green's trial, Green tried to introduce testimony from another party, Pasby, who had overheard Moore say that he (Moore) had killed Allen by shooting her twice after sending Green on an errand. The judge refused to introduce Pasby's testimony, which would have mitigated Green's role in Allen's murder. Green appealed and the SC overturned the death sentence, holding that it was improper for the judge to exclude exculpatory testimony from a witness during the sentencing phase, as such testimony was relevant to the critical issue of the death penalty. Thus, Green had been denied a fair trial in regard to his punishment.

Greenholtz v. Inmates of Nebraska, 442 U.S. 1, 99 S.Ct. 2100 (1979) [John B. GREENHOLTZ, etc., et al., Petitioners, v. INMATES OF the NEBRASKA Penal and Correctional Complex] (Corrections; Inmate Rights; Probation and Parole) The Nebraska prison system annually reviews files of inmates who are parole eligible, and the Nebraska Parole Board decides whether they should be released in a two-stage proceeding: one phase consists of an initial review, and the second phase is a final parole hearing. The parole board decides whether the inmate is a good or bad parole risk, partially on the basis of evidence presented at these hearings. Inmate rights given by the parole board include the right to present evidence, call witnesses, be represented by counsel, and receive a written statement of reasons in the event parole is denied. Inmates believed that they were entitled to more constitutional rights relating to their early release than those given by the parole board, and appealed to the SC. The Court upheld the Nebraska Parole Board and declared that inmates have no inherent constitutional rights to be released conditionally before the expiration of their valid sentences. Parole is a *privilege,* not a *right.* Furthermore, parole is optional with each state. For instance, Maine and the federal prison system have abolished parole. These jurisdictions currently use a form of supervised release.

Greer v. Spock, 424 U.S. 828, 96 S.Ct. 1211 (1976) [Thomas U. GREER, Commander, Fort Dix Military Reservation, et al., Petitioners, v. Benjamin SPOCK et al.] (Bifurcated Trials; Corrections; Fifth Amendment; Free Speech; Inmate Rights) Spock and others were members of a political party in 1972 seeking to make speeches on a government reservation, Fort Dix, NJ. They were prohibited from making such speeches on the reservation and appealed to a federal district court, where they argued that their First and Fifth Amendment rights had been violated. Injunctive relief was granted by a New Jersey court, and the government appealed. The SC reversed the injunction, declaring that Spock and others had no constitutional right to make political speeches and distribute leaflets on a military reservation, that regulations banning such political speeches and demonstrations and governing the distribution of literature were not constitutionally invalid on their face, and that regulations had not been unconstitutionally applied to Spock. Thus politicians have no constitutional right to campaign on military installations.

Gregg v. Georgia, 428 U.S. 153, 96 S.Ct. 2909 (1976) [Troy Leon GREGG, Petitioner, v. State of GEORGIA] (Aggravating and Mitigating Circumstances; Bifurcated Trials; Corrections; Death Penalty; Fourteenth Amendment) Gregg was convicted of robberies and murders in Atlanta and sentenced to death. According to newly enacted provisions by the Georgia legislature, death penalty cases required bifurcated trials (two-stage trials), in which guilt or innocence would be determined in the first stage, and the penalty would be assessed in the second stage. The provisions further required that in the penalty phase the jury was to consider and weigh aggravating and mitigating circumstances, and if the former outweighed the latter, the death penalty was to be imposed. An automatic appeal of the death sentence was also prescribed by law. Gregg appealed his death sentence, but the SC upheld it, saying that the procedures Georgia had instituted for applying the death penalty were constitutional and were not in violation of either the Eighth or Fourteenth Amendments.

Griffin v. California, 380 U.S. 609, 85 S.Ct. 1229 (1965) [Eddie Dean GRIFFIN, Petitioner, v. State of CALIFORNIA] (Corrections; Fifth Amendment; Inmate Rights) Griffin was accused of a crime in California and decided during the trial not to take the stand or answer questions in his own defense. However, the prosecutor commented on the fact that Griffin failed to speak on his own behalf and that this failure was interpreted to reflect the guilt of the defendant, when in fact Griffin did not want his prior criminal record exposed. He was convicted. Griffin appealed, protesting the constitutionality of the California statute allowing prosecutors (and judges) the privilege of commenting about a defendant's decision not to testify in his own behalf. The SC ruled the California statute unconstitutional. Thus, prosecutors and others may not comment on the refusal of a defendant to testify as a Fifth Amendment right to avoid making incriminating statements. (*See Adamson v. California* [1947] *for a similar case and prior ruling.*)

Griffin v. Illinois, 351 U.S. 12, 76 S.Ct. 585 (1956) [Judson GRIFFIN and James Crenshaw, Petitioners, v. The

People of the State of ILLINOIS] (**Indigent Clients**) Griffin and an accomplice were convicted of armed robbery in a Cook County court. Following their conviction, Griffin, who claimed to be indigent, requested a copy of the court transcript at no charge. Under existing Illinois law, only persons sentenced to death and indigent could make such requests. The request was denied by Illinois. Griffin appealed. The SC reversed the Illinois court, holding that the due-process rights of Griffin had been violated by denying him a transcript. The SC further stated that it did not hold that Illinois must purchase a stenographer's transcript in every case in which a defendant cannot buy it, but it believed the state should find other means of affording adequate and effective appellate review to indigent defendants.

Griffin v. Wisconsin, 483 U.S. 868, 107 S.Ct. 3164 (1987) [**Joseph G. GRIFFIN, Petitioner, v. WISCONSIN**] (**Corrections; Fourth Amendment; Probation and Parole**) Griffin was placed on probation after being convicted of resisting arrest, disorderly conduct, and obstructing a Wisconsin police officer in 1980. One condition of Griffin's probation was that he not possess a firearm. An informant advised Griffin's probation officer that Griffin had a weapon on his premises. Based on previous reliable information provided by the informant, the officer believed that reasonable grounds existed to conduct a warrantless search. He went to Griffin's home, searched it without a warrant, and discovered a gun. Griffin was subsequently arrested, prosecuted, and convicted for being a convicted felon in possession of a firearm. He was sentenced to two years. He appealed on the grounds that the search of his premises should have been conducted with a properly issued warrant and based on probable cause. The SC declared that probation officers are entitled to special consideration because of their demanding jobs. They should not be held to the more stringent standard of probable cause because they must often take immediate action to detect crimes or seize illegal contraband relating to their probationer or parolee clients. The reasonable grounds standard, a lesser standard than probable cause, is upheld to the extent that probation or parole agency policies make provisions for such warrantless searches of offenders' premises in their jurisdictions. The ruling was not intended as a blanket right to violate a person's Fourth Amendment rights on a whim.

Griffith v. Kentucky, 479 U.S. 314, 107 S.Ct. 708 (1987) [**Randall Lamont GRIFFITH, Petitioner, v. KENTUCKY. Willie Davis Brown, aka Will Brown, Petitioner, v. United States**] (**Corrections; Death Penalty; Peremptory Challenges**) Griffith, a black man, was arrested for conspiracy to distribute marijuana. During his 1982 trial in Jefferson County, the prosecutor used four out of five peremptory challenges to strike from jury duty four out of five prospective black jurors. Griffith was convicted. He later appealed, saying that the prosecutor had violated his right to due process by striking from jury duty most of the black candidates. He said the case of *Batson v. Kentucky* (1986) should be retroactively applied to his case. The SC overturned his conviction, holding that the *Batson* case, prohibiting prosecutors from using their peremptory challenges to give racial bias to a jury pool, should

be retroactively applied where a showing exists that such conduct has occurred. Thus, Griffith's case qualified for a retroactive application of *Batson.* The SC held that a new rule for the conduct of criminal prosecutions is to be applied retroactively to all cases, state or federal, pending on direct review or not yet final, with no exception for cases in which the new rule constitutes a "clear break" with the past.

Groh v. Ramirez, ___U.S.___, 124 S.Ct. 1284 (2004) [**Jeff GROH, Petitioner, v. Joseph R. RAMIREZ et al.**] (**Civil Rights, Section 1983 Claims; Fourth Amendment; Searches and Seizures**) Jeff Groh, an agent with the Bureau of Alcohol, Tobacco, and Firearms, prepared and signed a warrant to search a Montana ranch owned by Joseph Ramirez and his family. The search warrant was for "weapons, explosives, and records." A magistrate signed the warrant, even though it failed to describe the places to be searched or things to be seized. Local and federal law enforcement officers searched the ranch pursuant to the search warrant, and found no illegal weapons or explosives. Subsequently, Ramirez filed a Section 1983 claim against Groh and other officers, as well as alleging a Fourth Amendment violation, claiming the search warrant was invalid because it did not describe with particularity the place to be searched and the items to be seized. The U.S. district court dismissed all claims, concluding that Groh had qualified immunity from lawsuits and that a cursory inspection of the warrant led the judge to believe that he understood its scope and limitations and that it was obviously not defective. The Ninth Circuit upheld the district court judge's ruling and Ramirez appealed to the SC, who heard the case. The SC reversed the lower courts, holding that the warrant was plainly invalid because it did not meet the Fourth Amendment's unambiguous requirement that a warrant "particularly describe the persons or things to be seized." In fact, the warrant did not describe any items at all, and was thus presumptively unreasonable. Furthermore, the SC held that Groh was not entitled to qualified immunity despite the constitutional violation because it would be clear to a reasonable officer that his conduct was unlawful in the situation he confronted. Groh's claim that the magistrate's assurance that the warrant contained an adequate description of what was to be searched and seized also failed, because Groh himself had prepared the warrant, nor could a reasonable officer claim to be unaware of the basic rule that, absent consent or exigency, a warrantless search of a home is presumptively unconstitutional. (*See for comparison Bivens v. Six Unknown Fed. Narcotics Agents* [1971].)

Grunewald v. United States, 353 U.S. 391, 77 S.Ct. 963 (1957) [**Henry W. GRUNEWALD, Petitioner, v. UNITED STATES of America**] (**Corrections; Inmate Rights**) Grunewald was convicted of conspiring to defraud the United States government by influencing witnesses testifying in a grand jury hearing in a criminal case. The conspiracy was alleged to have occurred in 1948 and 1949, although prosecution for this conspiracy was not implemented until October 1954. Grunewald appealed, arguing that the statute of limitations had expired for prosecuting his case. The SC overturned his conviction, basically agreeing with Grunewald. The SC said that the government had failed to show that any overt acts had occurred since October 1951, three years prior to October 1954, the three-year statute-of-limitations period. In any case, government prosecutors must be mindful of the statute of limitations governing conspiracy cases, and even though they can demonstrate that a conspiracy might be continuing, their case fails if it cannot show any overt act associated with this conspiracy during the statute-of-limitations period.

Gustafson v. Florida, 414 U.S. 260, 94 S.Ct. 488 (1973) [James E. GUSTAFSON, Petitioner, v. State of FLORIDA] (Fourteenth Amendment; Fourth Amendment; Law Enforcement Officers or Agencies; Searches and Seizures; Searches Incident to Arrest) Gustafson was driving in Brevard County when he was stopped for a traffic violation. He did not have a valid driver's license, so the officer arrested him. Then he was searched. A cigarette package was recovered that contained marijuana cigarettes. He was charged for marijuana possession and convicted. He appealed, arguing that this search of his person had violated his rights against unreasonable searches and seizures under the Fourth Amendment. The SC upheld his conviction, saying that full searches of persons incident to lawful arrests do not violate Fourth or Fourteenth Amendment rights of arrestees. Thus, police may conduct a thorough search of a lawfully arrested person.

H

Hafer v. Melo, 502 U.S. 21, 112 S.Ct. 358 (1991) [Barbara HAFER, Petitioner, v. James C. MELO, Jr., et al.] (Civil Rights, Section 1983 Claims; Immunity) Melo was a government employee who was fired by Hafer, the auditor general of Pennsylvania. Melo sued Hafer under Title 42 U.S.C. Section 1983, seeking monetary damages. Hafer claimed immunity because of her official capacity. The suit was filed in federal court and Hafer was being sued in her personal capacity, not her official capacity. Thus, she was not immune from Section 1983 lawsuits. (*See Will v. Michigan Department of State Police* [1989] *for a comparable opinion about this issue.*) Currently, state officials cannot be sued in state or federal courts in their official capacity, but they may be sued in their personal capacity.

Hagen v. Utah, 510 U.S. 399, 114 S.Ct. 958 (1994) [Robert HAGEN, Petitioner, v. UTAH] (Jurisdiction) Hagen pleaded guilty to distributing drugs on a Utah Reservation for American Indians. He appealed, arguing that the State of Utah did not have jurisdiction over the reservation; rather, jurisdiction was properly placed in a United States district court. A Utah court of criminal appeals reversed Hagen's conviction on this ground, but the Utah Supreme Court reversed this reversal and reinstated Hagen's original conviction. He appealed to the SC, which upheld his conviction. The SC said that the reservation had once been a federally protected reservation, but it had been opened to non-Indians during the early 1900s; thus, it was no longer a federally protected area. There-

fore, Utah courts had exercised proper jurisdiction over Hagen.

Haines v. Kerner, 404 U.S. 519, 92 S.Ct. 594 (1972) [Francis HAINES, Petitioner, v. Otto J. KERNER, former Governor, State of Illinois, et al.] (Corrections; Inmate Rights) Haines, an inmate of the Illinois State Penitentiary, was involved in a fight with another inmate. He sustained various injuries and was placed in solitary confinement as a punishment. While in solitary confinement, he was forced to sleep on the floor with only a blanket. He had both a prior foot injury and circulatory ailments that were not treated by correctional officials during this time. He later sued the prison and state, but his case was dismissed outright by an appellate court without entitling Haines to show proof of his injuries or the harsh treatment. He appealed again. The SC reversed the decision of the lower court, holding that Haines had a right to show proof as a means of recovering damages from the state. This narrow SC holding means that prisoners seeking relief are entitled to show proof that they suffered damages. Courts may not bar them from showing such proof. The SC did not rule on the merits of Haines' arguments, only the procedural matter of being able to show proof in court to sustain his petition.

Haley v. Ohio, 332 U.S. 596, 68 S.Ct. 302 (1948) [John Harvey HALEY, Petitioner, v. State of OHIO] (Confessions; Juvenile Law; *Miranda* Warning; Right to Counsel) A 15-year-old youth, Haley, suspected of being involved in a store robbery, was taken into custody one night for interrogation. The police questioned Haley for five hours, rotating their interrogator teams in shifts. They showed Haley confessions from some of his friends that implicated him. Eventually, he confessed. At no time was he advised of his right to counsel; an attorney who tried to see him was rebuffed by police. Even his mother was unable to see him. Haley was subsequently convicted of murder and sentenced to life imprisonment. He appealed. Although this case occurred before the *Miranda* case and the defendant's rights were not considered by police officers while they conducted their interrogation, the SC detected considerable coercion in Haley's case. The conviction was overturned, and the SC concluded that juvenile suspects may not be coerced into confessing to crimes. Involuntary confessions cannot be used in court.

Ham v. South Carolina, 409 U.S. 524, 93 S.Ct. 848 (1973) [Gene HAM, Petitioner, v. State of SOUTH CAROLINA] (Jury Trials) Ham was convicted of a crime. When the jury was being selected, he was prohibited from asking prospective jurors if they harbored any sort of racial bias or any bias because Ham wore a beard. He was convicted. He appealed, arguing that he had the right to question jurors about their biases. The SC overturned Ham's conviction and declared that defendants have a right to inquire about possible juror bias against persons who wear beards. It is also permissible for *judges* to inquire of potential jurors whether they are racially prejudiced. (*See Ristaino v. Ross* [1976] *for a comparable case.*)

Hamilton v. Alabama, 368 U.S. 52, 82 S.Ct. 157 (1961) [Charles Clarence HAMILTON, Petitioner, v. State of ALABAMA] (Corrections; Indigent Clients; Probation and Parole; **Right to Counsel**) Hamilton, an indigent, was indicted for murder by a grand jury. At his arraignment following the indictment, he was not represented by counsel and he was subsequently convicted of murder. He appealed, contending that he had been disadvantaged by not having counsel present during the arraignment. The SC overturned his conviction, saying that arraignments are critical stages requiring the presence of a court-appointed attorney in indigent cases. In Alabama at the time, defendants were required to show that they were in need of counsel. Hamilton had not requested counsel at the time, but neither had counsel been offered.

Hammett v. Texas, 448 U.S. 725, 100 S.Ct. 2905 (1980) [**William Jack HAMMETT v. State of TEXAS**] (**Death Penalty; Mental Capacity**) Hammett was convicted of murder and sentenced to death. On his behalf, an appeal was filed by his attorney. Hammett moved to have the petition withdrawn, so that his execution could proceed without any legal delay. The SC held that Hammett withdrew the petition knowingly and intelligently, and therefore granted his motion. The significance of this case is that persons sentenced to death can waive their appeal rights if they desire, with full knowledge of the consequences, including execution.

Hampton v. United States, 425 U.S. 484, 96 S.Ct. 1646 (1976) [**Charles HAMPTON, Petitioner, v. UNITED STATES**] (**Entrapment**) Hampton was suspected of trafficking in narcotics. A paid government informant agreed to supply him with narcotics so that Hampton could, in turn, sell these drugs to another undercover agent, in this case a DEA agent. Hampton was arrested, charged with trafficking in narcotics, and convicted. He appealed, arguing that entrapment existed because the government had provided illegal narcotics to an acquaintance and that Hampton had never intended to sell heroin nor had even known that he was dealing in it at the time. The SC upheld Hampton's conviction, saying that entrapment does not exist, even when government agents supply heroin in arranging a situation meriting an arrest for narcotics trafficking. (*See United States v. Russell* [1973] *for a similar case and holding.*) The SC stressed the fact that Hampton had had a predisposition to traffic in narcotics at the time the government provided the illegal drugs to the paid informant. This was a very controversial case, because the government engaged in what many persons regarded as outrageous conduct by supplying a narcotic, heroin, to a paid informant to create its own crime scenario.

Harlow v. Fitzgerald, 457 U.S. 800, 102 S.Ct. 2727 (1982) [**Bryce N. HARLOW and Alexander P. Butterfield, Petitioners, v. A. Ernest FITZGERALD**] (**Immunity; Law Enforcement Officers or Agencies**) Harlow was an aide to President Richard Nixon, and Fitzgerald was an Air Force official who was dismissed, based on allegations by Harlow and others. Fitzgerald sued for unlawful discharge, alleging that Harlow was retaliating for Fitzgerald's intent to call attention to extravagant Air Force spending. Harlow claimed absolute immunity because of his position relative to President Nixon as a government official. The SC said that government officials are not entitled to absolute immunity, only to qualified immunity. It stressed the importance of official conduct relative to

employee dismissals and whether such conduct violates clearly established statutory or constitutional rights of which a reasonable person should have known.

Harmelin v. Michigan, 501 U.S. 957, 111 S.Ct. 2680 (1991) [**Ronald Allen HARMELIN, Petitioner, v. MICHIGAN**] (**Sentencing**) Harmelin, a convicted drug dealer, was apprehended with 672 grams of cocaine. He was convicted and a mandatory sentence of life imprisonment was imposed. Harmelin challenged the constitutionality of this sentence and also declared that it was disproportional to the crime. The SC disagreed and let his conviction and sentence stand, believing them not to have violated any of Harmelin's constitutional rights.

Harrington v. California, 395 U.S. 250, 89 S.Ct. 1726 (1969) [**Glen Martin HARRINGTON, Petitioner, v. State of CALIFORNIA**] (**Confessions; Confrontration Clause; Sixth Amendment**) Harrington was charged with murder. A codefendant made a confession implicating Harrington, and this confession was introduced as evidence against him. The codefendant also testified in court against Harrington and was cross-examined by Harrington's attorney. Confessions from two others involved in the murder were read into the record, but these two persons were not called to testify, inasmuch as there was already overwhelming evidence against Harrington. Harrington was convicted. He appealed, arguing that his Sixth Amendment right to cross-examine his accusers had been violated. In an unusual turn of events, the SC upheld Harrington's conviction, saying that because of the overwhelming inculpatory evidence against him, the judicial decision to disallow cross-examination of these other persons had not violated Harrington's Sixth Amendment rights. The SC considered not calling the accomplices to testify to be harmless error.

Harris v. Alabama, 513 U.S. 504, 115 S.Ct. 1031 (1995) [**Louise HARRIS, Petitioner, v. ALABAMA**] (**Aggravating and Mitigating Circumstances; Death Penalty; Juries; Jury Instructions**) Harris was convicted of capital murder. During the sentencing phase, the jury recommended life imprisonment to the judge, but the judge cited a preponderance of aggravating factors over mitigating ones and imposed the death penalty. Harris appealed, contending that the jury decision should have been honored by the judge. The SC upheld Harris' conviction and death penalty, saying that judges may impose the death penalty despite a recommendation by the jury for a sentence of life imprisonment. Juries only "recommend" to judges, who need only consider the recommendation; judges make the final sentencing decision. This case is significant, because it underscores the power of sentencing judges to consider and weigh aggravating and mitigating circumstances. If the aggravating circumstances in a capital case outweigh the mitigating ones, then the death penalty is justified. In this case, the jury had been emotionally persuaded to recommend a life sentence; however, the judge had determined that specific aggravating circumstances far outweighed any mitigating ones, and he had imposed the death penalty.

Harris v. New York, 401 U.S. 222, 91 S.Ct. 643 (1971) [**Viven HARRIS v. NEW YORK**] (**Fifth Amendment;** *Miranda* **Warning; Self-Incrimination**) Harris was indicted for selling heroin. During his trial, statements were admitted into evidence that Harris had made to police, both before and after he was told his *Miranda* rights. Some of these statements involved transactional details of his heroin sales. Harris was cross-examined by the prosecutor about these pre-*Miranda* statements. He was convicted. He sought to suppress these statements from his case and appealed to the SC. The SC affirmed Harris' conviction, saying that Harris could not invoke the Fifth Amendment concerning statements he had already made to police. Harris' past inconsistent and conflicting statements were within the proper scope of cross-examination by the prosecutor and unprotected by any Fifth Amendment claim.

Harris v. Oklahoma, 433 U.S. 682, 97 S.Ct. 2912 (1977) [**Thomas Leon HARRIS v. State of OKLAHOMA**] (**Double Jeopardy**) Harris and a companion robbed a grocery store, and the grocery store clerk was shot and killed by Harris' companion. Harris was charged with and convicted of felony murder. Subsequently, he was charged with robbery with a firearm and convicted. He appealed, alleging that his double-jeopardy rights had been violated, as he had already been convicted of felony murder, which included similar crime elements. The SC reversed his robbery conviction, holding that when conviction of a greater crime, murder, cannot be had without conviction of the lesser crime, robbery with firearms, the double-jeopardy clause bars prosecution for the lesser crime after conviction of the greater one.

Harris v. United States, 390 U.S. 234, 88 S.Ct. 992 (1968) [**James H. HARRIS, Petitioner, v. UNITED STATES**] (**Inventory Searches; Law Enforcement Officers or Agencies; Plain-View Rule; Searches and Seizures**) Harris' automobile had been observed leaving the scene of a bank robbery. Later, Harris was arrested by police and his car was impounded. The car was subjected to a routine search. Incriminating evidence was obtained from his car and later used against him in court, when he was convicted. He appealed, but the SC upheld his conviction, saying that anything in plain view in an automobile during an inventory search is subject to seizure and admissible in court later.

Harris v. United States, ___U.S.___, 122 S.Ct. 2406 (2002) [**William Joseph HARRIS, Petitioner, v. UNITED STATES**] (**Sentencing**) Harris was convicted in a U.S. district court of selling narcotics. Harris ran a pawnshop and carried an unconcealed semiautomatic pistol at his side during working hours. Although he was not charged with brandishing a firearm during the act of selling narcotics, the judge considered "brandishing" a firearm in relation to a drug-trafficking offense as a sentencing factor and imposed a mandatory minimum sentence of seven years. Harris objected, contending that "brandishing" a firearm was an element of a separate statutory offense for which he was neither indicted nor convicted. The district court judge and the Fourth Circuit rejected Harris' argument and upheld his sentence. The SC heard the case and affirmed, holding that the possession of a firearm during the commission of a criminal offense was a sentencing factor rather than an element of a crime, and that al-

lowing the judge to find that factor did not violate Harris' constitutional rights.

Hayes v. Florida, 470 U.S. 811, 105 S.Ct. 1643 (1985) [**Joe HAYES, Petitioner, v. FLORIDA**] (**Custodial Interrogations; Fourth Amendment; Law Enforcement Officers or Agencies; Searches and Seizures**) Hayes was a suspect in a criminal case. He was visited by police, who asked him if they could take his fingerprints. Hayes refused, at which time the police advised him that if he didn't go to the police station voluntarily, he would be arrested. He reluctantly agreed to go, and his fingerprints were taken. They matched those at the crime scene and Hayes was subsequently convicted of the crime. He appealed. The SC overturned his conviction, holding that there had been no probable cause to arrest Hayes, he had given no consent to go to the police station, and there had been no prior judicial authorization for such fingerprinting. The subsequent investigative detention at the police station had violated Hayes' Fourth Amendment rights against unreasonable searches and seizures. Police must have probable cause to take persons into custody for purposes of taking their fingerprints and subjecting them to interrogations.

Haynes v. Washington, 373 U.S. 503, 83 S.Ct. 1336 (1963) [**Raymond L. HAYNES, Petitioner, v. State of WASHINGTON**] (**Confessions**) In December 1957, Haynes was arrested by Spokane police shortly after a gasoline station had been robbed. On the way to the police station, Haynes admitted the robbery orally. He was subsequently interrogated by a Spokane detective and was placed in a lineup for identification by gas station attendants and other witnesses later that evening. The following morning, Haynes was again questioned by detectives for about one-and-one-half hours. He gave two confession statements, signing one but not the other. The next day he was taken before a magistrate for a preliminary hearing. Police continued to insist that Haynes should sign the second confession, as he had already signed the first one. He persistently refused to sign the second confession. He was later convicted, with the first signed confession used against him as evidence. He appealed. The SC overturned Haynes' conviction, holding that the police interrogation methods had been improper and that Haynes had been subjected to coercive methods in signing the first confession. Thus, such evidence would be inadmissible in a retrial of the case.

Heath v. Alabama, 474 U.S. 82, 106 S.Ct. 433 (1985) [**Larry Gene HEATH, Petitioner, v. ALABAMA**] (**Double Jeopardy**) Heath was charged by a Georgia jury for arranging to have his wife killed by two men from Alabama. They kidnapped his wife and transported her body across state lines into Georgia. Following his conviction in Georgia for murder with malice, an Alabama court also found him guilty of murder during a kidnapping and sentenced him to death. His convictions were affirmed by Alabama courts despite an appeal based on a double-jeopardy claim. He appealed again. The SC upheld his murder convictions in both states, saying that the inherent sovereignty of both Alabama and Georgia as states meant that Heath had not been subjected to double jeopardy by being convicted of the same murder in two different jurisdictions. When Heath committed murder, he had violated the laws of two separate state jurisdictions, and thus the double-jeopardy provision does not apply to him.

Heck v. Humphrey, 512 U.S. 477, 114 S.Ct. 2364 (1994) [Roy HECK v. James HUMPHREY et al.] (Civil Rights, Section 1983 Claims) Roy Heck was convicted of voluntary manslaughter for killing his wife, Rickie Heck, and sentenced to 15 years in an Indiana prison. Heck appealed his conviction. Shortly after filing this appeal, Heck filed a Section 1983 civil rights action against county prosecutors and state police alleging that under color of law, they had engaged in unlawful, unreasonable, and arbitrary investigations leading to Heck's arrest; that they had knowingly destroyed exculpatory evidence; and that they had caused an illegal and unlawful voice identification procedure to be used in court against Heck. The complaint sought compensatory and punitive monetary damages. However, Heck did not seek injunctive relief. The U.S. district court dismissed Heck's suit without prejudice, and the appellate court affirmed. Heck then appealed to the SC, who heard the case. The SC affirmed the lower courts and held that in order for Heck to recover damages under Section 1983 of Title 42 of the U.S. Code, he had to prove that conviction or sentence (1) had been reversed on direct appeal, (2) was expunged by executive order, (3) was declared invalid by a state tribunal authorized to make such a determination, or (4) was called into question by the federal court's issuance of a writ of *habeas corpus.* Heck failed to meet any of these standards with his Section 1983 claim.

Helling v. McKinney, 509 U.S. 25, 113 S.Ct. 2475 (1993) [Donald L. HELLING et al., Petitioners, v. William McKINNEY] (Civil Rights, Section 1983 Claims; Corrections; Cruel and Unusual Punishment; Eighth Amendment; Inmate Rights) McKinney was a prisoner in the Nevada state prison system. He filed suit against prison officials under Title 42 U.S.C. Section 1983, alleging that cigarette smoke from cellmates was jeopardizing his health and thus was subjecting him to cruel and unusual punishment under the Eighth Amendment. He also said officials had exhibited deliberate indifference to him when he asked for a smoke-free environment. The environmental tobacco smoke (ETS) could not be proved to cause future bodily harm or injury, although the SC declared that McKinney had plainly stated a case upon which relief could be granted. The SC remanded this case back to the originating court to determine whether deliberate indifference actually had been manifested by prison administrators. Since McKinney filed his suit, however, the Nevada prison system has created smoke-free areas and has implemented major policy changes regarding ETS throughout the Nevada prison system. These administrative changes may discourage any favorable decision for McKinney on the deliberate indifference issue.

Henderson v. Morgan, 426 U.S. 637, 96 S.Ct. 2253 (1976) [Robert J. HENDERSON, Superintendent, Auburn Correctional Facility, Petitioner, v. Timothy G. MORGAN] (*Habeas Corpus* Petitions; Plea Bargaining) Morgan was convicted following a plea of guilty to second-degree murder in New York. He later filed a writ of *habeas corpus,* alleging that

his plea had not been voluntary, as the nature and proof of actual charges were never explained to him and he had never admitted to committing the specific acts constituting the charge. The SC set aside the conviction, noting that Morgan was of unusually low mental capacity and had not admitted that he had intended to commit the crime. Further, the SC noted, neither defense counsel nor trial court had explained to Morgan that intent to cause the death of his victim was an essential element of the offense of second-degree murder. Thus, it was impossible to conclude that Morgan's plea to the unexplained charge of second-degree murder was voluntary.

Henderson v. United States, 339 U.S. 816, 70 S.Ct. 843 (1950) [Elmer W. HENDERSON, Petitioner, v. UNITED STATES et al.] (Corrections; Inmate Rights) In 1942, Henderson, a black man, attempted to dine in a railroad car that had been partitioned by curtains, with 10 tables reserved for white passengers and one table reserved for black passengers. He sought to be accommodated in the white dining area, was refused, and brought suit against the railroad. The case was ultimately heard by the SC, who decided in Henderson's favor, holding that such divisions of dining conveniences in railroad cars were discriminatory and violated the Interstate Commerce Act.

Henry v. United States, 361 U.S. 98, 80 S.Ct. 168 (1959) [John Patrick HENRY, Petitioner, v. UNITED STATES] (Fourth Amendment; Law Enforcement Officers or Agencies; Searches and Seizures; Vehicle Searches) FBI agents who were conducting surveillance in a case totally unrelated to Henry happened to observe him and another person load several boxes into Henry's automobile. At a distance of 300 feet, FBI agents could see "Admiral" on the boxes being loaded. They approached Henry and his friend, inquired about the boxes, searched them, and detained the two men while they determined whether the merchandise was stolen. It was, and Henry and his friend were arrested for interstate transportation of stolen radios. A federal district court convicted the two men and they appealed. They claimed that the FBI agents had lacked probable cause to conduct a warrantless search of Henry's vehicle, because a visual inspection of the boxes and their contents was not definitive proof of their status as stolen merchandise. The U.S. attorney argued that because the radios were indeed stolen, the end (the arrest and conviction of Henry and his friend) justified the means (the warrantless search and lack of probable cause). The SC ruled against the government, overturning Henry's conviction. It concluded that "an arrest is not justified by what the subsequent search discloses." It also said, "It is better, so the Fourth Amendment teaches, that the guilty sometimes go free than that citizens be subject to easy arrest." The case significance for police officers is that they cannot conduct warrantless searches lacking probable cause and justify their conduct if illegal contraband is uncovered as a result of their illegal search. (*See Terry v. Ohio* [1968] *and Sibron v. New York* [1968].)

Hernandez v. New York, 500 U.S. 352, 111 S.Ct. 1859 (1991) [Dionisio HERNANDEZ, Petitioner, v. NEW YORK] (Juries; Peremptory Challenges; Right to Counsel; Sixth Amendment) Hernandez was convicted of various crimes. During the selection of his jury, the prosecutor used several peremptory challenges to strike from potential jury duty four Latinos. Following his conviction, Hernandez filed an appeal, alleging that the prosecutor had deliberately deprived him of a fair trial by eliminating persons like Hernandez. The argument was similar to the one made in *Batson v. Kentucky* (1986), in which it was held that peremptory challenges cannot be used to create racially pure juries or to strike off members of a particular race. At the time, objections had been raised by defense counsel, but the prosecutor cited various valid reasons for using these challenges. The SC upheld his conviction, holding that an acceptable race-neutral explanation had been provided by the prosecutor for striking the Latino jurors in that case. No evidence to the contrary had been presented.

Herrera v. Collins, 506 U.S. 390, 113 S.Ct. 853 (1993) [Leonel Torres HERRERA, Petitioner, v. James A. COLLINS, Director, Texas Department of Criminal Justice, Institutional Division] (Death Penalty; *Habeas Corpus* Petitions) On the basis of a handwritten confession, two eyewitness accounts and identifications, and two additional and critical pieces of circumstantial evidence, Herrera was convicted of first-degree murder and sentenced to death in Texas in 1982. Ten years later, he initiated a *habeas corpus* petition alleging that he was innocent of these murders because of "newly discovered evidence." Texas statutes have provisions governing the time limits to bring new appeals on newly discovered evidence. Herrera had gone well beyond these limits, and considering his confession, eyewitnesses to the murders, and the incriminating circumstantial evidence, the threshold for questioning Herrera's original conviction had not been reached. The SC upheld Herrera's conviction and death sentence, although it did offer one other avenue of relief. The SC said that Herrera could appeal to the Texas governor for clemency on a posttrial demonstration of actual innocence. Thus, if Herrera could show that the newly discovered evidence was exonerating, then the governor could grant clemency.

Herring v. New York, 422 U.S. 853, 95 S.Ct. 2550 (1975) [Clifford HERRING, Appellant, v. State of NEW YORK] (Fourteenth Amendment; Sixth Amendment) In a bench trial, Herring's attorney was denied the opportunity to summarize the defense case before the New York judge. A New York statute gave the judge discretion to either hear a summation from the defense or not hear it. The judge convicted Herring after hearing the evidence. Herring appealed, saying that he had been denied the assistance of counsel because of this statute in violation of the Sixth Amendment and that his due-process rights had been violated under the Fourteenth Amendment. The SC overturned Herring's conviction, saying that the New York statute had violated Herring's Fourteenth Amendment rights by preventing defense counsel from presenting closing arguments.

Hester v. United States, 265 U.S. 57, 44 S.Ct. 445 (1924) [Charlie HESTER, Petitioner, v. UNITED STATES] (Fourth Amendment; Open-Fields Doctrine; Plain-View Rule) Hester was suspected of manufacturing illegal liquor. Revenue agents secreted themselves in bushes near Hester's house. When he emerged carrying a large jug, he saw them in the bushes, panicked, dropped the jug, and ran. The agents picked up the jug and determined that it contained illegal whiskey. Hester was convicted of manufacturing moonshine whiskey. He appealed, arguing that the officers were trespassing on his land at the time he observed them. The SC disagreed, saying that the fact that officers were trespassing did not by itself nullify their observations. The officers had no warrant, but they didn't need one, because Hester had dropped the whiskey jug in plain view. Rather, officers had merely examined the abandoned container when Hester and his companions attempted to elude officers. Thus, there had been no Fourth Amendment violation and the evidence was properly admitted against Hester.

Hewitt v. Helms, 459 U.S. 460, 103 S.Ct. 864 (1983) [Lowell D. HEWITT et al., Petitioners v. Aaron HELMS] (Civil Rights, Section 1983 Claims; Corrections) Following riots in a Pennsylvania prison, an inmate, Helms, was given several misconduct reports. He was placed in solitary confinement for a period of time. Subsequent misconduct reports resulted in his being placed in solitary confinement for six months. Helms filed suit under Title 42 U.S.C. Section 1983, alleging that his Fourteenth Amendment right to due process had been violated because he had been denied full hearings on the two punishments. The SC denied Helms relief, saying that administrative segregation (solitary confinement) requires no formal hearings and is often ordered to insure prisoner safety. Specifically, inmates are not entitled to hearings to determine whether administrative segregation should be imposed for *protection.* The SC stressed, however, that for purposes of *punishment,* inmates are entitled to hearings as set forth in *Wolff v. McDonnell* (1974). Thus, there is a difference between administrative segregation, where no hearing is required, and punitive segregation, where it is.

Hiibel v. Sixth Judicial Dist. Court of Nev., Humboldt Cty., 542 U.S. ___, ___S.Ct.___ (2004) [Larry D. HIIBEL, Petitioner, v. SIXTH JUDICIAL COURT OF NEVADA, HUMBOLDT COUNTY, et al.] (Fifth Amendment; Fourth Amendment; Self-Incrimination) Sheriff's department officers received a call reporting an assault in a small Nevada community. They went to the scene and discovered a red truck. A man was standing by the truck and a woman was seated inside it. Sheriff's deputies approached the man and asked him to identify himself and to produce a driver's license. The man, who appeared to be intoxicated, refused their request. The officers asked the man his name at least 11 times, and he refused to answer. Subsequently the man was arrested and charged with willfully resisting, delaying, or obstructing a public officer in discharging the legal duties of his office. The man was subsequently identified as Larry D. Hiibel, tried in a Justice Court of Union Township, convicted, and fined $250. Hiibel appealed, alleging violations of his Fourth and Fifth Amendment rights. The Nevada Supreme Court rejected his appeal and Hiibel sought relief with the SC, who heard the case. Because of the nature of the original report of an assault, the sheriff's deputies had reasonable suspicion to approach Hiibel and request identification from him. This satisfied the

Fourth Amendment requirement concerning the reasonableness of their investigation and request. The SC declared that it is an essential part of police investigations to ask persons for identification in the ordinary course of doing their jobs. The SC also held that Hiibel's Fifth Amendment right against self-incrimination was not violated because of the sheriff's deputies' asking for identification. In order to qualify as a Fifth Amendment violation, Hiibel's statements to police must be either testimonial, or incriminating, or compelled. The Nevada statute in question merely requires of persons to provide officers with their names. The SC declared that in this case, Hiibel's refusal to disclose his name was not based on any articulated real and appreciable fear that his name would be used to incriminate him, or that it would furnish a link in the chain of evidence needed to prosecute him. The significance of this case is that persons must identify themselves to law enforcement officers when asked to do so in the normal course of discharging their responsibilities as public officers. The SC declined to rule on the matter that might arise where there is a substantial allegation and furnishing one's identity at the time of a stop would give police a link in the chain of evidence needed to convict the person of a separate offense.

Hildwin v. Florida, 490 U.S. 638, 109 S.Ct. 2055 (1989) [**Paul C. HILDWIN, Petitioner v. FLORIDA**] (**Aggravating and Mitigating Circumstances; Death Penalty; Sixth Amendment**) Hildwin was convicted of first-degree murder. During the penalty phase of Hildwin's trial, the jury recommended the death penalty, citing four specific aggravating factors and no mitigating ones. Hildwin appealed the death sentence, contending that Florida's capital-sentencing scheme is unconstitutional because it permits the imposition of death without a specific finding by the jury that sufficient aggravating circumstances exist to merit it. The conviction and death sentence were upheld by the SC, which declared that Hildwin's rights had not been violated. The SC said that findings made by a judge rather than a jury did not violate the Sixth Amendment because there is no Sixth Amendment right to jury sentencing, even where the sentence turns on specific findings of fact.

Hill v. California, 401 U.S. 797, 91 S.Ct. 1106 (1971) [**Archie William HILL, Jr., Petitioner, v. State of CALIFORNIA**] (**Confessions; Exclusionary Rule; Law Enforcement Officers or Agencies; Searches and Seizures; Searches Incident to an Arrest**) Police in Los Angeles County arrested two men for narcotics possession. A search of the car in which they were driving disclosed incriminating evidence linking the men with an armed robbery and kidnapping that had occurred a few days earlier. The police obtained confessions from the two men implicating Hill, the owner of the car. On the basis of probable cause alone, the police went to Hill's apartment to arrest him, but they did not have an arrest or search warrant. A person answered the door who matched Hill's description but was not Hill and denied that he was. The police arrested him anyway, thinking he was Hill, and conducted a warrantless search of his apartment. They found guns, some stolen property, and some pages of Hill's diary, which contained incrimi-

nating information. The prosecutor used this seized evidence incident to an arrest to prosecute and convict the real Hill. Hill appealed, saying that the warrantless search of his apartment was not valid because the person in it was not the person police thought he was. Therefore, the wrong person had been arrested and this fact should have nullified any incriminating evidence later found by police. The SC heard Hill's appeal and upheld his conviction, using the good-faith exception to the exclusionary rule. Thus, the SC said, the police were entitled to do whatever the law would allow them to do, even under circumstances in which they had the wrong arrestee in custody. The SC upheld their subsequent search incident to lawful arrest based on probable cause to be valid and reasonable.

Hitchcock v. Dugger, 481 U.S. 279, 107 S.Ct. 1821 (1987) [**James Ernest HITCHCOCK, Petitioner, v. Richard L. DUGGER, Secretary, Florida Department of Corrections**] (**Aggravating and Mitigating Circumstances; Death Penalty; Eighth Amendment; Juries**) Hitchcock was convicted of capital murder in Florida. During the sentencing phase of his trial, the judge advised the jury on aggravating and mitigating circumstances, saying that certain nonstatutory mitigating circumstances "had no place" in the proceeding. Thus, the judge obligated jurors to disregard any nonstatutory mitigating factors when considering whether Hitchcock should receive the death penalty. They decided that he should. He appealed, arguing this point as violative of his Eighth Amendment right against cruel and unusual punishment. The SC vacated his sentence, holding that Hitchcock had been sentenced to death in proceedings that did not comport with the requirement that the sentencer may neither refuse to consider nor be precluded from considering any relevant mitigating evidence. Thus juries may consider nonstatutory mitigating factors when deciding to impose the death penalty in capital cases.

Hobby v. United States, 468 U.S. 339, 104 S.Ct. 3093 (1984) [**Wilbur HOBBY, Petitioner, v. UNITED STATES**] (**Discrimination; Grand Juries**) Hobby was charged with federal fraud charges in North Carolina. Prior to his trial, he was indicted by a grand jury. He moved to dismiss the indictment, alleging racial discrimination in the selection of the jury foreman. The motion was rejected and he was convicted. He again sought to overturn his conviction by claiming the grand-jury foreman had been selected on racially discriminatory grounds. Hobby, a white man, made a general allegation that none of the 15 grand juries convened in North Carolina in the past seven years had had black or female foremen, and that only six grand-jury members had been women. The SC observed that although discrimination is prohibited by law, there was insufficient evidence to support the idea that the grand jury in Hobby's indictment showed a purposeful discrimination pattern in regard to race or gender. Further, the SC declared, any discrimination evident in the grand jury had nothing whatever to do with his conviction in the fair trial that followed. Thus there was nothing presented by Hobby as evidence as to why his conviction should be overturned or his indictment dismissed.

Hoffa v. United States, 335 U.S. 293, 87 S.Ct. 408 (1966) [James R. HOFFA, Petitioner, v. UNITED STATES. Thomas Ewing Parks, Petitioner, v. United States. Larry Campbell, Petitioner, v. United States. Ewing King, Petitioner, v. United States] (Fourth Amendment; Right to Counsel) Hoffa was suspected of jury tampering when it was alleged that he attempted to bribe jurors. One of his close friends, Partin, who was a government informant, agreed to ask him incriminating questions at the request of FBI agents. Based in part on the testimony given by Partin, Hoffa was convicted. He appealed, alleging that his right to confidentiality under the Fourth Amendment had been violated. The SC upheld Hoffa's conviction, saying that he had had no reasonable expectation of privacy when he voluntarily confided his wrongdoing to a friend.

Holbrook v. Flynn, 475 U.S. 560, 106 S.Ct. 1340 (1986) [Terrance HOLBROOK, Superintendent, Massachusetts Correctional Institution, Norfolk, Massachusetts, et al., Petitioners, v. Charles FLYNN] (Prosecutorial Misconduct; Sixth Amendment) Flynn was indicted for armed robbery in Rhode Island and held without bail. Later in court, four uniformed state troopers were positioned behind him as a customary security force. He was convicted. Flynn appealed, alleging that the presence of the officers sitting behind him had prejudiced the jury, and thus his Sixth Amendment fair trial rights had been violated. Following a reversal of his conviction by a lower appellate court, the SC heard the case and reinstated Flynn's robbery conviction, holding that he had failed to show that the officers' presence in court prejudiced his case to the extent that his fair trial rights had been violated. The SC expressed serious doubts that the mere presence of these officers in court had posed an unacceptable threat to Flynn's right to a fair trial or that the jurors had regarded their presence as inherently prejudicial.

Holloway v. Arkansas, 435 U.S. 475, 98 S.Ct. 1173 (1978) [Winston M. HOLLOWAY et al., Petitioners, v. State of ARKANSAS] (Right to Counsel; Sixth Amendment) Holloway was accused of robbery with the use of a firearm and rape. Before his trial, he and several codefendants were being represented by the same counsel. Motions were made for appointment of separate counsel for each man because of confidential information one might give against another. The judge denied these motions, and Holloway was subsequently convicted. Holloway appealed on the grounds that he had been denied effective assistance of counsel and that the judge's ruling had created an unfair trial situation. The SC reversed Holloway's conviction and chided the judge for not having granted defense motions for separate attorney representation. The SC said that whenever judges improperly require joint representation of several defendants over a timely objection, reversal of the conviction is automatic. Thus, the SC declared, Holloway's case was unfairly prejudiced because the same counsel represented codefendants with conflicting interests.

Holloway v. United States, 526 U.S. 1, 119 S.Ct. 966 (1999) [Francois HOLLOWAY, aka Abdu Ali, Petitioner, v. UNITED STATES] (*Mens Rea*) Holloway was convicted in federal court of carjacking, defined as taking a motor vehicle from another by force and violence or by intimidation with the intent to cause death or serious bodily harm. Holloway appealed his conviction, alleging that he did not have the *mens rea* or criminal intent "to cause death or serious bodily harm" to satisfy a portion of the carjacking statute, and thus, the conviction should be set aside. Holloway's accomplice testified, however, that Holloway said he would have used his gun if any of his victims had given him a "hard time." The SC upheld Holloway's carjacking conviction, holding that the "with intent to cause death or serious bodily harm" phrase does not require the government to prove that Holloway had an unconditional intent to kill or harm in all events, but merely requires proof of an intent to kill or harm if necessary to effect a carjacking.

Hope v. Pelzer, ___U.S.___, 122 S.Ct. 2508 (2002) [Larry HOPE, Petitioner, v. Mark PELZER et al.] (Civil Rights, Section 1983 Claims; Cruel and Unusual Punishment; Eighth Amendment; Immunity; Inmate Rights) Hope was an Alabama prison inmate. In 1995, he was handcuffed twice to a hitching post for disruptive conduct. During one seven-hour period, he was given one or two water breaks but no bathroom breaks. A guard taunted him about his thirst. He was ordered to remove his shirt in the hot sun. Subsequently, Hope filed a civil rights claim in U.S. district court under Title 42, Section 1983 of the U.S. Code, alleging violations of his Eighth Amendment right against cruel and unusual punishment. The district court ruled against Hope and granted summary judgment for the guards on the ground of qualified immunity, and the Eleventh Circuit affirmed. Hope appealed next to the SC, who heard the case. The SC reversed, holding that Hope was subjected to cruel and unusual punishment in violation of the Eighth Amendment when prison guards handcuffed him to a hitching post for disruptive behavior, despite his already having been subdued. Furthermore, for purposes of qualified immunity, prison guards can still be on notice that their conduct violates established law even in novel factual circumstances. Also, Alabama prison guards are not entitled to qualified immunity on Hope's claim, particularly as the Alabama Department of Corrections was on notice from the U.S. Department of Justice that its hitching post punishment was unconstitutional and thus prohibited.

Horton v. California, 496 U.S. 128, 110 S.Ct. 2301 (1990) [Terry Brice HORTON, Petitioner, v. CALIFORNIA] (Exclusionary Rule; Law Enforcement Officers or Agencies; Plain-View Rule; Searches and Seizures) A suspect in an armed robbery, Horton, was visited by police armed with a valid search warrant, specifically authorizing them to look only for stolen property, not the weapons used in the robbery. No stolen property was found. However, the police discovered some weapons that were in plain view, and an officer seized them, correctly believing them to be the weapons used in the robbery. Horton was convicted. He appealed, contending that the weapons should have been excluded in the case against him, because the warrant had not specified them to be seized. The SC disagreed and said that an inadvertent discovery of incriminating evidence in plain view does not result in the exclusion of this evidence from trial later. Ordinarily, in plain-view cases as exceptions to the exclusionary rule, discovery by police of illegal contraband has to be "accidental." In the *Horton* case, however, the officers knew that they *might* find other incriminating evidence, such as weapons, even though weapons were not listed in the search warrant. The *Horton* case eliminated the "accidental" requirement for seizures of evidence in plain view known by police to be incriminating evidence for criminal suspects.

Houchins v. KQED, Inc., 438 U.S. 1, 98 S.Ct. 2588 (1978) [**Thomas L. HOUCHINS, Sheriff of the County of Alameda, California, Petitioner, v. KQED, INC., et al.**] (**Corrections; First Amendment; Inmate Rights; Media Rights**) A television station, KQED, reported the suicide of a jail inmate. Interviews were conducted with the sheriff and with a psychiatrist who was on call with the jail. KQED wanted a more extensive tour of the facility but was refused. However, the sheriff instituted a systematic tour of the jail for interested citizens, including the media. KQED was dissatisfied with this short tour and wanted a more extensive one. Sheriff Houchins denied this request, so KQED filed suit against him, alleging that he had violated the First Amendment rights of KQED by not granting it a more extensive tour of the jail. The SC upheld Houchins' decision and held that his policy had not violated the First Amendment rights of the media. (*See Saxbe v. Washington Post Co.* [1974] *and Pell v. Procunier* [1974] *for similar rulings on similar issues.*)

Hubbard v. United States, 514 U.S. 695, 115 S.Ct. 1754 (1995) [**John Bruce HUBBARD, Petitioner, v. UNITED STATES**] (**Jurisdiction**) Hubbard filed for bankruptcy in 1985. He gave various false statements in oral and written responses to the bankruptcy court. Later, when his false statements were disclosed, he was charged with violating a federal law prohibiting false statements made to any department or agency of the United States knowingly and willfully. Hubbard was convicted under the statute. He appealed. The SC overturned his conviction regarding false statements made, holding that such false statements do not pertain to judicial proceedings, such as bankruptcy courts. This was a technical interpretation and should not be taken to mean that defendants may routinely commit perjury during trial proceedings. Rather, this specific statute, Title 18 U.S.C. Section 1001, does not apply to judicial proceedings. The United States attorney should have sought other charges falling under more appropriate criminal statutes of Title 18.

Hudson v. Louisiana, 450 U.S. 40, 101 S.Ct. 970 (1981) [**Tracy Lee HUDSON, Petitioner, v. State of LOUISIANA**] (**Double Jeopardy; Fifth Amendment**) Hudson was convicted of first-degree murder. He filed a motion for a new trial with the original trial judge, who granted it, declaring that "the evidence presented by the prosecution in the first trial was legally insufficient to support the guilty verdict." Thus, a second trial was ordered. Hudson appealed, however, arguing that this would be double jeopardy. The SC agreed, stating that the double-jeopardy clause of the Fifth Amendment precludes a second trial once the reviewing court has found that

the evidence in the first trial was legally insufficient to support a guilty verdict. Hudson was therefore freed.

Hudson v. McMillian, 503 U.S. 1, 112 S.Ct. 995 (1992) [**Keith J. HUDSON, Petitioner, v. Jack McMILLIAN et al.**] (**Civil Rights, Section 1983 Claims; Corrections; Cruel and Unusual Punishment; Inmate Rights**) Hudson, a prison inmate in Louisiana, was beaten by two correctional officers as he was being transported between units on the penitentiary grounds. He suffered minor injuries and filed suit against the officers under Title 42 U.S.C. Section 1983. The trial court awarded Hudson damages, but a higher court reversed the trial court, ruling in favor of the officers by saying that the minor injuries to Hudson were not sufficient to constitute cruel and unusual punishment. The SC disagreed, saying that the excessive force used by the correctional officers had indeed been cruel and unusual punishment, even though only minor injuries to the prisoner had been sustained.

Hudson v. Palmer, 468 U.S. 517, 104 S.Ct. 3194 (1984) [**Ted S. HUDSON, Petitioner, v. Russell Thomas PALMER, Jr. Russell Thomas Palmer, Jr., Petitioner, v. Ted S. Hudson**] (**Corrections; Fourth Amendment; Searches and Seizures**) Palmer was an inmate at Bland Correctional Center in Virginia, serving sentences for forgery and bank robbery. During a cell shakedown, in which officers searched his cell, they discovered a torn pillow. They broke a few of Palmer's personal effects in the process of their search. Palmer sued the officers, alleging his Fourth Amendment right against an illegal search and seizure had been violated. He claimed that the officers needed probable cause and a search warrant to enter his cell and search it. The SC disagreed, saying that prisoners have no reasonable expectation of privacy; further, correctional officers do not need probable cause or a warrant to search inmate cells from time to time for illegal contraband. If personal items are broken, intentionally or unintentionally, this is not a violation of the inmate's due-process rights in violation of the Fourteenth Amendment.

Hudson v. United States, 522 U.S. 93, 118 S.Ct. 488 (1997) [**John HUDSON, Larry Baresel, and Jack Butler Rackley, Petitioners, v. UNITED STATES**] (**Double Jeopardy; Fifth Amendment**) Hudson and others were bank officers who were indicted for misapplication of bank funds. Previously, they had been subjected to civil sanctions, including monetary penalties and occupational debarment by the Office of Controller of Currency (OCC). Hudson appealed, contending that a prosecution for misapplication of bank funds would constitute double jeopardy in violation of his Fifth Amendment rights, as he had already been monetarily penalized and occupationally debarred. The SC heard his appeal and held that the double-jeopardy clause of the Fifth Amendment does not prohibit additional sanctions that are punishments *per se;* rather, it protects offenders against impositions of multiple criminal punishments for the same offense. The occupational debarment and monetary penalties were not criminal punishments, and thus, double jeopardy was not applicable in the present case.

Hughes v. Rowe, 449 U.S. 5, 101 S.Ct. 173 (1980) [**Russell B. HUGHES, Jr., Petitioner, v. Charles J. ROWE et al.**]

(Civil Rights, Section 1983 Claims; Corrections; Inmate Rights) Hughes was a prisoner in Illinois. He allegedly consumed some alcohol made on prison grounds in violation of prison regulations. Without a hearing in the matter or any emergency conditions, he was placed in isolation for 10 days, and he lost 30 days of statutory "good-time" credit. Hughes filed a Title 42 U.S.C. Section 1983 civil rights suit, alleging that his constitutional rights had been violated and that he had never been given a hearing before being penalized. Lawyers representing the attorney general for the State of Illinois were awarded $400 in counsel fees and Hughes was ordered to pay them. He appealed. The SC said that (1) no emergency conditions had existed to justify Hughes' isolation; (2) no hearing had been held; and (3) the assignment of $400 in fees was improper. Officials must give prisoners a hearing before administering punishments of any kind, barring any emergency conditions that might exist. In this case, administrators, as well as the district court judge, had acted improperly assessing counsel costs to Hughes.

Hurtado v. California, 110 U.S. 516, 4 S.Ct. 111 (1884) [Joseph HURTADO, Petitioner, v. People of the State of CALIFORNIA] (Death Penalty; Grand Juries) In 1879, California dropped the grand-jury system, replacing it with broad prosecutorial discretionary powers, such as filing information against minor offenders and felons. In 1884, absent an indictment, Hurtado was charged with murder through a piece of criminal information, convicted, and sentenced to death. He appealed. The SC upheld the death sentence, holding that the grand jury is merely a procedure that the states can abolish at will. The significance of this case is that grand juries are not required for death-penalty cases to be conducted in state courts.

Husty v. United States, 282 U.S. 694, 51 S.Ct. 240 (1931) [Richard HUSTY, Petitioner, v. UNITED STATES] (Law Enforcement Officers or Agencies; Stop and Frisk; Vehicle Searches) Husty was a known bootlegger of illegal whiskey. His automobile was searched without warrant by federal officers who knew Husty and his reputation. Incriminating evidence was seized and Husty was convicted. His sentence greatly exceeded the actual statutory sentence for the offense. Husty appealed, and the SC overturned his conviction and sentence, because the maximum sentence for the offense was exceeded by the sentence actually imposed. Nevertheless, the search of Husty's automobile was ruled reasonable under the circumstances, because a reliable informant had given police an accurate description of where the car would be parked and what it would contain. Essentially, the SC said that officers may search a vehicle for illegal liquor, if on probable cause, without a previous arrest, and if facts coming to their attention would lead a reasonably prudent man to believe that liquor was illegally possessed therein.

Hutto v. Davis, 454 U.S. 370, 102 S.Ct. 703 (1982) [Terrell Don HUTTO, Director, Virginia State Department of Corrections, et al. v. Roger Trenton DAVIS] (Corrections; Cruel and Unusual Punishment; *Habeas Corpus* Petitions; Inmate Rights) Davis was a Virginia inmate who had been sentenced to 40 years in prison and a $20,000 fine for a conviction for marijuana possession with intent to distribute. He sought *habeas corpus* relief, contending that the 40-year sentence was disproportionate to the crime and thus was cruel and unusual punishment. Ultimately, after considerable hearing and rehearing through the appellate process, the SC decided the matter by upholding Virginia authority to mandate sentences for crimes as they see fit without labeling such sentences "cruel and unusual." Davis' 40-year sentence had been legislatively mandated, and thus the SC believed that it would be improper to interfere with state legislative sanctions. Davis' sentence was therefore upheld.

Hutto v. Finney, 437 U.S. 678, 98 S.Ct. 2565 (1978) [Terrell Don HUTTO et al., Petitioners, v. Robert FINNEY et al.] (Corrections; Cruel and Unusual Punishment; Eighth Amendment) In 1970, the Arkansas prison system was declared unconstitutional on various grounds and its conditions of confinement cruel and unusual, in violation of the Eighth Amendment. Subsequently, a check by federal officials revealed that the reforms to be implemented had not been completed. The court issued additional orders for prison official compliance. These orders included (1) limiting the number of prisoners who could reasonably be confined in one cell, (2) discontinuing particular types of nonnutritious meals, (3) maximizing the days of solitary confinement as punishment at 30, and (4) obligating the state to pay for attorneys' fees and expenses. Hutto, the Arkansas commissioner of corrections, appealed, contending that the 30-day confinement standard was too lenient and that the court had wrongfully assigned attorneys' fees to the state. The SC upheld the lower court on the 30-day limitation on solitary confinement and the assessment of attorneys' fees against the state.

Hutto v. Ross, 429 U.S. 28, 97 S.Ct. 202 (1976) [Terrell Don HUTTO, Commissioner, Arkansas Department of Correction, v. Andrew Jackson ROSS] (Confessions; Fifth Amendment; Self-Incrimination; Sixth Amendment) Ross was charged in an Arkansas court with embezzlement. He entered into a plea-bargain agreement with prosecutors in which he would plead guilty in exchange for a 15-year sentence, with 10 years suspended. Before accepting the plea agreement, Ross was requested by prosecutors to make a statement confessing to the embezzlement, and Ross did so, after being advised by his attorney of his Fifth Amendment privilege against self-incrimination. Later, Ross withdrew from the plea bargain and demanded a jury trial, which he was granted. During the trial, the prosecutor admitted Ross' confession into evidence against him, and he was convicted. Ross appealed, contending that the confession "was a part of the plea bargain" and that as he had withdrawn from the plea bargain, the confession was thus inadmissible. The SC disagreed, holding that the existence of a plea bargain may well have entered into Ross' decision to give a confession, but Ross had been properly advised by his attorney of his Fifth Amendment right against self-incrimination. The plea agreement would be enforceable in any case, with or without Ross' confession. Thus, Ross confessed, and this confession was determined to be freely and voluntarily given, without any direct or implied promises or inducements or coercion from prosecutors. Ross' conviction stood.

I

Idaho v. Wright, 497 U.S. 805, 110 S.Ct. 3139 (1990) [IDAHO, Petitioner, v. Laura Lee WRIGHT] (Confrontation Clause; Fifth Amendment; Sixth Amendment) Wright was accused of lewd conduct with a minor. She and a boyfriend, Giles, had sodomized her two daughters, aged 5 and 2. Giles had sexual intercourse with both girls, while Wright held them down and covered their mouths. At Wright's trial, the older daughter testified directly. It had previously been stipulated that the younger daughter would not testify, as she was not "capable of communicating to the jury." Nevertheless, under an exception to the hearsay rule, the examining child-abuse specialist was able to relate what she had been told by the 2-year-old victim. Wright was convicted. She appealed later, maintaining that such hearsay was not admissible under the confrontation clause of the Fifth Amendment. A reliability requirement provided that hearsay should be supported by a showing of "particularized guarantees of trustworthiness." The Idaho Supreme Court overturned Wright's conviction and the case was appealed to the SC, which affirmed the Idaho decision. The SC determined that the statements given by the 2-year-old were not made under circumstances of reliability comparable to those required by law. The case was remanded for possible retrial.

Illinois v. Allen, 397 U.S. 337, 90 S.Ct. 1057 (1970) [State of ILLINOIS, Petitioner, v. William ALLEN] (Jury Trials; Right to Counsel; Sixth Amendment) Allen was charged with robbery. He waived his right to counsel and elected to represent himself. During the jury selection and trial, he was abusive and argued constantly with the trial judge until eventually he was ordered removed from the courtroom. The trial was held anyway and he was convicted. Later, Allen appealed to the SC, arguing that his Sixth Amendment right had been violated because he was not present at his own trial when convicted. The SC upheld his conviction, saying that repeated warnings to Allen from the judge had had no effect on his conduct, which was so disruptive as to prevent the jurors from properly considering the evidence. Thus, there was nothing unconstitutional about the judge's removing Allen from the courtroom.

Illinois v. Andreas, 463 U.S. 765, 103 S.Ct. 3319 (1983) [ILLINOIS, Petitioner, v. John ANDREAS] (Closed Container Searches; Fourth Amendment; Law Enforcement Officers or Agencies; Searches and Seizures) DEA agents in Illinois intercepted a large container from Calcutta and opened it. They found marijuana, resealed the container, and had it delivered to Andreas' home, where they placed the container under surveillance. Eventually, Andreas was seen with the container, and police moved in without a warrant. They seized it, arrested Andreas, and reopened the container, disclosing the marijuana. Andreas was convicted of possessing a controlled substance. He filed an appeal with the SC, arguing that his Fourth Amendment rights had been violated because police did not have a warrant when they reopened the container, which had been previously opened during a customs inspection. The SC upheld his conviction, saying that warrants to open containers are not needed if the containers have first been opened by customs agents according to their statutory duty and rights. The SC also said that there was no substantial likelihood that the contents of the container had changed during the brief period that it was out of the sight of a surveilling officer, and thus reopening the container did not intrude on any legitimate expectation of privacy and did not violate the Fourth Amendment rights of Andreas.

Illinois v. Condon, 507 U.S. 948, 113 S.Ct. 1359 (1993) [ILLINOIS, Petitioner, v. Timothy CONDON] (Fourth Amendment; Knock and Announce; Searches and Seizures) Condon was suspected of dealing in cocaine. An informant provided police in DuPage County with sufficient information to obtain a warrant to search Condon's home. One evening, a team of police officers stormed Condon's home without knocking or announcing their presence and found a large quantity of cocaine, marijuana, and several weapons. At a later trial, Condon was convicted. He appealed, alleging that police had not knocked and first announced their intentions before conducting the search. Police countered that their unannounced entry and search were caused by exigent circumstances. Condon's conviction was overturned by the Illinois Supreme Court, which held that the unannounced entry had not been prompted by exigent circumstances and conflicted with the protocol to be followed in such instances of searches and seizures. The Illinois prosecutor appealed the ruling to the SC. The SC declined to hear Illinois' appeal in this ruling. However, some dissenting SC members suggested that because of the present conflict among the states about search-and-seizure protocol, the SC should hear the case and resolve the conflict.

Illinois v. Fisher, ___U.S.___, 124 S.Ct. 1200 (2004) [ILLINOIS, Petitioner, v. Gregory FISHER] (Discovery; Due Process; Evidence Preservation) Gregory Fisher was arrested for and charged with cocaine possession following a routine traffic stop by police officers in Chicago, IL, in September 1988. In October 1988, Fisher filed a motion for discovery, requesting all physical evidence seized by police officers when he was arrested. Prosecutors stated that all evidence would be made available to Fisher at a reasonable date and time upon request and a trial date was set for July 1989. When the trial date occurred, it was discovered that Fisher had fled the jurisdiction, ultimately residing in Tennessee for the next 11 years. An outstanding arrest warrant for Fisher was subsequently executed in September 1999, and Chicago authorities reinstated the 1988 cocaine charges. Fisher renewed his demand to have access to the original evidence seized, but the prosecutor stated that according to established procedures, the substance seized from him had been destroyed after several years of preservation. Fisher moved to have the charges against him dismissed, as the evidence against him no longer existed. The trial court denied his motion and Fisher was convicted by a jury for cocaine possession, based in large part upon police testimony and the admission of four laboratory tests that confirmed the substance seized at the time of Fisher's 1988 arrest was cocaine.

Fisher was sentenced to one year in prison. Fisher appealed, alleging a violation of his right to due process, since the substance he was accused of possessing had been destroyed by police years earlier, and thus they had framed him for the crime. The appellate court reversed Fisher's conviction, holding that the due-process clause required the dismissal of the original charge in the absence of incriminating evidence. The government appealed and the SC heard the case. The SC reversed the Illinois Appellate Court, holding that due process did not require dismissal of cocaine possession charges on the ground that police, nearly 11 years after Fisher was charged, destroyed the cocaine seized. The SC held that unless a criminal defendant can show bad faith on the part of police, their failure to preserve potentially useful evidence does not constitute a denial of due process of law. Fisher failed to demonstrate bad faith on the part of police; thus, his claim of a violation of his due-process rights was dismissed. There is nothing in the record to indicate that the alleged cocaine was destroyed in bad faith.

Illinois v. Gates, 462 U.S. 213, 103 S.Ct. 2317 (1983) [ILLINOIS, Petitioner, v. Lance GATES et ux.] (**Fourth Amendment; Informants; Searches and Seizures**) Based on an anonymous letter received by police officers, a couple, Lance and Sue Gates, of Bloomingdale, was accused of selling drugs. A fairly detailed description of the Gateses' activities was contained in the letter. Police placed the Gateses under surveillance, and everything described in the letter was observed to occur. The Gateses were moving large quantities of drugs between Florida and Illinois by automobile and air. The police obtained a search warrant from a judge and searched the Gates home, discovering large quantities of drugs. The Gateses were convicted. They appealed to the SC, arguing that the reliability of the informant could not be determined; thus, no basis existed to support the search warrant leading to the drug discovery. The Gateses moved to suppress all drugs found as the result of this allegedly faulty search. The landmark decision in this case was that the totality of circumstances, not informant reliability (previously used in *Aguilar v. Texas* [1964]), justified the search warrant issued. Thus it is now easier for police to obtain search warrants when they allege that a totality of circumstances suggests a crime is or has been committed and specific suspects have been named.

Illinois v. Krull, 480 U.S. 340, 107 S.Ct. 1160 (1987) [ILLINOIS, Petitioner, v. Albert KRULL, George Lucas, and Salvatore Mucerino] (**Exclusionary Rule; Searches and Seizures**) Officers conducted a good-faith, warrantless search of an automobile in an auto-wrecking yard. The Illinois statute permitting such a search was unconstitutional, although the officers did not know that and were acting in good faith. The incriminating evidence obtained from the search was admissible in court, however, because of the good-faith conduct of the officers.

Illinois v. Lafayette, 462 U.S. 640, 103 S.Ct. 2605 (1982) [ILLINOIS, Petitioner, v. Ralph LAFAYETTE] (**Booking; Law Enforcement Officers or Agencies; Searches Incident to Arrest**) Lafayette was arrested for disturbing the peace. While being booked at the local jail, he was searched along with his personal effects. His shoulder bag contained drugs in violation of the Illinois Controlled Substances Act. Lafayette was convicted. He moved to suppress the drugs because they had been the subject of a warrantless search. The SC upheld Lafayette's conviction, contending that it is perfectly reasonable to search an arrestee's personal effects if he or she is under arrest based on probable cause. Further, the SC stressed the fact that it was administrative procedure for the jail to scan clothing and other personal possessions of arrestees to ensure that illegal contraband does not enter the inner jail facilities to become available to other inmates. Discoveries of illegal drugs during such searches are only incidental to these administrative searches.

Illinois v. Lidster, ___U.S.___, 124 S.Ct. 885 (2004) [ILLINOIS, Petitioner, v. Robert S. LIDSTER] (**Fourth Amendment; Searches and Seizures; Sobriety Checkpoints**) In late August 1997, Lombard, IL, police officers set up a highway checkpoint shortly after midnight. A week before, a 70-year-old bicyclist had been killed at about the same time at night on that highway in the same location by a hit-and-run driver who eluded police. Police cars with flashing lights blocked the eastbound lanes of the highway, leading to long lines of vehicles. As each vehicle approached the checkpoint, police stopped it for 10 to 15 seconds, gave the driver a flyer that said "ALERT . . . FATAL HIT-AND-RUN ACCIDENT," and requested the driver's assistance in locating the vehicle and driver in the fatal incident. When Robert Lidster drove his minivan toward the checkpoint, he swerved, nearly striking a police officer. Officers detected the odor of alcohol on Lidster's breath, and he was directed to a side street where other officers subjected him to a sobriety test. He was arrested, charged with DWI, and convicted. Lidster appealed, claiming that the highway checkpoint violated his Fourth Amendment right against unreasonable searches and seizures and that much of the government's evidence against him was the result of the illegal checkpoint stop. The Illinois Supreme Court heard the case and reversed Lidster's conviction. The government appealed and the SC heard the case. The SC reversed the Illinois Supreme Court and reinstated Lidster's conviction, holding that highway checkpoints where police officers stop motorists and ask them for information about recent hit-and-run accidents are reasonable and therefore constitutional. The checkpoint stop here differs significantly from that in *City of Indianapolis v. Edmond* (2000). The stop's primary law enforcement purpose was not to determine whether a vehicle's occupants were committing a crime, but to ask vehicle occupants, as members of the public, for their help in providing information about a crime in all likelihood committed by others. The police expected the information elicited to help them apprehend not the vehicle's occupants, but other individuals.

Illinois v. McArthur, 531 U.S. 326, 121 S.Ct. 946 (2001) [ILLINOIS, Petitioner, v. Charles McARTHUR] (**Fourth Amendment; Searches and Seizures**) In April 1997, Tera McArthur asked two police officers to accompany her to the trailer of Charles McArthur so that they could keep the peace while she removed her belongings from the premises. After she had collected her personal effects, she left and suggested to the officers that they should "check the trailer" because "Chuck had dope in there," and that she had seen him slide it under the couch. The officers knocked on the door and Charles McArthur answered. The officers requested permission to search the trailer but McArthur refused. By this time, McArthur, who was on the porch, turned to reenter the trailer but was prevented from doing so by one of the officers. The other officer left to obtain a search warrant. Later, when the search warrant was issued, the officers searched the trailer and discovered marijuana and a marijuana pipe. McArthur was arrested and subsequently charged with possessing marijuana and drug paraphernalia. McArthur moved to suppress this evidence because, he argued, the drugs were the fruit of an unlawful police seizure and that he had been prevented from reentering his own dwelling, which would have permitted him to destroy the marijuana. The trial court granted his motion and the government appealed. The Illinois Supreme Court denied the state's appeal and the SC was petitioned to hear the case. The SC reversed the Illinois Supreme Court, holding that the officers acted reasonably and did not violate the Fourth Amendment requirements. The SC reasoned that the officers were entitled to exercise reasonable means at their disposal to preserve any evidence of a jailable offense, and that the officers' refusal to allow McArthur the privilege of reentering his trailer was only minimally intrusive. The officers had probable cause to believe that the home contained contraband that was evidence of a crime. They imposed a restraint that was limited and tailored reasonably to secure law enforcement needs while protecting privacy interests.

Illinois v. Perkins, 496 U.S. 292, 110 S.Ct. 2394 (1990) [ILLINOIS, Petitioner, v. Lloyd PERKINS] (Custodial Interrogations; Informants; *Miranda* Warning) Perkins was being held in jail on an aggravated battery charge. An undercover officer entered the cell, pretending to be another arrestee. Soon Perkins gave him voluntary statements about an unrelated crime, a murder, and the statements were used later to obtain a murder conviction against Perkins. Perkins appealed, contending that the officer should have told him his *Miranda* rights before interrogating him. The SC said that *Miranda* warnings are not required whenever suspects give voluntary statements to persons they do not believe are law enforcement officers.

Illinois v. Rodriguez, 497 U.S. 177, 110 S.Ct. 2793 (1990) [ILLINOIS, Petitioner, v. Edward RODRIGUEZ] (Consent Searches; Law Enforcement Officers or Agencies; Plain-View Rule) A woman, Fischer, called police and reported that she had been beaten by her boyfriend, Rodriguez, who was living elsewhere. The police went with Fischer to Rodriguez's apartment. She allowed them entry, as she lived there with Rodriguez and had a key. Indeed, her clothes, furniture, and other personal effects were in the apartment as proof of her statements. When police entered, they saw in plain view containers of cocaine and drug paraphernalia and arrested Rodriguez. The seized evidence was used against him and he was convicted. He appealed, contending that Fischer had moved out weeks before she and the police came to his apartment, and that she did not have the right to permit police entry. In fact, Fischer had moved out. Nevertheless, the police were acting in

good faith that she did, indeed, have the authority to admit them. Thus, the court upheld Rodriguez's conviction, saying that a warrantless entry and search based on the consent of someone they believed to possess common authority over the premises was valid, even if the person actually lacked that authority.

Illinois v. Sommerville, 410 U.S. 458, 93 S.Ct. 1066 (1973) [State of ILLINOIS, Petitioner, v. Donald SOMMERVILLE] (Double Jeopardy; Fifth Amendment) Sommerville was tried for a crime. During the trial, a mistrial was declared and the original indictment was ruled defective. A new trial was scheduled and Sommerville appealed, contending that it represented double jeopardy in violation of his Fifth Amendment rights. The SC disagreed, saying that the first trial was never completed, and that therefore, double jeopardy was not an issue. The significance of this case is that it legitimizes mistrials of defendants and does not place them in double jeopardy.

Illinois v. Vitale, 447 U.S. 410, 100 S.Ct. 2260 (1980) [State of ILLINOIS, Petitioner, v. John M. VITALE] (Double Jeopardy) Vitale, driving his car, was convicted of "failing to reduce speed," resulting in the death of two children. Later, he was charged with involuntary manslaughter under a different Illinois statute. He sought to dismiss this charge on double-jeopardy grounds, as "failing to reduce speed" was an essential element of the manslaughter offense. The Illinois Supreme Court dismissed the charge, but prosecutors appealed to the SC. Vitale's case was remanded to the originating trial court in order to determine whether "failing to reduce one's speed" was an essential element of the manslaughter offense. If it was essential, then double jeopardy would attach and Vitale could not be prosecuted for manslaughter. This decision relied on the *Blockburger* test (*see Blockburger v. United States* [1932]), which said that the second of two successive prosecutions would be barred if the prosecution sought to establish an essential element of the second crime by proving the conduct for which the defendant had been convicted in the first prosecution.

Imbler v. Pachtman, 424 U.S. 409, 96 S.Ct. 984 (1976) [Paul Kern IMBLER, Petitioner, v. Richard PACHTMAN, District Attorney] (Civil Rights, Section 1983 Claims; *Habeas Corpus* Petitions; Immunity) Imbler was convicted of murder. He subsequently filed for *habeas corpus* relief, alleging that the prosecutor had suppressed material evidence at his earlier trial and that he had been unlawfully prosecuted as a result. Further, he filed a civil suit under Title 42 U.S.C. Section 1983, alleging his civil rights had been violated. The SC upheld his conviction, stating that the state prosecuting attorney had been acting within the scope of his authority and duties in initiating and pursuing a criminal prosecution. The prosecutor had not violated Imbler's constitutional rights and possessed absolute immunity from suits from Imbler.

Immigration and Naturalization Service v. St. Cyr, 533 U.S. 289, 121 S.Ct. 2271 (2001) [IMMIGRATION AND NATURALIZATION SERVICE, Petitioner, v. Enrico ST. CYR] (Deportation) St. Cyr was a permanent resident alien who was ordered deported by the Board of Immigration Appeals (BIA) after he pleaded guilty to an aggravated felony. St. Cyr filed a *habeas corpus* petition for relief from deportation in a federal district court. The basis of his appeal was that he entered into a plea-bargain agreement to plead guilty to a felony prior to the enactment of the Antiterrorism and Effective Death Penalty Act (AEDPA) and the Illegal Immigration Reform and Immigrant Responsibility Act (IIRIRA), and that these acts do not apply retroactively to aliens convicted of felonies. The federal district court granted the petition and ruled that the repeal of discretionary relief from deportation did not apply retroactively to aliens. The INS appealed, and the court of appeals affirmed. The INS further appealed to the SC, who heard the case. The SC upheld the previous rulings, holding that the AEDPA and IIRIRA, which repealed discretionary relief from deportation, did not apply retroactively to aliens who pleaded guilty to one or more felonies prior to the statutes' enactment.

Ingraham v. Wright, 430 U.S. 651, 97 S.Ct. 1401 (1977) [**James INGRAHAM, by his mother and next friend, Eloise Ingraham, et al., Petitioners, v. Willie J. WRIGHT I et al.**] (**Corrections; Cruel and Unusual Punishment; Eighth Amendment; Inmate Rights**) In January 1971 Ingraham and another junior high school student filed a complaint against the Drew Junior High School in Dade County, FL. They complained that "paddling" youths as a punishment was cruel and unusual and violative of their Eighth Amendment rights. The SC determined that the cruel-and-unusual-punishment clause of the Eighth Amendment does not apply to school discipline, whatever its form.

In re Blodgett, 502 U.S. 236, 112 S.Ct. 674 (1992) [**In re James BLODGETT, Superintendent, Washington State Penitentiary, et al.**] (**Death Penalty; Eighth Amendment**) Campbell was convicted of multiple murders and sentenced to death in the State of Washington. Numerous motions and appeals were filed to delay his execution while various issues were decided. The State of Washington filed a petition for a writ of *mandamus* (requiring officials to carry out the execution order) but did not file any appeals regarding a court of appeals order staying Blodgett's execution. Blodgett filed a motion to proceed *in forma pauperis.* The SC denied the writ of *mandamus,* holding that a *mandamus* to the court of appeals from Washington would not issue, where Washington had failed to file any objection to the court of appeals stay of execution order or to vacate or modify its order. Campbell's execution was thus stayed while he continued litigating various issues relative to his conviction and sentence.

In re Gault, 387 U.S. 1, 87 S.Ct. 1428 (1967) [**Application of Paul L. GAULT and Marjorie Gault, Father and Mother of Gerald Francis Gault, a Minor, Appellants**] (**Juvenile Law; Right to Counsel; Self-Incrimination**) Gault was a 15-year-old in Arizona who, with another boy, allegedly made an obscene telephone call to an adult neighbor, Mrs. Cook. Police arrested Gault and took him to jail for questioning. In several subsequent one-sided juvenile court proceedings, Gault was not permitted to cross-examine his accuser or to testify in his own behalf. He was not initially permitted counsel or advised of his rights. Later, the juvenile court judge

adjudicated his case and confined him in the Arizona State Industrial School until he reached age 21. He appealed, and the SC reversed the decision. This landmark case established a juvenile's right to have counsel, to confront and cross-examine accusers, to have protection from self-incrimination, and to have adequate notice of charges when there is the possibility of confinement as a punishment.

In re Kemmler, 136 U.S. 436, 10 S.Ct. 930 (1890) [**In re William KEMMLER**] (**Cruel and Unusual Punishment; Death Penalty; Eighth Amendment**) The SC declared that the use of the electric chair for administering the death penalty is not cruel and unusual punishment.

In re Sindram, 498 U.S. 177, 111 S.Ct. 596 (1991) [**In re Michael SINDRAM**] (**Corrections; Frivolous Lawsuits; Indigent Clients**) Sindram was convicted of speeding in Dorchester County, MD, in May 1987. Since then, he filed 43 separate petitions and motions with appellate courts, all of which were denied. The SC heard an extraordinary writ wherein Sindram requested the court to allow him to proceed *in forma pauperis.* Essentially, he asked the SC to declare him indigent so that the government would have to pay the costs and docket fees of his future petitions. Noting that this same motion had been made and denied on 12 previous occasions, the SC denied the writ, stating that Sindram had failed to show that no adequate relief could be had in any other form or from any other court and that there were no "drastic" circumstances that warranted extraordinary relief. The SC ordered the clerk of the SC not to accept any petitions from Sindram unless he paid the requisite docket fees. Further, the SC labeled his numerous motions and filings as "frivolous."

In re Winship, 397 U.S. 358, 90 S.Ct. 1068 (1970) [**In the Matter of Samuel WINSHIP, Appellant**] (**Juvenile Law**) Winship, age 12, purportedly entered a locker and stole $112 from a woman's pocketbook in New York City. He was charged with larceny. Under Section 712 of the New York Family Court Act, a juvenile delinquent is defined as "a person over seven and less than sixteen years of age who does any act, which, if done by an adult, would constitute a crime." Interestingly, the juvenile judge in the case acknowledged that the proof to be presented by the prosecution might be insufficient to establish the guilt of Winship beyond a reasonable doubt, although he did indicate that the New York Family Court Act provided that "any determination at the conclusion of [an adjudicatory hearing] that a [juvenile] did an act or acts must be based on a preponderance of the evidence" standard (397 U.S. at 360). Winship was adjudicated as a delinquent and ordered to a training school for 18 months, subject to annual extensions of his commitment until his 18th birthday. Appeals to New York courts were unsuccessful. The SC subsequently heard Winship's appeal and reversed the New York Family Court ruling because the beyond-a-reasonable-doubt standard had not been used in a case in which incarceration or loss of freedom was likely. The standard of proof of beyond a reasonable doubt applies to juvenile delinquency proceedings in which incarceration or incapacitation is a judicial adjudicatory option.

Iowa v. Tovar, ___U.S.___, 124 S.Ct. 1279 (2004) [IOWA, Petitioner, v. Felipe Edgardo TOVAR] (**Right to Counsel; Sixth Amendment**) Felipe Tovar was convicted of DWI (OWI in Iowa, which means "operating a vehicle while intoxicated") in 1996 following a guilty plea and after he waived his right to counsel. In that case, the judge offered all conventional warnings to defendants who wish to enter guilty pleas, including a determination that the plea was voluntary and that the right to counsel was knowingly and voluntarily waived. Tovar was subsequently convicted of a second DWI offense, this time with an attorney present. In 2000 Tovar was charged with a third DWI offense, and the prosecution sought to charge this offense as a class D felony, thus enhancing the offense from an aggravated misdemeanor to a third-offense felony. Tovar was convicted and appealed. Tovar's appeal claimed that his 1996 conviction without an attorney was constitutionally inadequate because the judge failed to advise Tovar that the guilty plea (1) entailed the risk that a viable defense might be overlooked if the right to an attorney was waived, and (2) deprived Tovar of the opportunity to obtain an independent opinion about whether, under the facts and applicable law, it was wise to plead guilty. The Iowa Supreme Court overturned Tovar's conviction on these grounds, remanding the case back to the trial court to recharge Tovar without using his 1996 conviction as a means of enhancing the 2000 charge. The government appealed and the SC heard the case. The SC reversed the Iowa court and held that neither warning ordered by the Iowa Supreme Court is mandated by the Sixth Amendment, and that the constitutional requirement is satisfied when the trial court informs the accused of the nature of the charges against him or her, of his or her right to be counseled regarding a plea, and of the range of allowable punishments attendant upon the entry of a guilty plea.

Irvine v. California, 374 U.S. 128, 74 S.Ct. 381 (1954) [IRVINE, Petitioner, v. People of CALIFORNIA] (**Electronic Surveillance, Wiretapping; Fourth Amendment; Law Enforcement Officers or Agencies**) Irvine was suspected of illegal gambling. Police officers, without a warrant, went to his home when he was not there and had a locksmith open the door. They placed various microphones throughout the home so they could record conversations later. They even bored a hole in the roof to install further wires, but no telephone lines were "tapped." Police reentered Irvine's home on several occasions and moved microphones about in order to listen to and record any incriminating statements. Later, at Irvine's trial, these statements were used as evidence against him and he was convicted. Irvine appealed. The SC affirmed and limited the *Rochin* exception to the *Wolf* doctrine in situations involving violence, brutality, or shocking conduct to the defendant; the SC severely criticized the authorities in this case for their behavior, but it did uphold the conviction. At no time in the appeal had Irvine mentioned his constitutional rights. This is significant. The SC cannot act on a constitutional question if it is not initiated by the convicted offender. Without a constitutional issue to consider, the SC affirmed Irvine's conviction. However, it noted that the statute of limitations had not expired and that the conduct of the police in entering Irvine's home without a warrant and plant-

ing microphones was inexcusable and in need of rectification. Thus it appears that if Irvine had raised a Fourth Amendment search-and-seizure issue with the SC, his conviction might have been overturned as the information yielded by these illegal microphone plants would have been declared inadmissible against him.

J

Jackson v. Denno, 378 U.S. 368, 84 S.Ct. 1774 (1966) [Nathan JACKSON, Petitioner, v. Wilfred DENNO, Warden] (**Confessions; Juries; Self-Incrimination**) Jackson was wounded in a gunfight following an August 28, 1996, robbery of a hotel desk clerk. At the hospital later, he gave incriminating statements that were introduced at his trial, where he was convicted. At his trial, he declared that his confession had been coerced. In New York, judges may exclude involuntary confessions, but they may allow confessions that are *questionably voluntary* and allow juries to decide whether or not they are voluntary. Jackson appealed, contending that the confession should have been suppressed outright, and that the jury should not have been shown it as evidence. The SC reversed his conviction, saying that Jackson is entitled to an evidentiary hearing to determine whether the incriminating confession was voluntarily given or whether it was coerced. Thus, judges may not decide to include or exclude a confession on their own authority, before allowing juries to hear it.

Jackson v. Indiana, 406 U.S. 715, 92 S.Ct. 1845 (1972) [Theon JACKSON, Petitioner, v. State of INDIANA] (**Mental Capacity**) Jackson was accused of two criminal offenses. He was a mentally defective deaf-mute who could not read, write, or virtually otherwise communicate. In Indiana, a statute declares that mentally incompetent criminal defendants may be committed to a state institution on more lenient standards than those applied to civil commitment cases. Further, the standards for release of committed criminal defendants are more stringent than those for the release of others who have been committed through civil process. The judge exercised his power in this case by declaring Jackson mentally unfit and incapable of standing trial, thus committing him to an institution until such time as "he is cured." Because this cure was not a reasonable expectation for Jackson, the commitment was tantamount to a life sentence in a mental institution. Jackson appealed. The SC intervened and rejected the judge's commitment order, thus remanding the case to the court to determine whether Jackson was criminally responsible for his alleged acts. The significance of this case is that Jackson's Fourteenth Amendment rights to due process and equal protection had been violated by the Indiana court, because Jackson had been committed by a more lenient standard than those of others, and his release conditions were more stringent than those of others. This inequality of treatment was in conflict with the Fourteenth Amendment provision.

Jacobson v. United States, 503 U.S. 540, 112 S.Ct. 1535 (1992) [Keith JACOBSON, Petitioner, v. UNITED STATES] (Entrapment) In early 1984, Jacobson ordered several books containing pictures of nude young boys from an adult book store. This was not illegal at the time, because the Child Protection Act of 1984 had not been passed. After the passage of this act, United States postal inspectors found Jacobson's name on an adult book store mailing list and began to send him fictitious catalogues and other materials, inviting him to subscribe. At the outset, however, Jacobson declared his interest in observing only young nudes, not sex acts between them. He responded to many of these solicitations over the next three years. All of this activity was generated by United States postal inspectors and the U.S. Customs Office, as some of the materials were sent from other countries. Finally, in May 1987, U.S. postal inspectors sent Jacobson a catalogue offering photos of young boys in sexually explicit poses. Jacobson ordered a magazine from the catalogue, and when it was delivered by the U.S. postal inspector, Jacobson was arrested for receiving child pornography through the mail. He was convicted. He appealed, arguing the defense of entrapment. The SC agreed and overturned his conviction, saying that the government may not originate a criminal design, implant in an innocent person's mind the disposition to commit the criminal act, and then induce commission of the crime so the government can prosecute.

Jago v. Van Curen, 454 U.S. 14, 102 S.Ct. 31 (1981) [A.R. JAGO, Former Superintendent, Southern Ohio Correctional Facility, et al., Petitioners, v. George D. VAN CUREN] (Corrections; Probation and Parole) Van Curen was convicted of embezzling $6 million. During his confinement, he was interviewed to see if he was possibly eligible for parole under a new shock parole program. The interview went well and he was notified that he would soon be paroled. However, it was then discovered that Van Curen had lied to the parole board about the amount of money he had embezzled (he told the board that he had embezzled $1 million, not $6 million), and that he had also lied about his parole plan and where he was going to live and with whom. His parole was rescinded by the parole board without a hearing. Van Curen appealed, alleging that he had a right to a hearing to answer the charges leading to the rescission. The SC declared that inmates do not have a right to be heard in a proceeding to rescind parole. This type of hearing is different from a parole hearing, in which inmates do have assorted rights.

James v. Illinois, 493 U.S. 307, 110 S.Ct. 648 (1990) [Darryl JAMES, Petitioner, v. ILLINOIS] (Exclusionary Rule; Fourth Amendment; *Miranda* Warning; Sixth Amendment) In August 1982, several boys were returning home from a party when they were confronted by three other boys who demanded money. A fight ensued, resulting in the shooting death of one boy and serious injury to another. Detectives from the Chicago Police Department discovered 15-year-old James in his mother's home under a hair dryer. They took him into custody as a suspect. His hair was black and curly. Detectives asked James about his prior hair color, and he said that the day before, his hair had been reddish brown and straight. He admitted to police that he deliberately changed his appear-

ance. James' statements were made without his being given the *Miranda* warning, and he had been arrested without a warrant. Eyewitnesses to the murder said the shooter had reddish, straight hair and identified James as the shooter, although his hair was now a different color. During the trial, James elected not to testify, and his prior statements about changing his hair color were not admitted into evidence, as they had been illegally obtained by police. However, James called a family friend, Henderson, who testified that on the day of the shooting, she had driven James to school so that he could register, and that his hair had been "black and curly." In an effort to counter this obvious perjury, the prosecutor used James' illegally obtained statements for impeachment purposes in confronting Henderson. Ordinarily, illegally obtained statements can be used to impeach a defendant who testifies under oath, as an important exception to the exclusionary rule. In this case, however, these illegally obtained statements were instead used to impeach a witness for the defense. James was subsequently convicted, and he appealed, alleging that his Fourth Amendment right had been violated. The SC agreed and overturned his conviction, holding that the impeachment exception to the exclusionary rule that permits the prosecution to introduce illegally obtained evidence to impeach a defendant's own testimony would not be expanded to impeach testimony of all defense witnesses.

Jenkins v. Anderson, 447 U.S. 23, 100 S.Ct. 2124 (1978) [Dennis Seay JENKINS, Petitioner, v. Charles ANDERSON, Warden] (Death Penalty; Fifth Amendment; Self-Incrimination) Dennis Jenkins was accused of manslaughter in a Michigan court. During his trial, he claimed self-defense. Further, the prosecutor questioned Jenkins on the witness stand about the fact that Jenkins had not surrendered himself to authorities for at least two weeks following the killing. This failure to turn himself in was referred to as prearrest silence. The prosecutor, therefore, used Jenkins' prearrest silence to impeach his credibility and truthfulness about alleging self-defense, suggesting that Jenkins would have spoken out had he actually killed the other person in self-defense. He was convicted. He appealed, claiming that the comments by the prosecutor about his "prearrest silence" were prejudicial remarks and violated his Fifth Amendment right against self-incrimination. The SC upheld his manslaughter conviction, holding that although prosecutors cannot comment on a defendant's silence during the trial, they may use prearrest silence as a means of impeaching a defendant's testimony on cross-examination. This does not violate the Fifth Amendment rights of defendants.

Johnson v. Avery, 393 U.S. 483, 89 S.Ct. 747 (1969) [William Joe JOHNSON, Petitioner, v. Harry S. AVERY, Commissioner of Correction, et al.] (Corrections; *Habeas Corpus* Petitions; Inmate Rights) The use of jailhouse lawyers may not be prohibited unless free counsel is provided by the state; in the absence of any adequate substitute, inmates should be allowed to use legal assistance of other inmates. Johnson was serving a life sentence in Tennessee. He studied the law diligently and on numerous occasions helped other inmates to prepare legal documents such as *habeas corpus* petitions, usually for a small fee or other reward. Tennessee had a statute prohibiting one prisoner providing legal aid to another.

The statute read in part, "no inmate will advise, assist or otherwise contract to aid another, either with or without a fee, to prepare writs or other legal matters. . . . Inmates are forbidden to set themselves up as practitioners for the purpose . . . of writing writs." Thus Johnson was violating a Tennessee law, but he was also assisting other prisoners, many of whom were illiterate and could not prepare petitions themselves, in having access to the courts under the 1941 (*Ex parte Hull*) SC declaration. As a punishment for his legal assistance to other prisoners, Tennessee authorities placed Johnson in solitary confinement for a year. He appealed. Eventually, his case was heard by the SC, which ruled that neither Tennessee nor any other state can prohibit the exercise of legal strategies by inmates, either on their own behalf or on the behalf of other prisoners, as a means of reaching the courts. All states are obligated to comply with this ruling unless they can demonstrate that prisoners have access to some alternative and equivalent form of legal assistance for those seeking *postconviction relief*. Such relief is an attempt by prisoners to obtain some satisfaction for a grievance such as a challenge about the nature of their confinement, their initial conviction, or some other matter. Thus, the SC ushered in the "new age in jailhouse lawyering."

Johnson v. Jones, 515 U.S. 304, 115 S.Ct. 2151 (1995) [Tyson JOHNSON et al., Petitioners, v. Houston JONES] (Civil Rights, Section 1983 Claims; Law Enforcement Officers or Agencies) Five police officers arrested Jones, thinking he was drunk, when in fact he was a diabetic suffering from an insulin seizure. He later found himself in a hospital with several broken ribs. He sued. His allegations that police officers had used excessive force when arresting him and beating him at the station house were substantiated by other collateral factual information. The police officers asked for a summary judgment in Jones' suit against them, and the motion was denied by a district court. The officers appealed. The SC affirmed the denial of the motion, holding that police officers may not appeal a district court's summary judgment order insofar as that order determines whether or not the pretrial record sets forth a "genuine" issue of fact for trial. Jones was therefore entitled to a trial on the issue of whether his Title 42 U.S.C. Section 1983 civil rights had been violated.

Johnson v. Louisiana, 406 U.S. 356, 92 S.Ct. 1620 (1972) [Frank JOHNSON, Appellant, v. LOUISIANA] (Juries; Jury Size; Jury Voting; Proof Standards) Johnson was arrested without a warrant at his home based on a photograph identification by a robbery victim. He was later subjected to a lineup, where he was identified again. Johnson was represented by counsel. He was subjected to trial by jury for the robbery offense and convicted in a jury vote of nine to three. Johnson appealed, contending that the jury verdict should be unanimous. The SC affirmed his conviction, saying, in effect, that states have the right to determine whether conviction requires unanimity of jury votes or only a majority vote. The SC concluded by saying that the verdicts rendered by nine out of 12 jurors are not automatically invalidated by the disagreement of the dissenting three. Johnson was not deprived of due process or a fair trial because of the 9–3 vote. (*See Apodaca v. Oregon* [1972] *for a comparable case.*) This SC decision applies to states only and does not affect federal juries, who must be unanimous in their verdicts. Federal criminal jury sizes of 12 may be reduced to 11 under special conditions with judicial approval; either size must be unanimous.

Johnson v. Mississippi, 486 U.S. 578, 108 S.Ct. 1981 (1988) [Samuel Bice JOHNSON, Petitioner v. MISSISSIPPI] (Aggravating and Mitigating Circumstances; Cruel and Unusual Punishment; Eighth Amendment) In December 1981, Johnson and several other men were stopped by a Mississippi highway patrolman for speeding. While the officer was searching the car, one of Johnson's companions stabbed the officer, seized his revolver, and shot him dead. Johnson and his companions were later arrested and charged with murder. They were convicted. During the penalty phase of the trial, the jurors found three aggravating circumstances, which, they said, outweighed the mitigating ones. One aggravating circumstance was an authenticated copy of a commitment order that showed Johnson's conviction and commitment to a Monroe County, NY, jail for the crime of second-degree assault in 1963. Although the New York Supreme Court had vacated Johnson's 1963 conviction, it had continued to function as an aggravating circumstance in the penalty phase of Johnson's 1988 trial. Johnson appealed and the SC reversed his conviction, holding that a death sentence that rests, in part, on a felony conviction that was later vacated violates the Eighth Amendment prohibition against cruel and unusual punishment.

Johnson v. Texas, 509 U.S. 350, 113 S.Ct. 2658 (1993) [Dorsie Lee JOHNSON, Jr., Petitioner, v. TEXAS] (Death Penalty) Johnson, age 19, was convicted of capital murder. During the sentencing phase of the trial, the judge instructed the jury to consider, in view of Johnson's age, his future dangerousness or threat to society. He was sentenced to death. Johnson appealed his conviction and death sentence on the grounds that the jury had been precluded from considering his youth because of the "future dangerousness" instruction. The SC rejected Johnson's appeal, as the jury had been instructed to consider all of the evidence, including Johnson's youthfulness. The future-dangerousness consideration was merely one additional factor to consider when recommending the death penalty.

Johnson v. United States, 520 U.S. 461, 117 S.Ct. 1544 (1997) [Joyce B. JOHNSON, Petitioner, v. UNITED STATES] (Jury Instructions; Jury Trials) Johnson was convicted of perjury in a federal court in Florida after falsely testifying before a grand jury about her boyfriend's drug trafficking. At her trial, Johnson did not object when the judge instructed the jury that materiality was for him to decide, and that he had determined that Johnson's statements were material. Subsequently, Johnson appealed on grounds articulated in *United States v. Olano* (1993) and *United States v. Gaudin* (1995), that plain error had been committed by the judge, because the jury, not the judge, should have determined the materiality of her testimony. The SC heard her appeal and affirmed her conviction, holding that although plain error was committed, it did not substantially affect the fairness, integrity, or public reputation of judicial proceedings. Furthermore, the SC added that Johnson presented no plausible argument that her false statements under oath were somehow not material to the grand-jury investigation. Also, there was no objection from Johnson's attorneys during the trial when the judge gave the jury instructions and remarked about who should determine materiality.

Johnson v. United States, 529 U.S. 694, 120 S.Ct. 1795 (2000) [**Cornell JOHNSON, Petitioner, v. UNITED STATES**] (*Ex Post Facto* **Laws; Probation and Parole**) In March 1994, Johnson was convicted of a Class D felony he committed in October 1993 and sentenced in federal court in Tennessee to 25 months' imprisonment to be followed by three years of supervised release. Johnson was released from prison on August 14, 1995, because of good-conduct credits and began serving his three-year supervised release term. However, after seven months on supervised release, Johnson was rearrested in Virginia and convicted of four state-related forgery offenses. These convictions violated the terms of his federal supervised release. An additional condition was that he could not leave the federal district in Tennessee without permission. Thus, Johnson was also in violation of this supervised release condition because he left Tennessee without permission and committed additional crimes in Virginia. The federal district court in Tennessee revoked his supervisory release program, imposed a prison term of 18 months, and ordered Johnson placed on supervised release for 12 months following his term of federal imprisonment. Between the time Johnson was originally convicted in 1994 and his subsequent resentencing in 1995, a new subsection was added to Title 18 U.S.C. Section 3583 in 1994, which empowered federal judges to impose an additional term of supervised release following reincarceration. Johnson protested and appealed, alleging that Section 3583 of Title 18 meant that the federal district judge was applying the law and additional supervised release following imprisonment in an *ex post facto* manner, a procedure that violated the *ex post facto* clause of the Constitution. The SC heard Johnson's appeal and rejected it. In a rather complex argument, the SC said that although Section 3583 of Title 18 cannot be applied retroactively to Johnson, this fact is unrelated to the punishment exacted for his original conviction offense and the conditions of his original supervised release program. Prior to the enactment of Title 18 U.S.C. Section 3583, federal judges were authorized and continue to be authorized to impose new terms of supervised release following reimprisonment and are not in violation of the *ex post facto* clause of the Constitution. However, new terms of imprisonment and supervised release cannot exceed the combined terms of imprisonment and supervised release provided for and stemming from the original offense.

Johnson v. Virginia, 373 U.S. 61, 83 S.Ct. 1053 (1963) [**Ford T. JOHNSON, Jr., v. State of VIRGINIA**] (**Corrections; Inmate Rights**) Johnson, a black man, was given a traffic citation. He appeared in traffic court, where he was supposed to be seated in a section reserved for black persons. He elected to stand instead and thus was cited for contempt by the judge. He appealed. The SC held that the segregation of public facilities is unconstitutional and violated Johnson's Four-

teenth Amendment rights to equal protection under the law. A state may not constitutionally require segregation of public facilities, including courtrooms.

Johnson v. Zerbst, 304 U.S. 458, 58 S.Ct. 1019 (1938) [**John A. JOHNSON, Petitioner, v. Fred G. ZERBST, Warden, United States Penitentiary, Atlanta, GA**] (**Indigent Clients; Sixth Amendment**) John A. Johnson and another man, both U.S. Marines, were arrested in Charleston, SC, on November 21, 1934, and charged with passing four counterfeit $20 federal reserve notes. Both entered not-guilty pleas at their preliminary hearing, and did not have counsel during the period their case was bound over to a federal grand jury. On January 21, 1935, they were indicted, and unable to make bail, they were arraigned, tried, and convicted on January 23, 1935, and sentenced to four and one-half years in the penitentiary. Johnson filed a *habeas corpus* petition, alleging that he had been denied assistance of counsel at his trial after making a timely request for such assistance. The SC ruled that in all *federal* trials of a serious nature, counsel must be appointed for an indigent defendant unless he or she intelligently waives this right. No evidence on the federal court record shows that Johnson or his associate waived his right to assistance of counsel.

Jones v. Barnes, 463 U.S. 745, 103 S.Ct. 3308 (1983) [**Everett W. JONES, Superintendent, Great Meadow Correctional Facility, et al., Petitioners, v. David BARNES**] (*Habeas Corpus* **Petitions; Right to Counsel; Sixth Amendment**) Barnes was convicted of robbery and assault in a New York jury trial. He attempted to launch several appeals through a court-appointed attorney. The attorney advised him that most of his claims were groundless. Defense counsel advised Barnes of at least seven claims of error that he considered including in his brief, but when the case was eventually appealed, the counsel focused primarily on three of the claims. Barnes filed a *habeas corpus* petition, alleging ineffective assistance of counsel. The SC rejected his argument that his counsel had been ineffective. Rather, the SC declared, defense counsel assigned to prosecute an appeal from a criminal conviction does not have a constitutional duty to raise every nonfrivolous issue requested by Barnes. In the SC's opinion, the counsel was effective and had supported Barnes' claims to the best of his ability, which was reasonable.

Jones v. North Carolina Prisoners' Labor Union, Inc., 433 U.S. 119, 97 S.Ct. 2532 (1977) [**David L. JONES, Secretary of the North Carolina Department of Correction, et al., Appellants, v. NORTH CAROLINA PRISONERS' LABOR UNION, INC., etc.**] (**Corrections; First Amendment; Free Speech; Inmate Rights**) A North Carolina Prisoners' Labor Union was established in 1974 for various purposes, such as charity work, the improvement of prison conditions, and resolutions of inmate grievances. A year later, prison officials sought to limit the activities of this prisoners' union and declared certain of its activities prohibited. The union filed suit against the prison system, specifically protesting that they had a right to solicit the membership of other inmates in their union through bulk mailings and group meetings. The SC upheld the North Carolina prison officials' action and declared that a ban on prisoner union activities is constitutional. It does not violate either the First Amendment right of free speech and assembly or the Fourteenth Amendment rights of equal protection and due process.

Jones v. United States, 357 U.S. 493, 78 S.Ct. 1253 (1958) [Roy JONES, Petitioner, v. UNITED STATES] (Fourth Amendment; Law Enforcement Officers or Agencies; Searches and Seizures) Federal alcohol agents received information from a reliable informant in April 1956 that Jones' farmhouse in Dawsonville, GA, was the site of an illicit distillery. In an area behind the house, they found mash and other discarded alcohol ingredients. The officers placed Jones' home under surveillance. During the evening hours, they observed a truck stop at the house and heard loud noises from the house. They approached the truck and saw Jones' wife and children. The truck appeared to be carrying illegal whiskey. Jones' wife ran to the house. Federal agents followed her, pushed by her, and entered the premises. When asked by Mrs. Jones if they had a warrant to search, the officers said a warrant was not required. They proceeded to conduct a thorough search and discovered considerable incriminating evidence later used in court against Jones. He was convicted of violating liquor laws and possessing an unregistered still. Jones appealed, arguing that the warrantless search of his home violated his Fourth Amendment right against an unreasonable search and seizure. The SC overturned Jones' conviction, saying that the federal officers could not make a warrantless search of one's premises regardless of whether they had probable cause to believe that the premises contained illegal contraband. Probable cause for belief that certain articles subject to seizure are in a dwelling cannot of itself justify a search without a warrant.

Jones v. United States, 362 U.S. 257, 80 S.Ct. 725 (1960) [Cecil JONES, Petitioner, v. UNITED STATES] (Exclusionary Rule; Law Enforcement Officers or Agencies) Officers in the District of Columbia executed a search warrant for drugs and entered an apartment where Jones was a guest. When the officers searched the apartment, they found illegal drugs on the premises and they also searched Jones and found drugs in his possession. Jones was convicted later after admitting that some of the drugs on the premises were his and that he had been living at the apartment for a time. Later, he sought to suppress the evidence against him, but his motion to do so was rejected, because he "lacked standing" as the owner of the apartment. Among other things, Jones had attacked the search warrant as being issued on the basis of "hearsay" and not probable cause, making it not a reliable or valid warrant. An appellate court denied his motion, but the SC decided in his favor that, at least, he had "standing" to file such a motion. The case was remanded back to the trial court where he could again challenge the admissibility of the original evidence.

Jones v. United States, 463 U.S. 354, 103 S.Ct. 3043 (1983) [Michael JONES, Petitioner, v. UNITED STATES] (Insanity Pleas) Jones was acquitted of a crime by reason of insanity and was committed to a mental hospital. Within 50 days, he was entitled to a hearing to show that he was eligible for release. The hearing disclosed that he was still mentally ill and should continue to be confined. He appealed. The SC af-

firmed the judgment of the lower courts, supporting Jones' continued confinement. The SC held that when a criminal defendant establishes by a preponderance of the evidence that he or she is not guilty of a crime by reason of insanity, the due-process clause permits the government, on the basis of the insanity judgment, to confine the defendant to a mental institution until such time as he or she regains his or her sanity or is no longer a danger to him- or herself or to society, and he or she can be confined to a mental hospital for a period longer than he or she could have been incarcerated had he been convicted.

Jones v. United States, 526 U.S. 227, 119 S.Ct. 1215 (1999) [Nathaniel JONES, Petitioner, v. UNITED STATES] (Sentencing) Jones and two others carjacked an automobile by force and intimidation. Eventually, they were apprehended by police and Jones was indicted under 18 U.S.C. 2119(1), which provided upon conviction for a sentence of not more than 15 years. However, following Jones' trial, Jones was sentenced to 25 years and appealed, contending that other carjacking elements under 18 U.S.C. 2119 were not charged in the indictment and thus the sentence was excessive. The SC heard Jones' appeal and examined the provisions of 18 U.S.C. 2119, which provides that a person possessing a firearm who takes a motor vehicle from the person or presence of another by force and violence or by intimidation shall (1) be imprisoned not more than 15 years; (2) if serious bodily injury results, be imprisoned not more than 25 years; and (3) if death results, be imprisoned for any number of years up to life. The indictment made no reference to Section 2119's numbered subsections. Furthermore, Jones was told at his arraignment that he faced a maximum 15-year sentence for carjacking, and that the jury instructions at his trial defined that offense only by referencing 18 U.S.C. 2119(1). The SC reversed Jones' conviction, holding that the additional subsections (2) and (3) of 18 U.S.C. 2119 constituted separate offenses, all elements of which must be proved beyond a reasonable doubt. As these offenses were not mentioned in the indictment, it was improper for the trial judge to sentence Jones to any term in excess of 15 years. The SC stressed that under the existing carjacking statute, 18 U.S.C. 2119, three distinct offenses are outlined rather than a single offense with a choice of three maximum penalties. The SC said, "we think the better reading is of three distinct offenses, particularly in light of the rule that any interpretive uncertainty should be resolved to avoid serious questions about the statute's constitutionality" (at 1217).

Judd v. United States District Court of Texas, 528 U.S. 5, 120 S.Ct. 1 (1999) [Keith Russell JUDD v. UNITED STATES DISTRICT COURT for the Western District OF TEXAS et al.] (Frivolous Lawsuits; *In Forma Pauperis* Motions; Inmate Rights) Keith Russell Judd, a Texas inmate, filed an *in forma pauperis* motion with the SC. The SC denied Judd's motion, noting that Judd had previously filed 12 frivolous petitions for *certiorari* or petitions for extraordinary writs in noncriminal matters since May 30, 1995, all of which were denied without recorded dissent. The SC chided Judd for filing frivolous claims and barred him from filing future noncriminal claims unless he paid the required docketing fees. According to the SC, Judd was not barred from filing petitions to challenge any criminal sanctions that might be imposed on him, but the order allowed the SC to devote its limited resources to the claims of petitioners who had not abused SC processes. (*See also Dempsey v. Martin* [1999] *and Prunty v. Brooks* [1999].)

Jurek v. Texas, 428 U.S. 262, 96 S.Ct. 2950 (1976) [**Jerry Lane JUREK, Petitioner, v. State of TEXAS**] (**Corrections; Cruel and Unusual Punishment; Death Penalty; Inmate Rights; Juries**) Jurek was convicted of murder and sentenced to death. He challenged the constitutionality of the sentence, arguing that it was capricious and arbitrary. Specifically, Texas statutes provide that juries must decide three questions: (1) whether the conduct of the defendant causing the death was deliberate and had the reasonable expectation that death would result; (2) whether the defendant's conduct was an unreasonable response to provocation, if any, by the deceased; and (3) whether it is probable that the defendant would commit criminal acts of violence constituting a continuing threat to society. Jurek challenged the constitutionality of these questions as *unconstitutionally vague.* The SC upheld his death sentence, holding that there is nothing in the Texas statutes that violates one's rights under the Eighth and Fourteenth Amendments. Further, the imposition of the death penalty is not *per se* cruel and unusual punishment.

Justices of Boston Municipal Court v. Lydon, 466 U.S. 294, 104 S.Ct. 1805 (1984) [**JUSTICES OF BOSTON MUNICIPAL COURT, Petitioners, v. Michael LYDON**] (**Double Jeopardy**) Lydon was convicted under the two-tiered trial system of breaking into an automobile and stealing property. Under Massachusetts law, the first tier consists of a bench trial, in which a police-court judge decides the case. Then, if the defendant is convicted, he or she may demand and receive a subsequent jury trial in the second tier. Lydon believed the evidence against him insufficient to warrant conviction. He appealed to a higher Massachusetts court, which denied his appeal, contesting the insufficiency of evidence. Lydon believed that as long as his insufficiency-of-evidence claim was under appeal by another court, it would be double jeopardy for him to be tried later by a jury. Ultimately, the SC heard Lydon's case and held that the procedures in place in Massachusetts were such that it would not be double jeopardy for Lydon to be convicted in one court and tried again in a jury trial in the second tier. It was constitutional that Lydon could be retried *de novo* without any judicial determination of the sufficiency of evidence at his prior bench trial.

K

Kalina v. Fletcher, 522 U.S. 118, 118 S.Ct. 502 (1997) [**Lynne KALINA, Petitioner, v. Rodney FLETCHER**] (**Immunity; Prosecutorial Misconduct**) Lynne Kalina was a deputy prosecuting attorney for King County, WA. She filed three documents in court against a suspect in a school burglary, Rodney Fletcher. The first two documents were a criminal information charging Fletcher with burglary (and theft of a school computer) and a motion for an arrest warrant, both unsworn pleadings. The third document was a "Certification for Determination of Probable Cause," which summarized the evidence against Fletcher and supported the first two documents. Kalina personally vouched for the truth of the facts set forth in the certification under penalty of perjury. Fletcher was subsequently arrested, held for one day in jail, and then released. The charges against Fletcher were subsequently dropped. Fletcher brought a Section 1983 civil rights action against Kalina, alleging that she deliberately made at least two false statements in the certification filed. Kalina responded that she was entitled to absolute immunity under the circumstances. The Washington Court of Appeals held that her filing of charges was protected by absolute immunity; however, she was not entitled to absolute immunity with respect to her actions in executing certification for determination of probable cause. Specifically, the two inaccurate statements were (1) that Fletcher's fingerprints were found on a school glass partition and that Fletcher had never been associated with the school in any manner, nor did he have permission to enter the school or take any property; and (2) that Fletcher had been identified by an electronics store employee as the person who had asked for an appraisal of a computer stolen from the school. In fact, the electronics store employee had *not* identified Fletcher. Further, Fletcher had assisted in installing glass partitions on the school premises and was authorized to enter the school. Kalina appealed and the SC upheld the Washington Court of Appeals, that she was not entitled to absolute immunity from lawsuits stemming from her actions in executing the certification for determination of probable cause. Thus, Fletcher had a cause of action through Section 1983 against Kalina for this specific prosecutorial misconduct.

Kansas v. Crane, ___U.S.___, 122 S.Ct. 867 (2002) [**KANSAS, Petitioner, v. Michael T. CRANE**] (**Sexual Predators**) Michael Crane was convicted of lewd and lascivious behavior and pleaded guilty to aggravated sexual battery for two incidents occurring in 1993. He exposed himself to a tanning salon attendant and a video store clerk. In the case of the video store clerk, he demanded oral sex and threatened to rape her. Subsequently, the state court evaluated Crane and adjudicated him a sexual predator under Kansas' Sexually Violent Predator Act (SVPA). This act permits the civil detention of a person convicted of any of several enumerated sexual offenses, if it is proven beyond a reasonable doubt that he or she suffers from a mental abnormality, a disorder affecting his or her emotional or volitional capacity, which predisposes the person to commit sexually violent acts, or which makes the person likely to engage in repeat acts of sexual violence. Crane was committed to civil custody. Crane appealed and the Kansas Supreme Court reversed the civil commitment of Crane, holding that the SVPA requires that the state must prove that the defendant cannot control his or her dangerous behavior, and that the trial court had made no such finding. Kansas appealed to the SC, who heard the case. The SC reversed the Kansas Supreme Court and held that (1) the SVPA does not require the state to prove the offender's total or complete lack of control over his or her dangerous behavior, and that (2) the federal constitution does not allow civil commitment under the act without any lack of control determination. The significance of the SC action is that a state must show that a defendant is likely to engage in sexually violent conduct in the future, but not in any absolute sense. There is no rule obligating the state to prove that any defendant must lack total control regarding violent sexual conduct. Rather, the phrase stressed is that the state must demonstrate that the defendant possesses an abnormality or disorder that makes it *difficult*, if not impossible, to control the dangerous behavior. (*See Kansas v. Hendricks* [1997] for a comparison.)

Kansas v. Hendricks, 521 U.S. 346, 117 S.Ct. 2072 (1997) [KANSAS, Petitioner, v. Leroy HENDRICKS. Leroy Hendricks, Petitioner, v. Kansas] (Double Jeopardy; Sexual Predators) Hendricks was convicted in 1984 of sexually molesting two 13-year-old boys. Hendricks had a lengthy history of child sexual abuse convictions. In 1994, Hendricks was scheduled to be released from prison to a halfway house, but Kansas had recently enacted the Sexually Violent Predator Act, which establishes procedures for the civil commitment of persons who, due to a mental abnormality or a personality disorder, are likely to engage in predatory acts of sexual violence. Kansas thus invoked the act against Hendricks and ordered his civil commitment to a mental hospital for an indeterminate period. Hendricks challenged the civil commitment on several grounds, including double jeopardy, the prohibited application of *ex post facto* laws, and a violation of his substantive due-process rights. The Kansas Supreme Court invalidated the act, finding that the precommitment condition of a mental abnormality did not satisfy what it perceived to be the substantive due-process requirement that involuntary civil commitment must be predicated on a mental illness finding. It did not address Hendricks' double-jeopardy or *ex post facto* claims. Kansas officials appealed to the SC, who heard the case. The SC reversed the Kansas Supreme Court, holding that the act's definition of mental abnormality satisfies "substantive" due-process requirements. Furthermore, the act does not violate Hendricks' rights against double jeopardy or its ban on *ex post facto* lawmaking, as the act does not establish criminal proceedings, and involuntary confinement under it is not punishment in any criminal context.

Kastigar v. United States, 406 U.S. 441, 92 S.Ct. 1653 (1972) [Charles Joseph KASTIGAR and Michael Gorean Stewart, Petitioners, v. UNITED STATES] (Fifth Amendment; Grand Juries; Immunity; Self-Incrimination) Kastigar was subpoenaed before a grand jury to give self-incriminating testimony, despite his invocation of the Fifth Amendment against self-incrimination under a grant of immunity from subsequent prosecution. The government was of course obligated to prove that the witness' testimony was sufficiently in furtherance of government interests. The witness objected. The SC upheld the right of the government to compel self-incriminating testimony from witnesses under a grant of immunity. They must answer questions of grand jurors. How-

ever, they have some protection. Should a prosecution be carried out against the same witnesses, it must be demonstrated that incriminating information was gleaned about them from sources other than their self-incriminating testimony.

Katz v. United States, 389 U.S. 347, 88 S.Ct. 507 (1967) [Charles KATZ, Petitioner, v. UNITED STATES] (Exclusionary Rule; Law Enforcement Officers or Agencies) Katz was a bookmaker suspected of transmitting wagering information by telephone. Federal agents bugged a public telephone booth that Katz was known to use frequently. No warrant was issued for such an action. He was convicted, and he appealed. The SC ruled that telephone booths are constitutionally protected areas designed to avoid the "uninvited ear." Thus warrants based on probable cause must be issued before any such intrusion can be made, and the requirements articulated in *Berger v. New York* (1967) must be observed. The *Katz* case overruled *Olmstead v. United States* (1928).

Kaufman v. United States, 394 U.S. 217, 89 S.Ct. 1068 (1969) [Harold KAUFMAN, Petitioner, v. UNITED STATES] (Corrections; Fourth Amendment; Searches and Seizures) Kaufman was convicted of armed robbery despite pleading insanity. He filed a motion to vacate the sentence because of evidence illegally seized in violation of his Fourth Amendment rights and because he had been denied the effective assistance of counsel. The lower appellate courts held that his claims were made too late and were not proper in a postconviction proceeding. The SC overturned the lower-court decision, saying that the claim of unconstitutional search and seizure was cognizable in postconviction proceedings.

Kaupp v. Texas, ___U.S.___, 123 S.Ct. 1843 (2003) [Robert KAUPP v. TEXAS] (Confessions; Fourth Amendment; *Miranda* Warning) Following the disappearance of a 14-year-old girl in Texas in January 1999, police focused their attention on the girl's half-brother, 19, and his friend, Robert Kaupp, 17. Both young men were interviewed by police and submitted to lie detector tests. Kaupp passed, denying involvement in the girl's disappearance. But the half-brother failed the test three times and eventually confessed and advised where the girl's body could be found, also implicating Kaupp as an accomplice. Shortly thereafter, police attempted to obtain an arrest warrant from a judge to seize Kaupp. In this case, they applied for a "pocket warrant" to take Kaupp into custody for interrogation instead of a conventional arrest warrant, because they did not have probable cause to arrest him. At approximately 3:00 a.m. one morning, they entered Kaupp's home with permission from Kaupp's father, awakened Kaupp from sleep, and took him to the police station in handcuffs, where he was interrogated. During the interrogation, after being Mirandized, Kaupp admitted to police to knowing about the crime but denied that he caused the fatal wound to the girl. Later, he was convicted of murder and sentenced to 55 years in prison. He appealed, seeking to suppress the confession he had given to police under those interrogation circumstances. Texas appellate courts denied his appeal and the SC heard the case. The SC overturned Kaupp's conviction and threw out his confession. The SC held that Kaupp's arrest was illegal, as police lacked probable cause to make it. Texas prosecutors explained that it was "routine" for police to handcuff those transported in police vehicles to and from the police station for interrogation purposes, and they claimed that Kaupp's interrogation was not the result of an official arrest. Further, they claimed Kaupp was agreeable to being questioned at that time. The SC decided otherwise, and using the Fourth Amendment as grounds for their decision, they declared that a confession obtained by exploitation of an illegal arrest may not be used against a criminal defendant. Given those circumstances, Kaupp was not free to leave at any time, and the demeanor of the officers and detectives who took Kaupp into custody was tantamount to a formal arrest, although it wasn't labeled as such.

Keeney v. Tamayo-Reyes, 504 U.S. 1, 112 S.Ct. 1715 (1992) [**J.C. KEENEY, Superintendent, Oregon State Penitentiary, Petitioner v. Jose TAMAYO-REYES**] (**Corrections;** *Habeas Corpus* **Petitions**) A prison inmate, Tamayo-Reyes, was a Cuban immigrant who entered a *nolo contendere* plea to a first-degree manslaughter charge. He claimed that the *mens rea* element of the crime had not been adequately explained to him in Spanish. Lower courts denied his *habeas corpus* petition to seek a hearing on whether he had fully understood when he entered the *nolo* plea. The SC held, however, that Tamayo-Reyes was entitled to a hearing and thus remanded his case to the trial court for further proceedings.

Kelly v. South Carolina, ___U.S.___, 122 S.Ct. 726 (2002) [**William Arthur KELLY, Petitioner, v. SOUTH CAROLINA**] (**Death Penalty; Parolee Rights**) Kelly was convicted of murder, kidnapping, armed robbery, and possession of a knife during the commission of a violent crime, and was sentenced to death. At his sentencing hearing, Kelly's defense counsel requested the judge to give the jury an instruction that Kelly would be ineligible for parole if given life imprisonment instead of the death penalty. The judge refused to give such a jury instruction, and the jury voted for the death penalty. Kelly's case was subsequently appealed to the SC, who heard the case. On appeal, the trial judge defended his refusal to instruct the jury about Kelly's parole ineligibility because, as he claimed, this instruction was only necessary if a convicted offender's future dangerousness was at issue, and in this particular case, the issue was not future dangerousness but rather Kelly's character and characteristics. The SC overturned Kelly's death sentence and remanded the case to the trial court, where the judge was ordered to issue the jury an instruction concerning his parole ineligibility under a life sentence. The significance of this case is that when life imprisonment is an option to the death penalty, juries must be instructed that the convicted offender is ineligible for parole if given life imprisonment rather than death.

Kennedy v. Mendoza-Martinez, 372 U.S. 144, 83 S.Ct. 554 (1963) [**Robert F. KENNEDY, Attorney General of the United States, Appellant, v. Francisco MENDOZA-MARTINEZ. Dean Rusk, Secretary of State, Appellant, v. Joseph Henry Cort**] (**Corrections; Inmate Rights; Sixth Amendment**) Mendoza-Martinez, born in the United States in 1922, went to Mexico in 1942 to evade military service. He returned voluntarily to the United States in 1946. In 1947, he was convicted of having violated the Selective Service Act of 1940. He served a year. In 1953, he was served with an arrest warrant and deported as an alien. He appealed the deportation order, and a lower court entered a judgment in his favor. The government appealed, but the SC affirmed the lower-court decision, holding that statutes divesting an American of his citizenship for leaving or remaining outside of the country in time of war and national emergency for the purpose of evading military service are unconstitutional because they do not afford procedural safeguards under the Fifth and Sixth Amendments.

Kent v. United States, 383 U.S. 541, 86 S.Ct. 1045 (1966) [**Morris A. KENT, Jr., Petitioner, v. UNITED STATES**] (**Insanity Pleas; Juvenile Law**) In 1959, Kent, a 14-year-old in the District of Columbia, was apprehended and charged with several housebreakings and attempted purse snatchings. He was judged delinquent and placed on probation. Subsequently, in 1961, an intruder entered the apartment of a woman, took her wallet, and raped her. Fingerprints at the crime scene were later identified as those of Kent, who had been fingerprinted in connection with his delinquency case in 1959. On September 5, 1961, Kent admitted the offense as well as other crimes, and the juvenile court judge advised him of his intent to waive Kent to criminal court. In the meantime, Kent's mother had obtained an attorney, who advised the court that he intended to oppose the waiver. The judge ignored the attorney's motion and transferred Kent to the United States district court for the District of Columbia, where Kent was tried and convicted of six counts of housebreaking by a federal jury, although the jury found him "not guilty by reason of insanity" on the rape charge. Kent appealed. His conviction was reversed by the SC. The SC held that a full hearing, with assistance of counsel, must be held concerning the question of transferring a juvenile case to an adult court; children or their attorneys must have full access to social records used to make determinations, and the judge must state in writing the reasons for the transfer. The majority held that his rights to due process and to the effective assistance of counsel had been violated when he was denied a formal hearing on the waiver and his attorney's motions were ignored. The SC said that the matter of a waiver to criminal court was a "critical stage" relating to the defendant's potential loss of freedoms, and thus attorney representation was fundamental to due process. Because of the *Kent* decision, waiver hearings are now considered critical stages.

Kentucky v. Stincer, 482 U.S. 730, 107 S.Ct. 2658 (1987) [**KENTUCKY, Petitioner, v. Sergio STINCER**] (**Sixth Amendment**) Sergio Stincer sodomized two minor girls and was arrested. In the early stages of his trial, the judge held an in-chambers hearing to determine whether the minor girls were competent to testify. Stincer's attorney was permitted to attend this hearing, but Stincer was not. The judge determined that both girls were competent to testify. Stincer was convicted. He appealed, alleging that his exclusion from the in-chambers hearing had violated his right to confront his accusers under the Sixth Amendment. The Kentucky Supreme Court reversed Stincer's conviction on these Sixth Amendment grounds, but the state appealed to the SC. The SC overruled the Kentucky high court and reinstated Stincer's sodomy convictions, holding that his exclusion from the competency in-chambers hearing had not violated his Sixth Amendment rights. There was no evidence to suggest that his attendance at the hearing would have affected the girls' testimony in any way to influence the trial outcome differently. It is not necessary that defendants be entitled to attend all in-chambers hearings between defense counsel, prosecutors, and judges as a means of preserving their due-process rights.

Kentucky Department of Corrections v. Thompson, 490 U.S. 454, 109 S.Ct. 1904 (1989) [**KENTUCKY DEPARTMENT OF CORRECTIONS et al., Petitioners, v. James M. THOMPSON et al.**] (**Corrections; Inmate Rights**) In a Kentucky prison, several prisoners were denied visits from three women on separate occasions. Reasons given were that such visits would constitute a clear and probable danger to the safety and security of the institution and would interfere with its orderly operation. No hearings were held to determine whether the prisoners should have these visits. The prisoners filed suit alleging that their Fourteenth Amendment rights had been violated. The SC upheld Kentucky prison policy, holding that a policy denying such visitation under those circumstances was not in violation of prisoner rights. The SC stressed the safety-and-security issue relative to maintaining prison orderliness and said that no hearings were required for such decision making.

Ker v. California, 374 U.S. 23, 83 S.Ct. 1623 (1963) [**George D. KER et al., Petitioners, v. State of CALIFORNIA**] (**Searches and Seizures**) Ker was suspected of unlawful possession of marijuana on the basis of various sales of marijuana to undercover officers and information from another man, Murphy, also a drug dealer. Police placed Ker under surveillance. One day, police went to Ker's apartment and asked the building manager to admit them. Without either an arrest or search warrant, they quickly entered the apartment and found large quantities of marijuana. Ker was subsequently arrested and convicted. He appealed, arguing that his right against unreasonable searches had been violated by the officers, who had failed to get a warrant. The SC upheld the warrantless search in Ker's case because, they reasoned, marijuana is a substance that is easily destroyed. Thus, drug dealers are known to dispose of these substances quickly if they are alerted to a possible arrest and search. They can flush narcotics down their toilets or sinks or dispose of them in other ways. Thus, because of exigent circumstances, it was important for police to act quickly in Ker's case.

Khanh Phuong Nguyen v. United States, ___U.S.___, 123 S.Ct. 2130 (2003) [**KHANH PHUONG NGUYEN, Petitioner, v. UNITED STATES et al.**] (**Federal Appellate Judge Qualifications**) Nguyen and Phan, petitioners, were convicted in the U.S. District Court for the District of Guam of conspiracy to transport methamphetamine, knowingly aiding and abetting importation of methamphetamine, and attempting to possess over 50 grams of methamphetamine with intent to distribute. They appealed and the Ninth Circuit Court of Appeals affirmed their conviction. At that time, the three-judge panel consisted of two regular Article III circuit judges

and one Article IV territorial court judge from Guam. Alleging that the three-judge panel did not have the authority to rule in their appeal, Nguyen and Phan appealed to the SC, who heard the case. The SC vacated the Ninth Circuit affirmation and remanded the case for further proceedings. The SC held that the inclusion of the Article IV judge was improper, and that he was not eligible to sit and vote as a duly constituted member of the Ninth Circuit Court of Appeals. Only duly appointed circuit court of appeals judges can decide district court appeals.

Kimmelman v. Morrison, 477 U.S. 365, 106 S.Ct. 2574 (1986) [**Irwin I. KIMMELMAN, Attorney General of New Jersey, et al., Petitioners, v. Neil MORRISON**] (**Discovery;** *Habeas Corpus* **Petitions; Right to Counsel; Sixth Amendment**) In a bench trial in New Jersey, Morrison was accused of rape. During the trial, a police officer testified about a bedsheet found at the crime scene, which had been seized without a proper search warrant. The defense attorney objected and moved to suppress statements about the bedsheet. The judge, however, ruled that it was too late to register such an objection, that the proper time would have been during discovery, when the items seized and to be used as evidence against Morrison were disclosed to him. Morrison was convicted. He filed a *habeas corpus* petition, alleging incompetence of counsel relating to the bedsheet and the motion to suppress it. Because the defense attorney had not raised a motion at an earlier and more proper time, Morrison argued, he had been deprived of the effective assistance of counsel and thus had been convicted. An appellate court reversed his conviction on these grounds, and the state appealed to the SC. The SC affirmed the lower appellate court, concluding that Morrison's counsel had been ineffective due to his failure to conduct any pretrial discovery and determine what the state had planned to present as incriminating evidence. Further, the counsel clearly had failed to make a timely motion to suppress such evidence. On these grounds, Morrison's conviction was reversed.

Kirby v. Illinois, 406 U.S. 682, 92 S.Ct. 1877 (1972) [**Thomas KIRBY, etc., Petitioner, v. State of ILLINOIS**] (**Law Enforcement Officers or Agencies; Lineups; Right to Counsel**) Kirby was stopped on the street by a police officer and asked for his identification. The identification shown the officer was that of another man who had been robbed of his wallet a few days earlier. Suspicious of Kirby, the officer asked him to accompany him to police headquarters, where he would check the identification. This was not an arrest and the officer did not know of the earlier robbery. While checking records at the police station, the officer discovered the robbery report. He called the robbed man and asked him to come to the police station. When the victim saw Kirby in a police detention room, he identified Kirby as the robber. At that time, Kirby was arrested, charged, and subsequently convicted of the robbery. Kirby appealed, seeking to question the identification procedure used by police and claiming that he should have had an attorney present at such an identification. The SC disagreed with Kirby, holding that there is no right to counsel at police headquarters, at police lineups, or at identification sessions when suspects have not been formally charged with a crime. (*See United States v. Wade* [1967].)

Kirk v. Louisiana, ___U.S.___, 122 S.Ct. 2458 (2002) [**Kennedy D. KIRK v. LOUISIANA**] (**Exigent Circumstances; Knock and Announce; Fourth Amendment; Searches and Seizures**) Police were alerted by an anonymous citizen complaint that Kirk was conducting drug sales out of his apartment. After witnessing what appeared to be various drug sales at Kirk's premises, they stopped one of the buyers on the street and questioned him. Shortly thereafter, they knocked on Kirk's door, entered his apartment without either an arrest warrant or a search warrant, and searched the premises, eventually discovering cocaine and money. The officers claimed exigent circumstances that entitled them to conduct a warrantless search and seizure of Kirk's apartment and drugs. Although the officers sought and obtained a search warrant while they detained Kirk at his apartment, they only obtained this warrant after they had entered his home, arrested him, frisked him, found a drug vial in his underwear, and observed contraband in plain view in the apartment. Subsequently, Kirk sought to suppress the drugs, alleging that the warrantless search violated his Fourth Amendment rights. The Louisiana Supreme Court upheld his conviction, and he appealed to the SC, who heard the case. Kirk's conviction was reversed and remanded, with the SC holding that absent exigent circumstances, police officers' warrantless entry into Kirk's apartment and their arrest and search of the defendant violated his Fourth Amendment rights. Police officers need either a warrant or probable cause plus exigent circumstances in order to make a lawful entry into a home.

Klopfer v. North Carolina, 386 U.S. 213, 87 S.Ct. 988 (1967) [**Peter H. KLOPFER, Petitioner, v. State of NORTH CAROLINA**] (**Speedy Trials**) Klopfer was charged with criminal trespass. His case was eventually brought to court, at which time a mistrial was declared. Klopfer inquired as to whether the government was going to continue its prosecution, and it advised him that the state was filing a *nolle prosequi* with leave, which means that it was allowing itself an opportunity to retry Klopfer at a later date convenient for it. Klopfer sought relief from the SC, declaring that he believed that the *nolle prosequi* with leave left him in a vulnerable position relative to eventual prosecution, and that he was entitled to a speedy trial under the law according to the Sixth and Fourteenth Amendments. The SC agreed with Klopfer and endorsed a speedy-trial provision, saying that defendants are entitled to such because (1) witnesses are more credible through an early trial; (2) a defendant's ability to defend himself and trial fairness would not be jeopardized; and (3) a defendant's pretrial anxiety would be minimized.

Knowles v. Iowa, 525 U.S. 113, 119 S.Ct. 484 (1998) [**Patrick KNOWLES, Petitioner, v. IOWA**] (**Fourth Amendment; Searches and Seizures; Vehicle Searches**) Knowles was stopped for speeding and issued a citation but not placed under custodial arrest. The officer proceeded to conduct a full-scale search of Knowles' vehicle, under a "search incident to an arrest." Subsequently, marijuana and a pot pipe were discovered and Knowles was arrested and convicted of state drug

charges. The Iowa Supreme Court upheld Knowles' conviction, contending that as long as the officer had probable cause to make a custodial arrest, there need not in fact have been an arrest in order for the officer to search Knowles' car. The SC heard Knowles' appeal and reversed the Iowa Supreme Court, holding that despite Iowa state law to the contrary, the "search incident to an arrest" exception is without merit in this instance on two grounds. First, although concern for officer safety during a routine traffic stop may justify minimal additional intrusion by ordering the driver and passengers from the vehicle, it does not by itself justify a greater intrusion of a full-scale automobile search. Second, the need to discover and preserve evidence does not exist during a traffic stop, for once Knowles was stopped for speeding and issued a citation, all evidence necessary to prosecute that offense had been obtained. An officer may arrest a driver if he is not satisfied with the identification furnished, but the possibility that the officer may stumble onto other incriminating evidence, such as drugs unrelated to the traffic offense, is remote. The search of Knowles' automobile was unconstitutional and violated his Fourth Amendment rights under these circumstances.

Koon v. United States, 518 U.S. 81, 116 S.Ct. 2035 (1996) [**Stacey C. KOON, Petitioner, v. UNITED STATES. Laurence M. Powell, Petitioner, v. United States**] (**Law Enforcement Officers or Agencies; Sentencing**) Police officers Koon and Powell were convicted in federal court of violating the constitutional rights of a motorist, King, under color of law during an arrest, and sentenced to 30 months' imprisonment. The United States district court trial judge used U.S. Sentencing Guidelines and justified a downward departure of eight offense levels from "27" to "19" to arrive at a 30- to 37-month sentence. The government appealed, contending that a downward departure of eight offense levels from "27" was an abuse of judicial discretion and that the factors cited for the downward departure were not statutory. An original offense seriousness level of "27" would have meant imposing a sentence of 70 to 87 months. The Ninth Circuit Court of Appeals rejected all of the trial court's reasons for the downward departure and Koon and Powell petitioned the SC. The SC upheld the circuit court of appeals in part and reversed it in part. Specifically, the SC said that the primary question to be answered on appeal is whether the trial judge abused his discretion by the downward departure in sentencing. The reasons given by the trial judge for the downward departure from an offense level of "27" to "19" were that (1) the victim's misconduct provoked police use of force; (2) Koon and Powell had been subjected to successive state and federal criminal prosecutions; (3) Koon and Powell posed a low risk of recidivism; (4) Koon and Powell would probably lose their jobs and be precluded from employment in law enforcement; and (5) Koon and Powell would be unusually susceptible to abuse in prison. The SC concluded that a five-level downward departure based on the victim's misconduct that provoked officer use of force was justified, because victim misconduct is an encouraged (by the U.S. Sentencing Commission) basis for a guideline departure. The SC said that the remaining three-level departure was an abuse of judicial discretion. Federal district judges may not consider a convicted offender's career loss as a downward departure factor. Further, trial judges may not consider an offender's low likelihood of recidivism, because this factor is already incorporated into the Criminal History Category in the sentencing guideline table. Considering this factor to justify a downward departure, therefore, would be tantamount to counting the factor *twice*. The SC upheld the trial judge's reliance on the offenders' susceptibility to prison abuse and the burdens of successive state and federal prosecutions, however. The SC remanded the case to the district court, where a new sentence could be determined. Thus, a new offense level must be chosen on the basis of the victim's own misconduct that provoked the officers and where offender susceptibility to prison abuse and the burden of successive state and federal prosecutions could be considered. The significance of this case for criminal justice is that specific factors are identified by the SC to guide federal judges in imposing sentences on police officers convicted of misconduct and violating citizen rights under color of law. Victim response that provokes police use of force, an officer's susceptibility to abuse in prison, and the burden of successive state and federal prosecutions are acceptable factors to be considered to justify downward departures in offense seriousness, whereas one's low recidivism potential and loss of employment opportunity in law enforcement are not legitimate factors to justify downward departure in offense seriousness.

Kremen v. United States, 353 U.S. 346, 77 S.Ct. 828 (1957) [Shirley KREMEN, Samuel Irving Coleman, and Sidney Steinberg, Petitioners, v. UNITED STATES] (Law Enforcement Officers or Agencies; Searches Incident to Arrest) Kremen owned a cabin in Twain Harte, CA. Two men, Steinberg and Thompson, were fugitives from federal justice. They were in the company of Kremen and another person, Coleman. FBI agents conducted surveillance of Kremen's cabin for some 24 hours, observing Thompson and Steinberg. When Thompson and Steinberg left the cabin, they were placed under arrest by FBI agents. The agents then entered the cabin and arrested Kremen and Coleman for "relieving, comforting, and assisting a fugitive from justice." Without a warrant they proceeded to search the cabin and remove all the contents, including incriminating evidence that was used to convict Kremen. He appealed, contending that the search had been illegal. The SC overturned his conviction, saying that the seizure of the entire contents of a house and its removal some 200 miles away to the FBI offices for the purpose of examination were beyond the sanction of any of its cases (at 829). It is invalid to conduct a warrantless search and seize a home's entire contents. Such action renders guilty verdicts as a result of the seized evidence illegal.

Kuhlman v. Wilson, 477 U.S. 436, 106 S.Ct. 2616 (1986) [R.H. KUHLMAN, Superintendent, Sullivan Correctional Facility, Petitioner, v. Joseph Allan WILSON] (Custodial Interrogations; *Habeas Corpus* Petitions; Informants; Law Enforcement Officers or Agencies; Right to Counsel; Sixth Amendment) Wilson was charged with robbery and murder following a 1970 robbery of a taxi company and murder of the night dispatcher in the Bronx, NY. Following his arraignment, he was placed in a cell with Lee, a paid government informant.

Wilson made various incriminating statements to Lee, which were reported to police and used against Wilson later in his trial. According to Lee, Wilson's incriminating statements to him were "unsolicited" and "spontaneous." Wilson was convicted. He filed a *habeas corpus* petition alleging that his incriminating statements to Lee should have been suppressed. He claimed that his Sixth Amendment right to counsel had been violated when police deliberately elicited statements from him through Lee acting on their behalf (*see Massiah v. United States* [1964]). The state court failed to vacate his conviction on those grounds, and Wilson appealed to federal court. The Circuit Court of Appeals reversed his conviction on these grounds. New York appealed this ruling to the SC, which reversed the lower appellate court ruling, thus *reinstating* Wilson's murder and robbery convictions. The SC held that apart from any information derived from the informant, Lee, there was sufficient additional inculpatory evidence against Wilson to support his conviction anyway. Further, New York courts had determined that a police officer had merely instructed Lee to "listen" to Wilson and not to elicit statements from him. Thus, unsolicited statements or statements made voluntarily do not violate a person's Sixth Amendment right to counsel during "interrogations" by police-paid sponsored informants.

Kyles v. Whitley, 514 U.S. 419, 115 S.Ct. 1555 (1995) [Curtis Lee KYLES, Petitioner, v. John P. WHITLEY, Warden] (Death Penalty; Discovery) Kyles was accused in Louisiana of first-degree murder. During the trial, the prosecution failed to disclose to Kyles favorable and exculpatory evidence under discovery. For instance, eyewitness testimony and statements favorable to Kyles were withheld, as were statements made to police by an informant, Beanie. A computer printout of all car license numbers at or near the murder scene, which did not include Kyles' car license number, was in the possession of the prosecution but was not made available to Kyles or his attorney when they demanded discovery. Kyles was convicted and sentenced to death. Appeals by Kyles to higher state courts resulted in affirmation of his original conviction and sentence. Then he sought relief by an appeal to the SC. The SC overturned Kyles' conviction, holding that the prosecution had violated Kyles' *Brady* rights (*see Brady v. Maryland* [1963]) to have relevant exculpatory information made available to him by the prosecution. The significance of this case is that it is the constitutional duty of prosecutors to disclose favorable evidence to defendants in criminal prosecutions.

Kyllo v. United States, 533 U.S. 27, 121 U.S. 2038 (2001) [Danny Lee KYLLO, Petitioner, v. UNITED STATES] (Fourth Amendment; Thermal Imaging Equipment) Kyllo was suspected of growing marijuana in his home in Florence, OR. U.S. Department of the Interior agents used a thermal imaging device to scan the triplex in which Kyllo lived, in order to determine the amount of heat emanating from it and whether the heat was consistent with high-intensity lamps used for indoor marijuana growth. The thermal scan disclosed that Kyllo's garage roof and a side wall were relatively hot compared with the rest of his home and warmer than neighboring units. Based in part on the thermal imaging evidence, a federal magistrate issued a search warrant of Kyllo's premises, where marijuana was found. Kyllo was successfully indicted on a charge of manufacturing marijuana and entered a conditional guilty plea, which was immediately appealed. The Ninth Circuit Court of Appeals upheld the search as valid, because Kyllo had made no attempt to conceal the heat escaping from his home, and even if he had, there was no objectively reasonable expectation of privacy because the thermal imager did not expose any intimate details of Kyllo's life, only amorphous hot spots on his home's exterior. Kyllo appealed to the SC, who heard the case. The SC reversed the Ninth Circuit, holding that if the government uses a device that is not in general public use to explore details of a private home that would previously have been unknowable without physical intrusion, the surveillance is a Fourth Amendment search and is presumptively unreasonable without a warrant. Thermal imaging disclosures cannot form the basis for a valid search warrant of one's home without additional evidence to support probable cause.

L

Lackawanna County District Attorney v. Coss, 532 U.S. 394, 121 S.Ct. 1567 (2001) [**LACKAWANNA COUNTY DISTRICT ATTORNEY et al., Petitioners, v. Edward R. COSS, Jr.**] (*Habeas Corpus* **Petitions; Ineffective Assistance of Counsel; Sixth Amendment**) Edward Coss was convicted in a Pennsylvania court in 1986 for simple assault, institutional vandalism, and criminal mischief. A subsequent appeal alleging ineffective assistance of counsel was lodged by Coss, but the Pennsylvania courts never ruled on the appeal. Subsequently, Coss served the full sentences for his 1986 convictions, but he was convicted again in 1990 for aggravated assault and sentenced to from six to 12 years. He successfully challenged his 1990 conviction on a direct appeal and was resentenced on remand because of some prejudicial errors of fact in a presentence investigation report that had been filed. At the time, although the sentencing judge mentioned his 1986 convictions, these convictions played no part in his new sentence. Rather, the judge noted other factors, including Coss' extensive criminal record, and reimposed a new six- to 12-year sentence. Coss filed a writ of *habeas corpus,* claiming that his 1986 convictions were constitutionally invalid, and thus he had been in custody from 1986–1990 in violation of his constitutional rights. A federal district court denied Coss' petition and said that he had not been prejudiced by his 1986 counsel's ineffectiveness. However, the Third Circuit Court of Appeals remanded, holding that although the district court had jurisdiction, there was a "reasonable probability" that but for Coss' counsel's ineffectiveness, Coss would not have been convicted in 1986. Further, the Third Circuit declared that indeed, the sentencing court for the 1990 conviction took into account Coss' 1986 convictions and that the reference to these convictions prejudiced his case and subsequent sentence. The Lackawanna County District Attorney's Office appealed to

the SC, who heard the case. The SC reversed the Third Circuit, holding that any consideration the trial court may have given to Coss' 1986 convictions in reimposing a sentence of his 1990 conviction did not actually affect his new sentence. The SC noted that Coss' substantial criminal background, excluding his 1986 convictions, regardless of their validity, more than justified the sentence Coss received for his 1990 crime.

Lackey v. Texas, 514 U.S. 1045, 115 S.Ct. 1421 (1995) [**Clarence Allen LACKEY, Petitioner, v. TEXAS**] (**Cruel and Unusual Punishment; Death Penalty; Eighth Amendment**) Lackey was convicted of murder and remained on death row for 17 years. He filed an appeal to the SC, arguing that 17 years on death row was cruel and unusual punishment in violation of his rights under the Eighth Amendment. The SC denied Lackey's writ of *certiorari,* commenting that this particular question was a "novel one" that should benefit from further study (at 1422). Justice Breyer commented that the issue was "an important *undecided* one" [emphasis added]. The SC further elaborated that often, death-row inmates cause long delays because of frivolous filings of motions or through escape or other delays. In short, the 17-year death-row period was not decided either way as cruel and unusual punishment in this particular case.

Lakeside v. Oregon, 435 U.S. 333, 98 S.Ct. 1091 (1978) [**Ensio Ruben LAKESIDE, Petitioner, v. State of OREGON**] (**Death Penalty**) Lakeside escaped from the Multnomah County Correctional Institution. During his trial on the escape charges, his attorney introduced evidence to show that he was not responsible for his actions because he was mentally ill. Lakeside did not testify in his own behalf. The judge advised the jury that no adverse inference should be drawn from that fact. However, before giving his jury instructions, the judge had been asked by the defense counsel not to mention the fact that Lakeside did not have to testify. The judge ignored this request and gave the instruction anyway. Lakeside was convicted. He appealed, alleging that his right against compulsory self-incrimination had been violated when the judge gave the jury that instruction despite the request from defense counsel. The SC rejected Lakeside's appeal, saying that although it may be wise for a trial judge not to give such a cautionary instruction over defense counsel's objection, trial judges may do so as a matter of law, unless their state instructs otherwise. Thus, Lakeside's Fifth and Fourteenth Amendment rights had not been infringed.

Lambrix v. Singletary, 520 U.S. 518, 117 S.Ct. 1517 (1997) [**Cary Michael LAMBRIX, Petitioner, v. Harry K. SINGLETARY, Jr., Secretary, Florida Department of Corrections**] (**Aggravating and Mitigating Circumstances; Fifth Amendment;** *Habeas Corpus* **Petitions; Self-Incrimination**) Lambrix was convicted of murdering two women. The Florida jury rendered an advisory verdict recommending death sentences in both cases, finding numerous aggravating circumstances, and no mitigating circumstances. Lambrix sought *habeas corpus* relief after his convictions were upheld by the Florida Supreme Court. Lambrix argued that a case, *Espinosa v. Florida* (1992), had recently been decided and had held that where invalid aggravating circumstances are cited, and where fundamental fairness and the accuracy of the criminal proceeding are jeopardized, neither the judge nor the jury is constitutionally permitted to weigh invalid aggravating circumstances. Specifically, Lambrix challenged that the jury was improperly instructed on the "especially heinous, atrocious, or cruel" aggravators. The Florida Supreme Court said Lambrix was procedurally barred from basing appeals on SC cases decided after his own conviction. The SC heard Lambrix's appeal and affirmed the Florida Supreme Court, holding that a prisoner whose conviction became final before *Espinosa* is foreclosed from relying on that decision in a federal *habeas corpus* proceeding. The SC added that there was no error for the trial judge to cure, because under Florida law the trial court, not the jury, is the sentencer. Further, the trial court's weighing of properly narrowed aggravators and mitigators was sufficiently independent of the jury to cure any error in the jury's consideration of a vague aggravator.

Lamont v. Postmaster General, 381 U.S. 301, 85 S.Ct. 1493 (1965) [**Corliss LAMONT, dba Basic Pamphlets, Appellant, v. POSTMASTER GENERAL of the United States. John F. Fixa, Individually and as Postmaster, San Francisco, California, et al., Appellants, v. Leif Heilberg**] (**Corrections; First Amendment; Free Speech; Inmate Rights**) Mail from Communist countries, in the form of propaganda-like literature and leaflets, was being routinely destroyed by the United States Post Office and letter carriers under a statute that permitted that agency to destroy unsealed foreign mail determined to be Communist political propaganda. This statute was challenged, and the SC ruled it unconstitutional in violation of the First Amendment right of free speech.

Lanier v. South Carolina, 474 U.S. 25, 106 S.Ct. 297 (1985) [**Kenneth Dale LANIER v. SOUTH CAROLINA**] (**Confessions; Fifth Amendment; Fourth Amendment; Law Enforcement Officers or Agencies;** *Miranda* **Warning**) Lanier was suspected in a robbery and arrested, although no arrest warrant had been prepared beforehand. During police interrogation, he gave a voluntary confession after being told his *Miranda* rights. He was convicted. Lanier appealed, contending that because no arrest warrant had been issued, his arrest was illegal; thus, his confession, tainted by the illegal arrest, had also been illegally obtained and should not have been admissible in court against him. Further review by the South Carolina Supreme Court led the court to conclude that Lanier's confession was admissible, despite the illegal arrest, because it was voluntarily given. He appealed again. The SC reversed the conviction, holding that voluntariness is insufficient on its own to purge the taint of an illegal arrest. Voluntariness is merely a threshold requirement for Fourth Amendment analysis.

Lankford v. Idaho, 500 U.S. 110, 111 S.Ct. 1723 (1991) [**Bryan Stuart LANKFORD, Petitioner, v. IDAHO**] (**Aggravating and Mitigating Circumstances; Corrections; Death Penalty**) In this rather complicated case, Lankford and his brother were charged with first-degree murder but entered a guilty plea in exchange for a minimum 10-year term. The judge refused to approve the plea agreement and the case went to trial. The defense and prosecuting attorneys proceeded as though the 10-year minimum term was being sought as a pun-

ishment and the death penalty was not contemplated. When the brothers were convicted of the murder, the judge asked whether either party wished to cite aggravating or mitigating circumstances to determine the type of sentence imposed. Neither side indicated this, and in the sentencing phase, the two brothers were recommended for long prison terms. The judge, however, decided that the punishment was too lenient and imposed the death penalty on both brothers, citing several aggravating circumstances in justification. The brothers appealed. The SC overturned the death penalty because neither side had been permitted to argue the merits of aggravating or mitigating circumstances. The judge's personal feelings in the matter had come too late in the proceeding for either side to address the aggravating and mitigating circumstances. Thus, the SC ruled that the sentences of death were unconstitutional because the judge had failed to provide adequate notice that they would be imposed.

Lanza v. State of New York, 370 U.S. 139, 82 S.Ct. 1218 (1962) [**Harry LANZA, Petitioner, v. STATE OF NEW YORK**] (**Fourth Amendment; Inmate Rights**) Lanza had a visit from his brother in a local jail. At the time, an electronic device was installed in the meeting room, where their conversation was intercepted. Subsequently, a transcript was made of their conversation. A state legislative committee investigating corruption in the state parole system called Lanza to testify concerning the remarks he made to his brother during the jail visit, and Lanza refused. He was convicted for failing to testify and appealed, alleging that it was improper for jail officials to electronically record his conversations with family members in jail visiting rooms. The SC upheld his conviction, holding that a jail room is not the equivalent of a house or car, where there might be a reasonable expectation of privacy. A jail is not a constitutionally protected area.

Lascelles v. Georgia, 148 U.S. 537, 13 S.Ct. 687 (1893) [**Sidney LASCELLES, Petitioner, v. State of GEORGIA**] (**Law Enforcement Officers or Agencies**) Lascelles was a former resident of Georgia who was living in New York. While in New York, he was served with an extradition order to Georgia to face indictments for larceny and fraud. After he was extradited to Georgia on these charges, another Georgia grand jury indicted him on other charges, for which he was subsequently tried and convicted. He contested this new conviction, saying that he should have been permitted to return to New York rather than face new indictments in Georgia. The SC affirmed his conviction, noting that there is no requirement for any state to bar trying a defendant for new offenses after he has been extradited to that state for earlier alleged offenses. Defendants may be tried for any other offenses than those specified in the requisition in the extradition, and no constitutional right is thereby denied. In short, if a person is extradited to a state for a specific charge, nothing exists to prevent the extraditing state from bringing new charges against him.

Lawrence v. Texas, ___U.S.___, 123 S.Ct. 2472 (2003) [**John Geddes LAWRENCE and Tyron Garner, Petitioners, v. TEXAS**] (**Sodomy Laws**) Texas police officers responded to a reported weapons disturbance in a private residence and observed John Lawrence and Tyron Garner engaging in a private, consensual sexual act. Lawrence and Garner were arrested and convicted of deviate sexual intercourse in violation of a Texas statute that prohibited two persons of the same sex from engaging in certain intimate sexual conduct. Lawrence and Garner appealed, but their convictions were upheld by higher Texas courts. An appeal was thus directed to the SC, who heard the case. The SC reversed the Texas courts and set aside these convictions, holding that the Texas statute making it a crime for two persons of the same sex to engage in certain intimate sexual conduct violates the due-process clause of the Fourteenth Amendment. The SC further overturned the case of *Bowers v. Hardwick* (1986), which had previously upheld state statutes prohibiting sodomy between consenting adults. The SC declared that the *Bowers* case was wrong in that it prohibited intimate acts between consenting adults when such acts were not intended to produce offspring. The view that an act is immoral is not sufficient for upholding a law prohibiting a sexual practice. Furthermore, individual decisions about physical relationships, even when not intended to produce offspring, are a form of liberty protected by due process. This analysis should have controlled *Bowers,* and it controls here. *Bowers* was not correct when it was decided, it is not correct today, and it is hereby overruled. This case does not involve minors, persons who might be injured or coerced, those who might not easily refuse consent, or public conduct or prostitution. It does involve two adults who, with full and mutual consent, engaged in sexual practices common to a homosexual lifestyle. Petitioners' right to liberty under the due-process clause gives them the full right to engage in private conduct without government intervention.

Lee v. Illinois, 476 U.S. 530, 106 S.Ct. 2056 (1986) [**Millie R. LEE, Petitioner, v. ILLINOIS**] (**Confrontation Clause; Sixth Amendment**) Lee and Thomas had killed Lee's aunt and a friend by stabbing them to death. Later, Thomas confessed to police about his role in the murders and implicated Lee. During their subsequent joint trial, neither testified in his or her own behalf. However, portions of Thomas' confession implicating Lee were read to the jury over the objections of Lee's attorney. They were both convicted. Lee appealed, arguing that she had been denied her Sixth Amendment right to confront her accuser, Thomas, as he had not testified. The SC held that an uncorroborated confession from a codefendant cannot suffice to satisfy the confrontation-clause requirements of the Sixth Amendment. Because Lee had not been permitted to cross-examine Thomas about the veracity of his confession, her right to a fair trial and to confront the witness against her had been violated. Hence, her conviction was overturned.

Lee v. Kemna, ___U.S.___, 122 S.Ct. 877 (2002) [**Remon LEE, Petitioner, v. Mike KEMNA, Superintendent, Crossroads Correctional Center**] (**Due Process;** *Habeas Corpus* **Petitions**) Remon Lee was tried for first-degree murder and a related crime in a Missouri court. According to prosecutor allegations, Lee was the driver of a getaway car when a passenger, Reginald Rhodes, shot and killed Steven Shelby in Kansas City, MO, on August 27, 1992. Lee's trial took place within a three-day time span in February 1994. Lee claimed that he wasn't in Missouri at the time of the crime and had been a victim of mistaken identity. His alibi witnesses included several of his family members, who had traveled to Missouri to testify during his trial. When it came time for them to testify, the family members could not be located. Lee's attorney attempted to obtain a continuance, but the trial judge denied the motion. The motion was denied because the judge's daughter was going to be in the hospital the next day and the judge wanted to be with her. The judge further declared that another trial commitment the following day prevented him from granting a continuance for Lee's trial. Without his alibi witnesses, Lee was convicted and sentenced to life without the possibility of parole. Two of the witnesses against Lee included William Sanders, who was unable to pick Lee out of a photographic array on the day of the shooting, but who later identified Lee as the driver for the first time 18 months after the murder. The second witness admitted that he had first identified Lee as a passenger and not the driver of the vehicle involved in the murder. These irregularities were ignored by the court. Subsequently, Lee determined from his family members that an officer of the court advised them that they were not needed and could leave the courthouse shortly before they were supposed to testify in Lee's case. Furthermore, the prosecutor declared in his closing argument before the jury that Lee had promised witnesses as his alibi, but he said, "Where are those alibi witnesses that [defense counsel] promised you from opening? They're not here." After deliberating three hours, the jury found Lee guilty. Lee appealed, arguing that his due-process rights had been violated because he had been denied the right to put on an alibi defense. The Missouri Supreme Court denied Lee's request for postconviction relief, partly on the grounds that Lee's appeal was procedurally flawed in that it was not in writing and unaccompanied by an affidavit. Lee appealed to the SC, who heard the case. Lee appended his appeal with written statements from his alibi witnesses. The SC, mildly implying prosecutorial misconduct in the case because of the court officer's instruction to Lee's alibi witnesses on the day of his trial that they were no longer needed, vacated Lee's conviction and remanded the case to the trial court for further proceedings. The significance of this case is that trial courts must ensure due process to defendants offering timely claims of alibi defenses and that continuances because of extraordinary circumstances should be granted to enable the defense to present a full and fair hearing on the anticipated evidence and testimony.

Lee v. Washington, 390 U.S. 333, 88 S.Ct. 994 (1968) [**Frank LEE, Commissioner of Corrections of Alabama, et al., Appellants, v. Caliph WASHINGTON et al.**] (**Corrections; Inmate Rights**) In the early 1960s, the Alabama prison system was segregated racially, with black prisoners in one section and white prisoners in another. Prisoners filed suit alleging racial discrimination relative to where they were placed in the prison. The SC decided that the Alabama prison system practice of segregating prisoners was in direct violation of the Fourteenth Amendment and therefore unconstitutional.

Lefkowitz v. Turley, 414 U.S. 70, 94 S.Ct. 316 (1973) [Louis J. LEFKOWITZ, Attorney General of New York, et al., Appellants, v. M. Russell TURLEY et al.] (Corrections; Fifth Amendment; Immunity; Inmate Rights; Self-Incrimination) New York statutes provided that contractors must waive their immunity to testify concerning their state contracts in such hearings as grand-jury proceedings. If contractors refuse to testify, then their contracts with the state are subject to cancellation. This statute was appealed by Turley and others as unconstitutional on various grounds, including the Fifth Amendment right against self-incrimination. A circuit court of appeals held the statute unconstitutional, and New York appealed. The SC affirmed the unconstitutionality of the statute, saying that a state may not insist that public employees or government contractors waive their Fifth Amendment privilege against self-incrimination and consent to the use of the fruits of the interrogation in any later proceeding. A significant infringement of constitutional rights, such as the right against compelled self-incrimination, cannot be justified by the speculative ability of those affected to cover the damage.

Lego v. Twomey, 404 U.S. 477, 92 S.Ct. 619 (1972) [Don Richard LEGO, Petitioner, v. John TWOMEY, Warden] (Self-Incrimination) Lego confessed to a crime after interrogation by police in Illinois. Some dispute arose during the trial to suggest that his confession was not voluntarily given. Lego was convicted. He appealed, alleging that the confession had not been voluntary. The SC upheld his conviction, saying that despite the fact that the voluntariness of the confession had been questioned, if the jury believed that it was freely given, then it might consider the confession in deciding Lego's guilt or innocence. In this case, the SC said it was only sufficient to demonstrate by a preponderance of the evidence whether Lego's confession was indeed voluntary, although states other than Illinois can establish stricter standards if they wish to do so.

Lewis v. Casey, 518 U.S. 343, 116 S.Ct. 2174 (1996) [Samuel A. LEWIS, Director, Arizona Department of Corrections, et al., Petitioners, v. Fletcher CASEY, Jr., et al.] (Inmate Rights) Casey and others filed a class-action suit against the Arizona Department of Corrections (ADOC) alleging that the state was providing prisoners with inadequate legal research facilities and thereby depriving them of their right of access to the courts, in violation of *Bounds v. Smith* (1977). The allegations included charges that some inmates were either illiterate or non-English speakers and were disenfranchised by the legal assistance available in Arizona prisons, and that inmates in lockdown were unreasonably deprived of timely access to legal materials and thus their subsequent appeals were jeopardized. A federal court ruled against the ADOC, and the state appealed. The SC reversed, holding (1) that inmates claiming denial of access to the courts cannot establish actual injury simply by showing that the prison law library is sub par in some theoretical sense; (2) that finding only two inmates who had suffered actual injury as the result of an inability to receive adequate legal assistance because they were illiterate or non-English speakers is insufficient to support a systemwide injunction mandating detailed changes in the state's provisions for inmate legal services; and (3) that prisoners under lockdown do not have their rights violated by delays of up to 16 days in receiving legal materials or legal assistance, even if such delays result in actual injury, especially if the lockdown relates to and is the product of prison regulations that relate to legitimate penological interests.

Lewis v. Jeffers, 497 U.S. 764, 110 S.Ct. 3092 (1990) [Samuel A. LEWIS, Director, Arizona Department of Corrections, et al., Petitioners, v. Jimmie Wayne JEFFERS] (Aggravating and Mitigating Circumstances; Death Penalty; Eighth Amendment) Jeffers and his girlfriend, Cheney, were arrested and held in the Pima County Jail on charges of possessing narcotics and stolen property. While on bail, Jeffers determined that Cheney was cooperating with police and made arrangements to kill her. Under false pretenses, he invited her to his apartment, gave her an overdose of heroin, and when she didn't die immediately, used his belt to strangle her. Following her death, Jeffers and a friend injected her body with considerably more heroin and took numerous photographs of her dead body, wrapped her in newspapers and plastic bags, and buried her in a shallow grave. Later, when Jeffers was arrested, tried, and convicted of her murder, the judge gave instructions to the jury during the penalty phase of the trial. The jury found two aggravating circumstances and no mitigating ones and recommended the death penalty for Jeffers. Jeffers appealed, alleging that the jury instruction containing the phrase "especially heinous . . . and depraved" was overly broad and unconstitutionally vague. The SC heard Jeffers' appeal and upheld his conviction and death sentence, thus rejecting his various claims. The statutory circumstance that the crime was committed in "an especially heinous, cruel, or depraved manner" was not unconstitutionally vague, and further, the jury, a rational body, could have found that Jeffers had committed the murder in this manner. Thus, Jeffers' Eighth and Sixth Amendment rights had not been violated.

Lewis v. United States, 385 U.S. 206, 87 S.Ct. 424 (1966) [Duke Lee LEWIS, Petitioner, v. UNITED STATES] (Fourth Amendment; Informants; Searches and Seizures) An undercover agent purchased marijuana from Lewis on two different occasions. In one instance, he entered Lewis' home and bought marijuana. Lewis was subsequently convicted, partially by the testimony given by the undercover agent. Lewis appealed, alleging his Fourth Amendment right against unreasonable searches and seizures had been violated. The SC disagreed and upheld his conviction, saying that the misrepresentation of the undercover agent's identity and Lewis' willingness to sell marijuana were insufficient to show that a Fourth Amendment rights violation had occurred.

Lewis v. United States, 518 U.S. 322, 116 S.Ct. 2163 (1996) [Ray A. LEWIS, Petitioner, v. UNITED STATES] (Jury Trials; Sixth Amendment) Lewis was a mail handler for the U.S. Postal Service. Lewis was observed by other postal workers opening some mail and removing and pocketing the contents. They next placed some "test mail" containing marked currency in a place where Lewis would have access to it, and Lewis opened it and removed the currency. Postal inspectors subsequently arrested Lewis, and he was charged with two counts of obstructing the mail, with each count carrying a maximum six-month sentence. Lewis requested a jury trial but was denied one, because according to the judge, the crimes were petty and did not require a jury trial. Furthermore, the judge advised Lewis that he would not sentence him to any term of jail longer than six months. A bench trial was conducted and Lewis was convicted and sentenced to a six-month jail term. Lewis appealed, contending that the aggregate amount of time for the two separate charges of obstructing the mail exceeded the six-month minimum, and that therefore his Sixth Amendment right to a jury trial was violated. The SC heard the case and affirmed Lewis' conviction, holding that a defendant who is prosecuted for multiple petty offenses does not have a Sixth Amendment right to a jury trial where the aggregate prison term authorized for the offenses exceeds six months. The right to a jury trial is reserved for defendants accused of serious offenses and does not extend to petty offenses. Petty offenses are not transformed into serious ones because their aggregate terms of punishment exceed six months.

Libretti v. United States, 516 U.S. 29, 116 U.S. 356 (1995) [**Joseph LIBRETTI, Petitioner, v. UNITED STATES**] (**Asset Forfeiture**) Libretti was convicted in federal court of various drug, money-laundering, and firearms offenses. He entered a guilty plea and was convicted. The government then seized all his criminal-tainted assets, including assets Libretti believed were beyond the scope of forfeiture. He appealed the more extensive forfeiture, contending that he had not been advised of it during his plea-bargain hearing and that he should have been so advised by the judge and prosecutor. The SC upheld the conviction and the more extensive asset forfeiture, holding that a plea agreement does not obligate the judge to set forth all material possessions subject to forfeiture, and that the plea agreement itself is designed to determine the voluntariness of the plea, among other things, and whether the offender is knowingly and intelligently waiving his rights to trial, confronting witnesses against him, and other provisions. When Libretti waived his right to a jury trial, he gave up the right to have a subsequent separate jury determination of which of his assets ought to be seized.

Lilly v. Virginia, 527 U.S. 116, 119 S.Ct. 1887 (1999) [**Benjamin Lee LILLY, Petitioner, v. VIRGINIA**] (**Confrontation Clause; Death Penalty; Sixth Amendment**) Benjamin Lilly, his brother Mark, and Gary Barker were arrested following a two-day crime spree, in which they stole liquor and guns, and abducted and murdered Alex DeFilippis. Mark Lilly confessed to stealing, but claimed his brother Benjamin killed DeFilippis. Later, at Benjamin Lilly's trial, Mark Lilly was called as a witness against him; however, Mark invoked his Fifth Amendment right against self-incrimination. Nevertheless, the trial court allowed the government to admit into evidence against Benjamin Lilly the confession given by Mark Lilly implicating his brother in the murder. Benjamin Lilly was convicted, sentenced to death, and appealed, contending that he was denied the right of confronting his accuser in court under his Sixth Amendment right. The Virginia Supreme Court upheld Lilly's murder conviction and death sentence and Lilly appealed to the SC for relief. The SC heard the case

and reversed his conviction on the grounds that his Sixth Amendment right to confront his accuser had been violated. The SC held that introducing Mark Lilly's tape-recorded statements to police at trial without making him available for cross-examination was a confrontation-clause violation.

Linkletter v. Walker, 381 U.S. 618, 85 S.Ct. 1731 (1965) [**Victor LINKLETTER, Petitioner, v. Victor G. WALKER, Warden**] (**Exclusionary Rule;** *Habeas Corpus* **Petitions**) Linkletter was arrested without a warrant in Louisiana. Police took him to the police station, where they searched him. Then the police went to his home and seized certain property and papers. Subsequently, they searched his place of business, finding incriminating information. All of these searches were conducted without a warrant. The searches were subsequently upheld as valid, based on probable cause, and incident to an arrest. Linkletter was convicted of burglary. Some time later, in June 1961, *Mapp v. Ohio* was decided, thereby extending the exclusionary rule to all states to deter police misconduct in conducting warrantless searches of a defendant's premises similar to the searches of Linkletter's business and dwelling. Linkletter filed a *habeas corpus* petition, claiming that the evidence police seized in his case ought to have been suppressed, given the decision in the *Mapp* case. The SC heard his appeal and upheld his conviction, saying that the exclusionary rule cannot be applied retroactively because his conviction occurred prior to the *Mapp* decision. The significance of this case is that it demonstrates that subsequent SC decisions are not retroactively applied to prior cases. The exclusionary rule does not apply to cases decided before *Mapp*. The SC was careful to note, however, that such retrospective applications of rules *may* be made in future cases, depending on the issue and law.

Lisenba v. People of the State of California, 314 U.S. 219, 62 S.Ct. 280 (1941) [**Major Raymond LISENBA v. PEOPLE OF THE STATE OF CALIFORNIA**] (**Corrections; Death Penalty**) Lisenba was accused of murder in California. He used an alias, Robert S. James. He was questioned extensively when he was first arrested. He confessed and was convicted. Later he appealed, claiming that his confession had been coerced. However, the SC noted that Lisenba had showed a self-possession, a coolness, and an acumen throughout his questioning and at his trial that negated the view that he had so lost his freedom of action that the statements made were not his but were the result of the deprivation of his free choice to admit, to deny, or to refuse to answer. Accordingly, the SC upheld his murder conviction and dismissed his allegations of coercion.

Liteky v. United States, 510 U.S. 540, 114 S.Ct. 1147 (1994) [**John Patrick LITEKY, Charles Joseph Liteky, and Roy Lawrence Bourgeois, Petitioners, v. UNITED STATES**] (**Discrimination**) Liteky and other persons were arrested for willfully injuring federal property. The indictment charged that Liteky and others had committed acts of vandalism, including the spilling of human blood on walls and various objects, at the Fort Benning Military Reservation. During the trial, the judge made frequent remarks interpreted as caustic, critical, or disapproving of, or hostile to, Liteky's counsel, Liteky, and his codefendants. Liteky was convicted. He appealed, arguing that the judge should have excused himself from the case because of his bias and prejudicial remarks made during the trial. The SC rejected Liteky's argument, holding that the fact that the presiding judge may, upon completion of the evidence, be exceedingly ill-disposed toward the defendant, who has been shown to be a thoroughly reprehensible person, does not make the judge excusable for bias or prejudice, as his knowledge and the opinion it produced were properly and necessarily acquired in the course of the proceedings and might be necessary to completion of the judge's task. The significance of this case, in part, is that federal judges have considerable latitude in their remarks made during criminal trials. It takes more than expressions of hostility or impatience or animosity to create conditions under which federal judges must excuse themselves from a federal district court criminal proceeding.

Lockett v. Ohio, 438 U.S. 586, 98 S.Ct. 2954 (1978) [Sandra LOCKETT, Petitioner, v. State of OHIO] (Corrections; Death Penalty) Lockett was convicted of aggravated murder and robbery and sentenced to death. Because she had been primarily an "aider and abettor" rather than the perpetrator of the crime, she challenged her conviction on various grounds. She alleged that it was improper for the prosecutor to make remarks to the jury to the effect that the state's evidence was "unrefuted" and "uncontradicted"; that exclusion of prospective jurors who indicated that they could not be trusted to decide the death penalty because of their particular views was improper; that she had not been given adequate notice of the meaning of the statute under which she was convicted; and that the death penalty statute did not permit consideration of aggravating and mitigating circumstances. The SC heard the appeal and ruled negatively on the first three allegations. However, it overturned her death sentence on the fourth allegation, noting that Ohio had an unusual means of considering aggravating and mitigating circumstances in its present death-penalty sentencing procedures. Specifically, the limited range of mitigating circumstances that might be considered was in violation of both the Eighth and Fourteenth Amendments.

Lockhart v. Fretwell, 506 U.S. 364, 113 S.Ct. 838 (1993) [A.L. LOCKHART, Director, Arkansas Department of Correction, Petitioner, v. Bobby Ray FRETWELL] (Aggravating and Mitigating Circumstances; Right to Counsel; Sixth Amendment) Fretwell was convicted of capital murder in Arkansas and sentenced to death. Subsequently, the death penalty was vacated and Fretwell was sentenced to life without parole. That sentence was imposed after it was determined that there were several errors involving Fretwell's counsel. One of these "errors" involved failing to make a motion protesting the inclusion of an aggravating factor that duplicated one of the elements of the capital murder offense. Arkansas appealed and the SC heard the case. The SC reinstated the death sentence, holding that the defense attorney's actions had not been sufficiently prejudicial to warrant setting aside the death sentence. Prejudice in this instance referred to specific trial unreliability or irregularities, not to weighing aggravating and mitigating circumstances. Further, Fretwell would have had to show that the defense counsel's errors had been so prejudicial as to render the trial fundamentally unfair or unreliable. Fretwell had failed to demonstrate this.

Lockhart v. McCree, 476 U.S. 162, 106 S.Ct. 1758 (1986) [A.L. LOCKHART, Director, Arkansas Department of Correction, Petitioner, v. Ardia V. McCREE] (Corrections; Death Penalty; Death-Qualified Juries) McCree was charged with capital murder. During jury selection at McCree's trial, the judge dismissed for cause various jurors who voiced their opposition to the death penalty, which was a consideration in McCree's case. The jury eventually convicted McCree of murder, but they recommended life without parole. McCree appealed the sentence, contending that the judge had had no right to remove prospective jurors simply because they opposed the death penalty. The SC upheld McCree's conviction, holding that it is constitutional in a capital murder case for jurors to be excused who oppose the death penalty in such a way that their performance as jurors would substantially be impaired. This case upholds the right of the judge and prosecutors to strike prospective jurors who oppose the death penalty and whose judgment would be impaired as a result, without violating the constitutional rights of the accused to enjoy a fair and impartial trial. Thus, the notion of a death-qualified jury was upheld here (*compare this case with Witherspoon v. Illinois* [1968] *on a similar issue*).

Lockyer v. Andrade, ___U.S.___, 123 S.Ct. 1166 (2003) [Bill LOCKYER, Attorney General of California, Petitioner, v. Leandro ANDRADE] (Cruel and Unusual Punishment; Eighth Amendment; Habitual Offender Statutes) In November 1995, Leandro Andrade stole five videotapes worth $85 from a Kmart store in Ontario, CA. About two weeks later, Andrade stole four additional videotapes from another Kmart store, but he was apprehended by a security guard. California authorities determined that Andrade had several previous felony convictions and they charged him with theft. Furthermore, under California's three-strikes law, any felony can constitute the third strike, and this third strike can subject an offender to a term of 25 years to life. The prosecutor charged Andrade with two felony counts in the tape thefts and sought imprisonment for Andrade of 25 years to life under the three-strikes law. Andrade was subsequently convicted of each of the thefts and sentenced to two consecutive terms of 25 years to life. Andrade appealed, alleging disproportionality of punishment in violation of the Eighth Amendment prohibition against cruel and unusual punishment. The Ninth Circuit Court of Appeals heard Andrade's appeal and reversed his convictions. California appealed and the SC heard the case. The SC reversed the circuit court and reinstated Andrade's convictions and sentences, holding that Andrade's sentences do not violate the Eighth Amendment prohibition against cruel and unusual punishment. Compelling evidence in supporting the SC's decision was Andrade's record of numerous state and federal convictions for serious felonies.

Logue v. United States, 412 U.S. 521, 93 S.Ct. 2215 (1973) [Orval C. LOGUE et al., Petitioners, v. UNITED STATES] (Federal Tort Claims; Inmate Rights) Logue, an arrestee who was taken into custody by U.S. Marshals on charges that he had smuggled marijuana into the United

States, was placed in the Nueces County Jail in Texas to await trial. While in jail, he committed suicide by hanging himself. Logue's family sued under the Federal Tort Claims Act. The SC eventually heard the case and rejected the family's claim against the U.S. government, holding that the Federal Tort Claims Act requires that any negligent action must be committed by a federal agency, and that although the Neuces County Jail was under contract with the federal government, it was not a federal agency. Thus, the Tort Claims Act had excluded a contractor with the United States from the definition of a federal agency. The Federal Tort Claims Act protects the United States from liability arising from the negligent acts or omissions by jail employees who are not employed by a federal agency.

Lo-Ji Sales, Inc., v. New York, 442 U.S. 319, 99 S.Ct. 2319 (1979) [LO-JI SALES, INC., Petitioner, v. State of NEW YORK] (Fourth Amendment; Law Enforcement Officers or Agencies; Obscenity Laws; Searches and Seizures) A New York police investigator purchased two films from Lo-Ji Sales, an "adult" bookstore. He concluded that such films were in violation of a New York obscenity ordinance. He obtained a general search warrant, authorizing officers to seize anything "similar" to the first two films. A subsequent six-hour search by officers yielded numerous films, projectors, magazines, and other "adult" paraphernalia. Lo-Ji Sales was charged with and convicted of violating the state obscenity ordinance. A motion to suppress the seized materials was denied. An appeal was subsequently directed to the SC, where the obscenity conviction was overturned. Although police argued that the Lo-Ji Sales "adult" bookstore was a "public place" and thus open to inspection, including searches and seizures, and that the attendant at the store "gave his consent" for the subsequent search, the SC rejected these rationales as invalid. The store clerk had been placed under arrest and thus was not in a position to give his consent. Furthermore, the search warrant had failed to specify the places to be searched and the items to be seized; it failed because of its lack of specificity. Thus, the items seized as the result of the unreasonable and illegal search were suppressed and the Lo-Ji conviction reversed.

Long v. District Court of Iowa, 385 U.S. 192, 87 S.Ct. 362 (1966) [Lawrence LONG, Petitioner, v. The DISTRICT COURT OF IOWA, in and for Lee County, Fort Madison, Iowa] (*Habeas Corpus* Petitions; Indigent Clients) Long was convicted of larceny. He was sentenced to a term "not to exceed five years." While serving his sentence in prison, Long filed for *habeas corpus* relief, alleging that his due-process rights had been violated because he had not been represented by counsel during his preliminary hearing and because the court would not give him, as an indigent, a free transcript of the *habeas corpus* proceeding. The Iowa court denied him the right to a free transcript and found his lack of attorney representation groundless. Long appealed to the SC, which overturned the Iowa court's decision denying him the right to a transcript. The SC said that to interpose any financial consideration between an indigent prisoner and his exercise of a state right to sue for his liberty is to deny that prisoner the equal protection of the laws.

Lopez v. Davis, 531 U.S. 230, 121 S.Ct. 714 (2001) [Christopher A. LOPEZ, Petitioner, v. Randy J. DAVIS, Warden, et al.] (Supervised Release Regulations; U.S. Bureau of Prisons Discretion) Randy Davis was convicted in federal court of possession with intent to distribute methamphetamine and the possession of a firearm during the commission of that offense. Davis was placed under the supervision of the Federal Bureau of Prisons (BOP) and incarcerated. He participated in and completed a drug-treatment program. Under a statute followed by the BOP, prisoners convicted of nonviolent crimes who complete a drug-treatment program may have their sentences reduced. However, the BOP refused to grant Davis early release, concluding that his prior involvement with a firearm in connection with another felony suggested a readiness to resort to life-endangering violence that was relevant to the early release decision. Davis filed a *habeas corpus* petition that was granted by the U.S. District Court. However, the Eighth Circuit Court of Appeals reversed that decision. Davis appealed therefore to the SC, which heard his case. The SC affirmed the circuit court and the decision of the BOP to deny Davis early release, holding that the BOP had discretion to promulgate a regulation that categorically denied early release to prisoners whose felonies involved the use of a firearm.

Lopez v. United States, 373 U.S. 427, 83 S.Ct. 1381 (1963) [German S. LOPEZ, Petitioner, v. UNITED STATES] (Electronic Surveillance, Wiretapping; Law Enforcement Officers or Agencies) Lopez was under investigation by the IRS for income-tax evasion. An IRS agent called Lopez and recorded a conversation during which Lopez offered the agent a bribe to ignore undeclared income. The incriminating statement was subsequently admitted into evidence against Lopez, and he was convicted. He appealed, contending that no warrant had been obtained to conduct such electronic surveillance and that his incriminating statements ought to have been excluded. The SC heard the case and upheld Lopez's conviction, saying that the IRS agent, as a participant in the conversation, had been entitled to record it, without giving notice to the other party that such a recording was being made. The importance of this case is that it authorizes warrantless recordings of conversations, wherein *one* of the parties *consents* to the recording despite the other party's ignorance of the fact that the conversation is being recorded. Thus, if anyone wishes to tape-record a telephone conversation without the knowledge or consent of the other party, the recording will be admissible as evidence as long as *one* of the parties consents to the recording. This does not mean, however, that conversations between two parties can be recorded by a third party without a warrant based on probable cause. (*See* **Berger v. New York** [1967] *for a specific statement on intercepted recordings of conversations and lawful wiretaps.*)

Los Angeles v. Lyons, 461 U.S. 95, 103 S.Ct. 1660 (1983) [City of LOS ANGELES, Petitioner, v. Adolph LYONS] (Law Enforcement Officers or Agencies) Lyons was stopped by Los Angeles police officers for a traffic violation. During the stop, police seized him and placed him in a choke hold. He offered no resistance, and the choke hold was applied without provocation or justification. It damaged Lyons' larynx. Lyons sued Los Angeles, but the city denied him relief. The SC heard the case and ruled that Lyons had failed to satisfy the case-or-controversy requirement to show that he had sustained immediate danger from the challenged official conduct (the choke hold). The case significance is that the federal court cannot entertain claims by any or all citizens who do no more than assert that certain practices of law enforcement officers are unconstitutional.

Louisiana ex rel. Francis v. Resweber, 329 U.S. 459, 67 S.Ct. 374 (1947) [**State of LOUISIANA EX REL. Willie FRANCIS, Petitioner, v. E. L. RESWEBER**] (**Corrections; Death Penalty; Double Jeopardy; Inmate Rights**) Francis was convicted of murder and sentenced to death in the state electric chair. On the appointed date, he was strapped in the electric chair and received a current of electricity designed to cause death. However, a chair malfunction caused the electrocution to be insufficient to kill Francis. Thus, Francis was returned to his prison cell and a new execution date was set, pending repair of the electric chair. Francis appealed, contending that a failed execution attempt made unconstitutional any subsequent execution attempt by the state. In short, Francis was declaring a case of double jeopardy. The SC disagreed, saying that a failed attempt to carry out a valid death sentence does not nullify or render unconstitutional any subsequent application of the death penalty as prescribed by law. This was not a case of double jeopardy.

Lowenfield v. Phelps, 484 U.S. 231, 108 S.Ct. 546 (1988) [**Leslie LOWENFIELD, Petitioner, v. C. Paul PHELPS, Secretary, Louisiana Department of Corrections, et al.**] (**Aggravating and Mitigating Circumstances; Death Penalty**) Lowenfield murdered a woman with whom he lived, her three children, and one of her male friends. A trial was held in Louisiana, and a conviction resulted. During the sentencing phase of the trial, the judge gave the jury instructions about weighing the aggravating and mitigating circumstances. One element of the offense was that Lowenfield "intended to kill or inflict great bodily harm upon more than one person." The jury deliberated for many hours and could not arrive at a decision as to the recommended sentence. A note was sent to the judge for additional instructions, and the judge complied. The judge advised the jurors that one aggravating circumstance was the fact that death resulted to more than one person as the result of the defendant's actions. With this instruction, the jury quickly decided that the death penalty should be imposed and recommended it to the judge. Lowenfield was sentenced to death. He appealed, alleging that his due-process rights had been violated when one of the crime elements was the same as an aggravating circumstance. Further, he alleged that the judge's subsequent clarification instruction was inherently coercive. The SC heard the case and rejected both of Lowenfield's arguments. The SC determined that the judge's instruction was not so coercive as to deprive Lowenfield of any constitutional right. Further, the SC said that the death sentence was not invalidated merely because one element of the crime happened to coincide with one of the statutory aggravating circumstances.

Lozada v. Deeds, 498 U.S. 430, 111 S.Ct. 860 (1991) [**Jose M. LOZADA v. George DEEDS, Warden**] (*Habeas Corpus* **Petitions; Right to Counsel; Sixth Amendment**) Lozada was convicted in Nevada on four counts of possession and sale of controlled substances. Following the trial proceedings, Lozada's attorney failed to notify him of his right to appeal, of the procedures and time limitations of an appeal, and of his right to court-appointed counsel. Further, Lozada alleged that his attorney had failed to file a notice of appeal or to ensure that Lozada received court-appointed counsel on appeal. Finally, he alleged that the attorney had misled Lozada's sister, and hence, Lozada, when he told her that the case had been forwarded to the public defender's office, which it hadn't. Lozada appealed on a subsequent *habeas corpus* petition on the grounds that he had had ineffective assistance of counsel as the result of these alleged events. Lower appellate courts dismissed his appeal. The SC found otherwise, however, and reversed his convictions, holding that Lozada had made a substantial showing that he had been denied the right to effective assistance of counsel.

Ludwig v. Massachusetts, 427 U.S. 618, 96 S.Ct. 2781 (1976) [**Richard I. LUDWIG, Appellant, v. Commonwealth of MASSACHUSETTS**] (**Double Jeopardy;** *Habeas Corpus* **Petitions; Speedy Trials**) Ludwig was convicted first in a nonjury trial, and later in a new six-person jury trial *de novo,* of negligently operating a motor vehicle so that public safety was endangered. Under Massachusetts law, a two-tiered trial system exists. The first tier consists of a nonjury trial. If the defendant is convicted, then he may appeal the case to an actual jury trial. Ludwig believed that the fact that he had initially requested a jury trial and had not been given one violated his speedy-trial rights, and that his subsequent conviction by the jury trial was double jeopardy stemming from the first nonjury trial conviction. The SC upheld the two-tiered trial system of Massachusetts and declared that Ludwig's right against double jeopardy and to a speedy trial had not been violated. Further, the SC noted that Massachusetts guarantees defendants a jury trial as the direct result of an appeal from a nonjury proceeding from which a conviction results. This fact is not held to be double jeopardy.

Lynce v. Mathis, 519 U.S. 433, 117 S.Ct. 891 (1997) [**Kenneth LYNCE, Petitioner, v. Hamilton MATHIS, Superintendent, Tomoka Correctional Institution**] (**Inmate Rights**) Lynce was convicted of attempted murder in 1986 in Florida and sentenced to 22 years. Under 1983 Florida legislative provisions, prison inmates were entitled to accumulate good-time credits of different types, including so many days off of their maximum sentences for certain numbers of days served. By 1992, Lynce had accumulated 5,668 days, including 1,860 days of provisional credits awarded as the result of prison overcrowding, and Lynce was released from prison. Shortly thereafter, the Florida legislature reduced the amount of good-time credits prison inmates could earn, and the Florida attorney general interpreted the statute as (1) cancelling all provisional credits awarded to inmates convicted of murder or attempted murder and (2) applying retroactively to all inmates previously awarded such credit. Thus, Lynce was rearrested and returned to prison. Lynce filed a *habeas corpus* petition alleging that the retroactive cancellation of his provisional credits violated the *ex post facto* clause of the constitution. Lower federal courts upheld Florida's actions and Lynce appealed to the SC for relief. The SC heard Lynce's case and reversed the denial of Lynce's early-release credits. To fall within the *ex post facto* prohibition, a law must be retrospective, in that it must apply to events occurring before its enactment and it must disadvantage offenders by either altering the definition of criminal conduct or increasing their punishment for crime. Because the challenged statute violated the *ex post facto* clause by increasing Lynce's punishment, it was unconstitutional.

M

Mabry v. Johnson, 467 U.S. 504, 104 S.Ct. 2543 (1984) [James MABRY, Commissioner, Arkansas Department of Correction, v. George JOHNSON] (Plea Bargaining) Johnson was convicted of burglary, assault, and murder in Arkansas. On appeal, the Arkansas Supreme Court set aside the murder conviction, and plea bargaining commenced between Johnson's defense counsel and the prosecution. In exchange for a guilty plea, the prosecution offered Johnson a 21-year sentence to be served *concurrently* with the other burglary and assault sentences. Johnson's attorney called the prosecutor a few days later to inform him that Johnson accepted the state's offer. However, the prosecutor withdrew that plea agreement offer because a mistake had been made. Instead, the prosecutor offered Johnson a modified plea agreement, wherein Johnson would serve a 21-year sentence to be served consecutive to the other sentences Johnson would receive. Johnson agreed to this offer, and the judge sentenced him to two 21-year sentences, to be served consecutively, meaning that when he finished one sentence, Johnson would have to begin the next 21-year sentence. He appealed in a *habeas corpus* finding, alleging that the first plea agreement containing the concurrent sentencing recommendation was enforceable in the present sentencing circumstance, and that the prosecutor should be held to honor that plea agreement. The SC heard Johnson's appeal and held that when Johnson ultimately accepted the prosecutor's first plea agreement, this did not create a constitutional right to have the bargain specifically enforced, and thus, he might not successfully attack his later guilty plea. The SC noted that prosecutors are obligated to honor their plea agreements; whenever defendants enter guilty pleas on false premises, they may withdraw their pleas and their convictions cannot stand. However, in this case, no such promises had been made to Johnson by the prosecutor, so the judge's ruling and sentencing were allowed to stand.

Maine v. Moulton, 474 U.S. 159, 106 S.Ct. 477 (1985) [MAINE, Petitioner, v. Perley MOULTON, Jr.] (Confessions; Law Enforcement Officers or Agencies) Moulton was

suspected of burglary and theft. When he was arrested, he obtained counsel. Later, a friend of Moulton's, Colson, agreed with police to record his telephone conversations with Moulton. Incriminating evidence was obtained in this fashion and introduced later against Moulton in court. Following his conviction, he appealed, and the SC heard the case. The SC held that the incriminating statements made by Moulton to Colson had been recorded by request of police; thus, this was an interrogation of sorts, at which Moulton's attorney should have been present. Because Moulton was being represented by counsel, the "interrogation" and the incriminating evidence it yielded had to be suppressed as evidence against Moulton. The SC overturned Moulton's conviction on this basis. (*See* **Massiah v. United States** [1964] *for a comparable case.*)

Maleng v. Cook, 490 U.S. 488, 109 S.Ct. 1923 (1989) [Norm MALENG, etc., et al., Petitioners v. Mark Edwin COOK] (Corrections; Frivolous Lawsuits; Inmate Rights) Cook was convicted of robbery in Washington and sentenced to 20 years. This term expired in 1978. While on parole in 1976, Cook was convicted of assault and was sentenced to two life terms. He was also sentenced to 30 years' imprisonment by a federal judge for bank robbery. In 1985, Cook filed a *habeas corpus* petition challenging his latest sentences and the enhancement of them resulting from his expired sentence from 1958. The SC ruled that Cook was entitled to file his petition because he was "in custody" through federal incarceration. This narrow ruling by the SC permitted Cook to proceed with his lawsuits against Washington and the federal government for their alleged illegal enhancements of his sentence.

Malinski v. New York, 324 U.S. 401, 65 S.Ct. 781 (1944) [Morris MALINSKI et al., Petitioners, v. People of the State of NEW YORK] (Confessions; Informants) Through informants close to him (his girlfriend and an old friend), Malinski was implicated in the murder of a police officer. He was later arrested and interrogated by police. He made a confession to police after being confronted by witness statements. Malinski was also humiliated by police, who kept him in a state of undress. His arraignment was delayed for four days. He was held without being permitted to speak to anyone other than police, who, he alleged, beat him during the interrogation sessions. He was convicted, and he appealed. The SC overturned his conviction, noting evident coercion and that other due-process rights had been violated during Malinski's processing.

Malley v. Briggs, 475 U.S. 335, 106 S.Ct. 1092 (1986) [Edward MALLEY and Rhode Island, Petitioners, v. James R. BRIGGS and Louisa Briggs] (Civil Rights, Section 1983 Claims; Immunity; Searches and Seizures) Malley was a police officer who obtained an arrest warrant against Briggs, a marijuana-dealing suspect. Briggs and others were arrested and charged with possession of marijuana. A grand jury subsequently failed to indict them, and the charges were dropped. At that point, Briggs filed a Title 42 U.S.C. Section 1983 civil rights suit against Malley, alleging that Malley had violated Briggs' constitutional rights against illegal searches and seizures. Malley raised the claim of absolute immunity, because he was a Rhode Island state trooper acting officially. The SC ruled that Malley was not entitled to absolute immunity but to qualified immunity in this case. The absolute-immunity defense does not extend to police officers when they are sued for damages under Title 42 U.S.C. Section 1983 claims.

Mallory v. United States, 354 U.S. 449, 77 S.Ct. 1356 (1957) [**Andrew R. MALLORY, Petitioner, v. UNITED STATES**] (**Confessions; Custodial Interrogations**) In an apartment house in the early morning hours of April 7, 1954, a woman doing laundry in the basement encountered trouble with the washing machine. She called the janitor, Mallory, who lived in the building with his wife and two sons. The janitor fixed the washing machine, left the laundry room, and later reappeared masked with his two sons. These men raped the woman and left the apartment shortly thereafter. The victim gave an account of the rape to police and named Mallory as a key suspect. Later that afternoon, Mallory and his sons were arrested and taken to police headquarters and questioned. Mallory was subjected to intensive questioning and a lie detector test. At about 10 p.m. that evening, he confessed. Because a magistrate could not be found, Mallory was brought before a commissioner the following morning and arraigned. Because of various delays, Mallory's trial occurred a year later. He was convicted. He appealed, arguing that he had not been brought before a magistrate without undue delay and that his extensive interrogation by police had been without probable cause and of unreasonable duration. The SC heard Mallory's case and overturned his conviction, holding that police had had only reasonable suspicion when Mallory was originally arrested, and that the subsequent detention and interrogation yielded probable cause for which rape charges could be filed against Mallory. The SC also noted that during the afternoon when Mallory was first arrested, numerous magistrates had been available to police. Thus Mallory had not been brought before them without undue delay, a violation of his due-process rights. The SC said that it is not the function of police to arrest, as it were, at large and to use an interrogating process at police headquarters to determine whom they should charge before a committing magistrate on "probable cause."

Malloy v. Hogan, 378 U.S. 1, 84 S.Ct. 1489 (1964) [**William MALLOY, Petitioner, v. Patrick J. HOGAN, Sheriff of Hartford County**] (**Fifth Amendment; Self-Incrimination**) Malloy was suspected of having knowledge about illegal gambling in Connecticut. He was subpoenaed to provide information about illegal gambling before a magistrate. He refused to testify on the grounds that his Fifth Amendment right against self-incrimination would be violated. He was jailed on a contempt citation for his refusal. He appealed. The SC overturned his contempt citation, saying that although Malloy was not a defendant in a criminal action, his testimony could have incriminated him in such illegal activity, and thus he had a right to invoke his Fifth Amendment right against self-incrimination.

Maness v. Meyers, 419 U.S. 492, 95 S.Ct. 584 (1976) [**Michael Anthony MANESS, Petitioner, v. James R. MEYERS, Presiding Judge**] (**Corrections; Fifth Amendment; Obscenity Laws; Probation and Parole; Self-Incrimination**) Maness is a lawyer in Temple, TX. His client was ac-

cused of selling obscene magazines. During the early investigative proceedings, Maness and a cocounsel represented his client and another man on the same obscenity charges and were served with a notice to produce numerous obscene magazines in court. Maness elected not to comply with the order because of his client's Fifth Amendment claim against self-incrimination. Maness was cited for contempt by the judge. He appealed. The SC heard Maness' case and decided the very narrow question of whether a lawyer may be held in contempt for advising his client, during the trial of a civil case, to refuse to produce material demanded by a subpoena *duces tecum* when the lawyer believes in good faith the material may tend to incriminate his client. The contempt order was set aside. The SC stressed the good faith of Maness in defending his client and justifying his conduct.

Manson v. Brathwaite, 432 U.S. 98, 97 S.Ct. 2243 (1977) [**John R. MANSON, Commissioner of Correction of Connecticut, Petitioner, v. Nowell A. BRATHWAITE**] (**Law Enforcement Officers or Agencies; Lineups**) An undercover officer, Glover, exchanged money for drugs with a man later described as Brathwaite. The exchange occurred in an apartment complex where Brathwaite was observed through a door open about 12 inches. Glover described the man to other officers, and they thought it might be Brathwaite, who fit that description and had a prior record of drug offenses. They showed a picture of Brathwaite to Glover, who identified Brathwaite as the drug dealer. Brathwaite was arrested and subsequently convicted. He appealed, seeking to suppress Glover's identification of him as biased, as other police officers had showed Glover Brathwaite's photograph and did not put him in a lineup. The SC upheld Brathwaite's conviction, holding that the identification procedure followed in Brathwaite's case was not a violation of due process, despite the suggestive nature of the photograph shown to Glover. Thus, the photograph as well as Glover's direct identification of Brathwaite in court were not suppressed as evidence against him.

Mapp v. Ohio, 367 U.S. 1081, 81 S.Ct. 1684 (1961) [**Dollree MAPP, etc., Appellant, v. OHIO**] (**Exclusionary Rule; Fourth Amendment; Law Enforcement Officers or Agencies; Searches and Seizures**) Police in Cleveland suspected someone of bomb making or possessing bomb materials. The suspect was believed to be at the home of Mapp, a woman friend. Officers went to Mapp's home and asked to come in. Mapp refused, suggesting that the officers get a warrant. The officers left and Mapp called her attorney. The officers returned later, waving a piece of paper and saying that they had a warrant to conduct their search of her premises. Mapp's attorney arrived at the same time. Neither he nor Mapp was permitted to see the "warrant." Mapp grabbed the piece of paper and shoved it down her bosom. A police officer quickly retrieved it and handcuffed her. A thorough search of her home disclosed no bomb materials. However, a trunk in Mapp's basement yielded pencil sketches and drawings depicting what officers believed to be "pornography." Mapp was subsequently convicted of possessing pornographic material. She appealed to the SC, claiming that the officers had had no right to search her home. The SC agreed with Mapp and overturned her conviction. No warrant had ever been issued and it was unknown what the piece of paper was that police waved in front of Mapp and her attorney preceding their unlawful search of her premises. This is a landmark SC case, because it established the *exclusionary rule* to deter police misconduct in search-and-seizure cases. It made the rule applicable to *both* state and federal law enforcement officers. Thus, any evidence seized illegally is inadmissible later in court against criminal suspects. The Fourth Amendment protects citizens from unreasonable searches and seizures by the states; this decision by the SC overturned the *Wolf* decision and made the Fourth Amendment applicable to states through the due-process clause of the Fourteenth Amendment.

Marbury v. Madison, 5 U.S. 137 (1803) [**William MARBURY v. James MADISON, Secretary of State of the United States**] (**Supreme Court Powers**) William Marbury was appointed by President John Adams as a justice of the peace shortly before the end of Adams' term. However, the new Jefferson administration delayed Adams' judicial appointments. Thus, Marbury sued James Madison, the secretary of state, in an effort to compel him to deliver Marbury's commission as a justice of the peace. The Supreme Court chief justice, John Marshall, understood that if the SC awarded Marbury a writ of *mandamus* to force Madison to deliver the commission, the Jefferson administration would ignore it, thus weakening the authority of the courts. However, if the SC denied the writ, it would appear that the justices acted out of fear. Marshall resolved the problem by declaring that Madison should have delivered the commission to Marbury; however, the SC also held that the section of the Judiciary Act of 1789 that gave courts the power to issue writs of *mandamus* exceeded court authority under the Constitution, and was therefore null and void. Therefore, Marshall was able to chastise the Jefferson administration and yet not create a situation in which a court order would be flouted. The significance of this case is that it established the right of the SC to interpret the Constitution and determine whether certain acts of Congress or the president were unconstitutional. The SC became the final arbiter of the Constitution and what it meant.

Marron v. United States, 275 U.S. 192, 48 S.Ct. 74 (1927) [**Joseph E. MARRON, Petitioner, v. UNITED STATES**] (**Fifth Amendment; Law Enforcement Officers or Agencies; Searches and Seizures**) Prohibition officers secured a search warrant for illegal liquors and entered Marron's premises. They found illegal liquor, but they continued their search and eventually discovered ledgers and other personal items unrelated to liquor. They arrested Marron and confiscated these materials, some of which were used to convict him of unlawfully selling liquor and operating a general nuisance. Marron appealed, arguing that the officers had had no right to seize his ledgers and that this evidence ought to have been suppressed. He also argued that his ledgers were a form of self-incrimination and that his Fifth Amendment right had been violated as a result of the officers violating his Fourth Amendment right against unreasonable searches and seizures. The SC heard the case and overturned his conviction, ruling that the illegal search warrant relating to his seized ledgers should have re-

sulted in suppression of these documents as evidence against him. The SC further noted that the Fifth Amendment protects every person against self-incrimination by evidence obtained through search and seizure in violation of rights under the Fourth Amendment.

Marshall v. Lonberger, 459 U.S. 422, 103 S.Ct. 843 (1983) [**R.C. MARSHALL, Superintendent, Southern Ohio Correctional Facility, Petitioner, v. Robert LONBERGER**] (**Aggravating and Mitigating Circumstances; Death Penalty**) Lonberger was accused of capital murder. During his Ohio trial, prosecutors introduced a document showing that he had entered a guilty plea to a crime in Illinois. He was convicted. Lonberger appealed on grounds that the Illinois conviction had been improperly introduced and that his guilty plea in the Illinois case had not been voluntary. The SC heard Lonberger's appeal and upheld his conviction, saying that the admission in the Ohio murder trial of Lonberger's Illinois conviction based on a guilty plea had not deprived Lonberger of a fair trial or violated any federal right.

Martin v. Hadix, 527 U.S. 343, 119 S.Ct. 1998 (1999) [**Bill MARTIN, Michigan Department of Corrections, et al., Petitioners, v. Everett HADIX et al.**] (**Prison Litigation Reform Act**) Hadix and others won a Section 1983 lawsuit against the Michigan Department of Corrections in 1987. Reasonable attorney's fees were awarded by a federal court for the purpose of enforcing compliance with remedial decrees. In 1995, the Prison Litigation Reform Act (PLRA) was passed, which reduced recoverable attorney's fees from $150 to $112.50 per hour. Subsequently, an appellate court ruled that the PLRA attorney fee cap did not apply to attorney's services performed for cases pending prior to but unpaid by 1995, when the PLRA was enacted. The SC held that the PLRA cannot be applied retroactively. Therefore, the PLRA limits attorney's fees for postjudgment monitoring services performed after the PLRA's effective date, but does not limit fees for monitoring performed before that date.

Martinez v. California, 444 U.S. 275, 100 S.Ct. 553 (1980) [**George MARTINEZ et al., Appellants, v. State of CALIFORNIA et al.**] (**Civil Rights, Section 1983 Claims; Corrections; Probation and Parole**) Thomas, a parolee, was convicted of rape in 1969 and sentenced to a 20-year term. He had previously been diagnosed as having mental problems and had spent some time in a state mental hospital. After serving only five years in prison, Thomas was paroled to the custody of his mother. While on parole, he murdered a 15-year-old girl. A wrongful death action under Title 42 U.S.C. Section 1983 was filed by the victim's family, alleging that California was liable for her death and that she had been deprived of her life without due process of law. Essentially, this case represents a challenge of whether or not a state is liable for the actions of paroled persons. Are parole officers exempted from liability when parolees commit crimes that harm others? The SC said that California authorities were not liable in this case; the death caused by Thomas was not caused by state action.

Maryland v. Buie, 494 U.S. 325, 110 S.Ct. 1093 (1990) [**MARYLAND, Petitioner, v. Jerome Edward BUIE**] (**Fourth Amendment; Plain-View Rule; Searches Incident to Arrest**)

Police suspected Buie of involvement in an armed robbery and went to his home with a valid arrest warrant. The officers fanned out and commenced searching the home for Buie, who was in the basement. He surrendered. While the police investigated the basement to see if anyone else was there who might pose a danger to them, they observed a red running suit like the one used in the armed robbery. This evidence was seized and used in a subsequent trial in which Buie was convicted of armed robbery. He appealed, arguing that the police had had no business entering parts of his home searching for evidence without a valid search warrant. The SC disagreed and said that in this case, officers were merely attempting to determine whether anyone else might be on the premises who would pose a danger to them. The SC stressed that this was a protective sweep for the safety of officers, and that contraband or evidence seen in plain view during such a sweep was not immune from a Fourth Amendment reasonable seizure.

Maryland v. Craig, 497 U.S. 836, 110 S.Ct. 3157 (1990) [MARYLAND, Petitioner, v. Sandra Ann CRAIG] (Confrontation Clause; Jury Trials; Sixth Amendment) Craig was suspected of sexual offenses, including assault and battery arising from her operation of a preschool and sexual abuse of a 6-year-old child. Under Maryland law, child witnesses may give testimony through one-way closed-circuit television, not directly in the courtroom in the presence of defendants, if it is believed that the child would suffer emotional distress from the courtroom appearance. This procedure is not regarded as denying defendants "the right to confront and cross-examine their accusers." Craig was convicted. She appealed, citing a violation of her Sixth Amendment right to confront and cross-examine her accuser as the result of the indirect, closed-circuit child testimony. The SC rejected her appeal, holding that the confrontation clause does not categorically prohibit child witnesses in child-abuse cases from testifying against defendants at their trials, outside of defendants' presence, by one-way closed-circuit television, especially given a finding of "necessity" (child trauma and mental distress) made on a case-specific basis.

Maryland v. Dyson, 527 U.S. 465, 119 S.Ct. 2013 (1999) [MARYLAND, Petitioner, v. Kevin Darnell DYSON] (Fourth Amendment; Searches and Seizures; Vehicle Searches) On the basis of a tip from a reliable informant, Maryland police stopped Dyson's vehicle and searched it without a warrant, believing that the vehicle contained cocaine. They discovered 23 grams of cocaine in a duffel bag in the trunk, and Dyson was convicted of conspiracy to possess cocaine with intent to distribute. Dyson appealed, alleging that the Maryland police required a warrant to search his vehicle, that they had ample time to obtain a search warrant, and that because they had failed to do so, the evidence they eventually discovered should be suppressed. The Maryland Court of Special Appeals reversed Dyson's conviction, noting that although there was abundant probable cause to search Dyson's car, the search violated the Fourth Amendment because there was no exigency that prevented or even made it significantly difficult for police to obtain a search warrant. The government appealed, and the SC heard the case. The SC reversed the Maryland Court of

Special Appeals and held that the finding of probable cause that the vehicle contained contraband satisfied the automobile exception to the search warrant requirement. Further, the SC noted that the separate finding of exigency in addition to a finding of probable cause is contrary to previous holdings. (*See United States v. Ross* [1982] *and Pennsylvania v. Labron* [1996].)

Maryland v. Garrison, 480 U.S. 79, 107 S.Ct. 1013 (1987) [MARYLAND, Petitioner, v. Harold GARRISON] (Exclusionary Rule; Fourth Amendment; Law Enforcement Officers or Agencies; Searches and Seizures) Armed with a valid search warrant into an apartment rented by McWebb, police mistakenly entered an apartment rented by Garrison, where they found illegal drugs. Garrison was subsequently convicted under the Controlled Substance Act. He appealed, contending that the police had not had a valid search warrant or probable cause to enter his apartment to look for contraband. The SC disagreed, saying that if officers happen to search the wrong dwelling in the reasonable but mistaken belief that they are in the right dwelling, this action does not violate Fourth Amendment rights of those in the wrongly invaded dwelling. In this instance, it was determined that the search warrant originally obtained was overbroad; however, even this ambiguity did not invalidate the warrant. This ruling is similar to the good-faith exception to the exclusionary rule. (*See United States v. Leon* [1984].)

Maryland v. Macon, 472 U.S. 463, 105 S.Ct. 2778 (1978) [MARYLAND, Petitioner v. Baxter MACON] (Fourth Amendment; Searches and Seizures) Macon was convicted of knowingly distributing obscene material. He appealed, claiming that government agents, in this case county detectives without a warrant, had entered his place of business for the purpose of looking at his obscene material and that this was tantamount to a search under the Fourth Amendment. The SC disagreed, upholding his conviction. The SC said that the county detectives' action in entering his business was not a "search" in the Fourth Amendment sense, because his place of business was open to the public, including county detectives. Further, the county detectives had arrested Macon following examination of the obscene material and had confiscated some of the material. The SC held that this material was not excludable as evidence against Macon, as it was a reasonable seizure incident to a lawful warrantless arrest.

Maryland v. Pringle, ___U.S.___, 124 S.Ct. 795 (2003) [MARYLAND, Petitioner, v. Joseph Jermaine PRINGLE] (Fourth Amendment; Searches and Seizures; Vehicle Searches) A Baltimore, MD, county police officer stopped a speeding automobile in the early morning hours on August 7, 1999. Police officers viewed three persons in the vehicle and asked the driver for his license and registration. He reached in the glove compartment for the registration, and officers saw a large wad of cash in plain view. The officers asked the driver if he had any drugs or weapons in the vehicle, which he denied, and after obtaining his consent, they searched the vehicle. They discovered cocaine in the back-seat armrest. Police arrested all three occupants, including Joseph Pringle, who was a front-seat passenger. They charged all three persons with cocaine possession, but Pringle subsequently confessed, admitting that the cocaine was his and that he planned to use it at a later party in exchange for sex. He was convicted, sentenced to 10 years in prison without the possibility of parole, and he appealed, contending that police lacked probable cause to arrest him initially, because it could not be determined from the scene who was the cocaine's owner. A Maryland appeals court reversed his conviction on the appeal, and Maryland prosecutors appealed to the SC, who heard the case. The SC reversed the appeals court, holding that police had probable cause to arrest all three persons, including Pringle. The SC stressed that a reasonable officer could conclude that there was probable cause to believe Pringle committed the crime of possession of cocaine, either solely or jointly, and that his subsequent confession was therefore admissible.

Maryland v. Wilson, 519 U.S. 408, 117 S.Ct. 882 (1998) [MARYLAND, Petitioner, v. Jerry Lee WILSON] (**Fourth Amendment; Searches and Seizures**) Wilson was a passenger in a car stopped by a Maryland state trooper for speeding. Wilson was ordered from the car and a quantity of cocaine fell onto the ground in plain view of the trooper. Wilson was arrested. Wilson moved to suppress the cocaine as evidence against him, and the Maryland Court of Appeals granted his motion, holding that an officer may as a matter of course order the driver of a lawfully stopped car to exit his vehicle, but this does not apply to passengers. The state appealed, and the SC heard the case. The SC reversed the Maryland decision, holding that police officers who make traffic stops may order other passengers to get out of the car pending completion of the stop.

Massachusetts v. Sheppard, 468 U.S. 981, 104 S.Ct. 3424 (1984) [MASSACHUSETTS, Petitioner, v. Osborne SHEPPARD] (**Exclusionary Rule; Law Enforcement Officers or Agencies**) Sheppard, a murder suspect, was investigated by police. Officers attempted to obtain a search warrant articulating the places to be searched and things or items to be seized. For some reason, conventional search warrants were not available, so the officers decided to use alternative warrants used for searching for controlled substances. These warrants were in a different form from those of conventional search warrants. The officers crossed out certain phraseology and wrote in other pertinent phraseology so that the warrant would be worded correctly. After further modification by a judge, the contrived search warrant against Sheppard was signed. Incriminating evidence was obtained as the result of executing the search warrant. Sheppard's attorney made a pretrial motion alleging that the contrived search warrant was invalid; thus, according to the exclusionary rule, the evidence obtained by its execution ought to be suppressed. The trial judge allowed the evidence against Sheppard, who was convicted of first-degree murder. He appealed, but the SC upheld his conviction, despite the faulty nature of the search warrant. The SC declared that in a manner similar to *United States v. Leon* (1984), the police officers executing the search warrant had done so in good faith. The difference between *United States v. Leon* and *Sheppard* is that in *Sheppard,* it was alleged that the officers *knew in advance* that the warrant was defective, as it had been

substantially revised and rewritten, whereas in *Leon,* officers *did not know* the defectiveness of the warrant. The SC concluded that the officers in *Sheppard believed* the warrant-issuing judge, who had advised them that the warrant was valid when, in fact, it wasn't.

Massaro v. United States, ___U.S.___, 123 S.Ct. 1690 (2003) [Joseph MASSARO, Petitioner, v. UNITED STATES] (**Ineffective Assistance of Counsel**) Massaro was indicted on federal racketeering charges in connection with a murder. The day before his trial began, prosecutors learned of a bullet recovered from the car in which the victim's body was found but did not inform Massaro's defense counsel until the trial had started. On several occasions during the trial, the defense counsel declined the trial court's offer for a continuance to allow time to examine the bullet as possible exculpatory evidence. Subsequently, Massaro was convicted and sentenced to life imprisonment. He appealed, and his new counsel argued that the court had erred in allowing the bullet into evidence. However, the ineffective-assistance-of-counsel claim was not raised at that time. The appeal was denied. Later, Massaro filed a new claim asserting ineffective assistance of counsel, citing the fact that his original attorney had failed to accept the trial court's offer to examine the bullet as evidence. This most recent appeal was rejected, with the appellate court holding that Massaro could have raised the ineffective-assistance-of-counsel issue on direct appeal but failed to do so. Therefore, this was a procedural default and barred Massaro from raising the issue on a new appeal. The SC heard the case and reversed the appellate court, holding that ineffective-assistance-of-counsel claims may be brought in collateral proceedings under 28 U.S.C. Section 2255, whether or not Massaro could have raised the claim on direct appeal. The procedural default rule's objectives are to conserve judicial resources and respect the law's important interest in the finality of judgments. Applying this rule to ineffective-assistance-of-counsel claims creates the risk that defendants would feel compelled to raise the issue before there has been an opportunity fully to develop the claim's factual predicate, and it would raise the issue for the first time in a forum not best suited to assess those facts, even if the record contains some indication of deficiencies in counsel's performance.

Massiah v. United States, 377 U.S. 201, 84 S.Ct. 1199 (1964) [Winston MASSIAH, Petitioner, v. UNITED STATES] (**Custodial Interrogations; Law Enforcement Officers or Agencies**) Massiah was believed to be transporting illegal drugs into the United States from South America. He was indicted by a federal grand jury on drug charges. While he was under indictment and awaiting trial, a friend of Massiah's was directed by FBI agents to sit in Massiah's car and elicit incriminating statements about the drugs from Massiah. Massiah's friend was wearing a wire transmitter, and an FBI agent was sitting in a car behind Massiah's car in order to record these incriminating statements. Massiah did make incriminating statements that were recorded and he was subsequently convicted. He appealed. The SC overturned his conviction, saying that the conversation he had with his friend in Massiah's car constituted an *interrogation,* because the friend was *acting on* *behalf of and at the instruction of the government.* Thus, because Massiah was under indictment and represented by counsel, who was entitled to be present during the interrogation but was not present, Massiah's constitutional rights had been violated.

Mathews v. United States, 485 U.S. 58, 108 S.Ct. 883 (1988) [**Frederick MATHEWS, Petitioner, v. UNITED STATES**] (**Entrapment**) Mathews allegedly provided a loan to a paid government informant who was sponsored by the FBI. The loan involved a kickback to Mathews for making the loan involving the Small Business Administration. The FBI arrested Mathews for accepting a bribe. At his trial, Mathews sought to raise the entrapment defense, but the judge ruled that Mathews could not do so unless he admitted to all elements of the bribery charge. Mathews wished to deny certain of these elements, but he also wanted to raise the entrapment defense. He was convicted. He appealed and the SC overturned his conviction, saying that defendants may raise the entrapment defense without admitting to one or more elements of the crimes with which they are charged. Previous courts had ruled narrowly that entrapment may be raised as an affirmative defense only if defendants admit to *all* elements of the offense initially. Thus the *Mathews* case broadened this entrapment issue and permitted defendants to raise the entrapment defense and deny certain elements of their alleged crimes.

Mathis v. United States, 391 U.S. 1, 88 S.Ct. 1503 (1968) [**Robert T. MATHIS, Sr., Petitioner, v. UNITED STATES**] (**Confessions; Law Enforcement Officers or Agencies;** *Miranda* **Warning**) Mathis was accused of filing false claims for income tax refunds. While he was awaiting his trial, IRS agents visited him at the jail and, without issuing a *Miranda* warning, asked Mathis various self-incriminating questions about his tax returns, who prepared them, and other matters. He was not warned to remain silent if he wished, or told he had the right to an attorney. He made various incriminating statements that were later used against him in court. He appealed, alleging that he should have been told his *Miranda* rights before IRS agents interrogated him. The SC agreed with Mathis, holding that under incarcerative interrogations such as these, investigators, even IRS agents, must inform suspects of criminal activity such as income tax evasion of their *Miranda* rights. Mathis' conviction was overturned.

Mayberry v. Pennsylvania, 400 U.S. 455, 91 S.Ct. 499 (1971) [**Richard MAYBERRY, Petitioner, v. PENNSYLVANIA**] (**Jury Trials**) Mayberry was convicted of a crime and was cited for 11 separate contempt-of-court charges by the judge. Mayberry had been verbally abusive to the judge and had engaged in continual disruptive behavior. The judge subsequently sentenced Mayberry to an additional 22 years for the contempt charges. Mayberry appealed. The SC reversed the contempt convictions and sentences, saying that another judge should have heard the inflammatory comments about the judge and the bases for contempt citations. The SC said that Mayberry's removal from the courtroom would have been the best remedy for his conduct, given the circumstances.

Mayer v. City of Chicago, 404 U.S. 189, 92 S.Ct. 410 (1971) [**Jack L. MAYER, Appellant, v. CITY OF CHI-**

CAGO] (**Corrections; Indigent Clients; Inmate Rights**) Mayer, an indigent, was arrested and charged with disorderly conduct in Chicago. He was convicted and requested a transcript of his trial proceeding. Illinois statutes provided for issuances of transcripts for indigents only for felony cases. Mayer appealed, alleging that his due-process rights had been violated. The SC heard the case and ordered Illinois to provide Mayer with a trial transcript. The SC said that the fact that the charges against Mayer involved fines only and not imprisonment were no excuse for the invidious discrimination against an indigent defendant.

Maynard v. Cartwright, 486 U.S. 356, 108 S.Ct. 1853 (1988) [**Gary D. MAYNARD, Warden, et al., Petitioners, v. William T. CARTWRIGHT**] (**Aggravating and Mitigating Circumstances; Eighth Amendment**) Cartwright shot and killed a man and slit his wife's throat. These victims had formerly employed him. An Oklahoma jury found Cartwright guilty of first-degree murder. When the judge gave the jury instructions during the penalty phase of the trial, he used the phrase "especially heinous, atrocious, or cruel" in describing various aggravating circumstances they were to consider. Cartwright challenged his death sentence on the grounds that such a statement was unconstitutionally vague. The SC agreed with Cartwright, and his death sentence was vacated, as the instruction, determined to be unconstitutionally vague, had not offered sufficient guidance to the jury in deciding whether to impose the death penalty.

McCarthy v. United States, 394 U.S. 459, 89 S.Ct. 1166 (1969) [**William J. McCARTHY, Petitioner, v. UNITED STATES**] (**Plea Bargaining**) McCarthy, a 65-year-old man, was charged with income tax evasion. He pleaded not guilty at first, but later, following a debilitating illness, entered a guilty plea in exchange for government leniency. The judge, however, sentenced McCarthy to one year's imprisonment and a $2,500 fine. The attorney for McCarthy objected strongly to the sentence and fine, and a subsequent appeal was filed, alleging the judge's violation of Rule 11 of the Federal Rules of Criminal Procedure. Among the crucial elements of Rule 11, which governs plea bargains and plea-bargain hearings, is the requirement that judges address defendants who wish to plead guilty in open court and determine the voluntariness of their plea. Further, judges are ordered by statute to determine whether there is a factual basis for the plea, meaning that judges must consider the evidence the prosecutor would have introduced against the defendant if the case had gone to trial. Thus, if the prosecutor fails to furnish the judge with evidence that would have resulted in the defendant's guilt beyond a reasonable doubt, then the judge would be compelled to reject the guilty plea and dismiss the case against the defendant. Because the judge in McCarthy's case had failed to inquire as to the factual basis for the plea, and failed to inquire of McCarthy whether he understood the nature of the charges against him, the SC overturned McCarthy's conviction.

McCleskey v. Kemp, 481 U.S. 279, 107 S.Ct. 1756 (1987) [**Warren McCLESKEY, Petitioner, v. Ralph KEMP, Superintendent, Georgia Diagnostic and Classification Center**] (**Death Penalty**) McCleskey, a black man, was convicted of murdering a police officer during a grocery store robbery in 1978. He was sentenced to death. McCleskey appealed, introducing evidence to show that statistically more black criminals receive the death penalty than white criminals and claiming that such disproportion is unconstitutional. The SC rejected McCleskey's claim. Georgia's death penalty, the SC said, was not arbitrary and capricious, nor was it being applied in a discriminatory manner, regardless of statistical evidence to the contrary.

McCleskey v. Zant, 499 U.S. 467, 111 S.Ct. 1454 (1991) [**Warren McCLESKEY, Petitioner v. Walter D. ZANT, Superintendent, Georgia Diagnostic and Classification Center**] (**Death Penalty;** *Habeas Corpus* **Petitions; Informants; Right to Counsel; Sixth Amendment**) McCleskey was charged with murder and armed robbery. A cellmate of McCleskey's, Evans, was called to testify against him. Evans said that McCleskey had boasted about the killing and admitted it. McCleskey was convicted and sentenced to death. He appealed, claiming that the cellmate-induced conversations had been made without the assistance of his counsel. The SC rejected his claim, stating that it could have been made in an earlier appeal proceeding. The fact that McCleskey was making it in a subsequent proceeding nullified the claim. Thus, in order for such claims to be considered, they must be made at the right time, shortly after they occur, not after several appeals have been unsuccessfully lodged with state and federal courts.

McCray v. Illinois, 386 U.S. 300, 87 S.Ct. 1056 (1967) [**George McCRAY, Petitioner, v. State of ILLINOIS**] (**Law Enforcement Officers or Agencies; Searches and Seizures; Searches Incident to an Arrest**) In this case, a warrantless search incident to a warrantless arrest was based on a reliable informant's information to police. Police refused to reveal the identity of the informant later at McCray's trial, at which he was convicted. McCray appealed, alleging that the identity of the informant should have been revealed and that a warrant based on probable cause should have been issued. The SC noted that in McCray's case, however, the use of the reliable informant was unrelated to McCray's guilt or innocence, a trial function. Rather, the informant had been used as a basis for investigating and conducting surveillance of McCray, who later exhibited sufficient incriminating conduct to justify his arrest by police. The Court upheld the conviction.

McDonald v. United States, 335 U.S. 451, 69 S.Ct. 191 (1948) [**Earl H. McDONALD et al., Petitioners, v. UNITED STATES**] (**Consent Searches; Law Enforcement Officers or Agencies; Searches and Seizures; Searches Incident to Arrest**) McDonald and others were suspected of operating a lottery from their home. Police conducted surveillance of them and then, without a warrant, entered McDonald's home through a window after hearing what they thought to be an "adding machine," a device often used in illegal lottery operations. Incriminating evidence was seized and McDonald was subsequently convicted because of it. Because the police had had no arrest or search warrants when they entered McDonald's residence and seized the illegal material and equipment, McDonald appealed, alleging his Fourth Amendment right against unreasonable searches and seizures had been vio-

lated. The SC summarily overturned McDonald's conviction, holding the evidence inadmissible, as it had been illegally seized without probable cause or an arrest or search warrant.

McGautha v. California, 402 U.S. 183, 91 S.Ct. 1454 (1971) [**Dennis Councle McGAUTHA, Petitioner, v. State of CALIFORNIA. James Edward Crampton, Petitioner, v. State of Ohio**] (**Bifurcated Trials; Death Penalty; Juries; Jury Trials; Jury Voting**) McGautha was convicted of first-degree murder during an armed robbery. During the penalty phase of the trial, the judge gave the jury instructions, saying that the jury would fix a penalty at their absolute discretion and that the vote for a particular punishment must be unanimous. The jury returned the death penalty and McGautha was sentenced. McGautha appealed, contending that standardless jury sentencing was unconstitutional. The SC rejected McGautha's argument and upheld the sentence as valid, despite an absence of specific standards by which to impose the death penalty, maintaining that juries have total discretion in deciding death penalty or life imprisonment. The decision was later modified in *Gregg v. Georgia* (1976).

McGinnis v. Royster, 410 U.S. 263, 93 S.Ct. 1055 (1972) [**Paul D. McGINNIS, Commissioner of Correction, et al., Appellants, v. James ROYSTER et al.**] (**Corrections; Probation and Parole**) A New York statute provides that jail prisoners may not accrue their time in jail as pretrial detainees to be used in calculating their prison good-time credit later. A circuit court of appeals ruled the statute unconstitutional, but the government appealed. The SC reversed the circuit court decision, saying that the New York statute denying certain state prisoners good-time credit for parole eligibility for the period of their presence county jail incarceration does not violate the equal-protection clause of the Fourteenth Amendment. Thus, there is no obligation for New York or any other state to provide prisoners with such credit for calculating good-time credit for parole eligibility.

McKeiver v. Pennsylvania, 403 U.S. 528, 91 S.Ct. 1976 (1971) [**Joseph McKEIVER and Edward Terry, Appellants, v. State of PENNSYLVANIA. In re Barbara Burrus et al., Petitioners**] (**Juvenile Law**) In May 1968, McKeiver, age 16, was charged with robbery, larceny, and receiving stolen goods. He was represented by counsel, who asked the court for a jury trial "as a matter of right." This request was denied. McKeiver was subsequently adjudicated delinquent. On appeal to the SC later, McKeiver's adjudication was upheld. The case is important because the SC said that jury trials for juveniles are not a matter of constitutional right but rather at the discretion of the juvenile court judge. In about one-fifth of the states today, jury trials for juveniles in juvenile courts are held under certain conditions.

McKoy v. North Carolina, 494 U.S. 433, 110 S.Ct. 1227 (1990) [**Dock McKOY, Jr., Petitioner, v. NORTH CAROLINA**] (**Aggravating and Mitigating Circumstances; Cruel and Unusual Punishment; Death Penalty; Eighth Amendment**) McKoy was convicted of first-degree murder. During the sentencing phase of his trial, the jury made a "binding" recommendation for the death penalty, after finding two statutory aggravating circumstances, two of eight possible mitigating circumstances, that the mitigating circumstances did not outweigh the aggravating circumstances, and that the aggravating circumstances were "substantial" enough to justify recommending the death penalty. North Carolina had a procedure whereby jurors must find unanimously that specific aggravating and mitigating circumstances exist. Some jurors believed that other mitigating circumstances may have existed, but the jury was not unanimous as to those mitigating circumstances, and thus, they were not considered as weight against the aggravating circumstances. McKoy appealed the death sentence on the grounds that the unanimity rule was unconstitutional and violative of his right against cruel and unusual punishment under the Eighth Amendment. The SC agreed with McKoy and overturned his conviction, holding that North Carolina's unanimity requirement impermissibly limited jurors' consideration of mitigating evidence and thus was contrary to prior case law decided by the SC. In effect, one holdout juror can exclude one or more mitigating circumstances from being weighed against the aggravating ones. Thus, the death sentence was vacated and the case was remanded.

McKune v. Lile, ___U.S.___, 122 S.Ct. 2017 (2002) [**David R. McKUNE, Warden, et al., Petitioners, v. Robert G. LILE**] (**Civil Rights, Section 1983 Claims; Fifth Amendment**) Robert Lile was convicted of rape and related crimes and incarcerated in a Kansas prison. A few years prior to his scheduled release, Lile was ordered by prison officials to participate in a Sexual Abuse Treatment Program (SATP), in which offenders are expected to sign an "Acceptance of Responsibility" form, accepting responsibility for their conviction offenses. Furthermore, they must complete a sexual history form detailing all prior sexual activities, regardless of whether the activities constitute uncharged criminal offenses. The information disclosed is not privileged, and thus, it could possibly be used against these offenders in future criminal proceedings. However, there is no evidence to indicate that such information has ever been disclosed under the SATP. If Lile refused to participate in the SATP, then his prison privileges would be reduced, resulting in the automatic curtailment of his visitation rights, earnings, work opportunities, ability to send money to family, canteen expenditures, access to a personal television, and other privileges. He would also be transferred to a potentially more dangerous maximum-security unit. Lile refused to participate in the SATP on Fifth Amendment self-incrimination grounds and sought relief by filing a Title 42 U.S.C. Section 1983 civil rights action. A U.S. district court granted him relief and the state appealed. The Tenth Circuit Court of Appeals upheld the lower-court ruling, holding that compelled self-incrimination prohibited by the Fifth Amendment can be established by penalties that do not constitute deprivations of potential liberty interests under due process, but that Kansas' imposition of a reduction in Lile's prison privileges and housing accommodations were improper punishments. Furthermore, compelled statements that incriminated Lile in other uncharged offenses would create a risk of a perjury prosecution. The state appealed this decision to the SC, who heard the case. The SC reversed the lower courts, holding that the SATP is supported by the legitimate penological objective of rehabil-

itation. The SATP and the consequences for nonparticipation in it do not combine to create a compulsion that encumbers the constitutional right not to incriminate oneself. Furthermore, Lile's movement to a more secure custody level in another part of the prison served the purpose of freeing space in the unit where the SATP was offered, and thus it was not intended as a punishment for nonparticipation.

McMann v. Richardson, 397 U.S. 759, 90 S.Ct. 1441 (1970) [**Daniel McMANN, Warden, et al., Petitioners, v. Willie RICHARDSON et al.**] (**Plea Bargaining**) The defendant knowingly and voluntarily pleaded guilty to murder. He was sentenced to 30 years in prison. He appealed, alleging that his guilty plea had been coerced. The SC upheld his conviction, saying that no evidence existed to show that the guilty plea was coerced. A mere allegation of coercion is insufficient to overturn a conviction resulting from a plea bargain.

McMillan v. Pennsylvania, 477 U.S. 79, 106 S.Ct. 2411 (1986) [**Dynel McMILLAN, Lorna Peterson, James J. Dennison, and Harold L. Smalls, Petitioners, v. PENNSYLVANIA**] (**Sentencing**) Dynel McMillan was convicted of aggravated assault by shooting another man in the right buttock during an argument over a debt. Under Pennsylvania's Mandatory Minimum Sentencing Act of 1982, anyone convicted of certain felonies and who "visibly possesses a firearm" during the commission of a felony is subject to a mandatory minimum sentence of five years. This fact may be determined by a preponderance of the evidence. McMillan appealed the conviction and five-year mandatory minimum sentence, arguing that such an issue ought to be decided by a jury trial, that the standard of proof should not be "preponderance of the evidence" but rather, "beyond a reasonable doubt," and that the act itself was invalid. The SC rejected all of McMillan's claims. First, the SC noted, the five-year mandatory minimum sentence is a *sentencing issue,* not a *jury issue.* Thus, a jury trial is not necessary for this factual determination. Further, because it is a sentencing issue, the standard of proof may be "preponderance of the evidence." The SC upheld the constitutionality of the mandatory minimum sentencing law.

McNabb v. United States, 318 U.S. 332, 63 S.Ct. 608 (1943) [**Benjamin McNABB et al., Petitioners, v. UNITED STATES**] (**Exclusionary Rule; Law Enforcement Officers or Agencies**) The McNabb family in Chattanooga, TN, was a clan of mountaineers dealing in illegal whiskey and operating an illegal still. Agents from the Alcohol Tax Unit raided their settlement one evening when it was learned that they planned to sell a large quantity of illegal liquor. During their raid, one federal officer was shot and killed. Later, federal agents visited the home of the McNabbs and arrested brothers Freeman and Raymond. They took the men to the federal building in Chattanooga, where they were not brought before any United States magistrate or other judicial official but kept in a small room for 14 hours and not permitted to see relatives or lawyers. There is no evidence that they requested counsel. Neither had passed the fourth grade in school. Following intensive questioning by agents, they eventually confessed to the killing and were tried, convicted of murder, and sentenced to 45 years in prison. They appealed. The SC reversed their convictions, holding that coerced confessions are not admissible. Further, the officers had erred by not providing suitable counsel for these defendants, and the interrogation conditions were inherently illegal and contrary to due process. Thus, their confessions had been improperly received as evidence against them.

McNeil v. Wisconsin, 501 U.S. 171, 111 S.Ct. 2204 (1991) [**Paul McNEIL, Petitioner, v. WISCONSIN**] (**Fifth Amendment;** *Miranda* **Warning; Right to Counsel; Sixth Amendment**) McNeil was charged with armed robbery in West Allis, WI. He requested and was represented by a public defender. While in police custody, McNeil signed a *Miranda* rights waiver and agreed to talk with police about the West Allis robbery; during that time, he made incriminating statements about his involvement in a murder in Caledonia, WI. He was then formally charged with the murder in Caledonia. In a pre-trial motion, he moved to suppress his former incriminating statements. This motion was denied, and he was convicted. He appealed on the grounds that his statements should have been barred from evidence, because he had requested counsel during his initial appearance and because police had initially told him his *Miranda* rights concerning an unrelated crime. McNeil believed he must be told his rights for *each* of the crimes with which he had been charged. The SC heard McNeil's appeal and rejected it, holding that the assertion of the Sixth Amendment right to counsel does not imply invocation of the *Miranda* Fifth Amendment right; such a rule would seriously impede effective law enforcement by precluding uncounseled but uncoerced admissions of guilt pursuant to valid *Miranda* warnings.

Meachum v. Fano, 427 U.S. 215, 96 S.Ct. 2532 (1976) [**Larry MEACHUM et al., Petitioners, v. Arthur FANO et al.**] (**Civil Rights, Section 1983 Claims; Corrections; Cruel and Unusual Punishment**) Fano was one of several inmates transferred from the Massachusetts prison at Norfolk to a prison at Bridgewater, following a period of fire setting at the institution at Norfolk. The Bridgewater prison was a lesser facility in regard to amenities, and it had maximum-security and medium-security designations compared with the medium-security-only designation at Norfolk. Thus prisoners transferred from Norfolk to Bridgewater would be deprived of many benefits they earlier enjoyed. Fano and others filed a civil rights suit under Title 42 U.S.C. Section 1983, alleging that they were entitled to due process when subjected to interstate prison transfers. The SC disagreed and ruled simply that prisoners have *no* rights concerning where they are placed within the prison system. Prisoners cannot have a say regarding where the prison system decides to place them, as long as cruel and unusual punishment conditions do not exist. Thus, many state prisoners are confined in local jails (because of prison overcrowding) with far fewer amenities than prisons. These jail-confined state prisoners are now governed by the *Meachum v. Fano* ruling and thus cannot dictate where they should be placed in the prison system.

Melendez v. United States, 518 U.S. 120, 116 S.Ct. 2057 (1996) [**Juan MELENDEZ, Petitioner, v. UNITED STATES**] (**Sentencing; U.S. Sentencing Guidelines**) Melendez was convicted of conspiring to distribute cocaine, a crime carrying a statutory minimum sentence of 10 years' imprisonment. However, in a plea agreement with the government, Melendez agreed to furnish valuable information leading to the arrest and conviction of other drug dealers. The government described the assistance rendered by Melendez to the court and recommended a lesser sentence than that provided under the sentencing guidelines. Under the sentencing guidelines, Melendez's sentence would have been from 135 to 168 months, and the government moved the court to grant a downward departure from this higher range. However, the government did *not* move to have the court reduce Melendez's sentence *below* the mandatory minimum of 120 months or 10 years. The federal district judge imposed the statutory minimum 10-year sentence and Melendez appealed, contending that the substantial assistance he rendered to the government and their implied promise of a downward departure should be honored. Melendez expected that his sentence would be less than the statutory 10-year minimum. The SC heard the case and affirmed the lower-court decision, holding that the district court lacked the authority to impose less than the minimum 10-year mandatory sentence where the government did not bring a motion requesting or authorizing such a departure below the 10-year minimum sentence based on substantial assistance from Melendez. Furthermore, the SC held that a motion by the government for departure from applicable guidelines based on substantial assistance does not authorize departure from statutory minimum sentences.

Mempa v. Rhay, 389 U.S. 128, 88 S.Ct. 254 (1967) [**Jerry Douglas MEMPA, Petitioner, v. B.J. RHAY, Superintendent, Washington State Penitentiary. William Earl Walkling, Petitioner, v. Washington State Board of Prison Terms and Paroles**] (**Corrections; Indigent Clients; Probation and Parole; Right to Counsel**) Mempa was convicted of joyriding in a stolen vehicle on June 17, 1959. He was placed on probation for two years by a Spokane, WA, judge. Several months later, on September 15, Mempa was involved in a burglary. Mempa admitted participating in the burglary. The county prosecutor in Spokane moved to have Mempa's probation revoked. At his probation revocation hearing, the sole testimony about his involvement in the burglary came from his probation officer. Mempa was not represented by counsel, was not asked if he wanted counsel, and was not given an opportunity to offer statements in his own behalf. Furthermore, there was no cross-examination of the probation officer about his statements. The court revoked Mempa's probation and sentenced him to 10 years in the Washington State Penitentiary. Six years later, in 1965, Mempa filed a writ of *habeas corpus*, alleging that he had been denied a right to counsel at the revocation hearing. The Washington Supreme Court denied his petition, but he appealed, and the SC elected to hear it. The SC overturned the Washington decision and ruled in Mempa's favor. Specifically, the SC said Mempa had been entitled to an attorney but had been denied one. Although the Court did not question Washington authority to defer sentencing in the probation matter, it said that any indigent (including Mempa) is entitled at every stage of a criminal proceeding to be represented by court-appointed counsel, where "substantial rights of a criminal accused may be affected." Thus, the SC considered a probation revocation hearing to be a "critical stage" that falls within the due-process provisions of the Fourteenth Amendment. In subsequent years, several courts also applied this decision to parole revocation hearings.

Menna v. New York, 423 U.S. 61, 96 S.Ct. 241 (1975) [Steve MENNA v. State of NEW YORK] (Double Jeopardy; Fifth Amendment; Immunity) A grand jury was investigating a murder conspiracy. On November 7, 1968, Steve Menna was summoned into the proceeding. He refused to answer questions after being granted immunity. He was summoned to the grand jury again in March 1969, where he again refused to answer grand-jury questions. He was held in contempt and sentenced to 30 days in jail. Menna served his sentence. Subsequently, he was indicted for his refusal to answer questions before the grand jury on the November 7, 1968, date. He moved to have the indictment dismissed under the double-jeopardy clause of the Fifth Amendment. However, he was unsuccessful and convicted on this second contempt charge. He appealed, again claiming double jeopardy, this time to the SC. The SC overturned Menna's contempt adjudication on the grounds that it violated his double-jeopardy rights. When a 30-day sentence has been imposed following a contempt adjudication, a subsequent conviction stemming from the same contempt incident is clearly double jeopardy and unconstitutional.

Michigan v. Chesternut, 486 U.S. 567, 108 S.Ct. 1975 (1988) [MICHIGAN, Petitioner, v. Michael Mose CHESTERNUT] (Fourth Amendment; Law Enforcement Officers or Agencies; Searches and Seizures; Stop and Frisk) Chesternut was walking down a road when he saw a police patrol unit and began to run. Police officers in the unit followed him to see where he was going. As they pulled alongside Chesternut, who continued to run, they saw him throw to the ground numerous bags containing a white substance. They stopped and examined the bags, concluding tentatively that they might be illegal drugs. They stopped Chesternut and found additional bags of the same substance. It turned out to be narcotics and he was arrested and charged with narcotics possession. He was convicted. He appealed to the SC, arguing that the police officers had violated his Fourth Amendment right against unreasonable searches and seizures by following him and investigating without probable cause. The SC upheld Chesternut's conviction, concluding that the officers' investigatory pursuit had not constituted a seizure in violation of the Fourth Amendment. The SC stressed the reasonable-man notion and the contextual circumstances surrounding Chesternut's arrest. Given the existing circumstances, investigatory pursuits of suspects by police do not constitute illegal seizures.

Michigan v. DeFillippo, 443 U.S. 31, 99 S.Ct. 2627 (1979) [State of MICHIGAN, Petitioner, v. Gary DeFILLIPPO] (Fourth Amendment; Law Enforcement Officers or Agencies; Searches Incident to an Arrest) One evening, Detroit police found DeFillippo in an alleyway with a woman who was in the process of lowering her slacks. DeFillippo was asked to produce identification, and when he gave vague replies, officers searched him and discovered illegal drugs in his pockets. Later, in court, his attorney moved to suppress the evidence seized by officers, contending that they had lacked probable cause to search DeFillippo. DeFillippo was subsequently convicted, but the Michigan Supreme Court held the Detroit ordinance, "which provides that a police officer may stop and question an individual if he has rerasonable cause to believe that the individual's behavior . . . warrants further investigation," to be unconstitutionally vague. The government appealed, and the SC heard the case. The SC ruled that DeFillippo's conviction should be upheld, because the officers were acting in good-faith reliance on the Detroit ordinance. DeFillippo had been observed engaged in an illegal act, and his lawful arrest had justified the subsequent search of his person, producing the incriminating drugs. It would be unreasonable to expect that officers would either know or have reason to know that the Detroit ordinance would subsequently be declared unconstitutionally vague. The fact of a lawful arrest, standing alone, authorizes a search. In this case, there was "abundant" probable cause to believe that DeFillippo had committed or was committing an illegal act.

Michigan v. Harvey, 494 U.S. 344, 110 S.Ct. 1176 (1990) [MICHIGAN, Petitioner, v. Tyris Lemont HARVEY] (Custodial Interrogations; Law Enforcement Officers or Agencies; Right to Counsel; Sixth Amendment) Harvey was arraigned on rape charges, and counsel was appointed for him. Initially, he wanted to make a statement to police but didn't know whether he ought to have his attorney present. The police advised Harvey that he could make a statement *without* his attorney present, as the attorney would eventually get a copy of his statement anyway. Subsequently, Harvey signed a rights waiver form and made incriminating statements to police without his attorney present. Later, in court, Harvey gave conflicting statements, and police used his earlier statement, given without the attorney present, to impeach his court testimony. Harvey was convicted of first-degree criminal sexual conduct. He appealed. A Michigan court overturned his conviction, saying that it is unconstitutional for prosecutors to use statements otherwise inadmissible under the *Jackson* rule (*see Michigan v. Jackson* [1986]) to impeach a defendant's later testimony in court. The State of Michigan appealed, and the SC reinstated Harvey's conviction, holding that a statement to police taken in violation of *Jackson* may be used to impeach a defendant's testimony (in court later). The important point here is that Harvey's statements had been initiated by Harvey, not by police, even though Harvey had invoked his Sixth Amendment right to counsel. This information *could not* be used by prosecutors in their case-in-chief against the defendant, but it *could* be used for impeachment purposes.

Michigan v. Jackson, 475 U.S. 625, 106 S.Ct. 1404 (1986) [MICHIGAN, Petitioner, v. Robert Bernard JACKSON. Michigan, Petitioner, v. Rudy Bladel] (Confessions; Custodial Interrogations; Law Enforcement Officers or Agencies; Sixth Amendment) A woman planned the murder of her husband and spoke to Jackson and several other men about possibly carrying out this crime. Jackson was arrested and made various incriminating statements about the conspiratorial nature of the planned murder. At his arraignment, Jackson requested that counsel be appointed for him. A lawyer was provided. The following day, police initiated another interrogation of Jackson, without his attorney present, in which he admitted that he had murdered the woman's husband. Jackson was charged with murder and convicted. He appealed. The SC overturned his conviction because his due-process right had been violated when he was interrogated without the counsel that had been provided for him. The prosecution argued that Jackson's statement was voluntary, and that he had waived his right to have counsel present when giving his murder confession. The SC disagreed and said that custodial interrogations that are police initiated require the presence of an attorney. Without an attorney present, the accused cannot effectively waive his or her right to be interrogated further. Thus, defendants cannot be interrogated by police once they have invoked their right to silence and have an attorney. However, interrogations and confessions initiated by the suspect are permissible. Thus, if Jackson had requested to speak with officers and had admitted the murder, the confession would have been valid. This case established the *Jackson* rule, which says that once a defendant invokes the Sixth Amendment right to counsel, any waiver of that right—even if voluntary, knowing, and intelligent under traditional standards—is presumed invalid if given in a police-initiated discussion, and that evidence obtained pursuant to that waiver is inadmissible in the prosecution's case-in-chief. However, suspect-initiated statements can be used to impeach testimony given by defendants on cross-examination.

Michigan v. Long, 463 U.S. 1032, 103 S.Ct. 3469 (1983) [MICHIGAN, Petitioner, v. David Kerk LONG] (Fourth Amendment; Law Enforcement Officers or Agencies; Searches and Seizures; Stop and Frisk; Vehicle Searches) Long was driving erratically in an automobile and swerved into a ditch. Police observed this action and approached him. Long appeared intoxicated, but he produced a driver's license. When returning to his vehicle to obtain the registration, police observed a large hunting knife on the floor of the car. At that point, they stopped Long and frisked him, finding no dangerous weapons. Nevertheless, one of the officers, for his own protection, shined his flashlight into Long's car and saw some marijuana. Long was arrested and his car trunk was then opened and searched, incident to an arrest. Approximately 75 pounds of marijuana were found in the trunk, and Long was convicted. Long appealed, arguing that his Fourth Amendment right against unreasonable searches and seizures had been violated when police looked in his car. However, the SC upheld his conviction, saying that protective searches are permissible when police have reason to believe a suspect may pose some danger to them.

Michigan v. Lucas, 500 U.S. 145, 111 S.Ct. 1743 (1991) [MICHIGAN, Petitioner, v. Nolan K. LUCAS] (Sixth Amendment) Lucas was charged with rape. Michigan's rape-shield law provides for exclusion of any testimony or evidence of a victim's past sexual conduct or history. In Lucas' case, however, he had had a prior sexual relationship with the victim and sought to introduce this evidence, which was excluded under the rape-shield law. Among other things, Lucas had failed to comply with a notice-and-hearing requirement of Michigan

law to determine the admissibility of such testimony. Lucas was convicted of third-degree sexual conduct, and appealed. The SC upheld Lucas' conviction, holding that the preclusion of evidence of Lucas' past sexual conduct with the victim for Lucas' failure to comply with notice-and-hearing requirements of Michigan's rape-shield law was not *per se* a violation of Lucas' Sixth Amendment rights adequately to confront and cross-examine his accuser on this past sexual relationship.

Michigan v. Mosley, 423 U.S. 96, 96 S.Ct. 321 (1975) [State of MICHIGAN, Petitioner, v. Richard Bert MOSLEY] (Confessions; Fifth Amendment; Law Enforcement Officers or Agencies; *Miranda* Warning) Mosley was a suspect in several robberies and was arrested by police. They advised Mosley of his *Miranda* rights, and he refused to talk to them. After two hours, another officer from another jurisdiction visited Mosley and asked him questions about a homicide, after giving him another *Miranda* warning. Mosley gave incriminating statements to the visiting detective and was subsequently convicted of murder. He appealed, alleging that his Fifth Amendment right had been violated because of the new questioning by the detective when he had said he didn't wish to discuss the robberies with police earlier. The SC disagreed, however, saying that Mosley had been properly told his *Miranda* rights and that in the first instance of questioning, officers had rigidly adhered to the letter of the *Miranda* warning and ceased questioning him. Further, the second interrogation by a visiting detective had been preceded by a new *Miranda* warning, and thus, Mosley's statements were considered voluntarily given.

Michigan v. Summers, 452 U.S. 692, 101 S.Ct. 2587 (1981) [State of MICHIGAN, Petitioner, v. George SUMMERS] (Law Enforcement Officers or Agencies; Searches Incident to an Arrest; Stop and Frisk) Summers was leaving a house believed by police to be a drug contact point. Police had it under surveillance. They detained Summers while they entered the house with a valid search warrant based on probable cause. They found large quantities of narcotics and also determined that Summers was the owner of the home. They arrested him and searched him, discovering a quantity of heroin. He was convicted of heroin possession, and he appealed, contending that his detention was a "seizure" because the police had lacked probable cause to detain him initially. The SC disagreed with Summers, noting that police officers had had a valid search warrant for Summers' premises, and that once contraband was found and it was determined that Summers was, indeed, the homeowner, sufficient probable cause existed to arrest him and conduct a more thorough search of his person.

Michigan v. Thomas, 458 U.S. 259, 102 S.Ct. 3079 (1983) [MICHIGAN, Petitioner, v. Lamont Charles THOMAS] (Fourth Amendment; Law Enforcement Officers or Agencies; Plain-View Rule; Searches and Seizures; Vehicle Searches) An automobile was routinely stopped by police for failing to give a left-turn signal. Thomas was a passenger in the vehicle. When officers approached the vehicle, they saw in plain view an open bottle of malt liquor on the floorboard between Thomas' feet. The driver of the car, a 14-year-old, was cited for not having a driver's license. Thomas claimed that he (Thomas) owned the car. He was taken to a patrol car and his automobile was ordered towed to a police impound lot. Before it was towed, however, an officer searched the vehicle, the standard operating procedure when inventorying a car's contents. Two bags of marijuana were found in the glove compartment, which prompted the officer to search further. He found a loaded .38 revolver in the air vents under the dashboard. Thomas was arrested and eventually convicted of concealing firearms. He appealed, claiming that the pistol had been discovered as the result of an unreasonable search and seizure in violation of his Fourth Amendment rights. The SC upheld the conviction, noting that when police officers have probable cause to believe there is contraband inside an automobile that has been stopped on the road, they may conduct a warrantless search of the vehicle, even after it has been impounded and is in police custody.

Michigan v. Tucker, 417 U.S. 433, 94 S.Ct. 2357 (1974) [**State of MICHIGAN, Petitioner, v. Thomas W. TUCKER**] (**Confessions; Fifth Amendment;** *Habeas Corpus* **Petitions; Indigent Clients;** *Miranda* **Warning; Right to Counsel; Self-Incrimination**) Tucker, an indigent, was arrested by police as a rape suspect. He was told that he could remain silent and had a right to counsel, but he was not advised of his right to counsel if indigent. Tucker told police, without the presence of counsel, that he was with a friend, Henderson, at the time of the alleged rape. However, the police later determined from questioning Henderson that Henderson only had incriminating information about Tucker and did not support his alibi. Henderson was later called to testify in court against Tucker and gave the incriminating statements, nullifying Tucker's alibi. Tucker was convicted of rape. He sought an appeal through a *habeas corpus* petition, alleging that his *Miranda* rights had not been observed by police, and that Henderson's testimony ought to have been suppressed, inasmuch as Henderson came to police attention only after Tucker brought up his name as an alibi witness. A lower court agreed and reversed the conviction. The government appealed, and the SC heard the case. The SC reinstated Tucker's rape conviction, holding that the failure of police to advise Tucker of his right to appointed counsel had no bearing on the reliability of Henderson's testimony, which was subjected to cross-examination in a fair trial later. The use of testimony of a witness discovered by police as the result of Tucker's statements under these circumstances did not violate Tucker's Fifth, Sixth, or Fourteenth Amendment rights. The SC further declared that although the police failed to afford Tucker the full measure of procedural safeguards later set forth in *Miranda*, this failure did not deprive Tucker of his privilege against self-incrimination, as the record clearly indicates that Tucker's statements during the police interrogation were not involuntary or the result of potential legal sanctions. The evidence derived from the police interrogation was therefore admissible.

Michigan v. Tyler and Tompkins, 436 U.S. 499, 98 S.Ct. 1942 (1978) [**State of MICHIGAN, Petitioner, v. Loren TYLER AND Robert TOMPKINS**] (**Fourth Amendment; Law Enforcement Officers or Agencies**) The state alleged that Tyler and his companion, Tompkins, conspired to burn some property they owned in order to collect insurance on the property, a fraudulent act. Evidence introduced at their subsequent trial included photographs taken by arson investigators, who arrived early at the site of the burning building. Also, firemen had entered the building, together with police and others, and several plastic containers of flammable liquid were retrieved. This evidence was also used against Tyler and Tompkins in convicting them of the conspiracy and arson charges. Tyler appealed, seeking to suppress the incriminating evidence under the theory that investigators had not first obtained a valid search warrant before entering the premises. An appellate court reversed their convictions on these grounds and ordered a second trial. The state appealed. The SC heard the case and ruled partly in favor of the state and partly in favor of Tyler and Tompkins, holding that official entries into premises to investigate fires must be preceded by warrants. However, a burning building presents an "exigent circumstance" in which a warrantless entry and search may be conducted; while on the premises and for a reasonable time thereafter, firemen and arson investigators may seize any evidence they believe relates to the fire's origin. Therefore, evidence seized the night of the fire in the course of extinguishing it and for a reasonable period afterward is admissible. However, evidence collected from the fire scene by arson investigators and police a day or so later must be prefaced by a proper search warrant. In this case, the postinvestigatory actions of police and investigators were warrantless, and therefore, the evidence obtained in these subsequent searches and seizures was inadmissible in a retrial of Tyler and Tompkins, which was ordered.

Michigan Department of State Police v. Sitz, 496 U.S. 444, 110 S.Ct. 2481 (1990) [**MICHIGAN DEPARTMENT OF STATE POLICE et al., Petitioners, v. Rick SITZ et al.**] (**Fourth Amendment; Law Enforcement Officers or Agencies; Searches and Seizures**) Michigan state police established various sobriety checkpoints to determine whether certain drivers were intoxicated. Sitz was stopped at one of these checkpoints and cited for driving while intoxicated. He was convicted, and he appealed. The SC heard his case, in which Sitz alleged that his Fourth and Fourteenth Amendment rights had been violated. Essentially, his argument was that sobriety checkpoints are unconstitutional because they constitute unreasonable searches and seizures. The SC said that although there was "slight" intrusion in Sitz's case, the checkpoint system used by Michigan was constitutional. It noted that when Sitz was stopped, he was one of approximately 125 other drivers who were inconvenienced by a delay averaging 25 seconds. The SC stressed the insignificance of the minor intrusion involved in sobriety checkpoints, which did not violate Fourth Amendment and Fourteenth Amendment guarantees.

Mickens v. Taylor, ___U.S.___, 122 S.Ct. 1237 (2002) [**Walter MICKENS, Jr., Petitioner, v. John TAYLOR, Warden**] (**Death Penalty; Sixth Amendment**) Walter Mickens was convicted of first-degree murder in the death of Timothy Hall in 1993 and sentenced to death in Virginia. The murder occurred during or following the commission of an attempted forcible sodomy. Subsequently, Mickens filed a *habeas corpus* petition in federal district court alleging ineffective assistance of counsel on the grounds that his defense attorneys had a conflict of interest during the trial. One of Mickens' attorneys, Bryan Saunders, had represented Hall on assault and concealed-weapons charges at the time of the murder. Also, a juvenile court judge who had dismissed the charges against Hall later appointed Saunders to represent Mickens. At the time of his appointment as counsel for Mickens, Saunders failed to disclose that he had earlier represented Hall, Mickens' victim, in another matter. The federal district court judge denied *habeas corpus* relief to Mickens, who appealed to the Fourth Circuit. The Fourth Circuit affirmed the federal judge's ruling and Mickens sought relief with the SC, who heard the case. The SC affirmed also, holding that in order to demonstrate a Sixth Amendment violation where the trial court fails to inquire into a potential conflict of interest about which it knew or reasonably should have known, a defendant must establish that a conflict of interest adversely affected his counsel's performance. Mickens had failed to establish this fact regarding Saunders' conduct as his defense counsel. The significance of this case for criminal justice is that whenever a defendant alleges ineffective assistance of counsel, the defendant must demonstrate a reasonable probability that, but for counsel's unprofessional errors, the result of the proceeding (trial) would have been different. (*See also Strickland v. Washington* [1984].)

Middleton v. McNeil, ___U.S.___, 124 S.Ct. 1830 (2004) [**Raymond L. MIDDLETON, Warden, v. Sally Marie MCNEIL**] (**Imperfect Self-Defense; Jury Instructions**) Sally Marie McNeil killed her husband after an argument over his infidelity and spending habits. She claimed that he tried to strangle her during the argument, that she escaped to the bedroom, fetched a shotgun from the bedroom, and shot him out of fear for her life. Finger and nail marks were found on her neck after the shooting, although forensic evidence introduced at her trial showed that these marks were not her husband's, and were likely self-inflicted. Furthermore, a 911 operator testified that she heard Sally McNeil tell her husband that she shot him because she would no longer tolerate his behavior. McNeil was convicted of second-degree murder despite the use of the imperfect self-defense standard her attorney used, which reduces a murder charge to voluntary manslaughter provided that the cause of death was the result of the belief, though unreasonable, that there was necessity to defend against imminent peril to one's life or great bodily injury. When the trial judge gave the jury instructions, he added that "an imminent peril is one that is apparent, present, immediate, and must be instantly dealt with, or must so appear at the time to the slayer as a reasonable person" (at 1831). The "as a reasonable person" part of this jury instruction was not a part of the relevant instruction, and was included in error. However, the prosecutor correctly stated the law in his closing argument to the jury. McNeil appealed on the basis of the erroneous jury instruction. The California Supreme Court upheld her conviction, but the Ninth Circuit Court of Appeals reversed, articulating its belief that the judge had misled the jury with the faulty instruction, and the state appealed. The SC heard the

case and reinstated McNeil's second-degree murder conviction, holding that although the trial judge may have given an erroneous jury instruction, it did not rise to the level of confusing the jurors or changing their original decision to convict McNeil of second-degree murder.

Miller v. California, 413 U.S. 15, 93 S.Ct. 2607 (1973) [**Marvin MILLER, Appellant, v. State of CALIFORNIA**] (**Obscenity Laws; Unconstitutionally Vague Ordinances**) Miller was convicted of breaking a California obscenity ordinance prohibiting the mailing of obscene materials, in this case, photographs of men and women in couples or groups performing sex acts. He appealed, alleging that the statute was unconstitutional because of its vagueness and because no one knew how to measure obscenity. The SC upheld his conviction, settling the question of obscenity standards by placing these standards in the hands of individual state legislatures. Thus, obscenity is defined according to individual state statutes.

Miller v. Fenton, 474 U.S. 104, 106 S.Ct. 445 (1985) [**Frank M. MILLER, Jr., Petitioner, v. Peter J. FENTON, Superintendent, Rahway State Prison, et al.**] (*Habeas Corpus* **Petitions; Self-Incrimination**) Miller was suspected of first-degree murder and subjected to a 58-minute interrogation in the New Jersey State Police Barracks. Eventually, he confessed and was convicted. He appealed, filing a *habeas corpus* petition challenging his conviction and his confession, which he alleged had been coerced. The SC overturned his conviction, saying that the *habeas corpus* petition was a proper means of challenging his conviction, and that the actions of police in obtaining Miller's confession had been inherently coercive. Substantial circumstances were prevalent in this case, and the conditions under which Miller confessed indicated that the confession had not been voluntary. The SC referred the case back to trial court, where it could be determined whether or not the confession was coercive or voluntary.

Miller-El v. Cockrell, ___U.S.___, 123 S.Ct. 1029 (2003) [**Thomas Joe MILLER-EL, Petitioner, v. Janie COCKRELL, Director, Texas Department of Criminal Justice, Institutional Division**] (**Fourteenth Amendment;** *Habeas Corpus* **Petitions; Juries; Peremptory Challenges**) Thomas Miller-El, his wife, Dorothy, and Kenneth Flowers robbed a Holiday Inn in Dallas, TX, in 1985. They bound and gagged two employees and then shot them. One employee died, but the other recovered and was able to identify Miller-El and his associates as his assailants. Subsequently, Miller-El was indicted and tried for capital murder in a Dallas criminal court in February and March 1986. During jury selection, the prosecutor used his peremptory challenges to exclude 10 of the 11 African-American prospective jurors, thus creating a largely white jury. Following the jury selection, Miller-El moved to strike the jury on the grounds that the prosecution had violated the equal-protection clause of the Fourteenth Amendment by excluding African Americans through the use of peremptory challenges. Miller-El's motion was denied. Upon his subsequent conviction for murder, Miller-El, a black, was sentenced to death. He began a lengthy series of appeals, contending that blacks had been systematically excluded from the jury. During his appeals, the case of *Batson v. Kentucky* (1986) was decided and established a three-part process for evaluating claims that a prosecutor used peremptory challenges in violation of the equal-protection clause. First, a defendant must make a *prima facie* showing that a peremptory challenge has been exercised on the basis of race. Second, if that showing has been made, the prosecution must offer a race-neutral basis for striking the juror in question. Third, in light of the parties' submissions, the trial court must determine whether the defendant has shown purposeful discrimination. Both Texas appellate courts and the federal Fifth Circuit Court of Appeals denied Miller-El's petitions, citing that insufficient evidence existed to show bias on the part of the prosecutor. The SC heard the case and disagreed. The SC overturned the circuit court, holding that Miller-El was entitled to appeal the issue of biased jury selection in his original trial, as there was evident unreasonableness associated with how the original jury was selected. Miller-El was entitled to appeal this issue in a Texas court in light of the holding in *Batson v. Kentucky.*

Mills v. Maryland, 486 U.S. 367, 108 S.Ct. 1860 (1988) [Ralph MILLS, Petitioner, v. MARYLAND] (Aggravating and Mitigating Circumstances; Death Penalty) Mills was an inmate of the Maryland Correctional Institution in Hagerstown. He stabbed his cellmate to death with a homemade knife and was charged with murder. A trial was held and the jury found Mills guilty. Instructions from the judge at the beginning of the sentencing phase led jurors to believe that they must agree unanimously on mitigating circumstances before they could consider them in Mills' case. If they could not agree, then they had to render a death-penalty decision. Because they were not unanimous regarding any mitigating circumstances, they decided on the death penalty as required by the judge's instructions. Thus, a mandatory element was introduced into the penalty phase, which is unconstitutional in relation to death-penalty decisions. Mills appealed, arguing this very point to the SC. The SC overturned Mills' conviction, concluding that there was a substantial probability that reasonable jurors, upon receiving the judge's instructions, might well have thought they were precluded from considering any mitigating evidence unless all 12 jurors agreed on the existence of a particular such circumstance. The SC said the jurors must consider all the mitigating evidence. The possibility that a single juror could block such consideration, and consequently require the jury to impose the death penalty, was not to be risked. Therefore, the death-penalty sentence was vacated.

Mincey v. Arizona, 437 U.S. 385, 98 S.Ct. 2408 (1978) [Rufus Junior MINCEY, Petitioner, v. State of ARIZONA] (Fourth Amendment; Law Enforcement Officers or Agencies) Mincey was involved in a raid on his apartment by undercover police officers. One police officer was shot and killed, and Mincey was seriously wounded and taken to a hospital. During the next four days, his apartment was searched extensively by police, who tore it apart. They also interrogated Mincey while he was in the hospital, drugged, and in great pain. Mincey continually asked the police to discontinue their questioning, but they persisted. He eventually gave incriminating statements to police under this debilitating condition in the hospital. These incriminating statements, as well as newly discovered evidence from his apartment, were used against him. He was convicted of murder, assault, and various narcotics offenses. He appealed. The SC held that Mincey's Fourth Amendment right against an unreasonable search and seizure had been violated when police searched his apartment for four days without a warrant. Further, statements he gave while hospitalized had been given under coercive circumstances and were therefore inadmissible. Because his due-process rights had been violated, his conviction was overturned.

Minnesota v. Carter, 525 U.S. 83, 119 S.Ct. 469 (1998) [MINNESOTA, Petitioner, v. Wayne Thomas CARTER] (Fourth Amendment; Inventory Searches; Searches and Seizures; Vehicle Searches) An informant advised James Thielen, a police officer in Eagan, MN, that he had passed an apartment building and observed through a window persons putting white powder into bags. Following up on this information, Carter and others were observed by the police officer, who merely looked through a gap in a closed blind in an apartment. Carter was bagging cocaine. Later, Carter and others left in an automobile, which was stopped by police. In plain view, officers observed a firearm on the vehicle's floor, together with a black bag. An inventory search of the car the following day revealed that the bag contained 47 grams of cocaine, scales, and pagers. After seizing the car, police returned to the apartment. A search revealed cocaine residue where the officer had observed the bagging operation the night before, together with several other plastic baggies similar to those found in the seized vehicle. It was determined that the apartment was leased by a Ms. Thompson, and that Carter and his associates were from Chicago. They were only in the apartment for two and one-half hours as temporary visitors, only for the purpose and period of time necessary to cut and bag the cocaine. Carter was convicted and appealed. Subsequently, the Minnesota Supreme Court reversed Carter's conviction, contending that although the apartment was not Carter's, Carter nevertheless had "standing" and a reasonable expectation of privacy. Thus, the police officer's observation of Carter and subsequent invasion of his privacy constituted an unreasonable search under the Fourth Amendment. The SC heard the case and reversed the Minnesota Supreme Court, holding that the transient nature of Carter's presence in the apartment—to package and distribute cocaine—did not vest him with Fourth Amendment protections ordinarily extended to persons who live in those places more permanently. The SC said that here, the purely commercial nature of the transaction, the relatively short period of time that Carter was on the premises, and the lack of any previous connection between him and the householder did not vest him with Fourth Amendment rights. Because Carter had no legitimate expectation of privacy, the police officer's observations did not constitute a "search." (*See Rakas v. Illinois* [1978] *for comparison.*)

Minnesota v. Dickerson, 508 U.S. 366, 113 S.Ct. 2130 (1993) [MINNESOTA, Petitioner, v. Timothy DICKERSON] (Law Enforcement Officers or Agencies; Stop and Frisk) Dickerson emerged from a known "crack house" and was observed by police officers walking down an alley. When he saw the officers approaching him, he reversed direction and walked away from them. They decided to stop him for an investigative pat-down. They discovered no weapons, but one of the officers thrust his hand into Dickerson's pocket and found a small quantity of crack cocaine in a glassine envelope. He claimed that he had "felt a small lump that felt like crack cocaine" through Dickerson's clothing after the initial pat-down and frisk. Dickerson was charged with cocaine possession and convicted. He appealed, and the SC overturned his conviction on the ground that the search of Dickerson went well beyond the scope specified in *Terry v. Ohio* (1968), which allows police officers to pat-down and frisk suspects exclusively for the purpose of determining whether suspects possess dangerous weapons that might be used to harm the police. This specific type of incident is directly on point and consistent with a SC ruling in another case involving excessive officer intrusion into a suspect's pocket in a search for contraband: *Sibron v. New York* (1968).

Minnesota v. Murphy, 465 U.S. 420, 104 S.Ct. 1136 (1984) [MINNESOTA, Petitioner, v. Marshall Donald MURPHY] (Confessions; Law Enforcement Officers or Agencies; *Miranda* Warning; Probation and Parole) Murphy was serving a three-year probation term for criminal sexual conduct. One of his probation conditions was that he was to report regularly to his probation officer and answer all questions truthfully. Another condition was that he seek sexual therapy and counseling. During one of these counseling sessions, Murphy confessed to one of his counselors that he had committed a rape and murder in 1974. The counselor told his probation officer, who, in turn, interrogated Murphy at his residence. Murphy admitted the crime (responding truthfully) after extensive interviewing and interrogation. The probation officer gave this incriminating information to police, who arrested Murphy later and charged him with the 1974 rape and murder. Murphy claimed later that the probation officer had not advised him of his *Miranda* rights, and thus, his confession should not be admitted later in court against him. As a general rule, criminal suspects who are the targets of a police investigation must be advised of their *Miranda* rights if undergoing an interrogation, whether or not they are in custody. A similar rule pertains to probationers. It might be argued, for instance, that the *fact* of their probation is a form of "custody." Thus, all probationers (and parolees) might be considered "in custody" during their program terms. However, "custody" implies being unable to leave the presence of the interrogator. When suspects conclude their interrogation, they may or may not be permitted to leave. If they leave, they are *not* considered to be in custody. Otherwise, they *are* in custody. Murphy was not in custody, however. Also, he had not been compelled to answer the probation officer's questions.

Minnesota v. Olson, 495 U.S. 91, 110 S.Ct. 1684 (1989) [MINNESOTA, Petitioner, v. Robert Darren OLSON] (Exclusionary Rule; Law Enforcement Officers or Agencies) Olson, a suspect in a robbery-murder, was believed to be staying at the home of two women, according to an anonymous tip. Police surrounded the house, called the women inside on a telephone, and advised them that Olson should surrender by stepping outside unarmed. A male voice was overheard to say, "Tell them I left." Hearing this, police officers forced entry into the house, without warrant or permission, and made a warrantless arrest of Olson, who was hiding in a closet. Later, incriminating statements made by Olson led to his conviction for the robbery-murder. He appealed, contending that the warrantless entry into the home of the women had been an unreasonable search and that exigent circumstances did not exist to justify it. The SC ruled that the search and subsequent arrest of Olson were invalid, and thus, his statements to police were inadmissible as evidence against him. This is an example of the fruits-of-the-poisonous-tree doctrine. (*See Wong Sun v. United States* [1963].)

Minnick v. Mississippi, 498 U.S. 146, 111 S.Ct. 486 (1990) [Robert S. MINNICK, Petitioner, v. MISSISSIPPI] (Custodial Interrogations; Law Enforcement Officers or Agencies; *Miranda* Warning; Right to Counsel) A day after escaping from a Mississippi county jail, Minnick and an accomplice killed two men during the burglary of a trailer. Minnick fled to California, where he was arrested on Friday, August 22, 1986, by Lemon Grove police. On August 23, FBI agents advised Minnick of his right to counsel and his right not to answer their questions. Minnick made a partial confession to FBI agents, although he advised them to "come back Monday" when he would have an attorney present. The same day, Minnick was appointed an attorney, who advised him to say nothing to police. On Monday, August 25, a deputy sheriff from Mississippi, Denham, flew to the San Diego jail where Minnick was being held. Minnick was reluctant to talk to Denham, but jailers told him he "had to talk." Minnick related all the incidents following his jail escape and admitted committing one of the murders. He was subsequently convicted on two counts of capital murder and sentenced to death. He appealed, moving to suppress his statements to FBI agents and to Denham. The SC reversed Minnick's conviction and sentence and remanded the case to a lower court, reasoning that once the *Miranda* warning had been given and an attorney appointed, further questioning by police might not resume without an attorney present, if the defendant had invoked the right to have counsel present.

Miranda v. Arizona, 384 U.S. 436, 86 S.Ct. 1602 (1966) [Ernesto A. MIRANDA, Petitioner, v. State of ARIZONA. Michael Vignera, Petitioner, v. State of New York. Carl Calvin Westover, Petitioner, v. United States. State of California, Petitioner, v. Roy Allen Stewart] (Confessions; Exclusionary Rule; Law Enforcement Officers or Agencies; *Miranda* Warning; Right to Counsel) Miranda was arrested on suspicion of rape and kidnapping. He was not permitted to talk to an attorney, nor was he advised of his right to one. He was interrogated by police for several hours, eventually confessing and signing a written confession. He was convicted. Miranda appealed, contending that his right to due process had been violated because he had not first been advised of his right to remain silent and to have an attorney present during a custodial interrogation. The SC agreed and set forth the *Miranda* warning. This monumental decision provided that confessions made by suspects who were not notified of their due-process rights cannot be admitted as evidence. Suspects must be advised of certain rights before they are questioned by police; these rights include the right to remain silent, the right to counsel, the right to free counsel if the suspect cannot afford it, and the right to terminate questioning at any time.

Mistretta v. United States, 488 U.S. 361, 109 S.Ct. 647 (1989) [**John M. MISTRETTA, Petitioner, v. UNITED STATES. United States, Petitioner, v. John M. Mistretta**] (**U.S. Sentencing Guidelines**) Mistretta was convicted of selling cocaine. The United States Sentencing Guidelines were officially in effect after November 1, 1987. Mistretta's criminal acts and conviction occurred after this date, and thus he was subject to guidelines-based sentencing rather than indeterminate sentencing, which the federal district courts had previously followed. Under the former sentencing scheme, Mistretta might have been granted probation. However, the new guidelines greatly restricted the use of probation as a sentence in federal courts, and thus, Mistretta's sentence involved serving an amount of time in prison. Mistretta appealed his conviction, arguing that the new guidelines violated the separation-of-powers doctrine, as several federal judges were members of the United States Sentencing Commission and helped to formulate laws and punishments, an exclusive function of Congress. The SC upheld Mistretta's conviction and declared the new guidelines to be constitutional, not in violation of the separation of powers doctrine.

Mitchell v. Esparza, ___U.S.___, 124 S.Ct. 7 (2004) [**Betty MITCHELL, Warden, v. Gregory ESPARZA**] (**Death Penalty;** *Habeas Corpus* **Petitions; Harmless Error Doctrine**) Gregory Esparza was convicted of aggravated murder during the commission of aggravated robbery. Esparza entered a convenience store alone in Toledo, OH, and shot and killed Melanie Gerschultz, a store employee. Esparza was subsequently convicted and sentenced to death, seven to 25 years for aggravated robbery, plus three years for a firearm charge. Esparza filed a *habeas corpus* action, alleging that Ohio prosecutors had failed to charge him as the "principal offender" in the robbery-murder, and that this omission of a critical element of a capital offense was contrary to clearly established federal law. Ohio courts upheld his conviction and rejected his argument, as he was the lone offender and no one else was named as an accomplice. Thus, it was deemed as harmless error for the trial court to charge him as the principal offender in the murder. A U.S. district court then granted Esparza *habeas corpus* relief and a circuit court of appeals affirmed. The SC heard the case and reversed, holding that the jury had been instructed on the elements of aggravated murder. The SC declared that the jury verdict would have been the same even if it had been instructed to find as well that Esparza was the "principal" in the offense. This omission was harmless error and thus the SC could not say that the state court's conclusion that Esparza was convicted of a capital offense was objectively unreasonable. Furthermore, the SC declared that the Ohio decision was not contrary to clearly established federal law.

Mitchell v. United States, 526 U.S. 314, 119 S.Ct. 1307 (1999) [**Amanda MITCHELL, Petitioner, v. UNITED STATES**] (**Fifth Amendment; Plea Bargaining**) Mitchell was convicted of conspiracy to distribute cocaine following a guilty plea entered during plea bargaining. Mitchell admitted that she had engaged in "some of" the conduct, but she reserved the right to clarify her guilty plea at the subsequent sentencing hearing. At the sentencing hearing, several of her codefendants testified that she had sold one to two ounces of cocaine per week for at least one and one-half years. Mitchell offered no witnesses, evidence, or statements in her own behalf, except to say that the government had proved only that she had sold two ounces of cocaine. The district court judge ruled that following her guilty plea during the plea bargaining phase, Mitchell had no right to remain silent about her crime's details. Thus, relying on her codefendants' testimony, the judge determined that Mitchell had conspired to distribute over five kilograms of cocaine and mandated a 10-year minimum sentence, noting that Mitchell's failure to testify was a factor in persuading the judge to rely on the codefendants' testimony in determining the quantity of cocaine sold. Mitchell appealed, contending that her Fifth Amendment right against self-incrimination had been violated by the federal district court judge. The SC heard the case and reversed Mitchell's conviction, holding that a defendant who waives the right against self-incrimination during plea bargaining does not automatically waive that same right during a sentencing hearing. Thus, if the sentencing judge draws adverse inferences from Mitchell's refusal to disclose the crime's details at the sentencing hearing when fixing the term of sentencing, this is unconstitutional and a violation of Mitchell's Fifth Amendment right against self-incrimination.

Monroe v. Pape, 365 U.S. 167, 81 S.Ct. 473 (1961) [**James MONROE et al., Petitioners, v. Frank PAPE et al.**] (**Civil Rights, Section 1983 Claims; Corrections; Inmate Rights**) Monroe was a suspect in a Chicago murder. Thirteen Chicago police officers broke into his home one evening and made him and several others stand naked in a room while the police ransacked his residence searching for incriminating information. During the search, officers tore up mattresses and furniture and emptied drawers. Monroe was taken to the police station, where he was held for several days on "open charges." Eventually, he was released without any charges being brought against him. He filed suit against the police department under Title 42 U.S.C. Section 1983, alleging that his civil rights had been violated. An Illinois court dismissed Monroe's complaint, and Monroe appealed. The SC declared that the Illinois police had acted improperly and had violated Monroe's rights under the Federal Civil Rights Act.

Montana v. Egelhoff, 518 U.S. 37, 116 S.Ct. 2013 (1996) [**MONTANA, Petitioner, v. James Allen EGELHOFF**] (**Intoxication Defense**) Egelhoff was convicted in Montana of two counts of deliberate homicide, or knowingly causing another's death. Egelhoff claimed he was intoxicated and that his condition rendered him incapable of committing the murders or recalling specific events of the night of the murders. Montana law prohibits consideration of intoxication as a defense in considering the existence of a mental state that is an element of the offense of deliberate homicide. Egelhoff appealed, claiming that when the court barred introduction of his intoxicated state as a defense, his right to due process was violated, because the jury did not have the opportunity to consider "all" relevant evidence in the issue. The Montana Supreme Court reversed the trial court, and the government appealed. The SC heard the case and reversed the Montana Supreme Court, holding that although the due-process clause does place limits on the restriction of the right to introduce evidence, that is only where the restriction offends some principle of justice so rooted in the traditions and conscience of our people as to be ranked as fundamental. Egelhoff has failed to meet the heavy burden of establishing that his right to have a jury consider voluntary intoxication as evidence in determining whether he possesses the requisite mental state is a fundamental principle of justice.

Montanye v. Haymes, 427 U.S. 236, 96 S.Ct. 2543 (1976) [**Ernest L. MONTANYE, former Superintendent, Attica Correctional Facility, et al., Petitioners, v. Rodney R. HAYMES**] (**Corrections; Inmate Rights**) Haymes, a prisoner at Attica Correctional Facility in New York, was involved in circulating a petition among other inmates protesting his removal as clerk in the Attica law library. Subsequently, he was transferred to Clinton Correctional Facility, another maximum-security prison. Haymes filed suit against the prison system in New York, alleging that his transfer to another prison had violated his due-process rights. The SC said that such a transfer had not violated the inmate's due-process rights, and that prisoners do not have a right to determine where they are confined. (*See Meachum v. Fano* [1976] for a similar scenario.)

Moody v. Daggett, 429 U.S. 78, 97 S.Ct. 274 (1976) [**Minor MOODY, Petitioner, v. Loren DAGGETT, Warden**] (**Corrections; Probation and Parole**) Moody was a convict serving time in prison for rape. He was subsequently paroled, and while on parole, he killed two persons. He received a concurrent 10-year sentence for both murders. These murders also violated one or more of his original parole conditions stemming from the rape conviction. Moody asked that a prompt revocation hearing be held on this parole violation so that any additional time imposed for this parole violation could run concurrently with his current 10-year sentence. The United States Parole Board rejected this request. Instead, it issued a *detainer warrant* such that whenever Moody was released subsequently, he would be returned to face the United States Parole Board and its own punishments imposed for the parole violation. Moody appealed this decision. The SC upheld the decision of the United States Parole Board. Thus, parole violators such as Moody are not entitled to a prompt revocation hearing in the event that they are incarcerated for other crimes.

Moore v. Illinois, 408 U.S. 786, 92 S.Ct. 2562 (1972) [**Lyman A. MOORE, Petitioner, v. State of ILLINOIS**] (**Discovery; Jury Trials**) Moore was accused of first-degree murder. Prior to his trial, written statements were obtained from witnesses by police. These statements as well as other information compiled by police were requested under discovery by Moore's attorney. Most information was given to Moore, with the exception of a diagram of the crime scene and several

witness statements unknown to Moore. Moore was convicted. He appealed, arguing that the exclusion of some pieces of information by the prosecution had violated his discovery rights. He claimed that a specific request from him about unknown statements was unnecessary because he should not have been expected to request that which he did not know was in existence. The SC upheld his conviction, saying that the suppression of evidence did not amount to a denial of discovery by the defendant and therefore did not constitute a denial of due process.

Moore v. Illinois, 434 U.S. 220, 98 S.Ct. 458 (1977) [**James Raymond MOORE, Petitioner, v. State of ILLINOIS**] (**Law Enforcement Officers or Agencies; Lineups**) Moore was suspected of rape and other crimes. He was arrested after police had shown the rape victim numerous photographs and she had picked out Moore's as that of a likely suspect. Moore was taken before a judge for a hearing. At the hearing, Moore was advised by the judge that he was being charged with rape and other crimes. At about the same time, the state's attorney brought the victim into the hearing, where she was advised in advance that a suspect was in custody and that she "ought to identify him if she could." The victim saw Moore and identified him as the rapist. Moore was not represented by counsel at any time from his arrest and through this hearing. Counsel for Moore was eventually appointed after a grand jury indicted him for the rape. Moore's attorney moved for suppression of the victim identification, but the motion was denied. Moore was convicted of rape. He appealed, arguing that admission of the identification testimony at trial had violated his Sixth and Fourteenth Amendment rights. The SC overturned Moore's conviction, saying that his Sixth and Fourteenth Amendment rights had, indeed, been violated because of an absence of counsel to represent him at these earlier critical stages. The identification had been conducted illegally, as the direct result of an illegal lineup.

Moore v. Michigan, 355 U.S. 155, 78 S.Ct. 191 (1957) [**Willie B. MOORE, Petitioner, v. State of MICHIGAN**] (**Corrections; Probation and Parole; Right to Counsel**) Moore was accused of murdering a woman in 1938. He entered a guilty plea through a plea-bargain agreement and was convicted and sentenced to life imprisonment. In 1950, he filed a motion for a new trial, alleging that his guilty plea had been entered without benefit of counsel. The SC overturned his conviction for the following reasons. When Moore entered his guilty plea, he was 17 years old and had a seventh-grade education. The trial judge had Moore come into his chambers, where he interviewed Moore for five or 10 minutes. The judge said that Moore had told him that he (Moore) just "wanted to get it over with" and that as far as the judge was concerned, Moore had intelligently, knowingly, and voluntarily given up his right to counsel and other rights normally waived during plea-bargain agreements. The SC observed that several different kinds of defenses, including insanity, could have been raised to account for Moore's conduct when committing the murder. The SC declared that under these circumstances, Moore's rights could not have been fairly protected without the assistance of counsel to help him with his defense. Essentially, the SC advised Michigan that the state should have provided him with counsel despite his waiver of his right to counsel.

Morales v. New York, 396 U.S. 102, 90 S.Ct. 291 (1969) [Melvin MORALES, Petitioner, v. State of NEW YORK] (Law Enforcement Officers or Agencies) In October 1964, a murder occurred in an apartment building where Morales lived. His mother informed police that Morales had wished to talk with them and that they should come to her place of business that evening to do so. Morales was subsequently arrested, confessed to the murder, and was convicted. He appealed, alleging that his arrest had been improper and therefore his confession was invalid. The SC reversed his conviction, reasoning that although his detention was not a formal "arrest," he was not free to leave the custody of officers at the police station when his confession was given. However, no hearing was conducted to determine whether the circumstances surrounding Morales' confession were coerced or voluntary. The SC vacated the conviction and remanded the case to the trial court, where the question of a coerced confession could be considered as a part of his due-process rights.

Moran v. Burbine, 475 U.S. 412, 106 S.Ct. 1135 (1986) [John MORAN, Superintendent, Rhode Island Department of Corrections, Petitioner, v. Brian K. BURBINE] (*Miranda* Warning; Self-Incrimination) Burbine, a murder suspect, was arrested by police and given the *Miranda* warning. The police, knowing that Burbine's sister had had counsel appointed for him and that the attorney was attempting to reach Burbine, elected to question Burbine for a few hours anyway, before he was allowed to see his counsel. Burbine did not know that his sister had appointed counsel for him or that his counsel was attempting to reach him. Further, the police had advised Burbine's attorney that no interrogation was planned for the evening and that the attorney could see him "in the morning." Burbine made a confession to police about the murder and was subsequently convicted. He appealed, alleging that his Fifth Amendment right against self-incrimination had been violated when police forbade the attorney to talk to him. The SC upheld Burbine's conviction, saying that he had been properly told his *Miranda* rights and was in the position of knowingly giving or not giving incriminating statements to police, regardless of other events occurring around him and of which he was unaware. The SC said that events outside the defendant's knowledge could have no bearing on the defendant's invocation of his right to silence. Thus, when Burbine decided to talk with police about the murder and confess, he was knowingly waiving his right to silence.

Morgan v. Illinois, 504 U.S. 719, 112 S.Ct. 2222 (1992) [Derrick MORGAN, Petitioner v. ILLINOIS] (Corrections; Death Penalty; Death-Qualified Juries; Juries) Morgan was suspected of capital murder. Prior to the trial, he wanted the judge to ask prospective jurors whether they would automatically impose the death penalty regardless of the facts, but the judge refused. Eventually, Morgan was convicted and sentenced to death. He appealed, arguing that his due-process rights had been violated. The SC reversed the conviction and sent the case back to the lower court for retrial. The explana-

tion was that it was unconstitutional for the judge *not* to ask such a question of jurors. Thus, Morgan's due-process rights had been violated. This case is distinguished from *Witherspoon v. Illinois* (1968), which had to do with a juror being impaired to function as a juror in view of his opposition to the death penalty. In *Morgan,* jurors who would automatically vote for the death penalty regardless of the facts would be excludable as jurors for cause.

Morris v. Mathews, 475 U.S. 237, 106 S.Ct. 1032 (1986) [T.L. MORRIS, Superintendent, Southern Ohio Correctional Facility, Petitioner, v. James Michael MATHEWS] (Double Jeopardy; *Habeas Corpus* Petitions) Mathews and another man, Dougherty, robbed a bank in Ohio and were pursued by police to a farmhouse, where they hid. Shortly thereafter, police heard shots from inside the house, and Mathews surrendered. Police found Dougherty dead and assumed he had committed suicide. Mathews pleaded guilty to the robbery and was convicted of aggravated robbery. A few days later, Mathews confessed to killing Dougherty and was indicted on aggravated murder charges stemming from the robbery incident. He moved to quash the indictment on the grounds of double jeopardy, as some of the aggravated murder elements were an integral part of the elements of the aggravated robbery of which he had been convicted. The state denied his motion. Later, the state concluded that the aggravated murder charge was indeed double jeopardy, and thus it reduced the charge to the lesser included offense of murder, which was clearly supported by independent elements not associated with the aggravated robbery conviction. Mathews sought *habeas corpus* relief from the SC, but the SC upheld his murder conviction, holding that because the state had changed his conviction from a jeopardy-barred offense to a non–jeopardy-barred offense, the burden would therefore shift to Mathews to prove that the trial outcome would have been somehow different. Thus, the SC declared that reducing Mathews' concededly jeopardy-barred conviction for aggravated murder to a conviction for murder that concededly was not jeopardy barred was an adequate remedy for the double-jeopardy violation.

Morris v. Schoonfield, 399 U.S. 508, 90 S.Ct. 2232 (1970) [Phillip MORRIS et al., Appellants, v. Hiram SCHOONFIELD, Warden, et al.] (Corrections; *Habeas Corpus* Petitions; Indigent Clients; Probation and Parole) Morris was convicted of a crime in Maryland, fined, and sentenced to a prison term. When his prison term expired, Morris, an indigent, couldn't pay the fine imposed, and thus authorities continued to imprison him. Morris filed a *habeas corpus* petition, alleging that he could not be held beyond the statutory imprisonment period simply because he was poor and couldn't pay the fine imposed by the sentencing court. The SC heard his case and vacated the sentence, holding that an indigent may not be imprisoned beyond the maximum term specified by statute solely because of his failure to pay a fine and court costs.

Morrissey v. Brewer, 408 U.S. 471, 92 S.Ct. 2593 (1972) [John J. MORRISSEY and G. Donald Booher, Petitioners, v. Lou B. BREWER, Warden, et al.] (Corrections; Parole Revocation; Probation and Parole) Morrissey was a parolee who allegedly violated several parole conditions. The violations included (1) failing to report his place of residence to his parole officer, (2) buying an automobile under an assumed name and operating it without parole officer permission, (3) obtaining credit under an assumed name, and (4) giving false statements to police after a minor traffic accident. The paroling authority summarily revoked his parole, and he was returned to prison. Morrissey appealed the summary revocation, and the SC heard his case. Among other things, the Court in this landmark case established the minimum due-process requirements for parole revocation: (1) Two hearings are required; the first is a preliminary hearing to determine whether probable cause exists that a parolee has violated any specific parole condition, and the second is a general revocation proceeding. (2) Written notice must be given to the parolee prior to the general revocation proceeding. (3) Disclosure must be made to the parolee concerning the nature of parole violation(s) and evidence obtained. (4) The parolee must be given the right to confront and cross-examine his or her accusers unless adequate cause can be given for prohibiting such a cross-examination. (5) A written statement must be provided containing the reasons for revoking the parole and the evidence used in making that decision. (6) The parolee is entitled to have the facts judged by a detached and neutral hearing committee.

Muhammad v. Close, ___U.S.___, 124 U.S. 1303 (2004) [Shakur MUHAMMAD, aka John E. Mease, Petitioner, v. Mark CLOSE] (Civil Rights, Section 1983 Claims) Muhammad was a Michigan inmate eating breakfast in the prison dining hall. A prison official, Close, stared at Muhammad through a hallway window, and Muhammad returned his stare. This staring prompted Close to approach Muhammad and ask him "What's up?" Muhammad stood up and faced Close, apparently exhibiting an angry facial expression. Close had Muhammad handcuffed, taken to a detention cell, and charged with threatening behavior and insolence. A hearing six days later absolved Muhammad of the "threatening behavior" charge, but he was found guilty of insolence, confined in detention for an additional seven days, and deprived of prison privileges for 30 days. Muhammad filed a Section 1983 civil rights claim alleging that Close was retaliating against Muhammad because of earlier grievances and lawsuits Muhammad had filed against Close. Muhammad sought $10,000 in compensatory and punitive damages arising from the incident and asked to have his misconduct charge expunged. Later, he amended his suit by abandoning his claim to have his misconduct record expunged. A summary judgment was entered against Muhammad on the ground that Muhammad had failed to come forward with sufficient evidence of retaliation to raise a genuine issue of material fact. An appellate court affirmed, but on different grounds, holding that an action by Muhammad under Section 1983 to have Muhammad's misconduct charge expunged could only be brought after satisfying the *Heck* rule and favorable termination requirement. Muhammad then appealed to the SC, who heard the case. The SC reversed the appellate court, noting that the *Heck* rule was inapplicable, and that the matter should be remanded to the dis-

trict court for consideration of summary judgment on the original ground adopted by that court. (*See Heck v. Humphrey* [1994].)

Mu'Min v. Virginia, 500 U.S. 415, 111 S.Ct. 1899 (1991) [Dawud Majid MU'MIN, Petitioner, v. VIRGINIA] (Publicity; Right to Counsel; Sixth Amendment) Mu'Min was charged with and convicted of a murder while he was out on a prison work detail (where he was serving a term on another charge). There was considerable news publicity surrounding the killing, and when the case came to trial, Mu'Min's attorney made a motion for the judge during *voir dire* to ask whether any specific jurors had any knowledge of the pretrial publicity and if so, what effect it would have on their ability to hear and decide the case fairly. The judge denied the motion, and Mu'Min was subsequently convicted. He appealed, alleging that his right to an impartial jury as provided by the Sixth Amendment had been violated. The SC upheld his conviction, holding that the refusal of the judge to question jurors about specific contents of news reports to which they had been exposed had not violated Mu'Min's Sixth or Fourteenth Amendment rights to due process.

Murphy v. Waterfront Commission, 378 U.S. 52, 84 S.Ct. 1594 (1964) [William MURPHY and John Moody, Sr., Petitioners, v. The WATERFRONT COMMISSION of New York Harbor] (Exclusionary Rule; Immunity; Law Enforcement Officers or Agencies; Self-Incrimination) Murphy and others were subpoenaed to appear before the Waterfront Commission of New York Harbor concerning a work stoppage. Murphy refused to answer questions on Fifth Amendment grounds against self-incrimination. Immunity was therefore granted to Murphy under New Jersey and New York law, but he continued to refuse to testify, claiming he had not been granted federal immunity. He was cited for contempt, and he appealed. The SC had previously held that federal immunity was not granted whenever states granted immunity to testifying witnesses. However, the SC overturned that particular decision, holding that the federal government may not make use of answers given by witnesses in state proceedings. Thus, Murphy was compelled to testify in New Jersey and New York hearings, but the federal government had to honor the immunity extended to Murphy by these states.

Murray v. Carrier, 477 U.S. 478, 106 S.Ct. 2639 (1986) [Edward W. MURRAY, Director, Virginia Department of Corrections, Petitioner, v. Clifford W. CARRIER] (*Habeas Corpus* Petitions; Indigent Clients; Right to Counsel; Sixth Amendment) Carrier was accused in a Virginia court of rape. Prior to his trial, Carrier demanded statements made by the rape victim, but the trial judge refused to disclose them. After Carrier was convicted of rape, his counsel filed an appeal but did not include the matter of the victim's testimony or the denial of the discovery motion pertaining to it. The appeal was denied. On his own, Carrier filed a *habeas corpus* petition alleging ineffective assistance of counsel and a failure of the prosecution to disclose the victim's statement. The SC held that the mere fact that counsel had failed to recognize the factual or legal basis for a claim or failed to raise it despite recognizing it did not constitute cause for procedural default. Nor did the fact that the defense counsel had inadvertently neglected to include the discovery matter in his later motion filed with the court. Thus, the SC rejected Carrier's appeal and dismissed his defaulted discovery claim.

Murray v. Giarrantano, 492 U.S. 1, 109 S.Ct. 2765 (1989) [Edward W. MURRAY, Director, Virginia Department of Corrections, et al., Petitioners, v. Joseph M. GIARRANTANO, Johnny Watkins, Jr., and Richard T. Boggs, et al.] (Corrections; Inmate Rights) Giarrantano was a Virginia prisoner sentenced to death for murder. He was indigent and sought postconviction relief, asking Virginia officials to appoint him an attorney to assist him in filing an appeal. Virginia denied him such appointed counsel, and he appealed on his own. The SC upheld the Virginia decision, saying that indigent death-row inmates are not entitled to prison-appointed counsel to pursue further appeals or other postconviction relief.

Murray v. United States, 487 U.S. 533, 108 S.Ct. 2529 (1988) [Michael F. MURRAY, Petitioner, v. UNITED STATES. James D. Carter, Petitioner, v. United States] (Closed-Container Searches; Exclusionary Rule; Law Enforcement Officers or Agencies; Plain-View Rule) DEA agents suspected Murray of dealing in illicit drugs. Placing him under surveillance, they observed him drive a camper into a warehouse. When Murray and an associate emerged from the warehouse 20 minutes later, other DEA agents observed a large tractor trailer with a long, dark container. When the truck departed, it was followed by DEA agents. They stopped the drivers and searched the truck, discovering marijuana. When the DEA agents watching the warehouse heard about the marijuana, they quickly, without a warrant, forced their way into Murray's warehouse, where they found several large burlap bags of marijuana "in plain view." They left the warehouse, obtained a valid search warrant from a judge, and reentered the warehouse, where they seized the previously viewed marijuana bales. They also confiscated notebooks detailing Murray's drug trafficking and other illicit dealings. Murray was ultimately arrested, tried, and convicted of trafficking in illegal drugs. He appealed. The SC rejected Murray's idea that the evidence should have been suppressed because officers had acted in an illegal manner when they first forced entry into the warehouse. While the SC declared this initial action by police to be misconduct, it concluded that the subsequent search in the context of a valid warrant was a valid search.

Muscarello v. United States, 524 U.S. 125, 118 S.Ct. 1911 (1998) [Frank J. MUSCARELLO, Petitioner, v. UNITED STATES. Donald E. Cleveland and Enrique Gray-Santana, Petitioners, v. United States] (Sentencing; Vehicle Searches) Muscarello was convicted of unlawfully selling marijuana, which he carried in his truck to the place of the sale. He also possessed a firearm, which was locked in his glove compartment. He was found guilty of carrying a firearm during the commission of a drug crime, and a mandatory five-year term was added to his sentence for drug possession. Muscarello sought to overturn his conviction on the weapons charge, as he alleged that he was not physically carrying the weapon when arrested. A U.S. district court judge granted Muscarello's motion to quash his conviction of carrying a firearm during and in relation to drug trafficking, but the Fifth Circuit Court of Appeals reversed and remanded. The case was appealed to the SC, who affirmed Muscarello's weapons conviction. The SC held that the phrase "carries a firearm" is not limited to carrying of firearms on one's person, but also applies to a person who knowingly possesses and conveys firearms in a vehicle that the person accompanies. Thus, carrying a firearm in the glove compartment of a truck while transporting drugs was within the "carrying a firearm" statute. In the *Cleveland* case, the circumstances were similar in that Cleveland transported drugs and weapons in the trunk of his vehicle. Thus, the same ruling of the SC applies to *Cleveland*, in which the firearms were carried in the locked trunk of the car rather than a locked glove compartment.

N

Neil v. Biggers, 409 U.S. 188, 93 S.Ct. 375 (1972) [William S. NEIL, Warden, v. Archie Nathaniel BIGGERS] (Law Enforcement Officers or Agencies; Showups) Biggers was suspected of rape. At the time the rape occurred, it was full moonlight, and the victim had an opportunity to look at the rapist clearly. Prior to Biggers' arrest, the victim had been subjected to showups and photographs of previous rape suspects. At no time did she identify any of them as her attacker. But when Biggers was presented in a showup with others, the victim immediately said she had "no doubt" that he was the rapist. He was convicted, largely on her testimony. He challenged the conviction, contending that his identification by the victim had been "suggestive." The SC upheld his conviction, noting the totality of circumstances under which the victim had made her positive identification. The SC concluded that weighing all the factors, it found no substantial likelihood of misidentification, and that the evidence was properly allowed to go to the jury.

Nelson v. Campbell, ___U.S.___, 124 S. Ct. 2117 (2004) [David L. NELSON, Petitioner, v. Donal CAMPBELL, Commissioner, Alabama Department of Corrections, et al.] (Cruel and Unusual Punishmnent; Civil Rights, Section 1983 Claims; Death Penalty; Eighth Amendment) Nelson was an Alabama prisoner convicted of capital murder in 1979 and sentenced to death. After numerous appeals and stays of execution, an execution date for Nelson was set for October 2003. During the period 1979–2003, Alabama modified its method of execution to include lethal injection besides electrocution. Because Nelson had not indicated a preference for either method of execution, he was scheduled for lethal injection. Nelson had been a former drug user and incurred serious vein damage because of long years of drug use. Therefore, Alabama officials advised Nelson that they would use a "cut down" procedure whereby a .5- to 2-inch incision would be made in Nelson's arm or leg a day prior to his execution in order to gain proper intravenous access. Nelson immediately filed a Section 1983 suit in U.S. district court seeking a permanent injunction against the use of the cut-down as an invasive procedure that constituted cruel and unusual punishment and deliberate indifference to his medical needs; a temporary stay of execution to allow the court to consider the merits of his claim; and that he should be furnished with a medical protocol of an alternative procedure whereby his veins could be accessed. Alabama officials fought the petition, contending that if granted, it would open Alabama to numerous suits from other death-row inmates seeking challenges to their method of execution and other death penalty-related claims. Further, Alabama claimed that Nelson was merely attempting to postpone his execution indefinitely and that his Section 1983 claim was frivolous. His suit was dismissed and the 11th Circuit Court of Appeals affirmed. Nelson asked the SC to hear his motion, and the SC reversed the 11th Circuit, holding that (1) Section 1983 was an appropriate vehicle for a prisoner to challenge the proposed use of the cut-down procedure, and (2) the prisoner's request for an injunction did not change his motion into a challenge of his death sentence. The result of this reversal obligates Alabama to proffer a less invasive, less painful, faster, cheaper, and safer alternative procedure of percutaneous central line placement as a preferred method for venous entry and that the cut-down procedure will only be used if absolutely necessary. The case was remanded to U. S. district court for a determination of the merits of the request. The SC noted that preliminary injunctive relief must be narrowly drawn, extend no further than necessary to correct the harm the Court finds requires preliminary relief, and be the least intrusive means necessary to correct that harm.

Nevada v. Hicks, 533 U.S. 353, 121 S.Ct. 2304 (2001) [NEVADA et al., Petitioners, v. Floyd HICKS et al.] (Immunity; Jurisdiction; Native American Tribal Law; Searches and Seizures) Hicks is a member of the Fallon Paiute-Shoshone Tribes of Western Nevada. In 1990, Hicks was suspected of killing a California bighorn sheep on nonreservation property, which is a gross misdemeanor under Nevada law. A state game warden obtained a search warrant from a state court to search Hicks' home, which was located on a reservation. The search warrant was served and received tribal-court authorization. The search yielded several heads of Rocky Mountain bighorn sheep, which is not a protected species. In 1991, an informant advised the state game warden that he observedtwo mounted bighorn sheep heads in Hicks' home . Another search warrant was obtained, again with the permission of the tribal council. Again, the search proved fruitless. Hicks filed suit against the State of Nevada, the tribal court, and various game wardens and other officials, claiming that state game wardens had no business searching his property on reservation land. He further alleged that the searches had damaged his sheep heads. The tribal court claimed that it had jurisdiction over the claims and asked the federal district court for a summary judgment. The federal court granted the tribal court a summary judgment, holding that it did have jurisdiction in the case. However, the district court held that the state officials would have to exhaust any claims of qualified immunity in the

tribal court. The Ninth Circuit Court of Appeals affirmed and Nevada appealed to the SC, who heard the case. The question to be answered was whether a tribal court may assert jurisdiction over civil claims against state officials who entered tribal land to execute a search warrant against a tribe member suspected of committing a crime outside the reservation. The SC reversed the appellate court, holding that the tribal court lacked legislative authority to restrict, condition, or otherwise regulate state officials in their investigations of violations of state law. Furthermore, the tribal courts cannot adjudicate Hicks' Section 1983 civil rights claim. Thus, state officials operating on a reservation to investigate off-reservation violations of state law are properly held accountable for tortious conduct and civil rights violations in either state or federal court, but not in tribal court.

New Jersey v. Portash, 440 U.S. 450, 96 S.Ct. 2737 (1976) [State of NEW JERSEY, Petitioner, v. Joseph S. PORTASH] (Immunity; Self-Incrimination) Portash was a public official who gave testimony before a grand jury investigating extortion and misconduct in office. He was granted immunity in exchange for his testimony. Later, he was charged with extortion and his grand-jury testimony was used against him. He was convicted. He appealed, saying that his Fifth Amendment rights had been violated and that he had been granted immunity, thus barring admission of his grand-jury statements, which were indeed incriminating. A New Jersey Supreme Court reversed his conviction on these grounds, and the government appealed to the SC. The SC upheld Portash's reversal of conviction, saying that his testimony in response to being granted immunity was the essence of coerced testimony and involved the Fifth Amendment in its most clear form.

New Jersey v. T.L.O., 469 U.S. 325, 105 S.Ct. 733 (1985) [NEW JERSEY v. T.L.O.] (Fourth Amendment; Juvenile Law; Searches and Seizures) A 14-year-old girl was caught smoking a cigarette in the school bathroom, violating school rules. When confronted by the principal, she denied that she had been smoking. The principal examined her purse and discovered a pack of cigarettes, some rolling papers, money, marijuana, and other drug materials. This information was turned over to police, who charged the girl with delinquency. She was convicted. The girl's attorney sought to exclude the seized evidence because it was believed to be in violation of her Fourth Amendment right against unreasonable searches and seizures. The SC heard the case and ruled in favor of school officials, declaring that they only need reasonable suspicion, not probable cause, in order to search students and their possessions while on school property. When students enter their schools, they are subject to a lower standard than that applied to adult suspects when suspected of wrongdoing or carrying illegal contraband in violation of school rules.

New York v. Belton, 453 U.S. 454, 101 S.Ct. 2860 (1981) [State of NEW YORK, Petitioner, v. Roger BELTON] (Fourth Amendment; Law Enforcement Officers or Agencies; Vehicle Searches) Police stopped a suspicious-looking car in which Belton was a passenger. When they approached the vehicle, the officers smelled marijuana, and they found that no occupant of the car had documents showing ownership of the car. They placed the occupants under arrest and proceeded to search the vehicle. The search turned up a jacket owned by Belton, which contained cocaine. Belton was convicted of cocaine possession. He appealed, arguing that the search of the vehicle had been a warrantless intrusion into his privacy and in violation of his Fourth Amendment rights. The SC upheld Belton's conviction, saying that searches of automobiles following arrests of suspects, based on probable cause, are proper.

New York v. Burger, 482 U.S. 691, 107 S.Ct. 2636 (1987) [NEW YORK, Petitioner, v. Joseph BURGER] (Fourth Amendment; Inventory Searches; Law Enforcement Officers or Agencies; Searches and Seizures; Vehicle Searches) Burger was in the automobile-wrecking business; he dismantled wrecked automobiles and sold parts for profit. In the course of his business, he dealt in stolen and unregistered vehicles. Following an investigation of his wrecking-yard activities, police visited the yard with the intent to conduct a routine, administrative inspection of a commercial enterprise. They discovered numerous stolen parts, which were seized and used later in court against Burger as evidence. Burger was convicted of criminal possession of stolen property. He appealed, alleging that the "search" for inventory purposes should have been preceded by a lawfully issued search warrant, and thus, items subsequently seized without such a warrant should have been suppressed as evidence against him. The SC disagreed, however, and upheld his conviction, noting that administrative inventory inspections and searches by police, which are authorized by statute, are legal and do not require search warrants.

New York v. Class, 475 U.S. 106, 106 S.Ct. 960 (1986) [NEW YORK, Petitioner, v. Benigno CLASS] (Fourth Amendment; Law Enforcement Officers or Agencies; Plain-View Rule; Vehicle Searches) Two New York City police officers stopped Benigno Class, who was speeding and driving with a cracked windshield. When they attempted to determine the vehicle identification number (VIN), it could not be seen directly. One of the officers reached into the automobile and moved some papers that were obscuring the VIN on the dashboard. In doing so, he saw the butt of a pistol protruding from underneath the driver's seat and seized the weapon. Class was arrested and convicted of criminal possession of a weapon. He appealed. Lower courts reversed Class' conviction. It was effectively argued that the search of the automobile by the officer had overstepped the officer's bounds of proper conduct. However, the SC heard the government's appeal and reinstated Class' conviction, holding that the movement of the papers was sufficiently unintrusive as to not violate his Fourth Amendment rights. Class had no reasonable expectation of privacy with respect to his VIN, and thus, when police attempted to see it, their conduct was reasonable. Thus they saw the pistol handle in plain view. Not only were two traffic violations committed by the offender, but officer safety became an immediate concern when the pistol handle was observed lawfully.

New York v. Harris, 495 U.S. 14, 110 S.Ct. 1640 (1990) [NEW YORK, Petitioner, v. Bernard HARRIS] (Exclusionary Rule; Law Enforcement Officers or Agencies; *Miranda*

Warning) Harris was suspected of committing second-degree murder in the death of Staton in New York City on January 11, 1984. Various facts gave police officers probable cause to believe that Harris was the perpetrator. Without an arrest warrant, police went to Harris' home, knocked, were admitted by Harris, read him his *Miranda* rights, and questioned him. Harris admitted killing Staton and was arrested. While at the police station, Harris made two additional inculpatory statements, one videotaped, and gave a written and signed confession to police, despite the fact that he had indicated he wanted to end their questioning of him. He was convicted. The SC said that because the police had acted without a warrant in the original arrest of Harris, his first statement made at home was inadmissible. Also, it ruled his third statement, which was videotaped, inadmissible, as Harris had declared his desire not to continue being interrogated but was interrogated anyway. The second statement, however, given at police headquarters, was ruled admissible, despite the fact that his arrest without a valid warrant was inconsistent with the SC's ruling in *Payton v. New York* (1980). The SC declared that when police have probable cause to arrest suspects, the exclusionary rule does not bar the state's use of a statement made by a defendant outside of his home, even though the statement is taken *after* an arrest made in the home in violation of *Payton*.

New York v. P.J. Video, 475 U.S. 868, 106 S.Ct. 1610 (1986) [NEW YORK, Petitioner, v. P.J. VIDEO, INC., dba Network Video, et al.] (Fourth Amendment; Law Enforcement Officers or Agencies; Obscenity Laws) Doing business as Network Video, P.J. Video was visited by investigators, who rented several videocassette movies and subsequently determined that they violated New York's obscenity laws. A search warrant was issued, and Network Video's premises were searched. Large quantities of movies were seized and introduced later in a trial against P.J. Video. P.J. Video attorneys moved for the dismissal of charges on the grounds that the search warrant should have been issued according to a "higher" probable-cause standard than is ordinarily used, as books and films were the subject matter under investigation. The motion was granted, and the state appealed. The SC heard the case and ruled that for purposes of the Fourth Amendment, there is no "higher" standard to which search warrants should adhere; a mere finding of probable cause is sufficient to authorize a valid search warrant, and thus the materials seized were legally admissible against P.J. Video. The videocassettes should not have been suppressed as evidence.

New York v. Quarles, 467 U.S. 649, 104 S.Ct. 2626 (1984) [NEW YORK v. Benjamin QUARLES] (Confessions; *Miranda* Warning) A woman reported that she had just been raped by an armed man, who ran into a supermarket. Police went to the market and saw Quarles. They approached him and had him place his hands on his head. A pat-down led to the discovery of an empty shoulder holster. Fearing that a firearm was near Quarles, making the issue of public safety of paramount concern, police asked Quarles where the gun was. He identified where he had thrown it among some empty cartons. The officers retrieved the gun and then read Quarles his *Miranda* rights. He was charged with rape and convicted. Quarles appealed, arguing that the initial statements he gave about the whereabouts of his gun should have been excluded as evidence against him, as officers had not told him his rights prior to questioning him about the gun's whereabouts. The SC upheld Quarles' conviction, saying that officer concern for public safety when a firearm is near a potentially dangerous suspect overrides the matter of advising suspects of their right to silence and other *Miranda* warnings. Thus, the SC created a public-safety exception to allow investigating officers to bypass the *Miranda* warning when public safety is believed to be in jeopardy.

Nix v. Williams, 467 U.S. 431, 104 S.Ct. 2501 (1984) [Crispus NIX, Warden, Petitioner, v. Robert Anthony WILLIAMS] (Exclusionary Rule; Law Enforcement Officers or Agencies; *Miranda* Warning) On Christmas Eve, a 10-year-old girl went missing from a YMCA building in Des Moines, IA. Eyewitnesses later reported observing Williams leaving the YMCA building carrying a large bundle wrapped in a blanket, with two skinny legs protruding. Officers found Williams' car the next day 160 miles east of Des Moines. At a rest stop between where the car was found and the YMCA building, they discovered items of clothing and other articles. They assumed that the girl's body was probably somewhere between Des Moines and where Williams' car was found. Williams was subsequently found in a nearby town and arrested. While he was being driven back to Des Moines in a police vehicle, police officers engaged him in conversation relating to the girl's whereabouts. Because it had recently snowed, finding her body would be difficult. Officers suggested to Williams that he ought to tell them where her body was so that they could give her a "Christian burial." (This became known as the "Christian burial case.") Williams confessed and directed officers to the girl's body. Williams was charged with and convicted of first-degree murder. He appealed, and his conviction was overturned inasmuch as police officers had not advised him of his *Miranda* rights. He was subjected to a second trial, in which his original confession was excluded. He was convicted again, but this time because the prosecutor showed that the girl's body would have been discovered eventually, thus providing the conclusive evidence against Williams. The significance of this case is that it introduced the inevitable-discovery exception to the exclusionary rule, whereby prosecutors may argue that inculpatory evidence may be introduced against criminal suspects if it can be shown that police would have eventually discovered the incriminating evidence anyway.

Nixon v. United States, 506 U.S. 224, 113 S.Ct. 732 (1993) [Walter L. NIXON, Petitioner, v. UNITED STATES et al.] (Judicial Misconduct) Nixon was a federal district court judge who was impeached following a Senate committee and testimony session that disclosed evidence of judicial misconduct. Nixon appealed, alleging that the Senate had not given him a full evidentiary hearing and thus had violated its constitutional duty to "try" all impeachments. The SC heard the appeal and upheld Nixon's impeachment, holding that the Senate had sole discretion to choose impeachment procedures, and thus, controversy was a nonjudiciable political question.

North v. Russell, 427 U.S. 328, 96 S.Ct. 2709 (1976) [Lonnie NORTH, Appellant, v. C.B. RUSSELL et al.] (Eighth Amendment) North was convicted of a DWI charge in Kentucky in July 1974 by a police-court judge. He had first demanded a jury trial and been denied one. Kentucky, like Massachusetts, has a two-tiered trial system, in which the first trial is a nonjury trial. Following a conviction, an offender may appeal to have a jury trial and must be granted one. North did not request a subsequent jury trial following his conviction for DWI in the nonjury situation. He was sentenced to and served 30 days in jail and lost his driver's license for a temporary period. He appealed the conviction, alleging that his due-process rights had been violated when he was tried before a police-court judge. Further, he alleged that his equal-protection rights had been violated, because some police-court judges have legal training and others do not. The SC upheld his conviction, holding that North had elected not to appeal his original conviction in a trial *de novo*, which was his right to do. The SC said that the Kentucky two-tiered trial court system, with judicial officers in the first tier in smaller cities and an appeal of right with a *de novo* trial before a traditionally law-trained judge in the second, does not violate either the due-process or equal-protection guarantees of the Constitution.

North Carolina v. Alford, 400 U.S. 25, 91 S.Ct. 160 (1970) [NORTH CAROLINA, Petitioner, v. Henry C. ALFORD] (Death Penalty; Plea Bargaining) Alford was indicted for first-degree murder. A subsequent plea agreement was approved wherein Alford entered a guilty plea to second-degree murder in exchange for life imprisonment (rather than the death penalty) in the event of a guilty verdict. The judge imposed a 30-year term. Alford appealed. A lower appellate court held that his plea of guilty had been involuntary, because it had been prompted by a fear of the death penalty, and vacated the sentence. The SC reversed the lower court, letting the 30-year term stand. The SC said that an accused may voluntarily, knowingly, and understandingly consent to the imposition of a prison sentence, even though he or she is unwilling to admit participation in the crime, or even if his or her guilty plea contains a protestation of innocence, when, as here, he or she intelligently concludes that his or her interests require a guilty plea and the record strongly evidences guilt. The significance of this case, known as the Alford plea, allows defendants to enter a *nolo contendere* plea that is in their best interests (e.g., avoiding a likely death penalty through a jury trial); thus, accused persons may be unwilling to admit guilt, but they may also waive their right to a jury trial and accept a sentence, such as that arranged through a plea bargain.

North Carolina v. Butler, 441 U.S. 369, 99 S.Ct. 1755 (1979) [State of NORTH CAROLINA, Petitioner, v. Willie Thomas BUTLER] (Custodial Interrogations; Law Enforcement Officers or Agencies; *Miranda* Warning; Right to Counsel) Butler was charged with kidnapping, armed robbery, and felonious assault. He made incriminating statements to police officers after they had given him the *Miranda* warning. He was convicted and appealed, arguing that he had not expressly waived his right to the presence of counsel. The North Carolina Supreme Court overturned his conviction.

Another appeal was made. The SC vacated the lower court's decision, saying that an explicit statement of waiver is not invariably necessary to support a finding that the defendant waived his right to remain silent or the right to counsel guaranteed by the *Miranda* case.

North Carolina v. Pearce, 395 U.S. 711, 89 S.Ct. 2072 (1969) [State of NORTH CAROLINA et al., Petitioners, v. Clifton A. PEARCE. Curtis M. Simpson, Warden, Petitioner, v. William S. Rice] (*Habeas Corpus* Petitions; Reconvictions and Resentencing) Pearce was convicted of assault with intent to commit rape and was sentenced to 12 to 15 years. Several years later, he filed a *habeas corpus* petition, alleging that an involuntary confession had been admitted as evidence against him at his trial. He was subsequently retried, was convicted, and this time was sentenced to eight years. This sentence, when added to the time he had already spent in prison, amounted to a term longer than his original sentence. Pearce appealed, arguing that the additional time imposed was a punishment for having his original conviction set aside. The SC heard this appeal and set aside the sentence, saying that although nothing prohibits judges from imposing harsher sentences in retrials than sentences imposed in earlier trials, constitutional guarantees obligate the government to give full credit of previous time served against the new sentence. The SC also said that any unexplained additional punishment is a violation of due process.

O

O'Connor v. Donaldson, 422 U.S. 536, 95 S.Ct. 2486 (1975) [J.R. O'CONNOR, Petitioner, v. Kenneth DONALDSON] (Civil Rights, Section 1983 Claims; Corrections; Immunity; Inmate Rights) Donaldson was confined in a mental health treatment facility for nearly 15 years. He petitioned for release but was denied. He sought a Title 42 U.S.C. Section 1983 action against hospital authorities, alleging that his civil rights were being violated because of what he alleged to be an unlawful detention. The SC ultimately heard his case and held that states may not lock up persons against their will merely based on a finding of "mental illness" and where there is no constitutional basis to continue to confine them after the basis for their original commitment no longer exists. A state cannot confine nondangerous individuals who are capable of surviving safely in freedom by themselves with the help of willing and responsible family. The state officials have only qualified immunity from suits brought by their patients.

O'Connor v. Ortega, 480 U.S. 709, 107 S.Ct. 1492 (1987) [Dennis M. O'CONNOR et al., Petitioners, v. Magno J. ORTEGA] (Corrections; Probation and Parole) A hospital administrator, Ortega, was suspected of sexual harassment of his employees. While he was on administrative leave during an investigation of these harassment allegations, officials invento-

ried and searched his property and computer. No warrant was ever obtained to conduct such a search, and Ortega's property was never properly inventoried following the search. Ortega filed suit, alleging that his Fourth Amendment rights had been violated. The SC heard his case and decided that the officials had needed a warrant to conduct such a search of his offices. The SC remanded the case to a lower court to decide the justification for the search and seizure and evaluate the reasonableness of both the inception of the search and its scope.

O'Dell v. Netherland, 521 U.S. 151, 117 S.Ct. 1969 (1997) [Joseph Roger O'DELL, III, Petitioner, v. J.D. NETHERLAND, Warden, et al.] (Death Penalty; *Habeas Corpus* Petitions; Sentencing) O'Dell was convicted of capital murder, rape, and sodomy in the Virginia case of Helen Schartner, whose body was found in February 1985. O'Dell's conviction occurred in 1988. At O'Dell's sentencing hearing, the state argued that O'Dell's future dangerousness should be considered in whether he should be given the death penalty. O'Dell sought to have the judge instruct the jury about his parole ineligibility if he should be given a life sentence, but the judge refused to give the jury such an instruction. The jury imposed the death penalty and the conviction and sentence were upheld by the Virginia Supreme Court. Subsequently, an SC case was decided in 1994 that entitled death penalty–eligible offenders the right to have the jury informed that the offender is not parole-eligible if a life sentence is imposed. (*See Simmons v. South Carolina* [1994].) O'Dell filed a *habeas corpus* appeal with the SC, contending that the judge violated his Fourteenth Amendment due-process right by failing to inform the sentencing jury about his parole ineligibility, particularly when the state introduced evidence about his future dangerousness insofar as making a decision about the death penalty was concerned. The SC heard O'Dell's appeal and affirmed the Virginia Supreme Court, holding that as the *Simmons* case was new and occurred after O'Dell's conviction, it could not, therefore, be used to disturb O'Dell's death sentence, which had been final for six years prior to *Simmons* being decided. Thus, *Simmons* could not be made retroactively applicable to O'Dell's conviction and death sentence. (There is an exception to this *ex post facto* prohibition that is found in *Teague v. Lane* [1989]. In *Teague,* the SC will not disturb a final state conviction or sentence unless it can be said that, at the time the conviction or sentence became final, a state court would have acted objectively unreasonably by not extending the relief later sought in federal court. *Teague* requires a federal *habeas* court to determine the date on which the conviction became final; to consider whether a state court considering the defendant's claim at the time it became final would have felt compelled by existing precedent to conclude that the rule he seeks was required by the constitution; and if not, to determine whether that new rule nonetheless falls within certain exceptions. In O'Dell's case, he did not satisfy the exceptions articulated under *Teague.*)

Ohio v. Roberts, 448 U.S. 56, 100 S.Ct. 2531 (1986) [State of OHIO, Petitioner, v. Herschel ROBERTS] (Confrontation Clause; Sixth Amendment) Roberts was suspected of a crime. At his trial, the prosecutor presented transcript testimony from a witness who had testified earlier at a preliminary hearing. In an effort to obtain the witness' presence in court to testify in person, the prosecutor had issued five different subpoenas over a five-month period, but the witness could not be located. Roberts was convicted. He appealed, arguing that his Sixth Amendment right to cross-examine his accuser had been denied. The SC upheld Roberts' conviction, saying that the state had made a good-faith effort to locate a state witness over several months by issuing five subpoenas, and that because the witness was constitutionally unavailable, the transcript of her testimony was admissible as evidence against Roberts. (Compare this case with *Harrington v. California* [1969], *Pointer v. Texas* [1965], and *Barber v. Page* [1968].)

Ohio v. Robinette, 519 U.S. 33, 117 S.Ct. 417 (1998) [OHIO, Petitioner, v. Robert D. ROBINETTE] (Fourth Amendment; Searches and Seizures; Vehicle Searches) After being stopped for speeding and issued a verbal warning by an Ohio deputy sheriff, Robinette was asked if he was carrying any illegal contraband, guns, or drugs in his car. He answered, "No." Then the officer asked Robinette if he could search the vehicle. Robinette consented, and the officer searched the car and discovered a small quantity of marijuana and a methamphetamine pill. Robinette was arrested and convicted of possessing a controlled substance, and he appealed. The Ohio Supreme Court reversed Robinette's conviction on the ground that the search was the result of an unlawful detention. The state appealed and the SC heard the case. The SC reversed the Ohio Supreme Court and reinstated Robinette's conviction, holding that Robinette had given his consent to search his vehicle. The SC also said that it would be unrealistic to require police to always inform detainees that they are free to go before a consent to search may be deemed voluntary.

Oklahoma City v. Tuttle, 471 U.S. 808, 105 S.Ct. 2427 (1985) [City of OKLAHOMA CITY, Petitioner, v. Rose Marie TUTTLE, etc.] (Civil Rights, Section 1983 Claims) Rose Marie Tuttle sued Oklahoma City officials because a police officer had shot and killed her husband outside a bar where he had been participating in a robbery. Her civil rights action, under Title 42 U.S.C. Section 1983, alleged negligence on the part of Oklahoma City officials in training their officers in the use of firearms. The SC ruled that Oklahoma City was not liable for Tuttle's death and that his shooting showed no sign of gross negligence, negligent training, or deliberate indifference.

Old Chief v. United States, 519 U.S. 172, 117 S.Ct. 644 (1997) [Johnny Lynn OLD CHIEF, Petitioner, v. UNITED STATES] (Judicial Misconduct; Prosecutorial Misconduct) Old Chief was convicted in federal court of being a felon in possession of a firearm, and he appealed. His appeal alleged that he had offered to stipulate to the federal court that he had previously been convicted of a crime punishable by a term exceeding one year, but that the court disallowed this stipulation. Rather, the prosecution admitted into evidence the specific prior conviction by name, which was assault causing serious bodily injury. Old Chief believed that the actual name of his crime would prejudice the jury in his case. The trial court and appellate court rejected his appeal, and the SC heard

his case. The SC reversed Old Chief's conviction, holding that it is an abuse of judicial discretion when the court spurns a defendant's offer to admit evidence of the prior conviction element of an offense and instead admits the full record of prior judgment of conviction when the name and nature of the prior offense raise the risk of a verdict, and that the evidence of the name and nature of the defendant's conviction was not admissible to show the prior felony conviction element of the offense of possession of a firearm by a felon.

Olden v. Kentucky, 488 U.S. 227, 109 S.Ct. 480 (1988) [James OLDEN v. KENTUCKY] (Confrontation Clause; Sixth Amendment) Olden and Harris, both black, were in a bar in Princeton, KY, that catered primarily to black customers. Earlier that evening, two white women, Matthews and her friend Patton, went to the same bar and began drinking. Matthews became nervous as more blacks entered the bar during the evening. She became intoxicated and lost track of her friend. Olden told her that her friend had left and had been involved in a car accident. He suggested that Matthews accompany him to the accident scene. When she left the bar, Olden and Harris threatened her with a knife and drove her to a remote location, where they allegedly raped her. She was later taken to a location near the home of a friend and released. She immediately advised her friend, a man named Russell, that she had just been raped by Olden, Harris, and two other men who had joined them later. Police subsequently arrested Olden and prosecuted him for sodomy. During the trial, Olden asserted the defense of consent, claiming that Matthews had wanted to have sex with him. Several men testified to corroborate Olden's version of events. During the trial, information came to the defense that Matthews had been having an extramarital affair with Russell. Thus, it was conjectured that she probably used the "rape" story to deceive Russell. The defense attempted to cross-examine Matthews about her living arrangement with Russell, but the judge barred such questioning. Olden was convicted of sodomy. He appealed, alleging that the trial court's refusal to allow him to impeach Matthews' testimony had deprived him of the right to confront and cross-examine his accuser. The SC overturned his conviction, holding that the trial court's refusal to permit Olden to cross-examine Matthews about her cohabitation arrangement with Russell had violated Olden's Sixth Amendment right to confront his accuser.

Olim v. Wakinekona, 461 U.S. 238, 103 S.Ct. 1741 (1983) [Antone OLIM et al., Petitioners, v. Delbert Kaahanui WAKINEKONA] (Corrections; Inmate Rights) Wakinekona was a Hawaiian prisoner transferred to a California prison and reclassified to a higher custody level. He appealed, alleging his due-process rights had been violated because no hearing had been held to determine his new classification. The appeal was rejected by a lower court, but a state court of appeals reversed the lower-court decision. The government appealed, and the SC heard the case. The SC reversed the state appellate court decision, holding that the transfer of the prisoner from Hawaii to California did not implicate the due-process clause of the Fourteenth Amendment. Hawaii's prison system does not create a protected liberty interest that must be considered by California prisons. Prisoners have no rights relating to where they are confined or at what custody level.

Oliver v. United States, 466 U.S. 170, 104 S.Ct. 1735 (1984) [**Ray E. OLIVER, Petitioner, v. UNITED STATES. Maine, Petitioner, v. Richard Thornton**] (**Law Enforcement Officers or Agencies; Open-Fields Doctrine; Plain-View Rule**) Oliver grew marijuana on some land near his home. He had fenced in the property and posted a "No Trespassing" sign. Acting on reports from an informant that Oliver was growing marijuana in the field, officers went to the field and found a footpath. Without an arrest warrant or a search warrant, they followed it about a mile until they came to some marijuana plants growing in the middle of the field. Oliver was arrested and convicted of marijuana manufacturing. He appealed, contending that the "No Trespassing" sign required police to obtain a search warrant before they trespassed on his property. The SC disagreed with Oliver and upheld the conviction, saying that "No Trespassing" signs are not sufficient to create the reasonable expectation of privacy that requires police to have a warrant; further, the open field was such that the privacy expectation that an owner would have relating to it does not exist. Police may "trespass" and search any such open area without a warrant and without probable cause.

Olmstead v. United States, 277 U.S. 438, 48 S.Ct. 564 (1928) [**Roy OLMSTEAD et al., Petitioners, v. UNITED STATES**] (**Electronic Surveillance, Wiretapping; Law Enforcement Officers or Agencies**) During Prohibition in the 1920s, Olmstead and others were involved in a conspiracy to distribute illegal liquor in violation of the National Prohibition Act. Federal agents had gathered most of their vital information about the conspiracy from wiretaps (telephone intercepts), from which information about the conspiracy could be easily obtained. The wiretaps had been installed in the telephone lines outside of suspects' homes. Olmstead and others were convicted. They appealed, arguing that the wiretaps were an invasion of their right to privacy under the Fourth Amendment. The SC upheld their conviction, declaring wiretaps by government agents legal. The SC stressed the fact that there was no trespass by authorities into any constitutionally protected area, such as the home's interior. Thus, an unreasonable search and seizure of "conversation" had not occurred. This was the landmark case ruling on wiretaps and their constitutionality. Subsequently, this case was overruled in *Katz v. United States* (1967), which held that any form of wiretapping or electronic surveillance that violates one's reasonable expectation of privacy is a search, and thus a warrant is required based on probable cause before such a "search" through electronic surveillance is conducted.

O'Lone v. Estate of Shabazz, 482 U.S. 342, 107 S.Ct. 2400 (1987) [**Edward O'LONE, etc., et al., Petitioners, v. ESTATE OF Ahmad Uthman SHABAZZ and Sadr-Ud-Din Nafis Mateen**] (**Civil Rights, Section 1983 Claims; Corrections; First Amendment; Inmate Rights**) Several Muslim prisoners in a New Jersey penitentiary filed suit under Title 42 U.S.C. Section 1983, alleging their First Amendment rights to religious freedom were being violated. Specifically, they ob-

jected to work assignments that interfered with their returning, during daytime hours, to buildings on prison grounds where religious services were observed. This was a prison policy based on security reasons. The SC disagreed with the men, saying that legitimate penological interests prevail over specific inmate religious interests, and that to accommodate the particular religious idiosyncrasies of inmates would jeopardize prison security in an unreasonable way. Thus, prison policies geared to maintain security of prisons, even though they prevent inmates from exercising their right to worship, are constitutional policies.

O'Neal v. McAninch, 513 U.S. 432, 115 S.Ct. 992 (1995) [**Robert O'NEAL, Petitioner, v. Fred McANINCH, Warden**] (**Jury Instructions**) O'Neal was accused of aggravated murder, kidnapping, and robbery. The trial judge gave the jury an incorrect instruction. O'Neal was convicted, and he appealed. An appellate court ruled that the judge's error was harmless. However, a federal appellate judge expressed grave doubt whether the trial error was indeed harmless or rather had had substantial and injurious effects or influences in determining the jury's verdict. O'Neal appealed again. The SC said that whenever a federal judge expresses "grave doubt" about a jury instruction and its constitutionality or effects, this is not harmless error and thus the petitioner must win. The significance of this case is the stress on "grave doubt." If there is a grave doubt that such an error is harmless, then it is not harmless. O'Neal's conviction was overturned and a new trial was ordered.

On Lee v. United States, 343 U.S. 747, 72 S.Ct. 967 (1952) [**ON LEE, Petitioner, v. UNITED STATES**] (**Electronic Surveillance, Wiretapping; Law Enforcement Officers or Agencies**) On Lee owned a laundry and also provided opium, a controlled substance, to others illegally. A friend and federal undercover agent visited On Lee and with a hidden electronic microphone engaged On Lee in incriminating conversations about his drug sales. Later, the evidence obtained, including the conversations the agent had with On Lee, was admitted against him in a trial, in which he was convicted. On Lee appealed, seeking to have the conversational evidence suppressed as a violation of his Fourth Amendment guarantees. The SC upheld his conviction. Its reasoning is significant, because it declared essentially that as long as one of the parties having a conversation with another "consents" to the recording of it, it is lawful under the Fourth Amendment. Thus, if someone called another person on the telephone and recorded the conversation without the other's knowledge, this would be lawful because the person recording the conversation was consenting to it. Therefore, *any* conversation between friends, even though one of the friends may be a police officer or informant, is subject to electronic surveillance as long as one of the parties agrees and if the recording is not in violation of state law.

Oregon v. Bradshaw, 462 U.S. 285, 103 S.Ct. 2830 (1988) [**OREGON, Petitioner, v. James Edward BRADSHAW**] (**Confessions; *Miranda* Warning; Right to Counsel**) Bradshaw wrecked his pickup truck, and a passenger in his truck was killed. During the police investigation, Bradshaw was told his *Miranda* rights, denied his involvement, and asked for an attorney. However, he continued to converse with the officer, eventually admitting that he had been driving the truck while intoxicated and under license suspension. In court later, Bradshaw moved to suppress the statements he had made to police, but his motion was denied and he was convicted. He appealed. The SC upheld his conviction, saying that his own continued conversation with officers constituted knowing and intelligent waiver of his right to counsel. Thus, voluntary statements made by arrestees after they have been told their *Miranda* rights may be used against them despite the absence of counsel that they have formerly requested.

Oregon v. Elstad, 470 U.S. 298, 105 S.Ct. 1285 (1985) [OREGON, Petitioner, v. Michael James ELSTAD] (Confessions; *Miranda* Warning) Elstad was suspected of burglary, and police officers went to his home with an arrest warrant. They entered the house at his mother's invitation and proceeded to Elstad's room, where they advised him that he was implicated in the burglary. Elstad told officers, "I was there," before being given his *Miranda* warning. He was placed under arrest and taken to the police station, where he requested to talk to officers. He gave a full and voluntary confession to the burglary and signed a typed statement. After he was convicted, he appealed, contending that his original statement was an inculpatory one, and because it had been given before he was told his *Miranda* rights, it should have been excluded as well as the confession he made later resulting from the incriminating statement. The SC disagreed with Elstad and upheld the burglary conviction. They noted that prior statements made by suspects before *Miranda* warnings are given are admissible so long as they are voluntary, especially if subsequent confessions are given following *Miranda* warnings, in which earlier statements are substantiated.

Oregon v. Hass, 420 U.S. 714, 95 S.Ct. 1215 (1975) [State of OREGON, Petitioner, v. William Robert HASS] (Confessions; *Miranda* Warning; Probation and Parole) Hass was accused of taking bicycles from two house garages in Klamath Falls, OR, in August 1972. An automobile license number enabled police officers preliminarily to identify Hass as the thief. Hass was told his *Miranda* rights, and he gave police statements about the bicycle thefts in a confession. Hass said he would probably want to see a lawyer when he got to jail, and he made other statements later to police. He was convicted of the theft and sentenced to two years' probation and a fine. He appealed, arguing that some of the testimony given by police officers should have been inadmissible, because of his statement about seeing an attorney after getting to jail. The SC upheld Hass' conviction, holding that his statements to Oregon police had been voluntary, despite the *Miranda* warning.

Oregon v. Kennedy, 456 U.S. 667, 102 S.Ct. 2083 (1982) [OREGON, Petitioner, v. Bruce Alan KENNEDY] (Double Jeopardy) Kennedy was accused of theft. During his trial, an expert witness for the state testified that he had never done business with Kennedy. The prosecutor asked him, "Is that because he is a crook?" Kennedy moved for a mistrial and was granted a new trial. In the retrial, a motion for dismissal on double-jeopardy grounds was rejected. Kennedy was con-

victed. Kennedy then appealed to the SC, asking it to consider whether the prosecution had deliberately provoked the mistrial by the remarks made to the witness. If these remarks reflected an intentional provocation, then a case of double jeopardy could be made and Kennedy could not be tried again on those same charges. The SC said that there was no apparent indication that the prosecutor intended to provoke a mistrial, and thus Kennedy was barred from making a double-jeopardy claim to prevent the retrial from occurring.

Oregon v. Mathiason, 429 U.S. 492, 97 S.Ct. 711 (1977) [State of OREGON v. Carl Ray MATHIASON] (Confessions; *Miranda* Warning; Probation and Parole) Mathiason, a parolee, was living at a residence where a burglary occurred. About a month later, a police officer left a card saying he would like to talk with Mathiason about the burglary. On his own volition, Mathiason went to the police station and entered voluntarily into a conversation with the officer and eventually confessed to the burglary. At no time prior to this confession did he receive a *Miranda* warning. He was convicted and appealed, arguing that he should have been given the warning before confessing. The SC rejected his appeal, saying that he went to the police station merely to answer questions. He was not in custody, he had not been arrested, and he had given statements to police freely and voluntarily, including his confession. Thus his conviction was proper.

Ornelas v. United States, 517 U.S. 690, 116 S.Ct. 1657 (1996) [Saul ORNELAS and Ismael Ornelas-Ledesma, Petitioners, v. UNITED STATES] (Fourth Amendment; Searches and Seizures; Vehicle Searches) Ornelas and others were observed at a Milwaukee, WI, motel on an early morning in December 1992. Their automobile had California plates and appeared to be one favored by drug dealers because it is easy to hide drugs in that model. Furthermore, California was known as a "source state" for illegal drugs. After the motel was placed under surveillance, Ornelas and others got into their car. The officers approached, identified themselves, and asked if they could search Ornelas' car. Subsequently, officers discovered a loose interior panel that, when removed, disclosed two kilograms of cocaine. Ornelas and others pleaded guilty later in federal court to various drug charges, but they reserved their right to appeal in order to contest the legality of the vehicle search. Subsequently, the SC heard the case and affirmed Ornelas' conviction, holding that police had reasonable suspicion to stop and question Ornelas and probable cause to remove one of the interior panels of the car after Ornelas gave officers permission to search it. Although Ornelas denied that he gave officers permission to search his vehicle, there is substantial supporting information from other defendants that permission had been given. The SC was also persuaded by the extensive experience of the investigating officers who initiated the surveillance and conducted the subsequent search of the vehicle. The SC noted that a reviewing court should view facts related to searches and seizures "according to the community's distinctive features and events, and by local police, who view the facts through the lens of their experience and expertise" (at 1659).

Orozco v. Texas, 394 U.S. 324, 89 S.Ct. 1095 (1969) [Reyes Arias OROZCO, Petitioner, v. TEXAS] (Confessions; *Miranda* Warning; Right to Counsel) Orozco was confined to a bed at the time he was questioned by police concerning his part in a crime. He gave incriminating statements about his part in the crime. Partial *Miranda* warnings had been given to him. He was convicted, and appealed. The SC declared that his bedridden condition and the presence of police had converted this "interview" into a full-fledged custodial interrogation in which Orozco's right attached, and thus he was entitled to the full *Miranda* warning apprising him of his right to counsel and to silence. His conviction was overturned.

Osborn v. United States, 385 U.S. 323, 87 S.Ct. 429 (1966) [Z.T. OSBORN, Jr., Petitioner, v. UNITED STATES] (Electronic Surveillance, Wiretapping; Law Enforcement Officers or Agencies) Osborn, a Nashville lawyer, had hired Vick, a Nashville police officer, to do some background checks on prospective jurors in a case Osborn was handing for Hoffa, a union official. Unknown to Osborn was the fact that Vick had agreed with the FBI to report any "illegal activities" in the case. Vick wore a recording device unknown to Osborn and was wearing it when Osborn made incriminating statements to Vick in Osborn's office. Osborn disclosed that one of the prospective jurors, Elliott, was his own cousin and that Vick ought to visit him and see whether he would be susceptible to receiving $5,000 for his prodefense jury work. Osborn was convicted, largely on Vick's testimony and the recording made of the conversation between Osborn and Vick. Osborn appealed his conviction, alleging entrapment. The SC heard the case and upheld Osborn's conviction, holding that it was proper for Vick to record his conversation with Osborn. There was significant overt action on Osborn's part to sustain his conviction. No warrant had been required for the wire worn by Vick, because Osborn himself was not presently under indictment when the conversations were recorded, and the conversation was consensually recorded, because Vick, one of the conversants, agreed to record it. This was *not* a third-party scenario in which the FBI was intentionally "listening in" to discover incriminating evidence; rather, Osborn had instructed Vick to offer Elliott the bribe.

O'Shea v. Littleton, 414 U.S. 488, 94 S.Ct. 669 (1974) [Michael O'SHEA, as Magistrate of the Circuit Court for Alexander County, Illinois, and Dorothy Spomer, as Associate Circuit Judge for Alexander County, Illinois, Petitioners, v. Ezell LITTLETON et al.] (Civil Rights, Section 1983 Claims; Corrections; Death Penalty) Littleton and 17 other black residents of Cairo, IL, brought a Title 42 U.S.C. Section 1983 action against judges and police for allegedly engaging in discriminatory practices relating to bail-setting, sentencing, and jury-free practices in criminal cases. The SC heard the case and rejected their claims, holding that these persons had failed to show any actual case or controversy in which such discrimination occurred, and that the simple assertions and inferences were only speculative and not grounded in fact. Further, Littleton had failed to show any likelihood of substantial and immediate irreparable injury, or the inadequacy of remedies under the law.

O'Sullivan v. Boerckel, 526 U.S. 838, 119 S.Ct. 1728 (1999) [William D. O'SULLIVAN, Petitioner, v. Darren BOERCKEL] (*Habeas Corpus* Petitions; *Miranda* Warning) Boerckel was convicted on state charges of rape, burglary, and aggravated battery of an 87-year-old woman in Illinois in 1977 and sentenced to serve 20 to 60 years' imprisonment in an Illinois penitentiary. Subsequently, Boerckel appealed his convictions to the Illinois Supreme Court, raising issues that his confession was coerced, that he had not knowingly and intelligently waived his rights under *Miranda,* that there had been prosecutorial misconduct, and that the evidence to convict him was insufficient. The Illinois Supreme Court rejected his claims and appeal, upholding his convictions and sentence. Later, Boerckel appealed for federal *habeas corpus* relief. The federal district court denied his *habeas corpus* petition, but the circuit court of appeals reversed and granted his petition. The government appealed to the SC, contending that Boerckel had not exhausted all of his state remedies. Neither had he properly exhausted his state remedies, the government said, because he excluded several allegations newly entered in his earlier state supreme court petition. The SC heard the case and held that Boerckel must present all of his claims in a state supreme court for discretionary review in order to satisfy the exhaustion requirement. The SC said that prisoners who fail to present all of their claims in a petition for discretionary review to a state court of last resort have not properly presented their claims to state courts. Boerckel had procedurally defaulted his claims and thus was not entitled to federal *habeas corpus* relief.

Overton v. Bazzetta, ___U.S.___, 123 S.Ct. 2162 (2003) [William OVERTON, Director, Michigan Department of Corrections, et al., Petitioners, v. Michelle BAZZETTA et al.] (Civil Rights, Section 1983 Claims) Bazzetta and other Michigan inmates filed suit against the Michigan Department of Corrections alleging that their civil rights were violated by newly implemented visitation policies that penalized prisoners for substance abuse and greatly restricted the numbers of close relatives and friends allowed for periodic visits. A district court judge entered a judgment for the plaintiffs, and the Sixth Circuit Court of Appeals affirmed. Michigan appealed the case, which was heard by the SC. The SC reversed the lower courts, holding that the new prison policies were rationally related to legitimate penological objectives and did not violate substantive due-process or free-association guarantees of the First Amendment. Furthermore, the two-year ban on visitation privileges for inmates with two substance-abuse violations did not violate the constitutional prohibition against cruel and unusual punishment. Four factors are relevant in deciding whether prison regulations are valid: (1) whether the regulation has a valid, rational connection to legitimate governmental interests; (2) whether alternative means are open to inmates to exercise the asserted right; (3) what impact on accommodation of right would have on guards, inmates, and prison resources; and (4) whether there are ready alternatives to the regulation. The SC stressed the importance of the good judgment of prison administrators who have a significant responsibility to define a correctional system's goals and determine the most appropriate means to accomplish them. The Michigan prison regulations satisfy all four requirements. Prisoners may communicate with their friends and relatives telephonically or in writing; although these conditions are not ideal, they need only be available. The two-year visitation restriction for those with two substance-abuse violations is consistent with prison discipline and functions as a deterrent to future drug abuse.

Owen v. City of Independence, Mo., 445 U.S. 622, 100 S.Ct. 1398 (1980) [George D. OWEN, Petitioner, v. CITY OF INDEPENDENCE, MISSOURI, et al.] (Civil Rights, Section 1983 Claims; Immunity) Owen, the chief of police in Independence, was fired without explanation by the city manager following citizen complaints about police misconduct. Owen sued the city under a Title 42 U.S.C. Section 1983 civil rights claim. He alleged that he had not been permitted a hearing or given a statement of charges against him; thus, his constitutional rights had been violated. Attorneys for the city manager claimed the city manager was acting in good faith and properly, according to existing city charter provisions. The SC declared that Independence did not have immunity from liability under the Section 1983 claim and might not assert the good-faith defense in response to such a Section 1983 complaint.

P

Palko v. Connecticut, 302 U.S. 319, 58 S.Ct. 149 (1937) [Frank PALKO, Petitioner, v. State of CONNECTICUT] (Corrections; Death Penalty; Double Jeopardy; Self-Incrimination) Palko was convicted of second-degree murder in Connecticut, and a life sentence was imposed. Because of procedural errors, the conviction was overturned and a new trial was held. In the second trial, Palko was again convicted of first-degree murder, and the death sentence was imposed. Palko appealed, saying that his second trial constituted double jeopardy and was in violation of his constitutional rights. The SC rejected his appeal, holding that none of his constitutional rights had been violated, when in fact, the state was merely seeking a fair trial for him.

Parke v. Raley, 506 U.S. 20, 113 S.Ct. 517 (1992) [Al C. PARKE, Warden, Petitioner, v. Ricky Harold RALEY] (Proof Standards) In 1986, Raley was charged with robbery and with being a persistent felony offender, having been previously convicted of various felonies in 1979 and 1981. These previous convictions were the result of guilty pleas entered by Raley in different courts, where records of such events were not made. He was convicted. Raley sought to challenge Kentucky's persistent-offender statute by showing that the other convictions ought to have been suppressed as considerations, because it could not be determined from the absence of records whether Raley's guilty pleas in those instances were voluntary. The SC ultimately heard Raley's appeal and rejected it, upholding the constitutionality of Kentucky's persistent-offender sentencing statute. Regarding Raley's earlier "guilty"

pleas, the SC held that prior factual determinations by previous court convictions are entitled to the presumption of correctness.

Parker v. Dugger, 498 U.S. 308, 111 S.Ct. 731 (1991) [Robert Lacy PARKER, Petitioner, v. Richard L. DUGGER, Secretary, Florida Department of Corrections, et al.] (Aggravating and Mitigating Circumstances; Bifurcated Trials; Death Penalty; Juries) Parker was convicted of a double first-degree murder in Florida. At the sentencing hearing, the jury found numerous aggravating circumstances, but they also found considerable mitigating circumstances that outweighed the aggravating factors. Therefore, they recommended to the judge a sentence of life imprisonment. However, the judge overrode the jury recommendation and sentenced Parker to death, citing several statutory aggravating factors and no statutory mitigating factors. There was also a question as to the validity of some of the aggravating circumstances cited by the judge and evidence of their existence. Parker appealed. The Florida Supreme Court affirmed the death penalty, so Parker appealed to the SC. The SC overturned the death sentence, holding that the Florida Supreme Court had acted arbitrarily and capriciously by failing to adequately treat Parker's nonstatutory mitigating evidence. The Florida court had also erred when it declared that the trial judge had found no "mitigating factors" when in fact he had found such factors, although they happened to be nonstatutory. The SC declared Parker's death sentence to be invalid because of these factors and because the court had deprived Parker of his right to individualized treatment and consideration.

Parker v. Randolph, 442 U.S. 62, 99 S.Ct. 2132 (1979) [Harry PARKER, Petitioner, v. James RANDOLPH et al.] (Confessions; Confrontation Clause; Sixth Amendment) Three defendants were tried and convicted of a crime in which they all participated. Some of them gave oral confessions, which were introduced as evidence against them. The judge instructed the jury to disregard any portion of those statements that implicated one or both of the other defendants. All three were convicted. They appealed, arguing that the interlocking nature of their cases and the confessions violated the Sixth Amendment. The SC overturned their convictions, saying that the accused's right to cross-examination had been violated in the joint trial at which some of the defendants did not testify, but where one or more of their confessions were read into the record, despite the judge's instructions to the jury to disregard portions of confessions implicating one or both defendants. The case's significance is that when codefendants are tried together, the admissibility of a confession is limited to the specific defendant who gives the confession. The court must be careful to control what portions of confessions may be used as evidence against specific defendants, if one or more defendants elect not to testify on their own behalf or subject themselves to cross-examination.

Parratt v. Taylor, 451 U.S. 527, 101 S.Ct. 1908 (1981) [Robert PARRATT and Francis Lugenbill, Petitioners, v. Bert TAYLOR, Jr.] (Civil Rights, Section 1983 Claims; Corrections; Inmate Rights) Taylor was an inmate at the Nebraska Penal and Correctional Complex. While confined, he ordered hobby materials from a company outside the prison. When his materials arrived, corrections officers signed for the package, but at that time, Taylor was in isolation and was not permitted to have these materials. Later, when Taylor was released from isolation, he sought to retrieve his package, but no one could locate it. He sued prison officials for the loss of his package under a Title 42 U.S.C. Section 1983 civil rights allegation. The SC heard the case and rejected Taylor's argument for the following reasons: In order to prevail in a Section 1983 action, the inmate must prove that (1) prison officials committed an act against an inmate in their official capacity; and (2) the conduct deprived the inmate of rights, privileges, or immunities under the United States Constitution. The SC found that the prison employees had acted in their official capacity as hobby shop employees, and there was not conduct apparent that caused Hughes to be deprived of his rights. In this case, what is apparent is that someone purloined Taylor's property, but no one could prove it. In any case, Taylor was advised that the "loss" he suffered did not constitute a violation of constitutional rights.

Patterson v. Illinois, 487 U.S. 285, 108 S.Ct. 2389 (1988) [Tyrone PATTERSON, Petitioner v. ILLINOIS] (Confessions; *Miranda* Warning; Right to Counsel; Self-Incrimination) Patterson was a murder suspect. He was interrogated twice, and on each occasion he signed a waiver of his *Miranda* rights in order to converse with police voluntarily. He gave several incriminating statements during these interrogations and was subsequently convicted of murder. He appealed, contending that he had not been specifically advised of his right to counsel during interrogation. The SC disagreed and upheld his conviction, saying that the waiver of a right to counsel is included in the *Miranda* warning, and that Patterson had waived his right to counsel in both instances when he signed this waiver. The *Miranda* warning is also a warning advising against self-incrimination.

Paul v. Davis, 424 U.S. 693, 96 S.Ct. 1155 (1976) [Edgar PAUL, etc., et al., Petitioners, v. Edward Charles DAVIS III] (Civil Rights, Section 1983 Claims; Corrections; Inmate Rights) Davis was a known shoplifter in Louisville, KY. His name and photo were distributed to various retail outlets in a flyer of suspected or known shoplifters. Davis found out about this circular from his boss and filed a class-action Title 42 U.S.C. Section 1983 civil rights suit against the chief of police of Louisville, alleging that he was being deprived of a liberty and property interest because of the circular. He asked the SC to declare unconstitutional the publication of such circulars as defamatory of his character and a violation of his right to privacy. The SC decided there was no constitutional basis for his claims against officials in Louisville, and his constitutional rights had not been violated by their circular actions.

Payne v. Tennessee, 501 U.S. 808, 111 S.Ct. 2597 (1991) [Pervis Tyrone PAYNE, Petitioner v. TENNESSEE] (Corrections; Death Penalty; Eighth Amendment; Victim Impact Statements) Payne was convicted of a double murder. At the sentencing hearing, he introduced various witnesses on his behalf to avoid the death penalty. During the same hearing, the victims' relatives introduced their victim impact statement, pressing the jury to impose the death penalty on Payne. The death penalty was imposed, and Payne appealed, contesting the introduction of damaging evidence and opinions expressed in the victim impact statement. The SC upheld Payne's death sentence, holding that victim impact statements do not violate an offender's Eighth Amendment rights. The significance of this case is that it supports and condones the use of victim impact statements against convicted offenders during sentencing hearings. (*See Booth v. Maryland* [1987] *for a comparable case in which victim impact statements were suppressed. In the present situation, however, victim impact statements were constitutional as a part of the sentencing hearing involving the death penalty and other crimes.*)

Payton v. New York, 445 U.S. 573, 100 S.Ct. 1371 (1980) [Theodore PAYTON, Applicant, v. NEW YORK. Obie Riddick, Applicant, v. New York] (Exclusionary Rule; Law Enforcement Officers or Agencies; Plain-View Rule) Payton was suspected of the death of a gas station manager. Police went to Payton's apartment to arrest him without a warrant, although they had plenty of time to obtain one. No one was home, and police forced their way in with a crowbar. They found a .30 caliber rifle shell casing on the floor "in plain view." This shell casing was incriminating evidence, and Payton was subsequently convicted of the murder. He appealed. The SC overturned Payton's conviction because police had not obtained a valid arrest warrant in a routine felony arrest situation. There were no exigent circumstances compelling police to act quickly. What evidence they later discovered as the result of their illegal entry into Payton's dwelling was inadmissible. The SC stressed that the governing factor here was whether there was reason for police to act quickly or whether the arrest of Payton was otherwise routine. The SC said the arrest was routine; thus, a lawful arrest warrant for Payton was required.

Peguero v. United States, 526 U.S. 23, 119 S.Ct. 961 (1999) [Manuel DeJesus PEGUERO, Petitioner, v. UNITED STATES] (*Habeas Corpus* Petitions) Peguero pleaded guilty to federal drug charges and was sentenced to prison. However, the U.S. District Court judge failed to advise Peguero of his right to appeal the sentence. Peguero filed a *habeas corpus* petition seeking to have his conviction overturned because of the absence of notification by the judge of the right of appeal. The SC upheld Peguero's conviction, holding that when Peguero was sentenced, he knew of his right to appeal; thus there was no prejudice exhibited by the judge when instructions relating to subsequent appeals were not mentioned at the time of sentencing. Convicted offenders who have full knowledge of their right to appeal are not entitled to collateral relief whenever trial judges fail to advise them of their right to appeal.

Pell v. Procunier, 417 U.S. 817, 94 S.Ct. 2800 (1974) [Eve PELL et al., Appellants, v. Raymond K. PROCUNIER, Director, California Department of Corrections, et al. Raymond K. Procunier, Director, California Department of Corrections, et al., Appellants, v. Booker T. Hillery, Jr., et al.] (Civil Rights, Section 1983 Claims; Corrections; First Amendment; Free Speech; Inmate Rights) Several professional journalists and California prison inmates filed suit against prison authorities under Title 42 U.S.C. Section 1983, alleging that they had been denied the First Amendment right of freedom of speech. Specifically, journalists had wanted to interview certain inmates following a prison riot. Prison policy was to refuse such interviews. The SC heard the case and decided in favor of prison authorities. Thus, a prison regulation prohibiting media interviews with inmates neither violates the First Amendment nor the rights of inmates to be heard by media personnel.

Pembaur v. Cincinnati, 475 U.S. 469, 106 S.Ct. 1292 (1986) [Bertold J. PEMBAUR, Petitioner, v. City of CINCINNATI et al.] (Civil Rights, Section 1983 Claims) A physician, Pembaur, filed suit against the City of Cincinnati, whose police officers allegedly violated his Fourth and Fourteenth Amendment rights by forcing their way into his clinic to serve a *capias* on two of his employees. He was subsequently charged with obstruction of justice and convicted. Pembaur continued his suit against county officials, and they alleged that they were immune from such suits. Pembaur's claim was rejected, and he appealed the case to the SC. The SC reinstated his claim against county officials, saying that the county is liable under Title 42 U.S.C., Section 1983.

Pennsylvania v. Bruder, 488 U.S. 9, 109 S.Ct. 205 (1988) [PENNSYLVANIA v. Thomas A. BRUDER, Jr.] (Custodial Interrogations; Law Enforcement Officers or Agencies; *Miranda* Warning; Sobriety Checkpoints) Bruder was stopped by police one evening because he appeared to be driving erratically and he ran a red light. Bruder left his vehicle and approached the police, who smelled alcohol. They also observed that Bruder was stumbling. He was administered several field sobriety tests, which he failed. Police asked Bruder if he had been drinking, and he said he had been drinking and was driving home. Police placed him under arrest and told him his *Miranda* rights. He was subsequently convicted of DWI. He appealed, alleging that his statements before the *Miranda* warning should not have been admitted against him in court. The SC asked the critical question whether or not he was in a coercive situation when answering police questions before his arrest. The SC determined that he was not entitled to a *Miranda* warning. His statements made before his arrest were admissible against him and his DWI conviction was upheld.

Pennsylvania v. Finley, 481 U.S. 551, 107 S.Ct. 1990 (1987) [PENNSYLVANIA, Petitioner, v. Dorothy FINLEY] (Corrections; Indigent Clients; Inmate Rights) Finley, an indigent, was convicted of second-degree murder in Pennsylvania. She appealed. An attorney was appointed to assist her in perfecting her appeal. The attorney inspected the trial record and other legal matters, concluded that there was nothing worth arguing in the appeal, and withdrew. A new lawyer was appointed to represent Finley. Her appeal efforts were fruitless, so she demanded a new attorney for a new appeal, alleging that the first attorney who withdrew had been incompetent and objecting to the conduct of the second lawyer. Finley appealed to the SC, alleging that her due-process rights had been violated by the attorney withdrawal and other attorney conduct. The SC rejected her appeal, holding that indigent prisoners have no equal-protection right to appointed counsel in postconviction proceedings after exhaustion of the appellate process or in postconviction relief proceedings after exhaustion of appellate process. States have no obligation to provide postconviction relief for collateral attack upon judgment, and when they do, fundamental fairness mandated by due process does not require them to supply a lawyer.

Pennsylvania v. Labron, 518 U.S. 938, 116 S.Ct. 2485 (1996) [PENNSYLVANIA, Petitioner, v. Edwin LABRON] (Fourth Amendment; Searches and Seizures; Vehicle Searches) Labron and others were observed by police engaging in a series of drug transactions on a street in Philadelphia. Police arrested Labron and searched the trunk of his car, finding bags of cocaine. He was convicted of cocaine possession for resale and he appealed, contending that police violated his Fourth Amendment rights when they failed to obtain a search warrant before searching his vehicle. The Pennsylvania Supreme Court reversed Labron's drug conviction, holding that as exigent circumstances did not exist, police had time to obtain a search warrant and did not obtain one; thus, their search of Labron's vehicle was unconstitutional, violating his Fourth Amendment rights. The government appealed and the SC heard the case. The SC overturned the Pennsylvania Supreme Court and reinstated Labron's drug conviction, holding that if a car is readily mobile and probable cause exists to believe it contains contraband, the Fourth Amendment permits police to search the vehicle without more. The Pennsylvania Supreme Court incorrectly read the automobile exception requirement, erroneously believing that exigent circumstances must be present in order for a warrantless search of a vehicle to be made. (*See Maryland v. Dyson* [1999] *for comparison.*)

Pennsylvania v. Mimms, 434 U.S. 106, 98 S.Ct. 330 (1977) [Commonwealth of PENNSYLVANIA, Petitioner, v. Harry MIMMS] (Law Enforcement Officers or Agencies; Searches and Seizures) Mimms was stopped in his vehicle for having expired license plates. Officers observed a "bulge" in his clothing when he got out of the vehicle, and they patted him down, discovering a firearm. He was subsequently arrested and convicted of carrying a concealed weapon and possessing a firearm without a license. He appealed. The SC upheld his conviction, citing *Terry v. Ohio* (1968) and the fact that the officers did indeed have reasonable suspicion and exercised reasonable caution when they observed the bulge in his jacket. The officers were entitled to act in a manner to ensure their safety and security.

Pennsylvania v. Muniz, 496 U.S. 582, 110 S.Ct. 2638 (1990) [PENNSYLVANIA, Petitioner, v. Inocencio MUNIZ] (Confessions; *Miranda* Warning; Sobriety Checkpoints) Muniz was stopped by police on suspicion of drunken driving. He was given various field sobriety tests and failed all of them. He even admitted to police that he failed because he had been drinking. The officers arrested Muniz. Later, they asked if Muniz would submit to taking these same tests again, but this time, the police would videotape his actions. He agreed, and again he failed the tests. Next, police asked Muniz to take a Breathalyzer test and Muniz refused. The police then read Muniz his *Miranda* rights for the first time and he admitted again that he had been drinking and driving. This evidence was admitted against him later in court, including the video-taped failing of the sobriety tests. He was convicted. He appealed, contending that the videotapings had been done before he had been told his *Miranda* rights. However, the SC upheld Muniz's DWI conviction, saying that the videotaping and questioning of Muniz before the *Miranda* warning was given constituted routine questioning and other procedures common to DWI stops and questioning. Police may videotape suspected drunken drivers and ask them routine questions, such as age, residence, and hair color, without specifically giving them the *Miranda* warning. Routine information of this sort may be used as evidence against them.

Pennsylvania v. Ritchie, 480 U.S. 39, 107 S.Ct. 989 (1987) [**PENNSYLVANIA, Petitioner, v. George F. RITCHIE**] (**Sixth Amendment**) Ritchie was accused of rape, corruption of a minor, and involuntary sexual intercourse. Prior to trial, defense counsel sought to examine certain juvenile records maintained by Children and Youth Services (CYS). CYS policy forbade inspection by others, including defense counsel, of confidential juvenile information. Ritchie was tried and convicted. He appealed, alleging that he should have been allowed to examine the juvenile records, and thus he had been deprived of a fair trial. The Pennsylvania Supreme Court overturned his conviction on these grounds, and the state appealed to the SC. The SC reinstated Ritchie's convictions but remanded the case to a lower court to resolve other issues. The SC declared that under the rules of discovery, defendants are not authorized to have unsupervised authority to search state records to make a determination of the materiality of confidential information. Thus, the state's compelling interest in safeguarding and protecting its child-abuse information outweighed Ritchie's discovery interests. The SC agreed that Ritchie was entitled to know whether the CYS information might have changed the outcome of his trial had it been disclosed. For this reason alone, a remand was necessary. But the SC disagreed with the notion that defense counsel is entitled to access to CYS files. Thus, an *in camera* review of file information would determine whether the information was relevant to Ritchie's case.

Pennsylvania Board of Probation and Parole v. Scott, 524 U.S. 357, 118 S.Ct. 2014 (1998) [**PENNSYLVANIA BOARD OF PROBATION AND PAROLE, Petitioner, v. Keith M. SCOTT**] (**Fourth Amendment; Probation and Parole; Searches and Seizures**) Scott, a parolee, was suspected of possessing firearms in violation of his parole conditions. Parole officers conducted a warrantless search of his premises and discovered firearms. Scott's parole was revoked on the basis of the discovered evidence, and he was recommitted to prison. Scott appealed, alleging that his Fourth Amendment right against unreasonable searches and seizures had been violated and that evidence thus seized was not admissible in parole revocation hearings. The SC held that a parolee's Fourth Amendment rights do not apply in parole revocation hearings, and that incriminating evidence discovered and seized in violation of a parolee's Fourth Amendment rights may be introduced at parole revocation proceedings.

Pennsylvania Department of Corrections v. Yeskey, 524 U.S. 206, 118 S.Ct. 1952 (1998) [**PENNSYLVANIA DE-PARTMENT OF CORRECTIONS** et al., **Petitioners, v. Ronald R. YESKEY**] (**Americans With Disabilities Act**) Yeskey was a Pennsylvania prison inmate who was sentenced to 18 to 36 months in a correctional facility but was recommended for placement in a Motivational Boot Camp that, if successfully completed, would have led to his parole in just six months. Yeskey was rejected by the boot camp officials because of a medical history of hypertension. Yeskey sued the Pennsylvania Department of Corrections, alleging that the exclusion violated the Americans With Disabilities Act (ADA), and the federal court rejected his claim, contending that the ADA was inapplicable to state prison inmates. The Third Circuit Court of Appeals reversed and remanded, and the government appealed to the SC, who heard the case. The SC affirmed the appellate court, declaring that the ADA provision prohibiting a public entity from discriminating against a qualified individual with a disability on account of that person's disability applied to inmates in state prisons.

Penry v. Johnson, 532 U.S. 782, 121 S.Ct. 1910 (2001) [**Johnny Paul PENRY, Petitioner, v. Gary L. JOHNSON, Director, Texas Department of Criminal Justice, Institutional Division**] (*Habeas Corpus* **Petitions; Jury Instructions; Sentencing**) Penry was convicted of first-degree murder in 1989 in a Texas court and sentenced to death. However, the conviction was overturned because it violated the Eighth Amendment. Penry was retried in 1990 and again found guilty of capital murder. During the penalty phase of the proceedings, the defense put on extensive evidence of Penry's mental impairments and childhood abuse. Prosecutors introduced and read into the record over a defense objection a 1977 psychiatric evaluation of Penry prepared at his attorney's request in another court matter unrelated to the murder at issue. The report concluded in part that if Penry were released, he would be dangerous to others. Subsequently, the judge gave the jury detailed instructions including a consideration of mitigating circumstances, and Penry was again sentenced to death. However, the judge provided jurors a document with the original special issues from Penry's first trial. Again a question arose about whether the judge had adequately permitted the jury to consider and give effect to the particular mitigating evidence. Penry appealed through a *habeas corpus* action, claiming in part that the introduction into evidence of his earlier psychiatric report was a violation of his Fifth Amendment right against self-incrimination. Further, Penry contended that the judge's jury instructions were inadequate because they did not permit the jury to consider and give effect to his particular mitigating evidence. The state denied Penry *habeas corpus* relief and Penry appealed to the U.S. District Court, which affirmed the Texas trial court. An appeal to the circuit court of appeals resulted in a similar affirmation of the sentence, and Penry appealed to the SC seeking *habeas corpus* relief. The SC heard the case and held that the introduction of the earlier psychiatric examination during Penry's sentencing phase did not warrant *habeas corpus* relief. However, the SC also held that the judge's instructions on mitigating circumstances failed to provide the jury with a vehicle to give effect to mitigating circumstances of mental retardation and childhood abuse as required by the

Eighth and Fourteenth Amendments. Thus, the SC reversed in part, and affirmed in part, the decision of the trial court. (*See Penry v. Lynaugh* [1989] *for selected details of Penry's 1989 conviction and death sentence and the reasons for the SC's reversal.*)

Penry v. Lynaugh, 492 U.S. 302, 109 S.Ct. 2934 (1989) [Johnny Paul PENRY, Petitioner, v. James A. LYNAUGH, Director, Texas Department of Corrections] (Corrections; Death Penalty) Penry was a mentally retarded inmate convicted of capital murder in Texas. He had an IQ of 54 and a mental age of 6 years. He was 22 when the capital murder was committed, and he was sentenced to death. During the sentencing phase of Penry's trial, the judge failed to advise the jury that it could consider evidence of Penry's mental retardation and childhood abuse. Penry appealed his death sentence, contending that mentally retarded persons cannot be executed and that the judge had failed to give the jury proper instructions concerning mitigating circumstances including his mental retardation and childhood abuse. The SC overturned Penry's death sentence as unconstitutional, largely because the jury had not been adequately instructed with respect to the mitigating evidence. Penry was retried in 1990 and again found guilty of capital murder and sentenced to death. (*See Penry v. Johnson* [2001] *for a discussion of Penry's subsequent appeal of his 1990 conviction and death sentence.*)

Penson v. Ohio, 488 U.S. 75, 109 S.Ct. 346 (1988) [Steven A. PENSON, Petitioner, v. OHIO] (Indigent Clients; Right to Counsel; Sixth Amendment) Penson, an indigent, was convicted of several serious crimes. He was appointed a new attorney for his appeal to a higher court, but his attorney filed a Certification of Meritless Appeal and Motion, which indicated that he had thoroughly examined the trial record and could find no sound basis for an appeal. The attorney asked to be removed as counsel for Penson. Later, Penson asked for but was denied a new attorney to launch yet another appeal. Subsequently, on its own, the Ohio Supreme Court discovered that Penson had several arguable claims in his case, and in fact, one of these claims might have resulted in reversible error. Nevertheless, the court rejected Penson's new request for counsel and his appeal, justifying its decision because the court had thoroughly examined the record and received the benefit of arguments from counsel who had represented Penson and a codefendant. Eventually, Penson's case reached the SC. The SC scolded the Ohio Supreme Court in various ways, by noting that it had erred in several respects. When Ohio judges determined that there were "arguable" issues in Penson's case, they erred when they decided not to hear his appeal. They also erred when they permitted Penson's counsel to withdraw, after he submitted a statement claiming that no arguable issues could be found. The SC noted that the most glaring error was the failure of the Ohio Supreme Court to appoint a new counsel for Penson after it had determined that there were several "arguable issues." Thus, the SC said, Penson's due-process rights had been violated, and it overturned his convictions.

Perry v. Leeke, 488 U.S. 272, 109 S.Ct. 594 (1989) [Donald Ray PERRY, Petitioner, v. William D. LEEKE, Commis-sioner, South Carolina Department of Corrections, et al.] (*Habeas Corpus* Petitions; Right to Counsel; Sixth Amendment) Perry was accused of murder, kidnapping, and sexual assault in South Carolina. During his trial, a 15-minute recess was declared by the judge, who advised Perry not to speak with anyone, including Perry's attorney. Subsequently, Perry was convicted of these crimes. He appealed through a *habeas corpus* petition, alleging that his Sixth Amendment right to counsel had been violated because of the prohibition against seeing his attorney during the recess. The SC upheld Perry's conviction, holding that the state trial court's order directing Perry not to consult his attorney during the afternoon recess had not violated Perry's Sixth Amendment right to assistance of counsel.

Pierson v. Ray, 386 U.S. 547, 87 S.Ct. 1213 (1967) [Robert L. PIERSON et al., Petitioners, v. J.L. RAY et al. J.L. Ray et al., Petitioners, v. Robert L. Pierson et al.] (Civil Rights, Section 1983 Claims) Fifteen white and black clergymen attempted to use white facilities at an interstate bus terminal in Jackson, MS. Police officers arrested them for disturbing the peace. They waived a jury trial and were convicted, being sentenced to four months. Subsequently, they appealed the case and filed a civil rights suit against the police officers who arrested them, alleging false imprisonment and civil rights violations. Early appellate decisions resulted in favorable verdicts for the officers, so the clergymen appealed to the SC. The SC decided that the clergymen did indeed have standing to seek damages against the Jackson police officers. Their claim under Title 42 U.S.C. Section 1983 was thus upheld and sent back to a civil trial court for further proceedings.

Plessy v. Ferguson, 163 U.S. 537, 16 S.Ct. 1138 (1896) [PLESSY v. John H. FERGUSON, Judge] (Discrimination) Plessy, a man who had one-eighth African-American ancestry and seven-eighths Caucasian ancestry, boarded an all white railroad car. He refused to leave when asked by the railroad conductor. At the time, "separate, but equal" facilities were the governing doctrine relating to white and black accommodations, particularly in Southern states. Plessy filed suit against the railroad, alleging discrimination. The SC heard the case and declared that as long as equal facilities were provided for blacks, separate accommodations for them did not violate the "separate, but equal" concept. The significance of this case is that it set a precedent for racial discrimination patterns for the next 50 years, in virtually every social activity involving different races: separate but equal restrooms, bus seating, drinking fountains, and housing. The doctrine was set aside on a piecemeal basis, beginning with *Brown v. Board of Education* (1954), in which this separate, but equal doctrine was determined *not* to apply to education. Thereafter, individual SC decisions addressed the separate, but equal issue in each of the areas to which it applied. The SC never overturned the original decision rendered in *Plessy v. Ferguson.* This fact demonstrates an important principle of SC decision making—it is narrow in its scope, and subsequent SC decisions almost never result in a total abandonment of prior SC decisions.

Pointer v. Texas, 380 U.S. 400, 85 S.Ct. 1065 (1965) [Bob Granville POINTER, Petitioner, v. State of TEXAS] (Confrontation Clause; Sixth Amendment) Pointer was accused of armed robbery. At a preliminary hearing where Pointer was not represented by counsel, a victim, Phillips, testified against him. Pointer did not cross-examine the victim. Later, at Pointer's trial, the prosecutor offered for the record the transcript of testimony of Phillips during the preliminary hearing as evidence against Pointer, because the victim had left the state and indicated no intention to return to give testimony directly in Pointer's trial. Pointer was convicted. He appealed, arguing that he had not had an opportunity to cross-examine Phillips. The Texas Supreme Court rejected his argument and upheld his conviction. The SC eventually heard Pointer's case and overturned his conviction because his Sixth Amendment rights had been violated. The SC said that the statements given by Phillips during the preliminary hearing had afforded no defense attorney an opportunity to cross-examine Phillips. The use of Phillips' transcript of testimony had offered Pointer no right of cross-examination, and thus the conviction could not be proper unless Pointer were allowed the right to cross-examine his accuser. The significance of this case is that a transcript of testimony from an available witness and victim is insufficient as a basis for a conviction, because the right of cross-examination is denied.

Poland v. Arizona, 476 U.S. 147, 106 S.Ct. 1749 (1986) [**Patrick Gene POLAND, Petitioner, v. ARIZONA. Michael Kent Poland v. Arizona**] (**Double Jeopardy**) Patrick Poland and his brother, Michael, had robbed a bank and killed the bank guards, dumping them in a nearby lake and weighting them down with rocks. A trial resulted in their conviction of first-degree murder, and the death penalty was imposed. Subsequently, they appealed; their convictions were reversed, the death penalties were set aside, and a new trial was ordered. A second trial had the identical result, with new death penalties imposed. The Polands sought to overturn their second convictions on the grounds of double jeopardy stemming from their first trial. The SC upheld their convictions and death sentences, declaring that when a conviction is reversed on appeal, it is nullified and the "slate is wiped clean," so that if the defendant is convicted again, he or she may be constitutionally subjected to whatever punishment is lawful, including the death penalty. There was no "death penalty" acquittal in the first trial. Thus double jeopardy was not a consideration in the Polands' case.

Polk County v. Dodson, 454 U.S. 312, 102 S.Ct. 445 (1981) [**POLK COUNTY et al., Petitioners, v. Russell Richard DODSON**] (**Civil Rights, Section 1983 Claims; Cruel and Unusual Punishment; Sixth Amendment**) Dodson was convicted of a crime after being defended by a public defender lawyer from Polk County, IA. Dodson filed suit under Title 42 U.S.C. Section 1983 that his Sixth, Eighth, and Fourteenth Amendment rights had been violated. First, he said, his attorney had failed to represent him adequately, and he was suing her under state law. Second, he further alleged that his attorney had subjected him to cruel and unusual punishment as the result of her desire to withdraw from the case, and that this withdrawal in turn had violated his due-process rights. Considering all claims against his lawyer and Polk County, the SC dismissed all of them, holding that Dodson had failed to show any right that was violated. The SC con-

cluded that withdrawals from frivolous cases by attorneys do not in and of themselves violate a person's right to due process.

Ponte v. Real, 471 U.S. 491, 105 S.Ct. 2192 (1985) [**Joseph PONTE, Superintendent, Massachusetts Correctional Institution, Walpole, Petitioner, v. John REAL**] (**Corrections; Inmate Rights**) Real was a prisoner at the Massachusetts Correctional Institution at Walpole. He was charged with various prison regulation violations. During his disciplinary hearing, Real said that he wanted to call four witnesses. Only one of the witnesses appeared to offer testimony against Real. The other witnesses were not called, and the board did not advise Real why they were not called. Real was found guilty and given 30 days in isolation and had 150 days deducted from his good-time credit. He appealed, contending that the board should have provided its reasons in writing for refusing to call these other witnesses. The SC disagreed, saying that the board need not reduce to writing the reasons for not calling specific witnesses at prison disciplinary hearings.

Porter v. Nussle, ___U.S.___, 122 S.Ct. 983 (2002) [**Correction Officer PORTER et al., Petitioners, v. Ronald NUSSLE**] (**Civil Rights, Section 1983 Claims; Prison Litigation Reform Act**) Ronald Nussle was an inmate in the Connecticut Department of Corrections. Despite a prison administrative grievance procedure already in place, Nussle bypassed this procedure and filed a Section 1983 civil rights claim in U.S. district court against several corrections officers, including Porter, for alleged harassment, intimidation, and physical injuries sustained from a severe beating. The officers moved to dismiss the suit on the grounds that Nussle had failed to exhaust his administrative remedies prior to filing the district court action. The Prison Litigation Reform Act (PLRA) directs that no inmate shall file a Section 1983 or any other claim until such administrative remedies as are available are exhausted. The district court dismissed the suit and Nussle appealed. The Second Circuit Court of Appeals reversed and remanded, holding that exhaustion of administrative remedies is not required for a claim of the kind Nussle asserted. The officers appealed the ruling to the SC, who heard the case. The SC reversed the Second Circuit Court, holding that the PLRA's exhaustion requirement applies to all inmate suits about prison life, whether they involve general circumstances or particular episodes, and whether they allege excessive force or some other wrong. Inmates of state and federal prisons must exhaust all administrative remedies before they can file suit in federal court asserting rights violations or any other complaint about prison life and treatment.

Portuondo v. Agard, 529 U.S. 61, 120 S.Ct. 1119 (2000) [**Leonard PORTUONDO, Superintendent, Fishkill Correctional Facility, Petitioner, v. Ray AGARD**] (**Habeas Corpus Petitions; Prosecutorial Misconduct**) Agard was convicted of anal sodomy and several weapons charges in a New York state court. During the summation, the prosecutor commented about Agard's opportunity to sit in the courtroom and listen to witnesses, and then to easily fabricate stories to fit his own version of events when he testified in his own behalf. Agard filed a writ of *habeas corpus* with the federal district court, contending that the prosecutor's comments were unconstitutional and in violation of his Fifth and Sixth Amendment rights to be present at trial and confront his accusers, and his Fourteenth Amendment right to due process. The federal district court denied Agard's motion, but the Second Circuit Court reversed his conviction. The government appealed, and the SC heard the case. The SC reversed the Second Circuit, reinstating Agard's conviction, holding that the prosecutor's comments did not violate Agard's Fifth and Sixth Amendment rights. The SC noted that the prosecutor's comments were intended to challenge Agard's credibility. The SC added that no promise of impunity is implicit in a statute requiring a defendant to be present at trial, and there is no authority whatever for the proposition that the impairment of credibility, if any, caused by mandatory presence at trial violates due process.

Powell v. Alabama, 287 U.S. 45, 53 S.Ct. 55 (1932) [Ozie POWELL et al., Petitioners, v. State of ALABAMA] (Right to Counsel) During a train trip in Alabama, two white women were allegedly raped by several young black men. At an unscheduled stop, the train was searched by police, who arrested nine young black men and charged them with rape. Not until the trial date did the judge assign an attorney to represent each man. In one-day trials, each young man was convicted and sentenced to death. They appealed. The SC overturned their convictions, citing several violations of constitutional rights. Among other things, the men had not been permitted the assistance of counsel in their own defense until the trial date. In addition, unreliable and incompetent evidence had been admitted against the men, evidence that would not have been admitted in other courts. The charges had not been properly formulated or delivered to the men, so that they did not understand fully what it was they were supposed to have done and when. Considering the time of the incident, the early 1930s, and race relations in the State of Alabama, their treatment by authorities was consistent with inequities against blacks in the South generally during that time period.

Powell v. Nevada, 511 U.S. 79, 114 S.Ct. 1280 (1994) [Kitrich POWELL, Petitioner, v. NEVADA] (Searches and Seizures) Powell was arrested on November 3, 1989, for felony child abuse. However, it was not until November 7 that a magistrate found probable cause to hold him for a preliminary hearing. Subsequently, the child, his girlfriend's 4-year-old daughter, died, and Powell was accused of murder and convicted. He appealed, alleging that the four-day delay between his warrantless arrest and the finding of probable cause to conduct a preliminary hearing violated the 48-hour rule set forth in a subsequent case, *County of Riverside v. McLaughlin* (1991). The Nevada Supreme Court upheld his conviction, saying that because the *McLaughlin* 48-hour rule came about *after* Powell's conviction, it could not be retroactively applied to affect his case and conviction. Powell appealed to the SC, which overturned Powell's conviction and set aside his death sentence, saying that the *McLaughlin* rule had indeed been violated by the excessive delay between arrest and a finding of probable cause. The significance of this case is that certain rules, such as the *McLaughlin* 48-hour rule, may be retroactively applied in capital cases. Thus, the Nevada court had erred by allowing the presumptively unreasonable delay of four days between a warrantless arrest, detention, and finding of probable cause. The SC did not say, however, that Powell

was automatically entitled to be set free. Rather, Nevada courts were encouraged to explore other remedies for their error and in violating the 48-hour rule under *McLaughlin.*

Powell v. Texas, 392 U.S. 514, 88 S.Ct. 2145 (1963) [Leroy POWELL, Appellant, v. State of TEXAS] (Cruel and Unusual Punishment) Powell was convicted of public drunkenness. He appealed, arguing that his "status" of being a chronic alcoholic should remove his public drunkenness from that of criminal conduct. The SC heard his case, upheld his conviction, and held that presently, the state of drunkenness is substantially different from that of being addicted to a narcotic.

Powell v. Texas, 492 U.S. 680, 109 S.Ct. 3146 (1989) [David Lee POWELL v. TEXAS] (Right to Counsel; Sixth Amendment) Powell was suspected of capital murder. When Powell was first arrested, the trial court ordered a psychiatric examination to determine his future dangerousness. Neither Powell nor his attorney was advised on at least four occasions that doctors would be examining Powell on the issue of his future dangerousness. During his trial, and during the penalty phase following a jury verdict of guilty, doctors for the state testified about Powell's future dangerousness and elaborated on their reports. Powell's attorney introduced the testimony of one doctor who examined Powell on the defense's behalf. Powell was convicted and sentenced to death. He appealed, alleging that his Sixth Amendment rights had been violated when he and his attorney were not notified about the state psychiatric examinations and their intended purposes. The state countered that because Powell had introduced psychiatric testimony of his own, his appeal should be rejected. The SC overturned Powell's conviction, saying that Powell had been deprived of his Sixth Amendment right to counsel when psychiatric examinations were performed by state experts, without notice to him or his attorney that the examinations would encompass the issue of future dangerousness, and that Powell's introduction of psychiatric testimony on his own behalf did not effectively waive his Sixth Amendment right to notification.

Powell v. United States, 518 U.S. 81, 116 S.Ct. 2035 (1996) [Stacey C. Koon, Petitioner, v. United States. Laurence M. POWELL, Petitioner, v. UNITED STATES] (Law Enforcement Officers or Agencies; Sentencing) *See Koon v. United States* (1996).

Powers v. Ohio, 499 U.S. 400, 111 S.Ct. 1364 (1991) [Larry Joe POWERS, Petitioner, v. OHIO] (Peremptory Challenges; Right to Counsel; Sixth Amendment) Powers was charged with murder, aggravated murder, and attempted aggravated murder, all with firearm specifications (calling for mandatory minimum sentences). A white man, he objected to the government's use of peremptory challenges to strike seven black prospective jurors from the jury. Subsequently, Powers was convicted. He appealed, alleging that his Fourteenth Amendment right had been violated under the equal-protection clause because of the alleged discriminatory use of peremptory challenges. The matter of excluding prospective black jurors by the use of peremptory challenges had already been decided in *Batson v. Kentucky* (1986), in which it was declared unconstitutional to use peremptory challenges to achieve a racially pure jury. In the *Batson* case, however, the defendant was black, and government prejudice was obvious in the use of these peremptory challenges. In the *Powers* case, the defendant was white, and prospective black jurors had been excluded. The SC heard Powers' appeal and overturned his conviction on the same grounds as *Batson,* holding that criminal defendants may object to race-based exclusions of jurors effected through peremptory challenges whether or not defendants and excluded jurors share the same race.

Preiser v. Rodriguez, 411 U.S. 475, 93 S.Ct. 1827 (1973) [Peter PREISER, Commissioner of Correctional Services, et al., Petitioners, v. Eugene RODRIGUEZ et al.] (Civil Rights, Section 1983 Claims; Corrections; *Habeas Corpus* Petitions; Inmate Rights) Rodriguez and others were state prisoners who were deprived of good-time credits by the New York Department of Correctional Services because of disciplinary proceedings. Rodriguez appealed under a *habeas corpus* petition. The lower courts dismissed the petition, saying that it was not relevant for challenging the fact and duration of one's confinement. The SC overturned the lower-court decision, holding that when state prisoners are challenging the very fact or duration of their physical confinement, and the relief sought is a determination that they are entitled to immediate release from that imprisonment, the sole federal remedy is a writ of *habeas corpus*. Although Section 1983 of the Civil Rights Act can be used by prisoners for constitutional claims against state prison officials or employees for the *conditions* of prison life, it cannot be used to challenge the *fact* and *length* of confinement.

Press-Enterprise Company v. Superior Court of California, 478 U.S. 1, 106 S.Ct. 2735 (1986) [PRESS-ENTERPRISE COMPANY, etc., Petitioner, v. SUPERIOR COURT OF CALIFORNIA for the County of Riverside] (First Amendment; Free Press; Jury Trials; Media Rights) A newspaper sought to be present at a preliminary hearing in a criminal proceeding in a California court. The court declared that there is no First Amendment right of access to preliminary hearings. The SC overturned this opinion by the California court and said that the media have a right under the First Amendment to attend preliminary hearings.

Preston v. United States, 376 U.S. 364, 84 S.Ct. 881 (1964) [John Brenton PRESTON, Petitioner, v. UNITED STATES] (Law Enforcement Officers or Agencies; Searches and Seizures; Searches Incident to an Arrest; Vehicle Searches) Preston was arrested for vagrancy. His car was towed from the arrest scene and searched. Police found two loaded revolvers in the glove compartment. Unable to open the trunk of the car, they entered it by removing the back seat, where they found additional incriminating evidence leading to Preston's conviction for various offenses. He appealed, alleging a violation of his Fourth Amendment right against an unreasonable search and seizure of contraband or illegal items. The government said that the warrantless search of his vehicle was incident to an arrest and therefore valid. Preston appealed again. The SC overturned Preston's conviction, saying that the warrantless search of Preston's vehicle had been too remote in time to be considered a search incident to an arrest. Therefore, the incriminating evidence should be suppressed.

Price v. Vincent, ___U.S.___, 123 S.Ct. 1848 (2003) [Janette PRICE, Warden, Petitioner, v. Duyonn Andre VINCENT] (Double Jeopardy; *Habeas Corpus* Petitions) Duyonn Vincent was convicted of first-degree murder in Michigan. Prior to his conviction and at the conclusion of the trial, out of earshot of the jury, the defense counsel moved for a directed verdict of acquittal on the first-degree murder charge by the judge, which was granted. The judge said that "second-degree murder was a more appropriate charge." However, the judge did not advise the jury as to his decision and directed the prosecutor to provide contrary arguments the following day. Following these prosecutorial arguments as to why first-degree murder should be retained as the primary charge against Vincent, the defense counsel objected, contending that the judge had already granted a motion for a directed verdict and that to permit the jury to consider first-degree murder would violate Vincent's right against double jeopardy. However, the judge said, "Oh, I granted that motion but I have not directed a verdict." The judge permitted the jury to deliberate on the first-degree murder charge. The jury found Vincent guilty of first-degree murder. Later, Vincent appealed, and higher courts in Michigan were mixed on the issue of double jeopardy. Eventually, from a Michigan prison, Vincent filed a *habeas corpus* petition with a U.S. district court, alleging double jeopardy in his case. The court granted his motion, which was appealed by Michigan. The SC eventually heard the case and overturned the lower court, holding that Vincent had failed to meet the statutory requirements for *habeas corpus* relief. The judge's actions lacked finality to the extent that his ruling on the original motion for a directed verdict on the first-degree murder charge was tentative, pending the prosecutor's argument. Furthermore, no formal judgment or order had been entered into the court record. Although formal motions or rulings are not required to demonstrate finality as a matter of Michigan law, a judgment must bear sufficient indicia of finality, which were not present in Vincent's case. Thus, Vincent's right against double jeopardy had not been violated.

Printz v. United States, 521 U.S. 898, 117 S.Ct. 2365 (1997) [Jay PRINTZ, Sheriff/Coroner, Ravalli County, Montana, Petitioner, v. UNITED STATES. Richard Mack, Petitioner, v. United States] (Gun Control Bill) The Brady Handgun Violence Prevention Act was passed in 1993, which required the attorney general to establish a national system for instantly checking prospective handgun purchasers' backgrounds and commanded the "chief law enforcement officer" (CLEO) to conduct such checks and perform related tasks on an interim basis until the national system should become operative. Printz and Mack, two county sheriffs, sought to prevent enforcement provisions of the act, arguing that requiring a federally mandated background check of prospective gun purchasers by CLEOs of state counties was unconstitutional. A federal district court held that the background check requirement for CLEOs was unconstitutional. The Ninth Circuit Court of Appeals reversed the federal district court ruling, and the sheriffs appealed to the SC, who heard the case. The SC reversed the Ninth Circuit, holding that obligation to conduct background checks on prospective handgun purchasers imposed an unconstitutional obligation on state officers to execute federal laws.

Procunier v. Martinez, 416 U.S. 396, 94 S.Ct. 1800 (1974) [**Raymond K. PROCUNIER, Director, California Department of Corrections, et al., Appellants, v. Robert MARTINEZ et al.**] (**Corrections; Inmate Rights**) Several California prison inmates brought a class-action suit against the California Department of Corrections alleging unreasonable mail censorship, specifically censorship of mail containing inmate complaints, grievances, and inflammatory views or beliefs. The SC agreed with the inmates and ruled that the mail censorship provisions used by the California Department of Corrections were unconstitutional, although any mail that is potentially disruptive of inmate discipline may be censored. Further, any censorship policy must demonstrate that such censorship furthers a particular government interest unrelated to such suppression. Thus authorities may not censor mail simply because it contains unflattering opinions about them or their staffs.

Procunier v. Navarette, 434 U.S. 555, 98 S.Ct. 855 (1978) [**Raymond K. PROCUNIER et al., Petitioners, v. Apolinar NAVARETTE, Jr.**] (**Civil Rights, Section 1983 Claims; Corrections; Immunity**) A class-action civil rights claim was filed by Navarette and other California inmates under Title 42 U.S.C. Section 1983 that correctional officers had failed to mail various letters and documents to legal aid groups, media, and other addressees. The prisoners alleged violations of their First and Fourteenth Amendment rights. The correctional officers sought protection under an absolute-immunity defense. The SC said that the officers were not entitled to *absolute* immunity, but rather to *qualified* immunity. According to the SC, qualified immunity is any action in the good-faith fulfillment of officers' responsibilities, and that such action will not be punished. Furthermore, at the time this case was filed, there was no existing or prevailing constitutional right specifically protecting a prisoner's correspondence. Thus, this case set a precedent for the current good-faith standard of immunity used in correctional settings.

Proffitt v. Florida, 428 U.S. 242, 96 S.Ct. 2960 (1976) [**Charles William PROFFITT, Petitioner, v. State of FLORIDA**] (**Aggravating and Mitigating Circumstances; Corrections; Cruel and Unusual Punishment; Death Penalty; Eighth Amendment**) Proffitt was convicted of first-degree murder and sentenced to death. He appealed, saying that the Florida statute outlining eight statutory aggravating factors and seven statutory mitigating factors was flawed, because the aggravating and mitigating circumstances "lacked precision" of definition. The SC upheld his conviction and death sentence, maintaining that under Florida law, judges are required to impose the death penalty on all first-degree murderers if statutory aggravating factors outweigh the mitigating ones. Further, the death penalty is not *per se* cruel and unusual punishment in violation of the Eighth Amendment, as originally alleged by Proffitt.

Prunty v. Brooks, 528 U.S. 9, 120 S.Ct. 3 (1999) [**Robert E. PRUNTY v. W. BROOKS et al.**] (**Frivolous Lawsuits; *In Forma Pauperis* Motions; Inmate Rights**) Robert E. Prunty, an inmate, filed an *in forma pauperis* motion with the SC, which was denied. The SC noted that Prunty had failed to pay previous docketing fees required for such motions. The SC ordered the clerk of the SC not to accept any further petitions from Prunty unless the required docketing fee was paid. The SC also observed that the present petition brought the total number of Prunty's frivolous filings to 10. However, the SC did not prevent Prunty from filing petitions challenging criminal sanctions that might be imposed on him. (*See also Judd v. U.S. Dist. Court of Texas* [1999] *and Dempsey v. Martin* [1999].) Contemporaneous with this decision, the SC also denied motions from Michael C. Antonelli (*Antonelli v. Caridine,* 528 U.S. 3, 120 S.Ct. 4 [1999]), who had filed 57 previous frivolous motions, Donald H. Brancato (*Brancato v. Gunn,* 528 U.S. 1, 120 S.Ct. 5 [1999]) who had filed eight previous frivolous motions, and Frederick W. Bauer (*In re Bauer,* 528 U.S. 16, 120 S.Ct. 6 [1999]), who had filed 12 previous frivolous motions. All denials were based on the same grounds as *Prunty.*

Pulley v. Harris, 465 U.S. 37, 104 S.Ct. 871 (1984) [**R. PULLEY, Warden, Petitioner, v. Robert Alton HARRIS**] (**Corrections; Death Penalty**) Harris was convicted of murder in a California court and sentenced to death. He appealed the sentence, alleging that the court had not considered his sentence of death in comparison with other similar situations in which the death penalty was not imposed. Thus, Harris claimed, the California death-penalty statute was unconstitutional because it did not require judges to make such a comparison. The SC upheld Harris' death sentence, holding that the Eighth Amendment is not violated when states do not consider other sentences imposed in other capital cases to determine whether a particular sentence is proportionate.

Purkett v. Elem, 514 U.S. 765, 115 S.Ct. 1769 (1995) [**James PURKETT, Superintendent, Farmington Corrections Center, v. Jimmy ELEM**] (**Habeas Corpus Petitions; Juries; Peremptory Challenges**) Elem, a black man, was accused of second-degree robbery. During the selection of jurors, the prosecutor used one of his peremptory challenges to strike from the jury pool a prospective black juror. Elem appealed, alleging that this use of a peremptory challenge was in violation of a policy set forth in *Batson v. Kentucky* (1986) prohibiting the use of peremptory challenges for racial purposes. The SC heard Elem's *habeas corpus* petition and argument. It upheld Elem's conviction when it determined that the prosecutor had used the peremptory challenge in a racially neutral fashion. The reason given for striking this black prospective juror was that the man had long, unkempt hair and a mustache and beard. The SC accepted this explanation as being race-neutral. It held that opponents of peremptory challenges must carry the burden of proving that purposeful discrimination has occurred. The explanation given by those exercising their peremptory challenges need not be persuasive or even plausible; rather, these explanations are considered only in determining whether opponents have carried their burden of proof by showing that the peremptory strikes were discriminatory. In this case, the peremptory challenge was satisfactorily explained and Elem's conviction was upheld.

R

Rakas v. Illinois, 439 U.S. 128, 99 S.Ct. 421 (1978) [RAKAS et al. v. ILLINOIS] (Law Enforcement Officers or Agencies; Open-Fields Doctrine; Plain-View Rule; Searches and Seizures; Stop and Frisk; Vehicle Searches) Rakas was a passenger in a car believed by police to be the getaway vehicle in a recent robbery. They stopped the car and conducted a warrantless search of it. They found incriminating evidence, including a sawed-off shotgun and ammunition, later used as evidence against Rakas, who was convicted of the robbery. Rakas appealed, attempting to suppress the evidence found in the vehicle because it was a result of a violation of his Fourth Amendment right against unreasonable searches and seizures. The SC upheld the conviction, saying that Rakas did not own the vehicle; thus, he could not interfere with the police search of it. In the SC's words, Rakas did not have a possessory interest in the car, and therefore, he could not claim a reasonable expectation of privacy in it.

R.A.V. v. City of St. Paul, Minn., 505 U.S. 377, 112 S.Ct. 2538 (1992) [R.A.V., Petitioner, v. CITY OF ST. PAUL, MINNESOTA] (Discrimination; First Amendment; Freedom of Religion) R.A.V. allegedly burned a cross on a black family's lawn. He was charged under a St. Paul ordinance that forbids such acts that "arouse anger, alarm, or resentment in others on the basis of race, color, creed, religion or gender." Following conviction, R.A.V. challenged the St. Paul ordinance as being invalid under the First Amendment. The SC reversed his conviction, saying that such an ordinance was overbroad and was facially invalid under the First Amendment.

Rawlings v. Kentucky, 448 U.S. 98, 100 S.Ct. 2556 (1980) [David RAWLINGS, Petitioner, v. Commonwealth of KENTUCKY] (Law Enforcement Officers or Agencies; Searches Incident to Arrest) Rawlings placed illegal drugs in the purse of a female friend. He later was convicted of possession of illegal drugs. He appealed, saying that the police had no right to search his friend's purse. The SC disagreed and upheld his conviction, saying that Rawlings had no reasonable expectation of privacy relative to putting illegal contraband into someone else's purse or personal property.

Reid v. Georgia, 448 U.S. 438, 100 S.Ct. 2752 (1980) [Tommy REID, Jr. v. State of GEORGIA] (Law Enforcement Officers or Agencies; Searches and Seizures) Reid was observed at the Atlanta airport with another person. They fit a profile of a particular drug carrier and were approached by a suspicious DEA agent. The agent asked them if they would accompany him to another airport area; during this walk, Reid fled, discarding his luggage. The DEA agent inspected the luggage and found that it contained drugs. Reid was arrested and eventually convicted. He appealed, alleging his Fourth Amendment rights had been violated. The SC overturned his conviction, noting that the DEA agent had had no reasonable suspicion, based on the totality of circumstances, to believe that Reid and the other person were engaging in any criminal activity. The SC said that the DEA agent's suspicions were more in the nature of an inchoate and unparticularized suspicion or hunch. This was too slender a reed to support the seizure in this case. Reid's case was vacated and remanded to the trial court. DEA agents need more than the factual information in this case to require persons in airports to stop and accompany them for further investigation.

Reno v. Koray, 515 U.S. 50, 115 S.Ct. 2021 (1995) [Janet RENO, Attorney General, et al., Petitioners, v. Ziya K. KORAY] (Corrections) Koray was arrested for laundering monetary instruments in violation of a federal statute. He was convicted and sentenced to 41 months in prison. Between his arrest and conviction, Koray was ordered "confined to the premises" of the Volunteers of America community treatment center, without authorization to leave unless accompanied by a government special agent. Koray appealed his 41-month sentence, arguing that he should be given credit for the time he had spent "in detention" in the community treatment program. The Third Circuit Court of Appeals reversed his conviction on those grounds, and the government appealed. The SC reversed the Third Circuit, upholding Koray's original 41-month sentence. The SC said that ordinarily, defendants might be entitled to time spent in official detention. However, the assignment of Koray to the community agency did not constitute official detention in the formal sense, and thus, the time he spent in this agency could not be counted as time against his 41-month sentence. This decision may seem like hairsplitting, but the SC said that official detention pertains only to those defendants placed in a penal or correctional facility and subject to the control of the Federal Bureau of Prisons (at 2021).

Rhode Island v. Innis, 446 U.S. 291, 100 S.Ct. 1682 (1981) [State of RHODE ISLAND, Petitioner, v. Thomas J. INNIS] (Confessions; Law Enforcement Officers or Agencies; *Miranda* Warning) Innis was suspected of the abduction and murder of a taxi driver. He was arrested by police, taken into custody, and told his *Miranda* rights. Two other officers arrived at that point and gave Innis his *Miranda* warning again. He was then driven to the police station. Both times after receiving the *Miranda* warning, Innis was asked if he wanted to speak with officers about the crime. Innis said he wanted an attorney and did not want to speak with the officers. While the officers were driving to the station, they talked among themselves, not with Innis. They spoke of how a shotgun was used in the murder and that it would be too bad if schoolchildren might find the shotgun and hurt themselves, as the murder occurred near a school. Innis interrupted the officers and asked them to drive him back to the murder scene, where subsequently he showed them where the shotgun was found. This evidence helped to convict Innis of the murder. He appealed, contending that his statements were inadmissible against him, as he had already asked for an attorney and had not wished to speak to police. The SC disagreed, saying that Innis had initiated the conversation on his own, that it had not been coerced by police, and that they had been talking among themselves, not to Innis. Thus, the conversation among the officers was not the functional equivalent of an interrogation, because the officers did not know that Innis would make a self-incriminating response and there was no express questioning of him.

Rhodes v. Chapman, 452 U.S. 337, 101 S.Ct. 2392 (1981) [James A. RHODES et al., Petitioners, v. Kelly CHAPMAN et al.] (Corrections; Cruel and Unusual Punishment; Eighth Amendment; Inmate Rights) Kelly Chapman and Richard Jaworski, two inmates of the Southern Ohio Correctional Facility, were housed in the same cell. They objected, contending that double-celling violated their constitutional rights. Furthermore, in support of their claim, they cited the facts that their confinement was *long-term* and not *short-term* as it was in *Bell v. Wolfish* (1979), that physical and mental injury would be sustained through such close contact and limited space for movement, and that the Ohio facility was housing 38 percent more inmates than its design capacity specified. The SC ruled that double-celling in this long-term prison facility was neither cruel and unusual punishment nor unconstitutional *per se.* The court based its holding on the "totality of circumstances" associated with Chapman's and Jaworski's confinement. The "cruel and unusual" provisions of the Eighth Amendment must be construed in a "flexible and dynamic" manner. Thus, when all factors were considered, no evidence existed that Ohio authorities were wantonly inflicting pain on these or other inmates. These conditions, considered in their totality, did not constitute serious deprivation. Double-celling, made necessary by the unanticipated increase in prisoners in the facility, had not resulted in food deprivations, a decrease in the quality of medical care, or a decrease in sanitation standards.

Richards v. Wisconsin, 520 U.S. 385, 117 S.Ct. 1416 (1997) [Steiney RICHARDS, Petitioner, v. WISCONSIN] (Fourth Amendment; Knock and Announce; Searches and Seizures) Richards was in a Madison, WI, hotel room and was targeted for investigation by police in an ongoing drug investigation. Police obtained a search warrant and knocked on Richards' hotel door, pretending to be repairmen. When Richards saw police, he slammed the door shut, and police rammed their way into his room, discovering drugs and related drug paraphernalia. Richards was convicted of drug offenses and appealed, contending that his Fourth Amendment right had been violated when police failed to announce their presence prior to forcing entry into his room. The SC upheld Richards' conviction and the seizure of evidence used against him. The SC held that (1) the Fourth Amendment does not permit a blanket exception to knock-and-announce requirements for felony drug investigations, and (2) that police officers' no-knock entry into Richards' hotel room did not violate his Fourth Amendment rights. The SC added that under the circumstances, police officers had suspicion to believe that Richards might destroy evidence if given further opportunity to do

so. Thus, exigency was a circumstantial factor further justifying the no-knock entry into Richards' hotel room.

Richardson v. Marsh, 481 U.S. 200, 107 S.Ct. 1702 (1987) [Gloria RICHARDSON, Warden, Petitioner, v. Clarissa MARSH] (Confrontation Clause; *Habeas Corpus* Petitions; Sixth Amendment) Clarissa Marsh was charged, with a companion, Benjamin Williams, and a third person, Martin, with assaulting Cynthia Knighton and murdering Knighton's 4-year-old son, and her aunt, Ollie Scott, at Scott's home. During Marsh's trial, Knighton testified as to Marsh's involvement in the murders. Furthermore, a confession, given by Williams, implicating Marsh, was read into the record shortly after his arrest. Williams did not take the stand to have his testimony rebutted by defense counsel. However, the judge instructed the jury to ignore references to Marsh in Williams' confession. Marsh was convicted of felony murder. She appealed by filing a writ of *habeas corpus* with the United States district court, alleging that her due-process right had been violated. Further, she alleged, her right to confront her accuser had been denied, when only Williams' confession was read without Williams actually testifying to authenticate it. The U.S. district court denied the writ, but the Sixth Circuit Court of Appeals granted it and reversed Marsh's conviction on grounds that she had been unable to confront and cross-examine her accuser. The state appealed to the SC, which reinstated Marsh's murder conviction. The SC held that the admission of a nontestifying codefendant's confession had not violated Marsh's rights under the confrontation clause because the judge had instructed the jury not to use the confession in any way against Marsh. Further, an inspection of the confession showed that it was not incriminating directly, but only indirectly, only when linked with other evidence introduced at Marsh's trial.

Richardson v. McKnight, 521 U.S. 399, 117 S.Ct. 2100 (1997) [Daryll RICHARDSON and John Walker, Petitioners, v. Ronnie Lee McKNIGHT] (Civil Rights, Section 1983 Claims; Corrections; Immunity) McKnight was a prisoner at Tennessee's South Central Correctional Center (SCCC), a private correctional facility, and brought suit against two prison guards for injuring him by placing upon him extremely tight physical restraints. The guards claimed that because of their qualified immunity as guards, they were not subject to lawsuits such as the one filed against them by McKnight. A U.S. district court ruled that they do not have qualified immunity, as they are employees of a private prison management firm. The immunity doctrine would only apply to state-employed prison guards. The guards appealed to the SC, who heard the case. The SC affirmed the lower court decision, declaring that prison guards who are employees of a private prison management firm are not entitled to qualified immunity from suits by prisoners charging a violation of Title 42 U.S.C. Section 1983. Thus, mere performance of a governmental function does not entitle a private person to qualified immunity under Section 1983, especially one who performs a job without government supervision or direction.

Richardson v. United States, 526 U.S. 813, 119 S.Ct. 1707 (1999) [Eddie RICHARDSON, Petitioner, v. UNITED

STATES] (Juries; Jury Instructions) Richardson was convicted in federal court for engaging in a "continuing criminal enterprise" (CCE). In deciding the case, the jury considered several different drug violations alleged against Richardson, each of which occurred at a different point in time. The judge instructed the jury that it must unanimously agree that Richardson committed a series of violations, and that he committed at least three of the numerous violations alleged, although he also instructed the jury that they did not have to unanimously agree as to which three violations made up the CCE. Jurors unanimously agreed that Richardson was guilty of committing a continuous series of violations, although they were not unanimous about any specific three violations that made up the continuing series. Richardson appealed to the SC, who heard the case. The SC vacated Richardson's conviction on the CCE charges, holding that a jury must not only unanimously agree that the defendant committed some continuing series of violations but must also unanimously agree about which specific violations make up that continuing series.

Richmond v. Lewis, 506 U.S. 40, 113 S.Ct. 528 (1992) [Willie Lee RICHMOND, Petitioner, v. Samuel A. LEWIS, Director, Arizona Department of Corrections, et al.] (Aggravating and Mitigating Circumstances; Death Penalty) Richmond was convicted of first-degree murder and given the death penalty. He appealed, arguing that one of the aggravating factors used by the judge in sentencing was vague and constituted a violation of his Eighth Amendment rights. At the time, the aggravating circumstance in question in Arizona courts was "especially heinous, cruel, or depraved." The SC heard the case and reversed Richmond's conviction and sentence, holding that the aggravating circumstance was indeed unconstitutionally vague.

Richmond Newspapers, Inc., v. Virginia, 448 U.S. 555, 100 S.Ct. 2814 (1978) [RICHMOND NEWSPAPERS, INC., v. Commonwealth of VIRGINIA et al.] (First Amendment; Free Press; Jury Trials; Media Rights) A murder case was being tried in a Virginia court. The court closed the proceedings to the public, including newspaper coverage. The Richmond Newspapers, Inc., filed suit to gain access to the trial proceedings under the First Amendment. The SC ruled that the right of the public to criminal trials is fundamental, including a right of access by the media, such as newspaper reporters. The press cannot be prevented from publishing truthful information about trial proceedings as long as the information has been obtained lawfully.

Ricketts v. Adamson, 483 U.S. 1, 107 S.Ct. 2680 (1987) [James G. RICKETTS, Director, Arizona Department of Corrections, et al., Petitioners, v. John H. ADAMSON] (Double Jeopardy; Plea Bargaining) Adamson was charged with murder. He entered into a plea bargain whereby he would plead guilty to second-degree murder and testify against his codefendants. The prosecutor indicated that if Adamson refused to cooperate, the terms of his plea agreement would be null and void. Adamson was convicted of second-degree murder, but during the later trial of his codefendants, he refused to testify. The Arizona Supreme Court reversed his conviction on the grounds outlined by the prosecutor, and Adamson was

tried again for first-degree murder. He was convicted and appealed, contending that this retrial was a violation of his double-jeopardy rights. The SC disagreed and upheld his first-degree murder conviction. The SC said that his prosecution for first- degree murder did not violate double-jeopardy principles, because his breach of the plea agreement removed the double-jeopardy bar that otherwise would have prevailed, assuming that under state law second-degree murder is a lesser included offense of first-degree murder.

Riggs v. California, 525 U.S. 1114, 119 S.Ct. 890 (1999) [Michael Wayne RIGGS, Petitioner, v. CALIFORNIA] (Eighth Amendment; Cruel and Unusual Punishment; Habitual Offender Statutes) Riggs was convicted in 1995 of stealing a bottle of vitamins from a supermarket. Because he had a prior criminal record, the misdemeanor offense of petty theft was elevated to a felony, and the three-strikes law became effective. Riggs was sentenced to a minimum of 25 years. Riggs appealed, alleging that the punishment was grossly disproportionate to his crime and that it violated the Eighth Amendment cruel and unusual punishment provision. The SC upheld Riggs' conviction and punishment, reaffirming the constitutionality of the three-strikes law enacted by California. The SC said that Riggs is not again punished for the first offense because the punishment is for the last offense committed, and it is rendered more severe in consequence of the situation into which Riggs has previously brought himself, referencing eight prior felony convictions.

Ring v. Arizona, ___U.S.___, 122 S.Ct. 2428 (2002) [Timothy Stuart RING, Petitioner, v. ARIZONA] (Bifurcated Trials; Death Penalty; Sixth Amendment) Ring was convicted by an Arizona jury of first-degree murder, conspiracy to commit armed robbery, and armed robbery. Following Ring's conviction, the judge determined by himself the existence of aggravating factors, and sentenced Ring to death. Ring appealed, contending that his Sixth Amendment right was violated when the jury was not permitted to determine the presence of mitigating or aggravating factors. According to Arizona law, judges were permitted to determine aggravating factors independent of the jury when the jury found a defendant guilty of first-degree murder. Ring's appeal was rejected by the Arizona Supreme Court, and he appealed to the SC, who heard the case. The SC reversed and remanded Ring's death sentence, finding that indeed, Ring's Sixth Amendment right to a jury trial and jury determination of aggravating and mitigating circumstances was violated. Juries, not judges, must determine the presence of any mitigating or aggravating factors.

Ristaino v. Ross, 424 U.S. 589, 96 S.Ct. 1017 (1976) [Theodore RISTAINO et al., Petitioners, v. James ROSS, Jr.] (Jury Trials) A black defendant was convicted of violent crimes against a white security guard. The defendant made a motion to question jurors about their racial prejudice during *voir dire.* An appeal was directed to the SC, where it was argued that the defendant had a constitutional right to ask jurors about racial prejudice. The SC upheld his conviction, saying that defendants do not have a constitutional right to question jurors about their racial prejudice. Judges may ask jurors about their racial prejudice; defendants may not.

Rivera v. Florida Department of Corrections, 526 U.S. 135, 119 S.Ct. 1167 (1999) [**Vincent F. RIVERA, Petitioner, v. FLORIDA DEPARTMENT OF CORRECTIONS**] (**Frivolous Lawsuits;** *In Forma Pauperis* **Motions**) Rivera was convicted of various crimes in Florida and subsequently filed at least 13 *in forma pauperis* petitions for *certiorari* to the SC. All filings were held by the SC to be frivolous; hence the clerk of the Court was ordered not to accept any subsequent petitions from Rivera unless he paid the docketing fees required under Rule 39.8 of the Federal Rules of Criminal Procedure.

Robbins v. California, 453 U.S. 420, 101 S.Ct. 2841 (1981) [**Jeffrey Richard ROBBINS, Petitioner, v. State of CALIFORNIA**] (**Closed Container Searches; Consent Searches; Law Enforcement Officers or Agencies; Vehicle Searches**) Officers stopped Robbins in his automobile for driving "erratically." They smelled marijuana when Robbins got out of the vehicle, and they placed him under arrest and searched the vehicle incident to an arrest. This warrantless search yielded a container in the trunk of Robbins' vehicle. The officers opened this container and discovered marijuana. They used this evidence against Robbins to secure a conviction of possession of marijuana. He appealed, arguing that the search of the container in his trunk had required a valid search warrant. The SC agreed with Robbins and overturned his conviction, holding that a closed container may not be opened without a warrant, even if found during a lawful search of an automobile. This case was modified by a later case entitling officers to search containers in automobiles.

Roberts v. LaVallee, 389 U.S. 40, 88 S.Ct. 194 (1967) [**Louis ROBERTS v. LaVALLEE, Warden**] (**Corrections; Indigent Clients; Inmate Rights**) Roberts was an indigent who was convicted in New York of various crimes incurring a 15- to 20-year prison sentence. Roberts appealed and demanded a free copy of the trial court transcript so that he could formulate an intelligent appeal of his sentence. His appeal was denied. The court declared that he was not entitled, as an indigent, to a free copy of the trial record for appeal purposes. The SC heard his petition and ruled in his favor, concluding that there was no doubt that the denial of a free transcript to the indigent Roberts was repugnant to his federal constitutional rights. Roberts had fully exhausted his state remedies and it was incumbent on the state to furnish Roberts with a free copy of the trial record because of his indigence.

Roberts v. Louisiana, 431 U.S. 633, 97 S.Ct. 1993 (1977) [**Harry ROBERTS, Petitioner, v. State of LOUISIANA**] (**Aggravating and Mitigating Circumstances; Death Penalty; Mandatory Death Penalty**) Roberts was convicted of killing a police officer in Louisiana, where there was a mandatory death penalty for such an offense. The death penalty was imposed and Roberts appealed. The SC overturned the sentence, holding that mandatory death penalties are unconstitutional because they do not allow consideration of aggravating and mitigating circumstances.

Robinson v. California, 370 U.S. 660, 82 S.Ct. 1417 (1962) [**Lawrence ROBINSON, Appellant, v. State of CALIFORNIA**] (**Corrections; Inmate Rights**) Robinson was convicted in Los Angeles of being addicted to narcotics. On appeal, the SC overturned his conviction, saying that the status of narcotic addiction is not a crime and thus cannot be treated as a crime by a California trial court.

Robinson v. United States, 516 U.S. 137, 116 S.Ct. 501 (1995) [**Roland J. Bailey, Petitioner, v. United States. Candisha Summerita ROBINSON, aka Candysha Robinson, Petitioner, v. UNITED STATES**] (**Law Enforcement Officers or Agencies; Searches and Seizures**) Robinson sold some crack cocaine to an undercover officer in a "controlled buy" set up in advance. The officer observed her obtain the crack cocaine from the bedroom of her one-bedroom apartment. A search warrant was obtained and her apartment was searched, disclosing more crack cocaine in a locked trunk in her bedroom closet together with an unloaded .22-caliber Derringer pistol. She was convicted of selling crack cocaine, and her sentence was enhanced because a weapon had been discovered in close proximity to the cocaine. The SC overturned the sentence enhancement, concluding that there was no evidence, other than mere proximity of the weapon to the cocaine itself, to indicate that Robinson intended actively to employ the weapon in the commission of the offense (*See Bailey v. United States* [1995] *for a similar opinion*). Offenders must *actively use* a weapon or have it readily available while committing their conviction offenses in order for sentence enhancements to be made.

Rochin v. California, 342 U.S. 165, 72 S.Ct. 205 (1952) [**Antonio Richard ROCHIN, Petitioner, v. People of CALIFORNIA**] (**Exclusionary Rule; Law Enforcement Officers or Agencies**) Rochin, a suspect allegedly trafficking in narcotics, was visited by sheriff's deputies one evening. Officers found him sitting on his bed partially dressed. Several white capsules were on a nearby nightstand in plain view. When officers attempted to seize them, Rochin grabbed the capsules and swallowed them. Officers immediately brought Rochin to a nearby hospital and ordered physicians to give him an emetic solution to cause him to vomit. The capsules were obtained through a stomach pump and turned out to be morphine. These capsules were used against him later in court, and he was convicted. He appealed. His conviction was overturned because of the unreasonableness of the manner of the officers' search and seizure of the capsules. In a written opinion, the SC labeled the police tactics offensive and "conduct that shocks the conscience."

Rock v. Arkansas, 483 U.S. 44, 107 S.Ct. 2704 (1987) [**Vickie Lorene ROCK, Petitioner, v. ARKANSAS**] (**Sixth Amendment**) Rock was charged with shooting her husband. She underwent tape-recorded hypnosis sessions as a means of refreshing her memory. During her trial, she attempted to testify and provide details about the shooting that had been elicited under hypnosis, but the court prevented her from doing so. Instead, she was limited to testifying about the events as she recalled them before being subjected to hypnosis. Following her conviction, she appealed, alleging that her right to give testimony in her own behalf had been infringed by the judge's ruling limiting her testimony. The SC heard the case and reversed her conviction, holding that the Arkansas rule prohibiting hypnotically refreshed testimony was unconstitutional. Rock should have been permitted to give all relevant testimony, whether or not it had been induced hypnotically.

Roe v. Wade, 410 U.S. 113, 93 S.Ct. 705 (1973) [**Jane ROE, et al., Appellants, v. Henry WADE**] (**Abortion; Fourteenth Amendment**) A pregnant single woman, Jane Roe, brought a class-action suit challenging the constitutionality of Texas criminal abortion laws, which prohibited procuring or attempting to procure an abortion except on medical advice for the purpose of saving the mother's life. Roe sought declaratory and injunctive relief. Roe wished to terminate her pregnancy by an abortion performed by a licensed doctor under safe, clinical conditions; also, she declared that she was unable to get a legal abortion because her life did not appear to be threatened by a continuation of her pregancy, and that she could not afford to travel to another jurisdiction in order to secure a legal abortion under safe conditions. Among her other claims were that the Texas statutes regarding abortion were unconstitutionally vague so as to deprive her of her right of personal privacy protected by the First, Fourth, Fifth, Ninth, and Fourteenth Amendments. A three-judge U.S. district court entered a judgment declaring the Texas abortion laws unconstitutional, and Texas appealed. The SC heard the case and held that the Texas criminal abortion statutes prohibiting abortions at any stage of pregnancy except to save the life of the mother were unconstitutional; that prior to approximately the end of the first trimester the abortion decision and its effectuation must be left to the medical judgment of the pregnant woman's attending physician; that subsequent to approximately the end of the first trimester the state may regulate abortion procedure in ways reasonably related to maternal health; and that at the stage subsequent to viability (i.e., where the fetus has the capability of meaningful life outside the mother's womb) the state may regulate and even prohibit abortion except where necessary in appropriate medical judgment for preservation of the life or health of the mother.

Rogers v. Richmond, 365 U.S. 534, 81 S.Ct. 735 (1961) [**Harold D. ROGERS, Petitioner, v. Mark S. RICHMOND, Warden**] (**Confessions; *Habeas Corpus* Petitions; Law Enforcement Officers or Agencies**) Rogers was arrested on robbery charges. While jailed, he was subjected to a grueling intensive interrogation. Further, his lawyer was turned away when trying to reach him. There was considerable evidence that police used psychological tactics on Rogers and eventually secured a confession of murder from him. He was convicted. He appealed, contending that his confession had been coerced. His murder conviction was overturned, largely on procedural grounds, because the state trial court had misconstrued the applicable law relating to confessions, and it had erred in affirming a lower-court denial of Rogers' *habeas corpus* petition alleging the coercion.

Rogers v. Tennessee, 532 U.S. 451, 121 S.Ct. 1693 (2001) [**Wilbert K. ROGERS, Petitioner, v. TENNESSEE**] (**Common Law; Due Process; Retroactive Rules**) Wilbert Rogers was convicted of the second-degree murder of James Bowdery. Bowdery was stabbed by Rogers, but Bowdery didn't die until

15 months later. Rogers appealed to the Tennessee Court of Criminal Appeals, claiming that under Tennessee common law, he could not be convicted of murder unless his victim died within a year and a day following the act. Since Bowdery had died 15 months later, the common-law rule was cited by Rogers to justify why his conviction should be overturned. The Tennessee Court of Criminal Appeals disagreed and affirmed Rogers' conviction. At the same time, the Tennessee Supreme Court abolished the common-law rule, finding that the reasons for recognizing the rule at common law no longer existed. Rogers appealed to the SC, who heard his case. Rogers claimed that the Tennessee Supreme Court action was an unconstitutional retroactive abolition of a common law that denied Rogers due process of law under the Fourteenth Amendment. The SC affirmed the Tennessee Supreme Court, holding that retroactive application to Rogers of its decision abolishing the year-and-a-day rule did not deny Rogers due process of law in violation of the Fourteenth Amendment. The SC declared that Tennessee's abolition of the year-and-a-day rule was not unexpected or indefensible. Advances in medical and related sciences have so undermined the rule's usefulness that it has been legislatively or judicially declared obsolete or abolished in the vast majority of jurisdictions.

Rosales-Lopez v. United States, 451 U.S. 182, 101 S.Ct. 1629 (1981) [**Humberto ROSALES-LOPEZ, Petitioner, v. UNITED STATES**] (**Corrections; Death Penalty**) Rosales-Lopez was suspected of conspiracy to admit illegal aliens into the United States. Prior to his trial, he asked the judge and prosecutor to conduct a *voir dire* to determine whether any prospective jurors were prejudiced against him and Mexicans generally. The judge refused to question jurors about potential racial or ethnic bias. Rosales-Lopez was convicted. He appealed, alleging that the failure of the judge to ask these questions had deprived him of significant due-process rights and a fair trial. The SC upheld his conviction, noting that the role of Rosales-Lopez in the smuggling operation had nothing to do with a racial or ethnic bias question, and thus, the judge was not obligated to confront prospective jurors with this issue of prejudice.

Rose v. Clark, 478 U.S. 570, 106 S.Ct. 3101 (1986) [**Jimmy C. ROSE, Warden, Petitioner, v. Stanley Barham CLARK**] (**Jury Instructions**) Charles Browning and Joy Faulk were shot to death while they sat in Browning's pickup truck in Rutherford County, TN. Stanley Clark, Faulk's former boyfriend, became a suspect and was subsequently charged with murder. During his trial, Clark attempted to blame Faulk's ex-husband for the murders. Also, Clark claimed that at the time, he (Clark) was insane or incapable of forming the requisite criminal intent. The prosecution rejected both claims. During the issuance of instructions to the jury, the judge defined the elements of the crimes alleged, including malice, which involved a killing "upon sudden impulse" if committed with intent to harm another. Clark was convicted, and he appealed. The Tennessee Supreme Court reversed Clark's conviction because the court believed that the jury instruction shifted the burden of proof to the defendant regarding the question of "malice." Thus, the court argued, the prosecution did not have to prove *all* criminal elements beyond a reasonable doubt. Eventually, the SC heard the case and reversed the lower court, reinstating Clark's conviction. In a carefully worded opinion, the SC said that the lower court would have to determine whether the error committed in this case (i.e., the jury instruction as to malice) was harmless beyond a reasonable doubt.

Rose v. Lundy, 455 U.S. 509, 102 S.Ct. 1198 (1982) [**Jim ROSE, Warden, Petitioner, v. Noah Harrison LUNDY**] (Corrections; *Habeas Corpus* Petitions) Lundy was a Tennessee prison inmate who had been convicted of rape and crimes against nature. He filed a writ of *habeas corpus* in federal court, seeking to overturn his conviction on various grounds, including the allegation that he had not been permitted to cross-examine his accusers adequately, that his fair trial chances had been impaired by the prosecutor's closing remarks, and that the trial judge had given improper jury instructions. The SC upheld Lundy's conviction, saying that Lundy had not exhausted all state remedies before bringing his action to federal courts. The significance of this case is that it obligates any state prisoner first to exhaust all state appeals before bringing a case to a federal court. *Habeas corpus* petitions challenge several things, including the fact, nature, and length of confinement. In Lundy's case, such a filing was tantamount to challenging his entire trial scenario, such that a new trial would have to be granted depending on the SC's action. One intent of this ruling is to lessen the sheer numbers of prisoner petitions that are processed by federal courts.

Rose v. Mitchell, 443 U.S. 545, 99 S.Ct. 2993 (1979) [**Jim ROSE, Warden, Petitioner, v. James E. MITCHELL and James Nichols, Jr.**] (Grand Juries; *Habeas Corpus* Petitions) James Mitchell, a black man, was accused of murder following an indictment from an all white county grand jury in Tennessee. The trial itself was properly conducted and a jury determined Mitchell to be guilty. Later, as an inmate of the Tennessee State Prison, Mitchell filed a *habeas corpus* petition, alleging that the grand jury had been racially discriminatory because it excluded blacks. The SC overturned his conviction, noting that racial discrimination in the selection of a grand jury is a valid ground for setting aside a guilty verdict, even where a defendant has been found guilty beyond a reasonable doubt by a petit jury at a trial that was free of other constitutional error. Further, the SC declared that such claims of discrimination are rightly included as a part of a *habeas corpus* petition.

Rosenberg v. United States, 346 U.S. 273, 73 S.Ct. 1152 (1953) [**Julius ROSENBERG et ux., Petitioners, v. UNITED STATES**] (Corrections; Death Penalty) Julius Rosenberg and his wife, Ethel, were convicted of violating the Espionage Act and sentenced to death. Rosenberg appealed, desiring a stay of execution; the appeal was rejected. The issue was whether a district judge had the power to impose the death sentence without a jury recommendation to that effect. The SC upheld the Rosenbergs' death sentence, holding that judges do have the right to impose death sentences.

Ross v. Moffitt, 417 U.S. 600, 94 S.Ct. 2437 (1974) [**Fred R. ROSS and North Carolina, Petitioners, v. Claude Franklin MOFFITT**] (Corrections; Indigent Clients; Inmate Rights) This case involved a convicted indigent offender who desired to have court-appointed counsel in order to lodge an appeal with the North Carolina Supreme Court. The SC declared that indigent defendants are not entitled, as a matter of right, to court-appointed counsel for discretionary appeals to higher courts. Thus, it is not a violation of due process to deny attorneys to convicted offenders for making such appeals.

Ross v. Oklahoma, 487 U.S. 85, 108 S.Ct. 2273 (1988) [**Bobby Lynn ROSS, Petitioner, v. OKLAHOMA**] (Corrections; Death Penalty) Ross was accused of first-degree murder in Oklahoma. During the impaneling of a jury, a juror was not eliminated for cause, but should have been. Ross' lawyer had to use one of his peremptory challenges to excuse this particular juror. Ross' attorney regarded this as a "waste" of a perfectly good peremptory challenge, thus limiting the favorableness of the jury for Ross' benefit. Ross was convicted; he appealed, contesting this point. The SC upheld his conviction, holding that a failure to exclude a prospective juror for cause and causing the defense to use one of its peremptory challenges to do so does not deprive defendants of due process of law. Ross' right to an impartial jury was not violated when his lawyer was required to use a peremptory challenge to excuse a juror who should have been rejected for cause anyway.

Roth v. United States, 345 U.S. 476, 77 S.Ct. 1304 (1957) [**Samuel ROTH, Petitioner, v. UNITED STATES**] (First Amendment; Free Press; Free Speech; Obscenity Laws) Roth was convicted of violating a federal obscenity statute prohibiting the distribution of a periodical magazine containing nude photographs of persons through the United States mail. He appealed, contending that the statute under which he was convicted was a violation of his First Amendment right to free speech and free press. The SC disagreed, saying that the obscenity ordinance in question was not violative of any particular constitutional right. Thus, United States Post Office authorities may utilize the federal obscenity statute as the proper exercise of their power.

Roviaro v. United States, 353 U.S. 53, 77 S.Ct. 623 (1957) [**Albert ROVIARO, Petitioner, v. UNITED STATES**] (Informants) Roviaro was convicted of illegally selling heroin and transporting it. His conviction was based in part on information supplied by an unknown informant who remained unknown throughout Roviaro's trial. The government sought to keep the informant's identity confidential. Roviaro appealed, alleging that he had not had the Fifth Amendment right to cross-examine his accuser. Thus, it was conceivable that the informant might have had exculpatory evidence to give that might have been favorable to Roviaro. The SC reversed Roviaro's conviction, saying that if an informer's testimony may be relevant and helpful to the accused's defense, such informant identity should be disclosed and the informant should be compelled to testify through cross-examination. Thus the government had been wrong to withhold the identity of its undercover employee in the face of repeated demands by the accused for his disclosure.

Ruffin v. Commonwealth, 62 Va. (21 Gratt) 790 (1871) (Corrections; Inmate Rights) A Virginia judge declared that "prisoners have no more rights than slaves." This remark became infamous as the beginning of the hands-off era of the SC toward corrections. The SC declined to hear most corrections cases because of its belief that corrections personnel and administrators are in the best position to understand, and know what is best for, the prisoners they supervise.

Rufo v. Inmates of Suffolk County Jail, 502 U.S. 367, 112 S.Ct. 748 (1992) [Robert C. RUFO, Sheriff of Suffolk County, et al., Petitioners, v. INMATES OF the SUFFOLK COUNTY JAIL et al. Thomas C. Rapone, Commissioner of Corrections of Massachusetts, Petitioner, v. Inamtes of the Suffolk County Jail et al.] (Corrections; Inmate Rights) Suffolk County Jail was under a consent decree to improve jail conditions through new construction that would create several single-occupancy cells for pretrial detainees. Construction delays prevented the jail from being redesigned as planned, the jail inmate population escalated, and the sheriff made a motion to the court to modify the original consent decree temporarily to allow double-bunking because of overcrowding. The court denied the motion, and the sheriff appealed. The SC overruled the lower-court decision, indicating that whenever factual conditions of original consent decrees change in ways that make it impossible to comply with such consent decree provisions, some relief of a temporary nature can be granted. Thus, consent decrees may be modified, provided there are circumstances that justify such modifications.

Rugendorf v. United States, 376 U.S. 528, 84 S.Ct. 825 (1964) [Samuel Joseph RUGENDORF, Petitioner, v. UNITED STATES] (Informants) FBI agents obtained a search warrant for Rugendorf's residence, where they believed that a large quantity of stolen furs were stored. Information from reliable informants and from hearsay from other informants led to the issuance of the warrant. Furs were found matching descriptions of those that were stolen, and Rugendorf was convicted. He appealed, saying that "hearsay evidence" was an insufficient basis for probable cause to obtain a valid search warrant. The SC upheld his conviction, saying that reliable-informant information had been supplemented with hearsay information, but that the hearsay information had merely corroborated the reliable-informant information. The search warrant, therefore, had been valid, and thus the evidence seized as the result of the warrant could be used against Rugendorf at his subsequent trial.

Rummel v. Estelle, 445 U.S. 263, 100 S.Ct. 1133 (1980) [William James RUMMEL, Petitioner, v. W.J. ESTELLE, Jr., Director, Texas Department of Corrections] (Cruel and Unusual Punishment; Eighth Amendment) Rummel had previously been convicted of two nonviolent felonies. Under a Texas recidivist statute, he was convicted and given a life sentence. He appealed to the SC, which upheld the sentence. The SC said that life sentences for violating habitual-offender statutes are *not* cruel and unusual in violation of the Eighth Amendment. (*See Solem v. Helm* [1983] *for a comparable case.*)

Rushen v. Spain, 464 U.S. 114, 104 S.Ct. 453 (1983) [Ruth RUSHEN, Director, California Department of Corrections, et al. v. Johnny SPAIN] (Corrections; Eighth Amendment; *Habeas Corpus* Petitions; Jury Instructions) Spain was an inmate at San Quentin prison in California during a prison riot in 1971, in which three prisoners and three corrections officers were killed. Spain was one of six prisoners tried for the murders of these persons, and he was convicted. During the *voir dire,* jurors were asked if they knew any members of the Black Panther Party, blacks who aggressively supported government reform on racial issues. No jurors indicated such knowledge. However, during the trial, one juror, Fagan, reported to the judge that she was familiar with someone involved in a murder case that was mentioned but was not one involving any of the specific defendants, including Spain. She went to the judge's chambers on several occasions to indicate her emotional concern over the mentioned case. The judge asked Fagan if her judgment would be impaired in deciding the guilt or innocence of the six defendants. She said that she could make an impartial judgment. Subsequently, they were convicted of murder, and Spain was sentenced to life imprisonment. Spain appealed and filed a *habeas corpus* petition with the federal district court, noting that he had not been permitted to be a party to the various exchanges between the juror, Fagan, and the judge during the trial. Thus, he argued, he had been deprived of a fair trial. The U.S. district court as well as the Ninth Circuit Court of Appeals held that an unrecorded *ex parte* communication between the trial judge and a juror can never be harmless error, and Spain's conviction was reversed. However, the government appealed. The SC heard the case and reinstated Spain's conviction and life sentence. The SC held that communications between the trial judge and the juror, as transpired in this particular case, were harmless. The judge had assured himself that the juror would maintain her impartiality throughout the trial, and the integrity of the proceeding had not been compromised.

Rutledge v. United States, 517 U.S. 292, 116 S.Ct. 1241 (1996) [Tommy L. RUTLEDGE, Petitioner, v. UNITED STATES] (Double Jeopardy) Rutledge was convicted in federal court of charges relating to conspiracy to distribute controlled substances and one count of conducting a continuing criminal enterprise in concert with others. Both convictions stemmed from the conspiracy to distribute cocaine. The court sentenced Rutledge to two concurrent life-without-parole terms and imposed special assessments of $50 for each count. Rutledge appealed on double-jeopardy grounds, and the SC heard his case. The SC held that Congress intended to authorize only one punishment. Thus, because Rutledge was convicted, based on the same underlying conduct, of both the offense of conducting a continuing criminal enterprise and of conspiracy to distribute controlled substances, which was a lesser included offense of the "continuing criminal enterprise" offense, one of his convictions and concurrent sentences had to be vacated. Courts cannot impose multiple punishments for the same criminal activity, as that would violate the defendant's right against double jeopardy.

S

Sandin v. Conner, 515 U.S. 472, 115 S.Ct. 2293 (1995) [Cinda SANDIN, Unit Team Manager, Halawa Correctional Facility, Petitioner, v. Demont R.D. CONNER et al.] (Corrections; Inmate Rights) A Hawaiian prisoner, Conner, was placed in solitary confinement following a disciplinary hearing pertaining to a charge of misconduct. Conner wanted to call certain prisoners as witnesses on his behalf during the adjustment committee hearing, but the authorities denied his request. He appealed, arguing that his due-process rights had been violated because of this committee action. The SC heard Conner's case and determined that he did not have a liberty interest in committee proceedings. Further, it determined that the committee action had not affected his parole eligibility date or sentence length. The SC said that in Conner's case, discipline in segregated confinement did not present the type of atypical, significant deprivation in which a state might conceivably create a liberty interest. In addition, his confinement did not present a case in which the state's action would inevitably affect the duration of his sentence, because the chance that the misconduct finding would affect his parole status was simply too attenuated to invoke the due-process clause's procedural guarantee.

Santobello v. New York, 404 U.S. 257, 92 S.Ct. 495 (1971) [Rudolph SANTOBELLO, Petitioner, v. NEW YORK] (Plea Bargaining) Santobello was charged with two felony counts and pleaded guilty to a lesser included offense following a promise by the prosecutor not to make a sentence recommendation at the plea bargain hearing. Several months lapsed, and in the meantime, a new prosecutor was appointed and represented the government at Santobello's plea hearing. At this time, the prosecutor recommended the maximum sentence under the law, and Santobello moved to withdraw his guilty plea. The judge refused to allow the withdrawal of the guilty plea, and Santobello was sentenced to the maximum sentence. The SC heard Santobello's appeal. Santobello alleged that the prosecutor was honor bound to stand by his statement not to make a sentence recommendation, despite the fact that the judge said that he was "uninfluenced" by the prosecutor's recommendation. The SC overturned Santobello's conviction and allowed him to withdraw his guilty plea, saying that when a guilty plea rests to a significant degree on a promise or agreement by the prosecutor, such a promise must be fulfilled. The significance of this case is that prosecutors cannot make promises to defendants to elicit guilty pleas unless they fulfill their promises.

Satterwhite v. Texas, 486 U.S. 249, 108 S.Ct. 1792 (1988) [John T. SATTERWHITE, Petitioner, v. TEXAS] (Death Penalty; Juries) Satterwhite was charged in the murder of Mary Davis during a robbery in Texas. He was arrested and several psychiatric evaluations were made of him at the request of the court. A psychiatrist, Dr. Grigson, conducted some of these evaluations and delivered an opinion to the court that he regarded Satterwhite as having "a severe antisocial personality disorder" and that he was "extremely dangerous and will commit future acts of violence." Subsequently, Satterwhite was convicted by a jury. During the penalty phase of his trial, Dr. Grigson was called over defense objections to testify about his "future dangerousness." It was also noted that Dr. Grigson's findings had not been delivered to defense counsel prior to the penalty phase of Satterwhite's trial. Following the imposition of the death sentence, Satterwhite appealed, alleging that his Sixth Amendment right to effective assistance of counsel had been violated. He further argued that Dr. Grigson's testimony about his "future dangerousness" should not have been allowed. The Texas Supreme Court heard the case and decided that although the testimony might be error, it was harmless. Satterwhite then appealed to the SC, which held that the finding of future dangerousness is critical in a sentence of death. Dr. Grigson was the only person to testify on this issue, and the prosecution had placed great weight on this testimony. The SC found it impossible to say beyond a reasonable doubt that Grigson's testimony about Satterwhite's future dangerousness had not influenced the jury in their sentence recommendation. Therefore, the SC reversed the Texas Supreme Court regarding the death sentence and remanded the case to the trial court for further proceedings.

Saucier v. Katz, 533 U.S. 194, 121 S.Ct. 2151 (2001) [Donald SAUCIER, Petitioner, v. Elliot M. KATZ and In Defense of Animals] (Excessive Force; Fourth Amendment; Free Speech; Immunity; Police Misconduct) During a speech by Vice President Al Gore in 1994 delivered at the Presidio Army Base in San Francisco, a protestor, Elliot Katz, attempted to unfurl a cloth banner in the direction of the vice president, which read, "Please Keep Animal Torture Out of Our National Parks." Office Donald Saucier was a military police officer at the time who saw Katz and identified him as a potential protestor. When Saucier saw what Katz was about to do, he moved in and intercepted him. Officer Saucier took Katz into custody and placed him in a nearby military van. Katz was driven to a military police station where he was held for a brief period and then released. Katz filed suit against Office Saucier for allegedly violating his Fourth Amendment rights by using excessive force to arrest him. Saucier moved for a summary judgment, citing qualified immunity on all claims. The federal district court denied the motion, and Saucier appealed. The Ninth Circuit Court of Appeals affirmed the federal district court decision, and Saucier appealed to the SC, who heard the case. The SC reversed the Ninth Circuit and held that Saucier was entitled to qualified immunity. The SC also held that the force used, dragging Katz from the area and shoving him while placing him in the van, was not so excessive that he suffered hurt or injury.

Saxbe v. Washington Post Co., 417 U.S. 843, 94 S.Ct. 2811 (1974) [William B. SAXBE, Attorney General of the United States, et al., Petitioners, v. The WASHINGTON POST CO. et al.] (Corrections; Free Press; Inmate Rights) The *Washington Post* wished to conduct interviews with various federal prison inmates. At the time, the Federal Bureau of Prisons had a policy prohibiting such interviews. The *Post* filed a lawsuit challenging the constitutionality of this regulation.

The SC upheld the right of the Federal Bureau of Prisons to forbid or prohibit interviews by the press or media generally with particular inmates. (*See the related case of Pell v. Procunier* [1974] *for a similar decision affecting state prisons and their regulations.*)

Schad v. Arizona, 501 U.S. 624, 111 S.Ct. 2491 (1991) [Edward Harold SCHAD, Jr., Petitioner, v. ARIZONA] (Death Penalty) Schad was charged with the death of a 74-year-old motorist when he was apprehended by police in the victim's stolen vehicle in Prescott, AZ. The prosecutor advanced various theories about first-degree murder and felony murder. Schad attempted to persuade the judge to instruct the jury on a lesser included offense of theft or robbery, because Schad believed that only circumstantial evidence linked him to the death of the victim. The judge denied Schad's request but did instruct the jury to consider first-degree and felony-murder charges and their elements in their deliberations. Schad appealed, alleging that his due-process rights had been violated when the judge failed to instruct the jury on the lesser included offense. The SC rejected Schad's appeal on the grounds that the failure of the judge to instruct the jury on the lesser included offense of robbery had not rendered the first-degree murder verdict the result of impermissible choice because sufficient evidence existed to support a second-degree murder conviction anyway.

Schall v. Martin, 467 U.S. 253, 104 S.Ct. 2403 (1984) [Ellen SCHALL, Commissioner of New York City Department of Juvenile Justice, v. Gregory MARTIN et al. Robert Abrams, Attorney General of New York, v. Gregory Martin et al.] (Juvenile Law; Preventive Detention) Martin, age 14, was arrested at 11:30 p.m. on December 13, 1977, in New York City. He was charged with first-degree robbery, second-degree assault, and criminal possession of a weapon. Martin lied to police at the time, giving a false name and address. Between the time of his arrest and December 29, when a fact-finding hearing was held, Martin was detained (a total of 15 days). His detention was based largely on the false information he had supplied to police and the seriousness of the charges pending against him. Subsequently, he was adjudicated a delinquent and placed on two years' probation. Later, his attorney filed an appeal, contesting his preventive detention as violative of the due-process clause of the Fourteenth Amendment. The SC eventually heard the case and upheld the detention as constitutional.

Scher v. United States, 305 U.S. 251, 59 S.Ct. 174 (1938) [Hyman SCHER, aka William Scher, Petitioner, v. UNITED STATES] (Law Enforcement Officers or Agencies; Searches and Seizures) A reliable informant advised police of a particular liquor transaction that would occur on a certain evening, and police conducted surveillance. At one point, they saw Scher move his automobile from one location to another, and they followed him. When he parked in an open garage, police moved in and told Scher that he was suspected of carrying illegal liquor. Scher admitted that he was carrying "a little" for a party, and he told police that the liquor was in the trunk. Police arrested him and conducted a warrantless search of his trunk, where they discovered illegal whiskey. Scher was con-

victed. He appealed, contending that officers had needed a search warrant to search his trunk. The SC disagreed and upheld his conviction, holding that the officers had seen and heard suspicious activity. The officers properly could have stopped Scher's car and made a search when putting him under arrest. Passage of the car into the open garage had not destroyed this right. Thus, examination of an automobile accompanied by an arrest, without objection and upon admission of probable guilt, was such that the officers had done nothing either unreasonable or oppressive.

Scheuer v. Rhodes, 416 U.S. 232, 94 S.Ct. 1683 (1974) [Sarah SCHEUER, Administratrix, etc., Petitioner, v. James RHODES et al. Arthur Krause, Administrator of the Estate of Allison Krause, et al., Petitioners, v. James Rhodes et al.] (Civil Rights, Section 1983 Claims) Initial complaints filed by families or victims involved in the Kent State University shootings of students by national guardsmen in May 1970 were dismissed by lower courts, which accepted the good-faith argument that national guardsmen were acting consistently with statutes and governor orders to quell riots and campus disturbances. The SC reinstated the complaints, ordering consideration of further proceedings to determine the merits of the filings. The SC held that it was erroneous to accept the guardsmen's actions as good-faith behaviors. The courts had to determine whether those issues had merit.

Schick v. Reed, 419 U.S. 256, 95 S.Ct. 379 (1974) [Maurice SCHICK, Petitioner, v. George J. REED, Chairman of the United States Board of Parole, et al.] (Death Penalty) Schick was a United States Army sergeant in Japan, where he was convicted of murdering an 8-year-old girl and sentenced to death in 1954. He alleged insanity when he was originally court-martialed, but the court rejected his defense. In March 1960, his case was sent to President Eisenhower, who commuted his death sentence to life imprisonment for the "term of his natural life." Subsequently, Schick learned that had he originally been given a simple sentence of life imprisonment, he would currently be eligible for parole. Thus, he petitioned the parole board for early release. His parole was denied. Schick appealed, alleging that it was "unfair" *not* to be eligible for parole, because many prisoners in the early 1970s were having their death sentences changed to simple life sentences and were becoming "parole eligible." The SC heard his case and determined that the fact of a presidential commutation order is not the equivalent of cases involving death penalties being changed to life sentences for prisoners when the case of *Furman v. Georgia* was decided in 1972. Thus, the "no-parole" decision of President Eisenhower was binding on Schick's case.

Schilb v. Kuebel, 404 U.S. 357, 92 S.Ct. 479 (1971) [John SCHILB et al., Applicants, v. Vincent P. KUEBEL et al.] (Bail) In a case in Illinois in which a defendant was ultimately acquitted, 1 percent of the bail amount was forfeited to the bail bond company, which by Illinois law is permitted to make a small amount of money as a commission for posting bail for criminal suspects. Schilb and others filed a class-action suit against the bail bond company as being discriminatory and unconstitutional in its procedures. They further challenged the release-on-own-recognizance scheme as discriminatory. The SC upheld the Illinois bail law, saying that its fee of 1 percent of bail was not excessive and that there had been no discrimination between the poor and the rich; in short, the Illinois law did not violate any constitutional amendment.

Schmerber v. California, 384 U.S. 757, 86 S.Ct. 1826 (1966) [**Armando SCHMERBER, Petitioner, v. State of CALIFORNIA**] (**Law Enforcement Officers or Agencies; Searches and Seizures**) Schmerber was arrested in California for driving under the influence of alcohol following an accident. He was brought to a hospital, where a nurse drew a sample of his blood against his will while he was being treated for injuries. The blood specimen became inculpatory evidence against him later in court, and he was convicted of DWI. He appealed, contending that the seizure of his blood had been unreasonable and had violated his Fourth Amendment rights. Furthermore, he argued that his own blood used against him was tantamount to self-incrimination and thus violated his Fifth Amendment rights. The SC disagreed on both counts, declaring that drawing blood without one's consent, when done by medical personnel, does not violate one's constitutional rights against unreasonable search and seizure. The SC rejected the Fifth Amendment violation argument by noting that this right pertained only to testimony, not blood evidence. The court added that exigent circumstances existed in that situation, because a delay would have prevented officers from obtaining a valid sample of Schmerber's blood to show its true alcohol content at or near the time of the accident.

Schneckloth v. Bustamonte, 412 U.S. 218, 93 S.Ct. 2041 (1973) [**Merle R. SCHNECKLOTH, Superintendent, California Conservation Center, Petitioner, v. Robert Clyde BUSTAMONTE**] (**Consent Searches; Fourth Amendment; Law Enforcement Officers or Agencies; Searches and Seizures; Vehicle Searches**) One evening, police observed an automobile with a broken tail light and stopped it. The driver had no driver's license and was asked to step out of the car together with several other occupants. One passenger, Alcala, had a driver's license and told police that the automobile belonged to his brother. The officers asked if they could search the vehicle and Alcala consented. While conducting their search, the officers discovered stolen checks from a car wash and arrested one of the passengers, Bustamonte. Bustamonte was later convicted of possessing checks with intent to defraud. He appealed, seeking to have the checks suppressed as evidence against him. The SC disagreed, saying that Alcala, who had constructive possession of the vehicle, was in a position to give police consent to conduct their search. Therefore, the evidence they later discovered as the result of that search was valid and had not violated Bustamonte's Fourth Amendment rights.

Schwartz v. Texas, 344 U.S. 199, 73 S.Ct. 232 (1952) [**SCHWARTZ, Petitioner, v. State of TEXAS**] (**Electronic Surveillance, Wiretapping; Law Enforcement Officers or Agencies**) Schwartz was a pawnbroker who entered into a conspiracy with thieves Jarrett and Bennett to dispose of stolen property through the pawnshop. The thieves and Schwartz eventually had a falling out in which one of the thieves informed on Schwartz. An agreement between Jarrett, Bennett, and the police set in motion a telephone call to Schwartz designed to implicate him. Jarrett called Schwartz and obtained various incriminating statements from him. Schwartz was later convicted based in part on incriminating evidence from those conversations. Schwartz appealed, contending that warrants were required for such telephonic interceptions of his conversations. The SC upheld his conviction, holding that one of the persons making the telephone call, Jarrett, had consented to the conversation being recorded. Thus, a participant who initiates a telephone call may record the conversation without violating the unreasonable-search-and-seizure provision of the Fourth Amendment. As third parties, however, police officers need a warrant in order to intercept telephonic conversations between two or more other individuals. That was not the situation here, as Jarrett had authorized the recording of the call to Schwartz, and Jarrett was one of the parties involved in the conversation. This type of recording is perfectly constitutional.

Scott v. Illinois, 440 U.S. 367, 99 S.Ct. 1158 (1979) [**Aubrey SCOTT, Petitioner, v. State of ILLINOIS**] (**Indigent Clients; Sixth Amendment**) Scott, an indigent, was convicted of shoplifting and fined $50 following a bench trial. Scott appealed this conviction, contending that he had been deprived of court-appointed counsel. The SC rejected Scott's appeal outright, noting that only if a defendant faces a real term of incarceration of any duration can the court be obligated to furnish court-appointed counsel. In this case, the penalty was a simple fine of $50, and the fact that the offense included a statute with a fine of "up to $500" and an incarcerative term of "up to one year" was irrelevant, because the Sixth and Fourteenth Amendments require only that no indigent criminal defendant shall be sentenced to a term of imprisonment unless the state has afforded him the right to assistance of court-appointed counsel in his defense.

Scott v. United States, 436 U.S. 128, 98 S.Ct. 1717 (1978) [**Frank R. SCOTT, etc., and Bernis L. Thurmon, etc., Petitioners, v. UNITED STATES**] (**Electronic Surveillance, Wiretapping**) Under the Omnibus Crime Control and Safe Streets Act of 1968, the government is required in wiretapping situations to conduct such electronic surveillance in a way that minimizes interception of extraneous or irrelevant communication. During an investigation of Frank Scott concerning allegations of narcotics distribution, considerable incriminating evidence was obtained against Scott as the result of government electronic surveillance. However, about 40 percent of the recorded telephonic information was irrelevant to the narcotics issue, and Scott's attorney moved to suppress all incriminating telephonic conversations, as their use did not comply with the act's provisions to minimize interceptions of irrelevant conversations. The SC heard Scott's appeal and decided against him. The intercepted conversations had been collected "in good faith" by federal agents, and the general conduct of the agents had complied with the spirit of the act and was reasonable and not violative of any Fourth Amendment provision.

See v. Seattle, 387 U.S. 541, 87 S.Ct. 1737 (1967) [**Norman SEE, Appellant, v. City of SEATTLE**] (**Law Enforcement Officers or Agencies; Searches and Seizures**) A fire inspector wished to inspect See's residence in Seattle. See objected, saying that the inspector needed a properly executed search warrant. The inspector discovered the violation of a city ordinance. See was charged and convicted. He appealed, and the SC overturned his conviction, holding that searches of the type authorized by the Seattle ordinance required warrants under the Fourth Amendment. Thus, administrative entry, without consent, upon portions of commercial premises not open to the public, may only be compelled through prosecution or physical force within the framework of a warrant procedure. This holding does not pertain to licensing requirements, such as firearms inspections of firearms dealers and the like.

Segura v. United States, 468 U.S. 796, 104 S.Ct. 3380 (1984) [**Andres SEGURA and Luz Marina Colon, Petitioners, v. UNITED STATES**] (**Exclusionary Rule; Law Enforcement Officers or Agencies**) A New York task force on drug-law enforcement suspected Segura of trafficking in cocaine. Other suspects were followed to their apartment, where Segura appeared and purchased cocaine. The agents obtained a search warrant for the apartment and entered it the following day. Then they went to Segura's apartment house, arrested Segura in the lobby, and took him to his apartment, where a man, Colon, opened the door. Standing in the doorway, officers could see in plain view drug paraphernalia and other incriminating items. They forced entry into the apartment and conducted a warrantless search of the premises. Later, at Segura's trial, all evidence was admitted, including that seized as the result of the warrantless search. He was convicted. He appealed, alleging his Fourth Amendment right against unreasonable searches and seizures had been violated. The SC upheld his conviction but held that the incriminating evidence seized without a warrant should have been suppressed. However, there was sufficient incriminating evidence without this other evidence to convict Segura. Thus, the Fourth Amendment violation in his case was irrelevant and did not affect his lawful conviction.

Seling v. Young, 531 U.S. 250, 121 S.Ct. 727 (2001) [**Mark SELING, Superintendent, Special Commitment Center, Petitioner, v. Andre Brigham YOUNG**] (**Sex Offender Laws**) Andre Young was convicted of six rapes over three decades and was scheduled for release from prison in October 1990 in Washington State. One day prior to his release, the State filed a petition to commit Young as a sexually violent offender. A commitment hearing was held, and it was determined that Young posed a threat as a sexually violent offender under Washington State's Community Protection Act of 1990, which authorizes civil commitment of such offenders. Young appealed, arguing that his civil commitment constituted double jeopardy and that the law was unconstitutional. Furthermore, Young alleged that the conditions of his confinement were incompatible with rehabilitation and too restrictive. Washington State courts rejected his arguments, and he appealed to the SC, which heard the case. The SC upheld Young's civil commitment and rejected his double jeopardy argument. It further held that the Washington State law was constitutional. The SC did not address whether the mental health center where Young was being housed and treated was operating properly. Rather, the SC left this determination to the Washington State courts. The SC noted that offenders have a cause of action at the state level if the mental health center fails to fulfill its statutory duty to adequately care and provide individualized treatment for sex offenders.

Sell v. United States, ___U.S.___, 123 S.Ct. 2174 (2003) [**Charles Thomas SELL, Petitioner, v. UNITED STATES**] (**Forced Medication of Mentally Ill Defendants**) Sell was a dentist who was charged with filing fraudulent insurance claims. A U.S. magistrate held a hearing to determine Sell's mental state because of several instances of bizarre behavior. The U.S. magistrate held that Sell posed a danger to himself or others and ordered Sell to be forcibly medicated through the administration of antipsychotic drugs by physicians. This forcible medication would enable Sell to remain competent to stand trial and understand the proceedings. Sell appealed, contending that he should not be forcibly medicated. The U.S. district court reversed the magistrate's finding that Sell posed a danger to himself and others, although the court affirmed that forcible medication was warranted in order to restore Sell to competency. Sell appealed, and the Eighth Circuit affirmed. The SC subsequently heard the case. The SC vacated the appellate decision and remanded the case for further proceedings. The SC said that under the Fifth Amendment due-process clause, the government is permitted to administer antipsychotic drugs for a mentally ill defendant facing serious criminal charges in order to render the defendant competent to stand trial, but only if the treatment is medically appropriate, is substantially unlikely to have side effects that may undermine the fairness of a trial, and is necessary significantly to further important government interests. In this instance, Sell was not considered dangerous to himself or others; therefore, he could not be ordered involuntarily to take antipsychotic drugs solely to render him competent to stand trial without consideration of other important questions.

Serfass v. United States, 420 U.S. 377, 95 S.Ct. 1055 (1975) [**David Emery SERFASS, Petitioner, v. UNITED STATES**] (**Double Jeopardy**) Serfass was indicted for failing to register for the draft for the United States Armed Forces in Pennsylvania. Subsequently, he successfully had the indictment dismissed by a motion, but the government appealed and an appellate court reversed the dismissal. Serfass appealed this reversal on the grounds that it constituted double jeopardy, because he believed that he was "being tried twice for the same offense." The SC upheld his indictment, holding that it is not double jeopardy to be first indicted without a trial to decide the case. The double-jeopardy clause does not bar an appeal by the government from dismissal of an indictment or information with respect to a criminal defendant who has not been put to trial. Persons must be placed on trial for an offense before they can claim double jeopardy, if they are subsequently charged again with that same offense.

Sgro v. United States, 287 U.S. 206, 53 S.Ct. 138 (1932) [**Cesara SGRO, Petitioner, v. UNITED STATES**] (**Elec-**

tronic Surveillance, Wiretapping; Law Enforcement Officers or Agencies) A liquor search warrant was issued for searching Sgro's premises. However, the search warrant was not executed within 10 days following its issuance. Thus, it became void. Officers then used the void warrant to search Sgro's premises. Evidence seized was used to convict Sgro of violating federal liquor laws, and he appealed. The SC overturned the conviction, holding that the expired and void warrant was an illegal device with which to initiate a new search of a constitutionally protected area. A new search warrant had to be obtained in order to conduct a reasonable search under the Fourth Amendment.

Shafer v. South Carolina, 532 U.S. 36, 121 S.Ct. 1263 (2001) [**Wesley Aaron SHAFER, Jr., Petitioner, v. SOUTH CAROLINA**] (**Death Penalty; Jury Instructions**) Shafer was convicted in a South Carolina criminal court of murder, attempted murder, and conspiracy, and he was sentenced to death. When the sentencing judge issued jury instructions, he did not advise the jury about Shafer's future dangerousness, as this fact had not been raised during the trial or in the prosecutor's or defense's summation. Shafer's defense counsel wanted the judge to instruct the jury that a life sentence carried no possibility of parole, but the judge refused to issue such an instruction to the jury. However, the judge twice told the jury that "life imprisonment means until the death of the defendant" (at 1265). Although the jury asked the judge under what circumstances someone convicted of murder could be paroled, the judge responded by saying that parole eligibility or ineligibility is not for their consideration. The jury thus recommended the death penalty for Shafer. Shafer's attorney appealed, but the South Carolina Supreme Court upheld the trial court, and Shafer directed his next appeal to the SC. The SC heard the case and reversed and remanded the capital sentence. The SC held that the South Carolina Supreme Court and sentencing judge had incorrectly interpreted another case (*Simmons v. South Carolina* [1994]), which it relied on in rejecting the request for a specific jury instruction about Shafer's parole ineligibility. In *Simmons,* when a capital jury begins deliberations, three alternative sentences are usually available: (1) death, (2) life without the possibility of parole, or (3) a mandatory 30-year sentence. The South Carolina courts incorrectly concluded that because *Simmons* contained an alternative sentence other than life without the possibility of parole (e.g., the mandatory 30-year sentence) and that this was not an option in Shafer's case, *Simmons* was not relevant to his particular circumstances. But the SC noted that South Carolina had recently changed its sentencing scheme, which now requires jurors who find an aggravating circumstance to recommend either death or life without parole. Because the jury was not specifically informed that a life sentence carries no possibility of parole, and because they had sought clarification in this matter from the judge but were denied such clarification, the jury was conceivably misled as to its options, whether to recommend death or life without parole. The SC referred the case back to the trial court, where such a clarifying instruction must be presented to subsequent deliberating jurors. Sentencing judges must inform jurors in capital cases about the parole in-

eligibility of convicted offenders in life-without-parole sentences as alternatives to the death penalty.

Shaw v. Murphy, 532 U.S. 223, 121 S.Ct. 1475 (2001) [**Robert SHAW et al., Petitioners, v. Kevin MURPHY, Respondent**] (**Civil Rights, Section 1983 Claims; First Amendment; Free Speech**) Kevin Murphy was an inmate law clerk at the Montana State Prison, and he provided legal assistance to fellow inmates. He learned that another inmate, Pat Tracy, had been charged with assaulting a correctional officer and wrote a letter to Tracy giving him legal advice. The letter was intercepted by Robert Shaw, an officer at the maximum-security unit, who reviewed it and did not deliver it to Tracy. Tracy was subsequently found guilty of violating prison rules and given a suspended sentence of 10 days' detention and demerits, which could affect his custody level. Murphy brought a Section 1983 civil rights action against Shaw and other prison officials for violating his First Amendment right of free speech by failing to deliver his letter to Tracy. Prison officials countered by arguing that Murphy's letter was withheld from Tracy in the interests of prison order, security, and inmate rehabilitation. A U.S. district court rejected Murphy's claim of a First Amendment infringement. However, the Ninth Circuit Court of Appeals overturned the district court, holding that inmates have a First Amendment right to assist other inmates with their legal claims, and that withholding correspondence from one inmate to another relating to a legal claim violated Murphy's First Amendment right. Prison officials appealed to the SC, who heard the case. The SC reversed the appellate court, holding that Murphy's attempt to offer legal assistance to Tracy is not a right protected by the First Amendment. Murphy did not specifically challenge the prison's policy of intercepting prisoner-to-prisoner correspondence. Murphy did question the prison rule forbidding insolence and interference with due-process hearings as being vague and overbroad. However, this issue was not addressed by the circuit court. Murphy was not prevented from raising this particular issue in another subsequent appeal if he chose.

Shea v. Louisiana, 470 U.S. 51, 105 S.Ct. 1065 (1985) [**Kevin Michael SHEA, Petitioner, v. LOUISIANA**] (*Miranda* **Warning; Self-Incrimination**) IRS agents interviewed Shea regarding an income-tax liability. During the same interview, Shea made various incriminating statements that led to his indictment and conviction for income-tax fraud. Shea appealed the conviction, alleging that he had not been told his *Miranda* rights during his interview, that he had not been advised that statements he made could be used against him later in court, and that therefore, his Fifth Amendment right against self-incrimination had been violated. The SC disagreed, holding that Shea was not in custody and was not being interrogated while in custody. If he had been arrested and taken into custody for interrogation purposes, then the *Miranda* warning would have had to be given. Under other circumstances, however, the IRS had no obligation to tell Shea his rights. Thus, his conviction was upheld.

Sheppard v. Maxwell, 384 U.S. 333, 86 S.Ct. 1507 (1966) [**Samuel H. SHEPPARD, Petitioner, v. E.L. MAXWELL, Warden**] (**Jury Trials; Publicity**) Sheppard claimed that someone unknown to him entered his home in Bay Village, OH, and hit him on the head. When he awakened, he saw his wife had been injured and was sitting in a chair, bleeding and not moving. Early in the case, police suspected Sheppard of killing his wife and diverting attention from himself to so-called unknown assailants. The police made known their views to the media, which dramatized the event, as Sheppard was a well-respected physician in the community. Front-page headlines in the local newspapers created a media frenzy, with Sheppard at its center. During his subsequent trial, Sheppard was subjected to considerable media attention, and cameras and other media agents and apparatuses were admitted into the courtroom to witness the proceedings. This action by the court further intensified the media frenzy. In this milieu, Sheppard was convicted of murder. He appealed, and the SC overturned his murder conviction, holding that the failure of the state trial judge to protect Sheppard from inherently prejudicial publicity, which saturated the community, and to control disruptive influences in court had deprived Sheppard of a fair trial consistent with due process.

Sherman v. United States, 356 U.S. 369, 78 S.Ct. 819 (1958) [**Joseph George SHERMAN**, Petitioner, v. **UNITED STATES**] (**Entrapment**) A paid government informant was instructed to meet Sherman, a drug addict, in a doctor's office and inquire about possible sources of drugs. Sherman repeatedly declined to provide the informant with drug information or sources of drugs. At some point, however, he eventually provided small quantities of drugs to the informant at his own cost plus expenses. Eventually, after several transactions, government agents arrested Sherman and he was convicted of drug offenses. Sherman appealed, alleging entrapment. The SC agreed and overturned his conviction. The SC stressed the significance of the phrase "entrapment occurs whenever the government induces persons to commit crimes they otherwise would never have committed." The persistence of the government informant in requesting drugs and Sherman's repeated avoidance and denials of involvement in drug trafficking were clear evidence to the SC that Sherman had never intended to traffic in drugs, without the substantial inducement and entrapment by the government and their paid informant.

Sibron v. New York, 392 U.S. 40, 88 S.Ct. 1889 (1968) [**Nelson SIBRON**, Appellant, v. State of **NEW YORK**. John Francis Peters, Appellant, v. State of New York] (**Law Enforcement Officers or Agencies; Stop and Frisk**) Sibron, a convicted drug user and ex-convict, was observed by a police officer in a New York diner conversing with other persons, also known to be involved with drugs. Sibron was sitting at a table while as many as six or eight persons approached him and conversed over a period of a few hours. Nothing was observed exchanged between them, according to the observing officer. However, when Sibron left the diner, the officer approached and said, "Sibron, you know what I want." Sibron began to place his hand in his pocket, but the officer moved quickly and thrust his hand in it instead. The search yielded several glassine envelopes containing heroin. Sibron was subsequently convicted of heroin possession. However, he appealed to the SC, and his conviction was overturned. The court reasoned that

officers should be able to protect themselves against possibly armed suspects. Thus, a "pat-down" and "frisk" are warranted under certain suspicious conditions. However, Sibron had not been observed doing anything illegal, and therefore his pocket search by the observing officer was unreasonable according to the Fourth Amendment. In short, the officer was entitled to pat Sibron down to detect a possible weapon; the officer would not have detected small glassine envelopes of heroin in such a pat-down, however, so the heroin evidence illegally obtained by the officer was excluded. This landmark case limited the scope of a police officer's search of suspicious persons to pat-downs and frisks, unless other special circumstances apply. Sibron's case did not involve special circumstances.

Silverman v. United States, 365 U.S. 505, 81 S.Ct. 679 (1961) [**Julius SILVERMAN et al.**, Petitioners, v. **UNITED STATES**] (**Electronic Surveillance, Wiretapping; Law Enforcement Officers or Agencies**) In the spring of 1958, Washington, DC, police placed microphones throughout a house suspected of headquartering an illegal gambling operation. On the basis of information obtained by police from conversations overheard from such microphone placements, convictions were obtained against Silverman and others. Silverman appealed. The SC overturned his conviction, holding that the warrantless search and placement of microphones illegally throughout his residence had violated the unreasonable-search provisions of the Fourth Amendment. The SC held that these microphones represented a nonconsensual intrusion, without warrant, into a constitutionally protected area, a private home.

Silverthorne Lumber Co. v. United States, 251 U.S. 385, 40 S.Ct. 182 (1920) [**SILVERTHORNE LUMBER CO., Inc., et al.**, v. **UNITED STATES**] (**Exclusionary Rule; Law Enforcement Officers or Agencies**) Silverthorne Lumber Co. officials were arrested after being indicted on various charges. Following their arrest, federal agents without a search warrant went to the business premises and seized all records, effects, and personnel, directing that the personnel should present themselves at the Department of Justice as soon as possible. New indictments were secured against Silverthorne officials based on the newly seized evidence. Silverthorne protested. The SC ruled that the evidence against Silverthorne Lumber Co. had been seized illegally and in violation of the Fourth Amendment and was therefore inadmissible. Also, it overturned contempt charges against the Silverthorne officials for not producing such materials. Corporations are protected, just as are individuals, against illegal and/or unreasonable warrantless searches as specified in the Fourth Amendment.

Simmons v. South Carolina, 512 U.S. 154, 114 S.Ct. 2187 (1994) [**Jonathan Dale SIMMONS**, Petitioner, v. **SOUTH CAROLINA**] (**Death Penalty**) Simmons was convicted of first-degree murder. During the penalty phase of Simmons' trial, the state argued that Simmons' future dangerousness should be considered as an aggravating circumstance in whether he should receive the death penalty. In his own behalf, Simmons argued that his future dangerousness only related to elderly women, and that he was also ineligible for parole. The judge refused to give the jury an instruction about Simmons' parole eligibility or lack of it, and Simmons was subsequently sentenced to death. Simmons appealed, and his conviction and sentence were upheld by the South Carolina Supreme Court. Simmons appealed to the SC, contending that his Fourteenth Amendment due-process rights were violated when the judge refused to instruct the jury about his ineligibility for parole if a life sentence were imposed. The SC reversed Simmons' conviction and sentence, holding that Simmons was entitled to inform the jury about his parole ineligibility. The SC also noted that the state's commentary about Simmons' future dangerousness was confusing to the jury without a specific instruction from the judge about Simmons' ineligibility for parole if given a life sentence. The judge's refusal to instruct the jury accordingly violated Simmons' right to due process under the Fourteenth Amendment.

Simmons v. United States, 390 U.S. 377, 88 S.Ct. 967 (1968) [**Thomas Earl SIMMONS et al., Petitioners, v. UNITED STATES**] (**Law Enforcement Officers or Agencies; Lineups**) Simmons was suspected of armed robbery of a federally insured savings and loan association. Following the robbery, witnesses were shown photographs of various suspects, including Simmons. A description of the getaway car yielded information leading to Simmons' mother's residence, which FBI visited and entered. They found inculpatory evidence in the home, including a gun holster, a sack similar to the one used in the robbery, and several bill wrappers from the bank that had been robbed. Simmons was charged with and convicted of the armed robbery. He appealed, arguing that the search of his mother's home had not been by consent or warrant, and that the photograph lineup of him was suggestive. The SC rejected Simmons' contention that the lineup was suggestive and noted that at the trial, five of the witnesses had positively identified Simmons. Simmons' conviction was upheld as valid.

Simpson v. United States, 435 U.S. 6, 98 S.Ct. 909 (1978) [**Michael Lee SIMPSON and Tommy Wayne Simpson, Petitioners, v. UNITED STATES**] (**Sentencing**) Simpson and his brother were charged in Kentucky in federal court with two separate bank robberies in which dangerous weapons were used. They were convicted of a bank-robbery charge (including the possession of a dangerous weapon) and also of the charge of using a dangerous weapon during the commission of a felony. Thus, the district judge sentenced Simpson to two consecutive prison terms for each of the statute violations. Simpson appealed. The SC reversed Simpson's conviction, declaring that sentence enhancements may not be permitted where different offenses are alleged and have stemmed from the same crime. In this case, there was a single transaction of "bank robbery with firearms." The prosecution added a second statute governing the use of weapons during the commission of felonies. The significance of the SC decision is that sentences may not be compounded or enhanced through the misapplication of two or more different statutes. Thus, where a prosecution grows out of a single transaction, such as bank robbery with firearms, defendants may not be sentenced according to two or more different statutes covering different dimensions of the offense.

Singer v. United States, 380 U.S. 24, 85 S.Ct. 783 (1965) [**Mortimer SINGER, Petitioner, v. UNITED STATES**] (**Jury Trials**) Singer, charged with a federal crime, requested to have a bench trial instead of a jury trial. His request was denied, and he was subsequently convicted of the crime by a federal jury. He appealed, arguing that he should have been entitled to a bench trial. The SC disagreed and said that although Singer had a right to a jury trial under the circumstances, the constitutional requirement did not entitle a citizen to the opposite of that right, namely, a bench trial. Thus, defendants cannot elect to have a bench trial as a matter of right if jury trials are prescribed in federal proceedings. (*See Duncan v. Louisiana* [1968].)

Skinner v. Oklahoma, 316 U.S. 535, 62 S.Ct. 1110 (1942) [**Jack T. SKINNER, Petitioner, v. State of OKLAHOMA ex rel. Williamson, Atty. Gen. of Oklahoma**] (**Corrections; Sterilization**) Skinner was a third-felony offender who had been convicted of stealing chickens in 1926, robbery with firearms in 1929, and robbery with firearms in 1934. An Oklahoma law proclaimed that persons who had committed such felonies should be sterilized, and, therefore, the court ordered Skinner sterilized. Skinner appealed, alleging that his equal-protection rights were being violated. Persons convicted on multiple occasions for embezzlement, for instance, would not be sterilized, whereas persons convicted on multiple occasions for larceny would be. Thus, Oklahoma was sterilizing convicted offenders selectively. The SC heard his case and ruled in Skinner's favor. It held that the Oklahoma law requiring sterilization of certain types of criminals was unconstitutional because the Oklahoma classification scheme determining who should or should not be sterilized denied equal protection under the law.

Skipper v. South Carolina, 476 U.S. 1, 106 S.Ct. 1669 (1986) [**Ronald DeRay SKIPPER, Petitioner, v. SOUTH CAROLINA**] (**Aggravating and Mitigating Circumstances; Bifurcated Trials; Death Penalty**) Skipper was convicted of rape and murder following a jury trial. During the sentencing phase of the trial, the jury considered aggravating and mitigating circumstances. Skipper planned to introduce testimony from jailers and a "regular visitor" that he had exhibited good conduct and made a good adjustment while confined. The court refused to allow him to introduce such testimony during this phase of his trial. He was sentenced to death, and he appealed. The SC overturned his conviction by noting that the sentencing jury must hear all relevant evidence in mitigation of punishment.

Smalis v. Pennsylvania, 476 U.S. 140, 106 S.Ct. 1745 (1986) [**Despina SMALIS and Ernest Smalis, Petitioners, v. PENNSYLVANIA**] (**Double Jeopardy**) Smalis and her husband were owners of a building housing a restaurant. The building caught fire and two tenants died as the result. The Smalises were charged with various crimes, including murder, voluntary manslaughter, and causing a catastrophe. They entered a demurrer, which acknowledged the facts of the fire but claimed that the state's case against them was insufficient to support a cause of action. The trial court sustained the demurrer, and the state appealed. An appellate court quashed the government's appeal on the grounds that it was barred by the double-jeopardy clause. However, the Pennsylvania Supreme Court reversed that decision, saying that a demurrer is not the functional equivalent of an acquittal. The SC heard the Smalises' case and held that when the trial judge granted their demurrer, it was an "acquittal" under the double-jeopardy clause. Thus, the state would be barred from further criminal proceedings against the Smalises.

Smith v. Bennett, 365 U.S. 708, 81 S.Ct. 895 (1961) [Neal Merle SMITH, Petitioner, v. John E. BENNETT, Warden. Richard W. Marshall, Petitioner, v. John E. Bennett, Warden] (Corrections; Inmate Rights) Smith, an indigent, was convicted of burglary and sentenced to 10 years in the Iowa State Penitentiary. He was paroled and violated one or more of his parole conditions. He was returned to prison and filed a motion to the Iowa Supreme Court. A $4 filing fee was required to accompany his motion. Because he didn't have $4, his petition was denied. He appealed. The SC heard Smith's case and overruled the Iowa Supreme Court, saying that indigents cannot be barred from access to the court because they cannot afford filing fees. To do so was a clear violation of Smith's Fourteenth Amendment rights.

Smith v. Daily Mail Publishing Co., 443 U.S. 97, 99 S.Ct. 2667 (1979) [Robert K. SMITH, etc., et al., Petitioners, v. DAILY MAIL PUBLISHING CO., etc., et al.] (Juvenile Law; Media Rights) A 15-year-old Virginia student was killed at a junior high school. A 14-year-old classmate was charged with the crime. Reporters for local newspapers were monitoring police broadcasts and went to the arrest scene, where they learned the name of the juvenile suspect. The suspect's picture and name were published in the local newspaper following the murder. Suit was brought against the newspaper, the *Gazette,* for illegally publishing the name and photograph of the juvenile without permission of the juvenile court. The SC upheld the right of the juvenile to confidentiality and ruled against the newspaper. Juvenile court permission is required before any names or photographs of juveniles are published relative to crimes alleged. The newspaper's action was a violation of the First and Fourteenth Amendments.

Smith v. Doe, ___U.S.___, 123 S.Ct. 1140 (2003) [Delbert W. SMITH and Bruce M. Botelho, Petitioners, v. John DOE I et al.] (Civil Rights, Section 1983 Claims; Retroactive Rules) Alaska enacted the Alaska Sex Offender Registration Act on May 12, 1994. The new law provided that current and previous sex offenders or child molesters must register within a day of entering the state, providing their name, address, and other specific information. All sex-offender information is transmitted to the Alaska Department of Public Safety, which maintains a central registry of sex offenders. Furthermore, offenders must provide annual verification of the submitted information for 15 years. Respondent Doe and others were convicted of aggravated sex offenses, released from prison, and completed rehabilitative programs for sex offenders. Although their convictions occurred prior to the act's passage, they are covered by the act. Doe and others filed a civil rights Section 1983 claim against Alaska, contending that the act cannot be made to be retroactive and encompass prior sex

offenders. An appellate court held that the Alaska act violated the *ex post facto* provision and thus did not pertain to Doe et al. The state appealed, and the SC heard the case. The SC reversed, holding that the *ex post facto* clause does not preclude a state from making reasonable categorical judgments that conviction of specified crimes should entail particular consequences. The *ex post facto* clause prohibits retroactive punishment for prior offenders based on newly established laws or acts. Alaska's determination to legislate with respect to convicted sex offenders as a class in the state's Sex Offender Registration Act (SORA), rather than require individual determination of their dangerousness, did not make the statute a punishment under the *ex post facto* clause. Because the Alaska SORA is nonpunitive, its retroactive application does not violate the civil rights of Doe et al. or the *ex post facto* clause.

Smith v. Hooey, 393 U.S. 374, 89 S.Ct. 575 (1969) [Richard M. SMITH, Petitioner, v. Fred M. HOOEY, Judge, Criminal District Court of Harris County, Texas] (Speedy Trials) A federal prisoner sought a writ of *mandamus* to compel authorities to bring him to trial in a Texas court on state-related charges. The Texas Supreme Court said that it did not have the power to compel the presence of federal prisoners in Texas for a state trial. The SC disagreed and said that Texas must make a good-faith effort to bring the defendant to court for trial.

Smith v. Illinois, 390 U.S. 129, 88 S.Ct. 748 (1968) [Fleming SMITH, Petitioner, v. State of ILLINOIS] (Confrontation Clause; *Habeas Corpus* Petitions) Smith was accused in Cook County, Illinois, of the unlawful sale of narcotics. During Smith's trial, a confidential informant testified. On cross-examination, the informant gave his name as "James Jordan," acknowledged to be false. The defense counsel sought to determine "Jordan's" real name, but a prosecutor's objection was sustained. The defense also sought to determine where "Jordan" lived, but again, the court refused to allow an answer to this question. The prosecution gave as its reason, "witness safety and protection," but the process did not entitle Smith's attorney to cross-examine the adverse witness fully. Smith was convicted. He filed an appeal, alleging that he had been denied the privilege of cross-examining his accuser under the Sixth Amendment. The SC heard the case and reversed Smith's conviction, holding that the Sixth Amendment entitles defendants to cross-examine their accusers, and to elicit from them information that may discredit them. The SC noted, however, that cross-examination that is intended to annoy, harass, or humiliate informants is unwarranted. In any event, Smith's conviction was reversed because of the Sixth Amendment right violation.

Smith v. Illinois, 469 U.S. 91, 105 S.Ct. 490 (1984) [Steven SMITH v. ILLINOIS] (*Miranda* Warning; Right to Counsel; Sixth Amendment) Smith was suspected of armed robbery. Shortly after his arrest, he was taken to police headquarters for interrogation. He was told his *Miranda* rights but was ambivalent about whether he wanted an attorney to be present during questioning. Specifically, Smith said, "I wanna get a lawyer" prior to his questioning by police. However, he said "Yeah and no" when asked whether he wanted to talk with police at that time. In any event, Smith admitted to the crime. During his trial, his attorney attempted to have the incriminating statements against him suppressed but was unsuccessful. Smith was convicted. He appealed to the SC, which overturned his conviction. The SC holding was a narrow one, not necessarily exploring the meticulous circumstances of Smith's confession or the conditions under which it was given. Rather, the SC reasoned that on several occasions during police questioning, Smith had indicated his intent to have an attorney present. Police were to *cease* their questioning at that point and obtain an attorney for Smith. They had failed to do so. Suspects who are in custody but invoke their right to counsel must be provided counsel before further interrogation is conducted.

Smith v. Maryland, 442 U.S. 735, 99 S.Ct. 2577 (1975) [**Michael Lee SMITH, Petitioner, v. State of MARYLAND**] (**Electronic Surveillance, Wiretapping**) In this warrantless seizure case, police used a pen register to record telephone numbers dialed from a particular location. Subsequent incriminating information resulted from a knowledge of these other telephone numbers. Smith was convicted. He appealed, contending that police had had no right to "seize" these telephone numbers without a warrant. The SC declared that telephone numbers by themselves do not constitute conversation, incriminating or otherwise. Thus they are not protected by the Fourth Amendment. Furthermore, telephone numbers are freely available through the telephone company, and therefore persons have no reasonable expectation of privacy regarding interceptions of telephone numbers.

Smith v. Murray, 477 U.S. 527, 106 S.Ct. 2661 (1986) [**Michael Marnell SMITH, Petitioner, v. Edward W. MURRAY, Director, Virginia Department of Corrections**] (**Corrections; Inmate Rights**) Smith was accused of murder in a Virginia court. At the defense counsel's request before Smith's trial, a psychiatrist examined Smith, and Smith told him about various events involving deviant sexual conduct. A jury trial followed. Neither side called the psychiatrist to testify. Smith was convicted. During the sentencing phase of the trial, the psychiatrist was called to testify and gave incriminating statements made to him by Smith. The defense objected without effect. Smith appealed to higher courts, alleging many issues. At no time during these state appeals, however, was the psychiatrist's testimony mentioned. Subsequently, after having exhausted his state remedies, Smith filed a *habeas corpus* petition in which the psychiatric testimony issue was raised. The SC summarily rejected Smith's claim, inasmuch as he had failed to state such a claim during any of his state appeals. The SC ruled in Smith's case that when the alleged error was unrelated to Smith's innocence, and when Smith was represented by competent counsel and had a full and fair opportunity to press his claim in the state system but had failed to do so, Smith had failed to carry the burden of showing how the psychiatrist's testimony would have affected his sentence.

Smith v. Ohio, 494 U.S. 541, 110 S.Ct. 1288 (1990) [**Danny SMITH, Petitioner, v. OHIO**] (**Fourth Amendment; Law Enforcement Officers or Agencies; Searches Incident to an Arrest**) Smith was leaving a YMCA building with a companion in Ashland, OH, one evening, carrying a brown

paper bag. Two police officers observed him and his friend. Neither Smith nor his companion was known to police. They approached the two men and said, "Come here a minute." Smith was standing by his car and threw the brown paper bag on the hood of the car and turned to face police. They immediately seized his bag, which he attempted to protect, and opened it, discovering drug paraphernalia. They placed Smith under arrest for possession of drug paraphernalia, and he was subsequently convicted. Smith appealed. The police and the state reasoned that the discovery of the drug paraphernalia had given them probable cause to arrest Smith. They contended that the search of the bag and seizure of its contents were made incident to an arrest and so were properly admissible against Smith during his subsequent trial. The state further argued that Smith had abandoned his property (the bag) when he tossed it on the hood of his car. Thus, the abandoned property fell within the purview of police to investigate it and its contents. The SC rejected these arguments and overturned Smith's conviction, holding that justifying a search by an arrest and an arrest by the search "will not do" (at 1290). A citizen who attempts to protect his private property from inspection has clearly not abandoned that property. The police had lacked probable cause to search the bag, and thus the sheer fact that drug paraphernalia was discovered was irrelevant and did not justify the arrest. Searches of areas in the immediate vicinity of persons arrested on the basis of probable cause are legitimately within the scope of police authority, but no search can be justified without probable cause. This case is a good example of how the SC treats the matter of the ends justifying the means. Finding illegal contraband without first having probable cause to make an arrest does not justify the search of a person or his personal effects, regardless of whatever is found.

Smith v. Phillips, 455 U.S. 209, 102 S.Ct. 940 (1982) [**Harold J. SMITH, Superintendent, Attica Correctional Facility, v. William R. PHILLIPS**] (**Corrections; Death Penalty**) Phillips was convicted of murder in a New York court. During his trial, one of his jurors had submitted a job application to the district attorney's office for employment as an investigator. When prosecutors learned of it, they withheld the information from the defense. Later, Phillips' attorney found out about it and moved to vacate Phillips' conviction on grounds of prosecutorial misconduct. The judge denied the motion, and Phillips appealed to the SC. The SC held that a new trial is not required every time a juror has been placed in a potentially compromising situation. In the present case, it was determined that the juror's ability to make an impartial judgment had not been impaired. The critical question was whether Phillips had had a fair trial, not whether the conduct of the prosecutor in withholding the information about the juror was wrong. In this case, a fair trial had been conducted, and Phillips' conviction was affirmed.

Smith v. United States, 508 U.S. 223, 113 S.Ct. 2050 (1993) [**John Angus SMITH, Petitioner, v. UNITED STATES**] (**Sentencing**) Smith was convicted in federal court of using a firearm during a drug sale. Essentially, he had traded a firearm for narcotics. The firearm was treated as a part of a drug transaction for purposes of sentence enhancement (e.g., if a person uses a gun, he does two years in prison). Smith appealed, alleging that he wasn't "using" the firearm but rather "trading" it. The SC heard his case and upheld his conviction with the enhancement for use of the firearm by declaring that "use" and "in relation to" are for all intents and purposes the same within the meaning of the statute.

Smith v. Wade, 461 U.S. 30, 103 S.Ct. 1625 (1983) [**William H. SMITH, Petitioner, v. Daniel R. WADE**] (**Corrections**) Wade was a youthful first offender in a prison. He had requested protective isolation because of previous violent incidents committed against him. He was initially placed in a cell with another inmate. Eventually, Smith, a corrections officer, placed a third inmate known for fighting in the cell with Wade and the other prisoner. Subsequently, Wade was sexually assaulted by one or both of the other cell occupants. He filed suit against Smith for disregarding his safety by placing these persons in the same cell with him. Damages were awarded to Wade, who had been placed in protective isolation at his request. Smith appealed, contending that the wrong instructions had been given to the jury by the judge about what damages should be imposed. The SC upheld the judge's decision and indicated that Smith had indeed acted in callous disregard for Wade's safety, and that his behavior could be interpreted as being actually malicious or having malicious intent. Thus, punitive damages can be awarded to inmates against corrections officers and other officials who act with callous disregard for the rights and safety of others.

Solem v. Helm, 463 U.S. 277, 103 S.Ct. 3001 (1983) [**Herman SOLEM, Warden, Petitioner, v. Jerry Buckley HELM**] (**Cruel and Unusual Punishment; Eighth Amendment**) A life sentence was imposed on a convicted offender after he had been convicted of six prior nonviolent offenses. The offender appealed, contending that a life sentence was disproportionate punishment, given the offense, and was thus cruel and unusual. The SC upheld the sentence, saying that a life sentence for a habitual offender was not cruel and unusual in violation of the Eighth Amendment.

Solem v. Stumes, 465 U.S. 638, 104 S.Ct. 1338 (1984) [**Herman SOLEM, Warden, Petitioner, v. Norman STUMES**] (**Confessions; Law Enforcement Officers or Agencies;** *Miranda* **Warning**) Stumes was a suspect in a woman's death in Sioux Falls, SD. Subsequently, he was arrested in Green Bay, WI, on unrelated charges (check forgery and perjury). While he was in jail awaiting trial, he talked to his attorney, who told him not to make any statements before returning to South Dakota. Sioux Falls police officers went to Wisconsin and brought Stumes back in an automobile. During the trip, Stumes was told his *Miranda* rights but talked with police. At one point, he admitted killing the woman. He was charged with and convicted of murder, based on the confession he gave to police in the car and other incriminating evidence. He appealed. Without offering an opinion as to Stumes' guilt or innocence, the SC remanded the case to the trial court to determine whether police had acted properly when they initiated further conversation with Stumes on the auto trip back to South Dakota. Stumes' appeal alleged that the conduct of police who interrogated him ought to be evalu-

ated in view of a decision in a contemporaneous case as yet unsettled. In this case, as in *Edwards v. Arizona* (1981), it was held that once a suspect has invoked his or her silence privilege, police may not initiate new conversation with the suspect. The suspect, however, may initiate new conversation, and any incriminating statements uttered may be used against the suspect later in court. In the present case, the SC held that retroactive application of the *Edwards* case was not proper.

Solesbee v. Balkcom, 339 U.S. 9, 70 S.Ct. 457 (1950) [**George W. SOLESBEE, Petitioner, v. R.P. BALKCOM, Jr., Warden of the State Penitentiary, Tattnall, Georgia**] (**Corrections; Death Penalty**) Solesbee was convicted of murder. He filed a writ of *habeas corpus,* seeking to have a hearing on whether he was insane. Then he was sentenced to death. At the time, Georgia governors had the power of determining whether or not such a hearing should be convened, and determining on their own authority whether convicts were mentally competent. The SC rejected Solesbee's claim that he had a constitutional right to a postconviction proceeding to determine his sanity. The SC said that persons legally convicted and sentenced to death have no statutory or constitutional right to a judicially conducted or supervised trial or inquisition on the question of insanity subsequent to sentence.

Sorrells v. United States, 287 U.S. 435, 53 S.Ct. 210 (1932) [**C.V. SORRELLS, Petitioner, v. UNITED STATES**] (**Entrapment**) Sorrells was a resident of a North Carolina county. A revenue agent, undercover, approached him on numerous occasions, asking him repeatedly if he would supply the agent with illegal liquor. Sorrells was a war veteran, and the undercover agent used this information to become closer to Sorrells by stating that he, himself, was also a war veteran. After repeated requests to supply illegal liquor, Sorrells finally did so. He was arrested and convicted. He appealed on the grounds of entrapment. The SC heard his case and overturned his conviction. It said it was of the opinion that on the evidence produced in this case, the defense of entrapment was available and that the trial court was in error by holding that there was no entrapment and in refusing to submit this issue to the jury. Entrapment was generally defined as government enticement for persons to engage in criminal activities when such persons initially have no such inclinations for engaging in these criminal activities.

South Carolina v. Gathers, 490 U.S. 805, 109 S.Ct. 2207 (1989) [**SOUTH CAROLINA, Petitioner, v. Demetrius GATHERS**] (**Corrections; Death Penalty**) Gathers and some friends encountered a man, Haynes, in a public park and killed him. Specifically, Gathers beat Haynes with an umbrella, which Gathers subsequently shoved into Haynes' anus. During the trial, the prosecutor's closing remarks included reading various passages from a religious book Haynes had been carrying when he was killed. The prosecutor also engaged in extensive commentary about a voting card Haynes had carried, as well as commentary about his religious convictions and mental condition. Gathers was convicted of murder and first-degree sexual assault. He appealed, alleging prosecutorial misconduct and a violation of his due-process rights. The South Carolina Supreme Court heard Gathers' appeal and reversed his conviction. The state appealed. The SC affirmed the South Carolina Supreme Court, holding that the contents of Haynes' personal papers could not be said to relate directly to the circumstances of the crime. Thus, the "contents" of whatever religious tracts victims are carrying are not directly relevant to the "circumstances of the crime."

South Dakota v. Neville, 499 U.S. 553, 103 S.Ct. 916 (1983) [SOUTH DAKOTA, Petitioner, v. Mason Henry NEVILLE] (Confessions; Self-Incrimination) Neville was arrested and charged with driving while intoxicated. He was asked to take a blood-alcohol test and was advised that if he did not take such a test, his license would be revoked. Officers did not warn Neville, however, that his refusal could be used against him later in court, if the case went to trial. He refused to take the test and the case went to trial, where the prosecutor used Neville's refusal as evidence. Neville was convicted of DWI. He appealed, alleging that his refusal to take such a test ought to have been excluded because it was a violation of his right against self-incrimination under the Fifth Amendment. The SC upheld his conviction, saying that the blood-alcohol test is simple and not coercive; thus it does not violate the Fifth Amendment right against self-incrimination.

South Dakota v. Opperman, 428 U.S. 364, 96 S.Ct. 3092 (1976) [SOUTH DAKOTA, Petitioner, v. Donald OPPERMAN] (Inventory Searches; Law Enforcement Officers or Agencies; Searches Incident to Arrest; Vehicle Searches) Opperman's car had been impounded for various parking violations. Following customary procedures, police inventoried the car's contents and found marijuana in the glove compartment. Opperman was arrested, charged, and convicted of marijuana possession. He appealed, and his conviction was overturned by the South Dakota Supreme Court; then the prosecution appealed. The SC overturned the South Dakota Supreme Court, reinstating Opperman's conviction, saying that the police inventory of his vehicle had been a routine procedure followed by that particular police department. Thus, there had been no attempt to discover contraband known in advance to be in the vehicle.

Spaziano v. Florida, 468 U.S. 447, 104 S.Ct. 3154 (1984) [Joseph Robert SPAZIANO, Petitioner, v. FLORIDA] (Corrections; Death Penalty; Jury Instructions) Judges in Florida are required to consider jury recommendations, whatever they may be, and to give them *great weight.* In Alabama, in contrast, judges are required to give jury recommendations *proper weight.* Spaziano was convicted of first-degree murder in a Florida trial court, and following their deliberations, a majority of jurors recommended life imprisonment. However, the judge imposed the death penalty as punishment for Spaziano after weighing the aggravating and mitigating circumstances. The judge provided specific written findings in support of the death sentence he imposed. Spaziano appealed the judge's ruling, contending that among other things, the judge had failed to instruct the jury about lesser included offenses that may have provided the jurors with more alternative sentencing options. Further, Spaziano argued that his Eighth Amendment right against cruel and unusual punishment was violated when the judge imposed a death sentence after the

jury had recommended life imprisonment. The SC heard the case and upheld the death sentence imposed, holding that it was not error for the judge to refuse to instruct the jury on lesser included offenses. Also, the SC said that there is no constitutional requirement that a jury's recommendation of life imprisonment in a capital case be final so as to preclude the trial judge from overriding the jury's recommendation and imposing the death sentence. The fundamental issue in a capital sentencing proceeding is the determination of the appropriate punishment to be imposed on an individual, and the Sixth Amendment does not guarantee a right to a jury determination of that issue.

Spevack v. Klein, 385 U.S. 511, 87 S.Ct. 625 (1967) [Samuel SPEVACK, Petitioner, v. Solomon A. KLEIN] (Right to Counsel; Self-Incrimination) Spevack, an attorney, was served with a subpoena *duces tecum* and refused to comply by not surrendering financial documents or testifying at a judicial inquiry. The grounds he cited were that the information would be incriminating, and thus he had exercised his Fifth Amendment right against self-incrimination. A New York higher court ordered Spevack disbarred, because, it said, the privilege against self-incrimination was not available to attorneys. He appealed. The SC reversed his disbarment, saying that the privilege against self-incrimination was not applicable to *records,* the basis on which the New York court had disbarred him. The court could not disbar Spevack because of noncompliance with producing records.

Spinelli v. United States, 394 U.S. 410, 89 S.Ct. 584 (1972) [William SPINELLI, Petitioner, v. UNITED STATES] (Law Enforcement Officers or Agencies; Searches and Seizures) An informant alerted the FBI to Spinelli's allegedly illegal bookmaking activities in St. Louis. Spinelli was placed under FBI surveillance. During this surveillance, FBI agents observed Spinelli enter an apartment where a telephone was located, one supposedly used in this bookmaking activity. The FBI filed an affidavit with a United States magistrate, detailing its observations of Spinelli and its belief that he was engaged in illegal interstate bookmaking. Little information was relayed to the magistrate about the informant and the basis for the informant's reliability. FBI agents entered Spinelli's apartment, searched, and found materials implicating Spinelli in illegal bookmaking. He was convicted. He appealed, and the SC overturned the conviction primarily because the FBI agents had not met the two-pronged test established by *Aguilar v. Texas* (1964). The two-pronged test is (1) how well is the informant known by the law enforcement officer? and (2) how reliable has been previous information furnished by the informant? The SC also rejected a totality-of-circumstances test, concluding in part that it "paints too broad a brush," making an affidavit too vague to substantiate probable cause. Subsequently, in the case of *Illinois v. Gates* (1983), the SC modified the two-pronged test established in *Aguilar* and created an additional totality-of-circumstances test, making it currently unnecessary for law enforcement officers to detail the nature of their relations with informants and informant reliability.

Springfield v. Kibbe, 480 U.S. 257, 107 S.Ct. 1114 (1987) [City of SPRINGFIELD, Massachusetts, Petitioner, v. Lois

Thurston KIBBE, Administratrix of Estate of Clinton Thurston] (Law Enforcement Officers or Agencies) In September 1981, Springfield, MA, police received a telephone call that Thurston was assaulting a woman with a knife in an apartment. Later, police discovered that Thurston had fled in an automobile. His automobile was seen on a highway and followed by police, who attempted to stop it. Thurston would not stop, even after police had erected roadblocks along the highway. At some point, an officer, Perry, gave chase and fired his weapon at Thurston, who was allegedly attempting to run Perry off the road. One bullet struck Thurston in the head, and he died shortly thereafter in a hospital. His relatives filed suit against Springfield police for negligent training, alleging that it had led an officer wrongfully to shoot and kill Thurston. The SC heard the case and decided the question of whether a city can be held liable for the inadequate training of its employees. The SC held that there was no evidence on the record of deliberate indifference or recklessness in the apprehension of Thurston's fleeing vehicle. Thus, Thurston's relatives failed to prove essential elements of their claim, and therefore, the suit was dismissed as being improvidently granted.

Stack v. Boyle, 342 U.S. 1, 72 S.Ct. 1 (1951) [**Loretta S. STACK et al., Petitioners, v. BOYLE, U.S. Marshal**] (**Bail**) Stack was charged with conspiracy to commit a crime, and bail was set at $50,000. She protested, saying that the bail was excessive and that no hearing was ever held to determine how much bail should be set. The SC agreed with Stack and remanded the case back to the district court, where a hearing could be held on the bail issue. The Court held that bail had not been fixed by proper methods in this case. It did not try to determine or define "proper methods," however.

Stanford v. Kentucky, 492 U.S. 361, 109 S.Ct. 2969 (1989) [**Kevin N. STANFORD, Petitioner, v. KENTUCKY. Heath A. Wilkins, Petitioner, v. Missouri**] (**Death Penalty; Juvenile Law**) Stanford was charged with murder committed when he was 17 years old. He was transferred to criminal court to stand trial for murder as an adult. He was convicted and sentenced to death. He appealed, contending that he was too young to receive the death penalty and that the death penalty would be cruel and unusual punishment. The SC upheld his death sentence and ruled that it is not unconstitutional to apply the death penalty to persons who are convicted of murders they committed when they were 17. (*See Wilkins v. Missouri* [1989] *for a comparable case.*)

Stanford v. Texas, 379 U.S. 476, 85 S.Ct. 506 (1965) [**John W. STANFORD, Jr., Petitioner, v. State of TEXAS**] (**Law Enforcement Officers or Agencies; Searches Incident to Arrest**) Stanford was suspected of possessing and distributing Communist materials. A search warrant was issued ordering officers to go to Stanford's home and seize any materials relevant to Communism. He was convicted. He appealed, alleging that the statute under which the search warrant was issued was unconstitutionally vague about the place to be searched and the things to be seized. The SC agreed and reversed his conviction on those grounds.

Staples v. United States, 511 U.S. 600, 114 S.Ct. 1793 (1994) [**Harold E. STAPLES III, Petitioner, v. UNITED STATES**] (*Mens Rea*) Staples was convicted in federal court for possessing a machine gun. He appealed, arguing that he did not know that the semiautomatic rifle he had purchased had been modified so that it was capable of firing multiple rounds from one trigger pull, thus making it function as a machine gun. He argued that the government was required to prove, beyond a reasonable doubt, that he had known such a weapon was in fact a machine gun. The SC overturned Staples' conviction, saying that the government had not proved beyond a reasonable doubt that Staples had known the weapon had been modified. The statute prohibiting possession of a machine gun did not have a statement of *mens rea* or intent to commit a crime. Therefore, the SC relied upon common law to resolve such a question and directed the case back to the originating trial court to retry, this time using the *mens rea* condition as an important crime element. The prosecution was required to prove that Staples had known the firearm was automatic rather than semiautomatic as he claimed.

Steagald v. United States, 451 U.S. 204, 101 S.Ct. 1642 (1981) [**Gary Keith STEAGALD, Petitioner, v. UNITED STATES**] (**Law Enforcement Officers or Agencies; Searches and Seizures**) Police agents had been advised by a confidential informant that a wanted fugitive would be at a particular house in Atlanta. They obtained an arrest warrant and proceeded to the house, which belonged to Gaultney. Police saw Gaultney and Steagald standing in front of the house, conversing. Mistaking one of them for the fugitive, the agents drew their weapons, approached Steagald and Gaultney, and frisked them, determining that neither was the fugitive they sought. Then they proceeded to the house, where Mrs. Gaultney met them. They ordered her to place her hands against the wall and proceeded to search the premises thoroughly for their wanted fugitive, who was not there. Instead, they discovered a small quantity of cocaine. They obtained a search warrant for a subsequent search, which uncovered 43 pounds of cocaine. Steagald was charged with and convicted of possession of cocaine. He appealed, contending that a search warrant should have been obtained before officers entered the house initially, and that their subsequent search of the premises had been unreasonable and unlawful. The police contended that their arrest warrant had "entitled" them to search the premises to hunt for their fugitive, and that as the result of their search, the illegal contraband was discovered lawfully. The SC strongly disagreed, saying that neither exigent circumstances nor consent existed to entitle these officers to search the premises. Steagald's conviction was overturned, because a valid search warrant was required, based on probable cause, and the officers conducting the search had possessed no such warrant. Thus, all evidence subsequently seized was inadmissible in court against Steagald. The SC specifically noted that arrest warrants do not authorize searches of premises in any absolute sense. Search warrants are necessary for the types of searches conducted in this Atlanta residence. Otherwise, such searches are unlawful and violative of the Fourth Amendment provision against unreasonable searches and seizures.

Stewart v. LaGrand, 526 U.S. 115, 119 S.Ct. 1018 (1999) [Terry STEWART, Director, Arizona Department of Corrections, et al. v. Walter LaGRAND] (Cruel and Unusual Punishment; Death Penalty; Eighth Amendment) Walter LaGrand and his brother, Karl, were convicted of first-degree murder in Arizona and sentenced to death. LaGrand was given a choice of execution either by lethal gas or lethal injection. LaGrand chose lethal gas. Subsequently, LaGrand appealed on the grounds that execution by lethal gas violated his constitutional right against cruel and unusual punishment. The SC upheld LaGrand's conviction and sentence of death by lethal gas, holding that LaGrand had waived his claim that execution by lethal gas violated his Eighth Amendment right when he chose lethal gas over lethal injection.

Stinson v. United States, 508 U.S. 36, 113 S.Ct. 1913 (1993) [Terry Lynn STINSON, Petitioner, v. UNITED STATES] (U.S. Sentencing Guidelines) Stinson pleaded guilty to a five-count indictment resulting from a bank robbery. He was sentenced according to the U.S. Sentencing Guidelines and the statutory language that the instant offense of conviction be a crime of violence. Later, the statutory language was changed to expressly exclude the felon-in-possession offense from the crime-of-violence definition. The sentencing court ignored this language change, however, and sentenced Stinson to the more serious penalty range. Stinson appealed, and the SC overturned his sentence, saying that the lower court had erred when it ignored the Sentencing Commission language change. Such commentary by the Sentencing Commission is binding on federal court judges.

Stogner v. California, ___U.S.___, 123 S.Ct. 2446 (2003) [Marion Reynolds STOGNER, Petitioner, v. CALIFORNIA] (*Ex Post Facto* Laws; Sex Offender Laws) In 1998, a California jury indicted Marion Stogner on several counts of sex-related child abuse committed several decades earlier, from 1955 through 1973. The statute of limitations on these crimes was three years during that particular time interval. However, California enacted an *ex post facto* statute in 1993 governing sex-related offenses, which was amended with additional provisions in 1996. The new law provided for prosecutions of sex-related crimes where the statute of limitations had already expired, provided that authorities prosecuted defendants within one year following a victim's first complaint of the crime to police. Stogner moved to dismiss the complaint on grounds that the *ex post facto* nature of the new law was unconstitutional. The trial court agreed and dismissed the complaint. However, a California appeals court reversed, thus permitting Stogner's prosecution for these prior crimes. Stogner persisted in his appeal to the SC who heard his case. The SC reversed the California court, holding that California's law subjects individuals such as Stogner to prosecution long after the state has, in effect, granted amnesty, telling them that they are at liberty to return to their country and may cease to preserve the proofs of their innocence. The statute is unfairly retroactive. A law enacted after the expiration of a previously applicable limitations period violates the *ex post facto* clause of the U.S. Constitution when it is applied to revive a previously time-barred prosecution.

Stone v. Immigration and Naturalization Service, 514 U.S. 386, 115 S.Ct. 1537 (1995) [Marvin STONE, Petitioner, v. IMMIGRATION AND NATURALIZATION SERVICE] (Statute of Limitations) Stone was a Canadian who was convicted on January 3, 1983, of conspiracy and mail fraud. He served 18 months of a three-year term. In 1987, the INS issued a show-cause order as to why Stone should not be deported. In January 1988, a judge ordered his deportation. In July 1991, Stone appealed to the Board of Immigration to reconsider his deportation. The motion was denied as frivolous. Stone then appealed to the SC, which upheld the deportation order. The reason given was that a 90-day period for hearing appeals to final deportation orders had expired. It probably wouldn't have mattered if Stone's motion had been timely within the 90-day period, because persons convicted of mail fraud are barred from establishing "good moral character" for legal immigrant status.

Stone v. Powell, 428 U.S. 465, 96 S.Ct. 3037 (1976) [W. T. STONE, Warden, Petitioner, v. Lloyd Charles POWELL. Charles L. Wolff, Jr., Warden, Petitioner, v. David L. Rice] (Corrections; Inmate Rights; Searches and Seizures) An inmate filed a *habeas corpus* petition in a federal court seeking release from prison. The prisoner had already filed the same petition in a state court and the petition had been denied. The SC heard the appeal and rejected the argument of the inmate, concluding that a *habeas corpus* petition will not be heard in federal court after it has already been rejected in a state court. The SC stressed the fact that the inmate had a full and fair opportunity to argue the case in a state appellate court.

Stoner v. California, 376 U.S. 364, 84 S.Ct. 889 (1964) [Joseph Lyle STONER, Petitioner, v. State of CALIFORNIA] (Consent Searches; Law Enforcement Officers or Agencies) Stoner became a suspect in an armed-robbery investigation when police discovered a checkbook on the ground near the robbery scene. The checkbook had Stoner's name in it and checks made out to a hotel in another city. They went to the hotel and learned that Stoner was staying there. Although Stoner wasn't in his room, the hotel clerk admitted the officers into Stoner's room without an arrest or search warrant. The police found evidence linking Stoner with the robbery, and he was arrested and convicted. Later, he appealed, arguing that the police officers had lacked a valid search warrant to enter and search his room. The SC agreed, overturning Stoner's conviction and suppressing the discovered evidence. Hotel clerks are not in the position of granting consent to police for warrantless searches of hotel guest rooms. There is a reasonable expectation of privacy, and thus Stoner's Fourth Amendment right against an unreasonable search of his premises and seizure of personal effects had been violated.

Stovall v. Denno, 388 U.S. 293, 87 S.Ct. 1967 (1967) [Theodore STOVALL, Petitioner, v. Wilfred DENNO, Warden] (Law Enforcement Officers or Agencies; Lineups) Stovall was a murder suspect. The victim's wife was so severely injured that she was hospitalized in critical condition. Stovall was brought by police to the hospital, where the victim's wife identified him as the murderer. He was convicted. He appealed, alleging that he should have been subjected to a lineup with other black persons, and that he was the only black suspect shown to the victim's wife. The SC upheld Stovall's conviction, saying that under the circumstances, the victim's wife was the only person in the world who could actually exonerate Stovall, by simply saying, "He is not the man." In this case, and under these circumstances, police identification methods had been proper. The usual police lineup believed by Stovall to be appropriate was totally out of the question, given the victim's wife's condition in the hospital. Thus, traditional lineups may be circumvented depending on the circumstances.

Strickland v. Washington, 466 U.S. 668, 104 S.Ct. 2052 (1984) [**Charles E. STRICKLAND, Superintendent, Florida State Prison, et al., Petitioners, v. David Leroy WASHINGTON**] (**Sixth Amendment**) Conduct in Washington's case of whether ineffective assistance of counsel was rendered was measured according to the following standards: Was the counsel's conduct such that it undermined the functioning of the adversarial process so much that a trial could not be relied on to render a just result? Did the counsel's behavior fall below the objective standard of reasonableness? There must be a reasonable probability that, but for counsel's unprofessional errors, the result of the proceedings would have been different.

Strickler v. Greene, 527 U.S. 263, 119 S.Ct. 1936 (1999) [**Tommy David STRICKLER, Petitioner, v. Fred W. GREENE, Warden**] (**Discovery**) Strickler was convicted of capital murder in Virginia and sentenced to death. During his trial, Strickler's attorney was permitted to examine prosecutors' files for exculpatory evidence. However, the prosecutor did not advise defense counsel that police files may have contained exculpatory information favorable to Strickler, which may have impeached the veracity of one of the witnesses against Strickler. Strickler filed a *habeas corpus* petition, alleging that the prosecutor had a duty to reveal police documents that may have impeached witnesses against him. Presently, there are three components of a true *Brady* violation: (1) the evidence at issue must be favorable to the accused, either because it is exculpatory, or because it is impeaching; (2) the evidence must have been suppressed by the state, either willfully or inadvertently; and (3) prejudice must have ensued. The SC heard Strickler's case and decided that although the *Brady* rule had been violated in part, the materiality of the evidence would not have affected the trial outcome. The SC held that (1) undisclosed documents impeaching eyewitness testimony as to circumstances of abduction of victim were favorable to Strickler for purposes of *Brady,* and (2) Strickler reasonably relied on prosecution's open-file policy and established cause for procedural default in raising a *Brady* claim, but (3) Strickler could not show either materiality under *Brady* or prejudice that would excuse Strickler's procedural default.

Stringer v. Black, 503 U.S. 222, 112 S.Ct. 1130 (1992) [**James R. STRINGER, Petitioner, v. Lee Roy BLACK, Commissioner, Mississippi Department of Corrections, et al.**] (**Aggravating and Mitigating Circumstances; Death Penalty; Eighth Amendment**) Stringer was convicted of capital murder in Mississippi. The penalty phase following conviction contained judicial instructions to the jury about the aggravating circumstance of finding the crime "especially heinous, atrocious, or cruel." He was sentenced to death. At the time of Stringer's conviction, two important cases had not yet been decided that would ultimately declare the phrase "especially heinous, atrocious, or cruel" to be unconstitutionally vague. These cases were, respectively, *Clemons v. Mississippi* (1990) and *Maynard v. Cartwright* (1988). Thus Stringer, in a *habeas corpus* petition filed after these cases had been decided, sought to have his death sentence vacated because of the new rule established in these cases. Lower courts of appeals denied Stringer any relief, and he appealed to the SC. The SC vacated Stringer's death sentence, holding that it had become final prior to cases establishing that a statute making the "especially heinous, atrocious, or cruel" nature of a crime an aggravating circumstance violated the Eighth Amendment, and was not precluded from relying on cases on the ground that they represented a new rule.

Strunk v. United States, 412 U.S. 434, 93 S.Ct. 2260 (1973) [**Clarence Eugene STRUNK, Petitioner, v. UNITED STATES**] (**Speedy Trials**) Strunk was arrested for interstate transportation of a stolen vehicle from Wisconsin to Illinois, and Strunk's case was eventually sent to the grand jury. In the meantime, Strunk, who had committed another crime in Nebraska, was tried and convicted on those charges, and sentenced to one to three years by a state court. Subsequently, a federal grand jury indicted Strunk on the federal charges, although a 10-month interval lapsed between Strunk's indictment and arraignment. He was subsequently convicted of the federal crime and sentenced to five years to run concurrently with his state one- to three-year sentence. He appealed, arguing that the 10-month delay relating to the federal charges against him violated his speedy-trial rights. Strunk asked the court not only to reverse his conviction, but also to dismiss the charges against him. The appeals court reversed Strunk's conviction but did not dismiss the criminal charges, arguing that the "extreme" remedy of dismissal of the charges was not warranted. Rather, the appellate court remanded the case back to the trial court with orders to reduce Strunk's original sentence by 259 days in order to compensate him for the unnecessary delay. The government did not challenge the appellate decision. Strunk was dissatisfied with this result and appealed directly to the SC, who heard the case. The SC noted several considerations in determining whether speedy-trial rights of suspects have been violated: (1) whether there are overcrowded court dockets and understaffed prosecutor's offices; (2) whether defendants suffered substantial emotional distress because of long delays; and (3) whether an accused is released pending a trial and whether there is little or no immediate interest in having a trial. The SC also noted that the government did not challenge the appellate holding that Strunk had been denied a speedy trial and that this was indeed a constitutional rights violation. The SC declared that in view of this rights violation, the only possible remedy was to dismiss the charges against Strunk. It was so ordered.

Sullivan v. Louisiana, 508 U.S. 275, 113 S.Ct. 2078 (1993) [**John SULLIVAN, Petitioner, v. LOUISIANA**] (**Death Penalty; Jury Instructions**) Sullivan was convicted of first-degree murder and given the death penalty. He appealed to the SC, alleging that his Sixth Amendment right to a trial by jury had been violated when the jury was given unconstitutional instructions about the meaning of reasonable doubt. The SC agreed and reversed Sullivan's conviction and death sentence. The basis for the reversal of conviction was the improper and unconstitutional phraseology used by the judge for the jury instructions about how to evaluate reasonable doubt. (*See Cage v. Louisiana* [1990] *for a comparable case and the unconstitutional phraseology.*)

Sumner v. Shuman, 483 U.S. 66, 107 S.Ct. 2716 (1987) [George SUMNER, Director, Nevada Department of Prisons, et al., Petitioners, v. Raymond Wallace SHUMAN] (Aggravating and Mitigating Circumstances; Corrections; Death Penalty; Mandatory Death Penalty) In Nevada, Shuman was convicted of first-degree murder and sentenced to life without parole. While in prison, he murdered another inmate and was convicted of this second murder. This time, he was sentenced to the death penalty. He appealed. Nevada had a statute imposing a mandatory death penalty on prisoners who commit murder while imprisoned and already serving life terms. The SC overturned Shuman's death sentence, indicating that mandatory death penalties are unconstitutional because they do not consider aggravating and mitigating circumstances.

Superintendent, Massachusetts Correctional Institution, Walpole, v. Hill, 472 U.S. 445, 105 S.Ct. 2768 (1985) [SUPERINTENDENT, MASSACHUSETTS CORRECTIONAL INSTITUTION, WALPOLE, Petitioner, v. Gerald HILL and Joseph Crawford] (Corrections; Inmate Rights) Hill, an inmate at the Massachusetts State Prison at Walpole, received a disciplinary report charging that he had assaulted another inmate. Evidence consisted solely of an inmate's word that he saw three inmates moving away from an area where an inmate was subsequently found who had been beaten. An inference was made that Hill had assaulted the injured inmate, but no eyewitnesses had been present. The board decided in the absence of strong evidence that Hill was guilty and it placed him in isolation for 15 days with a loss of 100 days of good-time credit. Hill appealed. The SC upheld Hill's "sentence" imposed by the board because a lesser evidentiary standard exists in prison disciplinary hearings compared with evidentiary standards in court. From the limited factual evidence presented, a reasonable inference could have been drawn that Hill had been involved in the assault.

Swain v. Alabama, 380 U.S. 202, 85 S.Ct. 824 (1965) [Robert SWAIN, Petitioner, v. State of ALABAMA] (Peremptory Challenges) Robert Swain, a black man, was indicted and convicted of rape in Talladega County, AL, and sentenced to death. Swain exhausted all of his state criminal appeals and petitioned the SC, contending that he was denied a fair trial because there were no blacks on the jury that convicted him. Swain supported his allegations with statistical information showing that no blacks had served on petit juries since 1950. Furthermore, he alleged that the prosecution excluded several prospective black jurors in his case through the use of peremptory challenges. The SC affirmed Swain's conviction, holding that Swain had failed to demonstrate that

there was invidious discrimination in the selection of his jurors. The SC noted that since the early 1950s, petit and grand juries have always included one or more black persons. The grand jury that indicted Swain included two black grand jurors. Furthermore, among the petit jury pool from which the jurors were selected in Swain's case, there were eight blacks, two being exempt and six being struck by the prosecutor in the process of selecting the jury. There was no evidence presented to indicate that the prosecutor had engaged in a systematic action designed to prevent persons from serving on juries merely because they were black.

T

Tate v. Short, 401 U.S. 395, 91 S.Ct. 668 (1971) [Preston A. TATE, Petitioner, v. Herman SHORT] (Corrections; Probation and Parole) An indigent, Tate was unable to pay fines to a Houston traffic court. The court imposed cumulative fines of $425, which it ordered Tate to pay at the rate of $5 per day while incarcerated. He appealed. The SC overturned Tate's conviction and ruled such a method of fine repayment to be obviously unconstitutional. It was a violation of Tate's Fourteenth Amendment right to equal protection under the law to impose such a fine and incarceration repayment method. Fines cannot be converted to imprisonment in the event indigents cannot pay these fines. This would be tantamount to debtor's prisons, where debtors, unable to earn money, would be incarcerated until they could pay.

Taylor v. Alabama, 457 U.S. 687, 102 S.Ct. 2664 (1982) [Omar TAYLOR, Petitioner, v. ALABAMA] (Exclusionary Rule; Law Enforcement Officers or Agencies) Taylor was suspected of robbery. An uncorroborated tip from an informant led to his warrantless arrest without probable cause, following which he was subjected to a grueling interrogation and lineup. Eventually, Taylor signed a confession, which was admitted into trial against him, and he was convicted. He appealed. The SC reversed Taylor's conviction, holding that the confession had been extracted illegally, through coercion, and could not be used against him. The confession should have been suppressed because it was the fruit of an illegal arrest.

Taylor v. Illinois, 484 U.S. 400, 108 S.Ct. 646 (1988) [Ray TAYLOR, Petitioner, v. ILLINOIS] (Discovery; Eighth Amendment) In 1984, Taylor had a street fight with Bridges, and Taylor attempted to kill him. Taylor had prepared for the fight by bringing a pipe and a gun. He beat Bridges with the pipe and shot him in the back. Taylor attempted to shoot Bridges in the head while Bridges was lying on the ground, but the gun misfired. All of this testimony and other incriminating evidence was presented at Taylor's trial. During the trial, Taylor's attorney attempted to introduce a late witness, Wormley, who allegedly had exculpatory information. The judge listened to Wormley's testimony outside the presence of the jury, and decided that Wormley should not be called as a defense witness because he lacked veracity and because the defense counsel had violated the rules of discovery by failing to notify the prosecution about Wormley in advance. Taylor was convicted. He appealed, alleging that his right to a fair trial had been violated when Wormley was not permitted to testify. The SC heard the case and rejected Taylor's arguments. It was not constitutional error to prohibit Wormley from testifying, said the SC. Further, the *voir dire* examination of Wormley had probably protected the prosecution from undue prejudice resulting from *surprise*. Further, it was not unfair to hold Taylor responsible for his lawyer's misconduct. The defense has full authority to manage the conduct of the trial, and the client must accept the consequences of the lawyer's trial decisions.

Taylor v. Kentucky, 436 U.S. 478, 98 S.Ct. 1930 (1978) [Michael TAYLOR, Petitioner, v. Commonwealth of KENTUCKY] (Jury Instructions) Taylor was accused of second-degree robbery. At the conclusion of his trial, the judge issued several jury instructions, but he failed to advise the jury about the "presumption of innocence" to which the defendant was entitled, which could be overcome by proof beyond a reasonable doubt. Taylor was convicted. He appealed to the SC, which overturned his conviction. The SC said that the judge's omission of the presumption-of-innocence statement had resulted in a violation of Taylor's right to a fair trial.

Taylor v. Louisiana, 419 U.S. 522, 95 S.Ct. 692 (1975) [Billy J. TAYLOR, Appellant, v. State of LOUISIANA] (Corrections; Death Penalty) Taylor was convicted of aggravated kidnapping by a jury consisting entirely of men, because Louisiana had a statute prohibiting females from jury service. He appealed. The SC overturned Taylor's conviction on the grounds that his due-process rights had been violated when women were systematically excluded from the jury. Thus, Louisiana's law excluding women from jury duty is unconstitutional.

Taylor v. United States, 286 U.S. 1, 52 S.Ct. 466 (1932) [John Vance TAYLOR, Petitioner, v. UNITED STATES] (Law Enforcement Officers or Agencies) Revenue agents received complaints over a period of one year about a residence where illegal whiskey was allegedly being manufactured. One evening, agents went to the address. Finding no one home, they went around the house to a garage, which was locked. They smelled what seemed to be whiskey coming from within the garage, and they shined their flashlights inside and saw cardboard boxes, which they assumed contained illegal whiskey. They broke into the garage and searched the boxes, retrieving illegal whiskey. They charged Taylor with having untaxed and illegal whiskey, and he was convicted. He appealed. The SC held the actions of the investigating agents to have been unreasonable. It declared that agents cannot base their reasons for search on odor of whiskey alone, without more supporting factual information. Their purpose was to secure evidence so that they could support some future arrest of Taylor. The conviction against Taylor was overturned.

Teague v. Lane, 489 U.S. 288, 109 S.Ct. 1060 (1989) [Frank Dean TEAGUE, Petitioner, v. Michael LANE, Director, Illinois Department of Corrections, et al.] (Double Jeopardy) Teague, a black man, was accused of attempted murder. During jury selection, the prosecutor used all of his 10 peremptory challenges to exclude blacks from the jury. He was eventually convicted by an all white jury. In the meantime, *Batson v. Kentucky* (1986) had recently been decided, which established that blacks could not be excluded from jury duty by use of peremptory challenges. Teague sought to make this rule retroactive in his case, thus causing his conviction to be overturned and a new trial conducted. The SC rejected the retroactive principle relating to *Batson,* holding that convicted offenders are barred from making retroactive claims involving racial discrimination in jury selection. Further, Teague had failed to make a convincing case that the peremptory challenges had been used in a discriminatory fashion.

Tennessee v. Garner, 471 U.S. 1, 105 S.Ct. 1694 (1985) [TENNESSEE, Appellant, v. Cleamtee GARNER, etc., et al. Memphis Police Department et al., Petitioners, v. Cleamtee Garner, etc., et al.] (Deadly Force; Law Enforcement Officers or Agencies) A 15-year-old boy, Edward Garner, and a friend were in an empty home in Memphis late at night when neighbors reported the "breaking and entering" to police. Police officers approached the home and saw someone fleeing. They shouted warnings to the fleeing suspects and finally shot at them. One bullet struck Garner in the back of the head, killing him instantly. The standard governing the use of deadly force was that *any* force could be employed, even deadly force, to prevent the escape of fleeing felons. Because burglary is a felony, those fleeing from the empty home were felony suspects and police believed they were entitled to shoot at them. Many years later, in 1985, the SC declared that deadly force had not been warranted in this case, as burglary is punishable with a few years in prison, not the death penalty. This landmark case was significant because it effectively nullified the fleeing-felon standard for using deadly force. Since then, deadly force may be applied to fleeing suspects only (1) if they pose a threat to the lives of officers, or (2) if they pose a threat to the lives of others.

Terry v. Ohio, 392 U.S. 1, 88 S.Ct. 1868 (1968) [John W. TERRY, Petitioner, v. State of OHIO] (Law Enforcement Officers or Agencies; Stop and Frisk) A 35-year veteran police officer observed Terry and two companions standing on a Cleveland street corner. They moved up and down the street, looking in store windows, returning frequently to the corner and conversing. The officer was suspicious of this behavior and confronted them about their identities and business. He patted down Terry and discovered a revolver. Terry was charged with carrying a concealed weapon and convicted. Terry appealed, and the SC eventually heard the case. The argument was whether police officers may "pat down and frisk" suspicious persons if they have reasonable suspicion that a crime is being contemplated. The SC upheld Terry's conviction, determining that police officers may pat down suspects as a means of protecting themselves and determining whether suspicious persons may be armed and pose a danger to them. (*See Sibron v. New York* [1968] *as a limitation to the pat-down-and-frisk ruling in* Terry.)

Texas v. Brown, 460 U.S. 730, 103 S.Ct. 1535 (1983) [TEXAS, Petitioner, v. Clifford James BROWN] (Law Enforcement Officers or Agencies; Searches and Seizures; Vehicle Searches) Brown was a motorist stopped by police at a routine driver's license checkpoint. Brown was asked to show officers his driver's license, and while he was fumbling for it, a party balloon dropped out of his pocket. It appeared to be tied at one end. Officers knew or had strong reason to believe that such balloons were often receptacles for drugs, such as cocaine. Brown continued to search for his license, and he reached into his glove compartment. When he did so, the officer shined his flashlight into the glove box and saw in plain view other party balloons, as well as glassine envelopes containing a white substance. One balloon was retrieved by an officer and examined more closely. The balloon contained cocaine, and Brown was subsequently convicted of cocaine possession. He appealed, arguing that the search of his vehicle had violated his Fourth Amendment rights, because the cocaine had not been in plain view. In this case, the SC upheld the validity of the officer's search of these balloons, saying that the police do not have to be absolutely certain that an object contains contraband in order for it to be inspected and seized under the plain-view rule. The plain-view rule states that officers may seize any apparent illegal contraband if it is in plain view and if they are in a place they are entitled to be at the time they view it. Thus, police officers might accompany paramedics to a rescue of a heart attack victim and observe illegal drugs on the victim's nightstand. The contraband is subject to seizure, because the police are in a place they have a right to be when they see it in plain view.

Texas v. Cobb, 532 U.S. 162, 121 S.Ct. 1335 (2001) [TEXAS, Petitioner, v. Raymond Levi COBB] (Confessions; *Miranda* Warning; Sixth Amendment) Cobb was indicted for a home burglary, and counsel was appointed to represent him. While in police custody, he received the *Miranda* warning concerning the burglary but waived his right to remain silent. During his interrogation concerning the burglary, Cobb was also Mirandized and questioned by police concerning the disappearance of a woman and her baby daughter from the home he was accused of burglarizing. Cobb said that he knew nothing about the disappearance of the woman and child. Later, while Cobb was out on bond awaiting the burglary trial, he confessed to his father that he had murdered the woman and child, and his father notified the police. Although he had not been charged with murder, he confessed to police anyway. Subsequently, he was convicted of the two murders and sentenced to death. Cobb appealed, contending that his confession to police about the two murders should have been suppressed because it was obtained without the presence of his attorney while he was under indictment for the unrelated charge of burglary. The Texas Supreme Court reversed and remanded his capital murder conviction to the lower court. State prosecutors appealed to the SC, who heard the case. The SC reversed the Texas Supreme Court, holding that the Sixth Amendment right to counsel does not bar police from interrogating suspects about other crimes while they are under indictment for other offenses that are factually related.

Texas v. McCullough, 475 U.S. 134, 106 S.Ct. 976 (1986) [TEXAS, Petitioner, v. Sanford James McCULLOUGH]

(Double Jeopardy; Plea Bargaining) McCullough was convicted of murder in a Texas court and sentenced to 20 years by a jury. Because of prosecutorial misconduct, however, the judge declared that McCullough should receive a new trial. This time, a new trial also resulted in his conviction for murder, but McCullough elected to have the judge fix his sentence. The judge imposed a sentence of 50 years rather than the 20-year sentence imposed in the earlier trial. McCullough appealed, arguing that the increased sentence length was the result of judicial vindictiveness. The SC disagreed and upheld the judge's 50-year sentence, saying that the judge was the same one who had detected prosecutorial misconduct and ordered the new trial for McCullough. Thus, an interpretation of vindictiveness was overcome by the judge's behavior of fairness in supporting a new trial for McCullough.

Thigpen v. Roberts, 468 U.S. 27, 104 S.Ct. 2916 (1984) [Morris THIGPEN, Commissioner, Mississippi Department of Corrections, et al., Petitioner, v. Barry Joe ROBERTS] (Sixth Amendment) Roberts had been intoxicated while driving a pickup truck carrying a passenger, and the passenger was subsequently killed in an accident Roberts caused. He was convicted of several misdemeanors, including reckless driving, driving while his license was revoked, driving on the wrong side of the road, and driving while intoxicated. He appealed. A subsequent trial *de novo* was granted under Mississippi law. Before the trial could take place, an indictment was issued against Roberts for manslaughter, arising out of the same incident for which he had been earlier convicted. Roberts appealed the new indictment as unconstitutional, while his case was under appeal to a higher court. He was nevertheless tried on the manslaughter charge, convicted, and sentenced to a 20-year prison term. He filed a *habeas corpus* petition, alleging that it was unconstitutional for the state to try him on a manslaughter charge before his appeal could be heard on the previous misdemeanor charges. The SC heard his case and agreed with Roberts, because of the violation of his due-process rights. The SC declared that the prosecution of Roberts for manslaughter, following his invocation of his statutory right to appeal his misdemeanor convictions, had been unconstitutional. The resulting conviction could not stand.

Thompson v. Keohane, 516 U.S. 99, 116 S.Ct. 457 (1995) [Carl THOMPSON, Petitioner, v. Patrick KEOHANE, Warden, et al.] (Confessions; Custodial Interrogations; Law Enforcement Officers or Agencies; *Miranda* Warning) Two moose hunters in Alaska discovered the body of a woman who had been stabbed 29 times. A bulletin was issued by state troopers to the public at large for assistance in determining her identity. Thompson informed police that his missing wife, Dixie, seemed to fit the description of the victim. Thompson drove to the troopers' headquarters in his truck and identified certain of the victim's items as belonging to his wife. While at the headquarters, he was told by investigating officers that although he was free to leave at any time, they *knew* he had killed his wife and suggested that he confess. Thompson was further advised during his presumed "noncustodial interrogation" that officers were preparing search warrants for his truck and home, and that they would probably discover something in-

criminating anyway. Thompson was being held in a small interview room with a tape recorder. He broke down and confessed. Following his confession, he was allowed to leave the
troopers' headquarters. The police impounded his truck, but
they gave him a ride home. Two hours later, after obtaining an
arrest warrant, they arrived and arrested him for first-degree
murder. Thompson was convicted of murder. He appealed.
The SC was asked to determine whether Thompson had or
had not been in custodial interrogation at the time his confession was made. If he had been in custody, then police would
have had to tell him his *Miranda* rights first in order for his
confession to be properly admissible later in court. In this instance, the SC used the following two-pronged standard: (1)
What were the circumstances surrounding the interrogation?
and (2) Given those circumstances, would a reasonable person
have felt he or she was not at liberty to terminate the interrogation and leave? Without providing a direct answer to this question, the SC vacated Thompson's murder conviction and remanded the case to a lower federal court for a *habeas corpus*
action to determine the custody question. In essence, a subsequent court would determine whether Thompson had been in
custody at the time he was interrogated; pending the outcome
of this determination, his murder conviction was temporarily
vacated.

Thompson v. Louisiana, 469 U.S. 17, 105 S.Ct. 409
(1984) [**Lillian THOMPSON v. LOUISIANA**] (**Fourth
Amendment; Law Enforcement Officers or Agencies**) In
May 1982, Jefferson Parish police officers responded to a report of a homicide made by the daughter of Lillian Thompson. They went to the house and found Thompson's husband
dead of a gunshot wound and Thompson lying unconscious
nearby, apparently having recently ingested a drug overdose in
a suicide attempt. The daughter reported that her mother had
shot the father and then ingested a quantity of pills to attempt
suicide. The officers transported Thompson to the hospital,
where she was treated for a drug overdose, and they secured the
crime scene. Homicide investigators, without a warrant, arrived a few hours later and conducted a thorough search of every room in the house, discovering a pistol and other evidence.
Because the search had been warrantless, Thompson sought to
suppress the evidence (e.g., the gun and a suicide note, among
other things) from the trial proceedings. Nevertheless, all evidence was subsequently admitted against her in a trial, and she
was convicted of second-degree murder. She appealed. The SC
said that a nonconsensual and warrantless search of the premises had been conducted by police who had had time to get a
valid search warrant but had not done so. Therefore, the evidence against Thompson they had seized was inadmissible.
The conviction was overturned.

Thompson v. Oklahoma, 487 U.S. 815, 108 S.Ct. 2687
(1988) [**William Wayne THOMPSON, Petitioner, v.
OKLAHOMA**] (**Death Penalty; Juvenile Law**) Thompson
was 15 years old when his brother-in-law was brutally murdered. Thompson was suspected. Under Oklahoma law, the
district attorney filed a statutory petition to have him waived
to criminal court, where he could be tried for murder as an
adult. The waiver was granted, and Thompson was tried, con-

victed, and sentenced to death. Thompson appealed, and his
case was eventually reviewed by the SC. The SC concluded
that "the Eighth and Fourteenth Amendments prohibit the execution of a person who was under 16 years of age at the time
of his or her offense" (108 S.Ct. at 2700). Thompson's death
sentence was overturned. Thompson's attorney had originally
requested the Court to draw a line so that all those under age
18 would be exempt from the death penalty as a punishment,
regardless of their crimes. The SC refused to do this. (*See also
Stanford v. Kentucky* [**1989**] *and Wilkins v. Missouri* [1989].)

Thornburgh v. Abbott, 490 U.S. 401, 109 S.Ct. 1874
(1989) [**Richard L. THORNBURGH, Attorney General of
the United States, et al., Petitioners, v. Jack ABBOTT, et al.**]
(**Corrections; Inmate Rights**) Several federal prisoners filed
suit against the Federal Bureau of Prisons (FBP) to contest the
regulations pertaining to the receipt of publications from different publishers. The FBP policy disallowed inmates to receive publications that were deemed detrimental to institutional order or discipline. The SC agreed with the FBP and its
policy, saying that the government, in disallowing certain publications, must show (1) that there is a rational connection between the policy and the government interest put forward to
justify it; (2) that there is a potential impact of the policy on
correctional staff and inmates alike; (3) whether there are alternative means of asserting rights available to prisoners; and (4)
the existence of available alternatives to the regulation. (*See
Turner v. Safley* [**1987**] *for a comparable ruling.*)

Thornton v. United States ___U.S.___, 124 S. Ct. 2127
(2004) [**Marcus THORNTON, Petitioner, v. UNITED
STATES**] (**Fourth Amendment; Searches and Seizures;
Searches Incident to an Arrest**) Thornton was a Norfolk, VA,
motorist who was noticed driving slowly by a police officer
driving an unmarked vehicle. The officer's suspicion of
Thornton's vehicle was confirmed when a license plate check
revealed that the license plates did not match the car Thornton
was driving. Thornton was stopped and quickly exited his vehicle. The police officer asked Thornton if Thornton had any
illegal narcotics on his person and whether the officer could
search him. Thornton admitted to possessing drugs and was
arrested and placed in the officer's cruiser. Shortly thereafter,
the officer searched Thornton's car and found a handgun under the driver's seat. A grand jury later indicted Thornton on
charges of possessing cocaine with intent to distribute and
with possessing a firearm after having been previously convicted of another felony. Thornton sought to suppress the firearm as the result of an unconstitutional search in violation of
the Fourth Amendment. He contended that the officer could
not search his car, as he had recently exited it. His motion to
suppress was denied, and he was convicted of these crimes and
sentenced to 180 months' imprisonment and 8 years of supervised release. He appealed and the SC eventually heard the
case. The state claimed that the officer lawfully conducted a
search of Thornton's vehicle as a search incident to an arrest,
despite the fact that Thornton had exited his vehicle prior to
the search. Furthermore, the state argued, a subsequent inventory search of the vehicle would have disclosed the presence of
the handgun regardless. The SC upheld Thornton's convic-

tion and rejected his Fourth Amendment violation claim, holding that the Fourth Amendment allows a police officer to search a vehicle's passenger compartment as a contemporaneous incident to an arrest, even when the officer does not make contact until the person arrested has already left the vehicle.

Tison v. Arizona, 481 U.S. 137, 107 S.Ct. 1676 (1987) [**Ricky Wayne TISON and Raymond Curtis Tison, Petitioners, v. ARIZONA**] (**Corrections; Death Penalty**) Tison was the son of a convicted murderer. He and his brother planned the escape of their father from prison by entering it with an ice chest filled with guns. They armed their father and another convicted murderer, who escaped with their father. Later, in Tison's presence, the father and the other convicted murderer abducted, robbed, and killed a family of four. Tison did nothing to prevent his father and the other man from killing the family. In fact, when apprehended later, Tison expressed surprise that the murders had occurred and denied any direct culpability. All four men were convicted. Under the felony-murder statute in Arizona, Tison and his brother were sentenced to death as the result of the felony-murder conviction. They appealed their death sentences, contending that they had not specifically killed anyone; therefore, they should receive a less serious sentence. The SC disagreed and upheld their death sentences, holding that their participation in the felony murder was major, and their mental state was one of reckless indifference to human life. Persons who do not actually kill others but participate in their killing may receive the death penalty.

Tollett v. Henderson, 411 U.S. 258, 93 S.Ct. 1602 (1973) [**Lewis S. TOLLETT, Warden, Petitioner, v. Willie Lee HENDERSON**] (**Plea Bargaining**) Willie Lee Henderson was indicted for first-degree murder in the robbery of a Nashville liquor store in Davidson County, TN, in 1948. Three weeks after he was arrested, Henderson voluntarily signed a confession admitting his involvement in the shooting and robbery. He entered a guilty plea through a plea bargain on the advice of counsel in order to avoid the death penalty. The indictment was from a grand jury consisting entirely of whites and from which blacks were automatically excluded. He was sentenced to 99 years in prison. Twenty-five years later, Henderson filed numerous *habeas corpus* petitions, alleging that his confession to the murder had been coerced and that he had been denied effective assistance of counsel. Both claims were rejected. Later, Henderson filed another *habeas corpus* petition alleging that he was deprived of his constitutional rights because blacks had been excluded from the grand jury that originally indicted him in 1948. A federal district court granted his *habeas corpus* motion, and it was affirmed by a federal court of appeals. The SC reversed this decision and reinstated Henderson's murder conviction. The sole question considered by the SC was whether a state prisoner, pleading guilty with the advice of counsel, may later obtain release through federal *habeas corpus* by proving only that the indictment to which he pleaded was returned by an unconstitutionally selected grand jury. The SC said that Henderson was not entitled to release from custody solely by reason of the fact that the grand jury that indicted him was unconstitutionally selected.

The SC added that Henderson was not precluded from challenging the voluntariness and intelligent nature of his guilty plea.

Tower v. Glover, 467 U.S. 914, 104 S.Ct. 2820 (1984) [**Bruce TOWER, etc., et al., Petitioners, v. Billy Irl GLOVER**] (**Civil Rights, Section 1983 Claims**) Glover was charged with robbery. Tower represented Glover at his trial. Glover suspected that Tower had conspired with various state officials in negotiating his conviction. Glover appealed. Tower countered by alleging that he was immune from Title 42 U.S.C. Section 1983 suits. Also, a lower appellate court said that Glover had failed to make a valid argument concerning any conspiracy to convict him. Glover appealed again. The SC heard the case and ruled in Glover's favor. The SC said that Glover's complaint adequately alleged conduct under "color of state law" for purposes of a Section 1983 action. Also, state public defenders are not immune from liability under this same section. The SC did not rule on the factual accuracy of the allegations; it merely said that Glover had a right to pursue his case in court.

Townsend v. Burke, 334 U.S. 736, 68 S.Ct. 1252 (1948) [**Frank TOWNSEND, Petitioner, v. C.J. BURKE, Warden**] (**Confessions; Corrections; Sixth Amendment**) Townsend was a fugitive who had been indicted for burglary and armed robbery in 1945. Several of his accomplices had made confessions to police implicating him. He was arrested later in 1945, and he pleaded guilty to two charges of robbery and two charges of burglary. He was sentenced to a long prison term. He appealed on various grounds. First, he alleged that he had not been represented by counsel when he pleaded guilty in court. Second, he argued that his long detention by police without access to an attorney was unreasonable. He had also not been advised of the particularity of his crimes or the punishments associated with them. Thus, he alleged that his due-process rights had been violated. The SC overturned his conviction and remanded the case for a new trial, holding that although counsel might not have changed the sentence, he could have taken steps to see that the conviction and sentence were not predicated on misinformation or misreading of court records, a requirement of fair play that absence of counsel withheld from this prisoner. Convicted offenders have the right to counsel at the time of their sentencing.

Townsend v. Sain, 372 U.S. 293, 83 S.Ct. 745 (1963) [**Charles TOWNSEND, Petitioner, v. Frank G. SAIN, Sheriff of Cook County, et al.**] (**Confessions; Law Enforcement Officers or Agencies; Probation and Parole**) Townsend was suspected of murder in Cook County, IL. Following his arrest, he was subjected to intensive questioning by police. A doctor from the police department administered Townsend an injection of phenobarbital, known as "truth serum." Under this drug, Townsend gave a confession. He was convicted. He appealed, recanting his confession and saying it had been given involuntarily. He asked to have his confession testimony excluded. His request was rejected, and the doctor who administered the truth serum was not required to testify, although Townsend's attorney had made such a request. Townsend appealed to the SC, which overturned his conviction and remanded the case for retrial, not intending to question the factual evidence but rather to allow the originating trial court the opportunity of hearing the evidence concerning the concealment of testimony by the doctor about the phenobarbital and other matters. Factual discrepancies would be resolved through further court action.

Trammel v. United States, 445 U.S. 40, 100 S.Ct. 906 (1980) [**Otis TRAMMEL, Jr., Petitioner, v. UNITED STATES**] (**Immunity; Self-Incrimination**) Otis Trammel was charged with importing and conspiring to import heroin in the U.S. district court of Colorado. Before the trial, government prosecutors indicated their intention to call Trammel's wife to testify against him. Trammel objected on the grounds that people cannot be compelled to make incriminating statements to others about their spouses. Trammel's wife was granted immunity and testified against Trammel voluntarily. He was convicted. Trammel appealed, moving to suppress her testimony. The SC upheld Trammel's conviction, holding that people may voluntarily act as witnesses against their spouses. Trammel's wife had been granted immunity from prosecution and thus had testified freely. The fact that she was the defendant's wife was immaterial to whether she testified voluntarily. She could have refused to testify. Thus, Trammel's claim of spousal privilege was rejected.

Trop v. Dulles, 356 U.S. 86, 78 S.Ct. 590 (1958) [**Albert L. TROP, Petitioner, v. John Foster DULLES, as Secretary of State of the United States and United States Department of State**] (**Corrections; Inmate Rights**) Trop was an American citizen stationed in French Morocco during World War II. He escaped from a stockade where he had been confined briefly for a breach of discipline, and later in the day he was picked up by military authorities as he was walking back to the military compound. He was charged with desertion and given a general court-martial. His sentence was three years' hard labor and a dishonorable discharge, among other things. In 1952, Trop applied for a passport but was denied one because he had lost his citizenship as the result of the conviction and dishonorable discharge. Trop appealed. He contended that the loss of citizenship was cruel and unusual punishment. The SC agreed and reinstated Trop's citizenship. Loss of citizenship may constitute cruel and unusual punishment in view of the offense.

Tuggle v. Netherland, 516 U.S. 10, 116 S.Ct. 283 (1995) [**Lem Davis TUGGLE, Jr., v. J.D. NETHERLAND, Warden**] (**Aggravating and Mitigating Circumstances; Death Penalty; Jury Instructions**) Tuggle was accused of first-degree murder in a Virginia court. During the trial, unrebutted testimony was given by a psychiatrist indicating Tuggle's future dangerousness and "vileness" as an aggravating circumstance. He was convicted. He appealed, alleging that the state had not afforded him, as an indigent, the opportunity of rebutting the "dangerousness" prediction made by the state psychiatrist. The SC remanded the case (*Tuggle v. Virginia,* 471 U.S. 1096, 105 S.Ct. 2315 [1985]) to the Virginia Supreme Court, which invalidated the "future dangerousness" aggravating circumstance but nevertheless upheld Tuggle's death sentence. Then Tuggle sought to invalidate the death sentence on grounds that a constitutional error had been committed and that a new trial should be granted. The SC heard Tuggle's appeal and remanded the case to the Fourth Circuit Court of Appeals. The SC concluded by saying that invalidation of one aggravator does not necessarily require that the death sentence should be set aside, but existence of a valid aggravator does not always excuse constitutional error in admission or exclusion of evidence. Essentially, the Fourth Circuit Court was to determine whether such error was "harmless" or "reversible."

Turner v. Louisiana, 379 U.S. 466, 85 S.Ct. 546 (1965) [**Wayne TURNER, Petitioner, v. State of LOUISIANA**] (**Jury Trials**) In a three-day murder trial, deputy sheriffs were in continuous contact with jurors, eating meals with them and chatting with them informally about the trial. Later, the deputies testified against Turner, and he was convicted. Turner appealed, arguing that substantial prejudice against him had been created by the deputy sheriff–juror relation. The SC agreed and reversed his conviction, holding that the credibility attached to the deputy sheriffs' testimony by the jury was such that the jury could not have been impartial in their deliberations.

Turner v. Murray, 476 U.S. 28, 106 S.Ct. 1683 (1986) [**Willie Lloyd TURNER, Petitioner, v. Edward W. MURRAY, Director, Virginia Department of Corrections**] (**Juries; Jury Trials**) Turner was accused of an interracial crime. During *voir dire,* he asked the judge to insist that prospective jurors be advised of the victim's race and questioned about their possible racial bias. The judge denied this request and Turner was convicted. He appealed to the SC, which overturned the conviction, saying that defendants under the Sixth and Fourteenth Amendments are entitled to insist that prospective jurors be advised of the victim's race as well as whether the jurors have racial bias. (*See Ristaino v. Ross* [1986] *and Ham v. South Carolina* [1976].)

Turner v. Safley, 482 U.S. 78, 107 S.Ct. 2254 (1987) [**William R. TURNER et al., Petitioners, v. Leonard SAFLEY et al.**] (**Corrections; Inmate Rights**) Prison inmates filed a class-action suit against the Missouri Division of Corrections, alleging that prison regulations forbidding or restricting mail between family members who are inmates at other institutions are unconstitutional. Further, the inmates alleged that a rule that permitted inmates to marry only when there were compelling circumstances, such as pregnancy or the birth of an illegitimate child, was unconstitutional. The SC declared that regulations prohibiting inmate marriages are unconstitutional. However, regulations regarding mail exchanges between related inmates in different prisons, as well as other inmate rights, should be determined as follows: such regulations are valid as long as they are related reasonably to legitimate penological interests, such as prison security, rehabilitation, security, and the orderly running of the institution. Thus, this case sets specific standards that declare the difference between inmate and institutional rights. Institutional regulations will prevail under the conditions specified above. One example of why prisons would *not* want to permit certain types of mail exchanges between prisoners in different institutions is the potential for institutional disruption and the perpetuation of inmate gang activities. Gang members of different institutions would be in a better position to establish regular mail networks between other gang members elsewhere. This is a legitimate concern and penological interest that would suffice to prohibit such prisoner information exchanges.

Tuyet Mai Thi Phan v. United States, ___U.S.___, 123 S.Ct. 2130 (2003) *See Khanh Phuong Nguyen v. United States* (2003).

Tyler v. Cain, 533 U.S. 656, 121 S.Ct. 2478 (2001) [Melvin TYLER, Petitioner, v. Burl CAIN, Warden] (*Habeas Corpus* Petitions; Retroactive Rules) Tyler was convicted of second-degree murder following a fight with his girlfriend. Tyler shot and killed their 20-day-old baby. Tyler launched numerous appeals for postconviction relief. His appeals were rejected. In 1997, Tyler filed a *habeas corpus* petition with the federal district court, claiming that the judge in his case had issued improper jury instructions defining reasonable doubt in his trial. The claim asked the court to retroactively apply a new rule that makes a new rule of constitutional law retroactive in cases on collateral review by the SC. Furthermore, the Antiterrorism and Effective Death Penalty Act (AEDPA) of 1996 provided some basis for Tyler's claim. However, the federal district judge held that a state prisoner can only prevail if the state court's decision was contrary to or involved an unreasonable application of clearly established federal law as determined by the SC. Concluding that Tyler could not overcome this barrier, the district court denied his petition, and the appellate court affirmed. Tyler then appealed to the SC, who heard the case. The SC affirmed the lower-court decisions, but clarified the issue of retroactivity addressed by the AEDPA. The SC also referred to lower-court interpretations of *Cage v. Louisiana* (1990), which dealt with the issue of the unconstitutionality of a jury instruction where there is a reasonable likelihood that the jury understood it to allow conviction without proof beyond a reasonable doubt. Some lower courts have interpreted *Cage* to mean that the issue of the unconstitutional jury instruction could be made retroactive to cases that are on collateral review by the SC. The SC held that this is not the case, and that "a new rule is made retroactive to cases on collateral review only if the Supreme Court holds it to be retroactively applicable to cases on collateral review." Tyler had failed to meet the standard that would lead the SC to retroactively apply the new rule.

U

United States v. Aguilar, 515 U.S. 593, 115 S.Ct. 2357 (1995) [UNITED STATES, Petitioner, v. Robert P. AGUILAR] (Judicial Misconduct) A grand jury had convened to investigate a crime. A wiretap had been placed on a suspect's telephone. Following the expiration of the wiretap, Aguilar, a federal judge, advised certain persons outside the United States Department of Justice that such a wiretap had

been placed, thus potentially obstructing justice. The FBI interviewed Judge Aguilar, in order to report back to the grand jury, and he gave false statements to it. Aguilar was charged with and convicted of (1) obstructing justice by disclosing the fact that a wiretap had been placed on a suspect's telephone, and (2) giving false statements to the FBI during a grand-jury investigation. Aguilar appealed, contending that the fact that the wiretap order had expired had removed any obligation on his part to remain quiet about it. Further, he contended that he had had no idea that the FBI would report his false statements to the grand jury. The SC heard Aguilar's appeal. The SC upheld the obstruction-of-justice charge, holding that the expiration of the wiretap order did not relieve Aguilar of the obligation to refrain from telling anyone about it. However, it overturned his conviction for making false statements to the FBI, because, they reasoned, the judge did not know such false statements were intended for grand-jury purposes.

United States v. Agurs, 427 U.S. 97, 96 S.Ct. 2392 (1976) [UNITED STATES, Petitioner, v. Linda AGURS] (Discovery) Agurs was charged with first-degree murder in the killing of her boyfriend, Sewell. Sewell was known to carry knives. Agurs took one away from him and stabbed him repeatedly. During her trial, information about Sewell's prior criminal record of assault and carrying a deadly weapon and his bad character were excluded from the prosecution's case against Agurs. Agurs was convicted. She appealed, arguing that this information about the victim would have helped her own case. The SC upheld Agurs' conviction, holding that the prosecutor was under no constitutional duty to disclose or volunteer any exculpatory information in the case against Agurs. The SC adopted a standard for evaluating the materiality of evidence. If such evidence would have been persuasive and produced reasonable doubt about the guilt of the defendant, then it would have been material. Under the circumstances, however, such disclosures would have been irrelevant.

United States v. Alvarez-Machain, 504 U.S. 655, 112 S.Ct. 2188 (1992) [UNITED STATES, Petitioner, v. Humberto ALVAREZ-MACHAIN] (Law Enforcement Officers or Agencies) A Mexican citizen, Alvarez-Machain, was indicted in the United States by federal authorities for his role in the murder of a DEA agent. Alvarez-Machain was abducted by federal agents in Mexico and taken back to the United States by force to face trial. He was convicted. He appealed, contending that his abduction by federal agents had violated the extradition treaty between Mexico and the United States, which therefore lacked the authority to try him. The SC disagreed and upheld his conviction. The SC said that no violation of the treaty existed, and that simple abduction of a criminal suspect by force from another country did not deprive the United States of jurisdiction over that criminal case.

United States v. A Parcel of Land in Rumson, N.J., 507 U.S. 111, 113 S.Ct. 1126 (1993) [UNITED STATES, Petitioner, v. A PARCEL OF LAND, Buildings, Appurtenances and Improvements, Known as 92 Buena Vista Avenue, RUMSON, NEW JERSEY, et al.] (Asset Forfeiture) The SC declared that in asset-forfeiture cases, innocent parties cannot have their property seized by the government as the result of criminal activities committed by others. Thus, if assets associated with drug transactions are later acquired by a new and innocent owner, the government cannot seize this property from the new and innocent owner.

United States v. Apfelbaum, 445 U.S. 115, 100 S.Ct. 948 (1980) [UNITED STATES, Petitioner, v. Stanley APFELBAUM] (Immunity; Self-Incrimination) Apfelbaum was granted immunity by the government in exchange for his testimony before a grand jury. He testified falsely at the grand-jury proceeding and was later indicted and convicted of a crime, at which time his grand-jury testimony was used against him. He appealed, contending that his Fifth Amendment right against self-incrimination had been violated when the government used his "immune" grand-jury testimony. The SC upheld Apfelbaum's conviction, saying that the Fifth Amendment right against self-incrimination does not protect false testimony given before grand juries. Thus, any false testimony before a grand jury may be used as evidence against someone, regardless of whether immunity had previously been granted in exchange for that testimony.

United States v. Armstrong, 517 U.S. 456, 116 S.Ct. 1480 (1996) [UNITED STATES, Petitioner, v. Christopher Lee ARMSTRONG et al.] (Discovery; Prosecutorial Misconduct) Armstrong and others were indicted for selling crack cocaine and using a firearm in connection with drug trafficking. Following their indictment for these crimes, Armstrong moved for discovery on a claim of selective prosecution, contending that because he was black, he was singled out for prosecution. The court granted the motion for discovery, but the government refused to comply with the motion. Therefore, the district-court judge dismissed the case. The government appealed, but the Ninth Circuit Court of Appeals affirmed. The SC was petitioned and heard the case. The SC reversed the Ninth Circuit, holding that Armstrong had failed to provide a convincing case that he was singled out for prosecution on the basis of his race. Armstrong had earlier presented a "study" listing 24 other drug defendants and their race, and whether they were prosecuted. Criminal defendants must present clear evidence of selective prosecution on the basis of their race, and in this instance, they failed to do so.

United States v. Arvizu, ___U.S.___, 122 S.Ct. 744 (2002) [UNITED STATES, Petitioner, v. Ralph ARVIZU] (Border Searches; Fourth Amendment; Searches and Seizures; Vehicle Searches) Arvizu was stopped by a Border Patrol agent in Arizona on an infrequently traveled dirt road near a Border Patrol checkpoint on a major highway. The stop was for investigatory purposes, and reasonable suspicion was created when Arvizu was observed sitting in a stiff manner and driving as though the Border Patrol agent was not there. Arvizu was traveling with a woman and two children. At one point, the children began waving mechanically at the Border Patrol agent, as though they were instructed to do so. They continued waving for four or five minutes. This further aroused the officer's suspicions. When the agent stopped the vehicle, he asked Arvizu if he could inspect the vehicle. With Arvizu's permission, the agent searched the vehicle and discovered a large quantity of marijuana in a black duffel bag under

the children's feet in the back seat. A further search revealed over 100 pounds of marijuana, and Arvizu was arrested and charged with intent to distribute marijuana for resale. Arvizu's attorney attempted to suppress the marijuana from Arvizu's subsequent trial, but the incriminating evidence was permitted and Arvizu was convicted. On appeal, the Ninth Circuit Court of Appeals reversed his conviction, holding that the search of his vehicle was unreasonable, largely on the basis that the Border Patrol agent lacked reasonable suspicion to stop his vehicle in the first place. The government appealed, and the SC heard the case. The SC reversed the circuit court and reinstated Arvizu's conviction, holding that the stop was permissible on the basis of the totality of circumstances. The SC said that the road's use by smugglers, the use of minivans by smugglers, and Arvizu's suspicious behavior while driving were sufficient factors to justify an investigatory stop.

United States v. Ash, 413 U.S. 300, 93 S.Ct. 2568 (1973) [UNITED STATES, Petitioner, v. Charles J. ASH, Jr.] (Lineups; Right to Counsel) Ash, a black man, was suspected of robbing a federally insured bank. A government informant, McFarland, brought Ash's name to the attention of the FBI, and color photographs of Ash and other blacks were shown to witnesses at the bank. They made uncertain identifications of Ash. Subsequently, Ash was indicted for the robbery and arrested. Color photographs were again shown to witnesses, but a black-and-white photograph of Ash was included. Again, witnesses were uncertain about Ash's identity. Trial was held almost three years following the robbery. Most witnesses could not positively identify Ash, but testimony was presented against him by McFarland. Ash was convicted and sentenced to concurrent sentences of 80 months to 12 years. Ash appealed. He contended that his attorney should have been present at the photo ID sessions. The SC did not specifically rule on the merits of Ash's conviction, but it did remand the case to the trial court for further proceedings on other issues. The SC said, however, that the Sixth Amendment does not grant the right to counsel in photographic displays conducted by the government for the purpose of allowing the witness to attempt to identify offenders.

United States v. Bagley, 473 U.S. 667, 105 S.Ct. 3375 (1985) [UNITED STATES, Petitioner, v. Hughes Anderson BAGLEY] (Discovery) As a result of an undercover investigation by the Bureau of Alcohol, Tobacco, and Firearms (BATF), Bagley was indicted in the United States District Court in Washington for breaking various narcotics and firearms statutes. His attorney filed a motion for discovery, obligating the government to disclose evidentiary materials it planned to use in court against Bagley, specifically, any documents that might be interpreted as "inducements, deals, or promises" made to government informants. The government supplied his attorney with various documents, including writings from various government witnesses. A trial was held, and Bagley was convicted. Later, he filed for additional government documentation under the Freedom of Information Act. New materials he received indicated that some of the government witnesses had received payment for their services and informant work. Bagley sought to overturn his conviction with this new information, alleging that the government had not complied with the discovery requirement. The SC heard Bagley's appeal and upheld his conviction, ruling that the "newly discovered" information would be materially relevant only if the introduction of this new evidence would have resulted in a different trial outcome. Other evidence was more than sufficient to establish Bagley's guilt beyond any reasonable doubt. The SC acknowledged that the defense's case had been hampered to an extent by the nondisclosure of this information. Nevertheless, the SC said that the new information would not have affected the conviction significantly.

United States v. Banks, ___U.S.___, 124 S.Ct. 521 (2003) [UNITED STATES, Petitioner, v. Lashawn Lowell BANKS] (Exigent Circumstances; Fourth Amendment; Knock and Announce; Searches and Seizures) An informant advised the North Las Vegas Police Department that Lashawn Banks was selling cocaine from his two-bedroom apartment. FBI agents and North Las Vegas police officers obtained a search warrant and went to Banks' apartment, positioning themselves at the front and back doors. The police knocked loudly on the front door to Banks' apartment, so that officers at the back door heard the knock. After a 15- to 20-second interval without a response from anyone inside, police battered their way into Banks' apartment, where they confronted Banks, who was emerging from a shower. They found crack cocaine, weapons, and other evidence of drug dealing. Banks was convicted of narcotics trafficking and weapons charges pursuant to a plea bargain, but he appealed the conviction, contending among other things that (1) the police violated the "refused admittance" requirement of a federal statute governing breaking of doors or windows to gain admittance to premises in execution of search warrants, and (2) the 15- to 20-second time interval between knocking and breaking his front door was an unreasonably short time interval to execute their search warrant. The government countered, arguing that the police acted under exigent circumstances, believing that a longer time interval before entering Banks' premises would enable Banks to destroy incriminating evidence. The Ninth Circuit Court of Appeals reversed Banks' conviction and the government appealed to the SC, who heard the case. The SC reversed the Ninth Circuit, holding that (1) the 15- to 20-second interval between the officers' knock and announcement of a search warrant and their forced entry was reasonable, given exigency of possible destruction of evidence; and (2) entry did not violate the "refused admittance" requirement of the federal statute governing breaking of doors or windows in execution of search warrants. The fact that Banks was in the shower and did not hear police knocking on his door was irrelevant compared with the inference by police that their reasonable suspicion of exigency was heightened as the result of no response to their knock and verbal announcement of their search warrant.

United States v. Benchimol, 471 U.S. 453, 105 S.Ct. 2103 (1985) [UNITED STATES, Petitioner, v. Joseph BENCHIMOL] (Plea Bargaining) Following a conviction pursuant to a plea agreement, the offender appealed, saying that the prosecutor did not make a recommendation enthusiastically. The SC upheld the conviction, saying that prosecu-

tors are under no obligation to make recommendations or to make them enthusiastically.

United States v. Biswell, 408 U.S. 311, 92 S.Ct. 1593 (1972) [UNITED STATES, Petitioner, v. Loarn Anthony BISWELL] (Corrections; Probation and Parole) Biswell was a firearms dealer. Under the Gun Control Act of 1968, a police officer and a Treasury agent visited Biswell at his place of business. They asked to inspect his books and a locked gun locker. When Biswell asked if they had a search warrant, they replied that they didn't need one. A subsequent search yielded illegal weapons, including sawed-off shotguns that Biswell was not licensed to possess. He was convicted of violating firearms laws. He appealed, and the SC heard his case, in which he alleged that the agents had needed a search warrant to search his premises. The SC upheld his conviction, holding that regulatory inspections of businesses may proceed without warrants where specifically authorized by statute. Thus, they held the search of Biswell's business by these officers and agents to be reasonable and not violative of his Fourth Amendment rights.

United States v. Brignoni-Ponce, 422 U.S. 873, 95 S.Ct. 2574 (1975) [UNITED STATES, Petitioner, v. Felix Humberto BRIGNONI-PONCE] (Border Searches; Law Enforcement Officers or Agencies) The Border Patrol stopped a vehicle containing persons apparently of Mexican descent. Officers asked about their illegal-alien status and other concerns and searched the vehicle, which yielded contraband. The result was a conviction. An appeal to the SC resulted in a declaration that the Border Patrol may not stop automobiles simply because of the apparent Mexican ancestry of the occupants. Border Patrol stops are justified only by consent, probable cause, or an awareness of specifically articulable facts, together with rational inferences therefrom.

United States v. Broce, 488 U.S. 563, 109 S.Ct. 757 (1989) [UNITED STATES, Petitioner, v. Ray C. BROCE and Broce Construction Co., Inc.] (Plea Bargaining) Broce and another person entered guilty pleas in U.S. district court to two separate charges of conspiracy, specifically to rig bids on certain state highway projects. Following their conviction on the two charges, Broce attempted to have their two conspiracies treated as one conspiracy and thus to have the earlier convictions set aside. He claimed, among other things, that the "two" conspiracies resulted from a common deal or incident and that there was truly only one conspiracy. Thus the second conspiracy conviction was double jeopardy under the law. The SC heard Broce's case and determined that their plea bargains had been voluntarily entered into and their pleas of guilty to the two charges had been accepted by the court. The guilty pleas and convictions foreclosed the double-jeopardy challenge, and the convictions stood.

United States v. Calandra, 414 U.S. 338, 94 S.Ct. 613 (1974) [UNITED STATES, Petitioner, v. John P. CALANDRA] (Searches and Seizures) Calandra became a suspect in a loan-shark operation when his name was found on a card possessed by others involved in this activity. When he was summoned to appear before a grand jury investigating the matter, he refused to testify, saying that this was an "illegal search and seizure" in violation of his Fourth Amendment rights. The SC disagreed, saying that this privilege may not be invoked for purposes of testifying to the grand jury.

United States v. Chadwick, 433 U.S. 1, 97 S.Ct. 2476 (1977) [UNITED STATES, Petitioner, v. Joseph A. CHADWICK et al., Respondents] (Law Enforcement Officers or Agencies; Searches and Seizures; Searches Incident to an Arrest; Vehicle Searches) The DEA established a "courier profile" of persons in the 1970s who trafficked in narcotics. Such profiles were used to stop and search suspicious persons at ports of entry into the United States, in airports, bus terminals, and rail stations. Chadwick was a train passenger in San Diego traveling to Boston. San Diego DEA officials observed that he was carrying a large footlocker, which appeared to be leaking talcum powder, a substance often used to disguise the odor of marijuana. DEA agents in Boston intercepted Chadwick, in the company of two others, just as he was about to place the footlocker in the trunk of an automobile. The agents arrested Chadwick and his companions and took them and the footlocker to a nearby federal building, where the footlocker was subsequently opened without warrant or permission from Chadwick, yielding a large quantity of marijuana. The DEA agents justified their warrantless search of the footlocker by citing "exigent circumstances"; they had had to act quickly to prevent Chadwick and his friends from disposing of the illegal contraband. Chadwick was subsequently convicted on drug-related charges. He appealed, moving to suppress the footlocker evidence by contending that police had lacked a valid search warrant. The SC overturned Chadwick's conviction, noting that the footlocker was "luggage" and thus its warrantless search was unjustified. The SC stressed the fact that the footlocker was only "incidentally" about to be loaded into a vehicle; although police officers were ordinarily entitled to search a vehicle and its contents in a "search incident to an arrest," a warrant must be obtained to search any luggage found. This holding was modified in *United States v. Ross* (1982), in which officers needed no warrant to search paper bags, leather pouches, and glove compartments of cars when arresting suspects, because of the lesser standard applying to them pertaining to an expectation of privacy. *California v. Acevedo* (1991) greatly modified the *Chadwick* holding.

United States v. Chavez, 416 U.S. 562, 94 S.Ct. 1849 (1974) [UNITED STATES, Petitioner, v. Umberto Jose CHAVEZ et al.] (Electronic Surveillance, Wiretapping) Chavez was indicted for conspiracy to distribute cocaine. As a part of the RICO statute, wiretaps may be ordered on request from the U.S. attorney general or the assistant attorney general. Wiretaps were ordered for Chavez's telephone line by the executive assistant to the U.S. attorney general. They disclosed considerable incriminating information. Chavez's attorneys moved to suppress this information on the grounds that procedurally, the person who ordered the wiretaps was not authorized to do so. The trial court granted the motion to suppress and the government appealed. The SC reversed the motion to suppress. It held, however, that when it is clearly established that authorization for a wiretap has been given by the attorney general, but the application and interception order incorrectly states that approval has instead been given by a specially designated executive assistant to the attorney general, the misidentification, by itself, will not render telephonic interceptions "unlawful." Thus the granted motion to suppress was in error. However, it is appropriate to recommend in the future that "strict adherence" by the government to the provisions for authorizing wiretaps be more in keeping with congressional intent of the RICO statute whenever wiretaps are ordered. (*See United States v. Giordano* [1974] *for a comparable case.*)

United States v. Cortez, 449 U.S. 411, 101 S.Ct. 690 (1981) [UNITED STATES, Petitioner, v. Jesus E. CORTEZ and Pedro Hernandez-Loera] (Border Searches; Law Enforcement Officers or Agencies; Searches and Seizures) Border Patrol officers were investigating trafficking in illegal aliens across the Mexico–United States border. They discovered a path that appeared to be one used by illegal aliens entering the United States. There were some distinctive shoe prints and tire tracks indicative of a particular kind of truck. Watching officers saw an approaching truck similar to the one they suspected had left the tire tracks. They stopped the truck and questioned Cortez, the truck driver, and his passenger, who happened to be wearing shoes matching prints made at the illegal border crossing. The officers opened the truck and discovered six illegal aliens. Cortez was convicted of transporting illegal aliens. He appealed, protesting unlawful search. The SC upheld the conviction, saying that the totality-of-circumstances test applied in this case. Objective facts and particular circumstances may lead police to make investigatory stops and subsequent arrests, if the totality of circumstances suggests that a crime has been committed.

United States v. Cotton, ___U.S.___, 122 S.Ct. 1781 (2002) [UNITED STATES, Petitioner, v. Leonard COTTON, Marquette Hall, Lamont Thomas, Matilda Hall, Jowan Powell, Jesus Hall, and Stanley Hall, Jr.] (Indictments; Plain Error) Cotton and others were convicted of conspiring to distribute and to possess with intent to distribute a "detectable amount" of cocaine and cocaine base. A federal grand jury initially issued the indictment that led to their conviction. The indictment failed to specify the quantity of drugs involved in the conspiracy, although a subsequent drug quantity of "at least 50 grams of cocaine" was used by the prosecution and court for a sentence enhancement under the U.S. Sentencing Guidelines. The defendants appealed, alleging that their sentences were invalid because the drug quantity issue was neither alleged in the indictment nor submitted to the petit jury. Thus, the error seriously affected the fairness, integrity, and public reputation of the judicial proceedings, as the defendants alleged. The circuit court upheld their convictions but ruled their enhanced sentences as invalid on the ground that the federal district court had no jurisdiction to impose a sentence for an offense not charged in the indictment. The government appealed to the SC, who heard the case. The SC reversed the circuit court ruling and remanded the case to the trial court, holding that a defective indictment does not deprive a federal court of jurisdiction. The government conceded the fact that the indictment's failure to allege a fact that increased the sentences was plain error. However, the evidence that the conspiracy involved at least 50 grams of cocaine base was overwhelming and essentially uncontroverted. Regarding the fairness allegation, the SC declared that "the real threat to the fairness, integrity, or public reputation of judicial proceedings would be if respondents, despite the overwhelming and uncontroverted evidence that they were involved in a vast drug conspiracy, were to receive a sentence prescribed for those committing less substantial drug offenses because of an error that was never objected to at trial."

United States v. Crews, 445 U.S. 463, 100 S.Ct. 1244 (1980) [UNITED STATES, Petitioner, v. Keith CREWS] (Exclusionary Rule; Law Enforcement Officers or Agencies) A woman was assaulted and robbed at gunpoint. She notified police and described the assailant. Crews was later seen in the vicinity by police, who stopped him, took him to the police station briefly, photographed him, and released him. Later, the woman was shown Crews' photograph and she identified him as the man who had attacked her. Crews was later arrested and placed in a lineup. The victim again identified him as her attacker. Crews was later charged and tried for armed robbery. During the trial, the victim again identified Crews. He was convicted. He appealed, contending that his initial detention by police and photographing had been unwarranted and not supported by probable cause. Further, he argued that the lineup identification evidence should have been considered inadmissible for the same reason. The SC ruled that the actions by police officers in detaining and arresting Crews constituted police misconduct. This misconduct also applied to the photograph and lineup identification of Crews by the victim. However, his conviction was upheld. The SC held that the in-court identification of Crews by the victim did not have to be suppressed as the fruits of Crews' unlawful arrest, where the robbery victim's presence in court was not the result of any police misconduct, and where the illegal arrest did not infect her ability to give accurate identification testimony.

United States v. Dionisio, 410 U.S. 1, 93 S.Ct. 764 (1973) [UNITED STATES, Petitioner, v. Antonio DIONISIO] (Law Enforcement Officers or Agencies; Lineups) Dionisio and about 20 others were advised that they were suspects in an illegal-gambling investigation. They were subpoenaed before a grand jury and ordered to submit vocal recordings of themselves for comparison with various messages police had intercepted through telephonic wiretapping. Dionisio refused and was held in contempt of court. He was ordered to jail for 18 months. He appealed, arguing that no one could compel him to give evidence against himself in violation of his Fifth Amendment rights and that the "seizure" of his voice pattern through a vocal recording was unreasonable in violation of his Fourth Amendment rights. The SC disagreed with Dionisio, saying that grand juries may compel a person to give vocal recordings and that such an intrusion is not an unreasonable seizure under Fourth Amendment protection. (*See Schmerber v. California* [1966] *and Winston v. Lee* [1985] *for comparable cases.*)

United States v. Di Re, 332 U.S. 581, 68 S.Ct. 222 (1948) [UNITED STATES, Petitioner, v. Michael DI RE] (Law Enforcement Officers or Agencies; Stop and Frisk) During

World War II, it was illegal to have counterfeit gasoline ration coupons. Buffalo, NY, police received information from an informant, Reed, that someone named Buttitta was selling counterfeit coupons. A detective with the Buffalo police department followed Buttitta's car. When it finally came to an appointed place, the police went to the car and found the informer, Reed. They asked Reed if he had illegal coupons, and he said yes and that he had obtained them from the driver, Buttitta. Di Re was sitting next to Buttitta. All persons were taken to the police station, where Di Re was ordered to turn out his pockets and place the contents on the table. Gasoline coupons fell out, and he was thoroughly searched, which yielded another 100 concealed in his underwear. These coupons were counterfeit, and Di Re was convicted of possession of counterfeit gasoline coupons. He appealed, contesting that his unreasonable search and seizure had violated his Fourth Amendment rights. The SC held that Di Re's mere presence with Buttitta had not entitled police to presume that he, too, was guilty of possessing fraudulent coupons. Nothing had been said or done by Buttitta to incriminate Di Re. Therefore, the police had had no justification to search Di Re. Thus, the warrantless search of Di Re was not based on any reasonable suspicion or probable cause, so his conviction was overturned.

United States v. Dixon, 509 U.S. 688, 113 S.Ct. 2849 (1993) [UNITED STATES, Petitioner, v. Alvin J. DIXON and Michael Foster] (Fifth Amendment; Self-Incrimination) Dixon was arrested for second-degree murder and released on bond. While on bond, he was "forbidden [to] commit any criminal offense." During this period, Dixon was arrested again and charged with cocaine possession. He was convicted shortly thereafter of contempt, and of the cocaine possession, and was sentenced to 180 days in jail. Later, he moved to dismiss the cocaine indictment, because his "contempt" conviction involved the identical drug charges. The trial court granted his motion and dismissed the indictment. The government appealed to the SC. The SC upheld the indictment dismissal, holding that where a criminal contempt sanction was imposed on Dixon for violating an order of conditional release by violating a drug offense which was incorporated into his release conditions, the later attempt to prosecute him for the drug offense itself was barred as an instance of double jeopardy.

United States v. Doe, 465 U.S. 553, 104 S.Ct. 1237 (1983) [UNITED STATES, Petitioner v. John DOE] (Fifth Amendment; Immunity; Self-Incrimination) John Doe was owner of several sole proprietorships. In late 1980, a grand-jury investigation of corruption in awarding county and municipal contracts resulted in subpoenas served on Doe and his proprietorships. The subpoenas sought various financial and business records. Doe filed a motion to have these records suppressed under the theory that his right against self-incrimination would be violated by disclosing those records to government prosecutors. The SC heard the appeal and said that the records sought in the subpoenas were not privileged communications of the Fifth Amendment variety, and thus their production before a grand jury would not violate Doe's Fifth Amendment rights. However, the "act" of compelling the submission of incriminating records by court order requires a statutory grant-of-use immunity. Thus, Doe's records were subject to subpoena, but a grant of immunity had to be made to him so that the incriminating information disclosed by the records could not be used against him later in a criminal prosecution.

United States v. Dominguez Benitez, ___U.S.___, 124 S.Ct. 2333 (2004) [UNITED STATES, Petitioner, v. Carlos DOMINGUEZ BENITEZ] (Plain Error; Plea Bargaining) Carlos Dominguez Benitez (hereafter known as Dominguez) was indicted by a federal grand jury on two counts: conspiracy to possess more than 500 grams of methamphetamine and possession of 1,391 grams of methamphetamine mixture. Dominguez faced a statutory mandatory minimum sentence of 10 years with a maximum of life. Pursuant to a plea agreement, Dominguez agreed to plead guilty to the conspiracy charge and the possession charge was dismissed. Although the government recommended a sentence less than the statutory 10-year minimum, it warned Dominguez in the written plea agreement that the court would not be bound by the plea agreement and could impose a tougher sentence, and that Dominguez would not be able to withdraw his guilty plea if the judge did in fact impose a greater sentence than contemplated by the plea agreement and prosecutor recommendation. At a subsequent plea-agreement hearing, the federal district court judge orally advised Dominguez of the plea-agreement conditions and the potential court response, which included the non-binding nature of the plea agreement; however, the court failed to advise Dominguez that he could not withdraw his guilty plea if a harsher sentence were imposed. This omission was considered a plain error in view of the Federal Rules of Criminal Procedure articulated by Rule 11. According to Rule 11, federal judges are required to advise defendants that they have no right to withdraw their guilty pleas if the court does not follow the prosecutor's sentencing recommendation or request. However, not every Rule 11 violation calls for reversal of conviction by entitling defendants to withdraw their guilty pleas. A variance with the requirements of this rule is harmless error if it does not affect substantial rights. The Ninth Circuit reversed Dominguez's conviction because of the judge's failure to properly instruct Dominguez, and the government appealed. The SC heard the case and reversed the appeals court, holding that the Rule 11 warning had been made in writing to Dominguez by the prosecution. Furthermore, the fact that the federal judge failed to orally advise Dominguez that he could not withdraw his guilty plea if the court refused to accept the government's recommendations did not materially affect the outcome. The Rule 11 error in this case made no difference in the sentencing outcome also in view of the standard of reasonable probability and Dominguez's assessment of his strategic position. The plea agreement containing all important elements of Rule 11 was read to Dominguez in both English and Spanish, specifically the warning that he could not withdraw his guilty plea if the court refused to accept the government's recommendation. This fact was uncontested by Dominguez and thus supported the SC's holding that the Rule 11 error made no difference to the sentencing outcome.

United States v. Donovan, 429 U.S. 413, 97 S.Ct. 658 (1977) [UNITED STATES, Petitioner, v. Thomas W. DONOVAN et al.] (Electronic Surveillance, Wiretapping; Law Enforcement Officers or Agencies) Donovan was one of several defendants indicted for illegal gambling on the basis of information gleaned from an authorized wiretap by the FBI. Because the identities of many of the persons involved in this conspiracy were unknown, and thus could not be inventoried in the wiretap authorization, the defendants moved to suppress these indictments. A lower court granted the motion, but the SC overturned this decision and reinstated the indictments, holding that it is not necessary to identify each and every person subject to a wiretap.

United States v. Drayton, ___U.S.___, 122 S.Ct. 2105 (2002) [UNITED STATES, Petitioner, v. Christopher DRAYTON and Clifton Brown, Jr.] (Fourth Amendment, Searches and Seizures) Defendants were convicted separately in a U.S. district court in Florida for conspiracy to distribute cocaine and possession of cocaine with intent to distribute. Drayton and Brown were bus passengers traveling through Florida. The bus driver stopped and permitted three plain-clothes police officers to board the bus as a part of a routine drug and weapons interdiction effort. One officer stationed himself at the front of the bus, while another officer positioned himself at the rear of the bus. The third officer, Lang, worked his way from the back of the bus to the front, speaking with individual passengers as he went. When Lang reached Drayton and Brown, he asked if they were carrying any bags. The said "yes," and Lang asked if he could search their bags. Drayton and Brown permitted Lang to search their bags. He found nothing. Next, Lang asked Drayton and Brown if he could search their persons. They consented, and as the result of a patdown, Lang found several packages of cocaine taped against their legs. Subsequently, Drayton and Brown were charged with cocaine possession for the purpose of resale and conspiracy to distribute cocaine. They sought to suppress the cocaine seizure on the ground that their consent to search was invalid and coerced. The trial court refused to suppress the cocaine seizure, and Drayton and Brown were convicted. They appealed, and a circuit court of appeals overturned their convictions, holding that based on prior SC holdings, bus passengers who do not feel free to disregard police officers' requests to search absent some positive indication that consent may be refused are coerced as a result, and thus contraband discovered as a result of such a search must be suppressed. The United States appealed to the SC, who heard the case. The SC reversed the circuit court and reinstated Drayton's and Brown's convictions, holding that the Fourth Amendment does not require police officers to advise bus passengers of their right not to cooperate and to refuse consent to searches. The SC said that when Lang asked the respondents if he could search their persons, he inquired first if they objected, thus indicating to a reasonable person that he or she was free to refuse. Although Lang did not give a warning that Drayton and Brown could refuse to be searched, the totality of circumstances indicated that respondents' consent was voluntary, and the searches were reasonable.

United States v. Dunn, 480 U.S. 294, 107 S.Ct. 1134 (1987) [UNITED STATES, Petitioner, v. Ronald Dale DUNN] (Law Enforcement Officers or Agencies; Open-Fields Doctrine; Plain-View Rule) Drug agents investigated Dunn, who was suspected of manufacturing drugs in large quantities in a private laboratory located on his property. With a properly executed warrant, police placed a beeper in a container used by Dunn to transport drugs. Eventually, the officers located Dunn's farm. Passing through several gates, fences, and other perimeter guards, they shined their flashlights into a large barn about 50 yards from Dunn's house. They could hear a motor running, and they saw drug equipment through the side boards. They secured a search warrant and entered the barn, where they seized a quantity of illegal drugs. Dunn was convicted of drug manufacturing. He appealed, seeking to suppress the barn evidence because he believed that police had had no legal authority to observe his barn in the middle of a heavily protected area. The SC upheld Dunn's conviction, saying that because the barn itself was not part of the curtilage of Dunn's home but rather was separately fenced, police were not required to obtain a search warrant to look at it or through its side boards. The SC stressed how close the barn was to Dunn's house; whether it was in a separate enclosure; the nature and uses of the area; and any evident concealment attempts. These guidelines gave greater parameters for police when conducting searches of open fields or yards. (See *Oliver v. United States* [1984] for comparison.)

United States v. Dunnigan, 507 U.S. 87, 113 S.Ct. 1111 (1993) [UNITED STATES, Petitioner, v. Sharon DUNNIGAN] (Sentencing) Dunnigan was accused of conspiracy to distribute cocaine. She testified in her own behalf, but it was subsequently determined that she had committed perjury during her testimony. She was convicted, and the judge enhanced her sentence because of her perjury. Dunnigan appealed, arguing that her testimony was self-incriminating and that she should not be further punished because of her perjury statements. The SC disagreed and upheld her sentence enhancement. Under the U.S. Sentencing Commission Guidelines, if the court finds the defendant committed perjury at the trial, the sentence can be enhanced.

United States v. Edwards, 415 U.S. 800, 94 S.Ct. 1234 (1974) [UNITED STATES, Petitioner, v. Eugene H. EDWARDS and William T. Livesay] (Law Enforcement Officers or Agencies; Searches Incident to Arrest) Edwards was arrested for attempting to break into a U.S. post office and was taken to jail. Jail officials exchanged Edwards' clothes for jail garments and searched his clothes for evidence of the break-in. Paint chips matching those from the U.S. post office window were found in Edwards' clothing, and this, as well as other incriminating evidence, led to his conviction. Edwards appealed, moving to suppress the paint chips and other evidence from his clothing, contending that the search had been a violation of his Fourth Amendment right against unreasonable searches and seizures. The SC disagreed, saying that whenever a suspect is arrested, it is not violative of his Fourth Amendment rights for police to conduct a more thorough search of his or her clothes and seize what is believed to be evidence of a crime. (See *United States v. Robinson* [1973].)

United States v. Felix, 503 U.S. 378, 112 S.Ct. 1377 (1992) [UNITED STATES, Petitioner, v. Frank Dennis FELIX] (Double Jeopardy) Felix was charged with various drug offenses in 1987, including an attempt to manufacture an illegal drug, methamphetamine, in Oklahoma. He was convicted. Subsequently, he was indicted on charges of conspiracy to manufacture, possess, and distribute methamphetamines. He claimed that this charge was a case of double jeopardy, because he had already been convicted on other charges stemming from the same offense. The SC upheld his conviction and held that the double-jeopardy clause did not bar the government's prosecution of Felix because essentially different conduct was being alleged in different indictments. Double jeopardy *would* have attached if two prosecutions had stemmed from the same conduct.

United States v. Flores-Montano, ___U.S.___, 124 S.Ct. 1582 (2004) [UNITED STATES, Petitioner, v. Manuel FLORES-MONTANO] (Fourth Amendment; Searches and Seizures; Vehicle Searches) At an international border between Mexico and California, customs officials seized 37 kilograms (81 pounds) of marijuana from the gas tank of an automobile driven by Manuel Flores-Montano. Flores-Montano had approached the Otay Mesa Port of Entry in Southern California and a customs inspector referred the car to a secondary inspection, where another customs inspector, on tapping the gas tank, believed that it sounded solid. A contract mechanic was called and within 15 to 25 minutes, the car was hoisted on a lift and the gas tank was removed and disassembled, yielding the illegal marijuana. Flores-Montano was subsequently convicted and appealed, alleging that his Fourth Amendment right against unreasonable searches and seizures was violated because no reasonable suspicion or probable cause could be articulated to justify the intrusive search of his vehicle. Also alleged was that Flores-Montano had a privacy interest in his gas tank, and that it was an invasion of his privacy for the customs officials to disassemble that gas tank. Further, he claimed that the search deprived him of his property and thus violated his property interest. The Ninth Circuit Court of Appeals agreed with Flores-Montano and reversed his conviction. The government appealed, and the SC heard the case. The SC reversed the Ninth Circuit ruling, declaring that reasonable suspicion and/or probable cause is not required to conduct an extensive and intrusive search of a vehicle. While reasonable suspicion would apply to more intrusive searches of persons, it does not apply to vehicles. Furthermore, suspicionless border inspections in an effort to prevent the entry of unwanted persons and effects and contraband into the country are warranted. The SC added that motorists have no privacy interest in their automobile gas tanks, particularly at international border crossings, and that Flores-Montano had failed to show that he was deprived of his property or that it was damaged as the result of the gas tank search.

United States v. Gaudin, 515 U.S. 506, 115 S.Ct. 2310 (1995) [UNITED STATES, Petitioner, v. Michael E. GAUDIN] (Jury Trials) Gaudin was convicted in a U.S.

district court on charges of making false statements on federally insured mortgages. He appealed to the SC, arguing, in part, that certain statements he made had been considered by the *judge*, not the *jury*, as materially relevant to his case. He believed that the jury should decide the materiality of these statements, rather than the judge. Thus the judge's jury instructions and conduct were at issue. The SC declared that the jury must decide whether every element of a crime has been proved beyond a reasonable doubt. In Gaudin's case, the judge had preempted the jury's right by determining the materiality of one of the crime elements. The SC overturned Gaudin's conviction, holding that the judge's refusal to submit the question of "materiality" to the jury was unconstitutional. The significance of the case is that juries, not presiding judges, must be given the right to determine the materiality of each and every crime element.

United States v. Giordano, 416 U.S. 505, 94 S.Ct. 1820 (1974) [UNITED STATES, Petitioner, v. Dominic Nicholas GIORDANO et al.] (Electronic Surveillance, Wiretapping) According to a RICO statute, federal judges were authorized to approve wiretaps of telephones of those suspected of violating federal laws. An application for a wiretap was authorized by a specially designated executive assistant to the attorney general for the purpose of investigating Dominic Giordano. Once Giordano was arrested and charged with various narcotics violations, the wiretap was removed. Nevertheless, the wiretap revealed considerable incriminating information, which was intended to be used against Giordano at his later federal trial. He was convicted. His attorney moved successfully to suppress this incriminating information. The government appealed, and the SC heard the case. The SC upheld the suppression decision, holding that primary or derivative evidence secured by wiretaps pursuant to court order issued in response to an application that was not in fact authorized by the attorney general, or an assistant attorney general specifically designated by him or her, must be suppressed upon proper motion. In Giordano's case, it developed that the executive assistant to the attorney general was not empowered by statute to authorize applications for wiretap orders.

United States v. Gonzales, 520 U.S. 1, 117 S.Ct. 1032 (1997) [UNITED STATES, Petitioner, v. Miguel GONZALES, Orlenis Hernandez-Diaz, and Mario Perez] (Sentencing) Gonzales, Hernandez-Diaz, and Perez were convicted in a New Mexico state court on drug-trafficking crimes and firearms violations following a drug sting operation, and the trial court sentenced them to a prison term of 13 to 17 years. Subsequently, they were convicted in federal court on charges arising from the same drug-trafficking offenses, including a mandatory five-year federal prison term to be served consecutively with the state and federal sentences. The district court also directed that the drug sentences should run concurrently with the state sentences being served. The Tenth Circuit Court of Appeals vacated these offenders' federal sentences for the firearms violations and drug charges, holding that the federal sentences, including the mandatory five-year firearms sentence, should have run concurrently with the state sentences. This finding was based on the assumption that mandatory

sentences for violating federal laws were applicable only to federal and not state crimes. The government appealed, and the SC heard the case. The SC reversed the circuit court, holding that a mandatory five-year sentence for firearms use in violation of a federal criminal statute is not limited to federal sentences but is also applicable to state sentences. Thus, U.S. district courts may impose mandatory sentences for firearms use, and these sentences may run consecutively with state sentences. Further, federal courts may order drug-trafficking convictions to run concurrently or consecutively with state-imposed sentences arising from the same crimes.

United States v. Goodwin, 457 U.S. 368, 102 S.Ct. 2485 (1982) [UNITED STATES, Petitioner, v. Learley Reed GOODWIN] (Prosecutorial Misconduct; Sixth Amendment) Goodwin was stopped by a U.S. park policeman on the Baltimore–Washington Parkway for speeding. When Goodwin stepped from his car, the officer observed a clear plastic bag underneath the armrest next to the driver's seat. The officer asked Goodwin to return to his car and retrieve the bag. When Goodwin got into his car, he placed the car in gear and accelerated rapidly. Goodwin's car struck the officer but did not seriously injure him. The officer got into his own car and pursued Goodwin, but Goodwin eluded him in a high-speed chase. Because of license information, Goodwin's identity was known and a warrant was issued for his arrest. Goodwin was arrested and arraigned before a U.S. magistrate, and a trial date was set. Before trial, Goodwin fled to Virginia. Three years later, he was found in custody in Virginia and returned to Maryland to stand trial on the earlier charges. Through a plea agreement, he entered a guilty plea but later changed his mind, insisting on a jury trial instead. About six weeks later, the prosecutor obtained a four-count indictment including one felony count of assaulting a federal officer. A jury trial resulted in Goodwin's conviction on these charges. Goodwin appealed, alleging that raising the original misdemeanor charge of assaulting an officer to the higher level of a felony-assault charge was vindictiveness on the prosecutor's part and thus had violated Goodwin's due-process rights. The SC found no evidence of vindictiveness on the prosecutor's part and therefore no due-process violation.

United States v. Gouveia, 467 U.S. 180, 104 S.Ct. 2292 (1984) [UNITED STATES, Petitioner, v. William GOUVEIA et al.] (Corrections; Inmate Rights) At the federal prison in Lompoc, CA, Gouveia and four other inmates were suspected of murdering a fellow inmate. These prisoners were placed temporarily in the Administrative Detention Unit at Lompoc, where they were isolated from one another. In the meantime, prison authorities conducted a hearing and determined that these prisoners were involved in the murder. Later, a grand jury indicted them, and at their arraignments they were provided court-appointed counsel, as they were indigent. They were convicted of the murder. Gouveia appealed, alleging that he should have been permitted access to a court-appointed attorney while he was in administrative detention. The SC upheld his conviction, saying that inmates under investigation for a crime and held in administrative detention are not automatically entitled to court-appointed counsel before any judicial proceedings have been launched against them. The rights of prisoners do not include court-appointed counsel until they are indicted.

United States v. Granderson, 511 U.S. 39, 114 S.Ct. 1259 (1994) [**UNITED STATES, Petitioner, v. Ralph Stuart GRANDERSON, Jr.**] (**Probation and Parole; Sentencing; U.S. Sentencing Guidelines**) Granderson, a letter carrier for the U.S. Postal Service, was convicted of destruction of mail and sentenced to five years' probation, although the U.S. Sentencing Guidelines provided for a zero- to six-month incarcerative term. Subsequently, Granderson's probation was revoked when it was discovered that he possessed a controlled substance. U.S.C. Section 3565(a) of Title 18, the criminal code, provides that one-third of the original sentence should be imposed as a punishment when revoking a federal probation. Thus, relying on the five-year (60-month) probationary term, the judge sentenced Granderson to 20 months of imprisonment. Granderson appealed, contending that the U.S. Sentencing Guidelines govern incarcerative terms, not probationary sentences. A circuit court of appeals reversed this sentence and ordered Granderson released. Its logic was that the original sentence was the U.S. Sentencing Guidelines of zero to six months, not the original probationary sentence. Because Granderson had already served 11 months of imprisonment at the time of the appellate decision, his immediate release was ordered. The government appealed, and the SC heard the case. The SC upheld the circuit court of appeals, concluding that indeed, the U.S. Sentencing Guidelines governed this situation, not the probationary sentence imposed by the federal judge.

United States v. Hale, 422 U.S. 71, 95 S.Ct. 2133 (1975) [**UNITED STATES, Petitioner, v. William G. HALE**] (*Miranda* **Warning; Self-Incrimination**) Hale was accused of a crime. During his trial, the prosecutor commented about the fact that Hale had remained silent after being given the *Miranda* warning at the time of his arrest. The fact of silence was interpreted as incriminating by the prosecutor, and Hale was convicted. He appealed. The SC declared that prosecutors are forbidden to comment about whether a defendant's invocation of his or her right to silence is potentially incriminating. Prosecutors are barred from inferring something nefarious or incriminating from a defendant's refusal to answer police questions following a *Miranda* warning.

United States v. Halper, 490 U.S. 435, 109 S.Ct. 1892 (1989) [**UNITED STATES, Appellant, v. Irwin HALPER**] (**Double Jeopardy**) Halper was a medical service manager convicted of filing 65 inflated Medicare claims. He was sentenced to prison and given a fine of $5,000. Subsequently, in a civil action, the United States government filed a civil suit against him, asking the court for a summary judgment under the False Claims Act. Halper appealed. The monetary punishment associated with false claims is $2,000 per claim, or a total of $130,000. In view of the actual amount of money involved in the fraudulent claims for which Halper had already been convicted and the government's expenses of $16,000, the difference between $16,000 and $130,000 was so dramatic as to be violative of Halper's right against double jeopardy. The SC

vacated the judgment against Halper and sent the case back to a lower court where the government could determine more reasonable monetary sanctions against Halper without violating his double-jeopardy rights.

United States v. Harris, 403 U.S. 573, 91 S.Ct. 2075 (1971) [**UNITED STATES, Petitioner, v. Roosevelt Hudson HARRIS**] (**Informants; Searches and Seizures**) An informant provided incriminating information about Harris to a government tax collector. Harris was later arrested and charged with possession of untaxed liquor. He moved to suppress the evidence on the ground that the search warrant had been insufficient in establishing adequate facts to search for and seize the untaxed liquor. The SC upheld Harris' conviction, concluding that the affidavit supporting the warrant had been sufficient. The informant was deemed credible, in part because the information he provided the federal tax collector implicated the informant himself. There was also sufficient factual basis for believing the informant.

United States v. Havens, 446 U.S. 620, 100 S.Ct. 1912 (1980) [**UNITED STATES, Petitioner, v. J. Lee HAVENS**] (**Fourth Amendment; Law Enforcement Officers or Agencies**) Havens was suspected of importing and conspiring to import cocaine. During his trial and under direct examination, he denied various facts pertaining to the cocaine allegations. While cross-examining him, the prosecutor used illegally obtained evidence to contradict Havens, who was subsequently convicted. He appealed to the SC, alleging that because the evidence used against him had been illegally seized and was otherwise inadmissible, it should have been excluded. The SC disagreed and upheld his conviction, holding that evidence that is otherwise inadmissible as the result of a Fourth Amendment violation may be used to impeach the credibility of the defendant when the defendant gives testimony that is contradicted by such illegally seized evidence. Thus, when defendants testify, they must testify truthfully "or suffer the consequences" (at 1912).

United States v. Henry, 447 U.S. 264, 100 S.Ct. 2183 (1980) [**UNITED STATES, Petitioner, v. Billy Gale HENRY**] (**Right to Counsel**) Henry was accused of armed robbery and indicted by a grand jury. While in jail awaiting trial, he acquired a new cellmate, who was a paid informant of the government. Acting on the government's instructions, the informant was supposed to elicit incriminating statements from Henry so that the government could have better evidence against him. Henry made such statements and was convicted. He appealed. The SC overturned Henry's conviction on the grounds that the conversations he had with the informant constituted an interrogation because the informant was acting as an extension of the government, which had paid him to conduct an interrogation of Henry, although the government didn't interpret the situation in that context. Nevertheless, the significance of this case is that whenever defendants are in custody and are questioned by police or their agents (e.g., paid informants), that situation simulates an interrogation and requires the presence of the defendant's attorney. (*See Massiah v. United States* [1964] *for a similar case and SC holding.*)

United States v. Hensley, 469 U.S. 221, 105 S.Ct. 675 (1985) [UNITED STATES, Petitioner, v. Thomas J. HENSLEY] (Law Enforcement Officers or Agencies; Searches Incident to an Arrest; Stop and Frisk) A motorist, Hensley, was a convicted felon from St. Bernard, OH, traveling through Kentucky. A recent robbery in Kentucky led police officers to suspect Hensley, although there was no evidence linking him to the crime. A "wanted" poster of Hensley was circulated among contiguous states, and a Covington, KY, police officer observed Hensley on a highway. He stopped and questioned Hensley and then arrested him, largely because of the "wanted" poster he had seen. In a search incident to the arrest, the officer found weapons in Hensley's automobile. Hensley was never charged with the robbery, but he was charged with and convicted of being a felon in possession of firearms, a prohibited act. He appealed, arguing that the police had lacked probable cause to stop him initially, and therefore, the weapons subsequently found in his car should have been excluded as evidence. The SC upheld the conviction of Hensley, contending that the "wanted" poster had provided police with sufficient grounds to stop and question Hensley. The SC stressed the increasing mobility of U.S. citizens and the greater importance of information exchanges about felons and crimes among the states.

United States v. Hyde, 520 U.S. 670, 117 S.Ct. 1630 (1997) [UNITED STATES, Petitioner, v. Robert E. HYDE] (Plea Bargaining) Hyde pleaded guilty to several federal fraud counts in accordance with a plea agreement contemplated by the government. The federal judge accepted the plea but deferred judgment on acceptance of the plea agreement until a presentence investigation could be prepared. During the period in which a presentence investigation was ordered for Hyde, he sought to withdraw his guilty plea. The federal judge denied his motion to withdraw the guilty plea and found Hyde guilty of the crimes. The Ninth Circuit Court of Appeals reversed Hyde's conviction, holding that if a court defers acceptance of a plea or of a plea agreement, then a defendant may withdraw his plea for any or no reason, until the court accepts both the plea and plea agreement. The government appealed, and the SC heard the case. The SC reversed the Ninth Circuit, holding that under the circumstances presented here, a defendant may not withdraw a guilty plea unless a "fair and just reason" is demonstrated under Federal Rules of Criminal Procedure 11 and 32(e). Hyde failed to demonstrate any compelling reason for withdrawing his guilty plea.

United States v. Inadi, 475 U.S. 387, 106 S.Ct. 1121 (1986) [UNITED STATES, Petitioner, v. Joseph INADI] (Confrontation Clause; Sixth Amendment) Inadi was convicted of a crime, partly on the basis of the evidence of coconspirators who gave statements to the prosecutor implicating Inadi. At no time did the prosecutor actually call the coconspirators to testify; rather, he introduced their inculpatory statements into the record. Inadi appealed, saying that his Sixth Amendment right to cross-examine his accusers had been violated, and that the prosecutor had not shown that these witnesses were unavailable. The SC upheld Inadi's conviction, saying that it did not intend for its ruling in *Ohio v.*

Roberts (1980) to be interpreted to mean that no out-of-court statements could ever be read into trial records. The SC said that prosecutors are not required to show the unavailability of coconspirators. Thus, prior testimony may be introduced without actually calling coconspirators to testify against a defendant. The confrontation clause of the Sixth Amendment allows for the introduction of such out-of-court statements as a part of its mission in the truth-determining process.

United States v. Jackson, 428 U.S. 153, 88 S.Ct. 1209 (1976) [UNITED STATES, Appellant, v. Charles JACKSON et al.] (Death Penalty) Jackson was indicted by a federal district court bench trial on charges of kidnapping a person in violation of the Federal Kidnapping Act. He sought to dismiss the indictment, arguing that the capital-punishment clause of this act is unconstitutional. The SC held that the capital-punishment clause violates the Fifth and Sixth Amendments, but its elimination does not jeopardize the act in other respects. Thus, the indictment against Jackson was valid despite the capital-punishment clause being declared unconstitutional.

United States v. Jakobetz, 747 F.Supp. 250, 113 S.Ct. 104 (cert. denied) (1992) [UNITED STATES, Petitioner, v. Randolph JAKOBETZ] (DNA Profiling) The SC held that DNA profiling is admissible as evidence in criminal trials.

United States v. Janis, 428 U.S. 433, 96 S.Ct. 3021 (1976) [UNITED STATES et al., Petitioners, v. Max JANIS] (Searches and Seizures) Janis was suspected by Los Angeles police of illegal betting. They obtained a search warrant and searched two of his apartments. The searches yielded betting slips, wagering records, and nearly $5,000 in cash. Janis was arrested and charged with bookmaking. He moved to have the seized evidence suppressed because there were defects in the warrant. A judge agreed and ordered all materials returned to Janis, with the exception of the currency. In the meantime, IRS agents with the Criminal Investigation Division commenced an investigation of Janis' records seized by Los Angeles police and calculated that he owed the government considerable money on his illegal betting activity. The judge ordered Janis' money held until a civil court determination could be made, because IRS levies were in effect concerning the money. Janis' attorney argued that the money ought to be returned as well, because the original IRS investigation was prompted by illegally seized evidence; if the evidence were suppressed, then the IRS would have no foundation to continue their action against Janis. The Ninth Circuit Court of Appeals ordered the return of Janis' money. The government appealed. The SC overturned the decision of the circuit court, holding that although the warrant may have been defective, the IRS had not participated in its issuance. The Los Angeles police officers had been acting in good faith when they advised the IRS of Janis' bookmaking documents. Thus, the IRS, an independent agency, came by this information properly, despite the warrant's defects. Therefore, the SC said, the IRS had not violated Janis' Fourth Amendment rights. The significance of this case is that although warrants may be defective and officers proceed in good faith, independent agencies, such as the IRS, are entitled to use illegally seized evidence against suspects for their own agency purposes in federal civil tax proceedings.

United States v. Jeffers, 342 U.S. 48, 72 S.Ct. 93 (1951) [UNITED STATES, Petitioner, v. Jesse W. JEFFERS, Jr.] (Consent Searches; Law Enforcement Officers or Agencies) In September 1949, Roberts came to the Dunbar Hotel in Washington, DC, and requested that the house detective, Scott, let him into Jeffers' room, where, Roberts said, some "stuff was stashed." Scott told Roberts to check back later. In the meantime, Scott called the police, who came to the hotel. With the assistance of a house key, the officers and Scott opened the room door and searched for narcotics. They discovered cocaine. Jeffers was subsequently charged with and convicted of cocaine possession. He appealed, arguing that his Fourth Amendment right against unreasonable searches and seizures had been violated. He claimed that the officers had needed a warrant to search his locked premises. The government said that it had not invaded Jeffers' privacy, because he wasn't in the room when the police searched it. The SC heard the case and overturned Jeffers' conviction, holding that police were required to obtain a search warrant in order to search his premises; therefore, the illegal cocaine was suppressed as evidence against him. In a related matter, Jeffers filed a motion to get his illegal cocaine back. The SC said that illegal contraband, no matter how it is seized, legally or otherwise, is not subject to return to those from whom it was taken.

United States v. Jimenez Recio, ___U.S.___, 123 S.Ct. 819 (2003) [UNITED STATES, Petitioner, v. Francisco JIMENEZ RECIO and Adrian Lopez-Meza] (Conspiracy) In November 1997, Nevada police stopped a truck and seized a large stash of illegal drugs. However, with the assistance of the truck's drivers, the police set up a sting operation designed to lure additional persons involved in the illegal distribution of drugs to the truck's location for the purpose of arresting them. Two persons, Francisco Jimenez Recio and Adrian Lopez-Meza, were contacted by the truck's drivers, who described the truck's location and contents. Jimenez Recio and Lopez-Meza subsequently appeared in an automobile and Recio drove the truck away, followed by Lopez-Meza. Nevada police stopped the truck a short while later and arrested all four persons (including the two original truck drivers), who were charged with conspiracy to distribute illegal drugs. They were convicted and appealed, alleging that once the conspiracy had been terminated by Nevada police, by stopping the truck and arresting the drivers, subsequent police action involving Jimenez Recio and Lopez-Meza did not make them a part of the conspiracy, as the conspiracy had already been terminated by police interdiction. The defendants also claimed entrapment, as the government had induced others to involve them in the illegal drug distribution. The Ninth Circuit Court of Appeals reversed the possession and conspiracy convictions of Jimenez Recio and Lopez-Meza on these grounds, and the government appealed. The SC heard the case and overturned the Ninth Circuit, holding that conspiracy does not automatically terminate simply because the government has defeated its object, namely the conspiracy to possess and distribute illegal drugs. The SC cited the fact that a conspiracy is an agreement to commit an unlaw-

ful act, an agreement which is a distinct evil, and which may exist and be punished whether or not the substantive crime ensues. Furthermore, no evidence was presented to show that the defendants, Jimenez Recio and Lopez-Meza, abandoned, withdrew from, or disavowed the conspiracy or defeated its purpose. Entrapment was also rejected as an affirmative defense for similar reasons.

United States v. Johns, 469 U.S. 478, 105 S.Ct. 881 (1985) [UNITED STATES, Petitioner, v. Lyle Gerald JOHNS et al.] (Aerial Surveillance; Law Enforcement Officers or Agencies; Vehicle Searches) Johns and others were believed by federal authorities to be involved in drug smuggling. U.S. customs officers conducted surveillance of Johns' movements, tracking him and his associates to an airfield about 50 miles from the Mexican border. Johns and a companion off-loaded cargo and left in their aircraft. Customs officers conducted surveillance of the aircraft in their own aircraft, following it to its final destination, which was Tucson, AZ. Customs officers approached trucks on the airfield and smelled marijuana. They also observed several large packages wrapped in dark green plastic. Their prior experience led them to believe that the packages contained marijuana, so they arrested all suspects and seized the packages. Johns was indicted and convicted of smuggling marijuana, after the trucks were searched, without warrant, at a customs headquarters three days later. Johns sought to suppress the evidence, arguing that the three-day delay in searching the trucks for marijuana should have required officers to obtain a search warrant first. The SC heard the appeal and upheld Johns' conviction, holding that although the officers could have searched the packages in the trucks lawfully incident to an arrest at the airfield, there is no requirement that the warrantless search of the vehicles should occur contemporaneously with the seizure of the unlawful contraband.

United States v. Johnson, 529 U.S. 53, 120 S.Ct. 1114 (2000) [UNITED STATES, Petitioner, v. Roy Lee JOHNSON] (Sentencing) Johnson was convicted of multiple drug and firearms felonies in 1990. A sentence of 171 months was imposed, consisting of three concurrent 51-month terms, to be followed by two consecutive 60-month terms. In addition, a three-year mandatory term of supervised release was ordered to be served for the drug possession offenses. After serving several years in prison, two of Johnson's convictions were held to be invalid. As a result, Johnson was ordered to be set free, as he had served two and one-half years too much prison time. Nevertheless, a three-year term of supervised release was yet to be served on the remaining conviction. Johnson filed a motion to reduce his supervised release time by the amount of extra prison time he had served. The motion was denied in a federal district court, but the Sixth Circuit Court reversed and granted the motion. The government appealed and the SC heard the case. The SC reversed the Sixth Circuit, holding that the term of Johnson's supervised release commenced upon his actual release from prison, not on the date when he should have been released. The SC said that supervised release periods do not run while a prisoner remains in the Bureau of Prisons' custody. The SC added, however, that the trial court was at liberty, "as it sees fit," to modify or terminate Johnson's supervised release obligations after one year of completed service according to 18 U.S.C. Section 3583(e)(1).

United States v. Jorn, 400 U.S. 70, 91 S.Ct. 547 (1971) [UNITED STATES, Appellant, v. Milton C. JORN] (Double Jeopardy) Jorn was tried in federal district court for income tax fraud. After the trial, the judge dismissed the jury, aborted the trial so that witnesses could consult with their attorneys, and ordered a new trial. Jorn contended on appeal that another trial on the same charges would constitute double jeopardy. A circuit court of appeals dismissed the case, but the government appealed. The SC agreed with Jorn and upheld the case dismissal, contending that this was a clear instance of double jeopardy.

United States v. Kahn, 415 U.S. 143, 94 S.Ct. 977 (1974) [UNITED STATES, Petitioner, v. Irving KAHN and Minnie Kahn] (Law Enforcement Officers or Agencies) As the result of government-authorized wiretaps in Kahn's home, incriminating information was obtained not only against Kahn, but also against Kahn's wife. Both were convicted. They appealed, alleging that the purpose of the wiretaps had been to intercept Kahn's calls, not those of Mrs. Kahn. The SC said that the search warrant authorizing the wiretaps was constitutional. Further, the phraseology of the wiretap order, "others as yet unknown," covered persons such as Mrs. Kahn. The ruling applied that legally intercepted conversations not necessarily involving Mr. Kahn did not have to be suppressed as evidence. Therefore, the convictions were upheld.

United States v. Karo, 468 U.S. 705, 104 S.Ct. 3296 (1984) [UNITED STATES, Petitioner, v. James Connors KARO et al.] (Electronic Surveillance, Wiretapping; Law Enforcement Officers or Agencies) Karo was suspected of being a coconspirator in an enterprise to distribute cocaine. A court order was obtained by DEA agents to install a beeper in a clothing container allegedly used by Karo and others to smuggle cocaine. The agents tracked the container by monitoring the beeper, and they discovered various addresses of homes and businesses that appeared to be involved in the cocaine distribution conspiracy. The beeper monitoring had been done without a specific search warrant. DEA agents eventually obtained a search warrant based on probable cause and entered several of the homes and businesses previously monitored through the concealed beeper. Karo and others were eventually convicted of this conspiracy, and they appealed. The SC overturned Karo's conviction on other grounds but declared that in order for beepers to be installed and monitored, especially in private dwellings, a valid search warrant based on probable cause must first be obtained. (*See United States v. Knotts* [1983] *for a comparable case.*)

United States v. Knights, ___U.S.___, 122 S.Ct. 587 (2001) [UNITED STATES, Petitioner, v. Mark James KNIGHTS] (Fourth Amendment; Probation and Parole; Searches and Seizures) Knights was convicted on a drug offense in California and placed on probation. His probation conditions included the provision that Knights should submit to warrantless searches of his premises at any time by a probation officer or a law enforcement officer. Subsequently, Knights became a suspect in the arson of a power transformer owned by the Pacific Gas & Electric Company. A sheriff's deputy had seen Knights and another person near the arson scene earlier. Several suspicious objects were observed in the truck Knights was driving, and a county detective later decided with reasonable suspicion to conduct a search of Knights' apartment. A search revealed detonation cord, ammunition, liquid chemicals, instruction manuals on chemistry and electrical circuitry, bolt cutters, pole-climbing equipment, drug paraphernalia, and a brass padlock stamped "PG & E." Knights was arrested and indicted by a federal grand jury on arson charges. He sought to suppress the evidence obtained against him, claiming the search was unreasonable and unlawful. The district court granted Knights' motion to suppress the evidence obtained on the grounds that the search was for investigatory rather than probationary purposes. The government appealed and the Ninth Circuit Court affirmed the decision of the district court. The government appealed to the SC, who heard the case. The SC reversed the circuit court, holding that the search of Knights' premises was reasonable in that it was authorized by a condition of his probation and within the scope of the Fourth Amendment. The significance of this case is that when probationers consent to warrantless searches of their premises by probation or law enforcement officers as a probation condition, such searches may be conducted at any time, particularly with reasonable suspicion, regardless of whether the search is for probationary or investigatory purposes. The SC also declared the search to be reasonable under the totality of circumstances approach.

United States v. Knotts, 460 U.S. 276, 103 S.Ct. 1081 (1983) [UNITED STATES, Petitioner v. Leroy Carlton KNOTTS] (Electronic Surveillance, Wiretapping; Law Enforcement Officers or Agencies) Knotts was suspected of trafficking in a narcotic ingredient. He was under surveillance at a cabin. Also, police installed a beeper inside a container of the drug ingredient sold to Armstrong, a friend of Knotts'. The beeper was used to track Armstrong's movements, as well as the container. Knotts and Armstrong unloaded the container into Knotts' cabin in plain view of watching officers. The officers obtained a search warrant and searched his premises for the illegal drug ingredient. Knotts was convicted. He appealed, contending that the beeper was an illegal intrusion into his privacy and in violation of his Fourth Amendment right against illegal searches and seizures. The SC disagreed, saying that beepers used as surveillance enhancements are neither "searches" nor "seizures" and therefore do not violate a person's right to privacy or Fourth Amendment rights.

United States v. LaBonte, 520 U.S. 751, 117 S.Ct. 1673 (1997) [UNITED STATES, Petitioner, v. George LaBONTE, Alfred Lawrence Hunnewell, and Stephen Dyer] (Habitual-Offender Statutes) LaBonte and others were convicted of federal drug felonies and sentenced as career offenders. Maximum or near-maximum sentences, including sentencing enhancements for career offenders, are prescribed for those convicted of their felony drug offense or violent crime in accordance with guidelines articulated by the U.S. Sentencing Commission. Several federal circuit courts of appeal were divided on the issue as to whether the sentencing guidelines were ambiguous concerning the phrase "specify a prison sentence at or near the maximum term authorized for categories of adult offenders who commit their third felony drug offense or violent crime." The government appealed those cases in which circuit appellate courts reduced sentences of convicted offenders. The SC heard the case and declared that the phrase "maximum term authorized" is unambiguous and means the maximum prison term available for the offense of conviction, including any applicable statutory sentencing enhancements. The circuit court cases in which prison sentences had been reduced were reversed accordingly, and those cases that did not involve sentence reductions were affirmed.

United States v. Lanier, 520 U.S. 259, 117 S.Ct. 1219 (1997) [**UNITED STATES, Petitioner, v. David W. LANIER**] (**Judicial Misconduct**) Tennessee state chancery court judge Lanier was convicted in federal district court for violating the constitutional rights of five women by sexually assaulting them while serving as a state judge. The women were orally raped and groped by Lanier on different occasions, and under a variety of circumstances. In each case, the women were in positions subordinate to Lanier, as either parties to lawsuits in court cases presided over by Lanier, or as employees under Lanier's direct administrative authority. Lanier was sentenced to several 10-year terms of imprisonment and appealed, contending that the "fair-warning requirement" under which no person may be held criminally liable for conduct that he or she could not reasonably understand to be proscribed, had not been sustained by the trial court. The Sixth Circuit Court of Appeals vacated Lanier's convictions on the basis that there was a "lack of any notice to the public that this ambiguous criminal statute (Title 18 U.S.C. Section 242) includes simple or sexual assault crimes within its coverage." The government appealed, and the SC heard the case. The SC reversed the circuit court and reinstated Lanier's convictions, holding that the Sixth Circuit had applied an incorrect standard in determining whether the "fair-warning requirement" was satisfied regarding the sexual assaults and their punishments. The SC added that it was not necessary that the right in question had previously been held to apply in a factual situation "fundamentally similar" to the one at bar; rather, all that can usefully be said is that it may be imposed for deprivation of a constitutional right if, but only if, in light of preexisting law, unlawfulness under the constitution is apparent. In sum, Title 18 U.S.C. Section 242 makes it criminal to act willfully and under color of state law to deprive a person of rights protected by the constitution or laws of the United States encompassed by the due-process clause of the Fourteenth Amendment.

United States v. Lanza, 260 U.S. 377, 43 S.Ct. 141 (1922) [**UNITED STATES, Petitioner, v. Vito LANZA**] (**Double Jeopardy**) Lanza was convicted of violating a Prohibition law of the State of Washington. The federal government moved to charge him with the same offense, but the SC said that to do so would be a case of double jeopardy and threw out the federal case.

United States v. Lee, 274 U.S. 559, 47 S.Ct. 746 (1927) [**UNITED STATES, Petitioner, v. James M. LEE**] (**Law Enforcement Officers or Agencies; Searches Incident to an Arrest**) On February 16, 1925, a United States Coast Guard cutter spotted a 30-foot motorboat in Gloucester Harbor in Massachusetts. The cutter lost sight of the boat, but later spotted it again, making furtive movements, about 20 miles off the Massachusetts coast near Boston. Coast Guardsmen boarded the vessel and found Lee and two associates with 71 cases of pure grain alcohol. Lee and his associates were later prosecuted for violating Prohibition statutes and were convicted. Their boat was seized as an instrument of the crime. Lee, the registered owner of the boat, appealed both the search and the seizure, claiming that they were illegal because they had taken place beyond the 12-mile limit of the territorial waters of the United States. Thus, Lee claimed, his Fourth Amendment right against unreasonable searches and seizures had been violated. The SC heard the case and upheld Lee's conviction and boat seizure, saying that the search and seizure of the boat were incident to an arrest. That the arrest was made on the high seas did not violate the U.S. Constitution, inasmuch as the persons violating the law were U.S. citizens and had been observed earlier within the 12-mile limit. The theory of "hot pursuit" might be applicable here, although the SC did not articulate it. However, the SC did indicate that probable cause existed for the search undertaken.

United States v. Leon, 468 U.S. 897, 104 S.Ct. 3405 (1984) [**UNITED STATES, Petitioner, v. Alberto Antonio LEON et al.**] (**Exclusionary Rule; Law Enforcement Officers or Agencies**) Leon, a suspected drug trafficker, was placed under surveillance by Burbank, CA, police. Subsequently, police obtained search warrants for three residences and several automobiles under Leon's control. Acting on the search warrants, they seized large quantities of inculpatory drug evidence, which was used against Leon at a trial in which he was convicted. He appealed to the SC, which upheld his conviction. Although the SC declared the search warrants invalid, they noted in a rambling and extensive opinion that the officers who abided by the directives outlined by the invalid warrants had been acting in good faith, presuming that the issued warrants were valid. The SC also noted that this decision was not to be interpreted as a blanket generalization authorizing officers to act in all instances in which defective warrants are issued. The SC simply weighed the benefits of suppressing the evidence obtained in Leon's case against the costs of exclusion. The significance of this case is that it creates a good-faith exception to the exclusionary rule. The SC's message is that evidence may be admissible if the fault for defective warrants rests with judges, not police officers. The target of the exclusionary rule is police misconduct, not judicial misconduct.

United States v. Loud Hawk, 474 U.S. 302, 106 S.Ct. 648 (1986) [**UNITED STATES, Petitioner, v. Kenneth Moses LOUD HAWK et al.**] (**Speedy Trials**) Loud Hawk was indicted for possession of firearms and dynamite. For various reasons, the indictment was dismissed. During a 46-month period when Loud Hawk was free, various appeals by the government were dismissed or affirmed by higher appellate courts. Subsequently, a circuit court of appeals upheld a dismissal of an indictment against Loud Hawk, but the government appealed. The SC reinstated Loud Hawk's indictment, holding that his right to a speedy trial had not been violated because he was not under indictment and had remained free during the period when it was being appealed. Thus, with no indictment, there was no urgency to bring about his trial. The SC concluded that based on the facts, the delays in question were not sufficiently long to justify dismissal of the case against Loud Hawk on speedy-trial grounds.

United States v. Lovasco, 431 U.S. 783, 97 S.Ct. 2044 (1977) [UNITED STATES, Petitioner, v. Eugene LOVASCO, Sr.] (Speedy Trials) Lovasco was indicted for various federal offenses. During the next 17 months, the government prepared an investigative report. Lovasco appealed to the circuit court of appeals, where his indictment was dismissed. The government appealed to the SC, who reversed the lower court, reinstating Lovasco's indictment. The SC held that there is no constitutional requirement for the prosecution to file charges promptly once it has assembled sufficient evidence to prove guilt beyond a reasonable doubt, even if the investigation of Lovasco was incomplete. Such a requirement might impair prosecutors by preventing them from filing additional indictments against suspects for other crimes, and it might pressure prosecutors into resolving doubtful cases in favor of early and possibly unwarranted prosecution. Thus, prosecutors are not under a duty to file charges as soon as probable cause exists but before they are satisfied that they will be able to establish guilt of a suspect beyond a reasonable doubt.

United States v. MacDonald, 456 U.S. 1, 102 S.Ct. 1497 (1982) [UNITED STATES, Petitioner, v. Jeffrey R. MacDONALD] (Speedy Trials) MacDonald was charged with several murders under military law in May 1970. Later that year, charges were dismissed. In 1974, the U.S. Department of Justice renewed the case against MacDonald, and a federal grand jury indicted him. MacDonald appealed, alleging that the government had violated his speedy-trial rights by waiting four years to bring an indictment against him. The SC disagreed, saying that the speedy-trial provision has no application after the government drops charges and decides to reopen a case several years later.

United States v. Mara, 410 U.S. 19, 93 S.Ct. 774 (1973) [UNITED STATES, Petitioner, v. Richard J. MARA aka Richard J. Marasovich] (Fifth Amendment; Self-Incrimination) Mara was compelled to give a handwriting sample to compare with words written on paper during the commission of a crime. He was convicted partially on the basis of this handwriting comparison. He appealed. The SC upheld the conviction, saying that handwriting specimens are not violations of the right against self-incrimination in the Fifth Amendment.

United States v. Marion, 404 U.S. 307, 92 S.Ct. 455 (1971) [UNITED STATES, Appellant, v. William R. MARION and Samuel C. Cratch] (Sixth Amendment; Speedy Trials) In April 1970, indictments were issued against Marion and Cratch on 19 counts of operating a business engaged in fraudulent activity. The acts covered by the indictment were alleged to have been committed between March 1965 and February 1967. Marion alleged that because there was a three-year delay between the overt acts alleged and the

indictment, his speedy-trial rights under the Sixth Amendment had been violated. The SC heard the case and disagreed. The speedy-trial provision of the Sixth Amendment begins when an indictment is delivered, not when overt acts are alleged. Furthermore, the allegations were within the proper statute of limitations for prosecuting such offenses. Thus, Marion's rights had not been violated.

United States v. Martinez-Fuerte, 428 U.S. 543, 96 S.Ct. 3074 (1976) [UNITED STATES, Petitioner, v. Amado MARTINEZ-FUERTE et al. Rodolfo Sifuentes, Petitioner, v. United States] (Border Searches; Fourth Amendment) The Border Patrol established checkpoints for illegal Mexican aliens at various places along a major interstate highway. Martinez-Fuerte was apprehended in one of these roving checkpoints and was convicted of transporting illegal aliens. He appealed to the SC, which upheld the convictions. The SC said that such checkpoint stops, particularly in view of their location and notoriety for illegal alien trafficking, are not in violation of any Fourth Amendment right. Such checkpoints are permissible and need not be prefaced by a judicial warrant. Even if stops are conducted because persons appear to have Mexican ancestry, that does not make such checkpoints and searches unconstitutional.

United States v. Matlock, 415 U.S. 164, 94 S.Ct. 988 (1974) [UNITED STATES, Petitioner, v. William Earl MATLOCK] (Consent Searches; Law Enforcement Officers or Agencies) Matlock was a robbery suspect. Based on probable cause, officers went to Matlock's residence, where they arrested Matlock in his front yard. A Mrs. Graff also lived in the home and admitted officers at their request, although they did not have a search warrant. They asked Mrs. Graff if they could look in various rooms, and she agreed. Eventually, money from the robbery was recovered from a closet in Matlock's bedroom. Police did not know that the bedroom they were searching was Matlock's. On the basis of the evidence, Matlock was indicted for robbery and convicted later at trial. He moved to suppress the evidence obtained because he claimed that the search had been invalid without a proper search warrant. An appeals court granted his motion and the evidence was excluded. The government appealed, and the SC heard the case. The SC upheld Matlock's conviction, concluding that consensual searches of premises by persons sharing the premises with a suspect are valid. Thus Mrs. Graff was in a position to grant officers permission to conduct a warrantless search of the premises, because she shared them with Matlock.

United States v. Mendenhall, 446 U.S. 544, 100 S.Ct. 1870 (1980) [UNITED STATES, Petitioner, v. Sylvia L. MENDENHALL] (Law Enforcement Officers or Agencies; Searches and Seizures) Mendenhall was approached by DEA agents at a Detroit airport and asked to accompany them to a room where she could be searched. Mendenhall did not refuse but said that she had a plane to catch. The agents advised her that if she were carrying no narcotics, she would be free to leave. Her original detention was based on a profile of drug couriers that the DEA had devised. She consented to a strip search, which yielded incriminating heroin, and she was convicted. She appealed, arguing that her Fourth Amendment right against unreasonable search and seizure had been violated. The SC upheld Mendenhall's conviction, holding that she had freely consented to the search of her person, and that expressing the need to "catch a plane" did not obligate officers to secure an arrest warrant or a search warrant to search her further. The SC stressed the "totality of circumstances" surrounding her investigative detention and subsequent search. She had also been advised that she did not have to consent to the search. The SC said that "nothing in the record suggests that [Mendenhall] had any objective reason to believe that she was not free to end the conversation in the concourse and proceed on her way." Perhaps this case suggests that citizens ought to be aware of their rights when approached by police officers or DEA agents in airports and other public transportation facilities, and of the citizen's right simply to "walk away" when no grounds exist otherwise for a search of one's person.

United States v. Miller, 425 U.S. 435, 96 S.Ct. 1619 (1976) [UNITED STATES, Petitioner, v. Mitchell MILLER] (Law Enforcement Officers or Agencies) Miller was convicted in Georgia of violating various liquor laws (e.g., operating an unregistered still) and of intent to defraud the government. During his trial, Miller's bank records were used as evidence against him. He was convicted. He appealed, moving to suppress the incriminating bank records. A circuit court of appeals reversed his conviction. The government appealed the case to the SC, where Miller's conviction was reinstated. The SC held that Miller had no Fourth Amendment interest in the bank records, which were business records, not private papers.

United States v. Monsanto, 491 U.S. 600, 109 S.Ct. 2657 (1989) [UNITED STATES, Petitioner, v. Peter MONSANTO] (Asset Forfeiture; Right to Counsel; Sixth Amendment) Peter Monsanto was indicted by a federal grand jury for RICO violations, including large-scale heroin dealing and distribution. Following the indictment, a government motion to freeze Monsanto's assets was granted. Monsanto objected, claiming that there should have been an exemption freeing his assets so that he could retain counsel. The SC heard Monsanto's appeal and declared that the federal drug forfeiture statute authorizes the federal district court to enter pretrial orders that freeze assets of indicted persons, even when they seek to use these assets to pay attorney fees.

United States v. Montoya de Hernandez, 473 U.S. 531, 105 S.Ct. 3304 (1985) [UNITED STATES, Petitioner, v. Rosa Elvira MONTOYA DE HERNANDEZ] (Border Searches; Searches and Seizures) Montoya de Hernandez was a female drug smuggler who operated as a "mule." Mules are persons who swallow large quantities of heroin or cocaine in glassine envelopes or rubber containers. Later, after they have entered the United States, they defecate the containers and recover the smuggled drug. Based on a reliable informant's tip, DEA agents established surveillance and intercepted Montoya de Hernandez at the airport when she exited a flight from Colombia. They detained her for 16 hours, until eventually, she defecated. The United States customs officials and DEA agents recovered the drugs, which were used as evidence to convict her of drug smuggling. She appealed, alleging that the lengthy airport detention had been unreasonable and violative

of her Fourth Amendment search-and-seizure rights. The SC disagreed, concluding that at border crossings, drug couriers who are profiled based on compelling information from reliable informants may be intercepted and held, considering the reasonable suspicion existing that they might be using their alimentary canal as a repository for smuggled drugs. This case illustrates the fact that different search-and-seizure standards exist in different locations throughout the United States. Thus at international borders, especially at ports of entry known for illegal drug trafficking, such searches and seizures are not unreasonable, whereas they might be considered unreasonable if attempted in cities such as Kansas City, MO; Lima, OH; Wheeling, WV; or Oklahoma City, OK.

United States v. Muniz, 374 U.S. 150, 83 S.Ct. 1850 (1963) [UNITED STATES, Petitioner, v. Carlos MUNIZ and Henry Winston] (Corrections; Federal Tort Claims Act) A federal prison inmate got in a fight with another inmate. A prison guard viewing the fight chose not to intercede and locked the door to the area where the fight was occurring, thus confining it to a limited space. Serious injuries were incurred by the first inmate, including a fractured skull and partial loss of vision in one eye. Lower courts denied the prisoner relief when he filed suit. However, the SC declared that the prisoner could file a suit under the Federal Tort Claims Act of 1946 to recover damages from the federal government and from the negligence of the prison guard, who was also a government employee.

United States v. Nachtigal, 507 U.S. 1, 113 S.Ct. 1072 (1993) [UNITED STATES v. Jerry J. NACHTIGAL] (Jury Trials) Nachtigal was convicted of DUI in a national park while driving a motor vehicle under the influence of alcohol. When he appeared before the U.S. magistrate, Nachtigal asked for a jury trial but was denied one. His offense carried a penalty of six months in prison; thus, the offense was a petty one for which jury trials are not available. He appealed the conviction on the grounds that he had been denied a jury trial. The SC upheld his conviction, saying that jury trials may not be granted in petty-offense cases. (*See Blanton v. North Las Vegas* [1989] *for a comparable case.*)

United States v. New York Telephone Co., 434 U.S. 159, 98 S.Ct. 364 (1977) [UNITED STATES, Petitioner, v. NEW YORK TELEPHONE COMPANY] (Electronic Surveillance, Wiretapping; Law Enforcement Officers or Agencies) The FBI suspected that illegal gambling was occurring at a specified New York City address. It requested the assistance of the telephone company in order to install listening devices on telephones at the location. The telephone company refused to comply with the FBI request, and a court opinion was delivered in favor of the telephone company. The SC reversed this order, however, and declared that it is proper to direct that a communication common carrier should furnish the applicant forthwith all information, facilities, and technical assistance as are necessary to accomplish the interception unobtrusively. Thus, telephone companies are subject to such orders and requests from official government agencies, such as the FBI.

United States v. Nobles, 422 U.S. 225, 95 S.Ct. 2160 (1975) [UNITED STATES, Petitioner, v. Robert Lee NO-

BLES] (**Fifth Amendment; Self-Incrimination**) Nobles was accused of bank robbery in a California U.S. district court. During his trial, the defense attempted to introduce an investigator's statements and interviews with prosecution witnesses for impeachment purposes. The judge ruled such statements would be admissible to the extent that the entire copy of the investigator's report should also be introduced. The defense declared that portions of the report were confidential and their introduction thus might violate the Fifth Amendment rights of Nobles. The judge declared that none of the report could be introduced if only selected portions of it were to be used for impeachment purposes. In view of this all-or-nothing declaration, the investigator was not called to testify. Following Nobles' conviction, he appealed, arguing that his right to a fair trial had been denied. The SC upheld his conviction, saying that the Fifth Amendment privilege against self-incrimination applies *only* to defendants, and not to third parties, such as investigators, who may or may not present incriminating information in their court testimony. Thus it was basically a defense choice to include the potentially incriminating testimony of the investigator, part of which may have helped to impeach a government witness, or to exclude the entirety of such testimony under court discovery provisions.

United States v. Ojeda Rios, 495 U.S. 257, 110 S.Ct. 1845 (1990) [**UNITED STATES, Petitioner, v. Filiberto OJEDA RIOS et al.**] (**Electronic Surveillance; Wiretapping**) Ojeda Rios was under electronic surveillance for alleged illegal activity. Tape recordings were made telephonically from his residence. The government secured the tapes but did not "seal" them. Ojeda Rios sought to suppress these tapes, because they had not been sealed in a timely manner and the government gave no satisfactory explanation for why they had not been sealed. Under the Omnibus Crime Control and Safe Streets Act, recordings of intercepted communications must be sealed immediately upon expiration of the period of order authorizing such interceptions. The SC held that the sealing rule had, indeed, been violated and ruled the tape recordings inadmissible against Ojeda Rios. The case was returned to the trial court for a determination to be made as to whether or not the government's explanation for the sealing delay of 82 days was reasonable.

United States v. Olano, 507 U.S. 725, 113 S.Ct. 1770 (1993) [**UNITED STATES, Petitioner, v. Guy W. OLANO, Jr., and Raymond M. Gray**] (**Jury Instructions**) Olano and Gray were convicted in federal court in Washington State on charges relating to loan kickbacks. During the jury deliberations, two alternate jurors were permitted to sit in the jury room during the deliberations, although they were not permitted to actually participate in those deliberations. Olano's attorneys did not object to the presence of these alternate jurors during juror deliberations. Subsequently, Olano appealed, contending that plain error was committed by the federal judge when he permitted the alternate jurors to sit in on the jury deliberations. Under Federal Rule of Criminal Procedure 24(c), it is required that alternate jurors be discharged after the jury retires to consider its verdict. The Ninth Circuit Court of Appeals reversed Olano's conviction, citing the plain error

rule. The government appealed and the SC heard the case. The SC reversed the Ninth Circuit, holding that the presence in the jury room during deliberations of alternates who had been instructed that they could sit in on the deliberations but were not to participate was not plain error, as it did not affect substantial rights of Olano and Gray. The *Olano* test requires (1) that there be error, (2) that is plain, and (3) that affects substantial rights. Thus, if all three of these elements exist, then an appellate court may exercise its discretion to notice a forfeited error, but only if (4) the error seriously affects the fairness, integrity, or public reputation of the judicial proceedings. In this instance, Olano and Gray failed to show that fairness was affected by the plain error committed by the judge.

United States v. Ortiz, 422 U.S. 891, 95 S.Ct. 2585 (1975) [**UNITED STATES, Petitioner, v. Luis Antonio ORTIZ**] (**Border Searches; Law Enforcement Officers or Agencies; Searches and Seizures; Vehicle Searches**) Ortiz was stopped at a Border Patrol checkpoint about 66 miles north of the Mexican border. Officers requested to search Ortiz's vehicle, but Ortiz refused. The officers searched it anyway, discovering illegal aliens. Ortiz was convicted of transporting them. He appealed. His conviction was overturned, however, when the SC ruled that a checkpoint so far removed from the Mexican border was unreasonable. Further, the Border Patrol agents had had no probable cause or even reasonable suspicion to arrest Ortiz or search his vehicle without warrant or permission. Thus, checkpoints are like "roving patrols" of Border Patrol officers—there must be probable cause, consent, or warrant before an automobile is searched. (*See Almeida-Sanchez v. United States* [1973] *for a comparable case.*)

United States v. Owens, 484 U.S. 554, 108 S.Ct. 838 (1988) [**UNITED STATES, Petitioner, v. James Joseph OWENS**] (**Confrontation Clause; Sixth Amendment**) In a federal prison, a correctional counselor was severely assaulted by an inmate. An FBI investigation followed, in which Foster, the counselor, disclosed that his memory was not too good. Nevertheless, he was able to describe his attack, name his attacker, Owens, and identify Owens from a photograph. During the subsequent trial, however, defense counsel cross-examined Foster and determined that he could not remember seeing his assailant or other details of the assault. Nevertheless, Foster's prior out-of-court statements became a part of the court record against Owens, who was convicted. He appealed to the SC, alleging that his Sixth Amendment right to cross-examine his accuser had been infringed because only out-of-court statements had been used against him, and that Foster, his accuser, could not recall details of the assault during the trial. Owens further alleged that Foster's prior out-of-court statements to FBI agents were nothing more than hearsay. The SC disagreed and upheld Owens' conviction. The SC said that Owens' confrontation rights had not been violated by the introduction of out-of-court statements from Foster, even though Foster admitted he could not recall specific details of the assault. Also, the SC said that Foster's out-of-court identification of Owens as his assailant was admissible against Owens, as Foster was present in court to be cross-examined about those statements.

United States v. Paradise, 480 U.S. 149, 107 S.Ct. 1053 (1987) [UNITED STATES, Petitioner, v. Phillip PARA-DISE, Jr., et al.] (Discrimination; Law Enforcement Officers or Agencies) The NAACP filed a class-action suit against the Alabama Department of Public Safety, alleging that although the department hired blacks as troopers, no blacks held officer ranks. The suit was initiated in 1972 and continued until 1981, when it was shown that the department had not complied with federal court orders to obtain a certain proportion of black highway patrol officers. The SC said that out of 232 state troopers at the rank of corporal or above, there were no black ones as of November 1978. It ordered Alabama officials to fill at least 50 percent of their promotions with black officers until such time that at least 25 percent of black proportionate representation in officer ranks was achieved. The SC said that this measure would fulfill the equal-protection clause of the Fourteenth Amendment.

United States v. Place, 462 U.S. 696, 103 S.Ct. 2637 (1983) [UNITED STATES, Petitioner, v. Raymond J. PLACE] (Law Enforcement Officers or Agencies; Stop and Frisk) Place was suspected of narcotics possession. His luggage was the subject of a 90-minute detention while a trained narcotics-detection dog sniffed it. Place was convicted, and he appealed. A circuit court of appeals reversed Place's conviction because the 90-minute investigative detention of his luggage was unreasonable in violation of his Fourth Amendment rights. The government appealed. The SC affirmed the reversal of Place's conviction.

United States v. Ramirez, 523 U.S. 65, 118 S.Ct. 992 (1998) [UNITED STATES, Petitioner, v. Hernan RA-MIREZ] (Fourth Amendment; Fresh Pursuit; Knock and Announce; Searches and Seizures) A reliable informant in Oregon told police that a dangerous suspect and escaped prisoner, Alan Shelby, was at the home of Hernan Ramirez, and that he had vowed "never to do federal time." Federal agents observed the home for several hours and saw a man resembling Shelby outside of the home. After obtaining a valid search warrant, police officers converged on Ramirez's house, broke a window into Ramirez's garage, where it was believed dangerous weapons were stashed, and advised by loud speaker that they were police. Ramirez was awakened by the noise and grabbed a pistol and fired it into the garage ceiling. Upon learning that police were outside, Ramirez surrendered and was taken into custody. Since Ramirez was a convicted felon, he was charged with and convicted of being a felon in possession of firearms. Ramirez appealed, moving to suppress the evidence regarding the weapons possession. A U.S. district court granted Ramirez's motion, because there were "insufficient exigent circumstances" to justify their destruction of property when executing the warrant. The Ninth Circuit Court of Appeals affirmed the district court decision. The government appealed, and the SC heard the case. The SC reversed the Ninth Circuit Court ruling, holding that the Fourth Amendment does not hold officers to a higher standard when a "no-knock" entry results in the destruction of property. Further, the SC said that officers did not violate Ramirez's Fourth Amendment rights when they broke the garage window, and that the statute

authorizing officers to damage property in executing search warrants under certain circumstances includes an exigent circumstances exception. This case has contributed a variation on the term "hot pursuit," known as "fresh pursuit."

United States v. Ramsey, 431 U.S. 606, 97 S.Ct. 1972 (1977) [UNITED STATES, Petitioner, v. Charles W. RAMSEY and James W. Kelly] (Law Enforcement Officers or Agencies) Ramsey had been receiving large envelopes from Thailand. A warrantless search of these envelopes by customs officials yielded large quantities of narcotics. Ramsey was convicted of various narcotics offenses. An appeal to the SC was of no avail; the SC held that border search exceptions to searches of letters and other items are within the guidelines of customs statutes. Thus customs officials do not require a search warrant to conduct inspections of suspicious mail in international commerce.

United States v. Robinson, 414 U.S. 218, 94 S.Ct. 467 (1973) [UNITED STATES, Petitioner, v. Willie ROBINSON, Jr.] (Law Enforcement Officers or Agencies; Searches Incident to Arrest) Robinson was stopped for operating a motor vehicle without a valid operator's license. It was known that Robinson's license had previously been revoked. Robinson was formally arrested on the basis of probable cause. While arrested, Robinson was searched extensively by police, who found heroin capsules in a crumpled cigarette package. These capsules became evidence against Robinson later when he was subsequently convicted of possession of heroin. Robinson appealed, contending that the scope of an officer's search was limited to "pat-downs and frisks" in view of the *Terry v. Ohio* (1968) and *Sibron v. New York* (1968) rulings. The SC heard the case and upheld Robinson's conviction, noting that the difference between *Terry* and the *Robinson* case was that Terry was not in custody when a police officer conducted a pat-down and frisk of Terry's outer clothing. Further, the *Sibron* case, which suppressed heroin found in Sibron's pocket when he was not under arrest, also differed from the *Robinson* case because Robinson had been placed under arrest, with probable cause, and then searched. Police have a right to search suspects extensively whenever suspects have been arrested, based on probable cause. A custodial arrest of a suspect based on probable cause is a reasonable intrusion under the Fourth Amendment.

United States v. Robinson, 485 U.S. 25, 108 S.Ct. 864 (1988) [UNITED STATES, Petitioner v. Thomas O. ROBINSON, Jr.] (Fifth Amendment; Self-Incrimination) Robinson had been investigated by insurance agents on arson-related insurance claims using the U.S. mails. He was indicted for mail fraud. At his trial in a U.S. district court in Tennessee, Robinson chose *not* to testify in his own behalf. In summation, defense counsel claimed that the government had not allowed Robinson to testify in his own behalf. Upon hearing this, the prosecutor demanded a sidebar conference out of the jury's presence to raise the issue of improper statements from the defense counsel. During this hearing, the judge agreed that the defense had "opened the door" by commenting about Robinson's failure to testify. Thus, when the jury reconvened, the prosecutor advised them that Robinson could have taken the stand and told his side of the story. Because he didn't, the jury was urged to make an adverse inference about Robinson's guilt. The judge gave the jury instructions at the trial's conclusion, instructing them *not* to make inferences about the fact that Robinson had not testified. Despite these admonitions, the jury found Robinson guilty. He appealed, alleging that the prosecutorial conduct was prejudicial and that his right against compulsory self-incrimination had been violated. The SC rejected Robinson's arguments, basically concluding that Robinson could have taken the stand and given testimony in his own behalf. Furthermore, it was *his* counsel, *not* the prosection, who first mentioned the fact that he didn't testify. Thus, the prosecution's reference to the defendant's opportunity to testify, ordinarily prohibited, was acceptable as a response to the defense assertion that Robinson was barred from testifying. There were no constitutional-rights violations in this process.

United States v. Rodriguez-Moreno, 526 U.S. 275, 119 S.Ct. 1239 (1999) [**UNITED STATES, Petitioner, v. Jacinto RODRIGUEZ-MORENO**] (**Jurisdiction**) Rodriguez-Moreno and others kidnapped a middleman, Avendano, during a drug transaction in Texas and drove to New York in an effort to find a New York drug dealer who stole 30 kilograms of cocaine from a Texas drug dealer. Traversing various states, Rodriguez-Moreno drove through Maryland. At a house in Maryland, Rodriguez-Moreno pulled out a .357 Magnum revolver and threatened to kill Avendano if the Texas drug dealer could not be found. At some point Avendano escaped, and Maryland police eventually arrested Rodriguez-Moreno and his cohorts, taking custody of the .357 Magnum pistol. Rodriguez-Moreno was charged in a federal district court in New Jersey with kidnapping, as well as using and carrying a firearm in relation to the kidnapping. He was convicted and sentenced to 87 months' imprisonment on the kidnapping charge and a mandatory consecutive term of 60 months on the weapons charge. He appealed, alleging that the only proper venue for charging the weapons offense was Maryland, not New Jersey. A circuit court of appeals reversed Rodriguez-Moreno's weapons conviction. The government appealed to the SC. The SC reversed the circuit court and reinstated the original 60-month mandatory sentence for the weapons charge, holding that the federal statutes under which Rodriguez-Moreno was charged do not define a "point-in-time" offense when a firearm is used during and in relation to a continuing crime of violence, which began in Texas and ended in Maryland. Thus, the kidnapping occurred in all the places in which any part of it took place, and the venue for the kidnapping charge was appropriate in any of them. This holds also for the weapons charge, which was directly connected with the kidnapping charge.

United States v. Ross, 456 U.S. 798, 102 S.Ct. 2157 (1982) [**UNITED STATES, Petitioner, v. Albert ROSS, Jr.**] (**Closed Container Searches; Consent Searches; Law Enforcement Officers or Agencies; Vehicle Searches**) A reliable informant advised police that Ross was dealing drugs out of his car in a designated location. Police went to the location, observed Ross as described by the informant, and made a warrantless arrest. Then they searched his vehicle, where they found heroin and other illegal substances in containers in the trunk. He was convicted, but he appealed, arguing that police had violated his Fourth Amendment rights against unreasonable searches and seizures. The SC upheld Ross' conviction, saying that following a lawful arrest based on probable cause, a person's car may be searched without warrant, as well as bags and other containers found within it. (*See **United States v. Chadwick*** [1977], *which prohibits warrantless searches of large footlockers, even if found in vehicles being searched incident to an arrest, if the police have time to get a warrant.*)

United States v. Ruiz, ___U.S.___, 122 S.Ct. 2450 (2002) [**UNITED STATES, Petitioner, v. Angela RUIZ**] (**Plea Bargaining; U.S. Sentencing Guidelines**) Ruiz was convicted in a U.S. district court of importing marijuana. The U.S. Attorney's Office attempted to formulate a plea agreement with Ruiz wherein she would plead guilty, waive indictment and a trial, as well as an appeal, in exchange for a reduced sentence recommendation. However, the prosecutor specified that Ms. Ruiz must waive her right to any impeachment information relating to any informants or other witnesses, as well as information supporting any affirmative defense she might raise if the case were to go to trial. Ruiz refused to waive this right, although she subsequently pleaded guilty absent a plea agreement. At sentencing, she asked the judge to grant her the same reduced sentence that the government had offered if she had accepted the plea agreement. The prosecutor opposed her request and it was denied. The Ninth Circuit vacated Ms. Ruiz's sentence, and the government appealed to the SC, who heard the case. The SC reversed the Ninth Circuit and reinstated Ms. Ruiz's conviction, holding that the constitution does not require the government to disclose impeachment information prior to entering into a plea agreement with a criminal defendant. Furthermore, a plea agreement requiring the defendant to waive her right to receive information from the government relating to any affirmative defense she would raise at trial does not violate the constitution.

United States v. Russell, 411 U.S. 423, 93 S.Ct. 1637 (1973) [**UNITED STATES, Petitioner, v. Richard RUSSELL**] (**Entrapment**) Russell and several other persons were suspected of selling methamphetamine, an illegal drug. Government drug agents met with Russell and his friends and offered to manufacture and market the drug and share the profits with them. One agent, Shapiro, offered to provide an essential, hard-to-get chemical component necessary for the manufacturing process. Russell and his partners agreed to participate. They were convicted. Russell appealed, contending that he had been the victim of entrapment, as the government supplied the essential chemical in the furtherance of the illegal activity. The SC disagreed and upheld Russell's conviction. The SC said that entrapment was not proved merely because a government agent supplied an essential chemical leading to the production of an illegal drug that Russell would have manufactured anyway. Russell was already predisposed to commit the illegal act of manufacturing these drugs. Predisposition, stressed by the SC, is one significant determinant of whether entrapment exists.

United States v. Salerno, 481 U.S. 739, 107 S.Ct. 2095 (1987) [UNITED STATES, Petitioner, v. Anthony SALERNO and Vincent Cafaro] (Preventive Detention) Salerno and others were arrested for several serious crimes and held without bail as dangerous under the Bail Reform Act of 1984. Salerno was convicted and sentenced to 100 years in prison. He appealed, being among the first to challenge the constitutionality of the new Bail Reform Act and its provision that specifies that dangerous persons may be detained prior to trial until such time as their case may be decided. He objected that the new act violated the Eighth Amendment provision against "cruel and unusual" punishment. The SC upheld the constitutionality of pretrial detention and declared that it did not violate the defendant's rights under the Eighth Amendment if a specific defendant was found to be dangerous.

United States v. Santana, 427 U.S. 38, 96 S.Ct. 2406 (1976) [UNITED STATES, Petitioner, v. Dominga SANTANA and William Alejandro] (Law Enforcement Officers or Agencies) An undercover police officer offered a woman, McCafferty, money to buy heroin. She accepted the money, drove to the home of Santana, went inside, and came back out with heroin, which she delivered to the officer. When asked about the money given to her, McCafferty said that Santana had it. McCafferty was placed under arrest, while other officers placed Santana's house under surveillance. Later, they observed Santana in the front doorway holding a brown paper bag. Officers approached and Santana attempted to flee back into her home. In hot pursuit, officers caught her, and two bags of heroin fell from her hands. The undercover "buy" money was found in her purse. She was arrested and subsequently convicted of possessing heroin with intent to distribute. Santana appealed, and the case was heard by the SC. She claimed the warrantless arrest and search of her belongings was a violation of her Fourth Amendment rights. The SC disagreed, contending that she was in a public place when she was standing in her doorway. The totality-of-circumstances rule also governed here, because her appearance and identification followed closely a situation in which drugs were purchased by undercover officers. Further, the police had engaged in "hot pursuit" when they followed her into her own home and therefore had not violated her privacy. Thus, a retreating suspect from a public place into a private one precludes pursuing police officers from having to first obtain an arrest or search warrant. (*See especially* **Warden v. Hayden** [1967].)

United States v. Scott, 437 U.S. 82, 98 S.Ct. 2187 (1978) [UNITED STATES, Petitioner, v. John Arthur SCOTT] (Double Jeopardy) Scott was indicted on three narcotics counts. Two of the counts were dismissed on a motion by the defense. After a federal trial was held and Scott was convicted of the one remaining narcotics count, federal prosecutors sought to reindict him on the two narcotics counts that had been dismissed. They alleged that the indictments had been sound but had been prejudiced by a preindictment delay. Scott objected to these new indictments and claimed that he could not be tried on charges stemming from dismissed indictments. The SC heard Scott's appeal and ruled against him, saying that because he had initiated the motions to dismiss the indict-

ments against him, that act did not preclude the government from seeking new indictments on the same charges. Scott's right against double jeopardy had not been violated.

United States v. Sharpe, 470 U.S. 675, 105 S.Ct. 1568 (1985) [UNITED STATES, Petitioner, v. William Harris SHARPE and Donald Davis Savage] (Law Enforcement Officers or Agencies; Stop and Frisk) Sharpe was following an overloaded truck in his own automobile when DEA agents, suspicious of possible drug trafficking, stopped him. They called for highway patrol officers to watch Sharpe while they investigated the overloaded truck. An initial encounter with the truck driver, Savage, led to an uninvited search of the truck's contents after DEA agents "smelled marijuana." Considerable quantities of marijuana were discovered in the truck, and both Savage and Sharpe were arrested and subsequently convicted of possessing a controlled substance. An appeal eventually reached the SC, arguing that the DEA agents had had no right to detain Sharpe for more than 20 minutes while other agents pursued and stopped Savage's truck. The SC avoided setting a specific time limit regarding how long criminal suspects may be stopped and detained under these circumstances. It held that because of the purpose of the stop, the reasonableness of it, and the reasonableness of the means of investigation by the DEA officers, such warrantless intrusion into Savage's truck and the length of Sharpe's detention had not violated the Fourth Amendment. The significance of this case is that no set time limit is placed on officers to stop and detain suspicious persons while others connected with them are also being investigated. However, the SC also said that police officers must be able to justify the length of particular stops and detentions if the case reaches court.

United States v. Sokolow, 490 U.S. 1, 109 S.Ct. 1581 (1989) [UNITED STATES, Petitioner, v. Andrew SOKOLOW] (Law Enforcement Officers or Agencies; Searches and Seizures) The Drug Enforcement Administration has developed a drug-courier profile for use at ports of entry, airports, and bus and train depots. On the basis of this profile, Sokolow and a companion were observed at an airport purchasing with cash two round-trip tickets to Hawaii. Both men appeared nervous and possessed only carry-on luggage. They were stopped by DEA agents and taken to a private airport office, where their luggage was examined by narcotics-detecting dogs. The dogs reacted as though the luggage contained drugs. Officers obtained a search warrant, and the bags were searched. The search yielded more than 1,000 grams of cocaine. Sokolow was subsequently convicted. He appealed, arguing that DEA agents had lacked probable cause to stop initially and search his personal effects. Essentially, he was contesting use of the drug courier profile. The SC downplayed the significance of profiling, favoring the totality-of-circumstances justification for stopping, questioning, and subsequently searching persons who fit profiles as drug couriers.

United States v. Ursery, 518 U.S. 267, 116 S.Ct. 2135 (1996) [UNITED STATES, Petitioner, v. Guy Jerome URSERY] (Asset Forfeiture; Double Jeopardy; Fifth Amendment) Michigan police discovered marijuana growing on some property owned by Ursery and determined that the grounds and home had been the site for illegal marijuana manufacture and distribution for several years. The federal government instituted civil asset forfeiture proceedings against Ursery, and he subsequently settled the forfeiture claims by paying the government $13,250. Shortly thereafter, the federal government indicted Ursery for manufacturing marijuana in violation of 18 U.S.C. Section 841(a)(1). A jury found him guilty, and he was sentenced to 63 months in prison. His conviction was overturned by the Sixth Circuit Court of Appeals on double-jeopardy grounds. The appellate court ruled that any civil forfeiture constitutes punishment for purposes of the double-jeopardy clause of the Fifth Amendment. The government appealed, and the SC heard the case. The SC reversed the appellate court, reinstating Ursery's conviction, holding that civil forfeitures are not punishment for purposes of the double-jeopardy clause of the Fifth Amendment. Thus, government actions to seize assets when crimes have been alleged do not bar subsequent criminal convictions for crimes arising from the circumstances under which the assets were originally forfeited.

United States v. Valenzuela-Bernal, 458 U.S. 858, 102 S.Ct. 3440 (1982) [**UNITED STATES, Petitioner, v. Ricardo VALENZUELA-BERNAL**] (**Confrontation Clause; Sixth Amendment**) Valenzuela-Bernal was charged with transporting illegal aliens. During his trial, he attempted to compel several prior passengers and illegal aliens to appear in court as witnesses in his behalf. It was concluded that these other witnesses would have nothing relevant to contribute. He appealed, alleging that his Fifth and Sixth Amendment rights had been violated because of the government "failure" to produce these other witnesses in his behalf. The SC ruled otherwise and held that there were no Fifth and Sixth Amendment rights violations. The SC stressed the materiality requirement in its decision, noting that sanctions against the government can be sustained only if there is a reasonable likelihood that the testimony of the illegal aliens could have affected the jury decision. The SC declared that in this case such testimony would have no perceptible effect.

United States v. Van Leeuwen, 397 U.S. 249, 90 S.Ct. 1029 (1970) [**UNITED STATES, Petitioner, v. Gerritt Johannes VAN LEEUWEN**] (**Law Enforcement Officers or Agencies; Searches and Seizures**) Van Leeuwen arranged to send coins from different addresses in Seattle, WA, and Van Nuys, CA, to Nashville, TN. A postal clerk became suspicious of the mailed packages, partly because they appeared to be mailed from a fictitious address (the postal worker knew that the address was a vacant lot), and alerted police. A search warrant was obtained, but police were unable to search the packages immediately because of various delays. The next day, the packages were searched and yielded illegal gold coins from Canada. The packages were resealed and forwarded. Van Leeuwen was arrested when he picked them up in Nashville. He was convicted. He appealed, alleging that his Fourth Amendment rights had been violated because of the lengthy delay between the police obtaining search warrants and actually searching the packages. The SC upheld his conviction, saying that no interest protected by the Fourth Amendment

had been violated by forwarding the packages the following day rather than the day they were deposited. There had also been sufficient probable cause upon which to obtain a search warrant, because Van Leeuwen had given a fictitious address and had a car with Canadian license plates.

United States v. Ventresca, 380 U.S. 102, 85 S.Ct. 741 (1965) [**UNITED STATES, Petitioner, v. Giacomo VENTRESCA**] (**Law Enforcement Officers or Agencies; Searches and Seizures**) Ventresca was suspected of operating an illegal distillery. Police conducting surveillance of Ventresca's property discovered deliveries of large amounts of sugar and numerous empty tin containers. Subsequently, they saw numerous filled tin containers being loaded into automobile trunks and driven off. They detected the odor of fermenting mash when they walked along the sidewalk in front of Ventresca's home. On the basis of these observations and impressions, officers obtained a search warrant and raided Ventresca's premises, finding an illegal still and a large quantity of illegal alcohol. Ventresca was convicted. He appealed, seeking to suppress the incriminating evidence seized, on the grounds that the officers had lacked probable cause when obtaining their search warrant. The SC heard the case and upheld Ventresca's conviction, holding that the officers had acted properly by first securing a search warrant based on probable cause, supported by oath or affirmation, describing the place to be searched and the things to be seized.

United States v. Verdugo-Urquidez, 494 U.S. 259, 110 S.Ct. 1056 (1990) [**UNITED STATES, Petitioner, v. Rene Martin VERDUGO-URQUIDEZ**] (**Law Enforcement Officers or Agencies**) Verdugo-Urquidez was arrested by Mexican police, who delivered him to U.S. authorities. Subsequently, U.S. authorities conducted a warrantless search of Verdugo-Urquidez's residence in Mexico and obtained incriminating information against him, which was used to convict him in a U.S. court. He appealed. A lower appellate court ruled to suppress the evidence seized in Mexico because the Fourth Amendment right against unreasonable search and seizure had been violated. The SC upheld Verdugo-Urquidez's conviction, saying that the Fourth Amendment does not apply in Mexico against persons who are Mexican residents, who are not U.S. citizens, and who have no voluntary attachment to the United States.

United States v. Villamonte-Marquez, 462 U.S. 579, 103 S.Ct. 2573 (1983) [**UNITED STATES, Petitioner, v. Jose Reynaldo VILLAMONTE-MARQUEZ**] (**Law Enforcement Officers or Agencies; Searches and Seizures**) U.S. customs officials were patrolling a water channel connecting Lake Charles, LA, with the Gulf of Mexico, when they observed an anchored boat caused to be upset by a passing sailboat. The boat rocked violently, and when customs officers went aboard to see if the occupants of the boat were all right, they smelled marijuana and saw through an open hatch a large quantity of marijuana wrapped in burlap. Further searching produced more marijuana, and Villamonte-Marquez, captain of the boat, was charged and convicted of conspiring to import, possess, and distribute marijuana. He appealed, saying that the search and seizure had been unreasonable, in violation of his

Fourth Amendment rights. The case went through various levels of appeals, eventually reaching the SC, where it was decided that U.S. customs officials are authorized to board any vessel located in waters providing easy access to the open sea, in order to examine the ship's manifest and other documents, even without suspecting any wrongdoing. The SC reinstated Villamonte-Marquez's original conviction.

United States v. Vonn, ___U.S.___, 122 S.Ct. 1043 (2002) [UNITED STATES, Petitioner, v. Alphonso VONN] (Reversible Error) Vonn was convicted in federal district court of armed bank robbery and using and carrying a firearm in relation to a crime of violence. Vonn entered the plea as a part of a plea bargain in accordance with Rule 11 of the Federal Rules of Criminal Procedure governing plea bargain agreements. At several stages prior to his conviction, Vonn was asked by a magistrate, and subsequently by the trial judge, whether he understood his rights, and that he was entitled to counsel. On each occasion, Vonn indicated that he understood his rights. In the meantime, Vonn was indicted on additional charges, including conspiracy to commit bank robbery. On at least two occasions when Vonn appeared before the district court judge for arraignment, he was advised of his rights. However, the judge failed to mention Vonn's right to assistance of counsel if the case went to trial. But Vonn was represented by counsel at the time, both on the prior bank robbery and firearms charges and the conspiracy charge. At no time did Vonn object to these proceedings or to what the district judge told him. On June 22, 1998, Vonn was sentenced to 97 months in prison. Several months later, Vonn filed an appeal of all of his convictions, contending that the district court judge's failure to advise him of his right to counsel, as required by Rule 11, was an error and warranted reversal of his convictions. An appellate court vacated Vonn's convictions and remanded the cases to federal court. The government appealed, and the SC heard the case. The SC reversed the circuit court of appeals, holding that unobjected-to error in the trial court's guilty plea colloquy was reversible only upon a showing that such error was plain and that it affected the defendant's substantial rights. Furthermore, the appellate court could have looked at the entire court record when determining whether Vonn's substantial rights had been affected. Vonn had failed to show that the judicial error in his case affected his substantial rights. It is insufficient for a defendant to merely demonstrate that a judge committed plain error during a plea agreement hearing.

United States v. Wade, 388 U.S. 218, 87 S.Ct. 1926 (1967) [UNITED STATES, Petitioner, v. Billy Joe WADE] (Law Enforcement Officers or Agencies; Lineups) Wade was a participant in a bank robbery. He drove away from the bank with an accomplice. Eyewitnesses saw them in the bank and gave descriptions to police. Subsequently, Wade was arrested and indicted for robbery. A lawyer was appointed for him. Later, at the jail, police placed Wade in a lineup with other men for two bank workers to view. Both bank workers identified Wade as the robber. Wade's attorney was not notified of the lineup. Later, at Wade's trial, the same bank employees reidentified Wade as the robber and he was convicted, in some

part, on the testimony of these eyewitnesses. Wade appealed, moving to suppress the testimony of the eyewitnesses, because he had been subjected to a lineup without his attorney present. The SC agreed and overturned Wade's conviction, saying that lineups are critical stages, and whenever indicted offenders have counsel appointed for them, those attorneys should be present at these critical stages. In Wade's case, because he was represented by counsel and his counsel was not present at his lineup, his right to counsel had been violated.

United States v. Washington, 431 U.S. 181, 97 S.Ct. 1814 (1977) [UNITED STATES, Petitioner, v. Gregory V. WASHINGTON] (Grand Juries) Washington was indicted for receiving stolen property on the basis of his self-incriminating testimony before a grand jury in a related matter. Washington sought to dismiss the indictment, contending that he had not waived his right against self-incrimination when he appeared before the grand jury. The SC upheld his indictment, holding that when a witness suspected of wrongdoing gives self-incriminating testimony before a grand jury, this information may be used against him or her in later criminal prosecution even though the witness is not informed in advance of his or her testimony that he or she is a potential defendant in danger of indictment.

United States v. Watson, 423 U.S. 411, 96 S.Ct. 820 (1976) [UNITED STATES, Petitioner, v. Henry Ogle WATSON] (Law Enforcement Officers or Agencies; *Miranda* Warning; Vehicle Searches) A postal inspector was advised by a reliable informant that Watson possessed stolen credit cards, had given the informant some cards, and planned to give him more cards in the future. The inspector arranged for the informant to meet with Watson later where the credit-card exchange could be observed by police. The informant was supposed to give police a signal whenever Watson gave him stolen credit cards. A signal was given by the informant and Watson was stopped, arrested, told his *Miranda* rights, and searched by police, who found no stolen credit cards. They asked Watson if they could search his vehicle, which was nearby. Watson agreed, and an envelope with stolen credit cards was found. Watson was charged with and convicted of possession of stolen credit cards. He appealed, arguing that police had had no business arresting him in a public place without first obtaining a valid arrest warrant. The SC upheld Watson's conviction, saying that sufficient probable cause had existed that a crime had been committed (on the basis of the reliable informant's information) for police officers to investigate and make an arrest. The significance of this case is that it permits officers to make warrantless arrests of suspects in a public place and with probable cause.

United States v. Wheeler, 435 U.S. 313, 98 S.Ct. 1079 (1978) [UNITED STATES, Petitioner, v. Anthony Robert WHEELER] (Double Jeopardy) Wheeler was a Navajo tribe member who was convicted in tribal court of contributing to the delinquency of a minor. Later, a federal grand jury indicted Wheeler on statutory rape charges arising from the same incident. Wheeler sought to dismiss the indictment on the grounds of double jeopardy. The SC refused to dismiss the indictment, holding that the Navajo tribal court was not an arm of the federal government but rather an independent sovereign. Thus, a federal prosecution arising from the same incident for which Wheeler was convicted by a tribal court did not violate his right against double jeopardy.

United States v. White, 401 U.S. 745, 91 S.Ct. 1122 (1971) [**UNITED STATES, Petitioner, v. James A. WHITE**] (**Electronic Surveillance, Wiretapping; Law Enforcement Officers or Agencies**) A criminal suspect, White, was under police surveillance. An informant, a friend of White's, wore an electronic transmitter and engaged White in incriminating conversations at his restaurant, home, and automobile. No warrant had been issued for such electronic surveillance. The informant was never called to testify, but the incriminating recorded conversations were admitted later at White's trial, where he was convicted. White appealed, alleging that a warrant should have been issued for such recordings, and that his Fourth Amendment rights had been violated as a result. The SC disagreed and said that voluntary statements made by a criminal suspect to a paid government informant are admissible as evidence against the suspect, even if the informant does not testify and if the information is introduced at trial through the testimony of FBI agents who did the original recording of the conversation. Compare this case with the same situation in *Massiah v. United States* (1964). Massiah was previously indicted and represented by counsel, but in Massiah's case, the incriminating information provided through an informant was inadmissible because Massiah's attorney was not present during the "interrogation." The "interrogation" was considered such because the informant was acting on behalf of the FBI investigating Massiah. The crucial element was whether Massiah was represented by counsel. If White had been previously indicted and represented by counsel, then the *Massiah* ruling would have governed his case, and the incriminating evidence could have been suppressed effectively.

United States v. Williams, 504 U.S. 36, 112 S.Ct. 1735 (1992) [**UNITED STATES, Petitioner, v. John H. WILLIAMS, Jr.**] (**Grand Juries**) Williams was indicted by a federal grand jury for various crimes, including making false statements for the purpose of influencing the action of a federally insured financial institution. During the presentation of the case, federal prosecutors omitted various exculpatory statements to the grand jury. Williams later saw the entire grand-jury record and moved to have the indictment dismissed because of the government failure to introduce these exculpatory statements. His motion was granted, and the indictment was dismissed. The government appealed. The SC heard the case and ruled in the government's favor, holding that prosecutors are not under any particular duty to present exculpatory evidence during grand-jury proceedings. The indictment was reinstated.

United States v. Wilson, 420 U.S. 332, 95 S.Ct. 1013 (1975) [**UNITED STATES, Petitioner, v. George J. WILSON, Jr.**] (**Self-Incrimination**) Wilson was indicted on charges of embezzling money from a labor organization. He was convicted. He filed several motions, including one to dismiss the indictment. The motion to dismiss the indictment was granted. Then he sought to have his embezzlement conviction set aside because of the lack of a valid indictment. The government appealed to have the original indictment upheld. The SC upheld the original indictment and Wilson's conviction.

United States v. Wong, 431 U.S. 174, 97 S.Ct. 1823 (1977) [**UNITED STATES, Petitioner, v. Rose WONG**] (**Grand Juries**) Wong testified before a grand jury in a criminal matter. She was indicted for perjury. She moved to have the indictment suppressed, alleging that she had not understood the warning of her right not to answer self-incriminating questions before the grand jury. The U.S. district court granted the suppression motion. The government appealed. The SC thought otherwise and reinstated her indictment on perjury charges. The SC held that a witness who is called to testify before a grand jury while under investigation for criminal activity, and who is later indicted for perjury relating to that grand-jury testimony, is not entitled to have false testimony suppressed on the ground that no effective warning of the Fifth Amendment privilege to remain silent was given.

United States Department of Justice v. Landano, 508 U.S. 165, 113 S.Ct. 2014 (1993) [**UNITED STATES DEPARTMENT OF JUSTICE et al., Petitioners, v. Vincent James LANDANO**] (**Corrections; Inmate Rights**) Landano, convicted of murder, sought to obtain investigative files from the FBI under the Freedom of Information Act (FOIA). The FBI gave Landano only partial files and withheld other files. Landano appealed to the SC, where the case was heard. The government claimed that it had denied certain files to Landano because of confidential sources. The SC declared that the FBI is not entitled to the presumption that all sources supplying information to the FBI in the course of a criminal investigation are confidential and thus exempted from FOIA requests. Thus, Landano was entitled to those files. The SC declared, however, that if it can be shown, through *in camera* affidavits, that some of the confidential informants might be jeopardized by such disclosures, then some of this information may be exempted from FOIA requests.

Uveges v. Pennsylvania, 335 U.S. 437, 69 S.Ct. 184 (1948) [**Elmer UVEGES, Petitioner, v. Commonwealth of PENNSYLVANIA**] (**Right to Counsel; Sixth Amendment**) In October 1938, Elmer Uveges, a 17-year-old, was charged in four separate indictments for different burglaries. He entered guilty pleas to all four charges and was sentenced to four consecutive terms totaling 80 years in prison. Later, he filed a *habeas corpus* petition, alleging that his due-process rights had been violated when he was not informed of his right to counsel and had not been offered counsel during the period between his arrest and conviction. Uveges also alleged that he had been intimidated by prosecutors, who threatened him and coerced a guilty plea from him on the promise that he would be sentenced for a short term to a nearby reformatory. The SC heard Uveges' case and reversed his convictions. Indigents are entitled to counsel whether they elect to stand trial or plead guilty, where the seriousness of the proceedings would otherwise render the proceedings fundamentally unfair. The SC held that under the requirements of due process, Uveges' case required the presence of counsel at his trial. He should not have pleaded guilty without having an offer of the advice of counsel. The fact that he was young and inexperienced was clearly advantageous to prosecutors. Thus, Uveges had been denied a fair hearing, and his sentences had to be vacated in this light and a new trial granted with counsel provided.

V

Vale v. Louisiana, 399 U.S. 30, 90 S.Ct. 1969 (1970) [Donald J. VALE, Appellant, v. State of LOUISIANA] (Law Enforcement Officers or Agencies; Searches and Seizures; Searches Incident to an Arrest) Vale, a suspected drug user, was under police surveillance. One evening while police were observing his home, a known drug addict spoke with Vale on his front porch and some object was exchanged between them. The police intercepted the drug addict as he left Vale, and arrested Vale outside his front door. Without a warrant, police proceeded to enter Vale's home and search it incident to the arrest. While searching, they discovered heroin and other narcotics in Vale's bedroom. Vale was convicted. He appealed, contending that police had needed a valid search warrant to search his premises and that a search incident to his arrest had violated his Fourth Amendment right against an unreasonable search and seizure. The SC agreed with Vale and overturned his conviction. No exigent circumstances existed in this case, because Vale didn't know that his activities were being observed or that he would have time to dispose of his illegal drugs. Arrests of suspects must occur in their homes, not outside of them, and even in this instance, police should have limited their search to areas immediately under the suspect's control, such as the room he was arrested in, not other rooms, such as bedrooms, kitchens, garages, and attics. (*See Chimel v. California* [1969] *for a specific SC statement on the scope of searches incident to arrests.*)

Vasquez v. Hillery, 474 U.S. 254, 106 S.Ct. 617 (1986) [Daniel VASQUEZ, Warden, Petitioner v. Booker T. HILLERY, Jr.] (Discrimination; Fourteenth Amendment) Hillery, a black man, was indicted in 1962 for murder in a California court. He sought to dismiss the indictment on the grounds that black persons had been deliberately excluded from the grand jury that issued it. He was unsuccessful and was ultimately convicted of first-degree murder. Sixteen years later, Hillery filed a *habeas corpus* suit alleging that the racial composition of the grand jury had adversely affected his conviction in violation of the equal-protection clause of the Fourteenth Amendment. The state countered that the fair trial Hillery was ultimately given had removed any taint of the racially biased grand jury that had issued the original indictment. The SC granted Hillery's petition, thus reversing his conviction, rejecting the idea that the biased racial composition of the grand jury had been a "harmless error." Rather, the SC declared, discrimination in grand-jury selections under-

mines the structural integrity of criminal tribunals, and fair trials cannot correct such problems. The SC ruled that convictions of any defendants indicted by grand juries from which members of their race have been systematically excluded must be reversed.

Victor v. Nebraska, 511 U.S. 1, 114 S.Ct. 1239 (1994) [Clarence VICTOR, Petitioner, v. NEBRASKA. Alfred Arthur Sandoval, Petitioner, v. California] (Jury Instructions) Victor was convicted in a Nebraska court of first-degree murder and sentenced to death. In the judge's instructions to the jury, he said that *reasonable* doubt can be equated with a *substantial* doubt. Victor sought to have his conviction reversed on the grounds that "substantial doubt" was an overstatement of the amount of doubt jury members would need to deliver an acquittal. The SC heard the case and declared that the matter of "substantial doubt" compared with "beyond a reasonable doubt" was an unexceptional proposition. In fact, the SC had upheld the constitutionality of the phrase "substantial doubt" in the case of *Cage v. Louisiana* (1990). Victor's murder conviction and death sentence were upheld.

Vitek v. Jones, 445 U.S. 480, 100 S.Ct. 1254 (1980) [Joseph VITEK, etc., et al., Applicants, v. Larry D. JONES] (Civil Rights, Section 1983 Claims; Corrections; Inmate Rights) Jones was a Nebraska inmate transferred from a prison cell to the penitentiary hospital for mental illness. This transfer was made without a hearing. Jones later was placed in solitary confinement and set his mattress on fire, suffering burns. Subsequently, he was transferred, again without a hearing, to a state mental hospital for commitment for an indefinite period. Jones sued under Title 42 U.S.C. Section 1983, alleging that his due-process rights had been violated when he was transferred to a mental hospital without a hearing. The SC agreed with Jones and held that before prisoners may be transferred to a mental institution from a prison, they are entitled to a hearing on the transfer. This is to insure that their due-process rights are observed. (*See Morrissey v. Brewer* [1972] *for a comparable case in due-process rights of probationers and parolees.*)

W

Wainwright v. Goode, 464 U.S. 78, 104 S.Ct. 378 (1983) [Louie L. WAINWRIGHT, Secretary, Florida Department of Corrections, v. Arthur Frederick GOODE III] (Aggravating and Mitigating Circumstances; Death Penalty; Sixth Amendment) Goode kidnapped a 10-year-old boy in Florida, sexually assaulted him, and then strangled him with a belt. Goode fled to Maryland and later to Virginia, where he committed another murder. He was convicted of murder in Virginia and then returned to Florida, where he was again convicted of murder and given the death penalty. The judge cited three aggravating factors and two mitigating ones and imposed the death penalty. Later, Goode appealed, alleging ineffective assistance of counsel, because his counsel had failed to challenge the judge's remarks, especially some that made reference to nonstatutory aggravating factors, such as predicting Goode's future dangerousness. Goode appealed to the Florida Supreme Court, which affirmed and upheld his sentence. Later Goode filed another motion contending that the judge in his case relied on an impermissible aggravating factor (i.e., future dangerousness) under Florida law. The motion was denied and the Florida Supreme Court said that Goode should have raised that motion with his first appeal. Next, Goode filed a *habeas corpus* petition with the federal court alleging that the original trial judge acted improperly when imposing the death penalty. The motion was denied, and Goode appealed to the 11th Circuit, which granted Goode's motion for a stay of execution. The 11th Circuit concluded that the trial judge had imposed the death penalty on Goode in an arbitrary and capricious manner, and reversed Goode's death sentence. Florida appealed and the SC heard the case. The SC reversed and reinstated Goode's death sentence, stating that (1) as regards the issue of whether the state trial court relied on an impermissible aggravating factor such as Goode's future dangerousness, the 11th Circuit erred when it substituted its view of the facts for those of the Florida Supreme Court, and (2) even if the sentencing judge relied on an aggravating factor unavailable under state law, the procedures followed did not produce an arbitrary or freakish sentence forbidden by the Eight Amendment.

Wainwright v. Greenfield, 474 U.S. 284, 106 S.Ct. 634 (1986) [Louie L. WAINWRIGHT, Secretary, Florida Department of Corrections, Petitioner, v. David Wayne GREENFIELD] (*Miranda* Warning; Self-Incrimination) Greenfield was suspected of sexual battery. At the time of his arrest, he was told his *Miranda* rights, and he refused to answer questions about the alleged crime. He pleaded not guilty by reason of insanity. During his trial, the prosecutor commented about the fact that Greenfield refused to answer police questions, and that this was evidence of his "sanity." Greenfield was subsequently convicted, and he appealed. The SC overturned Greenfield's conviction, saying that it is fundamentally unfair for prosecutors to comment on a defendant's silence invoked as the result of a *Miranda* warning. This is a violation of the due-process clause of the Fourteenth Amendment. (*See Doyle v. Ohio* [1976] *for a comparable case.*)

Wainwright v. Witt, 469 U.S. 412, 105 S.Ct. 844 (1985) [Louie L. WAINWRIGHT, Secretary, Florida Department of Corrections, Petitioner, v. Johnny Paul WITT] (Death-Qualified Juries) Witt was convicted of first-degree murder by a Florida jury and sentenced to death. He appealed, arguing that it was wrong of the trial judge to exclude a prospective juror because of her views on the death penalty. A lower court set aside the conviction, remanding the case to the lower court for a new trial. The government appealed, and the SC reinstated the original conviction and death penalty, saying that the finding of juror bias by the trial judge had been made under the proper standard. The proper standard is whether a juror's attitudes about the death penalty would substantially impair his or her ability to determine the proper penalty in the punishment phase of a two-phase trial. Potential jurors in capital murder cases may be excluded if their views would prevent or substantially impair the performance of their duties in accordance with their instructions and oath. (*See Witherspoon v. Illinois* [1968].)

Walder v. United States, 347 U.S. 62, 74 S.Ct. 354 (1954) [WALDER v. UNITED STATES] (Corrections; Searches and Seizures) In May 1950, Walder was indicted for possessing cocaine. He moved to have the evidence suppressed, because the search-and-seizure tactics used by police were questionable. His motion was granted, and his case was dismissed. Later, he was indicted in January 1952 for four additional narcotics transactions. During his trial, he was asked whether he had ever dealt in narcotics, and he said no. An officer who arrested him in 1950 gave impeaching testimony, which Walder sought to suppress. He was convicted. He appealed, contending that the original cocaine seized from him was the result of an illegal search and seizure. The SC upheld his conviction, saying that impeachment evidence may come from formerly illegal searches and seizures from those involved in the seizures of cocaine. Thus it was not improper to introduce testimony that Walder had engaged formerly in cocaine sales, even though the evidence was subsequently excluded and the charges against him were dismissed.

Walton v. Arizona, 497 U.S. 639, 110 S.Ct. 3047 (1990) [Jeffrey Alan WALTON, Petitioner, v. ARIZONA] (Aggravating and Mitigating Circumstances; Death Penalty; Eighth Amendment; Self-Incrimination) Walton and two friends, while at a bar in Arizona, determined they would steal someone's car at random. They encountered Thomas Powell, an off-duty Marine, kidnapped him, stole his car, and shot him to death, execution-style, in the desert. Following their arrest, they all made inculpatory statements suggesting that the killing was especially cruel and heinous. Walton told his friends, for instance, that after he shot Powell in the back of the head, he saw Powell "pee in his pants" and that he had never seen someone do that before. Walton was convicted of first-degree murder, armed robbery, kidnapping, and theft. At his sentencing hearing, the jury was given instructions by the judge, including one that two aggravating circumstances were present if the jury found the murder was committed (1) in "an especially heinous, cruel, or depraved manner" and (2) for pecuniary gain. The jury found that such circumstances existed and recommended the death penalty for Walton. Walton appealed, alleging that these instructions and the nature of weighing aggravating circumstances in relation to mitigating ones were "facially vague." Therefore, he alleged his Sixth and Eighth Amendment rights had been violated. The SC heard his case and upheld his murder conviction and death penalty, holding that Arizona was not required to call aggravating circumstances "elements" of offense or permit only the jury to determine the existence of such circumstances; the "especially heinous, cruel, or depraved" aggravating circumstance as construed by the Arizona Supreme Court furnished sufficient guidance to jurors to satisfy the Eighth and Fourteenth Amendments. Subsequently, the SC overruled this case in the 2002 case of *Ring v. Arizona*, to the extent that a judge, sitting without a jury, is not permitted to find aggravating circumstances in order for the death penalty to be imposed. The Sixth Amendment requires that aggravating and mitigating factors should be determined by a jury, not a judge. (*See Ring v. Arizona* [2002].)

Warden v. Hayden, 387 U.S. 294, 87 S.Ct. 1642 (1967) [WARDEN, Maryland Penitentiary, Petitioner, v. Bennie Joe HAYDEN] (Exclusionary Rule; Law Enforcement Officers or Agencies; Searches and Seizures) A cab company robbery was reported to police, and a description of the man was provided by eyewitnesses. A pedestrian followed the man to his home and reported immediately to police. They went to the house and a woman answered the door. They asked if they could come in and look around. She consented. They found Hayden "pretending to be asleep." Further, they found a shotgun and pistol in a toilet water tank, clothes fitting the robber's description in a washing machine, and a bag containing money with the cab company name imprinted on it. Hayden was arrested and convicted. He appealed, alleging that the police had had no right to enter his home without a valid warrant based on probable cause. The SC disagreed and said that police in hot pursuit of a criminal suspect do not need a search warrant to enter his home. Even more important was the fact that Mrs. Hayden had given police permission to enter the home and conduct a search of it. Thus, consent provides an additional exception to the exclusionary rule that would ordinarily require a search warrant before incriminating evidence can be searched for and seized.

Washington v. Chrisman, 455 U.S. 1, 102 S.Ct. 812 (1982) [WASHINGTON, Petitioner, v. Neil Martin CHRISMAN] (Fourth Amendment; Law Enforcement Officers or Agencies; *Miranda* Warning; Searches Incident to an Arrest) In late January 1978, the Washington State University campus police observed a student, Overdahl, carrying a half-gallon bottle of gin as he was leaving his dormitory. Campus regulations forbade the possession of alcoholic beverages by students, so the campus police stopped Overdahl and asked for ID. He told police that his ID was in his dorm room and they accompanied him back to his room to obtain it. When they entered the room, another student, Chrisman, was placing a small box in a medicine cabinet. Officers observed in plain view several seeds and a pipe lying on a nearby table. One of the officers, based on his experience, believed the seeds to be marijuana and the pipe to be one used for smoking marijuana. He entered the room, inspected the seeds, and smelled the pipe, confirming his suspicions. Both students were told their *Miranda* rights and questioned. They admitted to possessing and smoking marijuana. Also, they voluntarily consented to permit the officers to search their room. The officers found more marijuana, LSD, and other controlled substances. Chrisman was charged with and convicted of marijuana possession. He appealed, alleging that the officers had had no right to enter his room and seize anything without first obtaining a warrant. The Washington Supreme Court reversed Chrisman's conviction on various grounds, particularly because it believed the officers had not been entitled to accompany Overdahl into the room while he secured his ID. There-

fore, the Washington Supreme Court reasoned, the evidence seized ought to have been suppressed, and it overturned Chrisman's conviction. The government appealed. The SC disagreed and reinstated Chrisman's conviction. The SC argued that from the first officer's vantage point in the doorway of the dorm room, the seeds and suspicious pipe were in plain view, which created probable cause to investigate further by entering the room. The officers were in a place where they had a right to be, and therefore their seizure of the drugs and drug paraphernalia was lawful. Furthermore, after being told their *Miranda* rights, the students had consented to a further search of their room. Thus the seizure of controlled substances was justified, the evidence admissible, and the convictions upheld.

Washington v. Harper, 494 U.S. 210, 110 S.Ct. 1028 (1990) [WASHINGTON et al., Petitioners, v. Walter HARPER] (Civil Rights, Section 1983 Claims; Confessions; Inmate Rights) Harper was a psychologically disturbed inmate in prison for robbery. He was eventually paroled but on condition that he participate in psychiatric treatment at a hospital. About a year later, Harper assaulted two nurses in a Seattle hospital, and his parole was revoked. When he returned to prison, prison psychiatrists determined that he should be administered antipsychotic medication. Harper agreed for a time to take this medication, but a while later, he refused to continue. The medicine was forcibly administered thereafter. Harper filed a Title 42 U.S.C. Section 1983 claim, alleging that he had not been given a hearing to determine whether due process was violated by having to take such medication forcibly. The SC disagreed with Harper, saying that it is proper whenever inmates have serious mental illnesses for treatment to be administered with antipsychotic drugs against their will and without a judicial hearing.

Washington v. Texas, 388 U.S. 14, 87 S.Ct. 1920 (1967) [Jackie WASHINGTON, Petitioner, v. State of TEXAS] (Jury Trials) Washington was charged with a crime in a Texas court. He demanded that the prosecutors obtain witnesses in his favor who were available to testify. The prosecution refused to serve these witnesses with subpoenas because defendants had a right to such witnesses only in federal proceedings, not in state proceedings. Washington was convicted. He appealed, arguing that he had not received a fair trial, as exculpatory witnesses had not been called by the prosecution at the defendant's request. The SC overturned Washington's conviction, saying that under the Sixth Amendment, compulsory process for obtaining witnesses in one's favor is so fundamental and essential to a fair trial that it should be incorporated into the due-process clause of the Fourteenth Amendment and thus would be applicable to both federal and state courts. The significance of this case is that compulsory process is guaranteed in state as well as federal trials, so that witnesses favorable to the defense must be called by the prosecution.

Watts v. Indiana, 338 U.S. 49, 69 S.Ct. 1347 (1949) [Robert A. WATTS v. State of INDIANA] (Confessions) Watts was suspected of murder while attempting to commit rape. He was arrested and subjected to lengthy and grueling interrogation, which several witnesses characterized as inquisitional. Subsequently, he confessed, but he recanted the confession in court later. He was convicted. He appealed, alleging that his confession had been coerced. Rejecting his confession, the SC scolded the trial court by saying that it was naive to think that this protective custody had been less than an inquisition. Coerced confessions are inadmissible in court; therefore, the SC overturned his conviction.

Wayte v. United States, 470 U.S. 598, 105 S.Ct. 1524 (1985) [**David Alan WAYTE, Petitioner, v. UNITED STATES**] (**Corrections; Death Penalty; First Amendment; Free Speech**) Wayte was charged with willfully failing to register for the Selective Service System ("draft"). The government subsequently invoked a passive enforcement policy, where the rules governing such prosecutions of draft dodgers were relaxed. However, Wayte sent letters and other forms of communication to the government, declaring that he never intended to register for the draft. Wayte was prosecuted. He appealed, arguing that the government was discriminating against him by such a prosecution. The SC rejected Wayte's arguments, saying that the government regulation was within its constitutional power, that such regulation furthered an important or substantial government interest, that the government interest was unrelated to the suppression of free speech, and that the incidental restriction on alleged First Amendment freedoms was no greater than was essential to the furtherance of that interest.

Weatherford v. Bursey, 429 U.S. 545, 97 S.Ct. 837 (1977) [**Jack M. WEATHERFORD, etc., et al., Petitioners, v. Brett Allen BURSEY**] (**Civil Rights, Section 1983 Claims; Law Enforcement Officers or Agencies; Right to Counsel; Sixth Amendment**) Weatherford was an undercover officer in Columbia, SC, "playing along" with Brett Bursey and other associates to learn what they intended to do in connection with vandalizing Selective Service offices. When all were arrested for vandalism of Selective Service offices, Weatherford was taken into custody with the others. Bursey retained counsel. Weatherford did so as well, to maintain the pretense of conspiring with Bursey. Before the trial was held, Weatherford, continuing his undercover role, met frequently with Bursey and his counsel and discussed with them Bursey's plans for defense. At no time did Weatherford ask Bursey for information; rather, Bursey volunteered information about his defense plans. Weatherford also advised Bursey and his attorney that Weatherford planned to sever his case from Bursey's. Even under these changed circumstances and anticipated severance, however, Bursey continued to disclose details of his defense to Weatherford. Later, at Bursey's trial, Weatherford gave incriminating testimony, which led to Bursey's conviction. Bursey filed a Title 42 U.S.C. Section 1983 civil rights suit against Weatherford. Bursey alleged that his Sixth Amendment rights had been violated when he was deprived of effective assistance of counsel in his meetings with undercover agent Weatherford. Thus Bursey claimed that he had had a fundamentally unfair trial, although Weatherford denied that he had given any of Bursey's plans or defense strategy to the prosecution. The SC upheld Bursey's conviction and rejected his civil rights claim against Weatherford, holding that Bursey had not been deprived of his right to effective assistance of counsel or been denied a fair trial, and that the Sixth Amendment does not establish a rule *per se* forbidding an undercover agent from meeting with a defendant's counsel. In short, incriminating statements given voluntarily to an undercover officer who does nothing to elicit such statements are admissible against criminal defendants, despite the fact that these defendants are represented by counsel at the time.

Weeks v. United States, 232 U.S. 383, 34 S.Ct. 341 (1914) [**Fremont WEEKS, Plff., in Err., v. UNITED STATES**] (**Exclusionary Rule; Law Enforcement Officers or Agencies; Searches and Seizures**) Weeks was suspected of using the mails to send lottery tickets, a form of prohibited gambling. U.S. marshals entered Weeks' home without a warrant, conducted a search, and discovered lottery tickets, which were used as evidence against Weeks in his later trial. Weeks was convicted of unlawful use of the mail. He appealed, arguing that law enforcement officers should have obtained a search warrant before entering his home and seizing materials later used in his conviction. The SC agreed with Weeks and overturned his conviction. Weeks had been gainfully employed at the time and was an unlikely flight risk, and the U.S. marshals had had plenty of time to obtain a valid search warrant. They simply failed to do so. This case set a precedent, at least for *federal* law enforcement officers. It established the *exclusionary rule,* which says that evidence seized illegally is inadmissible in court. Subsequently, some states chose to abide by the exclusionary rule, whereas other states chose not to abide by it, citing various exceptions or special circumstances. These became known as *exclusionary* and *nonexclusionary* states. An unusual situation developed following *Weeks,* whereby states would obtain evidence against criminal suspects illegally and turn over this information to federal authorities for their own prosecutions of these same suspects. The reasoning behind the practice became known as the *silver-platter doctrine,* because state officers were delivering illegally obtained evidence to federal prosecutors on a "silver platter," so to say. Ultimately, in *Elkins v. United States* (1960) and *Mapp v. Ohio* (1961), the silver-platter doctrine was eliminated, and both state and federal laws were harmonized relative to protocol to be followed in searches and seizures conducted against criminal suspects.

Weems v. United States, 217 U.S. 349, 30 S.Ct. 544 (1910) [**Paul A. WEEMS, Plff. in Err., v. UNITED STATES**] (**Corrections; Probation and Parole**) Weems was a government officer stationed in the Philippine Islands convicted of falsifying a public and official document. He was sentenced to 15 years' hard labor. Weems appealed, contending that his sentence was excessive and disproportionate to the offense committed. Thus, he argued, the sentence violated his Eighth Amendment right against cruel and unusual punishment. The SC agreed with Weems and said that any sentence that is disproportionate to the offense committed violates the Eighth Amendment prohibition against cruel and unusual punishment.

Welsh v. Wisconsin, 466 U.S. 740, 104 S.Ct. 2091 (1984) [**Edward G. WELSH, Petitioner, v. WISCONSIN**] (**Searches and Seizures**) Welsh was a motorist whom a witness observed driving erratically. He swerved off a road and stopped in a field, later abandoning his vehicle and going into his home nearby. Welsh had damaged no property, and thus, from all outward appearances, he had not committed a jailable offense. The witness advised police that Welsh appeared to be either "drunk" or "very sick." Police discovered Welsh's address from the automobile registration, went to his home, and arrested him for driving while intoxicated. He was convicted. Welsh appealed, and the SC heard his case. The SC reversed Welsh's DWI conviction, noting that police were in violation of Welsh's Fourth Amendment rights by intruding into his home at night to arrest him for a nonjailable offense. The SC stressed the minor nature of the infraction leading to Welsh's arrest and said that this minor event was insufficient to establish probable cause to justify such an intrusion into his home.

West v. Atkins, 487 U.S. 42, 108 S.Ct. 2250 (1988) [**Quincy WEST, Petitioner, v. Samuel ATKINS**] (**Civil Rights, Section 1983 Claims; Corrections; Inmate Rights**) West was an inmate in a North Carolina prison. He injured his leg and was transported outside the prison to a hospital in Raleigh, where he could be treated by a private physician under contract with the prison system. The doctor placed West's leg in a cast and repeated this procedure over several months. Eventually, West was released but still evidenced some leg swelling. He filed suit against the doctor and others under a Title 42 U.S.C. Section 1983 civil rights action, alleging that he was subject to cruel and unusual punishment because of continuing leg pain. The doctor claimed that he was not a state employee and thus could not be sued under a Section 1983 action. The SC disagreed, saying that when doctors are treating prison inmates, even though they are not actually corrections employees, they are acting on behalf of the system under the authority of state law. Thus, they are conceivably liable for their actions when sued by prisoners.

Wheat v. United States, 486 U.S. 153, 108 S.Ct. 1692 (1988) [**Mark Erick WHEAT, Petitioner, v. UNITED STATES**] (**Right to Counsel; Sixth Amendment**) Wheat was suspected of conspiracy to possess and distribute 1,000 pounds of marijuana. In a U.S. district court in California, he and several other persons were indicted in a far-flung interstate conspiracy. Several defendants wished to enter guilty pleas, others wished to go to trial. Wheat was represented by counsel, but he wished to change his counsel to another lawyer who was also representing one of the coconspirators. The judge denied his request to change counsel, holding that the proposed substitution would create conflict-of-interest problems, because the codefendants might have to give adverse testimony against each other. Wheat was convicted. He appealed, alleging that the federal trial judge's refusal to allow him to change attorneys had violated his Sixth Amendment right to counsel of his choice. The SC rejected Wheat's argument, saying that it was not a violation of Wheat's Sixth Amendment rights to refuse the counsel substitution, in view of the irreconcilable and unavoidable conflicts that would have arisen had counsel been switched. In multiple-defendant actions, judges must take appropriate actions and measures, including the issuance of separate representation orders, that protect criminal defendants against counsel's conflicts of interest.

White v. Illinois, 502 U.S. 346, 112 S.Ct. 736 (1992) [**Randall D. WHITE, Petitioner, v. ILLINOIS**] (**Confrontation Clause; Jury Trials**) White was charged with molesting a 4-year-old girl, S.G. S.G. gave statements incriminating White to the police and to her mother and babysitter. S.G. was not required to testify against White, but her statements to the others were permitted under an exception to a hearsay rule. White was convicted. He appealed, contending that because he had been unable to confront his accuser, his due-process rights to a fair trial had been violated. The SC upheld White's conviction, holding that spontaneous statements made under medical circumstances at hospitals are exceptions to the hearsay rule and may be used against White in the absence of any testimony from a 4-year-old witness-accuser.

White v. Maryland, 373 U.S. 59, 83 S.Ct. 1050 (1963) [**Robert Galloway WHITE, Petitioner, v. State of MARYLAND**] (**Corrections; Probation and Parole; Right to Counsel**) White, an indigent, was suspected of murder. At his arraignment, he entered a not-guilty plea, but later at a preliminary hearing, he pleaded guilty. He was not represented by counsel at the preliminary hearing, and his guilty plea was introduced later in the trial as evidence against him. He was convicted. White appealed, contending that the preliminary hearing was a critical stage requiring appointment of counsel to represent him. Thus, the guilty plea he entered should have been inadmissible in court later. The SC agreed with White and overturned his conviction, saying that preliminary hearings are critical stages in which indigent defendants must be represented by counsel.

White v. Texas, 310 U.S. 530, 60 S.Ct. 1032 (1939) [**WHITE v. State of TEXAS**] (**Confessions**) White was accused of rape in Texas. Prior to his trial, Texas Rangers allegedly took White from the county jail into the nearby woods and beat him, attempting to get a confession from him. Subsequently, he signed a confession but recanted it during his trial. He was convicted and sentenced to death, and he appealed. The SC overturned his conviction, holding that the confession had indeed been coerced by the Texas Rangers. Coerced confessions are inadmissible in court.

Whiteley v. Warden, Wyoming State Penitentiary, 401 U.S. 560, 91 S.Ct. 1031 (1971) [**Harold WHITELEY, Petitioner, v. WARDEN, WYOMING STATE PENITENTIARY**] (**Law Enforcement Officers or Agencies; Searches Incident to an Arrest; Vehicle Searches**) In November 1964, various business establishments in Saratoga, WY, were burglarized, and two suspects were identified. Information was transmitted to law enforcement agencies around the state to be on the lookout for persons of a particular description driving a particular type of car. Officers in Casper, WY, spotted a car one evening that seemed like the one described in the radio bulletin and stopped it. They immediately arrested the suspects without a warrant and proceeded to search the vehicle without a warrant, not knowing whether the persons in the vehicle were the actual perpetrators of the burglary. They discovered some stolen rare coins, and an arrest warrant was issued after the fact of the arrest. It was eventually revealed that the basis for the complaint leading to the radio announcement was a tip by an unknown informant to a sheriff, and that fact and other supporting factual evidence were omitted from the original complaint. Thus, the justice of the peace issuing the original complaint had no basis for properly doing so. Whiteley, the suspect, moved to have such evidence removed from the record but was denied. He was convicted of breaking and entering and of being a habitual criminal. He appealed to the SC through a *habeas corpus* petition, claiming that his right against unreasonable searches and seizures had been violated and thus, his conviction should be vacated. The SC heard Whiteley's appeal and reversed his conviction, holding that the complaint upon which the arrest warrant was issued could not be supported by a finding of probable cause or of any factual data tending to corroborate an informant's tip about Whiteley. Thus Whiteley's arrest had violated his constitutional rights under the Fourth and Fourteenth Amendments, and the evidence obtained as the result of the illegal arrest had to be excluded as incriminating evidence against Whiteley.

Whitley v. Albers, 475 U.S. 312, 106 S.Ct. 1078 (1986) [Harold WHITLEY, Individually and as Assistant Superintendent, Oregon State Penitentiary, et al., Petitioners, v. Gerald ALBERS] (Civil Rights, Section 1983 Claims; Corrections; Inmate Rights) During a riot in the Oregon penitentiary, a corrections officer was taken hostage. After officials conferred about what to do in the situation, it was agreed that force should be used to effect the rescue of the officer; therefore, other correctional officers were armed and entered the riot area. They were instructed to "shoot low" in the event that they saw any prisoner who might pose a risk to them. As they entered the riot area, they saw a prisoner on a stairwell, and they fired, wounding the prisoner in the knee. The correctional officer was rescued and the riot was quelled. Afterward, the wounded prisoner filed a Title 42 U.S.C. Section 1983 civil rights action against the prison staff participating in the shooting. The SC decided in favor of the prison staff and their forceful methods, indicating that the infliction of pain in the course of prison security measures does not violate the Eighth Amendment protecting persons from cruel and unusual punishment. Thus, prison officials may use forceful means to quell prison riots, and any resultant injuries to prisoners are neither "cruel and unusual" nor unconstitutional.

Whitmore v. Arkansas, 495 U.S. 149, 110 S.Ct. 1717 (1990) [Jonas H. WHITMORE, Individually and as Next Friend of Ronald Gene Simmons, Petitioner, v. ARKANSAS et al.] (Corrections; Death Penalty) Simmons was convicted of capital murder and sentenced to death. He made statements under oath that he wanted no action taken on his behalf and no appeals of the death sentence. Nevertheless, another death-row inmate, Whitmore, interceded and appealed Simmons' death sentence. The SC rejected this appeal, as the person bringing the appeal lacked standing. This decision makes it extremely difficult for those organizations that oppose the death penalty to file appeals for prisoners sentenced to death.

Whitus v. Georgia, 385 U.S. 598, 87 S.Ct. 643 (1967) [Phil WHITUS and Leon Davis, Petitioners, v. State of GEORGIA] (Corrections; Death Penalty) Whitus and another person were convicted of murder in 1960. Several ap-

peals later, Whitus alleged that the jury composition was unconstitutionally discriminatory because a disproportionately lower number of blacks were on the jury compared with the list of candidates. The SC overturned Whitus' conviction, holding that sufficient evidence existed to show that Georgia had indeed engaged in questionable jury-selection practices. Nevertheless, the SC held that a prisoner whose conviction is reversed by the SC need not go free if he or she is in fact guilty, for Georgia may indict and try him or her again by a procedure that conforms to constitutional requirements.

Whren v. United States, 517 U.S. 806, 116 S.Ct. 1769 (1996) [Michael A. WHREN and James L. Brown, Petitioners, v. UNITED STATES] (Fourth Amendment; Searches and Seizures) In June 1993, two plainclothes vice-squad officers of the District of Columbia Police Department, Officer Soto and another, were patrolling in a high-drug area of the District in an unmarked car. Their suspicions were aroused when they passed a dark Pathfinder with temporary license tags and youthful occupants who were waiting at a stop sign for what police considered an unusually long time, more than 20 seconds. When the police traveled further, they did a U-turn and as they headed back toward the Pathfinder, it turned and sped off at an unreasonable speed. When it stopped behind other traffic at a red light, the officers pulled alongside the vehicle and one stepped out and approached. Officer Soto walked to the driver's window, identified himself as a police officer, and intended to admonish the driver about the city's traffic laws. But Officer Soto observed two large plastic bags of what appeared to be crack cocaine in the passenger's (Whren's) hands. The driver, Brown, and the passenger, Whren, were arrested and charged with four counts of various federal drug offenses. Whren sought to suppress the drugs later at a pretrial hearing, contending that their stop by officers was unreasonable, and that no probable cause, even reasonable suspicion, existed to cause officers to believe that they were involved in any illegal activity. The court admitted the drugs into evidence and Whren was convicted. He appealed, and the SC heard the case. The SC affirmed the lower and appellate courts, holding that (1) the reasonableness of traffic stops does not depend on the actual motivations of the individual officers involved; (2) temporary detentions of motorists who the police have probable cause to believe have committed traffic violations are consistent with the reasonableness of the Fourth Amendment prohibition against unreasonable seizures regardless of whether the reasonable officer would have been motivated to stop the automobile by a desire to enforce the traffic laws; and (3) balancing inherent in the Fourth Amendment inquiry does not require the court to weigh governmental and individual interests implicated in a traffic stop. Thus, temporary detentions of motorists based on probable cause that a traffic violation has occurred are reasonable, even if a reasonable officer would not have stopped the motorist absent some additional law enforcement objective.

Wiggins v. Smith, ___U.S.___, 123 S.Ct. 2527 (2003) [Kevin WIGGINS, Petitioner, v. Sewall SMITH, Warden] (*Habeas Corpus* Petitions; Ineffective Assistance of Counsel; Sixth Amendment) Wiggins was convicted of capital murder in Maryland in 1989. His public defenders remarked outside of earshot of the jury during Wiggins' trial that they would introduce mitigating evidence of Wiggins' difficult life and upbringing, although this evidence was never introduced. In a bifurcated trial, Wiggins was found guilty of murder and sentenced to death. Wiggins' counsels failed to introduce this mitigating evidence during the sentencing phase of the trial as well. A Maryland appeals court affirmed the verdict and sentence. Wiggins appealed through a *habeas corpus* petition in federal district court, contending that the failure of his attorneys to explore mitigating factors related to his background and childhood prejudiced his case and was ineffective assistance of counsel. A U.S. district court judge granted his *habeas corpus* motion, but the circuit court of appeals reversed. Wiggins therefore sought relief with the SC, who heard his case. The SC reversed the court of appeals, holding that the failure of Wiggins' attorneys to explore Wiggins' childhood and present this information to the jury, specifically the physical abuse he had suffered at the hands of his mother and various foster parents, was sufficient to show ineffective assistance of counsel and violated his Sixth Amendment rights. Furthermore, Wiggins' counsels' failure to present such evidence about his personal background prejudiced the jury concerning mitigation issues, and thus he was denied a fair hearing on these issues during the sentencing phase of his trial.

Wilkerson v. Utah, 99 U.S. 130 (1878) (**Death Penalty; Firing Squads**) The SC decided that public execution by firing squads is not cruel and unusual punishment under the Eighth Amendment.

Wilkins v. Missouri, 492 U.S. 361, 109 S.Ct. 2969 (1989) [**Heath A. WILKINS, Petitioner, v. MISSOURI; Kevin N. Stanford, Petitioner, v. Kentucky**] (**Death Penalty; Juvenile Law**) Wilkins was 16 when he stabbed to death a woman who was managing a convenience store. There was evidence of aggravating circumstances and torture of the woman. Wilkins was transferred to criminal court and prosecuted as an adult. He was convicted of the murder and sentenced to death. He appealed, arguing that 16 is too young an age for execution, which is therefore cruel and unusual punishment. This landmark case set a minimum age at which juveniles can be executed. The SC ruled that if juveniles are 16 or older at the time they commit a capital crime, they can suffer execution in those jurisdictions with death penalties. The year before, in *Thompson v. Oklahoma,* the SC had said that persons who were 15 at the time they committed murder could not be executed. The *Wilkins* case effectively drew this line at age 16. (*See Stanford v. Kentucky* [1989] *for a similar ruling.*)

Will v. Michigan Department of State Police, 491 U.S. 58, 109 S.Ct. 2304 (1989) [**Ray WILL, Petitioner, v. MICHIGAN DEPARTMENT OF STATE POLICE et al.**] (**Civil Rights, Section 1983 Claims; Immunity**) Wills, a Michigan police officer, was denied a promotion. He sued the State of Michigan under Title 42 U.S.C., Section 1983, alleging that authorities were holding against him the record of his brother, who had a prior history as a student activist. The SC declared that state law enforcement officials, acting in their official capacity, have absolute immunity. However, they may be sued in

their personal capacity. The SC also distinguished between state officials and municipal officials, such as local police, who do not enjoy the same type and degree of immunity enjoyed by state officials.

Williams v. Florida, 399 U.S. 78, 90 S.Ct. 1893 (1970) [**Johnny WILLIAMS, Petitioner, v. State of FLORIDA**] (**Juries**) Williams was arrested and charged with robbery. At his subsequent trial, a six-member jury found him guilty. Williams appealed, alleging among other things that he should have had a jury of 12 members rather than six. Florida law proclaimed that 12-member juries would be convened in capital cases, but that juries with only six members would hear all other types of cases. The SC heard Williams' appeal and affirmed the Florida provision, saying that the "jury . . . composed of 12 is a historical accident, unnecessary to effect the purposes of the jury system and wholly without significance except to mystics."

Williams v. Illinois, 399 U.S. 235, 90 S.Ct. 2018 (1970) [**Willie E. WILLIAMS, Appellant, v. State of ILLINOIS**] (**Corrections; Inmate Rights; Probation and Parole**) Williams was convicted of petty theft and sentenced to one year in jail, a $500 fine, and $5 court costs. State law provided that at the end of one year of imprisonment, if offenders could not pay their fines and court costs, they must "work off" these payments at the rate of $5 per day. Thus Williams would be required to be incarcerated an additional 101 days before he could pay the fine and court costs. He appealed. The SC ruled that this additional time served behind bars to "work off" such fines is unconstitutional, because it violates the equal-protection clause of the Fourteenth Amendment.

Williams v. Taylor, 529 U.S. 420, 120 S.Ct. 1479 (2000) [**Michael Wayne WILLIAMS, Petitioner, v. John TAYLOR, Warden**] (**Death Penalty; Discovery;** *Habeas Corpus* **Petitions; Juries; Prosecutorial Misconduct**) Williams was convicted of two capital murders in Virginia and sentenced to death. During his trial, Williams sought to discover the results of a psychiatric examination of Jeffrey Cruse, his accomplice and the main witness against him. The court refused to permit him access to these psychiatric records, and he was convicted. The Virginia Supreme Court subsequently dismissed Williams' *habeas corpus* petition requesting an evidentiary hearing on three claims: (1) that Williams and his counsel were denied access to a psychiatric evaluation of Cruse; (2) that a juror was possibly biased; and (3) that the prosecutor knew about the biased juror and the nature of the bias and permitted the juror to be seated anyway. The Virginia Supreme Court dismissed Williams' *habeas corpus* claims. Williams appealed to the SC, where the case was heard. The SC upheld the lower court denial of access to Cruse's psychiatric reports, because Williams had failed to develop a factual basis for the claim that the prosecutor's nondisclosure of the report violated the *Brady* discovery rule. However, the SC overruled the lower courts and held that Williams had been wrongfully denied an evidentiary hearing on the biased juror and the prosecutor's misconduct resulting from a knowledge of the biased juror. The juror issue was that the seating of one juror, Ms. Stinnett, was unfair because during *voir dire,* Stinnett denied knowing Deputy Sheriff

Meinhard, who had investigated the crime, interrogated Cruse, and later became the prosecution's first witness. Stinnett had a previous 17-year marriage to Sheriff Meinhard and four children with him. Further, Stinnett denied knowing the prosecutor, Woodson, when in fact Stinnett had retained Woodson as her attorney to represent her in her divorce from Meinhard. Later, Woodson admitted that he knew Stinnett and Meinhard had been married and divorced, but stated that he did not consider divorced people to be related and that he had no recollection of having been hired by Stinnett as her private attorney in the divorce action. Stinnett's reticence to admit that she knew either Meinhard or Woodson, and Woodson's failure to divulge this same information, disclose the need for an evidentiary hearing, according to the SC.

Wilson v. Layne, 526 U.S. 603, 119 S.Ct. 1692 (1999) [Charles H. WILSON, et ux., et al., Petitioners, v. Harry LAYNE, Deputy United States Marshal, etc., et al.] (Fourth Amendment; Immunity; Media Rights) U.S. marshals and local sheriff's deputies executed a search warrant for a fugitive, Dominic Wilson, son of Charles and Geraldine Wilson, as a part of "Operation Gunsmoke," a program targeting armed individuals wanted on federal and/or state and local warrants for serious drug and other violent felonies. Several television and newspaper reporters and photographers were invited to accompany the federal marshals when they entered the Wilson home and videotape the search. Following an early morning intrusion into the Wilson home in Rockville, MD, and a protective sweep, Dominic Wilson was not there. However, in the process, Charles and Geraldine Wilson were rousted from bed by police and subdued temporarily at gunpoint as the search for their son progressed. The Wilsons sued the U.S. marshals, deputies, and news media, contending that their Fourth Amendment rights had been violated because the media were involved in the search and were not authorized by the search warrant to be involved. The SC heard the case and held that the Wilsons' Fourth Amendment rights had been violated, but because the laws governing media ride-alongs were not "clearly established," the officers involved in the search were entitled to qualified immunity.

Wilson v. Seiter, 501 U.S. 294, 111 S.Ct. 2321 (1991) [Pearly L. WILSON, Petitioner, v. Richard SEITER et al.] (Civil Rights, Section 1983 Claims; Corrections; Inmate Rights) Wilson was a felon incarcerated in the Hocking, OH, Correctional Facility. Filing a Title 42 U.S.C. Section 1983 civil rights claim against prison officials, he alleged that the conditions of his confinement violated his constitutional rights under the Eighth and Fourteenth Amendments. These conditions were improper ventilation, inadequate heating and cooling, excessive noise, unclean and inadequate restrooms, unsanitary dining facilities and food preparation, and housing with mentally and physically abusive inmates. The suit was rejected by the SC, which declared that prison officials must exhibit deliberate indifference to prisoner needs and living conditions before inmates will successfully prevail in their suits. Further, a culpable state of mind must be demonstrated on the part of prison officials. These difficult criteria mean that suits by prisoners alleging poor prison conditions will be difficult to sustain.

Winston v. Lee, 470 U.S. 753, 105 S.Ct. 1611 (1985) [Andrew J. WINSTON, Sheriff, and Aubrey M. Davis, Jr., Petitioners, v. Rudolph LEE, Jr.] (Searches and Seizures) Lee claimed to have been shot in the left side of his chest and robbed by someone fleeing down the street. Police officers were simultaneously investigating a robbery and shooting in which a store owner had been shot but had wounded the assailant in return. The store owner advised police that he thought he had shot his assailant in the chest. While both men were being treated at the same hospital in town, the store owner recognized Lee as the robber. The officers obtained a court order for doctors to remove a bullet from Lee's chest, but the doctors advised police that the surgery might be dangerous. Lee sought to bar doctors from removing the bullet because the act would be an unwarranted bodily intrusion. The SC agreed with Lee, saying that such surgery was unwarranted, as it would violate his Fourth Amendment right. The SC said that states cannot compel surgical intrusions into one's body, even if that intrusion would produce evidence of a crime.

Wisconsin v. Mitchell, 508 U.S. 476, 113 S.Ct. 2194 (1993) [WISCONSIN, Petitioner, v. Todd MITCHELL] (First Amendment; Free Speech; Sentencing) Mitchell was convicted of aggravated battery and theft, and his sentence was enhanced under a Wisconsin statute because he targeted his victim by reason of the victim's race. Mitchell appealed, arguing that he should not be punished more because he had selected a person of a particular race to attack. Thus, Mitchell declared, the Wisconsin statute was unconstitutional because it violated his free-speech rights. The SC heard Mitchell's case and upheld the constitutionality of the Wisconsin statute, whereby offenders may have their sentences enhanced if it is proved that they attacked their victim because of the victim's race.

Witherspoon v. Illinois, 391 U.S. 510, 88 S.Ct. 1770 (1968) [William C. WITHERSPOON, Petitioner, v. State of ILLINOIS et al.] (Corrections; Death Penalty; Death-Qualified Juries) Witherspoon was charged and convicted of capital murder in Arkansas. During the *voir dire,* the judge asked prospective jurors their views on the death penalty and whether they could vote for it if it were the prescribed punishment. Witherspoon appealed, saying that persons who said that they could not vote for the death penalty had been excluded as jurors, and thus prosecutors had deprived Witherspoon of a fair trial by generating a death-qualified jury. The SC reversed Witherspoon's conviction, saying that a sentence of death cannot be carried out if the jury that imposed or recommended it was chosen by excluding veniremen for cause simply because they voiced general objections to the death penalty or expressed conscientious or religious scruples against its infliction. Prospective jurors may not be excluded from death-penalty cases despite their beliefs about the death penalty, provided that they can make a fair and impartial decision to apply it if it is justified by evidence of guilt beyond a reasonable doubt. Prospective jurors who were thus excluded because of their expressed opposition to the death penalty, despite whether they could render a fair judgment and subsequently impose it if justified, became known as Witherspoon-excludables.

Withrow v. Williams, 507 U.S. 680, 113 S.Ct. 1745 (1993) [Pamela WITHROW, Petitioner, v. Robert Allen WILLIAMS, Jr.] (Corrections; *Miranda* Warning; Self-Incrimination) Williams, an inmate in a Michigan prison, was suspected of a double murder. During the investigation, he was interrogated by police, who did not immediately tell him his *Miranda* rights. He made several pre-*Miranda* warning statements that were inculpatory and several more after the warning by police. Williams admitted to providing a weapon to the man who actually did the killing. A bench trial resulted in Williams' conviction, and he was given two concurrent life sentences for the two felony-murder convictions. Williams appealed, alleging that his *Miranda* rights had been violated by police. Williams alleged that police had told him throughout all pre- and post-*Miranda* questioning that if he confessed, he would be given lenient treatment, and that that inducement was sufficient to overcome his will against giving incriminating information to them. Williams claimed that his admissions had been involuntarily made throughout the entire interrogation, and thus, the admissions should have been suppressed. The SC heard his case and ruled that Williams' statements to police were involuntary and thus excludable as evidence against him, in view of the violation of the *Miranda* warning.

Witte v. United States, 515 U.S. 389, 115 S.Ct. 2199 (1995) [Steven Kurt WITTE, Petitioner, v. UNITED STATES] (Double Jeopardy) Witte was a drug trafficker convicted on federal marijuana charges. Simultaneously, Witte, together with several other coconspirators, was also named as trafficking in cocaine, although no charges had been brought against him before his conviction for the marijuana offense. When the presentence investigation report of Witte had been completed by the federal probation officer, the uncharged criminal conduct of cocaine distribution was added to Witte's base offense to yield a score higher than that yielded by using only the marijuana charge. Consequently, Witte was sentenced to a longer term. Subsequently, he was indicted for conspiring to distribute cocaine, and he moved to quash this indictment on the grounds of double jeopardy. The federal district court dismissed the indictment following a motion by Witte's attorney. The government appealed, and the circuit court of appeals reinstated the indictment. Witte appealed. The SC heard Witte's case and upheld the circuit court of appeals' decision to reinstate the indictment. The SC argued that because consideration of relevant conduct in determining a defendant's sentence within the legislatively authorized punishment range does not constitute punishment for that conduct within the meaning of the double-jeopardy clause, Witte's prosecution on cocaine charges did not violate the prohibition against multiple punishments. In other words, current indictable conduct (conspiracy to distribute cocaine) may serve to enhance present sentences in federal criminal convictions, and subsequent charges may be brought against these same persons citing the same indictable conduct.

Wolf v. Colorado, 338 U.S. 25, 69 S.Ct. 1359 (1949) [Julius A. WOLF, Petitioner, v. People of the State of COLORADO] (Exclusionary Rule; Law Enforcement Officers or Agencies; Searches and Seizures) Wolf was a physician in Colorado, a nonexclusionary state (*see Weeks v. United States* [1914]). He was suspected of performing illegal abortions. State officers entered his office illegally and seized numerous papers and documents implicating him in such activity. Despite the fact that this evidence was obtained in an unreasonable manner, with several procedural errors and warrant defects, he was convicted. Because the governing case at the time was *Weeks,* forbidding the admissibility of evidence seized by federal law enforcement officers without a valid search warrant, Wolf sought to apply the same standard to the officers who seized his property and papers from his Colorado office. He sought to declare the evidence inadmissible by citing the Fourteenth Amendment equal-protection clause, suggesting that the states should follow the federal precedent set in *Weeks.* The SC decided to uphold Wolf's conviction and avoid obligating states to adhere to an exclusionary rule applicable only to federal officers and those states that chose to adopt it.

Wolff v. McDonnell, 418 U.S. 539, 94 S.Ct. 2963 (1974) [Charles WOLFF, Jr., etc., et al., Petitioners, v. Robert O. McDONNELL, etc.] (Corrections; Inmate Rights) Basic elements of a procedural due process must be present when decisions are made concerning the discipline of a prison inmate. In this Nebraska case, the SC ruled that in procedures resulting in loss of good time or in solitary confinement, due process requires the following: advance written notice of the violation, a written statement of fact findings, the prisoner's right to call witnesses and present evidence where it will not be hazardous to the operation of the institution, mail from attorneys to be opened and inspected in the presence of inmates, and prison records to be expunged if not in accord with required procedures. This case also dealt with the question of whether letters determined to be from attorneys may be opened by prison authorities in the presence of the inmate or whether such mail must be delivered unopened if normal detection techniques fail to indicate contraband. The SC did not add a great deal of clarity to this issue in their decision. It indicated that attorneys must clearly identify themselves by placing their names and addresses in plain view on envelopes and that the letters should show that they came from lawyers. In any event, prison authorities may inspect and read any document leaving and entering the institution in an effort to determine whether inmates are abusing their rights by communicating about "restricted matters."

Wong Sun v. United States, 371 U.S. 471, 83 S.Ct. 407 (1961) [WONG SUN and James Wah Toy, Petitioners, v. UNITED STATES] (Exclusionary Rule; Law Enforcement Officers or Agencies) Wong Sun was a suspected drug dealer. Federal narcotics agents learned from various informants the identity of a drug dealer named Sea Dog, who was Wong Sun. The agents went to where Wong Sun lived, arrested him, and searched his premises, discovering no narcotics. He was released. Several days later Wong Sun and another suspect, an associate, gave statements to federal officers but did not sign these statements. Subsequently, Wong Sun returned to the federal offices and admitted to the accuracy of his statement given a few days earlier. He and the associate were subsequently convicted of transportation and concealment of heroin. Wong Sun appealed, alleging that his statements were inadmissible as evidence against him, because several illegal acts had been perpetrated by federal officers earlier against him and his associate. The SC agreed to the extent that, indeed, illegal acts by federal officers had nullified certain evidence against Wong Sun and his associate. However, when Wong Sun revisited the federal offices and admitted to the accuracy of his previous statements, this admission removed the taint overshadowing the illegally obtained evidence. The significance of this complex case is that it articulated the fruits-of-the-poisonous-tree doctrine, which says that if the tree (a police search, for instance) is poisoned (by an illegal search), the fruit from the tree (the evidence obtained from the illegal search) is also poisoned (made inadmissible). Thus, Wong Sun's original statements were inadmissible because they were fruits of the poisonous tree; however, his later admission about the accuracy of his previous statements had removed the "taint" from the poisonous tree and rendered his statements admissible against him.

Wood v. Bartholomew, 516 U.S. 1, 116 S.Ct. 7 (1995) [Tana WOOD, Superintendent, Washington State Penitentiary, v. Dwayne Earl BARTHOLOMEW] (Death Penalty; Jury Trials) Dwayne Bartholomew was charged with murdering a laundromat attendant during a robbery in August 1981. Bartholomew's brother, Randy, and his girlfriend, Dormady, testified against him during his trial. Randy testified that while sitting with Dwayne in a car outside the laundromat, Dwayne told him that he intended to rob it and "leave no witnesses." Subsequently, Bartholomew perpetrated the robbery, firing two shots into the head of the laundromat operator. Dormady testified that Bartholomew told her that he had "put two bullets in the kid's head." Bartholomew testified in his own behalf; he declared that the murder was *not* premeditated, as his pistol had accidentally discharged twice (the pistol was a single-action revolver and could only be fired by pulling back the hammer for each shot). Dormady and Randy Bartholomew both took lie detector tests, with Dormady's having questionable results. Although her testimony in court was incriminating against Bartholomew, her lie detector results were not admitted into evidence. Bartholomew was convicted. He appealed because the prosecutor had failed to produce these polygraph results. The SC rejected Bartholomew's appeal, holding that evidence is "material" to the extent that its admission at trial would have a reasonable probability of affecting the trial outcome. In this case, the SC said it would not have affected the outcome because of other evidence. To acquit Bartholomew of aggravated murder, the jury would have had to believe that Bartholomew's single-action revolver discharged accidentally, not once but twice, by tragic coincidence depositing a bullet to the back of the victim's head, execution style, as the victim lay face down on the floor.

Woodford v. Garceau, ___U.S.___, 123 S.Ct. 1398 (2003) [Jeanne WOODFORD, Warden, Petitioner, v. Robert Frederick GARCEAU] (Antiterrorism and Effective Death Pen-

alty Act of 1996; Death Penalty; *Habeas Corpus* Petitions) Robert Garceau was convicted in California for the murders of Maureen Bautista and her 14-year-old son and sentenced to death. Garceau filed several petitions asserting various claims, and his petitions were denied. On May 12, 1995, Garceau filed a motion for the appointment of a federal *habeas* counsel and a stay of execution in a U.S. district court. On June 26, 1995, counsel was appointed and a stay of execution was granted. Subsequently, Garceau filed a *habeas corpus* petition on July 2, 1996. In the meantime, the Antiterrorism and Effective Death Penalty Act (AEDPA) was passed on April 24, 1996, prior to Garceau's *habeas* filing. The purpose of the act was to reduce delays in execution of state and federal criminal sentences, particularly in capital cases, and to further principles of comity, finality, and federalism. A U.S. district court denied Garceau's new motion on the basis that Garceau had a pending appeal prior to passage of the AEDPA, and that *habeas* petitions pending prior to the passage of the AEDPA were not affected by it. However, the Ninth Circuit Court reversed for reasons unrelated to the AEDPA. The SC heard the case and overturned the Ninth Circuit decision, holding that Garceau's *habeas* filing was not "pending" at the time of the AEDPA's passage, and thus his *habeas* motion was affected by the AEDPA. The significance of this case is the timeliness of appeals, especially of inmates convicted of capital crimes, and whether the AEDPA affects such appeals. Any petition filed by a condemned offender following the AEDPA's passage is affected by the act.

Woodford v. Visciotti, ___U.S.___, 123 S.Ct. 357 (2002) [Jeanne WOODFORD, Warden, Petitioner, v. John Louis VISCIOTTI] (*Habeas Corpus* Petitions; Sixth Amendment) John Visciotti and a coworker, Brian Hefner, attempted to rob fellow employees Timothy Dykstra and Michael Wolbert in California on November 8, 1982. During the robbery, Visciotti pulled a gun and shot Dykstra, killing him instantly with a shot to the chest. Visciotti then shot Wolbert three times, thinking he had killed him. Wolbert survived his wounds and identified his attackers, who were convicted of first-degree murder, attempted murder, and armed robbery, with a special-circumstance finding that the murder was committed during a robbery. The jury determined that Visciotti should be sentenced to death. The California Supreme Court affirmed the conviction and sentence. However, Visciotti filed a writ of *habeas corpus*, alleging ineffective assistance of counsel, especially during the penalty phase of the trial. The defense counsel was accused of failing to note Visciotti's brain damage, his dysfunctional family, and resulting psychological abuse as mitigating circumstances. Further, the defense counsel made numerous concessions during his summation to the jury in final argument, failing to mention that Visciotti had a troubled family background, was berated constantly by others, was born with club feet, had feelings of inadequacy, incompetency, and inferiority, possibly suffered from seizures while growing up, and had moved more than 20 times to different locations during his childhood. The Ninth Circuit Court of Appeals granted Visciotti's petition as to the sentence of death but denied it as to the conviction, and California appealed to the SC, who heard the case. The SC reversed the Ninth Circuit, holding that trial counsel's assumed inadequate representation did not prejudice Visciotti sufficiently to set aside his death sentence. The SC further noted that the circumstances of the crime, its cold-blooded nature, killing one victim and the attempted execution-style killing of another, both during the course of a preplanned armed robbery, together with the aggravating evidence of other prior offenses (the knifing of one man and the stabbing of a pregnant woman as she lay in bed trying to protect her unborn baby) were devastating. Thus, the aggravating circumstances were so severe that Visciotti suffered no prejudice from the trial counsel's assumed inadequacy.

Woodson v. North Carolina, 428 U.S. 280, 96 S.Ct. 2978 (1980) [**James Tyrone WOODSON and Luby Waxton, Petitioners, v. State of NORTH CAROLINA**] (**Aggravating and Mitigating Circumstances; Corrections; Death Penalty; Mandatory Death Penalty**) Woodson and others were convicted of first-degree murder. Woodson was a lookout and did not participate in the actual murder. However, the death penalty for such an offense was mandatory in North Carolina. He appealed to the SC, which overturned his death penalty sentence, declaring that mandatory death-penalty statutes are unconstitutional. The major reason they are unconstitutional is that aggravating and mitigating circumstances cannot be considered.

Wyoming v. Houghton, 526 U.S. 295, 119 S.Ct. 1297 (1999) [**WYOMING, Petitioner, v. Sandra HOUGHTON**] (**Closed-Container Searches; Fourth Amendment; Searches and Seizures**) A routine traffic stop by a Wyoming Highway Patrol officer resulted in the officer's observation of a hypodermic syringe in the driver's shirt pocket. The driver admitted to taking drugs. The officer proceeded to search the car and its contents, including the purse of a passenger, Sandra Houghton. Drug paraphernalia and a quantity of methamphetamine were found, and Houghton was arrested on drug charges. She was subsequently convicted and appealed, contending that her Fourth Amendment right against unreasonable search and seizure had been violated. The Wyoming Supreme Court reversed Houghton's drug conviction, holding that an officer may search a car and any container that may conceal the objects of the search; but if the officer knows or should know that a container belongs to a passenger who is not suspected of criminal activity, then that container is outside the scope of the search. Wyoming prosecutors appealed to the SC, who reversed the Wyoming Supreme Court and reinstated Houghton's conviction. The SC held that police officers with probable cause to search a car may inspect any passenger's belongings found in the car that are capable of concealing the object of the search.

Wyrick v. Fields, 459 U.S. 42, 103 S.Ct. 394 (1982) [**Donald W. WYRICK, Warden, v. Edward FIELDS**] (**Law Enforcement Officers or Agencies;** *Miranda* **Warning; Right to Counsel**) Fields was a soldier stationed at Fort Leonard Wood, MO. He was charged with raping an 81-year-old woman. Following his arrest in September 1974, Fields requested a polygraph examination. This request was granted,

and Fields signed a written consent document containing his *Miranda* rights. Further, an officer read those rights aloud to Fields and asked him if he wished to have his attorney present. Fields said no. Following the polygraph test, the examiner indicated to Fields that there had been some deceit. At that time, Fields admitted to having intercourse with the woman but claimed it was consensual. He also made similar admissions to Missouri police, who also had told him his *Miranda* rights before questioning. Fields was convicted. He filed a *habeas corpus* petition, alleging that his confessions had been "coerced." The SC rejected Fields' claim and upheld his conviction, noting that Fields had been repeatedly and amply advised of his rights and had voluntarily, knowingly, and intelligently had waived those rights. Thus there was no rights violation as a reason for overturning his conviction.

Y

Yarborough v. Alvarado, ___U.S.___, 124 S.Ct. 2140 (2004) [**Michael YARBOROUGH, Warden, Petitioner, v. Michael ALVARADO**] (**Custodial Interrogations;** *Miranda* **Warning**) Alvarado was a Los Angeles 17-year-old who helped another man steal a truck, which eventually led to the death of the truck's owner. Initially Alvarado was called in for an interview by Los Angeles detectives, accompanied by his parents. He was not Mirandized during a two-hour interview, but he was frequently asked if he needed a break. During the interview, however, Alvarado admitted to assisting another man, Soto, try to steal the victim's truck and to hide a gun following the truck owner's murder. Alvarado was allowed to leave with his parents following the interview. Subsequently Alvarado was apprehended and charged with murder and robbery. His earlier interview statements were used against him in court and he was convicted of second-degree murder and robbery. During the trial. Alvarado's attorney had tried unsuccessfully to suppress Alvarado's earlier statements, contending that Alvarado was "in custody" and subject to being Mirandized before the interview was conducted. However his motion to suppress was denied. Alvarado launched an appeal and the California Supreme Court affirmed his conviction. Later Alvarado appealed to the U.S. district court where his petition was denied. However, the 9th Circuit Court of Appeals reversed his conviction, holding that the state appellate court unreasonably applied the standard governing his status of custody at the time he was interrogated. The state appealed and the SC heard the case. The SC reversed and reinstated Alvarado's conviction, holding that Alvarado was not in police custody at the time of his interrogation, and therefore a *Miranda* warning was unwarranted. The facts that Alvarado was not required to appear at the police station at a particular time, that police were not coercive or threatening and twice asked Alvarado if he needed a break, and that he went home following the interview would allow reasonable persons to conclude that Alvarado was not in police custody during this period of interrogation.

Yarborough v. Gentry, ___U.S.___, 124 S.Ct. 1 (2003) [Michael YARBOROUGH, Warden, et al. v. Lionel E. GENTRY] (*Habeas Corpus* Petitions; Ineffective Assistance of Counsel; Sixth Amendment) Lionel Gentry was convicted in a California court of assault with a deadly weapon for stabbing his girlfriend. At his subsequent trial, Gentry claimed that the stabbing was accidental. His victim, Tanaysha Handy, was a pregnant, drug-addicted mother of three who had been using drugs in the evening of the stabbing. Witnesses testified that they saw parts of the incident, but that their vision was obscured because of darkness or the amount of lighting in the area. Gentry's defense counsel's summation stressed conflicting testimony and accounts of what had been observed. Further, defense counsel declared that no one had seen what had happened clearly, and that the jury would have to decide whether Gentry's testimony was truthful. Gentry was convicted and filed a *habeas corpus* petition, alleging ineffective assistance of counsel on grounds that his counsel had failed to mention various exculpatory facts. A California appeals court rejected Gentry's claim, but the Ninth Circuit Court of Appeals reversed, faulting the defense counsel for not arguing explicitly that the government had failed to prove Gentry's guilt beyond a reasonable doubt. The SC heard the case and reversed the Ninth Circuit, holding that the California appellate court's judgment that the defense counsel's performance was neither deficient nor unreasonable was proper. The SC also said that although defense counsel did not insist that the existence of reasonable doubt would require the jury to acquit Gentry, defense counsel could reasonably rely on judicial instructions to the jury to that effect.

Ybarra v. Illinois, 444 U.S. 85, 100 S.Ct. 338 (1979) [Ventura E. YBARRA, Appellant, v. State of ILLINOIS] (Law Enforcement Officers or Agencies; Searches Incident to Arrest) A reliable informant advised police officers that a bartender in a certain bar was selling heroin in small tinfoil packets to customers. Further, the informant said that the bartender had told him that heroin would be available for purchase on a given date. With this information, police obtained a search warrant authorizing a "search of the tavern for evidence of the offense of possession of a controlled substance." They entered the bar and advised all present, including customers, that they would be searched. A pat-down of Ybarra, a customer, disclosed a cigarette package, which the searching officer said contained "objects." He retrieved the cigarette package and found heroin in six tinfoil packets. Ybarra was convicted. He appealed, contending that the search had been unreasonable and violative of the Fourth Amendment and the equal-protection clause of the Fourteenth Amendment. The SC agreed with Ybarra and overturned his conviction, noting that police officers had had no reason to suspect him individually as a person in possession of controlled substances. Their warrant was confined to a tavern search, not specific persons in the tavern who were unknown to the police and their informant.

Young v. Harper, 520 U.S. 143, 117 S.Ct. 1148 (1997) [Leroy L. YOUNG, et al., Petitioners, v. Ernest Eugene HARPER] (*Habeas Corpus* Petitions; Probation and Parole) Harper was an Oklahoma prisoner serving a life sentence for two murders. After serving five years, Harper was conditionally released into Oklahoma's Preparole Conditional Supervision Program, in which an inmate may be placed on preparole after serving 15 percent of his or her sentence. After five months outside of prison, Harper's preparole was summarily denied by the Oklahoma governor, and Harper was ordered back to prison. Harper filed a petition for *habeas corpus* relief, stating that his summary return to prison had deprived him of liberty without due process. The Oklahoma Court of Criminal Appeals upheld the governor's decision, and Harper's appeal to a federal district court for *habeas corpus* relief resulted in the same decision. The rationale used was that preparole was not like parole, and thus, inmates on preparole were not entitled to the same liberty constitutional protections as other parolees as set forth in *Morrissey v. Brewer* (1972). However, the Tenth Circuit Court of Appeals reversed and held that preparole was sufficiently like parole and that Harper had indeed been deprived of his due-process rights as set forth under the Fourteenth Amendment. Oklahoma appealed, and the SC heard the case. The SC affirmed the circuit court's decision, ruling that preparole, as it existed when Harper was released, was equivalent to parole within the meaning of *Morrissey v. Brewer.*

Youngberg v. Romeo, 457 U.S. 307, 102 S.Ct. 2452 (1982) [Duane YOUNGBERG, etc., et al., Petitioners, v. Nicholas ROMEO, an Incompetent, by His Mother and Next Friend, Paula Romeo] (Corrections; Inmate Rights) Romeo was a mentally retarded man with a history of violence. He was involuntarily committed to a state mental hospital, where he sustained numerous physical injuries at the hands of others. His mother filed a suit on his behalf, alleging that her son was entitled to safe conditions of confinement, freedom from bodily restraints, and training or rehabilitation. The SC heard the case and declared that Romeo was entitled to conditions of reasonable care and safety, reasonably nonrestrictive confinement conditions, and such training as might be required by these interests. The judge had given an improper jury instruction in Romeo's commitment proceeding when he advised the jury to consider the standard of cruel and unusual punishment as set forth in the Eighth Amendment.

Younger v. Gilmore, 404 U.S. 15, 92 S.Ct. 250 (1971) [Evelle J. YOUNGER et al., Appellants, v. Robert O. GILMORE, Jr., et al.] (Corrections; Inmate Rights) Gilmore and other inmates filed suit against the California Department of Corrections, alleging that the law library in the prison contained rules that were unconstitutionally restrictive and limited Gilmore's access to the courts. Almost every book was a single issue, and many pages were either lost or stolen. The rules governing inmate access to books were also greatly restrictive. The SC declared that in this particular case, California had indeed violated prisoner rights of access to the courts by the greatly restrictive library rules and also their right to equal protection under the Fourteenth Amendment. The

SC required the California system (and any other similar system within the United States) to beef up the law library selections and develop law library guidelines that would not violate prisoner rights and deny them access to courts or effective legal assistance.

Z

Zafiro v. United States, 506 U.S. 534, 113 S.Ct. 933 (1993) [Gloria ZAFIRO, Jose Martinez, Salvador Garcia, and Alfonso Soto, Petitioners, v. UNITED STATES] (Jury Trials) Various defendants, including Zafiro, opposed being tried together in federal court on various drug charges, alleging that such a joinder would violate Rule 14 of the Federal Rules of Criminal Procedure, and that the defenses to be offered by these defendants would be mutually antagonistic. The SC rejected their appeal, saying that joinders do not make mutually exclusive defenses unconstitutional *per se,* and that defendants are required to show where prejudice might occur. There was no prejudice in this particular case.

Zant v. Stephens, 462 U.S. 862, 103 S.Ct. 2733 (1983) [Walter ZANT, Warden, Petitioner, v. Alpha Otis O'Daniel STEPHENS] (Aggravating and Mitigating Circumstances; Corrections; Cruel and Unusual Punishment; Death Penalty; Eighth Amendment) Stephens was convicted of murder. The jury considered three aggravating circumstances and sentenced him to death. Stephens appealed, arguing that the third aggravating circumstance was so vague that it should have nullified the imposition of the death penalty. The SC said that the third aggravating circumstance was immaterial and irrelevant, as there were two other clear aggravating circumstances that sufficed to warrant imposition of the death penalty.

Zap v. United States, 328 U.S. 624, 66 S.Ct. 1277 (1946) [Edward F. ZAP, Petitioner, v. UNITED STATES] (Consent Searches; Law Enforcement Officers or Agencies) Zap was a government contractor who did experimental work on government airplane wings. He was convicted of making false claims against the United States on the basis of information obtained in a search of his offices by FBI agents. This inspec-

tion was done as a part of the Department of Navy agreement authorizing such records inspections. Zap appealed, alleging that the search of his offices had violated his Fourth Amendment rights, and that evidence obtained against him resulting from this search should have been suppressed. The SC upheld Zap's conviction, holding that inspections of one's offices pursuant to government contractual agreements do not violate the Fourth Amendment search-and-seizure provision.

Zicarelli v. New Jersey State Commission of Investigation, 406 U.S. 472, 92 S.Ct. 1670 (1972) [Joseph Arthur ZICARELLI, Appellant, v. The NEW JERSEY STATE COMMISSION OF INVESTIGATION] (Immunity; Self-Incrimination) Zicarelli was subpoenaed to testify in a case involving organized crime. New Jersey prosecutors offered him immunity from prosecution in exchange for his testimony. Despite this immunity, Zicarelli refused to answer some of the questions. He was cited for contempt and jailed, and he appealed. The SC heard his case and affirmed the contempt citation, concluding that there is no legal reason justifying nonresponse if immunity has been granted.

Zurcher v. Stanford Daily, 436 U.S. 547, 98 S.Ct. 1970 (1978) [James ZURCHER, etc., et al., Petitioners, v. The STANFORD DAILY et al. Louis P. Bergna, District Attorney, and Craig Brown, Petitioners, v. The Stanford Daily et al.] (Law Enforcement Officers or Agencies; Searches and Seizures) In the aftermath of a college campus disturbance, police searched for those who were demonstrating and who had attacked and injured several police officers. Photographs of the incident had been taken by the student newspaper staff on the scene, and some of them were subsequently published in the *Stanford Daily.* The district attorney's office obtained a search warrant for the newspaper's premises to locate photos and other materials that might help to identify those who had injured the police officers. Over the objections of newspaper staffers, police searched the offices and seized various photographs of the incident. The student newspaper filed suit, alleging that the search warrant was unconstitutional and that their photographs had been unlawfully seized. The SC disagreed, concluding that it is constitutional under the Fourth Amendment to issue search warrants for premises of nonsuspects if it is believed on the basis of probable cause that fruits, instrumentalities, or evidence of a crime might be found there. ✦

Summary of Case Index Topics

Case Index by Topic

Freedom of Religion

Free Press

Free Speech

Fresh Pursuit

Frivolous Lawsuits

Gas Chamber

Good-Faith Exception

Grand Juries

Gun Control Bill

References

Abadinsky, Howard. 2004. *Drugs: An Introduction,* 5th ed. Belmont, CA: Wadsworth Publishing Company.

——. 2003. *Organized Crime,* 7th ed. Belmont, CA: Wadsworth Publishing Company.

Adams, Thomas F., Alan G. Caddell, and Jeffrey L. Krutsinger. 2004. *Crime Scene Investigation,* 2nd ed. Upper Saddle River, NJ: Prentice Hall.

Anderson, James F., and Laronistine Dyson. 2001. *Legal Rights of Prisoners: Cases and Comments.* Lanham, MD: University Press of America.

Bilchik, Shay. 1996. *State Responses to Serious and Violent Juvenile Crime.* Washington, DC: U.S. Department of Justice, Office of Juvenile Justice and Delinquency Prevention.

Black, Henry Campbell. 1990. *Black's Law Dictionary,* 6th ed. St. Paul, MN: West Publishing Company.

Bonczar, Thomas P., and Tracy L. Snell. 2003. *Capital Punishment, 2002.* Washington, DC: U.S. Department of Justice.

Britz, Marjie T. 2004. *Computer Forensics and Cyber Crime: An Introduction.* Upper Saddle River, NJ: Prentice Hall.

Champion, Dean J. 2004. *Corrections in the United States: A Contemporary Perspective,* 3rd ed. Upper Saddle River, NJ: Prentice Hall.

——. 1998. *Criminal Justice in the United States,* 2nd ed. Belmont, CA: Wadsworth.

——. 2004. *The Juvenile Justice System: Delinquency, Processing, and the Law,* 3rd ed. Upper Saddle River, NJ: Prentice Hall.

——. 2002. *Probation, Parole, and Community Corrections,* 4th ed. Upper Saddle River, NJ: Prentice Hall.

——. 2000. *Research Methods for Criminal Justice and Criminology,* 2nd ed. Upper Saddle River, NJ: Prentice Hall.

Chesney-Lind, Meda, and Randall G. Shelden. 2004. *Girls, Delinquency, and Juvenile Justice.* Belmont, CA: Wadsworth Publishing Company.

Ching, James. 1997. "Credits as Personal Property: Beware of the New *Ex Post Facto* Clause." *Corrections Compendium* 22:1–16.

Clear, Todd R., and George F. Cole. 2003. *American Corrections,* 6th ed. Belmont, CA: Wadsworth Publishing Company.

Del Carmen, Rolando V. 2004. *Criminal Procedure: Law and Practice* 6th ed. Belmont, CA: Wadsworth Publishing Company.

Egger, Steven A. 2002. *The Killers Among Us,* 2nd ed. Upper Saddle River, NJ: Prentice Hall.

Florida Department of Corrections. 2003. *Probation Guidelines.* Tallahassee, FL: Florida Department of Corrections.

Gardner, Thomas J., and Terry M. Anderson. 2004. *Criminal Evidence: Principles and Cases.* Belmont, CA: Wadsworth Publishing Company.

Glaze, Lauren E. 2003. *Probation and Parole in the United States, 2002.* Washington, DC: Bureau of Justice Statistics.

Harrison, Paige M., and Allen J. Beck. 2003. *Prisoners in 2002.* Washington, DC: U.S. Department of Justice.

Harrison, Paige M., and Jennifer C. Karberg. 2003. *Prison and Jail Inmates at Midyear 2002.* Washington, DC: U.S. Department of Justice.

Hess, Karen M., and Robert W. Drowns. 2004. *Juvenile Justice,* 6th ed. Belmont, CA: Wadsworth Publishing Company.

Hess, Karen M., and Henry Wrobleski. 2003. *Police Operations: Theory and Practice,* 3rd ed. Belmont, CA: Wadsworth Publishing Company.

Howell, James C., Arlen Egley, Jr., and Debra K. Gleason. 2002. *Modern-Day Youth Gangs.* Washington, DC: U.S. Department of Justice.

Icove, David J., and John D. DeHaan. 2004. *Forensic Fire Scene Reconstruction.* Upper Saddle River, NJ: Prentice Hall.

Karmen, Andrew. 2004. *Crime Victims: An Introduction to Victimology.* Belmont, CA: Wadsworth Publishing Company.

Kunz, Christina L., Deborah A. Schmedemann, Matthew P. Downs, and Ann L. Bateson. *The Process of Legal Research,* 5th ed. New York: Aspen Publishers.

Metropolitan Police Department, Planning and Development Division. "The Shadow of the Past—The Light of the Future: 1974 Annual Report." Washington, DC: Metropolitan Police Department.

National Advisory Committee on Criminal Justice Standards and Goals. 1967. *Juvenile Justice and Delinquency Prevention.* Washington, DC: U.S. Government Printing Office.

Ohio Parole Board. 2003. *Ohio Parole Program and Requirements.* Columbus, OH: Ohio Parole Board.

Peoples, Edward E. 2003. *Basic Criminal Procedures,* 2nd ed. Upper Saddle River, NJ: Prentice Hall.

Rennison, Callie Marie, and Michael R. Rand. 2003. *Criminal Victimization, 2002.* Washington, DC: U.S. Department of Justice.

Ross, Jeffrey Ian, and Stephen C. Richards. 2003. *Convict Criminology.* Belmont, CA: Wadsworth Publishing Company.

Roth, Mitchel P. 2004. *Crime and Punishment: A History of the Criminal Justice System.* Belmont, CA: Wadsworth Publishing Company.

Samaha, Joel. 2003. *Criminal Justice,* 6th ed. Belmont, CA: Wadsworth Publishing Company.

Senna, Joseph J., and Larry J. Siegel. 2002. *Introduction to Criminal Justice.* Belmont, CA: Wadsworth Publishing Company.

Siegel, Larry J. 2004. *Criminology: Theories, Patterns, and Typologies.* Belmont, CA: Wadsworth Publishing Company.

Smith, Christopher E. 2004. *Constitutional Rights in Criminal Justice.* Belmont, CA: Wadsworth Publishing Company.

Stojkovic, Stan, David Kalinich, and John Klofas. 2003. *Criminal Justice Organizations: Administration and Management.* Belmont, CA: Wadsworth Publishing Company.

Sweet, Kathleen M. 2004. *Aviation and Airport Security.* Upper Saddle River, NJ: Prentice Hall.

U.S. Department of Justice, Federal Bureau of Investigation. 1999. *Crime in the United States.* Washington, DC: U.S. Government Printing Office.

Weisburd, David, and Chester Britt. 2003. *Statistics in Criminal Justice.* Belmont, CA: Wadsworth Publishing Company.

Wrightsman, Lawrence S. 2001. *Forensic Psychology.* Belmont, CA: Wadsworth Publishing Company.

Wrobleski, Henry M., and Karen M. Hess. 2003. *Introduction to Law Enforcement and Criminal Justice,* 7th ed. Belmont, CA: Wadsworth Publishing Company. ◆

APPENDICES

Ph.D. Programs in Criminal Justice

University of Albany, SUNY
School of Criminal Justice
125 Western Avenue
Albany, NY 12222
(518) 442-5214
Internet: http://www.albany.edu/scj/
   prog-phd.html

American University
School of Public Affairs
4400 Massachusetts Avenue, NW
Washington, DC 20016
(202) 885-2940
Internet: http://www.american.edu/spa

University of Arkansas–Little Rock
Department of Criminal Justice
2801 South University Avenue
Little Rock, AR 72204-1099
(501) 569-3206
Fax: (501) 569-3039
Internet: http://www.ualr.edu/
   %7Ecjdept/courses.html

Bowling Green State University
Criminal Justice Program
222 Williams Hall
Bowling Green, OH 43403
(419) 372-2294
Internet: http://bgsu.edu/departments/
   crju/CJmain.htm

University of California–Berkeley
Jurisprudence and Social Policy
2240 Piedmont Avenue #2150
Berkeley, CA 94720-2150
(510) 642-3771
Fax: (510) 642-2951
Internet: http://www.law.berkeley.edu/
   academics/jsp

University of California–Irvine
Department of Criminology, Law, and
   Society
203 Social Ecology

PO Box 6050
Irvine, CA 92697-7065
(949) 824-5917
Fax: (949) 824-9843
Internet: http://www.seweb.uci.edu/cls

Capella University (Online)
School of Human Services
222 South 9th Street, 20th Floor
Minneapolis, MN 55402
(888) 227-3552
Internet: http://www.capella.edu/
   reborn/html/schools/humanserv/
   crim_just_phd.aspx

University of Cincinnati
Division of Criminal Justice
600 Dyer Hall
PO Box 210389
Cincinnati, OH 45221-0389
(513) 556-5827
Internet: http://www.uc.edu/
   criminaljustice

University of Delaware
Department of Sociology and Criminal
   Justice
342 Smith Hall
Newark, DE 19716
(302) 831-1236
Fax: (302) 831-2607
Internet: http://www.udel.edu/soc

Florida State University
School of Criminology and Criminal
   Justice
Hecht House
634 West Call Street
Tallahassee, FL 32306-1127
(850) 644-4050
Fax: (850) 644-9614
Internet: http://
   www.criminology.fsu.edu

Georgia State University
Department of Criminal Justice
PO Box 4018
33 Gilmer Street SE
Atlanta, GA 30302-4018
(404) 651-0747
Internet: http://www.cjgsu.net

University of Illinois at Chicago
Department of Criminal Justice
1007 West Harrison
M/C 141
Chicago, IL 60607-7140
(312) 996-2383
Internet: http://www.uic.edu/depts/
   cjus

Indiana University
Department of Criminal Justice
Sycamore Hall 302
Bloomington, IN 47405
(504) 388-6760
Internet: http://www.indiana.edu/
   ~crimjust

Indiana University of Pennsylvania
IUP Graduate School
101 Stright Hall
Indiana, PA 15705-1081
(412) 357-2222
Fax: (412) 357-4862
Internet: http://www.chss.iup.edu/cr

John Jay College of Criminal Justice
899 Tenth Avenue
New York, NY 10019
(212) 237-8866
Internet: http://www.jjay.cuny.edu

Louisiana State University
Criminal Justice and Sociology
271 Pleasant Hall
Baton Rouge, LA 70803-1530
(504) 388-6760

Internet: http://www.lsu.edu/sociology/
grad

University of Maryland–Baltimore
Forensic Sciences
515 West Lombard Street, Room 208
Baltimore, MD 21201
(410) 706-7131
Fax: (410) 706-3473
Internet: http://
graduate.umaryland.edu

University of Maryland–College Park
Department of Criminology and
Criminal Justice
University Boulevard at Adelphi Road
College Park, MD 20742-5121
(301) 405-4699
Internet: http://www.bsos.umd.edu/
ccjs

Michigan State University
School of Criminal Justice
560 Baker Hall
East Lansing, MI 48824-1118
(517) 355-2197
Internet: http://www.cj.msu.edu

University of Missouri
Criminology and Criminal Justice
Department
324 Lucas Hall
8001 Natural Bridge Road
St. Louis, MO 63121-4499
(314) 516-5031
Fax: (314) 516-5048
Internet: http://www.umsl.edu/~ccj

University of Nebraska–Omaha
Department of Criminal Justice
Durham Science Center, Room 208
6001 Dodge Street
Omaha, NE 68182-0149
(402) 554-2610
Fax: (402) 554-2326
Internet: http://www.unomaha.edu/
~crimjust

City University of New York
365 Fifth Avenue at 34th Street
Manhattan
New York, NY 10016
(212) 817-7000
Internet: http://www.cuny.edu

Pennsylvania State University
Crime, Law, and Justice Program
Department of Sociology
211 Oswald Tower
University Park, PA 16802-6207
(814) 865-6222
Fax: (814) 863-7216
Internet: http://sociology.la.psu.edu/
best.htm

Prairie View A&M University
Juvenile Justice Ph.D. Program
PO Box 3089
Prairie View, TX 77446
(936) 857-2626
Fax: (936) 857-2699
Internet: http://www.pvamu.edu

Rutgers University
School of Criminal Justice
123 Washington Street, Room 568
Newark, NJ 07102
(973) 353-3311
Fax: (973) 353-5896
Internet: http://www.rutgers-
newark.rutgers.edu/rscj

Sam Houston State University
College of Criminal Justice
George J. Beto Criminal Justice Center
Huntsville, TX 77341-2478
(936) 294-1702
Fax: (936) 294-1271
Internet: http://www.shsu.edu/
cjcenter/College/graduate/phd.htm

University of South Carolina
Department of Criminology and
Criminal Justice
Columbia, SC 29208
(803) 777-7088
Internet: http://www.cla.sc.edu/crju

University of Southern Mississippi
Administration of Justice
Office of Graduate Studies
USM Box 10066
Hattiesburg, MS 39406-0066
(601) 266-4509
Fax: (601) 266-5138
Internet: http://www.usm.edu/cj

University of South Florida
Department of Criminology
College of Arts and Sciences
4202 East Fowler Avenue, SOC 107

Tampa, FL 33620-8100
(813) 974-2815
Fax: (813) 974-2803
Internet: http://www.cas.usf.edu/
criminology

Temple University
College of Arts and Sciences
5th Floor, Gladfelter Hall
1115 W. Berks Street
Philadelphia, PA 19122
(215) 204-7918
Fax: (215) 204-3872
Internet: http://www.temple.edu/cjus

University of Tennessee–Knoxville
Department of Sociology
Criminology and Criminal Justice
901 McClung Tower
1115 Volunteer Boulevard
Knoxville, TN 37996
(865) 974-6021
Fax: (865) 974-1000
Internet: http://web.utk.edu/~utsoc
dep/other/criminal_justice.html

University of Texas–Austin
Center for Criminology and Criminal
Justice
Deparment of Sociology
Burdine Hall, Room 336
Austin, TX 78712-1088
(512) 471-1122
Internet: http://www.la.utexas.edu/
research/cccjr/index.htm

Walden University (Online)
Human Services–Criminal Justice
1001 Fleet Street
Baltimore, MD 21202
Internet: http://www.elearners.com/
online-degree/3485.htm

Washington State University
Department of Political Science/
Criminal Justice Program
Program in Criminal Justice
Johnson Tower 801
PO Box 644880
Pullman, WA 99164-4880
(509) 335-2544
Internet: http://libarts.wsu.edu/polisci/
overview/index.html ✦

Internet Connections

Prosecution and the Courts

Abuse of Judicial Discretion
http://www.constitution.org/abus/
discretion/judicial/
judicial_discretion.htm

Administrative Office of U.S. Courts
http://www.uscourts.gov

American Arbitration Association
http://www.adr.org/index2.1.jsp

American Bar Association
http://www.abanet.org/crimjust/
links.html

American Civil Liberties Union
http://www.aclu.org

Association of Pretrial Professionals of Florida
http://www.appf.org

Bureau of Justice Statistics
http://www.ojp.usdoj.gov/bjs/
correct.htm

Bureau of Justice Statistics Courts and Sentencing Statistics
http://www.ojp.usdoj.gov/bjs/
stssent.htm

Center for Court Innovation
http://www.courtinnovation.org

Criminal justice links
http://www.lawguru.com/ilawlib/
96.htm

Federal Judicial Center
http://www.fjc.gov

Legal Resource Center
http://www.crimelynx.com/
research.html

National Association of Pretrial Services
http://www.napsa.org

National Association of State Judicial Educators
http://nasje.unm.edu

National Center for State Courts
http://www.ncsconline.org

National Center for Youth Law
http://www.youthlaw.org

National Center on Institutions and Alternatives
http://www.sentencing.org

National Clearinghouse for Judicial Educational Information
http://jeritt.msu.edu

National Council of Juvenile and Family Court Judges
http://www.ncjfcj.org

National Institute of Justice
http://www.ojp.usdoj.gov/nij

Pretrial Procedures
http://www.uaa.alaska.edu/just/
just110/courts2.html

Pretrial Services Resource Center
http://www.pretrial.org

Punishment and Sentencing
http://www.fsmlaw.org/chuuk/code/
title12/T12_CH11.htm

Sentencing Advisory Panel
http://www.sentencing-advisory-
panel.gov.uk

Sentencing Project
http://www.sentencingproject.org

State court links
http://www.uscourts.gov/links.html

State criminal justice links
http://www.criminology.fsu.edu/cjlinks

U.S. Courts
http://www.uscourts.gov/links.html

U.S. Department of Justice
http://www.usdoj.gov/02organizations/
02_1.html

U.S. Sentencing Commission
http://www.ussc.gov

Vera Institute of Justice
http://www.vera.org

Vera Institute of Justice Projects: State Sentencing and Corrections Program
http://www.vera.org/project/
project1_1.asp?section_id=3&projec
t_id=26&archive=NO

Corrections

American Civil Liberties Union
http://www.aclu.org

American Community Corrections Institute
http://www.accilifeskills.com

American Correctional Association
http://www.aca.org

American Correctional Association: Past, Present, and Future
http://www.aca.org/pastpresentfuture/principles.asp

American Correctional Chaplains Association
http://www.correctionalchaplains.org

American Correctional Health Services Association
http://www.corrections.com/achsa/index1.html

American Jail Association
http://www.corrections.com/aja

American Probation and Parole Association
http://www.appa-net.org

Amnesty International
http://www.amnesty.org

BI Incorporated
http://www.bi.com

Boot Camps
http://www.boot-camps-info.com

Boot Camps for Juvenile Offenders
http://www.ncjrs.org/txtfiles/bootjuv.txt

Boot Camps for Struggling Teens
http://www.juvenile-boot-camps.com

Building Blocks for Youth
http://www.buildingblocksforyouth.org/issues/girls/resources.html

Bureau of Justice Statistics
http://www.ojp.usdoj.gov/bjs

Bureau of Prisons
http://www.bop.gov

Burnout in Billings
http://www.cannabisnews.com/news/16/thread16603.shtml

California Board of Prison Terms
http://www.bpt.ca.gov

Center for Community Corrections
http://www.communitycorrectionsworks.org/aboutus.htm

Center for Restorative Justice
http://ssw.che.umn.edu/rjp

Citizens for Effective Justice
http://www.okplus.com/fedup

Citizens for Legal Responsibility
http://www.clr.org

Colorado Council of Mediators
http://www.coloradomediation.org

Colorado Judicial Department Probation Program
http://www.courts.state.co.us/panda/statrep/ar2000/probnarr.pdf

Cook County Boot Camp
http://www.cookcountysheriff.org/bootcamp

Correctional Medical Services
http://www.cmsstl.com

Corrections Corporation of America
http://www.correctionscorp.com

Corrections industries links
http://www.corrections.com/industries

Corrections.Com
http://www.corrections.com/index.aspx

CounterPunch
http://www.counterpunch.org

CPR Institute for Dispute Resolution
http://www.cpradr.org

Crawford County Intensive Supervised Probation
http://www.crawfordcocpcourt.org/ISProbation.htm

Crime Watch
http://www.misterfixit.com/CrimeWatch.htm

Criminal Justice: Corrections
http://www.lib.msu.edu/harris23/crimjust/correct.htm

CSS Special Supervision Services
http://www.csosa.gov/txt_css_SpecialSupervision.htm

Death Row Speaks
http://www.deathrowspeaks.net

Department of Justice
http://www.usdoj.gov

Fairfax County, VA, Public Safety
http://www.co.fairfax.va.us/living/safety/default.htm

Faith to Faith Friends
http://www.f2ff.com

Federal Bureau of Prisons
http://www.bop.gov

Federal Bureau of Prisons Library
http://bop.library.net

Federal Prison Consultants
http://www.federalprisonconsultants.com

Federal Probation System Persons on Supervision
http://www.ca7.uscourts.gov/rpt/report00/proba.pdf

Female inmate pen pals
http://www.thepamperedprisoner.com

Fugitive Apprehension Unit
http://www.doc.missouri.gov/Horizon/fugitive05_k03.htm

Furlough programs
http://www.xpay.net/SevFurloughPrograms.htm

Gang unit resources
http://www.officer.com/special_ops/gang.htm

George A. Keene, Inc.
http://www.keenjailequip.com

Georgia Parolee Database
http://www.pap.state.ga.us/
parolee_database.htm

Grundy County Probation
Department
http://www.grundyco.com/
probation.htm

History of American Probation and
Parole Associaton
http://www.appa-net.org/
about%20appa/history.htm

History of the Federal Bureau of
Prisons
http://www.bop.gov/ipapg/ipahist.html

Home Confinement Program: Court
and Community
http://uscourts.gov/misc/2003-
home.PDF

International Association of
Correctional Training Personnel
http://www.iactp.org

International Community Corrections
Association
http://www.iccaweb.org

International Corrections and Prisons
Association
http://www.icpa.ca/home.html

International Community Corrections
Association
http://www.health.gov/NHIC/
NHICScripts/
Entry.cfm?HRCode=HR0353

Jail management
http://www.mmmicro.com/
jail_management.htm

Jail management system
http://www.sunridgesystems.com/
jail_management.html

Koch Crime Institute (KCI: The
Website)
http://www.kci.org/

Massachusetts Council on Family
Mediation
http://www.divorcenet.com/ma-
mediators.html

Massachusetts State Police Violent
Fugitive Apprehension Section
http://www.state.ma.us/msp/unitpage/
violent.htm

McHenry County Department of
Probation and Court Services
http://www.co.mchenry.il.us/
CountyDpt/CourtServ/
CSerAdult.asp

Meet-an-Inmate.Com
http://www.meet-an-inmate.com

Michigan 36th District Court
Probation Programs
http://www.36thdistrictcourt.org/
probation-programs.html

Montana Mediation Association
http://www.mtmediation.org

Naber Technical Enterprises:
Correctional training, correctional
consulting, jail research for
criminal justice and public safety
http://www.nteusa.org/

NaphCare, Inc.
http://www.naphcare.com

National Association of Probation
Executives
http://www.napehome.org/

National Corrections Corporation
http://www.nationalcorrections.com

National Corrections Industries
Association
http://www.nationalcia.org

National Crime Prevention Council
http://www.ncpc.org

National Criminal Justice Reference
Service
http://www.ncjrs.org

National Institute of Corrections
http://www.nicic.org

National Institute of Corrections Jail
Administration Training Program
http://www.nicic.org/services/training/
programs/jails/jail-admin.htm

National Institute on Drug Abuse
http://www.nida.nih.gov

National Institute of Corrections
http://www.nicic.org

National State History of Halfway
Houses
http://www.ni-cor.com/
halfwayhouses.html

New Jersey State Parole Board
http://www.state.nj.us/parole

New York Correction History Society
http://www.correctionhistory.org/

New York State Parole Department
http://www.parole.state.ny.us/
specialrelease.html

New York State Probation Officer's
Association
http://www.nyspoa.com

North Carolina Study Release
Program
http://www.doc.state.nc.us/DOP/
Program/studyrel.htm

Objective jail classification
http://www.corrections.com/aja/
training

Online friends to death-row inmates
http://www.freeworldfriends.com

Organizations for inmates
http://www.4lbb.com/sf/
organizations.htm

PACER Service Center
http://www.pacer.psc.uscourts.gov

Paraprofessionals: ERIC
http://ericec.org/faq/paraprof.html

Parole links
http://www.appa-net.org/links.htm

Parole officer stress
http://www.enlightenedsentencing.org/
what-probation-officers-say.htm

Parole sites
http://www.tbcnet.com/~salsberry/
ParoleSites.htm

Parole violators
http://www.bottomlinestudios.com/
ParoleViolators.html

Probation agency links
http://www.cppca.org

Probation and Parole Compact Administrators Association
http://www.ppcaa.net

Probation and parole sites: Web of Justice
http://www.co.pinellas.fl.us/bcc/
juscoord/eprobation.htm

Probation in the new century
http://www.dcor.state.ga.us/pdf/
proFY01.pdf

Probation officer recruitment
http://www.wvmccd.cc.ca.us/wvmccd/
police/officer_hire.html

Probation philosophy
http://www.appa-net.org/
about%20appa/probatio.htm

The Program for Female Offenders, Inc.
http://www.fcnetworks.org/Dir98/
dir98front.html

Reynolds Work Release Second Chance Program
http://www.wa.gov/doc/
REYN02DSWRdescription.htm

State parole boards
http://www.peace-officers.com/
catparo.shtml

Street Time
http://www.post-gazette.com/tv/
20020623tvweek2p2.asp

Support staff probation
http://www.kyrene.k12.az.us/policy/
gdg.htm

Thunder Road Probation Program
http://www.thunder-road.org/
programs_acp.html

Unauthorized federal prison manual
http://www.bureauofprisons.com

U.S. Parole Commission
http://www.usdoj.gov/uspc

U.S. Probation Department of the Southern District of Ohio
http://www.ohsp.uscourts.gov/pdfs/
psi.pdf

Ventura County Probation Agency
http://
www.probation.countyofventura.org

Volunteer Management Bibliography
http://www.energizeinc.com/art/
biblio5.html

Volunteers in Prevention, Probation, and Prisons, Inc.
http://www.vipmentoring.org/
about_vip/page3.html

Volunteers of America
http://www.voa.org

Women Behind Bars
http://www.womenbehindbars.com

Women in Criminal Justice
http://www.wicj.com

Women's Prison Association
http://www.wpaonline.org/WEBSITE/
home.htm

Worcester County, MA, Gang Unit
http://www.worcesterda.com/daunits/
gangst.html

Work furlough programs
http://www.dcn.davis.ca.us/YoloLINK/
services/S0026.html

Work-release program
http://www.legis.state.la.us/tsrs/RS/15/
RS_15_1111.htm

Criminological Theory

Advances in criminological theory
http://www.newark.rutgers.edu/rscj/
journals/advances.htm

Criminological theory on the web
http://www.wku.edu/~john.faine/
soc332/diane.pdf

Criminological Theory: Past to Present
http://www.roxbury.net/
crimtheorypast2.html

North Carolina Department of Corrections Offender Treatment Programs
http://www.doc.state.nc.us/DOP/
health/mhs/special/soar.html

Sex-offenders treatment program
http://www.auditor.leg.state.mn.us/
sexoff.htm

Sex-offender treatment programs
http://www.auditor.leg.state.mn.us/
ped/1994/sexoff.htm

Understanding criminological theory
http://www.faculty.ncwc.edu/
toconnor/301/crimtheo.htm

Special-Needs Offenders and Programs

Adcare Correctional Drug and Alcohol Treatment Programs
http://www.adcare.com/correc

Addictions page
http://www.well.com/user/woa

Alcoholics Anonymous
http://www.aa.org

Connections: A Correctional Education Program Serving Offenders With Special Learning Needs
http://
www.theconnectionsprogram.com/
MainPageText.htm

Domestic Violence Project of Silicon Valley, CA
http://www.growing.com/nonviolent/index.htm

Female special-needs offenders
http://stars.csg.org/slc/special/2000/female_offenders.pdf

Gamblers Anonymous
http://www.gamblersanonymous.org

The William Glasser Institute on Reality Therapy
http://www.wglasser.com

Gurley House Women's Recovery Center
http://www.thegurleyhouse.com

International Institute on Special-Needs Offenders
http://www.iisno.org.uk

Narcotics Anonymous
http://www.na.org

Narcotics Complete Recovery Center
http://www.drugrehab.net

National Association for Community Mediation
http://www.nafcm.org

National Association of Social Workers
http://www.naswdc.org

Recovery resources online
http://www.soberrecovery.com

Sex Offender.Com
http://www.sexoffender.com

Shadow Track Technologies
http://www.shadowtrack.com/?sources=Overture

Smart Recovery
http://www.smartrecovery.org

Social workers
http://www.stats.bls.gov/oco/ocos060.htm

Texas Correctional Office on Offenders with Medical or Mental Impairments
http://www.tdcj.state.tx.us/tcomi/tcomi-home.htm

2003 International Conference on Special-Needs Offenders (Canada)
http://www.specialneedsoffenders.org/aboutus.html

Juvenile Justice

ABA Juvenile Justice Center
http://www.abanet.org/crimjust/juvjus/home.html

Action Without Borders
http://www.idealist.org

Youth Activism Project
http://www.youthactivism.com

American Bar Association's Juvenile Justice Center
http://www.abanet.org/crimjust/juvjus/home.html

Aspen Youth Services
http://www.aspenyouth.com

Boot camp information
http://www.ncjrs.org/txtfiles/evalboot.txt

Boot camps
http://www.boot-camps-info.com

Building Blocks for Youth
http://www.buildingblocksforyouth.org/issues/jjdpa/factsheet.html

Campaign Against Wrongful Executions
http://www.justice.policy.net

Center for the Prevention of School Violence
http://www.ncdjjdp.org/cpsv

Center on Crime, Communities, and Culture
http://www.rgs.uci.edu/research/fundopp/msg00681.html

Center on Juvenile and Criminal Justice
http://www.cjcj.org

Children and Family Justice Center
http://www.law.northwestern.edu/depts/clinic/cfjc

Children Now
http://www.childrennow.org

Children's Defense Fund
http://www.childrensdefense.org

Children's legal protection center
http://www.childprotect.org

Close Cheltenham Now!
http://www.closecheltenham.com

Communication Works
http://www.communicationworks.com

CompassPoint nonprofit services
http://www.compasspoint.org

Correctional educational connections
http://www.io.com/~ellie

Corrections connection
http://www.corrections.com

Council of Juvenile Correctional Administrators
http://www.corrections.com/cjca

Criminal Justice Distance Learning Consortium
http://www.cjcentral.com/cjdlc

Criminal Justice Policy Foundation
http://www.cjpf.org

CURE-NY
http://users.bestweb.net/~cureny/cure-ny.htm

Debt to society
http://www.motherjones.com/prisons

Drug Reform Coordination Network
http://www.drcnet.org

DrugSense
http://www.drugsense.org

Empowerment resources
http://
www.empowermentresources.com

Engaged Zen Foundation
http://www.engaged-zen.org

Families Against Mandatory Minimums
http://www.famm.org/index2.htm

Families and Corrections Network
http://www.fcnetwork.org

Federal Bureau of Prisons
http://www.bop.gov/bopmain.html

Federal Gang Violence Act
http://www.feinstein.senate.gov/
booklets/gangs.pdf

Fight Crime, Invest in Kids
http://www.fightcrime.org

Fortune Society
http://www.fortunesociety.org

Gangs: A bibliography
http://www-lib.usc.edu/~anthonya/
gang.htm

Gangs in the schools
http://ericfacility.net/ericdigests/
ed372175.html

General Victim's Assistance Information
http://www.ncjrs.org/victhome.htm

Georgia Alliance for Children
http://www.gac.org

HandsNet
http://www.handsnet.org

Helping.org
http://www.helping.org

Howard League
http://www.howardleague.org

Human rights and the drug war
http://www.hr95.org

Idaho Youth Ranch
http://www.youthranch.org

Institute for Global Communications
http://www.bapd.org/ginbns-1.html

Intensive aftercare for high-risk juveniles
http://www.ncjrs.org/pdffiles/juvcc.pdf

John Howard Association
http://www.johnhowardassociation.org

Justice Policy Institute
http://www.justicepolicy.org/
article.php?id=118

Juvenile boot camp directory
http://www.kci.org/publication/
bootcamp/prerelease.htm

Juvenile boot camps
http://www.juvenile-boot-camps.com/
?source=overture

Juvenile intensive probation supervision
http://www.nal.usda.gov/pavnet/yf/
yfjuvpro.htm

Juvenile Justice Evaluation Center
http://www.jrsa.org/jjec/programs/
publications.html

Juvenile justice reform initiatives
http://www.ojjdp.ncjrs.org/pubs/
reform/ch2_k.html

Juvenile Law Center
http://www.jlc.org

Marijuana Policy Project
http://www.mpp.org

Moratorium2000
http://www.moratorium2000.org

National Center on Institutions and Alternatives
http://www.vard.org/register/ieo_files/
frame.htm

National Center for Missing and Exploited Children
http://www.ncmec.org

National Center for Youth Law
http://www.youthlaw.org

National Center on Education, Disability, and Juvenile Justice
http://www.edjj.org

National Clearinghouse on Child Abuse and Neglect Information
http://www.nccanch.acf.hhs.gov

National Coalition to Abolish the Death Penalty
http://www.ncadp.org

National Council of Juvenile and Family Court Judges
http://www.ncjfcj.org

National Council on Crime and Delinquency
http://www.nccd-crc.org

National Institute of Corrections
http://www.nicic.org

National Organization for the Reform of Marijuana Laws
http://www.norml.org

National Youth Court Center
http://www.youthcourt.net

National Youth Gang Center
http://www.iir.com/nygc

NetAction
http://www.netaction.org

Nonprofit Consultants ONTAP
http://www.ontap.org

Nonprofit GENIE
http://www.genie.org

North Carolina IMPACT boot camps
http://www.doc.state.nc.us/impact

Office of Juvenile Justice and Delinquency Prevention
http://www.ojjdp.ncjrs.org

Other Side of the Wall
http://www.prisonwall.org

Out-of-control gangs
http://www.freerepublic.com/focus/
  f-news/807681/posts

PACE Center for Girls, Inc.
http://www.pacecenter.org

Peacefire.org
http://www.peacefire.org

Penal reform
http://www.penalreform.org

Prison industry
http://www.corpwatch.org

Prison-issues desk
http://www.prisonactivist.org

REALJUSTICE
http://www.realjustice.org

Resources for youth
http://www.preventviolence.org

Rights for All
http://www.amnesty-usa.org/
  rightsforall/juvenile/dp/
  section2.html

**Riker's Island High-Impact
  Incarceration Program**
http://www.correctionhistory.org/html/
  chronicl/nycdoc/html/hiip.html

Safe and Responsive Schools Project
http://www.indiana.edu/~safeschl

Schools, Not Jails
http://www.schoolsnotjails.com

Sentencing Project
http://www.sentencingproject.org

ServiceLeader
http://www.serviceleader.org

**State of California Youthful Offender
  Parole Board**
http://www.yopb.ca.gov

Stop Prison Rape
http://www.spr.org/index.html

Teenage CURFEW
http://www.fromdebbieskitchen.com/
  TeenCurfewQR.htm

Teen boot camps
http://www.teenbootcamps.com/
  resources/BootCamps.html

Teen court
http://www.teen-court.org

Teens, crime, and the community
http://www.nationalaltcc.org

Texas Juvenile Probation Commission
http://www.tjpc.state.tx.us

Unusual Suspects Theatre Company
http://www.theunusualsuspects.org/
  index.html

Urban Institute
http://www.urban.org

Vera Institute of Justice
http://www.vera.org

**Victim-Offender Mediation
  Association**
http://www.igc.org/voma

Wilderness Programs, Inc.
http://www.wildernessprogramsetc
  .com

Youth Alternatives, Inc.
http://www.volunteersolutions.org/
  volunteer/agency/one_177937.html

**Youth Change (problem-youth
  problem solving)**
http://www.youthchg.com

Youth defense counsels
http://www.juveniledefense.com

Youth Law Center
http://www.youthlawcenter.com

**Youth on Trial: A Developmental
  Perspective on Juvenile Justice**
http://www.mac-adoldev-juvjustice.org

Recidivism Research

Abstract on recidivism
http://www.stat.washington.edu/www/
  seminars/archive/2003/winter/
  sirakaya.shtml

Basic guide to program evaluation
http://www.eval.org/Evaluation
  Documents/progeval.html

**Bureau of Data and Research Program
  Accountability Measures**
http://www.djj.state.fl.us/RnD/
  r_digest/issue37/issue37.pdf

Expert program evaluation services
http://www.statistics-talk.com

FBI Academy
http://fbi.gov/hq/td/academy/
  academy.htm

FBI Laboratory
http://fbi.gov/hq/lab/labhome.htm

**Guidelines for state parole program
  evaluation**
http://www.csulb.edu/~ddowell/
  guidelines.htm

The NIJ Research Review
http://www.ncjrs.org/rr/vol1_1/
  17.html

**Oregon Department of Corrections
  Recidivism of New Parolees**
http://www.doc.state.or.us/research/
  Recid.pdf

Recidivism of adult felons
http://www.auditor.leg.state.mn.us/
  ped/1997/pe9701.htm

Recidivism of adult probationers
http://www.co.hennepin.mn.us/
  commcorr/reports/
  RecidivismofAdultProbationers.htm

Selected Professional Organizations and Agencies

Academy of Criminal Justice Sciences
http://www.acjs.org

American Academy of Forensic Sciences
http://aafs.org

American Bar Association
http://www.abanet.org

American Correctional Association
http://www.aca.com

American Judges Association
http://aja.ncsc.dni.us

American Probation and Parole Association
http://www.appa-net.org

American Psychological Association
http://www.apa.org

American Service Group, Inc.
http://www.asgr.com

American Society of Criminology
http://asc41.com

American Sociological Association
http://asanet.org

Federal Bureau of Investigation
http://fbi.gov

Federation of Law Societies of Canada
http://flsc.ca

Freedom of Information Act
http://www.usdoj.gov/04foia

Law and Society Association
webmaster@lawandsociety.org

Midwestern Criminal Justice Association
http://www.geocities.com/midwestcja/home.html

National Association of Counsel for Children
http://naccchildlaw.org

National Association for Court Management
http://nacm.ncsc.dni.us

National Association of Drug Court Professionals
http://www.nadcp.org

National Criminal Justice Reference Service
http://www.ncjrs.org

National District Attorneys Association
http://www.ndaa.org

National Institute of Corrections
http://nicic.org/inst

National Institute of Justice
http://www.ojp.usdoj.gov/nij

National Institute of Justice Data Resources Program
nacjd@icpsr.umich.edu

National Law Enforcement and Corrections Technology Center
http://www.nlectc.org/

Office of Justice Programs
http://ojp.usdoj.gov/

Office of Juvenile Justice and Delinquency Prevention (OJJDP)
http://www.ojjdp.ncjrs.org

OJP Drug Court Clearinghouse and Technical Assistance Project: Drug Testing in a Drug Court Environment
http://www.american.edu/spa/justice/publications/drugtesting.pdf

Pacific Sociological Association
http://www.csus.edu/psa

Sentencing Project
http://www.sentencingproject.org

Sourcebook of Criminal Justice Statistics
http://albany.edu/sourcebook

Southern Sociological Society
http://www.msstate.edu/org/sss

State Justice Institute
http://www.statejustice.org

U.S. Citizenship and Immigration Services
http://www.uscis.gov

U.S. Customs Service and Border Protection
http://www.customs.ustreas.gov

U.S. Federal Judiciary
http://www.uscourts.gov

U.S. Government Printing Office
http://www.access.gpo.gov

U.S. Marshals Service
http://www.usdoj.gov/marshals

U.S. Parole Commission
http://www.usdoj.gov/uspc

U.S. Sentencing Commission
http://www.ussc.gov

U.S. Supreme Court
http://www.supremecourtus.gov

Vera Institute of Justice
http://www.vera.org

Victim-Offender Reconciliation Project (VORP)
http://vorp.com

Western and Pacific Association of Criminal Justice Educators
http://cja.boisestate.edu/wpacje

Internet Addresses for Selected Publishers

Addison-Wesley
http://awprofessional.com

Allyn and Bacon
http://www.abacon.com

American Law and Economics
Association
alea@pantheon.yale.edu

American Society of International Law
http://asil.org

American Sociological Association
http://asanet.org

Anderson Publishing Company
http://www.andersonpublishing.com

Arnold Publishers
http://arnoldpublishers.com

William C. Brown
http://www.mhhe.com/catalogs/sem/

Butterworth-Heinemann
http://books.elsevier.com

Cambridge University Press
http://www.cup.org

Carolina Academic Press
http://www.cap-press.com

Close Up Publishing
http://www.closeup.org

Constitutional Rights Foundation
Chicago
http://www.crfc.org

Copperhouse Publishers
http://copperhouse.com

Cornell Companies
www.cornellcompanies.com

Dryden Press
http://www.thomson.com/learning/
learning.jsp

Durrant Justice
http://www.durrant.com

Dushkin Publishing Company
http://dushkin.com

Educational Testing Service
http://www.ets.org/hea

FBI Law Enforcement Bulletin
http://www.fbi.gov/publications/leb/
leb.htm

Gilbane
http://www.gilbaneco.com

Greenhaven Press
http://www.galegroup.com/greenhaven

Harcourt
http://www.harcourt.com

Harrow and Heston Publishers
http://crimeprevention.rutgers.edu/
resources/publishers.htm

Heery International
http://www.heery.com

Holt, Rinehart, and Winston
http://www.hrw.com

Justice Research and Statistics
Association
http://jrsainfo.org

Law and Society Association
http://www.lawandsociety.org

Macmillan Computer Publishing
http://wwwiz.com/books/mcp.html

McGraw-Hill
http://www.mhhe.com/socscience/
crimjustice

Microcase Corporation
http://www.microcase.com

National Clearinghouse for Judicial
Educational Information
http://jeritt.msu.edu

National Law Enforcement and
Corrections Technology Center
http://www.nlectc.org

NCOVR: National Consortium on
Violence Research
http://www.ncovr.org

Northeastern University Press
http://www.neu.edu/nupress

Pacific Sociological Association
psa@csus.edu

Prentice Hall
http://prenhall.com

Rosser Justice Systems/Rosser
International, Inc.
jmatthews@rosser.com

Roxbury Publishing Company
http://www.roxbury.net

Rowman Littlefield
http://rowmanlittlefield.com

R.R. Brink Locking Systems, Inc.
http://www.rrbrink.com

Sage Publications, Inc.
http://www.sagepub.com

Southern Illinois University Press
http://www.siu.edu/~siupress

Southern Sociological Society
levin@soc.msstate.edu

Street Law, Inc.
http://www.streetlaw.org

Uniform Crime Reports
http://fbi.gov/ucr/ucr.htm

U.S. Government Printing Office
http://access.gpo.gov

University of Chicago Press
http://www.press.uchicago.edu

Wackenhut Corrections Corporation
http://www.wackenhut.com

Wadsworth Thomson Learning
http://cj.wadsworth.com

Waveland Press, Inc.
http://www.waveland.com

West Publishing Company
http://westgroup.com

Western and Pacific Association of
Criminal Justice Educators
http://cja.boisestate.edu/wpacje

Western Criminology Review
http://wcr.sonoma.edu

Westview Press
http://perseusbooksgroup.com

John Wiley
http://www.wiley.com ✦

Names, Addresses, and Telephone Numbers of Federal and State Probation and Parole Agencies, Adult and Juvenile

Alabama—Adult Probation/Parole
Board of Pardons and Paroles
500 Monroe St.
PO Box 302405
Montgomery, AL 36130
(334) 242-8700

Alabama—Juvenile Probation/Parole
Administrative Office of Courts
300 Dexter Ave.
Montgomery, AL 37104
(334) 242-0300

Alaska—Adult Parole
Board of Parole
802 3rd St., Ste. 212-A
PO Box 112000
Juneau, AK 99811
(907) 465-3384

Alaska—Adult Probation
Department of Corrections
Division of Community Corrections
4500 Diplomacy Dr., Rm. 219
Anchorage, AK 99508
(907) 269-7370

Alaska—Juvenile Probation/Parole
Department of Health and Social
   Services
Division of Juvenile Justice
350 Main St., Rm. 404
PO Box 110635
Juneau, AK 99811
(907) 465-2212

**Arizona—Adult and Juvenile
   Probation**
Administrative Office of the Courts

1501 W. Washington St.
Phoenix, AZ 85007
(602) 542-9300

Arizona—Adult Parole
Board of Executive Clemency
1645 W. Jefferson, Ste. 326
Phoenix, AZ 85007
(602) 542-5656

Arizona—Juvenile Parole
Department of Juvenile Corrections
1624 W. Adams St.
Phoenix, AZ 85007
(602) 542-3987

Arkansas—Adult Probation/Parole
Post-Prison Transfer Board
PO Box 34085
Little Rock, AR 72203
(501) 682-3850

Arkansas—Adult Probation/Parole
Board of Correction and Community
   Punishment
PO Box 5900
Pine Bluff, AR 71611
(870) 247-0052

Arkansas—Adult Probation/Parole
Department of Community
   Punishment
105 W. Capitol, 2nd. Floor
Little Rock, AR 72201
(501) 682-9511

Arkansas—Juvenile Probation/Parole
Department of Human Services
Division of Youth Services

PO Box 1437, Slot 450
Little Rock, AR 72203
(501) 682-9400

Arkansas—Juvenile Probation/Parole
Administrative Office of the Courts
625 Marshall St., Rm. 1100
Little Rock, AR 72160
(501) 682-9400

California—Adult/Juvenile Probation
Judicial Council of California/
   Administrative Office of the Courts
455 Golden Gate Ave.
San Francisco, CA 94102
(415) 865-4200

California—Adult Parole
Board of Prison Terms
428 J St., Ste. 600
Sacramento, CA 95814
(916) 324-0557

California—Adult Parole
Parole and Community Services
   Division
1515 S. St., Rm. 212N
Sacramento, CA 95814
(916) 323-0576

California—Juvenile Parole
Youthful Offender Parole Board
1029 "J" St., 500
Sacramento, CA 95814
(916) 322-9800

California—Juvenile Parole
Department of Youth Authority
4241 Williamsbourgh Dr.

504

Sacramento, CA 95823
(916) 262-1467

Colorado—Adult and Juvenile Probation
Office of State Court Administrator
1301 Pennsylvania St., Ste. 300
Denver, CO 80203
(303) 861-1111

Colorado—Adult and Juvenile Probation
Office of Probation Services
1301 Pennsylvania St. Ste., 300
Denver, CO 80203
(303) 861-1111

Colorado—Adult Parole
Board of Parole
1600 W. 24th St., Bldg. 54
Pueblo, CO 81003
(719) 583-5800

Colorado—Adult Parole
Department of Corrections
Division of Adult Parole Supervision
10403 W. Colfax Ave., Ste. 700
Lakewood, CO 80215
(303) 238-5967

Colorado—Juvenile Parole
Juvenile Parole Board
1575 Sherman St.
Denver, CO 80203
(303) 866-5793

Connecticut—Adult and Juvenile Probation
Judicial Branch
Office of the Chief Court
   Administrator
231 Capitol Ave.
Hartford, CT 06106
(860) 757-2100

Connecticut—Adult and Juvenile Probation
Court Support Services Division
2275 Silas Deane Hwy.
Rocky Hill, CT 06067
(860) 563-1332

Connecticut—Adult Parole
Board of Parole
21 Grand St., 3rd Floor
Hartford, CT 06106
(860) 692-7400

Connecticut—Juvenile Parole
Department of Children and Families
505 Hudson St.
Hartford, CT 06106
(860) 550-6300

Delaware—Adult Parole
Board of Parole
820 N. French St.
Wilmington, DE 19801
(302) 577-5233

Delaware—Adult Probation/Parole
Bureau of Community Corrections
Division of Probation and Parole
26 Parkway Circle
New Castle, DE 19720
(302) 323-6050

Delaware—Juvenile Probation/Parole
Division of Youth Rehabilitative
   Services
Community Services
1825 Faulkland Rd.
Wilmington, DE 19805
(302) 995-8334

District of Columbia—Adult and Juvenile Probation
D.C. Superior Court
Social Services Division
Superior Court, 409 "E" St. NW
Washington, DC 20001
(202) 508-1800

District of Columbia—Juvenile Parole
Department of Human Services
Youth Services Administration
8300 Riverton Ct.
Laurel, MD 20707
(301) 497-8100

Florida—Adult Parole
Parole Commission
2601 Blair Stone Rd., Bldg. C
Tallahassee, FL 32399
(850) 487-1980

Florida—Adult Probation/Parole
Department of Corrections
Office of Community Corrections
2601 Blair Stone Rd.
Tallahassee, FL 32399
(850) 487-3865

Florida—Juvenile Probation/Parole
Department of Juvenile Justice

2737 Centerview Dr., Ste. 307
Tallahassee, FL 32399
(850) 921-0904

Georgia—Adult Parole
Board of Pardons and Paroles
2 Martin Luther King Jr. Dr., 4th
   Floor E
Atlanta, GA 30334
(404) 651-6638

Georgia—Adult Probation
Department of Corrections
Probation Division
2 Martin Luther King Jr. Dr. SE, Rm.
   954-E
Atlanta, GA 30334
(404) 656-4747

Georgia—Juvenile Probation/Parole
Department of Juvenile Justice
2 Peachtree St., 5th Floor
Atlanta, GA 30303
(404) 657-2400

Hawaii—Adult Parole
Paroling Authority
1177 Alakea St., Ground Floor
Honolulu, HI 96813
(808) 587-1300

Hawaii—Adult Probation
Judiciary Department
Adult Probation Division
777 Punchbowl St.
Honolulu, HI 96813
(808) 539-4910

Hawaii—Juvenile Parole
Department of Human Services
Office of Youth Services
820 Mililani St., Ste. 817
Honolulu, HI 96813
(808) 587-5700

Hawaii—Juvenile Probation
Youth Correctional Facility
42-477 Kalanianaole Hwy.
Kailua, HI 96734
(808) 266-9514

Idaho—Adult Parole
Commission of Pardons and Parole
3215 Shoshone St., Ste. A
PO Box 83720
Boise, ID 83720
(208) 334-2520

Idaho—Adult Probation/Parole
Department of Corrections
Division of Field and Community
    Services
129 N. Orchard, Ste. 110
PO Box 83720
Boise, ID 83720
(208) 658-2123

Idaho—Juvenile Probation/Parole
Department of Juvenile Corrections
400 N. 10th, 2nd Floor
PO Box 83720
Boise, ID 83720
(208) 334-5102

Idaho—Juvenile Probation/Parole
Administrative Office of the Courts
451 State St.
PO Box 83720
Boise, ID 83720
(208) 334-2246

Illinois—Adult Parole
Prisoner Review Board
319 Madison St., Ste. A
Springfield, IL 62701
(217) 782-7273

Illinois—Adult Parole
Department of Corrections
Community Services Division/Field
    Operations
1 Doris Ave.
Joliet, IL 60433
(815) 740-8794

Illinois—Juvenile Parole
Department of Corrections
Juvenile Division
1301 Concordia Ct.
PO Box 19277
Springfield, IL 62794
(217) 522-2666

Illinois—Juvenile Probation
Administrative Office of the Courts
Probation Services Division
816 S. College St.
Springfield, IL 62704
(217) 785-0413

Indiana—Adult/Juvenile Parole
Department of Corrections
Division of Programs and Community
    Service
302 W. Washington St., E., 334

Indianapolis, IN 46204
(317) 232-5711

Indiana—Adult/Juvenile Probation
Supreme Court
Judicial Center
115 W. Washington St., S. Tower, Ste.
    1075
Indianapolis, IN 46204
(317) 232-1313

Indiana—Adult Parole
Parole Board
302 W. Washington St.
Indianapolis, IN 64204
(317) 232-5737

Iowa—Adult Parole
Board of Parole
420 Keo
Des Moines, IA 50309
(515) 242-5757

Iowa—Adult Probation/Parole
Iowa Department of Corrections
Division of Community Correctional
    Services
420 Watson Powell Jr. Way
Des Moines, IA 50309
(515) 242-5708

Iowa—Juvenile Probation/Parole
Department of Human Services
Division of Adult, Children and
    Family Services
Hoover State Office Bldg.
Des Moines, IA 50319
(515) 281-4597

**Kansas—Adult and Juvenile
    Probation/Parole**
Supreme Court/Judicial Branch
301 W. 10th
Topeka, KS 66612
(785) 291-3223

Kansas—Adult Parole
Parole Board
900 SW Jackson, 4th Floor
Topeka, KS 66612
(785) 296-4523

Kansas—Adult Parole
Department of Corrections
Division of Community Corrections
900 SW Jackson St.
Topeka, KS 66612

(785) 296-4520

Kansas—Juvenile Parole
Juvenile Justice Authority
714 SW Jackson, Ste. 300
Topeka, KS 66612
(785) 296-4213

Kentucky—Adult Parole
Parole Board
State Office Bldg., 5th Floor
Frankfort, KY 40601
(502) 564-3620

Kentucky—Adult Probation/Parole
Department of Corrections
275 E. Main St.
Frankfort, KY 40601
(502) 564-4726

Kentucky—Juvenile Probation/Parole
Department of Juvenile Justice
1025 Capital Center Dr.
Frankfort, KY 40601
(502) 573-2738

Louisiana—Adult Parole
Board of Parole
504 Mayflower St.
PO Box 94304
Baton Rouge, LA 70804
(225) 342-6622

Louisiana—Adult Probation/Parole
Department of Public Safety and
    Corrections
Division of Probation and Parole
504 Mayflower St.
Baton Rouge, LA 70802
(225) 342-6609

Lousiana—Juvenile Probation/Parole
Office of Youth Development
504 Mayflower St.
Baton Rouge, LA 70802
(225) 342-6001

Maine—Adult and Juvenile Parole
Parole Board
111 State House Station
Augusta, ME 04333
(207) 287-2711

**Maine—Adult and Juvenile
    Probation/Parole**
Department of Corrections
Division of Probation and Parole

111 State House Station
Augusta, ME 04333
(207) 287-4384

Maryland—Adult Parole
Parole Commission
6776 Riesterstown Rd., Ste. 307
Baltimore, MD 21215
(410) 585-3200

Maryland—Adult Probation/Parole
Department of Public Safety and
    Correctional Services
Division of Parole and Probation
6776 Reisterstown Rd. Ste. 305
Baltimore, MD 21215
(410) 585-3500

Maryland—Juvenile Probation/Parole
Department of Juvenile Justice
1 Center Plaza
120 W. Fayette St.
Baltimore, MD 21201
(410) 230-3100

**Massachusetts—Adult and Juvenile
    Probation**
Massachusetts Trial Court
Office of the Commissioner of
    Probation
1 Ashburton Pl., Rm. 305
Boston, MA 02108
(617) 727-5300

Massachusetts—Adult Parole
Parole Board
27 Wormwood St., Ste. 300
Boston, MA 02210
(617) 727-3271

Massachusetts—Juvenile Parole
Executive Office of Health and Human
    Services
Department of Youth Services
27-43 Wormwood St.
Boston, MA 02210
(617) 727-7575

Michigan—Adult Parole
Parole Board
206 E. Michigan Ave.
PO Box 30003
Lansing, MI 48909
(517) 373-0270

Michigan—Adult Probation
State Court Administrative Office

PO Box 30003
Lansing, MI 48909
(517) 373-0130

Michigan—Adult Probation/Parole
Department of Corrections
Field Operations Administration
PO Box 30003
Lansing, MI 48909
(517) 373-0720

Michigan—Juvenile Probation/Parole
Family Independence Agency
Bureau of Juvenile Justice
235 S. Grand Ave.
Lansing, MI 48909
(517) 335-3489

**Minnesota—Adult and Juvenile
    Parole**
Board of Pardons
1450 Energy Park Dr., Ste. 200
St. Paul, MN 55108
(651) 642-0284

**Minnesota—Adult and Juvenile
    Probation/Parole**
Department of Corrections
1450 Energy Park Dr., Ste. 200
St. Paul, MN 55108
(651) 642-0282

Mississippi—Adult Parole
Parole Board
201 W. Capitol St., Ste. 800
Jackson, MS 39201
(601) 354-7716

Mississippi—Adult Probation/Parole
Department of Corrections
723 N. President St.
Jackson, MS 39202
(601) 359-5622

**Mississippi—Juvenile Probation/
    Parole**
Department of Human Services
Division of Youth Services
720 N. State St.
PO Box 352
Jackson, MS 39202
(601) 359-4972

Missouri—Adult Probation/Parole
Department of Corrections
Board of Probation and Parole
1511 Christy Dr.

Jefferson City, MO 65101
(573) 751-8488

Missouri—Juvenile Parole
Department of Social Services
Division of Youth Services
PO Box 447
Jefferson City, MO 65102
(573) 751-3324

Missouri—Juvenile Probation
Office of State Courts Administrator
2112 Industrial Dr.
PO Box 104480
Jefferson City, MO 65110
(573) 751-4377

Montana—Adult Parole
Board of Pardons and Parole
300 Maryland Ave.
Deer Lodge, MT 59722
(406) 846-1404

Montana—Adult Probation/Parole
Department of Corrections
1539 11th Ave.
Helena, MT 59620
(406) 444-4936

Montana—Juvenile Parole
Department of Family Services
Division of Juvenile Corrections
1539 11th Ave.
Helena, MT 59620
(406) 444-5900

Montana—Juvenile Probation
Office of Court Administration
215 N. Sanders St., Rm. 315
Helena, MT 59620
(406) 444-2621

**Nebraska—Adult and Juvenile
    Probation**
Supreme Court
Probation Administration
State Capitol
PO Box 98910
Lincoln, NE 68509
(402) 471-3730

Nebraska—Adult Parole
Board of Parole
PO Box 94754
State House Station
Lincoln, NE 68509
(402) 471-2156

Nebraska—Adult Parole
Adult Parole Administration
Folsom and W. Prospector Pl.
PO Box 94661
Lincoln, NE 68509
(402) 479-5771

Nebraska—Juvenile Parole
Health and Human Services
Protection and Safety Division
PO Box 95044
Lincoln, NE 68509
(402) 471-8410

Nevada—Adult Parole
Board of Parole Commissioners
1445 Hot Springs Rd., Ste. 108-B
Carson City, NV 89711
(702) 687-5049

Nevada—Adult Probation/Parole
Department of Motor Vehicles and
    Public Safety
Division of Parole and Probation
1445 Hot Springs Rd. Ste 104
Carson City, NV 89706
(775) 687-5040

Nevada—Juvenile Parole
Department of Human Resources/
    Youth Correctional Services
Nevada Youth Parole Bureau
620 Belrose, Ste. C
Las Vegas, NV 89107
(702) 486-5080

Nevada—Juvenile Probation
Carson City Juvenile Probation
1545 E. 5th St.
Carson City, NV 89701
(775) 688-1421

New Hampshire—Adult Parole
Board of Parole
281 N. State St.
PO Box 14
Concord, NH 03302
(603) 271-2569

**New Hampshire—Adult Probation/
    Parole**
Department of Corrections
Division of Field Services
105 Pleasant St., 3rd Floor
PO Box 1806
Concord, NH 03302
(603) 271-5662

New Hampshire—Juvenile Parole
Juvenile Parole Board
1056 N. River Rd.
Manchester, NH 03104
(603) 625-5471

**New Hampshire—Juvenile Probation/
    Parole**
Department of Youth Development
    Services
1056 N. River Rd.
Manchester, NH 03104
(603) 625-5471

**New Jersey—Adult and Juvenile
    Parole**
Parole Board
Whittlesey Rd.
PO Box 862
Trenton, NJ 08625
(609) 292-4257

**New Jersey—Adult and Juvenile
    Parole**
Department of Corrections
Division of Parole and Community
    Corrections
Whittlesey Rd. and Stuyvesant Ave.
Trenton, NJ 08625
(609) 292-9980

**New Jersey—Adult and Juvenile
    Probation**
Administrative Office of the Courts
Richard J. Hughes Justice Complex
PO Box 037
Trenton, NJ 08625
(609) 984-0275

New Mexico—Adult Parole
Adult Parole Board
4351 State Rd. 14
Santa Fe, NM 87505
(505) 827-8825

New Mexico—Adult Probation/Parole
Corrections Department
Probation and Parole Division
PO Box 27116
Santa Fe, NM 87502
(505) 827-8830

New Mexico—Juvenile Parole
Juvenile Parole Board
3411 Pan American Freeway NE
Albuquerque, NM 87107
(505) 841-2457

**New Mexico—Juvenile Probation/
    Parole**
Department of Children, Youth, and
    Families
Juvenile Justice Division
PO Drawer 5160
Santa Fe, NM 87502
(505) 827-7629

New York—Adult and Juvenile Parole
Division of Parole
97 Central Ave.
Albany, NY 12206
(518) 473-9548

New York—Adult Parole
Board of Parole
97 Central Ave.
Albany, NY 12206
(518) 473-9548

New York—Adult Probation
Probation Commission
4 Tower Pl., 3rd Floor
Albany, NY 12203
(518) 485-2395

New York—Adult Probation
Division of Probation and Correctional
    Alternatives
4 Tower Pl.
Albany, NY 12203
(518) 485-2395

New York—Juvenile Probation
Office of Children and Family Services
52 Washington St.
Rensselaer, NY 12144
(518) 473-8437

North Carolina—Adult Parole
Post-Release Supervision and Parole
    Commission
2020 Yonkers Rd.
Raleigh, NC 27626
(919) 716-3010

**North Carolina—Adult Probation/
    Parole**
Department of Correction
Division of Community Corrections
2020 Yonkers Rd.
4250 MSC
Raleigh, NC 27669
(919) 716-3105

**North Carolina—Juvenile Probation/
Parole**
Administrative Office of the Courts
Juvenile Services Division
PO Box 2448
Raleigh, NC 27602
(919) 733-3388

North Dakota—Adult Pardons
Pardon Advisory Board
PO Box 5521
Bismarck, ND 58506
(701) 328-6190

North Dakota—Adult Parole
Parole Board
PO Box 5521
Bismarck, ND 58506
(701) 328-6199

**North Dakota—Adult Probation/
Parole**
Department of Corrections and
Rehabilitation
Division of Field Services
PO Box 5521
Bismarck, ND 58506
(701) 328-6192

North Dakota—Juvenile Parole
Division of Juvenile Services
PO Box 1898
Bismarck, ND 58202
(701) 328-6390

North Dakota—Juvenile Probation
Court Administration
600 E. Boulevard Ave.
Bismarck, ND 58505
(701) 224-4216

Ohio—Adult Parole
Adult Parole Authority
1050 Freeway Dr. N
Columbus, OH 43229
(614) 752-1254

Ohio—Adult Probation/Parole
Department of Rehabilitation and
Correction
Division of Parole and Community
Services
1050 Freeway Dr. N.
Columbus, OH 43229
(614) 752-1230

Ohio—Juvenile Parole
Department of Youth Services
Division of Parole and Community
Services
51 N. High St.
Columbus, OH 43215
(614) 466-3576

Ohio—Juvenile Probation
Bureau of Community-Based Programs
51 N. High St.
Columbus, OH 43215
(614) 752-2546

Oklahoma—Adult Parole
Pardon and Parole Board
4040 N. Lincoln Ave., Ste. 219
Oklahoma City, OK 73105
(405) 427-8601

Oklahoma—Adult Parole
Board of Parole and Post-Prison
Supervision
2575 Center St. NE Ste. 100
Salem, OK 97301
(503) 945-0919

Oklahoma—Adult Probation/Parole
Department of Corrections
Division of Probation and Parole/
Community Corrections
1219 Classen Dr.
Oklahoma City, OK 73103
(405) 218-4200

Oklahoma—Juvenile Parole
Juvenile Parole Board
3814 N. Santa Fe
PO Box 268812
Oklahoma City, OK 73126
(405) 530-2800

**Oklahoma—Juvenile Probation/
Parole**
Office of Juvenile Affairs
Department of Juvenile Justice
PO Box 268812
Oklahoma City, OK 73216
(405) 530-2800

Oregon—Adult Parole
Board of Parole and Post-Prison
Supervision
2575 Center St. NE
Salem, OR 97310
(503) 945-9064

Oregon—Adult Probation/Parole
Department of Corrections
Division of Community Corrections
2575 Center St. NE
Salem, OR 97310
(503) 945-9050

Oregon—Juvenile Probation/Parole
Youth Authority
Community Resources and State
Parole/Probation Administration
530 Center St. NE, Ste. 200
Salem, OR 97301
(503) 373-7238

**Pennsylvania—Adult and Juvenile
Probation/Parole**
Administrative Office of Courts
1515 Market St., Ste. 1414
Philadelphia, PA 19102
(215) 560-6300

**Pennsylvania—Adult Probation/
Parole**
Board of Probation and Parole
1101 S. Front St., Ste. 5100
Harrisburg, PA 17104
(717) 787-5100

**Pennsylvania—Juvenile Probation/
Parole**
Juvenile Court Judges' Commission
Finance Bldg., Rm. 401
Harrisburg, PA 17120
(717) 787-6910

Rhode Island—Adult Parole
Parole Board
1 Center Pl.
Providence, RI 02903
(401) 222-3262

**Rhode Island—Adult Probation/
Parole**
Department of Corrections
Division of Rehabilitative Services/
Probation and Parole
Bernadette Bldg.
PO Box 8276
Cranston, RI 02920
(401) 462-1619

**Rhode Island—Juvenile Probation/
Parole**
Department of Children, Youth, and
Families
Probation and Parole Services

101 Friendship St.
Providence, RI 02903
(401) 528-3520

South Carolina—Adult Parole
Board of Paroles and Pardons
2221 Divine St.
PO Box 50666
Columbia, SC 29250
(803) 734-9278

South Carolina—Adult Probation/ Parole
Department of Corrections
Department of Probation, Parole, and
    Pardon Services
2221 Devine St.
PO Box 50666
Columbia, SC 29204
(803) 734-9278

South Carolina—Juvenile Parole
Juvenile Parole Board
100 Executive Center, Ste. 103
Columbia, SC 29210
(803) 896-5614

South Carolina—Juvenile Probation/ Parole
Department of Juvenile Justice
4900 Broad River Rd.
PO Box 21069
Columbia, SC 29221
(803) 896-9791

South Dakota—Adult and Juvenile Probation/Parole
Unified Judicial System
500 E. Capitol
Pierre, SD 57501
(605) 773-3474

South Dakota—Adult Parole
Board of Pardons and Paroles
PO Box 5911
Sioux Falls, SD 57117
(605) 367-5040

South Dakota—Juvenile Parole
Division of Juvenile Corrections
415 N. Dakota Ave.
Pierre, SD 57104
(605) 367-5547

Tennessee—Adult Probation/Parole
Board of Probation and Parole
404 James Robertson Pkwy., Ste. 1300

Nashville, TN 37243
(615) 741-1673

Tennessee—Juvenile Probation/Parole
Department of Children's Services
436 6th Ave. N., 7th Floor
Nashville, TN 37243
(615) 741-9701

Texas—Adult Parole
Board of Pardons and Paroles
209 W. 14th St., Ste. 500
Austin, TX 78701
(512) 463-1679

Texas—Adult Probation
Department of Criminal Justice
Community Justice Assistance Division
209 W. 14th St., Ste. 400
Austin, TX 78701
(512) 305-9300

Texas—Juvenile Parole
Texas Youth Commission
4900 N. Lamar
Austin, TX 78765
(512) 424-6000

Texas—Juvenile Probation
Juvenile Probation Commission
4900 N. Lamar
Austin, TX 78765
(512) 424-6682

Utah—Adult Parole
Board of Pardons and Parole
448 East 6400 S., Ste. 300
Murray, UT 84107
(801) 261-6464

Utah—Adult Probation/Parole
Department of Corrections
Division of Adult Probation and Parole
155 East 6100 S.
Murray, UT 84107
(801) 264-4300

Utah—Juvenile Parole
Department of Human Services
Division of Youth Corrections
120 North 200 West
Salt Lake City, UT 84103
(801) 538-4330

Utah—Juvenile Probation
Board of Juvenile Court Judges
Juvenile Court

230 South 500 East
Salt Lake City, UT 84102
(801) 578-3800

Utah—Juvenile Probation
Administrative Office of the Courts
450 S. State
PO Box 140241
Salt Lake City, UT 84114
(801) 578-3800

Vermont—Adult Parole
Board of Parole
103 S. Main St.
Waterbury, VT 05671
(802) 241-2312

Vermont—Adult Probation/Parole
Department of Corrections
103 S. Main St.
Waterbury, VT 05676
(802) 241-2442

Vermont—Juvenile Probation/Parole
Department of Social and
    Rehabilitation Services
Divison of Social Services
103 S. Main St., 3rd Floor
Waterbury, VT 05671

Virginia—Adult Parole
Parole Board
6900 Atmore Dr.
Richmond, VA 23225
(804) 674-3081

Virginia—Adult Probation/Parole
Department of Corrections/Division
of Community Corrections
6900 Atmore Dr.
Richmond, VA 23225
(804) 674-3119

Virginia—Juvenile Probation/Parole
Department of Juvenile Justice
700 Centre, 4th Floor
PO Box 1110
Richmond, VA 23218
(804) 371-2555

Washington—Adult Parole
Indeterminate Sentence Review Board
4317 6th Ave. SE
PO Box 40907
Olympia, WA 98504
(360) 493-9271

Washington—Adult Probation
Office of the Administrator for the
  Courts
1206 S. Quince St. SE
Olympia, WA 98504
(360) 753-3365

Washington—Adult Probation/Parole
Department of Corrections
Office of Correctional Operations
410 W. 5th Ave.
PO Box 41118
Olympia, WA 98504
(360) 753-4616

Washington—Juvenile Parole
Department of Social and Health
  Services
Juvenile Rehabilitation Administration
14th and Jefferson Sts.
PO Box 45045
Olympia, WA 98504
(509) 902-7804

**Washington—Juvenile Probation/
  Parole**
Adams County Juvenile Court Services
120 S. Broadway Ave., Ste. B
Othello, WA 99344
(509) 488-5646

West Virginia—Adult Parole
Parole Board
112 California Ave., Bldg. 4, Rm. 307
Charleston, WV 25305

(304) 558-6366

**West Virginia—Juvenile Parole/Adult
  and Juvenile Probation**
Supreme Court of Appeals
Administrative Office of the Courts
E-100 State Capitol Bldg. 1
Charleston, WV 25305
(304) 558-0145

Wisconsin—Adult Parole
Parole Commission
149 E. Wilson St.
PO Box 7825
Madison, WI 53707
(608) 266-2957

Wisconsin—Adult Probation/Parole
Department of Corrections
Division of Community Corrections
PO Box 7925
Madison, WI 53707
(608) 266-4548

**Wisconsin—Juvenile Probation/
  Parole**
Division of Juvenile Corrections
Office of Juvenile Offender Review
149 E. Wilson St.
PO Box 8930
Madison, WI 53708
(608) 266-9342

Wyoming—Adult Parole
Board of Parole

700 W. 21st St.
Cheyenne, WY 82002
(307) 777-7208

Wyoming—Adult Probation/Parole
Department of Corrections
Division of Field Services
700 W. 21st St.
Cheyenne, WY 82002
(307) 777-7208

Wyoming—Juvenile Probation/Parole
Department of Family Services
Hathaway Bldg., 3rd Floor
Cheyenne, WY 82002
(307) 777-7564

United States—Adult Parole
Department of Justice
U.S. Parole Commission
5550 Friendship Blvd., Ste. 420
Chevy Chase, MD 20815
(301) 492-5990

**United States—Adult Probation/
  Parole**
Administrative Office of the U.S.
  Courts
Division of Probation and Pretrial
  Services
1 Columbia Circle NE
Washington, DC 20544
(202) 273-1600 ✦

Regional Departments of Corrections Telephone, Fax, and Internet Contacts

Region	Phone	Fax	Internet
Alabama	(334) 353-3870	(334) 353-3891	http://www.agencies.state.al.us/doc
Alaska	(907) 465-4652	(907) 456-3390	http://www.correct.state.ak.us
Arizona	(602) 542-5497	(602) 542-1728	http://adcprisoninfo.az.gov
Arkansas	(870) 267-6200	(870) 627-6244	http://www.state.ar.us/doc
California	(916) 445-7688	(916) 322-2877	http://www.cdc.state.ca.us
Colorado	(719) 579-9580	(719) 540-4755	http://www.doc.state.co.us
Connecticut	(860) 692-7482	(860)692-7483	http://www.state.ct.us/doc
Delaware	(302) 539-7601	(302) 739-8221	http://www.state.de.us/correct
District of Columbia	(202) 673-7316	(202) 332-1470	http://doc.dc.gov
Florida	(850) 488-7480	(850) 922-2848	http://www.dc.state.fl.us
Georgia	(404) 656-6002	(404) 651-6818	http://www.dcor.state.ga.us
Hawaii	(808) 587-1350	(808) 587-1282	http://www.state.hi.us/csd/psd/psd.html
Idaho	(208) 658-2000	(208) 327-7404	http://www.corr.state.id.us
Illinois	(217) 522-2666	(217) 522-5089	http://www.idoc.state.il.us
Cook County	(773) 869-2859	(773) 869-2562	http://www.cookcountysheriff.org/doc
Indiana	(317) 232-5715	(317) 232-6798	http://www.state.in.us/indcorrection
Iowa	(515) 242-5703	(515) 281-7345	http://www.doc.state.ia.us
Kansas	(785) 296-3317	(785) 296-0014	http://docnet.dc.state.ks.us
Kentucky	(502) 564-4726	(502) 564-5037	http://www.cor.state.ky.us
Louisiana	(225) 342-6741	(225) 342-3095	http://www.corrections.state.la.us
Maine	(207) 287-4360	(207) 287-4370	http://www.janus.state.me.us/corrections
Maryland	(410) 585-3300	(410) 764-4373	http://www.dpscs.state.md.us/doc
Massachusetts	(508) 422-3339	(508) 422-3386	http://www.state.ma.us/doc
Michigan	(517) 373-0720	(517) 373-6883	http://www.state.mi.us/mdoc
Minnesota	(651) 642-0282	(651) 642-0223	http://www.doc.state.mn.us
Mississippi	(601) 359-5600	(601) 359-5680	http://www.mdoc.state.ms.us
Missouri	(573) 751-2389	(573) 751-4099	http://www.corrections.state.mo.us

Region	Phone	Fax	Internet
Montana	(406) 444-3930	(406) 444-4920	http://www.cor.state.mt.us
Nebraska	(402) 471-2654	(402) 479-5623	http://www.corrections.state.ne.us
Nevada	(775) 887-3216	(775) 687-6715	http://www.prisons.state.nv.us
New Hampshire	(603) 271-5600	(603) 271-5643	http://www.state.nh.us/doc
New Jersey	(609) 292-4036	(609) 292-9083	http://www.state.nj.us/corrections
New Mexico	(505) 827-8709	(505) 827-8220	http://www.state.nm.us/corrections
New York State	(518) 457-8126	(518) 457-7252	http://www.docs.state.ny.us
New York City	(212) 266-1212	(212) 266-1219	http://www.ci.nyc.ny.us/html.doc/home.html
North Carolina	(919) 716-3700	(919) 716-3794	http://www.doc.state.nc.us
North Dakota	(701) 328-6390	(701) 328-6651	http://www.state.nd.us/docr
Ohio	(614) 752-1164	(614) 752-1171	http://www.drc.state.oh.us
Oklahoma	(405) 425-2505	(405) 425-2578	http://www.doc.state.ok.us
Oregon	(503) 945-0920	(503) 373-1173	http://www.doc.state.or.us
Pennsylvania	(717) 975-4918	(717) 731-0486	http://www.cor.state.pa.us
Philadelphia	(215) 685-8201	(215) 685-8577	http://www.phila.gov/departments/prisons
Rhode Island	(401) 462-2611	(401) 462-2630	http://www.doc.state.ri.us
South Carolina	(803) 896-8555	(803) 896-3972	http://www.state.sc.us/doc
South Dakota	(605) 773-3478	(605) 773-3194	http://www.state.sd.us/corrections/corrections.html
Tennessee	(615) 741-1000	(615) 532-8281	http://www.state.tn.us/correction
Texas	(936) 437-2101	(936) 537-2123	http://www.tdcj.state.tx.us
Utah	(801) 265-5500	(801) 265-5726	http://www.udc.state.ut.us
Vermont	(802) 241-2442	(802) 241-2565	http://www.doc.state.vt.us
Virginia	(804) 674-3119	(804) 674-3509	http://www.vadoc.state.va.us
Washington	(360) 753-1573	(360) 664-4056	http://www.wa.gov/doc
West Virginia	(304) 558-2036	(304) 558-5934	http://www.state.wv.us/wvdoc
Wisconsin	(608) 266-4548	(608) 267-3661	http://www.wi-doc.com
Wyoming	(307) 777-7208	(307) 777-7459	http://doc.state.wy.us